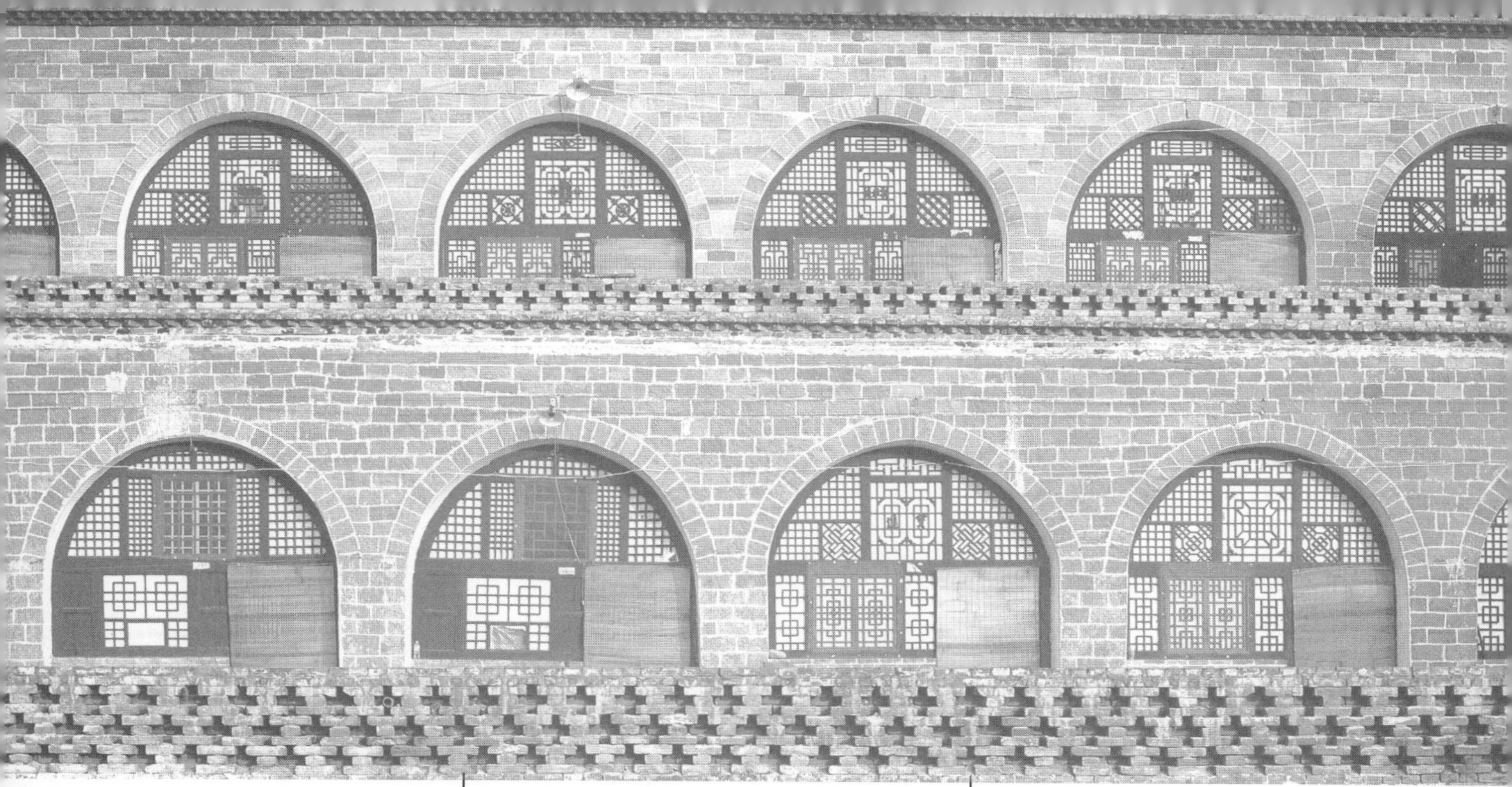

统计年鉴2017

SHANXI STATISTICAL YEARBOOK

山　西　省　统　计　局
国家统计局山西调查总队　编

Compiled by Shanxi Provincial Bureau of Statistics &
Survey Office of the NationalBureau of Statisticsin Shanxi

总 第35期

© 中国统计出版社 2017
版权所有。未经许可，本书的任何部分不得以任何方式在世界任何地区以任何文字翻印、拷贝、仿制或转载。

© 2017 China Statistics Press
All rights reserved. No part of the publication may be reproduced or transmitted in any form or by any means, electronic or mechanical, including photocopying, recording, or any information storage and retrieval system, without written permission from the publisher.

图书在版编目（CIP）数据

山西统计年鉴. 2017：汉英对照 / 山西省统计局，国家统计局山西调查总队编. -- 北京：中国统计出版社，2017.9
ISBN 978-7-5037-8173-5

Ⅰ. ①山… Ⅱ. ①山… ②国… Ⅲ. ①统计资料－山西－2017－年鉴－汉、英 Ⅳ. ①C832.25-54

中国版本图书馆 CIP 数据核字(2017)第 157192 号

山西统计年鉴—2017

作　　者/山西省统计局　国家统计局山西调查总队
责任编辑/佘竞雄　李潇潇
责任校对/董晓玲　樊梅洁　李　静　田　甜
装帧设计/黄　晨　王　芳
出版发行/中国统计出版社
通信地址/北京市丰台区西三环南路甲 6 号　邮政编码/100073
电　　话/邮购（010）63376909　书店（010）68783171
网　　址/ http://www.zgtjcbs.com
印　　刷/河北鑫兆源印刷有限公司
经　　销/新华书店
开　　本/890mm×1240mm　1/16
字　　数/1420 千字
印　　张/48.25
版　　别/2017 年 9 月第 1 版
版　　次/2017 年 9 月第 1 次印刷
定　　价/390.00 元

本书附同版本 CD-ROM 一张，光盘内容以书面文字为准。
如有印装差错，由本社发行部调换。

编辑委员会

主　　任

翟振新　刘顺国

副 主 任

卢永良　张晓东　王德才　荆红社　李春泽　窦志达
包超英　程海营　张继德　王润拴　王续孔　刘建业

编　　委（以姓氏笔画为序）

卫永杰　马　忠　王育民　白日成　刘文斌　刘雪琴
闫立铭　李永章　李俊鹏　李冠玲　杨玉云　杨生广
杨志刚　杨艳文　吴世明　张　胜　张明峰　张俊霞
陈培文　赵天胜　赵满仓　郝　海　郝玉成　侯晓远
耿爱莲　高青山　剡建国　董晓玲　韩亚彪　景　伟
程建平　解长金　潘会玲　穆永梅

编辑工作人员

总 编 辑

张晓东

副总编辑

董晓玲　刘海滨　郝增国　樊梅洁

编辑人员

樊梅洁　李　静　田　甜　李　婷

版式设计

董晓玲　樊梅洁

英文校译

李　静　张奇科

Editorial Board

Chairmen : Zhai Zhenxin, Liu Shunguo

Vice-chairmen : Lu Yongliang, Zhang Xiaodong, Wang Decai, Jing Hongshe, Li Chunze, Dou Zhida, Bao Chaoying, Cheng Haiying, Zhang Jide, Wang Runshuan, Wang Xukong, Liu Jianye

Editorial Board : (in order of strokes of Chinese surname)

Wei Yongjie, Ma Zhong, Wang Yumin, Bai Richeng, Liu Wenbin, Liu Xueqin, Yan Liming, Li Yongzhang, Li Junpeng, Li Guanling, Yang Yuyun, Yang Shengguang, Yang Zhigang, Yang Yanwen, Wu Shiming, Zhang Sheng, Zhang Mingfeng, Zhang Junxia, Chen Peiwen, Zhao Tiansheng, Zhao Mancang, Hao Hai, Hao Yucheng, Hou Xiaoyuan, Geng Ailian, Gao Qingshan, Yan Jianguo, Dong Xiaoling, Han Yabiao, Jing Wei, Cheng Jianping, Xie Changjin, Pan Huiling, Mu Yongmei

Editorial Staffs

Editor-in-chief : Zhang Xiaodong

Deputy Editors-in-chief : Dong Xiaoling, Liu Haibin, Hao Zengguo, Fan Meijie

Editors : Fan Meijie, Li Jing, Tian Tian, Li Ting

Format Designers : Dong Xiaoling, Fan Meijie

English Proofreaders : Li Jing, Zhang Qike

编者说明

一、《山西统计年鉴—2017》收录了全省和各地市、县（市、区）2016年经济、社会、科技等方面的统计数据，以及多个重要历史年份主要统计数据，是一部全面反映山西省国民经济和社会发展情况的资料性年刊。为便于国际交流，内文全部采用中英文对照。

二、全书共分20个篇章，1. 综合；2. 人口、劳动工资和社会保障；3. 物价；4. 人民生活；5. 财政、金融和保险；6. 能源；7. 固定资产投资；8. 对外经济贸易；9. 农业；10. 工业；11. 建筑业；12. 房地产；13. 批发和零售业；14. 住宿、餐饮业和旅游；15. 交通运输、邮电通信业；16. 教育、科技；17. 文化、体育、卫生、环保；18. 城市概况；19. 地市篇；20. 县（市、区）篇。为方便读者使用，各篇章前绘制了反映总体趋势的统计图，篇末附有《主要统计指标解释》，对主要统计指标的涵义、统计范围和统计方法以及历史沿革予以简要说明。

三、与《山西统计年鉴—2016》相比，本年鉴内容主要做了如下修订："物价"篇中居民消费价格指数采用了新的行业分类标准，"工业"篇中增加了"规模以上主要工业产品产量"表。

四、本年鉴统计指标口径范围及解释以国家现行统计报表制度为准。资料主要来源于统计年报，部分资料来自于抽样调查和有关部门。

五、为方便读者使用，对个别有变动的指标在表下作了简要注释。本年鉴中涉及到的历史数据，均以最新出版的本年鉴数据为准。

六、本年鉴所使用的度量衡单位，均采用国际统一标准计量单位。部分数据合计数或相对数由于单位取舍不同而产生的计算误差，均未作机械调整。

七、年鉴符号使用说明："空格"表示该项统计指标数据不足本表最小单位数、数据不详或无数据；"#"表示该指标其中的主要项。

COMPILER'S NOTES

Ⅰ . *Shanxi Statistical Yearbook 2017* is an annual statistics publication, which reflects comprehensively the national economic and social development of Shanxi province. It covers data for 2016 and key statistical data in some historically important years at the provincial level and the local levels of prefecture and county. To meet the need of international exchange, this yearbook is made in both Chinese and English.

Ⅱ . The yearbook contains the following twenty parts: 1. General Survey; 2. Population, Labor Wages and Social Security; 3. Price; 4. People's Livelihood; 5. Public Finance, Banking and Insurance; 6. Energy; 7. Investment in Fixed Assets; 8. Foreign Trade and Economic Cooperation; 9. Agriculture; 10. Industry; 11. Construction; 12. Real Estate; 13. Wholesale and Retail Trade; 14. Hotels, Catering Services and Tourism; 15. Transportation, Post and Telecommunication Services; 16. Education, Science and Technology; 17. Culture, Sports, Public Health and Environmental Protection; 18. General Survey of Cities; 19. Cities at Prefecture Level; 20. Counties, Cities and Districts at County Level. To facility readers, Statistical Charts reflecting total trend are attached at the beginning of each chapter, and Explanatory Notes on Main Statistical Indicators, a brief introduction about the meaning, statistical coverage, statistical methods and historical changes of main statistical indicators, are provided at the end of each chapter.

Ⅲ . Comparing with *Shanxi Statistical Yearbook 2016*, following revision has been made in this new version: Consumer price indices adopts new industrial classification standard in the chapter of Price; Table of Output of Major Industrial Products above Designated Size is added in the chapter of Industry.

Ⅳ . The statistical coverage and explanation of indicators in this yearbook is the same as the current national statistical report system. The data in this yearbook are mainly obtained from annual statistical reports, and some are from sample surveys and related departments.

Ⅴ . For the convenience of the readers, brief notes concerning some indicators about their changes in meaning or coverage are given at the lower part of relevant tables. According to international practice, some main indicators need to check and revise regularly by statistical census. In case of some statistical data issued before being inconsistent with this publication, take the data in this publication as correction.

Ⅵ . The units of measurement used in this yearbook are international standard measurement units. Statistical discrepancies due to rounding are not adjusted in this yearbook.

Ⅶ . Notations used in this book: " (blank) " indicates that the figure is not large enough to be measured with the smallest unit in the table or is not available; "#"indicates the major items of the total.

目　　录

CONTENTS

一、综　合

GENERAL SURVEY

统计图 ……………………………………………………………………………………………………（3）
CHARTS

1-1　行政区划(2016 年)……………………………………………………………………………（5）
ADMINISTRATIVE DIVISION(2016)

1-2　国民经济和社会发展总量与速度指标……………………………………………………………（6）
PRINCIPAL AGGREGATE INDICATORS ON NATIONAL ECONOMIC AND SOCIAL DEVELOPMENT AND GROWTH RATES

1-3　山西省水资源总量(2015 年)…………………………………………………………………（10）
TOTAL VOLUME OF WATER RESOURCES(2015)

1-4　山西省实际用水量(2015 年)…………………………………………………………………（10）
ACTUAL CONSUMPTION OF WATER(2015)

1-5　平均每天主要社会经济活动 …………………………………………………………………（11）
MAJOR INDICATORS OF AVERAGE DAILY SOCIAL AND ECONOMIC ACTIVITIES

1-6　社会经济主要指标人均水平 …………………………………………………………………（12）
MAJOR PER CAPITA INDICATORS OF SOCIETY AND ECONOMY

1-7　国民经济与社会发展结构指标 ………………………………………………………………（13）
MAJOR COMPOSITION INDICATORS ON NATIONAL ECONOMIC AND SOCIAL DEVELOPMENT

1-8　人民物质文化生活情况…………………………………………………………………………（14）
CONDITIONS OF PEOPLE'S MATERIAL AND CULTURAL LIFE

1-9　主要年份地区生产总值…………………………………………………………………………（15）
GROSS DOMESTIC PRODUCT IN MAJOR YEARS

1-10　主要年份地区生产总值构成 …………………………………………………………………（16）
COMPOSITION OF GROSS DOMESTIC PRODUCT IN MAJOR YEARS

1-11　主要年份地区生产总值指数(1952 年=100) ………………………………………………（17）
INDICES OF GROSS DOMESTIC PRODUCT IN MAJOR YEARS (year of 1952=100)

1-12　主要年份地区生产总值指数(上年=100)……………………………………………………（18）
INDICES OF GROSS DOMESTIC PRODUCT IN MAJOR YEARS (last year=100)

1-13　支出法地区生产总值……………………………………………………………………………（19）
GROSS DOMESTIC PRODUCT BY EXPENDITURE APPROACH

1-14　支出法地区生产总值构成 ……………………………………………………………………（19）
COMPOSITION OF GROSS DOMESTIC PRODUCT BY EXPENDITURE APPROACH

1-15　总产出 …………………………………………………………………………………………（20）
TOTAL OUTPUT

1-16　资本形成总额 …………………………………………………………………………………（20）
GROSS CAPITAL FORMATION

1-17 地区生产总值构成项目(2016 年)…… (21)
COMPONENTS OF GROSS DOMESTIC PRODUCT(2016)
1-18 按三次产业、行业(门类)划分的法人单位数、产业活动单位数及从业人数(2016 年)…… (22)
NUMBER OF CORPORATION UNITS, ACTIVE UNITS AND EMPLOYEES BY TYPE OF INDUSTRY AND SECTOR(2016)
1-19 按登记注册类型划分的法人单位数、产业活动单位数及从业人数(2016 年)…… (24)
NUMBER OF CORPORATION UNITS, ACTIVE UNITS AND EMPLOYEES BY REGISTRATION STATUS(2016)
1-20 按登记注册类型、从业人数组距划分的法人单位数(2016 年)…… (26)
NUMBER OF CORPORATION UNITS BY REGISTRATION STATUS AND QUANTITY OF EMPLOYEES(2016)
主要统计指标解释…… (28)
EXPLANATORY NOTES ON MAIN STATISTICAL INDICATORS

二、人口、劳动工资和社会保障

POPULATION, LABOR WAGES AND SOCIAL SECURITY

统计图…… (35)
CHARTS
2-1 主要年份总户数、常住人口数…… (37)
TOTAL HOUSEHOLD AND RESIDENT POPULATION IN MAJOR YEARS
2-2 主要年份人口自然变动…… (37)
NATURAL CHANGE OF POPULATION IN MAJOR YEARS
2-3 城乡人口情况…… (38)
URBAN AND RURAL POPULATION
2-4 主要年份人口年龄构成和抚养比…… (39)
AGE COMPOSITION AND DEPENDENCY RATIO OF POPULATION IN MAJOR YEARS
2-5 主要年份全社会从业人员年末人数…… (39)
TOTAL EMPLOYEES AT YEAR-END IN MAJOR YEARS
2-6 全社会劳动力资源配置情况…… (40)
LABOR RESOURCES ALLOCATION IN THE WHOLE SOCIETY
2-7 非私营单位从业人员(2016 年)…… (41)
NUMBER OF EMPLOYEES IN NON-PRIVATE UNITS(2016)
2-8 非私营单位从业人员劳动报酬(2016 年)…… (42)
REWARD OF EMPLOYEES IN NON-PRIVATE UNITS(2016)
2-9 国有单位从业人员(2016 年)…… (43)
NUMBER OF EMPLOYEES IN STATE-OWNED UNITS(2016)
2-10 国有单位从业人员劳动报酬(2016 年)…… (44)
REWARD OF EMPLOYEES IN STATE-OWNED UNITS(2016)
2-11 城镇集体单位从业人员(2016 年)…… (45)
NUMBER OF EMPLOYEES IN URBAN COLLECTIVE-OWNED UNITS(2016)
2-12 城镇集体单位从业人员劳动报酬(2016 年)…… (46)
REWARD OF EMPLOYEES IN URBAN COLLECTIVE-OWNED UNITS(2016)
2-13 其他单位从业人员(2016 年)…… (47)
NUMBER OF EMPLOYEES IN OTHER-OWNED UNITS(2016)

2-14 其他单位从业人员劳动报酬(2016 年) …… (48)
REWARD OF EMPLOYEES IN OTHER-OWNED UNITS(2016)
2-15 私营单位从业人员和劳动报酬(2016 年) …… (49)
NUMBER AND REWARD OF EMPLOYEES IN PRIVATE UNITS(2016)
2-16 主要年份在岗职工平均工资及指数 …… (50)
AVERAGE WAGE AND RELATED INDICES OF FULLY EMPLOYED STAFF AND WORKERS IN MAJOR YEARS
2-17 城镇职工社会保障基本情况 …… (51)
BASIC SOCIAL SECURITY OF STAFF AND WORKERS IN URBAN UNITS
主要统计指标解释 …… (52)
EXPLANATORY NOTES ON MAIN STATISTICAL INDICATORS

三、物 价

PRICE

统计图 …… (59)
CHARTS
3-1 主要年份各类物价总指数 …… (60)
GENERAL PRICE INDICES IN MAJOR YEARS
3-2 主要年份城市居民消费价格总指数 …… (61)
GENERAL URBAN RESIDENTS CONSUMER PRICE INDICES IN MAJOR YEARS
3-3 主要年份商品零售价格总指数 …… (61)
GENERAL RETAIL PRICE INDICES IN MAJOR YEARS
3-4 居民消费价格分类指数(2016 年) …… (62)
GENERAL RESIDENTS CONSUMER PRICE INDICES BY CATEGORY OF COMMODITIES(2016)
3-5 商品零售价格分类指数(2016 年) …… (65)
GENERAL RETAIL PRICE INDICES BY CATEGORY OF COMMODITIES(2016)
3-6 调查市县居民消费价格指数(2016 年) …… (67)
RESIDENTS CONSUMER PRICE INDICES IN CITIES AND COUNTIES SURVEYED(2016)
3-7 调查市县商品零售价格指数(2016 年) …… (68)
RETAIL PRICE INDICES IN CITIES AND COUNTIES SURVEYED(2016)
3-8 农业生产资料价格分类指数 …… (69)
INDICES OF AGRICULTURAL PRODUCTIVE MATERIALS BY CATEGORY OF COMMODITIES
3-9 工业生产者购进价格指数 …… (69)
PURCHASING PRICE INDICES OF INDUSTRIAL PRODUCER
3-10 工业生产者出厂价格指数 …… (70)
EX-FACTORY PRICE INDICES OF INDUSTRIAL PRODUCER
3-11 工业生产者分行业出厂价格指数 …… (71)
EX-FACTORY PRICE INDICES OF INDUSTRIAL PRODUCER BY SECTOR
3-12 固定资产投资价格指数 …… (72)
PRICE INDICES OF INVESTMENT IN FIXED ASSETS
主要统计指标解释 …… (73)
EXPLANATORY NOTES ON MAIN STATISTICAL INDICATORS

四、人民生活

PEOPLE'S LIVELIHOOD

统计图 …… (77)
CHARTS

4-1 全省居民家庭生活基本情况 …… (78)
BASIC LIVING CONDITIONS OF THE PROVINCIAL HOUSEHOLDS

4-2 城镇居民家庭生活基本情况 …… (78)
BASIC LIVING CONDITIONS OF URBAN HOUSEHOLDS

4-3 城镇家庭人口状况 …… (79)
POPULATION CONDITIONS OF URBAN HOUSEHOLDS

4-4 城镇家庭劳动力状况 …… (80)
LABOR FORCE OF URBAN HOUSEHOLDS

4-5 城镇居民家庭人均全年总收入 …… (81)
PER CAPITA ANNUAL INCOME OF URBAN HOUSEHOLDS

4-6 城镇居民家庭人均全年总支出 …… (82)
PER CAPITA ANNUAL EXPENDITURE OF URBAN HOUSEHOLDS

4-7 城镇居民家庭人均可支配收入及构成 …… (83)
PER CAPITA DISPOSABLE INCOME AND COMPOSITION OF URBAN HOUSEHOLDS

4-8 城镇居民家庭人均消费支出及构成 …… (83)
PER CAPITA LIVING EXPENDITURE AND COMPOSITION OF URBAN HOUSEHOLDS

4-9 城镇家庭平均每人家庭经营净收入 …… (84)
PER CAPITA NET INCOME FROM HOUSEHOLD BUSINESS OF URBAN HOUSEHOLDS

4-10 主要年份城镇居民人均可支配收入增长情况 …… (85)
PER CAPITA DISPOSABLE INCOME GROWTH OF URBAN HOUSEHOLDS IN MAJOR YEARS

4-11 主要年份城镇居民人均消费支出增长情况 …… (85)
PER CAPITA LIVING EXPENDITURE GROWTH OF URBAN HOUSEHOLDS IN MAJOR YEARS

4-12 城镇居民家庭平均每人食品消费量 …… (86)
PER CAPITA FOOD CONSUMPTION OF URBAN HOUSEHOLDS

4-13 城镇居民家庭平均每百户年末耐用消费品拥有量 …… (86)
DURABLE CONSUMER GOODS OWNED PER 100 URBAN HOUSEHOLDS AT YEAR-END

4-14 城镇居民家庭年末居住情况 …… (87)
LIVING CONDITIONS OF URBAN HOUSEHOLDS AT YEAR-END

4-15 城镇居民家庭五等分分组基本情况(2016 年) …… (90)
BASIC CONDITIONS OF URBAN HOUSEHOLDS BY INCOME QUINTILE(2016)

4-16 城镇居民家庭五等分分组人均收支情况(2016 年) …… (92)
PER CAPITA INCOME AND EXPENDITURE OF URBAN HOUSEHOLDS BY INCOME QUINTILE(2016)

4-17 农村居民家庭生活基本情况 …… (94)
BASIC LIVING CONDITIONS OF RURAL HOUSEHOLDS

4-18 农村家庭人口状况 …… (94)
POPULATION CONDITIONS OF RURAL HOUSEHOLDS

4-19 农村居民家庭劳动力状况 …… (95)
LABOR FORCE OF RURAL HOUSEHOLDS

4-20 农村居民家庭人均全年总收入 …… (96)
PER CAPITA ANNUAL INCOME OF RURAL HOUSEHOLDS
4-21 农村居民家庭人均全年总支出 …… (97)
PER CAPITA ANNUAL EXPENDITURE OF RURAL HOUSEHOLDS
4-22 农村居民家庭平均每户土地经营情况 …… (98)
LAND MANAGEMENT OF RURAL HOUSEHOLDS
4-23 农村居民家庭人均可支配收入及构成 …… (99)
PER CAPITA DISPOSABLE INCOME AND COMPOSITION OF RURAL HOUSEHOLDS
4-24 农村居民家庭人均消费支出及构成 …… (99)
PER CAPITA LIVING EXPENDITURE AND COMPOSITION OF RURAL HOUSEHOLDS
4-25 农村居民家庭平均每人家庭经营净收入 …… (100)
PER CAPITA NET INCOME FROM HOUSEHOLD BUSINESS OF RURAL HOUSEHOLDS
4-26 主要年份农村居民人均可支配收入增长情况 …… (101)
PER CAPITA DISPOSABLE INCOME GROWTH OF RURAL HOUSEHOLDS IN MAJOR YEARS
4-27 主要年份农村居民人均消费支出增长情况 …… (101)
PER CAPITA LIVING EXPENDITURE GROWTH OF RURAL HOUSEHOLDS IN MAJOR YEARS
4-28 农村居民家庭平均每人食品消费量 …… (102)
PER CAPITA FOOD CONSUMPTION OF RURAL HOUSEHOLDS
4-29 农村居民家庭平均每百户耐用消费品拥有量 …… (102)
DURABLE CONSUMER GOODS OWNED PER 100 RURAL HOUSEHOLDS
4-30 农村居民家庭年末居住情况 …… (103)
LIVING CONDITIONS OF RURAL HOUSEHOLDS AT YEAR-END
4-31 农村居民家庭五等分分组基本情况(2016 年) …… (106)
BASIC CONDITIONS OF RURAL HOUSEHOLDS BY INCOME QUINTILE(2016)
4-32 农村居民家庭五等分分组人均收支情况(2016 年) …… (108)
PER CAPITA INCOME AND EXPENDITURE OF RURAL HOUSEHOLDS BY INCOME QUINTILE(2016)
主要统计指标解释 …… (110)
EXPLANATORY NOTES ON MAIN STATISTICAL INDICATORS

五、财政、金融和保险

PUBLIC FINANCE, BANKING AND INSURANCE

统计图 …… (115)
CHARTS
5-1 主要年份财政收支情况 …… (116)
FINANCIAL REVENUE AND EXPENDITURE IN MAJOR YEARS
5-2 政府性基金收支额(2016 年) …… (117)
REVENUE AND EXPENDITURE OF GOVERNMENT FUNDS(2016)
5-3 一般公共预算收入(2016 年) …… (118)
GENERAL PUBLIC BUDGET REVENUE(2016)
5-4 一般公共预算支出(2016 年) …… (119)
GENERAL PUBLIC BUDGET EXPENDITURE(2016)
5-5 税收分经济类型情况(2016 年) …… (120)
TAXES REVENUE BY FORM OF OWNERSHIP(2016)

5-6 金融机构信贷收支余额(2016 年) (122)
BALANCE OF CREDIT FUNDS OF FINANCIAL INSTITUTIONS(2016)
5-7 金融机构人民币各项存款和贷款余额 (123)
BALANCE OF DEPOSITS AND LOANS IN RENMINBI OF FINANCIAL INSTITUTIONS
5-8 金融机构法定存款利率 (124)
OFFICIAL INTEREST RATES OF DEPOSITS OF FINANCIAL INSITITUTIONS
5-9 保险业基本情况(分险种) (126)
BASIC STATISTICS ON INSURANCE BUSINESS BY TYPE
5-10 原保险保费收入情况(山西分公司) (127)
BASIC STATISTICS ON INCOME OF PREMIUMS BY COMPANY(SHANXI BRANCH)
5-11 证券业基本情况 (131)
BASIC STATISTICS ON SECURITY
主要统计指标解释 (132)
EXPLANATORY NOTES ON MAIN STATISTICAL INDICATORS

六、能 源

ENERGY

统计图 (139)
CHARTS
6-1 能源生产、外调、使用平衡表 (140)
BALANCE SHEET OF ENERGY PRODUCTION, TRANSFER AND USE
6-2 煤炭生产、外调、使用平衡表 (141)
BALANCE SHEET OF COAL PRODUCTION, TRANSFER AND USE
6-3 焦炭生产、外调、使用平衡表 (142)
BALANCE SHEET OF COKE PRODUCTION, TRANSFER AND USE
6-4 电力生产、外调、使用平衡表 (143)
BALANCE SHEET OF ELECTRICITY PRODUCTION, TRANSFER AND USE
6-5 石油制品生产、外调、使用平衡表 (144)
BALANCE SHEET OF PETROLEUM PRODUCTS PRODUCTION, TRANSFER AND USE
6-6 主要年份一、二次能源生产量及构成 (145)
PRODUCTION AND COMPOSITION OF PRIMARY AND SECONDARY ENERGY IN MAJOR YEARS
6-7 主要年份煤炭消费量 (145)
COAL CONSUMPTION IN MAJOR YEARS
6-8 主要年份石油制品、焦炭消费量 (146)
PETROLEUM PRODUCTS AND COKE CONSUMPTION IN MAJOR YEARS
6-9 主要年份社会用电量 (146)
TOTAL ELECTRICITY CONSUMPTION IN MAJOR YEARS
6-10 主要年份能源生产弹性系数 (147)
ELASTICITY RATIO OF ENERGY PRODUCTION IN MAJOR YEARS
6-11 主要年份能源消费弹性系数 (147)
ELASTICITY RATIO OF ENERGY CONSUMPTION IN MAJOR YEARS

6-12 主要年份能源加工转换投入产出情况 …… (148)
EFFICIENCY OF ENERGY CONVERSION IN MAJOR YEARS
6-13 终端能源消费量和构成(2016 年) …… (150)
CONSUMPTION AND COMPOSITION OF TERMINAL ENERGY(2016)
6-14 分行业能源消费总量(2016 年) …… (152)
TOTAL ENERGY CONSUMPTION BY SECTOR(2016)
主要统计指标解释 …… (156)
EXPLANATORY NOTES ON MAIN STATISTICAL INDICATORS

七、固定资产投资

INVESTMENT IN FIXED ASSETS

统计图 …… (161)
CHARTS
7-1 全社会固定资产投资主要指标 …… (162)
MAJOR INDICATORS OF TOTAL INVESTMENT IN FIXED ASSETS
7-2 全社会固定资产投资 …… (163)
TOTAL INVESTMENT IN FIXED ASSETS
7-3 按登记注册类型和控股情况分全社会固定资产投资 …… (164)
TOTAL INVESTMENT IN FIXED ASSETS BY REGISTRATION STATUS AND SHARE HOLDING
7-4 按国民经济行业分全社会固定资产投资(2016 年) …… (165)
TOTAL INVESTMENT IN FIXED ASSETS BY ECONOMIC SECTOR(2016)
7-5 固定资产投资 …… (166)
INVESTMENT IN FIXED ASSETS
7-6 工业固定资产投资 …… (168)
INDUSTRY INVESTMENT IN FIXED ASSETS
7-7 按国民经济行业分固定资产投资 …… (170)
INVESTMENT IN FIXED ASSETS BY ECONOMIC SECTOR
7-8 固定资产投资主要指标 …… (173)
MAJOR INDICATORS OF INVESTMENT IN FIXED ASSETS
7-9 固定资产投资规模(2016 年) …… (174)
SCALE OF FIXED ASSETS INVESTMENT(2016)
7-10 按登记注册类型分固定资产投资(2016 年) …… (176)
INVESTMENT IN FIXED ASSETS BY REGISTRATION STATUS(2016)
7-11 按构成分固定资产投资(2016 年) …… (188)
INVESTMENT IN FIXED ASSETS BY COMPOSITION(2016)
7-12 按建设性质分固定资产投资(2016 年) …… (194)
INVESTMENT IN FIXED ASSETS BY TYPE OF CONSTRUCTION(2016)
7-13 按控股情况分固定资产投资(2016 年) …… (200)
INVESTMENT IN FIXED ASSETS BY SHARE HOLDING(2016)
7-14 按资金来源分固定资产投资(2016 年) …… (206)
INVESTMENT IN FIXED ASSETS BY SOURCE OF FUNDS(2016)
7-15 固定资产投资规模及新增生产能力(2016 年) …… (212)
SCALE OF INVESTMENT IN FIXED ASSETS AND NEWLY INCREASED PRODUCTION CAPACITY(2016)

7-16 固定资产投资总规模及新增固定资产(2016 年)……(216)
SCALE OF INVESTMENT AND NEWLY INCREASED FIXED ASSETS(2016)
7-17 农户固定资产投资主要指标……(222)
MAJOR INDICATORS OF RURAL HOUSEHOLDS INVESTMENT IN FIXED ASSETS
7-18 主要年份农户固定资产投资……(223)
INVESTMENT IN FIXED ASSETS OF RURAL HOUSEHOLDS IN MAJOR YEARS
主要统计指标解释……(224)
EXPLANATORY NOTES ON MAIN STATISTICAL INDICATORS

八、对外经济贸易

FOREIGN TRADE AND ECONOMIC COOPERATION

统计图……(231)
CHARTS
8-1 主要年份海关进出口贸易总额……(232)
TOTAL VALUE OF IMPORTS AND EXPORTS OF CUSTOMS IN MAJOR YEARS
8-2 海关进出口贸易总额(2016 年)……(232)
TOTAL VALUE OF IMPORTS AND EXPORTS OF CUSTOMS(2016)
8-3 海关进出口主要商品分类总额(2016 年)……(233)
TOTAL VALUE OF IMPORTS AND EXPORTS OF CUSTOMS BY CATEGORY OF MAIN COMMODITIES(2016)
8-4 海关分国别(地区)进出口贸易总额(2016 年)……(234)
TOTAL VALUE OF IMPORTS AND EXPORTS OF CUSTOMS BY COUNTRY(REGION)(2016)
8-5 实际利用外资额……(235)
ACTURAL UTILIZATION OF FOREIGN CAPITAL
8-6 主要年份实际利用外资额……(235)
ACTURAL UTILIZATION OF FOREIGN CAPITAL IN MAJOR YEARS
8-7 主要年份合同利用外资金额(外商直接投资)……(236)
CONTRACT UTILIZATION OF FOREIGN CAPITAL IN MAJOR YEARS(DIRECT INVESTMENT)
8-8 按行业分利用外商直接投资额(2016 年)……(237)
UTILIZATION OF FOREIGN DIRECT INVESTMENT CAPITAL BY SECTOR(2016)
8-9 按国别(地区)分利用外商直接投资额(2016 年)……(237)
UTILIZATION OF FOREIGN DIRECT INVESTMENT CAPITAL BY COUNTRY(REGION)(2016)
8-10 主要年份对外承包工程和劳务合作……(238)
CONTRACTED PROJECTS AND LABOR COOPERATION WITH FOREIGN COUNTRIES OR REGIONS IN MAJOR YEARS
8-11 高新经济技术开发区综合情况……(238)
KEY STATISTICS OF HIGH-TECH DEVELOPMENT ZONES
8-12 各开发区综合发展情况(2016 年)……(239)
KEY STATISTICS OF DEVELOPMENT ZONES(2016)
8-13 人民币对主要外币年末汇价(中间价)……(240)
YEAR-END EXCHANGE RATE OF RMB YUAN AGAINST MAIN CONVERTIBLE CURRENCIES (MIDDLE RATE)

主要统计指标解释 …… (241)
EXPLANATORY NOTES ON MAIN STATISTICAL INDICATORS

九、农　业
AGRICULTURE

统计图 …… (245)
CHARTS

9-1 农村基层组织情况 …… (246)
BASIC CONDITIONS OF RURAL GRASS-ROOTS UNITS

9-2 主要年份农林牧渔业总产值 …… (247)
GROSS OUTPUT VALUE OF FARMING, FORESTRY, ANIMAL HUSBANDRY AND FISHERY IN MAJOR YEARS

9-3 农林牧渔业总产值及增加值(按当年价格计算) …… (247)
GROSS OUTPUT VALUE AND VALUE ADDED OF FARMING, FORESTRY, ANIMAL HUSBANDRY AND FISHERY(AT CURRENT PRICE)

9-4 主要年份耕地情况 …… (248)
CULTIVATED AREA IN MAJOR YEARS

9-5 主要年份主要农作物播种面积 …… (248)
SOWN AREAS OF MAJOR FARM CROPS IN MAJOR YEARS

9-6 农作物播种面积 …… (249)
SOWN AREA OF FARM CROPS

9-7 主要年份主要农作物产量 …… (250)
OUTPUT OF MAJOR FARM CROPS IN MAJOR YEARS

9-8 主要年份主要油料作物产量 …… (251)
OUTPUT OF MAJOR OIL-BEARING CROPS IN MAJOR YEARS

9-9 主要年份主要农作物单位面积产量 …… (252)
MAJOR FARM CROPS OUTPUT PER HECTARE IN MAJOR YEARS

9-10 主要年份造林和果园面积 …… (253)
AREA OF AFFORESTATION AND ORCHARDS IN MAJOR YEARS

9-11 造林和果园面积 …… (253)
AREA OF AFFORESTATION AND ORCHARDS

9-12 主要林产品和水果产量 …… (254)
OUTPUT OF MAJOR FOREST PRODUCTS AND FRUITS

9-13 主要年份肉类产量和猪羊数量 …… (254)
OUTPUT OF MEAT AND NUMBER OF HOGS, SHEEP AND GOATS IN MAJOR YEARS

9-14 畜牧业生产情况 …… (255)
NUMBER OF LIVESTOCK AND LIVESTOCK PRODUCTS

9-15 渔业生产情况 …… (256)
PRODUCTION OF FISHERY

9-16 农业现代化情况 …… (256)
AGRICULTURAL MODERNIZATION

9-17 主要年份化肥施用量、小水电站和农村用电量 …… (257)
CONSUMPTION OF CHEMICAL FERTILIZER, NUMBER OF SMALL HYDROPOWER STATION AND ELECTRICITY CONSUMPTION IN RURAL AREAS IN MAJOR YEARS

9-18 农民家庭平均每户生产性固定资产原值 …… (258)
ORIGINAL VALUE OF PRODUCTIVE FIXED ASSETS PER RURAL HOUSEHOLD
9-19 农民家庭平均每百户拥有主要生产性固定资产数量 …… (259)
MAJOR PRODUCTIVE FIXED ASSETS PER 100 RURAL HOUSEHOLDS
9-20 农民家庭平均每人生产和销售的主要农林产品 …… (259)
PER CAPITA MAJOR FARM AND FOREST PRODUCTS PRODUCED AND SOLD BY RURAL HOUSEHOLDS
主要统计指标解释 …… (260)
EXPLANATORY NOTES ON MAIN STATISTICAL INDICATORS

十、工　业

INDUSTRY

统计图 …… (265)
CHARTS
10-1 主要年份工业企业单位数 …… (266)
NUMBER OF INDUSTRIAL ENTERPRISES IN MAJOR YEARS
10-2 主要年份主要工业产品产量 …… (267)
OUTPUT OF MAJOR INDUSTRIAL PRODUCTS IN MAJOR YEARS
10-3 规模以上主要工业产品产量 …… (269)
OUTPUT OF MAJOR INDUSTRIAL PRODUCTS ABOVE DESIGNATED SIZE
10-4 工业增加值(2016 年) …… (270)
VALVE ADDED OF INDUSTRY(2016)
10-5 工业企业主要经济指标(2016 年) …… (272)
MAIN ECONOMIC INDICATORS OF INDUSTRIAL ENTERPRISES(2016)
10-6 国有控股工业企业主要经济指标(2016 年) …… (290)
MAIN INDICATORS OF STATE-HOLDING INDUSTRIAL ENTERPRISES(2016)
10-7 外商投资和港澳台投资工业企业主要经济指标(2016 年) …… (302)
MAIN ECONOMIC INDICATORS OF INDUSTRIAL ENTERPRISES WITH HONG KONG, MACAO, TAIWAN AND FOREIGN FUNDS(2016)
10-8 大中型工业企业主要经济指标(2016 年) …… (314)
MAIN ECONOMIC INDICATORS OF LARGE AND MEDIUM-SIZE INDUSTRIAL ENTERPRISES(2016)
10-9 工业企业主要经济效益指标(2016 年) …… (332)
MAIN ECONOMIC BENEFIT INDICATORS OF INDUSTRIAL ENTERPRISES(2016)
10-10 国有控股工业企业主要经济效益指标(2016 年) …… (338)
MAIN ECONOMIC BENEFIT INDICATORS OF STATE-HOLDING INDUSTRIAL ENTERPRISES(2016)
10-11 外商投资和港澳台投资工业企业主要经济效益指标(2016 年) …… (342)
MAIN ECONOMIC BENEFIT INDICATORS OF INDUSTRIAL ENTERPRISES WITH HONG KONG, MACAO, TAIWAN AND FOREIGN FUNDS(2016)
10-12 大中型工业企业主要经济效益指标(2016 年) …… (346)
MAIN ECONOMIC BENEFIT INDICATORS OF LARGE AND MEDIUM-SIZE INDUSTRIAL ENTERPRISES (2016)
主要统计指标解释 …… (352)
EXPLANATORY NOTES ON MAIN STATISTICAL INDICATORS

十一、建筑业

CONSTRUCTION

统计图 ……………………………………………………………………………………………（359）

CHARTS

11-1 建筑施工企业主要经济指标 ……………………………………………………………（360）

MAJOR ECONOMIC INDICATORS OF CONSTRUCTION ENTERPRISES

11-2 建筑业企业总产值和竣工产值(2016 年)……………………………………………（361）

GROSS OUTPUT VALUE AND COMPLETED VALUE OF CONSTRUCTION ENTERPRISES(2016)

11-3 按主要用途分的房屋建筑竣工面积(2016 年)………………………………………（362）

FLOOR SPACE OF BUILDINGS COMPLETED BY MAJOR USE(2016)

11-4 按主要用途分的房屋建筑竣工价值(2016 年)………………………………………（364）

VALUE OF BUILDINGS COMPLETED BY MAJOR USE(2016)

11-5 建筑业企业房屋建筑面积(2016 年) ………………………………………………（366）

FLOOR SPACE OF BUILDINGS CONSTRUCTED BY CONSTRUCTION ENTERPRISES(2016)

11-6 建筑业企业机械设备情况(2016 年) ………………………………………………（367）

MACHINARY AND EQUIPMENT OF CONSTRUCTION ENTERPRISES(2016)

11-7 建筑业企业劳动生产率(2016 年) …………………………………………………（368）

LABOR PRODUCTIVITY OF CONSTRUCTION ENTERPRISES(2016)

11-8 建筑业企业资本金及资产(2016 年) ………………………………………………（369）

CAPITAL AND ASSETS OF CONSTRUCTION ENTERPRISES(2016)

11-9 建筑业企业负债及所有者权益(2016 年)……………………………………………（370）

LIABILITIES AND CREDITORS' EQUITY OF CONSTRUCTION ENTERPRISES(2016)

11-10 建筑业企业收入及成本情况(2016 年) ……………………………………………（371）

REVENUE AND COST OF CONSTRUCTION ENTERPRISES(2016)

11-11 建筑业企业费用情况(2016 年) ……………………………………………………（372）

EXPENSES OF CONSTRUCTION ENTERPRISES(2016)

11-12 建筑业企业薪酬及利润情况(2016 年) ……………………………………………（373）

REMUNERATION AND PROFITS OF CONSTRUCTION ENTERPRISES(2016)

11-13 建筑业企业利润及税金情况(2016 年) ……………………………………………（374）

PROFITS AND TAXES OF CONSTRUCTION ENTERPRISES(2016)

主要统计指标解释 ………………………………………………………………………（375）

EXPLANATORY NOTES ON MAIN STATISTICAL INDICATORS

十二、房地产

REAL ESTATE

统计图……………………………………………………………………………………………（381）

CHARTS

12-1 房地产开发企业主要指标 ……………………………………………………………（382）

MAJOR INDICATORS OF REAL ESTATE DEVELOPMENT ENTERPRISES

12-2 房地产开发企业完成投资 …… (383)
COMPLETED INVESTMENT OF REAL ESTATE ENTERPRISES
12-3 房地产开发企业施工、销售和待售情况(2016 年) …… (384)
BUILDINGS UNDER CONSTRUCTION, SELLING AND FOR SALE OF REAL ESTATE DEVELOPMENT ENTERPRISES(2016)
12-4 房地产开发企业投资完成情况(2016 年) …… (386)
COMPLETED INVESTMENT OF REAL ESTATE DEVELOPMENT ENTERPRISES(2016)
12-5 房地产开发企业资金来源情况(2016 年) …… (392)
SOURCE OF FUNDS FOR REAL ESTATE DEVELOPMENT ENTERPRISES(2016)
12-6 房地产开发企业土地购置、开发和待售情况(2016 年) …… (394)
LAND PURCHASING, DEVELOPING AND FOR SALE OF REAL ESTATE DEVELOPMENT ENTERPRISES(2016)
12-7 房地产开发企业施工和销售情况(2016 年) …… (396)
CONSTRUCTION AND SALES OF REAL ESTATE DEVELOPMENT ENTERPRISES(2016)
12-8 房地产开发企业财务状况(2016 年) …… (408)
FINANCIAL CONDITION OF REAL ESTATE DEVELOPMENT ENTERPRISES(2016)
主要统计指标解释 …… (414)
EXPLANATORY NOTES ON MAIN STATISTICAL INDICATORS

十三、批发和零售业

WHOLESALE AND RETAIL TRADE

统计图 …… (419)
CHARTS
13-1 主要年份社会消费品零售总额 …… (420)
TOTAL RETAIL SALES OF CONSUMER GOODS IN MAJOR YEARS
13-2 社会消费品零售总额 …… (421)
TOTAL RETAIL SALES OF CONSUMER GOODS
13-3 限额以上连锁批发零售业经营情况(2016 年) …… (421)
MANAGEMENT OF CHAIN ENTERPRISES ABOVE DESIGNATED SIZE IN WHOLESALE AND RETAIL TRADE(2016)
13-4 限额以上批发和零售业法人企业商品购销存情况(2016 年) …… (422)
TOTAL VALUE OF COMMODITIES' PURCHASING, SELLING AND INVENTORY OF CORPORATION ENTERPRISES ABOVE DESIGNATED SIZE IN WHOLESALE AND RETAIL TRADE(2016)
13-5 限额以上批发和零售业法人企业财务状况(2016 年) …… (438)
FINANCIAL CONDITION OF CORPORATION ENTERPRISES IN WHOLESALE AND RETAIL TRADE ABOVE DESIGNATED SIZE(2016)
13-6 限额以上批发零售业商品销售类值(2016 年) …… (470)
SALES VALUE OF ENTERPRISES ABOVE DESIGNATED SIZE IN WHOLESALE AND RETAIL TRADE BY CATEGORY OF COMMODITIES(2016)
13-7 亿元以上商品交易市场基本情况(2016 年) …… (472)
BASIC STATISTICS ON COMMODITY EXCHANGE MARKETS OF TRANSACTION VOLUME OVER 100 MILLION YUAN(2016)

13-8 亿元以上商品交易市场按摊位分类成交情况(2016 年) (473)
CLASSIFICATION OF COMMODITY EXCAHNGE MARKETS OF TRANSACTION VOLUME OVER 100 MILLION YUAN(2016)
13-9 私营企业基本情况(2016 年) (474)
BASIC STATISTICS ON PRIVATE-OWNED ENTERPRISES(2016)
13-10 个体工商业基本情况(2016 年) (475)
BASIC STATISTICS ON INDIVIDUAL BUSSINESS(2016)
主要统计指标解释 (476)
EXPLANATORY NOTES ON MAIN STATISTICAL INDICATORS

十四、住宿、餐饮业和旅游

HOTELS, CATERING SERVICES AND TOURISM

统计图 (481)
CHARTS
14-1 限额以上住宿和餐饮业法人企业经营情况(2016 年) (482)
MANAGEMENT OF HOTELS AND CATERING CORPORATION ENTERPRISES ABOVE DESIGNATED SIZE (2016)
14-2 限额以上住宿和餐饮业法人企业主要财务状况(2016 年) (490)
FINANCIAL CONDITION OF HOTELS AND CATERING CORPORATION ENTERPRISES ABOVE DESIGNATED SIZE(2016)
14-3 限额以上连锁住宿餐饮业经营情况(2016 年) (506)
MANAGEMENT OF CHAIN ENTERPRISES ABOVE DESIGNATED SIZE IN HOTELS AND CATERING SERVICES(2016)
14-4 主要年份旅游接待人数 (506)
NUMBER OF TOURISTS IN MAJOR YEARS
14-5 主要年份旅游收入 (507)
TOTAL INCOME OF TOURISM IN MAJOR YEARS
14-6 旅游外汇收入(2016 年) (507)
FOREIGN EXCHANGE EARNINGS FROM INTERNATIONAL TOURISM(2016)
14-7 旅游四星级以上饭店(2016 年) (508)
TOURIST HOTELS ABOVE FOUR STAR GRADE(2016)
主要统计指标解释 (511)
EXPLANATORY NOTES ON MAIN STATISTICAL INDICATORS

十五、交通运输、邮电通信业

TRANSPORTATION, POST AND TELECOMMUNICATION SERVICES

统计图 (515)
CHARTS
15-1 主要年份运输线路长度 (516)
LENGTH OF TRANSPORT ROUTES IN MAJOR YEARS

15-2 主要年份货运量 …… (516)
FREIGHT TRAFFIC IN MAJOR YEARS
15-3 主要年份货物周转量 …… (517)
TURNOVER VOLUME OF FREIGHT TRAFFIC IN MAJOR YEARS
15-4 主要年份旅客运输量和周转量 …… (517)
PASSENGER TRAFFIC AND TURNOVER VOLUME IN MAJOR YEARS
15-5 主要年份民用汽车拥有量 …… (518)
NUMBER OF CIVIL MOTOR VEHICLES IN MAJOR YEARS
15-6 民用汽车拥有量(2016 年) …… (518)
NUMBER OF CIVIL MOTOR VEHICLES(2016)
15-7 民用航空航线(2016 年) …… (519)
CIVIL AVIATION ROUTES(2016)
15-8 国家铁路分货类运输量(2016 年) …… (521)
NATIONAL RAILWAY FREIGHT TRAFFIC BY CATEGORY OF CARGO(2016)
15-9 地方铁路营运概况(2016 年) …… (522)
BASIC STATISTICS ON LOCAL RAILWAYS(2016)
15-10 邮电业务总量(2016 年) …… (523)
BUSINESS VOLUME OF POST AND TELECOMMUNICATION SERVICES(2016)
15-11 主要年份邮电通信网 …… (524)
NETWORK OF POST AND TELECOMMUNICATION IN MAJOR YEARS
15-12 邮政邮路 …… (524)
POSTAL ROUTES
15-13 邮政局所、房屋、服务点 …… (525)
NUMBER OF POSTAL OFFICES, BUILDINGS AND SERVICE PLACES
主要统计指标解释 …… (526)
EXPLANATORY NOTES ON MAIN STATISTICAL INDICATORS

十六、教育、科技

EDUCATION, SCIENCE AND TECHNOLOGY

统计图 …… (531)
CHARTS
16-1 主要年份各类学校数 …… (532)
SCHOOLS BY LEVEL IN MAJOR YEARS
16-2 主要年份各类学校专任教师数 …… (532)
NUMBER OF FULL-TIME TEACHERS BY LEVEL OF SCHOOL IN MAJOR YEARS
16-3 主要年份各类学校在校学生数 …… (533)
STUDENTS ENROLLMENT BY LEVEL OF SCHOOL IN MAJOR YEARS
16-4 主要年份各类学校招生数 …… (533)
NEW STUDENTS ENROLLMENT BY LEVEL OF SCHOOL IN MAJOR YEARS
16-5 主要年份各类学校毕业生数 …… (534)
GRADUATES BY LEVEL OF SCHOOL IN MAJOR YEARS

16-6 普通本科分形式、分学科学生数(2016 年)……（534）
STUDENTS OF REGULAR UNDERGRADUATE COURSES BY FORM AND BY FIELD OF STUDY(2016)
16-7 主要年份研究生数……（535）
NUMBER OF POSTGRADUATES IN MAJOR YEARS
16-8 研究生数(2016 年)……（535）
NUMBER OF POSTGRADUATES(2016)
16-9 高等教育学校学生数(2016 年)……（536）
NUMBER OF STUDENTS IN HIGHER EDUCATION INSTITUTIONS(2016)
16-10 普通高校分类别专任教师数(2016 年)……（538）
FULL-TIME TEACHERS OF HIGHER EDUCATION INSTITUTIONS BY TYPE(2016)
16-11 普通高校分科专任教师数(2016 年)……（539）
FULL-TIME TEACHERS OF HIGHER EDUCATION INSTITUTIONS BY FIELD OF STUDY(2016)
16-12 中等职业教育分科类学生情况(2016 年)……（539）
STUDENTS IN SECONDARY VOCATIONAL EDUCATION BY FIELD OF STUDY(2016)
16-13 普通中学学校数、班数(2016 年)……（540）
NUMBER OF REGULAR SECONDARY SCHOOLS AND CLASSES(2016)
16-14 普通中学学生数(2016 年)……（541）
STUDENTS OF REGULAR SECONDARY SCHOOLS(2016)
16-15 中学学校教职工数(2016 年)……（542）
TEACHERS AND STAFF OF SECONDARY SCHOOLS(2016)
16-16 职业高中分科类学生数(2016 年)……（543）
STUDENTS OF VOCATIONAL HIGH SCHOOLS BY FIELD OF STUDY(2016)
16-17 职业高中分课程专任教师数……（544）
FULL-TIME TEACHERS OF VOCATIONAL HIGH SCHOOLS BY COURSE OF STUDY
16-18 小学学生情况(2016 年)……（545）
BASIC STATISTICS ON PRIMARY SCHOOLS(2016)
16-19 小学学校教职工数(2016 年)……（546）
TEACHERS AND STAFF OF PRIMARY SCHOOLS(2016)
16-20 小学学龄人口入学率(2016 年)……（547）
RATE OF SCHOOL-AGED CHILDREN ENROLLMENT(2016)
16-21 主要年份幼儿园基本情况……（547）
BASIC STATISTICS ON KINDERGARTENS IN MAJOR YEARS
16-22 幼儿园基本情况(2016 年)……（548）
BASIC STATISTICS ON KINDERGARTENS(2016)
16-23 特殊教育学校基本情况(2016 年)……（549）
BASIC STATISTICS ON SPECIAL EDUCATION SCHOOLS(2016)
16-24 科学研究机构及人员(2016 年)……（550）
INSTITUTIONS AND PERSONNELS OF SCIENTIFIC RESEARCH(2016)
16-25 主要年份县级以上自然科学研究与技术开发机构数……（551）
NATURAL SCIENTIFIC RESEARCH AND TECHNOLOGICAL DEVELOPMENT INSTITUTIONS AT COUNTY LEVEL AND ABOVE IN MAJOR YEARS
16-26 县级以上自然科学研究与技术开发机构人员数(2016 年)……（551）
PERSONNELS OF NATURAL SCIENTIFIC RESEARCH AND TECHNOLOGICAL DEVELOPMENT INSTITUTIONS AT COUNTY LEVEL AND ABOVE(2016)

16-27 主要年份自然科学技术人员数 ……………………………………………… (552)
PERSONNELS OF NATURAL SCIENCE AND TECHNOLOGY IN MAJOR YEARS
16-28 省科学技术协会及所属学会工作情况(2016 年) ……………………………………… (553)
PROVINCIAL SCIENCE AND TECHNOLOGY ASSOCIATION AND ITS BRANCHES(2016)
16-29 规模以上工业企业的科技活动基本情况 ……………………………………… (554)
BASIC STATISTICS ON SCIENCE AND TECHNOLOGY ACTIVITIES OF INDUSTRIAL ENTERPRISES ABOVE DESIGNATED SIZE
16-30 按登记注册类型分规模以上工业企业研究与试验发展(R&D)活动及专利情况(2016 年) ……… (555)
STATISTICS ON R&D ACTIVITIES AND PATENTS OF INDUSTRIAL ENTERPRISES ABOVE DESIGNATED SIZE BY REGISTRATION STATUS(2016)
16-31 按行业分规模以上工业企业研究与试验发展(R&D)活动及专利情况(2016 年) ……… (556)
STATISTICS ON R&D ACTIVITIES AND PATENTS OF INDUSTRIAL ENTERPRISES ABOVE DE SIGNATED SIZE BY INDUSTRIAL SECTOR(2016)
16-32 按登记注册类型分规模以上工业企业新产品开发及生产情况(2016 年) ……… (558)
NEW PRODUCTS DEVELOPMENT AND PRODUCTION OF INDUSTRIAL ENTERPRISES ABOVE DESIGNATED SIZE BY REGISTRATION STATUS(2016)
16-33 按行业分规模以上工业企业新产品开发及生产情况(2016 年) ……… (559)
NEW PRODUCTS DEVELOPMENT AND PRODUCTION OF INDUSTRIAL ENTERPRISES ABOVE DESIGNATED SIZE BY INDUSTRIAL SECTOR(2016)
主要统计指标解释 ……………………………………………… (562)
EXPLANATORY NOTES ON MAIN STATISTICAL INDICATORS

十七、文化、体育、卫生、环保

CULTURE, SPORTS, PUBLIC HEALTH AND ENVIRONMENTAL PROTECTION

统计图 ……………………………………………… (567)
CHARTS
17-1 主要年份广播、电视台(站)数 ……………………………………… (568)
NUMBER OF RADIO AND TELEVISION STATIONS IN MAJOR YEARS
17-2 文化艺术机构和人员数(2016 年) ……………………………………… (568)
INSTITUTIONS AND PERSONNELS OF CULTURE AND ART(2016)
17-3 主要年份广播剧、电视剧、电影故事片制作情况 ……………………………… (569)
PRODUCTION OF RADIO PLAYS, TELEVISION PLAYS AND FEATURE FILMS IN MAJOR YEARS
17-4 主要年份国有文化艺术、文物单位数 ……………………………… (569)
INSTITUTION NUMBER OF STATE-OWNED CULTURE, ART AND CULTURAL RELICS IN MAJOR YEARS
17-5 国有艺术表演团体演出情况(2016 年) ……………………………… (570)
PERFORMANCE OF STATE-OWNED ART TROUPES(2016)
17-6 国有艺术表演团体收入和支出(2016 年) ……………………………… (570)
REVENUE AND EXPENDITURE OF STATE-OWNED ART TROUPES(2016)
17-7 群众艺术馆、文化馆(站)业务活动及经费(2016 年) ……………………… (571)
ACTIVITIES AND FUNDS OF MASS ART CENTERS AND CULTURAL CENTERS(2016)
17-8 公共图书馆业务活动及经费(2016 年) ……………………………… (571)
ACTIVITIES AND FUNDS OF PUBLIC LIBRARIES(2016)

17-9 出版发行、文物、图书馆、群众文化事业机构和人员数(2016 年) …… (572)
INSTITUTIONS AND PERSONNELS OF PUBLISHING, CULTURAL RELICS, LIBRARY AND MASS CULTURE(2016)
17-10 博物馆、文物机构业务活动及经费(2016 年) …… (572)
ACTIVITIES AND FUNDS OF MUSEUMS AND CULTURAL RELICS INSTITUTIONS(2016)
17-11 主要年份图书、期刊和报纸总印数 …… (573)
TOTAL PRINTED COPIES OF BOOKS, MAGAZINES AND NEWSPAPERS IN MAJOR YEARS
17-12 体育局系统从业人员数(2016 年) …… (574)
EMPLOYEES OF SPORTS BUREAU(2016)
17-13 体育场地情况(2016 年) …… (575)
STATISTICS ON SPORTS GROUND(2016)
17-14 主要年份体育场地数 …… (576)
STADIUMS AND GYMNASIUMS IN MAJOR YEARS
17-15 分项目等级运动员发展人数(2016 年) …… (577)
CERTIFIED ATHLETES BY TYPE OF SPORTS(2016)
17-16 分项目等级裁判员发展人数(2016 年) …… (578)
CERTIFIED REFEREES BY TYPE OF SPORTS(2016)
17-17 主要年份运动员打破纪录情况 …… (579)
RECORDS BROKEN BY ATHLETES IN MAJOR YEARS
17-18 体育彩票、福利彩票发行情况 …… (579)
ISSUE OF SPORTS LOTTERY AND WELFARE LOTTERY
17-19 主要年份卫生机构数 …… (580)
HEALTH CARE INSTITUTIONS IN MAJOR YEARS
17-20 主要年份卫生机构床位数 …… (581)
NUMBER OF BEDS IN HEALTH CARE INSTITUTIONS IN MAJOR YEARS
17-21 主要年份卫生技术人员数 …… (581)
NUMBER OF MEDICAL TECHNICAL PERSONNELS IN MAJOR YEARS
17-22 卫生机构、床位、人员数(2016 年) …… (582)
INSTITUTIONS, BEDS AND PERSONNELS IN HEALTH CARE INSTITUTIONS(2016)
17-23 卫生机构分类人员数 …… (584)
NUMBER OF PERSONNELS IN HEALTH CARE INSTITUTIONS BY CATEGORY
17-24 医疗机构医疗服务量情况(2016 年) …… (585)
SERVICES QUANTITY IN HEALTH CARE INSTITUTIONS(2016)
17-25 公证工作和调解 …… (585)
STATISTICS ON NOTARIZATION AND MEDIATION
17-26 律师工作 …… (586)
STATISTICS ON LAWYERS
17-27 主要年份婚姻登记数 …… (586)
MARRIAGE REGISTRATION IN MAJOR YEARS
17-28 妇联组织状况(2016 年) …… (587)
WOMEN'S FEDERATION ORGANIZATION(2016)
17-29 全省工业企业“三废”排放与治理情况 …… (587)
DISCHARGE AND TREATMENT OF WASTE WATER, WASTE GAS AND SOLID WASTES BY INDUSTRIAL ENTERPRISES

主要统计指标解释 ······ (588)
EXPLANATORY NOTES ON MAIN STATISTICAL INDICATORS

十八、城市概况

GENERAL SURVEY OF CITIES

18-1 地级城市主要经济指标(2016 年) ······ (593)
MAJOR ECONOMIC INDICATORS OF CITIES AT PREFECTURE LEVEL(2016)
18-2 地级城市公用事业及设施水平(2016 年) ······ (601)
LEVEL OF PUBLIC FACILITIES IN CITIES AT PREFECTURE LEVEL(2016)
主要统计指标解释 ······ (605)
EXPLANATORY NOTES ON MAIN STATISTICAL INDICATORS

十九、地市篇

CITIES AT PREFECTURE LEVEL

19-1 国民经济核算主要指标(2016 年) ······ (609)
MAJOR INDICATORS OF NATIONAL ECONOMIC ACCOUNTING(2016)
19-2 国民经济核算主要指标指数(2016 年) ······ (610)
INDICES OF MAJOR INDICATORS OF NATIONAL ECONOMIC ACCOUNTING(2016)
19-3 基本单位数(2016 年) ······ (612)
NUMBER OF BASIC UNITS (2016)
19-4 按登记注册类型分基本单位数(2016 年) ······ (612)
NUMBER OF BASIC UNITS BY REGISTRATION STATUS(2016)
19-5 按产业分基本单位数及从业人数(2016 年) ······ (613)
NUMBER OF BASIC UNITS AND EMPLOYEES BY INDUSTRY(2016)
19-6 按行业分法人单位数(2016 年) ······ (614)
NUMBER OF CORPORATION UNITS BY SECTOR(2016)
19-7 总户数、常住人口数(2016 年) ······ (616)
NUMBER OF HOUSEHOLDS AND RESIDENT POPULATION(2016)
19-8 城镇人口增加来源(2016 年) ······ (616)
INCREASE SOURCES OF URBAN POPULATION(2016)
19-9 非私营单位从业人员(2016 年) ······ (617)
NUMBER OF EMPLOYEES IN NON-PRIVATE UNITS(2016)
19-10 非私营单位从业人员劳动报酬(2016 年) ······ (617)
REWARD OF EMPLOYEES IN NON-PRIVATE UNITS(2016)
19-11 国有单位从业人员(2016 年) ······ (618)
NUMBER OF EMPLOYEES IN STATE-OWNED UNITS(2016)
19-12 国有单位从业人员劳动报酬(2016 年) ······ (618)
REWARD OF EMPLOYEES IN STATE-OWNED UNITS(2016)
19-13 城镇集体单位从业人员(2016 年) ······ (619)
NUMBER OF EMPLOYEES IN URBAN COLLECTIVE-OWNED UNITS(2016)

19-14　集体单位从业人员劳动报酬(2016 年) ………………………………………………………… (619)
REWARD OF EMPLOYEES IN COLLECTIVE-OWNED UNITS(2016)
19-15　其他单位从业人员(2016 年)………………………………………………………… (620)
NUMBER OF EMPLOYEES IN OTHER-OWNED UNITS(2016)
19-16　其他单位从业人员劳动报酬(2016 年) ………………………………………………………… (620)
REWARD OF EMPLOYEES IN OTHER-OWNED UNITS(2016)
19-17　私营单位从业人员和劳动报酬(2016 年) ………………………………………………………… (621)
NUMBER AND REWARD OF EMPLOYEES IN PRIVATE UNITS(2016)
19-18　居民家庭生活基本情况(2016 年)………………………………………………………… (621)
BASIC LIVING CONDITIONS OF HOUSEHOLDS(2016)
19-19　财政收支情况(2016 年) ………………………………………………………… (622)
FINANCIAL REVENUE AND EXPENDITURE(2016)
19-20　金融机构本外币各项存款和贷款余额(2016 年)………………………………………………………… (623)
BALANCE OF DEPOSITS AND LOANS IN FINANCIAL INSTITUTIONS(2016)
19-21　原保险保费收入(2016 年) ………………………………………………………… (624)
PREMIUM OF PRIMARY INSURANCE(2016)
19-22　单位地区生产总值能源消耗(等价值)情况………………………………………………………… (624)
ENERGY CONSUMPTION PER UNIT OF GDP(EQUIVALENT VALUE)
19-23　固定资产投资主要指标(2016 年)………………………………………………………… (625)
MAJOR INDICATORS OF INVESTMENT IN FIXED ASSETS(2016)
19-24　固定资产投资房屋面积(2016 年)………………………………………………………… (626)
FLOOR SPACE OF BUILDINGS UNDER INVESTMENT IN FIXED ASSETS(2016)
19-25　海关进出口情况………………………………………………………… (627)
IMPORTS AND EXPORTS OF CUSTOMS
19-26　利用外商直接投资额………………………………………………………… (627)
UTILIZATION OF FOREIGN DIRECT INVESTMENT
19-27　乡村基本情况(2016 年) ………………………………………………………… (628)
BASIC CONDITIONS OF RURAL AREAS (2016)
19-28　农林牧渔业总产值(2016 年)………………………………………………………… (629)
GROSS OUTPUT VALUE OF FARMING, FORESTRY, ANIMAL HUSBANDRY AND FISHERY(2016)
19-29　农林牧渔业中间消耗(2016 年)………………………………………………………… (629)
INTERMEDIATE CONSUMPTION OF FARMING, FORESTRY, ANIMAL HUSBANDRY AND FISHERY(2016)
19-30　粮食播种面积 ………………………………………………………… (630)
SOWN AREAS OF GRAIN
19-31　油料和棉花播种面积………………………………………………………… (630)
SOWN AREAS OF OIL-BEARING CROPS AND COTTON
19-32　粮食产量 ………………………………………………………… (631)
OUTPUT OF GRAIN
19-33　油料和棉花产量………………………………………………………… (631)
OUTPUT OF OIL-BEARING CROPS AND COTTON
19-34　水果、林业及渔业生产情况(2016 年) ………………………………………………………… (632)
OUTPUT OF FRUITS, FORESTRY AND FISHERY(2016)
19-35　畜牧业生产情况(2016 年) ………………………………………………………… (633)
NUMBER OF LIVESTOCK AND LIVESTOCK PRODUCTS(2016)

19-36 农业生产条件(2016 年) …… (634)
CONDITIONS OF AGRICULTURAL PRODUCTION(2016)
19-37 规模以上主要工业产品产量(2016 年) …… (635)
OUTPUT OF MAJOR INDUSTRIAL PRODUCTS OF ENTERPRISES ABOVE DESIGNATED SIZE(2016)
19-38 工业企业主要经济指标(2016 年) …… (637)
MAIN ECONOMIC INDICATORS OF INDUSTRIAL ENTERPRISES(2016)
19-39 国有控股工业企业主要经济指标(2016 年) …… (640)
MAIN ECONOMIC INDICATORS OF STATE-HOLDING INDUSTRIAL ENTERPRISES(2016)
19-40 外商投资和港澳台投资工业企业主要经济指标(2016 年) …… (643)
MAIN INDICATORS OF INDUSTRIAL ENTERPRISES WITH HONG KONG, MACAO, TAIWAN AND FOREIGN FUNDS(2016)
19-41 大中型工业企业主要经济指标(2016 年) …… (646)
MAIN ECONOMIC INDICATORS OF LARGE AND MEDIUM-SIZE INDUSTRIAL ENTERPRISES(2016)
19-42 建筑业企业总产值和竣工产值(2016 年) …… (649)
GROSS OUTPUT VALUE AND COMPLETED VALUE OF CONSTRUCTION ENTERPRISES(2016)
19-43 按主要用途分的房屋建筑竣工面积(2016 年) …… (649)
FLOOR SPACE OF BUILDINGS COMPLETED BY MAJOR USE(2016)
19-44 按主要用途分的房屋建筑竣工价值(2016 年) …… (650)
VALUE OF BUILDINGS COMPLETED BY MAJOR USE(2016)
19-45 建筑业企业房屋建筑面积(2016 年) …… (650)
FLOOR SPACE OF BUILDINGS CONSTRUCTED BY CONSTRUCTION ENTERPRISES(2016)
19-46 建筑业企业机械设备情况(2016 年) …… (651)
MACHINARY AND EQUIPMENT OF CONSTRUCTION ENTERPRISES(2016)
19-47 建筑业企业劳动生产率(2016 年) …… (651)
LABOR PRODUCTIVITY OF CONSTRUCTION ENTERPRISES(2016)
19-48 建筑业企业负债及所有者权益(2016 年) …… (652)
LIABILITIES AND CREDITORS' EQUITY OF CONSTRUCTION ENTERPRISES(2016)
19-49 建筑业企业收入及成本情况(2016 年) …… (652)
REVENUE AND COST OF CONSTRUCTION ENTERPRISES(2016)
19-50 建筑业企业资产(2016 年) …… (653)
ASSETS OF CONSTRUCTION ENTERPRISES(2016)
19-51 建筑业企业费用情况(2016 年) …… (654)
EXPENSES OF CONSTRUCTION ENTERPRISES(2016)
19-52 建筑业企业薪酬及利润情况(2016 年) …… (654)
REMUNERTION AND PROFITS OF CONSTRUCTION ENTERPRISES(2016)
19-53 建筑业企业利润及税金情况(2016 年) …… (655)
PROFITS AND TAXES OF CONSTRUCTION ENTERPRISES(2016)
19-54 房地产开发投资(2016 年) …… (655)
INVESTMENT IN REAL ESTATE DEVELOPMENT(2016)
19-55 房地产开发房屋销售额(2016 年) …… (656)
SALES OF BUILDINGS IN REAL ESTATE DEVELOPMENT(2016)
19-56 房地产开发房屋销售面积(2016 年) …… (657)
FLOOR SPACE OF BUILDINGS SOLD IN REAL ESTATE DEVELOPMENT(2016)

19-57 房地产开发施工、竣工面积及价值(2016 年)…………………………………………………………(658)
FLOOR SPACE AND VALUE OF BUILDINGS UNDER CONSTRUCTION AND COMPLETED IN REAL ESTATE DEVELOPMENT(2016)
19-58 社会消费品零售总额(2016 年)…………………………………………………………(658)
TOTAL RETAIL SALES OF CONSUMER GOODS(2016)
19-59 旅游事业发展情况(2016 年)…………………………………………………………(659)
DEVELOPMENT OF TOURISM(2016)
19-60 公路通车里程(2016 年)…………………………………………………………(659)
LENGTH OF HIGHWAYS(2016)
19-61 公路等级里程(2016 年)…………………………………………………………(660)
LENGTH OF HIGHWAYS BY CLASS(2016)
19-62 公路路面里程(2016 年)…………………………………………………………(660)
LENGTH OF PAVED HIGHWAYS(2016)
19-63 公路绿化里程(2016 年)…………………………………………………………(661)
LENGTH OF AFFOREST HIGHWAYS(2016)
19-64 公路客货运输量(2016 年)…………………………………………………………(661)
HIGHWAY PASSENGER AND FREIGHT TRAFFIC(2016)
19-65 镇(乡)村通公路、通油路情况(2016 年)…………………………………………………………(662)
TRAFFIC CONNECTION OF TOWNS, TOWNSHIPS AND VILLAGES(2016)
19-66 邮电业务总量及电话数(2016 年)…………………………………………………………(663)
BUSINESS VOLUME OF POST AND TELECOMMUNICATION SERVICES AND NUMBER OF TELEPHONE SUBSCRIBERS(2016)
19-67 小学基本情况(2016 年)…………………………………………………………(663)
BASIC STATISTICS ON PRIMARY SCHOOLS(2016)
19-68 普通中学基本情况(2016 年)…………………………………………………………(664)
BASIC STATISTICS ON REGULAR SECONDARY SCHOOLS(2016)
19-69 村卫生室情况(2016 年)…………………………………………………………(665)
MAIN INDICATORS OF RURAL CLINICS (2016)
19-70 卫生机构数(2016 年)…………………………………………………………(666)
HEALTH CARE INSTITUTIONS(2016)
19-71 卫生机构床位数和人员情况(2016 年)…………………………………………………………(666)
BEDS AND PERSONNELS IN HEALTH CARE INSTITUTIONS(2016)
19-72 主要城市空气质量情况 (2016 年)…………………………………………………………(667)
AIR QUALITY IN MAJOR CITIES(2016)

二十、县(市、区)篇

COUNTIES, CITIES AND DISTRICTS AT COUNTY LEVEL

20-1 常住人口数(2016 年)…………………………………………………………(671)
RESIDENT POPULATION(2016)
20-2 非私营单位从业人员和在岗职工工资(2016 年)…………………………………………………………(674)
NUMBER OF EMPLOYEES AND WAGE OF FULLY EMPLOYED STAFF AND WORKERS IN NON-PRIVATE UNITS(2016)

20-3 地区生产总值(2016 年) …… (680)
GROSS DOMESTIC PRODUCT(2016)
20-4 城乡居民收入(2016 年) …… (683)
INCOME OF URBAN AND RURAL HOUSEHOLDS(2016)
20-5 财政收支情况(2016 年) …… (686)
FINANCIAL REVENUE AND EXPENDITURE(2016)
20-6 固定资产投资 …… (689)
INVESTMENT IN FIXED ASSETS
20-7 乡村基本情况(2016 年) …… (692)
BASIC CONDITIONS OF RURAL AREAS(2016)
20-8 农林牧渔业总产值(2016 年) …… (698)
GROSS OUTPUT VALUE OF FARMING, FORESTRY, ANIMAL HUSBANDRY AND FISHERY(2016)
20-9 农林牧渔业中间消耗(2016 年) …… (701)
INTERMEDIATE CONSUMPTION OF FARMING, FORESTRY, ANIMAL HUSBANDRY AND FISHERY(2016)
20-10 主要粮食作物播种面积(2016 年) …… (704)
SOWN AREAS OF MAJOR GRAIN CROPS(2016)
20-11 主要粮食作物产量(2016 年) …… (710)
OUTPUT OF MAJOR GRAIN CROPS(2016)
20-12 棉花生产基本情况(2016 年) …… (716)
BASIC STATISTICS ON COTTON PRODUCTION(2016)
20-13 油料生产基本情况(2016 年) …… (717)
BASIC STATISTICS ON OIL-BEARING CROPS(2016)
20-14 药材、蔬菜、瓜果生产情况(2016 年) …… (720)
PRODUCTION OF MEDICINAL MATERIALS, VEGETABLES AND MELONS(2016)
20-15 农业生产条件(2016 年) …… (723)
CONDITIONS OF AGRICULTURAL PRODUCTION(2016)
20-16 畜牧业生产情况(2016 年) …… (726)
NUMBER OF LIVESTOCK AND LIVESTOCK PRODUCTS(2016)
20-17 水果、林业及渔业生产情况(2016 年) …… (732)
PRODUCTION OF FRUITS, FORESTRY AND FISHERY(2016)
20-18 社会消费品零售总额(2016 年) …… (735)
TOTAL RETAIL SALES OF CONSUMER GOODS(2016)
20-19 工业主要指标(2016 年) …… (738)
MAJOR INDUSTRIAL INDICATORS(2016)

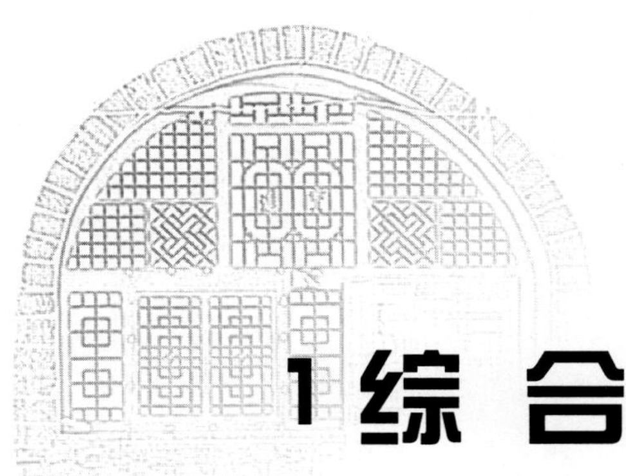

1 综　合

GENERAL SURVEY

资料整理人员

樊梅洁　李　静　田　甜　高春堂　贺彩虹　张淑虹

综　合
GENERAL SURVEY

地区生产总值	Gross Domestic Product	12966.2	亿元	(100 million yuan)
第一产业	Primary Industry	784.8	亿元	(100 million yuan)
第二产业	Secondary Industry	4963.3	亿元	(100 million yuan)
第三产业	Tertiary Industry	7218.1	亿元	(100 million yuan)

地区生产总值构成(%)
Composition of Gross Domestic Product (%)

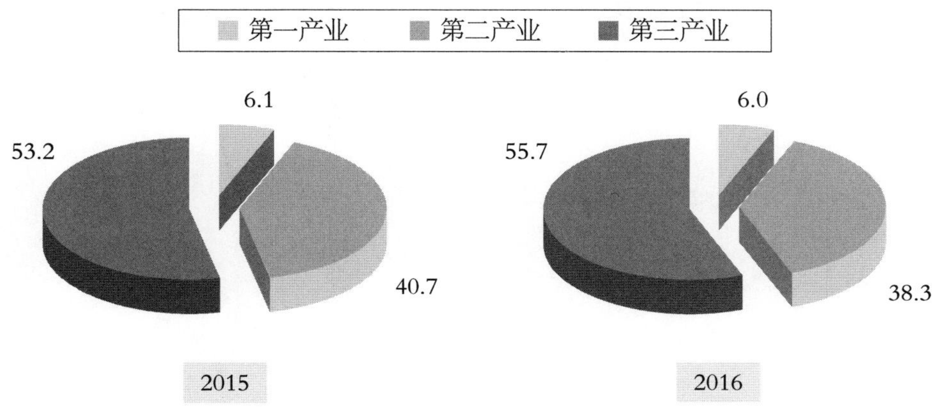

地区生产总值(亿元)
Gross Domestic Product (100 million yuan)

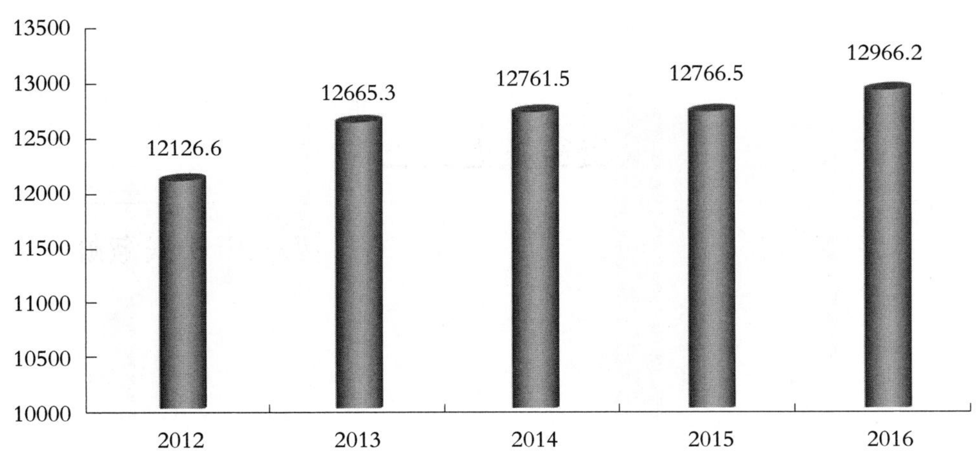

综　合
GENERAL SURVEY

人均地区生产总值	Per Capita Gross Domestic Product	35303	元	(yuan)
支出法地区生产总值	Gross Domestic Product by Expenditure Approach	12966.2	亿元	(100 million yuan)
最终消费	Final Consumption Expenditure	7454.7	亿元	(100 million yuan)
资本形成总额	Gross Capital Formation	9371.7	亿元	(100 million yuan)
货物和服务净出口	Net Export of Goods and Services	-3860.2	亿元	(100 million yuan)

支出法地区生产总值构成（%）

Composition of Gross Domestic Product by Expenditure Approach (%)

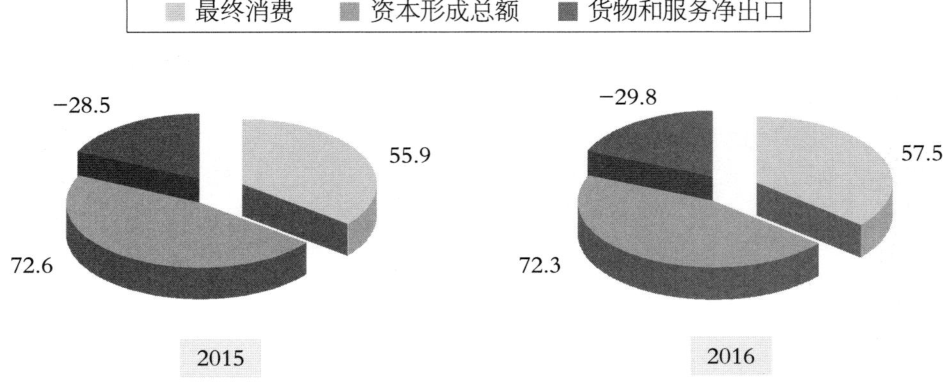

人均地区生产总值（元）

Per Capita Gross Domestic Product (yuan)

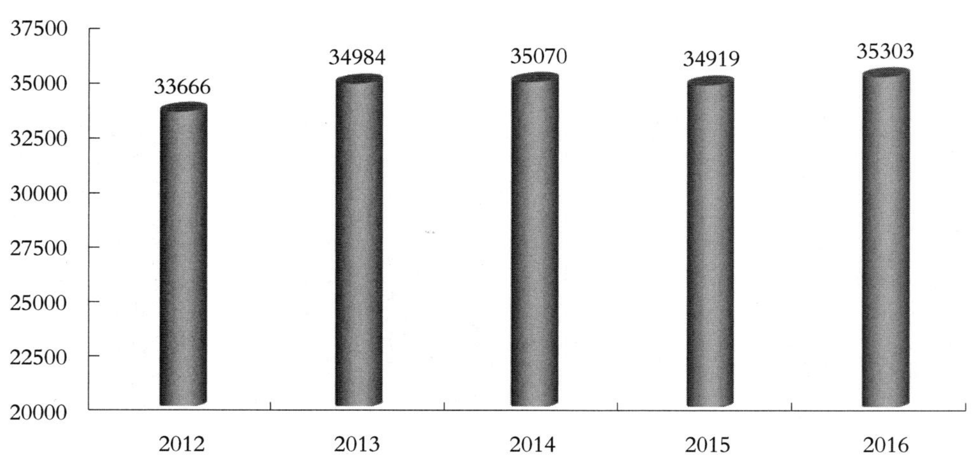

1-1 行政区划(2016年)

ADMINISTRATIVE DIVISION(2016)

市 名 City	城 市 City			市辖区 District under Jurisdiction of Cities	县 County	镇 Town	乡 Township
	合 计 Total	地级市 City at Prefecture Level	县级市 City at County Level				
	22	11	11	23	85	564	632

市 名 City	区、县、市
太原市 Taiyuan	小店区 Xiaodian　迎泽区 Yingze　杏花岭区 Xinghualing　尖草坪区 Jiancaoping　万柏林区 Wanbailin　晋源区 Jinyuan　清徐县 Qingxu　阳曲县 Yangqu　娄烦县 Loufan　古交市 Gujiao
大同市 Datong	城　区 Chengqu　矿　区 Kuangqu　南郊区 Nanjiao　新荣区 Xinrong　阳高县 Yanggao　天镇县 Tianzhen　广灵县 Guangling　灵丘县 Lingqiu　浑源县 Hunyuan　左云县 Zuoyun　大同县 Datong
阳泉市 Yangquan	城　区 Chengqu　矿　区 Kuangqu　郊　区 Jiaoqu　平定县 Pingding　盂　县 Yuxian
长治市 Changzhi	城　区 Chengqu　郊　区 Jiaoqu　长治县 Changzhi　襄垣县 Xiangyuan　屯留县 Tunliu　平顺县 Pingshun　黎城县 Licheng　壶关县 Huguan　长子县 Zhangzi　武乡县 Wuxiang　沁　县 Qinxian　沁源县 Qinyuan　潞城市 Lucheng
晋城市 Jincheng	城　区 Chengqu　沁水县 Qinshui　阳城县 Yangcheng　陵川县 Lingchuan　泽州县 Zezhou　高平市 Gaoping
朔州市 Shuozhou	朔城区 Shuocheng　平鲁区 Pinglu　山阴县 Shanyin　应　县 Yingxian　右玉县 Youyu　怀仁县 Huairen
晋中市 Jinzhong	榆次区 Yuci　榆社县 Yushe　左权县 Zuoquan　和顺县 Heshun　昔阳县 Xiyang　寿阳县 Shouyang　太谷县 Taigu　祁　县 Qixian　平遥县 Pingyao　灵石县 Lingshi　介休市 Jiexiu
运城市 Yuncheng	盐湖区 Yanhu　临猗县 Linyi　万荣县 Wanrong　闻喜县 Wenxi　稷山县 Jishan　新绛县 Xinjiang　绛　县 Jiangxian　垣曲县 Yuanqu　夏　县 Xiaxian　平陆县 Pinglu　芮城县 Ruicheng　永济市 Yongji　河津市 Hejin
忻州市 Xinzhou	忻府区 Xinfu　定襄县 Dingxiang　五台县 Wutai　代　县 Daixian　繁峙县 Fanshi　宁武县 Ningwu　静乐县 Jingle　神池县 Shenchi　五寨县 Wuzhai　岢岚县 Kelan　河曲县 Hequ　保德县 Baode　偏关县 Pianguan　原平市 Yuanping
临汾市 Linfen	尧都区 Yaodu　曲沃县 Quwo　翼城县 Yicheng　襄汾县 Xiangfen　洪洞县 Hongtong　古　县 Guxian　安泽县 Anze　浮山县 Fushan　吉　县 Jixian　乡宁县 Xiangning　大宁县 Daning　隰　县 Xixian　永和县 Yonghe　蒲　县 Puxian　汾西县 Fenxi　侯马市 Houma　霍州市 Huozhou
吕梁市 Lvliang	离石区 Lishi　文水县 Wenshui　交城县 Jiaocheng　兴　县 Xingxian　临　县 Linxian　柳林县 Liulin　石楼县 Shilou　岚　县 Lanxian　方山县 Fangshan　中阳县 Zhongyang　交口县 Jiaokou　孝义市 Xiaoyi　汾阳市 Fenyang

1-2 国民经济和社会发展总量与速度指标

指 标	Item	总量指标	
		1990	2000
一、人口与从业人员（万人）	**Population and Employment (10 000 persons)**		
年末常住人口	Resident Population at Year-end	2899.0	3247.8
全社会从业人员	Total Employees	1304.0	1392.4
#非私营单位在岗职工人数	Fully Employed Staff and Workers in Non-private Units	438.7	370.2
二、国民经济核算（亿元）	**National Economic Accounting (100 million yuan)**		
地区生产总值	Gross Domestic Product	429.3	1868.1
第一产业	Primary Industry	80.8	202.2
第二产业	Secondary Industry	210.1	858.4
第三产业	Tertiary Industry	138.4	807.5
三、物价总指数（上年=100）	**Price Indices (last year=100)**		
居民消费价格总指数	General Consumer Price Index	102.2	103.9
商品零售价格总指数	General Retail Price Index	102.1	97.1
四、财 政（亿元）	**Public Finance (100 million yuan)**		
一般公共预算收入	General Public Budget Revenue	51.7	114.5
一般公共预算支出	General Public Budget Expenditure	54.9	225.1
五、固定资产投资（亿元）	**Investment in Fixed Assets (100 million yuan)**		
全社会固定资产投资	Total Investment in Fixed Assets	123.4	625.2
#住 宅	Residential Buildings	22.0	111.3
第一产业	Primary Industry	5.2	12.0
第二产业	Secondary Industry	75.6	289.6
第三产业	Tertiary Industry	42.6	323.6
六、对外贸易（亿美元）	**Foreign Trade (USD 100 million)**		
海关进出口总额	Total Value of Exports and Imports of Customs	3.5	17.6
出 口	Total Value of Exports	2.6	12.4
进 口	Total Value of Imports	0.9	5.3
七、农 业	**Agriculture**		
主要农产品产量（万吨）	Output of Major Farm Products (10 000 tons)		
粮 食	Grain	969.0	853.4
蔬 菜	Vegetables	347.4	920.3
油 料	Oil-bearing Crops	39.4	44.8
猪牛羊肉 （万吨）	Output of Pork, Beef and Mutton (10 000 tons)	29.3	59.2
猪年末存栏 （万头）	Hogs at Year-end (10 000 heads)	363.1	519.5
羊年末存栏 （万只）	Sheep and Goats at Year-end (10 000 heads)	709.6	1058.4
八、房地产开发投资（亿元）	**Investment in Real Estate Development (100 million yuan)**		
本年完成投资	Investment Completed This Year	2.8	39.5
#住 宅	Residential Buildings	2.5	27.2

PRINCIPAL AGGREGATE INDICATORS ON NATIONAL ECONOMIC AND SOCIAL DEVELOPMENT AND GROWTH RATES

Aggregate Data			速 度 指 标 Indices and Growth Rates						
2010	2015	2016	指数(2016为以下各年%) Index (2016 as percentage of the following years)				平均增长速度 (%) Average Annual Growth Rate (%)		
			1990	2000	2010	2015	1991–2016	2001–2016	2011–2016
3574.1	3664.1	3681.6	127.0	113.4	103.0	100.5	0.9	0.8	0.5
1685.9	1872.8	1908.2	146.3	137.0	113.2	101.9	1.5	2.0	2.1
384.5	421.9	412.4	94.0	111.4	107.2	97.7	–0.2	0.7	1.2
9188.8	12766.5	12966.2	1279.8	487.1	153.0	104.5	10.3	10.4	7.3
554.5	783.2	784.8	223.8	177.1	128.7	102.8	3.1	3.6	4.3
5202.4	5194.3	4963.3	1401.7	515.3	146.4	101.5	10.7	10.8	6.6
3432.0	6789.1	7218.1	1639.2	546.1	163.6	107.0	11.4	11.2	8.5
103.0	100.6	101.1	308.9	143.7	115.0	101.1	4.4	2.3	2.4
102.3	99.3	100.5	218.1	126.7	109.1	100.5	3.0	1.5	1.5
969.7	1642.4	1557.0	3008.7	1360.1	160.6	94.8	14.0	17.7	8.2
1931.4	3423.0	3428.9	6246.1	1523.6	177.5	100.2	17.2	18.6	10.0
6352.6	14137.2	14285.0	11574.9	2285.0	224.9	101.0	20.9	23.7	17.0
900.3	2106.8	1882.8	8544.2	1690.9	209.1	89.4	19.9	21.8	18.9
281.3	1563.7	1870.4	35995.2	15632.4	665.0	119.6	23.6	36.8	36.4
2628.1	5206.0	4909.6	6491.4	1695.2	186.8	94.3	18.8	22.8	15.9
3443.2	7367.5	7505.0	17623.5	2319.4	218.0	101.9	23.1	23.5	15.7
125.8	147.2	166.4	4755.5	943.4	132.3	113.1	16.0	15.1	4.8
47.1	84.2	99.3	3776.5	803.0	210.9	117.9	15.0	13.9	13.2
78.7	62.9	67.1	7715.1	1272.4	85.3	106.6	18.2	17.2	–2.6
1085.1	1259.6	1318.5	136.1	154.5	121.5	104.7	1.2	2.8	3.3
909.1	1302.2	1294.5	372.6	140.7	142.4	99.4	5.2	2.2	6.1
17.6	15.3	15.4	39.2	34.4	87.8	100.9	–3.5	–6.4	–2.2
63.6	73.0	70.9	242.1	119.6	111.4	97.1	3.5	1.1	1.8
474.8	485.9	449.7	123.8	86.6	94.7	92.5	0.8	–0.9	–0.9
734.7	1001.5	910.4	128.3	86.0	123.9	90.9	1.0	–0.9	3.6
592.2	1494.9	1597.4	56075.0	4048.5	269.7	106.9	27.6	26.0	18.0
457.4	1098.3	1141.1	46319.5	4190.8	249.5	103.9	26.6	26.3	16.5

1-2 续表

指　　标	Item	总 量 指 标	
		1990	2000
九、工　业	**Industry**		
主要工业产品产量(全社会)	Output of Major Industrial Products (Total Society)		
原　煤　(万吨)	Coal (10 000 tons)	28597	25152
发电量　(亿千瓦小时)	Electricity (100 million kwh)	314.2	624.7
粗　钢　(万吨)	Crude Steel (10 000 tons)	238.6	472.7
钢　材　(万吨)	Steel Products (10 000 tons)	128.8	392.6
水　泥　(万吨)	Cement (10 000 tons)	612.5	1434.0
十、国内贸易 (亿元)	**Domestic Trade (100 million yuan)**		
社会消费品零售总额	Total Retail Sales of Consumer Goods	158.0	722.7
十一、交通运输、邮电	**Transportation, Post and Telecommunication Services**		
货物运输量　(万吨)	Freight Traffic (10 000 tons)	50111	86624
#铁　路	Railways	23332	28779
旅客客运量　(万人)	Passenger Traffic (10 000 persons)	15960	31818
#铁　路	Railways	3226	2953
邮电业务总量　(亿元)	Business Volume of Post and Telecommunication Services (100 million yuan)		
移动电话用户　(万户)	Number of Mobile Telephone Subscribers (10 000 subscribers)		126
十二、教育、科技、文化、卫生	**Education, Science and Technology, Culture and Public Health**		
教　育	**Education**		
高等学校数(所)	Number of Institutions of Higher Education (unit)	26	24
高等学校在校学生数(万人)	Student Enrollment of Institutions of Higher Education (10 000 persons)	5.1	12.6
普通中学在校学生数(万人)	Student Enrollment of Regular Secondary Schools (10 000 persons)	145.1	199.8
小学在校学生数 (万人)	Student Enrollment of Primary Schools (10 000 persons)	297.4	343.6
科　技	**Science and Technology**		
自然科学技术人员数 (万人)	Personnels of Natural Science and Technology (10 000 persons)	32.4	32.9
文　化	**Culture**		
图书总印数　(万册)	Total Printed Copies of Books (10 000 copies)	12166	10105
期刊总印数　(万份)	Total Printed Copies of Magazines (10 000 copies)	2815	2657
报纸总印数　(万份)	Total Printed Copies of Newspapers (10 000 copies)	54361	58825
卫　生	**Public Health**		
医　院　(个)	Number of Hospitals (unit)		716
执业(助理)医师　(人)	Number of Licensed (Assitant) Docotors (person)	60185	64900

continued

Aggregate Data			速 度 指 标 Indices and Growth Rates						
2010	2015	2016	指数(2016为以下各年%) Index (2016 as percentage of the following years)				平均增长速度 (%) Average Annual Growth Rate (%)		
			1990	2000	2010	2015	1991–2016	2001–2016	2011–2016
74096	96680	83044	290.4	330.2	112.1	85.9	4.2	7.8	1.9
2150.6	2457.5	2510.5	799.1	401.9	116.7	102.2	8.3	9.1	2.6
3048.8	3847.0	3936.1	1649.8	832.6	129.1	102.3	11.4	14.2	4.3
2866.4	4267.3	4279.0	3322.7	1089.9	149.3	100.3	14.4	16.1	6.9
3670.3	3786.1	3851.5	628.9	268.6	104.9	101.7	7.3	6.4	0.8
3318.2	6033.7	6480.5	4100.5	896.8	195.3	107.4	15.4	14.7	11.8
124677	161772	167082	333.4	192.9	134.0	103.3	4.7	4.2	5.0
63836	70509	64861	278.0	225.4	101.6	92.0	4.0	5.2	0.3
39059	30676	27619	173.1	86.8	70.7	90.0	2.1	−0.9	−5.6
5746	7393	7530	233.4	255.0	131.0	101.9	3.3	6.0	4.6
260	511	386			148.5	75.5			6.8
2225	3337	3366		2666.7	151.3	100.9		22.8	7.1
65	79	80	307.7	333.3	123.1	101.3	4.4	7.8	3.5
56.3	74.0	75.6	1474.0	601.8	134.3	102.2	10.9	11.9	5.0
253.7	192.1	184.7	127.3	92.4	72.8	96.1	0.9	−0.5	−5.2
291.1	227.0	227.1	76.4	66.1	78.0	100.1	−1.0	−2.6	−4.1
42.7	46.1	47.0	145.2	142.9	110.1	102.0	1.4	2.3	1.6
13183	12439	9860	81.0	97.6	74.8	79.3	−0.8	−0.2	−4.7
4000	2573	2421	86.0	91.1	60.5	94.1	−0.6	−0.6	−8.0
206698	203549	201619	370.9	342.7	97.5	99.1	5.2	8.0	−0.4
1201	1274	1393		194.6	116.0	109.3		4.2	2.5
85376	90216	91748	152.4	141.4	107.5	101.7	1.6	2.2	1.2

1-3 山西省水资源总量(2015年)
TOTAL VOLUME OF WATER RESOURCES(2015)

单位：亿立方米 (100 million cu.m)

市　名 City		水资源总量 Water Resources	地表水资源量 Surface Water Resources	地下水资源量 Ground Water Resources	重复计算量 Repetition Statistical Amount	年降水量 Annual Precipitation
全　省	**Total**	**93.95**	**53.83**	**86.39**	**46.27**	**751.04**
太原市	Taiyuan	4.27	1.32	4.44	1.50	31.07
大同市	Datong	7.31	3.75	5.86	2.30	65.86
阳泉市	Yangquan	2.93	3.53	2.84	3.44	25.13
长治市	Changzhi	9.32	5.78	7.96	4.41	69.83
晋城市	Jincheng	9.99	7.22	8.93	6.16	51.29
朔州市	Shuozhou	5.03	1.80	4.85	1.62	45.92
晋中市	Jinzhong	9.53	5.82	8.20	4.49	82.20
运城市	Yuncheng	11.70	4.36	10.55	3.21	77.00
忻州市	Xinzhou	14.20	6.79	13.67	6.26	121.39
临汾市	Linfen	8.17	5.75	8.88	6.45	87.26
吕梁市	Lvliang	11.51	7.71	10.21	6.41	94.10

1-4 山西省实际用水量(2015年)
ACTUAL CONSUMPTION OF WATER(2015)

单位：亿立方米 (100 million cu.m)

市　名 City		总　计 Total	农田灌溉 Farmland Irrigation	工　业 Industry	城镇生活 Urban Living	农村生活 Rural Living	林牧渔畜 Forestry, Animal Husbandry, Fishery and Livestock	生　态 Ecological Utilization
全　省	**Total**	**73.59**	**42.84**	**13.75**	**9.05**	**3.27**	**2.34**	**2.35**
太原市	Taiyuan	7.47	1.64	2.70	2.48	0.28	0.11	0.25
大同市	Datong	6.21	3.54	1.36	0.75	0.28	0.11	0.17
阳泉市	Yangquan	1.94	0.23	0.76	0.48	0.13	0.12	0.23
长治市	Changzhi	5.34	2.42	1.42	0.75	0.33	0.22	0.21
晋城市	Jincheng	4.31	1.36	1.71	0.68	0.21	0.27	0.08
朔州市	Shuozhou	4.87	3.50	0.61	0.36	0.15	0.19	0.06
晋中市	Jinzhong	7.36	4.77	1.18	0.69	0.35	0.19	0.18
运城市	Yuncheng	16.20	12.92	1.34	1.03	0.50	0.36	0.04
忻州市	Xinzhou	6.65	4.42	0.78	0.40	0.26	0.29	0.49
临汾市	Linfen	7.54	4.77	1.00	0.78	0.39	0.28	0.31
吕梁市	LvLiang	5.72	3.28	0.88	0.65	0.39	0.19	0.33

1-5 平均每天主要社会经济活动
MAJOR INDICATORS OF AVERAGE DAILY SOCIAL AND ECONOMIC ACTIVITIES

指　　标	Item	2010	2015	2016
地区生产总值(万元)	Gross Domestic Product (10 000 yuan)	251749	349767	355238
全社会固定资产投资额(万元)	Total Investment in Fixed Assets (10 000 yuan)	174044	387319	391369
社会消费品零售总额(万元)	Total Retail Sales of Consumer Goods (10 000 yuan)	90908	165306	177549
海关进出口总额(万美元)	Total Value of Exports and Imports of Customs (USD 10 000)	3446	4032	4560
一般公共预算收入(万元)	General Public Budget Revenue (10 000 yuan)	26566	44996	42657
一般公共预算支出(万元)	General Public Budget Expenditure (10 000 yuan)	52914	93780	93941
主要农产品产量(吨)	Output of Major Farm Products (ton)			
粮　食	Grain	29729	34509	36124
油　料	Oil-bearing Crops	482	419	423
蔬　菜	Vegetables	24907	35677	35466
主要工业产品产量(全社会)	Output of Major Industrial Products (Total Society)			
原　煤　(万吨)	Coal (10 000 tons)	203	265	228
发电量　(万千瓦小时)	Electricity (10 000 kwh)	58919	67327	68781
钢　材　(吨)	Steel Products (ton)	78530	116911	117232
焦　炭　(万吨)	Coke (10 000 tons)	23	22	22
水　泥　(吨)	Cement (ton)	100556	103728	105522
货运量(万吨)	Freight Traffic (10 000 tons)	342	443	458
客运量(万人)	Passenger Traffic (10 000 persons)	107	84	76
图书出版　(万册)	Books Published (10 000 copies)	36.12	34.08	27.01
期刊出版　(万份)	Magazines Issued (10 000 copies)	10.96	7.05	6.63
报纸出版　(万份)	Newspapers Issued (10 000 copies)	566.30	557.67	552.38
出　生　(人)	Births (person)	1043	1000	1035
死　亡　(人)	Deaths (person)	525	557	555
结　婚　(对)	Marriages (couple)	988	950	822
离　婚　(对)	Divorces (couple)	73	148	162

1-6 社会经济主要指标人均水平
MAJOR PER CAPITA INDICATORS OF SOCIETY AND ECONOMY

指　标	Item	2010	2015	2016
一、地区生产总值 (元)	**Gross Domestic Product (yuan)**	**26249**	**34919**	**35303**
二、主要农产品产量 (公斤)	**Output of Major Farm Products (kg)**			
粮　食	Grain	310	345	359
油　料	Cotton	5.0	4.2	4.2
甜　菜	Beetroots	6.4	1.5	0.9
蔬　菜	Vegetables	259.7	356.2	352.5
猪牛羊肉	Pork, Beef and Mutton	18.2	20.0	19.3
三、主要工业产品产量 (全社会)	**Output of Major Industrial Products (Total Society)**			
原　煤　(吨)	Coal (ton)	21.17	26.44	22.61
发电量　(千瓦小时)	Electricity (kwh)	6143.2	6721.6	6835.3
粗　钢　(公斤)	Crude Steel (kg)	870.9	1052.2	1071.7
钢　材　(公斤)	Steel Products (kg)	818.8	1167.2	1165.0
焦　炭　(吨)	Coke (ton)	2.43	2.20	2.23
水　泥　(公斤)	Cement (kg)	1048.4	1035.6	1048.6
布　(米)	Cloth (m)	2.1	2.1	1.1
四、社会消费品零售额 (元)	**Total Retail Sales of Consumer Goods (yuan)**	**9478**	**16503**	**17644**
五、人民生活 (元)	**People's Livelihood (yuan)**			
在岗职工平均工资	Average Wage of Fully Employed Staff and Workers	33544	52960	54975
国　有	State-owned Units	33119	54953	58952
集　体	Collective-owned Units	21993	44114	45794
城镇居民可支配收入	Disposable Income of Urban Residents	15648	25828	27352
城镇居民消费支出	Living Expenditure of Urban Residents	9793	15819	16993
农村居民可支配收入	Disposible Income of Rural Residents	4736	9454	10082
农村居民消费支出	Living Expenditure of Rural Residents	3664	7421	8029
住户存款	Households Deposits	26346	42877	46634

1-7 国民经济与社会发展结构指标
MAJOR COMPOSITION INDICATORS ON NATIONAL ECONOMIC AND SOCIAL DEVELOPMENT

单位：%　　(%)

指　标	Item	2010	2015	2016
男女人口比例	**Sex Ratio**			
男　性	Male	51.4	51.3	51.2
女　性	Female	48.6	48.7	48.8
人口抚养比	**Dependency Ratio of Population**			
总抚养比	Gross Dependency Ratio	32.8	32.6	33.2
少儿抚养比	Children Dependency Ratio	22.7	20.6	20.6
老年抚养比	Old People Dependency Ratio	10.1	12.1	12.6
地区生产总值构成(生产法)	**Composition of GDP**			
第一产业	Primary Industry	6.0	6.1	6.0
第二产业	Secondary Industry	56.6	40.7	38.3
第三产业	Tertiary Industry	37.3	53.2	55.7
地区生产总值构成(支出法)	**Compositon of GDP**			
最终消费	Final Consumption	44.9	55.9	57.5
资本形成总额	Cross Capital Formation	67.8	72.6	72.3
货物和服务净出口	Net Export of Goods and Services	-12.7	-28.5	-29.8
一般公共预算支出构成	**Compositon of General Public Budget Expenditure**			
#教　育	Education	17.0	17.6	17.7
社会保障和就业	Social Security and Employment	14.2	15.6	15.8
医疗卫生与计划生育	Expenditure for Medical and Health Care and Family Planning	5.9	8.5	8.8
能源使用比例	**Structure of Energy Consumption**			
第一产业	Primary Industry	2.4	2.0	2.0
第二产业	Secondary Industry	75.9	76.1	75.8
第三产业	Tertiary Industry	12.0	12.2	12.5
人民生活	People's Livelihood	9.6	9.7	9.7
全社会固定资产投资构成	**Composition of Total Investment in Fixed Assets**			
第一产业	Primary Industry	4.4	11.1	13.1
第二产业	Secondary Industry	41.4	36.8	34.4
第三产业	Tertiary Industry	54.2	52.1	52.5
工业增加值构成(规模以上)	**Composition of Value Added of Industry (above designated size)**			
轻工业	Light Industry	4.9	8.5	7.8
重工业	Heavy Industry	95.1	91.5	92.2
城乡居民人均收入比(农民=1)	**Ratio of Per Capita Income of Urban and Rural Households(rural income=1)**	**3.30**	**2.73**	**2.71**

1-8 人民物质文化生活情况
CONDITIONS OF PEOPLE'S MATERIAL AND CULTURAL LIFE

指　标	Item	2010	2015	2016
一、城乡居民收入 (元)	**Income of Urban and Rural Residents (yuan)**			
城镇居民人均可支配收入	Per Capita Disposable Income of Urban Residents	15648	25828	27352
农村居民人均可支配收入	Per Capita Disposable Income of Rural Residents	4736	9454	10082
在岗职工平均工资	Average Wage of Fully Employed Staff and Workers	33544	52960	54975
二、平均每人住房面积 (平方米)	**Per Capita Floor Space of Residential Buildings (sq.m)**			
城镇居民住房面积	Urban Residents	28.0	32.0	33.2
农村居民住房面积	Rural Residents	28.7	33.5	37.5
三、生活、文化、教育、卫生	**Livelihood, Culture, Education and Public Health**			
每百户拥有 (抽 样)	Number of Durable Consumer Goods Owned Per 100 Households by Sample			
彩色电视机 (台)	Color Television Sets (unit)			
城镇居民	Urban Residents	111.8	107.2	106.0
农村居民	Rural Residents	109.0	104.6	105.9
洗衣机(台)	Washing Machines (unit)			
城镇居民	Urban Residents	100.7	98.9	99.1
农村居民	Rural Residents	81.0	83.2	88.4
移动电话 (部)	Mobile Telephones (unit)			
城镇居民	Urban Residents	146.6	220.6	230.6
农村居民	Rural Residents	107.7	201.2	215.5
每人每年拥有期刊 (份)	Number of Magazines per Person per Year (copy)	1.1	0.7	0.7
每百人每天拥有报纸 (份)	Newspapers per 100 Persons per Day (copy)	16.2	15.3	15.0
每万人拥有在校大学生 (人)	Number of Enrollment Students of Regular Institutions of Higher Education per 10 000 Persons (person)	160.8	202.5	205.9
每千人拥有医院床位数 (张)	Number of Hospital Beds per 1 000 persons (unit)	3.1	3.8	4.0
每千人拥有卫生技术人员 (人)	Number of Medical Technical Personnels Per 1 000 Persons (person)	5.5	5.8	6.1

1-9 主要年份地区生产总值
GROSS DOMESTIC PRODUCT IN MAJOR YEARS

按当年价格计算 (at current prices)

年 份 Year	地区生产总值 (万元) Gross Domestic Product (10 000 yuan)	第一产业 Primary Industry	第二产业 Secondary Industry	工 业 Industry	建筑业 Construction	第三产业 Tertiary Industry	人均地区生产总值 (元) Per Capita GDP (yuan)
1952	159978	93831	27484	23447	4037	38663	116
1957	291594	115415	93994	71745	22249	82185	186
1962	324083	110666	121848	109126	12722	91569	188
1965	439158	127041	205199	185889	19310	106918	238
1970	576900	151931	302600	279549	23051	122369	277
1975	698101	208009	346700	321978	24722	143392	301
1978	879946	182040	514685	481225	33460	183221	365
1980	1087619	206348	635098	582107	52991	246173	442
1985	2189896	422629	1200573	1021192	179381	566694	838
1990	4292736	808080	2100746	1866110	234636	1383910	1528
1991	4685100	687700	2362800	2108100	254700	1634600	1592
1992	5511200	829400	2702800	2404400	298400	1979000	1862
1993	6804100	972700	3350300	2960100	390200	2481100	2271
1994	8266600	1238400	3965700	3471800	493900	3062500	2729
1995	10760300	1686900	4944500	4385000	559500	4128900	3515
1996	12968122	2029822	6002100	5327300	674800	4936200	4193
1997	14852068	2010468	7075800	6263600	812200	5765800	4753
1998	16261771	2223471	7612500	6585500	1027000	6425800	5152
1999	16828221	1756821	7854700	6845500	1009200	7216700	5279
2000	18680826	2022226	8583700	7486500	1097200	8074900	5791
2001	20553640	1969240	9560100	8324500	1235600	9024300	6305
2002	23600662	2330662	11343100	9914400	1428700	9926900	7189
2003	28995998	2595698	14633800	12919400	1714400	11766500	8775
2004	36362566	3411866	19194000	17113000	2081000	13756700	10936
2005	42998417	3317317	23570400	21176800	2393600	16110700	12854
2006	49600091	3581691	27556600	24850600	2706000	18461800	14739
2007	61257757	4132957	34544900	31418900	3126000	22579900	18104
2008	74271005	4252805	42423600	38685400	3738200	27594600	21834
2009	73563828	4775900	39819711	35052137	4767574	28968217	21516
2010	91888284	5544800	52023556	46218598	5804958	34319928	26249
2011	112141991	6414200	65739573	58907889	6831684	39988219	31292
2012	121265818	6983200	66495493	59305186	7190306	47787126	33666
2013	126652500	7410100	66130600	58421400	7745000	53111800	34984
2014	127614900	7888900	62939100	54710100	8269500	56786900	35070
2015	127664900	7831600	51942700	43596000	8472000	67890600	34919
2016	129662000	7847800	49633000	40831400	8956300	72181200	35303

注：2013年起采用了新的三次产业划分标准，后同。
Note: New division of three industry has been used since 2013. The same applies to the following.

1-10 主要年份地区生产总值构成
COMPOSITION OF GROSS DOMESTIC PRODUCT IN MAJOR YEARS

单位：%　　(%)

年 份 Year	地区生产总值 Gross Domestic Product	第一产业 Primary Industry	第二产业 Secondary Industry	工 业 Industry	建筑业 Construction	第三产业 Tertiary Industry
1952	100.0	58.6	17.2	14.6	2.5	24.2
1957	100.0	39.6	32.2	24.6	7.6	28.2
1962	100.0	34.2	37.6	33.7	3.9	28.3
1965	100.0	28.9	46.7	42.3	4.4	24.3
1970	100.0	26.3	52.5	48.4	4.0	21.2
1975	100.0	29.8	49.7	46.1	3.5	20.5
1978	100.0	20.7	58.5	54.7	3.8	20.8
1980	100.0	19.0	58.4	53.5	4.9	22.6
1985	100.0	19.3	54.8	46.6	8.2	25.9
1990	100.0	18.8	48.9	43.5	5.5	32.3
1991	100.0	14.7	50.4	45.0	5.4	34.9
1992	100.0	15.0	49.0	43.6	5.4	35.9
1993	100.0	14.3	49.2	43.5	5.7	36.5
1994	100.0	15.0	48.0	42.0	6.0	37.0
1995	100.0	15.7	46.0	40.8	5.2	38.4
1996	100.0	15.7	46.3	41.1	5.2	38.1
1997	100.0	13.5	47.6	42.2	5.5	38.8
1998	100.0	13.7	46.8	40.5	6.3	39.5
1999	100.0	10.4	46.7	40.7	6.0	42.9
2000	100.0	10.8	45.9	40.1	5.9	43.2
2001	100.0	9.6	46.5	40.5	6.0	43.9
2002	100.0	9.9	48.1	42.0	6.1	42.1
2003	100.0	9.0	50.5	44.6	5.9	40.6
2004	100.0	9.4	52.8	47.1	5.7	37.8
2005	100.0	7.7	54.8	49.3	5.6	37.5
2006	100.0	7.2	55.6	50.1	5.5	37.2
2007	100.0	6.7	56.4	51.3	5.1	36.9
2008	100.0	5.7	57.1	52.1	5.0	37.2
2009	100.0	6.5	54.1	47.6	6.5	39.4
2010	100.0	6.0	56.6	50.3	6.3	37.3
2011	100.0	5.7	58.6	52.5	6.1	35.7
2012	100.0	5.8	54.8	48.9	5.9	39.4
2013	100.0	5.9	52.2	46.1	6.1	41.9
2014	100.0	6.2	49.3	42.9	6.5	44.5
2015	100.0	6.1	40.7	34.1	6.6	53.2
2016	100.0	6.0	38.3	31.5	6.9	55.7

1-11 主要年份地区生产总值指数

INDICES OF GROSS DOMESTIC PRODUCT IN MAJOR YEARS

1952年=100 (year of 1952=100)

年 份 Year	地区生产总值 Gross Domestic Product	第一产业 Primary Industry	第二产业 Secondary Industry	工 业 Industry	建筑业 Construction	第三产业 Tertiary Industry
1952	100.0	100.0	100.0	100.0	100.0	100.0
1957	174.0	106.1	371.3	326.7	629.9	198.2
1962	169.2	92.7	404.4	411.5	335.5	194.3
1965	248.5	123.3	705.2	725.5	538.1	251.0
1970	304.2	129.3	982.4	1026.3	648.5	291.6
1975	378.4	160.0	1264.7	1348.3	636.2	334.6
1978	485.1	131.7	1893.0	2034.9	821.4	434.3
1980	543.3	124.4	2117.4	2241.3	1169.7	555.9
1985	939.1	188.3	3565.9	3519.2	3454.5	1119.2
1990	1252.9	220.3	4689.7	4850.7	3266.6	1651.7
1991	1305.5	192.6	4985.2	5185.4	3309.1	1831.7
1992	1468.7	217.4	5453.8	5698.8	3355.4	2090.0
1993	1660.5	237.2	6149.5	6463.6	3605.5	2371.3
1994	1831.2	247.9	6857.3	7220.4	4006.0	2612.8
1995	2051.6	257.3	7776.8	8225.8	4257.2	2939.8
1996	2292.8	287.7	8659.5	9106.0	5087.5	3289.7
1997	2552.8	273.3	9813.2	10282.3	5999.4	3732.8
1998	2805.9	302.0	10714.2	11071.8	7664.6	4112.8
1999	3009.6	251.5	11771.9	12115.6	8691.0	4508.7
2000	3292.0	278.4	12757.1	13197.9	9084.2	4957.9
2001	3624.7	268.4	14133.6	14631.4	10045.3	5580.6
2002	4091.7	304.9	16248.1	16836.0	11437.4	6206.4
2003	4700.1	326.0	18963.8	19648.8	13171.2	7168.1
2004	5416.1	340.6	22291.8	23157.7	15011.5	8304.3
2005	6147.2	322.2	25947.7	27071.3	16797.9	9408.8
2006	6934.1	338.7	29995.5	31402.7	18830.4	10349.7
2007	8036.6	338.0	35154.8	37118.0	20449.8	12036.7
2008	8719.7	346.5	37404.7	39679.1	20613.4	13553.3
2009	9197.6	361.0	38098.2	39248.4	26839.0	15084.7
2010	10481.0	383.0	44915.2	46719.6	29394.7	16549.1
2011	11830.3	407.4	52168.1	54686.2	32026.2	18040.0
2012	13027.7	433.2	57615.8	60876.1	32969.3	19880.0
2013	14187.2	453.6	63274.3	67085.0	35066.0	21477.3
2014	14882.3	474.9	65552.2	69231.7	37555.7	23002.2
2015	15343.7	479.7	64765.5	67985.5	39508.6	25302.4
2016	16034.1	493.1	65737.0	68733.3	41167.9	27073.6

1-12 主要年份地区生产总值指数

INDICES OF GROSS DOMESTIC PRODUCT IN MAJOR YEARS

上年=100 (last year=100)

年 份 Year	地区生产总值 Gross Domestic Product	第一产业 Primary Industry	第二产业 Secondary Industry	工 业 Industry	建筑业 Construction	第三产业 Tertiary Industry
1953	116.7	105.6	125.7	124.6	132.0	137.2
1957	107.6	89.6	133.0	122.2	181.5	108.4
1962	91.3	105.7	85.2	84.2	93.9	84.7
1965	118.8	103.1	135.2	136.6	124.5	117.4
1970	124.4	99.2	147.0	150.5	120.0	121.7
1975	107.9	108.1	112.0	113.4	93.0	97.9
1978	117.6	89.8	131.2	130.7	140.9	109.9
1980	102.0	87.6	102.9	104.6	82.6	111.1
1985	107.1	82.2	113.1	110.2	133.3	115.8
1990	105.0	112.6	101.4	100.4	110.7	108.6
1991	104.2	87.4	106.3	106.9	101.3	110.9
1992	112.5	112.9	109.4	109.9	101.4	114.1
1993	113.1	109.1	112.8	113.4	107.5	113.5
1994	110.3	104.5	111.5	111.7	111.1	110.2
1995	112.0	103.8	113.4	113.9	106.3	112.5
1996	111.8	111.8	111.4	110.7	119.5	111.9
1997	111.3	95.0	113.3	112.9	117.9	113.5
1998	109.9	110.5	109.2	107.7	127.8	110.2
1999	107.3	83.3	109.9	109.4	113.4	109.6
2000	109.4	110.7	108.4	108.9	104.5	110.0
2001	110.1	96.4	110.8	110.9	110.6	112.6
2002	112.9	113.6	115.0	115.1	113.9	111.2
2003	114.9	106.9	116.7	116.7	115.2	115.5
2004	115.2	104.5	117.5	117.9	114.0	115.9
2005	113.5	94.6	116.4	116.9	111.9	113.3
2006	112.8	105.1	115.6	116.0	112.1	110.0
2007	115.9	99.8	117.2	118.2	108.6	116.3
2008	108.5	102.5	106.4	106.9	100.8	112.6
2009	105.5	104.2	101.9	98.9	130.2	111.3
2010	114.0	106.1	117.9	118.9	109.5	109.7
2011	112.9	106.1	116.1	117.1	109.0	109.0
2012	110.1	106.3	110.4	111.3	102.9	110.2
2013	108.9	104.7	109.8	110.2	106.4	108.0
2014	104.9	104.7	103.6	103.2	107.1	107.1
2015	103.1	101.0	98.8	98.2	105.2	110.0
2016	104.5	102.8	101.5	101.1	104.2	107.0

1-13 支出法地区生产总值
GROSS DOMESTIC PRODUCT BY EXPENDITURE APPROACH

单位：万元 (10 000 yuan)

指 标	Item	按当年价格计算 at Current Prices		2016年为2015年% 2016 as Percentage of 2015
		2015	2016	
总 计	**Total**	**127664900**	**129662000**	**104.5**
一、最终消费	Final Consumption Expenditure	71347000	74547100	101.3
居民消费	Residents Consumption Expenditure	52514200	55332500	104.2
农村居民	Rural Residents	14681400	15037200	101.4
城镇居民	Urban Residents	37832800	40295300	105.3
政府消费	Government Consumption Expenditure	18832800	19214600	93.3
二、资本形成总额	Gross Capital Formation	92699400	93717300	100.6
固定资本形成总额	Gross Fixed Capital Formation	80077300	82767600	102.4
存货增加	Changes in Inventories	12622100	10949700	89.1
三、货物和服务净出口	Net Export of Goods and Services	−36381500	−38602400	

1-14 支出法地区生产总值构成
COMPOSITION OF GROSS DOMESTIC PRODUCT BY EXPENDITURE APPROACH

单位：% (%)

指 标	Item	按当年价格计算 at Current Prices	
		2015	2016
总 计	**Total**	**100.0**	**100.0**
一、最终消费	Final Consumption Expenditure	55.9	57.5
居民消费	Residents Consumption Expenditure	41.1	42.7
农村居民	Rural Residents	11.5	11.6
城镇居民	Urban Residents	29.6	31.1
政府消费	Government Consumption Expenditure	14.8	14.8
二、资本形成总额	Gross Capital Formation	72.6	72.3
固定资本形成总额	Gross Fixed Capital Formation	62.7	63.8
存货增加	Changes in Inventories	9.9	8.4
三、货物和服务净出口	Net Export of Goods and Services	−28.5	−29.8

1-15 总产出
TOTAL OUTPUT

单位：万元 (10 000 yuan)

指　　标	Item	按当年价格计算 at Current Prices	
		2015	2016
总　　计	**Total**	**325431000**	**329147500**
按国民经济行业分	**Grouped By Sector**		
农、林、牧、渔业	Farming, Forestry, Animal Husbandry and Fishery	15226400	15340200
工　业	Industry	154732600	142065200
建筑业	Construction	43224900	45695184
交通运输、仓储和邮政业	Transportation, Storage and Post	19590000	21518100
批发和零售业	Wholesale and Retail Trade	14531800	14577300
其　他	Others	78125300	89951516
按三次产业分	**By Type of Industry**		
第一产业	Primary Industry	14359300	14445000
第二产业	Secondary Industry	197630000	187363800
第三产业	Tertiary Industry	113441700	127338700

1-16 资本形成总额
GROSS CAPITAL FORMATION

单位：万元 (10 000 yuan)

指　　标	Item	2015	2016
总　　计	**Total**	**92699400**	**93717300**
固定资本形成总额	Gross Fixed Capital Formation	80077300	82767600
住　宅	Residential Buildings	11041800	12001400
非住宅建筑物	Nonresidential Buildings	36440700	38664000
机器和设备	Machinery and Equipment	23536700	22008000
其　他	Others	9058100	10094200
存货增加	Changes in Inventories	12622100	10949700
第一产业	Primary Industry	279100	287000
第二产业	Secondary Industry	3045800	2991100
第三产业	Tertiary Industry	9297200	7671600

1-17 地区生产总值构成项目(2016年)
COMPONENTS OF GROSS DOMESTIC PRODUCT(2016)

单位：万元 (10 000 yuan)

指 标	Item	总 计 Total	劳动者报 酬 Compensation of Employees	生产税净 额 Net Taxes on Production	固定资产折 旧 Depreciation of Fixed Assets	营业盈余 Operating Surplus
地区生产总值	**Gross Domestic Product**	**129662000**	**62097900**	**20950000**	**22682100**	**23932000**
按国民经济行业分	**Grouped By Sector**					
农、林、牧、渔业	Farming, Forestry, Animal Husbandry and Fishery	8273200	6440800	–565600	776400	1621600
#农、林、牧、渔服务业	Farming, Forestry, Animal Husbandry and Fishery Service	425400	324600	–900	47400	54300
工 业	Industry	40831400	17142800	10989300	9072300	3627000
#金属制品、机械和设备修理业	Metal Products, Machinery and Equipment Repair	154700	108600	28700	8200	9200
建筑业	Construction	8956300	4737800	1931800	569700	1717000
批发和零售业	Wholesale and Retail Trade	10581200	2815100	3237000	1077500	3451600
交通运输、仓储和邮政业	Transport, Storage and Post	9307500	4332000	625800	1562800	2786900
住宿和餐饮业	Hotels and Catering Services	3757500	1289500	413000	384200	1670800
信息传输、软件和信息技术服务业	Information Transmission, Software and Information Technology Services	5300200	2151200	389500	1460500	1299000
金融业	Financial Industry	12073500	5067800	1668300	727200	4610200
房地产业	Real Estate	6985300	936700	1497800	4397800	153000
租赁和商务服务业	Lease and Business Affairs Services	2528800	994000	231600	557500	745700
科学研究和技术服务业	Scientific Research and Technical Services	1096300	698500	105700	123500	168600
水利、环境和公共设施管理业	Water, Environmental Protection and Public Facility Management	625900	455700	23500	159000	–12300
居民服务、修理和其他服务业	Resident Services, Repair and Other Services	3393900	1663700	158100	177800	1394300
教 育	Education	4815400	4110000	75300	575400	54700
卫生和社会工作	Health Care and Social Work	2156500	1508700	47900	221000	378900
文化、体育和娱乐业	Culture, Sports and Recreation	1558000	994800	103500	222700	237000
公共管理、社会保障和社会组织	Public Management, Social Security and Social Organization	7421100	6758800	17500	616800	28000
按三次产业分	**By Type of Industry**					
第一产业	Primary Industry	7847800	6116200	–564700	729000	1567300
第二产业	Secondary Industry	49633000	21772000	12892400	9633800	5334800
第三产业	Tertiary Industry	72181200	34209700	8622300	12319300	17029900

1-18 按三次产业、行业(门类)划分的法人单位数、产业活动单位数及从业人数(2016年)

项　目	Item	单位数 (个) Number of Units (unit)
总　计	**Total**	**498902**
按三次产业分	**By Industry**	
第一产业	Primary Industry	87165
第二产业	Secondary Industry	62498
第三产业	Tertiary Industry	349239
按行业(门类)分	**By Sector**	
农、林、牧、渔业	Farming , Forestry , Animal Husbandry and Fishery	94596
采矿业	Ming	6965
制造业	Manufacturing	32151
电力、热力、燃气及水生产和供应业	Production and Supply of Electricity, Heat, Gas and Water	3662
建筑业	Construction	20372
批发和零售业	Wholesale and Retail Trade	139240
交通运输、仓储和邮政业	Transport, Storage and Post	11375
住宿和餐饮业	Hotels and Catering Services	7109
信息传输、软件和信息技术服务业	Information Transmission, Software and Information Technology Services	11529
金融业	Financial Industry	2883
房地产业	Real Estate	12856
租赁和商务服务业	Lease and Business Affairs Services	36562
科学研究和技术服务业	Scientific Reseach and Technical Services	13141
水利、环境和公共设施管理业	Management of Water Conservancy, Environment and Public Facilities	3848
居民服务、修理和其他服务业	Resident Services, Repair and Other Services	15397
教　育	Education	11769
卫生和社会工作	Health Care and Social Work	6400
文化、体育和娱乐业	Culture, Sports and Recreation	10128
公共管理、社会保障和社会组织	Public Management, Social Security and Social Organization	58919

NUMBER OF CORPORATION UNITS, ACTIVE UNITS AND EMPLOYEES BY TYPE OF INDUSTRY AND SECTOR(2016)

法人单位 Corporation Units			产业活动单位 Active Units		
单产业法人 Single Industry	多产业法人 Multi-industry	从业人数 (人) Employees (person)	单位数 (个) Number of Units (unit)	#多产业法人所属的产业活动单位 Units Belong to Multi-industry Corporation	从业人数 (人) Employees (person)
471982	**26920**	**9963653**	**602197**	**130215**	**10725975**
87004	161	939976	87465	461	943486
60506	1992	3847514	68328	7822	3986956
324472	24767	5176163	446404	121932	5795533
94404	192	1014393	95016	612	1018384
6759	206	1240101	7422	663	1169143
31260	891	1697481	33645	2385	1785354
3497	165	171706	4752	1255	234227
19624	748	757861	23271	3647	838833
135452	3788	1228967	158294	22842	1346841
10860	515	471853	16142	5282	559715
6764	345	184973	8242	1478	217082
11301	228	128946	14581	3280	154023
2316	567	152185	12277	9961	249392
12090	766	205282	14196	2106	231553
35701	861	378485	41245	5544	438420
12712	429	175256	15574	2862	199452
3744	104	107802	4705	961	113930
15197	200	129190	16633	1436	147313
10620	1149	610277	21617	10997	664595
5657	743	238226	29662	24005	290969
9989	139	112662	10805	816	117836
44035	14884	958007	74118	30083	948913

1-19 按登记注册类型划分的法人单位数、产业活动单位数及从业人数(2016年)

项　目	Item	单位数(个) Number of Units (unit)
总　计	**Total**	**498902**
一、内　资	**Civil Funded Enterprises**	**498382**
国　有	State-owned Enterprises	45525
集　体	Collective Owned Enterprises	4587
股份合作	Share Cooperative Enterprises	432
国有联营	State-owned Joint Owned Enterprises	78
集体联营	Collective-owned Joint Owned Enterprises	117
国有与集体联营	State-owned and Collective-owned Joint Owned Enterprises	28
其他联营	Other Joint Owned Enterprises	42
国有独资公司	Company Exclusively with Investment from State	840
其他有限责任公司	Other Limited Responsibility Company	31423
股份有限公司	Share Holding Limited Company	2446
私营独资	Enterprise Exclusively with Investment from Private	33740
私营合伙	Private Partner Enterprises	5681
私营有限责任公司	Privately Owned Limited Responsibility Company	239262
私营股份有限公司	Privately Owned Share Holding Limited Company	5741
其　他	Others	128440
二、港澳台商投资	**Enterprises Funded by Hong Kong, Macao and Taiwan**	**214**
与港澳台商合资经营	Joint Venture	111
与港澳台商合作经营	Cooperative Enterprise	5
港澳台商独资	Ventures Exclusively with Hong Kong, Macao and Taiwan Investment	82
港澳台商投资股份有限公司	Share Holding Limited Company	9
其他港澳台商投资	Others	7
三、外商投资	**Foreign Funded Enterprises**	**306**
中外合资经营	Joint Venture	166
中外合作经营	Cooperative Enterprises	20
外资企业	Enterprises Funded By Foreign Investments	84
外商投资股份有限公司	Limited Company Funded by Foreign Investment	17
其他外商投资	Others	19

NUMBER OF CORPORATION UNITS, ACTIVE UNITS AND EMPLOYEES BY REGISTRATION STATUS(2016)

法人单位 Corporation Units			产业活动单位 Active Units		
单产业法人 Single Industry	多产业法人 Multi-industry	从业人数 (人) Employees (person)	单位数 (个) Number of Units (unit)	#多产业法人所属的产业活动单位 Units Belong to Multi-industry Corporation	从业人数 (人) Employees (person)
471982	**26920**	**9963653**	**602197**	**130215**	**10725975**
471548	**26834**	**9732320**	**600690**	**129142**	**10476999**
38558	6967	2113509	86367	47809	2708624
3836	751	191303	14692	10856	218746
400	32	15700	869	469	19842
69	9	7158	207	138	11985
106	11	3028	173	67	3531
25	3	832	47	22	3506
42		1079	77	35	1340
680	160	320026	1098	418	254043
29727	1696	1859383	37305	7578	1704677
1998	448	418215	8043	6045	530896
33288	452	362889	35999	2711	379419
5616	65	56539	6010	394	59398
234118	5144	2923989	258145	24027	3077743
5598	143	115412	6563	965	120339
117487	10953	1343258	145095	27608	1382910
177	**37**	**146506**	**658**	**481**	**148383**
97	14	78757	185	88	80056
3	2	2009	19	16	2272
63	19	61287	401	338	60817
7	2	4301	36	29	4203
7		152	17	10	1035
257	**49**	**84827**	**849**	**592**	**100593**
143	23	40317	252	109	47136
16	4	7861	23	7	8446
72	12	29839	452	380	38439
9	8	4413	90	81	2021
17	2	2397	32	15	4551

1-20 按登记注册类型、从业人数组距划分的法人单位数(2016年)

单位：个

项　目	Item	9人以下 9 Persons Below
总　计	**Total**	**344182**
一、内　资	**Civil Funded Enterprises**	**344083**
国　有	State-owned Enterprises	17208
集　体	Collective Owned Enterprises	2067
股份合作	Share Cooperative Enterprises	226
国有联营	State-owned Joint Owned Enterprises	27
集体联营	Collective-owned Joint Owned Enterprises	62
国有与集体联营	State-owned and Collective-owned Joint Owned Enterprises	15
其他联营	Other Joint Owned Enterprises	17
国有独资公司	Company Exclusively with Investment from State	245
其他有限责任公司	Other Limited Responsibility Company	18941
股份有限公司	Share Holding Limited Company	1051
私营独资	Enterprise Exclusively with Investment from Private	24851
私营合伙	Private Partner Enterprises	4235
私营有限责任公司	Privately Owned Limited Responsibility Company	174839
私营股份有限公司	Privately Owned Share Holding Limited Company	4047
其　他	Others	96252
二、港澳台商投资	**Enterprises Funded by Hong Kong, Macao and Taiwan**	**33**
与港澳台商合资经营	Joint Venture	18
与港澳台商合作经营	Cooperative Enterprise	1
港澳台商独资	Ventures Exclusively with Hong Kong,Macao and Taiwan Investment	10
港澳台商投资股份有限公司	Share Holding Limited Company	1
其他港澳台商投资	Others	3
三、外商投资	**Foreign Funded Enterprises**	**66**
中外合资经营	Joint Venture	24
中外合作经营	Cooperative Enterprises	4
外资企业	Enterprises Funded By Foreign Investments	23
外商投资股份有限公司	Limited Company Funded by Foreign Investment	5
其他外商投资	Others	10

NUMBER OF CORPORATION UNITS BY REGISTRATION STATUS AND QUANTITY OF EMPLOYEES(2016)

(unit)

10-49人 10-49 Persons	50-99人 50-99 Persons	100-299人 100-299 Persons	300-499人 300-499 Persons	500-999人 500-999 Persons	1000-4999人 1000-4999 Persons	5000人以上 5000 Persons Above
126497	**15630**	**9286**	**1555**	**1052**	**632**	**68**
126336	**15556**	**9192**	**1523**	**1023**	**606**	**63**
18830	5367	3322	448	232	106	12
1812	347	255	68	23	13	2
139	26	34	3	4		
27	11	6	3	2	2	
38	12	4		1		
11		1	1			
15	8	2				
278	112	88	33	37	36	11
8725	1474	1262	368	387	246	20
787	195	212	64	76	51	10
7776	721	367	15	9	1	
1315	106	24	1			
56729	4578	2378	403	203	126	6
1376	182	100	18	9	7	2
28478	2417	1137	98	40	18	
75	**33**	**30**	**16**	**13**	**11**	**3**
32	21	22	10	6	1	1
1		2			1	
36	11	5	5	5	8	2
3	1		1	2	1	
3		1				
86	**41**	**64**	**16**	**16**	**15**	**2**
53	25	36	13	7	7	1
4	6	3		1	2	
22	7	20	3	5	3	1
4	2	2		2	2	
3	1	3		1	1	

主要统计指标解释

地区生产总值 是按市场价格计算的一个地区所有常住单位在一定时期内生产活动的最终成果。地区生产总值有三种表现形态，即价值形态、收入形态和产品形态。从价值形态看，它是所有常住单位在一定时期内所生产的全部货物和服务价值与同期投入的全部非固定资产货物和服务价值的差额，即所有常住单位的增加值之和；从收入形态看，它是所有常住单位在一定时期内所创造并分配给常住单位和非常住单位的初次分配收入之和；从产品形态看，它是最终使用的货物和服务价值与货物和服务价值净出口之和。在核算中，地区生产总值的三种表现形态表现为三种计算方法，即生产法、收入法和支出法。三种方法分别从不同的方面反映地区生产总值及其构成。

三次产业 我国的三次产业划分是：

第一产业是指农、林、牧、渔业（不含农、林、牧、渔服务业）。

第二产业是指采矿业（不含开采辅助活动），制造业（不含金属制品、机械和设备修理业），电力、热力、燃气及水生产和供应业，建筑业。

第三产业即服务业，是指除第一产业、第二产业以外的其他行业。第三产业包括：批发和零售业，交通运输、仓储和邮政业，住宿和餐饮业，信息传输、软件和信息技术服务业，金融业，房地产业，租赁和商务服务业，科学研究和技术服务业，水利、环境和公共设施管理业，居民服务、修理和其他服务业，教育，卫生和社会工作，文化、体育和娱乐业，公共管理、社会保障和社会组织，国际组织，以及农、林、牧、渔业中的农、林、牧、渔服务业，采矿业中的开采辅助活动，制造业中的金属制品、机械和设备修理业。

总产出 指一定时期内一个地区常住单位生产的所有货物和服务的价值，既包括新增价值，也包括被消耗的货物和服务价值以及固定资产的转移价值。总产出按生产者价格计算，它反映常住单位生产活动的总规模。

增加值 指常住单位生产过程创造的新增价值和固定资产的转移价值。它可以按生产法计算，也可以按收入法计算，按生产法计算，它等于总产出减去中间投入；按收入法计算，它等于劳动者报酬、生产税净额、固定资产折旧和营业盈余之和。

劳动者报酬 指劳动者因从事生产活动所获得的全部报酬。包括劳动者获得的各种形式的工资、奖金和津贴，既有货币形式的，也有实物形式的，还包括劳动者所享受的公费医疗和医药卫生费、上下班交通补贴、单位支付的社会保险费、住房公积金等。对于个体经济来说，其所有者所获得的劳动报酬和经营利润不易区分，这两部分统一作为劳动者报酬处理。

生产税净额 指生产税减生产补贴后的差额。生产税指政府对生产单位从事生产、销售和经营活动以及因从事生产活动使用某些生产要素（如固定资产、土地、劳动力）所征收的各种税、附加费和规费。生产补贴与生产税相反，指政府对生产单位的单方面转移支付，因此视为负生产税，包括政策性亏损补贴、价格补贴等。

固定资产折旧 指一定时期内为弥补固定资产损耗按照规定的固定资产折旧率提取的固定资产折旧，或按国民经济核算统一规定的折旧率虚拟计算的固定资产折旧。它反映了固定资产在当期生产中的转移价值。各类企业和企业化管理的事业单位的固定资产折旧是指实际计提的折旧费；不计提折旧的政府机关、非企业化管理的事业单位和居民住房的固定资产折旧是按照统一规定的折旧率和固定资产原值计算的虚拟折旧。原则上，固定资产折旧应按固定资产的重置价值计算，但是目前我国尚不具备对全社会固定资产进行重估价的基础，所以暂时还不能采用这种办法。

营业盈余 指常住单位创造的增加值扣除劳动者报酬、生产税净额和固定资产折旧后的余额。它相当于企业的营业利润加上生产补贴，但要扣除从利润中开支的工资和福利等。

支出法地区生产总值 指一个地区所有常住单位在一定时期内用于最终消费、资本形成总额，以及货物和服务净出口的总额，它反映本期生产的地区生产总值的使用情况。

最终消费 指常住单位在一定时期内对于货物和服务的全部最终消费支出，也就是说常住单位为满足物质、文化和精神生活的需要，从本地区经济领土和地区外购买的货物和服务的支出，不包括非常住单位在本地区经济领土内的消费支出。最终消费分为居民消费和政府消费。

居民消费 指常住住户在一定时期内对货物和服务的全部最终消费支出。它除了常住住户直接以货币形式购买货物和服务的消费之外，还包括以其他方式获得的货物和服务的消费，即单位以实物报酬及实物转移的形式提供给劳动者的货物和服务；住户生产并由住户自己消费的货物和服务，其中的服务仅指住户的自有住房服务和付酬的家庭服务；金融机构提供的金融媒介服务；保险公司提供的保险服务。

政府消费 指政府部门为全社会提供公共服务的消费支出和免费或以较低价格向住户提供的货物和服务的净支出。前者等于政府服务的产出价值减去政府单位所获得的经营收入后的价值,政府服务的产出价值等于它的经常性业务支出加上固定资产折旧；后者等于政府部门免费或以较低价格向住户提供的货物和服务的市场价值减去向住户收取的价值。

资本形成总额 指常住单位在一定时期内获得的减去处置的固定资产加存货的净变动额,包括固定资本形成总额和存货增加。

固定资本形成总额 指生产者在一定的时期内获得的固定资产减处置的固定资产的价值总额。固定资产是通过生产活动生产出来的，其使用年限在一年以上，单位价值在规定标准以上的资产，不包括自然资产。固定资本形成总额分有形固定资本形成总额和无形固定资本形成总额。有形固定资本形成总额包括一定时期内完成的建筑工程、安装工程、设备工器具购置（减处置）价值以及土地改良、新增役、种、奶、毛、娱乐用牲畜和新增经济林木价值。无形固定资本形成总额包括矿藏的勘探、计算机软件等获得减处置。

存货增加 指常住单位存货实物量变动的市场价值，即期末价值减期初价值的差额，再扣除当期由于价格变动而产生的持有收益。存货增加可以是正值，也可以是负值；正值表示存货增加，负值表示存货减少。它包括生产单位购进的原材料、燃料和储备物资等存货，以及生产单位生产的产成品、在制品存货等。

货物和服务净出口 指货物和服务出口减货物和服务进口的差额。出口包括常住单位向非常住单位出售或无偿转让的各种货物和服务的价值；进口包括常住单位从非常住单位购买或无偿得到的各种货物和服务的价值。由于服务活动的提供与使用同时发生，因此服务的进出口业务并不发生出入境现象，一般把常住单位从国外得到的服务作为进口，常住单位向国外提供的服务作为出口。

法人单位 指有权拥有资产、承担负债，并独立从事社会经济活动（或与其他单位进行交易）的组织。

产业活动单位 指位于一个地点，从事一种或主要从事一种社会经济活动的组织或组织的一部分。

Explanatory Notes on Main Statistical Indicators

Gross Domestic Product refers to the final products of all resident units calculated at market prices, in a region during a certain period of time. Gross domestic product is expressed in three different forms i.e. value, income and products respectively. The form of value refers to the total value of all products and services produced by all resident units during a certain period of time minus total value of intermediate input of materials and services of the nature of non-fixed assets or the summation of the value-added of all resident units; the form of income includes all the income created by all resident units and distributed primarily to all resident and non-resident units; the form of products refers to the value of all final goods and services for final use by all resident units plus the value of net exports of goods and services during given period of time. In the practice of national accounting, gross domestic product is calculated with three approaches, i.e. production approach, income approach, and expenditure approach, which reflect gross domestic product and its composition from different aspects.

Three Industries Industry in China comprises:

Primary industry refers to farming, forestry, animal husbandry and fishery, excluding services supported these industries.

Secondary industry refers to mining (excluding auxiliary activities), manufacturing (excluding repair of metal products, machinery and equipment), production and supply of electricity, heat, gas and water, construction.

Tertiary industry refers to all other industries not included in primary or secondary industry. It includes wholesale and retail trade, transport, storage and post, hotels and catering services, information transmission, software and information technology services, financial industry, real estate, lease and business affairs services, scientific research and technical services, management of water conservancy, environment and public facilities, residents services, repair and other services, education, health care and social work, culture, sports and recreation, public management, social security and social organization, international organization, services of farming, forestry, animal husbandry and fishery, auxiliary activities of mining, repair of metal products, machinery and equipment of manufacturing.

Total Output refers to value of all goods and services produced by resident units in a certain period of time, including new increasing value, also including value of goods and services consumed and transfer value of fixed assets. It is calculated at producer price, reflecting total production scale of resident units.

Intermediate Input refers to total non-fixed assets goods and services consumed and used by resident units during producing or supplying goods and services. Intermediate input is also called intermediate consumption, calculated at price of buyer.

Value Added refers to new increasing value and transfer value of fixed assets created by resident units during production. It is calculated in production way, also in income way. It equals total output minus intermediate consume when in production way. It equals compensation of laborers plus net tax on production, depreciation of fixed assets and operating surplus when in income way.

Laborers' Remuneration refers to the whole payment of various forms earned by the laborers from the productive activities they are engaged in. It includes wages, bonuses and allowances the laborers earned in monetary form and in kind. It also includes the free medical services provided to the laborers and the medicine expenses, traffic subsidies and social insurance fee paid by the laborers working units for them. As the individual economy is concerned, since the laborers remuneration is not easily distinguished from the operating profit, both are treated as laborers remuneration.

Net Taxes on Production refers to the residual of the taxes on production minus the subsidies on production. The taxes on production refers to the various taxes, extra charges and fees levied on the production units on their production, sale and business activities as well as on some factors pf production, such as fixed assets, land and labor force, used in the production activities they are engaged in. In contrast to the taxes on production, the subsidies on production refer to the unilateral transfer of part of the government's revenue to the production units and is therefore regarded as negative taxes on production. They include subsidies on the loss due to implementation of government policies and price subsidies etc.

Depreciation of Fixed Assets refers to the depreciation of fixed assets of a given period, drawn in accordance with the stipulated depreciation rate for the purpose of compensating the wear loss of the fixed assets of the depreciation of fixed assets calculated in a fictitious way in accordance with the stipulated unified depreciation rate in the national economic accounting It reflects the value of transfer of the fixed assets in the production of the current period. The depreciation of fixed assets in various enterprises and institutions managed as enterprises which do not drawn and calculated as part of the cost. In government agencies and institution not managed as enterprises which do not draw the depreciation expenses, as well as for the houses of residents, the depreciation of fixed assets is the imputed depreciation, which is calculated in accordance with the stipulated unified depreciation rate. In principle, the depreciation of fixed assets should be calculated on the basis of the repurchased value of the fixed assets.

However, there is no actual condition to reevaluate all the fixed assets in China. Therefore, the method can't be adopted temporarily at present.

Operating Surplus refers to the balance of the value added created by the resident units deducting the laborers remuneration, net taxes on production and the depreciation of fixed assets. It is equivalent to the business profit of the enterprises plus subsidies on production, but the wages and welfare expenses paid from the profits should be deducted.

GDP Calculated by Expenditure Approach refers to total expenditure on final consumption, total capital formation and net export of goods and services by resident units of a region in a certain period of time. It reflects the composition of GDP by its use.

Final Consumption refers to the total expenditure of resident units on final consumption of goods and services in a certain period, namely the expenditure of the resident units for purchases of goods and services from domestic economic territory and other regions to meet the requirements of material, cultural and spiritual life. It excludes the expenditure of non-resident units on consumption in the economic territory. The final consumption is classified into household consumption and government consumption.

Households Consumption refers to the total expenditure of resident households on the final consumption of goods and services during a certain period of time. In addition to the consumption of goods and services bought by the households directly with money, the expenditure on goods and services obtained by the households in other ways, i.e. the so-called imputed expenditure on consumption, is also include in the households consumption. The imputation expenditure of the households on consumption includes the following types: (a) the goods and services provided to the households themselves, in the form of payment in kind and transfer in kind; (b) the goods and services produced and consumed by the households themselves, in which the services refer only to the services provided by the residential buildings owned by the households; (c) the services of financial intermediary provided by the financial institutions; (d) the insurance services provided by the insurance companies.

Government Consumption refers to the expenditure on the consumption of the public services provided by the government to the whole society and the net expenditure on the goods and services provided by the government to the households at free charge or lower prices. The former equals to the output value of the government services minus the value of operating income obtained by the government departments.(The output value of the government services equals to its current operating expenditure plus depreciation of fixed assets). The latter equals to the market value of the goods and services provided by the government free of charge or at low prices to the households minus the value received by the government from the households.

Total Capital Formation refers to the fixed assets acquired minus those disposed and the change in inventory, including the total fixed assets formation and the increase in inventory.

Total Fixed Capital Formation refers to the value of fixed assets purchased, transferred in by the resident units and those produced and used by themselves deducting the value of fixed assets sold and transferred out. It can be classified into total tangible assets formation and total intangible assets formation. The total tangible assets formation include the value of the construction projects, installation projects completed and the equipment, apparatus and instruments purchased as well as the value of land improved, the value of draught animals, breeding stock, milk, wool and recreational animals and the newly increased economic forest in a certain period. The total intangible assets formation includes the prospecting of minerals, the acquisition of computer software, the originals of recreational works and works of literature and arts minus the disposal of them.

Increase in Inventory refers to the market value of the charge in inventory, i.e. the difference of value between the beginning and the end of the period. The increase in inventory can be positive or negative. A positive value indicates the increase in inventory while negative value indicates the decrease in stock. The inventory includes the raw materials, fuels, reserve materials purchased by the production units as well as the inventory of finished products, semi-finished products, work-in-progress, etc.

Net Export of Goods and Services refers to the difference of the exports of goods and services minus the imports of goods and services. The exports include the value of various goods and services sold or gratuitously transferred by the resident units to the non-resident units. The imports include the value of various goods and services purchased or gratuitously acquisition by the resident units from the non-resident units. Because the provision of services and the use of them happen simultaneously, the import and export of services do not appear to have the phenomena of crossing the border of country. The acquisition of services by the resident units from abroad is usually treated as import while the acquisition of services by non-resident units in this country is usually treated as export.

Corporation Units refer to organizations which are entitled to possess assets, assume liabilities and carry out social economic activities (or can trade with other units) independently.

Active Units refer to organizations or a part of it which carry out one or mainly one social economic activities in certain places.

2 人口、劳动工资和社会保障

POPULATION, LABOR WAGES AND SOCIAL SECURITY

资料整理人员

周俊英　栗金荣　李渔翔

人 口
POPULATION

总户数	Number of Households	1304.35	万户	(10 000 households)
常住人口	Resident Population	3681.64	万人	(10 000 persons)
男 性	Male	1885.96	万人	(10 000 persons)
女 性	Female	1795.68	万人	(10 000 persons)
出生人口	Birth Population	37.79	万人	(10 000 persons)
死亡人口	Death Population	20.27	万人	(10 000 persons)

城乡人口构成 (%)

Composition of Urban and Rural Population (%)

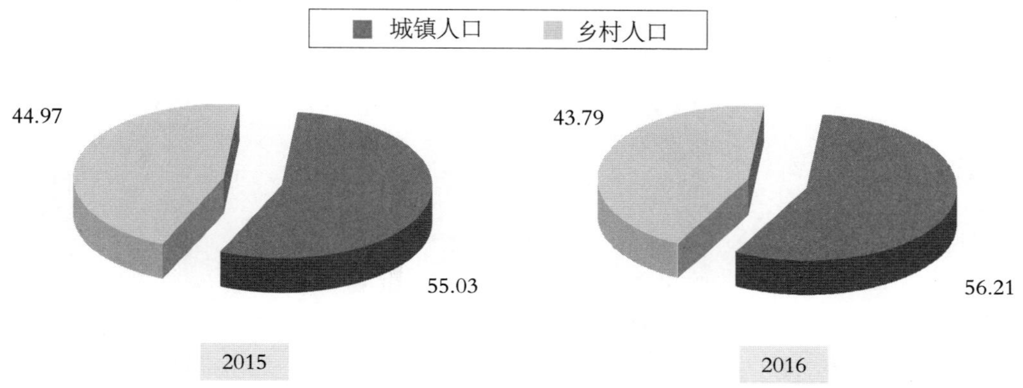

人口出生率、死亡率、自然增长率 (‰)

Birth Rate, Death Rate and Natural Growth Rate of Population (‰)

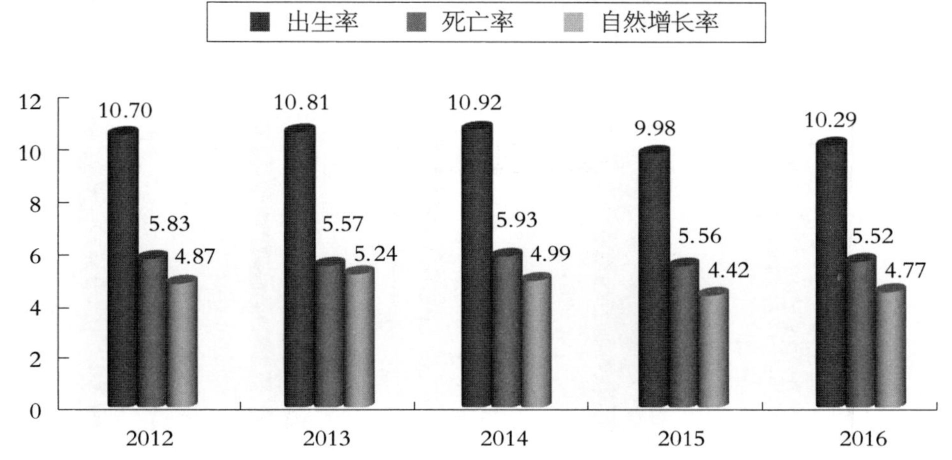

全社会从业人员和劳动报酬
TOTAL EMPLOYEES AND PAYMENT

全社会从业人员	Total Employees	1908.2	万人	(10 000 persons)
第一产业	Primary Industry	670.5	万人	(10 000 persons)
第二产业	Secondary Industry	481.1	万人	(10 000 persons)
第三产业	Tertiary Industry	756.6	万人	(10 000 persons)

全社会从业人员和在岗职工人数（万人）

Number of Total Employees and Fully Employed Staff and Workers (10 000 persons)

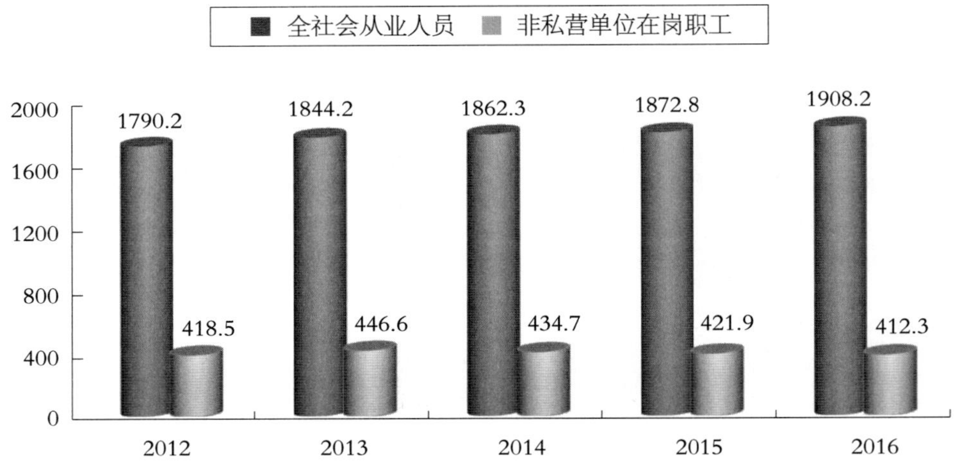

非私营单位在岗职工平均工资（元）

Average Wage of Fully Employed Staff and Workers in Non-private Units (yuan)

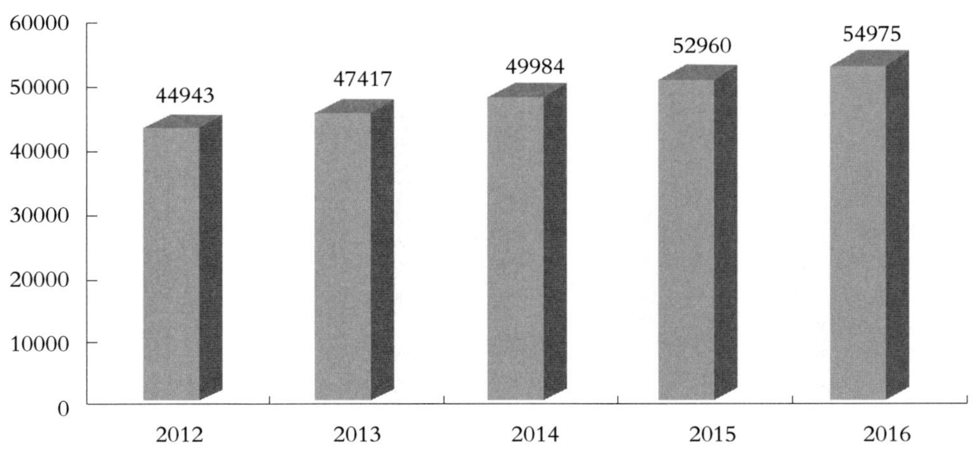

2-1 主要年份总户数、常住人口数
TOTAL HOUSEHOLD AND RESIDENT POPULATION IN MAJOR YEARS

单位：万人 (10 000 persons)

年 份 Year	总户数(万户) Number of Households (10 000 Households)	常住人口 Resident Population	按性别分 By Sex		按农业非农业分 By Registered Residence	
			男 性 Male	女 性 Famle	非农业人口 Non-agriculture	农业人口 Agriculture
1978	558.01	2423.60	1273.07	1150.53	393.79	2029.81
1980	579.71	2476.46	1299.32	1177.14	439.81	2036.65
1985	631.69	2673.51	1403.33	1270.18	536.84	2136.67
1990	740.63	2898.96	1508.62	1390.34	639.22	2259.74
1995	815.23	3077.28	1606.34	1470.94	748.39	2328.89
2000	885.55	3247.80	1680.91	1566.89	861.84	2334.34
2005	1008.04	3355.21	1719.33	1635.88	1010.46	2283.97
2010	1188.84	3574.11	1835.37	1738.75	1144.45	2329.18
2011	1233.13	3593.28	1843.75	1749.52	1162.44	2334.79
2012	1282.40	3610.83	1850.96	1759.87	1171.99	2326.73
2013	1313.25	3629.80	1865.40	1764.40	1189.51	2333.93
2014	1313.35	3647.96	1872.97	1774.99	1192.72	2329.46
2015	1297.74	3664.12	1879.09	1785.03		
2016	1304.35	3681.64	1885.96	1795.68		

注：本表2000年及以后年份农业、非农业人口和2005年及以后年份总户数为公安年报数；2015年起，取消农业户口和非农业户口。

Note: Data of agriculture and non-agriculture population since 2000 and number of households since 2005 are all from public security department. The indicators of agriculture and non-agreculture have been cancelled since 2015.

2-2 主要年份人口自然变动
NATURAL CHANGE OF POPULATION IN MAJOR YEARS

单位：万人 (10 000 persons)

年 份 Year	出 生 Birth		死 亡 Death		自然增长 Natural Growth	
	人 数 Population	出生率 (‰) Birth Rate	人 数 Population	死亡率 (‰) Death Rate	人 数 Population	增长率 (‰) Natural Growth Rate
1978	37.76	15.66	15.80	6.55	21.96	9.11
1980	41.74	16.95	15.98	6.49	25.76	10.46
1985	56.65	21.36	16.87	6.36	39.78	15.00
1990	64.82	22.54	18.87	6.56	45.95	15.98
1995	50.82	16.60	18.73	6.12	32.09	10.48
2000	42.72	13.25	18.59	5.77	24.13	7.48
2005	40.21	12.02	20.07	6.00	20.14	6.02
2010	38.06	10.68	19.18	5.38	18.88	5.30
2011	37.50	10.47	20.10	5.61	17.41	4.86
2012	38.53	10.70	20.99	5.83	17.55	4.87
2013	39.15	10.81	20.17	5.57	18.98	5.24
2014	39.74	10.92	21.58	5.93	18.16	4.99
2015	36.49	9.98	20.33	5.56	16.16	4.42
2016	37.79	10.29	20.27	5.52	17.52	4.77

2-3 城乡人口情况
URBAN AND RURAL POPULATION

单位：万人 (10 000 persons)

年份 Year	城 镇 Urban Area		乡 村 Rural Area	
	人口数 Population	比 重(%) Proportion	人口数 Population	比 重(%) Proportion
1978	464.85	19.18	1958.75	80.82
1979	484.79	19.81	1962.41	80.19
1980	502.72	20.30	1973.74	79.70
1981	517.06	20.61	1991.71	79.39
1982	546.63	21.47	1999.37	78.53
1983	577.73	22.32	2010.67	77.68
1984	610.77	23.21	2020.71	76.79
1985	645.65	24.15	2027.86	75.85
1986	682.72	25.16	2030.81	74.84
1987	721.80	26.17	2036.31	73.83
1988	763.01	27.18	2044.23	72.82
1989	806.54	28.27	2046.44	71.73
1990	837.80	28.90	2061.16	71.10
1991	854.90	29.06	2086.96	70.94
1992	872.04	29.27	2107.27	70.73
1993	889.93	29.54	2122.69	70.46
1994	908.08	29.82	2137.13	70.18
1995	926.57	30.11	2150.71	69.89
1996	945.53	30.41	2163.73	69.59
1997	964.57	30.71	2176.32	69.29
1998	984.33	31.03	2187.87	68.97
1999	1004.34	31.35	2199.29	68.65
2000	1165.31	35.88	2082.49	64.12
2001	1147.92	35.09	2123.71	64.91
2002	1254.56	38.09	2039.15	61.91
2003	1286.28	38.81	2028.01	61.19
2004	1321.65	39.63	2013.42	60.37
2005	1412.81	42.11	1942.40	57.89
2006	1451.39	43.01	1923.16	56.99
2007	1493.75	44.03	1898.83	55.97
2008	1538.58	45.11	1872.06	54.89
2009	1576.09	45.99	1851.27	54.01
2010	1717.43	48.05	1856.68	51.95
2011	1785.31	49.68	1807.97	50.32
2012	1851.08	51.26	1759.75	48.74
2013	1907.92	52.56	1721.88	47.44
2014	1962.32	53.79	1685.64	46.21
2015	2016.37	55.03	1647.75	44.97
2016	2069.63	56.21	1612.01	43.79

2-4 主要年份人口年龄构成和抚养比

AGE COMPOSITION AND DEPENDENCY RATIO OF POPULATION IN MAJOR YEARS

单位：% (%)

年 份 Year	年龄构成 Age Composition			抚养比 Dependency Ratio		
	0—14岁 Age 0-14	15—64岁 Age 15-64	65岁及以上 Age 65 and Over	总抚养比 Gross Dependency Ratio	少儿抚养比 Children Dependency Ratio	老年抚养比 Old People Dependency Ratio
1953	33.89	61.37	4.74	62.95	55.22	7.72
1964	40.43	55.22	4.35	81.09	73.22	7.88
1982	33.36	61.65	4.99	62.21	54.11	8.09
1990	28.15	66.46	5.39	50.47	42.36	8.11
2000	25.73	67.94	6.33	47.19	37.87	9.32
2005	21.30	71.55	7.15	39.76	29.77	9.99
2010	17.10	75.33	7.58	32.75	22.70	10.06
2011	16.47	75.62	7.91	32.24	21.78	10.46
2012	16.44	75.59	7.97	32.29	21.75	10.54
2013	15.83	75.80	8.37	31.93	20.88	11.04
2014	15.67	75.65	8.68	32.19	20.71	11.47
2015	15.50	75.40	9.10	32.63	20.56	12.07
2016	15.45	75.06	9.49	33.23	20.58	12.64

注：1953、1964、1982、1990、2000、2010年为六次人口普查数据，其余年份为人口抽样调查推算数。

Note: Data of 1953,1964,1982,1990,2000 and 2010 in this table are obtained from six National Population Census, and the rest are caculated from the Sample Survey of Population .

2-5 主要年份全社会从业人员年末人数

TOTAL EMPLOYEES AT YEAR-END IN MAJOR YEARS

单位：万人 (10 000 persons)

年 份 Year	从业人员合计 Total Employees	在岗职工 Fully Employed Staff and Workers	国有单位 State-Owned Units	城镇集体单位 Urban Collective-Owned Units	其他单位 Other-Owned Units	其他从业人员 Other Employees	城镇私营企业及个体 Urban Private Enterprises and Self-employed Individuals	农村及乡镇企业 Rural, Township and Village Enterprises
1978	965.23	268.30	227.34	40.96			0.12	696.81
1980	1002.64	298.98	246.24	52.74			1.08	702.58
1985	1154.11	377.09	291.49	85.27	0.33		8.18	768.84
1990	1304.01	438.68	340.94	97.41	0.33		11.84	853.49
1995	1424.52	463.51	370.14	88.14	5.23	15.41	34.48	911.12
2000	1392.40	370.16	276.62	48.24	45.30	11.64	48.66	961.94
2005	1500.20	352.11	247.50	29.83	74.78	8.38	80.15	1059.56
2010	1685.90	384.48	231.90	22.79	129.79	9.93	171.50	1100.01
2011	1738.89	398.62	237.25	23.72	137.65	11.07	199.66	1129.53
2012	1790.17	418.48	232.44	23.75	162.29	17.52	216.47	1137.70
2013	1844.20	446.56	201.36	20.35	224.85	17.48	233.45	1146.71
2014	1862.29	434.72	197.32	18.61	218.79	17.37	250.20	1160.00
2015	1872.76	421.90	193.81	16.54	211.55	18.37	272.29	1160.20
2016	1908.21	412.35	190.33	15.92	206.10	18.20	317.10	1160.56

2-6 全社会劳动力资源配置情况
LABOR RESOURCES ALLOCATION IN THE WHOLE SOCIETY

单位：万人 (10 000 persons)

指　　标	Item	2015	2016
年末劳动力资源总数	**Labor Resources at Year-end**	**2762.8**	**2724.0**
年末劳动力配置	**Labor Allocation at Year-end**		
一、从业人员	**Number of Employees**	**1872.8**	**1908.2**
按经济类型分	**By Ownership**		
1.国有经济	State-Owned Economy	201.9	199.9
2.集体经济	Colletive-Owned Economy	952.6	948.1
3.私营经济	Private Economy	234.4	241.4
4.个体经济	Indivdual Economy	262.9	306.0
5.联营经济	Joint-Owned Economy	0.4	0.3
6.股份制经济	Share Holding Ecnonmy	27.0	25.5
7.外商投资经济	Foreign Funded Economy	8.4	7.5
8.港、澳、台投资经济	Economy Funded By Entrepreneurs from Hongkong, Macao and Taiwan	10.8	12.5
9.其他经济	Other Types of Ownership	174.3	167.1
按国民经济行业分	**By Sector**		
1.农、林、牧、渔业	Farming, Forestry, Animal Husbandry and Fishery	666.6	670.5
2.采矿业	Mining	170.0	144.3
3.制造业	Manufacturing	168.1	187.2
4.电力、热力、燃气及水生产和供应业	Production and Supply of Electricity, Heat, Gas and Water	12.6	13.7
5.建筑业	Construction	141.1	136.0
6.批发和零售业	Wholesale and Retail Trade	211.6	230.8
7.交通运输、仓储和邮政业	Transport, Storage and Post	97.3	99.7
8.住宿和餐饮业	Hotels and Catering Services	71.2	81.8
9.信息传输、软件和信息技术服务业	Information Transmission, Software and Information Technology Services	27.3	27.6
10.金融业	Financial Industry	19.2	20.2
11.房地产业	Real Estate Trade	8.2	8.4
12.租赁和商务服务业	Lease and Business Services	20.0	20.9
13.科学研究和技术服务业	Scientific Reseach and Technical Services	10.5	10.4
14.水利、环境和公共设施管理业	Water, Environmental Protection and Public Facility Management	11.3	11.5
15.居民服务、修理和其他服务业	Resident Services, Repair and Other Services	23.3	30.3
16.教　育	Education	52.1	51.7
17.卫生和社会工作	Health Care and Social Work	21.4	22.1
18.文化、体育和娱乐业	Culture, Sports and Recreation	7.5	8.3
19.公共管理、社会保障和社会组织	Public Management, Social Security and Social Organization	58.0	58.2
20.其他行业	Others	75.7	74.9
按三次产业分	**By Type of Industry**		
1.第一产业	Primary Industry	666.6	670.5
2.第二产业	Secondry Industry	491.7	481.1
3.第三产业	Tertiary Industry	714.4	756.6
二、城镇登记失业人员	**Urban Unemployed Registered**	**25.6**	**26.1**
三、16岁以上在校学生	**Student Enrollment Over Age 16**	**182.1**	**172.8**
四、其他劳动者	**Others**	**682.4**	**616.9**

2-7 非私营单位从业人员(2016年)
NUMBER OF EMPLOYEES IN NON-PRIVATE UNITS(2016)

单位：人 (person)

项目	Item	从业人员 Number of Employees	#女性 Female	在岗职工 Fully Employed	其他从业人员 Other Employees
总计	**Total**	**4305525**	**1477117**	**4123482**	**182043**
一、按企业、事业、机关分	**Grouped By Enterprises, Institutions and Government Agencies**				
#1.企业	Enterprises	2787132	753153	2675591	111541
2.事业	Institutions	1052238	574136	997192	55046
3.机关	Government Agencies	454900	143954	440080	14820
二、按国民经济行业分	**Grouped By Sector**				
1.农、林、牧、渔业	Farming, Forestry, Animal Husbandry and Fishery	17389	4950	17210	179
2.采矿业	Mining	910853	156358	898866	11987
3.制造业	Manufacturing	637631	201854	625548	12083
4.电力、热力、燃气及水生产和供应业	Production and Supply of Electricity, Heat, Gas and Water	125355	37463	123145	2210
5.建筑业	Construction	294152	46993	273884	20268
6.批发和零售业	Wholesale and Retail Trade	170781	68905	163790	6991
7.交通运输、仓储和邮政业	Transport, Storage and Post	234470	56055	228380	6090
8.住宿和餐饮业	Hotels and Catering Services	39338	21790	34514	4824
9.信息传输、软件和信息技术服务业	Information Transmission, Software and Information Technology Services	49690	21713	46750	2940
10.金融业	Financial Industry	178822	90678	142225	36597
11.房地产业	Real Estate	34821	13624	32172	2649
12.租赁和商务服务业	Lease and Business Services	90796	23874	85972	4824
13.科学研究和技术服务业	Scientific Reseach and Technial Services	72279	23380	70499	1780
14.水利、环境和公共设施管理业	Water, Environmental Protection and Public Facility Management	97995	42725	80432	17563
15.居民服务、修理和其它服务业	Resident Services, Repair and Other Services	6249	2458	6009	240
16.教育	Education	512600	320360	498218	14382
17.卫生和社会工作	Health Care and Social Work	204858	133858	193798	11060
18.文化、体育和娱乐业	Culture, Sports and Recreation	45774	21273	43638	2136
19.公共管理、社会保障和社会组织	Public Management, Social Security and Social Organization	581672	188806	558432	23240
总计中:国有控股	**Share Controlled by State**	**2025915**	**514290**	**1944938**	**80977**

注：在岗职工包含劳务派遣工，后同。

Note: Dispatching workers are included in fully employed workers. The same applies to the tables following.

2-8 非私营单位从业人员劳动报酬(2016年)
REWARD OF EMPLOYEES IN NON-PRIVATE UNITS(2016)

单位：万元 (10 000 yuan)

项 目	Item	从业人员劳动报酬 Total Reward of Employees	在岗职工工资总额 Wages of Fully Employed	其他从业人员劳动报 酬 Reward of Other Employees	在岗职工平均工资(元) Average Wages of Fully Employed (yuan)
总 计	**Total**	**23032647**	**22575147**	**457500**	**54975**
一、按企业、事业、机关分	**Grouped By Enterprises, Institutions and Government Agencies**				
#1.企 业	Enterprises	14665653	14344218	321435	53833
2.事 业	Institutions	5777662	5670392	107270	57150
3.机 关	Government Agencies	2536856	2509576	27280	57161
二、按国民经济行业分	**Grouped By Sector**				
1.农、林、牧、渔业	Farming, Forestry, Animal Husbandry and Fishery	79825	79438	387	46118
2.采矿业	Mining	5116737	5082715	34022	56413
3.制造业	Manufacturing	2670062	2638404	31658	42578
4.电力、热力、燃气及水生产和供应业	Production and Supply of Electricity, Heat, Gas and Water	904539	900054	4485	74696
5.建筑业	Construction	1363970	1272347	91623	46893
6.批发和零售业	Wholesale and Retail Trade	660622	647237	13386	39909
7.交通运输、仓储和邮政业	Transport, Storage and Post	1624827	1605727	19100	69884
8.住宿和餐饮业	Hotels and Catering Services	113598	106427	7171	30795
9.信息传输、软件和信息技术服务业	Information Transmission, Software and Information Technology Services	329700	315341	14359	65876
10.金融业	Financial Industry	1323810	1239052	84758	87737
11.房地产业	Real Estate	148127	141964	6162	44731
12.租赁和商务服务业	Lease and Business Services	337050	326414	10636	38689
13.科学研究和技术服务业	Scientific Reseach and Technial Services	435444	429143	6301	61031
14.水利、环境和公共设施管理业	Water, Environmental Protection and Public Facility Management	286812	259528	27284	32411
15.居民服务、修理和其它服务业	Resident Services, Repair and Other Services	22892	22359	533	36872
16.教 育	Education	3190451	3165648	24803	63826
17.卫生和社会工作	Health Care and Social Work	1038050	1009498	28552	52650
18.文化、体育和娱乐业	Culture, Sports and Recreation	225544	218970	6574	49987
19.公共管理、社会保障和社会组织	Public Management, Social Security and Social Organization	3160588	3114881	45707	55916
总计中:国有控股	**Share Controlled by State**	**11477958**	**11242175**	**235783**	**57661**

2-9 国有单位从业人员(2016年)
NUMBER OF EMPLOYEES IN STATE-OWNED UNITS(2016)

单位：人 (person)

项　目	Item	从业人员 Number of Employees	#女性 Female	在岗职工 Fully Employed	其他从业人员 Other Employees
总　计	**Total**	**1998589**	**848224**	**1903284**	**95305**
一、按隶属关系分	**Grouped By Administrative Relationship**				
1.中　央	Central Government	243262	63478	238464	4798
2.省、自治区、直辖市	Province	326840	122004	306842	19998
3.地　区	Prefecture	359121	153072	341221	17900
4.县及县以下	County and Below	1069366	509670	1016757	52609
二、按企业、事业、机关分	**Grouped By Enterprises, Institutions and Government Agencies**				
#1.企　业	Enterprises	525954	148727	498692	27262
#地　方	Local	308199	94558	285480	22719
2.事　业	Institutions	1016581	555084	963450	53131
#地　方	Local	1005817	551374	952783	53034
3.机　关	Government Agencies	453641	143333	438892	14749
#地　方	Local	439102	137872	424511	14591
三、按国民经济行业分	**Grouped By Sector**				
1.农、林、牧、渔业	Farming, Forestry, Animal Husbandry and Fishery	15440	4394	15261	179
2.采矿业	Mining	21724	4882	21081	643
3.制造业	Manufacturing	37616	12489	36753	863
4.电力、热力、燃气及水生产和供应业	Production and Supply of Electricity, Heat, Gas and Water	64697	19659	63598	1099
5.建筑业	Construction	58602	10453	55021	3581
6.批发和零售业	Wholesale and Retail Trade	41881	14536	40869	1012
7.交通运输、仓储和邮政业	Transport, Storage and Post	174069	37643	170657	3412
8.住宿和餐饮业	Hotels and Catering Services	13737	7215	13039	698
9.信息传输、软件和信息技术服务业	Information Transmission, Software and Information Technology Services	8503	3178	7828	675
10.金融业	Financial Industry	62793	28493	50177	12616
11.房地产业	Real Estate	8160	3052	7720	440
12.租赁和商务服务业	Lease and Business Services	51153	9841	47971	3182
13.科学研究和技术服务业	Scientific Reseach and Technial Services	56860	19278	55536	1324
14.水利、环境和公共设施管理业	Water, Environmental Protection and Public Facility Management	84298	36011	67809	16489
15.居民服务、修理和其它服务业	Resident Services, Repair and Other Services	3048	1125	2987	61
16.教　育	Education	495248	310749	481390	13858
17.卫生和社会工作	Health Care and Social Work	180103	118517	170006	10097
18.文化、体育和娱乐业	Culture, Sports and Recreation	39615	18128	37779	1836
19.公共管理、社会保障和社会组织	Public Management, Social Security and Social Organization	581042	188581	557802	23240

2-10 国有单位从业人员劳动报酬(2016年)
REWARD OF EMPLOYEES IN STATE-OWNED UNITS(2016)

单位：万元 (10 000 yuan)

项　目	Item	从业人员劳动报酬 Total Reward of Employees	在岗职工工资总额 Wages of Fully Employed	其他从业人员劳动报酬 Reward of Other Employees	在岗职工平均工资(元) Average Wages of Fully Employed (yuan)
总　计	**Total**	**11379609**	**11178725**	**200884**	**58952**
一、按隶属关系分	**Grouped By Administrative Relationship**				
1.中　央	Central Government	2101536	2084529	17007	87579
2.省、自治区、直辖市	Province	2012765	1968361	44404	63987
3.地　区	Prefecture	1862402	1817535	44868	53885
4.县及县以下	County and Below	5402906	5308301	94605	52387
二、按企业、事业、机关分	**Grouped By Enterprises, Institutions and Government Agencies**				
#1.企　业	Enterprises	3206797	3137188	69609	63055
#地　方	Local	1264029	1210858	53171	42528
2.事　业	Institutions	5632757	5528899	103858	57677
#地　方	Local	5564639	5461093	103546	57608
3.机　关	Government Agencies	2530552	2503367	27185	57174
#地　方	Local	2440862	2413934	26928	57002
三、按国民经济行业分	**Grouped By Sector**				
1.农、林、牧、渔业	Farming, Forestry, Animal Husbandry and Fishery	73894	73508	387	48110
2.采矿业	Mining	123363	120652	2711	57008
3.制造业	Manufacturing	138554	136591	1963	36845
4.电力、热力、燃气及水生产和供应业	Production and Supply of Electricity, Heat, Gas and Water	481462	479556	1906	78259
5.建筑业	Construction	236325	219850	16475	39051
6.批发和零售业	Wholesale and Retail Trade	189699	187503	2196	45553
7.交通运输、仓储和邮政业	Transport, Storage and Post	1361310	1350680	10630	78485
8.住宿和餐饮业	Hotels and Catering Services	42130	40075	2055	30782
9.信息传输、软件和信息技术服务业	Information Transmission, Software and Information Technology Services	56026	52949	3077	67970
10.金融业	Financial Industry	442647	421509	21138	84206
11.房地产业	Real Estate	27945	27290	655	35762
12.租赁和商务服务业	Lease and Business Services	178176	170944	7232	37399
13.科学研究和技术服务业	Scientific Reseach and Technial Services	342097	337997	4100	60954
14.水利、环境和公共设施管理业	Water, Environmental Protection and Public Facility Management	253874	228289	25585	33842
15.居民服务、修理和其它服务业	Resident Services, Repair and Other Services	12324	12165	159	40686
16.教　育	Education	3128575	3105295	23280	64803
17.卫生和社会工作	Health Care and Social Work	933579	907276	26303	53955
18.文化、体育和娱乐业	Culture, Sports and Recreation	203602	198275	5327	52169
19.公共管理、社会保障和社会组织	Public Management, Social Security and Social Organization	3154028	3108321	45707	55862

2-11 城镇集体单位从业人员(2016年)

NUMBER OF EMPLOYEES IN URBAN COLLECTIVE-OWNED UNITS(2016)

单位：人　　(person)

项　目	Item	从业人员 Number of Employees	#女性 Female	在岗职工 Fully Employed	其他从业人员 Other Employees
总　计	**Total**	**167947**	**71459**	**159179**	**8768**
一、按企业、事业、机关分	**Grouped By Enterprises, Institutions and Government Agencies**				
#1.企　业	Enterprises	137302	55293	130357	6945
2.事　业	Institutions	29512	15667	27689	1823
3.机　关	Government Agencies	601	231	601	
二、按国民经济行业分	**Grouped By Sector**				
1.农、林、牧、渔业	Farming, Forestry, Animal Husbandry and Fishery	476	126	476	
2.采矿业	Mining	8358	909	7939	419
3.制造业	Manufacturing	33802	17583	33035	767
4.电力、热力、燃气及水生产和供应业	Production and Supply of Electricity, Heat, Gas and Water	599	252	599	
5.建筑业	Construction	19692	3902	16384	3308
6.批发和零售业	Wholesale and Retail Trade	24201	7908	23875	326
7.交通运输、仓储和邮政业	Transport, Storage and Post	2498	762	2478	20
8.住宿和餐饮业	Hotels and Catering Services	1528	807	1474	54
9.信息传输、软件和信息技术服务业	Information Transmission, Software and Information Technology Services	159	65	154	5
10.金融业	Financial Industry	40136	19742	38407	1729
11.房地产业	Real Estate	1016	419	975	41
12.租赁和商务服务业	Lease and Business Services	3982	1732	3824	158
13.科学研究和技术服务业	Scientific Reseach and Technial Services	563	195	528	35
14.水利、环境和公共设施管理业	Water, Environmental Protection and Public Facility Management	7028	3556	6117	911
15.居民服务、修理和其它服务业	Resident Services, Repair and Other Services	1325	619	1172	153
16.教　育	Education	2560	1282	2525	35
17.卫生和社会工作	Health Care and Social Work	18383	10972	17645	738
18.文化、体育和娱乐业	Culture, Sports and Recreation	1293	522	1224	69
19.公共管理、社会保障和社会组织	Public Management, Social Security and Social Organization	348	106	348	

2-12 城镇集体单位从业人员劳动报酬(2016年)
REWARD OF EMPLOYEES IN URBAN COLLECTIVE-OWNED UNITS(2016)

单位：万元 (10 000 yuan)

项　目	Item	从业人员劳动报酬 Total Reward of Employees	在岗职工工资总额 Wages of Fully Employed	其他从业人员劳动报　酬 Reward of Other Employees	在岗职工平均工资(元) Average Wages of Fully Employed (yuan)
总　计	**Total**	**751047**	**732277**	**18770**	**45794**
一、按企业、事业、机关分	**Grouped By Enterprises, Institutions and Government Agencies**				
#1.企　业	Enterprises	627199	611594	15606	46589
2.事　业	Institutions	118547	115383	3164	41965
3.机　关	Government Agencies	3181	3181		52925
二、按国民经济行业分	**Grouped By Sector**				
1.农、林、牧、渔业	Farming, Forestry, Animal Husbandry and Fishery	2558	2558		53407
2.采矿业	Mining	47552	47321	230	59984
3.制造业	Manufacturing	101995	100185	1809	29968
4.电力、热力、燃气及水生产和供应业	Production and Supply of Electricity, Heat, Gas and Water	1318	1318		25696
5.建筑业	Construction	66874	59040	7834	34004
6.批发和零售业	Wholesale and Retail Trade	49089	48667	422	20511
7.交通运输、仓储和邮政业	Transport, Storage and Post	6608	6580	28	26564
8.住宿和餐饮业	Hotels and Catering Services	4385	4292	94	28899
9.信息传输、软件和信息技术服务业	Information Transmission, Software and Information Technology Services	569	563	6	36532
10.金融业	Financial Industry	330923	326281	4642	85620
11.房地产业	Real Estate	2109	2017	92	20705
12.租赁和商务服务业	Lease and Business Services	16709	16485	223	42719
13.科学研究和技术服务业	Scientific Reseach and Technial Services	2251	2201	50	41131
14.水利、环境和公共设施管理业	Water, Environmental Protection and Public Facility Management	16443	15082	1361	24660
15.居民服务、修理和其它服务业	Resident Services, Repair and Other Services	3040	2712	329	22673
16.教　育	Education	12715	12617	98	50426
17.卫生和社会工作	Health Care and Social Work	79338	77999	1339	44479
18.文化、体育和娱乐业	Culture, Sports and Recreation	3801	3588	213	29583
19.公共管理、社会保障和社会组织	Public Management, Social Security and Social Organization	2772	2772		79647

2-13 其他单位从业人员(2016年)
NUMBER OF EMPLOYEES IN OTHER-OWNED UNITS(2016)

单位：人 (person)

项目	Item	从业人员 Number of Employees	#女性 Female	在岗职工 Fully Employed	其他人员 Other Employees
总计	**Total**	**2138989**	**557434**	**2061019**	**77970**
一、按登记注册类型分	**Grouped by Registered Kind**				
内资	Civil Funded Enterprises	1939077	485377	1867280	71797
1.股份合作	Share Cooperative Enterprises	6885	3328	6623	262
2.联营	Joint Owned Enterprises	3646	781	3563	83
#国有联营	State-owned Joint Owned Enterprises	1506	185	1431	75
集体联营	Collective-owned Joint Owned Enterprises	1292	363	1284	8
3.有限责任公司	Limited Liability Company	1645732	380531	1602156	43576
#国有独资	Company Exclusively with Investment from State	353759	96475	344162	9597
4.股份有限公司	Share Holding Limited Company	255301	88473	228345	26956
5.其他	Others	27513	12264	26593	920
港、澳、台商投资	Enterprises Funded by HongKong, Macao and Taiwan	123095	44067	121888	1207
外商投资	Foreign Funded Enterprises	76817	27990	71851	4966
二、按企业、事业、机关分	**Grouped By Enterprises, Institutions and Government Agencies**				
#1.企业	Enterprises	2123876	549133	2046542	77334
2.事业	Institutions	6145	3385	6053	92
三、按国民经济行业分	**Grouped By Sector**				
1.农、林、牧、渔业	Farming, Forestry, Animal Husbandry and Fishery	1473	430	1473	
2.采矿业	Mining	880771	150567	869846	10925
3.制造业	Manufacturing	566213	171782	555760	10453
4.电力、热力、燃气及水生产和供应业	Production and Supply of Electricity, Heat, Gas and Water	60059	17552	58948	1111
5.建筑业	Construction	215858	32638	202479	13379
6.批发和零售业	Wholesale and Retail Trade	104699	46461	99046	5653
7.交通运输、仓储和邮政业	Transport, Storage and Post	57903	17650	55245	2658
8.住宿和餐饮业	Hotels and Catering Services	24073	13768	20001	4072
9.信息传输、软件和信息技术服务业	Information Transmission, Software and Information Technology Services	41028	18470	38768	2260
10.金融业	Financial Industry	75893	42443	53641	22252
11.房地产业	Real Estate	25645	10153	23477	2168
12.租赁和商务服务业	Lease and Business Services	35661	12301	34177	1484
13.科学研究和技术服务业	Scientific Reseach and Technial Services	14856	3907	14435	421
14.水利、环境和公共设施管理业	Water, Environmental Protection and Public Facility Management	6669	3158	6506	163
15.居民服务、修理和其它服务业	Resident Services, Repair and Other Services	1876	714	1850	26
16.教育	Education	14792	8329	14303	489
17.卫生和社会工作	Health Care and Social Work	6372	4369	6147	225
18.文化、体育和娱乐业	Culture, Sports and Recreation	4866	2623	4635	231
19.公共管理、社会保障和社会组织	Public Management, Social Security and Social Organization	282	119	282	

2-14 其他单位从业人员劳动报酬(2016年)
REWARD OF EMPLOYEES IN OTHER-OWNED UNITS(2016)

单位：万元 (10 000 yuan)

项目	Item	从业人员劳动报酬 Total Reward of Employees	在岗职工工资总额 Wages of Fully Employed	其他从业人员劳动报酬 Reward of Other Employees	在岗职工平均工资(元) Average Wages of Fully Employed (yuan)
总计	**Total**	**10901991**	**10664144**	**237847**	**52013**
一、按登记注册类型分	**Grouped by Registered Kind**				
内资	Civil Funded Enterprises	9946875	9723826	223049	52210
1.股份合作	Share Cooperative Enterprises	42180	41684	496	63456
2.联营	Joint Owned Enterprises	17953	17694	259	49703
#国有联营	State-owned Joint Owned Enterprises	11318	11198	119	76180
集体联营	Collective-owned Joint Owned Enterprises	4014	3928	86	31227
3.有限责任公司	Limited Liability Company	8363617	8222161	141456	51461
#国有独资	Company Exclusively with Investment from State	1917882	1899851	18031	55481
4. 股份有限公司	Share Holding Limited Company	1433967	1355596	78372	59173
5. 其他	Others	89158	86691	2467	34034
港、澳、台商投资	Enterprises Funded by HongKong, Macao and Taiwan	518667	512961	5706	44868
外商投资	Foreign Funded Enterprises	436449	427357	9092	58115
二、按企业、事业、机关分	**Grouped By Enterprises, Institutions and Government Agencies**				
#1.企业	Enterprises	10831656	10595436	236220	52046
2.事业	Institutions	26359	26110	249	42845
三、按国民经济行业分	**Grouped By Sector**				
1.农、林、牧、渔业	Farming, Forestry, Animal Husbandry and Fishery	3372	3372		22988
2.采矿业	Mining	4945823	4914742	31080	56367
3.制造业	Manufacturing	2429513	2401628	27885	43733
4.电力、热力、燃气及水生产和供应业	Production and Supply of Electricity, Heat, Gas and Water	421759	419179	2580	71404
5.建筑业	Construction	1060771	993457	67314	50259
6.批发和零售业	Wholesale and Retail Trade	421834	411067	10768	42252
7.交通运输、仓储和邮政业	Transport, Storage and Post	256909	248467	8442	45013
8.住宿和餐饮业	Hotels and Catering Services	67083	62060	5023	30943
9.信息传输、软件和信息技术服务业	Information Transmission, Software and Information Technology Services	273105	261829	11276	65580
10.金融业	Financial Industry	550239	491262	58978	92590
11.房地产业	Real Estate	118073	112657	5416	48702
12.租赁和商务服务业	Lease and Business Services	142166	138984	3181	39937
13.科学研究和技术服务业	Scientific Reseach and Technial Services	91096	88945	2151	62069
14.水利、环境和公共设施管理业	Water, Environmental Protection and Public Facility Management	16496	16157	338	24850
15.居民服务、修理和其它服务业	Resident Services, Repair and Other Services	7528	7482	45	39841
16.教育	Education	49162	47737	1425	33408
17.卫生和社会工作	Health Care and Social Work	25133	24223	911	40064
18.文化、体育和娱乐业	Culture, Sports and Recreation	18140	17106	1034	37301
19.公共管理、社会保障和社会组织	Public Management, Social Security and Social Organization	3789	3789		134355

2-15 私营单位从业人员和劳动报酬(2016年)
NUMBER AND REWARD OF EMPLOYEES IN PRIVATE UNITS(2016)

项　目	Item	从业人员(人) Number of Employees (person)	劳动报酬总额(万元) Total Reward of Employees (10 000 yuan)	平均劳动报酬(元) Average Reward of Employees (yuan)
总　计	**Total**	**2168433**	**6600416**	**30501**
按国民经济行业分	**Grouped By Sector**			
1.农、林、牧、渔业	Farming, Forestry, Animal Husbandry and Fishery	63710	137200	21144
2.采矿业	Mining	135751	518521	38096
3.制造业	Manufacturing	621415	1909252	30736
4.电力、热力、燃气及水生产和供应业	Production and Supply of Electricity, Heat, Gas and Water	19731	57341	31722
5.建筑业	Construction	320292	1118334	35151
6.批发和零售业	Wholesale and Retail Trade	411257	1111519	26948
7.交通运输、仓储和邮政业	Transport, Storage and Post	106395	316435	30365
8.住宿和餐饮业	Hotels and Catering Services	83492	209231	25721
9.信息传输、软件和信息技术服务业	Information Transmission, Software and Information Technology Services	34433	116027	33433
10.金融业	Financial Industry	12416	40544	34297
11.房地产业	Real Estate	106867	354170	33398
12.租赁和商务服务业	Lease and Business Services	84956	226148	26511
13.科学研究和技术服务业	Scientific Reseach and Technical Services	35171	109039	30892
14.水利、环境和公共设施管理业	Water, Environmental Protection and Public Facility Management	17484	51672	25904
15.居民服务、修理和其他服务业	Resident Services, Repair and Other Services	46970	132761	28188
16.教　育	Education	25957	71825	27957
17.卫生和社会工作	Health Care and Social Work	19423	67215	35466
18.文化、体育和娱乐业	Culture, Sports and Recreation	22650	53004	23396
19.公共管理、社会保障和社会组织	Public Management, Social Security and Social Organization	63	178	28317

2-16 主要年份在岗职工平均工资及指数

AVERAGE WAGE AND RELATED INDICES OF FULLY EMPLOYED STAFF AND WORKERS IN MAJOR YEARS

单位：元 (yuan)

年 份 Year	在岗职工平均工资 Average Wage of Fully Employed	指 数 (1952年＝100) Indices (year of 1952=100)		国有单位平均工资 Average Wage of State-owned Units
		货币工资 Money Wage	实际工资 Real Wage	
1952	375	100.0	100.0	394
1978	632	168.5	145.8	655
1980	754	201.1	163.2	795
1985	1122	299.2	201.9	1200
1990	2111	562.9	228.3	2263
1995	4721	1258.9	258.2	5094
2000	6918	1844.8	323.5	7249
2005	15645	4172.0	702.3	16027
2010	33544	8945.1	1301.2	33119
2011	39903	10640.8	1470.0	37164
2012	44943	11984.8	1616.7	41561
2013	47417	12644.5	1655.3	43228
2014	49984	13329.1	1717.4	47001
2015	52960	14122.7	1807.1	54953
2016	54975	14650.0	1856.7	58952

年 份 Year	指 数 (1952年＝100) Indices (year of 1952=100)		集体单位平均工资 Average Wage of Collective -owned Units	指 数(1952年＝100) Indices (year of 1952=100)	
	货币工资 Money Wage	实际工资 Real Wage		货币工资 Money Wage	实际工资 Real Wage
1952	100.0	100.0	307	100.0	100.0
1978	166.2	143.8	519	169.1	146.2
1980	201.8	163.8	581	189.3	153.6
1985	304.6	205.5	856	278.8	188.1
1990	574.4	232.9	1565	509.8	206.7
1995	1292.9	265.2	3108	1012.4	207.6
2000	1839.8	322.7	4193	1365.8	239.5
2005	4067.8	684.7	10157	3308.4	556.9
2010	8405.8	1222.7	21993	7163.8	1046.1
2011	9432.5	1303.0	27669	9012.7	1245.0
2012	10548.5	1423.0	33355	10864.8	1465.6
2013	10971.6	1436.3	37152	12101.2	1584.2
2014	11929.2	1537.0	39887	12992.5	1674.4
2015	13881.5	1776.2	44114	14369.4	1838.6
2016	14962.4	1895.0	45794	14916.6	1889.2

2-17 城镇职工社会保障基本情况
BASIC SOCIAL SECURITY OF STAFF AND WORKERS IN URBAN UNITS

年 份 Year	参加保险人数(万人) Active Contributors (10 000 persons)				基金收入(亿元) Fund Revenue(100 million yuan)		
	城镇在岗职工养老保险 Basic Pension Insurance of Fully Employed		失业保险 Unempl-oyment Insurance	医疗保险 Basic Medical Insurance	城镇在岗职工养老保险 Basic Pension Insurance of Fully Employed		失业保险 Unemployment Insurance
	企 业 Enterprises	机关事业 Government Agencies and Institutions			企 业 Enterprises	机关事业 Government Agencies and Institutions	
2000	358.81		254.80		53.87		2.43
2001	365.57		286.10	156.00	58.05		2.94
2002	361.24		278.90	217.00	75.91		3.42
2003	364.42	67.13	284.10	272.00	86.27	7.09	3.80
2004	376.08	68.71	286.50	295.00	109.30	9.04	4.22
2005	383.43	80.08	288.50	325.00	118.90	11.96	5.53
2010	494.92	96.11	305.05	935.00	357.13	48.24	13.52
2011	523.93	99.84	309.35	1005.06	516.78	56.93	18.62
2012	548.67	100.02	380.88	1055.90	602.26	64.68	25.05
2013	570.21	102.22	400.98	1086.30	563.51	75.53	34.13
2014	588.73	103.30	407.68	1100.70	580.56	83.35	36.07
2015	604.23	110.00	411.29	1113.81	586.07	102.52	30.61
2016	620.57	139.64	415.15	1121.16	652.11	135.92	27.51

年 份 Year		基金支出(亿元) Fund Expenditure(100 million yuan)				城 镇 低保人数 (万人) Persons Receiving Lowest Cost of Living (10 000 persons)
	医疗保险 Basic Medical Insurance	城镇在岗职工养老保险 Basic Pension Insurance of Fully Employed		失业保险 Unemployment Insurance	医疗保险 Basic Medical Insurance	
		企 业 Enterprises	机关事业 Government Agencies and Institutions			
2000		50.62		1.34		3.06
2001	1.32	51.22		1.49	0.68	28.53
2002	4.13	60.32		2.12	1.53	62.21
2003	10.19	65.18	8.19	3.17	4.80	84.21
2004	17.88	76.30	12.40	2.58	10.98	84.86
2005	25.60	78.37	14.75	2.78	15.75	84.97
2010	86.74	226.81	43.61	6.56	69.65	91.51
2011	106.32	367.39	51.79	5.64	84.07	91.69
2012	141.04	437.23	58.24	4.96	104.24	89.04
2013	160.93	411.31	66.49	5.22	128.25	85.03
2014	163.22	480.56	75.36	13.44	146.54	72.60
2015	178.60	554.76	102.20	13.79	154.17	59.90
2016	187.17	614.57	132.31	11.87	170.25	53.10

主要统计指标解释

人口数 指一定时点、一定地区范围内有生命的个人总和。

年度统计的年末人口数指每年 12 月 31 日 24 时的常住人口数。

常住人口 包括：1、住本乡（镇）街道，户口登记地在本乡（镇）街道；2、住本乡（镇）街道半年以上，户口登记地在其他乡（镇）街道；3、住本乡（镇）街道不满半年，但是已离开户口登记地半年以上；4、户口登记地在本乡（镇）街道，离开不满半年；5、住本乡（镇）街道，户口待定。6、户口登记地在本乡（镇）街道，现居住国外。

城镇人口和乡村人口 城镇人口是指居住在城镇范围内的全部常住人口；乡村人口是除上述人口以外的全部人口。

城镇包括城区和镇区。城区是指在市辖区和不设区的市中，街道办事处所辖的居民委员会地域；城市公共设施、居住设施等连接到的其他居民委员会地域和村民委员会地域。

镇区是指在城区以外的镇和其他区域，其包括镇所辖的居民委员会地域；镇的公共设施、居住设施等连接到的村民委员会地域。

出生率（又称粗出生率） 指在一定时期内（通常为一年）一定地区的出生人数与同期内平均人数（或期中人数）之比，用千分率表示。本资料中的出生率指年出生人数，其计算公式为：

出生率=年出生人数/年平均人数×1000‰

式中：出生人数指活产婴儿，即胎儿脱离母体时（不管怀孕月数），有过呼吸或其他生命现象。年平均人数指年初、年底人口数的平均数，也可用年中人口数代替。

死亡率（又称粗死亡率） 指在一定时期内（通常为一年）一定地区的死亡人数与同期内平均人数（或期中人数）之比，用千分率表示。本资料中的死亡率指年死亡率，其计算公式为：

死亡率=年死亡人数/年平均人数×1000‰

人口自然增长率 指在一定时期内（通常为一年）人口自然增加数（出生人数减死亡人数）与该时期内平均人数（或期中人数）之比，用千分率表示。计算公式为：

人口自然增长率=（本年出生人数-本年死亡人数）/年平均人数×1000‰=人口出生率-人口死亡率

总抚养比 也称总负担系数。指人口总体中非劳动年龄人口数与劳动年龄人口数之比。通常用百分比表示。用以表明每 100 名劳动年龄人口大致要负担多少名非劳动年龄人口。用于从人口角度反映人口与经济发展的基本关系。计算公式为：

$$GDR=(P_{0-14}+P_{65^+})/P_{15-64}\times 100\%$$

其中：GDR 为总抚养比；

P_{0-14} 为 0-14 岁少年儿童人口数；

P_{15-64} 为 15-64 岁的劳动年龄人口数；

P_{65^+} 为 65 岁及 65 岁以上的老年人口数。

老年人口抚养比 也称老年人口抚养系数。指某一人口中老年人口数与劳动年龄人口数之比。通常用百分比表示。用以表明每 100 名劳动年龄人口要负担多少名老年人。老年人口抚养比是从经济角度反映人口老龄化社会后果的指标之一。计算公式为：

$$ODR=P_{65^+}/P_{15-64}\times 100\%$$

其中：ODR 为老年人口抚养比；

P_{15-64} 为 15-64 岁的劳动年龄人口数；

P_{65^+} 为 65 岁及 65 岁以上的老年人口数。

少年儿童抚养比 也称少年儿童抚养系数。指某一人口中少年儿童人口数与劳动年龄人口数之比。通常用百分比表示。以反映每 100 名劳动年龄人口要负担多少名少年儿童。计算公式为：

$$CDR=P_{0-14}/P_{15-64}\times 100\%$$

其中：CDR 为少年儿童抚养比；

P_{0-14} 为 0-14 岁少年儿童人口数；

P_{15-64} 为 15-64 岁的劳动年龄人口数。

劳动力资源总数 指在劳动年龄内，具有劳动能力，在正常情况下，可能或实际参加社会劳动的人口数。劳动力资源的范围为：劳动年龄内（16 周岁以上），有劳动能力，实际参加社会劳动和未参加社会劳动的人员。劳动力资源也可划分为经济活动人口和非经济活动人口。劳动力资源不包括下列人员：

(1)在押犯人；

(2)劳动年龄内丧失劳动能力的人员；

(3)16岁以下实际参加社会劳动的人员。

从业人员期末人数 指报告期末最后一日24时在本单位工作，并取得工资或其他形式劳动报酬的人员数。该指标为时点指标，不包括最后一日当天及以前已经与单位解除劳动合同关系的人员，是在岗职工、劳务派遣人员及其他从业人员之和。从业人员不包括：

(1)离开本单位仍保留劳动关系，并定期领取生活费的人员；

(2)利用课余时间打工的学生及在本单位实习的各类在校学生；

(3)本单位因劳务外包而使用的人员，如：建筑业整建制使用的人员。

私营企业和个体从业人员 指在私营企业或个体经营者所经营的机构中劳动，并领取劳动报酬的人员，包括在私营或个体经营机构中劳动的帮工、学徒、雇用人员。

在岗职工 指在本单位工作且与本单位签订劳动合同，并由单位支付各项工资和社会保险、住房公积金的人员，以及上述人员中由于学习、病伤、产假等原因暂未工作仍由单位支付工资的人员。在岗职工还包括：

(1)应订立劳动合同而未订立劳动合同人员（如使用的农村户籍人员）；

(2)处于试用期人员；

(3)编制外招用的人员，如临时人员；

(4)派往外单位工作，但工资仍由本单位发放的人员（如挂职锻炼、外派工作等情况）。

在岗职工不包括：

(1)本单位使用的且由本单位直接支付工资的劳务派遣人员，应统计在本单位“劳务派遣人员”指标中；

(2)本单位因劳务外包而使用的人员，由承包劳务的单位统计为在岗职工。

在岗职工工资总额 指本单位在报告期内直接支付给本单位全部在岗职工的劳动报酬总额。在岗职工工资总额由基本工资、绩效工资、工资性津贴和补贴、其他工资四部分组成。工资总额不包括病假、事假等情况的扣款。

各单位在填报在岗职工工资总额四项构成时，应根据实际情况调整对应项目；如不能确定调整项，可扣减基本工资项。

在岗职工平均工资 指本单位在岗职工在报告期内平均每人所得的工资额。计算公式为：

$$\text{在岗职工平均工资}=\frac{\text{在岗职工工资总额}}{\text{在岗职工平均人数}}$$

在岗职工平均实际工资 指扣除物价变动因素后的在岗职工平均工资。计算公式为：

$$\text{在岗职工平均实际工资}=\frac{\text{报告期在岗职工平均工资}}{\text{报告期职工生活费价格指数}}\times 100\%$$

在岗职工平均工资指数 指报告期平均工资与基础平均工资的比率，是反映不同时期职工货币工资水平变动情况的相对数。它表明报告期平均工资比基期平均工资提高或降低的程度。计算公式为：

$$\text{在岗职工平均工资指数}=\frac{\text{报告期在岗职工平均工资}}{\text{基期在岗职工平均工资}}\times 100\%$$

城镇登记失业人员 指有非农业户口，在劳动年龄内（16周岁至退休年龄），有劳动能力，无业而要求就业，并在当地劳动保障部门进行失业登记的人员。

城镇登记失业率 指城镇期末实有登记失业人数与城镇期末就业人员总数加城镇期末实有登记失业人数之比。计算公式为：

$$\text{城镇登记失业率}=\frac{\text{城镇期末实有登记失业人数}}{\text{城镇期末就业人员总数}+\text{城镇期末实有登记失业人数}}\times 100\%$$

Explanatory Notes on Main Statistical Indicators

Total Population refers to the total number of people alive at a certain point of time within a given area.

The annual statistics on total population is taken at midnight, the 31st of December.

Resident Population includes (1) population residing in the township or sub-district office area with residence registered here, (2) population residing in the township or sub-district office area more than half a year with residence registered in other places, (3) population residing in the township or sub-district office area less than half a year, but having left place of residence registration more than half a year, (4) population having left the place for less than half a year with residence registered in the township or sub-district office, (5) population residing in the township or sub-district office area with pending residence registration, (6) population now residing in foreign countries with residence registered in the township or sub-district office.

Urban Population and Rural Population Urban population refer to all people residing in cities and towns, while rural population refer to population other than urban population.

City and town include city area and town area. City area refers to the area of residence committees ruled by sub-district office in municipal district or cities with no district, and area of other residence committees which joined by urban public establishment and residence establishment.

Town area refers to the area of township and other areas besides the city zone, including the area of residence committees ruled by town government, and the area of villager's committees which joined by township public establishment and residence establishment.

Birth Rate (Crude Birth Rate) refers to the ratio of the number of birth to the average population (or mid-period population) during a certain period of time (usually a year), expressed in ‰. Birth rate in the chapter refers to annual birth rate. The following formula is used:

Birth Rate=(Number of Births/Average Number of Population)*1000‰

Number of births in the formula refers to live births, i.e. when a baby has breathed or shown any vital phenomena regardless of the length of pregnancy. Annual average number of population is the average of the beginning of the year and that at the end of the year. Sometimes it is substituted by the mid-year population.

Death Rate (Crude Death Rate) refers to the ratio of the number of deaths to the average population (or mid-period population) during a certain period of time (usually a year), expressed in ‰. Death rate in the chapter refers to annual death rate. The following formula is used:

Death Rate=(Number of Deaths/Annual Average Number of Population)*1000‰.

Natural Growth Rate of Population refers to the ratio of natural increase in population (number of births minus number of deaths) in a certain period of time (usually a year) to the average population (or mid-period population) of the same period, expressed in ‰. The following formula is applied:

Natural Growth Rate of Population=[(Number of Birth-Number of Death)/Average Number of Population]*1000‰=Birth Rate-Death Rate

Gross Dependency Ratio also called gross dependency coefficient, refers to the ratio of non-working-age population to the working-age population, express in ‰. Describing in general the number of non-working-age population that every 100 people at working ages will take care of, this indicator reflects the basic relation between population and economic development from the demographic perspective. The gross dependency ratio is calculated with the following formula:

$GDR=P_{0\text{-}14}+P_{65}^{+}/P_{15\text{-}64}\times100\%$

Where: GDR is the gross dependency ratio;

$P_{0\text{-}14}$ is the population of children aged 0-14;

$P_{15\text{-}64}$ is the working-age population aged 15-64;

P_{65}^{+} is the elderly population aged 65 and over.

Old Dependency Ratio also called old dependency coefficient, refers to the ratio of the elderly population to the working-age population, express in ‰. It describes the number of the elderly population that every 100 people at working ages will take care of. Old dependency ratio is one of the indicators reflecting the social implication of population aging from the economic perspective. The old dependency ratio is calculated with the following formula:

$ODR=P_{65}^{+}/P_{15\text{-}64}\times 100\%$

Where: ODR is the old dependency ratio;

$P_{15\text{-}64}$ is the working-age population aged 15-64;

P_{65}^{+} is the elderly population aged 65 and over.

Children Dependency Ratio also called children dependency coefficient, refers to the ratio of the children population to the working-age population, express in ‰. It describes the number of children population that every 100 people at working ages will take care of. The children dependency ratio is calculated with the following formula:

$CDR=P_{0\text{-}14}/P_{15\text{-}64}\times 100\%$

Where: CDR is the children dependency ratio;

$P_{0\text{-}14}$ is the children population aged 0-14;

$P_{15\text{-}64}$ is the working-age population aged 15-64.

Labor Resources refer to the persons, under normal condition, who are capable to labor within age of the total population. The coverage of labor resources includes: laborers within the working age (16 and over 16) and those who are capable to labor, and actually engaged in or not engaged in social labor. Labor resources also may be divided into economically active population and non-economically active population.

The following persons are not included in the labor resources;

(1)Prisoners in custody;

(2)Persons with the working age but disabled;

(3)Persons actually engaged in social labor under aged 16.

Employed Persons at the End of Period refer to the number of employees working and receiving wages or other form of payments in the units. It is a point data, which doesn't include the number of employees who dissolve labor contract relationship in the last day and before. It equals to the sum of the number of employed staff and workers, labor dispatch persons and other employed persons.

The following persons cannot be included:

(1)Staff and workers who get living expenses regularly from the units, while left the unit and retain labor relation;

(2)Students and undergraduate trainees who work in the units in their spare time;

(3) Labor outsourcing persons working in the units.

Private Enterprises and Self-employed Individuals refer to the persons work in and receive payment from the private enterprises and individual agencies including self-employed persons as well as helper and hired laborers.

Fully Employed Staff and Workers refer to persons who work in, and receive wages, social insurance and housing funds from their working units, as well as persons who have their work posts, but are temporarily absent from work for reasons of study or on sick, injury or maternal leave and still receive wages from their working units. Fully Employed Staff and Workers also include:

(1)Persons who should have signed the labor contracts but not, such as persons with rural household registration;

(2)Employees on probation;

(3)Employees beyond the staffing quota;

(4)Employees who are sent to other working units but still receive wages from the original units. (Situations like on-the-job placement, expatriated assignment, etc.)

Fully Employed Staff and Workers do not include:

(1)Dispatched persons who work and are paid directly by the working units should be counted into "labor dispatch persons" of the units;

(2)Persons through labor outsourcing who should be counted into fully employed staff and workers by the contracted units.

Total Wages of Fully Employed Staff and Workers refer to the total remuneration payment paid directly to the fully employed staff and workers by the units during a certain period of time. Total wages include four parts which include base wages, performance wages, allowances and subsidies and other wages. Total Wages do not include leave deductions.

Units can adjust the wage composition in according to the actual situation while filling the forms of total wages. When it doesn't confirm the adjustment items, the units can deduct the base wages.

Average Wages of Fully Employed Staff and Workers refers to the average wage in money terms per person during a certain period of time for fully employed staff and workers in enterprises, institutions and government agencies, which reflects the general level of wage income during a certain period of time and is calculated as follows:

$$\text{Average Wages of Fully Employed Staff and Workers} = \frac{\text{Total Wages of Fully Employed Staff and Workers}}{\text{Average Number of Fully Employed Staff and Workers}}$$

Average Real Wage of Fully Employed Staff and Workers refers to average wage of staff and workers after removing the effects of price changes, which is calculated as follows:

Average Real Wage of Fully Employed Staff and Workers

$$= \frac{\text{Average Wage of Fully Employed Staff and Workers in Reference Period}}{\text{Consumer Price Index of Urban Residents in Reference Period}} \times 100\%$$

Average Wage Indices of Fully Employed Staff and Workers refers to the ratio of average wage of stuff and workers at reference period to that at base period, which reflects the change of wage of staff and workers at different period and shows the increasing or decreasing level of average wage. It is calculated as follows:

Average Wage Indices of Fully Employed Staff and Workers

$$= \frac{\text{Average Wage of Fully Employed Staff and Workers in Reference Period}}{\text{Average Wage of Fully Employed Staff and Workers in Base Period}} \times 100\%$$

Registered Unemployed Persons in Urban Areas refer to the persons with non-agricultural household registration at certain working ages (16 years old to retirement age), who are capable of working, unemployed and willing to work, and have been registered at the local employment service agencies to apply for a job.

Registered Unemployment Rate in Urban Areas refers to the ratio of the number of the registered unemployed persons to the sum of the number of the registered unemployed persons and the number of registered employed persons in urban areas.

The formula is as follows:

Registered Unemployment Rate in Urban Areas

$$= \frac{\text{Number of Registered Urban Unemployed Persons}}{\text{Number of Registered Urban Employed Persons} + \text{Number of Registered Urban Unemployed Persons}} \times 100\%$$

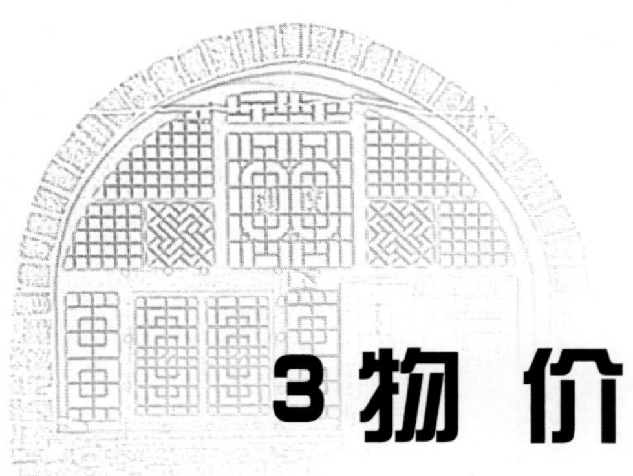

3 物 价

PRICE

资料整理人员

高　晋　陈　中

物　价
PRICE

居民消费价格总指数	General Residents Consumer Price Index	101.1
城　市	General Urban Residents Consumer Price Index	101.1
农　村	General Rural Residents Consumer Price Index	101.1
商品零售价格总指数	General Retail Price Index	100.5
工业生产者出厂价格指数	Ex-factory Price Index of Industrial Producer	96.8
工业生产者购进价格指数	Purchasing Price Index of Industrial Producer	98.1

物价总指数(上年=100)
General Price Index (last year=100)

居民消费价格总指数　商品零售价格总指数

工业生产者价格指数(上年=100)
Price Index of Industrial Producer (last year=100)

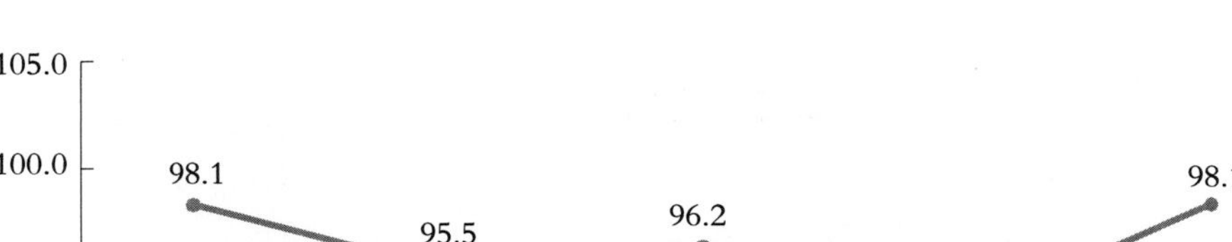

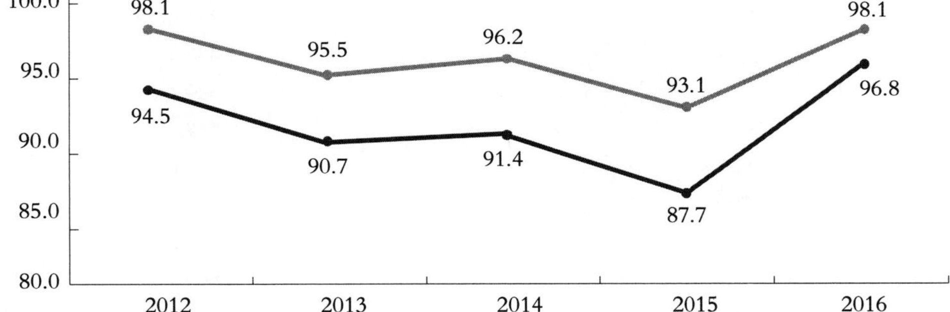

3-1 主要年份各类物价总指数
GENERAL PRICE INDICES IN MAJOR YEARS

上年=100 (last year=100)

年 份 Year	全省居民消费价格总指数 General Residents Consumer Price Index	城市居民消费价格总指数 General Urban Residents Consumer Price Index	农村居民消费价格总指数 General Rural Residents Consumer Price Index	全省商品零售价格总指数 General Retail Price Index
1978		100.0		100.0
1980	103.4	105.5	101.3	103.5
1985	108.5	109.1	107.8	107.6
1990	102.2	101.5	103.0	102.1
1995	116.9	116.7	117.2	115.6
2000	103.9	104.7	103.0	97.1
2005	102.3	101.7	103.7	100.3
2010	103.0	103.1	102.8	102.3
2011	105.2	105.1	105.4	104.9
2012	102.5	102.4	102.6	101.8
2013	103.1	103.0	103.2	101.8
2014	101.7	101.8	101.4	100.6
2015	100.6	100.6	100.7	99.3
2016	101.1	101.1	101.1	100.5

3-1 续表 continued

1978年=100 (year of 1978=100)

年 份 Year	全省居民消费价格总指数 Ceneral Residents Consumer Price Index	城市居民消费价格总指数 General Urban Residents Consumer Price Index	农村居民消费价格总指数 General Rural Residents Consumer Price Index	全省商品零售价格总指数 General Retail Price Index
1978	100.0	100.0	100.0	100.0
1980	104.0	106.6	101.5	104.0
1985	123.4	128.2	118.4	122.0
1990	206.6	213.4	200.5	203.2
1995	391.3	421.6	354.6	356.7
2000	444.2	488.5	391.6	349.9
2005	472.9	508.9	437.4	354.3
2010	554.9	589.6	529.4	406.1
2011	583.8	619.7	558.0	426.0
2012	598.4	634.8	572.6	433.7
2013	617.0	653.8	590.9	441.5
2014	627.5	665.6	599.2	444.1
2015	631.3	669.6	603.4	441.0
2016	638.2	677.0	610.0	443.2

3-2 主要年份城市居民消费价格总指数
GENERAL URBAN RESIDENTS CONSUMER PRICE INDICES IN MAJOR YEARS

年 份 Year	1950年 价格=100 Year of 1950=100	1957年 价格=100 Year of 1957=100	1965年 价格=100 Year of 1965=100	1970年 价格=100 Year of 1970=100	1978年 价格=100 Year of 1978=100	1980年 价格=100 Year of 1980=100	1985年 价格=100 Year of 1985=100	1990年 价格=100 Year of 1990=100	上年=100 Last Year=100
1978	141.3	104.1	98.6	100.0	100.0				100.0
1980	150.6	110.9	102.1	106.5	106.6	100.0			105.5
1985	181.1	133.5	123.0	128.2	128.2	120.3	100.0		109.1
1990	301.4	222.2	204.7	213.4	213.4	200.2	166.4	100.0	101.5
1995	595.6	439.3	404.6	421.6	421.6	395.8	328.9	197.6	116.7
2000	690.0	508.8	468.7	488.5	488.5	458.6	380.9	229.0	104.7
2005	718.8	530.1	488.3	508.9	508.9	477.7	396.8	238.7	101.7
2010	832.6	614.2	565.8	589.6	589.6	553.4	459.7	276.5	103.1
2011	875.1	645.5	594.7	619.7	619.7	581.6	483.1	290.6	105.1
2012	896.5	661.3	609.2	634.8	634.8	595.8	494.9	297.7	102.4
2013	923.4	681.1	627.5	653.9	653.8	613.7	509.7	306.6	103.0
2014	940.0	693.4	638.8	665.7	665.6	624.7	518.9	312.1	101.8
2015	945.6	697.6	642.6	669.7	669.6	628.4	522.0	314.0	100.6
2016	956.0	705.3	649.7	677.1	677.0	635.3	527.7	317.5	101.1

3-3 主要年份商品零售价格总指数
GENERAL RETAIL PRICE INDICES IN MAJOR YEARS

年 份 Year	1950年 价格=100 Year of 1950=100	1957年 价格=100 Year of 1957=100	1965年 价格=100 Year of 1965=100	1970年 价格=100 Year of 1970=100	1978年 价格=100 Year of 1978=100	1980年 价格=100 Year of 1980=100	1985年 价格=100 Year of 1985=100	1990年 价格=100 Year of 1990=100	上年=100 Last Year=100
1978	143.1	104.2	95.4	99.6	100.0				100.0
1980	148.8	108.4	99.3	103.6	104.0	100.0			103.5
1985	174.5	127.0	116.3	121.5	122.0	117.3	100.0		107.6
1990	290.6	211.5	193.8	202.4	203.2	195.4	166.6	100.0	102.1
1995	510.1	371.3	340.3	355.5	356.7	343.1	292.5	175.6	115.6
2000	500.5	364.1	333.7	348.6	349.9	336.5	286.8	172.2	97.1
2005	506.8	368.8	337.9	353.0	354.3	340.6	290.3	174.3	100.3
2010	580.8	422.6	387.4	404.5	406.1	390.4	332.6	199.7	102.3
2011	609.3	443.3	406.4	424.3	426.0	409.5	348.9	209.5	104.9
2012	620.3	451.3	413.7	431.9	433.7	416.9	355.2	213.3	101.8
2013	631.5	459.4	421.1	439.7	441.5	424.4	361.6	217.1	101.8
2014	635.3	462.2	423.6	442.3	444.1	426.9	363.8	218.4	100.6
2015	630.9	459.0	420.6	439.2	441.0	423.9	361.3	216.9	99.3
2016	634.1	461.3	422.7	441.4	443.2	426.0	363.1	218.0	100.5

3-4 居民消费价格分类指数(2016年)

GENERAL RESIDENTS CONSUMER PRICE INDICES BY CATEGORY OF COMMODITIES(2016)

上年=100 (last year=100)

指 标	Item	全 省 Total Province Indices	城 市 Urban Indices	农 村 Rural Indices
居民消费价格总指数	**General Consumer Price Index**	**101.1**	**101.1**	**101.1**
一、食品烟酒	Food, Tobacco and Liquor	102.8	102.8	102.8
1.食 品	Food	103.3	103.4	103.3
粮 食	Grain	99.7	99.6	99.8
薯 类	Tubers	111.2	111.7	110.3
豆 类	Beans	101.2	100.2	103.2
食用油	Oil	100.3	100.6	99.8
菜	Vegetables	111.1	111.1	111.1
鲜 菜	Fresh Vegetables	111.6	111.7	111.6
干菜及菜制品	Dried Vegetables and Processed Products	104.5	104.9	103.1
畜肉类	Meat	111.0	110.2	112.7
猪 肉	Pork	120.1	120.5	119.5
禽肉类	Poultry	100.3	100.5	99.6
水产品	Aquatic Products	103.0	103.8	100.9
蛋 类	Poultry Eggs	94.8	95.3	94.1
鸡 蛋	Eggs	94.6	95.0	93.9
奶 类	Milk	99.6	99.5	99.9
干鲜瓜果类	Dried and Fresh Melons and Fruits	95.8	95.9	95.4
鲜瓜果	Fresh Melons and Fruits	94.3	94.3	94.4
坚 果	Dried Fruits	98.3	98.8	96.4
糖果糕点类	Candy and Cake	100.4	100.8	99.4
调味品	Flavouring	101.5	101.5	101.7
其他食品类	Other Foods	102.8	103.8	101.1
2.茶及饮料	Tea and Beverages	100.6	100.5	100.8
茶 叶	Tea	101.2	100.5	102.9
固体咖啡	Solid Coffee	101.2	100.9	102.7
其他固体饮料	Other Solid Drinks	100.9	101.1	100.6
饮用水	Potable Water	101.1	99.7	103.7
果汁饮料	Fruit Juice	101.5	102.2	100.0
3.烟 酒	Tobacco and Liquor	101.4	101.7	101.1
烟 草	Tobacco	102.1	102.3	101.9
酒 类	Liquor	100.2	100.7	99.6
4.在外餐饮	Dining Out	101.9	101.8	102.4
正 餐	Dinner	102.4	102.0	104.5
快 餐	Snack	101.2	101.5	100.2
地方小吃	Local Snack	101.4	101.6	100.2

3-4 续表1 continued

上年=100 (last year=100)

指 标	Item	全 省 Total Province Indices	城 市 Urban Indices	农 村 Rural Indices
二、衣 着	Clothing	101.0	101.0	101.3
1.服 装	Garments	101.2	101.1	101.7
男式服装	Man's Garments	102.1	102.2	101.8
女式服装	Woman's Garments	100.9	100.9	100.8
儿童服装	Children's Garments	100.4	99.2	104.5
2.服装材料	Garment Material	100.0	99.4	102.2
3.其他衣着及配件	Other Clothing and Accessories	101.1	100.8	102.5
4.衣着加工服务费	Fees for Clothing Manufacturing Services	102.3	102.2	102.7
5.鞋 类	Footwear	100.3	100.5	99.7
鞋	Shoes	100.3	100.5	99.6
鞋类加工服务	Shoes Manufacturing Services	102.7	102.6	102.9
三、居 住	Residence	99.9	99.7	100.2
1.租赁房房租	Rent	100.9	101.0	100.3
2.住房保养维修及管理	Household Maintenance, Renovation and Management	99.8	99.9	99.7
3.水电燃料	Water, Electricity and Fuels	100.2	99.8	101.0
4.自有住房	Private Housing	99.7	99.5	100.0
四、生活用品及服务	Articles for Daily Use and Services	100.0	100.1	99.7
1.家具及室内装饰品	Furniture and Interior Decorations	99.5	99.8	98.3
家 具	Furniture	99.4	99.8	98.1
室内装饰品	Interior Decorations	100.3	100.5	99.8
2.家用器具	Household Appliances	99.1	99.1	99.1
3.家用纺织品	Household Textiles	100.0	100.2	99.4
4.家庭日用杂品	Daily Use Household Articles	100.6	100.4	101.1
5.个人护理用品	Personal Care Articles	100.6	100.9	99.1
6.家庭服务	Household Services	102.2	102.5	101.5
五、交通和通信	Transportation and Communication	98.3	98.5	97.8
1.交 通	Transportation	98.8	98.8	98.6
交通工具	Transportation Facility	99.3	99.2	99.7
交通工具用燃料	Fuels of Transportation Facility	95.4	95.4	95.5
交通工具使用和维修	Use and Repairment of Transportation Facility	101.0	101.5	100.1
交通费	Traffic Fare	100.8	101.4	99.4
市内公共交通	Incity Public Transportation	98.2	100.0	94.9
出租汽车	Taxi	100.7	101.0	100.0
飞机票	Plane Ticket	107.0	107.0	106.8
火车票	Train Ticket	100.0	100.0	100.0
长途汽车	Coach	100.6	101.3	99.5

3-4 续表2 continued

上年=100 (last year=100)

指 标	Item	全 省 Total Province Indices	城 市 Urban Indices	农 村 Rural Indices
2.通 信	Communication	97.5	97.9	96.5
通信工具	Communication Facility	91.3	92.6	88.1
通信服务	Communication Service	99.8	99.8	100.0
邮递服务	Postal Service	100.3	100.8	98.4
六、教育文化和娱乐	Education, Culture and Recreation	101.3	101.4	100.9
1.教 育	Education	101.6	101.9	101.2
教育用品	Education Articles	101.5	101.4	101.6
教育服务	Education Services	101.6	101.9	101.2
2.文化娱乐	Culture and Recreation	100.6	100.7	99.9
文娱耐用消费品	Durable Consumer Goods for Cultural and Recreational Use	97.5	96.7	99.4
其他文娱用品	Other Cultural and Recreational Articles	100.8	100.7	100.9
文化娱乐服务	Cultural and Recreational Services	101.0	101.1	100.2
旅 游	Touring	102.6	102.9	98.1
七、医疗保健	Health Care	102.4	102.4	102.3
1.药品及医疗器具	Medicine and Medical Appliances	104.7	104.8	104.7
中 药	Traditional Chinese Medicine	104.2	105.0	102.7
西 药	Western Medicine	104.7	104.4	105.4
滋补保健品	Health Care Products	108.3	108.6	107.5
医疗卫生器具	Medical Appliances	100.6	100.6	100.7
保健器具	Health Care Appliances	100.3	100.3	100.4
2.医疗服务	Medical Services	100.8	100.7	101.1
综合医疗类	General Practice	102.2	101.7	103.0
诊断类	Diagnosis	99.3	99.9	98.4
治疗类	Treatment	101.3	100.6	102.5
康复类	Rehabilitation	100.8	100.0	102.4
中医医疗服务类	Traditional Chinese Medical Services	101.1	100.1	102.6
其他医疗服务	Other Medical Services	101.1	100.0	102.9
八、其他用品和服务	Other Articles and Services	101.2	101.1	101.6
1.其他用品类	Other Articles	100.5	100.5	100.6
首饰手表	Jewelry and Watch	100.9	100.9	101.0
其他杂项用品	Other Miscellaneous Articles	100.0	100.0	100.2
2.其他服务类	Other Services	101.8	101.6	102.4
旅馆住宿	Touring Accomodation	98.4	98.4	98.3
美容美发洗浴	Hairdressing, Beauty and Bath	102.3	101.2	104.6
养老服务	Pension Services	100.0	100.0	100.0
金融保险	Financial Insurance	102.7	102.7	102.5
其他服务类	Other Services	100.0	100.0	100.0

3-5 商品零售价格分类指数(2016年)

GENERAL RETAIL PRICE INDICES BY CATEGORY OF COMMODITIES(2016)

上年=100 (last year=100)

指 标	Item	全 省 Total Province Indices	城 市 Urban Indices	农 村 Rural Indices
商品零售价格总指数	**General Retail Price Indices**	**100.5**	**100.5**	**100.4**
一、食 品	Food	102.9	102.9	103.1
1.粮 食	Grain	99.6	99.5	99.8
2.薯 类	Starches and Its Products	111.5	111.8	110.4
3.豆 类	Bean and Its Prodrcts	100.8	100.3	102.5
4.食用油	Oil or Fat	100.1	100.5	99.2
5.菜	Meat, Poultry and their Products	111.1	111.2	111.0
6.畜肉类	Eggs	110.8	110.2	112.9
7.禽肉类	Aquatic Products	100.3	100.5	99.6
8.水产品	Vegetables	103.2	103.7	100.6
9.蛋 类	Condiments	94.9	95.2	94.0
10.奶 类	Sugar	99.5	99.4	99.8
11.干鲜瓜果类	Fresh and Dried Fruits	95.9	96.0	95.3
12.糖果糕点类	Cake, Biscuit and Bread	100.6	100.8	99.2
13.调味品	Milk and Its Products	101.4	101.5	101.3
14.其他食品类	Food Eating out	102.9	103.6	101.0
15.在外餐饮	Others	101.7	101.6	102.2
二、饮料、烟酒	Drinking, Tobacco and Liquor	101.4	101.5	101.1
1.茶及饮料	Tea and Drinking	100.5	100.5	100.4
2.烟 草	Tobacco	102.4	102.5	102.0
3.酒 类	Liquor	100.2	100.4	99.4
三、服装、鞋帽	Garments, Shoes and Hats	100.9	100.9	101.2
1.服 装	Garments	101.1	101.0	101.7
2.鞋帽袜	Shoes, Socks and Stockings, Hats	100.6	100.7	99.9
3.其他衣着配件	Others	100.3	99.7	102.3
四、纺织品	Textiles	100.0	100.1	99.6
1.服装材料	Clothing Material	100.3	99.5	103.0
2.床上用品	Bed Articles	100.0	100.3	98.9
五、家用电器及音像器材	Household Appliances and Audiovisual Equipment	98.6	98.4	99.3
1.家庭设备	Household Facilities	99.1	99.1	99.2
2.文娱用耐用消费品	Durable Consumer Goods for Cultural and Recreational Use	97.0	96.3	99.5
3.专业音像器材	Professional Audiovisual Equipment	100.5	100.6	100.4

3-5 续表 continued

上年=100 (last year=100)

指标	Item	全省 Total Province Indices	城市 Urban Indices	农村 Rural Indices
六、文化办公用品	Culture and Office Articles	98.9	98.7	99.8
七、日用品	Daily Use Articles	100.3	100.3	100.4
1.日用百货	Daily Use Articles	100.2	100.4	99.4
2.厨具餐具茶具	Daily Use Sundry Goods	101.5	100.8	104.3
3.清洗用品	Washing Goods	100.4	100.3	100.7
4.其他日用品	Others	100.1	100.1	99.8
八、体育娱乐用品	Sports and Recreational Articles	100.9	101.1	100.1
1.体育户外用品	Sports Articles	100.4	100.6	100.0
2.娱乐用品	Recreational Articles	101.0	101.2	100.1
九、交通、通信用品	Transportation and Communication Appliances	98.1	98.3	97.1
1.交通运输机械	Transportation Machinery	99.4	99.3	100.1
2.通信器材	Communication Equipment	93.4	94.5	89.4
十、家　具	Furniture	99.7	99.9	98.8
十一、化妆品	Cosmetics	100.6	100.9	99.3
十二、金银饰品	Gold, Silver and Jewelry	101.1	101.2	100.8
十三、中西药品及医疗保健用品	Traditional, Western Medicines and Health Care Products	104.7	104.7	104.7
1.医疗卫生器具	Medical Appliances and Articles	100.5	100.5	100.4
2.中　药	Traditional Chinese Medicine	104.3	104.7	102.7
3.西　药	Western Medicine	104.7	104.5	105.8
4.保健器具及用品	Health Care Equipment and Articles	107.2	107.5	105.8
十四、书报杂志及电子出版物	Newspapers, Magazines and Electronic Publication	101.0	101.0	101.2
1.教材及参考书	Teaching Materials and Reference Books	101.6	101.4	102.1
2.书报杂志	Newspapers and Magazines	100.6	100.7	100.2
3.计算机办公软件	Computer Office Software	100.2	100.2	100.0
十五、燃　料	Fuels	97.9	98.0	97.3
1.煤炭及制品	Coal and Coal Products	100.3	100.5	99.4
2.石油及制品	Petroleum and its Products	97.0	97.2	95.9
十六、建筑材料及五金电料	Building Materials, Hardware and Electrical Materials	99.5	99.7	99.0
1.建筑装璜材料	Decoration Materials	99.4	99.5	98.9
2.五金水暖	Hardware and Electrical Materials	100.0	100.2	99.2

3-6 调查市县居民消费价格指数(2016年)

RESIDENTS CONSUMER PRICE INDICES IN CITIES AND COUNTIES SURVEYED(2016)

上年=100 (last year=100)

市 县	Region	居民消费价格总指数 General Index	食品烟酒 Food,Tobacco and Liquor	衣 着 Clothing	居 住 Residence	生活用品及服务 Articles for Daily Use and Services
全 省	**Total**	**101.1**	**102.8**	**101.0**	**99.9**	**100.0**
太原市	Taiyuan	101.2	103.3	101.4	99.4	100.3
大同市	Datong	101.1	102.8	101.3	100.3	99.1
阳泉市	Yangquan	100.7	102.3	100.1	99.3	100.3
长治市	Changzhi	100.9	102.5	98.8	99.9	100.3
晋城市	Jincheng	100.7	101.9	100.8	100.4	99.4
朔州市	Shuozhou	100.8	102.5	101.0	98.2	99.9
晋中市	Jinzhong	101.2	103.3	98.9	100.2	100.8
运城市	Yuncheng	101.5	102.6	105.0	99.9	100.9
忻州市	Xinzhou	100.9	102.4	97.9	103.6	99.4
临汾市	Linfen	100.5	101.9	99.9	99.9	100.8
吕梁市	Lvliang	100.6	102.6	101.1	97.1	100.1
浑源县	Hunyuan	101.4	101.4	103.3	102.0	99.6
平遥县	Pingyao	101.1	102.5	102.0	98.6	98.9
永济市	Yongji	101.1	102.7	103.6	99.9	101.4
洪洞县	Hongtong	101.0	103.3	101.8	100.0	99.9
兴 县	Xingxian	101.1	103.7	98.1	100.8	99.6
汾阳市	Fenyang	101.2	103.1	97.7	101.1	99.1

市 县	Region	交通和通信 Transportation and Communication	教育文化和娱乐 Education, Culture and Recreation	医疗保健 Health Care	其他用品和服务 Other Articles and Services
全 省	**Total**	**98.3**	**101.3**	**102.4**	**101.2**
太原市	Taiyuan	98.6	102.0	102.2	101.4
大同市	Datong	98.1	101.3	102.5	101.2
阳泉市	Yangquan	98.5	99.8	103.4	101.8
长治市	Changzhi	97.8	103.3	102.7	101.1
晋城市	Jincheng	97.3	99.7	104.3	100.9
朔州市	Shuozhou	99.0	100.9	103.8	102.0
晋中市	Jinzhong	99.3	99.7	104.9	101.0
运城市	Yuncheng	99.0	101.6	101.4	101.0
忻州市	Xinzhou	97.5	99.2	100.8	100.3
临汾市	Linfen	99.1	100.2	100.6	98.8
吕梁市	Lvliang	99.1	102.9	100.4	101.7
浑源县	Hunyuan	98.2	100.6	104.2	100.9
平遥县	Pingyao	96.5	102.4	105.1	104.8
永济市	Yongji	97.6	101.1	101.2	100.7
洪洞县	Hongtong	98.6	100.3	100.0	101.2
兴 县	Xingxian	96.4	100.1	102.6	101.5
汾阳市	Fenyang	98.6	100.7	102.5	99.0

3-7 调查市县商品零售价格指数(2016年)
RETAIL PRICE INDICES IN CITIES AND COUNTIES SURVEYED(2016)

上年=100 (last year=100)

市 县 Region		商品零售价格总指数 General Index	食 品 Food	服装鞋帽 Garments,Shoes and Hats	纺织品 Textiles	家用电器及音像器材 Household Appliances and Audiovisual Equipment
全 省	**Total**	**100.5**	**102.9**	**100.9**	**100.0**	**98.6**
太原市	Taiyuan	100.8	103.4	101.4	99.2	98.3
大同市	Datong	100.4	102.9	101.4	99.9	98.4
阳泉市	Yangquan	100.2	102.3	100.1	101.6	98.3
长治市	Changzhi	100.3	102.5	98.8	100.0	99.7
晋城市	Jincheng	100.0	102.1	100.8	99.8	95.0
朔州市	Shuozhou	101.0	102.8	100.8	100.0	100.1
晋中市	Jinzhong	101.3	103.7	98.8	100.0	99.3
运城市	Yuncheng	100.9	102.7	105.2	106.6	96.3
忻州市	Xinzhou	99.4	102.5	97.9	99.6	97.3
临汾市	Linfen	100.0	102.2	99.9	100.6	99.7
吕梁市	Lvliang	101.0	102.8	101.1	99.8	100.3
浑源县	Hunyuan	101.3	101.3	103.3	100.1	99.3
平遥县	Pingyao	99.6	102.8	102.1	98.9	99.3
永济市	Yongji	100.8	102.9	103.5	102.8	99.9
洪洞县	Hongtong	100.4	103.6	101.7	99.6	99.2
兴 县	Xingxian	100.3	104.8	98.0	101.0	98.2
汾阳市	Fenyang	100.6	103.6	97.5	96.2	99.2

市 县 Region		日用品 Daily Use Articles	中西药品及医疗保健用品类 Traditional,Western Medecines and Health Care Products	燃 料 Fuels	建筑材料及五金电料 Building Materials, Hardware and Electrical Materials
全 省	**Total**	**100.3**	**104.7**	**97.9**	**99.5**
太原市	Taiyuan	101.0	103.1	98.4	100.7
大同市	Datong	99.3	106.3	99.0	97.3
阳泉市	Yangquan	99.8	107.8	94.1	99.0
长治市	Changzhi	100.7	105.8	98.5	99.2
晋城市	Jincheng	99.8	110.5	97.2	100.3
朔州市	Shuozhou	100.1	108.8	97.6	100.2
晋中市	Jinzhong	99.1	111.0	98.0	100.7
运城市	Yuncheng	100.6	101.7	97.6	98.1
忻州市	Xinzhou	98.6	101.9	99.0	99.4
临汾市	Linfen	100.5	101.4	96.8	99.6
吕梁市	Lvliang	100.3	101.0	99.9	100.0
浑源县	Hunyuan	99.8	109.0	103.0	100.0
平遥县	Pingyao	98.7	106.8	93.3	96.4
永济市	Yongji	100.7	102.4	97.4	99.6
洪洞县	Hongtong	101.7	100.1	96.2	99.0
兴 县	Xingxian	100.6	107.7	97.6	99.3
汾阳市	Fenyang	100.2	107.5	99.4	99.9

3-8 农业生产资料价格分类指数
INDICES OF AGRICULTURAL PRODUCTIVE MATERIALS BY CATEGORY OF COMMODITIES

上年=100 (last year=100)

类 别	Category	2010	2015	2016
农业生产资料价格指数	**Price Indices of Agricultural Pruductive Materials**	**102.0**	**99.6**	**99.8**
一、农用手工工具	Manipulative Tools for Agruiculture	103.3	100.6	102.9
二、饲 料	Forage	109.7	98.7	90.8
三、产品畜	Commodity Animals	96.1	105.9	134.9
四、半机械化农具	Semi-mechanized Farm Implements	100.0	99.7	97.5
五、机械化农具	Mechanized Farm Implements	99.6	98.7	98.1
六、化学肥料	Chemical Fertilizer	94.7	99.5	99.2
七、农药及农药械	Pesticide and Its Appliances	101.3	99.9	99.6
化学农药	Chemical Pesticide	101.1	99.9	99.4
农药器械	Chemical Pesticide Appliances	102.2	100.0	100.4
八、农用机油	Oil for Farm Machinery	109.8	88.9	96.7
九、其他农业生产资料	Other Agricultural Pruductive Material	105.7	100.1	101.0
十、农业生产服务	Agricultural Pruductive Service	107.2	101.1	101.4

3-9 工业生产者购进价格指数
PURCHASING PRICE INDICES OF INDUSTRIAL PRODUCER

上年=100 (last year=100)

名 称	Item	2010	2015	2016
总 指 数	**Total Price Index**	**109.0**	**93.1**	**98.1**
一、燃料动力类	Fuels	104.9	93.2	100.5
二、黑色金属材料类	Ferrous Metal Materials	110.1	90.6	94.4
钢 材	Steel	103.6	94.0	94.0
其 他	Others	115.7	88.3	94.7
三、有色金属材料和电线类	Non-ferrous Metals	119.9	93.0	94.0
四、化工原料类	Chemical Raw Materials	112.2	90.0	97.7
五、木材及纸浆类	Timber and Paper Pulp	103.5	99.3	99.7
六、建筑材料及非金属矿类	Building Materials and Non-metal Mineral	98.2	94.7	98.6
七、其他工业原材料及半成品类	Other Industrial Raw Materials and Half-products	102.5	99.6	98.6
八、农副产品类	Farm Products	118.8	98.8	98.8
九、纺织原料类	Textile Raw Materials	111.4	93.4	97.7

3-10 工业生产者出厂价格指数
EX-FACTORY PRICE INDICES OF INDUSTRIAL PRODUCER

上年=100 (last year=100)

指　标	Item	2010	2015	2016
全部工业品	**Total Industrial Products**	**109.5**	**87.7**	**96.8**
1.轻工业	Light Industry	101.8	98.1	99.8
以农产品为原料	Using Farm Products as Raw Materials	106.7	98.1	100.2
以非农产品为原料	Using Non-farm Products as Raw Materials	98.4	98.0	97.5
重工业	Heavy Industry	110.2	87.2	96.7
采掘工业	Ming and Quarrying	112.1	82.2	97.8
原料工业	Raw Material Industry	109.8	86.4	95.6
加工工业	Manufacturing Industry	109.6	90.8	97.6
2.生产资料	Productive Materials	109.7	87.2	96.7
采掘工业	Ming and Quarrying	110.7	82.2	97.8
原料工业	Raw Material Industry	110.1	86.3	95.6
加工工业	Manufacturing Industry	107.9	90.9	97.5
生活资料	Living Materials	104.9	99.3	99.0
食　品	Food	105.0	98.6	101.0
衣　着	Clothing	104.9	99.8	97.5
一般日用品	Daily Articles	105.2	101.1	94.2
耐用消费品	Durable Consumer Goods	101.7	99.7	97.5
按工业部门分	**By Department of Industry**			
1.冶金工业	Metallurgical Industry	114.3	85.9	96.1
2.电力工业	Power Industry	105.7	101.0	95.5
3.煤炭及炼焦工业	Coal and Coking Industry	110.5	81.6	97.4
4.石油工业	Petroleum Industry	101.2	96.4	92.3
5.化学工业	Chemical Industry	102.8	98.3	95.9
6.机械工业	Machine Industry	98.9	98.2	97.1
7.建筑材料工业	Building Materials Industry	98.5	97.5	97.1
8.森林工业	Forestry Industry	104.8	100.1	96.9
9.食品工业	Food Industry	105.4	98.3	100.7
10.纺织工业	Textile Industry	116.9	94.7	97.0
11.缝纫工业	Tailoring Industry	104.9	99.8	97.5
12.皮革工业	Leather Industry	104.2	103.5	86.7
13.造纸工业	Paper Making Industry	105.5	98.1	97.5
14.文教艺术用品工业	Cultural, Education & Handicrafts Article	101.8	100.0	97.6
15.其他工业	Other Industry	102.5	98.9	96.4

3-11 工业生产者分行业出厂价格指数
EX-FACTORY PRICE INDICES OF INDUSTRIAL PRODUCER BY SECTOR

上年=100 (last year=100)

指 标	Item	2015	2016
煤炭开采和洗选业	Coal Mining and Dressing	81.9	96.8
石油和天然气开采业	Petroleum and Natural Gas Extraction	99.4	90.7
黑色金属矿采选业	Ferrous Metals Mining and Dressing	89.7	89.9
有色金属矿采选业	Non-ferrous Metals Mining and Dressing	92.5	108.3
非金属矿采选业	Non-metal Minerals Mining and Dressing	99.5	97.5
其他采矿业	Other Minings		
农副食品加工业	Farm Products Processing	97.0	103.2
食品制造业	Food Manufacturing	99.3	97.5
饮料制造业	Beverage Manufacturing	98.8	97.7
烟草制品业	Tobacco Products	100.9	98.6
纺织业	Textile Industrial	94.8	97.0
纺织服装、鞋、帽制造业	Garments, Shoes and Hats Manufacturing	100.0	97.5
皮革、毛皮、羽毛(绒)及其制品业	Leather, Furs, Down and Related Products	103.5	86.7
木材加工及木、竹、藤、棕、草制品业	Timber Processing, Bamboo, Cane, Plam, Fiber and Straw Products	100.1	96.1
家具制造业	Furniture Manufacturing	99.9	98.7
造纸及纸制品业	Papermaking and Paper Products	98.1	97.5
印刷业和记录媒介的复制	Printing and Record Medium Reproduction	100.0	98.0
文教体育用品制造业	Cultural, Educational and Sports Goods	99.7	97.1
石油加工、炼焦及核燃料加工业	Petroleum Processing, Coking and Nuclear Fuel Processing	80.6	99.9
化学原料及化学制品制造业	Raw Chemical Materials and Chemical Products	97.9	96.2
医药制造业	Medical and Pharmaceutical Products	102.3	95.4
化学纤维制造业	Chemical Fiber	100.0	
橡胶制品业	Rubber Products	93.9	95.1
塑料制品业	Plastic Products	98.2	95.1
非金属矿物制品业	Non-metal Mineral Products	97.6	96.7
黑色金属冶炼及压延加工业	Smelting and Pressing of Ferrous Metals	84.3	98.4
有色金属冶炼及压延加工业	Smelting and Pressing of Non-ferrous Metals	91.9	89.3
金属制品业	Metal Prodcuts	95.1	97.1
通用设备制造业	Ordinary Machinery Manufacturing	98.8	97.4
专用设备制造业	Special Purpose Equipment Manufacturing	98.7	97.5
交通运输设备制造业	Transport Equipment Manufacturing	98.8	95.1
电气机械及器材制造业	Electric Equipment and Machinery	97.7	97.7
通信设备、计算机及其他电子设备制造业	Telecommunications Equipments , Computer and Other Electronic Equipments Manufacturing	95.2	97.1
仪器仪表及文化、办公用机械制造业	Instrument, Meters, Cultural and Office Machinery Manufacturing	99.7	99.6
工艺品及其他制造业	Handicraft Articles and Others Manfacturing	97.1	99.6
废弃资源和废旧材料回收加工业	Resources Discarded & Waste Materials Recovering and Processing		
电力、热力的生产和供应业	Production & Supply of Electric Power and Heating Power	101.0	95.5
燃气生产和供应业	Production and Supply of Gas	103.6	93.2
水的生产和供应业	Production and Supply of Water	102.7	99.3

3-12 固定资产投资价格指数
PRICE INDICES OF INVESTMENT IN FIXED ASSETS

上年=100 (last year=100)

指 标	Item	2010	2015	2016
固定资产投资	**Investment in Fixed Assets**	**103.7**	**98.2**	**100.0**
建筑安装、装饰工程	**Construction, Installation and Decoration**	**105.5**	**97.7**	**100.5**
人工费	Labour	109.1	102.8	101.9
工程管理人员	Manager	109.6	100.4	101.8
工程技术人员	Engineer	107.2	100.4	102.1
普通工人	Ordinary Labour	109.4	103.9	101.9
材料费	Material	104.5	93.9	99.6
钢 材	Steel	105.0	87.7	99.2
木 材	Timber	102.4	97.8	96.0
水 泥	Cement	104.9	95.9	99.3
地方建筑材料	Local Construction Material	104.1	98.4	100.3
化工材料	Chemical Material	104.4	98.2	97.9
电 料	Electric Material	104.4	100.2	100.2
其他材料	Others	104.4	99.8	99.1
机械费	Machinery	104.9	100.3	100.3
土石方及筑路机械	Earthwork and Road Building Machinery	104.4	100.1	100.9
打桩机械	Piling	103.1	92.6	99.9
起重机械	Hoist	102.9	100.1	98.9
运输机械	Transporting	107.7	101.6	100.7
混凝土及砂浆机械	Concrete and Sand Starch	104.2	100.2	99.4
加工机械	Processing	102.7	99.4	100.4
泵类机械	Pumping	102.3	101.1	99.9
船舶机械	Shipping			
其他机械	Others	105.6	99.9	99.1
设备、工器具购置	**Purchase of Equipment, Tools and Instruments**	**100.3**	**99.3**	**98.9**
其他费用	**Others**	**100.9**	**99.3**	**99.9**
土地取得费	Land Obtaining	100.3	99.9	100.1
前期工程费	Prophase Project	100.1	99.2	98.8
施工工作费	Construction	101.8	99.7	99.7
建设单位其他费用	Other fees of Construction Unit	101.3	98.5	100.8

主要统计指标解释

居民消费价格指数 反映居民生活消费品及服务项目价格变动趋势和变动程度的相对数，采用链式拉斯贝尔公式，加权平均计算。根据抽样调查方法在全省抽取 17 个调查市、县为填报单位。

商品零售价格指数 反映市场商品零售价格变动趋势和变动程度的相对数，计算方法及样本单位同上。

农业生产资料价格指数 反映农业生产资料价格变动趋势和变动程度的相对数，计算方法同上，根据抽样调查方法在全省抽取 6 个县、市为填报单位。

工业生产者出厂价格指数 是反映全部工业产品出厂价格总水平的变动趋势和程度的相对数，根据全省部分重点企业的产品出厂价格的定期调查资料，按加权算术平均公式计算。

工业生产者购进价格指数 是反映工业企业购进主要原材料、燃料、动力价格水平变动趋势和程度的相对数。根据全省部分重点企业主要原材料、燃料、动力购进价格的定期调查资料，按加权算术平均公式计算。

Explanatory Notes on Main Statistical Indicators

Residents Consumer Price Indices reflect the trend and degree of changes in prices of consumer goods and services purchased by urban and rural residents. They are calculated by the weighted arithmetic mean, using Byes formula. According to sampling survey, draw 17 survey cities and counties in total Province as report units.

Retail Price Indices reflect the general change and degree in retail prices of market commodities. The calculating method and sample unit are the same as above.

Indices of Agricultural Productive Materials refer the trend and degree of changes in price of agricultural productive materials. The calculating method is same as above, and drawing 6 survey cities and counties as report units.

Ex-factory Price Indices of Industrial Producer reflect the trend and degree of changes in ex-factory prices of all industrial products. They are calculated by the weighted arithmetic mean, according to regular survey data of ex-factory price in part of important enterprises in the province.

Purchasing Price Indices of Industrial Producer reflect the trend and degree of changes in prices of industrial enterprises purchasing raw materials and fuels. They are calculated by the weighted arithmetic mean, according to regular survey data of major raw materials and fuels purchasing price in part of important enterprises in the province.

4 人民生活

PEOPLE'S LIVELIHOOD

资料整理人员

任启龙　李艳旭　康小梅

人民生活
PEOPLE'S LIVELIHOOD

城镇居民人均可支配收入	Per Capita Disposable Income of Urban Households	27352.3	元 (yuan)
城镇居民人均消费支出	Per Capita Living Expenditure of Urban Households	16992.8	元 (yuan)
农村居民人均可支配收入	Per Capita Disposable Income of Rural Households	10082.5	元 (yuan)
农村居民人均消费支出	Per Capita Living Expenditure of Rural Households	8028.8	元 (yuan)

城乡居民恩格尔系数 (%)

Engel's Coefficient of Urban and Rural Households (%)

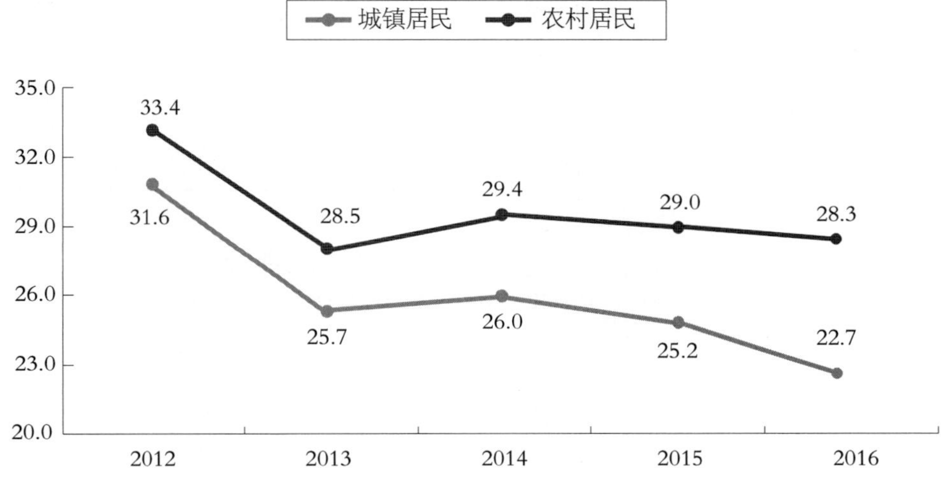

城乡居民家庭人均收入（元）

Per Capita Disposable Income of Urban and Rural Households (yuan)

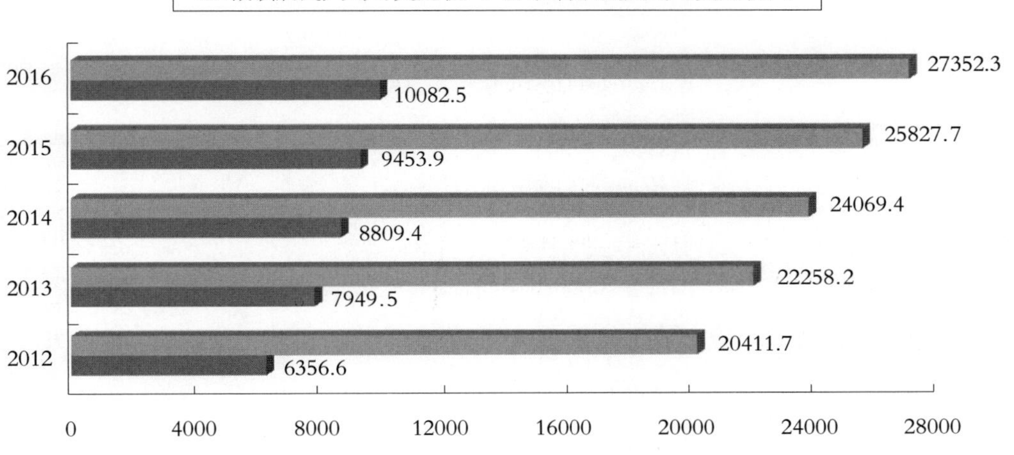

4-1 全省居民家庭生活基本情况
BASIC LIVING CONDITIONS OF THE PROVINCIAL HOUSEHOLDS

指　标	Item	2015	2016
一、调查户数 (户)	Number of Households Surveyed (household)	4536	4543
二、调查户常住人口(人)	Number of Resident Population Surveyed (person)	13623	13382
三、平均每户常住人口数 (人)	Average Number of Resident Population per Household (person)	3.00	2.95
四、平均每户从业人口 (人)	Average Number of Employees per Household (person)	1.66	1.73
五、平均每一从业者负担人数 (人)	Average Number of Persons Supported by Each Employee (person)	1.81	1.77
六、平均每人全年可支配收入 (元)	Per Capita Annual Disposable Income (yuan)	17854	19049
七、平均每人全年消费支出 (元)	Per Capita Annual Living Expenditure (yuan)	11729	12683

4-2 城镇居民家庭生活基本情况
BASIC LIVING CONDITIONS OF URBAN HOUSEHOLDS

指　标	Item	2015	2016
一、调查户数 (户)	Number of Households Surveyed (household)	2304	2383
二、调查户常住人口(人)	Number of Resident Population Surveyed (person)	6880	7069
三、平均每户常住人口数 (人)	Average Number of Resident Population per Household (person)	2.99	2.97
四、平均每户从业人口数 (人)	Average Number of Employees per Household (person)	1.44	1.45
五、平均每一从业者负担人数 (人)	Average Number of Persons Supported by Each Employee (person)	2.07	2.08
六、平均每人全年可支配收入 (元)	Per Capita Annual Disposable Income (yuan)	25828	27352
七、平均每人全年消费支出 (元)	Per Capita Annual Living Expenditure (yuan)	15819	16993
八、平均每人期末住房面积 (平方米)	Per Capita Living Space at Year-end (sq.m)	31.96	33.21

4-3 城镇家庭人口状况
POPULATION CONDITIONS OF URBAN HOUSEHOLDS

指　标	Item	2015	2016
一、调查户数 (户)	**Number of Households Surveyed (household)**	**2304**	**2383**
二、调查户常住人口(人)	**Number of Resident Population Surveyed (person)**	**6880**	**7069**
#劳动力数	Labors	4918	5091
#从业人数	Employees	3327	3343
#在校学生	Students Enrollment	1373	1403
按年龄分组	**Grouped by Age**		
5岁及以下	Aged 5 and Under	243	257
6–15岁	Aged 6–15	782	781
16–19岁	Aged 16–19	379	377
20–24岁	Aged 20–24	462	499
25–29岁	Aged 25–29	420	382
30–34岁	Aged 30–34	490	457
35–40岁	Aged 35–40	607	617
41–50岁	Aged 41–50	1429	1466
51–60岁	Aged 51–60	1148	1222
61–65岁	Aged 61–65	373	422
66岁及以上	Aged 66 and Above	534	563

4-4 城镇家庭劳动力状况
LABOR FORCE OF URBAN HOUSEHOLDS

单位：人 (person)

指　标	Item	2015	2016
一、劳动力文化状况	**Cultural Level of Labor Force**		
未上过学	Illiteracy or little literacy	44	42
小　学	Level of Primary School	390	415
初　中	Level of Junior Middle School	1964	2028
高　中	Level of Senior Middle School	1201	1252
大学专科	Level of Specialized Secondary School	755	766
大学本科	Level of Undergraduate	533	546
研究生	Level of Master and Doctor	32	41
二、劳动力从业情况	**Employment of Labor Force**		
(一)第一产业	Primary Industry	226	241
(二)第二产业	Secondary Industry	926	897
采矿业	Mining	347	356
制造业	Manufacturing	303	232
电力、热力、燃气及水生产供应业	Production and Supply of Power, Heat, Gas and Water	95	126
建筑业	Construction	181	183
(三)第三产业	Tertiary Industry	2176	2205
批发和零售业	Wholesale and Retail Trade	351	368
交通运输、仓储和邮政业	Transportation, Storage and Post	253	220
住宿和餐饮业	Hotels and Catering Services	138	153
信息传输、软件业和信息技术服务业	Information Transmission, Software and Information Technology	43	40
金融业	Financial Industry	78	80
房地产业	Real Estate	16	21
租赁和商务服务业	Leasing and Business Services	53	40
科学研究和技术服务业	Scientific Research and Technical Services	12	6
水利、环境和公共设施管理业	Management of Water Conservancy, Environment and Public Facilities	28	39
居民服务、修理和其他服务业	Services to Households, Repair and Other Services	434	454
教　育	Education	228	249
卫生和社会工作	Health and Social Service	125	137
文化、体育和娱乐业	Culture, Sports and Entertainment	48	48
公共管理、社会保障和社会组织	Public Management, Social Security and Social Organization	370	350
国际组织	International Organization		

4-5 城镇居民家庭人均全年总收入
PER CAPITA ANNUAL INCOME OF URBAN HOUSEHOLDS

单位：元 (yuan)

指标	Item	2015	2016
总收入	**Total Income**	**28242.82**	**29838.26**
一、工资性收入	Income of Wages and Salaries	16561.81	16954.36
二、经营性收入	Business Income	3664.31	3458.83
(一)第一产业	Primary Industry	424.15	699.85
农　业	Farming	146.94	246.94
林　业	Forestry	42.91	16.63
牧　业	Animal Husbandry	234.30	431.03
渔　业	Fishery		5.25
(二)第二产业	Secondary Industry	444.93	691.44
采矿业	Mining		0.65
制造业	Manufacturing	351.75	507.75
电力、热力、燃气及水生产和供应业	Production and Supply of Power, Heat, Gas and Water		
建筑业	Construction	93.18	183.04
(三)第三产业	Tertiary Industry	2795.24	2067.53
批发和零售业	Wholesale and Retail Trade	1323.34	907.23
交通运输、仓储和邮政业	Transportation, Storage and Post	664.35	522.54
住宿和餐饮业	Hotels and Catering Services	178.66	217.75
房地产业	Real Estate	13.60	10.72
租赁和商务服务业	Leasing and Business Services	211.07	33.79
居民服务、修理和其他服务业	Resident Services, Repair and Other Services	325.38	238.30
农林牧渔服务业	Services of Agriculture, Forestry, Animal Husbandry and Fishery	14.55	5.62
其　他	Others	64.30	131.58
三、财产性收入	Property Income	1813.45	2043.19
#利息收入	Interest	63.37	142.57
红利收入	Dividend and Bonus	161.04	148.91
储蓄性保险净收益	Net Savings Insurance	17.65	7.69
出租房屋财产性净收入	Net Income of Property Rental	477.07	455.25
四、转移性收入	Transfer Income	6203.24	7381.88
#养老金或离退休金	Pension or Retirement Payments	5549.97	6537.84
社会救济和补助	Social Relief and Subsidy	54.90	59.96
政策性生活补贴	Policy Living Allowances	57.87	30.93
赡养收入	Old Alimony	81.38	88.43
报销医疗费	Reimbursement of Medical Expenses	261.51	410.86
从政府和组织得到的实物产品和服务折价	Goods and Services Discount Received from Governments and Organizations	28.52	29.17
现金政策性惠农补贴	Cash Benefits Policy of Aagricultural Subsidies	5.97	7.36

4-6 城镇居民家庭人均全年总支出
PER CAPITA ANNUAL EXPENDITURE OF URBAN HOUSEHOLDS

单位：元 (yuan)

项　　目	Item	2015	2016
总支出	**Total Expenditure**	**22833.98**	**24250.44**
#通过互联网购买的商品和服务	Commodities and Services Purchased by the Internet	163.38	187.83
一、消费支出	Living Expenditure	15818.61	16992.82
二、生产经营费用支出	Production and Operation Expenses	692.35	668.22
(一)第一产业	Primary Industry	208.16	284.92
农　业	Farming	51.95	40.17
林　业	Forestry	0.96	1.05
牧　业	Animal Husbandry	155.24	243.07
渔　业	Fishery		0.63
(二)第二产业	Secondary Industry	28.20	15.35
采矿业	Mining		0.21
制造业	Manufacturing	18.95	5.46
电力、热力、燃气及水生产和供应业	Production and Supply of Power, Heat, Gas and Water		
建筑业	Construction	9.24	9.69
(三)第三产业	Tertiary Industry	456.00	367.94
批发和零售业	Wholesale and Retail Trade	129.84	104.62
交通运输、仓储和邮政业	Transportation, Storage and Post	250.50	174.62
住宿和餐饮业	Hotels and Catering Services	26.12	37.06
房地产业	Real Estate	0.15	
租赁和商务服务业	Leasing and Business Services	3.58	13.43
居民服务、修理和其他服务业	Resident Services, Repair and Other Services	23.65	18.25
农林牧渔服务业	Services of Agriculture, Forestry, Animal Husbandry and Fishery	4.25	2.12
其　他	Others	17.91	17.84
三、财产性支出	Property Expenditure	24.88	39.73
生活贷款利息支出	Living Loans Interest Expense	21.59	35.30
其他财产性支出	Other Property Expenditure	3.29	4.43
四、转移性支出	Transfer Expenditure	1515.01	1646.52
个人所得税	Individual Income Tax	77.92	71.65
社会保障支出	Social Security Expenditures	1247.26	1378.63
外来从业人员寄给家人的支出	Expenses of Foreign Employees Sent to The Family	10.73	0.12
赡养支出	Alimony Expenses	86.43	108.19
其他转移性支出	Other Property Expenditure	92.66	87.93
五、部分商业保险支出	Part of the Commercial Insurance Expenses	127.74	122.60
六、购置资产及非经常性转移支出	Acquisition of Assets and Non-recurring Transfer Expenditures	3213.20	3366.69
七、借贷性支出	Borrowing Expenditure	1442.18	1413.86

4-7 城镇居民家庭人均可支配收入及构成
PER CAPITA DISPOSABLE INCOME AND COMPOSITION OF URBAN HOUSEHOLDS

指　　标	Item	2015	2016
可支配收入(元)	**Disposable Income (yuan)**	**25827.72**	**27352.33**
一、工资性收入	Income of Wages and Salaries	16561.81	16954.36
二、经营净收入	Net Business Income	2789.82	2659.14
三、财产净收入	Net Property Income	1788.57	2003.46
四、转移净收入	Net Transfer Income	4687.51	5735.37
可支配收入构成(%)	**Composition of Disposable Income (%)**	**100.00**	**100.00**
一、工资性收入	Income of Wages and Salaries	64.12	61.99
二、经营净收入	Net Business Income	10.80	9.72
三、财产净收入	Net Property Income	6.93	7.32
四、转移净收入	Net Transfer Income	18.15	20.97

4-8 城镇居民家庭人均消费支出及构成
PER CAPITA LIVING EXPENDITURE AND COMPOSITION OF URBAN HOUSEHOLDS

项　　目	Item	2015	2016
消费支出(元)	**Living Expenditure (yuan)**	**15818.61**	**16992.82**
一、食品烟酒	Food, Tobacco and Liquor	3981.03	3862.79
二、衣　着	Clothing	1705.09	1602.96
三、居　住	Residence	3019.53	3633.80
四、生活用品及服务	Household Living Facilities, Articles and Services	947.93	951.65
五、交通通信	Transportation and Communication	2148.07	2401.01
六、教育文化娱乐服务	Education, Culture and Recreation Services	2207.93	2438.96
七、医疗保健	Health Care	1394.09	1651.55
八、其他商品和服务	Other Commodities and Services	414.94	450.09
消费支出构成 (%)	**Composition of Living Expenditure (%)**	**100.00**	**100.00**
一、食品烟酒	Food, Tobacco and Liquor	25.17	22.73
二、衣　着	Clothing	10.78	9.43
三、居　住	Residence	19.09	21.38
四、生活用品及服务	Household Living Facilities, Articles and Services	5.99	5.60
五、交通通信	Transportation and Communication	13.58	14.13
六、教育文化娱乐服务	Education, Culture and Recreation Services	13.96	14.35
七、医疗保健	Health Care	8.81	9.72
八、其他商品和服务	Other Commodities and Services	2.62	2.65

4-9 城镇家庭平均每人家庭经营净收入
PER CAPITA NET INCOME FROM HOUSEHOLD BUSINESS OF URBAN HOUSEHOLDS

单位：元 (yuan)

指　标	Item	2015	2016
家庭经营净收入	**Net Income from Household Business**	**2789.82**	**2659.14**
农　业	Farming	92.61	205.19
林　业	Forestry	41.95	15.58
牧　业	Animal Husbandry	72.23	185.31
渔　业	Fishery		4.61
采矿业	Mining		–0.86
制造业	Manufacturing	329.89	501.60
电力、热力、燃气及水生产和供应业	Production and Supply of Power, Heat, Gas and Water		
建筑业	Construction	68.49	158.89
批发和零售业	Wholesale and Retail Trade	1131.41	762.75
交通运输、仓储和邮政业	Transportation, Storage and Post	376.75	301.56
住宿和餐饮业	Hotels and Catering Services	148.33	172.17
房地产业	Real Estate	13.45	10.72
租赁和商务服务业	Leasing and Business Services	173.70	16.61
居民服务、修理和其他服务业	Resident Services, Repair and Other Services	289.60	213.41
农林牧渔服务业	Services of Agriculture, Forestry, Animal Husbandry and Fishery	9.41	3.50
其　他	Others	42.01	108.09

4-10 主要年份城镇居民人均可支配收入增长情况
PER CAPITA DISPOSABLE INCOME GROWTH OF URBAN HOUSEHOLDS IN MAJOR YEARS

单位：元 (yuan)

年 份 Year	可支配收入 Disposable Income	比上年增加额 Increase Value over Last Year	比上年增长(%) Increase Rate over Last Year	城镇居民消费价格指数(上年=100) Consumer Price Index of Urban Residents (last year=100)	扣除物价上涨因素后 Deducting Price Rising	
					实际收入 Real Income	比上年增长% Increase Rate over Last Year
1978	301.4					
1980	379.7			105.5	359.9	
1985	595.3	78.4	15.2	109.1	545.6	5.6
1990	1290.9	114.8	9.8	101.5	1271.8	8.2
1995	3301.9	736.2	28.7	116.7	2829.4	10.3
2000	4724.1	381.5	8.8	104.7	4512.0	3.9
2005	8913.9	1011.0	12.8	101.7	8764.9	10.9
2010	15647.7	1651.1	11.8	103.1	15177.2	8.4
2011	18123.9	2476.2	15.8	105.1	17244.4	10.2
2012	20411.7	2287.8	12.6	102.4	19933.3	10.0
2013	22455.6	2043.9	10.0	103.0	21801.6	6.8
2013(新口径)	22258.2			103.0	21609.9	
2014	24069.4	1811.2	8.1	101.8	23643.8	6.2
2015	25827.7	1758.3	7.3	100.6	25673.7	6.7
2016	27352.3	1524.6	5.9	101.1	27054.7	4.8

4-11 主要年份城镇居民人均消费支出增长情况
PER CAPITA LIVING EXPENDITURE GROWTH OF URBAN HOUSEHOLDS IN MAJOR YEARS

单位：元 (yuan)

年 份 Year	消费支出 Living Expenditure	比上年增加额 Increase Value over Last Year	比上年增长(%) Increase Rate over Last Year	城镇居民消费价格指数(上年＝100) Consumer Price Index of Urban Residents (last year=100)	扣除物价上涨因素后 Deducting Price Rising	
					实际支出 Real Expenditure	比上年增长% Increase Rate over Last Year
1978	275.4					
1980	356.6	51.8	17.0	105.5	338.0	10.8
1985	533.4	100.1	23.1	109.1	488.9	12.8
1990	1047.7	54.2	5.5	101.5	1032.2	3.9
1995	2640.7	597.4	29.2	116.7	2262.8	10.7
2000	3941.9	448.9	12.9	104.7	3764.9	7.8
2005	6342.6	688.4	12.2	101.7	6236.6	10.3
2010	9792.7	437.6	4.7	103.1	9498.2	1.5
2011	11354.3	1561.7	15.9	105.1	10803.3	10.3
2012	12211.5	857.2	7.6	102.4	11925.3	5.0
2013	13166.2	954.7	7.8	103.0	12782.7	4.7
2013(新口径)	13762.7			103.0	13361.8	
2014	14636.9	874.2	6.4	101.8	14378.1	4.5
2015	15818.6	1221.5	8.1	100.6	15724.3	7.4
2016	16992.8	1174.2	7.4	101.1	16807.9	6.3

注：2013年起，国家统计局实施城乡一体化住户调查改革，居民收支相关指标采用新口径。

Note: The NBS has conducted the integrated household survey reform and related indicators of household income and expenditure have adopted a new coverage since 2013.

4-12 城镇居民家庭平均每人食品消费量
PER CAPITA FOOD CONSUMPTION OF URBAN HOUSEHOLDS

单位：公斤 (kg)

指　标	Item	2015	2016
粮　食	Grain	110.67	109.00
油脂类	Oil or Fat	8.25	8.00
蔬菜及菜制品	Vegetables and Processed Products	85.24	87.58
肉　类	Meat	16.65	16.20
禽　类	Poultry	2.65	2.55
水产品	Aquatic Product	4.89	3.08
蛋类及蛋制品	Eggs and Processed Products	11.41	10.65
奶和奶制品	Milk and Processed Products	20.64	18.89
干鲜瓜果类	Fresh and Dried Fruits	60.05	57.79
糖果糕点类	Sweets and Pastry	6.43	5.29
饮　料	Beverage	0.16	0.18
酒	Liquor	3.39	3.09

4-13 城镇居民家庭平均每百户年末耐用消费品拥有量
DURABLE CONSUMER GOODS OWNED PER 100 URBAN HOUSEHOLDS AT YEAR-END

名　称	Item	2015	2016
家用汽车(辆)	Automobile (unit)	29.13	33.77
摩托车(辆)	Motorcycle (unit)	22.32	20.21
洗衣机(台)	Washing Machine (set)	98.91	99.12
电冰箱(台)	Refrigerator (set)	91.91	94.32
微波炉(台)	Microwave oven (set)	36.36	38.31
彩色电视机(台)	Color Television (set)	107.15	106.01
空　调(台)	Air conditioner (set)	32.79	33.88
固定电话(部)	Fixed Telephone (set)	39.21	32.17
移动电话(部)	Mobile Telephone (set)	220.58	230.56
#接入互联网	Mobile Telephone with Internet Access	117.74	137.33
计算机(台)	Computer (set)	73.14	73.09
#接入互联网	Computer with Internet Access	60.12	60.09
照相机(台)	Camera (set)	22.22	19.36
组合音响(套)	Hi-Fi Stereo Componet System (set)	4.08	3.57

4-14 城镇居民家庭年末居住情况
LIVING CONDITIONS OF URBAN HOUSEHOLDS AT YEAR-END

单位：% (%)

指　标	Item	2015	2016
一、居住空间样式	Style of Residential Space	100.0	100.0
单栋楼房	Dependent Resident	9.5	11.6
单栋平房	Dependent Bungalow	21.1	20.8
四居室及以上单元房	Apartment with Four and More Bedrooms	1.3	1.2
三居室单元房	Apartment with Three Bedrooms	24.9	25.7
二居室单元房	Apartment with Two Bedrooms	32.5	30.4
一居室单元房	Apartment with One Bedrooms	2.8	2.8
筒子楼或连片平房	Tube-Shaped Apartment or Contiguous Bungalow	7.3	7.3
其　他	Others	0.5	0.2
二、主要建筑材料	Major Building Materials	100.0	100.0
钢筋混凝土	Reinforced Concrete	24.4	28.3
砖混材料	Brick and Concrete Material	62.5	58.9
砖瓦砖木	Tile and Brick	12.2	12.2
竹草土坯	Bamboo, Grass and Adobe	0.3	0.1
其　他	Others	0.5	0.5
三、现住房房屋来源	Current Housing Sources	100.0	100.0
租赁公房	Rent Public Houses	2.3	2.0
租赁私房	Rent Private Houses	7.2	5.5
自建住房	Self-Build Housing	30.6	31.1
购买商品房	Purchased Commercial Housing	28.1	30.1
购买房改住房	Purchased Housing-Reform Houses	19.4	18.1
购买保障性住房	Purchased Security Housing	4.3	4.2
拆迁安置房	Resettlement Housing	2.6	3.8
继承或获赠住房	Inherited or receive Housing	1.2	1.0
免费借用房	Free Rental Housing	1.0	1.3
雇主提供免费住房	Employer-Provided Free Housing	0.6	0.5
其他来源	Other Sources	2.7	2.5

4–14 续表1 continued

单位：% (%)

指 标	Item	2015	2016
四、现住房建筑面积	Current Housing Construction Area	100.0	100.0
10平方米以内	Within 10 sq. m		0.1
10–20平方米	10 – 20 sq. m	1.4	1.5
20–30平方米	20 – 30 sq. m	2.4	1.9
30–60平方米	30 – 60 sq. m	21.1	19.8
60–90平方米	60 – 90 sq. m	30.1	30.6
90–120平方米	90 – 120 sq. m	25.1	25.7
120–200平方米	120 – 200 sq. m	16.9	17.0
200平方米以上	Above 200 sq. m	2.9	3.4
五、住宅外道路路面情况	Road Conditions Outside Houses	100.0	100.0
水泥或柏油路面	Cement or Asphalt Road	90.5	91.4
沙石或石板等硬质路面	Sand, Stone and Other Hard Surfacing Road	7.9	7.5
其 他	Others	1.6	1.1
六、住宅有管道供水情况	House Water Supply	100.0	100.0
管道供水入户	Piped Water Supply Inlet	97.7	98.8
管道供水至公共取水点	Piped Water Supply to Public Water Draw–off	1.1	0.3
没有管道设施	No Pipeline Facilities	1.2	0.9
七、住户主要饮用水来源情况	Major Sources of Drinking Water for Households	100.0	100.0
经过净化处理的自来水	Purified Running Water	85.1	87.4
受保护的井水和泉水	Protected Wells and Springs	12.4	10.1
不受保护的井水和泉水	Unprotected Wells and Springs	1.0	1.4
江河湖泊水	River and Lake Water		
收集雨水	Collected rainwater		
桶装水	Bottled water	0.7	0.3
其他水源	Other Water sources	0.8	0.8
八、住户厕所类型	Household Toilet Type	100.0	100.0
水冲式卫生厕所	Clean Flush Toilets	70.1	69.4
水冲式非卫生厕所	Non–clean Flush Toilets	0.7	0.8
卫生旱厕	Clean Pit Latrines	4.4	7.6
普通旱厕	General Pit Latrines	21.9	20.2
无厕所	No Toilet	3.0	2.0

4-14 续表2 continued

单位：% (%)

指 标	Item	2015	2016
九、住户主要取暖设备状况	Major Heating Equipments for Households	100.0	100.0
由市政或小区集中供暖	Central Heating Supplied by Municipal or Residential Area	69.4	70.3
自行供暖	Self Heating	29.4	29.5
无取暖设备	No Heating Equipments	1.2	0.1
十、住户主要取暖用能源状况	Major Heating Energy for Households	100.0	100.0
柴 草	Firewood	0.4	0.8
煤 炭	Coal	27.3	25.8
罐装液化石油气	Bottled Liquefied Petroleum Gas	0.1	
管道液化石油气	Pipelined Liquefied Petroleum Gas		0.1
管道煤气	Pipelined Gas	1.5	5.5
管道天然气	Pipelined Natural Gas	1.8	3.4
电	Electricity	1.9	3.7
燃料用油	Fuel oil		
沼 气	Biogas		
其 他	Others	3.6	7.5
无取暖行为	None	63.5	53.3
十一、主要炊用能源状况	Major Cooking Energy	100.0	100.0
柴 草	Firewood	0.3	0.2
煤 炭	Coal	16.6	14.6
罐装液化石油气	Bottled Liquefied Petroleum Gas	5.4	4.9
管道液化石油气	Pipelined Liquefied Petroleum Gas	0.5	0.5
管道煤气	Pipelined Gas	17.1	14.9
管道天然气	Pipelined Natural Gas	37.7	41.7
电	Electricity	21.8	22.9
燃料用油	Fuel oil		
沼 气	Biogas		
其 他	Others	0.4	0.4
无炊用行为	None	0.2	

4-15 城镇居民家庭五等分分组基本情况(2016年)

按可支配收入分组

指　　标	Item	低收入户 (20%) Low Income Households
一、调查户数(户)	Number of Households Surveyed (household)	477
二、调查户常住人口(人)	Number of Resident Population Surveyed (person)	1674
三、劳动力数(人)	Number of Labors	1057
#从业人数	Number of Employees	690
四、人均期末住房面积(平方米)	Per Capita Housing Area at the Year-end (sq.m)	27.65
五、平均每百户期末耐用品拥有量	Durable Goods Owned Per 100 Households at the Year-end	
家用汽车(辆)	Automobile (unit)	22.41
摩托车(辆)	Motorcycle (unit)	32.03
洗衣机(台)	Washing Machine (set)	96.44
电冰箱(台)	Refrigerator (set)	83.57
微波炉(台)	Microwave Oven (set)	16.97
彩色电视机(台)	Color Television (set)	105.24
空　调(台)	Air Conditioner (set)	14.87
固定电话(部)	Fixed Telephone (set)	20.74
移动电话(部)	Mobile Telephone (set)	231.42
#接入互联网	Mobile Telephone with Internet Access	125.64
计算机(台)	Computer (set)	56.55
#接入互联网	Computer with Internet Access	44.41
照相机(台)	Camera (set)	4.82
组合音响(套)	Hi-Fi Stereo Componet System (set)	1.47
六、平均每人食品消费情况(公斤)	Per Capita Food Consumption (kg)	
粮　食	Grain	105.19
油脂类	Oil and Fat	7.56
蔬菜及菜制品	Vegetables and Processed Products	64.16
肉　类	Meat	11.21
禽　类	Poultry	1.67
水产品	Aquatic Product	1.69
蛋类及蛋制品	Eggs and Processed Products	8.38
奶和奶制品	Milk and Processed Products	13.23
干鲜瓜果类	Fresh and Dried Fruits	39.54
糖果糕点类	Sweets and Pastry	4.10
饮　料	Beverage	0.12
酒	Liquor	2.41

BASIC CONDITIONS OF URBAN HOUSEHOLDS BY INCOME QUINTILE(2016)

(by the group of disposible income)

中低收入户 (20%) Lower Middle Income Households	中等收入户 (20%) Middle Income Households	中高收入户 (20%) Higher Middle Income Households	高收入户 (20%) High Income Households
477	477	478	473
1575	1479	1255	1087
1098	1093	962	882
781	770	607	495
29.71	32.03	34.29	44.09
30.20	36.59	37.32	42.40
26.83	19.08	12.54	10.49
98.85	101.10	99.16	100.04
94.13	98.39	96.86	98.70
26.22	41.62	47.56	59.34
106.71	105.71	104.18	108.24
25.10	35.56	37.42	56.65
26.78	33.74	35.33	44.37
247.97	249.78	215.26	208.26
143.79	148.58	134.36	134.30
73.07	76.88	78.29	80.70
60.33	64.93	63.03	67.83
10.85	20.32	23.83	37.14
2.72	3.56	3.76	6.37
101.73	108.94	122.04	111.46
7.77	7.73	9.37	8.04
73.93	86.13	112.82	119.61
14.49	16.65	21.48	21.10
2.36	2.79	3.34	3.32
2.50	3.13	4.30	4.79
9.61	10.37	12.94	13.75
16.32	18.71	24.21	26.43
53.57	57.60	72.10	80.44
5.04	5.79	6.24	6.25
0.09	0.30	0.22	0.21
3.28	2.94	4.49	2.95

4-16 城镇居民家庭五等分分组人均收支情况(2016年)

按可支配收入分组

指　　标	Item	低收入户 (20%) Low Income Households
一、总收入(元)	**Total Income (yuan)**	**12721.32**
(一)工资性收入	Income of Wages and Salaries	8582.78
(二)经营性收入	Business Income	2125.22
第一产业	Primary Industry	504.93
第二产业	Secondary Industry	114.42
第三产业	Tertiary Industry	1505.87
(三)财产性收入	Property Income	759.73
#利息收入	Interest	45.16
红利收入	Dividend and Bonus	37.39
储蓄性保险净收益	Net Savings Insurance	2.79
出租房屋财产性净收入	Net Income of Property Rental	64.25
(四)转移性收入	Transfer Income	1253.60
#养老金或离退休金	Pension or Retirement Payments	749.13
社会救济和补助	Social Relief and Subsidy	126.34
政策性生活补贴	Policy Living Allowances	42.43
赡养收入	Old Alimony	51.93
报销医疗费	Reimbursement of Medical Expenses	47.87
从政府和组织得到的实物产品和服务折价	Goods and Services Discount Received from Governments and Organizations	18.99
现金政策性惠农补贴	Cash Benefits Policy of Aagricultural Subsidies	12.04
二、总支出(元)	**Total Expenditure (yuan)**	**12985.45**
(一)生活消费支出	Living Expenditure	9170.94
食品烟酒	Food, Tobacco and Liquor	2354.37
衣　着	Clothing	848.62
居　住	Residence	2115.92
生活用品及服务	Household Living Facilities,Articles and Services	409.33
交通通信	Transportation and Communication	1188.72
教育文化娱乐服务	Education, Culture and Recreation Services	1607.54
医疗保健	Health Care	497.41
其他商品和服务	Other Commodities and Services	149.02
(二)生产经营费用支出	Production and Operation Expenses	610.08
第一产业	Primary Industry	292.80
第二产业	Secondary Industry	13.43
第三产业	Tertiary Industry	303.85
(三)财产性支出	Property Expenditure	8.01
(四)转移性支出	Transfer Expenditure	1023.93
(五)部分商业保险支出	Part of the Commercial Insurance Expenses	106.89
(六)购置资产及非经常性转移支出	Acquisition of Assets and Non-recurring Transfer Expenditures	1748.59
(七)借贷性支出	Borrowing Expenditure	317.00
三、可支配收入(元)	**Disposable Income (yuan)**	**10919.58**

PER CAPITA INCOME AND EXPENDITURE OF URBAN HOUSEHOLDS BY INCOME QUINTILE(2016)

(by the group of disposible income)

中低收入户 (20%) Lower Middle Income Households	中等收入户 (20%) Middle Income Households	中高收入户 (20%) Higher Middle Income Households	高收入户 (20%) High Income Households
20533.51	**28075.43**	**36683.26**	**58755.19**
13766.45	18314.06	20987.54	28897.68
2621.31	1865.90	1336.45	6570.60
150.48	250.23	58.68	2478.10
152.14	64.01	135.49	655.60
2318.70	1551.65	1142.28	3436.90
1430.27	1710.96	2373.01	4430.99
102.12	133.06	193.15	288.71
64.52	143.49	81.63	258.90
5.47	5.74	8.10	19.48
269.29	285.14	545.18	1266.73
2715.48	6184.51	11986.26	18855.93
2296.34	5453.79	11113.60	17050.77
51.08	35.01	3.17	29.64
33.13	20.34	20.55	29.40
57.39	128.77	78.31	144.97
70.93	238.02	567.13	1286.98
27.51	36.54	35.23	35.58
8.90	2.91	3.14	6.24
17540.21	**23994.45**	**25955.18**	**46595.59**
12960.22	16586.73	19238.90	31203.98
3291.95	3946.73	4800.40	5723.40
1340.51	1648.50	1885.70	2662.43
2793.43	3465.78	4135.42	6529.46
670.44	1003.05	1013.38	1919.18
1600.23	2290.88	2251.41	5270.15
1900.24	2717.54	2666.31	3801.99
945.50	1128.59	2062.27	4304.06
417.93	385.66	424.02	993.31
379.42	500.82	141.08	1538.84
49.65	99.51	5.17	892.36
47.04	13.60	0.56	4.72
282.73	387.72	135.35	641.75
12.69	71.76	56.16	71.06
1231.34	1653.30	2013.49	2734.62
86.36	98.55	134.31	196.68
2022.43	2986.59	3331.71	7501.30
847.75	2096.70	1039.52	3349.11
18776.59	**25782.24**	**34440.56**	**54190.64**

4-17 农村居民家庭生活基本情况
BASIC LIVING CONDITIONS OF RURAL HOUSEHOLDS

指　标	Item	2015	2016
一、调查户数(户)	Number of Households Surveyed (household)	2232	2160
二、调查户常住人口（人）	Number of Resident Population Surveyed (person)	6743	6312
三、平均每户常住人口数(人)	Average Number of Resident Population per Household (person)	3.02	2.92
四、平均每户从业人口数(人)	Average Number of Employees per Household (person)	1.89	2.04
五、平均每一从业者负担人数(人)	Average Number of Persons Supported by Each Employee (person)	1.60	1.54
六、平均每人全年可支配收入(元)	Per Capita Annual Disposable Income (yuan)	9454	10082
七、平均每人全年消费支出(元)	Per Capita Annual Living Expenditure (yuan)	7421	8029
八、人均期末住房面积(平方米)	Per Capita Living Space at Year-end (sq.m)	33.51	37.51

4-18 农村家庭人口状况
POPULATION CONDITIONS OF RURAL HOUSEHOLDS

指　标	Item	2015	2016
一、调查户数(户)	**Number of Households Surveyed (household)**	**2232**	**2160**
二、调查户常住人口(人)	**Number of Resident Population Surveyed (person)**	**6743**	**6312**
#劳动力数	Labors	4914	4632
#从业人数	Employees	4218	3924
#在校学生	Students Enrollment	1229	1158
按年龄分组	**Grouped by Age**		
5岁及以下	Aged 5 and Under	206	178
6-15岁	Aged 6-15	678	645
16-19岁	Aged 16-19	430	378
20-24岁	Aged 20-24	548	463
25-29岁	Aged 25-29	350	298
30-34岁	Aged 30-34	298	256
35-40岁	Aged 35-40	404	361
41-50岁	Aged 41-50	1321	1263
51-60岁	Aged 51-60	1438	1388
61-65岁	Aged 61-65	488	503
66岁及以上	Aged 66 and Above	520	518

4-19 农村居民家庭劳动力状况
LABOR FORCE OF RURAL HOUSEHOLDS

单位：人 (person)

指 标	Item	2015	2016
一、劳动力文化状况	**Cultural Level of Labor Force**		
未上过学	Illiteracy or little literacy	135	121
小 学	Level of Primary School	1171	1094
初 中	Level of Junior Middle School	2789	2687
高 中	Level of Senior Middle School	608	550
大学专科	Level of Specialized Secondary School	164	145
大学本科	Level of Undergraduate	44	34
研究生	Level of Master and Doctor	4	1
二、劳动力从业情况	**Employment of Labor Force**		
(一)第一产业	Primary Industry	2362	2238
(二)第二产业	Secondary Industry	703	652
采矿业	Mining	188	158
制造业	Manufacturing	243	225
电力、热力、燃气及水生产供应业	Production and Supply of Power, Heat, Gas and Water	43	50
建筑业	Construction	229	219
(三)第三产业	Tertiary Industry	1153	1034
批发和零售业	Wholesale and Retail Trade	182	168
交通运输、仓储和邮政业	Transportation, Storage and Post	214	181
住宿和餐饮业	Hotels and Catering Services	122	127
信息传输、软件业和信息技术服务业	Information Transmission, Software and Information Technology	16	15
金融业	Financial Industry	7	6
房地产业	Real Estate	2	5
租赁和商务服务业	Leasing and Business Services	16	11
科学研究和技术服务业	Scientific Research and Technical Services	1	1
水利、环境和公共设施管理业	Management of Water Conservancy, Environment and Public Facilities	24	15
居民服务、修理和其他服务业	Services to Households, Repair and Other Services	402	313
教 育	Education	57	60
卫生和社会工作	Health and Social Service	44	47
文化、体育和娱乐业	Culture, Sports and Entertainment	8	9
公共管理、社会保障和社会组织	Public Management, Social Security and Social Organization	59	77
国际组织	International Organization		

4-20 农村居民家庭人均全年总收入
PER CAPITA ANNUAL INCOME OF RURAL HOUSEHOLDS

单位：元 (yuan)

指　标	Item	2015	2016
总收入	**Total Income**	**11402.60**	**12167.18**
一、工资性收入	Income of Wages and Salaries	4921.83	5204.45
二、经营性收入	Business Income	4331.57	4480.89
(一)第一产业	Primary Industry	3433.78	3499.62
农　业	Farming	2672.36	2932.56
林　业	Forestry	113.61	93.19
牧　业	Animal Husbandry	647.64	473.80
渔　业	Fishery	0.17	0.08
(二)第二产业	Secondary Industry	23.59	56.63
采矿业	Mining		0.03
制造业	Manufacturing	17.32	30.87
电力、热力、燃气及水生产和供应业	Production and Supply of Power, Heat, Gas and Water		
建筑业	Construction	6.27	25.73
(三)第三产业	Tertiary Industry	874.20	924.64
批发和零售业	Wholesale and Retail Trade	321.96	288.66
交通运输、仓储和邮政业	Transportation, Storage and Post	301.80	390.89
住宿和餐饮业	Hotels and Catering Services	46.44	74.60
房地产业	Real Estate	0.32	
租赁和商务服务业	Leasing and Business Services	18.58	13.42
居民服务、修理和其他服务业	Resident Services, Repair and Other Services	66.39	63.46
农林牧渔服务业	Services of Agriculture, Forestry, Animal Husbandry and Fishery	75.41	67.44
其　他	Others	43.31	26.18
三、财产性收入	Property Income	150.03	161.28
#利息收入	Interest	20.69	22.57
红利收入	Dividend and Bonus	59.78	38.17
储蓄性保险净收益	Net Savings Insurance	0.46	0.35
出租房屋财产性净收入	Net Income of Property Rental	24.84	22.16
四、转移性收入	Transfer Income	1999.17	2320.57
#养老金或离退休金	Pension or Retirement Payments	772.38	881.72
社会救济和补助	Social Relief and Subsidy	98.36	120.62
政策性生活补贴	Policy Living Allowances	89.21	150.07
赡养收入	Old Alimony	146.13	146.16
报销医疗费	Reimbursement of Medical Expenses	164.70	120.16
从政府和组织得到的实物产品和服务折价	Goods and Services Discount Received from Governments and Organizations	53.00	90.25
现金政策性惠农补贴	Cash Benefits Policy of Aagricultural Subsidies	136.68	141.60

4-21 农村居民家庭人均全年总支出

PER CAPITA ANNUAL EXPENDITURE OF RURAL HOUSEHOLDS

单位：元　　(yuan)

项　目	Item	2015	2016
总支出	**Total Expenditure**	**11613.56**	**12487.10**
#通过互联网购买的商品和服务	Commodities and Services Purchased by the Internet	12.47	15.43
一、消费支出	Living Expenditure	7421.16	8028.77
二、生产经营费用支出	Production and Operation Expenses	1554.12	1609.27
(一)第一产业	Primary Industry	1333.13	1305.09
农　业	Farming	933.83	987.21
林　业	Forestry	6.11	20.32
牧　业	Animal Husbandry	393.12	297.53
渔　业	Fishery	0.08	0.04
(二)第二产业	Secondary Industry	1.35	13.61
采矿业	Mining		
制造业	Manufacturing	0.43	11.13
电力、热力、燃气及水生产和供应业	Production and Supply of Power, Heat, Gas and Water		
建筑业	Construction	0.92	2.49
(三)第三产业	Tertiary Industry	219.63	290.56
批发和零售业	Wholesale and Retail Trade	84.92	36.96
交通运输、仓储和邮政业	Transportation, Storage and Post	93.16	210.23
住宿和餐饮业	Hotels and Catering Services	2.37	4.95
房地产业	Real Estate		
租赁和商务服务业	Leasing and Business Services	3.42	5.86
居民服务、修理和其他服务业	Resident Services, Repair and Other Services	7.57	7.39
农林牧渔服务业	Services of Agriculture, Forestry, Animal Husbandry and Fishery	15.20	16.60
其　他	Others	13.00	8.58
三、财产性支出	Property Expenditure	8.28	12.26
生活贷款利息支出	Living Loans Interest Expense	8.09	11.93
其他财产性支出	Other Property Expenditure	0.19	0.34
四、转移性支出	Transfer Expenditure	233.18	321.43
个人所得税	Individual Income Tax	0.17	1.30
社会保障支出	Social Security Expenditures	206.20	265.73
外来从业人员寄给家人的支出	Expenses of Foreign Employees Sent to The Family		19.51
赡养支出	Alimony Expenses	12.83	11.11
其他转移性支出	Other Property Expenditure	13.97	23.78
五、部分商业保险支出	Part of the Commercial Insurance Expenses	29.23	45.89
六、购置资产及非经常性转移支出	Acquisition of Assets and Non-recurring Transfer Expenditures	1959.71	2143.26
七、借贷性支出	Borrowing Expenditure	407.88	326.22

4-22 农村居民家庭平均每户土地经营情况
LAND MANAGEMENT OF RURAL HOUSEHOLDS

单位：亩 (mu)

指　标	Item	2015	2016
一、期初实际经营土地面积	**Land Area Under Real Management at the Beginning of the Period**	**9.30**	**9.90**
耕　地	Cultivated Land	8.46	9.00
#有效灌溉面积	Effective Irrigated Area	2.59	2.92
林　地	Forest Land	0.27	0.27
园　地	Gardern Plot	0.57	0.63
二、期末实际经营土地面积	**Land Area Under Real Management at the End of the Period**	**9.37**	**9.80**
耕　地	Cultivated Land	8.45	8.93
#有效灌溉面积	Effective Irrigated Area	2.55	2.83
林　地	Forest Land	0.32	0.26
园　地	Orchards	0.60	0.62
三、期内主要粮食播种面积	**Sown Area of Major Crops within the Period**	**6.37**	**6.80**
小　麦	Wheat	0.89	1.00
水　稻	Rice		
玉　米	Corn	4.78	4.97
大　豆	Soybean	0.21	0.32
薯　类	Rubers	0.48	0.51
四、期内主要经济作物播种面积	**Sown Area of Major Commercial Crops within the Period**	**0.95**	**1.28**
棉　花	Cotton		
油　料	Oil-bearing Plants	0.48	0.65
糖料作物	Sugar-yileding Crops		
蔬　菜	Vegetables	0.11	0.14
#设施蔬菜	Greenhouse Vegetables	0.03	0.05
水　果	Fruit	0.36	0.49
#设施水果	Greenhouse Fruit	0.01	0.02
五、农业生产技术应用情况	**Application of Agriculture Production Technology**		
机耕面积	Area Cultivated by Machine	6.16	6.30
机播面积	Area Sown by Machine	4.97	4.71
机收面积	Area Harvested by Machine	2.73	2.66
机电灌溉面积	Area Irrigated by Machine	1.67	1.61

4-23 农村居民家庭人均可支配收入及构成
PER CAPITA DISPOSABLE INCOME AND COMPOSITION OF RURAL HOUSEHOLDS

指　　标	Item	2015	2016
可支配收入(元)	**Disposable Income (yuan)**	**9453.91**	**10082.45**
一、工资性收入	Income of Wages and Salaries	4921.83	5204.45
二、经营净收入	Net Business Income	2624.36	2729.85
三、财产净收入	Net Property Income	141.75	149.02
四、转移净收入	Net Transfer Income	1765.97	1999.14
可支配收入构成(%)	**Composition of Disposable Income (%)**	**100.00**	**100.00**
一、工资性收入	Income of Wages and Salaries	52.06	51.62
二、经营净收入	Net Business Income	27.76	27.08
三、财产净收入	Net Property Income	1.50	1.48
四、转移净收入	Net Transfer Income	18.68	19.83

4-24 农村居民家庭人均消费支出及构成
PER CAPITA LIVING EXPENDITURE AND COMPOSITION OF RURAL HOUSEHOLDS

项　　目	Item	2015	2016
消费支出(元)	**Living Expenditure (yuan)**	**7421.16**	**8028.77**
一、食品烟酒	Food, Tobacco and Liquor	2150.25	2272.44
二、衣　着	Clothing	558.51	565.25
三、居　住	Residence	1536.77	1798.29
四、生活用品及服务	Household Living Facilities, Articles and Services	382.40	385.88
五、交通通信	Transportation and Communication	820.27	961.76
六、教育文化娱乐服务	Education, Culture and Recreation Services	1017.11	1132.31
七、医疗保健	Health Care	794.33	769.58
八、其他商品和服务	Other Commodities and Services	161.53	143.25
消费支出构成 (%)	**Composition of Living Expenditure (%)**	**100.00**	**100.00**
一、食品烟酒	Food, Tobacco and Liquor	28.97	28.30
二、衣　着	Clothing	7.53	7.04
三、居　住	Residence	20.71	22.40
四、生活用品及服务	Household Living Facilities, Articles and Services	5.15	4.81
五、交通通信	Transportation and Communication	11.05	11.98
六、教育文化娱乐服务	Education, Culture and Recreation Services	13.71	14.10
七、医疗保健	Health Care	10.70	9.59
八、其他商品和服务	Other Commodities and Services	2.18	1.78

4-25 农村居民家庭平均每人家庭经营净收入
PER CAPITA NET INCOME FROM HOUSEHOLD BUSINESS OF RURAL HOUSEHOLDS

单位：元 (yuan)

指　标	Item	2015	2016
家庭经营净收入	**Net Income from Household Business**	**2624.36**	**2729.94**
农　业	Farming	1678.70	1882.10
林　业	Forestry	107.50	72.86
牧　业	Animal Husbandry	232.44	168.91
渔　业	Fishery	0.09	0.04
采矿业	Mining		
制造业	Manufacturing	16.58	18.17
电力、热力、燃气及水生产和供应业	Production and Supply of Power, Heat, Gas and Water		
建筑业	Construction	5.09	21.33
批发和零售业	Wholesale and Retail Trade	225.57	237.23
交通运输、仓储和邮政业	Transportation, Storage and Post	169.31	139.77
住宿和餐饮业	Hotels and Catering Services	39.61	67.09
房地产业	Real Estate	0.32	
租赁和商务服务业	Leasing and Business Services	13.41	6.68
居民服务、修理和其他服务业	Resident Services, Repair and Other Services	54.49	52.13
农林牧渔服务业	Services of Agriculture, Forestry, Animal Husbandry and Fishery	54.13	46.91
其　他	Others	27.11	16.72

4-26 主要年份农村居民人均可支配收入增长情况
PER CAPITA DISPOSABLE INCOME GROWTH OF RURAL HOUSEHOLDS IN MAJOR YEARS

单位：元 (yuan)

年 份 Year	可支配收入 Disposable Income	比上年增加额 Increase Value over Last Year	比上年增长(%) Increase Rate over Last Year	农村居民消费价格指数(上年=100) Consumer Price Index of Rural Residents (last year=100)	扣除物价上涨因素后 Deducting Price Rising	
					实际收入 Real Income	比上年增长% Increase Rate over Last Year
1978	101.6	8.0	8.6			
1980	155.8	10.4	7.1	101.3	153.8	5.8
1985	358.3	19.5	5.8	107.8	332.4	-1.9
1990	603.5	89.6	17.4	103.0	585.9	14.0
1995	1208.3	324.1	36.7	117.2	1031.0	16.6
2000	1905.6	133.0	7.5	103.0	1850.1	4.4
2005	2890.7	301.1	11.6	103.7	2787.5	7.6
2010	4736.2	492.2	11.6	102.8	4607.2	8.6
2011	5601.4	865.2	18.3	105.4	5314.4	12.2
2012	6356.6	755.2	13.5	102.6	6194.3	10.6
2013	7153.5	796.9	12.5	103.2	6931.7	9.0
2013(新口径)	7949.5			103.2	7703.0	
2014	8809.4	860.0	10.8	101.4	8685.4	9.2
2015	9453.9	644.5	7.3	100.7	9388.2	6.6
2016	10082.5	628.6	6.6	101.1	9968.9	5.5

4-27 主要年份农村居民人均消费支出增长情况
PER CAPITA LIVING EXPENDITURE GROWTH OF RURAL HOUSEHOLDS IN MAJOR YEARS

单位：元 (yuan)

年 份 Year	消费支出 Living Expenditure	比上年增加额 Increase Value over Last Year	比上年增长(%) Increase Rate over Last Year	农村居民消费价格指数(上年＝100) Consumer Price Index of Rural Residents (last year=100)	扣除物价上涨因素后 Deducting Price Rising	
					实际支出 Real Expenditure	比上年增长% Increase Rate over Last Year
1978	90.6					
1980	134.4	16.1	13.6	101.3	132.7	12.1
1985	272.7	48.4	21.6	107.8	253.0	12.8
1990	487.7	78.4	19.2	103.0	473.4	15.7
1995	928.0	254.4	37.8	117.2	791.8	17.5
2000	1149.0	101.8	9.7	103.0	1115.5	6.5
2005	1877.7	241.2	14.7	103.7	1810.7	10.6
2010	3663.9	359.1	10.9	102.8	3564.1	7.8
2011	4587.0	923.1	25.2	105.4	4352.0	18.8
2012	5566.2	979.2	21.3	102.6	5424.0	18.2
2013	6017.1	450.9	8.1	103.2	5830.5	4.7
2013(新口径)	6457.8			103.2	6257.6	
2014	6991.7	534.0	8.3	101.4	6895.2	6.8
2015	7421.2	429.5	6.1	100.7	7369.6	5.4
2016	8028.8	607.6	8.2	101.1	7938.4	7.0

4-28 农村居民家庭平均每人食品消费量
PER CAPITA FOOD CONSUMPTION OF RURAL HOUSEHOLDS

单位：公斤 (kg)

指　标	Item	2015	2016
粮　食	Grain	153.56	162.15
油脂类	Oil or Fat	7.64	7.85
蔬菜及菜制品	Vegetables and Processed Products	66.16	68.52
肉　类	Meat	10.48	10.36
禽　类	Poultry	1.44	1.65
水产品	Aquatic Product	1.01	1.17
蛋类及蛋制品	Eggs and Processed Products	9.08	9.26
奶和奶制品	Milk and Processed Products	8.40	8.91
干鲜瓜果类	Fresh and Dried Fruits	33.06	35.75
糖果糕点类	Sweets and Pastry	3.44	3.88
饮　料	Beverage	0.11	0.10
酒	Liquor	4.24	4.68

4-29 农村居民家庭平均每百户耐用消费品拥有量
DURABLE CONSUMER GOODS OWNED PER 100 RURAL HOUSEHOLDS

名　称	Item	2015	2016
家用汽车(辆)	Automobile (unit)	12.82	15.70
摩托车(辆)	Motorcycle (unit)	55.28	51.39
洗衣机(台)	Washing Machine (set)	83.22	88.38
电冰箱(台)	Refrigerator (set)	62.47	70.53
微波炉(台)	Microwave oven (set)	7.48	6.99
彩色电视机(台)	Color Television (set)	104.64	105.86
空　调(台)	Air conditioner (set)	10.20	12.85
固定电话(部)	Fixed Telephone (set)	22.64	19.38
移动电话(部)	Mobile Telephone (set)	201.24	215.46
#接入互联网	Mobile Telephone with Internet Access	80.39	99.02
计算机(台)	Computer (set)	31.80	33.58
#接入互联网	Computer with Internet Access	22.66	25.32
照相机(台)	Camera (set)	3.05	2.13
组合音响(套)	Hi-Fi Stereo Componet System (set)	1.84	1.30

4-30 农村居民家庭年末居住情况
LIVING CONDITIONS OF RURAL HOUSEHOLDS AT YEAR-END

单位：% (%)

指 标	Item	2015	2016
一、居住空间样式	Style of Residential Space	100.0	100.0
单栋楼房	Dependent Resident	10.7	11.6
单栋平房	Dependent Bungalow	69.3	70.1
四居室及以上单元房	Apartment with Four and More Bedrooms	0.2	0.1
三居室单元房	Apartment with Three Bedrooms	1.3	1.3
二居室单元房	Apartment with Two Bedrooms	0.3	0.2
一居室单元房	Apartment with One Bedrooms		
筒子楼或连片平房	Tube-Shaped Apartment or Contiguous Bungalow	8.7	8.2
其 他	Others	9.5	8.5
二、主要建筑材料	Major Building Materials	100.0	100.0
钢筋混凝土	Reinforced Concrete	7.5	8.4
砖混材料	Brick and Concrete Material	33.7	37.0
砖瓦砖木	Tile and Brick	45.3	45.2
竹草土坯	Bamboo, Grass and Adobe	5.9	4.2
其 他	Others	7.6	5.1
三、现住房房屋来源	Current Housing Sources	100.0	100.0
租赁公房	Rent Public Houses		
租赁私房	Rent Private Houses	2.2	2.3
自建住房	Self-Build Housing	90.5	90.1
购买商品房	Purchased Commercial Housing	1.7	1.4
购买房改住房	Purchased Housing-Reform Houses	0.4	0.6
购买保障性住房	Purchased Security Housing	0.2	0.3
拆迁安置房	Resettlement Housing	0.5	0.4
继承或获赠住房	Inherited or receive Housing	1.6	1.9
免费借用房	Free Rental Housing	1.2	1.5
雇主提供免费住房	Employer-Provided Free Housing	1.0	1.1
其他来源	Other Sources	0.6	0.5

4-30 续表1 continued

单位：% (%)

指 标	Item	2015	2016
四、现住房建筑面积	Current Housing Construction Area	100.0	100.0
10平方米以内	Within 10 sq. m		
10-20平方米	10 – 20 sq. m	1.6	1.6
20-30平方米	20 – 30 sq. m	2.8	2.6
30-60平方米	30 – 60 sq. m	22.6	20.2
60-90平方米	60 – 90 sq. m	24.8	24.6
90-120平方米	90 – 120 sq. m	24.5	24.7
120-200平方米	120 – 200 sq. m	17.8	19.6
200平方米以上	Above 200 sq. m	6.0	6.6
五、住宅外道路路面情况	Road Conditions Outside Houses	100.0	100.0
水泥或柏油路面	Cement or Asphalt Road	85.7	86.5
沙石或石板等硬质路面	Sand, Stone and Other Hard Surfacing Road	9.1	9.4
其 他	Others	5.2	4.1
六、住宅有管道供水情况	House Water Supply	100.0	100.0
管道供水入户	Piped Water Supply Inlet	78.9	80.9
管道供水至公共取水点	Piped Water Supply to Public Water Draw-off	4.2	4.7
没有管道设施	No Pipeline Facilities	17.0	14.4
七、住户主要饮用水来源情况	Major Sources of Drinking Water for Households	100.0	100.0
经过净化处理的自来水	Purified Running Water	41.7	46.5
受保护的井水和泉水	Protected Wells and Springs	45.5	42.6
不受保护的井水和泉水	Unprotected Wells and Springs	8.1	7.0
江河湖泊水	River and Lake Water		
收集雨水	Collected rainwater	2.2	1.9
桶装水	Bottled water		0.1
其他水源	Other Water sources	2.4	1.9
八、住户厕所类型	Household Toilet Type	100.0	100.0
水冲式卫生厕所	Clean Flush Toilets	4.1	4.2
水冲式非卫生厕所	Non-clean Flush Toilets	0.5	0.4
卫生旱厕	Clean Pit Latrines	11.3	13.3
普通旱厕	General Pit Latrines	83.2	81.3
无厕所	No Toilet	0.9	0.8

4-30 续表2 continued

单位：% (%)

指 标	Item	2015	2016
九、住户主要取暖设备状况	Major Heating Equipments for Households	100.0	100.0
由市政或小区集中供暖	Central Heating Supplied by Municipal or Residential Area	4.3	3.3
自行供暖	Self Heating	88.2	95.5
无取暖设备	No Heating Equipments	7.5	1.2
十、住户主要取暖用能源状况	Major Heating Energy for Households	100.0	100.0
柴 草	Firewood	9.9	11.0
煤 炭	Coal	80.7	77.3
罐装液化石油气	Bottled Liquefied Petroleum Gas		0.1
管道液化石油气	Pipelined Liquefied Petroleum Gas	0.1	
管道煤气	Pipelined Gas	1.0	1.2
管道天然气	Pipelined Natural Gas	0.1	0.3
电	Electricity	1.7	2.7
燃料用油	Fuel oil		
沼 气	Biogas		
其 他	Others	2.1	3.6
无取暖行为	None	4.3	3.8
十一、主要炊用能源状况	Major Cooking Energy	100.0	100.0
柴 草	Firewood	21.0	19.1
煤 炭	Coal	55.3	52.0
罐装液化石油气	Bottled Liquefied Petroleum Gas	2.2	2.4
管道液化石油气	Pipelined Liquefied Petroleum Gas		0.1
管道煤气	Pipelined Gas	1.9	2.0
管道天然气	Pipelined Natural Gas	1.0	1.6
电	Electricity	17.6	22.4
燃料用油	Fuel oil		
沼 气	Biogas		
其 他	Others	0.8	0.3
无炊用行为	None	0.1	

4-31 农村居民家庭五等分分组基本情况(2016年)

按可支配收入分组

指 标	Item	低收入户 (20%) Low Income Households
一、调查户数 (户)	Number of Households Surveyed (household)	431
二、调查户常住人口(人)	Number of Resident Population Surveyed (person)	1287
三、劳动力数	Number of Labors	894
#从业人数	Number of Employees	741
四、人均期末住房面积 (平方米)	Per Capita Housing Area at the Year–end (sq.m)	31.79
五、户均期末经营土地面积(亩)	Average Land Area under Management at the End of the Period (mu)	8.99
六、平均每百户期末耐用品拥有量	Durable Goods Owned Per 100 Households at the Year–end	
家用汽车(辆)	Automobile (unit)	7.19
摩托车(辆)	Motorcycle (unit)	44.65
洗衣机(台)	Washing Machine (set)	77.98
电冰箱(台)	Refrigerator (set)	53.24
微波炉(台)	Microwave Oven (set)	4.41
彩色电视机(台)	Color Television (set)	101.28
空 调(台)	Air Conditioner (set)	5.57
固定电话(部)	Fixed Telephone (set)	20.07
移动电话(部)	Mobile Telephone (set)	187.22
#接入互联网	Mobile Telephone with Internet Access	73.23
计算机(台)	Computer (set)	22.27
#接入互联网	Computer with Internet Access	16.24
照相机(台)	Camera (set)	0.23
组合音响(套)	Hi–Fi Stereo Componet System (set)	1.16
七、平均每人食品消费情况 (公斤)	Per Capita Food Consumption (kg)	
粮 食	Grain	163.86
油脂类	Oil and Fat	7.18
蔬菜及菜制品	Vegetables and Processed Products	58.77
肉 类	Meat	8.08
禽 类	Poultry	1.19
水产品	Aquatic Product	0.73
蛋类及蛋制品	Eggs and Processed Products	8.07
奶和奶制品	Milk and Processed Products	6.55
干鲜瓜果类	Fresh and Dried Fruits	27.64
糖果糕点类	Sweets and Pastry	3.17
饮 料	Beverage	0.07
酒	Liquor	4.00

BASIC CONDITIONS OF RURAL HOUSEHOLDS BY INCOME QUINTILE(2016)

(by the group of disposible income)

中低收入户 (20%) Lower Middle Income Households	中等收入户 (20%) Middle Income Households	中高收入户 (20%) Higher Middle Income Households	高收入户 (20%) High Income Households
432	431	433	432
1342	1322	1282	1079
929	955	964	890
799	804	834	746
33.40	34.67	41.54	46.80
9.72	9.87	10.31	10.13
11.57	16.46	21.72	21.51
52.75	56.38	54.07	49.07
85.89	90.96	94.24	92.81
65.90	73.71	78.99	80.74
4.40	5.56	8.78	11.80
106.94	107.19	107.41	106.46
7.36	11.13	17.79	22.36
19.20	16.23	20.08	21.34
208.25	222.02	232.58	227.14
93.08	96.43	113.92	118.37
28.19	34.77	41.83	40.81
21.98	25.96	31.20	31.21
1.16	1.62	3.00	4.63
0.46	1.39	1.16	2.31
143.56	169.55	162.67	174.23
6.93	8.20	7.94	9.27
65.19	65.11	72.85	83.03
8.64	9.62	11.66	14.53
1.17	1.51	2.08	2.51
0.88	0.98	1.55	1.86
8.12	8.79	9.79	11.93
6.69	8.84	10.79	12.66
30.54	32.43	40.12	50.41
3.29	3.81	4.45	4.98
0.07	0.14	0.07	0.13
3.94	4.91	4.80	6.00

4-32 农村居民家庭五等分分组人均收支情况(2016年)

按可支配收入分组

指　　标	Item	低收入户 (20%) Low Income Households
一、总收入(元)	**Total Income (yuan)**	**5936.90**
(一)工资性收入	Income of Wages and Salaries	1309.32
(二)经营性收入	Business Income	3385.10
第一产业	Primary Industry	2795.52
第二产业	Secondary Industry	88.64
第三产业	Tertiary Industry	500.94
(三)财产性收入	Property Income	27.74
#利息收入	Interest	12.92
红利收入	Dividend and Bonus	7.19
储蓄性保险净收益	Net Savings Insurance	1.44
出租房屋财产性净收入	Net Income of Property Rental	0.22
(四)转移性收入	Transfer Income	1214.74
#养老金或离退休金	Pension or Retirement Payments	214.38
社会救济和补助	Social Relief and Subsidy	128.90
政策性生活补贴	Policy Living Allowances	252.03
赡养收入	Old Alimony	158.91
报销医疗费	Reimbursement of Medical Expenses	53.49
从政府和组织得到的实物产品和服务折价	Goods and Services Discount Received from Governments and Organizations	84.85
现金政策性惠农补贴	Cash Benefits Policy of Aagricultural Subsidies	117.26
二、总支出(元)	**Total Expenditure (yuan)**	**9848.33**
(一)消费支出	Living Expenditure	5816.24
食品烟酒	Food, Tobacco and Liquor	1870.35
衣　着	Clothing	369.68
居　住	Residence	1238.01
生活用品及服务	Household Living Facilities,Articles and Services	224.32
交通通信	Transportation and Communication	529.24
教育文化娱乐服务	Education, Culture and Recreation Services	904.24
医疗保健	Health Care	597.16
其他商品和服务	Other Commodities and Services	83.24
(二)生产经营费用支出	Production and Operation Expenses	2222.10
第一产业	Primary Industry	1671.53
第二产业	Secondary Industry	42.11
第三产业	Tertiary Industry	508.46
(三)财产性支出	Property Expenditure	18.49
(四)转移性支出	Transfer Expenditure	205.01
(五)部分商业保险支出	Part of the Commercial Insurance Expenses	15.30
(六)购置资产及非经常性转移支出	Acquisition of Assets and Non-recurring Transfer Expenditures	1343.77
(七)借贷性支出	Borrowing Expenditure	227.43
三、可支配收入(元)	**Disposable Income (yuan)**	**3353.85**

PER CAPITA INCOME AND EXPENDITURE OF RURAL HOUSEHOLDS BY INCOME QUINTILE(2016)

(by the group of disposible income)

中低收入户 (20%) Lower Middle Income Households	中等收入户 (20%) Middle Income Households	中高收入户 (20%) Higher Middle Income Households	高收入户 (20%) High Income Households
8511.52	**10871.61**	**13757.68**	**23352.97**
3491.88	5223.73	7086.65	10018.68
3657.65	3910.29	4401.37	7277.41
3080.23	3126.91	3362.06	5248.58
3.24	16.14	40.67	132.84
574.18	767.25	998.64	1895.99
87.27	88.65	190.38	442.21
9.01	14.05	21.93	57.70
35.60	34.52	52.63	67.76
		0.16	
14.16	30.78	10.96	57.66
1274.72	1648.94	2079.28	5614.66
182.64	314.21	578.82	3231.36
122.39	117.87	122.46	110.20
111.70	93.45	154.50	127.29
147.93	143.15	127.44	148.11
47.27	112.81	90.50	311.71
83.79	66.36	103.67	114.95
134.95	143.37	130.06	184.98
9822.02	**11574.98**	**12545.20**	**19365.17**
6520.73	7873.82	8720.78	11850.32
1895.66	2167.28	2423.00	3136.38
456.15	576.92	647.91	833.47
1446.19	1784.76	2038.64	2653.16
267.70	390.28	513.59	594.85
627.87	930.22	1187.40	1679.25
1145.93	1150.09	1135.18	1357.54
560.79	741.24	637.22	1343.68
120.43	133.03	137.84	251.98
1233.12	1206.85	1181.43	2078.58
1090.13	982.46	961.83	1724.29
0.99	3.73	11.53	6.65
141.99	220.66	208.08	347.64
6.08	8.90	4.24	22.14
260.08	261.26	335.04	569.62
29.68	30.38	84.94	81.19
1548.55	1966.90	2006.31	4018.36
223.78	226.87	212.46	744.96
6880.81	**9258.22**	**12129.29**	**20490.88**

主要统计指标解释

可支配收入 指住户在调查期内获得的、可用于最终消费支出和储蓄的总和，即调查户可以用来自由支配的收入。可支配收入既包括现金，也包括实物收入。按照收入的来源，可支配收入包含四项，分别为：工资性收入、经营净收入、财产净收入和转移净收入。计算公式为：

可支配收入 = 工资性收入 + 经营净收入 + 财产净收入 + 转移净收入

工资性收入 指就业人员通过各种途径得到的全部劳动报酬和各种福利，包括受雇于单位或个人、从事各种自由职业、兼职和零星劳动得到的全部劳动报酬和福利。

经营净收入 指住户或住户成员从事生产经营活动所获得的净收入，是全部经营收入中扣除经营费用、生产性固定资产折旧和生产税之后得到的净收入。计算公式具体为：

经营净收入 = 经营收入 - 经营费用 - 生产性固定资产折旧 - 生产税

财产净收入 指住户或住户成员将其所拥有的金融资产、住房等非金融资产和自然资源交由其他机构单位、住户或个人支配而获得的回报并扣除相关的费用之后得到的净收入。财产净收入包括利息净收入、红利收入、储蓄性保险净收益、转让承包土地经营权租金净收入、出租房屋净收入、出租其他资产净收入和自有住房折算净租金等。

转移净收入 计算公式为：转移净收入 = 转移性收入 - 转移性支出

转移性收入 指国家、单位、社会团体对住户的各种经常性转移支付和住户之间的经常性收入转移。包括政府、非行政事业单位、社会团体对居民转移的养老金或退休金、社会救济和补助、惠农补贴、政策性生活补贴、救灾款、经常性捐赠和赔偿以及报销医疗费等；住户之间的赡养收入、经常性捐赠和赔偿以及农村地区（村委会）在外（含国外）工作的本住户非常住成员寄回带回的收入等。

转移性支出 指住户对国家、单位、住户或个人的经常性或义务性转移支付。包括缴纳的税款、各项社会保障支出、赡养支出、经常性捐赠和赔偿支出以及其他经常转移支出等。

消费支出 指住户用于满足家庭日常生活消费需要的全部支出，包括用于消费品的支出和用于服务性消费的支出。根据用途不同，消费支出可划分为食品烟酒、衣着、居住、生活用品及服务、交通通信、教育文化娱乐服务、医疗保健、其他商品及服务八大类。

Explanatory Notes on Main Statistical Indicators

Disposable Income refers to the disposable income of households which obtained during the survey period, and can be used for final consumption and savings. It includes cash and physical income. It can be divided into four categories, including income of wages and salaries, net business income, net property income and net transfer income by the sources of income. The formula is as follows:

Disposable Income = Income of Wages and Salaries + Net Business Income + Net Property Income + Net Transfer Income

Income of Wages and Salaries refers to total labor rewards and welfare employees received through various channels, including employed by units or individuals, engaged in free occupations, part-time jobs and sporadic jobs.

Net Business Income refers to net income the households or their members received through production and operation activities. It equals to total business income minus business expenses, depreciation of productive fixed assets and production taxes. The formula is as follows:

Net Business Income = Business Income – Business Expenses – Depreciation of Productive Fixed Assets – Production Taxes

Net Property Income refers to net income received as returns deducting related expenses by the households or their members, who owns the financial assets, non-financial assets such as housing and natural resources, by providing them to other institutional units, households or individuals. It includes net interest income, dividend and bonus, net savings insurance, net rental income from transferring management right of contracted land, net rental income from houses, net rental income from other assets, imputed net rental from owner occupied housing and etc.

Net Transfer Income is calculated by the following formula:

Net Transfer Income = Transfer Income – Transfer Expenditure

Transfer Income refers to current transfer payment the state, units, social organizations pay to households and current transfer income among households. It includes pensions or retirement payments, social relief and subsidies, agricultural subsidies, policy living allowances, relief funds, regular donations and compensations and reimbursement of medical expenses, which the government, non-administrative institutions, social organizations transferring to households. It also includes old alimony, regular donations and compensations and incomes that non-resident household members who work away from home including abroad sending or bringing back to the rural area, which transferring among households.

Transfer Expenditure refers to current or compulsory transfer payment households pay to the state, units, households and individuals. It includes taxes, social security expenditures, alimony payments, regular donations and compensations and other current transfer expenditures.

Living Expenditure refers to total expenditure households used to satisfy daily life consumption, which includes consumer goods and services expenditure. It can be classified into eight categories, including expenditure on food, tobacco and liquor, clothing, residence, living articles and services, transportation and communication, education, culture and recreation services, health care, other commodities and services.

5 财政、金融和保险

PUBLIC FINANCE, BANKING AND INSURANCE

资料整理人员

安爱萍　张艳君

财政、金融和保险
PUBLIC FINANCE, BANKING AND INSURANCE

一般公共预算收入	General Public Budget Revenue	1557.0	亿元	(100 million yuan)
一般公共预算支出	General Public Budget Expenditure	3428.9	亿元	(100 million yuan)
住户存款	Households Deposits	17128.0	亿元	(100 million yuan)
原保险保费收入	Income of Premiums	700.5	亿元	(100 million yuan)

金融机构人民币各项存款余额（亿元）
Deposits Balance in RMB of Financial Institutions (100 million yuan)

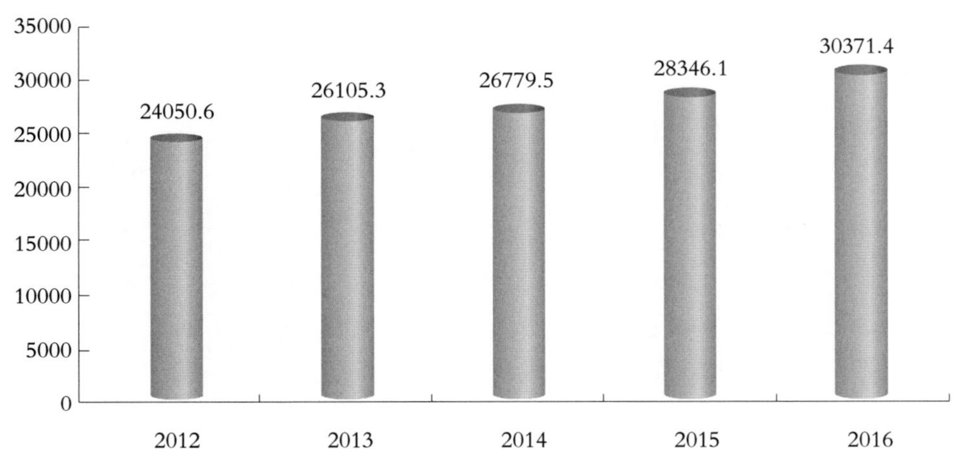

一般公共预算收入（亿元）
General Public Budget Revenue (100 million yuan)

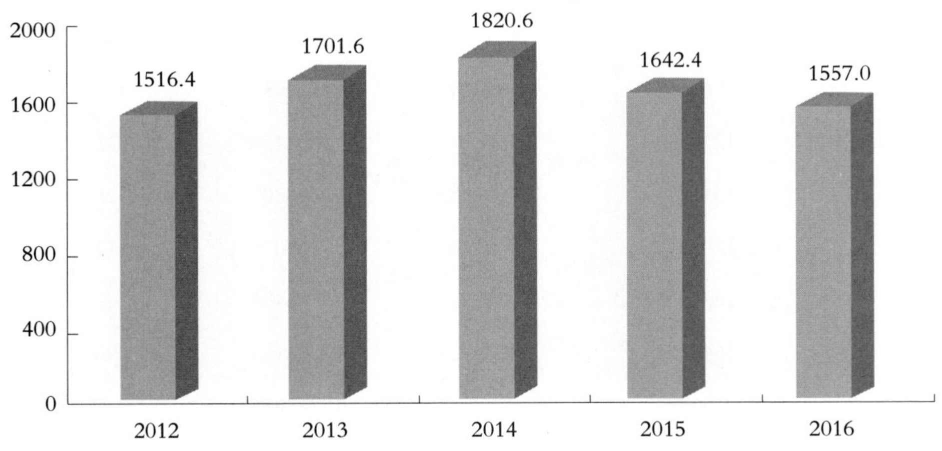

5-1 主要年份财政收支情况
FINANCIAL REVENUE AND EXPENDITURE IN MAJOR YEARS

单位：万元　　(10 000 yuan)

年 份 Year	财 政 总收入 Overall Revenue	一般公共 预算收入 General Public Budget Revenue	一般公共 预算支出 General Public Budget Expenditure	一般公共 预算收支差额 General Public Budget Balance	一般公共预算收支指数(上年=100) Genera Public Budget Revenue and Expenditure Indices (last year=100)	
					收 入 Revenue	支 出 Expenditure
1952	18276	18276	10913	7362	138	185
1957	35230	35230	28832	6398	109	95
1962	54001	54001	36423	17578	79	50
1965	68571	68571	51064	17507	115	103
1970	92081	92081	94164	-2083	181	150
1975	123934	123934	149779	-25845	113	98
1978	196419	196419	211118	-14699	148	129
1980	209555	209555	196099	13456	103	95
1985	249905	249906	355483	-105577	92	119
1990	517495	517495	548962	-31467	107	108
1995	1293837	722064	1128924	-406860	134	127
2000	1945545	1144762	2250554	-1105792	105	121
2005	7581168	3683437	6687508	-3004071	144	129
2006	10481656	5833752	9155698	-3321946	158	137
2007	12005356	5978870	10499228	-4520358	102	115
2008	15187825	7480047	13150175	-5670128	125	125
2009	15380230	8058279	15617047	-7558768	108	119
2010	18101830	9696652	19313641	-9616989	120	124
2011	22605379	12134340	23638476	-11504136	125	122
2012	26503326	15163780	27594582	-12430802	125	117
2013		17016227	30301263	-13285036	112	110
2014		18206350	30852826	-12646476	107	102
2015		16423546	34229731	-17806185	90	111
2016		15569972	34288617	-18718645	95	100

注：1994年以前一般预算收支为财政收支；2013年起，取消财政总收入。

Note: General budget revenue and expenditure refer to financial revenue and expenditure before 1994. Overall finance revenue has been canceled since 2013.

5-2 政府性基金收支额(2016年)
REVENUE AND EXPENDITURE OF GOVERNMENT FUNDS(2016)

单位：万元 (10 000 yuan)

项　目	Item	金　额 Value
收入合计	**Total Revenue**	**5349057**
支出合计	**Total Expenditure**	**6451518**
一、文化体育与传媒	Expenditure for Culture, Sports and Media	3795
二、社会保障和就业	Expenditure for Social Security and Employment	47760
三、节能环保	Expenditure for Energy Conservation and Environmental Protection	
四、城乡社区	Expenditure for Urban and Rural Community	4075162
五、农林水	Expenditure for Agriculture, Forestry and Water Conservancy	90100
六、交通运输	Expenditure for Transportation	1116868
七、资源勘探信息等	Expenditure for Resources Exploration and Information	19730
八、商业服务业等	Expenditure for Business and Services	1412
九、债务发行费用	Expenditure for Debts Issuance	2310
十、债务付息	Expenditure for Interest Payment on Debts	70187
十一、其他支出	Other Expenditures	1024194

5-3 一般公共预算收入(2016年)
GENERAL PUBLIC BUDGET REVENUE(2016)

单位：万元 (10 000 yuan)

项 目	Item	金 额 Value
收入总计	**Total Revenue**	**15569972**
一、税收收入	**Total taxes**	**10366653**
增值税	Value-added Taxes	3494456
营业税	Operation Taxes	1615596
企业所得税	Enterprises Income Taxes	1165517
个人所得税	Individual Income Taxes	351794
资源税	Resource Taxes	1403441
城市维护建设税	Taxes on Urban Construction and Maintenance	563937
房产税	House Property Taxes	333138
印花税	Stamp Taxes	174167
城镇土地使用税	Taxes on Use of Urban Land	341787
土地增值税	Land Value-added Taxes	316235
车船税	Taxes on Use of Vehicles and vessels	185618
耕地占用税	Taxes on Occuping Cultivated Land	117500
契 税	Contract Taxes	300544
烟叶税	Tobacco Taxes	2923
其他税收收入	Other Taxes	
二、非税收入	**Non-tax Revenue**	**5203319**
专项收入	Special Incomes	1494573
行政事业性收费收入	Incomes from Administrative Fees	757273
罚款收入	Penalty Incomes	481676
国有资本经营收入	Business Revenue of State-owned Properties	39175
国有资源(资产)有偿使用收入	Incomes from State-owned Resource Utilization	2015110
捐赠收入	Donation Incomes	28258
政府住房基金收入	Incomes from Government Housing Fund	214125
其他收入	Other Incomes	173129

5-4 一般公共预算支出(2016年)
GENERAL PUBLIC BUDGET EXPENDITURE(2016)

单位：万元 (10 000 yuan)

项　目	Item	金　额 Value
支出总计	**Total Expenditure**	**34288617**
一、一般公共服务	Expenditure for General Public Services	2662830
二、国　防	Expenditure for National Defence	48397
三、公共安全	Expenditure for Public Security	2035151
四、教　育	Expenditure for Education	6069733
五、科学技术	Expenditure for Science and Technology	345617
六、文化体育与传媒	Expenditure for Culture, Sports and Media	726432
七、社会保障和就业	Expenditure for Social Security and Employment	5422844
八、医疗卫生与计划生育	Expenditure for Medical and Health Care and Family Planning	3008622
九、节能环保	Expenditure for Energy Conservation and Environmental Protection	1155371
十、城乡社区	Expenditure for Urban and Rural Community	2567032
十一、农林水	Expenditure for Agriculture, Forestry and Water Conservancy	4320168
十二、交通运输	Expenditure for Transportation	1931715
十三、资源勘探信息等	Expenditure for Resources Exploration and Information	605472
十四、商业服务业等	Expenditure for Business and Services	159137
十五、金　融	Expenditure for Finance	79521
十六、援助其他地区	Expenditure for Other Regional Assistance	25350
十七、国土海洋气象等	Expenditure for Land, Ocean and Weather	911770
十八、住房保障	Expenditure for Housing Security	1487034
十九、粮油物资储备	Expenditure for Cereals, Oils and Material Reserves	178769
二十、债务付息	Expenditure for Interest Payment on Debts	302387
二十一、债务发行费用	Expenditure for Debts Issuance	5884
二十二、其　他	Other Expenditures	239381

5-5 税收分经济类型情况(2016年)

单位：万元

项　目	Item	合 计 Total	内　资			
			国有企业 Stated –owned Enterprise	集体企业 Collective –owned Enterprise	股份合作 企　业 Share Cooperative Enterprise	联营企业 Joint Enterprise
地税收入	**Local Tax Revenue**	**7431975**	**493731**	**77015**	**15615**	**1432**
国内增值税	Domestic Value–added Taxes	17323	14	2		
营业税	Operation Taxes	1764859	97366	35942	8379	153
企业所得税	Enterprises Income Taxes	1031399	83195	12753	499	248
个人所得税	Individual Income Taxes	879393	85974	7172	3606	17
资源税	Resource Taxes	1404505	56230	1026	1	870
城市维护建设税	Taxes on Urban Construction and Maintenance	562582	74065	7283	987	72
房产税	House Property Taxes	333136	29471	6062	846	18
印花税	Stamp Taxes	174166	10340	1715	192	11
城镇土地使用税	Taxes on Use of Urban Land	341791	34481	3212	219	43
土地增值税	Land Value–added Taxes	316240	3346	544	4	
车船税	Taxes on Use of Vehicles and vessels	185616	9942	5	84	
烟叶税	Tobacco Taxes	2922	1738			
耕地占用税	Taxes on Occuping Cultivated Land	117502	3190	21		
契　税	Contract Taxes	300541	4379	1278	798	
国税收入	**National Tax Revenue**	**10591571**	**1356527**	**130416**	**70710**	**991**
国内增值税	Domestic Value–added Taxes	7668242	789707	71513	12172	991
#一般纳税人	General Taxpayers	6953559	686493	65886	11587	972
国内消费税	Domestic Consumption Taxes	589885	338342	70	857	
企业所得税	Income Taxes of Enterprises	1623056	87790	58450	57597	
个人所得税	Individual Income Taxes	89				
车辆购置税	Vehicle Purchase Taxes	571834	2223	383	84	
其他税收	Other Taxes	138465	138465			

TAXES REVENUE BY FORM OF OWNERSHIP(2016)

(10 000 yuan)

Civil Funded Enterprises					港澳台投资企业 Enterprise Funded by Hongkong, Macao and Taiwan	外商投资企业 Foreign Funded Enterprise	个体经营 Individual
有限责任公司 Limited Responsibility Company	股份公司 Share Holding Limited Company	#国有控股 State Controlling Share	私营企业 Private Enterprise	其他企业 Other Enterprise			
4567847	**1185178**	**967158**	**199949**	**394052**	**50724**	**146724**	**299708**
3737	147	147	42	509			12872
1072948	352115	289762	48147	93266	4373	11307	40863
732003	148597	95010	26497	18918	146	8543	
326444	213987	182139	26561	73855	9652	26768	105357
1070768	198494	193585	24402	898	3197	48128	491
311369	99857	84988	14439	9988	12955	23725	7842
187529	51618	39364	10988	12591	6787	11714	15512
114565	26054	22468	7898	3156	4832	3289	2114
243757	27043	22143	14113	3151	7255	7803	714
274625	17615	3458	10679	1131	1048	3949	3299
39188	31710	28410	1396	100532	15	786	1958
348	836						
36732	2257	1169	2913	71239	41	416	693
153834	14848	4515	11874	4818	423	296	107993
4994617	**1724317**	**1423351**	**811372**	**30289**	**340756**	**497823**	**633753**
4366147	1006405	852628	689635	25131	214404	319781	172356
4010937	995821	852628	619235	16299	211610	317997	16722
20338	220597	219787	3915	7	715	4524	520
530214	496496	350449	93948	944	125055	172562	
							89
77918	819	487	23874	4207	582	956	460788

5-6 金融机构信贷收支余额(2016年)
BALANCE OF CREDIT FUNDS OF FINANCIAL INSTITUTIONS(2016)

单位：亿元 (100 million yuan)

项　　目	Item	本外币 RMB and Foreign Currency	人民币 RMB
一、各项存款	**Deposits**	**30869.07**	**30371.37**
境内存款	Domestic Deposits	30863.70	30366.35
住户存款	Households Deposits	17231.12	17128.05
#活期存款	Demand Deposits	4680.30	4628.70
非金融企业存款	Non-financial Enterprises Deposits	7843.18	7453.41
#活期存款	Demand Deposits	3824.41	3765.05
广义政府存款	Broad Government Deposits	5174.62	5171.33
非银行业金融机构存款	Deposits of Non-banking Financial Institutions	614.77	613.56
境外存款	Foreign Deposites	5.38	5.03
二、所有者权益	**Creditors' Equity**	**1155.55**	**1157.74**
三、各项贷款	**Loans**	**20356.50**	**20228.58**
境内贷款	Domestic Loans	20352.76	20225.01
住户贷款	Households Loans	3393.13	3392.90
#短期贷款	Short-term Loans	1387.87	1387.64
中长期贷款	Medium and Long-term Loans	2005.26	2005.26
非金融企业及机关团体贷款	Loans to Non-financial Enterprises, Government Departments and Orgnizations	16959.63	16832.11
#短期贷款	Short-term Loans	6463.58	6341.43
中长期贷款	Medium and Long-term Loans	8862.83	8858.63
票据融资	Bill Finance	1544.00	1544.00
境外贷款	Foreign Loans	3.74	3.57

5-7 金融机构人民币各项存款和贷款余额
BALANCE OF DEPOSITS AND LOANS IN RENMINBI OF FINANCIAL INSTITUTIONS

单位：万元 (10 000 yuan)

年 份 Year	各项存款合计 Balance of Deposits	#非金融企业存款 Non-financial Enterprises Deposits	#住户存款 Households Deposits	各项贷款合计 Balance of Loans	#短期贷款 Short-term	#中长期贷款 Medium and Long-term
1980	392088	125522	128705	591107	578830	12277
1981	447477	147220	166949	650669	631246	19189
1982	543771	160023	219636	712125	684031	27712
1983	673990	194255	288045	801843	767329	32372
1984	877119	269620	405322	1092897	1012969	68283
1985	1050817	401574	529220	1512441	1185224	247760
1986	1333530	496555	704837	1837204	1406768	347628
1987	1640576	562031	944179	2150614	1643114	403385
1988	1933480	642254	1244252	2382519	1995685	340744
1989	2480443	745858	1719554	2809278	2371858	397300
1990	3141354	847362	2313378	3569045	2877047	571351
1991	3809523	1034918	2915655	4328291	3262954	943164
1992	4607404	1224459	3636711	5148408	3712448	1274798
1993	5702498	1414515	4603533	6381035	4400154	1778957
1994	6854272	2062932	6159495	8020557	5081106	2756760
1995	12882737	2833481	8444641	12231107	7744271	3210760
1996	15699109	3681447	10738217	14201114	9259966	3910686
1997	17923626	4474154	12368354	15249840	11782869	2965442
1998	20811147	4948038	14370605	17417903	13022710	3360439
1999	23572121	5643636	16143945	19092096	13767722	3740309
2000	26283900	6772936	17484210	24531452	14224781	8212709
2001	30907287	8219315	19797268	24084029	14317608	7687055
2002	37087186	9602764	23073176	29031751	16331829	9587870
2003	46815142	12594164	27815374	35522883	19343085	12138826
2004	58116546	15579954	33423062	40161240	20362341	14893336
2005	70886971	17489745	41196865	42289987	21082074	16994250
2006	85774569	22553297	47961838	47885141	23096219	20234188
2007	100418455	26614242	54223930	53944680	26792518	22980302
2008	127667183	32744816	70486087	59603272	27912981	27300364
2009	156984678	42390374	80994287	78147390	33337917	39118456
2010	185756526	53338036	92229697	96343196	37425196	54092971
2011	209204319	93395109	104554604	111693542	42314059	63877414
2012	240505805	107851389	119970319	131062060	51960561	71455443
2013	261053489	111639664	133393743	148875306	59772430	80157833
2014	267794699	108700270	141451816	164327453	63715573	87589237
2015	283460992	69622303	156758537	184586645	59898305	79535966
2016	303713743	74534097	171280459	202285781	77290669	108638948

注：2015年，央行对金融机构存贷款统计口径进行了调整。本表非金融企业存款2015年以前数据为企事业存款口径；住户存款2015年以前数据为城乡居民储蓄存款口径；短期贷款、中长期贷款2015年数据为非金融企业及机关团体贷款。

Note: PBC adjusted the coverage of deposits and loans of financial institutions in 2015. Non-financial Enterprises deposits before 2015 uses the former data of corporate deposits; households deposits before 2015 uses the former data of saving deposits of urban and rural residents; the coverage of short-term, medium and long-term loans changes to non-financial enterprises, government departments and organizations after 2015.

5-8 金融机构法定存款利率
OFFICIAL INTEREST RATES OF DEPOSITS OF FINANCIAL INSITITUTIONS

单位：年利率% (annual interest rate %)

项　目	Item	2008.10.30 Oct.30,2008	2008.11.27 Nov.27,2008	2008.12.23 Dec.23,2008	2010.10.20 Oct.20,2010
城乡居民和单位存款	**Deposits of Urban and Rural Residents and Units**				
活　期	Demand Savings	0.72	0.36	0.36	0.36
定　期	Time Savings				
整存整取	Lump-sum Deposit and Withdrawing				
三个月	3 Months	2.88	1.98	1.71	1.91
半　年	6 Months	3.24	2.25	1.98	2.20
一　年	1 Year	3.60	2.52	2.25	2.50
二　年	2 Years	4.14	3.06	2.79	3.25
三　年	3 Years	4.77	3.60	3.33	3.85
五　年	5 Years	5.13	3.87	3.60	4.20
零存整取、整存零取、存本取息	Small Savings for Lump-sum Withdrawal, Big Money Saving and Small Withdrawing, Interest Withdrawal on a Principal Deposited				
一　年	1 Year	2.88	1.98	1.71	1.91
三　年	3 Years	3.24	2.25	1.98	2.30
五　年	5 Years	3.60	2.52	2.25	2.50
定活两便	Time-demand Optional Deposit				

项　目	Item	2010.12.26 Dec.26,2010	2011.2.9 Feb.9,2011	2011.4.6 Apr.6,2011	2011.7.7 Jul.7,2011
城乡居民和单位存款	**Deposits of Urban and Rural Residents and Units**				
活　期	Demand Savings	0.36	0.40	0.50	0.50
定　期	Time Savings				
整存整取	Lump-sum Deposit and Withdrawing				
三个月	3 Months	2.25	2.60	2.85	3.10
半　年	6 Months	2.50	2.80	3.05	3.30
一　年	1 Year	2.75	3.00	3.25	3.50
二　年	2 Years	3.55	3.90	4.15	4.40
三　年	3 Years	4.15	4.50	4.75	5.00
五　年	5 Years	4.55	5.00	5.25	5.50
零存整取、整存零取、存本取息	Small Savings for Lump-sum Withdrawal, Big Money Saving and Small Withdrawing, Interest Withdrawal on a Principal Deposited				
一　年	1 Year	2.25	2.60	2.85	3.10
三　年	3 Years	2.50	2.80	3.05	3.30
五　年	5 Years	2.75	3.00	3.25	3.50
定活两便	Time-demand Optional Deposit				

注：定活两便存款按一年期以内定期整存整取同档次利率打六折执行；2014年起不再公布5年期存款基准利率。

Note: Time-demand optional deposit enjoys a 60% preferential interest rate of lump-sum deposit and withdrawing in a year. Five-year benchmark deposit rate doesn't be announced from 2014.

5-8 续表 continued

单位：年利率% (annual interest rate %)

项 目	Item	2012.6.8 Jun.8,2012	2012.7.6 Jul.6,2012	2014.11.22 Nov.22,2014	2015.3.1 Mar.1,2015
城乡居民和单位存款	**Deposits of Urban and Rural Residents and Units**				
活 期	Demand Savings	0.40	0.35	0.35	0.35
定 期	Time Savings				
整存整取	Lump-sum Deposit and Withdrawing				
三个月	3 Months	2.85	2.60	2.35	2.10
半 年	6 Months	3.05	2.80	2.55	2.30
一 年	1 Year	3.25	3.00	2.75	2.50
二 年	2 Years	4.10	3.75	3.35	3.10
三 年	3 Years	4.65	4.25	4.00	3.75
五 年	5 Years	5.10	4.75		
零存整取、整存零取、存本取息	Small Savings for Lump-sum Withdrawal, Big Money Saving and Small Withdrawing, Interest Withdrawal on a Principal Deposited				
一 年	1 Year	2.85	2.60	2.35	2.10
三 年	3 Years	3.05	2.80	2.55	2.30
五 年	5 Years	3.25	3.00		
定活两便	Time-demand Optional Deposit				

项 目	Item	2015.5.11 May.11,2015	2015.6.28 Jun.28,2015	2015.8.26 Aug.26,2015	2015.10.24 Oct.24,2015
城乡居民和单位存款	**Deposits of Urban and Rural Residents and Units**				
活 期	Demand Savings	0.35	0.35	0.35	0.35
定 期	Time Savings				
整存整取	Lump-sum Deposit and Withdrawing				
三个月	3 Months	1.85	1.60	1.35	1.10
半 年	6 Months	2.05	1.80	1.55	1.30
一 年	1 Year	2.25	2.00	1.75	1.50
二 年	2 Years	2.85	2.60	2.35	2.10
三 年	3 Years	3.50	3.25	3.00	2.75
五 年	5 Years				
零存整取、整存零取、存本取息	Small Savings for Lump-sum Withdrawal, Big Money Saving and Small Withdrawing, Interest Withdrawal on a Principal Deposited				
一 年	1 Year	1.85	1.60	1.35	1.10
三 年	3 Years	2.05	1.80	1.55	1.30
五 年	5 Years				
定活两便	Time-demand Optional Deposit				

5-9 保险业基本情况(分险种)
BASIC STATISTICS ON INSURANCE BUSINESS BY TYPE

单位：万元 (10 000 yuan)

项　　目	Item	2015	2016
原保险保费收入	**Premium of Primary Insurance**	**5867255**	**7005480**
财产险	Property Insurance	1595491	1741487
企业财产保险	Enterprise Property Insurance	79774	74095
家庭财产保险	Family Property Insurance	3854	3317
机动车辆保险	Motor Vehicle Insurance	1352983	1481450
工程保险	Engineering Insurance	7302	15094
责任保险	Liability Insurance	54783	56819
信用保险	Export Credit Insurance	6750	8016
保证保险	Guarantee Insurance	19936	29313
船舶保险	Ship Insurance	433	79
货物运输保险	Freight Transport Insurance	10863	7682
特殊风险保险	Special Risks Insurance	742	796
农业保险	Agriculture Insurance	56612	63535
其他险	Other Insurance	1458	1292
人身险	Personal Insurance	4271764	5263994
意外险	Accident Insurance	91470	111710
健康险	Health Insurance	408496	598997
寿　险	Life Insurance	3771798	4553287
普通寿险	Ordinary Life Insurance	2079465	2667651
分红寿险	Participating Life Insurance	1671941	1862346
投资连结保险	Investment-linked Life Insurance	178	176
万能寿险	Universal Life Insurance	20214	23114
赔款及给付	**Claim and Payment**	**2002219**	**2390159**
财产险	Property Insurance	893710	924765
人身险	Personal Insurance	1108509	1465394
意外险	Accident Insurance	27083	30673
健康险	Health Insurance	114416	164974
寿　险	Life Insurance	967010	1269746

5-10 原保险保费收入情况(山西分公司)

BASIC STATISTICS ON INCOME OF PREMIUMS BY COMPANY(SHANXI BRANCH)

单位：万元 (10 000 yuan)

公司名称	Name of Company	2015	2016
合　计	**Total**	**5867255**	**7005480**
财产险公司	**Property Insurance Company**	**1673863**	**1839741**
中国人民财产保险股份有限公司山西省分公司	PICC Property and Casualty Insurance Co., Ltd. Shanxi Branch	578423	618958
中国太平洋财产保险股份有限公司山西分公司	China Pacific Property Insurance Co., Ltd. Shanxi Branch	114914	118567
永安财产保险股份有限公司山西分公司	Yong An Property Insurance Co., Ltd. Shanxi Branch	27981	48148
中国平安财产保险股份有限公司山西分公司	Ping An Property & Casualty Insurance Company of China, Ltd. Shanxi Branch	250386	288549
天安财产保险股份有限公司山西省分公司	Tianan Property Insurance Co., Ltd. of China Shanxi Branch	24193	24618
中国大地财产保险股份有限公司山西分公司	China Continent Property & Casualty Insurance Co., Ltd. Shanxi Branch	71055	78866
太平财产保险有限公司山西分公司	Taiping General Insurance Co., Ltd. Shanxi Branch	42550	46302
华安财产保险股份有限公司山西分公司	Sinosafe General Insurance Co., Ltd. Shanxi Branch	20532	30216
安邦财产保险股份有限公司山西分公司	Anbang Property & Casualty Insurance Company Ltd. Shanxi Branch	2946	3555
永诚财产保险股份有限公司山西分公司	Alltrust Property Insurance Co., Ltd. Shanxi Branch	14928	13397
阳光财产保险股份有限公司山西分公司	Sunshine Property & Casualty Insurance Co., Ltd. Shanxi Branch	52127	67760
中国人寿财产保险股份有限公司山西省分公司	China Life Property & Casualty Insurance Share Co., Ltd. Shanxi Branch	253912	256651

注：因虚拟总公司尚未设立各省分公司，分省数据按照业务来源进行统计。

Note: Provincial virtual data are calculated by the business sources because of the head company hasn't opened branches.

5-10　续表1　continued

单位：万元　　(10 000 yuan)

公司名称	Name of Company	2015	2016
渤海财产保险股份有限公司山西分公司	Bohai Property Insurance Co., Ltd. Shanxi Branch	2953	3710
都邦财产保险股份有限公司山西分公司	Dubon Property & Casualty Insurance Co., Ltd. Shanxi Branch	6535	7519
华泰财产保险有限公司山西省分公司	Huatai Property & Casualty Insurance Co., Ltd. Shanxi Branch	20786	20457
中国出口信用保险公司山西分公司	China Export & Credit Insurance Corporation, Shanxi Branch	5395	5673
安盛天平财产保险股份有限公司山西分公司	AXA Tianping Property & Casualty Insurance Co., Ltd. Shanxi Branch	26604	31254
安诚财产保险股份有限公司山西分公司	Ancheng Property & Casualty Insurance Co., Ltd. Shanxi Branch	5926	10000
信达财产保险股份有限公司山西分公司	Cinda Property and Casualty Insurance Co., Ltd. Shanxi Branch	10169	12170
中银保险有限公司山西分公司	Bank of China Insurance Co., Ltd. Shanxi Branch	6587	8748
中煤财产保险股份有限公司山西分公司	China Coal Insurance Co., Ltd. Shanxi Branch	74628	61455
英大泰和财产保险股份有限公司山西分公司	Yingda Taihe Property Insurance Co., Ltd. Shanxi Branch	17322	24563
紫金财产保险股份有限公司山西分公司	Zking Property & Casualty Insurance Co., Ltd. Shanxi Branch	10826	14595
中华联合财产保险股份有限公司山西分公司	China United Property Insurance Co., Ltd. Shanxi Branch	30001	39053
华农财产保险股份有限公司山西分公司	China Huanong Property & Casualty Insurance Co., Ltd. Shanxi Branch		242
众安在线财产保险股份有限公司山西分公司（虚拟）	Zhongan Online Property Insurance Co., Ltd. Shanxi Branch (Virtual)	2166	3089

5-10 续表2 continued

单位：万元 (10 000 yuan)

公司名称	Name of Company	2015	2016
中国铁路财产保险自保有限公司山西分公司（虚拟）	China Railway Captive Insurance Co., Ltd. Shanxi Branch (Virtual)	16	1609
泰康在线财产保险股份有限公司山西分公司（虚拟）	TK.CN Insurance Co., Ltd. Shanxi Branch (Virtual)	1	6
阳光渝融信用保证保险股份有限公司山西分公司（虚拟）	Sunshine Yurong Credit and Guarantee Insurance Co., Ltd. Shanxi Branch (Virtual)		7
安心财产保险有限责任公司山西分公司（虚拟）	Answern Property & Casualty Insurance Co., Ltd. Shanxi Branch (Virtual)		2
易安财产保险股份有限公司山西分公司（虚拟）	E An Property & Casualty Insurance Co., Ltd. Shanxi Branch (Virtual)		2
人身险公司	**Life Insurance Company**	**4193392**	**5165740**
中国人寿保险股份有限公司山西省分公司	China Life Insurance Co., Ltd. Shanxi Branch	1146883	1352283
中国太平洋人寿保险股份有限公司山西分公司	China Pacific Life Insurance Co., Ltd. Shanxi Branch	551234	675850
中国平安人寿保险股份有限公司山西分公司	Ping An Life Insurance Company of China, Ltd. Shanxi Branch	314190	434080
新华人寿保险股份有限公司山西分公司	New China Life Insurance Co., Ltd. Shanxi Branch	302148	303588
泰康人寿保险股份有限公司山西分公司	Taikang Life Insurance Co., Ltd. Shanxi Branch	198149	221783
平安养老保险股份有限公司山西分公司	Ping An Annuity Insurance Company of China, Ltd. Shanxi Branch	8167	9245
太平人寿保险有限公司山西分公司	Taiping Life Insurance Co., Ltd. Shanxi Branch	177084	220517
中国人民人寿保险股份有限公司山西省分公司	PICC Life Insurance Co., Ltd. Shanxi Branch	279370	375091
农银人寿保险股份有限公司山西分公司	ABC Life Insurance Co., Ltd. Shanxi Branch	63671	114473

5-10 续表3 continued

单位：万元 (10 000 yuan)

公司名称	Name of Company	2015	2016
中国人民健康保险股份有限公司	PICC Health Insurance Co., Ltd.	71353	115740
山西省分公司	Shanxi Branch		
英大泰和人寿保险股份有限公司	Yingda Taihe Life Insurance Co., Ltd.	7879	11833
山西分公司	Shanxi Branch		
合众人寿保险股份有限公司	Unionlife Insurance Co., Ltd.	46083	86028
山西分公司	Shanxi Branch		
民生人寿保险股份有限公司	Minsheng Life Insurance Co., Ltd.	54484	26948
山西分公司	Shanxi Branch		
阳光人寿保险股份有限公司	Sunshine Life Insurance Co., Ltd.	217576	102237
山西分公司	Shanxi Branch		
富德生命人寿保险股份有限公司	Funde Sino Life Insurance Co., Ltd.	170009	184563
山西分公司	Shanxi Branch		
光大永明人寿保险有限公司	Sun Life Everbright Life Insurance Co., Ltd.	10678	13346
山西分公司	Shanxi Branch		
国华人寿保险股份有限公司	Guohua Life Insurance Co., Ltd.	374752	275035
山西分公司	Shanxi Branch		
幸福人寿保险股份有限公司	Happy Life Insurance Co., Ltd.	46103	63275
山西分公司	Shanxi Branch		
泰康养老保险股份有限公司	Taikang Pension & Insurance Co., Ltd.	7593	10984
山西分公司	Shanxi Branch		
信诚人寿保险股份有限公司	Citic Prudential Life Insurance Co., Ltd.	1272	3276
山西分公司	Shanxi Branch		
安邦人寿保险股份有限公司	Anbang Life Insurance Co., Ltd.	111411	445520
山西分公司	Shanxi Branch		
百年人寿保险股份有限公司	Aeon Life Insurance Co., Ltd.	4520	29064
山西分公司	Shanxi Branch		
工银安盛人寿保险股份有限公司	ICBC-AXA Life Insurance Co., Ltd.	28783	90984
山西分公司	Shanxi Branch		

5-11 证券业基本情况
BASIC STATISTICS ON SECURITY

年 份 Year	境内上市公司(家) Number of Listed Companies in Mainland (unit)	上交所 Shanghai Stock Exchange	深交所 Shenzhen Stock Exchange	股票总发行股本(万股) Issued Capital (10 000 shares)	股票发行量(万股) Issued Share (10 000 shares)	#A股 A Shares
2000	17	7	10	663761	206471	188391
2001	18	8	10	714403	228688	210608
2002	19	9	10	733432	240216	222136
2003	21	12	9	809114	267920	249840
2004	22	13	9	907871	271920	253840
2005	22	13	9	907871	271920	253840
2006	25	16	9	2570003	761526	743446
2007	26	16	10	2734756	807626	789546
2008	27	16	11	3343555	851495	833415
2009	28	17	11	3483585	873895	855815
2010	31	18	13	4314023	1119875	898926
2011	34	18	16	4623996	1128522	907573
2012	34	18	16	4983495	1315198	1083249
2013	34	18	16	5268694	1514809	1282860
2014	35	19	16	5624837	1533841	1301892
2015	37	19	18	6944563	2328559	2086610
2016	38	20	18	7540697	2708300	2466351

年 份 Year	股票筹资额(万元) Raised Capital (10 000 yuan)	#A股 A Shares	保险公司保费收入(万元) Premium Income of Insurance Companies (10 000 yuan)	保险公司赔款及给付(万元) Indemnity Expenditure and Payment of Insurance Companies (10 000 yuan)
2000	1092835	1070061	283300	104200
2001	1234761	1211987	374100	104200
2002	1306661	1283887	694621	121023
2003	1505721	1482947	905101	156993
2004	1531281	1508507	1041413	197050
2005	1531281	1508507	1218039	200781
2006	4036272	4013498	1409766	252664
2007	4387204	4364430	1803611	525335
2008	4869204	4846430	2608864	735782
2009	5051201	5028427	2892495	785454
2010	8411601	7358740	3652983	798544
2011	8638229	7585368	3646684	1035325
2012	9168729	8111468	3846491	1193251
2013	9873152	8815892	4123840	1693188
2014	10451202	9393942	4653746	1824737
2015	13171489	12114229	5867255	2002219
2016	14122089	13064829	7005480	2390159

主要统计指标解释

一般公共预算收入 指按照现行财政体制规定列入地方预算，直接缴入地方金库的财政收入。具体由两部分组成：一是税收收入，包括增值税、企业所得税、个人所得税的地方分享部分，营业税、资源税、城市维护建设税、房产税、印花税、城镇土地使用税、土地增值税、车船税、契税、耕地占用税等；二是非税收入，包括专项收入、行政事业性收费收入、罚没收入、国有资本经营收入、国有资源（资产）有偿使用收入、其他收入等。

上划中央收入 指实行分税制财政体制后，增值税的75%部分和消费税划为中央收入，以及从2002年起实行所得税分享改革后，所得税（包括企业所得税、个人所得税）由中央分享部分，这部分收入直接缴入中央金库。根据《预算法》和财政体制规定，上划中央收入属于列入中央预算范围的收入，地方总预算中不予包括。

税收收入 反映政府税收收入。包括：增值税、营业税、企业所得税、个人所得税、城市维护建设税、房产税、印花税、城镇土地使用税、土地增值税、车船税、耕地占用税、契税、烟叶税以及其他税收收入等。

非税收入 反映政府非税收入。包括：专项收入、行政事业性收入、罚没收入、国有资本经营收入、国有资源（资产）有偿使用收入以及其他收入等。

一般公共预算支出 是指列入地方预算的财政支出，包括：一般公共服务支出、国防支出、公共安全支出、教育支出、科学技术支出、文化体育与传媒支出、社会保障和就业支出、医疗卫生与计划生育支出、节能环保支出、城乡社区支出、农林水支出、交通运输支出、资源勘探信息等支出、商业服务业等支出、金融支出、国土海洋气象等支出、住房保障支出、粮油物资储备支出、国债还本付息支出及其他支出等。其资金来源包括用地方当年财力安排的支出、上年结余、调入资金和中央一般性及专项转移支付补助收入安排的支出。

一般公共服务 反映政府提供一般公共服务的支出。具体包括人大、政协、政府办公厅（室）及相关机构、发展与改革、统计信息、财政、税收、审计、海关、人事、纪检监察、人口与计划生育、商贸、知识产权、工商行政管理、质量技术监督与检验检疫、民族、宗教、港澳台侨、档案、民主党派及工商联、群众团体事务、党委办公厅（室）其相关机构事务、组织事务、宣传事务、统战事务、对外联盟、其它共产党事务支出、其它一般公共服务支出。

公共安全支出 反映政府维护社会公共安全方面的支出。有关事务包括：武装警察、公安、国家安全、法院、司法、强制隔离戒毒、国家保密、缉私警察等。

教育支出 反映政府教育事务支出。有关事务包括：教育管理事务、学前教育、小学教育、初中教育、高中教育、高等教育、初等职业教育、中专教育、技校教育、职业高中教育、高等职业教育、成人教育、广播电视教育、留学生教育、特殊教育、进修及培训等。

科学技术支出 反映科学技术方面的支出。有关事务包括：科学技术管理事务、基础研究、应用研究、技术研究与开发、科技条件与服务、社会科学、科学技术普及、科技交流与合作等。

文化体育与传媒支出 反映政府在文化、文物、体育、广播影视、新闻出版等方面的支出。

社会保障和就业支出 反映政府在社会保障与就业方面的支出。有关事务包括：人力资源和社会保障管理事务、民政管理事务、财政对社会保险基金的补助、补充全国社会保障基金、行政事业单位离退休、企业改革补助、就业补助、抚恤、退役安置、社会福利、残疾人事业、城市居民最低生活保障、其他城市生活救助、自然灾害生活救助、农村最低生活保障、红十字事务等。

医疗卫生与计划生育支出 反映政府医疗卫生方面的支出。有关事务包括：医疗卫生管理事务、公立医院、公共卫生、基层医疗卫生机构、医疗保障、中医药、人口与计划生育事务、食品和药品监督管理事务等。

节能环保支出 反映政府节能环保支出。有关事务包括：环境保护管理事务、环境监测与监察、污染防治、自然生态保护、天然林保护、退耕还林、风沙荒漠治理、退牧还草、已垦草原退耕还草、能源节约利用、污染减排、可再生能源和资源综合利用等支出等。

城乡社区支出 反映政府城乡社区事务支出。有关事务包括：城乡社会管理事务、城乡社区规划与管理、城乡社区公共设施、城乡社区环境卫生、建设市场管理与监督等。

农林水支出 反映政府农林水事务支出。有关事务包括：农业、林业、水利、扶贫、农业综合开发等。

交通运输支出 反映交通运输和邮政业方面的支出。有关事务包括：公路水路运输、铁路运输、民用航空运输等。

资源勘探信息等支出 反映用于资源勘探、制造业、建筑业、信息等方面的支出。有关事务包括：资源勘探、制造业、建筑业、工业和信息产业监管、安全生产监管、国有资产监管、支持中小企业发展和管理支出等。

粮油物资储备支出 反映政府用于粮油物资储备方面的支出。有关事务包括：粮油事务、物资事务、能源储备、重要商品储备等。

金融支出 反映金融方面的支出。有关事务包括：金融部门行政支出、金融部门监管支出、金融发展支出、金融调控支出等。

国土海洋气象支出 反映政府用于国土资源、海洋、测绘、地震、气象等公益服务事务方面的支出。

商业服务业等支出 反映商业服务业等方面的支出。有关事务包括：商业流通事务、旅游业管理与服务支出、涉外发展服务支出等。

其他支出 反映不能划分到上述功能科目的其他政府支出。包括年初预留和其他支出。

当年可用财力 是指按照现行财政体制规定，在预算年度内可统筹安排使用的预算内资金，其来源包括当年公共财政收入、税收返还收入、下级上解收入、一般性转移支付补助，并从中扣减上解上级及补助下级的资金。当年可用财力不包括上年结余资金及中央专项转移支付补助。根据《预算法》的规定，当年支出预算应当小于或等于当年地方可用财力。

存款 企业、机关、团体或居民根据可以收回的原则，把货币资金存入银行或其他信用机构保管并取得一定利息的一种信用活动形式。根据存款对象的不同可划分：企业存款、财政存款、机关团体存款、城镇居民储蓄存款、农村存款等项目。

住户存款 银行业金融机构通过信用方式吸收的居民储蓄存款及通过其他方式吸收的由住户部门(由住户和为其服务的非营利机构组成的部门）支配的存款。其他方式吸收的存款主要有两部分：一是保证金存款；二是个人委托业务在银行沉淀资金。

非金融企业存款 银行业金融机构吸收的企业定活期存款、保证金存款、应解及临时存款以及企业委托银行业金融机构开展委托业务沉淀在银行的货币资金。

贷款 银行或其他信用机构根据必须归还的原则，按一定利率，为企业、个人等提供资金的一种信用活动形式。我国银行贷款，分流动资金贷款、农业贷款、固定资产贷款等科目。

境内贷款 银行业金融机构对非金融企业、个人、机关团体以贷款、票据贴现、垫款、押汇、福费廷等方式提供的融资总额。

住户贷款 银行业金融机构向住户部门（由住户和为其服务的非营利机构组成的部门）发放的贷款。

非金融企业及机关团体贷款 银行业金融机构向非金融企业及机关团体发放的贷款。

票据融资 银行业金融机构通过对客户持有的商业汇票、银行承兑汇票等票据进行贴现提供的融资。

保费收入 指投保人依据保险合同的约定向保险人缴付的保险费。

赔付支出 指保险人根据保险合同的约定，向被保险人或受益人支付的赔款、死伤医疗给付、满期给付和年金给付。

Explanatory Notes on Main Statistical Indicators

General Public Budget Revenue refers to financial revenue arranged to regional budget and directly paid to local treasury according to the current regulation of financial system. It consists of tax revenue and non-tax revenue. Tax revenue includes value-added tax, enterprise income tax, local share of individual income tax, operation tax, resource tax, urban construction and maintenance tax, house property tax, stamp tax, tax on use of urban land, land value-added tax, tax on use of vehicles and vessels, contract tax, tax on occupying cultivated land and etc. And non-tax revenue includes special incomes, incomes from administrative fees, penalty incomes, business revenue of state-owned properties, incomes from state-owned resource utilization and other incomes.

Revenue Turned Over to the State refers to 75 percent of value added tax and consumption tax turned over to the state after implement financial system of tax distribution, and part of income tax shared by state and directly paid to central treasury after implement reform of income tax share from 2002. According to budget law and rule of financial system, revenue turned over to the state belongs to state budget, excluded in local budget.

Tax Revenue reflects to the government's tax revenue, including value-added tax, operation tax, enterprise income tax, individual income tax, urban maintenance and construction tax, house property tax, stamp tax, tax on use of urban land, urban land value-added tax, tax on use of vehicles and vessels, tax on occupying cultivated land, contract tax, tobacco tax and etc.

Non-tax Revenue reflects to the government's non-tax revenue, including special revenue, incomes from administrative fees, penalty incomes, business revenue of state-owned properties, incomes form state-owned resource utilization and other incomes.

General Public Budget Expenditure refers to financial expenditure arranged to local budget, including expenditure for public services, national defence, public safety, education, science and technology, culture, sports and media, social security and employment, medical and health care, family planning, energy conservation and environmental protection, urban and rural community, agriculture, forest and water conservancy, transportation, resources exploration and information, business and services, finance, land, ocean and weather, housing security, cereals, oils and material reserves, government bond and its interest and other expenditures. The sources of funds include expenditure arranged from local disposable financial resources of the year, surplus of last year, funds transferred and subsides of general and special transfer payment from central government.

General Public Services reflect the government's provision of general public service expenditures, specifically including the NPC and CPPCC, government offices and related agencies, development and reform, statistics, finance, taxation, auditing, customs, personnel, discipline inspection and supervision, population and family planning, commerce, intellectual property rights, industrial and commercial administration, quality and technical supervision, inspection and quarantine, land and natural resources, marine management, surveying and mapping, earthquakes, weather, ethnic, religious, Hong Kong, Macao oversea Chinese affairs, files, democratic parties and the federation of industry and commerce, mass organizations, party committee offices and related agencies, organization affairs, publicity affairs, united front affairs, external alliances, other CPC affairs and other affairs.

Expenditure for Public Safety reflects the expenditure of government maintaining social public safety. Related affairs include armed police, public security, national security, justice, compulsory isolation for drug rehabilitation, state secrecy, anti-smuggling police, etc.

Expenditure for Education reflects the government's education expenditure. Related affairs include education administration affairs, pre-primary education, primary education, secondary education, high school education, higher education, primary vocational education, secondary education, technical school education, vocational high school education and higher vocational education, adult education, radio and television education, the international education, special education, further education and training.

Expenditure for Science and Technology reflects the expenditure used for science and technology. It includes science and technology management services, basic research, applied research, technology research and development, science and technology and service conditions, social science, science and technology popularization, scientific and technological exchanges and cooperation.

Expenditure for Culture, Sports and Media reflects the expenditures government used for culture, heritage, sports, radio, film and television, press, publishing and other aspects.

Expenditure for Social Security and Employment reflects expenditures government used in the aspects of employment and social security. Related affairs include human resources and social security management affairs, civil administration affairs, the financial allowance for social security fund, addition of the national social security fund, retirement of administrative and institution units, subsidies for enterprises reform, employment subsidies, pension, retirement and placement, social welfare, disabled cause, the minimum living guarantee for urban residents, other urban life assistance, life assistance for natural disaster, rural minimum living guarantee, the Red Cross affairs and so on.

Expenditure for Medical and Health Care, Family Planning, reflects expenditures government used in the aspects of medical and health care. Related affairs include management affairs of medical and health care, public hospitals, public health care, primary medical and health care institutions, medical security, traditional Chinese medicine, population and family planning affairs, supervision and management affairs of food and drugs.

Expenditure for Energy Conservation and Environmental Protection reflects government's expenditure on energy conservation and environmental protection, including expenditures on management of environmental protection, environmental monitoring and supervision, pollution control, natural and ecological protection, natural forests protection, returning farmland to forests, desertification control, restoring grassland from over-grazing and cultivating, energy conservation and utilization, pollution reduction, comprehensive utilization of renewable energy and resources.

Expenditure for Urban and Rural Community reflects the government's expenditure on urban and rural community affairs, including urban and rural social management affairs, planning and management of urban and rural communities, public facilities in rural and urban communities, urban and rural community sanitation, management and supervision of the construction market and so on.

Expenditure for Agriculture, Forestry and Water Conservancy reflects the government's expenditure on agriculture, forestry and water conservancy affairs. Related affairs include agriculture, forestry, water conservancy, poverty alleviation, comprehensive agricultural development, etc.

Expenditure for Transportation reflects transport and post expenditure. Related affairs include highway and waterway transport, railway transport and civil aviation transport, etc.

Expenditure for Resources Exploration and Information reflects the expenditure used on resources exploration, manufacture, construction and information. Related affairs include resources exploration, manufacture, construction, supervision of industry and information, supervision of safety production, supervision of national assets, development and management on supporting small and medium-sized enterprises, etc.

Expenditure for Cereals, Oils and Material Reserves reflects the government expenditure on the aspects of cereals, oils, and material reserves. Related affairs include cereals and oils affairs, materials affairs, energy reserves, critical commodities reserves, etc.

Expenditure for Finance reflects expenditure in banking areas. Related Affairs include administrative expenditure of financial department, supervision of financial department, financial development expenditure, financial regulation expenditure, etc.

Expenditure for Land, Ocean and Weather reflects expenditure used on the public service affairs, such as land resources, oceans, surveying and mapping, earthquake and weather affairs.

Expenditure for Business and Services reflects expenditure on business and services aspects. Related affairs include expenditure on commercial circulation affairs, management and service of tourism, foreign developing service and so on.

Other Expenditures reflect other government expenditures that cannot be subjected to the above mentioned functions, including reserve expenditures at the beginning of the year and other expenses.

Disposable Financial Resources in the Year refer to budgetary funds which can be overall arranged and used in the budget year according to current regulation of financial system. The sources of funds include public finance revenue, return revenue of taxes, revenue turned over from lower authorities, subsides of general transfer payment, deducing funds turning over to higher authorities and subsides to lower authorities. It excludes surplus of last year and subsides of transfer payment from special central funds. According to regulation of budgetary law, budget expenditure should be less than or equal to the local disposable financial resources of the year.

Deposit is a form of credit activities by which enterprises, institutions, organizations or households can put money into banks and other credit institutions for sake keeping and interest earning under the principle of free withdrawal. According to different depositors, deposits are divided into enterprise deposits, fiscal deposits, government agencies and institutions deposits, saving deposits of urban and rural residents, rural deposits and etc.

Households Deposits refer to the residents saving deposits banking financial institutions absorbed by credit and the deposits at household sector's (consisting of households and non-profit service institutions) disposal by other means. Other means of deposits mainly contain margin deposits and precipitation funds of individual entrusted business.

Non-financial Enterprises Deposits refer to enterprise demand and time deposits, margin deposits, remittances outstanding, temporary deposits and precipitation funds of enterprise entrusted business.

Loan is a form of credit activities by which banks and other credit institutions provide funds at certain interest rate to enterprises and individuals in the light of the principle of unconditional repayment. Loans from Chinese banks include circulating capital loans, agriculture loans, fixed assets loans, etc.

Domestic Loans refer to finance amount that banking institutions provide for non-financial enterprises, individuals, government organizations by loaning, bill discounting, advancing, bill exchanging, forfeiting.

Households Loans refer to loans banking institutions offer to the household sector (consisting of households and non-profit service institutions).

Loans to Non-financial Enterprises, Government Departments and Organizations refer to loans that banking institutions offer to non-financial banking enterprises, government departments and organizations.

Bill Finance refers to the discount bill financing that banking institutions offer customers by trade bill, bank acceptance, etc.

Income of Premiums refers to the fees paid by the insurant to the insurer according to contract agreed terms.

Indemnity Expenditure refers to the indemnity, payment for death, injury and medical treatment, payment at maturity and annuity payment that the insurer paid to the insurant according to the contract agreed terms.

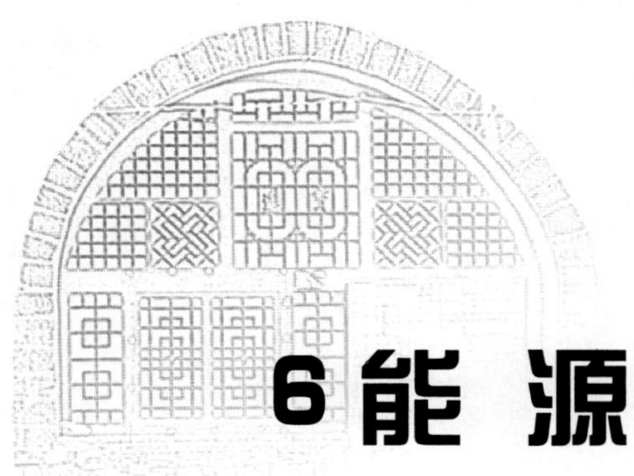

6 能 源

ENERGY

资料整理人员

郭骞擘　武鹏程　康秀芳　牛玉龙　李伟琨

能　源
ENERGY

能源消费总量	Total Energy Consumption	19400.6	万吨标准煤	(10 000 tons of SCE)
全社会发电装机容量	Total Installed Electricity Capacity	7640	万千瓦	(10 000 kw)
#6000千瓦及以上火电	Thermal Power of 6000 Kilowatt and Above	7599	万千瓦	(10 000 kw)
全社会用电量	Total Electricity Consumption	1797.2	亿千瓦小时	(100 million kwh)

全社会用电量（亿千瓦小时）

Total Electricity Consumption (100 million kwh)

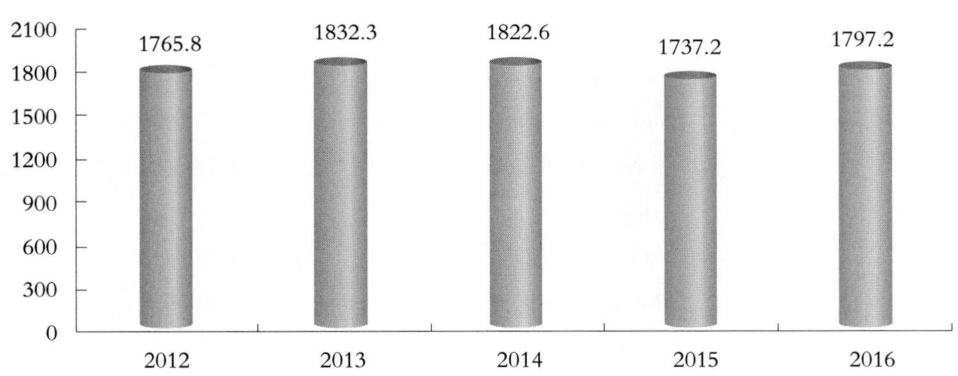

电力外调量（亿千瓦小时）

Electricity Transferred to Other Provinces and Exported (100 million kwh)

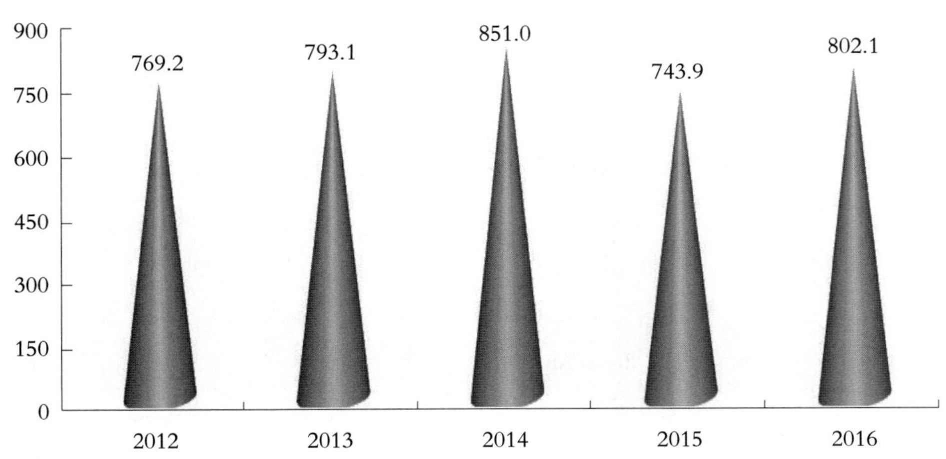

6-1 能源生产、外调、使用平衡表
BALANCE SHEET OF ENERGY PRODUCTION, TRANSFER AND USE

单位：万吨标准煤 (10 000 tons of SCE)

项　　目	Item	2010	2015	2016
一、资　源	Resources	65274.19	79138.84	72239.24
年初库存	Stock of Year Beginning	3377.39	6640.49	8221.40
一次能源生产量	Primary Energy Output	56098.74	67283.04	56480.85
外省市调入量	Transfer from Other Provinces	5466.26	4629.65	7020.81
回收能	Recvery of Energy	331.80	585.66	516.18
二、加工转换投入产出差数	Margin of Input and Output for Conversion	2734.44	3865.46	3679.26
加工转换投入量	Input for Conversion	34471.73	60696.06	56916.32
加工转换产出量	Output for Conversion	31737.29	56830.60	53237.07
三、外调出省、出口	Transfer to Other Provinces and Export	45730.99	50788.04	45533.32
调给外省市	Transfer to Other Provinces	45268.31	50788.04	45533.32
供应外贸出口	Export	462.68		
四、终端消费	Final Consumption	13820.47	15813.30	15958.30
(一)第一产业	Primary Industry	337.65	313.37	320.24
农林牧渔业	Farming, Forestry, Animal Husbandry And Fishery	337.65	313.37	320.24
(二)第二产业	Secondry Industry	10489.37	12041.17	12098.16
工　业	Industry	10343.91	11878.09	11934.86
轻工业	Light Industry	202.37	287.07	267.55
重工业	Heavy Industry	10141.54	11591.02	11667.31
建筑业	Construction	145.46	163.08	163.28
(三)第三产业	Tertiary Industry	1661.76	1930.67	1993.52
交通运输、仓储和邮政业	Transport, Storage and Post	887.83	1051.19	1086.92
批发、零售业和住宿、餐饮业	Wholesale and Retail Trade, Hotels and Catering Services	339.74	392.73	399.27
其　他	Others	434.19	486.75	507.34
(四)人民生活	Residential Consumption	1331.69	1528.09	1546.37
城　镇	Cities and Towns	774.12	940.16	946.06
乡　村	Rural Areas	557.57	587.93	600.31
五、损失量	Losses	253.12	290.43	279.23
#运输变电损失	Losses in Transmission	253.12	290.43	279.23
六、年末库存量	Stock of Year End	3956.72	8381.61	6789.14

6-2 煤炭生产、外调、使用平衡表
BALANCE SHEET OF COAL PRODUCTION, TRANSFER AND USE

单位：万吨 (10 000 tons)

项　　目	Item	2010	2015	2016
一、资　源	Resources	83330.02	110410.88	101710.43
年初库存	Stock of Year Beginning	3226.07	8813.12	10870.15
一次能源生产量	Primary Energy Product	74096.00	96680.00	83043.72
外省市调入量	Transfer from Other Provinces	6007.95	4917.76	7796.56
二、加工转换投入产出差数	Margin of Input and Output for Conversion	24186.40	30471.90	28781.42
加工转换投入量	Input for Conversion	42727.04	86168.36	83830.63
加工转换产出量	Output for Conversion	18540.64	55696.46	55049.21
三、外调出省、出口	Transfer to Other Provinces and Export	51197.64	62425.63	56567.07
调给外省市	Transfer to Other Provinces	50714.22	62425.63	56567.07
供应外贸出口	Export	483.42		
四、终端消费	Final Consumption	5678.70	6643.20	6839.61
(一)第一产业	Primary Industry	175.55	175.50	205.41
农林牧渔业	Farming, Forestry, Animal Husbandry And Fishery	175.55	175.50	205.41
(二)第二产业	Secondry Industry	3921.41	5075.55	5206.05
工　业	Industry	3849.34	5044.91	5174.50
轻工业	Light Industry	146.91	223.84	216.64
重工业	Heavy Industry	3702.43	4821.07	4957.86
建筑业	Construction	72.07	30.64	31.55
(三)第三产业	Tertiary Industry	499.28	460.95	491.44
交通运输、仓储和邮政业	Transport, Storage and Post	54.94	69.26	74.80
批发、零售业和住宿、餐饮业	Wholesale and Retail Trade, Hotels and Catering services	219.19	170.60	180.07
其　他	Others	225.15	221.09	236.57
(四)人民生活	Residential Consumption	1082.46	931.20	936.71
城　镇	Cities and Towns	421.46	277.50	309.34
乡　村	Rural Areas	661.00	653.70	627.37
五、损失量	Losses			
#运输变电损失	Losses in Transmission			
六、年末库存量	Stock of Year End	4267.28	10870.15	9522.33

6-3 焦炭生产、外调、使用平衡表
BALANCE SHEET OF COKE PRODUCTION, TRANSFER AND USE

单位：万吨 (10 000 tons)

项　目	Item	2010	2015	2016
一、资　源	Resources	916.71	760.08	815.22
年初库存	Stock of Year Beginning	916.71	760.08	815.22
二、加工转换投入产出差数	Margin of Input and Output for Conversion	8476.44	8039.88	8185.98
加工转换投入量	Input for Conversion			
加工转换产出量	Output for Conversion	8476.44	8039.88	8185.98
三、外调出省、出口	Transfer to Other Provinces and Export	6121.00	5901.29	7059.26
调给外省市	Transfer to Other Provinces	5954.93	5901.29	7059.26
供应外贸出口	Export	166.07		
四、终端消费	Final Consumption	2589.22	2083.45	2198.10
(一)第一产业	Primary Industry			
农林牧渔业	Farming, Forestry, Animal Husbandry And Fishery			
(二)第二产业	Secondry Industry	2586.93	2082.65	2197.94
工　业	Industry	2586.73	2082.51	2197.82
轻工业	Light Industry	0.24	0.11	0.01
重工业	Heavy Industry	2586.48	2082.40	2197.81
建筑业	Construction	0.20	0.14	0.12
(三)第三产业	Tertiary Industry	1.11	0.80	0.16
交通运输、仓储和邮政业	Transport, Storage and Post			
批发、零售业和住宿、餐饮业	Wholesale and Retail Trade, Hotels and Catering services	1.11	0.80	0.16
其　他	Others			
(四)人民生活	Residential Consumption	1.18		
城　镇	Cities and Towns	1.10		
乡　村	Rural Areas	0.08		
五、损失量	Losses			
运输变电损失	Losses in Transmission			
六、年末库存量	Stock of Year End	682.93	815.22	631.68

6-4 电力生产、外调、使用平衡表
BALANCE SHEET OF ELECTRICITY PRODUCTION, TRANSFER AND USE

单位：万千瓦小时 (10 000 kwh)

项 目	Item	2010	2015	2016
一、资 源	Resources	915400	1625200	2899600
一次能源生产量	Primary Energy Output	462100	1388500	2012200
外省市调入量	Transfer from Other Provinces	453300	236700	887400
二、加工转换投入产出差数	Margin of Input and Output for Conversion	21043500	23186000	23092900
加工转换投入量	Input for Conversion			
加工转换产出量	Output for Conversion	21043500	23186000	23092900
三、外调出省、出口	Transfer to Other Provinces and Export	7358400	7439100	8020700
调给外省市	Transfer to Other Provinces	7358400	7439100	8020700
四、终端消费	Final Consumption	13812500	16440900	17069400
(一)第一产业	Primary Industry	351400	409700	384500
农林牧渔业	Farming, Forestry, Animal Husbandry And Fishery	351400	409700	384500
(二)第二产业	Secondry Industry	11273900	12802100	13200900
工 业	Industry	11112100	12633657	13008100
轻工业	Light Industry	284300	342795	351700
重工业	Heavy Industry	10827800	12290862	12656400
建筑业	Construction	161800	168443	192800
(三)第三产业	Tertiary Industry	1132400	1630400	1780400
交通运输、仓储和邮政业	Transport, Storage and Post	456300	543100	584300
批发、零售业和住宿、餐饮业	Wholesale and Retail Trade, Hotels and Catering services	201700	350400	383800
其 他	Others	474400	736900	812300
(四)人民生活	Residential Consumption	1054800	1598700	1703600
城 镇	Cities and Towns	641200	999300	1057900
乡 村	Rural Areas	413600	599400	645700
五、损失量	Losses	788000	931200	902400
运输变电损失	Losses in Transmission	788000	931200	902400

6-5 石油制品生产、外调、使用平衡表
BALANCE SHEET OF PETROLEUM PRODUCTS PRODUCTION, TRANSFER AND USE

单位：万吨标准煤 (10 000 tons SCE)

项　　目	Item	2010	2015	2016
一、资　源	Resources	1183.83	1203.88	1250.80
年初库存	Stock of Year Beginning	64.27	72.76	68.81
外省市调入量	Transfer from Other Provinces	1119.56	1131.12	1181.99
二、加工转换投入产出差数	Margin of Input and Output for Conversion			11.49
加工转换投入量	Input for Conversion			16.41
加工转换产出量	Output for Conversion			27.91
三、外调出省、出口	Transfer to Other Provinces and Export			11.49
调给外省市	Transfer to Other Provinces			11.49
四、终端消费	Final Consumption	1103.77	1133.29	1188.01
(一)第一产业	Primary Industry	100.14	61.04	67.80
农林牧渔业	Farming, Forestry, Animal Husbandry And Fishery	100.14	61.04	67.80
(二)第二产业	Secondry Industry	172.23	208.98	243.95
工　业	Industry	131.31	147.95	173.29
轻工业	Light Industry	2.39	1.64	1.77
重工业	Heavy Industry	128.91	146.31	171.51
建筑业	Construction	40.92	61.02	70.66
(三)第三产业	Tertiary Industry	743.48	780.31	800.13
交通运输、仓储和邮政业	Transport, Storage and Post	643.12	738.65	754.02
批发、零售业和住宿、餐饮业	Wholesale and Retail Trade, Hotels and Catering services	47.06	14.75	24.19
其　他	Others	53.30	26.90	21.92
(四)人民生活	Residential Consumption	87.92	82.95	76.12
城　镇	Cities and Towns	54.25	37.16	34.40
乡　村	Rural Areas	33.68	45.79	41.72
五、损失量	Losses	1.76	1.79	0.88
运输变电损失及仓储	Losses in Transmission and Storage	1.76	1.79	0.88
六、年末库存量	Stock of Year End	78.30	68.81	61.91

6-6 主要年份一、二次能源生产量及构成
PRODUCTION AND COMPOSITION OF PRIMARY AND SECONDARY ENERGY IN MAJOR YEARS

年 份 Year	一次能源产量 (万吨标准煤) Primary Energy Production (10 000 tons of SCE)	占能源产量(%) Percentage			加工转换能源占一次能源产量(%) Conversion As Percentage of Primary Energy(%)			
		原 煤 Coal	水电和风电 Hydro Power and Wind Power	瓦 斯 Gas		火 电 Thermal Power	洗精煤 Washed Coal	焦 炭 Coke
1980	10310.32	99.71	0.18	0.04	11.28	4.68	3.02	3.57
1985	18237.45	99.82	0.16	0.02	8.85	4.06	2.23	2.56
1990	24341.19	99.86	0.13	0.01	17.08	5.37	5.29	6.42
1995	29760.94	99.88	0.10	0.02	38.73	6.77	14.67	17.29
2000	21457.60	99.63	0.31	0.06	53.72	11.44	19.79	22.50
2005	47233.52	99.74	0.17	0.09	47.04	11.05	19.58	16.41
2010	63326.74	99.45	0.23	0.32	47.20	13.43	20.77	13.00
2011	74481.77	99.55	0.26	0.19	45.31	12.46	21.05	11.80
2012	78182.88	99.30	0.47	0.23	45.89	12.62	22.57	10.70
2013	68925.26	98.95	0.45	0.60	70.36	11.44	46.13	12.79
2014	68426.78	98.83	0.52	0.65	71.69	11.54	47.71	12.44
2015	72488.91	98.76	0.60	0.64	64.86	9.95	44.14	10.77
2016	63030.18	98.21	0.99	0.80	74.80	11.36	50.82	12.62

注：2013年、2014年能源相关指标为三经普调整数据，后同。
Note: Energy data of 2013 and 2014 have been adjusted according to the Third Economic Census. The same applies to the following.

6-7 主要年份煤炭消费量
COAL CONSUMPTION IN MAJOR YEARS

单位：万吨 (10 000 tons)

年 份 Year	总 计 Total	生产建设消费 Production and Construction Consumption			生活用 Living Consumption
			#发 电 Electricity Generation	#炼 焦 Coking	
1980	4326	3378	727	642	948
1985	5566	4539	1028	1169	1027
1990	7292	6451	1692	2383	841
1995	13373	12757	2717	7264	616
2000	12704	12179	3128	6298	525
2005	22631	21811	6550	11208	820
2010	28180	27098	9968	11640	1082
2011	30896	29702	10980	12498	1194
2012	31085	29840	11547	11800	1245
2013	33062	32043	12271	12334	1019
2014	32056	31078	11597	11971	978
2015	29428	28497	10248	10914	931
2016	30061	29059	10324	10969	937

注：本表煤炭消费量包括终端消费量和用于加工转换消费量。
Note: Data of coal consumption in this table includes end-use consumption and consumption during the process of energy conversion.

6-8 主要年份石油制品、焦炭消费量
PETROLEUM PRODUCTS AND COKE CONSUMPTION IN MAJOR YEARS

单位：吨 (ton)

年 份 Year	石油制品(标准煤) Petroleum Products (SCE)	#工业交通 Industry And Transportation	#农 业 Agriculture	焦 炭 Coke	#工业生产 Industry	#建 筑 Construction
1980	1084440	684270	351519	2995572	2553669	9840
1985	1582990	913600	462500	3698900	3118000	17500
1990	1987500	1481400	380400	8326800	7611200	12100
1995	2581000	1828700	449300	12764800	10114700	40800
2000	2751900	1988800	455100	12769000	10103000	62000
2005	5374600	4169400	524300	21399000	20405000	89000
2010	11037700	7744300	1001400	25892200	25867300	2000
2011	11105000	8238700	1004700	25585500	25546900	1500
2012	11296100	8331900	1068700	29385500	29344200	1600
2013	11481700	8876600	597500	21455900	21435500	300
2014	10929900	8677400	583400	21776900	21772000	300
2015	11332800	8866160	610400	20834500	20825100	1400
2016	11880100	9273100	678000	21981000	21978200	1200

6-9 主要年份社会用电量
TOTAL ELECTRICITY CONSUMPTION IN MAJOR YEARS

单位：万千瓦小时 (10 000 kwh)

年 份 Year	社会用电量 Total Consumption	#农 业 Agriculture	#工 业 Industry	#电力工业 Electricity	#化学工业 Chemistry	#煤炭工业 Coal	#黑色金属 Ferrous Metal	#交通运输 Transportation	#市政生活 Civicism
1980	1185877	171092	962483	248288	218915	146197	131800	5502	46798
1985	1634743	159100	1343101	321440	268079	232152	173668	37281	85000
1990	2552179	146279	2127321	480095	403856	386180	272555	89230	157301
1995	3782338	232387	3280436	809643	547112	553580	391889	121693	298126
2000	5020917	261338	4114046	939969	684945	603963	493088	147750	392327
2005	9463268	356384	7873556	1704567	1380229	1101659	1223916	310704	701698
2010	14600467	351399	11900099	2725517	1323372	1718512	2096358	456362	1482910
2011	16504098	387461	13451317	2933961	1500490	1943094	2223308	507130	1651314
2012	17657848	373888	14340495	3261393	1646993	2129660	2491088	519249	1659972
2013	18323479	378267	14755243	3252894	1676244	2347403	2624159	557756	1824445
2014	18226274	378518	14521438	3416360	1548017	2339848	2543894	587914	1926674
2015	17372078	409692	13564889	3187532	1511069	2359723	2360362	543134	2012292
2016	17971804	384500	13910563	3334719	1501452	2374025	2166583	584274	2152262

6-10 主要年份能源生产弹性系数
ELASTICITY RATIO OF ENERGY PRODUCTION IN MAJOR YEARS

单位：%　　(%)

年 份 Year	能源生产 比上年增长 Growth Rate of Energy Production Over Preceding Year	电力生产 比上年增长 Growth Rate of Electricity Over Preceding Year	地区生产总值 比上年增长 Growth Rate of Gross Domestic Product Over Preceding Year	能源生产 弹性系数 Elasticity Ratio of Energy Production	电力生产 弹性系数 Elasticity Ratio of Electricity Production
1980	11.10	5.38	2.00	5.55	2.69
1985	14.46	10.18	7.10	2.04	1.43
1990	3.96	3.64	5.00	0.79	0.73
1995	5.26	10.73	12.00	0.44	0.89
2000	1.12	9.62	9.40	0.12	1.02
2005	10.85	21.59	13.50	0.80	1.60
2010	24.87	14.97	14.00	1.78	1.07
2011	15.75	9.01	12.90	1.22	0.70
2012	4.94	8.13	10.10	0.49	0.80
2013	5.62	3.57	8.90	0.63	0.40
2014	−3.22	0.22	4.90	−0.66	0.04
2015	3.95	−7.16	3.10	1.27	−2.31
2016	−16.05	2.16	4.50	−3.57	0.48

注：本表2014年为三经普调整后数据，下表同。

Note: Data of 2014 have been dajusted according to the Third Economic Census. The same applies to the following.

6-11 主要年份能源消费弹性系数
ELASTICITY RATIO OF ENERGY CONSUMPTION IN MAJOR YEARS

单位：%　　(%)

年 份 Year	能源消费 比上年增长 Growth Rate of Energy Consumption Over Preceding Year	煤炭消费 比上年增长 Growth Rate of Coal Consum-ption Over Preceding Year	电力消费 比上年增长 Growth Rate of Electricity Consumption Over Preceding Year	地区生产总值 比上年增长 Growth Rate of Gross Domestic Product Over Preceding Year	能源消费 弹性系数 Elasticity Ratio of Energy Consumption	煤炭消费 弹性系数 Elasticity Ratio of Coal Consumption	电力消费 弹性系数 Elasticity Ratio of Electricity Consumption
1980	3.92	8.31	−4.22	2.00	1.96	4.16	−2.11
1985	10.25	7.20	14.85	7.10	1.44	1.01	2.09
1990	−0.19	−12.57	2.98	5.00	−0.04	−2.51	0.60
1995	10.03	5.85	10.82	12.00	0.84	0.49	0.90
2000	3.60	2.44	11.61	9.40	0.38	0.26	1.24
2005	8.61	3.30	14.24	13.50	0.64	0.24	1.05
2010	7.91	−3.22	15.47	14.00	0.57	−0.23	1.11
2011	8.97	9.77	14.12	12.90	0.70	0.76	1.09
2012	5.57	3.03	6.10	10.10	0.55	0.30	0.60
2013	4.85	7.69	3.53	8.90	0.54	0.86	0.40
2014	0.51	−3.04	−0.31	4.90	0.10	−0.62	−0.06
2015	−2.41	−5.23	−4.75	3.10	−0.78	−1.69	−1.53
2016	0.09	−2.96	3.82	4.50	0.02	0.66	0.85

6-12 主要年份能源加工转换投入产出情况
EFFICIENCY OF ENERGY CONVERSION IN MAJOR YEARS

年 份 Year	投入及转换总效率 Total Efficiency		发电及供热投入原煤(万吨) Coal Input in Electricity And Heat (10 000 tons)	洗选加工投入原煤(万吨) Coal Input in Washing (10 000 tons)
	投入总量(万吨标准煤) Total Input (10 000 tons of SCE)	投入产出总效率(%) Efficiency(%)		
1980	1512.30	54.35	727.18	617.16
1985	2214.09	61.77	1108.00	802.00
1990	4792.46	73.22	1812.74	2162.71
1995	13076.80	82.56	2946.49	6864.89
2000	12867.25	81.44	3127.88	6958.75
2005	25291.10	79.72	6597.20	14652.96
2010	34407.94	80.18	9977.89	20225.00
2011	39760.22	80.86	11085.49	24827.28
2012	42285.31	81.08	11742.37	28952.95
2013	63122.88	86.20	12566.48	62776.72
2014	62427.14	86.40	12029.82	66236.01
2015	60696.06	86.49	10895.02	63383.77
2016	56916.32	86.02	10625.63	60609.49

年 份 Year	炼焦投入量 Input in Coking		制气投入原 煤(万吨) Coal Input in Making Gas (10 000 tons)	产出总量(万吨标准煤) Total Output (10 000 tons of SCE)
	原 煤(万吨) Coal (10 000 tons)	洗精煤(万吨) Cleaned Coal (10 000 tons)		
1980	474.00	168.00		821.90
1985	834.00	234.74		1367.69
1990	1772.80	610.24	72.59	3509.20
1995	3964.26	3298.52	63.97	10796.47
2000	3250.02	3045.74	58.03	10478.69
2005	2633.60	8571.16	136.14	20161.30
2010	223.61	11414.74	33.76	27587.12
2011	297.20	12180.33	55.57	32149.49
2012	67.32	11732.62	55.09	34283.93
2013	25.27	12309.16	52.79	54410.16
2014	26.23	11943.36	42.99	55508.26
2015	32.07	10882.20	24.80	52493.20
2016	32.99	10935.80	99.76	48959.49

注：本表炼焦产出的焦炉煤气从2005年起包括了加热炼焦炉用气；2013年以前洗精煤为炼焦洗精煤，以后为炼焦洗精煤加动力洗精煤。

Note: The gas output of coking in this table includes the gas used to heat up the coke ovens from 2005. Cleaned coal refers to coking coal and power coal after 2013, while it refers to coking coal in the previous years.

6-12 续表 continued

年 份 Year	发电及供热产出 Output of Electricity And Heat		炼焦产出 Output of Coking	
	电 力 (万千瓦小时) Electricity (10 000 kwh)	热 力 (万百万千焦) Heat (10 billion kilo-joule)	焦 炭 (万吨) Coke (10 000 tons)	焦炉煤气 (万立方米) Gas (10 000 cu.m)
1980	1156600		320.95	
1985	1777200	1297.88	568.66	55634
1990	3068800	2324.00	1586.57	81600
1995	4988500	3930.40	5294.97	159800
2000	6087300	2367.70	4967.22	179900
2005	12916500	6020.60	7981.04	1440000
2010	21043500	12089.93	8476.44	1607200
2011	22964500	14472.47	9047.91	1868200
2012	24429600	16014.55	8612.66	1674300
2013	25513000	17916.84	9022.40	1780300
2014	25460100	19810.66	8765.84	1709900
2015	23186000	23630.29	8039.88	1600600
2016	23092900	27215.90	8185.98	1595100

年 份 Year	洗选煤产出 Output of Washed Coal		制气产出 Output of Making Gas	
	洗精煤 (万吨) Cleaned Coal (10 000 tons)	其他洗煤 (万吨) Others (10 000 tons)	焦炉煤气 (万立方米) Coke Gas (10 000 cu.m)	其他煤气 (万立方米) Others (10 000 cu.m)
1980	409.00			
1985	518.55	158.91		
1990	1429.65	366.30	9400	136400
1995	4850.20	710.59	1100	230000
2000	4818.21	590.05		191800
2005	10275.88	1327.49		417900
2010	14863.17	3537.38		101600
2011	17426.68	4652.97		168300
2012	19604.71	5698.09		156000
2013	34615.00	24428.00		117900
2014	35974.94	24563.82		84600
2015	35577.81	19983.52		54200
2016	22458.30	32452.00		224700

6-13 终端能源消费量和构成(2016年)

单位：万吨标准煤

项　目	Ietm	合　计 Total
消费总计	**Total Consumption**	**15958.30**
一、第一产业	Primary Industry	320.24
农林牧渔业	Farming, Forestry, Animal Husbandry And Fishery	320.24
二、第二产业	Secondry Industry	12098.16
工　业	Industry	11934.86
轻工业	Light Industry	267.55
重工业	Heavy Industry	11667.31
建筑业	Construction	163.28
三、第三产业	Tertiary Industry	1993.52
交通运输、仓储及邮电通讯业	Transport, Storage, Post and Telecommunication	1086.92
批发、零售业和住宿、餐饮业	Wholesale and Retail Trade, Hotels and Catering Services	399.27
其　他	Others	507.34
四、人民生活	Residential Consumption	1546.37
部门构成 (%)	**Composition of Department(%)**	
消费总计	**Total Consumption**	**100.00**
一、第一产业	Primary Industry	2.01
农林牧渔业	Farming, Forestry, Animal Husbandry And Fishery	2.01
二、第二产业	Secondry Industry	75.81
工　业	Industry	74.79
轻工业	Light Industry	1.68
重工业	Heavy Industry	73.11
建筑业	Construction	1.02
三、第三产业	Tertiary Industry	12.49
交通运输、仓储及邮电通讯业	Transport, Storage, Post and Telecommunication	6.81
批发、零售业和住宿、餐饮业	Wholesale and Retail Trade, Hotels and Catering Services	2.50
其　他	Others	3.18
四、人民生活	Residential Consumption	9.69
品种构成 (%)	**Composition of Variety(%)**	
消费总计	**Total Consumption**	**100.00**
一、第一产业	Primary Industry	100.00
农林牧渔业	Farming,Forestry,Animal Husbandry And Fishery	100.00
二、第二产业	Secondry Industry	100.00
工　业	Industry	100.00
轻工业	Light Industry	100.00
重工业	Heavy Industry	100.00
建筑业	Construction	100.00
三、第三产业	Tertiary Industry	100.00
交通运输、仓储和邮政业	Transport,Storage and Post	100.00
批发、零售业和住宿、餐饮业	Wholesale and Retail Trade, Hotels and Catering Services	100.00
其　他	Others	100.00
四、人民生活	Residential Consumption	100.00

CONSUMPTION AND COMPOSITION OF TERMINAL ENERGY(2016)

(10 000 tons of SCE)

原 煤 Coal	洗精煤及其他洗煤 Washed Coal and Others	焦 炭 Coke	石油制品 Petroleum Products	电 力 Electricity	天然气煤气及其他 Natural Gas, Gas and Others
4083.13	**369.83**	**2135.23**	**1188.01**	**5265.14**	**2916.96**
133.72			67.80	118.60	0.12
133.72			67.80	118.60	0.12
3360.57	153.61	2135.08	243.95	4071.89	2133.07
3340.03	153.61	2134.96	173.28	4012.43	2120.55
141.33	0.44	0.01	1.77	108.48	15.52
3198.70	153.17	2134.95	171.51	3903.95	2105.03
20.54		0.12	70.66	59.47	12.49
319.93		0.16	800.13	549.17	324.13
48.69			754.02	180.23	103.97
117.23		0.16	24.19	118.39	139.31
154.01			21.92	250.56	80.85
268.91	216.22		76.12	525.48	459.64
100.00	**100.00**	**100.00**	**100.00**	**100.00**	**100.00**
3.27			5.71	2.25	
3.27			5.71	2.25	
82.30	41.54	99.99	20.53	77.34	73.13
81.80	41.54	99.99	14.59	76.21	72.70
3.46	0.12		0.15	2.06	0.53
78.34	41.42	99.99	14.44	74.15	72.17
0.50		0.01	5.95	1.13	0.43
7.84		0.01	67.35	10.43	11.11
1.19			63.47	3.42	3.56
2.87		0.01	2.04	2.25	4.78
3.77			1.85	4.76	2.77
6.59	58.46		6.41	9.98	15.76
25.59	**2.32**	**13.38**	**7.44**	**32.99**	**18.28**
41.76			21.17	37.03	0.04
41.76			21.17	37.03	0.04
27.78	1.27	17.65	2.02	33.66	17.63
27.99	1.29	17.89	1.45	33.62	17.77
52.82	0.17		0.66	40.55	5.80
27.42	1.31	18.30	1.47	33.46	18.04
12.58		0.07	43.28	36.42	7.65
16.05		0.01	40.14	27.55	16.26
4.48			69.37	16.58	9.57
29.36		0.04	6.06	29.65	34.89
30.36			4.32	49.39	15.94
17.39	13.98		4.92	33.98	29.72

6-14 分行业能源消费总量(2016年)

单位：万吨标准煤

行　业	Sector	能源消费总量 Total Energy Consumption
消费总计	**Total**	**19400.62**
农、林、牧、渔业	**Farming, Forestry, Animal Husbandry And Fishery**	**320.24**
工　业	**Industry**	**15376.33**
轻工业	Light Industry	306.96
重工业	Heavy Industry	15069.38
按工业行业分	Grouped by Industry Sector	
采矿业	Mining	4339.33
煤炭开采和洗选业	Coal Mining and Dressing	4137.65
石油和天然气开采业	Petroleum and Natural Gas Extraction	21.06
黑色金属矿采选业	Ferrous Metals Mining and Dressing	119.50
有色金属矿采选业	Nonferrous Metals Mining and Dressing	31.46
非金属矿采选业	Nonmetal Minerals Mining and Dressing	9.23
开采辅助活动	Mining Auxiliary Activities	
其他采矿业	Other Minerals Mining	20.42
制造业	Manufacturing	9719.73
农副食品加工业	Farm and Sideline Food Processing	35.65
食品制造业	Food Manufacturing	33.91
酒、饮料和精制茶制造业	Alcohol, Beverage and Refined Tea Manufacturing	29.61
烟草制品业	Tobacoo Manufaturing	0.74
纺织业	Textile Industry	21.14
纺织服装、服饰业	Manufacture of Garments and Accessories	2.71
皮革、毛皮、羽毛及其制品和制鞋业	Manufacture of Leather, Fur, Feather and their Products and Footwear	0.14
木材加工和木、竹、藤、棕、草制品业	Processing of Timber, Manufacture of Wood, Bamboo, Rattan, Palm, and Straw Products	4.13
家具制造业	Manufacture of Funiture	0.42
造纸和纸制品业	Manufacture of Paper and Paper Products	23.85
印刷和记录媒介复制业	Printing and Record Medium Reproduction	2.06
文教、工美、体育和娱乐用品制造业	Manufacture of Articles For Culture, Education and Sport Activity	1.68

TOTAL ENERGY CONSUMPTION BY SECTOR(2016)

(10 000 tons of SCE)

煤　炭 (万吨) Coal (10 000 tons)	电　力 (亿千瓦小时) Electricity (100 million kwh)	焦　炭 (万吨) Coke (10 000 tons)	汽　油 (万吨) Gasoline (10 000 tons)	柴　油 (万吨) Diesel Oil (10 000 tons)
30060.76	**1797.18**	**2198.10**	**228.29**	**536.10**
205.41	**38.45**		**21.50**	**24.82**
28330.38	**1391.05**	**2197.82**	**17.14**	**87.58**
357.40	43.38		0.83	0.41
27972.98	1347.67	2197.82	16.30	87.17
1759.12	291.35	21.65	10.02	61.48
1718.66	237.40	15.52	9.64	56.19
	5.91		0.21	0.02
39.72	28.91	6.10	0.16	4.42
0.68	9.67	0.03	0.01	0.79
0.07	2.84			0.07
	6.62			
16425.92	726.97	2176.17	6.54	24.20
24.20	5.88		0.19	0.03
29.76	2.64		0.17	0.04
25.05	2.84		0.09	0.08
	0.15			
18.73	2.71		0.02	0.01
1.49	0.38		0.05	0.04
0.07	0.03			
0.01	1.32			0.01
0.03	0.12		0.02	
24.08	2.61		0.04	0.04
0.19	0.52		0.05	0.06
0.86	0.13		0.03	0.01

6-14 续表

单位：万吨标准煤

行　业	Sector	能源消费总量 Total Energy Consumption
石油加工、炼焦和核燃料加工业	Petroleum Processing ,Coking and Nuclear Fuel Processing	1344.58
化学原料和化学制品制造业	Manufacture Raw Chemical Materials and Chemical Products	1941.60
医药制造业	Manufacture of Medical Products	100.51
化学纤维制造业	Manufacture of Chemical Fibers	11.92
橡胶和塑料制品业	Manufacture of Rubber and Plastic Products	27.12
非金属矿物制品业	Manufacture of Nonmetals Mineral Products	1039.33
黑色金属冶炼和压延加工业	Smelting and Pressing of Ferrous Metals	3581.65
有色金属冶炼和压延加工业	Smelting and Pressing of Nonferrous Metals	1241.62
金属制品业	Manufacture of Metal Products	71.96
通用设备制造业	Manufacture of Universal Purpose Equipment	29.57
专用设备制造业	Manufacture of Special Purpose Equipment	63.96
汽车制造业	Manufacture of Motor Vehicles	12.88
铁路、船舶、航空航天和其他运输设备制造业	Manufacture of Railways, Ships, Aviation, Aircrafts and Other Transportation Equipments	13.85
电气机械和器材制造业	Manufacture of Electrical Equipment and Machinery	9.35
通信设备、计算机和其他电子设备制造业	Manufacture of Computer, Telecommunication and Other Electronic Equipments	25.70
仪器仪表制造业	Manufacture of Measuring Instrument and Machinery	2.19
其他制造业	Other Manufacturing	42.62
废弃资源综合利用业	Comprehensive Utilization of Waste	3.21
金属制品、机械和设备修理业	Repair of Metal Products, Machinery and Equipment	0.07
电力、热力、燃气及水生产和供应业	Production and Supply of Electricity, Heat, Gas and Water	1317.28
电力、热力生产和供应业	Production and Supply of Electricity and Heat	1194.90
燃气生产和供应业	Production and Supply of Gas	75.99
水的生产和供应业	Production and Supply of Water	46.39
建筑业	**Construction**	**163.28**
交通运输、仓储和邮政业	**Transport, Storage and Post**	**1087.79**
批发、零售业和住宿、餐饮业	**Wholesale and Retail Trade, Hotels and Catering Services**	**399.27**
人民生活及其他	**Residential Consumption and Others**	**2053.71**

continued

(10 000 tons of SCE)

煤 炭 (万吨) Coal (10 000 tons)	电 力 (亿千瓦小时) Electricity (100 million kwh)	焦 炭 (万吨) Coke (10 000 tons)	汽 油 (万吨) Gasoline (10 000 tons)	柴 油 (万吨) Diesel Oil (10 000 tons)
10016.11	46.98	7.52	0.51	3.20
1678.95	150.15	41.70	1.51	1.29
92.17	12.26		0.15	0.08
	3.87			
2.81	7.12		0.10	0.11
1030.02	65.89	6.70	0.41	8.83
2011.15	216.67	2110.02	1.53	8.77
1352.19	142.18	1.42	0.09	0.91
16.18	14.11	8.55	0.24	0.17
3.97	8.38	0.18	0.27	0.08
9.36	16.45	0.05	0.45	0.19
4.54	2.24		0.05	0.16
5.59	1.69	0.01	0.09	0.03
0.51	2.37		0.11	0.02
1.19	6.36		0.19	0.02
	0.65		0.09	
141.95	9.25		0.01	0.03
	1.03	0.01		
			0.04	0.01
10145.34	372.73		0.58	1.90
10144.40	333.47		0.24	1.88
	24.48		0.23	
0.94	14.78		0.11	0.01
31.55	**19.28**	**0.12**	**16.25**	**31.56**
74.80	**58.43**		**113.46**	**377.10**
180.07	**38.38**	**0.16**	**8.13**	**8.39**
1173.28	**251.59**		**51.81**	**6.65**

主要统计指标解释

能源资源 指报告期全省各种能源资源总量。能源品种包括原煤、洗精煤、焦炭、原油、汽油、柴油、煤油、燃料油、天然气、焦炉煤气、其他煤气、其他焦化制品、热力、电力等品种。能源资源组成包括三部分:

1.期初、期末库存量是指一定时点各种能源的库存量，其中包括产成品库存量，各种能源库存量。

2.一次能源生产量是指报告期一次能源的生产量，其中包括原煤、水电、风电、天然气（煤矿瓦斯）的生产量。由一次能源加工转换产出的二次能源产量不包括在内。

3.外省市调入量是指报告期调入的各种能源数量。我省从外省市调入的能源主要是石油制品：汽油、柴油、煤油、燃料油及电网交界处输入部分电力和相邻省调入的部分煤炭。

能源消费总量 是指报告期全省用于生产、生活的各种能源消费量的总和。能源消费总量按标准煤折算。能源消费总量中包括：原煤、原油及其制品、天然气、电力，不包括生物能和太阳能等的利用。能源消费总量包括三部分:

1.能源终端消费量 指报告期全省物质生产部门、非物质生产部门的各种能源消费量。不包括加工转换损失量和运输、管理中的损失量。

2.能源加工转换损失量 指全省投入加工转换的各种能源数量和与产出能源及制品之和的差数，是能源加工转换过程的消费量，也称加工转换损失量。

3.损失量 指能源的运输、储存中发生的经营管理损失量，包括煤炭库存中的水冲、自燃等损失量。

能源生产弹性系数 是研究能源生产量的增长与国民经济增长之间关系的指标。国民经济年平均增长速度，可根据不同目的的需要，用工农业总产值、国内生产总值等指标来计算，本资料是采用国内生产总值指标计算的。其计算公式为:

$$\text{能源生产弹性系数}=\frac{\text{能源生产量年平均增长速度}}{\text{国内生产总值年平均增长速度}}\times 100\%$$

电力生产弹性系数 是研究电力生产的增长与国民经济增长之间关系的指标。其计算公式为:

$$\text{电力生产弹性系数}=\frac{\text{电力生产量年平均增长速度}}{\text{国内生产总值年平均增长速度}}\times 100\%$$

能源消费弹性系数 是反映能源消费增长速度与国民经济增长速度之间比例关系的指标。其计算公式为:

$$\text{能源消费弹性系数}=\frac{\text{能源消费年平均增长速度}}{\text{国内生产总值年平均增长速度}}\times 100\%$$

电力消费弹性系数 是反映电力消费增长速度与国民经济增长速度之间比例关系的指标。其计算公式为:

$$\text{电力消费弹性系数}=\frac{\text{电力消费年平均增长速度}}{\text{国内生产总值年平均增长速度}}\times 100\%$$

能源加工转换效率 是指报告期内一次能源产品经过加工转换后，产出的各种能源产品及其制品的数量，与同期投入加工转换的各种一次能源数量的比率。它是观察能源加工转换装置和生产工艺先进与落后、管理水平高低等的重要指标。

Explanatory Notes on Main Statistical Indicators

Energy Resources refers to total resources of all energy in the province in the reference period. It includes coal, washed coal, coke, crude oil, gasoline, diesel oil, kerosene, fuel oil, natural gas, gas and other gas, other coking products, heat and electricity, etc. It includes three parts:

1. Stock in the beginning and end of the year refers to stock of all kind of energy at a certain point of time, including products stock and energy stock.

2. Primary Energy Production refers to the total production of primary energy in the reference period, including production of coal, hydropower, wind power and gas, excluding secondary energy converted from the primary energy.

3. Energy Quantity Transferred from other Province refers to energy quantity transferred in a given period of time. Energy transferred from other province mostly is crude oil product including gasoline, diesel oil, kerosene, fuel oil, some electricity input in the juncture of electricity nets and some coals.

Total Energy Consumption refers to the total consumption of various kinds by production and households in the province in a given period of time. It is converted by SCE. The total energy includes that of coal, crude oil and their products, natural gas and electricity. It excludes bioenergy and solar energy. It can be divided into three parts:

1. Final energy consumption refers to total energy consumption by material production sectors, non-material production sectors in the province in a given period of time, but excludes the loss in the conversion and transportation.

2. Loss during the Process of Energy Conversion refers to the total input of various kinds of energy for conversion, minus total output of various kinds of energy in the province in a given period of time. It is energy consumption during the process of energy conversion, also called loss of energy conversation.

3. Loss refers to the loss of energy during the course of energy transportation and storage, include coal loss caused by washed away by the water and self-ignite in the storage.

Elasticity Ratio of Energy Production refers to indicators to show the relationship between the growth rate of energy production and the growth rate of the national economy. Average annual growth rate of national economy can be shown by the gross domestic product, gross output value of industry and agriculture, depending upon the purposes or need. The gross domestic product is used in calculation of the indicator in this chapter. The formula is:

$$\text{Elasticity Ratio of Energy Production} = \frac{\text{Average Annual Growth Rate of Energy Production}}{\text{Average Annual Growth Rate of Gross Demestic Product}} \times 100\%$$

Elasticity Ratio of Electricity Production refers to indicators to show the relationship between the growth rate of electricity production and the growth rate of the national economy. The formula is:

$$\text{Elasticity Ratio of Electricity Production} = \frac{\text{Average Annual Growth Rate of Electricity Production}}{\text{Average Annual Growth Rate of Gross Demestic Product}} \times 100\%$$

Elasticity Ratio of Energy Consumption refers to indicators to show the relationship between the growth rate of energy consumption and the growth rate of the national economy. The formula is:

$$\text{Elasticity Ratio of Energy Consumption} = \frac{\text{Average Annual Growth Rate of Energy Consumption}}{\text{Average Annual Growth Rate of Gross Demestic Product}} \times 100\%$$

Elasticity Ratio of Electricity Consumption refers to indicators to show the relationship between the growth rate of electricity consumption and the growth rate of the national economy. The formula is:

$$\text{Elasticity Ratio of Electricity Consumption} = \frac{\text{Average Annual Growth Rate of Electricity Consumption}}{\text{Average Annual Growth Rate of Gross Demestic Product}} \times 100\%$$

Efficiency of Energy Processing and Conversion refers to the ratio of the total output of energy products of various kinds after processing and conversion and the total input of energy of various kinds for processing and conversion in the same reference period. It is an important indicator to show the current conditions of energy processing and conversion equipment, production technique and management.

7 固定资产投资

INVESTMENT IN FIXED ASSETS

资料整理人员

邸慧东　宋雅静　任启龙

固定资产投资
INVESTMENT IN FIXED ASSETS

全社会固定资产投资	Total Investment in Fixed Assets	14285.0	亿元	(100 million yuan)
第一产业	Primary Industry	1870.4	亿元	(100 million yuan)
第二产业	Secondary Industry	4909.6	亿元	(100 million yuan)
第三产业	Tertiary Industry	7505.0	亿元	(100 million yuan)
全社会竣工房屋面积	Total Floor Space of Completed Buildings	9348	万平方米	(10 000 sq.m)
#住　宅	Residential Buildings	6266	万平方米	(10 000 sq.m)

全社会固定资产投资总额构成 (%)
Composition of Total Investment in Fixed Assets (%)

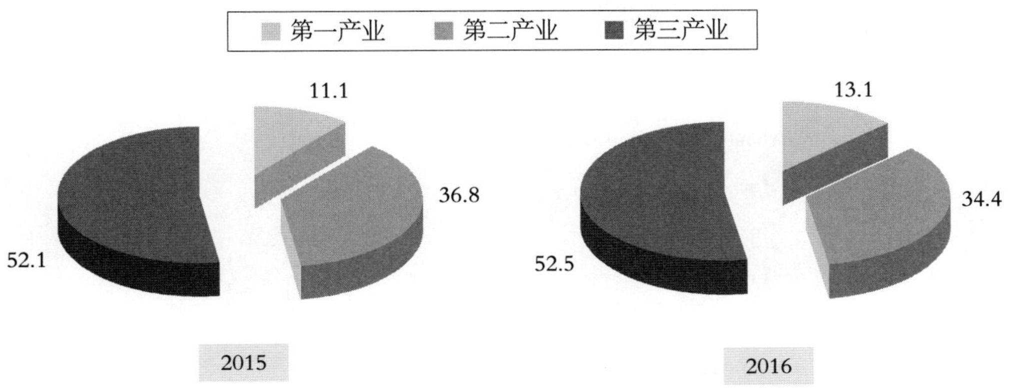

全社会固定资产投资（亿元）
Total Investment in Fixed Assets (100 million yuan)

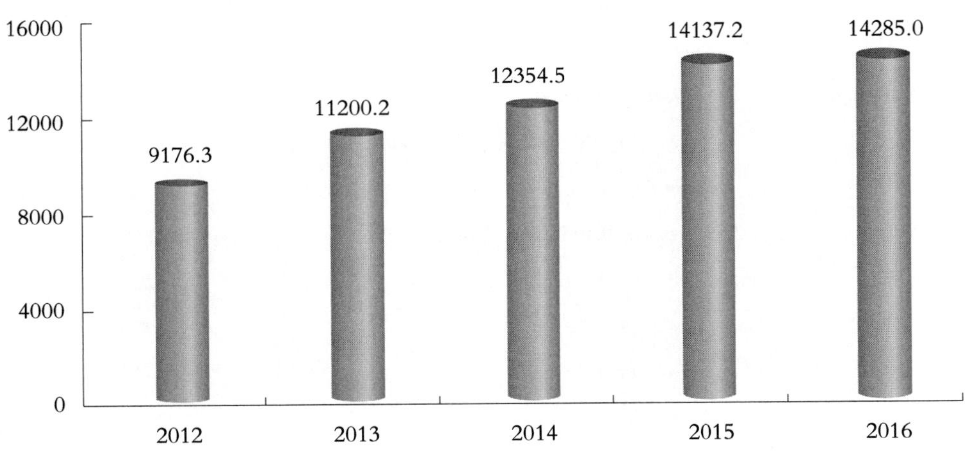

7-1 全社会固定资产投资主要指标
MAJOR INDICATORS OF TOTAL INVESTMENT IN FIXED ASSETS

单位：万元 (10 000 yuan)

指　标	Item	2015	2016
一、投资总额	**Total**	**141371594**	**142849820**
#房地产开发投资	Real Estate Investment	14948719	15973532
#农户投资	Rural Households Investment	3295638	3386310
#住　宅	Residential Buildings	21067639	18827570
按登记注册类型分	Grouped by Type of Registration Status		
内　资	Domestic-funded Enterprises	138983337	140029139
港、澳、台商投资	Enterprises with Investment from Hong Kong, Macao and Taiwan	1430078	1723126
外商投资	Enterprises with Foreign Investment	958179	1097555
按构成分	Grouped by Composition		
建筑工程	Construction	90469954	93466278
安装工程	Installation	13172744	13052403
设备工器具购置	Purchase of Equipment and Instruments	23621442	22104588
其他费用	Other Expenses	14107454	14226551
按三次产业分	Grouped by Type of Industry		
第一产业	Primary Industry	15636698	18703803
第二产业	Secondary Industry	52060392	49096362
第三产业	Tertiary Industry	73674504	75049655
二、新增固定资产	**Newly Increased Fixed Assets**	**111904731**	**100255975**
三、房屋建筑面积(万平方米)	**Floor Space of Buildings (10 000 sq.m)**		
本年施工房屋面积	Floor Space of Buildings Under Construction	31499	28566
#住　宅	Residential Buildings	19823	18240
本年竣工房屋面积	Floor Space of Buildings Completed This Year	10156	9348
#住　宅	Residential Buildings	6568	6266
四、本年资金来源小计	**Total Sources of Funds This Year**	**122071213**	**120182591**
国家预算内资金	State Budgetary Appropriation	7209721	7327910
国内贷款	Domestic Loans	6970349	7339778
利用外资	Foreign Investment	25069	55792
自筹资金	Self-Raised Funds	99503631	95227778
#企事业单位自有资金	Own Funds of Enterprises and Institutions	29050787	33743562
其　他	Others	8362442	10231334

7-2 全社会固定资产投资
TOTAL INVESTMENT IN FIXED ASSETS

单位：万元 (10 000 yuan)

年 份 Year	总 计 Total	#房地产开发 Real Estate Development	#农 户 Rural Households	#住 宅 Residential Buildings	第一产业 Primary Industry	第二产业 Secondary Industry	第三产业 Tertiary Industry
1978	214935		11313	15006	1645	132080	81210
1979	232713		14940	38261	10752	131838	90123
1980	281960		21173	59117	17560	162157	102243
1981	254719		38452	76511	13723	129473	111523
1982	345486		38244	95144	20698	186438	138350
1983	448347		57569	96277	26159	257200	164988
1984	688991		63475	114800	15352	384594	289045
1985	916918		87387	158060	11443	554744	350731
1986	970247		106473	176525	22578	600777	346892
1987	1062371	6207	136987	193745	25621	597032	439718
1988	1076779	5421	141201	169236	33359	662277	381143
1989	1079587	2370	136709	184680	28614	668424	382549
1990	1234137	28486	164556	220354	51962	756324	425851
1991	1495206	32642	202269	238231	56159	934621	504426
1992	1727858	51869	119330	240328	48795	1079071	599992
1993	2512628	129685	191765	415095	84534	1424294	1003800
1994	2909041	116512	201153	464303	63897	1427878	1417266
1995	2955570	150886	188798	456871	76160	1401945	1477465
1996	3334714	147893	302383	666374	90324	1587144	1657246
1997	3983959	181736	317673	708704	104368	2008130	1871461
1998	5346852	278653	331200	920980	83706	2135036	3128110
1999	5753507	350458	245781	1083149	103046	2261965	3388496
2000	6251628	394556	344392	1113447	119648	2896273	3235707
2001	7083468	466464	399594	1021534	205239	3090533	3787696
2002	8382683	674331	462572	1173468	334467	3793232	4254984
2003	11163486	950740	533216	1210898	359529	6127825	4676132
2004	14776985	1449898	621851	1551521	362856	8697815	5716314
2005	18593969	1779937	757098	2245567	501034	11304223	6788712
2006	23214735	2086231	933279	3503467	651894	13463726	9099115
2007	29271653	2589251	1157947	4619967	838947	16171517	12261189
2008	36351396	3279807	1443268	5651842	1119701	18688907	16542788
2009	50335333	4772748	1785790	7600820	2203844	21636020	26495469
2010	63526011	5922376	2179375	9003350	2812813	26281280	34431918
2011	73730582	7901982	2353725	11877169	2712048	33485814	37532720
2012	91763142	10104513	2784109	14670489	3660868	41354020	46748254
2013	112002376	13086275	2865426	16889560	7140003	46579278	58283095
2014	123545298	14035549	3190738	20045373	9462029	50040489	64042780
2015	141371594	14948719	3295638	21067639	15636698	52060392	73674504
2016	142849820	15973532	3386310	18827570	18703803	49096362	75049655

7-3 按登记注册类型和控股情况分全社会固定资产投资
TOTAL INVESTMENT IN FIXED ASSETS BY REGISTRATION STATUS AND SHARE HOLDING

单位：万元 (10 000 yuan)

指 标	Item	2015	2016
总 计	**Total**	**141371594**	**142849820**
按登记注册类型分	**Grouped by Type of Registration Status**		
内 资	Domestic-Funded Enterprises	138983337	140029139
国 有	State-owned Enterprises	40843760	29363837
集 体	Collective-owned Enterprises	8665498	4427425
股份合作	Share Cooperative Enterprises	221464	65668
国有联营	State Joint Ownership Enterprises	277978	23712
集体联营	Collective Joint Ownership Enterprises	57871	6182
国有与集体联营	Joint State-collective Enterprises	26292	54742
其他联营	Other Joint Ownership Enterprises	10035	55312
国有独资公司	State-funded Corporations	1849697	4992024
其他有限责任公司	Other Limited Liability Corporations	27658699	24665465
股份有限公司	Share-holding Corporations Ltd.	3751395	2158948
私 营	Private Enterprises	38679537	52481972
个体户	Self-employed Individuals	3759258	3915649
个人合伙	Individual Partnership Enterprises	260114	955879
其 他	Others	12921739	16862324
港澳台投资	Enterprises with Investment from Hong Kong, Macao and Taiwan	1430078	1723126
港澳台合资经营	Joint-venture Enterprises	601881	848871
港澳台合作经营	Cooperative Enterprises		1460
港澳台独资	Enterprises with Sole Investment	767495	764010
港澳台股份有限	Share-holding Corporations Ltd.	28412	104890
其 他	Others	32290	3895
外商投资	Enterprises with Foreign Investment	958179	1097555
外商合资经营	Joint-venture Enterprises	332821	436961
外商合作经营	Cooperative Enterprises	152829	66872
外商独资	Enterprises with Sole Foreign Investment	442290	338408
外商股份有限	Share Corporations Ltd.	9773	68508
其 他	Others	20466	186806
按控股情况分	**Grouped by Share Holding**		
国有控股	State-owned Enterprises	52432880	48546614
集体控股	Collective-owned Enterprises	11010208	10452696
私人控股	Private Enterprises	64397411	70225420
港澳台商控股	Enterprises with Investment from Hong Kong, Macao and Taiwan	994001	1297909
外商控股	Enterprises with Foreign Investment	677615	492426
其 他	Others	11859479	11834755

7–4 按国民经济行业分全社会固定资产投资(2016年)
TOTAL INVESTMENT IN FIXED ASSETS BY ECONOMIC SECTOR(2016)

单位：万元 (10 000 yuan)

行　业	Sector	全社会固定资产投资 Total Investment in Fixed Assets	#农户投资 Rural Households Investment
总　计	**Total**	**142849820**	**3386310**
农、林、牧、渔业	Farming, Forestry, Animal Husbandry and Fishery	19788459	729477
采矿业	Mining	10545566	
制造业	Manufacturing	26433613	3125
电力、热力、燃气及水生产和供应业	Production and Supply of Electricity, Heat, Gas and Water	12640199	
建筑业	Construction	141533	7982
批发和零售业	Wholesale and Retail Trade	3698270	61589
交通运输、仓储和邮政业	Transport, Storage and Post	9995997	308698
住宿和餐饮业	Hotels and Catering Services	756407	23259
信息传输、软件和信息技术服务业	Information Transmission, Software and Information Technology Services	1008837	
金融业	Banking and Insurance	92029	
房地产业	Real Estate Trade	29407807	2172577
租赁和商务服务业	Lease and Business Affairs Services	1648295	22500
科学研究和技术服务业	Scientific Reseach and Technical Services	1045745	
水利、环境和公共设施管理业	Management of Water Conservancy, Environmental and Public Facilities	18736035	
居民服务、修理和其他服务业	Resident Services, Repair and Other Services	452260	31295
教　育	Education	1885492	17848
卫生和社会工作	Health Care and Social Work	1673209	4875
文化、体育和娱乐业	Culture, Sports and Recreation	1929250	1653
公共管理、社会保障和社会组织	Public Management, Social Security and Social Organization	970817	1432

7-5 固定资产投资

单位：万元

年 份 Year	施工项目(个) Number of Projects Under Construction (unit)	新开工项目(个) Number of Newly Started Projects (unit)	本年投产项目(个) Number of Projects Put into Use (unit)	固定资产投资 Investment in Fixed Assets	#住 宅 Residential Buildings
1978	4477	548	2424	197409	11507
1979	2282	509	841	203476	21911
1980	3253	878	1204	227885	34960
1981	3398	878	1290	186890	33669
1982	4848	989	2172	263473	49408
1983	4354	848	2015	331972	46070
1984	4049	1216	1913	523864	51023
1985	5249	1656	2250	728498	68621
1986	4335	1063	2053	789593	98173
1987	4173	1071	1981	859390	94857
1988	4219	942	1863	861514	83192
1989	3618	542	1695	873928	90315
1990	3017	582	1401	981331	113872
1991	3417	582	1628	1187970	113389
1992	3702	819	1867	1490073	185171
1993	3833	841	1902	2144908	324911
1994	4124	2043	2043	2546950	341533
1995	3815	892	2004	2550276	367761
1996	4416	2713	2539	2859217	470490
1997	5718	3781	3678	3488553	508095
1998	4011	1481	1896	4812052	695634
1999	4497	2679	2627	5273575	885847
2000	4937	3343	3107	5518198	847573
2001	4851	3464	3148	6325861	751015
2002	5542	4264	3584	7526897	859174
2003	5419	4076	2948	10143163	898601
2004	5060	3323	2663	13490264	1302098
2005	5090	3764	2975	16992979	1723145
2006	5846	3902	3331	21214238	2741836
2007	6558	4336	3972	26659240	3525849
2008	6803	4571	3898	32985514	4435275
2009	9656	7389	6097	45999284	6112434
2010	12861	9425	8031	58160325	7316208
2011	9941	6621	6494	71376857	10348491
2012	10777	7285	6593	88979033	12810088
2013	12689	8458	8286	109136950	14982702
2014	12818	8444	9173	120354560	17909781
2015	17295	13421	13918	138075956	18897592
2016	23321	19717	18687	139463510	16654993

注：2010年以前为城镇固定资产投资，下同。

Note：Data coverage in the table is urban investment in fixed assets before 2010. The same applies to the following.

INVESTMENT IN FIXED ASSETS

(10 000 yuan)

第一产业 Primary Industry	第二产业 Secondary Industry	第三产业 Tertiary Industry	工业 Industry	轻工业 Light Industry	重工业 Heavy Industry	#能源工业 Energy Industry
1592	130133	65684	130534	3573	126961	66664
3392	127372	72712	127800	44571	83229	74156
4038	152567	71280	158672	10202	148470	88460
1891	119232	65767	118886	8224	110662	73167
2744	173884	86845	168500	12998	155502	98593
4167	236887	90918	235600	11440	224160	140591
3227	359278	161359	361794	16198	345596	214490
4961	506000	217537	503455	23596	479859	257108
5351	565154	219088	536314	31439	504875	330956
4993	566917	287480	544004	33077	510927	347642
4966	613805	242743	605667	43721	561946	381904
5146	628569	240213	621684	40844	580840	415226
7880	708513	264938	704105	25287	678818	489747
6740	876223	305007	868290	32581	835709	602208
6879	1017443	465751	1007817	38803	969014	638782
8971	1305601	830336	1292477	55174	1237303	733737
6515	1371463	1168972	1287314	34898	1252416	699372
7003	1300878	1242395	1259735	71793	1187942	727468
10983	1513878	1334356	1490037	87527	1402510	919671
45001	1918423	1525129	1811050	38473	1772577	1262414
21302	2015391	2775359	1974814	84854	1889960	1378520
33087	2194339	3046149	2143590	134705	2008885	1508720
72412	2593464	2852322	2532148	165447	2366701	1706272
103986	2836651	3385224	2766524	228006	2538518	1661777
215901	3577905	3733091	3527500	397139	3130361	1826431
235450	5833360	4074353	5795798	584801	5210997	3046474
192183	8306909	4991172	8269361	664565	7604796	4930625
253784	10701927	6037268	10660374	541604	10118770	6027304
353720	12846351	8014167	12782402	857080	11925322	6856405
485984	15443603	10729653	15348518	1162724	14185794	8627639
671437	17628300	14685777	17459436	836878	16622558	10231350
1477215	20640157	23881912	20423626	1286480	19137146	12194046
1609380	25367665	31183280	25201300	1990317	23210983	15207315
2227834	33478939	35670084	33389789	3228708	30161081	19190472
3134957	41348398	44495678	41296706	5416452	35880254	21126315
6599858	46567723	55969369	47004222	7089092	39915130	20978446
8872300	50030104	61452156	50524764	7941544	42583220	23133511
15000374	52050467	71025115	52831396	7777053	45054343	25831278
17974326	49085255	72403929	49616253	9341723	40274530	21209888

7-6 工业固定资产投资

单位：万元

年 份 Year	工业合计 Total Industry	煤炭工业 Coal Industry	食品工业 Food Industry	纺织工业 Textile Industry	炼焦工业 Coking Industry	医药工业 Medical Industry
1978	130534	42326	595	3731	2452	
1979	127800	44571	1273	3672	3159	301
1980	158672	61543	2700	6663	2584	1451
1981	118886	56227	1134	5417	1928	920
1982	168500	71532	3074	8297	1529	1534
1983	235600	98328	4601	7646	3615	1502
1984	361794	153277	9504	9122	6228	1609
1985	503455	179652	10790	14680	1856	4808
1986	536314	244082	9891	11892	1437	1044
1987	544004	250597	11898	9956	1465	2566
1988	605667	257214	7945	10549	3639	3879
1989	621684	270039	4871	11630	4321	2695
1990	704105	324577	10867	7944	1681	3281
1991	868290	377988	6560	11377	1201	2689
1992	1007817	407803	11047	16381	1874	3373
1993	1292477	435372	20448	30578	3728	4621
1994	1287314	405070	20562	14013	9622	4206
1995	1259735	473255	10174	29886	21173	7312
1996	1490037	598324	36195	26176	25246	8213
1997	1811050	671205	35400	17395	46370	8462
1998	1974814	480879	24755	8534	32066	6540
1999	2143590	421932	29734	9428	67568	13885
2000	2532148	365536	42995	15450	118894	15977
2001	2766524	466135	35928	13640	227631	57351
2002	3527500	674181	103161	33102	266173	97095
2003	5795798	903602	228361	26114	761553	119907
2004	8269361	1523924	237363	31665	1231811	217946
2005	10660374	2587510	234051	36801	940325	119171
2006	12782402	3056054	448909	60892	744919	114432
2007	15348518	3639235	630765	51605	923172	82769
2008	17459436	4640781	480582	44382	1014761	116958
2009	20423626	5986723	638705	136310	1025476	213235
2010	25201300	9295058	844184	87951	964168	266805
2011	33389789	12402352	1408809	159945	922900	560131
2012	41296706	13522238	2292109	214322	965519	618691
2013	47004222	11579546	2628882	297289	1135629	908555
2014	50524764	10780765	3544405	203606	643261	760721
2015	52831396	10481658	4212920	274255	719246	904008
2016	49616253	7691758	5328783	194814	729233	1023404

INDUSTRY INVESTMENT IN FIXED ASSETS

(10 000 yuan)

化学工业 Chemical Industry	建材工业 Building Materials Industry	冶金工业 Metallurgical Industry	机械工业 Machinery Industry	电力工业 Power Industry	其他工业 Others
14665	2827	19577	19225	21886	3250
7974	3366	11823	18336	26426	6899
8790	4402	12983	17229	24333	15994
7194	2010	7041	13131	15012	8872
12055	4397	18899	19895	25532	1756
12089	4569	20637	20584	38648	23381
41986	8416	29405	16561	54985	30701
75494	14595	59590	34519	70424	37047
58768	18490	55891	33104	80994	20721
32144	30402	66666	33664	87301	17345
37512	24226	77954	39492	112286	30971
36350	18079	80367	29048	136334	27950
46013	15541	69476	39446	154818	30461
68093	24920	94526	32441	206166	42329
66447	35103	150136	47118	200365	68170
39808	65250	264320	40015	273695	114642
32096	75502	355916	56577	266244	47506
54248	83759	228823	68076	213791	69238
88097	57404	228823	84496	264519	72544
27638	42921	179755	108587	524099	149218
92894	80906	228381	109525	823699	86635
78552	50793	234689	119146	933944	183919
125360	59112	359334	136555	1155472	137463
195203	95932	433812	143919	917135	179838
224754	159615	797834	135082	819672	216831
417828	266663	1411434	184932	1243865	231539
361725	258973	1558100	547290	1993540	307024
551373	311073	2565294	707231	2351865	255680
854895	399107	2834415	1049695	2859992	359092
1168096	575193	2383560	1533976	3559634	800513
1669419	795012	2402164	1379377	3860768	1055232
1356876	1350349	2167187	1826408	4084562	1637795
1301352	1823683	2514715	2299351	3628893	2175140
1987466	1989882	3516824	3762369	3973930	2705181
2720478	3435742	4756524	4747496	3826177	4197410
3287996	4048065	5229945	7175055	4201362	6511898
4865070	4613278	4457474	6652858	7089819	6913507
4178438	4561540	4001162	5751531	9562467	8184171
4323522	5123103	3531361	5443492	8210036	8016747

7-7 按国民经济行业分固定资产投资
INVESTMENT IN FIXED ASSETS BY ECONOMIC SECTOR

单位：万元　　(10 000 yuan)

行　业	Sector	2015	2016
总　计	**Total**	**138075956**	**139463510**
农、林、牧、渔业	Farming, Forestry, Animal Husbandry and Fishery	15677054	19058982
农　业	Farming	5350978	7468871
林　业	Forestry	2157474	2349342
畜牧业	Animal Husbandry	7384742	7982031
渔　业	Fishery	107180	174082
农、林、牧、渔服务业	Farming, Forestry, Animal Husbandry and Fishery Services	676680	1084656
采矿业	Mining	14120186	10545566
煤炭开采和洗选业	Coal Mining and Washsing	10481658	7691758
石油和天然气开采业	Extraction of Petroleum and Natural Gas	1240702	630077
黑色金属矿采选业	Mining and Dressing of Ferrous Metals	935648	835964
有色金属矿采选业	Mining and Dressing of Nonferrous Metals	209281	259345
非金属矿采选业	Mining and Dressing of Nonmetal Ores	429306	533270
开采辅助活动	Mining Auxiliary Activities	812176	542789
其他采矿业	Others	11415	52363
制造业	Manufacturing	25152005	26430488
农副食品加工业	Farm and Sideline Food Processing	2407003	3718849
食品制造业	Food Manufacturing	1037550	836751
酒、饮料和精制茶制造业	Alcohol, Beverage and Refined Tea Manufacturing	716458	702469
烟草制品业	Tobacoo Manufaturing	51909	70714
纺织业	Textile Industry	249630	178714
纺织服装、服饰业	Manufacture of Garments and Accessories	85435	86815
皮革、毛皮、羽毛及其制品和制鞋业	Manufacture of Leather, Fur, Feather and their Products and Footwear	35761	44007
木材加工和木、竹、藤、棕、草制品业	Processing of Timber, Manufacture of Wood, Bamboo, Rattan, Palm, and Straw Products	273814	428641
家具制造业	Manufacture of Funiture	136165	152299
造纸和纸制品业	Manufacture of Paper and Paper Products	208082	331508
印刷和记录媒介复制业	Printing and Record Medium Reproduction	70115	62041
文教、工美、体育和娱乐用品制造业	Manufacture of Articles For Culture, Education and Sport Activity	113808	160055
石油加工、炼焦和核燃料加工业	Petroleum Processing ,Coking and Nuclear Fuel Processing	1351178	1109023
化学原料和化学制品制造业	Manufacture Raw Chemical Materials and Chemical Products	3687856	3842813
医药制造业	Manufacture of Medical Products	904008	1023404
化学纤维制造业	Manufacture of Chemical Fibers	24625	16100
橡胶和塑料制品业	Manufacture of Rubber and Plastic Products	490582	480709
非金属矿物制品业	Manufacture of Nonmetals Mineral Products	4132234	4589833
黑色金属冶炼和压延加工业	Smelting and Pressing of Ferrous Metals	1301250	1036949
有色金属冶炼和压延加工业	Smelting and Pressing of Nonferrous Metals	1554983	1399103
金属制品业	Manufacture of Metal Products	1094136	957458
通用设备制造业	Manufacture of Universal Purpose Equipment	1071621	783633
专用设备制造业	Manufacture of Special Purpose Equipment	981518	853479
汽车制造业	Manufacture of Motor Vehicles	490349	642943

7-7 续表1 continued

单位：万元 (10 000 yuan)

行　业	Sector	2015	2016
铁路、船舶、航空航天和其他运输设备制造业	Manufacture of Railways, Ships, Aviation, Aircrafts and Other Transportation Equipments	224324	103870
电气机械和器材制造业	Manufacture of Electrical Equipment and Machinery	923780	1020819
计算机、通信和其他电子设备制造业	Manufacture of Computer, Telecommunication and Other Electronic Equipments	873073	921029
仪器仪表制造业	Manufacture of Measuring Instrument and Machinery	92730	38501
其他制造业	Other Manufacturing	138393	376560
废弃资源综合利用业	Comprehensive Utilization of Waste	363933	339639
金属制品、机械和设备修理业	Repair of Metal Products, Machinery and Equipment	65702	121760
电力、热力、燃气及水生产和供应业	Production and Supply of Electricity, Heat, Gas and Water	13559205	12640199
电力、热力生产和供应业	Production and Supply of Electricity and Heat	11258809	10040056
燃气生产和供应业	Production and Supply of Gas	1498931	1738974
水的生产和供应业	Production and Supply of Water	801465	861169
建筑业	Construction	96949	133551
房屋建筑业	Buildings Construction	35085	61931
土木工程建筑业	Civil Engineering	45653	19707
建筑安装业	Building Installation	3568	7920
建筑装饰和其他建筑业	Building Decoration and Other Construction	12643	43993
批发和零售业	Wholesale and Retail Trade	3432021	3636681
批发业	Wholesale Trade	1321012	1689542
零售业	Retail Trade	2111009	1947139
交通运输、仓储和邮政业	Transport, Storage and Post	9517880	9687299
铁路运输业	Railway Transport	2213788	1816588
道路运输业	Highway Transport	4481175	5040273
航空运输业	Air Transport	46687	2482
管道运输业	Transport Via Pipelines	137127	23908
装卸搬运和运输代理业	Loading, Unloading and Other Transport Services	82086	121809
仓储业	Storage	2548578	2662656
邮政业	Post	8439	19583
住宿和餐饮业	Hotels and Catering Services	774489	733148
住宿业	Hotels	561242	458881
餐饮业	Catering Services	213247	274267
信息传输、软件和信息技术服务业	Information Transmission, Software and Information Technology Services	1045132	1008837
电信、广播电视和卫星传输服务	Transimission Services of Telecommunication, Broadcast, Television and Satellite	640781	373430
互联网和相关服务	Internet and Relative Services	108151	454678
软件和信息技术服务业	Software and Information Technology Services	296200	180729
金融业	Banking and Insurance	44852	92029
货币金融服务	Monetary Banking	36732	69793

7-7 续表2 continued

单位：万元 (10 000 yuan)

行　业	Sector	2015	2016
资本市场服务	Capital Market		7147
保险业	Insurance	500	5669
其他金融业	Other Financial Activities	7620	9420
房地产业	Real Estate Trade	31145926	27235230
房地产业	Real Estate Trade	31145926	27235230
租赁和商务服务业	Lease and Business Affairs Services	696878	1625795
租赁业	Leasing	25909	109265
商务服务业	Business Affairs Services	670969	1516530
科学研究和技术服务业	Scientific Reseach and Technical Services	769117	1045745
研究和试验发展	Reserch and Experimental Development	171837	321645
专业技术服务业	Professional Technical Services	276528	427041
科技推广和应用服务业	Services of Science and Technology Exchanges and Promotion	320752	297059
水利、环境和公共设施管理业	Management of Water Conservancy, Environment and Public Facilities	16074140	18736035
水利管理业	Water Conservancy	2185811	2277188
生态保护和环境治理业	Ecological Protection and Environmental Management	1410921	1649800
公共设施管理业	Public Facilities	12477408	14809047
居民服务、修理和其他服务业	Resident Services, Repair and Other Services	461959	420965
居民服务业	Residence Services	343219	192792
机动车、电子产品和日用产品修理业	Repair of Motor Vehicles, Electronic Products and Daily Products	89811	181230
其他服务业	Other Services	28929	46943
教　育	Education	1810609	1867644
教　育	Education	1810609	1867644
卫生和社会工作	Health Care and Social Work	1255563	1668334
卫　生	Health Care	874122	991731
社会工作	Social Work	381441	676603
文化、体育和娱乐业	Culture, Sports and Recreation	1952159	1927597
新闻和出版业	Journalism and Publishing Activities		13791
广播、电视、电影和影视录音制作业	Broadcasting, Movies, Televisions and Audiovisual Activities	30271	69216
文化艺术业	Culture and Arts Activities	1051140	1021856
体　育	Sports Activities	280581	297773
娱乐业	Entertainment	590167	524961
公共管理、社会保障和社会组织	Public Management, Social Security and Social Organization	489832	969385
中国共产党机关	Organs of CPC	951	
国家机构	Government Agencies	280738	510116
社会保障	Social Security	20720	9865
群众团体、社会团体和其他成员组织	Mass Organizations, Social Organizations and Other Member Organizations	132624	315491
基层群众自治组织	Grass Roots Self-governing Organizations	54799	133913

7-8 固定资产投资主要指标

MAJOR INDICATORS OF INVESTMENT IN FIXED ASSETS

单位：万元 (10 000 yuan)

指　　标	Item	2015	2016
一、投资总额	**Total Investment**	**138075956**	**139463510**
#国有经济控股	State-Controlled Share Holding	52432880	48546532
#住　宅	Residential Buildings	18897592	16654993
按隶属关系分	Grouped by Administrative Relationship		
中　央	Central Investment	6332509	6251398
地　方	Local Investment	131743447	133212112
按登记注册类型分	Grouped by Type of Registration Status		
内　资	Domestic-Funded Enterprises	135687699	136642829
港、澳、台商投资	Enterprises with Investment from Hong Kong, Macao and Taiwan	1430078	1723126
外商投资	Enterprises with Foreign Investment	958179	1097555
按构成分	Grouped by Composition		
建筑工程	Construction	88182519	91168968
安装工程	Installation	13172744	13052403
设备工器具购置	Purchase of Equipment and Instruments	22758778	21169672
其他费用	Others	13961915	14072467
按建设性质分(不含房地产投资)	Grouped by Type of Construction		
新　建	New Construction	82823949	89574546
扩　建	Expansion	18757606	15778096
改建和技术改造	Reconstruction and Technical Reformation	13315758	11811368
单纯建造生活设施	Construction of Living Facilities	6579413	4011479
其　他	Others	1650511	2314489
按三次产业分	Grouped by Type of Industry		
第一产业	Primary Industry	15000374	17974326
第二产业	Secondary Industry	52050467	49085255
第三产业	Tertiary Industry	71025115	72403929
二、新增固定资产	**Newly Increased Fixed Assets**	**108412978**	**96652686**
三、建设项目(个)	**Construction Projects (unit)**		
施工项目	Projects Under Construction	17295	23321
#本年新开工	Projects Newly Started This Year	13421	19717
本年投产项目	Projects Put into Use This Yesr	13918	18687
四、房屋建筑面积(万平方米)	**Floor Space of Buildings (10 000 sq.m)**		
本年施工房屋面积	Floor Space Under Construction	28591.5	25557.8
#住　宅	Residential Buildings	17086.6	15342.9
本年竣工房屋面积	Floor Space Completed	7448.7	6496.7
#住　宅	Residential Buildings	4032.9	3579.8
五、投资资金来源合计	**Grouped by Source of Funds**	**125311967**	**123069088**
上年结余资金	Balance of Funds Last Year	6536392	6272807
本年资金来源小计	Subtotal Source of Funds This Year	118775575	116796281
国家预算内资金	State-budgetary Appropriation	7209721	7327910
国内贷款	Domestic Loans	6642501	6991775
利用外资	Foreign Investment	25069	55792
自筹资金	Self-raised Funds	96562905	92214849
#企事业单位自有资金	Own Funds of Enterprises and Institutions	29050787	33743562
其　他	Others	8335379	10205955

7-9 固定资产投资规模(2016年)

单位：万元

指　标	Item	计划总投资 Total Planned Investment	自开始建设至本年底累计完成投资 Accumulated Investment Completed This Year
总　计	**Total**	**282346181**	**206611469**
#本年新开工项目	Projects Newly Started This Year	59221667	55629504
#本年投产项目	Projects Put into Use This Year	56720597	57490504
按隶属关系分	Grouped By Administrative Relationship		
中　央	Central Investment	32843725	23096861
地　方	Local Investment	249502456	183514608
按登记注册类型分	Grouped by Type of Registration Status		
内　资	Domestic-Funded Enterprises	273903727	200696991
港、澳、台商投资	Enterprises with Investment from Hong Kong, Macao and Taiwan	4800154	3683267
外商投资	Enterprises with Foreign Investment	3642300	2231211
按建设性质分	Grouped by Type of Construction		
新　建	New Construction	216847197	154076636
扩　建	Expansion	31509957	25484759
改建和技术改造	Reconstruction and Technical Reforming	20849982	17316736
单纯建造生活设施	Construction of Living Facilities	8689967	7018761
其　他	Others	4449078	2714577
按控股情况分	Grouped by Share Holding		
国有控股	State-owned Enterprises	136878106	96411568
集体控股	Collective-owned Enterprises	19208090	15363936
私人控股	Private Enterprises	103061556	76663795
港澳台商控股	Enterprises with Investment from Hong Kong, Macao and Taiwan	3379975	2842412
外商控股	Enterprises with Foreign Investment	2312842	1344461
其　他	Others	17505612	13985297
按三次产业分	Grouped by Type of Industry		
第一产业	Primary Industry	22493959	19571689
第二产业	Secondary Industry	123076628	89575845
第三产业	Tertiary Industry	136775594	97463935
按投资总规模分	Grouped by Scale of Investment		
500 - 5000万元	5 million-50 million yuan	66116725	62500353
5000万元 - 1亿元	50 million-100 million yuan	7868626	6641979
1亿元 - 5亿元	100 million-500 million yuan	48653628	35900695
5亿元 - 10亿元	500 million-1 billion yuan	25956706	18591375
10亿元以上	1 billion yuan and Above	133750496	82977067

注：本表不含房地产开发投资。

Note：Data in this table excludes investment in real estate development.

SCALE OF FIXED ASSETS INVESTMENT(2016)

(10 000 yuan)

#本年完成投资 Investment Completed This Year	本年新增固定资产 Newly Increased Fixed Assets This Year	施工项目(个) Number of Projects under Construction (unit)	#本年新开工 Newly Started This Year	本年投产项目(个) Number of Projects Put into Use This Year (unit)
123489978	**88555506**	**23321**	**19717**	**18687**
55618623	49728581	17631	17631	15001
55338205	55669847	16773	15001	17203
5824590	3179169	396	285	313
117665388	85376337	22925	19432	18374
121027376	87598770	23181	19618	18594
1416762	587773	57	42	34
1045840	368963	83	57	59
89574546	60245168	16595	14083	12659
15778096	13337908	3590	3131	3064
11811368	10345276	2488	2055	2028
4011479	2852109	578	394	444
2314489	1775045	70	54	492
45132220	26671798	7062	5477	5220
10335081	8132902	2166	1936	1925
55444648	45118593	11526	10009	9558
1095007	544315	40	27	23
418771	69252	32	16	16
11064251	8018646	2495	2252	1945
17974326	15387317	5247	4729	4382
49085255	36203846	7645	6376	6214
56430397	36964343	10429	8612	8091
60215024	55727369	19602	17631	17203
5329541	4321385	1002	695	596
24825953	15576559	1925	1160	744
8705845	4598766	378	131	94
24413615	8331427	414	100	50

7-10 按登记注册类型分固定资产投资(2016年)

单位：万元

行　业	Sector	总　计 Total
总　计	**Total**	**139463510**
农、林、牧、渔业	Farming, Forestry, Animal Husbandry and Fishery	19058982
农　业	Farming	7468871
林　业	Forestry	2349342
畜牧业	Animal Husbandry	7982031
渔　业	Fishery	174082
农、林、牧、渔服务业	Farming, Forestry, Animal Husbandry and Fishery Services	1084656
采矿业	Mining	10545566
煤炭开采和洗选业	Coal Mining and Washsing	7691758
石油和天然气开采业	Extraction of Petroleum and Natural Gas	630077
黑色金属矿采选业	Mining and Dressing of Ferrous Metals	835964
有色金属矿采选业	Mining and Dressing of Nonferrous Metals	259345
非金属矿采选业	Mining and Dressing of Nonmetal Ores	533270
开采辅助活动	Mining Auxiliary Activities	542789
其他采矿业	Others	52363
制造业	Manufacturing	26430488
农副食品加工业	Farm and Sideline Food Processing	3718849
食品制造业	Food Manufacturing	836751
酒、饮料和精制茶制造业	Alcohol, Beverage and Refined Tea Manufacturing	702469
烟草制品业	Tobacoo Manufaturing	70714
纺织业	Textile Industry	178714
纺织服装、服饰业	Manufacture of Garments and Accessories	86815
皮革、毛皮、羽毛及其制品和制鞋业	Manufacture of Leather, Fur, Feather and their Products and Footwear	44007
木材加工和木、竹、藤、棕、草制品业	Processing of Timber, Manufacture of Wood, Bamboo, Rattan, Palm, and Straw Products	428641
家具制造业	Manufacture of Funiture	152299
造纸和纸制品业	Manufacture of Paper and Paper Products	331508
印刷和记录媒介复制业	Printing and Record Medium Reproduction	62041
文教、工美、体育和娱乐用品制造业	Manufacture of Articles For Culture, Education and Sport Activity	160055
石油加工、炼焦和核燃料加工业	Petroleum Processing ,Coking and Nuclear Fuel Processing	1109023
化学原料和化学制品制造业	Manufacture Raw Chemical Materials and Chemical Products	3842813
医药制造业	Manufacture of Medical Products	1023404
化学纤维制造业	Manufacture of Chemical Fibers	16100
橡胶和塑料制品业	Manufacture of Rubber and Plastic Products	480709
非金属矿物制品业	Manufacture of Nonmetals Mineral Products	4589833
黑色金属冶炼和压延加工业	Smelting and Pressing of Ferrous Metals	1036949
有色金属冶炼和压延加工业	Smelting and Pressing of Nonferrous Metals	1399103
金属制品业	Manufacture of Metal Products	957458
通用设备制造业	Manufacture of Universal Purpose Equipment	783633

INVESTMENT IN FIXED ASSETS BY REGISTRATION STATUS(2016)

(10 000 yuan)

内 资 Domestic-Funded Enterprises	国 有 State-owned Enterprises	集 体 Collective -owned Enterprises	股份合作 Share Cooperative Enterprises	国有联营 State Joint Ownership Enterprises	集体联营 Collective Joint Ownership Enterprises	国有与集体联营 Joint State-collective Enterprises	其他联营 Other Joint Ownership Enterprises
136642829	**29363837**	**4427425**	**65668**	**23712**	**6182**	**54742**	**55312**
19032862	1894647	723024	31269		722		3200
7468871	612308	413685	13630				
2349342	723991	56651					
7955911	253058	126734	17639		722		3200
174082	17488						
1084656	287802	125954					
10372603	1003063	28464	12230	212			
7575779	891601	6392	12230	212			
573093	92990	3678					
835964	10021						
259345							
533270		13479					
542789	6161	4915					
52363	2290						
25434821	1253399	180641		3113	1250		46400
3687766	68718	73883					
836751	61	18382					
687156	70						
70714	700						
178714							
86815	3850						
44007		3860					
428641	2685	3933					
152299	4710						
331508							
62041	4100						
160055	20361						
1034104	321635						46400
3754313	465130	4100					
998579	19269				1250		
16100							
480709	3700			3113			
4575503	70829	55073					
1015553	35314	500					
1281539	1320						
952958	11940						
777933	27283	3821					

7-10 续表1

单位：万元

行　业	Sector	总　计 Total
专用设备制造业	Manufacture of Special Purpose Equipment	853479
汽车制造业	Manufacture of Motor Vehicles	642943
铁路、船舶、航空航天和其他运输设备制造业	Manufacture of Railways, Ships, Aviation, Aircrafts and Other Transportation Equipments	103870
电气机械和器材制造业	Manufacture of Electrical Equipment and Machinery	1020819
计算机、通信和其他电子设备制造业	Manufacture of Computer, Telecommunication and Other Electronic Equipments	921029
仪器仪表制造业	Manufacture of Measuring Instrument and Machinery	38501
其他制造业	Other Manufacturing	376560
废弃资源综合利用业	Comprehensive Utilization of Waste	339639
金属制品、机械和设备修理业	Repair of Metal Products, Machinery and Equipment	121760
电力、热力、燃气及水生产和供应业	Production and Supply of Electricity, Heat, Gas and Water	12640199
电力、热力生产和供应业	Production and Supply of Electricity and Heat	10040056
燃气生产和供应业	Production and Supply of Gas	1738974
水的生产和供应业	Production and Supply of Water	861169
建筑业	Construction	133551
房屋建筑业	Buildings Construction	61931
土木工程建筑业	Civil Engineering	19707
建筑安装业	Building Installation	7920
建筑装饰和其他建筑业	Building Decoration and Other Construction	43993
批发和零售业	Wholesale and Retail Trade	3636681
批发业	Wholesale Trade	1689542
零售业	Retail Trade	1947139
交通运输、仓储和邮政业	Transport, Storage and Post	9687299
铁路运输业	Railway Transport	1816588
道路运输业	Highway Transport	5040273
水上运输业	Water Transport	
航空运输业	Air Transport	2482
管道运输业	Transport Via Pipelines	23908
装卸搬运和运输代理业	Loading, Unloading and Other Transport Services	121809
仓储业	Storage	2662656
邮政业	Post	19583
住宿和餐饮业	Hotels and Catering Services	733148
住宿业	Hotels	458881
餐饮业	Catering Services	274267
信息传输、软件和信息技术服务业	Information Transmission, Software and Information Technology Services	1008837
电信、广播电视和卫星传输服务	Transimission Services of Telecommunication, Broadcast, Television and Satellite	373430
互联网和相关服务	Internet and Relative Services	454678
软件和信息技术服务业	Software and Information Technology Services	180729

continued

(10 000 yuan)

内　资 Domestic-Funded Enterprises	国　有 State-owned Enterprises	集　体 Collective -owned Enterprises	股份合作 Share Cooperative Enterprises	国有联营 State Joint Ownership Enterprises	集体联营 Collective Joint Ownership Enterprises	国有与集体联　营 Joint State-collective Enterprises	其他联营 Other Joint Ownership Enterprises
850723	42924	3100					
640143	4010						
103870	4930						
1011012	30183						
354390	18326	3850					
38501	13293						
375025	62126						
325639	8398	8835					
121760	7534	1304					
11722981	3690842	247978	1133			49472	
9182690	2954133	161863				49472	
1701667	339901	32786					
838624	396808	53329	1133				
133551	23894					4420	
61931	10644						
19707	9390					4420	
7920	3860						
43993							
3636681	196777	233292	1954				
1689542	81155	112788					
1947139	115622	120504	1954				
9687299	3804015	226995	2240	3710			
1816588	974218	3512					
5040273	2714387	163799	2240				
2482							
23908	5067						
121809	8240	4865					
2662656	93436	54819		3710			
19583	8667						
733148	101293	27171					
458881	77342	24671					
274267	23951	2500					
743930	180047			11857			
288756	124666						
274445	45964			11857			
180729	9417						

7-10　续表2

单位：万元

行　业	Sector	总　计 Total
金融业	Banking and Insurance	92029
货币金融服务	Monetary Banking	69793
资本市场服务	Capital Market	7147
保险业	Insurance	5669
其他金融业	Other Financial Activities	9420
房地产业	Real Estate Trade	27235230
房地产业	Real Estate Trade	27235230
租赁和商务服务业	Lease and Business Affairs Services	1625795
租赁业	Leasing	109265
商务服务业	Business Affairs Services	1516530
科学研究和技术服务业	Scientific Reseach and Technical Services	1045745
研究和试验发展	Reserch and Experimental Development	321645
专业技术服务业	Professional Technical Services	427041
科技推广和应用服务业	Services of Science and Technology Exchanges and Promotion	297059
水利、环境和公共设施管理业	Management of Water Conservancy, Environment and Public Facilities	18736035
水利管理业	Water Conservancy	2277188
生态保护和环境治理业	Ecological Protection and Environmental Management	1649800
公共设施管理业	Public Facilities	14809047
居民服务、修理和其他服务业	Resident Services, Repair and Other Services	420965
居民服务业	Residence Services	192792
机动车、电子产品和日用产品修理业	Repair of Motor Vehicles, Electronic Products and Daily Products	181230
其他服务业	Other Services	46943
教　育	Education	1867644
教　育	Education	1867644
卫生和社会工作	Health Care and Social Work	1668334
卫　生	Health Care	991731
社会工作	Social Work	676603
文化、体育和娱乐业	Culture, Sports and Recreation	1927597
新闻和出版业	Journalism and Publishing Activities	13791
广播、电视、电影和影视录音制作业	Broadcasting, Movies, Televisions and Audiovisual Activities	69216
文化艺术业	Culture and Arts Activities	1021856
体　育	Sports Activities	297773
娱乐业	Entertainment	524961
公共管理、社会保障和社会组织	Public Management, Social Security and Social Organization	969385
中国共产党机关	Organs of CPC	
国家机构	Government Agencies	510116
人民政协、民主党派	PPCC and Democratic Parties	
社会保障	Social Security	9865
群众团体、社会团体和其他成员组织	Mass Organizations, Social Organizations and Other Member Organizations	315491
基层群众自治组织	Grass Roots Self-governing Organizations	133913

continued

(10 000 yuan)

内 资 Domestic-Funded Enterprises	国 有 State-owned Enterprises	集 体 Collective-owned Enterprises	股份合作 Share Cooperative Enterprises	国有联营 State Joint Ownership Enterprises	集体联营 Collective Joint Ownership Enterprises	国有与集体联营 Joint State-collective Enterprises	其他联营 Other Joint Ownership Enterprises
92029	16074	2243	3120				
69793	9330	2243	3120				
7147	1747						
5669							
9420	4997						
26839264	3302042	1578710	6170				
26839264	3302042	1578710	6170				
1625795	323063	58894		4820			
109265	3560						
1516530	319503	58894		4820			
1045745	383316	16902					
321645	124690						
427041	183489	5548					
297059	75137	11354					
18688195	9818534	713181	7552		4210		
2277188	1782076	161601			3990		
1611683	604192	70522					
14799324	7432266	481058	7552		220		
420965	77485	19384					
192792	64062	12216					
181230	4200	2518					
46943	9223	4650					
1867644	1147596	63153				850	
1867644	1147596	63153				850	
1668334	781599	64877					
991731	643000	14580					
676603	138599	50297					
1927597	677174	197203					
13791	1372						
69216	14305						
1021856	510019	138516					
297773	119919	19555					
524961	31559	39132					
969385	688977	45313					5712
510116	488194	5289					
9865	7302	2563					
315491	190931	14930					5712
133913	2550	22531					

7–10 续表3

单位：万元

行业	Sector	国有独资公司 State–funded Corporations
总计	**Total**	**4992024**
农、林、牧、渔业	Farming, Forestry, Animal Husbandry and Fishery	46009
农业	Farming	37314
林业	Forestry	4410
畜牧业	Animal Husbandry	4285
渔业	Fishery	
农、林、牧、渔服务业	Farming, Forestry, Animal Husbandry and Fishery Services	
采矿业	Mining	1168091
煤炭开采和洗选业	Coal Mining and Washsing	566925
石油和天然气开采业	Extraction of Petroleum and Natural Gas	31255
黑色金属矿采选业	Mining and Dressing of Ferrous Metals	68907
有色金属矿采选业	Mining and Dressing of Nonferrous Metals	15669
非金属矿采选业	Mining and Dressing of Nonmetal Ores	3778
开采辅助活动	Mining Auxiliary Activities	481557
其他采矿业	Others	
制造业	Manufacturing	199271
农副食品加工业	Farm and Sideline Food Processing	
食品制造业	Food Manufacturing	
酒、饮料和精制茶制造业	Alcohol, Beverage and Refined Tea Manufacturing	
烟草制品业	Tobacoo Manufaturing	
纺织业	Textile Industry	
纺织服装、服饰业	Manufacture of Garments and Accessories	
皮革、毛皮、羽毛及其制品和制鞋业	Manufacture of Leather, Fur, Feather and their Products and Footwear	
木材加工和木、竹、藤、棕、草制品业	Processing of Timber, Manufacture of Wood, Bamboo, Rattan, Palm, and Straw Products	
家具制造业	Manufacture of Funiture	
造纸和纸制品业	Manufacture of Paper and Paper Products	
印刷和记录媒介复制业	Printing and Record Medium Reproduction	
文教、工美、体育和娱乐用品制造业	Manufacture of Articles For Culture, Education and Sport Activity	
石油加工、炼焦和核燃料加工业	Petroleum Processing ,Coking and Nuclear Fuel Processing	11250
化学原料和化学制品制造业	Manufacture Raw Chemical Materials and Chemical Products	8500
医药制造业	Manufacture of Medical Products	
化学纤维制造业	Manufacture of Chemical Fibers	
橡胶和塑料制品业	Manufacture of Rubber and Plastic Products	
非金属矿物制品业	Manufacture of Nonmetals Mineral Products	11499
黑色金属冶炼和压延加工业	Smelting and Pressing of Ferrous Metals	14350
有色金属冶炼和压延加工业	Smelting and Pressing of Nonferrous Metals	43050
金属制品业	Manufacture of Metal Products	
通用设备制造业	Manufacture of Universal Purpose Equipment	1580

continued

(10 000 yuan)

其他有限责任公司 Other Limited Liability Corporations	股份有限公司 Share Co. Ltd.	私营 Private Enterprises	个体户 Self-employed Individuals	个体合伙 Individual Partnership Enterprises	其他 Others	港澳台商投资 Enterprises with Investment from HongKong, Macao and Taiwan	外商投资 Enterprises with Foreign Investment
24665465	**2158948**	**52481972**	**529339**	**955879**	**16862324**	**1723126**	**1097555**
1127220	63201	7863181	265578	711547	6303264		26120
463562	31428	2967064	75832	157788	2696260		
179357	23060	815082	11011	27073	508707		
421633	8713	3548736	164943	523393	2882855		26120
3800		88417	8194	3143	53040		
58868		443882	5598	150	162402		
4085716	558286	3427884	23589	9175	55893		172963
3548005	477158	2029806		4243	39207		115979
269543	71840	103787					56984
59574		695315	2147				
132901	4963	105812					
62362	4270	407915	19848	4932	16686		
13331		36825					
	55	48424	1594				
4668193	483714	16801941	166736	108432	1521731	908242	87425
394277	6344	2177678	59254	84109	823503		31083
97383	10276	653919		9033	47697		
185707	1698	458983		8370	32328		15313
66514		3500					
38845		134969			4900		
13388		66747			2830		
1599		38548					
28096	31411	331267	10546		20703		
22277		125312					
30238		287148	306		13816		
12918		38783	1260		4980		
7381	6287	117208	1200		7618		
227071	2519	420429	4800			59363	15556
875520	125556	2177547		5480	92480	88500	
152767	98392	626404			100497	24825	
6148		9952					
85453	15761	329338	6200		37144		
523996	33848	3578407	72274	1440	228137	8960	5370
228467		726663			10259	21396	
472030	4500	734459	4380		21800	115374	2190
163735	8000	748553			20730		4500
118358	31578	584692	1600		9021	4850	850

7-10 续表4

单位：万元

行 业	Sector	国有独资公司 State-funded Corporations
专用设备制造业	Manufacture of Special Purpose Equipment	14331
汽车制造业	Manufacture of Motor Vehicles	
铁路、船舶、航空航天和其他运输设备制造业	Manufacture of Railways, Ships, Aviation, Aircrafts and Other Transportation Equipments	
电气机械和器材制造业	Manufacture of Electrical Equipment and Machinery	39583
计算机、通信和其他电子设备制造业	Manufacture of Computer, Telecommunication and Other Electronic Equipments	
仪器仪表制造业	Manufacture of Measuring Instrument and Machinery	
其他制造业	Other Manufacturing	
废弃资源综合利用业	Comprehensive Utilization of Waste	4950
金属制品、机械和设备修理业	Repair of Metal Products, Machinery and Equipment	50178
电力、热力、燃气及水生产和供应业	Production and Supply of Electricity, Heat, Gas and Water	911042
电力、热力生产和供应业	Production and Supply of Electricity and Heat	820409
燃气生产和供应业	Production and Supply of Gas	51567
水的生产和供应业	Production and Supply of Water	39066
建筑业	Construction	
房屋建筑业	Buildings Construction	
土木工程建筑业	Civil Engineering	
建筑安装业	Building Installation	
建筑装饰和其他建筑业	Building Decoration and Other Construction	
批发和零售业	Wholesale and Retail Trade	15999
批发业	Wholesale Trade	7699
零售业	Retail Trade	8300
交通运输、仓储和邮政业	Transport, Storage and Post	983132
铁路运输业	Railway Transport	
道路运输业	Highway Transport	964367
水上运输业	Water Transport	
航空运输业	Air Transport	
管道运输业	Transport Via Pipelines	
装卸搬运和运输代理业	Loading, Unloading and Other Transport Services	
仓储业	Storage	18765
邮政业	Post	
住宿和餐饮业	Hotels and Catering Services	1500
住宿业	Hotels	
餐饮业	Catering Services	1500
信息传输、软件和信息技术服务业	Information Transmission, Software and Information Technology Services	27083
电信、广播电视和卫星传输服务	Transimission Services of Telecommunication, Broadcast, Television and Satellite	
互联网和相关服务	Internet and Relative Services	
软件和信息技术服务业	Software and Information Technology Services	27083

continued

(10 000 yuan)

其他有限责任公司 Other Limited Liability Corporations	股份有限公司 Share Co. Ltd.	私营 Private Enterprises	个体户 Self-employed Individuals	个体合伙 Individual Partnership Enterprises	其他 Others	港澳台商投资 Enterprises with Investment from HongKong, Macao and Taiwan	外商投资 Enterprises with Foreign Investment
185031	13125	574996	4916		12300		2756
275038	12171	348924				2800	
17293		81647					
196514	18190	706852			19690		9807
178715	141	150708			2650	566639	
6152		19056					
13449	6427	292883			140	1535	
43833	56280	195765			7578	14000	
	1210	60604			930		
3670090	360846	2574960		27534	189084	459252	457966
2989079	278010	1810965		27534	91225	429371	427995
565585	56832	575167			79829	14307	23000
115426	26004	188828			18030	15574	6971
21746	5690	77801					
8000		43287					
3930	730	1237					
3960		100					
5856	4960	33177					
437681	16532	2344890	18046	63459	308051		
113968		1127513	10786	58841	176792		
323713	16532	1217377	7260	4618	131259		
1476918	190165	2455865	17432	4429	522398		
461141	71940	305777					
519313	113605	422594	4585		135383		
332		2150					
10863		7978					
34021		74683					
451248	4620	1631767	12847	4429	387015		
		10916					
108745	1610	372298	5407	1140	113984		
60555	1610	231610	3997	1140	57956		
48190		140688	1410		56028		
134897	107498	282548				37468	227439
45450	95978	22662				16986	67688
63322	6420	146882				20482	159751
26125	5100	113004					

7-10 续表5

单位：万元

行　业	Sector	国有独资公司 State-funded Corporations
金融业	Banking and Insurance	9235
货币金融服务	Monetary Banking	9235
资本市场服务	Capital Market	
保险业	Insurance	
其他金融业	Other Financial Activities	
房地产业	Real Estate Trade	823799
房地产业	Real Estate Trade	823799
租赁和商务服务业	Lease and Business Affairs Services	8890
租赁业	Leasing	
商务服务业	Business Affairs Services	8890
科学研究和技术服务业	Scientific Reseach and Technical Services	8900
研究和试验发展	Reserch and Experimental Development	8900
专业技术服务业	Professional Technical Services	
科技推广和应用服务业	Services of Science and Technology Exchanges and Promotion	
水利、环境和公共设施管理业	Management of Water Conservancy, Environment and Public Facilities	693390
水利管理业	Water Conservancy	29960
生态保护和环境治理业	Ecological Protection and Environmental Management	
公共设施管理业	Public Facilities	663430
居民服务、修理和其他服务业	Resident Services, Repair and Other Services	
居民服务业	Residence Services	
机动车、电子产品和日用产品修理业	Repair of Motor Vehicles, Electronic Products and Daily Products	
其他服务业	Other Services	
教　育	Education	21284
教　育	Education	21284
卫生和社会工作	Health Care and Social Work	
卫　生	Health Care	
社会工作	Social Work	
文化、体育和娱乐业	Culture, Sports and Recreation	74399
新闻和出版业	Journalism and Publishing Activities	
广播、电视、电影和影视录音制作业	Broadcasting, Movies, Televisions and Audiovisual Activities	
文化艺术业	Culture and Arts Activities	72839
体　育	Sports Activities	
娱乐业	Entertainment	1560
公共管理、社会保障和社会组织	Public Management, Social Security and Social Organization	
中国共产党机关	Organs of CPC	
国家机构	Government Agencies	
人民政协、民主党派	PPCC and Democratic Parties	
社会保障	Social Security	
群众团体、社会团体和其他成员组织	Mass Organizations, Social Organizations and Other Member Organizations	
基层群众自治组织	Grass Roots Self-governing Organizations	

continued

(10 000 yuan)

其他有限责任公司 Other Limited Liability Corporations	股份有限公司 Share Co. Ltd.	私营 Private Enterprises	个体户 Self-employed Individuals	个体合伙 Individual Partnership Enterprises	其他 Others	港澳台商投资 Enterprises with Investment from HongKong, Macao and Taiwan	外商投资 Enterprises with Foreign Investment
6100	6263	43891			5103		
3300	6263	35622			680		
2800		2600					
		5669					
					4423		
5856165	155746	10177169			4939463	306364	89602
5856165	155746	10177169			4939463	306364	89602
104494	870	474075		3650	647039		
5034		65681		3650	31340		
99460	870	408394			615699		
226875		376923			32829		
114031		73920			104		
110244		121478			6282		
2600		181525			26443		
2385694	189377	3639996	11477	13700	1211084	11800	36040
122492	1924	96936			78209		
288760	53691	566386			28132	11800	26317
1974442	133762	2976674	11477	13700	1104743		9723
14893		215321	4840		89042		
2942		56301	2820		54451		
5834		136927	2020		29731		
6117		22093			4860		
33077		352325	1345		248014		
33077		352325	1345		248014		
106775	19150	488117	11349		196467		
12685	6650	227193	3500		84123		
94090	12500	260924	7849		112344		
193061		489382	3540	12813	280025		
		12419					
4750		39052	740		10369		
22847		122475			155160		
6675		83636	2800		65188		
158789		231800		12813	49308		
7125		23405			198853		
4735		11190			708		
2390		12215			89313		
					108832		

7-11 按构成分固定资产投资(2016年)

单位：万元

行　业	Sector	本年完成投资 Investment Completed This Year
总　计	**Total**	**139463510**
农、林、牧、渔业	Farming, Forestry, Animal Husbandry and Fishery	19058982
农　业	Farming	7468871
林　业	Forestry	2349342
畜牧业	Animal Husbandry	7982031
渔　业	Fishery	174082
农、林、牧、渔服务业	Farming, Forestry, Animal Husbandry and Fishery Services	1084656
采矿业	Mining	10545566
煤炭开采和洗选业	Coal Mining and Washsing	7691758
石油和天然气开采业	Extraction of Petroleum and Natural Gas	630077
黑色金属矿采选业	Mining and Dressing of Ferrous Metals	835964
有色金属矿采选业	Mining and Dressing of Nonferrous Metals	259345
非金属矿采选业	Mining and Dressing of Nonmetal Ores	533270
开采辅助活动	Mining Auxiliary Activities	542789
其他采矿业	Others	52363
制造业	Manufacturing	26430488
农副食品加工业	Farm and Sideline Food Processing	3718849
食品制造业	Food Manufacturing	836751
酒、饮料和精制茶制造业	Alcohol, Beverage and Refined Tea Manufacturing	702469
烟草制品业	Tobacoo Manufaturing	70714
纺织业	Textile Industry	178714
纺织服装、服饰业	Manufacture of Garments and Accessories	86815
皮革、毛皮、羽毛及其制品和制鞋业	Manufacture of Leather, Fur, Feather and their Products and Footwear	44007
木材加工和木、竹、藤、棕、草制品业	Processing of Timber, Manufacture of Wood, Bamboo, Rattan, Palm, and Straw Products	428641
家具制造业	Manufacture of Funiture	152299
造纸和纸制品业	Manufacture of Paper and Paper Products	331508
印刷和记录媒介复制业	Printing and Record Medium Reproduction	62041
文教、工美、体育和娱乐用品制造业	Manufacture of Articles For Culture, Education and Sport Activity	160055
石油加工、炼焦和核燃料加工业	Petroleum Processing ,Coking and Nuclear Fuel Processing	1109023
化学原料和化学制品制造业	Manufacture Raw Chemical Materials and Chemical Products	3842813
医药制造业	Manufacture of Medical Products	1023404
化学纤维制造业	Manufacture of Chemical Fibers	16100
橡胶和塑料制品业	Manufacture of Rubber and Plastic Products	480709
非金属矿物制品业	Manufacture of Nonmetals Mineral Products	4589833
黑色金属冶炼和压延加工业	Smelting and Pressing of Ferrous Metals	1036949
有色金属冶炼和压延加工业	Smelting and Pressing of Nonferrous Metals	1399103
金属制品业	Manufacture of Metal Products	957458
通用设备制造业	Manufacture of Universal Purpose Equipment	783633

INVESTMENT IN FIXED ASSETS BY COMPOSITION(2016)

(10 000 yuan)

#住　宅 Residential Buildings	建筑工程 Construction	安装工程 Installation	设备工器具购置 Purchase of Equipment and Instruments	其他费用 Others
16654993	**91168968**	**13052403**	**21169672**	**14072467**
26699	14217635	1167013	1876195	1798139
1382	5781758	373313	605834	707966
12965	1566080	111793	145908	525561
12232	5999294	606122	962565	414050
	139602	17349	11671	5460
120	730901	58436	150217	145102
11739	5637284	1355720	2765400	787162
11724	4013469	888050	2207450	582789
	408544	86114	87110	48309
	476095	119792	207091	32986
	108376	23223	35631	92115
15	343771	46937	117929	24633
	241771	190979	108479	1560
	45258	625	1710	4770
41169	14308261	2846809	7854474	1420944
3728	2602005	302704	656083	158057
1384	502909	83077	213415	37350
7503	502591	43411	133730	22737
	18094	7676	44244	700
	78120	18093	72179	10322
	48641	12477	20860	4837
	24455	1572	10837	7143
14012	259657	59166	77343	32475
	107865	13334	23132	7968
	134467	115267	71848	9926
	41889	7675	10572	1905
	114630	14453	25513	5459
	456009	203749	351843	97422
1429	1664073	438177	1454374	286189
	667001	80231	243824	32348
	4279	1633	9059	1129
2300	251410	44882	167629	16788
1731	2729704	417794	1220858	221477
25	496609	125023	354306	61011
	676430	259707	417827	45139
10	510662	89332	312284	45180
5910	447976	71167	234897	29593

7-11 续表1

单位：万元

行　业	Sector	本年完成投资 Investment Completed This Year
专用设备制造业	Manufacture of Special Purpose Equipment	853479
汽车制造业	Manufacture of Motor Vehicles	642943
铁路、船舶、航空航天和其他运输设备制造业	Manufacture of Railways, Ships, Aviation, Aircrafts and Other Transportation Equipments	103870
电气机械和器材制造业	Manufacture of Electrical Equipment and Machinery	1020819
计算机、通信和其他电子设备制造业	Manufacture of Computer, Telecommunication and Other Electronic Equipments	921029
仪器仪表制造业	Manufacture of Measuring Instrument and Machinery	38501
其他制造业	Other Manufacturing	376560
废弃资源综合利用业	Comprehensive Utilization of Waste	339639
金属制品、机械和设备修理业	Repair of Metal Products, Machinery and Equipment	121760
电力、热力、燃气及水生产和供应业	Production and Supply of Electricity, Heat, Gas and Water	12640199
电力、热力生产和供应业	Production and Supply of Electricity and Heat	10040056
燃气生产和供应业	Production and Supply of Gas	1738974
水的生产和供应业	Production and Supply of Water	861169
建筑业	Construction	133551
房屋建筑业	Buildings Construction	61931
土木工程建筑业	Civil Engineering	19707
建筑安装业	Building Installation	7920
建筑装饰和其他建筑业	Building Decoration and Other Construction	43993
批发和零售业	Wholesale and Retail Trade	3636681
批发业	Wholesale Trade	1689542
零售业	Retail Trade	1947139
交通运输、仓储和邮政业	Transport, Storage and Post	9687299
铁路运输业	Railway Transport	1816588
道路运输业	Highway Transport	5040273
水上运输业	Water Transport	
航空运输业	Air Transport	2482
管道运输业	Transport Via Pipelines	23908
装卸搬运和运输代理业	Loading, Unloading and Other Transport Services	121809
仓储业	Storage	2662656
邮政业	Post	19583
住宿和餐饮业	Hotels and Catering Services	733148
住宿业	Hotels	458881
餐饮业	Catering Services	274267
信息传输、软件和信息技术服务业	Information Transmission, Software and Information Technology Services	1008837
电信、广播电视和卫星传输服务	Transimission Services of Telecommunication, Broadcast, Television and Satellite	373430
互联网和相关服务	Internet and Relative Services	454678
软件和信息技术服务业	Software and Information Technology Services	180729

continued

(10 000 yuan)

#住　宅 Residential Buildings	建筑工程 Construction	安装工程 Installation	设备工器具购置 Purchase of Equipment and Instruments	其他费用 Others
1420	495342	106263	213126	38748
1530	318164	59660	186662	78457
35	54212	18255	27619	3784
	417843	84031	462856	56089
	245884	82399	588911	3835
	8595	5867	19156	4883
100	234873	22077	86384	33226
52	140576	36037	104341	58685
	53296	21620	38762	8082
15131	5110113	2110865	4564575	854646
3233	3586327	1656913	4062357	734459
5188	1034997	283028	335401	85548
6710	488789	170924	166817	34639
	85682	20192	26501	1176
	42247	10371	9313	
	6770	415	12186	336
	5480	2420	10	10
	31185	6986	4992	830
55094	2587780	332923	428160	287818
5615	1190890	180735	213569	104348
49479	1396890	152188	214591	183470
14546	7175228	412108	1067456	1032507
	1077022	77124	85525	576917
6256	4053693	101955	572527	312098
	2480			2
	9936	1870	3628	8474
	79618	4729	30044	7418
8290	1941563	226430	367065	127598
	10916		8667	
20389	511999	62293	82234	76622
2389	302212	44966	48141	63562
18000	209787	17327	34093	13060
	392087	183351	363956	69443
	136193	96811	91843	48583
	140051	75048	229108	10471
	115843	11492	43005	10389

7-11 续表2

单位：万元

行　业	Sector	本年完成投资 Investment Completed This Year
金融业	Banking and Insurance	92029
货币金融服务	Monetary Banking	69793
资本市场服务	Capital Market	7147
保险业	Insurance	5669
其他金融业	Other Financial Activities	9420
房地产业	Real Estate Trade	27235230
房地产业	Real Estate Trade	27235230
租赁和商务服务业	Lease and Business Affairs Services	1625795
租赁业	Leasing	109265
商务服务业	Business Affairs Services	1516530
科学研究和技术服务业	Scientific Reseach and Technical Services	1045745
研究和试验发展	Reserch and Experimental Development	321645
专业技术服务业	Professional Technical Services	427041
科技推广和应用服务业	Services of Science and Technology Exchanges and Promotion	297059
水利、环境和公共设施管理业	Management of Water Conservancy, Environment and Public Facilities	18736035
水利管理业	Water Conservancy	2277188
生态保护和环境治理业	Ecological Protection and Environmental Management	1649800
公共设施管理业	Public Facilities	14809047
居民服务、修理和其他服务业	Resident Services, Repair and Other Services	420965
居民服务业	Residence Services	192792
机动车、电子产品和日用产品修理业	Repair of Motor Vehicles, Electronic Products and Daily Products	181230
其他服务业	Other Services	46943
教　育	Education	1867644
教　育	Education	1867644
卫生和社会工作	Health Care and Social Work	1668334
卫　生	Health Care	991731
社会工作	Social Work	676603
文化、体育和娱乐业	Culture, Sports and Recreation	1927597
新闻和出版业	Journalism and Publishing Activities	13791
广播、电视、电影和影视录音制作业	Broadcasting, Movies, Televisions and Audiovisual Activities	69216
文化艺术业	Culture and Arts Activities	1021856
体　育	Sports Activities	297773
娱乐业	Entertainment	524961
公共管理、社会保障和社会组织	Public Management, Social Security and Social Organization	969385
中国共产党机关	Organs of CPC	
国家机构	Government Agencies	510116
人民政协、民主党派	PPCC and Democratic Parties	
社会保障	Social Security	9865
群众团体、社会团体和其他成员组织	Mass Organizations, Social Organizations and Other Member Organizations	315491
基层群众自治组织	Grass Roots Self-governing Organizations	133913

continued

(10 000 yuan)

#住　宅 Residential Buildings	建筑工程 Construction	安装工程 Installation	设备工器具购置 Purchase of Equipment and Instruments	其他费用 Others
	73051	7035	9600	2343
	58448	6440	3015	1890
	1747		5400	
	5669			
	7187	595	1185	453
16302727	19546381	3161958	431358	4095533
16302727	19546381	3161958	431358	4095533
9780	1400822	40014	143140	41819
600	58579	9767	37645	3274
9180	1342243	30247	105495	38545
120	746693	100624	87958	110470
	213476	48830	18125	41214
	283548	41944	48655	52894
120	249669	9850	21178	16362
72608	13986048	829435	820538	3100014
200	1885205	62882	117860	211241
5820	853502	98933	253888	443477
66588	11247341	667620	448790	2445296
	332258	17949	49634	21124
	165610	5443	14922	6817
	138866	11272	23902	7190
	27782	1234	10810	7117
43066	1486437	121797	163961	95449
43066	1486437	121797	163961	95449
34979	1244754	96254	226312	101014
2990	699721	58777	170742	62491
31989	545033	37477	55570	38523
6946	1492040	135310	171244	129003
	9450	4341		
	47739	4583	14916	1978
4376	857798	35351	51718	76989
1920	201145	21913	40780	33935
650	375908	69122	63830	16101
	834415	50753	36976	47241
	403062	40734	34046	32274
	9304	434	34	93
	292610	8208	1389	13284
	129439	1377	1507	1590

7-12 按建设性质分固定资产投资(2016年)

单位：万元

行 业	Sector	新 建 New Construction
总 计	**Total**	**89574546**
农、林、牧、渔业	Farming, Forestry, Animal Husbandry and Fishery	16255607
农 业	Farming	6606434
林 业	Forestry	2036971
畜牧业	Animal Husbandry	6550767
渔 业	Fishery	136478
农、林、牧、渔服务业	Farming, Forestry, Animal Husbandry and Fishery Services	924957
采矿业	Mining	5200123
煤炭开采和洗选业	Coal Mining and Washsing	3485597
石油和天然气开采业	Extraction of Petroleum and Natural Gas	405541
黑色金属矿采选业	Mining and Dressing of Ferrous Metals	394918
有色金属矿采选业	Mining and Dressing of Nonferrous Metals	119815
非金属矿采选业	Mining and Dressing of Nonmetal Ores	294794
开采辅助活动	Mining Auxiliary Activities	462632
其他采矿业	Others	36826
制造业	Manufacturing	18449625
农副食品加工业	Farm and Sideline Food Processing	2730973
食品制造业	Food Manufacturing	625020
酒、饮料和精制茶制造业	Alcohol, Beverage and Refined Tea Manufacturing	456441
烟草制品业	Tobacoo Manufaturing	70078
纺织业	Textile Industry	123180
纺织服装、服饰业	Manufacture of Garments and Accessories	50210
皮革、毛皮、羽毛及其制品和制鞋业	Manufacture of Leather, Fur, Feather and their Products and Footwear	11862
木材加工和木、竹、藤、棕、草制品业	Processing of Timber, Manufacture of Wood, Bamboo, Rattan, Palm, and Straw Products	306866
家具制造业	Manufacture of Funiture	105241
造纸和纸制品业	Manufacture of Paper and Paper Products	178296
印刷和记录媒介复制业	Printing and Record Medium Reproduction	56423
文教、工美、体育和娱乐用品制造业	Manufacture of Articles For Culture, Education and Sport Activity	126848
石油加工、炼焦和核燃料加工业	Petroleum Processing ,Coking and Nuclear Fuel Processing	875757
化学原料和化学制品制造业	Manufacture Raw Chemical Materials and Chemical Products	2945987
医药制造业	Manufacture of Medical Products	716489
化学纤维制造业	Manufacture of Chemical Fibers	16100
橡胶和塑料制品业	Manufacture of Rubber and Plastic Products	372861
非金属矿物制品业	Manufacture of Nonmetals Mineral Products	3088443
黑色金属冶炼和压延加工业	Smelting and Pressing of Ferrous Metals	566966
有色金属冶炼和压延加工业	Smelting and Pressing of Nonferrous Metals	601547
金属制品业	Manufacture of Metal Products	625953
通用设备制造业	Manufacture of Universal Purpose Equipment	567611

注：本表不含房地产开发投资。

Note: Investment in this table doesn't include investment in real estate development.

INVESTMENT IN FIXED ASSETS BY TYPE OF CONSTRUCTION(2016)

(10 000 yuan)

扩　建 Expansion	改建和技术改造 Reconstruction and Technical Reformation	单纯建造生活设施 Construction of Living Facilities	迁　建 Movement Construction	恢　复 Resumption Construction	单纯购置 Purchase of Equipment and Instruments
15778096	**11811368**	**4011479**	**345818**	**209537**	**1759134**
2600033	192922		550	4170	5700
823893	33844				4700
259379	52992				
1390112	39602		550		1000
37604					
89045	66484			4170	
1847726	2849640	14360	8684	9100	615933
1129726	2439953	14360	1900	9100	611122
201936	22600				
222619	218427				
95921	43609				
191574	42998		3904		
5950	66516		2880		4811
	15537				
4840579	2647565	30950	81354	8510	371905
872623	68765	21550	16000		8938
171288	24128				16315
207778	36850				1400
	614				22
38836	6372				10326
36605					
27239	4906				
112697	9078				
47058					
80355	69590				3267
5618					
33207					
78152	155114				
710980	102941	4900	7000	8510	62495
150076	91225		24825		40789
100485	7363				
1098230	343755		21281		38124
200233	260732		1300		7718
134752	662804				
170822	108743	4500			47440
94369	91148				30505

7-12 续表1

单位：万元

行 业	Sector	新 建 New Construction
专用设备制造业	Manufacture of Special Purpose Equipment	603428
汽车制造业	Manufacture of Motor Vehicles	455277
铁路、船舶、航空航天和其他运输设备制造业	Manufacture of Railways, Ships, Aviation, Aircrafts and Other Transportation Equipments	82798
电气机械和器材制造业	Manufacture of Electrical Equipment and Machinery	806374
计算机、通信和其他电子设备制造业	Manufacture of Computer, Telecommunication and Other Electronic Equipments	605903
仪器仪表制造业	Manufacture of Measuring Instrument and Machinery	32202
其他制造业	Other Manufacturing	331857
废弃资源综合利用业	Comprehensive Utilization of Waste	258545
金属制品、机械和设备修理业	Repair of Metal Products, Machinery and Equipment	54089
电力、热力、燃气及水生产和供应业	Production and Supply of Electricity, Heat, Gas and Water	9841532
电力、热力生产和供应业	Production and Supply of Electricity and Heat	7766789
燃气生产和供应业	Production and Supply of Gas	1481694
水的生产和供应业	Production and Supply of Water	593049
建筑业	Construction	91159
房屋建筑业	Buildings Construction	57111
土木工程建筑业	Civil Engineering	10267
建筑安装业	Building Installation	
建筑装饰和其他建筑业	Building Decoration and Other Construction	23781
批发和零售业	Wholesale and Retail Trade	2885204
批发业	Wholesale Trade	1336081
零售业	Retail Trade	1549123
交通运输、仓储和邮政业	Transport, Storage and Post	6965822
铁路运输业	Railway Transport	1713502
道路运输业	Highway Transport	2989971
水上运输业	Water Transport	
航空运输业	Air Transport	2482
管道运输业	Transport Via Pipelines	7767
装卸搬运和运输代理业	Loading, Unloading and Other Transport Services	118409
仓储业	Storage	2130831
邮政业	Post	2860
住宿和餐饮业	Hotels and Catering Services	526390
住宿业	Hotels	299357
餐饮业	Catering Services	227033
信息传输、软件和信息技术服务业	Information Transmission, Software and Information Technology Services	777959
电信、广播电视和卫星传输服务	Transimission Services of Telecommunication, Broadcast, Television and Satellite	307847
互联网和相关服务	Internet and Relative Services	289965
软件和信息技术服务业	Software and Information Technology Services	180147

continued

(10 000 yuan)

扩　建 Expansion	改建和技术改造 Reconstruction and Technical Reformation	单纯建造生活设施 Construction of Living Facilities	迁　建 Movement Construction	恢　复 Resumption Construction	单纯购置 Purchase of Equipment and Instruments
148954	92787				8310
123504	64162				
17537	587		2948		
92732	31277				90436
23785	277521		8000		5820
3440	2859				
22380	22323				
22951	58143				
13893	53778				
1626174	1074376		874		97243
1328922	847280		874		96191
190560	65668				1052
106692	161428				
22847	3860				15685
					4820
					9440
4060	3860				
18787					1425
531339	124191	48000	36587		11360
280768	34552		33261		4880
250571	89639	48000	3326		6480
848541	1448727	5967		1740	416502
13946	69844				19296
304060	1369367	900		1740	374235
8474		5067			2600
3400					
510605	9516				11704
8056					8667
154194	17696	4850			30018
111660	17496	4850			25518
42534	200				4500
52234	153262				25382
18774	46809				
33460	106453				24800
					582

7-12 续表2

单位：万元

行　业	Sector	新　建 New Construction
金融业	Banking and Insurance	56054
货币金融服务	Monetary Banking	39218
资本市场服务	Capital Market	1747
保险业	Insurance	5669
其他金融业	Other Financial Activities	9420
房地产业	Real Estate Trade	6717567
房地产业	Real Estate Trade	6717567
租赁和商务服务业	Lease and Business Affairs Services	1525025
租赁业	Leasing	92926
商务服务业	Business Affairs Services	1432099
科学研究和技术服务业	Scientific Reseach and Technical Services	983771
研究和试验发展	Reserch and Experimental Development	313756
专业技术服务业	Professional Technical Services	384508
科技推广和应用服务业	Services of Science and Technology Exchanges and Promotion	285507
水利、环境和公共设施管理业	Management of Water Conservancy, Environment and Public Facilities	14370411
水利管理业	Water Conservancy	1526077
生态保护和环境治理业	Ecological Protection and Environmental Management	978688
公共设施管理业	Public Facilities	11865646
居民服务、修理和其他服务业	Resident Services, Repair and Other Services	313127
居民服务业	Residence Services	170228
机动车、电子产品和日用产品修理业	Repair of Motor Vehicles, Electronic Products and Daily Products	120083
其他服务业	Other Services	22816
教　育	Education	1260340
教　育	Education	1260340
卫生和社会工作	Health Care and Social Work	1198927
卫　生	Health Care	635578
社会工作	Social Work	563349
文化、体育和娱乐业	Culture, Sports and Recreation	1544457
新闻和出版业	Journalism and Publishing Activities	12419
广播、电视、电影和影视录音制作业	Broadcasting, Movies, Televisions and Audiovisual Activities	55769
文化艺术业	Culture and Arts Activities	718564
体　育	Sports Activities	262389
娱乐业	Entertainment	495316
公共管理、社会保障和社会组织	Public Management, Social Security and Social Organization	611446
中国共产党机关	Organs of CPC	
国家机构	Government Agencies	340713
人民政协、民主党派	PPCC and Democratic Parties	
社会保障	Social Security	9315
群众团体、社会团体和其他成员组织	Mass Organizations, Social Organizations and Other Member Organizations	156929
基层群众自治组织	Grass Roots Self-governing Organizations	104489

continued

(10 000 yuan)

扩　建 Expansion	改建和技术改造 Reconstruction and Technical Reformation	单纯建造生活设施 Construction of Living Facilities	迁　建 Movement Construction	恢　复 Resumption Construction	单纯购置 Purchase of Equipment and Instruments
20405	10170				5400
20405	10170				
					5400
434137	210353	3855064	43877	700	
434137	210353	3855064	43877	700	
45909	11900			31797	11164
5175					11164
40734	11900			31797	
47768	6237		2490		5479
	2410				5479
39466	577		2490		
8302	3250				
1559780	2666344	52288	11500	71747	3965
145003	606108				
61093	547434		8500	54085	
1353684	1512802	52288	3000	17662	3965
84905	16217		1804		4912
14600	7964				
51873	4658		1804		2812
18432	3595				2100
365328	136534		27522	50312	27608
365328	136534		27522	50312	27608
221307	44689		106676		96735
129316	38426		106676		81735
91991	6263				15000
231436	122100			23761	5843
1372					
6260	2437				4750
166977	111971			23761	583
29392	5992				
27435	1700				510
243454	74585		23900	7700	8300
69371	67832		23900		8300
	550				
150862				7700	
23221	6203				

7-13 按控股情况分固定资产投资(2016年)

单位：万元

行 业	Sector	本年完成投资 Investment Completed This Year
总 计	**Total**	**139463510**
农、林、牧、渔业	Farming, Forestry, Animal Husbandry and Fishery	19058982
农 业	Farming	7468871
林 业	Forestry	2349342
畜牧业	Animal Husbandry	7982031
渔 业	Fishery	174082
农、林、牧、渔服务业	Farming, Forestry, Animal Husbandry and Fishery Services	1084656
采矿业	Mining	10545566
煤炭开采和洗选业	Coal Mining and Washsing	7691758
石油和天然气开采业	Extraction of Petroleum and Natural Gas	630077
黑色金属矿采选业	Mining and Dressing of Ferrous Metals	835964
有色金属矿采选业	Mining and Dressing of Nonferrous Metals	259345
非金属矿采选业	Mining and Dressing of Nonmetal Ores	533270
开采辅助活动	Mining Auxiliary Activities	542789
其他采矿业	Others	52363
制造业	Manufacturing	26430488
农副食品加工业	Farm and Sideline Food Processing	3718849
食品制造业	Food Manufacturing	836751
酒、饮料和精制茶制造业	Alcohol, Beverage and Refined Tea Manufacturing	702469
烟草制品业	Tobacoo Manufaturing	70714
纺织业	Textile Industry	178714
纺织服装、服饰业	Manufacture of Garments and Accessories	86815
皮革、毛皮、羽毛及其制品和制鞋业	Manufacture of Leather, Fur, Feather and their Products and Footwear	44007
木材加工和木、竹、藤、棕、草制品业	Processing of Timber, Manufacture of Wood, Bamboo, Rattan, Palm, and Straw Products	428641
家具制造业	Manufacture of Funiture	152299
造纸和纸制品业	Manufacture of Paper and Paper Products	331508
印刷和记录媒介复制业	Printing and Record Medium Reproduction	62041
文教、工美、体育和娱乐用品制造业	Manufacture of Articles For Culture, Education and Sport Activity	160055
石油加工、炼焦和核燃料加工业	Petroleum Processing ,Coking and Nuclear Fuel Processing	1109023
化学原料和化学制品制造业	Manufacture Raw Chemical Materials and Chemical Products	3842813
医药制造业	Manufacture of Medical Products	1023404
化学纤维制造业	Manufacture of Chemical Fibers	16100
橡胶和塑料制品业	Manufacture of Rubber and Plastic Products	480709
非金属矿物制品业	Manufacture of Nonmetals Mineral Products	4589833
黑色金属冶炼和压延加工业	Smelting and Pressing of Ferrous Metals	1036949
有色金属冶炼和压延加工业	Smelting and Pressing of Nonferrous Metals	1399103
金属制品业	Manufacture of Metal Products	957458
通用设备制造业	Manufacture of Universal Purpose Equipment	783633

INVESTMENT IN FIXED ASSETS BY SHARE HOLDING(2016)

(10 000 yuan)

国有控股 State-owned	集体控股 Collective-owned	私人控股 Private	港澳台商控股 Investment from Hong Kong, Mcao and Taiwan	外商控股 Foreign Investment	其　他 Others
48546614	**10452696**	**66839110**	**1297909**	**492426**	**11834755**
2121458	1094581	11559871		26120	4256952
764128	685911	4086599			1932233
789640	78341	1089278			392083
257343	186075	5724984		26120	1787509
17488		112875			43719
292859	144254	546135			101408
5338841	270571	4579198		70990	285966
4203720	248499	2957074		14355	268110
410347	3678	157617		56635	1800
114448		705460			16056
106089		153256			
3778	13479	516013			
498169	4915	39705			
2290		50073			
3041488	790959	20521500	760753	22070	1293718
151185	91704	2837678			638282
61	18382	777234			41074
29810	18480	621538	5090	6043	21508
67214		3500			
	1672	172142			4900
3850	4800	76150			2015
	3860	40147			
2685	13266	402970			9720
4710		147239			350
1983	9316	320209			
4100		45023			12918
20361	4660	132076			2958
389275		609570	57463		52715
1010867	76173	2691664			64109
60475	27704	765610	24825		144790
6148		9952			
13748	27411	431430			8120
169926	127172	4149229	8960	5370	129176
57565	500	950729	21396		6759
307786	207444	822628	48245		13000
18765	14521	868533	7750		47889
41095	21442	715396	4850	850	

7-13 续表1

单位：万元

行　　业	Sector	本年完成投资 Investment Completed This Year
专用设备制造业	Manufacture of Special Purpose Equipment	853479
汽车制造业	Manufacture of Motor Vehicles	642943
铁路、船舶、航空航天和其他运输设备制造业	Manufacture of Railways, Ships, Aviation, Aircrafts and Other Transportation Equipments	103870
电气机械和器材制造业	Manufacture of Electrical Equipment and Machinery	1020819
计算机、通信和其他电子设备制造业	Manufacture of Computer, Telecommunication and Other Electronic Equipments	921029
仪器仪表制造业	Manufacture of Measuring Instrument and Machinery	38501
其他制造业	Other Manufacturing	376560
废弃资源综合利用业	Comprehensive Utilization of Waste	339639
金属制品、机械和设备修理业	Repair of Metal Products, Machinery and Equipment	121760
电力、热力、燃气及水生产和供应业	Production and Supply of Electricity, Heat, Gas and Water	12640199
电力、热力生产和供应业	Production and Supply of Electricity and Heat	10040056
燃气生产和供应业	Production and Supply of Gas	1738974
水的生产和供应业	Production and Supply of Water	861169
建筑业	Construction	133551
房屋建筑业	Buildings Construction	61931
土木工程建筑业	Civil Engineering	19707
建筑安装业	Building Installation	7920
建筑装饰和其他建筑业	Building Decoration and Other Construction	43993
批发和零售业	Wholesale and Retail Trade	3636681
批发业	Wholesale Trade	1689542
零售业	Retail Trade	1947139
交通运输、仓储和邮政业	Transport, Storage and Post	9687299
铁路运输业	Railway Transport	1816588
道路运输业	Highway Transport	5040273
水上运输业	Water Transport	
航空运输业	Air Transport	2482
管道运输业	Transport Via Pipelines	23908
装卸搬运和运输代理业	Loading, Unloading and Other Transport Services	121809
仓储业	Storage	2662656
邮政业	Post	19583
住宿和餐饮业	Hotels and Catering Services	733148
住宿业	Hotels	458881
餐饮业	Catering Services	274267
信息传输、软件和信息技术服务业	Information Transmission, Software and Information Technology Services	1008837
电信、广播电视和卫星传输服务	Transimission Services of Telecommunication, Broadcast, Television and Satellite	373430
互联网和相关服务	Internet and Relative Services	454678
软件和信息技术服务业	Software and Information Technology Services	180729

continued

(10 000 yuan)

国有控股 State-owned	集体控股 Collective-owned	私人控股 Private	港澳台商控股 Investment from Hong Kong, Mcao and Taiwan	外商控股 Foreign Investment	其　他 Others
89651	34478	725650			3700
71547	20599	529604			21193
17715		82305			3850
142540	48804	773570		9807	46098
138276	3991	209473	566639		2650
18449		19216			836
66522	480	307883	1535		140
77467	12796	221338	14000		14038
57712	1304	61814			930
7875077	384831	3384207	268771	245795	481518
6694969	198713	2418593	256708	243010	228063
672925	100301	716620	12063		237065
507183	85817	248994		2785	16390
37685		95241			625
18644		43287			
13810		5897			
3860		3960			100
1371		42097			525
379178	379298	2668512			209693
175473	190882	1246331			76856
203705	188416	1422181			132837
5680922	401175	3115229			489973
1447960	3512	319754			45362
3969040	223793	697868			149572
332		2150			
15930		7978			
13190	4865	97424			6330
225803	169005	1987195			280653
8667		2860			8056
133611	117378	469173			12986
108160	66563	274842			9316
25451	50815	194331			3670
454437		336347	65483	12512	140058
282274		25222	16986	12512	36436
122395		188609	48497		95177
49768		122516			8445

7-13 续表2

单位：万元

行 业	Sector	本年完成投资 Investment Completed This Year
金融业	Banking and Insurance	92029
货币金融服务	Monetary Banking	69793
资本市场服务	Capital Market	7147
保险业	Insurance	5669
其他金融业	Other Financial Activities	9420
房地产业	Real Estate Trade	27235230
房地产业	Real Estate Trade	27235230
租赁和商务服务业	Lease and Business Affairs Services	1625795
租赁业	Leasing	109265
商务服务业	Business Affairs Services	1516530
科学研究和技术服务业	Scientific Reseach and Technical Services	1045745
研究和试验发展	Reserch and Experimental Development	321645
专业技术服务业	Professional Technical Services	427041
科技推广和应用服务业	Services of Science and Technology Exchanges and Promotion	297059
水利、环境和公共设施管理业	Management of Water Conservancy, Environment and Public Facilities	18736035
水利管理业	Water Conservancy	2277188
生态保护和环境治理业	Ecological Protection and Environmental Management	1649800
公共设施管理业	Public Facilities	14809047
居民服务、修理和其他服务业	Resident Services, Repair and Other Services	420965
居民服务业	Residence Services	192792
机动车、电子产品和日用产品修理业	Repair of Motor Vehicles, Electronic Products and Daily Products	181230
其他服务业	Other Services	46943
教 育	Education	1867644
教 育	Education	1867644
卫生和社会工作	Health Care and Social Work	1668334
卫 生	Health Care	991731
社会工作	Social Work	676603
文化、体育和娱乐业	Culture, Sports and Recreation	1927597
新闻和出版业	Journalism and Publishing Activities	13791
广播、电视、电影和影视录音制作业	Broadcasting, Movies, Televisions and Audiovisual Activities	69216
文化艺术业	Culture and Arts Activities	1021856
体 育	Sports Activities	297773
娱乐业	Entertainment	524961
公共管理、社会保障和社会组织	Public Management, Social Security and Social Organization	969385
中国共产党机关	Organs of CPC	
国家机构	Government Agencies	510116
人民政协、民主党派	PPCC and Democratic Parties	
社会保障	Social Security	9865
群众团体、社会团体和其他成员组织	Mass Organizations, Social Organizations and Other Member Organizations	315491
基层群众自治组织	Grass Roots Self-governing Organizations	133913

continued

(10 000 yuan)

国有控股 State-owned	集体控股 Collective-owned	私人控股 Private	港澳台商控股 Investment from Hong Kong, Mcao and Taiwan	外商控股 Foreign Investment	其　他 Others
26202	5363	56984			3480
19458	5363	44292			680
1747		2600			2800
		5669			
4997		4423			
7262602	4264392	12341963	202902	99372	3063999
7262602	4264392	12341963	202902	99372	3063999
348347	649489	572403			55556
5134	4000	75831			24300
343213	645489	496572			31256
505347	29230	462777			48391
220195		81120			20330
210015	5548	203766			7712
75137	23682	177891			20349
11787137	1225008	4589528		15567	1118795
1853358	182788	107842			133200
774213	75372	723230		7000	69985
9159566	966848	3758456		8567	915610
78132	92145	232576			18112
64709	58839	65566			3678
4200	27499	135097			14434
9223	5807	31913			
1173632	120157	504904			68951
1173632	120157	504904			68951
850474	148316	611937			57607
649735	56254	245380			40362
200739	92062	366557			17245
763067	419519	657946			87065
1372		12419			
14305	7615	47296			
594352	252011	122811			52682
119919	82443	93111			2300
33119	77450	382309			32083
688977	60284	78814			141310
488194	5289	15925			708
7302	2563				
190931	14930	62889			46741
2550	37502				93861

7-14 按资金来源分固定资产投资(2016年)

单位：万元

行　业	Sector	本年资金来源小计 Total Source of Funds
总　计	**Total**	**116796281**
农、林、牧、渔业	Farming, Forestry, Animal Husbandry and Fishery	16690135
农　业	Farming	6207617
林　业	Forestry	2126630
畜牧业	Animal Husbandry	7202297
渔　业	Fishery	170871
农、林、牧、渔服务业	Farming, Forestry, Animal Husbandry and Fishery Services	982720
采矿业	Mining	8972733
煤炭开采和洗选业	Coal Mining and Washsing	6475562
石油和天然气开采业	Extraction of Petroleum and Natural Gas	494413
黑色金属矿采选业	Mining and Dressing of Ferrous Metals	744965
有色金属矿采选业	Mining and Dressing of Nonferrous Metals	166621
非金属矿采选业	Mining and Dressing of Nonmetal Ores	502864
开采辅助活动	Mining Auxiliary Activities	535863
其他采矿业	Others	52445
制造业	Manufacturing	22615339
农副食品加工业	Farm and Sideline Food Processing	3223838
食品制造业	Food Manufacturing	731766
酒、饮料和精制茶制造业	Alcohol, Beverage and Refined Tea Manufacturing	557990
烟草制品业	Tobacoo Manufaturing	119474
纺织业	Textile Industry	143717
纺织服装、服饰业	Manufacture of Garments and Accessories	73116
皮革、毛皮、羽毛及其制品和制鞋业	Manufacture of Leather, Fur, Feather and their Products and Footwear	38097
木材加工和木、竹、藤、棕、草制品业	Processing of Timber, Manufacture of Wood, Bamboo, Rattan, Palm, and Straw Products	402857
家具制造业	Manufacture of Funiture	125181
造纸和纸制品业	Manufacture of Paper and Paper Products	256535
印刷和记录媒介复制业	Printing and Record Medium Reproduction	55833
文教、工美、体育和娱乐用品制造业	Manufacture of Articles For Culture, Education and Sport Activity	142885
石油加工、炼焦和核燃料加工业	Petroleum Processing ,Coking and Nuclear Fuel Processing	811746
化学原料和化学制品制造业	Manufacture Raw Chemical Materials and Chemical Products	2972058
医药制造业	Manufacture of Medical Products	935919
化学纤维制造业	Manufacture of Chemical Fibers	9630
橡胶和塑料制品业	Manufacture of Rubber and Plastic Products	433711
非金属矿物制品业	Manufacture of Nonmetals Mineral Products	4062442
黑色金属冶炼和压延加工业	Smelting and Pressing of Ferrous Metals	786532
有色金属冶炼和压延加工业	Smelting and Pressing of Nonferrous Metals	1209902
金属制品业	Manufacture of Metal Products	849246
通用设备制造业	Manufacture of Universal Purpose Equipment	723479

INVESTMENT IN FIXED ASSETS BY SOURCE OF FUNDS(2016)

(10 000 yuan)

国家预算内资金 State Budgetary Appropriation	国内贷款 Domestic Loans	利用外资 Foreign Investment	自筹资金 Self-raised Funds	#企事业单位自有资金 Own Funds of Enterprises and Institutions	其他资金 Others
7327910	**6991775**	**55792**	**92214849**	**33743562**	**10205955**
522629	324273		15517084	3919578	326149
125311	81987		5807168	1858685	193151
202433	16026		1860656	285863	47515
41905	211585		6900583	1598574	48224
10300	200		155383	16769	4988
142680	14475		793294	159687	32271
44393	404471	19000	8215239	3179984	289630
35345	389731		5844400	2611578	206086
9048	280	19000	451085	228326	15000
	7110		672090	154366	65765
	500		166121	61690	
	6850		494829	113959	1185
			535863	10010	
			50851	55	1594
72539	695985	100	21487084	8508657	359631
27558	86682		3076003	718675	33595
	19380		688082	224379	24304
	13300		541870	147547	2820
			119474	29722	
	2720		133417	32349	7580
			73116	11889	
	930		37167	10405	
	7917		391740	178130	3200
	1000		124181	40344	
	3140		235893	28477	17502
			54953	21450	880
19312	800		118127	33646	4646
	44070	100	763891	452442	3685
	194243		2665002	1279509	112813
6700	25926		897553	287290	5740
			7510	4610	2120
	3800		422206	136184	7705
1579	56310		3962997	1383332	41556
	8000		772343	258066	6189
	500		1208002	706633	1400
3204	17100		814559	381410	14383
	9190		710539	342631	3750

7-14 续表1

单位：万元

行　业	Sector	本年资金来源小计 Total Source of Funds
专用设备制造业	Manufacture of Special Purpose Equipment	764921
汽车制造业	Manufacture of Motor Vehicles	552840
铁路、船舶、航空航天和其他运输设备制造业	Manufacture of Railways, Ships, Aviation, Aircrafts and Other Transportation Equipments	89210
电气机械和器材制造业	Manufacture of Electrical Equipment and Machinery	1003370
计算机、通信和其他电子设备制造业	Manufacture of Computer, Telecommunication and Other Electronic Equipments	786651
仪器仪表制造业	Manufacture of Measuring Instrument and Machinery	35184
其他制造业	Other Manufacturing	307162
废弃资源综合利用业	Comprehensive Utilization of Waste	299017
金属制品、机械和设备修理业	Repair of Metal Products, Machinery and Equipment	111030
电力、热力、燃气及水生产和供应业	Production and Supply of Electricity, Heat, Gas and Water	9598106
电力、热力生产和供应业	Production and Supply of Electricity and Heat	7358814
燃气生产和供应业	Production and Supply of Gas	1536235
水的生产和供应业	Production and Supply of Water	703057
建筑业	Construction	126633
房屋建筑业	Buildings Construction	59077
土木工程建筑业	Civil Engineering	19688
建筑安装业	Building Installation	7922
建筑装饰和其他建筑业	Building Decoration and Other Construction	39946
批发和零售业	Wholesale and Retail Trade	3096735
批发业	Wholesale Trade	1495607
零售业	Retail Trade	1601128
交通运输、仓储和邮政业	Transport, Storage and Post	7766003
铁路运输业	Railway Transport	1829502
道路运输业	Highway Transport	3591654
水上运输业	Water Transport	
航空运输业	Air Transport	2667
管道运输业	Transport Via Pipelines	19872
装卸搬运和运输代理业	Loading, Unloading and Other Transport Services	99026
仓储业	Storage	2203698
邮政业	Post	19584
住宿和餐饮业	Hotels and Catering Services	561255
住宿业	Hotels	370173
餐饮业	Catering Services	191082
信息传输、软件和信息技术服务业	Information Transmission, Software and Information Technology Services	861716
电信、广播电视和卫星传输服务	Transimission Services of Telecommunication, Broadcast, Television and Satellite	320331
互联网和相关服务	Internet and Relative Services	344385
软件和信息技术服务业	Software and Information Technology Services	197000

continued

(10 000 yuan)

国家预算内资金 State Budgetary Appropriation	国内贷款 Domestic Loans	利用外资 Foreign Investment	自筹资金 Self-raised Funds	#企事业单位自有资金 Own Funds of Enterprises and Instiutions	其他资金 Others
671	22802		724897	320073	16551
	4900		537132	284946	10808
	2030		86810	23515	370
6549	68820		925246	281488	2755
	49245		735206	659837	2200
977	300		30928	10250	2979
	1380		277982	79934	27800
5989	51300		239428	66841	2300
	200		110830	72653	
483098	2238036	16257	6633983	2569060	226732
363242	2087469	16157	4710079	1779127	181867
35767	125345	100	1344454	543238	30569
84089	25222		579450	246695	14296
8223			118408	34948	2
			59077	23668	
4363			15325	260	
3860			4060	4060	2
			39946	6960	
21297	65096		2886501	773855	123841
16847	34142		1350498	222317	94120
4450	30954		1536003	551538	29721
1307671	957099	2019	4986731	1372934	512483
253500	719970		796032	103399	60000
1030554	205983	2019	1948164	461641	404934
367			2300		
			13952		5920
	2140		96886	47802	
23250	29006		2109813	760092	41629
			19584		
965	1430		539758	232729	19102
737			356072	145737	13364
228	1430		183686	86992	5738
16228			824438	322960	21050
5625			313856	177908	850
1186			343199	89569	
9417			167383	55483	20200

7-14 续表2

单位：万元

行　业	Sector	本年资金来源小计 Total Source of Funds
金融业	Banking and Insurance	86918
货币金融服务	Monetary Banking	66434
资本市场服务	Capital Market	7147
保险业	Insurance	5689
其他金融服务	Other Financial Activities	7648
房地产业	Real Estate Trade	25347304
房地产业	Real Estate Trade	25347304
租赁和商务服务业	Lease and Business Affairs Services	1227874
租赁业	Leasing	97121
商务服务业	Business Affairs Services	1130753
科学研究和技术服务业	Scientific Reseach and Technical Services	845087
研究和试验发展	Reserch and Experimental Development	165004
专业技术服务业	Professional Technical Services	404451
科技推广和应用服务业	Services of Science and Technology Exchanges and Promotion	275632
水利、环境和公共设施管理业	Management of Water Conservancy, Environment and Public Facilities	13423222
水利管理业	Water Conservancy	1993895
生态保护和环境治理业	Ecological Protection and Environmental Management	1435501
公共设施管理业	Public Facilities	9993826
居民服务、修理和其他服务业	Resident Services, Repair and Other Services	331965
居民服务业	Residence Services	149010
机动车、电子产品和日用产品修理业	Repair of Motor Vehicles, Electronic Products and Daily Products	142182
其他服务业	Other Services	40773
教　育	Education	1487889
教　育	Education	1487889
卫生和社会工作	Health Care and Social Work	1450776
卫　生	Health Care	851119
社会工作	Social Work	599657
文化、体育和娱乐业	Culture, Sports and Recreation	1512048
新闻和出版业	Journalism and Publishing Activities	13791
广播、电视、电影和影视录音制作业	Broadcasting, Movies, Televisions and Audiovisual Activities	47603
文化艺术业	Culture and Arts Activities	761652
体　育	Sports Activities	254174
娱乐业	Entertainment	434828
公共管理、社会保障和社会组织	Public Management, Social Security and Social Organization	794543
中国共产党机关	Organs of CPC	
国家机构	Government Agencies	388084
人民政协、民主党派	PPCC and Democratic Parties	
社会保障	Social Security	10618
群众团体、社会团体和其他成员组织	Mass Organizations, Social Organizations and Other Member Organizations	271454
基层群众自治组织	Grass Roots Self-governing Organizations	124387

continued

(10 000 yuan)

国家预算内资金 State Budgetary Appropriation	国内贷款 Domestic Loans	利用外资 Foreign Investment	自筹资金 Self-raisied Funds	#企事业单位自有资金 Own Funds of Enterprises and Instiutions	其他资金 Others
2020			84898	24788	
2020			64414	17563	
			7147	2600	
			5689		
			7648	4625	
530452	1066567	3650	16351782	7521787	7394853
530452	1066567	3650	16351782	7521787	7394853
40677	3080		1137447	241535	46670
	680		95461	8778	980
40677	2400		1041986	232757	45690
74700	28903		685027	178591	56457
13494	6438		143072	76083	2000
48317			349499	49178	6635
12889	22465		192456	53330	47822
3059820	1055974	14766	8757842	3398456	534820
749821	333907	2825	792347	174977	114995
192324	36242	5000	1176988	471949	24947
2117675	685825	6941	6788507	2751530	394878
18269	6800		288003	68166	18893
16184	4000		117294	20112	11532
			135591	40516	6591
2085	2800		35118	7538	770
402870	78964		904173	401000	101882
402870	78964		904173	401000	101882
281252	19380		1117678	349675	32466
236305	15080		576317	241794	23417
44947	4300		541361	107881	9049
190331	36717		1207904	537975	77096
			13791	8919	
9811			32242	9131	5550
144837	25857		562341	277889	28617
26362	6180		190886	75826	30746
9321	4680		408644	166210	12183
250476	9000		470869	106884	64198
243553	9000		108472	50604	27059
5962			4656	508	
			234315	48964	37139
961			123426	6808	

7-15 固定资产投资规模及新增生产能力(2016年)

生产能力(或效益)名称		Item	建设规模 Construction Scale
原煤开采	(万吨／年)	Coal Mining (10 000 tons/year)	18694
焦　炭	(万吨／年)	Coke (10 000 tons/year)	1521
天然气开采	(亿立方米／年)	Extraction of Natural Gas(100 million cu.m/year)	144
石油加工：裂化设备能力	(处理万吨／年)	Petroleum Processing: Capacity of Cracking Equipment (10 000 tons/year)	20
铁矿开采(原矿)	(万吨／年)	Iron-Ore Mining (10 000 tons/year)	1119
生　铁	(万吨／年)	Pig Iron (10 000 tons/year)	10
钢　材	(万吨／年)	Rolled Steel (10 000 tons /year)	166
铜采矿(原矿)	(万吨／年)	Copper Ore Mining (10 000 tons/year)	93
铜选矿：铜含量	(吨／年)	Copper Ore Dressing: Copper Content (ton/year)	2000
铅冶炼	(万吨／年)	Plumbum Smelting (10 000 tons /year)	24000
锌冶炼	(吨／年)	Zinc Smelting (ton/year)	216000
氧化铝	(吨／年)	Oxide Aluminium (ton/year)	4400000
铝加工	(吨／年)	Aluminium Fabrication (ton/year)	521302
黄　金	(公斤／年)	Gold (kg/year)	3250
发电机组容量	(万千瓦)	Capacity of Power Generating Sets (10 000 kw)	3453
火力发电	(万千瓦)	Fire Power (10 000 kw)	2758
风力发电	(万千瓦)	Wind Power (10 000 kw)	442
太阳能发电	(万千瓦)	Solar Power (10 000 kw)	224
其　他	(万千瓦)	Others (10 000 kw)	29
输电线路长度(11万伏及以上)	(公里)	Length of Power Transmission Line (≥110 kv) (km)	4040
水　泥	(万吨／年)	Cement (10 000 tons/year)	408
农用氮、磷、钾化学肥料	(吨／年)	Chemical Fertilizers (ton/year)	1952000
氮　肥	(吨／年)	Nitrogen Fertilizers (ton/year)	1396500
磷　肥	(吨／年)	Phosphate Fertilizers (ton/year)	48000
钾　肥	(吨／年)	Potash Fertilizers (ton/year)	507500
化学农药原药	(吨／年)	Chemical Pesticides (ton/year)	1006
塑料树脂及共聚物	(吨／年)	Plastic Colophony and Polymer (ton/year)	510500
合成橡胶	(吨／年)	Synthetic Rubber (ton/year)	44500
内燃机	(台／年)	Internal Combustion Engine (unit/year)	100009
内燃机	(万千瓦／年)	Internal Combustion Engine (10 000 kw/year)	40
汽车制造	(辆／年)	Motor Vehicles (unit/year)	25000
客车制造	(辆／年)	Passenger Motor Vehicles (unit/year)	5000
轿车制造	(辆／年)	Passenger Motor Vehicles (unit/year)	20000

SCALE OF INVESTMENT IN FIXED ASSETS AND NEWLY INCREASED PRODUCTION CAPACITY(2016)

本年施工规模 Construction Scale This Year	#本年新开工 Newly Started This Year	累计新增生产能力 Accumulated Newly Increased Production Capacity	#本年新增 Newly Increased This Year
13863	1815	4468	2805
1424	348	385	385
69	48	17	10
20	20	20	20
1062	1026	1034	1026
10	10	10	10
166	166	166	166
91	91	33	31
2000	2000	2000	2000
9000		9000	9000
81000		81000	81000
1400000	1000000	2800000	1400000
258747	258532	290222	258312
1957	1957	1750	1750
2570	586	719	530
1988	275	447	322
361	149	106	67
201	146	157	132
20	17	8	8
3312	2123	2864	2159
408	83	283	83
1706900	406900	136000	126000
1364200	164200	128500	118500
25200	25200		
317500	217500	7500	7500
1006	1006	1006	1000
510500	10500	10500	10500
44500	44500	44500	44500
9	9	30009	9
		12	
24000	20000	11000	10000
4000		1000	
20000	20000	10000	10000

7–15 续表

生产能力(或效益)名称		Item	建设规模 Construction Scale
化学纤维	(吨／年)	Chemical Fibre (ton/year)	1500
棉纺锭	(锭)	Cotton Spindles (unit)	1220000
酒	(万吨／年)	Alcoholic Drink (10 000 tons/year)	14.1
白　酒	(万吨／年)	White Spirit(10 000 tons/year)	11.6
其他酒	(万吨／年)	Other Alcohols (10 000 tons/year)	2.5
机制纸浆	(万吨／年)	Machine–made Paper Pulp (10 000 tons/year)	16
家用电冰箱	(万台／年)	Household Refrigerators (10 000 unit/year)	100
家用洗衣机	(万台／年)	Household Washing Machines (10 000 unit/year)	100
新建铁路投产里程	(公里)	Operating Length of Newly Built Railways (km)	556
复线里程	(公里)	Length of Mutiple Line (km)	1
电气化铁路里程	(公里)	Length of Electrified Railways (km)	79
新建高速铁路里程	(公里)	Length of Newly Built High Speed Railways (km)	147
新建公路	(公里)	Length of Newly Built Highways (km)	2073
#高速公路	(公里)	Express Way (km)	603
一级公路	(公里)	First Class (km)	86
二级公路	(公里)	Second Class (km)	361
改建公路	(公里)	Reconstructed Highways (km)	5518
#高速公路	(公里)	Express Way (km)	54
一级公路	(公里)	First Class (km)	53
二级公路	(公里)	Second Class (km)	1494
新建独立公路桥梁	(延长米)	Independent Highway Bridges Newly Built (extended m)	11284
新建独立公路桥梁	(座)	Independent Highway Bridges Newly Built (unit)	18
新建独立公路隧道	(延长米)	Independent Highway Tunnels Newly Built (extended m)	910
新建独立公路隧道	(座)	Independent Highway Tunnels Newly Built (unit)	1
新(扩)建公路客、货运站	(个)	Highway Passenger and Freight Station of Newly Built or Extended (unit)	11
新(扩)建公路客、货运站	(平方米)	Highway Passenger and Freight Station of Newly Built or Extended (sq.m)	27563
民航机场跑道	(条)	Runways of Civil Aviation Airport (unit)	2
民航机场跑道	(米)	Runways of Civil Aviation Airport (meter)	1500
候机楼	(座)	Terminal Buildings (unit)	1
候机楼	(平方米)	Terminal Buildings (sq.m)	7200
城市自来水供水能力	(万吨／日)	City Tap Water Supply Capacity (10 000 tons/day)	159
城市污水处理能力	(万吨／日)	City Sewage Treatment Capacity (10 000 tons/day)	129

continued

本年施工规模 Construction Scale This Year	#本年新开工 Newly Started This Year	累计新增生产能力 Accumulated Newly Increased Production Capacity	#本年新增 Newly Increased This Year
32		1500	32
1120000	1120000	1120000	1120000
13.6	3.1	3.5	3.5
11.1	1.1	1.0	1.0
2.5	2.0	2.5	2.5
16	16	16	16
35	35	35	35
52	52	52	52
227		183	3
1			
45		45	45
145	145	147	145
1811	1332	1436	1272
453	61	182	85
73	28	32	28
332	298	302	292
5279	4416	4263	4212
54			
25	6	13	13
1457	878	972	954
10185	7195	4754	4505
18	15	9	8
910	910	910	910
1	1	1	1
10	8	8	8
24869	21658	19855	19855
2			
1500			
1			
7200			
134	37	45	35
107	65	105	101

7-16 固定资产投资总规模及新增固定资产(2016年)

单位：万元

行 业	Sector	计划总投资 Total Planned Investment
总 计	**Total**	**371271960**
农、林、牧、渔业	Farming, Forestry, Animal Husbandry and Fishery	24286957
农 业	Farming	9317183
林 业	Forestry	2926214
畜牧业	Animal Husbandry	10052591
渔 业	Fishery	197971
农、林、牧、渔服务业	Farming, Forestry, Animal Husbandry and Fishery Services	1792998
采矿业	Mining	28664151
煤炭开采和洗选业	Coal Mining and Washsing	21487230
石油和天然气开采业	Extraction of Petroleum and Natural Gas	3694834
黑色金属矿采选业	Mining and Dressing of Ferrous Metals	1562965
有色金属矿采选业	Mining and Dressing of Nonferrous Metals	358341
非金属矿采选业	Mining and Dressing of Nonmetal Ores	716633
开采辅助活动	Mining Auxiliary Activities	690849
其他采矿业	Others	153299
制造业	Manufacturing	61911790
农副食品加工业	Farm and Sideline Food Processing	6066809
食品制造业	Food Manufacturing	1535585
酒、饮料和精制茶制造业	Alcohol, Beverage and Refined Tea Manufacturing	2037067
烟草制品业	Tobacoo Manufaturing	217726
纺织业	Textile Industry	450904
纺织服装、服饰业	Manufacture of Garments and Accessories	261698
皮革、毛皮、羽毛及其制品和制鞋业	Manufacture of Leather, Fur, Feather and their Products and Footwear	47574
木材加工和木、竹、藤、棕、草制品业	Processing of Timber, Manufacture of Wood, Bamboo, Rattan, Palm, and Straw Products	667322
家具制造业	Manufacture of Funiture	180090
造纸和纸制品业	Manufacture of Paper and Paper Products	579208
印刷和记录媒介复制业	Printing and Record Medium Reproduction	103919
文教、工美、体育和娱乐用品制造业	Manufacture of Articles For Culture, Education and Sport Activity	238843
石油加工、炼焦和核燃料加工业	Petroleum Processing ,Coking and Nuclear Fuel Processing	4934143
化学原料和化学制品制造业	Manufacture Raw Chemical Materials and Chemical Products	12758019
医药制造业	Manufacture of Medical Products	1833408
化学纤维制造业	Manufacture of Chemical Fibers	75928
橡胶和塑料制品业	Manufacture of Rubber and Plastic Products	582174
非金属矿物制品业	Manufacture of Nonmetals Mineral Products	6781667
黑色金属冶炼和压延加工业	Smelting and Pressing of Ferrous Metals	2157123
有色金属冶炼和压延加工业	Smelting and Pressing of Nonferrous Metals	4316387
金属制品业	Manufacture of Metal Products	1645201
通用设备制造业	Manufacture of Universal Purpose Equipment	1595864

注：本表项目个数不含房地产开发投资。

Note: Number of projects in this table doesn't include investment in real estate development.

SCALE OF INVESTMENT AND NEWLY INCREASED FIXED ASSETS(2016)

(10 000 yuan)

自开始建设至本年底累计完成投资 Accumulated Investment Completed This Year	#本年完成投资 Investment Completed This Year	施工项目(个) Number of Projects under Construction (unit)	#本年新开工 Newly Started This Year	本年投产项目(个) Number of Projects Put into Use This Year (unit)	本年新增固定资产 Newly Increased Fixed Assets This Year
267723741	**139463510**	**23321**	**19717**	**18687**	**96652686**
20879640	19058982	5617	5048	4665	16168462
8125497	7468871	2004	1779	1685	6204529
2495047	2349342	700	643	590	2091885
8769204	7982031	2487	2257	2060	6944572
181941	174082	55	50	47	146331
1307951	1084656	371	319	283	781145
22416987	10545566	1574	1307	1381	7891143
17363121	7691758	1051	869	974	5926595
2398282	630077	37	19	13	204191
1129905	835964	167	138	123	676799
265974	259345	32	28	20	94230
580822	533270	151	138	133	476031
603762	542789	131	115	115	492717
75121	52363	5		3	20580
45301586	26430488	4721	4049	3830	21287590
4419907	3718849	963	854	762	3086999
1290762	836751	205	181	169	687931
1630603	702469	127	106	104	575357
124699	70714	6	2	5	16087
360502	178714	39	30	33	174287
131440	86815	20	15	17	61260
46608	44007	13	12	12	43417
434350	428641	80	74	64	256430
171574	152299	46	43	40	155312
424861	331508	69	66	60	222252
74989	62041	15	13	9	33900
168007	160055	37	32	29	113959
3757025	1109023	105	85	78	512667
8157464	3842813	409	340	343	2544948
1238667	1023404	162	136	124	707965
66303	16100	3	2	2	9952
507558	480709	110	98	93	393615
5582910	4589833	1064	955	914	3964472
1792754	1036949	194	156	153	764318
3841683	1399103	108	86	82	2382236
1322659	957458	209	175	172	880011
1200453	783633	160	133	119	686494

7-16 续表1

单位：万元

行　业	Sector	计划总投资 Total Planned Investment
专用设备制造业	Manufacture of Special Purpose Equipment	1881656
汽车制造业	Manufacture of Motor Vehicles	2458031
铁路、船舶、航空航天和其他运输设备制造业	Manufacture of Railways, Ships, Aviation, Aircrafts and Other Transportation Equipments	579039
电气机械和器材制造业	Manufacture of Electrical Equipment and Machinery	2744723
计算机、通信和其他电子设备制造业	Manufacture of Computer, Telecommunication and Other Electronic Equipments	3195020
仪器仪表制造业	Manufacture of Measuring Instrument and Machinery	215125
其他制造业	Other Manufacturing	463082
废弃资源综合利用业	Comprehensive Utilization of Waste	1132585
金属制品、机械和设备修理业	Repair of Metal Products, Machinery and Equipment	175870
电力、热力、燃气及水生产和供应业	Production and Supply of Electricity, Heat, Gas and Water	33177299
电力、热力生产和供应业	Production and Supply of Electricity and Heat	28854903
燃气生产和供应业	Production and Supply of Gas	2479560
水的生产和供应业	Production and Supply of Water	1842836
建筑业	Construction	190107
房屋建筑业	Buildings Construction	84859
土木工程建筑业	Civil Engineering	42153
建筑安装业	Building Installation	17820
建筑装饰和其他建筑业	Building Decoration and Other Construction	45275
批发和零售业	Wholesale and Retail Trade	7646867
批发业	Wholesale Trade	3512559
零售业	Retail Trade	4134308
交通运输、仓储和邮政业	Transport, Storage and Post	40961338
铁路运输业	Railway Transport	22912721
道路运输业	Highway Transport	11772583
水上运输业	Water Transport	
航空运输业	Air Transport	6072
管道运输业	Transport Via Pipelines	61329
装卸搬运和运输代理业	Loading, Unloading and Other Transport Services	253723
仓储业	Storage	5893213
邮政业	Post	61697
住宿和餐饮业	Hotels and Catering Services	1542680
住宿业	Hotels	1180020
餐饮业	Catering Services	362660
信息传输、软件和信息技术服务业	Information Transmission, Software and Information Technology Services	1906292
电信、广播电视和卫星传输服务	Transimission Services of Telecommunication, Broadcast, Television and Satellite	522281
互联网和相关服务	Internet and Relative Services	707991
软件和信息技术服务业	Software and Information Technology Services	676020

continued

(10 000 yuan)

自开始建设至本年底累计完成投资 Accumulated Investment Completed This Year	#本年完成投资 Investment Completed This Year	施工项目(个) Number of Projects under Construction (unit)	#本年新开工 Newly Started This Year	本年投产项目(个) Number of Projects Put into Use This Year (unit)	本年新增固定资产 Newly Increased Fixed Assets This Year
1399021	853479	189	150	149	578732
1226003	642943	54	36	33	372775
224258	103870	22	14	10	68329
1592261	1020819	112	94	110	778315
2525065	921029	31	23	22	623674
131211	38501	16	10	5	28600
411215	376560	58	54	45	185660
915914	339639	74	55	54	265360
130860	121760	21	19	18	112276
22427523	12640199	1472	1128	1107	7517734
18950509	10040056	907	650	647	5488660
2030630	1738974	336	291	279	1221439
1446384	861169	229	187	181	807635
164371	133551	30	26	29	112372
81031	61931	11	10	11	53031
31427	19707	5	4	4	9440
7920	7920	3	3	2	7279
43993	43993	11	9	12	42622
4873543	3636681	891	796	722	2912919
2453083	1689542	392	359	303	1386805
2420460	1947139	499	437	419	1526114
29063962	9687299	1572	1303	1286	5934055
15303555	1816588	46	19	24	128740
9382557	5040273	960	815	798	3488363
3149	2482	2	1		
65844	23908	7	2	6	13045
193677	121809	28	22	23	94503
4095597	2662656	527	442	432	2200737
19583	19583	2	2	3	8667
860817	733148	175	148	137	547065
504822	458881	112	100	80	292785
355995	274267	63	48	57	254280
1261294	1008837	156	128	116	594313
411877	373430	75	68	50	222061
535687	454678	48	37	46	263367
313730	180729	33	23	20	108885

7-16　续表2

单位：万元

行　　业	Sector	计划总投资 Total Planned Investment
金融业	Banking and Insurance	93398
货币金融服务	Monetary Banking	71013
资本市场服务	Capital Market	7946
保险业	Insurance	5020
其他金融业	Other Financial Activities	9419
房地产业	Real Estate Trade	118723381
房地产业	Real Estate Trade	118723381
租赁和商务服务业	Lease and Business Affairs Services	2454423
租赁业	Leasing	197097
商务服务业	Business Affairs Services	2257326
科学研究和技术服务业	Scientific Reseach and Technical Services	2597297
研究和试验发展	Reserch and Experimental Development	1008362
专业技术服务业	Professional Technical Services	657769
科技推广和应用服务业	Services of Science and Technology Exchanges and Promotion	931166
水利、环境和公共设施管理业	Management of Water Conservancy, Environment and Public Facilities	34156486
水利管理业	Water Conservancy	5022372
生态保护和环境治理业	Ecological Protection and Environmental Management	2164463
公共设施管理业	Public Facilities	26969651
居民服务、修理和其他服务业	Resident Services, Repair and Other Services	468804
居民服务业	Residence Services	230052
机动车、电子产品和日用产品修理业	Repair of Motor Vehicles, Electronic Products and Daily Products	192534
其他服务业	Other Services	46218
教　育	Education	3326758
教　育	Education	3326758
卫生和社会工作	Health Care and Social Work	4061344
卫　生	Health Care	2638511
社会工作	Social Work	1422833
文化、体育和娱乐业	Culture, Sports and Recreation	3451471
新闻和出版业	Journalism and Publishing Activities	18850
广播、电视、电影和影视录音制作业	Broadcasting, Movies, Televisions and Audiovisual Activities	75567
文化艺术业	Culture and Arts Activities	1945982
体　育	Sports Activities	374745
娱乐业	Entertainment	1036327
公共管理、社会保障和社会组织	Public Management, Social Security and Social Organization	1651117
中国共产党机关	Organs of CPC	
国家机构	Government Agencies	903909
人民政协、民主党派	PPCC and Democratic Parties	
社会保障	Social Security	16023
群众团体、社会团体和其他成员组织	Mass Organizations, Social Organizations and Other Member Organizations	589261
基层群众自治组织	Grass Roots Self-governing Organizations	141924

continued

(10 000 yuan)

自开始建设至本年底累计完成投资 Accumulated Investment Completed This Year	#本年完成投资 Investment Completed This Year	施工项目(个) Number of Projects under Construction (unit)	#本年新开工 Newly Started This Year	本年投产项目(个) Number of Projects Put into Use This Year (unit)	本年新增固定资产 Newly Increased Fixed Assets This Year
92029	92029	24	22	22	85443
69793	69793	19	18	16	66390
7147	7147	1	1	2	5400
5669	5669	2	1	2	5206
9420	9420	2	2	2	8447
82386760	27235230	1458	1053	1062	14481180
82386760	27235230	1458	1053	1062	14481180
1952347	1625795	281	261	235	1128941
110385	109265	26	25	26	103267
1841962	1516530	255	236	209	1025674
1450616	1045745	222	184	167	769988
465441	321645	38	20	18	93947
492242	427041	127	115	110	365417
492933	297059	57	49	39	310624
25459840	18736035	3371	2831	2564	12301199
3932102	2277188	632	519	496	1535458
1923674	1649800	361	323	315	1385520
19604064	14809047	2378	1989	1753	9380221
449770	420965	130	116	113	382206
216526	192792	59	52	46	160870
186301	181230	57	50	53	176715
46943	46943	14	14	14	44621
2727399	1867644	536	425	427	1529833
2727399	1867644	536	425	427	1529833
2273586	1668334	361	286	275	829149
1467987	991731	211	159	170	470044
805599	676603	150	127	105	359105
2549997	1927597	492	418	393	1534426
14812	13791	3	2	2	4872
69266	69216	23	21	20	52646
1306130	1021856	289	240	231	786541
347723	297773	89	75	69	225966
812066	524961	88	80	71	464401
1131674	969385	238	188	156	644668
619218	510116	143	107	95	328550
14663	9865	12	6	7	10207
363878	315491	40	33	20	188142
133915	133913	43	42	34	117769

7-17 农户固定资产投资主要指标
MAJOR INDICATORS OF RURAL HOUSEHOLDS INVESTMENT IN FIXED ASSETS

单位：万元 (10 000 yuan)

指　　标	Item	2015	2016
一、本年新增固定资产原值	Original Value of Newly Increased Fixed Assets This Year	3491753	3603289
二、本年固定资产投资完成额	Completed Investment in Fixed Assets This Year	3295638	3386310
按投资来源分	Grouped by Source of Funds		
国内贷款	Domestic Loans	327848	348003
自筹资金	Self-raised Funds	2940726	3012929
其他资金	Others	27063	25379
按投资构成分	Grouped by Composition		
建筑工程	Construction	2287435	2297310
#水　利	Conservancy	1960	1809
房　屋	Buildings	2229316	2221473
#住　宅	Residential Buildings	2170047	2172577
安装工程	Installation		
设备工器具购置	Purchase of Equipment and Instruments	862664	934916
#生产设备	Production Equipment	862664	934916
其　他	Others	145539	154084
按具体投资项目分	Grouped by Investment Projects		
房　屋	Buildings	2229316	2221473
#住　宅	Residential Buildings	2170047	2172577
道　路	Roadway		
桥　梁	Bridge		
设　备	Equipment	862664	934916
水　利	Conservancy	1960	1809
其　他	Others	201697	228112
三、本年施工房屋面积(万平方米)	Floor Space of Buildings Under Construction This Year (10 000 sq.m)	2907	3008
#住　宅	Residential Buildings	2736	2897
#当年新开工	Newly Started in The Current Year	2387	2676
四、本年竣工房屋面积(万平方米)	Floor Space of Buildings Completed This Year (10 000 sq.m)	2708	2852
#住　宅	Residential Buildings	2535	2686
五、本年竣工房屋投资额	Investment in Buildings Completed This Year	2188411	2089957
#住　宅	Residential Buildings	2159373	2055069

7-18 主要年份农户固定资产投资
INVESTMENT IN FIXED ASSETS OF RURAL HOUSEHOLDS IN MAJOR YEARS

年 份 Year	竣工房屋面积 (万平方米) Floor Space of Buildings Completed (10 000 sq.m)	#住 宅 Residential Buildings	本年竣工房屋投资额 (万元) Investment in Buildings Completed This Year (10 000 yuan)	#住 宅 Residential Buildings	购置生产性固定资产投资(万元) Purchase of Productive Fixed Assets (10 000 yuan)
1985	1327	1165	67840	58794	19547
1990	1214	1192	152724	103171	10971
1995	406	403	85050	84528	97111
2000	793	765	236059	227276	58651
2001	862	826	258909	246602	49381
2002	954	932	304384	298523	91453
2003	1152	1023	332777	320480	131960
2004	1164	1077	377435	362733	158117
2005	1320	1298	456869	448930	158022
2006	1545	1507	596264	577144	205530
2007	1702	1666	783527	769298	176299
2008	1617	1554	869494	824246	357467
2009	1700	1599	960717	904851	413236
2010	1899	1714	1107868	1022321	451000
2011	1929	1815	1155259	1123754	473729
2012	2020	1907	1330340	1321667	489125
2013	2365	2264	1907906	1832392	727639
2014	2588	2505	2061461	2019725	805335
2015	2708	2535	2188411	2159373	862664
2016	2852	2686	2089957	2055069	934916

主要统计指标解释

全社会固定资产投资 是以货币形式表现的在一定时期内全社会建造和购置固定资产的工作量以及与此有关的费用的总称。该指标是反映固定资产投资规模、结构和发展速度的综合性指标,又是观察工程进度和考核投资效果的重要依据。全社会固定资产投资按登记注册类型可分为国有、集体、联营、股份制、私营和个体、港澳台商、外商、其他等。

固定资产投资（不含农户） 指城镇和农村各种登记注册类型的企业、事业、行政单位及城镇个体户进行的计划总投资500万元及500万元以上的建设项目投资和房地产开发投资,包含原口径的城镇固定资产投资加上农村企事业组织项目投资,该口径自2011年起开始使用。

固定资产投资的实际到位资金 根据固定资产投资的资金来源不同，分为国家预算资金、国内贷款、利用外资、自筹资金和其他资金。

(1)国家预算资金 国家预算包括一般预算、政府性基金预算、国有资本经营预算和社保基金预算。各类预算中用于固定资产投资的资金全部作为国家预算资金填报，其中一般预算中用于固定资产投资的部分包括基建投资、车购税、灾后恢复重建基金和其他财政投资。各级政府债券也应归入国家预算资金。

(2)国内贷款 指报告期固定资产项目投资单位向银行及非银行金融机构借入用于固定资产投资的各种国内借款,包括银行利用自有资金及吸收存款发放的贷款、上级主管部门拨入的国内贷款、国家专项贷款（包括煤代油贷款、劳改煤矿专项贷款等），地方财政专项资金安排的贷款、国内储备贷款、周转贷款等。

(3)利用外资 指报告期收到的境外（包括外国及港澳台地区）资金(包括设备、材料、技术在内)。包括对外借款(外国政府贷款、国际金融组织贷款、出口信贷、外国银行商业贷款、对外发行债券和股票)、外商直接投资、外商其他投资(包括利用外商投资收益在国内进行固定资产再投资活动的资金)。不包括我国自有外汇资金(国家外汇、地方外汇、留成外汇、调剂外汇和国内银行自有资金发放的外汇贷款等)。各类外资按报告期末的外汇牌价（中间价）折成人民币计算。

(4)自筹资金 指固定资产投资单位在报告期收到的，由各企、事业单位筹集用于固定资产投资的资金，包括各类企事业单位的自有资金和从其他单位筹集的用于固定资产投资的资金，但不包括各类财政性资金、从各类金融机构借入资金和国外资金。

(5)其他资金 指在报告期收到的除以上各种资金之外的用于固定资产投资的资金，包括社会集资、个人资金、无偿捐赠的资金及其他单位拨入的资金等。

固定资产投资按国民经济行业分 指根据其从事的社会经济活动性质对各类单位进行的分类。应根据建设项目建成投产后的主要产品种类或主要用途及社会经济活动种类来划分，不能根据项目单位本身的行业类别来划分。如果项目投产后有几种产品，应根据主要产品来确定行业类别。一般情况下，一个建设项目只能属于一种国民经济行业。

固定资产投资按隶属关系分 是按建设单位或企业、事业、行政单位的主管上级机关确定的。

(1)中央 是指中共中央、人大常委会和国务院各部、委、局、总公司以及直属机构直接领导的建设项目和企业、事业、行政单位。这些单位的固定资产投资计划由国务院各部门直接编制和下达，统一组织或委托下级实施。包括有中央垂直管理的部门（如国家统计局各级调查队）和中央直属企业、事业单位（如工商银行、中国电信、中国石油）等。

(2)地方 是由省（自治区、直辖市）、地（区、市、州、盟）、县（区、市、旗）三级政府及业务主管部门直接领导和管理的建设项目、企业、事业、行政单位。地方项目还包括不隶属以上各级政府及主管部门的建设项目和企业、事业单位，如外商投资企业和无主管部门的企业等。

固定资产投资按建设性质分 按整个建设项目情况来确定。建设项目的性质一般分为新建、扩建、改建和技术改造、单纯建造生活设施、迁建、恢复、单纯购置。房地产开发单位、农户投资不划分建设性质。

(1)新建 指从无到有“平地起家”开始建设的项目。现有企业、事业、行政单位投资的项目一般不属于新建。但如有的单位原有基础很小，经过建设后新增的固定资产价值超过该企业、事业、行政单位原有固定资产价值（原值）三倍以上的，也应作为新建。

(2)扩建 指在厂内或其他地点，为扩大原有产品的生产能力(或效益)或增加新的产品生产能力，而增建的生产车间(或主要工程)、分厂、独立的生产线的企业、事业单位。行政、事业单位在原单位增建业务性用房(如学校增建教学用房、医院增建门诊部、病房等)也作为扩建。

现有企、事业单位为扩大原有主要产品生产能力或增加新的产品生产能力，增建一个或几个主要生产车间(或主要工程)、分厂，同时进行一些更新改造工程的，也应作为扩建。

(3)改建和技术改造　指现有企业、事业单位对原有设施进行技术改造或更新(包括相应配套的辅助性生产、生活福利设施) 的建设项目。改建项目包括现有企业、事业单位为适应市场变化的需要，而改变企业的主要产品种类(如军工企业转民产品等) 的建设项目，原有产品生产作业线由于各工序(车间)之间能力不平衡，为填平补齐充分发挥原有生产能力而增建不增加本企业主要产品设计能力的车间的建设项目。技术改造是指企业、事业单位在现有基础上，用先进的技术代替落后的技术，用先进的工艺和装备代替落后的工艺和装备，以改变企业落后的技术经济面貌，实现以内涵为主的扩大再生产，达到提高产品质量、促进产品更新换代、节约能源、降低消耗、扩大生产规模、全面提高社会经济效益的目的。技术改造具体包括以下内容：机器设备和工具的更新改造；生产工艺改革、节约能源和原材料的改造；厂房建筑和公共设施的改造；保护环境进行的“三废”治理改造；劳动条件和生产环境的改造等。

固定资产投资按构成分

(1)建筑工程　指各种房屋、建筑物的建造工程，又称建筑工作量。这部分投资额必须兴工动料，通过施工活动才能实现，是固定资产投资额的重要组成部分。

(2)安装工程　指各种设备、装置的安装工程，又称安装工作量。

在安装工程中，不包括被安装设备本身价值。

(3)设备工具器具购置　指报告期内购置或自制的，达到固定资产标准的设备、工具、器具的价值。新建单位及扩建单位的新建车间，按照设计或计划要求购置或自制的全部设备、工具、器具，不论是否达到固定资产标准均计入“设备工具器具购置”中。

(4)其他费用　指在固定资产建造和购置过程中发生的，除建筑安装工程和设备、工器具购置投资完成额以外的应当分摊计入固定资产投资的费用，不指经营中财务上的其他费用。

施工项目个数　是指本年正式进行过建筑或安装施工活动的建设项目个数。包括本年新开工项目，以前年度开工跨入本年继续施工项目，本年全部建成投产项目、以前年度全部停缓建在本年恢复施工的项目，本年进行过施工又在本年内全部停缓建的项目。施工项目个数可以反映一定时期固定资产投资的实际规模，与同期全部建成投产项目个数相比，可以从建设速度的角度反映固定资产投资的效果。

本年投产项目个数　指报告期内按设计文件规定建成主体工程和相应配套的辅助设施，形成生产能力或工程效益，经过验收合格，并且已正式投入生产或交付使用的建设项目。

新增生产能力(或工程效益)　指通过固定资产投资活动而增加的设计能力(或工程效益)。主要指标包括建设规模、本年施工规模、自开始建设累计新增生产能力(或工程效益)、本年新增生产能力(或工程效益)等。

建设规模　指建设项目或工程设计文件中规定的全部设计能力(或工程效益)。包括已经建成投产和尚未建成投产的工程的生产能力(或工程效益)。

本年施工规模　指报告期内施工的单项工程（或更新改造项目）的设计能力(或工程效益)，包括报告期以前已开工跨入本年继续施工的工程的设计能力和报告期新开工工程的设计能力。也包括报告期内建成投产或报告期施工后又停缓建的单项工程设计能力。不包括在报告期以前建成投产或已经停、缓建的工程，以及报告期内尚未正式开工的工程的设计能力。

自开始建设累计新增生产能力(或工程效益)　指自开始建设至本年底止建成投产的全部单项工程累计新增生产能力(或工程效益)。

本年新增生产能力(或工程效益)　指在本年度内按照新增生产能力(或工程效益)的计算条件和标准，实际建成投入生产或交付使用的生产能力(或工程效益)。

新增固定资产　是指已经完成建造和购置过程，并已交付生产或使用单位的固定资产的价值，包括已经建成投入生产或交付使用的工程投资和达到固定资产标准的设备、工具、器具的投资及有关应摊入的费用。该指标是表示固定资产投资成果的价值指标，也是反映建设进度，计算固定资产投资效果的重要指标。

项目建成投产率　指一定时期内全部建成投产项目个数与同期施工项目个数的比率。该指标从建设单位建设速度的角度反映投资效果。

固定资产交付使用率　指一定时期新增固定资产与同期完成投资额的比率。该指标是反映固定资产动用速度，衡量建设过程中宏观投资效果的综合指标。由于新增固定资产是较长时期内形成的结果，而投资额则是当年完成的，因此，该指标一般适宜于反映较长时期内固定资产的动用情况。

Explanatory Notes on Main Statistical Indicators

Total Investment in Fixed Assets in the Whole Country refers to the volume of activities in construction and purchases of fixed assets of the whole country and related fees, expressed in monetary terms during the reference period. It is a comprehensive indicator which shows the size, structure and growth of the investment in fixed assets, providing a basis for observing the progress of construction projects and evaluating results of investment. Total investment in fixed assets in the whole country includes, by type of ownership, the investment by State-owned units, collective-owned units, joint ownership units, share-holding units, private units, individuals as well as investments by entrepreneurs from Hong Kong, Macao and Taiwan, foreign investors and others.

Investment in Fixed Assets (Excluding Rural Households) refers to the investment in construction projects with a total planned investment of 5 million yuan and over by enterprises of various ownerships, institutions, administrative units and urban self-employed individuals, and the investment in real estate development in both urban and rural areas. Since 2011, it covers the urban investment in fixed assets under the previous statistical coverage plus project investments by rural enterprises and institutions.

Actual Funds in Place for Investment in Fixed Assets are categorized as funds from the State budget, domestic loans, foreign investment, self-raised funds, and others, depending on the sources of investment.

(1) Fund from the State budget: State budget consists of general budget, government fund budget, operation budget of state-owned assets and social security fund budget. Funds for investment in fixed assets from various budgets are reported as fund from the state budget, of which, the general budget utilized on fixed assets investment includes investment on infrastructure construction, vehicle purchase tax, post-disaster restoration and reconstruction funds and other financial investment. Government bonds at all levels should also be included.

(2) Domestic loans refer to loans of various forms borrowed by investing units from banks and non-bank financial institutions during the reference period for the purpose of investment in fixed assets, including loans issued by banks from their self-owned funds and deposit, loans appropriated by higher responsible authorities, special loans by government (including loan for substituting petroleum with coal, special loans for reform-through-labour coal mines), loans arranged by local government from special funds, domestic reserve loan, and revolving loan, etc.

(3) Foreign investment refers to overseas (including foreign countries, Hongkong, Macao and Taiwan) funds received during the reference period (covering equipment, materials and technology), including foreign borrowings (loans from foreign governments and international financial institutions, export credit, commercial loans from foreign banks, issue of bonds and stocks overseas), foreign direct investment and other foreign investments (including funds from foreign direct investment income that are reinvested in fixed assets domestically). Excluded from this category is capital in foreign exchanges owned by China (foreign exchanges owned by the central and local governments, foreign exchanges retained by enterprises, foreign exchanges by enterprises through the regulating mechanism, loans in foreign exchanges issued by the Bank of China with its own fund, etc.). In calculating the utilization of foreign capital, foreign currencies are converted into Chinese Renminbi applying the exchange rate (central parity rate) at the end of the reference period.

(4) Self-raised funds refer to funds for investment in fixed assets received during the reference period by investing units, including investment in fixed assets using own funds of various enterprises and institutions or funds raised from other units other than financial funds, funds borrowed from financial institutions and overseas funds.

(5) Others refer to funds for investment in fixed assets received from sources other than those listed above, including funds raised from individuals and through donations, and funds transferred from other units.

Investment in Fixed Assets by Sector refers to the classification of investment by the nature of social economic activities the investing units are engaged in. The classification of construction projects by sector is determined by the major products or the purpose of the projects when they are put into production or use, and by the nature of their social economic activities, instead of being determined by industrial classification of the project enterprises. The project will be classified according to major product if there are several kinds of products yielded. In general, one project can only be classified into one sector.

Investment in Fixed Assets by Jurisdiction of Management refers to the classification of investment by the competent authorities under which investment is made by construction units, enterprises, institutions or administrative units.

(1) Central investment refers to the investment in projects or by enterprises, institutions or administrative units which are under the direct leadership and management of the State Council and of the national commissions, ministries, agencies and State-owned large corporations. Various ministries and departments of the State Council prepare and implement plans through unified organization or lower-level commissions, which include departments direct under central government (i.e. survey offices at all level of the National Bureau of Statistics) and enterprises and institutions directly under central government (like the Industrial and Commercial Bank of China, China Telecom and China National Petroleum Corporation)..

(2) Local investment refers to the investment in projects or by enterprises, institutions or administrative units which are under the direct leadership and management of competent departments and governments at the level of province (autonomous regions and municipalities directly under the Central Government), prefecture （prefectures, cities and leagues） and county (districts, cities and banners). Also included are projects by foreign-invested enterprises and enterprises without competent managing authorities.

Investment in Fixed Assets by Type of Construction Construction projects in general can be classified, by the type of construction, into new construction, expansion, reconstruction and technical transformation, purely construction of living facilities, moving, restoration and purely purchasing. However, investment by type of construction is not applied to investment by real-estate development units and investment by rural households.

(1) New construction in general refers to construction projects, which start from scratch. The existing projects invested by enterprises, institutions and administrative agencies cannot be classified as new construction. In case the size of the existing unit is quite small, and the value of newly added fixed assets is more than three times of the original value, the expansion will be considered as new construction.

(2) Expansion refers to construction of new production workshop, branch factory or independent production line within a factory or in other locations, for the purpose of increasing the production capacity (or improving efficiency) or adding new production capacity by enterprises and institutions. Newly constructed accommodation for the operation of institutions and administrative organizations (such as newly constructed buildings for teaching in schools, buildings for clinics or wards in hospitals, etc.) are also classified as expansion.

Also included in expansion are investments by existing enterprises or institutions in building major production line(s) or branch factory (ies) along with some work on innovation, for the purpose of expanding the production capacity of original products or producing new products.

(3) Reconstruction and technical transformation refers to construction projects by existing enterprises or institutions in innovation or technical transformation of the old facilities (including auxiliary production equipment and welfare facilities). Also considered as reconstruction is the construction of new workshops by the existing enterprises or institutions to change the variety of products to meet the market demand (such as the production of civil products by defence industries), or to bring the designed production capacity into full play through a more balanced production process on production lines. Technical transformation refers to replacement of old technology or equipment by new technology or equipment, in order to expand the reproduction through improvement of technology contents in production, to improve product quality, to promote new products, to save energy, to reduce consumption, to expand the production scale and to improve overall social-economic efficiency. Contents of technical transformation include: updating of machinery, equipment and tools; reforming production process by using energy or materials saving technology; construction of factory workshops and transformation of public facilities; treatment transformation of “three wastes” (waste gas, waste water and industrial residue) aiming at environmental protection; improvement of working conditions and environment, etc.

Investment in Fixed Assets by Structure

(1) Construction refers to the construction of houses and buildings, also known as work volume of construction. This part of investment can only be achieved through construction activities, it is the major component of the total investment in fixed assets.

(2) Installation refers to the installation of various kinds of equipment and instruments, also known as work volume of installation.

The value of equipment installed itself is not included in the value of installation projects.

(3) Purchase of equipment and instruments refers to the total value of equipment, tools, and instruments purchased or self-produced which come up to the cut-off point for fixed assets during the reference period. Equipment, tools and instruments purchased or self-produced for new workshops by newly established or expanded units are categorized as “purchase of equipment and instruments” no matter whether they come up to the cut-off point for fixed assets.

(4) Other expenses refer to expenses arising during the construction or purchase of fixed assets other than those expenses on

construction, installation and purchase of equipment and instruments. Other financial expenses arising in operation are not included.

Number of Projects under Construction refers to number of all projects with actual construction or installation activities in current year, including newly started projects, projects started previously and extended into the current year, projects completed and put into operation in current year, projects suspended previously and resumed in current year, and projects started this year but suspended or postponed in current year. The number of projects under construction can reflect the actual size of investment in fixed assets during a given period, and when compared with the number of projects completed and put into use during the same period, it demonstrates the results of investment in fixed assets from the angle of the speed of the construction.

Number of Projects Put into Use This Year refer to projects have completed the main construction and correspondent auxiliary facilities in accordance with the design documents, resulting in forming production capacity (efficiency) and have been checked and accepted after relevant tests, and have been formally delivered for use.

Newly Increased Production Capacity (or Project Efficiency) refers to the increase in design capacity (or project efficiency) through investment in fixed assets. The main indicators include: construction scale, scale of projects under construction in current year, the accumulated newly increased production capacity (project efficiency) since the start of the projects and the newly increased production capacity (project efficiency) of current year.

Construction Scale refers to the total designed production capacity (project efficiency) of the construction projects in accordance with the design document, including those have been put into operation and those that have not been completed.

Scale of Projects under Construction in Current Year refers to the designed production capacity (project efficiency) of a single project (or renovation project) under construction in the reference period, including the designed production capacity of projects that have been started previously and still under construction in the current year, the newly started projects, and projects that have been completed and put into operation in the reference period or those have been started but suspended or postponed in the reference period. Projects that have been completed and put into operation, suspended or postponed before the reference period, and projects that have not been officially started in the reference period are not included.

The Accumulated Newly Increased Production Capacity (project efficiency) since the Start of the Projects refers to the accumulated newly increased production capacity of all the single projects which have been put into use from the beginning of the projects till the end of current year.

The Newly Increased Production Capacity (project efficiency) of Current Year refers to the production capacity(project efficiency) that has been completed and put into operation in current year according to the calculation conditions and standards on newly increased production capacity (project efficiency).

Newly Increased Fixed Assets refer to the value of fixed assets that has completed the construction and purchase, and has been delivered to the production or owner units, including investment in projects that have been completed and put into operation in current year and the investment in equipment, tools and appliance that meet the standard of fixed assets and fees that should be apportioned. This is an indicator that demonstrates the results of investment in fixed assets in monetary terms, and an important indicator to reflect the speed of construction and to calculate the efficiency of investment.

Rate of Construction Projects Completed and Put into Use refers to the ratio of the number of construction projects completed and put into use in a certain period of time to the number of projects under construction in the same period. This reflects the investment efficiency from the perspective of the speed of projects construction.

Rate of Projects of Fixed Assets Completed and Put into Operation refers to the ratio of the newly increased fixed assets to the total investment made in the same period. This is a comprehensive indicator reflecting the speed of the employment of fixed assets and the investment efficiency at the macro-level. As the newly increase fixed assets is the result of a long period while the investment is completed in the current year, this indicator is expected to be used to reflect the employment of fixed assets over a long period of time.

8 对外经济贸易

FOREIGN TRADE
AND ECONOMIC COOPERATION

资料整理人员

王玉凤

对外经济贸易
FOREIGN TRADE AND ECONOMIC COOPERATION

海关进出口总额	Total Value of Imports and Exports of Customs	166.4	亿美元	(USD 100 million)
出口总额	Total Value of Exports	99.3	亿美元	(USD 100 million)
进口总额	Total Value of Imports	67.1	亿美元	(USD 100 million)
实际利用外资额	Actual Utilization of Foreign Capital	34.3	亿美元	(USD 100 million)

海关进出口总额（亿美元）

Total Value of Imports and Exports of Customs (USD 100 million)

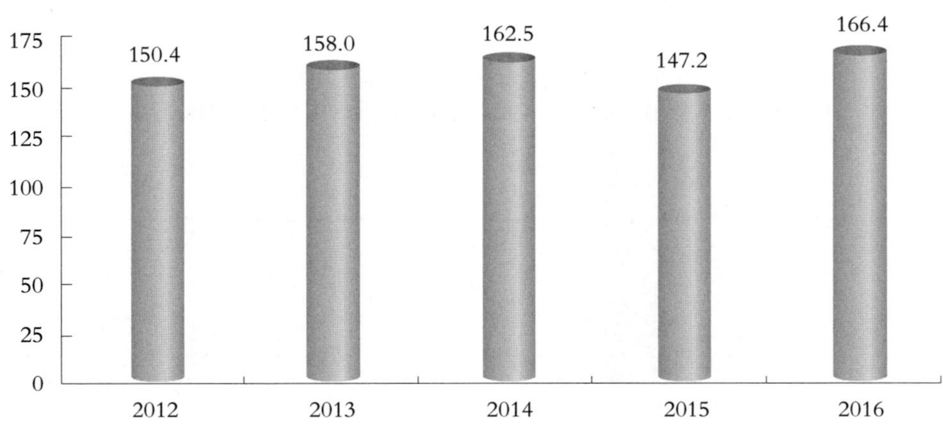

外商直接投资额（亿美元）

Foreign Direct Investment (USD 100 million)

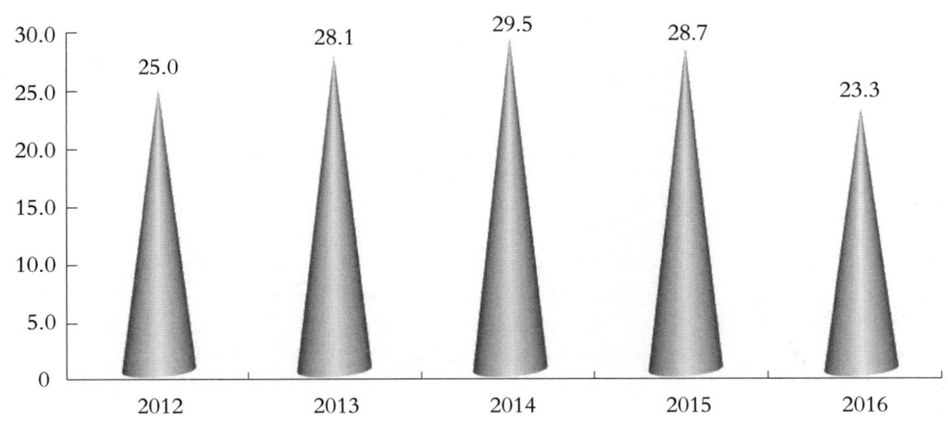

8-1 主要年份海关进出口贸易总额
TOTAL VALUE OF IMPORTS AND EXPORTS OF CUSTOMS IN MAJOR YEARS

单位：万美元 (USD 10 000)

年 份 Year	进出口总额 Total	出口总额 Exports	进口总额 Imports
1990	35000	26300	8700
1995	140769	114367	26402
2000	176438	123687	52751
2005	554597	352871	201726
2010	1257839	470930	786909
2011	1475981	542823	933158
2012	1504325	701620	802705
2013	1579785	799649	780136
2014	1624852	894222	730631
2015	1471541	842091	629449
2016	1664428	993219	671210

8-2 海关进出口贸易总额(2016年)
TOTAL VALUE OF IMPORTS AND EXPORTS OF CUSTOMS(2016)

单位：万元 (10 000 yuan)

项 目	Item	进出口总额 Total	出口总额 Exports	进口总额 Imports
总 额	**Total**	**10989659**	**6553289**	**4436370**
一、按企业性质分	**Grouped by Ownership**			
国有企业	State-Owned Enterprises	2538064	1217593	1320470
外商投资企业	Foreign Funded Enterprises	6765726	4297945	2467781
合作企业	Sino-Foreign Cooperative Operation Enterprises	10680	9895	785
合资企业	Sino-Foreign Joint Ventures Enterprises	6620714	4218113	2402601
独资企业	Solely Foreign-Funded Enterprises	134332	69937	64395
民营企业	Non-State-Owned Enterprises	1685868	1037748	648120
集体企业	Collective-owned Enterprises	76886	29758	47128
私人企业	Private-owned Enterprises	1600055	999063	600992
个体工商户	Self-employed Business	8927	8927	
二、按贸易方式分	**Grouped by The Mode of Trade**			
一般贸易	Original Trade	3377925	1757138	1620786
国家间、国际组织无偿援助和赠送的物资	Aid and Donation between Countries and from International	2248	2248	
加工贸易	Processing Trade	7533172	4764173	2768999
来料加工装配贸易	Processing and Assembly Trade for Income Material	944	476	469
进料加工贸易	Processing Trade for Imported Material	7532228	4763697	2768530
加工贸易进口设备	Processing Trade for Imported Equipment	36733		36733
对外承包工程出口货物	Exported Goods on Contracted Projects	29218	29218	
外商投资企业作为投资进口的设备、物品	Equipments and Goods Imported as Foreign Investment	3822		3822
保税仓库进出境货物	Goods of Bonded Warehouse	1630	52	1578
保税区进出境仓储或转口货物	Storage and Transit Goods of Bonded Area	2236		2236
其 他	Others	2675	460	2215

8-3 海关进出口主要商品分类总额(2016年)

TOTAL VALUE OF IMPORTS AND EXPORTS OF CUSTOMS BY CATEGORY OF MAIN COMMODITIES(2016)

单位：万元 (10 000 yuan)

项目	Item	出口总额 Exports	进口总额 Imports
合计	**Total**	**6553289**	**4436370**
1.活动物;动物产品	Live Animals; Animal Products	8947	965
2.植物产品	Vegetables Products	28206	122815
3.动,植物油,脂,蜡及其分解产品	Animal or Vegetable Oils, Fats and Waxes and their Cleavage Products	4	80
4.食品,饮料,酒及醋;烟草及制品	Foods, Beverages, Liquor and Vinegar; Tobacco and Its Products	23490	459
5.矿产品	Mineral Products	63964	871304
6.化学工业及其相关工业的产品	Chemicals and Related Products	382697	21188
7.塑料及其制品;橡胶及其制品	Plastics and Related Products; Rubber and Related Products	48228	62026
8.生皮,皮革,毛皮及其制品	Raw Hides, Leather, Furs and Related Products	1184	33
9.木及木制品;其他编结材料制品	Wood and Wooden Products; Plaited Products of Other Materials	2847	541
10.纸浆;纸,纸板及其制品	Paper Pulp; Paper, Paperboard and Their Products	3435	15470
11.纺织原料及纺织制品	Textile Materials and Products	74387	3627
12.鞋帽伞杖鞭;羽毛制品;人造花	Footwear, Headgear, Umbrellas, Canes, Whips; Feather Products; Artificial Flowers	1843	6
13.石料及其制品;陶瓷玻璃及制品	Building Stone and Its Products; Ceramics, Glass and Glassware	81288	9292
14.珍珠,宝石,贵金属;仿首饰;硬币	Pearls, Precious Stones, Precious Metals; Imitation Jewelery; Coins	139	17
15.贱金属及其制品	Base Metals and Related Products	1199399	784985
16.机器,电子产品,电气设备及零件	Machinery, Electronic Products, Electric Equipment and Accessoris	4421430	2383578
17.车辆,航空器,船舶及运输设备	Vehicles, Aircraft, Vessels and Trasportation Equipment	129730	68889
18.光学,检测,医疗设备;钟表,乐器	Optical, Testing, Medical Apparatus, Clocks and Watches, Musical Instruments	18723	90913
19.武器,弹药及其零件,附件	Arms, Ammunition and Related Parts and Accessories		
20.杂项制品	Miscellaneous Products	63121	170
21.艺术品,收藏品及古物	Works of Art, Collectors' Pieces and Antiques	190	
22.特殊交易品及未分类商品	Special Trading Goods and Non-classified Goods	39	13

8-4 海关分国别(地区)进出口贸易总额(2016年)

TOTAL VALUE OF IMPORTS AND EXPORTS OF CUSTOMS BY COUNTRY(REGION)(2016)

单位：万元 (10 000 yuan)

国 别 (地区)	Country (Region)	进出口总额 Total	出口总额 Exports	进口总额 Imports
总 计	**Total**	**10989659**	**6553289**	**4436370**
亚 洲	**Asia**	**5205592**	**2399658**	**2805934**
#韩 国	Republic of Korea	893506	244246	649260
日 本	Japan	800902	433665	367237
印 度	India	442089	406605	35484
中华人民共和国	China	757499	13	757486
哈萨克斯坦	Kazakhstan	190527	11525	179002
印度尼西亚	Indonesia	99289	44767	54522
香 港	Hong Kong	84806	84505	301
台湾省	Taiwan Province	714480	296502	417977
新加坡	Singapore	199456	167401	32055
土耳其	Turkey	221289	200170	21119
马来西亚	Malaysia	108665	62028	46637
泰 国	Thailand	107550	103915	3635
越 南	Vietnam	192263	75908	116355
阿联酋	United Arab Emirates	79408	79233	175
沙特阿拉伯	Saudi Arabia	57643	57641	2
菲律宾	Philippines	49766	16830	32936
非 洲	**Africa**	**313285**	**106770**	**206515**
#南 非	South Africa	202572	28705	173867
毛里塔尼亚	Mauritania	11540	265	11274
欧 洲	**Europe**	**2499184**	**2134348**	**364836**
#荷 兰	Netherlands	853596	852423	1173
德 国	Germany	405642	321747	83895
意大利	Italy	254444	176692	77752
俄罗斯联邦	Russia	337308	263098	74210
英 国	United Kingdom	283990	264409	19581
卢森堡	Luxembourg	79412	79370	42
比利时	Belgium	48741	48195	546
西班牙	Spain	28900	23225	5674
乌克兰	Ukraine	32260	2428	29832
捷 克	Czech	33876	31467	2409
拉丁美洲	**Latin America**	**842372**	**320072**	**522300**
#巴 西	Brazil	293120	93062	200058
墨西哥	Mexico	171490	122447	49043
智 利	Chile	162761	49829	112931
秘 鲁	Peru	106867	7877	98990
北美洲	**North America**	**1622790**	**1451143**	**171647**
#加拿大	Canada	234491	185495	48996
美 国	United States	1388299	1265648	122651
大洋洲	**Oceania**	**506387**	**141298**	**365089**
#澳大利亚	Australia	381697	123366	258331
新喀里多尼亚	New Caledonia	106862	151	106711
东盟组织	**ASEAN**	**833261**	**477300**	**355960**
欧盟组织	**EU**	**2098439**	**1866861**	**231578**
亚太经济合作组织	**APEC**	**6809436**	**3565834**	**3243602**
金砖国家(除中国)	**BRICKS (except China)**	**1275089**	**791469**	**483620**

8-5 实际利用外资额
ACTURAL UTILIZATION OF FOREIGN CAPITAL

单位：万美元　　(USD 10 000)

项　目	Item	2010	2015	2016
总　计	**Total**	**116512**	**325840**	**343355**
一、对外借款	**Foreign Loans**	**45091**	**38855**	**110113**
外国政府贷款	Government Loans	4874	4637	2034
国际金融组织贷款	Loans form International Financial Organizations	12480	5918	4279
一般商业贷款	General Commercial Loans	20589	28300	103800
买方信贷	Buyer Credit	7147		
二、外商直接投资	**Foreign Direct Investments**	**71421**	**286985**	**233242**
独资企业	Solely Foreign-Funded Enterprises	34009	96802	108080
合资企业	Joint Ventures Enterprises	34900	164537	122877
合作企业	Cooperative Operation Enterprises	2512	25646	
外商投资股份制	Foreign-funded Joint-stock			2284

注：2011年起，实际利用外资额为全口径，后同。
Note: The coverage of actural utilization of foreign capital has changed to whole society since 2011.The same applies to the following.

8-6 主要年份实际利用外资额
ACTURAL UTILIZATION OF FOREIGN CAPITAL IN MAJOR YEARS

单位：万美元　　(USD 10 000)

年　份 Year	利用外资总　额 Total	对外借款 Foreign Loans	外商直接投资 Foreign Direct Investments	外商其他投资 Other Foreign Investments
1985	176	55	43	78
1990	3763	3006	340	417
1995	16085	7662	6383	2040
2000	63188	40716	22472	
2005	106369	78853	27516	
2006	132438	85239	47199	
2007	191471	57188	134283	
2008	172174	69892	102282	
2009	82646	33331	49315	
2010	116512	45091	71421	
2011	249530	42252	207278	
2012	276711	26332	250379	
2013	299096	18429	280667	
2014	335672	40486	295186	
2015	325840	38855	286985	
2016	343355	110113	233242	

8-7 主要年份合同利用外资金额(外商直接投资)

CONTRACT UTILIZATION OF FOREIGN CAPITAL IN MAJOR YEARS(DIRECT INVESTMENT)

年 份 Year	项目投资总 额 Total Value of Project Investment	合同利用外资情况 Contract Utilization of Foreign Capital	独资企业 Solely Foreign -funded Enterprises	合资企业 Joint Venture Enterprises	合作企业 Cooperative Operation Enterprises	外商投资股份制 Foreign-funded Joint-stock
一、新批项目(企业)(个) New Projects and Enterprises (unit)						
1985		4		4		
1990		26		24	2	
1995		178	26	138	14	
2000		71	11	48	12	
2005		85	28	35	21	
2006		150	51	71	28	
2007		152	39	98	15	
2008		77	25	37	15	
2009		58	20	25	13	
2010		52	15	28	6	3
2011		62	35	21	6	
2012		39	12	18	7	2
2013		48	24	23	1	
2014		50	22	26	2	
2015		36	20	13	3	
2016		30	14	15	1	
二、合同金额(万美元) Contracted Value (USD10 000)						
1985	201	53		53		
1990	2160	1194		458	736	
1995	40058	23133	3206	17223	2704	
2000	44409	26174	732	15028	10414	
2005	244292	110208	30712	35877	43619	
2006	338880	134207	53339	37109	43759	
2007	834379	247174	50496	175153	21525	
2008	171644	107758	48949	30175	28634	
2009	109438	66893	22326	22548	22019	
2010	132039	100301	32528	56198	7436	4139
2011	291687	155636	50325	7157	11539	86615
2012	144834	35605	6734	24009	4574	288
2013	286998	96152	27089	64083	4980	
2014	262216	96785	67251	23791	5743	
2015	184554	98210	59577	21471	16450	712
2016	228154	83030	29899	28141	24990	

8-8 按行业分利用外商直接投资额(2016年)

UTILIZATION OF FOREIGN DIRECT INVESTMENT CAPITAL BY SECTOR(2016)

单位：万美元 (USD 10 000)

行业	Item	新批项目(企业)(个) New Projects and Enterprises (unit)	合同金额 Contract Value	实际使用金额 Actual Value
总　计	**Total**	**30**	**83030**	**233242**
农、林、牧、渔业	Farming, Forestry, Animal Husbandry and Fishery	1	304	3646
采矿业	Mining			9130
制造业	Manufacturing	8	22624	104491
电力、热力、燃气及水生产和供应业	Production and Supply of Electricity, Heat, Gas and Water	8	36315	83889
建筑业	Construction			
交通运输、仓储和邮政业	Transportation, Storage and Post			17070
信息传输、计算机服务和软件业	Information Transmission, Computer Services	1	5237	4900
批发和零售业	Wholesale and Retail Trade	5	1798	
住宿和餐饮业	Hotels and Catering Services	2	5	
金融业	Financial Industry		-2500	
房地产业	Real Estate Trade			
租赁和商务服务业	Lease and Business Affairs Services	2	245	
科学研究、技术服务和地质勘查业	Scientific Reseach, Technical Services and Geological Prospecting	1	12	
居民服务和其他服务业	Resident Services and Other Services	1	9990	
卫生、社会保障和社会福利业	Health Care, Socail Security and Social Welfare	1	9000	
其　他	Others			10115

8-9 按国别(地区)分利用外商直接投资额(2016年)

UTILIZATION OF FOREIGN DIRECT INVESTMENT CAPITAL BY COUNTRY(REGION)(2016)

单位：万美元 (USD 10 000)

国别(地区)	Country (Region)	新批项目(企业)(个) New Projects and Enterprises (unit)	合同金额 Contract Value	实际使用金额 Actual Value
合　计	**Total**	**30**	**83030**	**233242**
#香　港	Hong Kong	13	28081	131028
新加坡	Singapore	1	1124	3086
台湾省	Taiwan Province	2	337	1255
塞舌尔	Seychelles	1	737	1777
英　国	United Kingdom	1	300	152
德　国	Germany			5325
意大利	Italy			1259
英属维尔京群岛	British Virgin Is.	1	21240	579
加拿大	Canada			50
美　国	United States	2	9017	17907
巴哈马	Bahamas			14922
澳大利亚	Australia	1	60	7965
捷　克	Czech			283
荷　兰	Netherlands			3948
投资性公司投资	Investment Companies	2	21837	43025

8-10 主要年份对外承包工程和劳务合作

CONTRACTED PROJECTS AND LABOR COOPERATION WITH FOREIGN COUNTRIES OR REGIONS IN MAJOR YEARS

年 份 Year	新签合同份数 (个) Number of New Contracts (unit)	新签合同额 (万美元) New Contracted Value (USD 10 000)	完成营业额 (万美元) Value of Business (USD 10 000)	派出人数 (人) Persons Posted Abroad (person)	年末在外人数 (人) Persons Abroad at Year-end (person)
1985	1	101	132		
1990	12	186	118		73
1995	43	1537	728		574
2000	50	5563	3892		1518
2005	55	22187	20200	1195	2263
2010	8	48179	72228	1224	6147
2011	71	42187	70018	2447	5934
2012	42	64018	44927	3264	3513
2013	20	23599	76505	1816	4073
2014	14	34586	73542	1511	4232
2015	26	34875	73754	1595	5010
2016	20	22266	68641	2441	7587

8-11 高新经济技术开发区综合情况

KEY STATISTICS OF HIGH-TECH DEVELOPMENT ZONES

单位：亿元 (100 million yuan)

指 标	Item	2015	2016
当年工业总产值	Gross Industry Output Value	3862.0	4072.9
当年进出口总额(万美元)	Total Value of Imports and Exports(USD 10 000)	823538.0	1118144.2
出口总额	Total Value of Exports	523915.5	731589.4
进口总额	Total Value of Imports	299622.5	386554.8
当年财政收入	Financial Revenue	209.1	205.2
#税收收入	Tax Revenue	193.5	192.9
实际到位外资金额(万美元)	Paid-in Foreign Funds(USD 10 000)	93667.6	122124.4
实际到位境内省外资金额	Paid-in Funds from Other Provinces	800.6	799.7
全区从业人员 (万人)	Employees (10 000 persons)	57.3	59.4
企业主营业务收入	Major Business Revenue of Enterprises	6234.8	6508.1

8-12 各开发区综合发展情况(2016年)

KEY STATISTICS OF DEVELOPMENT ZONES(2016)

单位：亿元 (100 million yuan)

开 发 区	Development Zone	企业主营业务收入 Major Business Revenue of Enterprises	工 业 总产值 Gross Industry Output Value	税 收 收 入 Tax Revenue	进出口总额 (万美元) Total Value of Imports and Exports (USD 10 000)
总 计	**Total**	**6508.1**	**4072.9**	**192.9**	**1118144**
太原经济区	Taiyuan Economic Zone	891.0	713.5	43.3	971315
太原高新区	Taiyuan High-tech Zone	1760.0	1480.0	26.9	29300
太原民营区	Taiyuan Private Econimic Zone	210.0	9.4	6.1	2779
太原不锈钢	Taiyuan Stainless Steer Industrial Park	72.0	66.0	2.9	1011
清徐开发区	Qingxu Development Zone	38.9	38.1	1.5	2173
大同开发区	Datong Development Zone	138.1	82.8	9.2	20878
朔州开发区	Shuozhou Development Zone	82.9	60.2	3.0	246
忻州开发区	Xinzhou Development Zone	99.9	48.2	4.0	442
孝义开发区	Xiaoyi Development Zone	244.5	257.9	15.9	341
文水开发区	Wenshui Development Zone	37.8	38.6	1.0	4362
交城开发区	Jiaocheng Development Zone	105.3	106.6	3.5	12300
阳泉开发区	Yangquan Development Zone	210.3	42.9	3.5	3813
晋中开发区	Jinzhong Development Zone	463.5	87.8	17.6	3600
榆次工业园	Yuci Industrial Park	132.9	167.9	5.6	3219
祁县开发区	Qixian Development Zone	63.3	59.4	2.9	2960
长治高新区	Changzhi High-tech Zone	220.4	175.3	16.8	112
壶关开发区	Huguan Development Zone	6.5	7.1	0.6	330
晋城开发区	Jincheng Development Zone	200.8	135.3	11.4	31133
临汾开发区	Linfen Development Zone	350.5	29.1	3.9	5032
侯马开发区	Houma Development Zone	247.4	33.2	1.3	626
运城开发区	Yuncheng Development Zone	587.1	169.8	3.0	16074
空港开发区	Konggang Development Zone	145.1	90.4	2.3	892
盐湖工业园	Yanhu Industrial Park	87.1	76.7	0.9	1472
绛县开发区	Jiangxian Development Zone	56.6	61.3	1.0	2535
风陵渡开发区	Fenglingdu Development Zone	56.2	35.4	4.8	1198

8-13 人民币对主要外币年末汇价(中间价)

YEAR-END EXCHANGE RATE OF RMB YUAN AGAINST MAIN CONVERTIBLE CURRENCIES (MIDDLE RATE)

单位：人民币元 (RMB yuan)

年 份 Year	100美元 100 US Dollars	100日元 100 Japanese Yen	100港元 100 Hong Kong Dollars	100欧元 100 Euros
1985	293.66	1.25	37.57	
1986	345.28	2.07	44.22	
1987	372.21	2.58	47.74	
1988	372.21	2.91	47.70	
1989	376.51	2.74	48.28	
1990	478.32	3.32	61.39	
1991	532.33	3.96	68.45	
1992	551.46	4.36	71.24	
1993	576.20	5.20	74.41	
1994	861.87	8.44	111.53	
1995	835.10	8.92	107.96	
1996	831.42	7.64	107.51	
1997	828.98	6.86	107.09	
1998	827.91	6.35	106.88	
1999	827.83	7.29	106.66	
2000	827.84	7.69	106.18	
2001	827.70	6.81	106.08	
2002	827.70	6.62	106.07	800.58
2003	827.70	7.15	106.24	936.13
2004	827.68	7.66	106.23	1029.00
2005	819.17	7.45	105.30	1019.53
2006	797.18	6.86	102.62	1001.90
2007	760.40	6.46	97.46	1041.75
2008	694.51	6.74	89.19	1022.27
2009	682.78	7.68	88.11	1020.76
2010	662.27	8.11	85.09	878.96
2011	633.59	8.19	81.29	843.89
2012	630.00	7.67	81.30	816.73
2013	613.76	6.02	79.16	830.72
2014	611.62	5.14	78.85	745.22
2015	649.36	5.39	83.78	709.52
2016	693.70	5.96	89.45	730.68

主要统计指标解释

进出口总额 指实际进出我国国境的货物总金额。包括对外贸易实际进出口货物，来料加工装配进出口货物，国家间、联合国及国际组织无偿援助物资和赠送品，华侨、港澳台同胞和外籍华人捐赠品，租赁期满归承租人所有的租赁货物，进料加工进出口货物，边境地方贸易及边境地区小额贸易进出口货物(边民互市贸易除外)，中外合资经营企业、中外合作经营企业、外商独资经营企业进出口货物和公用物品，到、离岸价格在规定限额以上的进出口货样和广告品(无商业价值、无使用价值和免费提供出口的除外)，从保税仓库提取在中国境内销售的进出口货物，以及其他进出口货物。进出口总额用以观察一个国家在对外贸易方面的总规模。我国规定出口货物按离岸价格统计，进口货物按到岸价格统计。

实际利用外资 指我国各级政府、部门、企业和其他经济组织通过对外借款、吸收外商直接投资以及用其他方式筹措的境外现汇、设备、技术等。

对外借款 是我国利用外资的主要部分。包括我国通过外国政府贷款、国际金融组织贷款、外国银行商业贷款、出口信贷以及对外发行债券、股票等方式，从境外筹措的资金。

外商直接投资 是指外国企业和经济组织或个人(包括华侨、港澳台同胞以及我国在境外注册的企业)按我国有关政策、法规，用现汇、实物、技术等在我国境内开办外商独资企业，与我国境内的企业或经济组织共同举办中外合资经营企业、合作经营业或合作开发资源的投资(包括外商投资收益的再投资)以及经政府有关部门批准的项目投资总额内企业从境外借入的资金。

对外承包工程 包括各对外承包公司以招标议标承包方式承揽下列业务：(1)承包国外工程建设项目；(2)承包我国对外经援项目；(3)承包我国驻外机构的工程建设项目；(4)承包我国境内利用外资进行建设的工程项目；(5)与外国承包公司合营或联合承包工程项目时我国公司分包部分；(6)以服务成果向业主收费的技术服务项目(包括承揽地形地貌测绘；地质资源勘探与普查；建区域规划；提供设计文件、图纸、生产工艺技术资料和工程技术经济咨询；工程项目的可行性考察、研究和评估；进行技术指导和培训人员等)；(7)对外承包兼经营的房屋开发业务。对外承包工程的营业额是以货币表现的本期内完成的对外承包工程的工作量，包括以前年度签订的合同和本年度新签订的合同在报告期完成的工作量。

Explanatory Notes on Main Statistical Indicators

Total Value of Imports and Exports refers to the real value of commodities imported and exported across the border of China. They include the actual imports and exports through foreign trade, imported and exported goods under the processing and assembling trades and materials, supplies and gifts as aid given gratis between governments and by the United Nations and other international organizations, and contributions donated by overseas Chinese, compatriots in Hong Kong and Macao and Chinese with foreign citizenship, leasing commodities owned by tenant at the expiration of leasing period, the imported and exported commodities processed with imported materials, commodities trading in border areas (excluding mutual exchange goods), the imported and exported commodities and articles for public use of the Sino-foreign joint ventures, cooperative enterprises and ventures with sole foreign investment. Also included is import or export of samples and advertising goods for which CIF or FOB value are beyond the permitted ceiling (excluding goods of no trading or use value and free commodities for export), imported goods sold in China from bonded warehouses and other imported or exported goods. The indicator of the total imports and exports at customs can be used to observe the total size of external trade in a country. In accordance with the stipulation of the Chinese government, imports are calculated at CIF, while exports are calculated at FOB.

Actual Utilization of Foreign Capital refers to remittance, equipment and technology financed from abroad, by loans, foreign direct investment and other forms undertaken by the Chinese governments at all levels, by various departments, enterprises and other economic units.

Foreign Borrowings refer to funds borrowed from abroad through formal signing of borrowing agreements with foreign institutions, including loans of foreign governments, loans of international financial institutions, commercial loans of foreign banks, export credit, and funds raised by Chinese bonds (and shares before 1996) issued abroad. It is an important part of China's utilization of foreign capitals.

Foreign Direct Investment refers to the investments inside china by foreign enterprises and economic organizations or individuals (including overseas Chinese, compatriots from Hong Kong and Macao, and Chinese enterprises registered abroad), following the relevant policies and laws of china, for the establishment of ventures exclusively with foreign own investment, Sino-foreign joint ventures and cooperative enterprises or for cooperative exploration of resources with enterprises or economic organizations in China. It includes the re-investment of the foreign entrepreneurs with the profits gained from the investment and the funds that enterprises borrow from abroad in the total investment of projects which are approved by the relevant department of the government.

Contracted Projects with Foreign Countries or Regions refer to projects undertaken by Chinese contractors (project contracting companies) through bidding process. They include: (1)overseas civil engineering construction projects financed by foreign investors; (2)overseas projects financed by the Chinese government through its foreign aid programs; (3)construction projects of Chinese diplomatic missions, trade offices and other institutions stationed abroad; (4)construction projects in china financed by foreign investment; (5)sub—contracted projects to be taken by Chinese contractors through a joint umbrella project with foreign contractor(s); (6)projects with charges for technical services from overseas operators. it includes geographic and topographic mappings geological resource prospecting and survey planning of construction areas provision of design documents blueprints materials on production process and techniques as well as engineering technical and economic consultation feasibility study research and evaluation of projects technical supervising and staff training. (7)housing development projects. The business income from international contracted projects is the work volume of contracted projects completed during the reference period, expressed in monetary terms, including completed work on projects signed in previous years.

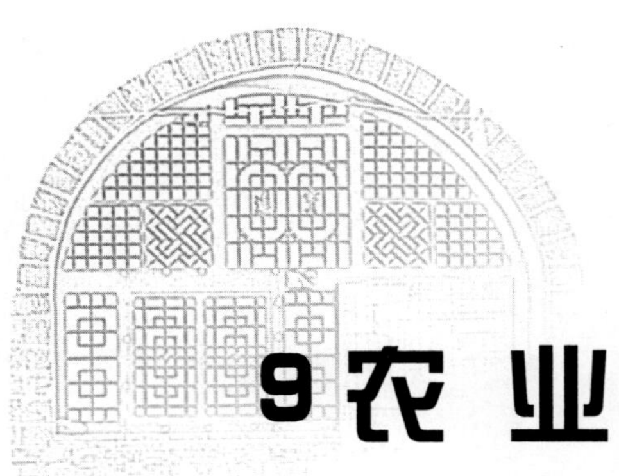

9 农 业

AGRICULTURE

资料整理人员

程英翠　郭俊德　李怀民　郝静敏　王翠翠
韩重远　陈　琰

农 业
AGRICULTURE

农作物播种面积	Sown Areas of Farm Crops	3720.8	千公顷	(1 000 ha)
#粮　食	Sown Areas of Grain	3241.4	千公顷	(1 000 ha)
粮食产量	Output of Grain	1318.5	万吨	(10 000 tons)
油料产量	Output of Oil-bearing Crops	15.4	万吨	(10 000 tons)
肉类产量	Output of Meat	84.4	万吨	(10 000 tons)

农林牧渔业总产值构成 (%)

Composition of Gross Output Value of Farming, Forestry, Animal Husbandry and Fishery (%)

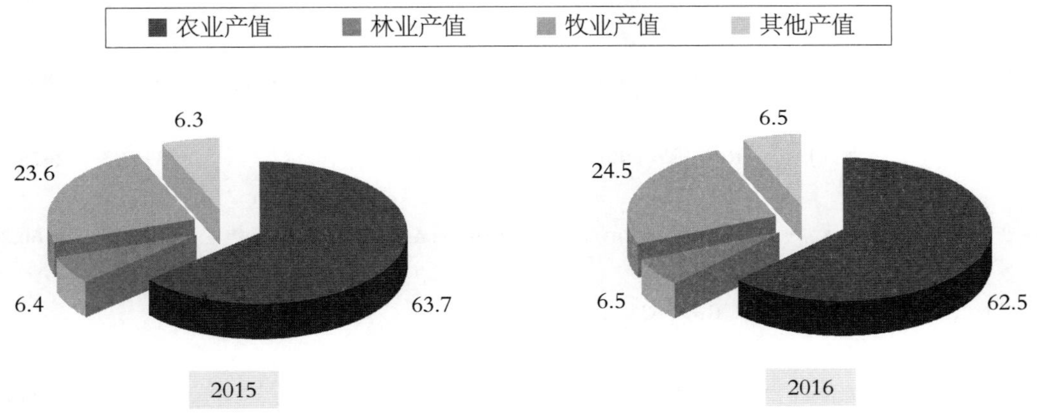

粮食总产量（万吨）

Output of Grain (10 000 tons)

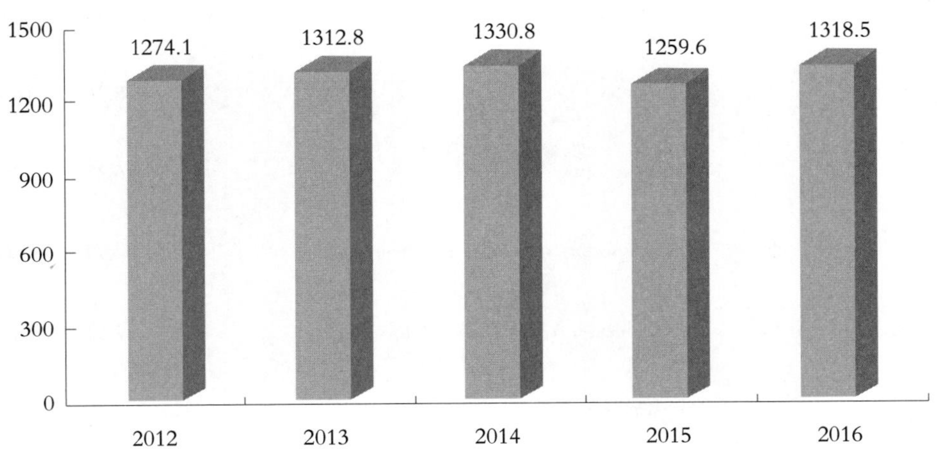

9-1 农村基层组织情况
BASIC CONDITIONS OF RURAL GRASS-ROOTS UNITS

指　　标	Item	2010	2015	2016
一、农村基层组织情况	**Basic Conditions of Rural Grass-roots Units**			
1.乡(镇)政府　(个)	Number of Township and Town Governments (unit)	1196	1196	1196
#镇政府	Number of Town Governments	563	564	564
2.村民委员会　(个)	Number of Villager Committees (unit)	28242	28122	28097
二、乡村户数　(万户)	**Number of Rural Households (10 000 households)**	**694.42**	**830.17**	**832.98**
三、乡村人口　(万人)	**Rural Population (10 000 persons)**	**2393.83**	**2426.97**	**2421.94**
四、乡村从业人员　(万人)	**Rural Employees (10 000 persons)**	**1100.01**	**1160.20**	**1160.56**
1.按性别分	Grouped by Sex			
男	Male	609.86	639.64	639.81
女	Female	490.15	520.56	520.75
2.按行业分	Grouped by Sector			
农、林、牧、渔业	Farming, Forestry, Animal Husbandry and Fishery	632.44	659.89	662.62
工　业	Industry	148.36	145.30	143.76
建筑业	Construction	86.31	95.78	95.22
交通运输、仓储和邮政业	Transportation, Storage and Post	64.97	66.66	65.91
批发、零售贸易业 、住宿和餐饮业	Wholesale, Retail Trade, Hotels and Catering Services	89.53	104.51	104.97
其他行业	Others	78.40	88.06	88.09

9-2 主要年份农林牧渔业总产值

GROSS OUTPUT VALUE OF FARMING, FORESTRY, ANIMAL HUSBANDRY AND FISHERY IN MAJOR YEARS

按当年价格计算 (at current price)

年 份 Year	农林牧渔业总产值(万元) Total (10 000 yuan)	农 业 Farming	林 业 Forestry	牧 业 Animal Husbandry	渔 业 Fishery	农林牧渔服务业 Farming, Forestry, Animal Husbandry and Fishery Service
1978	290133	239742	17391	32934	66	
1980	382302	286574	40154	55492	82	
1985	629163	484341	41218	102941	663	
1990	1247781	889037	78275	276170	4299	
1995	2996751	2033892	133136	817463	12260	
2000	3223544	2183303	127258	896667	16316	
2005	4837972	2817384	165153	1485882	26945	342608
2010	10478483	6689937	650089	2508360	61097	569000
2011	12075686	7671421	734651	2956927	75187	637500
2012	13042557	8474140	790686	2988314	84168	705250
2013	14470052	9321433	900699	3388152	94768	765000
2014	15304785	9840281	984743	3545724	98243	835794
2015	15226384	9695198	974234	3590442	99411	867100
2016	15340250	9581137	1003129	3761654	99131	895200

9-3 农林牧渔业总产值及增加值(按当年价格计算)

GROSS OUTPUT VALUE AND VALUE ADDED OF FARMING, FORESTRY, ANIMAL HUSBANDRY AND FISHERY(AT CURRENT PRICE)

单位：万元 (10 000 yuan)

指 标	Item	2015	2016
一、农林牧渔业总产值	**Gross Output Value**	**15226384**	**15340250**
农 业	Farming	9695198	9581137
林 业	Forestry	974234	1003129
牧 业	Animal Husbandry	3590442	3761654
渔 业	Fishery	99411	99131
农林牧渔服务业	Farming, Forestry, Animal Husbandry and Fishery Service	867100	895200
二、农林牧渔业中间消耗	**Intermediate Material Consumption**	**6985361**	**7066939**
农 业	Farming	4157628	4131468
林 业	Forestry	555929	571310
牧 业	Animal Husbandry	1769327	1849663
渔 业	Fishery	44765	44686
农林牧渔服务业	Farming, Forestry, Animal Husbandry and Fishery Service	457714	469811
三、农林牧渔业增加值	**Value Added**	**8241023**	**8273312**
农 业	Farming	5537570	5449669
林 业	Forestry	418306	431819
牧 业	Animal Husbandry	1821115	1911991
渔 业	Fishery	54646	54444
农林牧渔服务业	Farming, Forestry, Animal Husbandry and Fishery Service	409386	425389

9-4 主要年份耕地情况
CULTIVATED AREA IN MAJOR YEARS

单位：千公顷 (1 000 ha)

年 份 Year	耕地总资源 Resoruces of Cultivated Area	有效灌溉面积 Effective Irrigated Area	#机电排灌面积 Mechanical and Electrical Irrigated Area	机耕地面积 Area Cultivated by Machine
1978	3923.41	1092.48	766.30	1936.99
1980	3921.46	1115.14	775.22	1777.76
1985	3761.09	1079.10	776.98	1916.74
1990	3692.51	1134.45	836.74	1987.08
1995	3645.09	1201.99	891.74	2143.55
2000	4341.94	1105.04	939.07	2270.24
2005	3793.19	1088.59	946.39	2042.27
2010	4064.18	1274.15	961.90	2559.72
2011	4064.51	1324.78	1012.03	2525.92
2012	4064.19	1319.16	1042.43	2573.45
2013	4061.73	1382.79	1052.79	2609.24
2014	4056.84	1408.17	1072.83	2683.05
2015	4058.79	1460.28	1111.71	2737.03
2016		1487.21	1141.20	

9-5 主要年份主要农作物播种面积
SOWN AREAS OF MAJOR FARM CROPS IN MAJOR YEARS

单位：千公顷 (1 000 ha)

年 份 Year	总播种面积 Total Sown Area	#粮食作物 Grain Crops	#谷 物 Cereal	#油 料 Oil-bearing Crops	#棉 花 Cotton	#甜 菜 Beetroots	#蔬 菜 Vegetables
1978	4389.25	3692.43	3279.15	165.16	237.53	9.00	
1980	4266.60	3508.76	3117.22	231.46	224.31	9.69	92.37
1985	3978.23	3055.05	2634.17	505.61	121.14	10.79	104.94
1990	4016.89	3290.79	2755.55	356.33	130.34	16.89	110.59
1995	3895.55	3151.48	2425.09	342.42	127.10	21.76	156.79
2000	4042.42	3186.46	2326.74	417.06	43.04	7.56	242.13
2005	3795.35	3033.59	2333.37	273.38	97.45	1.22	244.93
2010	3763.92	3239.23	2714.82	156.95	58.72	4.89	228.47
2011	3797.42	3287.85	2774.28	149.97	53.32	5.61	228.58
2012	3796.43	3291.50	2776.91	145.86	37.36	8.55	247.81
2013	3782.44	3274.30	2763.53	140.32	23.44	4.60	252.77
2014	3783.43	3286.38	2772.85	129.70	18.72	1.76	257.06
2015	3767.71	3287.19	2779.22	121.19	10.62	1.18	256.69
2016	3720.81	3241.42	2716.19	114.70	7.05	0.65	256.96

9-6 农作物播种面积
SOWN AREA OF FARM CROPS

单位：千公顷 (1 000 ha)

指　　标	Item	2010	2015	2016
农作物总播种面积	**Total Sown Area**	**3763.92**	**3767.71**	**3720.81**
一、粮　食	**Grain**	**3239.23**	**3287.19**	**3241.42**
(一)谷　物	Cereal	2714.82	2779.22	2716.19
#稻　谷	Rice	1.04	0.70	0.70
小　麦	Wheat	728.47	675.09	672.94
玉　米	Corn	1548.93	1676.86	1624.75
谷　子	Millet	204.96	227.08	217.41
高　粱	Sorghum	34.09	22.99	23.13
燕　麦	Nakedoats	62.48	60.03	60.69
(二)豆　类	Beans	334.03	318.78	321.42
#大　豆	Soybean	195.07	189.41	191.61
(三)薯　类	Tubers	190.38	189.19	203.81
#马铃薯	Potato	170.19	167.14	182.81
二、油　料	**Oil-bearing Crops**	**156.95**	**121.19**	**114.70**
#花　生	Peanuts	9.04	6.57	6.41
油　菜	Rapeseeds	6.07	4.27	4.70
芝　麻	Sesame	4.45	2.31	2.25
胡　麻	Benne	62.81	55.68	46.96
葵花籽	Sunflower Seeds	43.04	28.52	32.69
三、棉　花	**Cotton**	**58.72**	**10.62**	**7.05**
四、生　麻	**Rough Bast Fiber**	**0.15**	**0.02**	
五、甜　菜	**Beetroots**	**4.89**	**1.18**	**0.65**
六、烟　叶	**Tobacco**	**3.38**	**2.81**	**2.82**
七、药　材	**Medicinal Materials**	**21.83**	**33.38**	**41.07**
八、蔬　菜	**Vegetables**	**228.47**	**256.69**	**256.96**
#设施蔬菜	Greenhouse Vegetables	**35.14**	51.63	48.25
九、瓜果类	**Melons**	**22.96**	**26.57**	**24.34**
十、其他作物	**Others**	**27.34**	**28.07**	**31.80**
#青饲料	Green feed	21.75	21.80	26.41

9-7 主要年份主要农作物产量
OUTPUT OF MAJOR FARM CROPS IN MAJOR YEARS

单位：吨 (ton)

年份 Year	粮食 Grain	1.谷物 Cereal	#稻谷 Rice	#小麦 Wheat	#玉米 Corn	#谷子 Millet
1978	7069560	6363715	58990	1288415	2711625	891140
1980	6857060	6201675	69290	1184780	2628820	960370
1985	8226767	7408051	58472	2950507	2098065	883671
1990	9690053	8643731	54429	3192990	3054441	876631
1995	9171000	8162190	41450	2701000	4035207	627530
2000	8533500	7029713	32770	2151500	3547500	602218
2005	9780000	8820582	8974	2022800	6161300	381889
2010	10851000	10351600	4615	2322400	7660000	203000
2011	11930000	11383900	5000	2403000	8546000	262000
2012	12741000	12146500	6000	2591800	9038700	312000
2013	13128000	12460000	6700	2307200	9554700	367600
2014	13307800	12602900	6200	2591100	9381100	389300
2015	12595700	11923000	4700	2714300	8627400	354200
2016	13185100	12329000	4900	2734100	8888900	427200

年份 Year	#高粱 Sorghum	2.豆类 Beans	#大豆 Soybean	3.薯类 Tubers	#马铃薯 Potato	油料 Oil-bearing Crops
1978	959400	137420	137420	568425		42290
1980	766805	130620	130620	524765		133672
1985	770607	176898	176898	641818	477197	444478
1990	767132	302242	302242	744080	585814	393810
1995	519119	366840	220104	641970	430120	222635
2000	299801	577822	359542	925965	704063	448259
2005	111894	366750	259806	592668	461451	212620
2010	53249	240500	154500	258900	212300	175892
2011	54000	244000	162400	302100	249300	187044
2012	62000	276000	182000	318500	261600	195672
2013	69900	307700	207600	360300	295800	194660
2014	75100	313600	207100	391300	317700	173246
2015	57200	305600	201700	367100	298300	153043
2016	63800	369300	238600	486800	416800	154346

9-7 续表 continued

单位：吨 (ton)

年 份 Year	棉 花 Cotton	生 麻 Rough Bast Fiber	甜 菜 Beetroots	烟 叶 Tobacco	蔬 菜 Vegetables
1978	69430	5000	54605	1650	
1980	77500	5792	117024	1001	1804220
1985	73455	3779	248541	4702	2915412
1990	111526	1048	431641	8860	3474121
1995	90817	2155	396978	10455	5428701
2000	44796	680	210313	16319	9203364
2005	102907	38	39617	6327	9015370
2010	69311	227	225768	12002	9090901
2011	63364	207	324347	11021	9819032
2012	46981	42	407752	9939	10733368
2013	30634	53	224571	9994	11984947
2014	23565	82	80408	10621	12714008
2015	14489	37	54780	9369	13022063
2016	10324	4	33244	8957	12945107

9-8 主要年份主要油料作物产量
OUTPUT OF MAJOR OIL-BEARING CROPS IN MAJOR YEARS

单位：吨 (ton)

年 份 Year	花 生 Peanuts	油菜籽 Rapeseeds	芝 麻 Sesame	胡麻籽 Benne Seeds	葵花籽 Sunflower Seeds
1978	888	2229	968	20437	3488
1980	5025	2800	2214	54932	31452
1985	50247	6766	11810	80071	164865
1990	48539	7758	23469	75102	139664
1995	48611	14759	11716	28820	78645
2000	41404	8638	19081	51279	257370
2005	28583	7676	4268	37889	102668
2010	21085	6360	4301	55026	57025
2011	21799	5888	4827	60302	56122
2012	20321	6570	3555	72553	53261
2013	18303	7174	3302	70263	53850
2014	16121	5772	2717	69847	48376
2015	11950	6674	1965	62889	41192
2016	13301	8293	2178	50708	54104

9-9 主要年份主要农作物单位面积产量
MAJOR FARM CROPS OUTPUT PER HECTARE IN MAJOR YEARS

单位：公斤/公顷 (kg/ha)

年 份 Year	粮 食 Grain	谷 物 Cereal	稻 谷 Rice	小 麦 Wheat	玉 米 Corn	谷 子 Millet	高 粱 Sorghum
1978	1915	1941	5207	1169	3419	1579	3171
1980	1954	1989	5670	1191	3541	1743	3269
1985	2693	2812	6871	2912	4221	2234	4315
1990	2945	3137	5923	3141	4797	2296	4532
1995	2910	3366	6436	2945	5253	2101	4430
2000	2678	3021	7234	2409	4470	2150	4393
2005	3224	3780	3349	2805	5205	1764	2903
2010	3350	3813	4438	3188	4945	990	1562
2011	3629	4103	4902	3384	5190	1272	1834
2012	3871	4374	5941	3762	5416	1508	2160
2013	4009	4509	6837	3406	5721	1750	2430
2014	4049	4545	6889	3845	5596	1800	2474
2015	3832	4290	6645	4020	5145	1560	2490
2016	4068	4545	6930	4063	5471	1965	2760

年 份 Year	豆 类 Beans	薯 类 Tubers	油 料 Oil-bearing Crops	棉 花 Cotton	生 麻 Rough Bast Fiber	甜 菜 Beetroots	烟 叶 Tobacco
1978	1188	1910	256	292	522	6067	851
1980	943	2074	578	346	695	12077	1125
1985	1066	2517	879	606	1050	23034	2387
1990	1200	2627	1105	856	1092	25556	1897
1995	884	2061	650	715	1390	18243	1700
2000	1194	2465	1075	1041	1236	27819	2042
2005	1059	1674	778	1056	760	32473	2379
2010	720	1360	1090	1112	1373	40099	3237
2011	760	1571	1209	1151	2045	43613	3293
2012	851	1674	1341	1257	602	47718	3197
2013	961	1891	1387	1307	790	48858	3035
2014	970	2056	1336	1259	858	45772	3246
2015	959	1940	1263	1365	2210	46467	3331
2016	1149	2388	1346	1464	1630	50980	3178

9-10 主要年份造林和果园面积
AREA OF AFFORESTATION AND ORCHARDS IN MAJOR YEARS

年 份 Year	当年造林面积 (千公顷) Afforestation Area in the year (1 000 ha)	#用材林 Timber Forest	零星植树 (万株) Planting Trees Piecemeal (10 000 unit)	年末果园面积 (千公顷) Area of Orchards (1 000 ha)	#苹果园面积 Area of Apple Orchards
1978	173.65	123.71	21992	64.00	37.57
1980	221.57	122.94	23129	68.21	40.80
1985	243.33	137.87	28764	111.47	56.98
1990	191.05	91.31	21057	184.71	101.15
1995	405.18	128.58	21418	286.34	188.47
2000	404.86	50.84	17176	288.89	177.98
2005	140.26	0.67	10596	279.69	151.40
2010	291.10	0.01	11098	294.38	137.63
2011	302.53	0.03	10803	322.57	144.73
2012	307.22	1.73	10415	342.36	150.69
2013	303.00	2.50	10504	348.34	154.12
2014	307.99	1.89	10062	360.33	158.62
2015	280.94	1.76	10023	362.76	155.46
2016	266.69	0.73	10131	355.82	150.31

9-11 造林和果园面积
AREA OF AFFORESTATION AND ORCHARDS

单位：千公顷 (1 000 ha)

指 标	Item	2010	2015	2016
一、当年造林面积	**Afforestation Area in the Year**	**291.1**	**280.9**	**266.7**
#用材林	Timber Forest		1.8	0.7
经济林	Economic Forest	52.3	56.9	31.1
防护林	Shelter Forest	223.7	131.7	196.3
薪炭林	Fuel Forest	6.3	30.6	31.6
二、育苗面积	**Area of Growing Seedings**	**40.0**	**71.3**	**72.8**
#本年新育	Area of Growing Seedings in the Year	19.2	21.8	18.9
三、零星植树(万株)	**Planting Trees Piecemeal (10 000 unit)**	**11098**	**10023**	**10131**
四、年末果园面积	**Area of Orchards at Year-end**	**294.4**	**362.8**	**355.8**
#苹果园	Apple Orchards	137.6	155.5	150.3
梨 园	Pears Orchards	28.1	36.5	37.4
葡萄园	Grapes Orchards	9.6	12.0	12.3

9-12 主要林产品和水果产量
OUTPUT OF MAJOR FOREST PRODUCTS AND FRUITS

单位：吨 (ton)

指　标	Item	2010	2015	2016
一、主要林产品产量	**Output of Major Forest Products**			
核　桃	Walnuts	65156	180572	217629
板　栗	Chinese Chestnut	1346	1991	1993
二、水果产量	**Output of Fruits**	**4084560**	**7556465**	**7539010**
#苹　果	Apples	2566472	4312091	4286152
梨	Pears	342202	733428	791462
葡　萄	Grapes	219513	266301	281597
红　枣(鲜枣)	Red Jujube(Fresh Jujube)	421167	815791	742398
柿　子(鲜柿)	Persimmon(Fresh Persimmon)	95516	166234	115404
桃	Peach	321002	984087	1027651

9-13 主要年份肉类产量和猪羊数量
OUTPUT OF MEAT AND NUMBER OF HOGS, SHEEP AND GOATS IN MAJOR YEARS

年　份 Year	猪牛羊肉产量 (万吨) Output of Pork, Beef and Mutton (10 000 tons)	肉猪出栏头数 (万头) Slaughtered Fattened Hogs (10 000 heads)	猪年末头数 (万头) Hogs at Year-end (10 000 heads)	羊年末只数 (万只) Sheep and Goats at Year-end (10 000 heads)		
					山　羊 Goats	绵　羊 Sheep
1978	18.23	274.10	578.50	872.04	532.45	339.59
1980	17.34	277.31	531.16	909.86	535.73	374.13
1985	20.85	270.56	372.12	414.28	174.06	240.22
1990	29.27	308.59	363.14	709.58	303.92	405.66
1995	56.09	569.36	560.99	915.01	408.03	506.98
2000	59.24	589.92	519.52	1058.42	474.86	583.56
2005	80.99	805.23	626.07	1196.35	488.82	707.52
2010	63.60	683.97	474.84	734.70	353.40	381.30
2011	62.30	672.10	446.10	778.70	369.20	409.50
2012	67.10	723.90	473.80	834.00	364.20	469.80
2013	72.57	786.16	502.18	877.97	387.45	490.52
2014	76.70	837.26	514.74	922.74	397.74	525.00
2015	73.00	783.67	485.91	1001.46	436.22	565.24
2016	70.87	748.86	449.68	910.41	363.56	546.85

9-14 畜牧业生产情况
NUMBER OF LIVESTOCK AND LIVESTOCK PRODUCTS

指 标	Item	2010	2015	2016
一、大牲畜年末存栏 (万头)	**Larger Animals at Year-end (10 000 heads)**	**127.64**	**122.00**	**125.50**
1.牛 (万头)	Cattle and Buffaloes (10 000 heads)	90.10	101.06	106.55
2.马 (万匹)	Horses (10 000 heads)	1.71	1.15	1.05
3.驴 (万头)	Donkeys (10 000 heads)	18.87	12.74	11.97
4.骡 (万头)	Mules (10 000 heads)	16.96	7.05	5.93
二、猪年末存栏 (万头)	**Hogs at Year-end (10 000 heads)**	**474.84**	**485.91**	**449.68**
#能繁殖的母猪	Reproducible Hogs	53.54	51.70	49.58
三、羊年末存栏 (万只)	**Sheep and Goats at Year-end (10 000 heads)**	**734.70**	**1001.46**	**910.41**
1.山 羊	Goats	353.40	436.22	363.56
2.绵 羊	Sheep	381.30	565.24	546.85
四、家禽年末存栏 (万只)	**Poultry at Year-end (10 000 heads)**	**5694.68**	**8857.73**	**9377.49**
五、养兔年末存栏 (万只)	**Rabbits at Year-end (10 000 heads)**	**322.09**	**206.84**	**178.58**
六、猪、牛、羊出栏	**Slaughtered Hogs, Cattle Buffaloes and Sheep**			
猪全年出栏 (万头)	Slaughtered Hog in the Year (10 000 heads)	683.97	783.67	748.86
牛全年出栏 (万头)	Slaughtered Cattle Buffaloes in the Year (10 000 heads)	34.98	40.23	40.27
羊全年出栏 (万只)	Slaughtered Mutton in the Year (10 000 heads)	405.60	484.35	517.78
七、当年肉类总产量 (万吨)	**Total Output of Meat (10 000 tons)**	**72.44**	**85.57**	**84.43**
#猪肉产量	Pork	53.09	60.25	57.52
牛肉产量	Beef	4.92	5.88	5.92
羊肉产量	Mutton	5.60	6.90	7.43
禽肉产量	Poultry	7.11	11.30	12.46
兔肉产量	Rabbit	0.75	0.57	0.50
八、畜禽产品产量 (吨)	**Output of Animal and Poulty Products (ton)**			
1.奶 类	Milk	749374	927397	958782
#牛 奶	Cow Milk	732250	918727	950883
2.绵羊毛产量	Sheep Wool	7094	9195	8979
3.山羊粗毛产量	Goat Wool	1285	1555	1638
4.羊绒产量	Cashmere	666	1217	1247
5.禽蛋产量	Poultry Eggs	706836	873897	892312
6.蜂蜜产量	Honey	3156	5082	5030
7.蚕茧产量	Silkworm Cocoons	5384	5503	2953

9-15 渔业生产情况
PRODUCTION OF FISHERY

指　标	Item	2010	2015	2016
淡水产品产量(吨)	**Freshwater Aquatic Products (ton)**	**31700**	**52427**	**52279**
#鱼类产量	Fish	30514	51850	50734
1.养殖产量	Aquiculture Products	30869	51264	51178
#池　塘	Pond	18933	34389	34672
湖　泊	Lakes	917	2114	2120
水　库	Reservoir	10682	14473	14051
河　沟	Brook	240	94	141
2.捕捞产量	Fishing Products	831	1163	1101
淡水养殖面积(公顷)	**Freshwater Aquatic Area (ha)**	**14840**	**15715**	**15937**

9-16 农业现代化情况
AGRICULTURAL MODERNIZATION

指　标	Item	2010	2015	2016
一、农田水利情况	**Farm Water Conservancy Condition**			
年末有效灌溉面积　(千公顷)	Effective Irrigated Area at Year–end (1 000 ha)	1274.15	1560.32	1487.21
#机电排灌面积　(千公顷)	Mechanical and Electrical Irrigated Area (1 000 ha)	961.90	1111.71	1141.20
灌溉机电井数量　(眼)	Electromechanical Well for Irrigation (unit)	81166	91276	92663
二、农村用电情况	**Electricity Consumed Condition**			
1.农村用电量　(万千瓦小时)	Electricity Consumed in Rural Areas (10 000 kwh)	811763	968311	975220
2.农村小型水电站个数　(个)	Small Hyrdopower Station in Rural Areas (unit)	72	60	61
装机容量　(千瓦)	Installed Capacity (kw)	29264	58607	59492
三、农用化肥情况	**Chemical Fertilizers Condition**			
农用化肥施用折纯量　(吨)	Effective Component of Chemical Fertilizers (ton)	1103663	1185472	1170719
1.氮　肥	Nitrogenous Fertilizer	400203	335291	315956
2.磷　肥	Phosphate Fertilizer	199996	160235	147966
3.钾　肥	Potash Fertilizer	85069	104235	103514
4.复合肥	compownd Fertilizer	418395	585710	603283

9-17 主要年份化肥施用量、小水电站和农村用电量

CONSUMPTION OF CHEMICAL FERTILIZER, NUMBER OF SMALL HYDROPOWER STATION AND ELECTRICITY CONSUMPTION IN RURAL AREAS IN MAJOR YEARS

年 份 Year	农用化肥施用量 (折纯量, 吨) Consumption of Chemical Fertilizer (ton)	农村小型水电站 Small Hydropower Station in Rural Areas		农村用电量 (万千瓦小时) Electricity Consumption in Rural Areas (10 000 kwh)
		个 数 (个) Number (unit)	装机容量 (千瓦) Installed Capacity (kw)	
1978	355990	401	18678	122683
1980	302904	407	23191	135870
1985	397907	231	26762	151085
1990	565624	197	30414	259437
1995	780568	142	31401	460583
2000	869882	106	24900	531441
2005	956999	87	22994	669390
2006	983000	69	22729	692109
2007	1008000	70	23880	759390
2008	1034042	74	25379	789864
2009	1043239	73	29000	811966
2010	1103663	72	29264	811763
2011	1145667	71	29177	865984
2012	1182795	71	28093	949517
2013	1210196	63	24963	997819
2014	1196138	60	28647	970811
2015	1185472	60	58607	968311
2016	1170719	61	59492	975220

9-18 农民家庭平均每户生产性固定资产原值
ORIGINAL VALUE OF PRODUCTIVE FIXED ASSETS PER RURAL HOUSEHOLD

单位：元 (yuan)

指　标	Item	2015	2016
一、农业生产性固定资产原价	**Original Value of Agricultural Productive Fixed Assets**		
生产性用房及建筑物	Productive Houses and Buildings	874.80	545.84
役　畜	Draught Animals	327.53	404.62
产品畜	Commodity Animals	625.13	208.30
农业设施	Agricultural Facilities	57.86	67.61
农业机械	Agricultural Machinery	1918.24	2160.81
农林牧渔服务业	Services of Farming, Forestry, Animal Husbandry and Fishery	434.08	269.19
二、非农产业固定资产原价	**Original Value of Nonagricultural Fixed Assets**		
采矿业	Mining		1.30
制造业	Manufacturing	84.22	413.00
电力、热力、燃气及水生产和供应业	Production and Supply of Power, Heat, Gas and Water	1.34	0.83
建筑业	Construction	124.62	143.58
批发和零售业	Wholesale and Retail Trade	672.23	863.08
交通运输、仓储和邮政业	Transportation, Storage and Post	3097.39	3890.06
住宿和餐饮业	Hotels and Catering Services	202.93	273.72
房地产业	Real Estate		
租赁和商务服务业	Leasing and Business Services	246.38	124.92
居民服务、修理和其他服务业	Resident Services, Repair and Other Services	253.75	322.05
其他行业	Others	109.30	43.75

9-19 农民家庭平均每百户拥有主要生产性固定资产数量
MAJOR PRODUCTIVE FIXED ASSETS PER 100 RURAL HOUSEHOLDS

指 标	Item	2015	2016
生产性用房及建筑物(平方米)	Productive Houses and Buildings (sq.m)	663.43	600.20
大中型农用拖拉机 (台)	Large and Medium-sized Agricultural Tractors (unit)	2.33	1.81
小型农用拖拉机 (台)	Small Agricultural Tractors (unit)	22.85	23.43
农用排灌动力机械 (台)	Machinery forAgricultural Drainage and Irrigation (unit)	0.90	1.44
插秧机 (台)	Rice Transplanters (unit)	0.31	0.05
收割机 (台)	Harvesters (unit)	1.03	0.60
脱粒机 (台)	Threshing Machines (unit)	1.43	1.30
役 畜 (头)	Draught Animals (head)	4.08	5.41
产品畜 (头)	Commodity Animals (head)	390.32	44.12

9-20 农民家庭平均每人生产和销售的主要农林产品
PER CAPITA MAJOR FARM AND FOREST PRODUCTS PRODUCED AND SOLD BY RURAL HOUSEHOLDS

单位：公斤 (kg)

指 标	Item	生产量 Output		出售量 Sales	
		2015	2016	2015	2016
谷 物	Cereal	873.71	1044.85	640.83	882.07
薯 类	Tubers	23.90	31.46	7.08	9.52
豆 类	Beans	17.50	25.68	12.64	17.77
棉 花	Cotton	0.30	0.11	0.04	0.03
油 料	Oil-bearing Crops	8.97	16.27	5.01	8.40

主要统计指标解释

乡村户数　指长期(一年以上)居住在乡镇(不包括城关镇)行政管理区域内的住户，还包括居住在城关镇所辖行政村范围内的农村住户。户口不在本地而在本地居住一年及以上的住户也包括在本地农村住户内；有本地户口，但举家外出谋生一年以上的住户，无论是否保留承包耕地都不包括在本地农村住户范围内。不包括乡村地区内的国有经济的机关、团体、学校、企业、事业单位的集体户。

乡村人口　乡村地区常住居民户数中的常住人口数，即经常在家或在家居住6个月以上，而且经济和生活与本户连成一体的人口。外出从业人员在外居住时间虽然在6个月以上，但收入主要带回家中，经济与本户连为一体，仍视为家庭常住人口；在家居住，生活和本户连成一体的国家职工、退休人员也为家庭常住人口，但是现役军人、中专及以上（走读生除外）的在校学生以及常年在外（不包括探亲、看病等）且已有稳定的职业与居住场所的外出从业人员，不应当作家庭常住人口。

乡村从业人员　指乡村人口中16岁以上实际参加生产经营活动并取得实物或货币收入的人员，既包括劳动年龄内经常参加劳动的人员，也包括超过劳动年龄但经常参加劳动的人员。但不包括户口在家的在外学生、现役军人和丧失劳动能力的人，也不包括待业人员和家务劳动者。从业人员年龄为16岁以上。从业人员按从事主业时间最长（时间相同按收入）分为农业从业人员、工业从业人员、建筑业从业人员、交运仓储及邮政从业人员、信息传输、计算机服务业和软件业从业人员、批发与零售业从业人员、住宿和餐饮业从业人员、其他行业从业人员。

农林牧渔业总产值　指以货币表现的农林牧渔业的全部产品总量和对农林牧渔业生产进行的各种支持性服务活动的价值。它反映一定时期内农林牧渔业生产总规模和总成果，是观察农林牧渔业生产水平和发展速度，研究农林牧渔业内部比例关系、农林牧渔业与工业、农林牧渔业与国家建设、人民生活比例关系的重要指标，同时也是计算农林牧渔业劳动生产率和农林牧渔业增加值的基础资料。

农林牧渔业增加值　指农、林、牧、渔业生产及农林牧渔服务业提供服务活动所增加的价值，为农林牧渔业现价总产值扣除农林牧渔业中间消耗后的余额。

耕地总资源　指种植农作物的土地。包括熟地，新开发、复垦、整理地，休闲地（含轮歇地、轮作地）；以种植农作物（含蔬菜）为主，间有零星果树、桑树或其他树木的土地；平均每年能保证收获一季的已是滩地和海涂。耕地中包括南方宽度<1.0米、北方宽度<2.0米固定的沟、渠、路和地坎（梗）；临时种植药材、草皮、花卉、苗木等的耕地，以及其他临时改变用途的耕地。

有效灌溉面积　具有一定水源，地块比较平整，灌溉工程或设备已经配套，在一般年景下当年能够进行正常灌溉的耕地面积。在一般情况下，有效灌溉面积应等于灌溉工程或设备已经配套，能够进行正常灌溉的水田和水浇地之和。

农作物播种面积　指实际播种或移植有农作物的面积。凡是实际种植有农作物的面积，不论种植在耕地上还是种植在非耕地上，均包括在农作物播种面积中。在播种季节基本结束后，因遭灾而重新改种和补种的农作物面积，也包括在内。

农作物总产量　指本年度内生产的各种农作物总产量，不论计划内外、数量多少，耕地与非耕地上的农作物产量，都应统计在内。包括粮食、棉花、油料、麻类、糖类、药材、蔬菜、瓜类及其他农作物。

期末畜禽存栏头(只)数　指报告期末农村各种合作组织和国营农场、农民个人、机关、团体、学校、工矿企业、部队等单位，以及城镇居民饲养的大牲畜、猪、羊、家禽等畜禽的数量。科学研究单位专门用于试验研究的牲畜和军马除外。

肉类总产量　指调查期内各种牲畜及家禽、兔等动物肉产量总计。猪、牛、羊、马、驴、骡、骆驼肉产量按去掉头蹄下水后带骨肉的胴体重量计算，兔及禽肉产量按屠宰后去毛和内脏后的重量计算。

禽蛋产量　指调查期内饲养的蛋用家禽生产的禽蛋总重量。包括出售的和农民自产自用的部分。品种主要为鸡鸭鹅。

奶类产量　指全社会产量，包括出售部分和农牧民自食部分。不包括牛犊和乳羊直接吮食部分。

农用化肥施用量　指本年内实际用于农业生产的化肥数量，包括氮肥、磷肥、钾肥和复合肥。化肥施用量要求按折纯量计算数量。折纯量是指把氮肥、磷肥、钾肥分别按含氮、含五氧化二磷、含氧化钾的百分之百成份进行折算后的数量。复合肥按其所含主要成分折算。公式为：折纯量=实物量×某种化肥有效成份含量的百分比

农村用电量　本年度内，扣除在农村中的国有工业、交通、基建等单位的用电量以后的农村生产和生活的全年用电总量。包括国家电网供电和农村自办电站供电量。

Explanatory Notes on Main Statistical Indicators

Number of Rural Households refers to households resident on a long term basis (i.e. 1 year or more) in administrative districts in townships (not including urban townships), including rural households resident in areas under the jurisdiction of urban townships. Households whose household registration is not in the locality yet resident for one year or more are included among the rural households. Households having local household registration yet the whole household having left for somewhere else for work for one year or more, whether still retaining contracted farmland, are not included among the local rural households. Also not included are collective households associated with institutions of the State economy, organizations, schools and enterprises.

Rural Population refers to residential population of residential households in rural areas, i.e. who stay at home usually or residing at home above 6 months and link closely to the household in economy and livelihood. Persons who engaged outside above 6 months while take their income back to home and link closely with the household in economy, are still calculated as rural population. National workers and retirees who reside at home at the same time link closely with the household are still calculated as rural population, while enlisted man, secondary specialized and above students (except day-students) and persons engaged outside (except family visit and medical treatment) for years having stable jobs and living places can't be calculated as rural population.

Rural Employees refer to rural persons aged over 16 years who are engaged in actual production and management activities and receive payment in kind or wages, including those covered within the labor force age bracket and regularly participating in production activities, and those who are out of the labor force age bracket yet also participating in production activities regularly. Students studying in other places with their permanent residence registered in local areas, servicemen and persons incapable of working are not included. Unemployed persons and domestic workers are also not included. Persons employed are classified as persons engaged in agriculture, forestry, animal husbandry or fishery activities; persons engaged in industrial activities; persons engaged in construction activities; persons engaged in transport, storage and telecommunications activities; persons engaged in information transmission, computer services and software industry; persons engaged in wholesale and retail trade and catering activities; and persons engaged in other non-agriculture activities. In case the person is engaged in more than one type of work, classification is according to the industry in which he works most of the time.

Gross Output of Farming, Forestry, Animal Husbandry and Fishery refers to the total volume of products of farming, forestry, animal husbandry and fishery and value of service for farming, forestry, animal husbandry and fishery productive activity in value terms. It reflects total scale and results of farming, forestry, animal husbandry and fishery productive in a period time. It's a important indicator to watch production level and rate, research interior percentage, percentage with industry, state construction and people's livelihood. It's also basic to calculate productivity and value added.

Value Added of Farming, Forestry, Animal Husbandry and Fishery refers to new increasing value through farming, forestry, animal husbandry and fishery and services activities, which equals to gross output of farming, forestry, animal husbandry and fishery minus their intermediate consumption.

Resources of Cultivated Area refers to farm land for growing crops, including cultivated land, newly cultivated land and land planted crops in the current year, fallow land including swidden and rotation land, land which are mainly planted with crops including vegetables and scattered with fruit trees, mulberry trees and other trees, beaches and shoal land which can gains at least one season. Cultivated Area includes channels, ditches, footpaths and ridges which are not wider than one meter in the south while 2 meters in the north, land temporarily plant with medical materials, turfs, flowers and nursery stocks, and other lands which temporarily change usage.

Effective Irrigated Area refers to area of land that are effectively irrigated, i.e. relatively level land, where there are water sources or complete sets of irrigation facilities to lift and move adequate water for irrigation purpose under normal conditions. Under normal institutions, irrigated area is the sum of watered fields and irrigated fields where irrigation systems or equipment have been installed for regular irrigation purpose.

Sown Area of Farm Crops refers to area of land sown or transplanted with crops regardless of being in cultivated area or non-cultivated area, area of land re-sown due to natural disasters is also included.

Total Output of Farm Crops refers to the total output of all kinds of crops this year. It does not matter if they are included in the plans the amount is large or small or the crops are grown on the cultivated land or on uncultivated land. The crops include grain cotton oil hemp sugar herbs vegetables melons and other crops.

Number of Livestock or Poultry in Stock at End of the Period refers to the total number of large animals, pigs, sheep, poultry, etc. raised by rural cooperative organizations, state farms, rural individuals, government agencies, groups, schools, industrial and mining enterprises, armies and urban residents at end of the reference period. Experimental Livestock used by the scientific research units and army horses are excepted.

Total Output of Meat refers to the total meat output of all kinds of livestock, poultry, rabbits, etc. at end of the period. Meat of hogs, cattle, sheep, horses, donkeys, mules and camels are calculated by the body weights without heads, feet and offal, while meat of rabbits and poultry are calculated by the slaughtered weights without hair and offal.

Output of Poultry Eggs refers to the total weight of poultry eggs produced by raised egg-laying poultry in the survey period, including eggs for sale and for peasants own use. The main products are chicken eggs, duck eggs and gooses eggs.

Output of Milk refers to the total society milk output, including sold milk and milk consumed by the peasants and herdsmen. Milk sucked by calves and lambs are excepted.

Consumption of Chemical Fertilizers refers to the quantity of chemical fertilizers applied in agriculture in the year, including nitrogenous fertilizer, phosphate fertilizer, potash fertilizer and compound fertilizer. It is calculated in terms of volume of effective components by means of converting the gross weight of the respective fertilizers into weight containing effective component (e.g. nitrogen content in nitrogenous fertilizer, phosphorous pentoxide contents in phosphate fertilizer and potassium oxide contents in potash fertilizer). Compound fertilizer is converted in regard to its major components. The formula is: Volume of effective component = physical quantity × effective component of certain chemical fertilizer (%)

Electricity Consumption in Rural Areas refers to the total electricity consumption for rural production and living in the year, which deduct consumption of national industry, transportation and capital construction units in rural areas. It includes the supply of national power grid and power station building by rural residents.

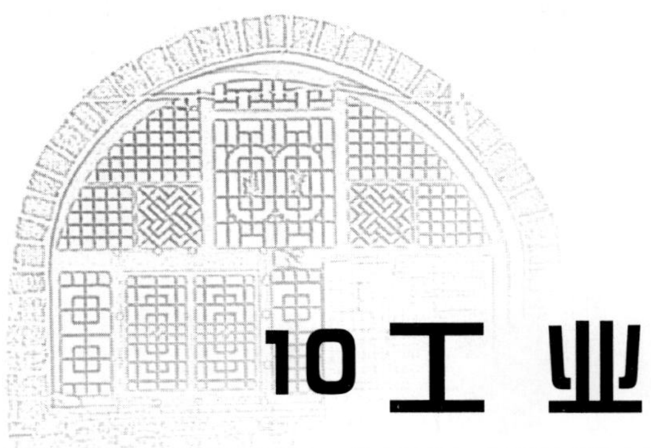

10 工 业

INDUSTRY

资料整理人员

刘香元　童　超　杨　健　刘肖余　黄岩峰

工　业
INDUSTRY

工业企业单位数	Number of Industrial Enterprises	3548	个	(unit)
工业增加值	Value Added of Industry	3948.9	亿元	(100 million yuan)
产品产量（全社会）	Output of Products(Total Socidty)			
原　煤	Coal	83044	万吨	(10 000 tons)
发电量	Electricity	2510.5	亿千瓦小时	(100 million kwh)
生　铁	Pig Iron	3641.1	万吨	(10 000 tons)
粗　钢	Crude Steel	3936.1	万吨	(10 000 tons)

工业增加值构成（%）
Composition of Value Added of Industry (%)

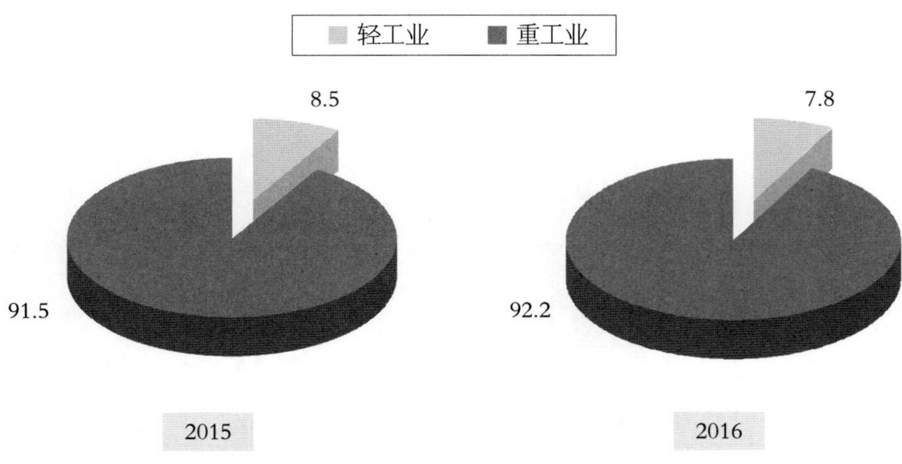

工业增加值（亿元）
Value Added of Industry (100 million yuan)

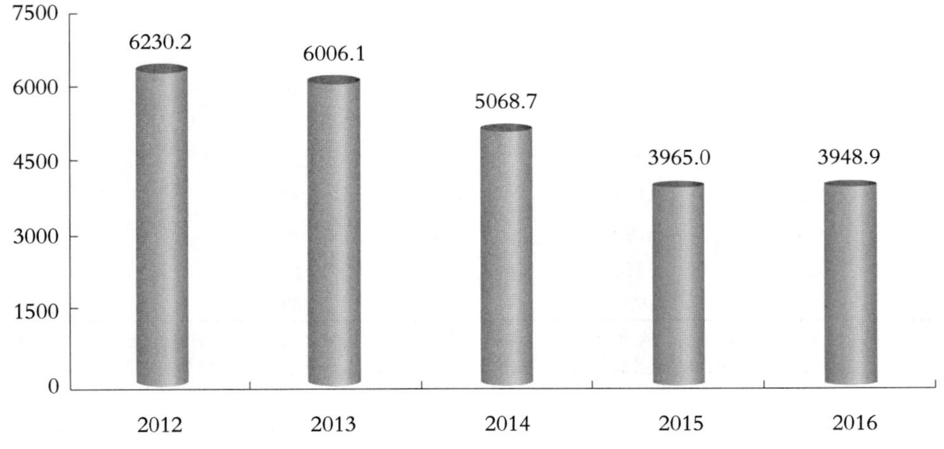

10-1 主要年份工业企业单位数
NUMBER OF INDUSTRIAL ENTERPRISES IN MAJOR YEARS

单位：个 (unit)

年份 Year	工业企业单位数 Number of Industrial Enterprises	按隶属关系分 Grouped by Jurisdiction of Management		按经济类型分 Grouped by Ownership		
		中央企业 Central Enterprise	地方企业 Local Enterprise	国有经济 State-owned Enterprise	集体经济 Collective-owned Enterprise	其他经济 Other Ownership
1978	9381	100	9281	2547	6834	
1980	9533	112	9421	2524	7009	
1985	11004	168	10836	2421	8577	6
1990	12122	187	11935	2776	9318	28
1995	12086	183	11903	3042	8698	346
2000	3275	110	3165	1537	766	972
2005	4441	95	4346	879	928	2634
2010	4240	120	4120	266	181	3793
2011	3673	135	3538	227	114	3332
2012	3905	150	3755	237	97	3571
2013	3979	148	3831	110	72	3797
2014	3906	144	3762	84	56	3766
2015	3845	147	3698	74	45	3726
2016	3548	148	3400	56	39	3453

年份 Year	按轻重工业分 Grouped by Light & Heavy Industry		按企业规模分 Grouped by Size of Enterprises			
	轻工业 Light Industry	重工业 Heavy Industry	大型企业 Large-size Enterprise	中型企业 Medium-size Enterprise	小型企业 Small-size Enterprise	微型企业 Micro-size Enterprises
1978	4463	4918	36	117	9228	
1980	4528	5005	50	94	9389	
1985	4875	6129	75	144	10785	
1990	4922	7200	97	169	11856	
1995	4080	8006	122	252	11712	
2000	944	2331	137	228	2910	
2005	761	3680	87	757	3597	
2010	737	3503	149	970	3121	
2011	546	3127	300	924	2297	152
2012	569	3336	295	889	2513	208
2013	586	3393	277	913	2542	247
2014	614	3292	246	898	2547	215
2015	625	3220	219	854	2476	296
2016	595	2953	223	843	2313	169

注：(1)工业企业统计范围1998-2006年为国有企业、大中型企业和年产品销售收入500万元及以上非国有企业；2007-2010年为年主营业务收入500万元以上的工业法人企业；2011年及以后为年主营业务收入2000万元以上的工业法人企业。

(2)2011年起企业规模划分采用新标准。

Notes: (1)Enterprises in this table contains enterprises which is state-owned, large & medium-sized and non-state-owned with sales above 5 million yuan from 1998 to 2006; enterprises whose major business revenue is above 5 million yuan from 2007 to 2010; enterprises whose major business revenue is above 20 million yuan since 2011.

(2)New standards of enterprise size have been used since 2011.

10-2 主要年份主要工业产品产量
OUTPUT OF MAJOR INDUSTRIAL PRODUCTS IN MAJOR YEARS

年 份 Year	原 煤 (万吨) Coal (10 000 tons)	发电量 (亿千瓦小时) Electricity (100 million kwh)	粗 钢 (万吨) Crude Steel (10 000 tons)	钢 材 (万吨) Steel Products (10 000 tons)	生 铁 (万吨) Pig Iron (10 000 tons)	焦 炭 (万吨) Coke (10 000 tons)	铜(吨) Copper(ton)
1978	9825	106.63	119.99	74.04	150.39	356.51	13583
1980	12103	120.24	149.38	86.42	171.39	320.95	26607
1985	21418	184.59	183.74	110.80	229.54	417.34	24400
1990	28597	314.16	238.58	128.78	454.88	1609.27	25147
1995	34731	505.97	339.80	217.09	1438.29	5297.62	27530
2000	25152	624.71	472.73	392.60	1628.00	4967.00	28544
2005	55426	1316.50	1654.72	1368.60	3229.80	7981.00	27225
2010	74096	2150.56	3048.82	2866.35	3402.43	8502.10	80610
2011	87228	2344.00	3490.42	3371.16	3786.08	9047.91	87785
2012	91333	2534.99	3950.17	3799.47	4009.64	8612.66	98134
2013	92167	2641.10	4671.44	4487.04	4310.66	9022.40	88564
2014	92794	2647.04	4325.39	4701.01	4059.29	8765.90	144489
2015	96680	2457.45	3846.96	4267.25	3576.38	8039.88	180935
2016	83044	2510.51	3936.13	4278.97	3641.09	8185.99	195596

年 份 Year	水 泥 (万吨) Cement (10 000 tons)	平板玻璃 (万重量箱) Plate Glass (10 000 weight cases)	化学肥料(折有效成份100%，万吨) Chemical Fertilizer (calculated on100% effictive content，10 000 tons)			化学农药 (万吨) Chemical Pesticide (10 000 tons)	初级形态的塑料(万吨) Primary Form of Plastics (10 000 tons)
			合 计 Total	#氮 肥 Nitrogenous	#磷 肥 Phosphate		
1978	255.87	47.09	32.33	30.24	2.09	0.90	0.57
1980	287.88	52.74	40.15	34.91	5.24	0.77	0.55
1985	458.68	113.33	39.31	37.41	1.89	0.29	0.94
1990	612.47	181.58	71.94	60.06	11.88	0.38	1.82
1995	1169.85	241.44	102.31	83.31	18.93	0.71	2.64
2000	1434.00	357.98	170.17	137.55	18.82	0.40	3.04
2005	2310.68	360.24	353.51	336.35	13.10	0.74	29.28
2010	3670.29	1673.37	331.84	321.60	10.24	0.17	20.24
2011	4101.47	1847.64	363.75	353.73	10.02	0.15	46.32
2012	5076.21	1975.81	389.07	379.23	9.84	0.08	51.86
2013	5269.09	2065.28	446.13	439.79	6.34	0.05	48.54
2014	4801.96	1758.92	461.67	453.36	8.02	0.03	49.36
2015	3786.09	1400.82	464.96	455.69	9.27	0.06	65.46
2016	3851.54	1648.08	443.54	431.16	7.58	0.06	67.24

注：本表产量为全社会口径。
Note: Coverage of products in the table is total society.

10-2 续表 continued

年 份 Year	轮胎外胎 (万条) Tires Cover (10 000 units)	矿山设备 (吨) Mining Equipment (ton)	金属切削机床(台) Metal-cutting Machine Tools (unit)	纱(吨) Yarn(ton)	布(万米) Cloth(10 000 m)
1978	9.97	18214	3131	72193	32756
1980	14.44	9349	1706	84145	38652
1985	29.25	16345	1288	77762	37555
1990	57.33	25717	1678	94237	42948
1995	112.45	23675	688	72165	35593
2000	154.30	6857	832	84765	33253
2005	135.11	109570	1813	149828	36256
2010	173.51	329442	1822	53913	7381
2011	164.86	354327	1937	54012	8139
2012	170.26	434304	834	61575	7499
2013	166.57	430963	466	56923	7553
2014	165.20	255155	330	55125	8172
2015	154.98	260185	109	52826	7720
2016	145.76	223304	13	53769	4176

年 份 Year	化学纤维 (吨) Chemical Fiber (ton)	糖(吨) Sugar(ton)	卷 烟 (万箱) Cigarettes (10 000 cases)	机制纸及纸板 (万吨) Machine-made Paper and Paperboard (10 000 tons)	合成洗涤剂 (吨) Synthetic Detergents (ton)
1978	1668	5319	16.77	9.35	14409
1980	3642	11111	18.62	11.55	18505
1985	14581	30118	18.72	18.75	60746
1990	19839	30514	24.17	35.44	68951
1995	25345	36850	28.43	59.69	135359
2000	28987	7660	30.34	27.00	189235
2005	27051	4111	25.00	40.49	162303
2010	10023	43547	29.50	21.78	119774
2011	6446	43480	31.00	20.48	98419
2012	4504	52607	31.20	33.39	101898
2013	2396	27436	31.70	34.17	108199
2014		10	32.70	25.87	92683
2015		3	32.70	35.34	87713
2016		4	31.10	41.67	79342

10-3 规模以上主要工业产品产量
OUTPUT OF MAJOR INDUSTRIAL PRODUCTS ABOVE DESIGNATED SIZE

指 标		Item	2015	2016
原 煤	(万吨)	Coal (10 000 tons)	94410.3	81641.5
发电量	(亿千瓦小时)	Electricity (100 million kwh)	2434.7	2498.7
粗 钢	(万吨)	Crude Steel (10 000 tons)	3847.0	3936.1
钢 材	(万吨)	Steel Products (10 000 tons)	4267.3	4279.0
生 铁	(万吨)	Pig Iron (10 000 tons)	3576.4	3641.1
原 铝	(万吨)	Electrolyzed Aluminum (10 000 tons)	66.0	86.8
氧化铝	(万吨)	Aluminum Oxide (10 000 tons)	1272.9	1414.1
焦 炭	(万吨)	Coke (10 000 tons)	8034.7	8186.0
铜	(万吨)	Copper (10 000 tons)	18.1	19.6
水 泥	(万吨)	Cement (10 000 tons)	3564.7	3595.4
平板玻璃	(万重量箱)	Plate Glass (10 000 weight cases)	1400.8	1648.1
硫 酸	(折纯，万吨)	Sulfuric Acid (10 000 tons)	53.4	53.6
化学肥料	(折纯，万吨)	Chemical Fertilizer (10 000 tons)	465.0	437.5
化学农药	(吨)	Chemical Pesticide (10 000 tons)	564.0	589.0
初级形态的塑料	(万吨)	Primary Form of Plastics (10 000 tons)	65.5	67.2
轮胎外胎	(万条)	Tires Cover (10 000 units)	155.0	145.8
矿山设备	(吨)	Mining Equipment (ton)	260185	223304
金属切削机床	(台)	Metal-cutting Machine Tools (unit)	109	13
工业锅炉	(蒸发量吨)	Industrial Boiler (ton)	14838	16430
变压器	(万千伏安)	Transformer (10 000 kva)	737.4	654.8
泵	(台)	Pump (unit)	148279	92547
纱	(吨)	Yarn (ton)	52826.2	53769.4
布	(万米)	Cloth (10 000 m)	4710.5	4175.9
白 酒	(千升)	White Spirit (kiloliter)	83568.2	103238.5
啤 酒	(千升)	Beer (kiloliter)	394745.8	339597.0
卷 烟	(万箱)	Cigarettes (10 000 cases)	32.7	31.1
机制纸及纸板	(万吨)	Machine-made Paper and Paperboard (10 000 tons)	35.3	41.7
合成洗涤剂	(吨)	Synthetic Detergents (ton)	87212.9	78342.1
煤层气	(亿立方米)	Coalbed Methane (100 million cu.m)	39.8	43.2
手 机	(万台)	Mobile Phones (10 000 unit)	2038.4	2693.4
化学药品原药	(吨)	Chemical Medicine (ton)	25349.7	27733.9
醋	(吨)	Vinegar (ton)	673052.0	626955.3
太阳能电池	(千瓦)	Solar Cell (kw)	764713	1441692
新能源汽车	(辆)	New Energy Motor Vehicles (unit)		12292

10-4 工业增加值(2016年)
VALVE ADDED OF INDUSTRY(2016)

单位：万元 (10 000 yuan)

指　　标	Item	2016
总　计	**Total**	**39488785**
按轻重工业分	Grouped by Light and Heavy Industry	
轻工业	Light Industry	3063800
重工业	Heavy Industry	36424986
按企业规模分	Grouped by Size of Enterprises	
大型企业	Large-size Enterprise	19954571
中型企业	Medium-size Enterprise	12597910
小型企业	Small-size Enterprise	6415501
微型企业	Micro-size Enterprise	520802
按行业大类分	Grouped by Sector	
采矿业	Mining	20258995
煤炭开采和洗选业	Coal Mining and Dressing	19079120
石油和天然气开采业	Petroleum and Natural Gas Extraction	253300
黑色金属矿采选业	Ferrous Metals Mining and Dressing	800398
有色金属矿采选业	Nonferrous Metals Mining and Dressing	122149
非金属矿采选业	Nonmetal Minerals Mining and Dressing	4028
开采辅助活动	Mining Auxiliary Activities	
其他采矿业	Other Mining Industry	
制造业	Manufacturing	14131663
农副食品加工业	Farm Products Processing	589464
食品制造业	Food Manufacturing	280876
酒、饮料和精制茶制造业	Wine, Beverages and Refined Tea Manufacturing	601775
烟草制品业	Tobacoo Products Manfacturing	337183
纺织业	Textile Industry	53273
纺织服装、服饰业	Textile, Wearing Apparel and Accessories	55581
皮革、毛皮、羽毛及其制品和制鞋业	Leather, Fur, Feather and Related Products and Footwear	1316
木材加工和木、竹、藤、棕、草制品业	Timber Processing,Bamboo,Cane,Palm Fiber and Straw Products	21402
家具制造业	Furniture Manufacturing	18486

10-4 续表 continued

单位：万元 (10 000 yuan)

指 标	Item	2016
造纸和纸制品业	Paper Making and Paper Products	25805
印刷和记录媒介复制业	Printing and Record Medium Reproduction	51825
文教、工美、体育和娱乐用品制造业	Culture, Education, Art and Crafts, Sport and Entertainment Products	24105
石油加工、炼焦和核燃料加工业	Petroleum Processing, Coking and Nuclear Fuel Processing	1812774
化学原料和化学制品制造业	Raw Chemical Materials and Chemical Products	774457
医药制造业	Medical and Pharmaceutical Products	647426
化学纤维制造业	Chemical Fiber Manufacturing	
橡胶和塑料制品业	Rubber and Plastic Products	95028
非金属矿物制品业	Nonmetal Mineral Products	922794
黑色金属冶炼和压延加工业	Smelting and Pressing of Ferrous Metals	2588940
有色金属冶炼和压延加工业	Smelting and Pressing of Non-ferrous Metals	1499547
金属制品业	Metal Prodcuts	270430
通用设备制造业	Ordinary Machinery Manufacturing	327108
专用设备制造业	Special Purpose Equipment Manufacturing	309346
汽车制造业	Automobile Manufacturing	225850
铁路、船舶、航空航天和其他运输设备制造业	Railroad, Marine, Aviation and Other Transport Equipment Manufacturing	210526
电气机械和器材制造业	Electrical Machinery and Equipment Manufacturing	304880
计算机、通信和其他电子设备制造业	Computers, Telecommunication and Other Electronic Equipments	1964395
仪器仪表制造业	Equipments and Instruments Manufacturing	41405
其他制造业	Other Manufacturing	23095
废弃资源综合利用业	Comprehensive Utilization of Waste Resources	17879
金属制品、机械和设备修理业	Metal products, Machinery and Equipment Repair Industry	34695
电力、热力、燃气及水生产和供应业	Production and Supply of Electricity, Heat, Gas and Water	5098128
电力、热力生产和供应业	Production and Supply of Electricity and Heat	4707116
燃气生产和供应业	Production and Supply of Gas	316945
水的生产和供应业	Production and Supply of Water	74067

10-5 工业企业主要经济指标(2016年)

单位：万元

指　标	Item	单位数(个) Number of Enterprises (unit)
总　计	**Total**	**3548**
一、按隶属关系分	Grouped by Jurisdiction of Management	
中央企业	Central Enterprises	148
省属企业	Province–owned Enterprises	341
市属企业	Cities–owned Enterprises	159
县(市、区)属企业	County–owned Enterprises	382
城市街道企业	Cities' Subdistrict–owned Enterprises	3
镇属企业	Town–owned Enterprises	18
乡属企业	Township Enterprises	10
居委会办企业	Neighbourhood Committee –run Enterprises	2
村办企业	Village Enterprises	24
其　他	Enterprises of Other Types of Ownership	2461
二、按登记注册类型分	Grouped by Registered Kind	
内资企业	Civil Funded Enterprises	3415
国有企业	State–owned Enterprises	56
集体企业	Collective–owned Enterprises	39
股份合作企业	Share Holding Cooperative Enterprises	1
联营企业	Joint Owned Enterprises	2
有限责任公司	Limited Responsibility Company	1177
国有独资公司	Company Exclusively with Investment from State	85
其他有限责任公司	Other Limited Responsibility Company	1092
股份有限公司	Share Holding Limited Company	123
私营企业	Privately Owned Enterprises	2015
私营独资企业	Enterprise Exclusively with Investment from Private	120
私营合伙企业	Private Partner Enterprises	11
私营有限责任公司	Privately Owned Limited Responsibility Company	1808
私营股份有限公司	Privately Owned Share Holding Limited Company	76
其他企业	Enterprises of Other Types of Ownership	2
港、澳、台商投资企业	Enterprises Funded by Hong Kong, Macao and Taiwan	52
合资经营企业(港或澳、台资)	Joint Venture	31
合作经营企业(港或澳、台资)	Cooperative Enterprise	1
港澳台商独资企业	Ventures Exclusively with Hong Kong, Macao and Taiwan Investment	15
港澳台商投资股份有限公司	Share Holding Limited Company	4
其他港澳台商投资企业	Others	1

MAIN ECONOMIC INDICATORS OF INDUSTRIAL ENTERPRISES(2016)

(10 000 yuan)

#亏损企业 Loss-making Enterprises	工业销售产值 Industrial Sales Output Value	资产总计 Total Assets	流动资产合计 Total Circulating Funds	固定资产合计 Total Fixed Assets	固定资产原价 Original Value of Fixed Assets
1234	**127572796**	**336219522**	**132904352**	**129013553**	**183644288**
37	19243570	42329308	9345427	24936997	42411405
147	32265229	143069339	55549444	52664356	72667472
76	5428161	17488168	6616488	6260457	8893852
146	10470459	30256462	11248758	11398211	14212647
2	22914	20965	15088	5877	12815
7	1334722	1744896	1055846	498207	759185
9	154708	1102523	480204	271218	379491
1	11952	15508	10194	4271	6457
4	590375	1129359	562154	382192	556813
805	58050707	99062994	48020750	32591768	43744152
1190	114735992	314692080	121526759	121093803	170674207
31	9372808	14442287	2439911	10671089	17486991
17	762439	1001594	574757	282107	613235
	2713	5220	4516	704	2619
2	42584	146078	54834	19329	65010
462	57118944	212215470	80548328	79758640	108148721
37	13305166	39289937	15131614	13758311	23395055
425	43813778	172925533	65416714	66000328	84753666
39	8317194	25868484	8172946	10577246	17556537
638	39091281	60737968	29538566	19710573	26730486
30	1712738	912143	571453	290387	432058
2	155213	64247	31868	14800	19921
587	34780065	55589837	26835825	17935753	24839595
19	2443266	4171742	2099421	1469634	1438913
1	28029	274978	192902	74114	70608
16	9064273	12523586	7735503	3985366	6175293
12	6934184	8796572	5887522	2523765	3841762
	221580	307519	236794	52680	175656
2	1656160	2625940	1251685	1030873	1639114
2	225233	712269	286359	370545	507221
	27117	81286	73143	7504	11540

10-5 续表1

单位：万元

指　标	Item	单位数 (个) Number of Enterprises (unit)
外商投资企业	Foreign Funded Enterprises	81
中外合资经营企业	Joint Venture	56
中外合作经营企业	Cooperative Enterprises	3
外资企业	Enterprises Funded By Foreign Investments	20
外商投资股份有限公司	Share Holding Limited Company	1
其他外商投资企业	Other Foreign Funded Enterprises	1
三、在总计中:亏损企业	Of the Total: Loss-making Enterprises	1234
在总计中:国有控股企业	Of the Total: State-Controlled Share Holding Enterprises	802
在总计中:农村工业	Of the Total: Rural Industry	34
在总计中:轻工业	Of the Total: Light Industry	595
重工业	Heavy Industry	2953
在总计中:大型企业	Of the Total: Large-size Enterprises	223
中型企业	Medium-size Enterprises	843
小型企业	Small-size Enterprises	2313
微型企业	Micro-size Enterprises	169
四、按工业行业大类分	Grouped by Sector	
采矿业	Mining	1228
煤炭开采和洗选业	Coal Mining and Dressing	1034
石油和天然气开采业	Petroleum and Natural Gas Extraction	16
黑色金属矿采选业	Ferrous Metals Mining and Dressing	154
有色金属矿采选业	Nonferrous Metals Mining and Dressing	18
非金属矿采选业	Nonmetal Minerals Mining and Dressing	6
开采辅助活动	Mining Auxiliary Activities	
其他采矿业	Other Mining Industry	
制造业	Manufacturing	2064
农副食品加工业	Farm Products Processing	162
食品制造业	Food Manufacturing	79
酒、饮料和精制茶制造业	Wine, Beverages and Refined Tea Manufacturing	60
烟草制品业	Tobacoo Products Manfacturing	1
纺织业	Textile Industry	28
纺织服装、服饰业	Textile, Wearing Apparel and Accessories	14
皮革、毛皮、羽毛及其制品和制鞋业	Leather, Fur, Feather and Related Products and Footwear	1
木材加工和木、竹、藤、棕、草制品业	Timber Processing,Bamboo,Cane,Palm Fiber and Straw Products	6

continued

(10 000 yuan)

#亏损企业 Loss-making Enterprises	工业销售产值 Industrial Sales Output Value	资产总计 Total Assets	流动资产合计 Total Circulating Funds	固定资产合计 Total Fixed Assets	固定资产原价 Original Value Of Fixed Assets
28	3772530	9003855	3642090	3934385	6794788
19	1967151	5698344	2287572	2433957	3205014
	745561	1598774	515699	735671	2263634
9	1037970	1548600	821108	627180	1178350
	7018	11265	6620	2709	6088
	14830	146873	11091	134868	141703
1234	30176810	127818457	48726888	51416318	65083169
333	60785946	221336883	76248782	91891872	133649185
13	745083	2231882	1042359	653410	936304
127	10436378	14257870	6870869	4708690	6373723
1107	117136419	321961652	126033484	124304863	177270565
65	61710139	182049517	80918790	61670096	91252773
366	35245646	101621413	30317998	45265974	64078500
754	29597923	47967816	20032148	20009963	26338311
49	1019087	4580775	1635416	2067520	1974705
512	44878408	176661923	69635614	58618040	75141876
438	41787726	169952008	67333354	56237792	72168391
6	426760	2857748	863707	947589	1139438
61	2409938	3485703	1291056	1327338	1705843
5	236411	321202	131364	93022	113796
2	17573	45262	16133	12299	14408
629	66501513	118872247	56467852	42095930	62439955
31	3302981	2545025	1169960	918348	1081395
4	1251623	1214821	589186	492412	652828
14	1174414	2245235	1246215	634869	824106
	422692	418993	272709	143319	148892
10	361201	537795	291603	170206	232949
2	198442	331701	214887	67050	105490
	14064	17412	8715	5881	7132
1	146467	229459	127949	68837	58374

10-5 续表2

单位：万元

指　标	Item	单位数(个) Number of Enterprises (unit)
家具制造业	Furniture Manufacturing	6
造纸和纸制品业	Paper Making and Paper Products	17
印刷和记录媒介复制业	Printing and Record Medium Reproduction	25
文教、工美、体育和娱乐用品制造业	Culture, Education, Art and Crafts, Sport and Entertainment Products	12
石油加工、炼焦和核燃料加工业	Petroleum Processing, Coking and Nuclear Fuel Processing	128
化学原料和化学制品制造业	Raw Chemical Materials and Chemical Products	198
医药制造业	Medical and Pharmaceutical Products	82
化学纤维制造业	Chemical Fiber Manufacturing	
橡胶和塑料制品业	Rubber and Plastic Products	55
非金属矿物制品业	Nonmetal Mineral Products	382
黑色金属冶炼和压延加工业	Smelting and Pressing of Ferrous Metals	168
有色金属冶炼和压延加工业	Smelting and Pressing of Non-ferrous Metals	96
金属制品业	Metal Prodcuts	125
通用设备制造业	Ordinary Machinery Manufacturing	88
专用设备制造业	Special Purpose Equipment Manufacturing	137
汽车制造业	Automobile Manufacturing	39
铁路、船舶、航空航天和其他运输设备制造业	Railroad, Marine, Aviation and Other Transport Equipments Manufacturing	28
电气机械和器材制造业	Electrical Machinery and Equipment Manufacturing	67
计算机、通信和其他电子设备制造业	Computers, Telecommunication and Other Electronic Equipments Manufacturing	27
仪器仪表制造业	Equipments and Instruments Manufacturing	15
其他制造业	Other Manufacturing	4
废弃资源综合利用业	Comprehensive Utilization of Waste Resources	3
金属制品、机械和设备修理业	Metal Products, Machinery and Equipment Repair	11
电力、热力、燃气及水生产和供应业	Production and Supply of Electricity, Heat, Gas and Water	256
电力、热力生产和供应业	Production and Supply of Electricity and Heat	203
燃气生产和供应业	Production and Supply of Gas	39
水的生产和供应业	Production and Supply of Water	14

continued

(10 000 yuan)

#亏损企业 Loss-making Enterprises	工业销售产值 Industrial Sales Output Value	资产总计 Total Assets	流动资产合计 Total Circulating Funds	固定资产合计 Total Fixed Assets	固定资产原价 Original Value Of Fixed Assets
3	47646	91349	47441	11680	16343
3	174165	207572	73455	114802	150788
9	158535	272484	126194	94126	168985
3	98138	153273	82217	50223	64212
70	9038948	23422713	11709039	6670104	10084764
67	4322243	11619002	4407633	4912727	6502277
17	1807004	3723394	1541294	1210906	1551879
17	542957	784364	388899	333881	480303
133	3645724	6599321	2858553	3196924	4358781
64	16722088	27590117	9152808	12331494	20754393
33	6518389	10356101	3429159	5501027	7985460
29	996848	1689348	1084481	414037	556071
24	1422140	2128358	1349358	587137	640809
39	1855782	6158465	4520678	1061661	1310910
14	1473199	2364407	1345178	690248	905628
9	900757	2039508	1350020	428557	675553
20	1733185	2564777	1518433	622282	811850
7	7772152	8787731	7039911	1219037	2093610
4	219596	470878	315484	55692	71951
	66070	121498	95395	21821	41790
	25148	78607	31150	41661	49705
2	88915	108539	79848	24981	52727
93	16192878	40685352	6800884	28299586	46062458
73	14560318	36259614	5662475	27428181	43937771
10	1448937	3568724	884300	437497	1370714
10	183623	857014	254109	433908	753973

10-5 续表3

单位：万元

指　标	Item	累计折旧 Total Depreciation
总　计	**Total**	**73600288**
一、按隶属关系分	Grouped by Jurisdiction of Management	
中央企业	Central Enterprises	18853085
省属企业	Province-owned Enterprises	30807944
市属企业	Cities-owned Enterprises	3324985
县(市、区)属企业	County-owned Enterprises	4542390
城市街道企业	Cities' Subdistrict-owned Enterprises	8937
镇属企业	Town-owned Enterprises	269362
乡属企业	Township Enterprises	109269
居委会办企业	Neighbourhood Committee -run Enterprises	2288
村办企业	Village Enterprises	253845
其　他	Enterprises of Other Types of Ownership	15428185
二、按登记注册类型分	Grouped by Registered Kind	
内资企业	Civil Funded Enterprises	67861818
国有企业	State-owned Enterprises	7913122
集体企业	Collective-owned Enterprises	330118
股份合作企业	Share Holding Cooperative Enterprises	1915
联营企业	Joint Owned Enterprises	45681
有限责任公司	Limited Responsibility Company	41804452
国有独资公司	Company Exclusively with Investment from State	9905622
其他有限责任公司	Other Limited Responsibility Company	31898830
股份有限公司	Share Holding Limited Company	8068918
私营企业	Privately Owned Enterprises	9678648
私营独资企业	Enterprise Exclusively with Investment from Private	150998
私营合伙企业	Private Partner Enterprises	6928
私营有限责任公司	Privately Owned Limited Responsibility Company	9037631
私营股份有限公司	Privately Owned Share Holding Limited Company	483091
其他企业	Enterprises of Other Types of Ownership	18965
港、澳、台商投资企业	Enterprises Funded by Hong Kong, Macao and Taiwan	2357775
合资经营企业(港或澳、台资)	Joint Venture	1508609
合作经营企业(港或澳、台资)	Cooperative Enterprise	122976
港澳台商独资企业	Ventures Exclusively with Hong Kong, Macao and Taiwan Investment	585477
港澳台商投资股份有限公司	Share Holding Limited Company	136676
其他港澳台商投资企业	Others	4036

continued

(10 000 yuan)

流动负债 Liquid Liabilities	负债合计 Total Liabilities	年末所有者权益 Creditors' Equity at Year-end	主营业务收入 Revenue of Major Business	主营业务成本 Costs of Major Business	主营业务税金及附加 Tax and Extra Charges of Major Business	营业费用 Costs of Business	管理费用 Costs of Administration
179011558	**255793619**	**80412180**	**142264467**	**119158298**	**2369920**	**4947885**	**7871158**
18151595	29784086	12545221	19747076	15485390	455666	914277	939598
73139506	112901713	30301532	49604339	41284649	1012913	1835251	3320011
9006701	12781665	4672204	5131438	4181134	110836	211592	514717
17941350	23680291	6576167	9745766	7462885	318875	368160	980632
12714	12714	8251	22984	21124	124	591	726
975896	1405059	339837	1165162	1018977	14298	25424	39106
490871	694045	408478	152664	96814	10234	4366	22867
13667	13667	1841	12182	10737	78	805	268
772433	799565	329793	579722	462963	10302	27592	44366
58506827	73720815	25228856	56103134	49133625	436594	1559826	2008867
166922127	240896617	73781740	129356683	107789663	2230899	4770698	7485413
6757138	10437524	4004763	9950697	8692227	52835	67141	439985
986372	1014239	−12645	915113	806230	18312	35703	69734
2098	2165	3055	2694	2244	13	31	423
244635	252649	−106571	47335	36993	3740		4081
112520760	168551837	43764567	73008031	59885375	1673020	2556596	5053959
18709821	26957057	12360339	15578963	12805445	335432	458774	1195734
93810939	141594780	31404228	57429068	47079930	1337588	2097822	3858225
10584198	15220900	10647582	7866402	5299007	257219	1062667	668939
35672290	45127284	15496029	37538106	33048220	223482	1048419	1242302
548873	592534	308467	1611879	1473809	14259	35014	27622
30240	39746	24501	138168	129747	429	470	3133
33128837	41791019	13695305	33409705	29535170	197619	948047	1119733
1964339	2703986	1467756	2378355	1909495	11175	64889	91815
154636	290019	−15042	28305	19367	2277	140	5989
8066836	9625747	2897839	9005777	8349472	34478	66466	163927
6748352	7528209	1268363	6953152	6578385	19536	41337	93990
92965	214336	93183	221580	220942		136	141
848117	1142252	1483687	1584803	1335189	13322	18257	50943
334428	664696	47574	216987	191694	1473	5725	18440
42974	76254	5032	29255	23262	147	1011	412

10-5 续表4

单位：万元

指 标	Item	累计折旧 Total Depreciation
外商投资企业	Foreign Funded Enterprises	3380695
中外合资经营企业	Joint Venture	1290810
中外合作经营企业	Cooperative Enterprises	1527962
外资企业	Enterprises Funded By Foreign Investments	551709
外商投资股份有限公司	Share Holding Limited Company	3379
其他外商投资企业	Other Foreign Funded Enterprises	6835
三、在总计中: 亏损企业	Of the Total: Loss-making Enterprises	25256395
在总计中: 国有控股企业	Of the Total: State-Controlled Share Holding Enterprises	55644957
在总计中: 农村工业	Of the Total: Rural Industry	363113
在总计中: 轻工业	Of the Total: Light Industry	2159040
重工业	Heavy Industry	71441248
在总计中: 大型企业	Of the Total: Large-size Enterprises	42159243
中型企业	Medium-size Enterprises	23427902
小型企业	Small-size Enterprises	7706672
微型企业	Micro-size Enterprises	306471
四、按工业行业大类分	Grouped by Sector	
采矿业	Mining	29910851
煤炭开采和洗选业	Coal Mining and Dressing	29153831
石油和天然气开采业	Petroleum and Natural Gas Extraction	245823
黑色金属矿采选业	Ferrous Metals Mining and Dressing	461413
有色金属矿采选业	Nonferrous Metals Mining and Dressing	46498
非金属矿采选业	Nonmetal Minerals Mining and Dressing	3286
开采辅助活动	Mining Auxiliary Activities	
其他采矿业	Other Mining Industry	
制造业	Manufacturing	25439517
农副食品加工业	Farm Products Processing	259477
食品制造业	Food Manufacturing	192097
酒、饮料和精制茶制造业	Wine, Beverages and Refined Tea Manufacturing	265474
烟草制品业	Tobacoo Products Manfacturing	72066
纺织业	Textile Industry	81180
纺织服装、服饰业	Textile, Wearing Apparel and Accessories	46302
皮革、毛皮、羽毛及其制品和制鞋业	Leather, Fur, Feather and Related Products and Footwear	1251
木材加工和木、竹、藤、棕、草制品业	Timber Processing,Bamboo,Cane,Palm Fiber and Straw Products	14535

continued

(10 000 yuan)

流动负债 Liquid Liabilities	负债合计 Total Liabilities	年末所有者权益 Creditors' Equity at Year-end	主营业务收入 Revenue of Major Business	主营业务成本 Costs of Major Business	主营业务税金及附加 Taxes and Extra Charges of Major Business	营业费用 Costs of Business	管理费用 Costs of Administration
4022595	5271255	3732601	3902006	3019163	104543	110722	221818
2648462	3717636	1980708	2088526	1657576	46838	89910	124470
735238	762515	836260	746024	472270	42487	11813	28546
561729	713939	834661	1045668	873290	15144	8772	65508
6235	6235	5030	6959	5098	32	227	1227
70931	70931	75943	14830	10929	42		2067
77529232	115489024	12393799	42044829	38363354	496915	1619807	2840618
111690534	171195462	50242216	78097611	63645549	1789916	3017144	5227177
1263304	1493610	738271	732386	559777	20536	31958	67233
6064473	7424665	6833239	11116343	8838025	339978	614888	593025
172947085	248368954	73578941	131148124	110320274	2029942	4332998	7278133
89988386	135242538	46806976	78122187	65294185	1277434	3192273	4369140
61783378	81852561	19746686	34824968	28227257	892110	901798	2457524
25402422	34945543	13022249	28272603	24814195	191025	831944	998863
1837373	3752976	836268	1044709	822661	9351	21870	45632
93338114	137546839	39127615	57591495	45274711	1749781	2716540	4084561
90249126	133128985	36843867	54629362	42743964	1712942	2691614	3845844
1203954	1750373	1107376	461475	390731	6557	3762	35101
1614356	2378284	1099105	2252452	1935664	22014	15465	190873
230242	248759	72443	221415	181969	7382	3941	11074
40436	40438	4824	26791	22383	886	1758	1669
70436931	88054342	30791655	67990466	59753580	544192	2107189	3213071
1070434	1279226	1265839	3109076	2791559	1629	53046	64214
499133	568299	646521	1172432	934822	2865	74622	56683
918697	1088629	1156605	2062590	1571434	124082	138860	116753
51468	51468	367525	420748	154001	187160	5106	26723
320945	350813	186981	362681	336849	507	4698	10548
187839	208885	122816	338754	307398	361	4976	17459
961	981	16432	14064	13469	118	59	59
77017	77419	152040	134344	114536	163	1747	1543

10-5 续表5

单位：万元

指　　标	Item	累计折旧 Total Depreciation
家具制造业	Furniture Manufacturing	4958
造纸和纸制品业	Paper Making and Paper Products	37448
印刷和记录媒介复制业	Printing and Record Medium Reproduction	86494
文教、工美、体育和娱乐用品制造业	Culture, Education, Art and Crafts, Sport and Entertainment Products	14009
石油加工、炼焦和核燃料加工业	Petroleum Processing, Coking and Nuclear Fuel Processing	4505297
化学原料和化学制品制造业	Raw Chemical Materials and Chemical Products	2720769
医药制造业	Medical and Pharmaceutical Products	492725
化学纤维制造业	Chemical Fiber Manufacturing	
橡胶和塑料制品业	Rubber and Plastic Products	152993
非金属矿物制品业	Nonmetal Mineral Products	1496230
黑色金属冶炼和压延加工业	Smelting and Pressing of Ferrous Metals	9218328
有色金属冶炼和压延加工业	Smelting and Pressing of Non-ferrous Metals	3041582
金属制品业	Metal Prodcuts	215258
通用设备制造业	Ordinary Machinery Manufacturing	196691
专用设备制造业	Special Purpose Equipment Manufacturing	570237
汽车制造业	Automobile Manufacturing	262556
铁路、船舶、航空航天和其他运输设备制造业	Railroad, Marine, Aviation and Other Transport Equipments Manufacturing	246978
电气机械和器材制造业	Electrical Machinery and Equipment Manufacturing	258514
计算机、通信和其他电子设备制造业	Computers, Telecommunication and Other Electronic Equipments Manufacturing	903860
仪器仪表制造业	Equipments and Instruments Manufacturing	25491
其他制造业	Other Manufacturing	19969
废弃资源综合利用业	Comprehensive Utilization of Waste Resources	8044
金属制品、机械和设备修理业	Metal Products, Machinery and Equipment Repair	28704
电力、热力、燃气及水生产和供应业	Production and Supply of Electricity, Heat, Gas and Water	18249921
电力、热力生产和供应业	Production and Supply of Electricity and Heat	17654078
燃气生产和供应业	Production and Supply of Gas	268640
水的生产和供应业	Production and Supply of Water	327203

continued

(10 000 yuan)

流动负债 Liquid Liabilities	负债合计 Total Liabilities	年末所有者权益 Creditors' Equity at Year-end	主营业务收入 Revenue of Major Business	主营业务成本 Costs of Major Business	主营业务税金及附加 Taxes and Extra Charges of Major Business	营业费用 Costs of Business	管理费用 Costs of Administration
48123	48292	43057	46679	40550	247	2470	2009
108848	144459	63113	177185	160550	426	4933	6608
118181	137896	134588	157777	131043	1032	5475	13334
146935	154165	-892	85433	71696	320	5804	5605
15935090	20954166	2461970	9121499	8050078	27941	548907	327199
8023587	9630224	1988777	5044934	4667288	20155	179675	316314
1363671	1884296	1839097	1790202	1122210	15315	271742	185512
358800	439020	345343	640608	584715	1607	13211	23237
3854051	5038667	1549552	3627487	3145909	16185	134652	199789
15137329	19729894	7860220	16858954	15030878	47962	300856	768003
5284188	7425313	2930786	6603868	6001163	28810	77566	174445
908464	1022869	657882	1028223	903838	4189	27873	64979
1153539	1423730	704628	1345434	1126521	4262	41605	95428
4033297	4715405	1443058	1990526	1758661	8573	63894	207683
1533582	1723457	640949	1470765	1255588	6325	54459	97380
1217147	1463411	576096	950179	764890	6929	28279	106052
1589542	1916438	648338	1280084	1042232	5971	35269	126065
6137358	6165802	2621929	7758676	7347880	28472	11684	158662
226516	247609	223269	217509	173572	1258	13613	24092
26171	38471	83027	61334	48989	119	745	3513
17298	35726	42881	23467	18097	338	395	5582
88720	89312	19228	94954	83164	871	968	7598
15236514	30192440	10492910	16682504	14130006	75946	124158	573528
13345502	27094513	9165100	15118292	12813880	70998	33322	480206
1616358	2676748	891975	1374960	1143972	3661	82118	55109
274654	421179	435835	189252	172154	1287	8718	38213

10-5 续表6

单位：万元

指　标	Item	财务费用 Costs of Finance
总　计	**Total**	**6096929**
一、按隶属关系分	Grouped by Jurisdiction of Management	
中央企业	Central Enterprises	765053
省属企业	Province-owned Enterprises	2795487
市属企业	Cities-owned Enterprises	219538
县(市、区)属企业	County-owned Enterprises	612458
城市街道企业	Cities' Subdistrict-owned Enterprises	277
镇属企业	Town-owned Enterprises	73774
乡属企业	Township Enterprises	41469
居委会办企业	Neighbourhood Committee -run Enterprises	274
村办企业	Village Enterprises	13751
其　他	Enterprises of Other Types of Ownership	1574848
二、按登记注册类型分	Grouped by Registered Kind	
内资企业	Civil Funded Enterprises	5892493
国有企业	State-owned Enterprises	217157
集体企业	Collective-owned Enterprises	20454
股份合作企业	Share Holding Cooperative Enterprises	1
联营企业	Joint Owned Enterprises	9125
有限责任公司	Limited Responsibility Company	4320957
国有独资公司	Company Exclusively with Investment from State	631596
其他有限责任公司	Other Limited Responsibility Company	3689361
股份有限公司	Share Holding Limited Company	333207
私营企业	Privately Owned Enterprises	963407
私营独资企业	Enterprise Exclusively with Investment from Private	11544
私营合伙企业	Private Partner Enterprises	262
私营有限责任公司	Privately Owned Limited Responsibility Company	872496
私营股份有限公司	Privately Owned Share Holding Limited Company	79105
其他企业	Enterprises of Other Types of Ownership	28185
港、澳、台商投资企业	Enterprises Funded by Hong Kong, Macao and Taiwan	85754
合资经营企业(港或澳、台资)	Joint Venture	59366
合作经营企业(港或澳、台资)	Cooperative Enterprise	315
港澳台商独资企业	Ventures Exclusively with Hong Kong, Macao and Taiwan Investment	3695
港澳台商投资股份有限公司	Share Holding Limited Company	19677
其他港澳台商投资企业	Others	2703

continued

(10 000 yuan)

#利息支出 Interest Expenditure	利润总额 Total Profits	亏损企业亏损额 Loss of Loss-making Enterprises	利税总额 Total Pre-tax Profits	应付薪酬总额 Total Wages Payable	应交所得税 Income Taxes Payable	应交增值税 Value Added Taxes Payable
6159242	**2947769**	**3986959**	**10517337**	**11702732**	**1038448**	**5010756**
693241	869874	335549	2215300	1064260	138505	885575
3158218	541776	1324549	3705025	5475300	446483	1987419
210400	–24925	310718	291526	788051	54874	203353
588358	57637	585369	897655	983516	85431	520369
40	93	70	578	1336	3	361
63529	6826	59442	30085	62070	537	8961
36209	–23613	36769	3250	19626	3264	16629
276	33	19	807	516		697
13225	22441	1351	67514	33342	5607	34770
1395745	1497627	1333125	3305597	3274715	303744	1352622
5910621	2227739	3768177	9298802	10214120	859367	4651654
200651	44213	173544	413746	403089	3942	313673
19621	–28998	36525	32779	97519	1648	43020
	116		237	152	16	108
2779	–6691	6691	468	3174		3419
4524016	857517	2580834	5646143	7267193	611935	2946663
678505	326908	443077	1305273	1468971	89591	632974
3845511	530609	2137757	4340871	5798221	522343	2313690
351967	379129	234535	1127962	997409	102920	490923
783552	1010273	708075	2099398	1441772	138906	850235
6984	63376	7935	130741	24611	7074	53106
77	4095	287	6658	2045	5	2134
742094	848754	676479	1821553	1319437	124359	759773
34396	94048	23374	140445	95679	7468	35222
28034	–27820	27974	–21930	3813		3613
141898	376203	85079	495709	928559	86152	85027
94353	212022	63581	290327	590189	52616	58769
315	46		1115	7127		1069
24697	177314	4558	226356	305087	33528	35720
19816	–14562	16940	–24537	25489	8	–11449
2717	1382		2448	667		919

10-5 续表7

单位：万元

指　标	Item	财务费用 Costs of Finance
外商投资企业	Foreign Funded Enterprises	118683
中外合资经营企业	Joint Venture	94281
中外合作经营企业	Cooperative Enterprises	10878
外资企业	Enterprises Funded By Foreign Investments	13466
外商投资股份有限公司	Share Holding Limited Company	58
其他外商投资企业	Other Foreign Funded Enterprises	-1
三、在总计中: 亏损企业	Of the Total: Loss-making Enterprises	3044051
在总计中: 国有控股企业	Of the Total: State-Controlled Share Holding Enterprises	4227264
在总计中: 农村工业	Of the Total: Rural Industry	55221
在总计中: 轻工业	Of the Total: Light Industry	161010
重工业	Heavy Industry	5935920
在总计中: 大型企业	Of the Total: Large-size Enterprises	3203539
中型企业	Medium-size Enterprises	2015309
小型企业	Small-size Enterprises	797346
微型企业	Micro-size Enterprises	80736
四、按工业行业大类分	Grouped by Sector	
采矿业	Mining	3363635
煤炭开采和洗选业	Coal Mining and Dressing	3282274
石油和天然气开采业	Petroleum and Natural Gas Extraction	30595
黑色金属矿采选业	Ferrous Metals Mining and Dressing	46919
有色金属矿采选业	Nonferrous Metals Mining and Dressing	3451
非金属矿采选业	Nonmetal Minerals Mining and Dressing	396
开采辅助活动	Mining Auxiliary Activities	
其他采矿业	Other Mining Industry	
制造业	Manufacturing	1861206
农副食品加工业	Farm Products Processing	45978
食品制造业	Food Manufacturing	12828
酒、饮料和精制茶制造业	Wine, Beverages and Refined Tea Manufacturing	12591
烟草制品业	Tobacoo Products Manfacturing	-4542
纺织业	Textile Industry	7876
纺织服装、服饰业	Textile, Wearing Apparel and Accessories	2309
皮革、毛皮、羽毛及其制品和制鞋业	Leather, Fur, Feather and Related Products and Footwear	132
木材加工和木、竹、藤、棕、草制品业	Timber Processing,Bamboo,Cane,Palm Fiber and Straw Products	3144

continued

(10 000 yuan)

#利息支出 Interest Expenditure	利润总额 Total Profits	亏损企业亏损额 Loss of Loss-making Enterprises	利税总额 Total Pre-tax Profits	应付薪酬总额 Total Wages Payable	应交所得税 Income Taxes Payable	应交增值税 Value Added Taxes Payable
106724	343828	133703	722826	560053	92929	274075
83647	70140	93632	230868	215939	25654	113526
11841	187767		310179	84870	54749	79925
11182	81361	40071	176040	257316	12478	79535
54	304		724	960	48	371
	4256		5016	968		717
2903088	−3986959	3986959	−2284499	4269394	76242	1051279
4489500	1153271	2409260	6457324	7885203	650544	3344322
49434	−1172	38120	70764	52968	8871	51399
165110	615165	111326	1281798	752723	100924	324770
5994133	2332604	3875634	9235538	10950008	937523	4685986
3603270	2021210	1306338	6265923	7787542	676892	2805094
1811281	40246	1897169	2496804	2863324	238244	1552697
680924	793372	740634	1645644	1035040	120213	646347
63767	92941	42818	108966	16825	3099	6618
3589779	1348387	1860656	6319417	6346593	572126	3049115
3521045	1211647	1771168	6051250	6219829	555779	2955445
23295	79334	17568	98822	39412	8549	12048
41463	47854	68047	137040	72046	5458	67138
3597	9976	3116	30310	12850	2325	12951
379	−424	757	1995	2456	15	1533
1763332	911102	1745395	2905046	4596334	341549	1439915
37751	158036	18683	178244	111817	2102	18546
11767	91148	2047	116604	79644	12176	22588
15062	96206	20016	305407	96946	39598	85120
	52233		285253	21619	13058	45860
7267	−1460	8434	3263	26145	1585	4216
1945	12196	139	19671	37080	2321	6498
120	228		466	622		121
3061	14507	2	14668	3649	770	−2

10-5 续表8

单位：万元

指 标	Item	财务费用 Costs of Finance
家具制造业	Furniture Manufacturing	1471
造纸和纸制品业	Paper Making and Paper Products	4503
印刷和记录媒介复制业	Printing and Record Medium Reproduction	3373
文教、工美、体育和娱乐用品制造业	Culture, Education, Art and Crafts, Sport and Entertainment Products	7790
石油加工、炼焦和核燃料加工业	Petroleum Processing, Coking and Nuclear Fuel Processing	431504
化学原料和化学制品制造业	Raw Chemical Materials and Chemical Products	228001
医药制造业	Medical and Pharmaceutical Products	39601
化学纤维制造业	Chemical Fiber Manufacturing	
橡胶和塑料制品业	Rubber and Plastic Products	14968
非金属矿物制品业	Nonmetal Mineral Products	121487
黑色金属冶炼和压延加工业	Smelting and Pressing of Ferrous Metals	513778
有色金属冶炼和压延加工业	Smelting and Pressing of Non-ferrous Metals	216824
金属制品业	Metal Prodcuts	12120
通用设备制造业	Ordinary Machinery Manufacturing	21013
专用设备制造业	Special Purpose Equipment Manufacturing	105176
汽车制造业	Automobile Manufacturing	8991
铁路、船舶、航空航天和其他运输设备制造业	Railroad, Marine, Aviation and Other Transport Equipments Manufacturing	14200
电气机械和器材制造业	Electrical Machinery and Equipment Manufacturing	48274
计算机、通信和其他电子设备制造业	Computers, Telecommunication and Other Electronic Equipments Manufacturing	-14117
仪器仪表制造业	Equipments and Instruments Manufacturing	1281
其他制造业	Other Manufacturing	-772
废弃资源综合利用业	Comprehensive Utilization of Waste Resources	1102
金属制品、机械和设备修理业	Metal Products, Machinery and Equipment Repair	322
电力、热力、燃气及水生产和供应业	Production and Supply of Electricity, Heat, Gas and Water	872092
电力、热力生产和供应业	Production and Supply of Electricity and Heat	826345
燃气生产和供应业	Production and Supply of Gas	39005
水的生产和供应业	Production and Supply of Water	6742

continued

(10 000 yuan)

#利息支出 Interest Expenditure	利润总额 Total Profits	亏损企业亏损额 Loss of Loss-making Enterprises	利税总额 Total Pre-tax Profits	应付薪酬总额 Total Wages Payable	应交所得税 Income Taxes Payable	应交增值税 Value Added Taxes Payable
908	347	1438	849	2119	8	255
4124	2226	323	6395	7666	159	3743
2285	5590	1601	11346	21673	281	4578
7995	–4972	6792	–773	6912	304	3877
357885	–149036	401300	63877	358267	28846	183653
236954	–340040	424304	–285430	358020	12771	34084
50095	166934	12404	279720	152806	22747	96758
13932	10147	11841	20200	34644	1697	8382
104514	22325	158045	153512	273081	16016	114428
436490	154377	258067	557353	873152	33119	354297
196726	189947	74384	389950	316557	47511	170905
15598	19301	12142	50416	94607	3277	26681
19403	79735	10875	112171	92183	3169	28162
109511	–147945	212880	–87215	231090	6582	51880
19407	85751	17208	118521	87343	10464	22343
14778	48351	24648	89204	128681	11764	33910
46065	33289	32730	67215	83164	7863	27712
46500	287997	26220	393025	1047343	58696	76476
1268	7119	8533	15528	18358	1306	7131
501	8838		9545	5550	1741	587
1089	5065		6261	3182	1253	858
331	2662	339	9800	22414	365	6268
806129	688281	380908	1292874	759807	124775	521729
761546	617550	336049	1202910	611420	96208	508526
38209	99888	14271	110211	90629	28348	5676
6374	–29157	30588	–20247	57758	219	7527

10-6 国有控股工业企业主要经济指标(2016年)

单位：万元

指　　标	Item	单位数(个) Number of Enterprises (unit)	#亏损企业 Loss-making Enterprises
总　计	**Total**	**802**	**333**
在总计中:	Of the Total:		
亏损企业	Loss-making Enterprises	333	333
按隶属关系分	Grouped by Jurisdiction of Management		
中央企业	Central Enterprises	142	33
地方企业	Local Enterprises	660	300
#省属企业	Province-owned Enterprises	325	140
市属企业	City-owned Enterprises	102	55
县属企业	County-owned Enterprises	171	77
在总计中:	Of the Total:		
轻工业	Light Industry	52	24
重工业	Heavy Industry	750	309
在总计中:	Of the Total:		
大型企业	Large-size Enterprises	127	42
中型企业	Medium-size Enterprises	381	189
小型企业	Small-size Enterprises	265	92
微型企业	Micro-size Enterprises	29	10
按工业行业大类分	Grouped by Sector		
采矿业	Mining	354	159
煤炭开采和洗选业	Coal Mining and Dressing	337	152
石油和天然气开采业	Petroleum and Natural Gas Extraction	9	3
黑色金属矿采选业	Ferrous Metals Mining and Dressing	4	2
有色金属矿采选业	Nonferrous Metals Mining and Dressing	4	2
非金属矿采选业	Nonmetal Minerals Mining and Dressing		
开采辅助活动	Mining Auxiliary Activities		
其他采矿业	Other Mining Industry		
制造业	Manufacturing	278	3
农副食品加工业	Farm Products Processing	2	
食品制造业	Food Manufacturing	2	
酒、饮料和精制茶制造业	Wine, Beverages and Refined Tea Manufacturing	9	2
烟草制品业	Tobacoo Products Manfacturing	1	
纺织业	Textile Industry	1	
纺织服装、服饰业	Textile, Wearing Apparel and Accessories	5	1

MAIN INDICATORS OF STATE-HOLDING INDUSTRIAL ENTERPRISES(2016)

(10 000 yuan)

工业销售产值 Industrial Sales Output Value	资产总计 Total Assets	流动资产合计 Total Circulating Funds	固定资产合计 Total Fixed Assets	固定资产原价 Original Value Of Fixed Assets	累计折旧 Total Depreciation
60785946	**221336883**	**76248782**	**91891872**	**133649185**	**55644957**
16561721	81578328	27191136	36452274	45969457	18700928
19126289	41839160	9298566	24551356	41989453	18800418
41659657	179497723	66950216	67340517	91659732	36844539
31919084	141949034	55197545	52332067	72003135	30450397
3589954	14778243	4995049	5501961	7889093	2937499
4856509	17333811	5563370	6831987	8465696	2635707
2031690	4182394	2118122	1309273	2035236	813874
58754257	217154489	74130661	90582600	131613949	54831083
36295338	142628250	59107296	49789575	73836684	34751909
19461611	59294366	12808916	30980402	45038443	16984659
4834843	16973630	3748455	9987498	13641199	3794306
194154	2440637	584116	1134397	1132859	114083
25065940	137341718	51572034	47060123	60175970	25087884
24373500	133725744	50709004	45772566	58721906	24863976
274633	2292929	689917	575386	657705	132891
357167	1297101	159115	707714	793457	90659
60640	25944	13998	4457	2902	358
20537110	47846772	19112548	19343065	30473300	12882009
16214	49225	25546	8447	17656	9209
45861	23646	15752	4134	18212	14079
628257	1294385	821037	221972	271838	58762
422692	418993	272709	143319	148892	72066
18635	27134	20594	6540	17914	12262
67320	146603	96469	17580	36155	18596

10-6 续表1

单位：万元

指　　标	Item	单位数(个) Number of Enterprises (unit)
皮革、毛皮、羽毛及其制品和制鞋业	Leather, Fur, Feather and its products and Footwear	
木材加工和木、竹、藤、棕、草制品业	Timber Processing, Bamboo, Cane, Palm Fiber and Straw Products	
家具制造业	Furniture Manufacturing	
造纸和纸制品业	Paper Making and Paper Products	
印刷和记录媒介复制业	Printing and Record Medium Reproduction	5
文教、工美、体育和娱乐用品制造业	Culture, Education, Art and Crafts, Sport and Entertainment Products	1
石油加工、炼焦和核燃料加工业	Petroleum Processing, Coking and Nuclear Fuel Processing	20
化学原料和化学制品制造业	Raw Chemical Materials and Chemical Products	46
医药制造业	Medical and Pharmaceutical Products	8
化学纤维制造业	Chemical Fiber	
橡胶和塑料制品业	Rubber and Plastic Products	8
非金属矿物制品业	Nonmetal Mineral Products	33
黑色金属冶炼和压延加工业	Smelting and Pressing of Ferrous Metals	11
有色金属冶炼和压延加工业	Smelting and Pressing of Non-ferrous Metals	18
金属制品业	Metal Prodcuts	9
通用设备制造业	Ordinary Machinery Manufacturing	16
专用设备制造业	Special Purpose Equipment Manufacturing	36
汽车制造业	Automobile Manufacturing	12
铁路、船舶、航空航天和其他运输设备制造业	Railroad, Marine, Aviation and Other Transport Equipments Manufacturing	8
电气机械和器材制造业	Electrical Machinery and Equipment Manufacturing	11
计算机、通信和其他电子设备制造业	Computers, Telecommunication and Other Electronic Equipments Manufacturing	2
仪器仪表制造业	Equipments and Instruments Manufacturing	5
其他制造业	Other Manufacturing	1
废弃资源综合利用业	Comprehensive Utilization of Waste Resources	
金属制品、机械和设备修理业	Metal Products, Machinery and Equipment Repair	8
电力、热力、燃气及水生产和供应业	Production and Supply of Electricity, Heat, Gas and Water	170
电力、热力生产和供应业	Production and Supply of Electricity and Heat	134
燃气生产和供应业	Production and Supply of Gas	24
水的生产和供应业	Production and Supply of Water	12

continued

(10 000 yuan)

#亏损企业 Loss-making Enterprises	工业销售产值 Industrial Sales Output Value	资产总计 Total Assets	流动资产合计 Total Circulating Funds	固定资产合计 Total Fixed Assets	固定资产原价 Original Value Of Fixed Assets	累计折旧 Total Depreciation
4	30632	70208	27886	21477	54783	34818
1	5748	49828	21673	22591	25904	3314
13	1700723	4548433	1849360	1629084	2443184	933303
26	2174398	7580207	2990786	3342362	4552794	1940564
5	447090	908088	308701	385161	543198	162190
2	252330	329058	119719	198869	262103	62678
16	673644	1389962	526149	757063	1069783	405792
5	6727113	13971547	2809701	6776924	12596798	5800154
4	3321560	6150149	1924115	3391083	5435438	2237881
3	218353	751061	460343	191288	185601	54584
6	375832	1140116	679960	380455	352461	96156
10	1113818	4676196	3517506	762946	871111	408273
5	245865	494640	279926	150306	284162	134256
3	543814	1577743	982320	363991	521972	157966
2	1260569	1671238	963574	458317	577519	181346
1	112734	337001	211357	63489	96963	33474
2	22801	56381	41828	11487	13744	8393
	30094	88529	75812	10610	26491	15881
	81013	96401	69725	23570	48624	26012
63	15182898	36148395	5564200	25488683	42999915	17675065
45	13832331	32197589	4609403	24830686	41130952	17141819
8	1171079	3155804	705772	251656	1154720	218207
10	179488	795002	249025	406341	714243	315039

10-6 续表2

单位：万元

指 标	Item	流动负债 Liquid Liabilities	负债合计 Total Liabilities
总 计	**Total**	**111690534**	**171195462**
在总计中:	Of the Total:		
亏损企业	Loss-making Enterprises	46732611	74228825
按隶属关系分	Grouped by Belongs		
中央企业	Central Enterprises	17959794	29397326
地方企业	Local Enterprises	93730739	141798136
#省属企业	Province-owned Enterprises	72514269	112245644
市属企业	City-owned Enterprises	7431082	11040897
县属企业	County-owned Enterprises	10499213	13945556
在总计中:	Of the Total:		
轻工业	Light Industry	1598108	2282836
重工业	Heavy Industry	110092426	168912625
在总计中:	Of the Total:		
大型企业	Large-size Enterprises	67619256	107833894
中型企业	Medium-size Enterprises	35263866	47460670
小型企业	Small-size Enterprises	8039174	13733160
微型企业	Micro-size Enterprises	768237	2167738
按工业行业大类分	Grouped by Sector		
采矿业	Mining	70455972	107686300
煤炭开采和洗选业	Coal Mining and Dressing	68921587	105419264
石油和天然气开采业	Petroleum and Natural Gas Extraction	1025394	1404938
黑色金属矿采选业	Ferrous Metals Mining and Dressing	493961	840718
有色金属矿采选业	Nonferrous Metals Mining and Dressing	15030	21380
非金属矿采选业	Nonmetal Minerals Mining and Dressing		
开采辅助活动	Mining Auxiliary Activities		
其他采矿业	Other Mining Industry		
制造业	Manufacturing	667973	36774677
农副食品加工业	Farm Products Processing	25605	30024
食品制造业	Food Manufacturing	7445	7667
酒、饮料和精制茶制造业	Wine, Beverages and Refined Tea Manufacturing	500086	597522
烟草制品业	Tobacoo Products Manfacturing	51468	51468
纺织业	Textile Industry	2040	9961
纺织服装、服饰业	Textile, Wearing Apparel and Accessories	81329	100158

continued

(10 000 yuan)

年末所有者权益 Creditors' Equity at Year-end	主营业务收入 Revenue of Major Business	主营业务成本 Costs of Major Business	主营业务税金及附加 Taxes and Extra Charges of Major Business	营业费用 Costs of Business	管理费用 Costs of Administration
50242216	**78097611**	**63645549**	**1789916**	**3017144**	**5227177**
7449109	28837796	26076053	348427	1107946	1986107
12441832	19623803	15382637	454467	906290	930606
37800384	58473809	48262912	1335449	2110854	4296571
29837296	49111562	40908744	994992	1800113	3271411
3703047	3547500	3018711	90969	101428	394112
3388253	4523126	3353281	208660	163132	503677
1899558	2917119	2115955	299252	154981	220477
48342659	75180492	61529594	1490664	2862163	5006700
34794355	53353050	43817024	1082382	2597029	3450294
11833693	19921950	15937605	643788	294580	1490810
3240468	4640141	3787803	61492	124044	256301
373700	182471	103118	2254	1491	29772
29756218	39401438	30390645	1322901	2186176	3097795
28407279	38694964	29792981	1312637	2182844	3035828
887991	308699	261757	6182	2120	24870
456383	355500	299072	2486		35582
4565	42275	36835	1596	1212	1515
11072089	23057809	19964314	397468	725009	1607435
19201	18713	13399	23	1189	4034
15979	50938	44261	133	3631	1509
696862	1527892	1169579	106386	97617	86143
367525	420748	154001	187160	5106	26723
17173	19227	16157	93	879	2370
46445	70362	59930	227	2659	8026

10-6 续表3

单位：万元

指 标	Item	流动负债 Liquid Liabilities
皮革、毛皮、羽毛及其制品和制鞋业	Leather, Fur, Feather and its products and Footwear	
木材加工和木、竹、藤、棕、草制品业	Timber Processing, Bamboo, Cane, Palm Fiber and Straw Products	
家具制造业	Furniture Manufacturing	
造纸和纸制品业	Paper Making and Paper Products	
印刷和记录媒介复制业	Printing and Record Medium Reproduction	41355
文教、工美、体育和娱乐用品制造业	Culture, Education, Art and Crafts, Sport and Entertainment Products	85241
石油加工、炼焦和核燃料加工业	Petroleum Processing, Coking and Nuclear Fuel Processing	3612395
化学原料和化学制品制造业	Raw Chemical Materials and Chemical Products	5704934
医药制造业	Medical and Pharmaceutical Products	311812
化学纤维制造业	Chemical Fiber	
橡胶和塑料制品业	Rubber and Plastic Products	159452
非金属矿物制品业	Nonmetal Mineral Products	801796
黑色金属冶炼和压延加工业	Smelting and Pressing of Ferrous Metals	6941774
有色金属冶炼和压延加工业	Smelting and Pressing of Non-ferrous Metals	2770623
金属制品业	Metal Prodcuts	421925
通用设备制造业	Ordinary Machinery Manufacturing	626073
专用设备制造业	Special Purpose Equipment Manufacturing	3094338
汽车制造业	Automobile Manufacturing	315859
铁路、船舶、航空航天和其他运输设备制造业	Railroad, Marine, Aviation and Other Transport Equipments Manufacturing	910883
电气机械和器材制造业	Electrical Machinery and Equipment Manufacturing	1005396
计算机、通信和其他电子设备制造业	Computers, Telecommunication and Other Electronic Equipments Manufacturing	273853
仪器仪表制造业	Equipments and Instruments Manufacturing	36935
其他制造业	Other Manufacturing	11636
废弃资源综合利用业	Comprehensive Utilization of Waste Resources	
金属制品、机械和设备修理业	Metal Products, Machinery and Equipment Repair	79291
电力、热力、燃气及水生产和供应业	Production and Supply of Electricity, Heat, Gas and Water	13361019
电力、热力生产和供应业	Production and Supply of Electricity and Heat	11674563
燃气生产和供应业	Production and Supply of Gas	1423826
水的生产和供应业	Production and Supply of Water	262630

continued

(10 000 yuan)

负债合计 Total Liabilities	年末所有者权益 Creditors' Equity at Year-end	主营业务收入 Revenue of Major Business	主营业务成本 Costs of Major Business	主营业务税金及附加 Taxes and Extra Charges of Major Business	营业费用 Costs of Business	管理费用 Costs of Administration
45518	24689	33909	27750	389	293	6761
85241	-35413	5748	4583		193	607
4398313	150120	1987241	1848687	4143	108529	76253
6653415	926791	2975405	2829143	14726	100165	214946
690776	217313	424961	322843	2625	24492	34123
214814	114244	332448	307602	640	5102	9945
1268652	121309	681122	570686	3015	30553	49480
9888304	4083243	7335026	6288434	36753	175516	545068
4477752	1672397	3450724	3133812	20339	44184	103694
484063	266998	273149	225702	1014	6839	31937
840060	300055	345656	285095	2280	14051	36620
3684775	991420	1212174	1104960	5355	45895	137755
374494	120146	253325	223367	1959	9887	28853
1151820	425922	607255	507066	4586	22017	80226
1300056	371182	804569	637258	4049	22976	96953
278854	58147	90842	78795	549	794	11350
38069	18312	27001	19629	160	1419	4843
23236	65293	22324	15028	68	55	2727
79665	16736	87050	76547	796	968	6489
26734486	9413909	15638368	13290590	69546	105961	521947
23910343	8287246	14348244	12197630	65874	26434	442289
2441761	714043	1110664	929473	2654	70809	42351
382382	412620	179460	163487	1018	8718	37307

10-6 续表4

单位：万元

指　标	Item	财务费用 Costs of Finance	#利息支出 Interest Expenditure
总　计	**Total**	**4227264**	**4489500**
在总计中:	Of the Total:		
亏损企业	Loss-making Enterprises	1998291	1957347
按隶属关系分	Grouped by Belongs		
中央企业	Central Enterprises	750195	678241
地方企业	Local Enterprises	3477070	3811260
#省属企业	Province-owned Enterprises	2780285	3142602
市属企业	City-owned Enterprises	187941	181358
县属企业	County-owned Enterprises	380357	367290
在总计中:	Of the Total:		
轻工业	Light Industry	36494	54982
重工业	Heavy Industry	4190770	4434518
在总计中:	Of the Total:		
大型企业	Large-size Enterprises	2762053	3168783
中型企业	Medium-size Enterprises	1041027	939589
小型企业	Small-size Enterprises	374141	338417
微型企业	Micro-size Enterprises	50043	42712
按工业行业大类分	Grouped by Sector		
采矿业	Mining	2455096	2770370
煤炭开采和洗选业	Coal Mining and Dressing	2421255	2736288
石油和天然气开采业	Petroleum and Natural Gas Extraction	21155	21392
黑色金属矿采选业	Ferrous Metals Mining and Dressing	12692	12690
有色金属矿采选业	Nonferrous Metals Mining and Dressing	-6	
非金属矿采选业	Nonmetal Minerals Mining and Dressing		
开采辅助活动	Mining Auxiliary Activities		
其他采矿业	Other Mining Industry		
制造业	Manufacturing	1003234	8294
农副食品加工业	Farm Products Processing	-337	22
食品制造业	Food Manufacturing	-22	26
酒、饮料和精制茶制造业	Wine, Beverages and Refined Tea Manufacturing	4483	7756
烟草制品业	Tobacoo Products Manfacturing	-4542	
纺织业	Textile Industry	-173	49
纺织服装、服饰业	Textile, Wearing Apparel and Accessories	384	441

continued

(10 000 yuan)

利润总额 Total Profits	亏损企业亏损额 Loss of Loss-making Enterprises	利税总额 Total Pre-tax Profits	应付薪酬总额 Total Wages Payable	应交所得税 Income Taxes Payable	应交增值税 Value Added Taxes Payable
1153271	**2409260**	**6457324**	**7885203**	**650544**	**3344322**
-2409260	2409260	-1152649	3344356	83530	766958
882796	319949	2242124	1049362	137752	900677
270475	2089311	4215200	6835842	512792	2443646
537826	1301825	3652733	5405020	441423	1957415
-163279	283265	63701	682176	29979	133957
-73694	392188	430080	593027	37986	294486
111223	54042	552115	237284	53423	141109
1042048	2355218	5905209	7647920	597122	3203213
891470	1135548	4354700	5908593	485322	2219768
133479	966599	1778343	1702767	117013	994004
107171	274005	304688	267513	47573	134363
21150	33109	19594	6331	637	-3813
908429	1088297	4560698	5402309	434220	2170106
838817	1075743	4442157	5354052	424507	2132356
59737	9140	77735	29116	8483	10933
9185	2774	36693	18202	982	24989
690	640	4113	939	248	1828
-350864	1013822	692180	1814097	100944	641912
775		832	1489		34
1644		2841	2024	-164	1065
65154	7332	240771	57809	33673	69231
52233		285253	21619	13058	45860
221		1125	5581		811
1155	71	3695	21133	6	2099

10-6 续表5

单位：万元

指 标	Item	财务费用 Costs of Finance
皮革、毛皮、羽毛及其制品和制鞋业	Leather, Fur, Feather and its products and Footwear	
木材加工和木、竹、藤、棕、草制品业	Timber Processing, Bamboo, Cane, Palm Fiber and Straw Products	
家具制造业	Furniture Manufacturing	
造纸和纸制品业	Paper Making and Paper Products	
印刷和记录媒介复制业	Printing and Record Medium Reproduction	332
文教、工美、体育和娱乐用品制造业	Culture, Education, Art and Crafts, Sport and Entertainment Products	6732
石油加工、炼焦和核燃料加工业	Petroleum Processing, Coking and Nuclear Fuel Processing	136720
化学原料和化学制品制造业	Raw Chemical Materials and Chemical Products	166455
医药制造业	Medical and Pharmaceutical Products	20668
化学纤维制造业	Chemical Fiber	
橡胶和塑料制品业	Rubber and Plastic Products	8577
非金属矿物制品业	Nonmetal Mineral Products	22699
黑色金属冶炼和压延加工业	Smelting and Pressing of Ferrous Metals	344725
有色金属冶炼和压延加工业	Smelting and Pressing of Non-ferrous Metals	159343
金属制品业	Metal Prodcuts	4785
通用设备制造业	Ordinary Machinery Manufacturing	9337
专用设备制造业	Special Purpose Equipment Manufacturing	85901
汽车制造业	Automobile Manufacturing	-5381
铁路、船舶、航空航天和其他运输设备制造业	Railroad, Marine, Aviation and Other Transport Equipments Manufacturing	10741
电气机械和器材制造业	Electrical Machinery and Equipment Manufacturing	33299
计算机、通信和其他电子设备制造业	Computers, Telecommunication and Other Electronic Equipments Manufacturing	-485
仪器仪表制造业	Equipments and Instruments Manufacturing	233
其他制造业	Other Manufacturing	-1267
废弃资源综合利用业	Comprehensive Utilization of Waste Resources	
金属制品、机械和设备修理业	Metal Products, Machinery and Equipment Repair	27
电力、热力、燃气及水生产和供应业	Production and Supply of Electricity, Heat, Gas and Water	768934
电力、热力生产和供应业	Production and Supply of Electricity and Heat	727183
燃气生产和供应业	Production and Supply of Gas	36185
水的生产和供应业	Production and Supply of Water	5566

continued

(10 000 yuan)

#利息支出 Interest Expenditure	利润总额 Total Profits	亏损企业亏损额 Loss of Loss-making Enterprises	利税总额 Total Pre-tax Profits	应付薪酬总额 Total Wages Payable	应交所得税 Income Taxes Payable	应交增值税 Value Added Taxes Payable
372	-670	892	1713	9326	53	1849
6731	-6372	6372	-5417	554		955
136700	-166160	194081	-110180	117437	1733	50584
185433	-330498	351831	-318404	243827	5054	-2992
29781	19578	7563	26489	33385	4231	4254
8235	4298	6735	8839	14972	432	3847
16402	13058	31820	45962	48375	7618	29582
306870	48020	125848	305920	557878	10045	220440
143655	60904	40344	190428	216756	12363	109072
9190	5283	3751	12642	18709	-233	6226
9423	-1141	6609	11733	43858	176	10588
92481	-168719	192751	-130404	163674	2444	32824
2879	-1497	6219	9287	34848	253	8703
12846	5652	20665	27428	98369	4374	17190
32758	37033	7175	61399	55796	3277	20318
48	443	413	1880	16564	231	809
258	168	3350	2534	7912	522	2187
	5734		6352	3099	1433	551
34	2840		9462	19103	365	5825
716740	595706	307140	1204444	668800	115382	532309
674000	551150	262586	1145202	532632	93373	522358
37514	74515	13966	81782	79705	21839	3645
5226	-29959	30588	-22540	56463	170	6306

10-7 外商投资和港澳台投资工业企业主要经济指标(2016年)

单位：万元

指　标	Item	单位数(个) Number of Enterprises (unit)	#亏损企业 Loss-making Enterprises
总　计	**Total**	**133**	**44**
港、澳、台商投资企业	Enterprises Funded by HongKong, Macao and Taiwan	52	16
合资经营企业(港或澳、台资)	Joint Venture	31	12
合作经营企业(港或澳、台资)	Cooperative Enterprise	1	
港澳台商独资经营企业	Ventures Exclusively with HongKong, Macao and Taiwan Investment	15	2
港澳台商投资股份有限公司	Share Holding Limited Company	4	2
其他港澳台商投资企业	Others	1	
外商投资企业	Foreign Funded Enterprises	81	28
中外合资经营企业	Joint Venture	56	19
中外合作经营企业	Cooperative Enterprises	3	
外资企业	Enterprises Funded By Foreign Investments	20	9
外商投资股份有限公司	Enterprises Invested By Foreign Investments	1	
其他外商投资企业	Others	1	
在总计中:亏损企业	Of the Total:Loss-making Enterprises	44	44
在总计中:国有控股企业	Of the Total:State Holding Enterprises	21	4
在总计中:轻工业	Of the Total:Light Industry	28	5
重工业	Heavy Industry	105	39
在总计中:大型企业	Of the Total:Large-size Enterprises	16	5
中型企业	Medium-size Enterprises	38	18
小型企业	Small-size Enterprises	74	20
微型企业	Micro-size Enterprises	5	1
按工业行业大类分	Grouped by Sector		
采矿业	Mining	17	6
煤炭开采和洗选业	Coal Mining and Dressing	13	4
石油和天然气开采业	Petroleum and Natural Gas Extraction	4	2
黑色金属矿采选业	Ferrous Metals Mining and Dressing		
有色金属矿采选业	Nonferrous Metals Mining and Dressing		
非金属矿采选业	Nonmetal Minerals Mining and Dressing		
开采辅助活动	Mining Auxiliary Activities		
其他采矿业	Other Mining Industry		
制造业	Manufacturing	93	34
农副食品加工业	Farm Products Processing	2	
食品制造业	Food Manufacturing	5	1
酒、饮料和精制茶制造业	Wine, Beverages and Refined Tea Manufacturing	13	3
烟草制品业	Tobacoo Products Manfacturing		

MAIN ECONOMIC INDICATORS OF INDUSTRIAL ENTERPRISES WITH HONG KONG, MACAO, TAIWAN AND FOREIGN FUNDS(2016)

(10 000 yuan)

工业销售产值 Industrial Sales Output Value	资产总计 Total Assets	流动资产合计 Total Circulating Funds	固定资产合计 Total Fixed Assets	固定资产原价 Original Value Of Fixed Assets	累计折旧 Total Depreciation
12836804	**21527442**	**11377593**	**7919750**	**12970081**	**5738470**
9064273	12523586	7735503	3985366	6175293	2357775
6934184	8796572	5887522	2523765	3841762	1508609
221580	307519	236794	52680	175656	122976
1656160	2625940	1251685	1030873	1639114	585477
225233	712269	286359	370545	507221	136676
27117	81286	73143	7504	11540	4036
3772530	9003855	3642090	3934385	6794788	3380695
1967151	5698344	2287572	2433957	3205014	1290810
745561	1598774	515699	735671	2263634	1527962
1037970	1548600	821108	627180	1178350	551709
7018	11265	6620	2709	6088	3379
14830	146873	11091	134868	141703	6835
1299267	4629317	1696334	2465783	3405489	1318780
1868157	4594053	952499	3033649	5669338	2740270
433089	514083	249544	212565	431577	219592
12403715	21013359	11128049	7707185	12538504	5518878
9072243	12963713	8464000	3220700	4863315	2142171
2631281	5961144	2094416	3029986	5553666	2663937
1111761	2427314	749180	1564802	2437575	920776
21518	175271	69998	104262	115525	11586
1051854	3835471	1178677	1611412	2279433	906492
947510	3361791	1027863	1303527	1881154	816099
104344	473680	150814	307885	398279	90393
10555159	13766332	9324071	3403716	5496515	2459443
30519	43673	26652	11319	13947	2627
82603	46851	25099	17445	35474	18084
144297	211345	81429	114644	225130	110089

10-7 续表1

单位：万元

指　标	Item	单位数(个) Number of Enterprises (unit)
纺织业	Textile Industry	1
纺织服装、服饰业	Textile, Wearing Apparel and Accessories	
皮革、毛皮、羽毛及其制品和制鞋业	Leather, Fur, Feather and Related Products and Footwear	
木材加工和木、竹、藤、棕、草制造业	Timber Processing,Bamboo,Cane,Palm Fiber and Straw Products	
家具制造业	Furniture Manufacturing	
造纸和纸制品业	Paper Making and Paper Products	
印刷和记录媒介复制业	Printing and Record Medium Reproduction	1
文教、工美、体育和娱乐用品制造业	Culture, Education, Art and Crafts, Sport and Entertainment Products	
石油加工、炼焦和核燃料加工业	Petroleum Processing, Coking and Nuclear Fuel Processing	11
化学原料和化学制品制造业	Raw Chemical Materials and Chemical Products	8
医药制造业	Medical and Pharmaceutical Products	2
化学纤维制造业	Chemical Fiber Manufacturing	
橡胶和塑料制品业	Rubber and Plastic Products	3
非金属矿物制品业	Nonmetal Mineral Products	8
黑色金属冶炼和压延加工业	Smelting and Pressing of Ferrous Metals	5
有色金属冶炼和压延加工业	Smelting and Pressing of Non-ferrous Metals	5
金属制品业	Metal Prodcuts	3
通用设备制造业	Ordinary Machinery Manufacturing	3
专用设备制造业	Special Purpose Equipment Manufacturing	7
汽车制造业	Automobile Manufacturing	3
铁路、船舶、航空航天和其他运输设备制造业	Railroad, Marine, Aviation and Other Transport Equipment Manufacturing	2
电气机械和器材制造业	Electrical Machinery and Equipment Manufacturing	2
计算机、通信和其他电子设备制造业	Computers, Telecommunication and Other Electronic Equipments Manufacturing	5
仪器仪表制造业	Equipments and Instruments Manufacturing	1
其他制造业	Other Manufacturing	1
废弃资源综合利用业	Comprehensive Utilization of Waste Resources	1
金属制品、机械和设备修理业	Metal products, Machinery and Equipment Repair	1
电力、热力、燃气及水生产和供应业	Production and Supply of Electricity, Heat, Gas and Water	23
电力、热力生产和供应业	Production and Supply of Electricity and Heat	18
燃气生产和供应业	Production and Supply of Gas	4
水的生产和供应业	Production and Supply of Water	1

continued

(10 000 yuan)

#亏损企业 Loss-making Enterprises	工业销售产值 Industrial Sales Output Value	资产总计 Total Assets	流动资产合计 Total Circulating Funds	固定资产合计 Total Fixed Assets	固定资产原价 Original Value Of Fixed Assets	累计折旧 Total Depreciation
1	4205	25167	21000	603	3878	3275
	3141	5858	3248	2609	5326	2717
9	902150	2445949	1409979	821623	1153059	635103
3	139562	211713	67230	133126	286951	153826
	45682	78411	46951	9872	17384	7512
2	29536	78983	37590	40736	86750	46057
7	166458	396802	51451	284845	387391	105702
2	97184	94699	58730	6869	76035	42246
1	814440	1674293	465380	799888	1023570	307969
	26922	33140	19719	12341	24010	11670
1	20695	22842	12699	9358	14861	6320
1	156644	219414	163599	45246	93448	48829
	19367	27505	20784	4236	8015	4130
	285142	291482	242643	38148	122271	84123
1	58039	60514	47177	5608	30546	24938
2	7407486	7626970	6443787	1001552	1831012	829460
	86254	105815	56675	4160	9825	5665
	13319	8240	7277	918	1081	163
	17420	47866	9385	36505	43378	6873
	4094	8800	5587	2065	3173	2065
4	1229792	3925642	874845	2904625	5194135	2372534
4	1133270	3737112	819993	2791039	5048059	2338557
	92847	156008	51949	86195	106798	22090
	3675	32522	2903	27391	39278	11887

10-7 续表2

单位：万元

指　标	Item	流动负债 Liquid Liabilities	负债合计 Total Liabilities
总　计	**Total**	**12089431**	**14897001**
港、澳、台商投资企业	Enterprises Funded by HongKong, Macao and Taiwan	8066836	9625747
合资经营企业(港或澳、台资)	Joint Venture	6748352	7528209
合作经营企业(港或澳、台资)	Cooperative Enterprise	92965	214336
港澳台商独资经营企业	Ventures Exclusively with HongKong, Macao and Taiwan Investment	848117	1142252
港澳台商投资股份有限公司	Share Holding Limited Company	334428	664696
其他港澳台商投资企业	Others	42974	76254
外商投资企业	Foreign Funded Enterprises	4022595	5271255
中外合资经营企业	Joint Venture	2648462	3717636
中外合作经营企业	Cooperative Enterprises	735238	762515
外资企业	Enterprises Funded By Foreign Investments	561729	713939
外商投资股份有限公司	Enterprises Invested By Foreign Investments	6235	6235
其他外商投资企业	Others	70931	70931
在总计中:亏损企业	Of the Total:Loss-making Enterprises	3058246	4272827
在总计中:国有控股企业	Of the Total:State Holding Enterprises	1947175	3075258
在总计中:轻工业	Of the Total:Light Industry	235496	254512
重工业	Heavy Industry	11853936	14642490
在总计中:大型企业	Of the Total:Large-size Enterprises	8049809	9038750
中型企业	Medium-size Enterprises	3078812	4364735
小型企业	Small-size Enterprises	889906	1359112
微型企业	Micro-size Enterprises	70905	134405
按工业行业大类分	Grouped by Sector		
采矿业	Mining	1651723	2157114
煤炭开采和洗选业	Coal Mining and Dressing	1511307	1871747
石油和天然气开采业	Petroleum and Natural Gas Extraction	140416	285367
黑色金属矿采选业	Ferrous Metals Mining and Dressing		
有色金属矿采选业	Nonferrous Metals Mining and Dressing		
非金属矿采选业	Nonmetal Minerals Mining and Dressing		
开采辅助活动	Mining Auxiliary Activities		
其他采矿业	Other Mining Industry		
制造业	Manufacturing	9297001	10190138
农副食品加工业	Farm Products Processing	13562	21434
食品制造业	Food Manufacturing	9893	11173
酒、饮料和精制茶制造业	Wine, Beverages and Refined Tea Manufacturing	139689	143811
烟草制品业	Tobacoo Products Manfacturing		

continued

(10 000 yuan)

年末所有者权益 Creditors' Equity at Year-end	主营业务收入 Revenue of Major Business	主营业务成本 Costs of Major Business	主营业务税金及附加 Taxes and Extra Charges of Major Business	营业费用 Costs of Business	管理费用 Costs of Administration
6630440	**12907783**	**11368635**	**139021**	**177187**	**385745**
2897839	9005777	8349472	34478	66466	163927
1268363	6953152	6578385	19536	41337	93990
93183	221580	220942		136	141
1483687	1584803	1335189	13322	18257	50943
47574	216987	191694	1473	5725	18440
5032	29255	23262	147	1011	412
3732601	3902006	3019163	104543	110722	221818
1980708	2088526	1657576	46838	89910	124470
836260	746024	472270	42487	11813	28546
834661	1045668	873290	15144	8772	65508
5030	6959	5098	32	227	1227
75943	14830	10929	42		2067
356490	1449717	1386620	12848	78686	83157
1518796	1834348	1391614	50288	26569	75851
259570	442263	320324	5277	39227	21529
6370870	12465520	11048311	133745	137960	364216
3924963	9181402	8407065	102083	49437	219929
1596408	2584057	2095390	20189	97262	109282
1068203	1118654	850153	16716	30435	55014
40866	23670	16027	34	53	1520
1678355	1052729	672517	71878	26232	84724
1490043	947728	586810	71657	24933	77744
188312	105001	85707	221	1299	6980
3576191	10622920	9752014	53400	143889	277321
22240	33698	28231		2168	1356
35678	77214	50446	225	4131	3281
67534	153682	115974	3833	18958	9870

10-7 续表3

单位：万元

指　标	Item	流动负债 Liquid Liabilities
纺织业	Textile Industry	22377
纺织服装、服饰业	Textile, Wearing Apparel and Accessories	
皮革、毛皮、羽毛及其制品和制鞋业	Leather, Fur, Feather and Related Products and Footwear	
木材加工和木、竹、藤、棕、草制造业	Timber Processing,Bamboo,Cane,Palm Fiber and Straw Products	
家具制造业	Furniture Manufacturing	
造纸和纸制品业	Paper Making and Paper Products	
印刷和记录媒介复制业	Printing and Record Medium Reproduction	768
文教、工美、体育和娱乐用品制造业	Culture, Education, Art and Crafts, Sport and Entertainment Products	
石油加工、炼焦和核燃料加工业	Petroleum Processing, Coking and Nuclear Fuel Processing	1849855
化学原料和化学制品制造业	Raw Chemical Materials and Chemical Products	98552
医药制造业	Medical and Pharmaceutical Products	23895
化学纤维制造业	Chemical Fiber Manufacturing	
橡胶和塑料制品业	Rubber and Plastic Products	13741
非金属矿物制品业	Nonmetal Mineral Products	310777
黑色金属冶炼和压延加工业	Smelting and Pressing of Ferrous Metals	38810
有色金属冶炼和压延加工业	Smelting and Pressing of Non-ferrous Metals	735418
金属制品业	Metal Prodcuts	10291
通用设备制造业	Ordinary Machinery Manufacturing	16969
专用设备制造业	Special Purpose Equipment Manufacturing	137421
汽车制造业	Automobile Manufacturing	20810
铁路、船舶、航空航天和其他运输设备制造业	Railroad, Marine, Aviation and Other Transport Equipment Manufacturing	152607
电气机械和器材制造业	Electrical Machinery and Equipment Manufacturing	68515
计算机、通信和其他电子设备制造业	Computers, Telecommunication and Other Electronic Equipments Manufacturing	5580432
仪器仪表制造业	Equipments and Instruments Manufacturing	39839
其他制造业	Other Manufacturing	6254
废弃资源综合利用业	Comprehensive Utilization of Waste Resources	4359
金属制品、机械和设备修理业	Metal products, Machinery and Equipment Repair	2167
电力、热力、燃气及水生产和供应业	Production and Supply of Electricity, Heat, Gas and Water	1140707
电力、热力生产和供应业	Production and Supply of Electricity and Heat	1070890
燃气生产和供应业	Production and Supply of Gas	63138
水的生产和供应业	Production and Supply of Water	6679

continued

(10 000 yuan)

负债合计 Total Liabilities	年末所有者权益 Creditors' Equity at Year-end	主营业务收入 Revenue of Major Business	主营业务成本 Costs of Major Business	主营业务税金及附加 Taxes and Extra Charges of Major Business	营业费用 Costs of Business	管理费用 Costs of Administration
22377	2790	2374	1973	7	29	356
2418	3440	2737	2359	17	102	219
2326121	119828	1033112	956838	8307	59287	33512
98700	113013	136820	130699	656	3262	8882
27829	50583	45607	15655	905	11238	3795
13909	65074	34486	30499	242	1907	3220
337402	59400	166622	145004	249	3477	14088
39048	55651	97390	73756	844	8101	8164
1015376	658917	763633	657762	6453	5503	12341
11514	21626	27793	19884	67	1882	2146
16992	5849	20694	17490	87	1267	1570
202108	17305	151099	130306	898	3123	18452
20810	6694	21729	16498	66	1415	2810
157604	133877	284994	205899	2183	6490	17596
72430	-11916	58059	30050	488	2575	3763
5580432	2046538	7396491	7039394	27129	4551	120229
43870	61945	80839	60373	405	4109	6320
6254	1986	13319	12037			98
16359	31506	16443	7201	277	314	4874
2167	6633	4085	3686	62		379
2549748	1375894	1232133	944103	13741	7070	23702
2465118	1271995	1134459	870217	13162	3	17330
63994	92014	92843	69170	504	7067	5998
20636	11885	4831	4716	75		374

10-7 续表4

单位：万元

指 标	Item	财务费用 Costs of Finance	#利息支出 Interest Expenditure
总 计	**Total**	**204437**	**248622**
港、澳、台商投资企业	Enterprises Funded by HongKong, Macao and Taiwan	85754	141898
合资经营企业(港或澳、台资)	Joint Venture	59366	94353
合作经营企业(港或澳、台资)	Cooperative Enterprise	315	315
港澳台商独资经营企业	Ventures Exclusively with HongKong, Macao and Taiwan Investment	3695	24697
港澳台商投资股份有限公司	Share Holding Limited Company	19677	19816
其他港澳台商投资企业	Others	2703	2717
外商投资企业	Foreign Funded Enterprises	118683	106724
中外合资经营企业	Joint Venture	94281	83647
中外合作经营企业	Cooperative Enterprises	10878	11841
外资企业	Enterprises Funded By Foreign Investments	13466	11182
外商投资股份有限公司	Enterprises Invested By Foreign Investments	58	54
其他外商投资企业	Others	-1	
在总计中:亏损企业	Of the Total:Loss-making Enterprises	103704	94916
在总计中:国有控股企业	Of the Total:State Holding Enterprises	86025	81956
在总计中:轻工业	Of the Total:Light Industry	4166	3597
重工业	Heavy Industry	200271	245025
在总计中:大型企业	Of the Total:Large-size Enterprises	59576	113615
中型企业	Medium-size Enterprises	103041	98258
小型企业	Small-size Enterprises	41379	36323
微型企业	Micro-size Enterprises	440	426
按工业行业大类分	Grouped by Sector		
采矿业	Mining	55835	43516
煤炭开采和洗选业	Coal Mining and Dressing	47019	41873
石油和天然气开采业	Petroleum and Natural Gas Extraction	8816	1643
黑色金属矿采选业	Ferrous Metals Mining and Dressing		
有色金属矿采选业	Nonferrous Metals Mining and Dressing		
非金属矿采选业	Nonmetal Minerals Mining and Dressing		
开采辅助活动	Mining Auxiliary Activities		
其他采矿业	Other Mining Industry		
制造业	Manufacturing	63446	120360
农副食品加工业	Farm Products Processing	449	462
食品制造业	Food Manufacturing	19	66
酒、饮料和精制茶制造业	Wine, Beverages and Refined Tea Manufacturing	1391	1345
烟草制品业	Tobacoo Products Manfacturing		

continued

(10 000 yuan)

利润总额 Total Profits	亏损企业亏损额 Loss of Loss-making Enterprises	利税总额 Total Pre-tax Profits	应付薪酬总额 Total Wages Payable	应交所得税 Income Taxes Payable	应交增值税 Value Added Taxes Payable
720030	**218782**	**1218534**	**1488612**	**179081**	**359102**
376203	85079	495709	928559	86152	85027
212022	63581	290327	590189	52616	58769
46		1115	7127		1069
177314	4558	226356	305087	33528	35720
-14562	16940	-24537	25489	8	-11449
1382		2448	667		919
343828	133703	722826	560053	92929	274075
70140	93632	230868	215939	25654	113526
187767		310179	84870	54749	79925
81361	40071	176040	257316	12478	79535
304		724	960	48	371
4256		5016	968		717
-218782	218782	-182434	160909	-6905	23257
222632	33405	410629	170648	62753	137709
44704	10449	67849	50925	3248	17869
675327	208333	1150685	1437687	175834	341234
413040	54861	734847	1237894	97668	219724
173626	135697	298659	166656	59313	104480
127664	28042	187881	83760	21689	43485
5701	182	-2852	301	411	-8587
166946	29722	350340	174177	47953	111515
147554	21529	330075	164512	47912	110863
19392	8193	20265	9665	41	652
384194	129136	624088	1211285	92948	186114
2023		2041	2124		18
16114	106	17748	22492	-197	1409
1958	5004	11628	18007	836	5837

10-7 续表5

单位：万元

指　　标	Item	财务费用 Costs of Finance
纺织业	Textile Industry	1006
纺织服装、服饰业	Textile, Wearing Apparel and Accessories	
皮革、毛皮、羽毛及其制品和制鞋业	Leather, Fur, Feather and Related Products and Footwear	
木材加工和木、竹、藤、棕、草制造业	Timber Processing,Bamboo,Cane,Palm Fiber and Straw Products	
家具制造业	Furniture Manufacturing	
造纸和纸制品业	Paper Making and Paper Products	
印刷和记录媒介复制业	Printing and Record Medium Reproduction	54
文教、工美、体育和娱乐用品制造业	Culture, Education, Art and Crafts, Sport and Entertainment Products	
石油加工、炼焦和核燃料加工业	Petroleum Processing, Coking and Nuclear Fuel Processing	35608
化学原料和化学制品制造业	Raw Chemical Materials and Chemical Products	1816
医药制造业	Medical and Pharmaceutical Products	319
化学纤维制造业	Chemical Fiber Manufacturing	
橡胶和塑料制品业	Rubber and Plastic Products	617
非金属矿物制品业	Nonmetal Mineral Products	12104
黑色金属冶炼和压延加工业	Smelting and Pressing of Ferrous Metals	-140
有色金属冶炼和压延加工业	Smelting and Pressing of Non-ferrous Metals	22138
金属制品业	Metal Prodcuts	153
通用设备制造业	Ordinary Machinery Manufacturing	141
专用设备制造业	Special Purpose Equipment Manufacturing	758
汽车制造业	Automobile Manufacturing	543
铁路、船舶、航空航天和其他运输设备制造业	Railroad, Marine, Aviation and Other Transport Equipment Manufacturing	2843
电气机械和器材制造业	Electrical Machinery and Equipment Manufacturing	1955
计算机、通信和其他电子设备制造业	Computers, Telecommunication and Other Electronic Equipments Manufacturing	-19495
仪器仪表制造业	Equipments and Instruments Manufacturing	472
其他制造业	Other Manufacturing	
废弃资源综合利用业	Comprehensive Utilization of Waste Resources	690
金属制品、机械和设备修理业	Metal products, Machinery and Equipment Repair	5
电力、热力、燃气及水生产和供应业	Production and Supply of Electricity, Heat, Gas and Water	85160
电力、热力生产和供应业	Production and Supply of Electricity and Heat	83032
燃气生产和供应业	Production and Supply of Gas	1684
水的生产和供应业	Production and Supply of Water	444

continued

(10 000 yuan)

#利息支出 Interest Expenditure	利润总额 Total Profits	亏损企业亏损额 Loss of Loss-making Enterprises	利税总额 Total Pre-tax Profits	应付薪酬总额 Total Wages Payable	应交所得税 Income Taxes Payable	应交增值税 Value Added Taxes Payable
997	-5339	5339	-5276	106		56
	1		164	433		145
29042	-39268	42848	-14220	32234	1181	16740
1746	-8575	15485	-4351	8806	1349	3568
318	14626		20474	3010	1977	4943
143	-1431	2321	-596	4069	222	593
10999	-7716	20654	-1142	18167	-20	6326
455	6288	221	9706	8345	40	2574
28366	62841	1258	104959	20901	16492	35665
151	3877		5463	3394	521	1398
3	266	161	800	974	107	448
692	2691	203	8346	30118	19	4757
712	458		850	3156	50	310
1948	44322		61081	14947	7434	14576
1513	1820	14050	6618	2953	3967	4068
40238	276510	21486	384384	1011405	56681	80745
458	8160		9924	2001	1224	1358
	1224		1224	472	306	
701	3043		3702	2506	750	382
5	301		561	665	9	198
84748	168891	59925	244106	103150	38180	61474
84299	159543	59925	233072	96054	35891	60368
34	8871		9903	6593	2282	527
415	477		1131	503	7	579

10-8 大中型工业企业主要经济指标(2016年)

单位：万元

指 标	Item	单位数(个) Number of Enterprises (unit)
总 计	**Total**	**1066**
一、按隶属关系分	Grouped by Jurisdiction of Management	
中央企业	Central Enterprises	82
省属企业	Province-owned Enterprises	229
市属企业	Cities-owned Enterprises	86
县(市、区)属企业	County-owned Enterprises	192
城市街道企业	Cities' Subdistrict-owned Enterprises	
镇属企业	Town-owned Enterprises	10
乡属企业	Township Enterprises	4
居委会办企业	Neighbourhood Committee -run Enterprises	
村办企业	Village Enterprises	7
其 他	Enterprises of Other Types of Ownership	456
二、按登记注册类型分	Grouped by Registered Kind	
内资企业	Civil Funded Enterprises	1012
国有企业	State-owned Enterprises	41
集体企业	Collective-owned Enterprises	13
股份合作企业	Share Holding Cooperative Enterprises	
联营企业	Joint Owned Enterprises	1
有限责任公司	Limited Responsibility Company	603
国有独资公司	Company Exclusively with Investment from State	54
其他有限责任公司	Other Limited Responsibility Company	549
股份有限公司	Share Holding Limited Company	62
私营企业	Privately Owned Enterprises	291
私营独资企业	Enterprise Exclusively with Investment from Private	1
私营合伙企业	Private Partner Enterprises	
私营有限责任公司	Privately Owned Limited Responsibility Company	274
私营股份有限公司	Privately Owned Share Holding Limited Company	16
其他企业	Enterprises of Other Types of Ownership	1
港、澳、台商投资企业	Enterprises Funded by Hong Kong, Macao and Taiwan	22
合资经营企业(港或澳、台资)	Joint Venture	13
合作经营企业(港或澳、台资)	Cooperative Enterprise	1
港澳台商独资企业	Ventures Exclusively with Hong Kong, Macao and Taiwan Investment	5
港澳台商投资股份有限公司	Share Holding Limited Company	3
其他港澳台商投资企业	Others	

MAIN ECONOMIC INDICATORS OF LARGE AND MEDIUM-SIZE INDUSTRIAL ENTERPRISES(2016)

(10 000 yuan)

#亏损企业 Loss-making Enterprises	工业销售产值 Industrial Sales Output Value	资产总计 Total Assets	流动资产合计 Total Circulating Funds	固定资产合计 Total Fixed Assets	固定资产原价 Original Value of Fixed Assets	累计折旧 Total Depreciation
431	**96955786**	**283670930**	**111236788**	**106936070**	**155331272**	**65587145**
25	17773578	36468600	8171670	20888076	36719952	17102123
101	30371915	134515273	54052009	47728546	66106466	29250561
44	4608520	15043185	5410812	5548067	7944345	3017898
84	7911656	25722106	9599545	9348240	11891496	3926778
5	1113868	1673966	1002731	483051	739224	261892
3	121672	989751	456020	244007	337718	94626
1	243529	429011	116443	188558	319434	132347
168	34811048	68829038	32427559	22507525	31272637	11800920
408	85252262	264746074	100678373	100685384	144914291	60781037
26	9242823	14201952	2333340	10593755	17384812	7881978
6	312375	764281	446206	239613	537011	296249
1	36041	144735	53824	19120	64800	45681
258	48642151	188155254	73259963	67769559	93011360	38051608
26	12901602	37180999	14602072	12634167	22070011	9752495
232	35740549	150974256	58657892	55135392	70941349	28299112
16	7587868	23474807	7490397	9234603	15701516	7466792
100	19407037	37742105	16908448	12759952	18146010	7020440
	99273	109084	79102	16116	49652	33536
96	17516649	35111798	15789473	11555149	16970643	6592914
4	1791116	2521223	1039874	1188687	1125715	393990
1	23967	262939	186195	68782	68782	18290
8	8466916	11007519	7285669	2953202	4580473	1765755
6	6501057	7964755	5684879	1914706	2748025	998423
	221580	307519	236794	52680	175656	122976
	1521896	2029150	1080486	618294	1154478	509563
2	222382	706096	283510	367522	502315	134793

10-8 续表1

单位：万元

指　标	Item	单位数(个) Number of Enterprises (unit)
外商投资企业	Foreign Funded Enterprises	32
中外合资经营企业	Joint Venture	24
中外合作经营企业	Cooperative Enterprises	3
外资企业	Enterprises Funded By Foreign Investments	5
外商投资股份有限公司	Share Holding Limited Company	
其他外商投资企业	Other Foreign Funded Enterprises	
三、在总计中: 亏损企业	Of the Total: Loss-making Enterprises	431
在总计中: 国有控股企业	Of the Total: State-Controlled Share Holding Enterprises	508
在总计中: 农村工业	Of the Total: Rural Industry	11
在总计中: 轻工业	Of the Total: Light Industry	135
重工业	Heavy Industry	931
在总计中: 大型企业	Of the Total: Large-size Enterprises	223
中型企业	Medium-size Enterprises	843
四、按工业行业大类分	Grouped by Sector	
采矿业	Mining	453
煤炭开采和洗选业	Coal Mining and Dressing	435
石油和天然气开采业	Petroleum and Natural Gas Extraction	4
黑色金属矿采选业	Ferrous Metals Mining and Dressing	11
有色金属矿采选业	Nonferrous Metals Mining and Dressing	3
非金属矿采选业	Nonmetal Minerals Mining and Dressing	
开采辅助活动	Mining Auxiliary Activities	
其他采矿业	Other Mining Industry	
制造业	Manufacturing	539
农副食品加工业	Farm Products Processing	15
食品制造业	Food Manufacturing	13
酒、饮料和精制茶制造业	Wine, Beverages and Refined Tea Manufacturing	12
烟草制品业	Tobacoo Products Manfacturing	1
纺织业	Textile Industry	6
纺织服装、服饰业	Textile, Wearing Apparel and Accessories	7
皮革、毛皮、羽毛及其制品和制鞋业	Leather, Fur, Feather and Related Products and Footwear	
木材加工和木、竹、藤、棕、草制品业	Timber Processing,Bamboo,Cane,Palm Fiber and Straw Products	1

continued

(10 000 yuan)

#亏损企业 Loss-making Enterprises	工业销售产值 Industrial Sales Output Value	资产总计 Total Assets	流动资产合计 Total Circulating Funds	固定资产合计 Total Fixed Assets	固定资产原价 Original Value Of Fixed Assets	累计折旧 Total Depredation
15	3236609	7917337	3272746	3297484	5836508	3040353
13	1574205	4952504	2003486	2030545	2568255	1039040
	745561	1598774	515699	735671	2263634	1527962
2	916843	1366060	753560	531268	1004619	473351
431	22562337	106547595	39800519	43388639	55268421	22282580
231	55756949	201922617	71916211	80769977	118875127	51736568
4	365201	1418762	572463	432565	657152	226974
33	6427686	9287891	4478490	2918388	4078094	1472406
398	90528099	274383039	106758299	104017683	151253178	64114739
65	61710139	182049517	80918790	61670096	91252773	42159243
366	35245646	101621413	30317998	45265974	64078500	23427902
197	30793774	158768762	61011199	53392615	69375451	28448552
192	29512163	155073054	60058265	52122613	67854440	28096321
	254140	1850490	611908	347505	419228	122239
5	922475	1786547	323045	882824	1048088	204209
	104996	58671	17981	39673	53695	25783
188	53327928	98837958	46050690	35297908	53300606	22433870
4	1640814	1139413	498475	378113	466557	126038
1	713468	621432	277368	271791	361101	95617
3	743342	1449571	860275	327802	367164	86134
	422692	418993	272709	143319	148892	72066
	257133	324362	172778	121085	163340	59568
1	179403	288076	194442	53208	98422	45236
	112751	183679	107318	45884	28405	5491

10-8 续表2

单位：万元

指　　标	Item	单位数(个) Number of Enterprises (unit)
家具制造业	Furniture Manufacturing	
造纸和纸制品业	Paper Making and Paper Products	2
印刷和记录媒介复制业	Printing and Record Medium Reproduction	4
文教、工美、体育和娱乐用品制造业	Culture, Education, Art and Crafts, Sport and Entertainment Products	2
石油加工、炼焦和核燃料加工业	Petroleum Processing, Coking and Nuclear Fuel Processing	97
化学原料和化学制品制造业	Raw Chemical Materials and Chemical Products	56
医药制造业	Medical and Pharmaceutical Products	22
化学纤维制造业	Chemical Fiber Manufacturing	
橡胶和塑料制品业	Rubber and Plastic Products	7
非金属矿物制品业	Nonmetal Mineral Products	72
黑色金属冶炼和压延加工业	Smelting and Pressing of Ferrous Metals	69
有色金属冶炼和压延加工业	Smelting and Pressing of Non-ferrous Metals	33
金属制品业	Metal Prodcuts	23
通用设备制造业	Ordinary Machinery Manufacturing	18
专用设备制造业	Special Purpose Equipment Manufacturing	26
汽车制造业	Automobile Manufacturing	19
铁路、船舶、航空航天和其他运输设备制造业	Railroad, Marine, Aviation and Other Transport Equipments Manufacturing	10
电气机械和器材制造业	Electrical Machinery and Equipment Manufacturing	10
计算机、通信和其他电子设备制造业	Computers, Telecommunication and Other Electronic Equipments Manufacturing	8
仪器仪表制造业	Equipments and Instruments Manufacturing	3
其他制造业	Other Manufacturing	2
废弃资源综合利用业	Comprehensive Utilization of Waste Resources	
金属制品、机械和设备修理业	Metal Products, Machinery and Equipment Repair	1
电力、热力、燃气及水生产和供应业	Production and Supply of Electricity, Heat, Gas and Water	74
电力、热力生产和供应业	Production and Supply of Electricity and Heat	53
燃气生产和供应业	Production and Supply of Gas	11
水的生产和供应业	Production and Supply of Water	10

continued

(10 000 yuan)

#亏损企业 Loss-making Enterprises	工业销售产值 Industrial Sales Output Value	资产总计 Total Assets	流动资产合计 Total Circulating Funds	固定资产合计 Total Fixed Assets	固定资产原价 Original Value Of Fixed Assets	累计折旧 Total Depredation
	91173	84149	21866	59615	84872	25257
1	37740	85955	32458	28390	62355	39049
	21766	44003	23580	15727	23316	7609
54	8506870	21999249	11120048	6071356	9213061	4186615
27	3072864	9488449	3516236	4217493	5498308	2350447
4	1311829	2928010	1174131	903194	1176810	389552
2	314750	346412	139192	195131	259317	69856
25	1568718	2860917	1154891	1450060	2040225	803010
27	15223174	25631635	7921881	11764789	19998551	8915672
8	5177501	9426614	2916575	5185048	7561294	2902259
3	467391	930405	610303	240584	302879	113961
4	972739	1348500	838929	420322	412683	118865
7	1208469	4899825	3657954	805298	955675	450160
6	1269228	2018677	1201708	533141	760533	236334
4	817334	1904430	1251756	405291	633961	228656
3	1336873	1771129	1055299	445966	575619	193231
3	7633377	8274604	6790588	1153055	2014505	873440
1	132641	225736	123055	39653	44096	13676
	49358	112336	87743	20355	39388	19032
	44530	31397	29132	2238	9277	7039
46	12834088	26064213	4174900	18245547	32655217	14704726
34	11585087	22649778	3305850	17695586	30931774	14208000
3	1075593	2630766	624458	149913	1022768	188961
9	173408	783669	244592	400048	700675	307765

10-8 续表3

单位：万元

指 标	Item	流动负债 Liquid Liabilities
总 计	**Total**	**151771763**
一、按隶属关系分	Grouped by Jurisdiction of Management	
中央企业	Central Enterprises	15959888
省属企业	Province-owned Enterprises	69461519
市属企业	Cities-owned Enterprises	7695477
县(市、区)属企业	County-owned Enterprises	15424505
城市街道企业	Cities' Subdistrict-owned Enterprises	
镇属企业	Town-owned Enterprises	938394
乡属企业	Township Enterprises	389685
居委会办企业	Neighbourhood Committee -run Enterprises	
村办企业	Village Enterprises	290682
其 他	Enterprises of Other Types of Ownership	41611614
二、按登记注册类型分	Grouped by Registered Kind	
内资企业	Civil Funded Enterprises	140643143
国有企业	State-owned Enterprises	6670032
集体企业	Collective-owned Enterprises	801064
股份合作企业	Share Holding Cooperative Enterprises	
联营企业	Joint Owned Enterprises	243011
有限责任公司	Limited Responsibility Company	100640198
国有独资公司	Company Exclusively with Investment from State	17563820
其他有限责任公司	Other Limited Responsibility Company	83076378
股份有限公司	Share Holding Limited Company	9772890
私营企业	Privately Owned Enterprises	22373163
私营独资企业	Enterprise Exclusively with Investment from Private	83677
私营合伙企业	Private Partner Enterprises	
私营有限责任公司	Privately Owned Limited Responsibility Company	21195078
私营股份有限公司	Privately Owned Share Holding Limited Company	1094408
其他企业	Enterprises of Other Types of Ownership	142785
港、澳、台商投资企业	Enterprises Funded by Hong Kong, Macao and Taiwan	7507244
合资经营企业(港或澳、台资)	Joint Venture	6395083
合作经营企业(港或澳、台资)	Cooperative Enterprise	92965
港澳台商独资企业	Ventures Exclusively with Hong Kong, Macao and Taiwan Investment	689271
港澳台商投资股份有限公司	Share Holding Limited Company	329925
其他港澳台商投资企业	Others	

continued

(10 000 yuan)

负债合计 Total Liabilities	年末所有者权益 Creditors' Equity at Year-end	主营业务收入 Revenue of Major Business	主营业务成本 Costs of Major Business	主营业务税金及附加 Taxes and Extra Charges of Major Business	营业费用 Costs of Business	管理费用 Costs of Administration
217095099	**66553663**	**112947155**	**93521442**	**2169544**	**4094071**	**6826664**
25181879	11286720	18301787	14381567	443679	907191	891614
105813225	28702046	47733973	39727540	984337	1818915	3209123
10972020	4071165	4515011	3656910	93694	186831	438286
20345666	5376438	7459892	5505347	303399	257623	871014
1355975	317991	973350	832035	13741	23657	38283
591863	397888	122720	70765	9863	2309	16598
292357	136654	234288	176651	7941	3956	27168
52542114	16264761	33606135	29170628	312890	893590	1334577
203691615	61032291	101181696	83018987	2047273	3947373	6497452
10274879	3927073	9819743	8591291	51351	57495	428850
817068	-52786	504753	419542	15745	26964	56994
251025	-106290	40792	29902	3695		4055
149401055	38754193	65253078	53335820	1588802	2326415	4637863
25165483	12015514	15172556	12477301	330074	453393	1165342
124235572	26738679	50080522	40858519	1258728	1873022	3472520
13774794	9700012	7196318	4752815	247604	1042501	621880
28894626	8825319	18342769	15873964	137811	493857	741873
83677	25407	91866	80014	549	5132	1812
27260170	7829467	16502278	14416740	132397	450449	684444
1550779	970444	1748625	1377210	4866	38276	55617
278168	-15229	24243	15654	2264	140	5939
8774730	2232789	8413542	7929535	29444	59318	141691
7093000	871755	6516076	6241258	15271	36801	78771
214336	93183	221580	220942		136	141
807225	1221925	1461751	1277872	12720	16734	44769
660169	45927	214136	189463	1453	5647	18011

10-8 续表4

单位：万元

指　　标	Item	流动负债 Liquid Liabilities
外商投资企业	Foreign Funded Enterprises	3621377
中外合资经营企业	Joint Venture	2436412
中外合作经营企业	Cooperative Enterprises	735238
外资企业	Enterprises Funded By Foreign Investments	449727
外商投资股份有限公司	Share Holding Limited Company	
其他外商投资企业	Other Foreign Funded Enterprises	
三、在总计中: 亏损企业	Of the Total: Loss-making Enterprises	63876642
在总计中: 国有控股企业	Of the Total: State-Controlled Share Holding Enterprises	102883122
在总计中: 农村工业	Of the Total: Rural Industry	680367
在总计中: 轻工业	Of the Total: Light Industry	3711158
重工业	Heavy Industry	148060605
在总计中: 大型企业	Of the Total: Large-size Enterprises	89988386
中型企业	Medium-size Enterprises	61783378
四、按工业行业大类分	Grouped by Sector	
采矿业	Mining	82252591
煤炭开采和洗选业	Coal Mining and Dressing	80744613
石油和天然气开采业	Petroleum and Natural Gas Extraction	696781
黑色金属矿采选业	Ferrous Metals Mining and Dressing	797968
有色金属矿采选业	Nonferrous Metals Mining and Dressing	13229
非金属矿采选业	Nonmetal Minerals Mining and Dressing	
开采辅助活动	Mining Auxiliary Activities	
其他采矿业	Other Mining Industry	
制造业	Manufacturing	59372216
农副食品加工业	Farm Products Processing	528292
食品制造业	Food Manufacturing	281583
酒、饮料和精制茶制造业	Wine, Beverages and Refined Tea Manufacturing	544456
烟草制品业	Tobacoo Products Manfacturing	51468
纺织业	Textile Industry	185610
纺织服装、服饰业	Textile, Wearing Apparel and Accessories	161616
皮革、毛皮、羽毛及其制品和制鞋业	Leather, Fur, Feather and Related Products and Footwear	
木材加工和木、竹、藤、棕、草制品业	Timber Processing,Bamboo,Cane,Palm Fiber and Straw Products	58344

continued

(10 000 yuan)

负债合计 Total Liabilities	年末所有者权益 Creditors' Equity at Year-end	主营业务收入 Revenue of Major Business	主营业务成本 Costs of Major Business	主营业务税金及附加 Tax and Extra Charges of Major Business	营业费用 Costs of Business	管理费用 Costs of Administration
4628755	3288582	3351916	2572919	92827	87381	187520
3271108	1681396	1689919	1332926	39200	72902	103230
762515	836260	746024	472270	42487	11813	28546
595133	770927	915974	767724	11140	2667	55745
96810563	9714871	34716753	31347500	435362	1375789	2403296
155294564	46628048	73275000	59754628	1726169	2891609	4941104
884220	534542	357007	247416	17804	6265	43765
4766946	4520943	7394632	5691873	318214	466297	427471
212328153	62032719	105552523	87829568	1851330	3627774	6399193
135242538	46806976	78122187	65294185	1277434	3192273	4369140
81852561	19746686	34824968	28227257	892110	901798	2457524
123162617	35583982	44356085	33453301	1623092	2278459	3748175
120917175	34133717	43051402	32426223	1609671	2269392	3583849
1048871	801619	284623	212268	5969	1478	21035
1175022	611524	935835	748581	5702	7242	139139
21549	37122	84225	66229	1750	347	4152
75056113	23781835	55220128	48425163	491371	1718815	2608752
656933	482480	1611041	1450119	79	14145	26254
321064	300368	650740	527051	1763	45061	25928
643258	806313	1675816	1275879	111251	119170	93477
51468	367525	420748	154001	187160	5106	26723
213458	110903	257267	238536	225	3406	8095
180463	107613	318333	290021	325	3992	16352
58515	125163	103795	89044		702	357

10-8 续表5

单位：万元

指　标	Item	流动负债 Liquid Liabilities
家具制造业	Furniture Manufacturing	
造纸和纸制品业	Paper Making and Paper Products	39026
印刷和记录媒介复制业	Printing and Record Medium Reproduction	33390
文教、工美、体育和娱乐用品制造业	Culture, Education, Art and Crafts, Sport and Entertainment Products	23820
石油加工、炼焦和核燃料加工业	Petroleum Processing, Coking and Nuclear Fuel Processing	14960909
化学原料和化学制品制造业	Raw Chemical Materials and Chemical Products	6814272
医药制造业	Medical and Pharmaceutical Products	949013
化学纤维制造业	Chemical Fiber Manufacturing	
橡胶和塑料制品业	Rubber and Plastic Products	147561
非金属矿物制品业	Nonmetal Mineral Products	1865016
黑色金属冶炼和压延加工业	Smelting and Pressing of Ferrous Metals	13645611
有色金属冶炼和压延加工业	Smelting and Pressing of Non-ferrous Metals	4740518
金属制品业	Metal Prodcuts	498599
通用设备制造业	Ordinary Machinery Manufacturing	778077
专用设备制造业	Special Purpose Equipment Manufacturing	3272887
汽车制造业	Automobile Manufacturing	1387799
铁路、船舶、航空航天和其他运输设备制造业	Railroad, Marine, Aviation and Other Transport Equipments Manufacturing	1137605
电气机械和器材制造业	Electrical Machinery and Equipment Manufacturing	1116665
计算机、通信和其他电子设备制造业	Computers, Telecommunication and Other Electronic Equipments Manufacturing	6004876
仪器仪表制造业	Equipments and Instruments Manufacturing	110709
其他制造业	Other Manufacturing	19898
废弃资源综合利用业	Comprehensive Utilization of Waste Resources	
金属制品、机械和设备修理业	Metal Products, Machinery and Equipment Repair	14596
电力、热力、燃气及水生产和供应业	Production and Supply of Electricity, Heat, Gas and Water	10146959
电力、热力生产和供应业	Production and Supply of Electricity and Heat	8693555
燃气生产和供应业	Production and Supply of Gas	1193579
水的生产和供应业	Production and Supply of Water	259825

continued

(10 000 yuan)

负债合计 Total Liabilities	年末所有者权益 Creditors' Equity at Year-end	主营业务收入 Revenue of Major Business	主营业务成本 Costs of Major Business	主营业务税金及附加 Tax and Extra Charges of Major Business	营业费用 Costs of Business	管理费用 Costs of Administration
71995	12154	91173	84655	262	2207	3728
38513	47441	46297	31609	606	4494	7001
25169	18834	28745	20859	195	3540	2967
19714322	2284926	8592929	7560038	21292	531010	297423
8030353	1458095	3831234	3595120	17599	135516	263350
1393783	1534228	1307898	749797	12183	230873	144729
195676	150735	369902	333908	459	8398	11016
2501004	359912	1533925	1319042	7022	60760	85124
18133864	7497771	15486533	13689169	46120	284276	739474
6803182	2623431	5268559	4728736	27582	59229	152080
562590	367815	525715	450232	1938	11130	39017
998208	350292	919754	764048	2772	28459	67444
3905561	994263	1333307	1193926	6322	50717	161388
1567513	451163	1285207	1103362	5976	49144	84619
1383730	520700	878125	707686	6465	26650	96540
1416935	354194	873238	675380	4578	25924	102197
6011637	2262967	7594143	7217904	27829	6957	136938
130825	94911	126552	101133	693	7204	10569
31498	80837	44622	33663	116	745	3356
14596	16801	44530	40245	559		2606
18876368	7187844	13370942	11642978	55081	96798	469737
16495922	6153855	12206445	10659642	51779	29571	398325
2001000	629767	991182	824805	2333	58509	34828
379446	404222	173315	158531	969	8718	36584

10-8 续表6

单位：万元

指 标	Item	财务费用 Costs of Finance
总 计	**Total**	**5218848**
一、按隶属关系分	Grouped by Jurisdiction of Management	
中央企业	Central Enterprises	619837
省属企业	Province-owned Enterprises	2588296
市属企业	Cities-owned Enterprises	197203
县(市、区)属企业	County-owned Enterprises	531725
城市街道企业	Cities' Subdistrict-owned Enterprises	
镇属企业	Town-owned Enterprises	72413
乡属企业	Township Enterprises	40987
居委会办企业	Neighbourhood Committee -run Enterprises	
村办企业	Village Enterprises	11377
其 他	Enterprises of Other Types of Ownership	1157011
二、按登记注册类型分	Grouped by Registered Kind	
内资企业	Civil Funded Enterprises	5056231
国有企业	State-owned Enterprises	215937
集体企业	Collective-owned Enterprises	19776
股份合作企业	Share Holding Cooperative Enterprises	
联营企业	Joint Owned Enterprises	9125
有限责任公司	Limited Responsibility Company	3869203
国有独资公司	Company Exclusively with Investment from State	596848
其他有限责任公司	Other Limited Responsibility Company	3272355
股份有限公司	Share Holding Limited Company	287279
私营企业	Privately Owned Enterprises	626857
私营独资企业	Enterprise Exclusively with Investment from Private	3589
私营合伙企业	Private Partner Enterprises	
私营有限责任公司	Privately Owned Limited Responsibility Company	561477
私营股份有限公司	Privately Owned Share Holding Limited Company	61790
其他企业	Enterprises of Other Types of Ownership	28054
港、澳、台商投资企业	Enterprises Funded by Hong Kong, Macao and Taiwan	60990
合资经营企业(港或澳、台资)	Joint Venture	45260
合作经营企业(港或澳、台资)	Cooperative Enterprise	315
港澳台商独资企业	Ventures Exclusively with Hong Kong, Macao and Taiwan Investment	-4126
港澳台商投资股份有限公司	Share Holding Limited Company	19541
其他港澳台商投资企业	Others	

continued

(10 000 yuan)

#利息支出 Interest Expenditure	利润总额 Total Profits	亏损企业亏损额 Loss of Loss-making Enterprises	利税总额 Total Pre-tax Profits	应付薪酬总额 Total Wages Payable	应交所得税 Income Taxes Payable	应交增值税 Value Added Taxes Payable
5414551	**2061456**	**3203507**	**8762726**	**10650867**	**915136**	**4357791**
569470	727346	282273	2031790	994285	108925	857153
2960452	559399	1176858	3625907	5351704	434451	1919789
195027	-9425	261474	262644	741480	48517	176511
524358	25155	495867	817587	886190	75370	488376
62455	6505	58256	28160	60370	535	7914
35944	-19013	32168	5988	16300	3264	15138
11377	7555	288	30679	25164	1945	15183
1055468	763934	896322	1959972	2575375	242129	877727
5202678	1474790	3012949	7729221	9246317	758155	4033586
199529	37160	169345	400134	386697	3090	308598
19129	-28991	30982	14482	85175	477	27283
2779	-6073	6073	1042	3136		3419
4131611	726657	2207632	5277949	6907586	563385	2795019
646290	323009	397120	1292859	1443910	84854	630025
3485321	403648	1810511	3985089	5463676	478531	2164994
308177	372146	188327	1080949	952732	95784	460782
513420	401864	382617	976906	907256	95420	435016
895	14458		18556	2048	2710	3550
488091	314256	373408	854382	850888	87800	405514
24434	73151	9209	103969	54321	4910	25952
28034	-27974	27974	-22241	3736		3469
119715	267975	69615	364896	885262	70008	67477
82154	152134	52675	201308	572394	38070	33903
315	46		1115	7127		1069
17429	130387		187061	280664	31937	43954
19816	-14592	16940	-24588	25078	1	-11449

10-8 续表7

单位：万元

指　　标	Item	财务费用 Costs of Finance
外商投资企业	Foreign Funded Enterprises	101627
中外合资经营企业	Joint Venture	79835
中外合作经营企业	Cooperative Enterprises	10878
外资企业	Enterprises Funded By Foreign Investments	10914
外商投资股份有限公司	Share Holding Limited Company	
其他外商投资企业	Other Foreign Funded Enterprises	
三、在总计中:亏损企业	Of the Total: Loss-making Enterprises	2657635
在总计中:国有控股企业	Of the Total: State-Controlled Share Holding Enterprises	3803080
在总计中:农村工业	Of the Total: Rural Industry	52364
在总计中:轻工业	Of the Total: Light Industry	92315
重工业	Heavy Industry	5126532
在总计中:大型企业	Of the Total: Large-size Enterprises	3203539
中型企业	Medium-size Enterprises	2015309
四、按工业行业大类分	Grouped by Sector	
采矿业	Mining	3137162
煤炭开采和洗选业	Coal Mining and Dressing	3083975
石油和天然气开采业	Petroleum and Natural Gas Extraction	25681
黑色金属矿采选业	Ferrous Metals Mining and Dressing	27274
有色金属矿采选业	Nonferrous Metals Mining and Dressing	232
非金属矿采选业	Nonmetal Minerals Mining and Dressing	
开采辅助活动	Mining Auxiliary Activities	
其他采矿业	Other Mining Industry	
制造业	Manufacturing	1585761
农副食品加工业	Farm Products Processing	25663
食品制造业	Food Manufacturing	6416
酒、饮料和精制茶制造业	Wine, Beverages and Refined Tea Manufacturing	5761
烟草制品业	Tobacoo Products Manfacturing	-4542
纺织业	Textile Industry	5563
纺织服装、服饰业	Textile, Wearing Apparel and Accessories	1912
皮革、毛皮、羽毛及其制品和制鞋业	Leather, Fur, Feather and Related Products and Footwear	
木材加工和木、竹、藤、棕、草制品业	Timber Processing,Bamboo,Cane,Palm Fiber and Straw Products	2111

continued

(10 000 yuan)

#利息支出 Interest Expenditure	利润总额 Total Profits	亏损企业亏损额 Loss of Loss-making Enterprises	利税总额 Total Pre-tax Profits	应付薪酬总额 Total Wages Payable	应交所得税 Income Taxes Payable	应交增值税 Value Added Taxes Payable
92159	318691	120943	668610	519288	86973	256728
71090	49363	86721	188420	188113	20520	99493
11841	187767		310179	84870	54749	79925
9228	81561	34223	170011	246304	11704	77310
2570649	-3203507	3203507	-1692435	3927859	79038	930923
4108371	1024950	2102147	6133042	7611360	602334	3213772
47321	-11458	32456	36667	41464	5209	30320
106913	444640	54890	1037508	543247	86250	272807
5307639	1616815	3148617	7725219	10107620	828886	4084983
3603270	2021210	1306338	6265923	7787542	676892	2805094
1811281	40246	1897169	2496804	2863324	238244	1552697
3408845	1033205	1517338	5480147	6102303	538317	2661076
3363137	922087	1502117	5298428	6030234	525926	2604764
18349	90818		115993	27830	9153	18371
26878	13445	15221	55693	37187	1871	36513
481	6855		10033	7052	1367	1428
1538132	751408	1402892	2474243	3927265	304620	1226098
23364	97989	6680	110105	75455	632	12037
6372	49015	133	67324	34994	8704	16546
9274	73446	7941	257728	67913	36392	73031
	52233		285253	21619	13058	45860
4979	1967		4631	19110	540	2439
1761	11604	71	18765	35690	2307	6220
2019	10606		10606	2105		

10-8 续表8

单位：万元

指　标	Item	财务费用 Costs of Finance
家具制造业	Furniture Manufacturing	
造纸和纸制品业	Paper Making and Paper Products	1518
印刷和记录媒介复制业	Printing and Record Medium Reproduction	816
文教、工美、体育和娱乐用品制造业	Culture, Education, Art and Crafts, Sport and Entertainment Products	259
石油加工、炼焦和核燃料加工业	Petroleum Processing, Coking and Nuclear Fuel Processing	416153
化学原料和化学制品制造业	Raw Chemical Materials and Chemical Products	198935
医药制造业	Medical and Pharmaceutical Products	29703
化学纤维制造业	Chemical Fiber Manufacturing	
橡胶和塑料制品业	Rubber and Plastic Products	8278
非金属矿物制品业	Nonmetal Mineral Products	54075
黑色金属冶炼和压延加工业	Smelting and Pressing of Ferrous Metals	496702
有色金属冶炼和压延加工业	Smelting and Pressing of Non-ferrous Metals	193384
金属制品业	Metal Prodcuts	5481
通用设备制造业	Ordinary Machinery Manufacturing	11184
专用设备制造业	Special Purpose Equipment Manufacturing	90861
汽车制造业	Automobile Manufacturing	4902
铁路、船舶、航空航天和其他运输设备制造业	Railroad, Marine, Aviation and Other Transport Equipments Manufacturing	13446
电气机械和器材制造业	Electrical Machinery and Equipment Manufacturing	34642
计算机、通信和其他电子设备制造业	Computers, Telecommunication and Other Electronic Equipments Manufacturing	-17486
仪器仪表制造业	Equipments and Instruments Manufacturing	829
其他制造业	Other Manufacturing	-800
废弃资源综合利用业	Comprehensive Utilization of Waste Resources	
金属制品、机械和设备修理业	Metal Products, Machinery and Equipment Repair	-5
电力、热力、燃气及水生产和供应业	Production and Supply of Electricity, Heat, Gas and Water	495926
电力、热力生产和供应业	Production and Supply of Electricity and Heat	456656
燃气生产和供应业	Production and Supply of Gas	33765
水的生产和供应业	Production and Supply of Water	5505

continued

(10 000 yuan)

#利息支出 Interest Expenditure	利润总额 Total Profits	亏损企业亏损额 Loss of Loss-making Enterprises	利税总额 Total Pre-tax Profits	应付薪酬总额 Total Wages Payable	应交所得税 Income Taxes Payable	应交增值税 Value Added Taxes Payable
1530	587		3236	2503	76	2387
60	2797	381	6119	12040	165	2571
324	1106		3050	3021	273	1749
343014	-128482	372477	73492	342994	27594	179389
214604	-348713	385665	-314541	300900	5864	16288
40494	148408	4560	240606	115759	19953	79301
8902	12112	2281	15780	18373	1227	3154
46194	13109	65852	75664	152020	12076	55087
423360	190880	209344	582963	831189	32188	345252
183183	186462	58435	375736	283206	45523	161579
10343	20617	2465	35551	46816	2306	12875
11390	67451	3660	88225	65741	2183	17991
98394	-167316	202884	-122705	179140	4443	38087
17031	77433	11967	103529	76644	10294	19789
14573	45397	23826	83102	116825	11648	31241
32898	38642	20951	68009	62691	7419	24545
42748	276518	22376	377094	1035478	56959	72667
846	8850	943	10988	7114	1361	1445
473	7600		8267	4719	1435	551
2	1090		5666	13206		4017
467575	276845	283276	808340	621299	72198	470618
427013	238167	248780	749903	495424	53164	454968
35399	68952	4131	81823	70495	19011	9826
5163	-30274	30365	-23386	55380	23	5824

10-9 工业企业主要经济效益指标(2016年)

单位：%

指 标	Item	亏损面 Range of Deficits
总 计	**Total**	**34.78**
一、按隶属关系分	Grouped by Jurisdiction of Management	
中央企业	Central Enterprises	25.00
省属企业	Province-owned Enterprises	43.11
市属企业	Cities-owned Enterprises	47.80
县(市、区)属企业	County-owned Enterprises	38.22
城市街道企业	Cities' Subdistrict-owned Enterprises	66.67
镇属企业	Town-owned Enterprises	38.89
乡属企业	Township Enterprises	90.00
居委会办企业	Neighbourhood Committee -run Enterprises	50.00
村办企业	Village Enterprises	16.67
其 他	Enterprises of Other Types of Ownership	32.71
二、按登记注册类型分	Grouped by Registered Kind	
内资企业	Civil Funded Enterprises	34.85
国有企业	State-owned Enterprises	55.36
集体企业	Collective-owned Enterprises	43.59
股份合作企业	Share Holding Cooperative Enterprises	
联营企业	Joint Owned Enterprises	100.00
有限责任公司	Limited Responsibility Company	39.25
国有独资公司	Company Exclusively with Investment from State	43.53
其他有限责任公司	Other Limited Responsibility Company	38.92
股份有限公司	Share Holding Limited Company	31.71
私营企业	Privately Owned Enterprises	31.66
私营独资企业	Enterprise Exclusively with Investment from Private	25.00
私营合伙企业	Private Partner Enterprises	18.18
私营有限责任公司	Privately Owned Limited Responsibility Company	32.47
私营股份有限公司	Privately Owned Share Holding Limited Company	25.00
其他企业	Enterprises of Other Types of Ownership	50.00
港、澳、台商投资企业	Enterprises Funded by Hong Kong, Macao and Taiwan	30.77
合资经营企业(港或澳、台资)	Joint Venture	38.71
合作经营企业(港或澳、台资)	Cooperative Enterprise	
港澳台商独资企业	Ventures Exclusively with Hong Kong,Macao and Taiwan Investment	13.33
港澳台商投资股份有限公司	Share Holding Limited Company	50.00
其他港澳台商独资企业	Others	

MAIN ECONOMIC BENEFIT INDICATORS OF INDUSTRIAL ENTERPRISES(2016)

(%)

总资产贡献率 Ratio of Profits, Taxes and Interests to Average Assets	资产负债率 Ratio of Debts to Assets	成本费用利润率 Ratio of Profits to Total Costs	利润率 Ratio of Profits to Revenue of Major Business	产品销售率 Ratio of Sales to Gross Output Value
4.79	**76.08**	**2.07**	**2.07**	**95.70**
6.82	70.36	4.71	4.41	98.17
4.40	78.91	1.05	1.09	93.05
2.76	73.09	–0.46	–0.49	94.88
4.87	78.27	0.60	0.59	96.14
3.08	60.64	0.41	0.40	100.00
5.40	80.52	0.57	0.59	96.39
3.59	62.95	–14.17	–15.47	104.46
7.00	88.13	0.27	0.27	172.17
7.13	70.80	4.08	3.87	98.09
4.80	74.42	2.71	2.67	96.35
4.64	76.55	1.71	1.72	95.17
4.19	72.27	0.46	0.44	99.78
5.17	101.26	–2.41	–3.17	98.50
4.54	41.47	4.30	4.31	100.00
2.22	172.95	–13.33	–14.14	100.00
4.53	79.42	1.15	1.17	94.26
4.83	68.61	2.05	2.10	95.99
4.46	81.88	0.90	0.92	93.74
5.58	58.84	5.01	4.82	96.19
4.78	74.30	2.73	2.69	95.17
15.07	64.96	4.08	3.93	97.51
10.49	61.86	3.07	2.96	87.97
4.59	75.18	2.57	2.54	95.36
5.00	64.82	4.02	3.95	91.57
2.22	105.47	–51.82	–98.29	95.32
5.33	76.86	4.31	4.18	102.49
4.86	85.58	3.11	3.05	105.01
0.47	69.70	0.02	0.02	100.00
9.09	43.50	12.54	11.19	94.75
–0.72	93.32	–5.95	–6.71	92.03
6.37	93.81	5.05	4.72	101.23

10-9 续表1

单位：%

指　标	Item	亏损面 Range of Deficits
外商投资企业	Foreign Funded Enterprises	34.57
中外合资经营企业	Joint Venture	33.93
中外合作经营企业	Cooperative Enterprises	
外资企业	Enterprises Funded By Foreign Investments	45.00
外商投资股份有限公司	Share Holding Limited Company	
其他外商投资企业	Other Foreign Funded Enterprises	
三、在总计中: 亏损企业	Of the Total: Loss-making Enterprises	100.00
在总计中: 国有控股企业	Of the Total: State-Controlled Share Holding Enterprises	41.52
在总计中: 农村工业	Of the Total: Rural Industry	38.24
在总计中: 轻工业	Of the Total: Light Industry	21.34
重工业	Heavy Industry	37.49
在总计中: 大型企业	Of the Total: Large-size Enterprises	29.15
中型企业	Medium-size Enterprises	43.42
小型企业	Small-size Enterprises	32.60
微型企业	Micro-size Enterprises	28.99
四、按工业行业大类分	Grouped by Sector	
采矿业	Mining	41.69
煤炭开采和洗选业	Coal Mining and Dressing	42.36
石油和天然气开采业	Petroleum and Natural Gas Extraction	37.50
黑色金属矿采选业	Ferrous Metals Mining and Dressing	39.61
有色金属矿采选业	Nonferrous Metals Mining and Dressing	27.78
非金属矿采选业	Nonmetal Minerals Mining and Dressing	33.33
开采辅助活动	Mining Auxiliary Activities	
其他采矿业	Other Mining Industry	
制造业	Manufacturing	30.47
农副食品加工业	Farm Products Processing	19.14
食品制造业	Food Manufacturing	5.06
酒、饮料和精制茶制造业	Wine, Beverages and Refined Tea Manufacturing	23.33
烟草制品业	Tobacoo Products Manfacturing	
纺织业	Textile Industry	35.71
纺织服装、服饰业	Textile,Wearing Apparel and Accessories	14.29
皮革、毛皮、羽毛及其制品和制鞋业	Leather, Fur, Feather and Related Products and Footwear	
木材加工和木、竹、藤、棕、草制品业	Timber Processing,Bamboo,Cane,Palm Fiber and Straw Products	16.67

continued

(%)

总资产贡献率 Ratio of Profits, Taxes and Interests to Average Assets	资产负债率 Ratio of Debts to Assets	成本费用利润率 Ratio of Profits to Total Costs	利润率 Ratio of Profits to Revenue of Major Business	产品销售率 Ratio of Sales to Gross Output Value
9.16	58.54	9.64	8.81	96.83
5.40	65.24	3.44	3.36	96.14
19.99	47.69	35.81	25.17	98.55
12.38	46.10	8.24	7.78	96.81
6.90	55.35	4.58	4.37	107.08
3.41	48.29	32.75	28.70	100.00
0.38	90.35	-8.39	-9.48	91.94
4.68	77.35	1.46	1.48	95.10
5.38	66.92	-0.16	-0.16	99.35
10.00	52.07	5.80	5.53	93.42
4.56	77.14	1.77	1.78	95.91
5.16	74.29	2.54	2.59	94.73
4.16	80.55	0.12	0.12	97.30
4.83	72.85	2.85	2.81	95.73
3.75	81.93	9.53	8.90	100.04
5.34	77.86	2.36	2.34	93.62
5.35	78.33	2.23	2.22	93.72
4.29	61.25	16.64	17.19	98.70
5.11	68.23	2.18	2.12	90.65
10.65	77.45	4.93	4.51	97.56
5.24	89.34	-1.62	-1.58	98.95
3.87	74.07	1.31	1.34	96.21
8.46	50.26	5.34	5.08	95.85
10.55	46.78	8.01	7.77	95.33
14.11	48.49	5.20	4.66	90.22
67.00	12.28	28.45	12.41	100.42
1.87	65.23	-0.41	-0.40	97.70
6.49	62.97	2.07	3.60	95.73
3.37	5.63	1.66	1.62	82.82
7.73	33.74	10.98	10.80	98.68

10-9 续表2

单位：%

指　标	Item	亏损面 Range of Deficits
家具制造业	Furniture Manufacturing	50.00
造纸和纸制品业	Paper Making and Paper Products	17.65
印刷和记录媒介复制业	Printing and Record Medium Reproduction	36.00
文教、工美、体育和娱乐用品制造业	Culture, Education, Art and Crafts, Sport and Entertainment Products	25.00
石油加工、炼焦和核燃料加工业	Petroleum Processing, Coking and Nuclear Fuel Processing	54.69
化学原料和化学制品制造业	Raw Chemical Materials and Chemical Products	33.84
医药制造业	Medical and Pharmaceutical Products	20.73
化学纤维制造业	Chemical Fiber Manufacturing	
橡胶和塑料制品业	Rubber and Plastic Products	30.91
非金属矿物制品业	Nonmetal Mineral Products	34.82
黑色金属冶炼和压延加工业	Smelting and Pressing of Ferrous Metals	38.10
有色金属冶炼和压延加工业	Smelting and Pressing of Non-ferrous Metals	34.38
金属制品业	Metal Prodcuts	23.20
通用设备制造业	Ordinary Machinery Manufacturing	27.27
专用设备制造业	Special Purpose Equipment Manufacturing	28.47
汽车制造业	Automobile Manufacturing	35.90
铁路、船舶、航空航天和其他运输设备制造业	Railroad, Marine, Aviation and Other Transport Equipments Manufacturing	32.14
电气机械和器材制造业	Electrical Machinery and Equipment Manufacturing	29.85
计算机、通信和其他电子设备制造业	Computers, Telecommunication and Other Electronic Equipments Manufacturing	25.93
仪器仪表制造业	Equipments and Instruments Manufacturing	26.67
其他制造业	Other Manufacturing	
废弃资源综合利用业	Comprehensive Utilization of Waste Resources	
金属制品、机械和设备修理业	Metal products, Machinery and Equipment Repair	18.18
电力、热力、燃气及水生产和供应业	Production and Supply of Electricity, Heat, Gas and Water	36.33
电力、热力生产和供应业	Production and Supply of Electricity and Heat	35.96
燃气生产和供应业	Production and Supply of Gas	25.64
水的生产和供应业	Production and Supply of Water	71.43

continued

(%)

总资产贡献率 Ratio of Profits, Taxes and Interests to Average Assets	资产负债率 Ratio of Debts to Assets	成本费用利润率 Ratio of Profits to Total Costs	利润率 Ratio of Profits to Revenue of Major Business	产品销售率 Ratio of Sales to Gross Output Value
1.90	52.86	0.75	0.74	81.09
5.04	69.59	1.26	1.26	96.77
4.99	50.61	3.61	3.54	98.07
4.59	100.58	–5.38	–5.82	78.24
1.77	89.46	–1.54	–1.63	96.51
–0.79	82.88	–6.17	–6.74	97.00
8.64	50.61	10.04	9.32	86.77
4.37	55.97	1.57	1.58	87.64
3.87	76.35	0.61	0.62	93.47
3.60	71.51	0.90	0.92	96.67
5.54	71.70	2.88	2.88	94.41
3.63	60.55	1.89	1.88	93.49
6.12	66.89	5.54	5.93	90.57
0.31	76.57	–6.66	–7.43	92.16
5.28	72.89	5.89	5.83	96.76
5.02	71.75	5.16	5.09	101.17
4.40	74.72	1.70	2.60	98.69
5.51	70.16	3.82	3.71	103.42
3.56	52.58	3.35	3.27	98.80
7.22	31.66	16.84	14.41	102.93
9.37	45.45	20.12	21.58	84.72
9.34	82.28	2.87	2.80	98.45
5.10	74.21	4.35	4.13	99.66
5.36	74.72	4.34	4.08	99.67
4.07	75.01	7.34	7.26	100.07
–1.68	49.14	–12.73	–15.41	96.14

10-10 国有控股工业企业主要经济效益指标(2016年)

单位：%

指　　标	Item	亏损面 Range of Deficits
总　计	**Total**	**41.52**
在总计中:	Of the Total:	
亏损企业	Loss-making Enterprises	100.00
在总计中:	Of the Total:	
中央企业	Central Enterprises	23.24
地方企业	Local Enterprises	
#省属企业	Province-owned Enterprises	43.08
地、市属企业	Prefectures, Cities-owned Enterprises	53.92
县(旗)属企业	County-owned Enterprises	45.03
在总计中:	Of the Total:	
轻工业	Light Industry	46.15
重工业	Heavy Industry	41.20
在总计中:	Of the Total:	
大型企业	Large-size Enterprises	33.07
中型企业	Medium-size Enterprises	49.61
小型企业	Small-size Enterprises	34.72
微型企业	Micro-size Enterprises	34.48
按工业行业大类分	Grouped by Sector	
采矿业	Mining	44.92
煤炭开采和洗选业	Coal Mining and Dressing	45.10
石油和天然气开采业	Petroleum and Natural Gas Extraction	33.33
黑色金属矿采选业	Ferrous Metals Mining and Dressing	50.00
有色金属矿采选业	Nonferrous Metals Mining and Dressing	50.00
非金属矿采选业	Nonmetal Minerals Mining and Dressing	
其他采矿业	Other Mining Industry	
制造业	Manufacturing	39.93
农副食品加工业	Farm Products Processing	
食品制造业	Food Manufacturing	
酒、饮料和精制茶制造业	Wine, Beverages and Refined Tea Manufacturing	22.22
烟草制品业	Tobacoo Products Manfacturing	
纺织业	Textile Industry	
纺织服装、服饰业	Textile, Wearing Apparel and Accessories	20.00

MAIN ECONOMIC BENEFIT INDICATORS OF STATE-HOLDING INDUSTRIAL ENTERPRISES(2016)

(%)

总资产贡献率 Ratio of Profits, Taxes and Interests to Average Assets	资产负债率 Ratio of Debts to Assets	成本费用利润率 Ratio of Profits to Total Costs	利润率 Ratio of Profits to Revenue of Major Business	产品销售率 Ratio of Sales to Gross Output Value
4.68	**77.35**	**1.46**	**1.48**	**95.10**
0.85	90.99	-7.45	-8.35	90.91
6.92	70.26	4.81	4.50	98.16
4.39	79.07	1.05	1.10	93.02
1.54	74.71	-4.26	-4.60	96.45
4.65	80.45	-1.66	-1.63	95.82
14.07	54.58	4.31	3.81	95.82
4.49	77.78	1.36	1.39	95.08
4.89	75.60	1.61	1.67	93.04
4.52	80.04	0.70	0.67	98.58
3.73	80.91	2.32	2.31	97.28
2.54	88.82	11.42	11.59	100.79
5.00	78.41	2.29	2.31	90.80
5.02	78.83	2.15	2.17	90.56
4.38	61.27	18.30	19.35	98.04
3.81	64.82	2.62	2.58	101.54
15.87	82.41	1.68	1.63	100.06
3.31	76.86	-1.44	-1.52	97.35
2.40	60.99	4.24	4.14	93.23
11.90	32.42	3.26	3.23	101.97
18.93	46.16	4.80	4.26	94.09
67.00	12.28	28.45	12.41	100.42
4.01	36.71	1.14	1.15	93.77
2.78	68.32	1.60	1.64	96.11

10-10 续表

单位：%

指　　标	Item	亏损面 Range of Deficits
皮革、毛皮、羽毛及其制品和制鞋业	Leather, Fur, Feather and its products and Footwear	
木材加工和木、竹、藤、棕、草制品业	Timber Processing, Bamboo, Cane, Palm Fiber and Straw Products	
家具制造业	Furniture Manufacturing	
造纸和纸制品业	Paper Making and Paper Products	
印刷和记录媒介复制业	Printing and Record Medium Reproduction	80.00
文教、工美、体育和娱乐用品制造业	Culture, Education, Art and Crafts, Sport and Entertainment Products	100.00
石油加工、炼焦和核燃料加工业	Petroleum Processing, Coking and Nuclear Fuel Processing	65.00
化学原料和化学制品制造业	Raw Chemical Materials and Chemical Products	56.52
医药制造业	Medical and Pharmaceutical Products	62.50
化学纤维制造业	Chemical Fiber	
橡胶和塑料制品业	Rubber and Plastic Products	25.00
非金属矿物制品业	Nonmetal Mineral Products	48.48
黑色金属冶炼和压延加工业	Smelting and Pressing of Ferrous Metals	45.45
有色金属冶炼和压延加工业	Smelting and Pressing of Non-ferrous Metals	22.22
金属制品业	Metal Prodcuts	33.33
通用设备制造业	Ordinary Machinery Manufacturing	37.50
专用设备制造业	Special Purpose Equipment Manufacturing	27.78
汽车制造业	Automobile Manufacturing	41.67
铁路、船舶、航空航天和其他运输设备制造业	Railroad, Marine, Aviation and Other Transport Equipments Manufacturing	37.50
电气机械和器材制造业	Electrical Machinery and Equipment Manufacturing	18.18
计算机、通信和其他电子设备制造业	Computers, Telecommunication and Other Electronic Equipments Manufacturing	50.00
仪器仪表制造业	Equipments and Instruments Manufacturing	40.00
其他制造业	Other Manufacturing	
废弃资源综合利用业	Comprehensive Utilization of Waste Resources	
金属制品、机械和设备修理业	Metal Products, Machinery and Equipment Repair	
电力、热力、燃气及水生产和供应业	Production and Supply of Electricity, Heat, Gas and Water	37.06
电力、热力生产和供应业	Production and Supply of Electricity and Heat	33.58
燃气生产和供应业	Production and Supply of Gas	33.33
水的生产和供应业	Production and Supply of Water	83.33

continued

(%)

总资产贡献率 Ratio of Profits, Taxes and Interests to Average Assets	资产负债率 Ratio of Debts to Assets	成本费用利润率 Ratio of Profits to Total Costs	利润率 Ratio of Profits to Revenue of Major Business	产品销售率 Ratio of Sales to Gross Output Value
2.98	64.83	-1.89	-1.97	97.14
2.64	171.07	-52.60	-110.86	80.64
0.49	96.70	-7.59	-8.36	101.23
-2.24	87.77	-9.66	-11.11	100.00
5.33	76.07	4.43	4.61	90.64
5.26	65.28	1.26	1.29	78.57
4.36	91.27	1.93	1.92	96.71
4.16	70.77	0.64	0.65	100.20
5.39	72.81	1.75	1.76	91.64
2.30	64.45	1.89	1.93	103.17
1.82	73.68	-0.33	-0.33	99.09
-0.86	78.80	-11.79	-13.92	90.11
0.69	75.71	-0.57	-0.59	99.87
2.47	73.00	0.88	0.93	102.85
5.62	77.79	2.51	4.60	99.75
0.41	82.75	0.49	0.49	100.74
4.94	67.52	0.64	0.62	99.41
5.74	26.25	34.66	25.68	98.16
9.86	82.64	3.35	3.26	98.30
5.25	73.96	4.03	3.81	99.80
5.59	74.26	4.09	3.84	99.78
3.68	77.37	6.72	6.71	100.27
-2.24	48.10	-13.73	-16.69	98.42

10-11 外商投资和港澳台投资工业企业主要经济效益指标(2016年)

单位：%

指　标	Item	亏损面 Range of Deficits
总　计	**Total**	**33.08**
港、澳、台商投资企业	Enterprises Funded by HongKong, Macao and Taiwan	30.77
合资经营企业(港或澳、台资)	Joint Venture	38.71
合作经营企业(港或澳、台资)	Cooperative Enterprise	
港澳台商独资经营企业	Ventures Exclusively with HongKong, Macao and Taiwan Investment	13.33
港澳台商投资股份有限公司	Share Holding Limited Company	50.00
外商投资企业	Foreign Funded Enterprises	34.57
中外合资经营企业	Joint Venture	33.93
中外合作经营企业	Cooperative Enterprises	
外资企业	Enterprises Funded By Foreign Investments	45.00
外商投资股份有限公司	Enterprises Invested By Foreign Investments	
其他外商投资企业	Others	
在总计中:亏损企业	Of the Total:Loss-making Enterprises	100.00
在总计中:国有控股企业	Of the Total:State Holding Enterprises	19.05
在总计中:轻工业	Of the Total:Light Industry	17.86
重工业	Heavy Industry	37.14
在总计中:大型企业	Of the Total:Large-size Enterprises	31.25
中型企业	Medium-size Enterprises	47.37
小型企业	Small-size Enterprises	27.03
微型企业	Micro-size Enterprises	20.00
按工业行业大类分	Grouped by Sector	
采矿业	Mining	35.29
煤炭开采和洗选业	Coal Mining and Dressing	30.77
石油和天然气开采业	Petroleum and Natural Gas Extraction	50.00
黑色金属矿采选业	Ferrous Metals Mining and Dressing	
有色金属矿采选业	Nonferrous Metals Mining and Dressing	
非金属矿采选业	Nonmetal Minerals Mining and Dressing	
开采辅助活动	Mining Auxiliary Activities	
其他采矿业	Other Mining Industry	
制造业	Manufacturing	36.56
农副食品加工业	Farm Products Processing	
食品制造业	Food Manufacturing	20.00
酒、饮料和精制茶制造业	Wine, Beverages and Refined Tea Manufacturing	23.08
烟草制品业	Tobacoo Products Manfacturing	

MAIN ECONOMIC BENEFIT INDICATORS OF INDUSTRIAL ENTERPRISES WITH HONG KONG, MACAO, TAIWAN AND FOREIGN FUNDS(2016)

(%)

总资产贡献率 Ratio of Profits, Taxes and Interests to Average Assets	资产负债率 Ratio of Debts to Assets	成本费用利润率 Ratio of Profits to Total Costs	利润率 Ratio of Profits to Revenue of Major Business	产品销售率 Ratio of Sales to Gross Output Value
6.93	**69.20**	**5.86**	**5.58**	**100.76**
5.33	76.86	4.31	4.18	102.49
4.86	85.58	3.11	3.05	105.01
0.47	69.70	0.02	0.02	100.00
9.09	43.50	12.54	11.19	94.75
−0.72	93.32	−5.95	−6.71	92.03
9.16	58.54	9.64	8.81	96.83
5.40	65.24	3.44	3.36	96.14
19.99	47.69	35.81	25.17	98.55
12.38	46.10	8.24	7.78	96.81
6.90	55.35	4.58	4.37	107.08
3.41	48.29	32.75	28.70	100.00
−1.89	92.30	−12.77	−15.09	95.88
10.70	66.94	13.80	12.14	98.21
13.88	49.51	11.28	10.11	83.64
6.76	69.68	5.68	5.42	101.48
6.83	69.72	4.68	4.50	102.50
6.47	73.22	7.05	6.72	98.35
9.23	55.99	12.87	11.41	93.21
−1.37	76.68	31.32	24.09	99.97
10.06	56.24	18.82	15.86	99.37
10.85	55.68	18.82	15.57	99.32
4.43	60.24	18.86	18.47	99.78
5.67	74.02	3.71	3.62	100.98
5.77	49.08	6.28	6.00	95.53
38.01	23.85	25.47	20.87	96.85
6.11	68.05	1.29	1.27	72.93

10-11 续表

单位：%

指　　标	Item	亏损面 Range of Deficits
纺织业	Textile Industry	100.00
纺织服装、服饰业	Textile, Wearing Apparel and Accessories	
皮革、毛皮、羽毛及其制品和制鞋业	Leather, Fur, Feather and Related Products and Footwear	
木材加工和木、竹、藤、棕、草制品业	Timber Processing,Bamboo,Cane,Palm Fiber and Straw Products	
家具制造业	Furniture Manufacturing	
造纸和纸制品业	Paper Making and Paper Products	
印刷和记录媒介复制业	Printing and Record Medium Reproduction	
文教、工美、体育和娱乐用品制造业	Culture, Education, Art and Crafts, Sport and Entertainment Products	
石油加工、炼焦和核燃料加工业	Petroleum Processing, Coking and Nuclear Fuel Processing	81.82
化学原料和化学制品制造业	Raw Chemical Materials and Chemical Products	37.50
医药制造业	Medical and Pharmaceutical Products	
化学纤维制造业	Chemical Fiber Manufacturing	
橡胶和塑料制品业	Rubber and Plastic Products	66.67
非金属矿物制品业	Nonmetal Mineral Products	87.50
黑色金属冶炼和压延加工业	Smelting and Pressing of Ferrous Metals	40.00
有色金属冶炼和压延加工业	Smelting and Pressing of Non-ferrous Metals	20.00
金属制品业	Metal Prodcuts	
通用设备制造业	Ordinary Machinery Manufacturing	33.33
专用设备制造业	Special Purpose Equipment Manufacturing	14.29
汽车制造业	Automobile Manufacturing	
铁路、船舶、航空航天和其他运输设备制造业	Railroad, Marine, Aviation and Other Transport Equipment Manufacturing	
电气机械和器材制造业	Electrical Machinery and Equipment Manufacturing	50.00
计算机、通信和其他电子设备制造业	Computers, Telecommunication and Other Electronic Equipments Manufacturing	40.00
仪器仪表制造业	Equipments and Instruments Manufacturing	
其他制造业	Other Manufacturing	
废弃资源综合利用业	Comprehensive Utilization of Waste Resources	
金属制品、机械和设备修理业	Metal products, Machinery and Equipment Repair	
电力、热力、燃气及水生产和供应业	Production and Supply of Electricity, Heat, Gas and Water	17.39
电力、热力生产和供应业	Production and Supply of Electricity and Heat	22.22
燃气生产和供应业	Production and Supply of Gas	
水的生产和供应业	Production and Supply of Water	

continued

(%)

总资产贡献率 Ratio of Profits, Taxes and Interests to Average Assets	资产负债率 Ratio of Debts to Assets	成本费用利润率 Ratio of Profits to Total Costs	利润率 Ratio of Profits to Revenue of Major Business	产品销售率 Ratio of Sales to Gross Output Value
-17.00	88.91	-158.74	-224.85	89.42
2.79	41.28	0.03	0.03	97.29
0.60	95.10	-3.49	-3.80	96.75
-0.88	46.62	-5.75	-6.27	93.43
26.49	35.49	47.17	32.07	66.04
-0.67	17.61	-3.92	-4.15	84.58
2.48	85.03	-4.42	-4.63	100.08
10.87	41.23	6.96	6.46	93.02
7.43	60.65	8.98	8.23	97.37
16.94	34.74	15.64	13.95	85.03
3.53	74.39	1.30	1.29	109.31
3.97	92.11	1.66	1.78	92.74
5.67	75.66	2.15	2.11	64.47
21.51	54.07	19.03	15.55	100.56
13.16	119.69	3.67	3.13	108.03
6.15	73.17	3.86	3.74	103.89
9.82	41.46	11.45	10.09	100.00
14.86	75.90	10.09	9.19	115.32
9.24	34.18	23.27	18.50	100.00
6.43	24.63	7.38	7.37	100.00
8.32	64.95	15.91	13.71	100.00
8.43	65.96	16.42	14.06	100.00
6.31	41.02	10.56	9.56	100.00
4.74	63.45	8.62	9.88	100.00

10-12 大中型工业企业主要经济效益指标(2016年)

单位：%

指 标	Item	亏损面 Range of Deficits
总 计	**Total**	**40.43**
一、按隶属关系分	Grouped by Jurisdiction of Management	
中央企业	Central Enterprises	30.49
省属企业	Province-owned Enterprises	44.10
市属企业	Cities-owned Enterprises	51.16
县(市、区)属企业	County-owned Enterprises	43.75
城市街道企业	Cities' Subdistrict-owned Enterprises	
镇属企业	Town-owned Enterprises	50.00
乡属企业	Township Enterprises	75.00
居委会办企业	Neighbourhood Committee -run Enterprises	
村办企业	Village Enterprises	14.29
其 他	Enterprises of Other Types of Ownership	36.84
二、按登记注册类型分	Grouped by Registered Kind	
内资企业	Civil Funded Enterprises	40.32
国有企业	State-owned Enterprises	63.41
集体企业	Collective-owned Enterprises	46.15
股份合作企业	Share Holding Cooperative Enterprises	
联营企业	Joint Owned Enterprises	100.00
有限责任公司	Limited Responsibility Company	42.79
国有独资公司	Company Exclusively with Investment from State	48.15
其他有限责任公司	Other Limited Responsibility Company	42.26
股份有限公司	Share Holding Limited Company	25.81
私营企业	Privately Owned Enterprises	34.36
私营独资企业	Enterprise Exclusively with Investment from Private	
私营合伙企业	Private Partner Enterprises	
私营有限责任公司	Privately Owned Limited Responsibility Company	35.04
私营股份有限公司	Privately Owned Share Holding Limited Company	25.00
其他企业	Enterprises of Other Types of Ownership	100.00
港、澳、台商投资企业	Enterprises Funded by Hong Kong, Macao and Taiwan	36.36
合资经营企业(港或澳、台资)	Joint Venture	46.15
合作经营企业(港或澳、台资)	Cooperative Enterprise	
港澳台商独资企业	Ventures Exclusively with Hong Kong, Macao and Taiwan Investment	
港澳台商投资股份有限公司	Share Holding Limited Company	66.67
其他港澳台商投资企业	Others	

MAIN ECONOMIC BENEFIT INDICATORS OF LARGE AND MEDIUM-SIZE INDUSTRIAL ENTERPRISES(2016)

(%)

总资产贡献率 Ratio of Profits, Taxes and Interests to Average Assets	资产负债率 Ratio of Debts to Assets	成本费用利润率 Ratio of Profits to Total Costs	利润率 Ratio of Profits to Revenue of Major Business	产品销售率 Ratio of Sales to Gross Output Value
4.80	**76.53**	**1.81**	**1.83**	**95.65**
7.09	69.05	4.24	3.97	98.01
4.48	78.66	1.12	1.17	92.78
2.91	72.94	-0.20	-0.21	94.99
5.18	79.10	0.35	0.34	96.11
5.45	81.00	0.65	0.67	96.00
4.25	59.80	-14.44	-15.49	106.07
9.78	68.15	3.42	3.22	99.40
4.45	76.34	2.29	2.27	96.98
4.66	76.94	1.44	1.46	94.89
4.15	72.35	0.40	0.38	99.63
4.31	106.91	-3.66	-5.74	97.37
2.64	173.44	-14.10	-14.89	100.00
4.70	79.40	1.08	1.11	93.85
4.99	67.68	2.08	2.13	95.99
4.63	82.29	0.79	0.81	93.10
5.76	58.68	5.40	5.17	96.06
4.02	76.56	2.19	2.19	94.87
17.83	76.71	15.08	15.74	96.66
3.80	77.64	1.91	1.90	95.27
6.46	61.51	4.24	4.18	91.03
2.20	105.79	-56.19	-115.39	94.85
4.67	79.72	3.25	3.19	102.77
4.09	89.05	2.36	2.33	105.37
0.47	69.70	0.02	0.02	100.00
9.46	39.78	9.75	8.92	94.77
-0.73	93.50	-6.03	-6.81	91.94

10-12 续表1

单位：%

指　标	Item	亏损面 Range of Deficits
外商投资企业	Foreign Funded Enterprises	46.88
中外合资经营企业	Joint Venture	54.17
中外合作经营企业	Cooperative Enterprises	
外资企业	Enterprises Funded By Foreign Investments	40.00
外商投资股份有限公司	Share Holding Limited Company	
其他外商投资企业	Others	
三、在总计中: 亏损企业	Of the Total: Loss-making Enterprises	100.00
在总计中: 国有控股企业	Of the Total: State-Controlled Share Holding Enterprises	45.47
在总计中: 农村工业	Of the Total: Rural Industry	36.36
在总计中: 轻工业	Of the Total: Light Industry	24.44
重工业	Heavy Industry	42.75
在总计中: 大型企业	Of the Total: Large-size Enterprises	29.15
中型企业	Medium-size Enterprises	43.42
四、按工业行业大类分	Grouped by Sector	
采矿业	Mining	43.49
煤炭开采和洗选业	Coal Mining and Dressing	44.14
石油和天然气开采业	Petroleum and Natural Gas Extraction	
黑色金属矿采选业	Ferrous Metals Mining and Dressing	45.45
有色金属矿采选业	Nonferrous Metals Mining and Dressing	
非金属矿采选业	Nonmetal Minerals Mining and Dressing	
开采辅助活动	Mining Auxiliary Activities	
其他采矿业	Other Mining Industry	
制造业	Manufacturing	34.88
农副食品加工业	Farm Products Processing	26.67
食品制造业	Food Manufacturing	7.69
酒、饮料和精制茶制造业	Wine, Beverages and Refined Tea Manufacturing	25.00
烟草制品业	Tobacoo Products Manfacturing	
纺织业	Textile Industry	
纺织服装、服饰业	Textile,Wearing Apparel and Accessories	14.29
皮革、毛皮、羽毛及其制品和制鞋业	Leather, Fur, Feather and Related Products and Footwear	
木材加工和木、竹、藤、棕、草制品业	Timber Processing,Bamboo,Cane,Palm Fiber and Straw Products	

continued

(%)

总资产贡献率 Ratio of Profits, Taxes and Interests to Average Assets	资产负债率 Ratio of Debts to Assets	成本费用利润率 Ratio of Profits to Total Costs	利润率 Ratio of Profits to Revenue of Major Business	产品销售率 Ratio of Sales to Gross Output Value
9.55	58.46	10.49	9.51	98.46
5.11	66.05	2.99	2.92	97.43
19.99	47.69	35.81	25.17	98.55
13.46	43.57	9.49	8.90	100.19
0.70	90.86	–8.16	–9.23	91.53
4.78	76.91	1.38	1.40	94.90
5.92	62.32	–3.25	–3.21	101.52
12.10	51.32	6.35	6.01	93.54
4.55	77.38	1.51	1.53	95.80
5.16	74.29	2.54	2.59	94.73
4.16	80.55	0.12	0.12	97.30
5.29	77.57	2.33	2.33	92.12
5.27	77.97	2.14	2.14	91.97
7.20	56.68	32.79	31.91	99.84
4.62	65.77	1.45	1.44	94.28
18.41	36.73	9.41	8.14	98.86
4.00	75.94	1.33	1.36	96.82
11.70	57.66	6.46	6.08	95.49
11.86	51.67	7.99	7.53	96.84
18.18	44.38	4.91	4.38	95.90
67.00	12.28	28.45	12.41	100.42
2.82	65.81	0.77	0.76	99.13
7.09	62.64	2.04	3.65	96.45
6.87	31.86	10.68	10.22	96.14

10-12 续表2

单位：%

指　标	Item	亏损面 Range of Deficits
家具制造业	Furniture Manufacturing	
造纸和纸制品业	Paper Making and Paper Products	
印刷和记录媒介复制业	Printing and Record Medium Reproduction	25.00
文教、工美、体育和娱乐用品制造业	Culture, Education, Art and Crafts, Sport and Entertainment Products	
石油加工、炼焦和核燃料加工业	Petroleum Processing, Coking and Nuclear Fuel Processing	55.67
化学原料和化学制品制造业	Raw Chemical Materials and Chemical Products	48.21
医药制造业	Medical and Pharmaceutical Products	18.18
化学纤维制造业	Chemical Fiber Manufacturing	
橡胶和塑料制品业	Rubber and Plastic Products	28.57
非金属矿物制品业	Nonmetal Mineral Products	34.72
黑色金属冶炼和压延加工业	Smelting and Pressing of Ferrous Metals	39.13
有色金属冶炼和压延加工业	Smelting and Pressing of Non-ferrous Metals	24.24
金属制品业	Metal Prodcuts	13.04
通用设备制造业	Ordinary Machinery Manufacturing	22.22
专用设备制造业	Special Purpose Equipment Manufacturing	26.92
汽车制造业	Automobile Manufacturing	31.58
铁路、船舶、航空航天和其他运输设备制造业	Railroad, Marine, Aviation and Other Transport Equipments Manufacturing	40.00
电气机械和器材制造业	Electrical Machinery and Equipment Manufacturing	30.00
计算机、通信和其他电子设备制造业	Computers, Telecommunication and Other Electronic Equipments Manufacturing	37.50
仪器仪表制造业	Equipments and Instruments Manufacturing	33.33
其他制造业	Other Manufacturing	
废弃资源综合利用业	Comprehensive Utilization of Waste Resources	
金属制品、机械和设备修理业	Metal products, Machinery and Equipment Repair	
电力、热力、燃气及水生产和供应业	Production and Supply of Electricity, Heat, Gas and Water	62.16
电力、热力生产和供应业	Production and Supply of Electricity and Heat	64.15
燃气生产和供应业	Production and Supply of Gas	27.27
水的生产和供应业	Production and Supply of Water	90.00

continued

(%)

总资产贡献率 Ratio of Profits, Taxes and Interests to Average Assets	资产负债率 Ratio of Debts to Assets	成本费用利润率 Ratio of Profits to Total Costs	利润率 Ratio of Profits to Revenue of Major Business	产品销售率 Ratio of Sales to Gross Output Value
5.66	85.56	0.64	0.64	99.36
7.16	44.81	6.32	6.04	96.22
7.50	57.20	3.79	3.85	65.35
1.87	89.61	-1.41	-1.50	96.54
-1.51	84.63	-8.11	-9.10	97.19
9.32	47.60	12.38	11.35	85.17
6.95	56.49	3.30	3.27	83.04
4.18	87.42	0.86	0.85	93.99
3.93	70.75	1.22	1.23	97.01
5.81	72.17	3.56	3.54	93.72
4.43	60.47	4.05	3.92	95.58
7.34	74.02	6.60	7.33	91.55
-0.56	79.71	-10.88	-12.55	90.75
5.34	77.65	6.04	6.02	97.39
5.04	72.66	5.23	5.17	101.78
5.67	80.00	2.52	4.43	99.88
5.61	72.65	3.75	3.64	103.64
5.25	57.95	7.39	6.99	99.95
6.65	28.04	20.56	17.03	100.15
18.10	46.49	2.54	2.45	100.00
4.85	72.42	2.16	2.07	99.78
5.16	72.83	2.05	1.95	99.78
4.35	76.06	7.06	6.96	100.00
-2.39	48.42	-14.25	-17.47	98.37

主要统计指标解释

工业 从事自然资源的开采，对采掘品和农产品进行加工和再加工的物质生产部门。具体包括：(1)对自然资源的开采，如采矿、晒盐、森林采伐等(但不包括禽兽捕猎和水产捕捞)；(2)对农副产品的加工、再加工，如粮油加工、食品加工、轧花、缫丝、纺织、制革等；(3)对采掘品的加工、再加工，如炼铁、炼钢、化工生产、石油加工、机器制造、木材加工等，以及电力、自来水、煤气的生产和供应等；(4)对工业品的修理、翻新，如机器设备的修理、交通运输工具(包括小卧车)的修理等。

1984 年以前农村的村及村以下办工业归属农业，1984 年以后划归工业。

工业统计调查单位 工业统计调查单位分为两类：独立核算法人工业企业和工业活动单位。

(1)独立核算法人工业企业 指从事工业生产经营活动的单位。独立核算法人工业企业应同时具备以下条件：①依法成立，有自己的名称、组织机构和场所，能够承担民事责任；②独立拥有和使用资产，承担负债，有权与其他单位签订合同；③独立核算盈亏，并能够编制资产负债表。

(2)工业活动单位 指在一个场所从事一种或主要从事一种工业生产活动的经济单位。它包括独立核算工业企业按主营业务活动(即工业生产活动)划分的主营业务活动单位和非工业企业所属的工业生产活动单位(即原非独立核算工业生产单位)。工业活动单位，一般应同时具备以下三个条件：①具有一个场所，从事一种或主要从事一种工业活动；②单独组织工业生产、经营或业务活动；③单独核算收入和支出。

本年鉴中涉及的企业登记注册类型：

国有控股企业 国有企业和国有控股企业。国有企业（即过去的全民所有制工业或国营工业）是指企业全部资产归国家所有，并按《中华人民共和国企业法人登记管理条例》规定登记注册的非公司制的经济组织。包括国有企业、国有独资公司和国有联营企业。1957 年以前的公私合营和私营工业，后均改造为国营工业，1992 年改为国有工业，这部分工业的资料不单独分列时，均包括在国有企业内。国有控股企业是对混合所有制经济的企业进行的“国有控股”分类。它是指这些企业的全部资产中国有资产（股份）相对其他所有者中的任何一个所有者占资（股）最多的企业。该分组反映了国有经济控股情况。

集体企业 企业资产归集体所有，并按《中华人民共和国企业法人登记管理条例》规定登记注册的经济组织。是社会主义公有制经济的组成部分。包括城乡所有使用集体投资举办的企业，以及部分个人通过集资自愿放弃所有权并依法经工商行政管理机关认定为集体所有制的企业。

股份有限公司 根据《中华人民共和国企业法人登记管理条例》规定登记注册，其全部注册资本由等额股份构成并通过发行股票筹集资本，股东以其认购的股份对公司承担有限责任，公司以其全部资产对其债务承担责任的经济组织。

港、澳、台商投资企业 企业注册登记类型中的港、澳、台资合资、合作、独资经营企业和股份有限公司之和。

外商投资企业 企业注册登记类型中的中外合资、合作经营企业、外资企业和外商投资股份有限公司之和。

本年鉴中主要年份工业企业单位数涉及的名称为“其他”的企业 指除国有企业、集体企业以外的其他类型工业企业（单位)。包括股份合作企业、联营企业、私营企业、股份有限公司、有限责任公司；外商投资企业(中外合资经营、中外合作经营、外资企业)；港、澳、台投资企业(与大陆合资经营、与大陆合作经营、港、澳、台独资企业)及其他企业。

轻工业 主要提供生活消费品和制作手工工具的工业。按其所使用的原料不同，可分为两大类：(1)以农产品为原料的轻工业，是指直接或间接以农产品为基本原料的轻工业。主要包括食品制造、饮料制造、烟草加工、纺织、缝纫、皮革和毛皮制作、造纸以及印刷等工业；(2)以非农产品为原料的轻工业，是指以工业品为原料的轻工业。主要包括文教体育用品、化学药品制造、合成纤维制造、日用化学制品、日用玻璃制品、日用金属制品、手工工具制造、医疗器械制造、文化和办公用机械制造等工业。

重工业 指为国民经济各部门提供物质技术基础的主要生产资料的工业。按其生产性质和产品用途，可以分为下列三类：(1)采掘工业，是指对自然资源的开采，包括石油开采、煤炭开采、金属矿开采、非金属矿开采和木材采伐等工业；(2)原材料工业，指向国民经济各部门提供基本材料、动力和燃料的工业。包括金属冶炼及加工、炼焦及焦炭、化学、化工原料、水泥、人造板以及电力、石油和煤炭加工等工业；(3)加工工业，是指对工业原材料进行再加工制造的工业。包括装备国民经济各部门的机械设备制造工业、金属结构、水泥制品等工业，以及为农业提供的生产资料如化肥、农药等工业。

根据上述划分原则，修理业中以重工业产品为修理作业对象的划为重工业，反之划为轻工业。从 2003 年起轻、重工业内部不再细划分。

工业增加值 指工业企业在报告期内以货币表现的工业生产活动的最终成果。

资产合计 企业拥有或控制的能以货币计量的经济资源。包括各种财产、债权和其他权利。资产按其流动性划分为流动资产、长期投资、固定资产、无形及递延资产和其他资产。

(1)流动资产　企业可以在一年内或者超过一年的一个生产周期内变现或耗用的资产合计。包括现金及各种存款、短期投资、应收及预付款项、存货等。

(2)固定资产　企业固定资产净值、固定资产清理、在建工程、待处理固定资产损失所占用的资金合计。

负债合计　企业承担的能以货币计量，将以资产或劳务偿付的债务。负债一般按偿还期长短分为流动负债和长期负债、递延税项等。

流动负债　企业在一年内或者超过一年的一个营业周期内需要偿还的债务合计，其中包括短期借款、应付及预收款项、应付工资、应交税金和应交利润等。

所有者权益　企业投资人对企业净资产的所有权。企业净资产等于企业全部资产减去全部负债后的余额，其中包括投资者对企业的最初投入，以及资本公积金、盈余公积金和未分配利润，股份制企业即为股东权益。

固定资产原价　企业在建造、购置、安装、改建、扩建、技术改造某项固定资产时所支出的全部货币总额。它一般包括买价、包装费、运杂费和安装费等。

主营业务收入　企业销售产品和提供劳务等主要经营业务取得的业务总额。

主营业务成本　企业销售产品和提供劳务等主要经营业务的实际成本。

主营业务税金及附加　企业销售产品和提供工业性劳务等主要经营业务应负担的城市维护建设税、消费税、资源税和教育费附加。

利润总额　企业在生产经营过程中各种收入扣除各种耗费后的盈余，反映企业在报告期内实现的亏盈总额，包括营业利润、补贴收入、投资净收益和营业外收支净额。

应交增值税　企业按税法规定，从事货物销售或提供加工、修理修配劳务等增加货物价值的活动报告期应交纳的增值税额。计算公式为：

应交增值税=销项税额-（进项税额-进项税额转出）-出口抵减内销产品应纳税额-减免税款+出口退税

总资产贡献率　反映企业全部资产的获利能力，是企业经营业绩和管理水平的集中体现，是评价和考核企业盈利能力的核心指标。计算公式为：

总资产贡献率(%)＝（利润总额+税金总额+利息支出）/平均资产总额×100%

资产负债率　指标既反映企业经营风险的大小，也反映企业利用债权人提供的资金从事经营活动的能力。计算公式：

资产负债率(%)＝负债总额/资产总额×100%

工业成本费用利润率　在一定时期内实现的利润与成本费用之比，是反映工业生产成本及费用投入的经济效益指标，同时也是反映降低成本的经济效益的指标。计算公式为：

工业成本费用利润率(%)＝利润总额/成本费用总额×100%

产品销售率　指报告期工业销售产值与同期工业总产值之比，是反映工业产品已实现销售的程度，分析工业产销衔接情况，研究工业产品满足社会需求程度的指标。计算公式为：

产品销售率(%)＝工业销售产值/工业总产值×100%

亏损面　指亏损企业单位数占全部工业企业单位数的比重。计算公式为：

亏损面(%)＝亏损企业单位数/全部工业企业单位数×100%。

销售收入利润率　指企业实现的总利润对同期的销售收入的比率，用以反映企业销售收入与利润之间的关系。计算公式为：

销售收入利润率＝利润总额/营业收入×100%

Explanatory Notes on Main Statistical Indicators

Industry refers to the material production sector which is engaged in extraction of natural resources and processing and reprocessing of minerals and agricultural products, including (1) extraction of natural resources, such as mining, salt production, logging (but not including hunting and fishing); (2) processing and reprocessing of farm and sideline produces, such as rice husking, flour milling, wine making, oil pressing, cotton ginning, silk reeling, spinning and weaving, and leather making; (3) manufacture of industrial products, such as steel making, iron smelting, chemicals manufacturing, petroleum processing, machine building, timber processing; water and gas production and electricity generation and supply; (4)repairing of industrial products such as the repairing of machinery and means of transport (including cars).

Prior to 1984, the rural industry run by villages and cooperative organizations under village was classified into agriculture. Since 1984, it has been grouped into industry.

Units of Industrial Statistics and Inquiry they are classified into two categories corporate industrial enterprises with independent accounting system and industrial establishments.

(1)**Corporate Industrial Enterprises with Independent Accounting System** refer to enterprises engaging in industrial production activities, which meet the following requirements: ①They are established legally, having their own names, organizations, location, able to take civil liability; ②They possess and use their assets independently, assume liabilities, and are entitled to sign contracts with other units; ③They are financially independent and compile their own balance sheets.

(2)**Industrial Establishments** refer to economic units which located in one single place and engaged entirely or primarily in one kind of industrial activity, including financially independent industrial enterprises and units engaged in industrial activities under the non industrial enterprises (or financially dependent). Industrial establishments generally meet the following requirements: ① They have each one location and are engaged in one kind of industrial activity each; ② They operate and manage their industrial production activities separately; ③ They have accounts of income and expenditures separately.

Types of registration status concerned in this yearbook:

State-holding Enterprises refer to state-owned enterprises and the enterprises which state holds majority shares. State-owned enterprises (industry ownership by the whole people or state-run industry) refers to non-corporation economic units, where the entire assets are owned by the state and which have registered in accordance with the Regulation of the People Republic of China on the Management of Registration of Corporate Enterprises, including the state-owned enterprise, sole state-funded corporation and state-owned joint ownership enterprise. Joint state-private industries and private industries, which existed before 1957, have been transformed into state-run industries. Since 1992, those were named state-owned industries. Statistics on these enterprises has been included in the state-industries since 1957 when separation of data was no longer necessary.

Collective-owned Enterprises refers to industrial enterprises where the means of production are owned collectively including urban and rural enterprises invested by collectives and some enterprises which were formerly owned privately but have been registered in industrial and commercial administration agency as collective units through raising fund from the public.

Share-holding Corporations Ltd. refer to economic units registered in accordance with the regulation of the people's republic of china on the management of registration of corporate enterprises with total registered capitals divided into equal shares and raised through issuing stocks. Each investor bears limited liability to the corporation depending on the holding of shares and the corporation bears liability to its debt to the maximum of its total assets.

Enterprises Funded by Hong Kong, Macao and Taiwan refer to all industrial enterprises as the joint-venture, cooperative, sole investment industrial enterprises and limited liability corporations with funds from Hong Kong, Macao and Taiwan.

Foreign Funded Enterprises refer to all industrial enterprises registered as the joint-venture, cooperative, sole investment industrial enterprises and limited liability corporations with foreign funds.

Other Enterprises Related in Number of Industrial Enterprises in Major Years refer to other types of industrial enterprises or units except for state-owned enterprises and collective enterprises, including share holding cooperative enterprises, joint-venture enterprises, private enterprises, share holding limited enterprises, foreign funded enterprises, enterprises funded by Hong Kong, Macao and Taiwan and other enterprises.

Light Industry refers to the industry that produces consumer goods and hand tools. It consists of two categories depending on the raw materials used:

(1)Industries using farm products as raw materials. These are branches of light industry which directly or indirectly use farm products as basic raw materials, including the manufacture of food and beverages, tobacco processing, textile, clothing, fur and leather manufacturing, paper making, printing, etc. (2)Industries using non farm products as raw materials. These are branches of light industry which use manufactured goods as raw materials, including the manufacture of cultural, educational articles and sports goods chemicals synthetic fiber chemical products for daily use glass products for daily use metal products for daily use hand tools medical apparatus and instruments and the manufacture of cultural and clerical machinery.

Heavy Industry refers to the industry which produces capital goods and provides various sectors of the national economy with necessary material and technical basis. It consists of the following three branches according to the purpose of production or the use of products: (1)Mining and Quarrying Industry refers to the industry that extracts natural resources including extraction of petroleum coal metal and non-metal ores and logging. (2)Raw Materials Industry refers to the industry that provides various sectors of the national economy with raw materials fuels and power. it includes smelting and processing of metals coking and coke chemistry chemical materials and building materials such as cement plywood and power petroleum refining and coal dressing. (3)Manufacturing Industry refers to the industry that processes raw materials. It includes machine building industry which equips sectors of the national economy industries of metal structure and cement products industries producing means of agricultural production such as chemical fertilizers and pesticides.

According to the above principle of classification the repairing trades which are engaged primarily in repairing products of heavy industry are classified into heavy industry while those engaged in repairing products of light industry are classified into light industry. It is not divided further in the interior of light industry and heavy industry from 2003.

Value Added of Industry refers to the final results of industrial production of the industrial trade in money terms during the reference period.

Total Assets refer to all economic resources owned or controlled by enterprises that could be measured in monetary terms including properties creditor equity and other economic rights of all forms. classified by the degree of equitability total assets include circulating assets long term investment fixed assets intangible assets and deferred assets and other assets.

(1)Circulating Assets refers to assets which can be cashed in or spent or consumed in an operating cycle of one year or over one year including cash all kinds of deposits short term investment receivables advance payment stock etc.

(2)Fixed Assets refers to the net value of fixed assets clearance of fixed assets project under construction fixed assets losses in suspense. these are corporations fund holdings.

Total Liabilities refers to the debts measured in monetary terms that enterprises are responsible for repayment in the form of cash assets or labor. Classified by terms of repayment liability include liquid liabilities and long-term liabilities.

Liquid Liabilities refers to enterprises total debt payable within an operating cycle of one year or over one year, including short term loans, payables and advance payments, wage payable, taxes payable and profit payable, etc.

Creditors' Equity refers to investors' ownership of net assets of the enterprise. It is equal to the total assets of the enterprise minus its total liabilities, including the primary input from investors, capital accumulation fund, surplus accumulation fund and undistributed profit. it is the shareholders equity in share—holding companies.

Original Value of Fixed Assets refers to the original value of all fixed assets owned by industrial enterprises calculated the cost paid at the time of purchase installation reconstruction expansion and technical innovation and transformation of at the said assets which includes expenses on purchase package transportation and installation etc.

Revenue of Major Business refers to the revenue from the sales of products by industrial enterprises and the revenue from services provided and etc.

Cost of Major Business refers to the actual cost of products of industrial enterprises and industrial services provided etc.

Taxes and Extra Charges of Major Business refer to the tax on city maintenance and construction consumption tax resources tax and extra charges for education which should be borne by the enterprises in selling products and providing industrial services.

Total Profits refer to the surplus gained by enterprises by deducting costs from all kinds of revenues in business, which reflects the total profits and losses of enterprises in reporting period, including business profits, subsidy revenue, net investment profit and net amount of non-business revenue and expenditure.

Value Added Taxes Payable refers to the amount of value-added tax which should be paid by enterprises which are engaged in value-added activities such as goods selling, processing and repairing according to the tax laws of enterprise. It is calculated as follows.

Value Added Taxes Payable = Tax on Sales - (Tax on Purchase-Transferred Tax on Purchase) - Tax Payable for the Exported Goods Sold on the Domestic Market - Derated Tax + Export Rebate.

Ratio of Profits, Taxes and Interests to Average Assets reflects the profit-making capability of all assets of the enterprise and is a key indicator manifesting the performance and management and evaluating the profit-making potential of the enterprise. It is calculated as follows:

Ratio of profits taxes and interests to average assets (%) = [(Total profits + total Taxes + interest payment) ÷ average assets]×100%

Ratio of Debts to Assets reflect both the operation risk and the capability of the enterprise in making use of the capital from the creditors. It is calculated as follows:

Ratio of debts to assets (%) = (Total debts ÷ total assets) ×100%

Ratio of Profits to Total Industrial Costs refers to the ratio of profits realized in a given period to the total costs in the same period, which reflects the economic efficiency of input cost and is calculated as follows:

Ratio of Profits to Total Industrial Cost (%) = (Total Profits ÷ Total Costs) ×100%

Ratio of Sales to Gross Output Value refers to the sales of industrial products to the gross industrial output value during the reference period and is important in reflecting the linkage between production and sales and the extent of the needs of the society that has been met by the supply of industrial products. It is calculated as follows:

Ratio of Sales to Gross Output Value = Industrial sales ÷ Gross industrial output value (at current prices) ×100%

Range of Deficits refers to the proportion of loss-making enterprises in the number of all industrial enterprises. The formula is as follows:

Range of Deficits (%) = (Number of loss-making enterprises ÷ Number of All Industrial Enterprises) ×100%

Ratio of Profits to Sales Revenue refers to the total profits to the business revenue in the same period, which reflects the linkage between sales revenue and profits. The formula is as follows:

Ratio of Profits to Sales Revenue (%) = (Total Profits ÷ Business Revenue) ×100%

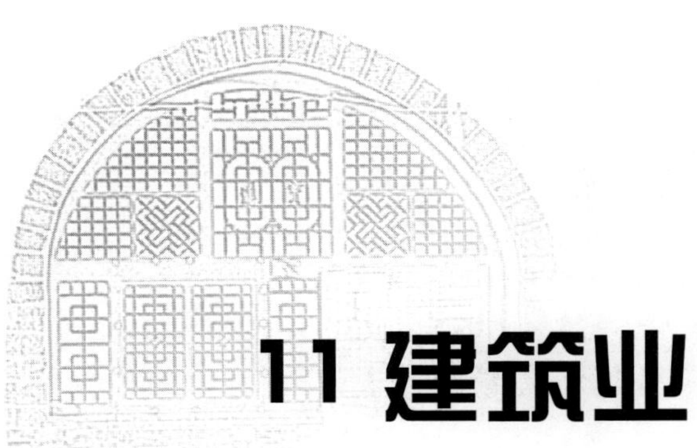

11 建筑业

CONSTRUCTION

资料整理人员

张利云　陈烨松

建筑业
CONSTRUCTION

建筑业施工企业个数	Number of Construction Enterprises	2532	个	(unit)
建筑业总产值	Gross Output Value of Construction	3318.5	亿元	(100 million yuan)
建筑业竣工产值	Completed Output Value of Costruction	1278.5	亿元	(100 million yuan)
建筑业房屋建筑竣工面积	Floor Space of Buildings Completed of Construction	3353	万平方米	(10 000 sq.m)

建筑业总产值构成 (%)
Composition of Total Output Value of Construction(%)

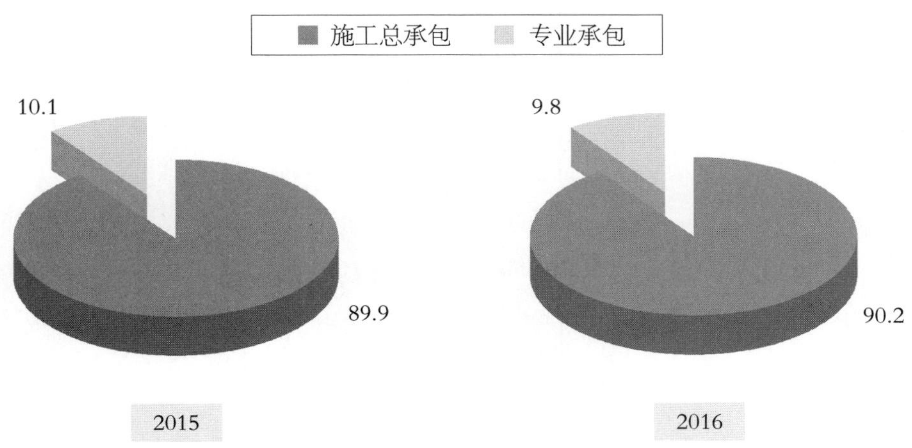

建筑业总产值（亿元）
Total Output Value of Construction (100 million yuan)

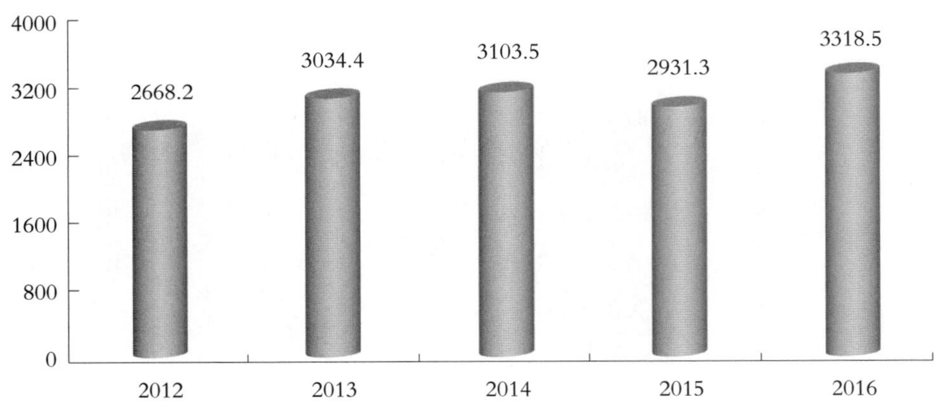

11-1 建筑施工企业主要经济指标
MAJOR ECONOMIC INDICATORS OF CONSTRUCTION ENTERPRISES

指 标	Item	2015	2016
施工企业个数 (个)	Number of Construction Enterprises (unit)	2285	2532
直接从事生产经营活动的平均人数 (万人)	Average Number of People Directly Engaged in Production and Operating Activities (10 000 persons)	99	112
建筑业企业期末人数 (万人)	Number of Employees at The End of Period (10 000 persons)	76	75
固定资产原价 (万元)	Original Value of Fixed Assets (10 000 yuan)	4592934	4806771
固定资产合计 (万元)	Total Fixed Assets (10 000 yuan)	2821926	2958614
自有机械设备总台数 (台)	Number of Machinery and Equipment Owned (set)	193051	197334
自有机械设备净值 (万元)	Net Value of Machinery and Equipment Owned (10 000 yuan)	1390530	1468913
自有机械设备总功率 (万千瓦)	Total Power of Machinery and Equipment Owned (10 000 kw)	692	697
建筑业总产值 (万元)	Output Value of Construction (10 000 yuan)	29312627	33184739
竣工产值 (万元)	Output Value of Buildings Completed (10 000 yuan)	15391066	12785480
固定资产折旧 (万元)	Depreciation of Fixed Assets (10 000 yuan)	302255	333113
施工面积 (万平方米)	Floor Space of Buildings under Construction (10 000 sq.m)	13943	14621
竣工面积 (万平方米)	Floor Space of Buildings Completed (10 000 sq.m)	3634	3353
营业利润 (万元)	Profits of Business (10 000 yuan)	920358	950924
管理费用 (万元)	Costs of Administration (10 000 yuan)	1397175	1565024
利润总额 (万元)	Total Profits (10 000 yuan)	938078	972077
上缴税金 (万元)	Tax Turned Over to the State (10 000 yuan)	853403	506539
按总产值计算的全员劳动生产率 (元/人)	Overall Labor Productivity in Terms of Total Output Value (yuan/person)	294641	295590
实收资本 (万元)	Capitals Hold (10 000 yuan)	6271056	7240168
资产总计 (万元)	Total Assets (10 000 yuan)	40337922	48453897
负债合计 (万元)	Total Liabilities (10 000 yuan)	30210940	37819762
所有者权益合计 (万元)	Total Creditors Equity (10 000 yuan)	10126944	10634135
竣工率(按产值计算) (%)	Rate of Completed (by Output Value) (%)	52.5	38.5
技术装备率 (元/人)	Value of Machines per Laborer (yuan/person)	18189	19473
动力装备率 (千瓦/人)	Power of Machines per Laborer (kw/person)	9.1	9.2
资产负债率 (%)	Ratio of Debts to Assets (%)	75.0	78.1
产值利润率 (%)	Ratio of Profit to Gross Output Value (%)	3.2	2.9

11-2 建筑业企业总产值和竣工产值(2016年)
GROSS OUTPUT VALUE AND COMPLETED VALUE OF CONSTRUCTION ENTERPRISES(2016)

单位：万元　　(10 000 yuan)

指　标	Item	建筑业总产值 Total Output Value	#建筑工程 Construction	#安装工程 Installation	竣工产值 Output Value of Buildings Completed
总　计	**Total**	**33184739**	**28780169**	**3475946**	**12785480**
#国有及国有控股	State Owned and State Controlling Share	20846911	18878315	1601085	6323372
按登记注册类型分	**Grouped by Registered Kind**				
内资企业	Civil Funded Enterprises	33125823	28725307	3475946	12755920
国有企业	State-owned Enterprises	3208902	2754835	392284	1746692
集体企业	Collective-owned Enterprises	377569	270112	60558	192906
股份合作企业	Share Cooperative Enterprises				
联营企业	Joint Ownership Enterprises				
有限责任公司	Limited Responsibility Corporations	20156843	18171195	1639398	6106980
国有独资公司	Company Exclusively with Investment from State	1607659	1404115	176429	437289
其他有限责任公司	Other Limited Responsibility Company	18549183	16767079	1462969	5669692
股份有限公司	Share-holding Limited Corporations	509068	403195	59254	136869
私营企业	Private-owned Enterprises	8873441	7125970	1324452	4572473
私营独资企业	Enterprise Exclusively with Investment from Private	448	444	4	368
私营合伙企业	Private Partnership Enterprises	4452	3627		1617
私营有限责任公司	Private Limited Responsibility Corporations	7243410	5882647	989926	4077050
私营股份有限公司	Private Share-holding Limited Corporations	1625131	1239253	334522	493439
其他企业	Other Enterprises				
港、澳、台商投资企业	Enterprises Funded by HongKong, Macao and Taiwan	36872	36872		7515
外商投资企业	Foreign Funded Enterprises	22044	17990		22044
按国民经济行业分	**Grouped by Economic Sector**				
房屋和土木工程建筑业	Housing and Civil Engineering Construction	30592357	27492042	2369069	11422319
房屋工程建筑	Housing	14155854	12857193	1087903	6087471
土木工程建筑	Civil Engineering	16436503	14634849	1281166	5334848
建筑安装业	Building Installation	1552476	545154	928237	710579
建筑装饰业	Building Fiting and Decoration	408090	305776	66225	282424
其他建筑业	Other Construction	631817	437197	112416	370157
按隶属关系分	**Grouped by Subordination**				
#中　央	Central	12159409	11173152	861969	2494185
省	Province	7107420	6388473	556490	2638041
地　区	Prefecture	2558827	2020358	429306	1550924
县	County	660607	536698	74266	463761
按企业资质等级分	**Grouped by Qualification Criteria**				
施工总承包	Overall Contract	29918265	26559902	2667924	11101160
专业承包	Specialized Contract	3266474	2220267	808022	1684320

11-3 按主要用途分的房屋建筑竣工面积(2016年)

单位：平方米

指标	Item	总计 Total	住宅房屋 Residential Buildings
总计	**Total**	**33532617**	**23662087**
#国有及国有控股	State Owned and State Controlling Share	13641163	9461289
按登记注册类型分	**Grouped by Registered Kind**		
内资企业	Civil Funded Enterprises	33532617	23662087
国有企业	State-owned Enterprises	4734030	3500775
集体企业	Collective-owned Enterprises	813941	734733
股份合作企业	Share Cooperative Enterprises		
联营企业	Joint Ownership Enterprises		
有限责任公司	Limited Responsibility Corporations	13877859	8596512
国有独资公司	Company Exclusively with Investment from State	1708970	1000356
其他有限责任公司	Other Limited Responsibility Company	12168889	7596156
股份有限公司	Share-holding Limited Corporations	84763	59649
私营企业	Private-owned Enterprises	14022024	10770418
私营独资企业	Enterprise Exclusively with Investment from Private	73	73
私营合伙企业	Private Partnership Enterprises		
私营有限责任公司	Private Limited Responsibility Corporations	12963144	10022017
私营股份有限公司	Private Share-holding Limited Corporations	1058807	748328
其他企业	Other Enterprises		
港、澳、台商投资企业	Enterprises Funded by HongKong, Macao and Taiwan		
外商投资企业	Foreign Funded Enterprises		
按国民经济行业分	**Grouped by Economic Sector**		
房屋和土木工程建筑业	Housing and Civil Engineering Construction	33011908	23520574
房屋工程建筑	Housing	31568854	22902047
土木工程建筑	Civil Engineering	1443054	618527
建筑安装业	Building Installation	354610	61666
建筑装饰业	Building Fiting and Decoration		
其他建筑业	Other Construction	166099	79847
按隶属关系分	**Grouped by Subordination**		
#中　央	Central	2569174	1774074
省	Province	9631593	5778435
地　区	Prefecture	2080956	1624717
县	County	2188597	1735968
按企业资质等级分	**Grouped by Qualification Criteria**		
施工总承包	Overall Contract	32952496	23584647
专业承包	Specialized Contract	580121	77440

FLOOR SPACE OF BUILDINGS COMPLETED BY MAJOR USE(2016)

(sq.m)

商业及服务用房屋 Commercial and Service Buildings	办公用房 Oiffices	科研、教育、医疗用房屋 Scientific Research, Education and Healthcare Buildings	文化、体育、娱乐用房屋 Culture, Sports and Entertaninment Buildings	厂房及建筑物 Factory Buildings	仓 库 Warehouses	其他未列明的房屋建筑物 Other Unlisted Buildings
1462378	**2650152**	**2332121**	**253489**	**2467081**	**112778**	**592531**
486887	1010144	1082227	155813	1226663	11176	206964
1462378	2650152	2332121	253489	2467081	112778	592531
166653	323258	448996	82187	177426	5539	29196
12163	4255	29292		29810	1100	2588
798955	1339939	1311089	83521	1414819	44946	288078
106170	126040	130793	28	261105		84478
692785	1213899	1180296	83493	1153714	44946	203600
600	418	1330		19700	2700	366
484007	982282	541414	87781	825326	58493	272303
282007	982282	528222	87781	736419	52113	272303
202000		13192		88907	6380	
1399530	2636856	2304683	221634	2228175	111846	588610
1340524	2545398	2285095	220296	1722767	106721	446006
59006	91458	19588	1338	505408	5125	142604
61400	11430	27070	6627	181930	932	3555
1448	1866	368	25228	56976		366
3338	222047	51852	1026	469460	4085	43292
693044	1058110	1263444	103733	703060	19819	11948
65292	90132	42962	30359	70016	2149	155329
34813	104045	135897	30590	117721	43	29520
1389860	2635599	2313185	244779	2088901	111728	583797
72518	14553	18936	8710	378180	1050	8734

11-4 按主要用途分的房屋建筑竣工价值(2016年)

单位：万元

指 标	Item	总 计 Total	住宅房屋 Residential Buildings
总 计	**Total**	**5480485**	**3563838**
#国有及国有控股	State Owned and State Controlling Share	2583605	1523117
按登记注册类型分	**Grouped by Registered Kind**		
内资企业	Civil Funded Enterprises	5480485	3563838
国有企业	State-owned Enterprises	802813	496576
集体企业	Collective-owned Enterprises	84517	74676
股份合作企业	Share Cooperative Enterprises		
联营企业	Joint Ownership Enterprises		
有限责任公司	Limited Responsibility Corporations	2545987	1454482
国有独资公司	Company Exclusively with Investment from State	314332	167132
其他有限责任公司	Other Limited Responsibility Company	2231655	1287351
股份有限公司	Share-holding Limited Corporations	18724	9064
私营企业	Private-owned Enterprises	2028445	1529041
私营独资企业	Enterprise Exclusively with Investment from Private	18	18
私营合伙企业	Private Partnership Enterprises		
私营有限责任公司	Private Limited Responsibility Corporations	1874365	1420874
私营股份有限公司	Private Share-holding Limited Corporations	154062	108148
其他企业	Other Enterprises		
港、澳、台商投资企业	Enterprises Funded by HongKong, Macao and Taiwan		
外商投资企业	Foreign Funded Enterprises		
按国民经济行业分	**Grouped by Economic Sector**		
房屋和土木工程建筑业	Housing and Civil Engineering Construction	5432491	3541598
房屋工程建筑	Housing	5011762	3419821
土木工程建筑	Civil Engineering	420729	121777
建筑安装业	Building Installation	30106	10497
建筑装饰业	Builing Fiting and Decoration		
其他建筑业	Other Construction	17889	11743
按隶属关系分	**Grouped by Subordination**		
#中 央	Central	705037	375000
省	Province	1613767	898103
地 区	Prefecture	364321	258913
县	County	307928	241623
按企业资质等级分	**Grouped by Qualification Criteria**		
施工总承包	Overall Contract	5446653	3557080
专业承包	Specialized Contract	33832	6758

VALUE OF BUILDINGS COMPLETED BY MAJOR USE(2016)

(10 000 yuan)

商业及服务用房屋 Commercial and Service Buildings	办公用房 Oiffices	科研、教育、医疗用房屋 Scientific Research, Education and Healthcare Buildings	文化、体育、娱乐用房屋 Culture, Sports and Entertaninment Buildings	厂房及建筑物 Factory Buildings	仓 库 Warehouses	其他未列明的房屋建筑物 Other Unlisted Buildings
240466	**495377**	**476824**	**65064**	**470317**	**23220**	**145379**
83134	238967	255458	53060	350734	1440	77695
240466	495377	476824	65064	470317	23220	145379
32368	84515	114432	28295	39048	279	7302
3186	250	3287		2633	155	330
132249	237908	256761	26397	337926	10975	89288
22873	28251	25720	7	45973		24376
109376	209657	231041	26389	291953	10975	64912
80	41	214		8999	290	37
72583	172663	102130	10372	81712	11522	48423
34390	172663	100278	10372	76599	10767	48423
38193		1852		5113	755	
237970	493811	470635	60970	459491	22984	145032
226051	468724	465488	60753	239232	22017	109677
11919	25088	5147	217	220259	968	35355
2200	1364	6113	306	9079	236	311
296	202	76	3788	1747		37
200	62447	17357	496	210504	800	38233
123292	181007	243545	45140	117292	2329	3059
9655	26777	10064	3981	19731	178	35021
7302	16853	20148	5075	11513	9	5405
237326	494175	474211	64134	453341	23187	143201
3140	1202	2613	930	16977	34	2178

11-5 建筑业企业房屋建筑面积(2016年)
FLOOR SPACE OF BUILDINGS CONSTRUCTED BY CONSTRUCTION ENTERPRISES(2016)

单位: 平方米 (sq.m)

指　标	Item	房屋建筑施工面积 Floor Space of Buildings under Construction	#本年新开工面积 Newly Started This Year	#投标承包的面积 Entered Bid Contracts
总　计	**Total**	**146205756**	**45322426**	**125671517**
#国有及国有控股	State Owned and State Controlling Share	93265718	22658452	88800225
按登记注册类型分	**Grouped by Registered Kind**			
内资企业	Civil Funded Enterprises	146205756	45322426	125671517
国有企业	State-owned Enterprises	18839181	4957675	18007360
集体企业	Collective-owned Enterprises	1905304	940716	666917
股份合作企业	Share Cooperative Enterprises			
联营企业	Joint Ownership Enterprises			
有限责任公司	Limited Responsibility Corporations	87089324	22860292	80546266
国有独资公司	Company Exclusively with Investment from State	10874165	1801395	10818120
其他有限责任公司	Other Limited Responsibility Company	76215159	21058897	69728146
股份有限公司	Share-holding Limited Corporations	3980543	590504	3830777
私营企业	Private-owned Enterprises	34391404	15973239	22620197
私营独资企业	Enterprise Exclusively with Investment from Private	75	75	
私营合伙企业	Private Partnership Enterprises	36460	36460	36460
私营有限责任公司	Private Limited Responsibility Corporations	29135034	14785788	17605847
私营股份有限公司	Private Share-holding Limited Corporations	5219835	1150916	4977890
其他企业	Other Enterprises			
港、澳、台商投资企业	Enterprises Funded by HongKong, Macao and Taiwan			
外商投资企业	Foreign Funded Enterprises			
按国民经济行业分	**Grouped by Economic Sector**			
房屋和土木工程建筑业	Housing and Civil Engineering Construction	144386288	44572888	125406299
房屋工程建筑	Housing	120955538	40019921	103131373
土木工程建筑	Civil Engineering	23430750	4552967	22274926
建筑安装业	Building Installation	926647	482862	167206
建筑装饰业	Building Fiting and Decoration			
其他建筑业	Other Construction	892821	266676	98012
按隶属关系分	**Grouped by Subordination**			
#中　央	Central	35574705	9388619	34175307
省	Province	53641580	11107841	51667021
地　区	Prefecture	10035187	3796974	8709746
县	County	4405602	1915975	3126637
按企业资质等级分	**Grouped by Qualification Criteria**			
施工总承包	Overall Contract	144541781	44550786	125284434
专业承包	Specialized Contract	1663975	771640	387083

11-6 建筑业企业机械设备情况(2016年)
MACHINARY AND EQUIPMENT OF CONSTRUCTION ENTERPRISES(2016)

指 标	Item	自有机械设备年末总台数(台) Number of Machinery and Equipment Owned(unit)	自有机械设备年末总功率(千瓦) Total Power of Machinery and Equipment Owned(kw)	自有机械设备净值(万元) Net Value of Machinery and Equipment Owned (10 000 yuan)
总 计	**Total**	**197334**	**6970480**	**1468913**
#国有及国有控股	State Owned and State Controlling Share	87302	4623143	846444
按登记注册类型分	**Grouped by Registered Kind**			
内资企业	Civil Funded Enterprises	196276	6952174	1465235
国有企业	State-owned Enterprises	19999	502002	80984
集体企业	Collective-owned Enterprises	9157	108685	15751
股份合作企业	Share Cooperative Enterprises			
联营企业	Joint Ownership Enterprises			
有限责任公司	Limited Responsibility Corporations	76834	4375356	841706
国有独资公司	Company Exclusively with Investment from State	7793	246800	71158
其他有限责任公司	Other Limited Responsibility Company	69041	4128556	770548
股份有限公司	Share-holding Limited Corporations	5183	123264	19720
私营企业	Private-owned Enterprises	85103	1842867	507074
私营独资企业	Enterprise Exclusively with Investment from Private	24	133	354
私营合伙企业	Private Partnership Enterprises	60	222	1895
私营有限责任公司	Private Limited Responsibility Corporations	79531	1698046	466397
私营股份有限公司	Private Share-holding Limited Corporations	5488	144466	38428
其他企业	Other Enterprises			
港、澳、台商投资企业	Enterprises Funded by HongKong, Macao and Taiwan	682	7328	668
外商投资企业	Foreign Funded Enterprises	376	10978	3010
按国民经济行业分	**Grouped by Economic Sector**			
房屋和土木工程建筑业	Housing and Civil Engineering Construction	174504	6511774	1351361
房屋工程建筑	Housing	90918	1701665	399611
土木工程建筑	Civil Engineering	83586	4810109	951750
建筑安装业	Building Installation	11327	270808	64661
建筑装饰业	Building Fiting and Decoration	7007	83164	12967
其他建筑业	Other Construction	4496	104734	39924
按隶属关系分	**Grouped by Subordination**			
#中 央	Central	39822	3380273	604013
省	Province	30339	726324	163723
地 区	Prefecture	16444	548506	87075
县	County	14182	236665	53226
按企业资质等级分	**Grouped by Qualification Criteria**			
施工总承包	Overall Contract	171357	6419538	1323127
专业承包	Specialized Contract	25977	550942	145785

11-7 建筑业企业劳动生产率(2016年)
LABOR PRODUCTIVITY OF CONSTRUCTION ENTERPRISES(2016)

指 标	Item	企业个数(个) Number of Enterprises (unit)	从事建筑业活动的从业人员平均人数(人) Average Number of Employees Engaged in Construction Activities(person)	按总产值计算的劳动生产率(元/人) Overall Labor Productivity in Terms of Total Output Value (yuan/person)	人均竣工产值(元/人) Per Capita Output Value of Buildings Completed (yuan/person)
总 计	**Total**	**2532**	**1122660**	**295590**	**113886**
#国有及国有控股	State Owned and State Controlling Share	308	637766	326874	99149
按登记注册类型分组	**Grouped by Registered Kind**				
内资企业	Civil Funded Enterprises	2525	1120351	295674	113856
国有企业	State-owned Enterprises	106	98520	325711	177293
集体企业	Collective-owned Enterprises	77	19842	190288	97221
股份合作企业	Share Cooperative Enterprises				
联营企业	Joint Ownership Enterprises				
有限责任公司	Limited Responsibility Corporations	475	637881	315997	95739
国有独资公司	Company Exclusively with Investment from State	32	46739	343965	93560
其他有限责任公司	Other Limited Responsibility Company	443	591142	313786	95911
股份有限公司	Share-holding Limited Corporations	27	11889	428184	115122
私营企业	Private-owned Enterprises	1840	352219	251930	129819
私营独资企业	Enterprise Exclusively with Investment from Private	2	58	77259	63483
私营合伙企业	Private Partnership Enterprises	2	162	274840	99802
私营有限责任公司	Private Limited Responsibility Corporations	1767	298132	242960	136753
私营股份有限公司	Private Share-holding Limited Corporations	69	53867	301693	91603
其他企业	Other Enterprises				
港、澳、台商投资企业	Enterprises Funded by HongKong, Macao and Taiwan	5	724	509285	103804
外商投资企业	Foreign Funded Enterprises	2	1585	139081	139081
按国民经济行业分组	**Grouped by Economic Sector**				
房屋和土木工程建筑业	Housing and Civil Engineering Construction	1476	1023174	298995	111636
房屋工程建筑	Housing	825	599941	235954	101468
土木工程建筑	Civil Engineering	651	423233	388356	126050
建筑安装业	Building Installation	485	52429	296110	135532
建筑装饰业	Building Fiting and Decoration	376	19979	204259	141361
其他建筑业	Other Construction	195	27078	233332	136700
按隶属关系分组	**Grouped by Subordination**				
#中 央	Central	53	263499	461459	94656
省	Province	111	312125	227711	84519
地 区	Prefecture	175	83949	304807	184746
县	County	140	41419	159494	111968
按企业资质等级分组	**Grouped by Qualification Criteria**				
施工总承包	Overall Contract	1283	989729	302287	112164
专业承包	Specialized Contract	1249	132931	245727	126706

11-8 建筑业企业资本金及资产(2016年)
CAPITAL AND ASSETS OF CONSTRUCTION ENTERPRISES(2016)

单位：万元 (10 000 yuan)

指 标	Item	实收资本 Capitals Hold	资产总计 Total Assets	#流动资产合计 Total Circul-ating Funds	#固定资产合计 Total Fixed Assets
总 计	**Total**	**7240168**	**48453897**	**40457188**	**2958614**
#国有及国有控股	State Owned and State Controlling Share	3038343	34456950	29060183	1283614
按登记注册类型分	**Grouped by Registered Kind**				
内资企业	Civil Funded Enterprises	7229764	48377437	40395893	2944366
国有企业	State-owned Enterprises	295109	3658285	2915091	312843
集体企业	Collective-owned Enterprises	98535	551569	451630	62605
股份合作企业	Share Cooperative Enterprises				
联营企业	Joint Ownership Enterprises				
有限责任公司	Limited Responsibility Corporations	3363316	33447367	28264679	1352111
国有独资公司	Company Exclusively with Investment from State	526059	6378019	4541913	79259
其他有限责任公司	Other Limited Responsibility Company	2837257	27069348	23722766	1272853
股份有限公司	Share-holding Limited Corporations	110144	962184	868992	54555
私营企业	Private-owned Enterprises	3362661	9758033	7895501	1162252
私营独资企业	Enterprise Exclusively with Investment from Private	1351	2719	1376	1215
私营合伙企业	Private Partnership Enterprises	1734	3763	3078	685
私营有限责任公司	Private Limited Responsibility Corporations	3210273	8894366	7132946	1104636
私营股份有限公司	Private Share-holding Limited Corporations	149303	857185	758102	55717
其他企业	Other Enterprises				
港、澳、台商投资企业	Enterprises Funded by HongKong, Macao and Taiwan	8804	54282	42462	10963
外商投资企业	Foreign Funded Enterprises	1600	22178	18833	3285
按国民经济行业分	**Grouped by Economic Sector**				
房屋和土木工程建筑业	Housing and Civil Engineering Construction	5997716	44207521	37003645	2422714
房屋工程建筑	Housing	2464952	14179760	12347876	1014096
土木工程建筑	Civil Engineering	3532765	30027761	24655769	1408618
建筑安装业	Building Installation	654893	2480428	2042938	313931
建筑装饰业	Building Fiting and Decoration	299553	656026	526642	91594
其他建筑业	Other Construction	288005	1109922	883964	130375
按隶属关系分	**Grouped by Subordination**				
#中 央	Central	1614825	18612051	16279066	626707
省	Province	1135927	13213127	10458532	439034
地 区	Prefecture	402654	3198252	2721528	317428
县	County	190151	1011096	838476	125287
按企业资质等级分	**Grouped by Qualification Criteria**				
施工总承包	Overall Contract	5887577	43534555	36355242	2400674
专业承包	Specialized Contract	1352591	4919342	4101946	557940

11-9 建筑业企业负债及所有者权益(2016年)
LIABILITIES AND CREDITORS' EQUITY OF CONSTRUCTION ENTERPRISES(2016)

单位：万元 (10 000 yuan)

指 标	Item	负债合计 Total Liabilities	#流动负债 Liquid Liabilities	#非流动负债合计 Illiquid Liabilities	所有者权益合计 Total Creditors' Equity
总 计	**Total**	**37819762**	**34841097**	**2443714**	**10634135**
#国有及国有控股	State Owned and State Controlling Share	29645921	27117231	2185350	4811029
按登记注册类型分	**Grouped by Registered Kind**				
内资企业	Civil Funded Enterprises	37752670	34774422	2443327	10624767
国有企业	State-owned Enterprises	3322464	3073988	188550	335820
集体企业	Collective-owned Enterprises	410076	399782	5163	141493
股份合作企业	Share Cooperative Enterprises				
联营企业	Joint Ownership Enterprises				
有限责任公司	Limited Responsibility Corporations	27924911	25671729	1966408	5522456
国有独资公司	Company Exclusively with Investment from State	5142051	3683139	1229637	1235969
其他有限责任公司	Other Limited Responsibility Company	22782861	21988590	736771	4286487
股份有限公司	Share-holding Limited Corporations	785131	669543	96307	177053
私营企业	Private-owned Enterprises	5310088	4959380	186900	4447945
私营独资企业	Enterprise Exclusively with Investment from Private	818	818		1901
私营合伙企业	Private Partnership Enterprises	2029	2026		1734
私营有限责任公司	Private Limited Responsibility Corporations	4681283	4409035	123829	4213082
私营股份有限公司	Private Share-holding Limited Corporations	625957	547500	63072	231228
其他企业	Other Enterprises				
港、澳、台商投资企业	Enterprises Funded by HongKong, Macao and Taiwan	47808	47391	387	6475
外商投资企业	Foreign Funded Enterprises	19284	19284		2894
按国民经济行业分	**Grouped by Economic Sector**				
房屋和土木工程建筑业	Housing and Civil Engineering Construction	35214092	32411227	2322720	8993429
房屋工程建筑	Housing	10559855	9997651	402668	3619905
土木工程建筑	Civil Engineering	24654237	22413575	1920052	5373525
建筑安装业	Building Installation	1604732	1462765	113140	875696
建筑装饰业	Building Fiting and Decoration	295684	289491	1985	360342
其他建筑业	Other Construction	705254	677615	5869	404668
按隶属关系分	**Grouped by Subordination**				
#中 央	Central	16363604	15690684	667163	2248447
省	Province	11201825	9758854	1442051	2011302
地 区	Prefecture	2401953	2288655	36127	796300
县	County	744026	460625	46750	267069
按企业资质等级分	**Grouped by Qualification Criteria**				
施工总承包	Overall Contract	34751556	31886882	2376764	8783000
专业承包	Specialized Contract	3068206	2954215	66950	1851136

11-10 建筑业企业收入及成本情况(2016年)
REVENUE AND COST OF CONSTRUCTION ENTERPRISES(2016)

单位：万元 (10 000 yuan)

指 标	Item	营业收入 Revenue of Business	#主营业务收入 Revenue of Major Business	主营业务成本 Cost of Major Business
总 计	**Total**	**33340063**	**33029335**	**29379325**
#国有及国有控股	State Owned and State Controlling Share	21017475	20900661	18595471
按登记注册类型分	**Grouped by Registered Kind**			
内资企业	Civil Funded Enterprises	33283595	32973588	29329178
国有企业	State-owned Enterprises	3170467	3148027	2948617
集体企业	Collective-owned Enterprises	379959	374839	319668
股份合作企业	Share Cooperative Enterprises			
联营企业	Joint Ownership Enterprises			
有限责任公司	Limited Responsibility Corporations	20273873	20110677	17805929
国有独资公司	Company Exclusively with Investment	1710669	1686720	1476162
其他有限责任公司	Other Limited Responsibility Company	18563205	18423956	16329768
股份有限公司	Share-holding Limited Corporations	552622	547520	475978
私营企业	Private-owned Enterprises	8906675	8792525	7778985
私营独资企业	Enterprise Exclusively with Investment from Private	1679	1679	1107
私营合伙企业	Private Partnership Enterprises	830	830	698
私营有限责任公司	Private Limited Responsibility Corporations	7168813	7099251	6181088
私营股份有限公司	Private Share-holding Limited Corporations	1735354	1690766	1596092
其他企业	Other Enterprises			
港、澳、台商投资企业	Enterprises Funded by HongKong, Macao and Taiwan	34424	33704	29227
外商投资企业	Foreign Funded Enterprises	22044	22044	20921
按国民经济行业分	**Grouped by Economic Sector**			
房屋和土木工程建筑业	Housing and Civil Engineering Construction	30663678	30443133	27154247
房屋工程建筑	Housing	13508448	13447643	11861851
土木工程建筑	Civil Engineering	17155230	16995491	15292396
建筑安装业	Building Installation	1641295	1562281	1347517
建筑装饰业	Building Fiting and Decoration	387764	381172	317961
其他建筑业	Other Construction	647327	642749	559600
按隶属关系分	**Grouped by Subordination**			
#中 央	Central	12398510	12353470	11240994
省	Province	6773279	6711828	5711110
地 区	Prefecture	2595313	2558798	2307860
县	County	718879	706572	623831
按企业资质等级分	**Grouped by Qualification Criteria**			
施工总承包	Overall Contract	29945258	29720898	26523569
专业承包	Specialized Contract	3394806	3308437	2855756

11-11 建筑业企业费用情况(2016年)
EXPENSES OF CONSTRUCTION ENTERPRISES(2016)

单位：万元 (10 000 yuan)

指　标	Item	销售费用 Sales Expenses	管理费用 Adminis-trative Expenses	财务费用 Financial Expenses
总　计	**Total**	**97429**	**1565024**	**214893**
#国有及国有控股	State Owned and State Controlling Share	8217	1097152	158404
按登记注册类型分	**Grouped by Registered Kind**			
内资企业	Civil Funded Enterprises	97429	1561382	214098
国有企业	State-owned Enterprises	3816	129786	10617
集体企业	Collective-owned Enterprises	1586	32080	443
股份合作企业	Share Cooperative Enterprises			
联营企业	Joint Ownership Enterprises			
有限责任公司	Limited Responsibility Corporations	16101	1043851	149771
国有独资公司	Company Exclusively with Investment from State	404	74780	65263
其他有限责任公司	Other Limited Responsibility Company	15697	969071	84508
股份有限公司	Share-holding Limited Corporations	2942	33591	8472
私营企业	Private-owned Enterprises	72984	322075	44795
私营独资企业	Enterprise Exclusively with Investment from Private	13	10	
私营合伙企业	Private Partnership Enterprises	27	73	
私营有限责任公司	Private Limited Responsibility Corporations	71552	298724	41115
私营股份有限公司	Private Share-holding Limited Corporations	1391	23268	3680
其他企业	Other Enterprises			
港、澳、台商投资企业	Enterprises Funded by HongKong, Macao and Taiwan	1	3182	796
外商投资企业	Foreign Funded Enterprises		460	-1
按国民经济行业分	**Grouped by Economic Sector**			
房屋和土木工程建筑业	Housing and Civil Engineering Construction	65311	1371823	198239
房屋工程建筑	Housing	45180	471518	71612
土木工程建筑	Civil Engineering	20131	900305	126627
建筑安装业	Building Installation	15315	112184	9074
建筑装饰业	Building Fiting and Decoration	5891	30722	3327
其他建筑业	Other Construction	10913	50296	4252
按隶属关系分	**Grouped by Subordination**			
#中　央	Central	2056	693223	53487
省	Province	1846	336137	99711
地　区	Prefecture	4270	120321	6270
县	County	7428	31683	2847
按企业资质等级分	**Grouped by Qualification Criteria**			
施工总承包	Overall Contract	59996	1323761	202961
专业承包	Specialized Contract	37433	241263	11932

11-12 建筑业企业薪酬及利润情况(2016年)
REMUNERATION AND PROFITS OF CONSTRUCTION ENTERPRISES(2016)

单位：万元 (10 000 yuan)

指　标	Item	应付职工薪酬 Remuneration Payable of Staff and Workers	营业利润 Business Profits	其他业务利润 Profits of Other Business
总　计	**Total**	**2513761**	**950924**	**33556**
#国有及国有控股	State Owned and State Controlling Share	1391905	607283	19325
按登记注册类型分	**Grouped by Registered Kind**			
内资企业	Civil Funded Enterprises	2507526	949689	32838
国有企业	State-owned Enterprises	241583	11077	9532
集体企业	Collective-owned Enterprises	59073	7937	1451
股份合作企业	Share Cooperative Enterprises			
联营企业	Joint Ownership Enterprises			
有限责任公司	Limited Responsibility Corporations	1369849	669719	11880
国有独资公司	Company Exclusively with Investment from State	97072	57469	3045
其他有限责任公司	Other Limited Responsibility Company	1272777	612250	8835
股份有限公司	Share-holding Limited Corporations	39805	16618	313
私营企业	Private-owned Enterprises	797216	244338	9663
私营独资企业	Enterprise Exclusively with Investment from Private	215	454	
私营合伙企业	Private Partnership Enterprises	72	-1	
私营有限责任公司	Private Limited Responsibility Corporations	706735	222631	7648
私营股份有限公司	Private Share-holding Limited Corporations	90194	21253	2015
其他企业	Other Enterprises			
港、澳、台商投资企业	Enterprises Funded by HongKong，Macao and Taiwan	4835	903	718
外商投资企业	Foreign Funded Enterprises	1400	332	1
按国民经济行业分	**Grouped by Economic Sector**			
房屋和土木工程建筑业	Housing and Civil Engineering Construction	2253884	882566	27880
房屋工程建筑	Housing	1012536	261282	12722
土木工程建筑	Civil Engineering	1241348	621284	15158
建筑安装业	Building Installation	160044	47300	4649
建筑装饰业	Building Fiting and Decoration	43919	15273	658
其他建筑业	Other Construction	55915	5785	370
按隶属关系分	**Grouped by Subordination**			
#中　央	Central	795996	451382	7126
省	Province	441161	115425	11208
地　区	Prefecture	215322	51303	1931
县	County	125950	13955	1059
按企业资质等级分	**Grouped by Qualification Criteria**			
施工总承包	Overall Contract	2184043	830629	26787
专业承包	Specialized Contract	329718	120295	6769

11-13 建筑业企业利润及税金情况(2016年)
PROFITS AND TAXES OF CONSTRUCTION ENTERPRISES(2016)

单位：万元 (10 000 yuan)

指 标	Item	利润总额 Total Profits	税金总额 Total Taxes	主营业务税金及附加 Taxes and Extra Charges of Major Business	管理费用中的税金 Taxes in Costs of Adminis-tration	应交增值税 Value-added Taxes Payable
总 计	**Total**	**972077**	**506539**	**477373**	**29166**	**396567**
#国有及国有控股	State Owned and State Controlling Share	628075	211446	200803	10643	232158
按登记注册类型分	**Grouped by Registered Kind**					
内资企业	Civil Funded Enterprises	970893	505786	476655	29131	395865
国有企业	State-owned Enterprises	20793	47885	44904	2981	48441
集体企业	Collective-owned Enterprises	8391	10881	9963	918	3680
股份合作企业	Share Cooperative Enterprises					
联营企业	Joint Ownership Enterprises					
有限责任公司	Limited Responsibility Corporations	682497	221768	210244	11524	214048
国有独资公司	Company Exclusively with Investment from State	58028	27527	26705	822	29442
其他有限责任公司	Other Limited Responsibility Company	624468	194241	183539	10702	184606
股份有限公司	Share-holding Limited Corporations	17361	6331	5584	747	5885
私营企业	Private-owned Enterprises	241852	218922	205960	12962	123812
私营独资企业	Enterprise Exclusively with Investment from Private	454	21	20	2	
私营合伙企业	Private Partnership Enterprises	-1	64	32	32	25
私营有限责任公司	Private Limited Responsibility Corporations	220198	181670	169890	11781	93720
私营股份有限公司	Private Share-holding Limited Corporations	21200	37166	36019	1147	30067
其他企业	Other Enterprises					
港、澳、台商投资企业	Enterprises Funded by HongKong, Macao and Taiwan	919	397	386	11	8
外商投资企业	Foreign Funded Enterprises	265	356	332	23	694
按国民经济行业分	**Grouped by Economic Sector**					
房屋和土木工程建筑业	Housing and Civil Engineering Construction	896178	454863	431377	23486	363584
房屋工程建筑	Housing	266417	251124	239044	12080	201667
土木工程建筑	Civil Engineering	629761	203739	192333	11406	161917
建筑安装业	Building Installation	51683	29992	26779	3213	23678
建筑装饰业	Building Fiting and Decoration	15332	10201	8805	1396	3223
其他建筑业	Other Construction	8885	11483	10411	1071	6082
按隶属关系分	**Grouped by Subordination**					
#中 央	Central	458548	88273	83812	4461	70531
省	Province	128135	84483	80430	4053	139677
地 区	Prefecture	53013	49864	47136	2728	28773
县	County	14461	20736	19560	1176	8414
按企业资质等级分	**Grouped by Qualification Criteria**					
施工总承包	Overall Contract	843653	439938	418003	21936	363102
专业承包	Specialized Contract	128424	66600	59370	7230	33465

主要统计指标解释

签订的合同额 指建筑业企业在报告期直接同建设单位签订合同的总价款和以前年度同建设单位签订的各种国内工程合同的未完工程跨入本年度继续施工工程合同的总价款余额。

本年新签合同额 指建筑业企业在报告期内同建设单位直接新签订的各种国内工程合同的总价款，不包括与其他建筑业企业新签的分包合同额。

建筑业总产值 指以货币表现的建筑业企业在一定时期内生产的建筑业产品和服务的总和。建筑业总产值包括建筑工程产值、安装工程产值和其他产值三部分内容。

竣工产值 一般是以单位工程为对象，当该工程按照设计所规定的工程内容全部完成，达到了设计规定的交工条件，经有关部门检查验收鉴定合格的单位工程价值，即为竣工产值。竣工产值包括范围应是报告期内竣工单位工程从开工到竣工的全部自行完成的价值，竣工产值不包括附属辅助企业或内部核算的其他单位为外单位生产和服务的价值。

房屋施工面积 指报告期内施工的全部房屋建筑面积，它包括本期新开工的房屋建筑面积、上期跨入本期继续施工的房屋建筑面积、上期停缓建在本期恢复施工的房屋建筑面积、本期竣工的房屋建筑面积以及本期施工后又停缓建的房屋建筑面积。

房屋竣工面积 指在报告期内房屋建筑按照设计要求已全部完工，达到住人和使用条件，经验收鉴定合格或达到竣工验收标准，可正式移交使用的各栋房屋建筑面积总和。

房屋竣工价值 指在报告期内按规定已经上报竣工的房屋本身的建造价值。一般按房屋设计和预算规定的内容计算。一般按结算价格（或中标价）计算。

固定资产合计 指企业为生产商品、提供劳务、出租或经营管理而持有的，使用寿命超过一个会计年度的有形资产。包括使用期限超过一年的房屋、建筑物、机器、机械、运输工具以及其他与生产、经营有关的设备、器具、工具等。

资产总计 指企业过去的交易或者事项形成的、由企业拥有或者控制的、预期会给企业带来经济利益的资源。资产一般按流动性分为流动资产和非流动资产。

执行 2006 年《企业会计准则》的企业：资产合计 ＝ 流动资产合计 ＋ 非流动资产合计；

未执行 2006 年《企业会计准则》的企业：资产合计 ＝ 流动资产合计 ＋ 长期投资 ＋ 固定资产合计 ＋ 无形及递延资产小计 ＋ 其他资产。

负债合计 指企业过去的交易或者事项形成的，预期会导致经济利益流出企业的现时义务。负债一般按偿还期长短分为流动负债和非流动负债。

所有者权益合计 指企业资产扣除负债后由所有者享有的剩余权益。公司的所有者权益又称股东权益。包括实收资本、资本公积、盈余公积、未分配利润等。

主营业务收入 指企业确认的销售商品、提供劳务等主营业务的收入。

执行 2006 年《企业会计准则》的企业，如未设置该科目，以“营业收入”代替填报。

销售费用 指企业从事施工生产活动过程中发生的各项费用，包括应由企业负担的运输费、装卸费、包装费、保险费、维修费、展览费、差旅费、广告费和其他经费。

营业利润 指企业从事生产经营活动所取得的利润。

执行 2006 年《企业会计准则》的企业，营业利润为营业收入减去营业成本、营业税金及附加、销售费用、管理费用、财务费用、资产减值损失，再加上公允价值变动收益和投资收益。

未执行 2006 年《企业会计准则》的企业，营业利润为主营业务收入减去主营业务成本、主营业务税金及附加，加上其他业务利润后，再减去销售费用、管理费用、财务费用后的金额。

利润总额 指企业在一定会计期间的经营成果，是生产经营过程中各种收入扣除各种耗费后的盈余，反映企业在报告期内实现的亏盈总额。

执行 2006 年《企业会计准则》的企业，利润总额为营业利润加上营业外收入，减去营业外支出后的金额。

未执行2006年《企业会计准则》的企业，利润总额为营业利润加上投资收益、政府补助、营业外收入，再减去营业外支出后的金额。

应付职工薪酬　指企业为获得职工提供的服务而给予各种形式的报酬以及其他相关支出。包括职工工资、奖金、津贴和补贴，职工福利费，医疗保险费、养老保险费、失业保险费、工伤保险费和生育保险费等社会保险费，住房公积金，工会经费和职工教育经费，非货币性福利，因解除与职工的劳动关系给予的补偿，其他与获得职工提供的服务相关的支出。

Explanatory Notes on Main Statistical Indicators

Contract Amount Signed refers to the contract total amount that construction enterprises signed directly with the constructed units in the reference period and the remaining sum of contract amount for domestic projects that construction enterprises signed in the previous years, with construction project are in process and extending to continue in current year.

Contract Amount Newly Signed This Year refers to total amount of domestic project contracts that construction enterprises newly signed directly with constructed units in the reference period, excluding subcontracts that construction enterprises newly signed with other construction enterprises.

Gross Output Value of Construction refers to total of construction products and services, expressed in money terms, completed by construction enterprises during a given period of time. It includes three parts: output value of construction projects, output value of installation projects and output value of others.

Output Value of Buildings Completed refers to the value of unit project that is completed in accordance with the requirements of the design, up to the standard for handing in, and has been checked and accepted by concerned departments as qualified one. It includes entire value of the completed project from start to completing in the reference period. If a project is under construction in two years, the output value of building completed should include completed value last year. Some large projects, such as large factory building, senior hotel, pipelines, roads, railways, which can be constructed by span, layer or fragment and can be put into use separately by contract, can calculate their output value separately. It excludes the value of products and services which affiliated enterprises or other inner accounting units provide to outer units.

Floor Space of Buildings under Construction refers to total floor space of buildings under construction during the reference period, including newly started buildings, buildings started earlier and continued during the reference period, and buildings suspended earlier but restarted during the reference period, buildings completed during the reference period, and buildings under construction and then suspended during the reference period.

Floor Space of Buildings Completed refers to the floor space of buildings that are completed in the reference period in accordance with the requirement of the design, up to the standard for being resided in and put into use, and have been checked and accepted by concerned departments as qualified ones or up to the standard of buildings completed and can be handed over fore putting into use.

Value of Buildings Completed refers to the constructing value of buildings which have reported completing in accordance with the requirement in reference period. Generally, it calculates by stipulated items in design and budget. It can report in term of settling value or value of attaining contract.

Total Fixed Assets refer to tangible assets enterprises possess for production, service supplying, leasing or management, with life operation is longer than a fiscal year. Total Fixed Assets include houses, buildings, machines, machineries, transport tools and other relevant equipments, appliances and tools which use longer than a year.

Total Assets refer to resources, formed by former transaction or events, owned or controlled by enterprises, and it can bring economic profits in future. Total assets normally include liquid assets and illiquid assets.

For enterprises implement Accounting Standards of 2006,

Total Assets = Liquid Assets + Illiquid Assets.

For enterprises don't implement Accounting Standards of 2006,

Total Assets = Liquid Assets + Long Term Investment + Fixed Assets + Intangible Assets + Deferred Assets + Other Assets.

Total Liabilities refer to the debts, formed by former transaction or events, and it can bring economic profits in future. The liabilities include liability include liquid liabilities and illiquid liabilities by terms of repayment.

Creditors' Equity refers to the residual equity enjoyed by the owners, which equals to assets deducting liabilities, including capital hold, capital accumulation fund, surplus accumulation fund and undistributed profit.

Revenue of Major Business refers to enterprises confirmed revenue of products sales, services supply and so on.

It is can be substituted by business revenue for enterprises implementing Accounting Standards of 2006 which don't set the account.

Sales Expenses refer to kinds of costs through constructing activities, which include costs of transport, loading and unloading, packing, insurance, maintaining, showing, business trip, advertisement and others.

Profits of Business refer to profits realized through the business of enterprises.

For enterprises implement Accounting Standards of 2006, profits of business equal to business revenue minus business costs, business taxes and extra charges, costs of sales, administrative expenses, fiscal costs, assets devaluation, and plus proceeds of changes in fair value and investment income.

For enterprises don't implement Accounting Standards of 2006, profits of business equal to business revenue of major business minus business costs of major business, taxes and extra charges of major business, plus other business profits, and minus costs of sales, administrative expenses, and fiscal costs.

Total Profits refer to business results of enterprises in a certain account period, i.e. enterprises' business surplus of income deduct losses in the production and operation process, reflecting total profits and losses during the reference period.

For enterprises implement Accounting Standards of 2006, total profits equal business profits plus non-business income, and minus non-business expenses.

For enterprises don't implement Accounting Standards of 2006, total profits equal business profits plus investment income, government subsidies, non-business income, and minus non-business expenses.

Remuneration Payable of Staff and Workers refers to all kinds of payments and other relevant expenditures that enterprises pay for getting services of staff and workers. It includes wages, bonus, allowances, subsides, welfare fees, health insurance premiums, endowment insurance premiums, unemployment insurance premiums, employment injury insurance premiums, birth insurance premiums, housing provident funds, labor union expenditures, educational expenditures, non-monetary welfare, compensation for terminal labor relations and other relevant expenditures.

12 房地产

REAL ESTATE

资料整理人员

郝志军　芦巧娟

房地产
REAL ESTATE

房地产开发投资	Investment in Real Estate Development	1597.4	亿元	(100 million yuan)
#住　宅	Residential Buildings	1141.1	亿元	(100 million yuan)
房地产施工面积	Floor Space of Buildings under Construction	17069.3	万平方米	(10 000 sq.m)
#住　宅	Residential Buildings	12222.3	万平方米	(10 000 sq.m)
房地产竣工面积	Floor Space of Buildings Completed	2683.6	万平方米	(10 000 sq.m)
#住　宅	Residential Buildings	2042.2	万平方米	(10 000 sq.m)

房地产开发投资构成（亿元）

Composition of Investment in Real Estate Development (100 million yuan)

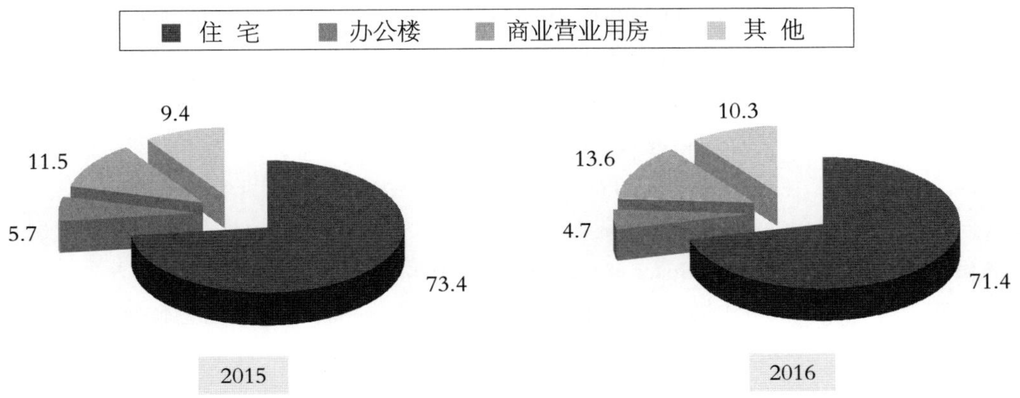

房地产开发投资（亿元）

Investment in Real Estate Development (100 million yuan)

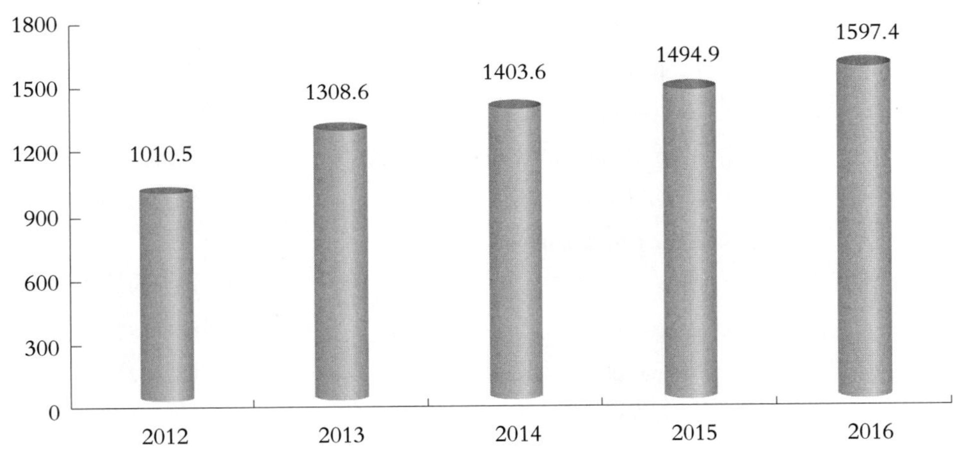

12-1 房地产开发企业主要指标
MAJOR INDICATORS OF REAL ESTATE DEVELOPMENT ENTERPRISES

单位：万元 (10 000 yuan)

指 标	Item	2015	2016
一、企业个数(个)	**Number of Enterprises (unit)**	**2430**	**2485**
二、本年完成投资	**Investment Completed This Year**	**14948719**	**15973532**
按工程用途分	Grouped by Use of Projects		
住 宅	Residential Buildings	10983176	11410813
办公楼	Office Buildings	855037	751536
商业营业用房	Buildings for Business Operation	1712127	2172920
其 他	Other Expenses	1398379	1638263
三、本年新增固定资产	**Newly Increased Fixed Assets This Year**	**6198568**	**8097180**
四、本年购置土地面积(平方米)	**Land Area Purchased This Year (sq.m)**	**4316647**	**3517434**
五、本年实际到位资金小计	**Total Actual Funds in Place This Year**	**14426669**	**15880181**
国内贷款	Domestic Loans	1088204	983256
自筹资金	Self-raised Fund	8093145	8110570
其他资金来源	Others	5245320	6786355
六、房屋建筑面积(平方米)	**Floor Space of Buildings (sq.m)**		
房屋施工面积	Floor Space of Buildings Under Construction	157344838	170692512
#住 宅	Residential Buildings	114499658	122223158
本年新开工面积	Floor Space of Buildings Newly Started Construction This Year	37006361	38547826
#住 宅	Residential Buildings	26246379	26542830
房屋竣工面积	Floor Space of Buildings Completed	21144870	26835885
#住 宅	Residential Buildings	15746777	20422192
七、商品房销售(平方米)	**Selling of Commercial Buildings (sq.m)**		
商品房销售面积	Floor Space of Commercial Buildings Sold	15925530	20610554
#住 宅	Residential Buildings	14811355	18815060
商品房销售额(万元)	Sales of Commercial Buildings (10 000 yuan)	7756381	10271364
#住 宅	Residential Buildings	7022858	9007879
八、经营状况	**Operation Condition**		
资产总计	Total Assets	70521791	81911104
营业收入	Business Revenue	6450182	9039089
#主营业务收入	Revenue of Major Business	6336522	8660816
营业利润	Business Profits	86751	304816
利润总额	Total Profits	94876	290414
九、从业人员平均人数(人)	**Average Number of Employees (person)**	**58757**	**56305**

12-2 房地产开发企业完成投资
COMPLETED INVESTMENT OF REAL ESTATE ENTERPRISES

单位：万元 (10 000 yuan)

年 份 Year	本年完成投资 Investement Completed This Year	住 宅 Residential Buildings	办公楼 Office Buildings	商业营业用房 Buildings for Business Operation	其 他 Others
1990	28486	24635	342	2108	1401
1991	32642	27132			5510
1992	51869	41963	1473	1451	6982
1993	129685	102732		2362	24591
1994	116512	87606	2964	6169	19773
1995	150866	101914	12353	13841	22758
1996	147893	107111	6442	7471	26869
1997	181736	151687	6258	6990	16801
1998	278653	199862	9774	21609	47408
1999	350458	270496	7771	30307	41884
2000	394556	272280	19201	48178	54897
2001	466464	288916	17639	67861	92048
2002	674331	369041	46104	88518	170668
2003	950740	473991	53641	211630	211478
2004	1449898	846989	110917	353485	138507
2005	1779937	1168931	107448	274199	229359
2006	2086231	1558224	83778	238224	206005
2007	2589251	1902509	51973	245495	389274
2008	3279807	2287311	81888	389808	520800
2009	4772748	3778904	106264	437877	449703
2010	5922376	4574340	125367	604588	618081
2011	7901982	6153199	172888	736434	839461
2012	10104513	7356137	227958	1392518	1127900
2013	13086275	9588469	484284	1825554	1187968
2014	14035549	10106901	692123	1913124	1323401
2015	14948719	10983176	855037	1712127	1398379
2016	15973532	11410813	751536	2172920	1638263

12-3 房地产开发企业施工、销售和待售情况(2016年)

指　标	Item	合计 Total	住宅 Residential Buildings
房屋施工面积 (平方米)	Floor Space of Buildings under Construction (sq.m)	170692512	122223158
#本年新开工面积	Buildings Newly Started Construction This Year	38547826	26542830
房屋竣工面积 (平方米)	Floor Space of Buildings Completed (sq.m)	26835885	20422192
#不可销售面积	Buildings Unable to be Sold	3274687	1955545
住宅竣工套数 (套)	Sets of Residential Buildings Completed (set)		178002
房屋竣工价值 (万元)	Value of Buildings Completed (10 000 yuan)	7855668	6057657
房屋出租面积 (平方米)	Floor Space of Buildings Leased (sq.m)	392750	20120
商品房销售面积(平方米)	Floor Space of Commercial Residential Buildings Sold (sq.m)	20610554	18815060
现　房	Completed Buildings	7969531	7046912
期　房	Forward Delivery Buildings	12641023	11768148
商品房销售额 (万元)	Sales of Commercial Buildings (10 000 yuan)	10271364	9007879
现　房	Completed Buildings	3153067	2672402
期　房	Forward Delivery Buildings	7118297	6335477
商品住宅销售套数(套)	Sets of Commercial Residential Buildings Sold (set)		166423
现　房	Completed Buildings		63080
期　房	Forward Delivery Buildings		103343
待售面积 (平方米)	Floor Space for Sale (sq.m)	17610298	12342732
#待售1-3年面积	Floor Space for Sale in 1-3 Years	7036040	4986551
待售3年以上面积	Floor Space for Sale More Than 3 Years	431982	334496

BUILDINGS UNDER CONSTRUCTION, SELLING AND FOR SALE OF REAL ESTATE DEVELOPMENT ENTERPRISES(2016)

#90平方米及以下住房 90 sq.m and Below	#144平方米以上住房 Above 144 sq.m	#别墅、高档公寓 Villas and High-grade Apartment Buildings	办公楼 Office Buildings	商业营业用房 Buildings for Business Operation	其 他 Others
27238318	21080384	1375477	6074722	21501258	20893374
5843888	3514569	183615	1577271	4942784	5484941
4066375	4428892	348217	420398	2984187	3009108
626873	246970	150568	49327	424305	845510
50716	24327	654			
1198367	1688165	191471	134403	971565	692043
15857			6306	331699	34625
3006168	3318801	188823	386227	986882	422385
1386775	1466250	15139	47742	599753	275124
1619393	1852551	173684	338485	387129	147261
1282270	2017101	188665	334819	798263	130403
454726	723892	10450	31374	382873	66418
827544	1293209	178215	303445	415390	63985
36977	19167	1307			
17052	8613	83			
19925	10554	1224			
2643306	2712477	129748	415393	3097638	1754535
1256660	1194743	57832	237328	1261585	550576
2465	188429	26700	6133	88064	3289

12-4 房地产开发企业投资完成情况(2016年)

单位：万元

指　标	Item	企业个数 (个) Number of Enterprises (unit)
总　计	**Total**	**2485**
按登记注册类型	**Grouped by Type of Registration Status**	
内　资	Domestic-Funded Enterprises	2465
国　有	State-owned Enterprises	63
集　体	Collective-owned Enterprises	7
股份合作	Share Cooperative Enterprises	
国有联营	State Joint Ownership Enterprises	
集体联营	Collective Joint Ownership Enterprises	
国有与集体联营	Joint State-collective Enterprises	
其他联营	Other Joint Ownership Enterprises	
国有独资公司	State-funded Corporations	38
其他有限责任公司	Other Limited Liability Corporations	468
股份有限公司	Share Corporations Ltd.	23
私营独资	Private-funded Enterprises	
私营合伙	Private Partnership Enterprises	
私营有限责任公司	Private Limited Liability Corporations	1813
私营股份有限公司	Private Share-holding Corporations Ltd.	53
其　他	Others	
港澳台投资	Enterprises with Investment from Hong Kong, Macao and Taiwan	13
合资经营	Joint-venture Enterprises	8
合作经营	Cooperative Enterprises	
独　资	Enterprises with Sole Investment	3
股份有限	Share Corporations Ltd.	1
其　他	Others	1
外商投资	Enterprises with Foreign Investment	7
合资经营	Joint-Venture Enterprises	3
合作经营	Cooperative Enterprises	
独　资	Enterprises with Sole Foreign Investment	3
股份有限	Share Corporations Ltd.	1
其　他	Others	
按控股情况分	**Grouped by Share Holding**	
国有控股	State Holding Enterprises	209
集体控股	Collective-owned Holding Enterprises	41
私人控股	Private Holding Enterprises	2110
港澳台商控股	Hongkong, Macao and Taiwan Holding Enterprises	7
外商控股	Foreign Holding Enterprises	6
其　他	Others	112

COMPLETED INVESTMENT OF REAL ESTATE DEVELOPMENT ENTERPRISES(2016)

(10 000 yuan)

计划总投资 Total Planned Investment	累计完成投资 Accumulative Investment Completed	本年完成投资 Investment Completed This Year	建筑工程 Construction	安装工程 Installation
88925779	**61112272**	**15973532**	**10516027**	**2419144**
86421708	59618126	15615453	10303935	2369941
1148266	895520	326484	243897	44198
57940	60207	5055	4600	
1683216	1332482	349111	173118	33163
30524975	19301601	5307716	3218607	640299
484930	442152	145681	113900	16600
51670307	37041208	9308677	6447860	1580239
852074	544956	172729	101953	55442
1661230	797262	306364	186736	30364
1317440	535934	266569	173118	4187
195516	115428	3680	3380	300
141000	142005	32220	6343	25877
7274	3895	3895	3895	
842841	696884	51715	25356	18839
59879	49640			
742962	605849	43728	17369	18839
40000	41395	7987	7987	
18316793	11712908	3414394	1932606	308906
864951	710947	117615	86026	5847
61894518	43425441	11394462	7908072	1906992
1127516	490435	202902	87180	26458
886032	736824	73655	34356	31779
5835969	4035717	770504	467787	139162

12-4 续表1

单位：万元

指　标	Item	设备工器具购置 Purchase of Equipment and Instruments
总　计	**Total**	**221372**
按登记注册类型	**Grouped by Type of Registration Status**	
内　资	Domestic-Funded Enterprises	213872
国　有	State-owned Enterprises	4526
集　体	Collective-owned Enterprises	
股份合作	Share Cooperative Enterprises	
国有联营	State Joint Ownership Enterprises	
集体联营	Collective Joint Ownership Enterprises	
国有与集体联营	Joint State-collective Enterprises	
其他联营	Other Joint Ownership Enterprises	
国有独资公司	State-funded Corporations	2726
其他有限责任公司	Other Limited Liability Corporations	56436
股份有限公司	Share Corporations Ltd.	900
私营独资	Private-funded Enterprises	
私营合伙	Private Partnership Enterprises	
私营有限责任公司	Private Limited Liability Corporations	149284
私营股份有限公司	Private Share-holding Corporations Ltd.	
其　他	Others	
港澳台投资	Enterprises with Investment from Hong Kong, Macao and Taiwan	
合资经营	Joint-venture Enterprises	
合作经营	Cooperative Enterprises	
独　资	Enterprises with Sole Investment	
股份有限	Share Corporations Ltd.	
其　他	Others	
外商投资	Enterprises with Foreign Investment	7500
合资经营	Joint-Venture Enterprises	
合作经营	Cooperative Enterprises	
独　资	Enterprises with Sole Foreign Investment	7500
股份有限	Share Corporations Ltd.	
其　他	Others	
按控股情况分	**Grouped by Share Holding**	
国有控股	State Holding Enterprises	36061
集体控股	Collective-owned Holding Enterprises	2180
私人控股	Private Holding Enterprises	166950
港澳台商控股	Hongkong, Macao and Taiwan Holding Enterprises	
外商控股	Foreign Holding Enterprises	7500
其　他	Others	8681

continued

(10 000 yuan)

其他费用 Other Expenses	#旧建筑物 购置费 Purchse of old Building	#土 地 购置费 Purchase of Land	住 宅 Residential Buildings	#90平方米及 以下住房 90 sq.m and Below
2816989	**59115**	**1695670**	**11410813**	**3360824**
2727705	59115	1624117	11306607	3327260
33863		22880	246128	116730
455			4875	2906
140104		127987	231030	70215
1392374	19202	662625	4190705	1368823
14281		11878	117562	50760
1131294	39813	783930	6365557	1675351
15334	100	14817	150750	42475
89264		71553	76439	16933
89264		71553	44480	16353
			2810	
			25754	
			3395	580
20			27767	16631
20			20978	16631
			6789	
1136821	15236	473293	2772668	1175208
23562	39	19523	96715	9715
1412448	41302	1016599	7831316	1986410
89264		71553	56691	
20			49707	18631
154874	2538	114702	603716	170860

12-4 续表2

单位：万元

指　标	Item	#144平方米以上住房 Above 144 sq.m
总　计	**Total**	**1686018**
按登记注册类型	**Grouped by Type of Registration Status**	
内　资	Domestic-Funded Enterprises	1630947
国　有	State-owned Enterprises	10325
集　体	Collective-owned Enterprises	
股份合作	Share Cooperative Enterprises	
国有联营	State Joint Ownership Enterprises	
集体联营	Collective Joint Ownership Enterprises	
国有与集体联营	Joint State-collective Enterprises	
其他联营	Other Joint Ownership Enterprises	
国有独资公司	State-funded Corporations	6126
其他有限责任公司	Other Limited Liability Corporations	568288
股份有限公司	Share Corporations Ltd.	16178
私营独资	Private-funded Enterprises	
私营合伙	Private Partnership Enterprises	
私营有限责任公司	Private Limited Liability Corporations	1009100
私营股份有限公司	Private Share-holding Corporations Ltd.	20930
其　他	Others	
港澳台投资	Enterprises with Investment from Hong Kong, Macao and Taiwan	54394
合资经营	Joint-venture Enterprises	28127
合作经营	Cooperative Enterprises	
独　资	Enterprises with Sole Investment	513
股份有限	Share Corporations Ltd.	25754
其　他	Others	
外商投资	Enterprises with Foreign Investment	677
合资经营	Joint-Venture Enterprises	
合作经营	Cooperative Enterprises	
独　资	Enterprises with Sole Foreign Investment	677
股份有限	Share Corporations Ltd.	
其　他	Others	
按控股情况分	**Grouped by Share Holding**	
国有控股	State Holding Enterprises	198939
集体控股	Collective-owned Holding Enterprises	12308
私人控股	Private Holding Enterprises	1308138
港澳台商控股	Hongkong, Macao and Taiwan Holding Enterprises	54394
外商控股	Foreign Holding Enterprises	18617
其　他	Others	93622

continued

(10 000 yuan)

#别墅、高档公寓 Villas and Highgrade Apartment Buildings	办公楼 Office Buildings	商业营业用房 Buildings for Business Operation	其 他 Others	本年新增固定资产 Newly Increased Fixed Assets This Year
94015	**751536**	**2172920**	**1638263**	**8097180**
68261	631330	2144198	1533318	7935188
	7988	20501	51867	158892
		96	84	
	50761	21863	45457	126804
47137	164173	480641	472197	2544757
10	1000	8016	19103	
16734	400668	1602447	940005	5063433
4380	6740	10634	4605	41302
25754	114206	18706	97013	154005
	114206	18028	89855	
		278	592	12000
25754			6466	142005
		400	100	
	6000	10016	7932	7987
	6000	8818	7932	
		1198		7987
18480	222247	204463	215016	1028654
	2525	12071	6304	101066
31882	476052	1853427	1233667	5698439
25754	36490	12808	96913	154005
	6000	10016	7932	7987
17899	8222	80135	78431	1107029

12-5 房地产开发企业资金来源情况(2016年)

单位：万元

指　标	Item	本年实际到位资金合计 Total Actual Funds in Place This Year	上年末结余资金 Remaining Funds at The End of Last Year
总　计	**Total**	**20308236**	**4428055**
按登记注册类型	**Grouped by Type of Registration Status**		
内　资	Domestic-Funded Enterprises	19874772	4268313
国　有	State-owned Enterprises	321669	34857
集　体	Collective-owned Enterprises	5180	572
股份合作	Share Cooperative Enterprises		
国有联营	State Joint Ownership Enterprises		
集体联营	Collective Joint Ownership Enterprises		
国有与集体联营	Joint State-collective Enterprises		
其他联营	Other Joint Ownership Enterprises		
国有独资公司	State-funded Corporations	739615	261625
其他有限责任公司	Other Limited Liability Corporations	6459066	1509487
股份有限公司	Share Corporations Ltd.	160484	10647
私营独资	Private-funded Enterprises		
私营合伙	Private Partnership Enterprises		
私营有限责任公司	Private Limited Liability Corporations	12021498	2448578
私营股份有限公司	Private Share-holding Corporations Ltd.	167260	2547
其　他	Others		
港澳台投资	Enterprises with Investment from Hong Kong, Macao and Taiwan	335999	110124
合资经营	Joint-venture Enterprises	295661	109981
合作经营	Cooperative Enterprises		
独　资	Enterprises with Sole Investment	4223	143
股份有限	Share Corporations Ltd.	32220	
其　他	Others	3895	
外商投资	Enterprises with Foreign Investment	97465	49618
合资经营	Joint-Venture Enterprises		
合作经营	Cooperative Enterprises		
独　资	Enterprises with Sole Foreign Investment	81397	37669
股份有限	Share Corporations Ltd.	16068	11949
其　他	Others		
按控股情况分	**Grouped by Share Holding**		
国有控股	State Holding Enterprises	3829073	1166193
集体控股	Collective-owned Holding Enterprises	242804	87774
私人控股	Private Holding Enterprises	14785185	2920579
港澳台商控股	Hongkong, Macao and Taiwan Holding Enterprises	207069	97701
外商控股	Foreign Holding Enterprises	119405	49618
其　他	Others	1124700	106190

SOURCE OF FUNDS FOR REAL ESTATE DEVELOPMENT ENTERPRISES(2016)

(10 000 yuan)

本年实际到位资金小计 Subtotal Actual Funds in Place This Year	国内贷款 Domestic Loans	自筹资金 Self-raised Funds	其他资金来源 Others	#定金及预付款 Deposit and Advanced Payment	#个人按揭贷款 Individual Mortgage
15880181	**983256**	**8110570**	**6786355**	**4248347**	**1880829**
15606459	955869	7983617	6666973	4138403	1871391
286812		255358	31454	13406	
4608		4608			
477990		232250	245740	167568	67472
4949579	456773	2231295	2261511	1489481	477907
149837	16400	68315	65122	60419	3213
9572920	445217	5124345	4003358	2352284	1318256
164713	37479	67446	59788	55245	4543
225875	13107	106943	105825	105825	
185680	3000	76855	105825	105825	
4080		4080			
32220	10107	22113			
3895		3895			
47847	14280	20010	13557	4119	9438
43728	14280	20010	9438		9438
4119			4119	4119	
2662880	234306	1353820	1074754	811611	145322
155030	2000	43055	109975	56925	39790
11864606	682136	6161296	5021174	3059397	1541173
109368	13107	81193	15068	15068	
69787	14280	41950	13557	4119	9438
1018510	37427	429256	551827	301227	145106

12-6 房地产开发企业土地购置、开发和待售情况(2016年)

单位：平方米

指　标	Item	待开发土地面积 Land Area Pending Development
总　计	**Total**	**6032882**
按登记注册类型	**Grouped by Type of Registration Status**	
内　资	Domestic-Funded Enterprises	5837108
国　有	State-owned Enterprises	
集　体	Collective-owned Enterprises	
股份合作	Share Cooperative Enterprises	
国有联营	State Joint Ownership Enterprises	
集体联营	Collective Joint Ownership Enterprises	
国有与集体联营	Joint State-collective Enterprises	
其他联营	Other Joint Ownership Enterprises	
国有独资公司	State-funded Corporations	264780
其他有限责任公司	Other Limited Liability Corporations	1568304
股份有限公司	Share Corporations Ltd.	
私营独资	Private-funded Enterprises	
私营合伙	Private Partnership Enterprises	
私营有限责任公司	Private Limited Liability Corporations	3974381
私营股份有限公司	Private Share-holding Corporations Ltd.	29643
其　他	Others	
港澳台投资	Enterprises with Investment from Hong Kong, Macao and Taiwan	195774
合资经营	Joint-venture Enterprises	195774
合作经营	Cooperative Enterprises	
独　资	Enterprises with Sole Investment	
股份有限	Share Corporations Ltd.	
其　他	Others	
外商投资	Enterprises with Foreign Investment	
合资经营	Joint-Venture Enterprises	
合作经营	Cooperative Enterprises	
独　资	Enterprises with Sole Foreign Investment	
股份有限	Share Corporations Ltd.	
其　他	Others	
按控股情况分	**Grouped by Share Holding**	
国有控股	State Holding Enterprises	634461
集体控股	Collective-owned Holding Enterprises	
私人控股	Private Holding Enterprises	4961865
港澳台商控股	Hongkong, Macao and Taiwan Holding Enterprises	195774
外商控股	Foreign Holding Enterprises	
其　他	Others	240782

LAND PURCHASING, DEVELOPING AND FOR SALE OF REAL ESTATE DEVELOPMENT ENTERPRISES(2016)

(sq.m)

本年购置土地面积 Land Area Purchased This Year	本年土地成交价款(万元) Deal Value of Land This Year (10 000 yuan)	待售面积 Land Area for Sale	#待售面积(一年至三年) Land Area for Sale in 1–3 Years	#待售面积(三年以上) Land Area for Sale More Than Three Years
3517434	**1279931**	**17610298**	**7036040**	**431982**
3321660	1173825	17546417	6984997	431982
65426	5960	252882	29485	
		6485		
390137	207349	70546	68531	
753543	448711	4260689	2372037	239214
		328159		
2085662	508439	12378004	4496965	192768
26892	3366	249652	17979	
195774	106106	59728	46890	
195774	106106	59728	46890	
		4153	4153	
		4153	4153	
803069	393305	1148852	583033	
		140278	129032	
2400309	691101	15281730	5737175	266686
195774	106106	12838		
		4153	4153	
118282	89419	1022446	582647	165296

12-7 房地产开发企业施工和销售情况(2016年)

单位：平方米

指 标	Item	房屋施工面积 Floor Space of Buildings under Construction	住 宅 Residential Buildings
总 计	**Total**	**170692512**	**122223158**
按登记注册类型	**Grouped by Type of Registration Status**		
内 资	Domestic-Funded Enterprises	166692758	120793171
国 有	State-owned Enterprises	3385539	2811396
集 体	Collective-owned Enterprises	395342	334178
股份合作	Share Cooperative Enterprises		
国有联营	State Joint Ownership Enterprises		
集体联营	Collective Joint Ownership Enterprises		
国有与集体联营	Joint State-collective Enterprises		
其他联营	Other Joint Ownership Enterprises		
国有独资公司	State-funded Corporations	3512849	2596636
其他有限责任公司	Other Limited Liability Corporations	49433839	36449305
股份有限公司	Share Corporations Ltd.	1368253	1110323
私营独资	Private-funded Enterprises		
私营合伙	Private Partnership Enterprises		
私营有限责任公司	Private Limited Liability Corporations	107042441	76279339
私营股份有限公司	Private Share-holding Corporations Ltd.	1554495	1211994
其 他	Others		
港澳台投资	Enterprises with Investment from Hong Kong, Macao and Taiwan	2735041	943969
合资经营	Joint-venture Enterprises	2149517	465080
合作经营	Cooperative Enterprises		
独 资	Enterprises with Sole Investment	309507	234560
股份有限	Share Corporations Ltd.	259036	229540
其 他	Others	16981	14789
外商投资	Enterprises with Foreign Investment	1264713	486018
合资经营	Joint-Venture Enterprises	156710	156710
合作经营	Cooperative Enterprises		
独 资	Enterprises with Sole Foreign Investment	1023772	257566
股份有限	Share Corporations Ltd.	84231	71742
其 他	Others		
按控股情况分	**Grouped by Share Holding**		
国有控股	State Holding Enterprises	28209146	20394595
集体控股	Collective-owned Holding Enterprises	1700324	1415402
私人控股	Private Holding Enterprises	127373801	91015896
港澳台商控股	Hongkong, Macao and Taiwan Holding Enterprises	1829143	830853
外商控股	Foreign Holding Enterprises	1340878	562183
其 他	Others	10239220	8004229

CONSTRUCTION AND SALES OF REAL ESTATE DEVELOPMENT ENTERPRISES(2016)

(sq.m)

#90平方米及以下住房 90 sq.m and Below	#144平方米以上住房 Above 144 sq.m	#别墅、高档公寓 Villas and High-grade Apartment Buildings	办公楼 Office Buildings	商业营业用房 Buildings for Business Operation	其　他 Others
27238318	**21080384**	**1375477**	**6074722**	**21501258**	**20893374**
26961747	20151531	1092688	4770416	20768489	20360682
1755727	48905		23848	162082	388213
190938				11495	49669
522772	21460		147224	294772	474217
7270386	6560786	524075	1615089	4580337	6789108
233811	452995			198152	59778
16615264	12871017	528590	2968808	15284027	12510267
372849	196368	40023	15447	237624	89430
113116	773931	229540	1104240	257406	429426
98327	346700		1104240	232845	347352
	197691			22807	52140
	229540	229540			29496
14789				1754	438
163455	154922	53249	200066	475363	103266
156710					
6745	154922	53249	200066	462874	103266
				12489	
5629184	3090518	385013	1732068	2326387	3756096
409740	98595		17390	91193	176339
19267220	15560175	604965	3555686	17585480	15216739
	773931	229540	417034	159255	422001
173455	164922	53249	200066	475363	103266
1758719	1392243	102710	152478	863580	1218933

12-7 续表1

单位：平方米

指 标	Item	本年新开工面积 Floor Space of Builings Newly Started Construction	住 宅 Residential Buildings
总 计	**Total**	**38547826**	**26542830**
按登记注册类型	**Grouped by Type of Registration Status**		
内 资	Domestic-Funded Enterprises	36988183	26121095
国 有	State-owned Enterprises	696730	533683
集 体	Collective-owned Enterprises		
股份合作	Share Cooperative Enterprises		
国有联营	State Joint Ownership Enterprises		
集体联营	Collective Joint Ownership Enterprises		
国有与集体联营	Joint State-collective Enterprises		
其他联营	Other Joint Ownership Enterprises		
国有独资公司	State-funded Corporations	612044	493958
其他有限责任公司	Other Limited Liability Corporations	13471973	10024746
股份有限公司	Share Corporations Ltd.	227083	187283
私营独资	Private-funded Enterprises		
私营合伙	Private Partnership Enterprises		
私营有限责任公司	Private Limited Liability Corporations	21426030	14537449
私营股份有限公司	Private Share-holding Corporations Ltd.	554323	343976
其 他	Others		
港澳台投资	Enterprises with Investment from Hong Kong, Macao and Taiwan	1234937	421735
合资经营	Joint-venture Enterprises	1167191	359677
合作经营	Cooperative Enterprises		
独 资	Enterprises with Sole Investment		
股份有限	Share Corporations Ltd.	50765	47269
其 他	Others	16981	14789
外商投资	Enterprises with Foreign Investment	324706	
合资经营	Joint-Venture Enterprises		
合作经营	Cooperative Enterprises		
独 资	Enterprises with Sole Foreign Investment	324706	
股份有限	Share Corporations Ltd.		
其 他	Others		
按控股情况分	**Grouped by Share Holding**		
国有控股	State Holding Enterprises	7102987	5635185
集体控股	Collective-owned Holding Enterprises	437569	328939
私人控股	Private Holding Enterprises	27021908	18205057
港澳台商控股	Hongkong, Macao and Taiwan Holding Enterprises	1152765	393969
外商控股	Foreign Holding Enterprises	324706	
其 他	Others	2507891	1979680

continued

(sq.m)

#90平方米及以下住房 90 sq.m and Below	#144平方米以上住房 Above 144 sq.m	#别墅、高档公寓 Villas and High-grade Apartment Buildings	办公楼 Office Buildings	商业营业用房 Buildings for Business Operation	其　他 Others
5843888	**3514569**	**183615**	**1577271**	**4942784**	**5484941**
5816122	3120600	136346	1084247	4652412	5130429
202607	28432		9380	56718	96949
227393	6753		17456	26978	73652
2335544	1205760	22731	430504	1106897	1909826
60245	10516			6313	33487
2926139	1784975	93572	611460	3309452	2967669
64194	84164	20043	15447	146054	48846
27766	393969	47269	389700	104568	318934
12977	346700		389700	102814	315000
	47269	47269			3496
14789				1754	438
			103324	185804	35578
			103324	185804	35578
1723245	587155		60710	419588	987504
10889	32846		13206	65565	29859
3756219	2401109	136346	996030	4017335	3803486
	393969	47269	389700	50600	318496
			103324	185804	35578
353535	99490		14301	203892	310018

12-7 续表2

单位：平方米

指 标	Item	房屋竣工面积 Floor Space of Buildings Completed	住宅 Residential Buildings
总 计	**Total**	**26835885**	**20422192**
按登记注册类型	**Grouped by Type of Registration Status**		
内 资	Domestic-Funded Enterprises	26480618	20108910
国 有	State-owned Enterprises	650725	506882
集 体	Collective-owned Enterprises		
股份合作	Share Cooperative Enterprises		
国有联营	State Joint Ownership Enterprises		
集体联营	Collective Joint Ownership Enterprises		
国有与集体联营	Joint State-collective Enterprises		
其他联营	Other Joint Ownership Enterprises		
国有独资公司	State-funded Corporations	446736	357376
其他有限责任公司	Other Limited Liability Corporations	7049162	5459204
股份有限公司	Share Corporations Ltd.		
私营独资	Private-funded Enterprises		
私营合伙	Private Partnership Enterprises		
私营有限责任公司	Private Limited Liability Corporations	18163516	13642848
私营股份有限公司	Private Share-holding Corporations Ltd.	170479	142600
其 他	Others		
港澳台投资	Enterprises with Investment from Hong Kong, Macao and Taiwan	271036	241540
合资经营	Joint-venture Enterprises		
合作经营	Cooperative Enterprises		
独 资	Enterprises with Sole Investment	12000	12000
股份有限	Share Corporations Ltd.	259036	229540
其 他	Others		
外商投资	Enterprises with Foreign Investment	84231	71742
合资经营	Joint-Venture Enterprises		
合作经营	Cooperative Enterprises		
独 资	Enterprises with Sole Foreign Investment		
股份有限	Share Corporations Ltd.	84231	71742
其 他	Others		
按控股情况分	**Grouped by Share Holding**		
国有控股	State Holding Enterprises	3261993	2422107
集体控股	Collective-owned Holding Enterprises	353565	292737
私人控股	Private Holding Enterprises	21012187	15805780
港澳台商控股	Hongkong, Macao and Taiwan Holding Enterprises	271036	241540
外商控股	Foreign Holding Enterprises	84231	71742
其 他	Others	1852873	1588286

continued

(sq.m)

#90平方米及以下住房 90 sq.m and Below	#144平方米以上住房 Above 144 sq.m	#别墅、高档公寓 Villas and High-grade Apartment Buildings	办公楼 Office Buildings	商业营业用房 Buildings for Business Operation	其 他 Others
4066375	**4428892**	**348217**	**420398**	**2984187**	**3009108**
4066375	4187352	118677	420398	2971698	2979612
192844	19609		10640	92087	41116
8172			13800	1155	74405
1030754	1277873	34897	74788	448279	1066891
2777035	2833978	63737	321170	2423477	1776021
57570	55892	20043		6700	21179
	241540	229540			29496
	12000				
	229540	229540			29496
				12489	
				12489	
577266	514485	34897	24440	202875	612571
47135	46586			7480	53348
3140943	3172576	83780	372225	2671914	2162268
	241540	229540			29496
				12489	
301031	453705		23733	89429	151425

12-7 续表3

单位：万元

指　标	Item	房屋竣工价值 Value of Buildings Completed	住宅 Residential Buildings
总　计	**Total**	**7855668**	**6057657**
按登记注册类型	**Grouped by Type of Registration Status**		
内　资	Domestic-Funded Enterprises	7702676	5912316
国　有	State-owned Enterprises	158444	123060
集　体	Collective-owned Enterprises		
股份合作	Share Cooperative Enterprises		
国有联营	State Joint Ownership Enterprises		
集体联营	Collective Joint Ownership Enterprises		
国有与集体联营	Joint State-collective Enterprises		
其他联营	Other Joint Ownership Enterprises		
国有独资公司	State-funded Corporations	117463	85615
其他有限责任公司	Other Limited Liability Corporations	2510771	2134316
股份有限公司	Share Corporations Ltd.		
私营独资	Private-funded Enterprises		
私营合伙	Private Partnership Enterprises		
私营有限责任公司	Private Limited Liability Corporations	4874696	3531982
私营股份有限公司	Private Share-holding Corporations Ltd.	41302	37343
其　他	Others		
港澳台投资	Enterprises with Investment from Hong Kong, Macao and Taiwan	145005	138539
合资经营	Joint-venture Enterprises		
合作经营	Cooperative Enterprises		
独　资	Enterprises with Sole Investment	3000	3000
股份有限	Share Corporations Ltd.	142005	135539
其　他	Others		
外商投资	Enterprises with Foreign Investment	7987	6802
合资经营	Joint-Venture Enterprises		
合作经营	Cooperative Enterprises		
独　资	Enterprises with Sole Foreign Investment		
股份有限	Share Corporations Ltd.	7987	6802
其　他	Others		
按控股情况分	**Grouped by Share Holding**		
国有控股	State Holding Enterprises	1014145	793143
集体控股	Collective-owned Holding Enterprises	99539	93453
私人控股	Private Holding Enterprises	5499307	3987759
港澳台商控股	Hongkong, Macao and Taiwan Holding Enterprises	145005	138539
外商控股	Foreign Holding Enterprises	7987	6802
其　他	Others	1089685	1037961

continued

(10 000 yuan)

#90平方米及以下住房 90 sq.m and Below	#144平方米以上住房 Above 144 sq.m	#别墅、高档公寓 Villas and High-grade Apartment Buildings	办公楼 Office Buildings	商业营业用房 Buildings for Business Operation	其 他 Others
1198367	**1688165**	**191471**	**134403**	**971565**	**692043**
1198367	1549626	55932	134403	970380	685577
44260	5582		2934	24195	8255
1315			12666	231	18951
455554	597908	16359	20211	160975	195269
687762	923574	17593	98592	783810	460312
9476	22562	21980		1169	2790
	138539	135539			6466
	3000				
	135539	135539			6466
				1185	
				1185	
249987	151312	16359	15600	63481	141921
10816	36929			1862	4224
778550	997368	39573	110488	874515	526545
	138539	135539			6466
				1185	
159014	364017		8315	30522	12887

12-7 续表4

单位：平方米

指　标	Item	商品房销售面积 Floor Space of Commercial Buildings Sold	住　宅 Residential Buildings
总　计	**Total**	**20610554**	**18815060**
按登记注册类型	**Grouped by Type of Registration Status**		
内　资	Domestic-Funded Enterprises	20423375	18730036
国　有	State-owned Enterprises	786217	755951
集　体	Collective-owned Enterprises	37848	37848
股份合作	Share Cooperative Enterprises		
国有联营	State Joint Ownership Enterprises		
集体联营	Collective Joint Ownership Enterprises		
国有与集体联营	Joint State-collective Enterprises		
其他联营	Other Joint Ownership Enterprises		
国有独资公司	State-funded Corporations	531434	517098
其他有限责任公司	Other Limited Liability Corporations	6012025	5303094
股份有限公司	Share Corporations Ltd.	151526	117222
私营独资	Private-funded Enterprises		
私营合伙	Private Partnership Enterprises		
私营有限责任公司	Private Limited Liability Corporations	12621689	11739071
私营股份有限公司	Private Share-holding Corporations Ltd.	282636	259752
其　他	Others		
港澳台投资	Enterprises with Investment from Hong Kong, Macao and Taiwan	133996	34324
合资经营	Joint-venture Enterprises	99672	
合作经营	Cooperative Enterprises		
独　资	Enterprises with Sole Investment	12000	12000
股份有限	Share Corporations Ltd.	22324	22324
其　他	Others		
外商投资	Enterprises with Foreign Investment	53183	50700
合资经营	Joint-Venture Enterprises		
合作经营	Cooperative Enterprises		
独　资	Enterprises with Sole Foreign Investment	53183	50700
股份有限	Share Corporations Ltd.		
其　他	Others		
按控股情况分	**Grouped by Share Holding**		
国有控股	State Holding Enterprises	2840273	2534913
集体控股	Collective-owned Holding Enterprises	269540	267619
私人控股	Private Holding Enterprises	15979166	14572155
港澳台商控股	Hongkong, Macao and Taiwan Holding Enterprises	34324	34324
外商控股	Foreign Holding Enterprises	53183	50700
其　他	Others	1434068	1355349

continued

(sq.m)

#90平方米及以下住房 90 sq.m and Below	#144平方米以上住房 Above 144 sq.m	#别墅、高档公寓 Villas and High-grade Apartment Buildings	办公楼 Office Buildings	商业营业用房 Buildings for Business Operation	其　他 Others
3006168	**3318801**	**188823**	**386227**	**986882**	**422385**
3006054	3273846	166499	287034	983920	422385
144222	15584		4514	24527	1225
33693	78720			7651	6685
835783	949828	143770	175069	364735	169127
15601	63859			26734	7570
1903351	2104863	22729	107451	541889	233278
73404	60992			18384	4500
	34324	22324	99193	479	
			99193	479	
	12000				
	22324	22324			
114	10631			2483	
114	10631			2483	
468297	371850	103754	162008	114043	29309
18821	70290				1921
2286805	2539295	42095	214448	817611	374952
	34324	22324			
114	10631			2483	
232131	292411	20650	9771	52745	16203

12-7 续表5

单位：万元

指 标	Item	商品房销售额 Sales of Commercial Buildings	住 宅 Residential Buildings
总 计	**Total**	**10271364**	**9007879**
按登记注册类型	**Grouped by Type of Registration Status**		
内 资	Domestic-Funded Enterprises	10122139	8951787
国 有	State-owned Enterprises	249787	227908
集 体	Collective-owned Enterprises	10352	10352
股份合作	Share Cooperative Enterprises		
国有联营	State Joint Ownership Enterprises		
集体联营	Collective Joint Ownership Enterprises		
国有与集体联营	Joint State-collective Enterprises		
其他联营	Other Joint Ownership Enterprises		
国有独资公司	State-funded Corporations	321414	310715
其他有限责任公司	Other Limited Liability Corporations	3459779	2922545
股份有限公司	Share Corporations Ltd.	71699	46553
私营独资	Private-funded Enterprises		
私营合伙	Private Partnership Enterprises		
私营有限责任公司	Private Limited Liability Corporations	5854450	5291676
私营股份有限公司	Private Share-holding Corporations Ltd.	154658	142038
其 他	Others		
港澳台投资	Enterprises with Investment from Hong Kong, Macao and Taiwan	129272	38491
合资经营	Joint-venture Enterprises	90781	
合作经营	Cooperative Enterprises		
独 资	Enterprises with Sole Investment	12000	12000
股份有限	Share Corporations Ltd.	26491	26491
其 他	Others		
外商投资	Enterprises with Foreign Investment	19953	17601
合资经营	Joint-Venture Enterprises		
合作经营	Cooperative Enterprises		
独 资	Enterprises with Sole Foreign Investment	19953	17601
股份有限	Share Corporations Ltd.		
其 他	Others		
按控股情况分	**Grouped by Share Holding**		
国有控股	State Holding Enterprises	1650301	1372436
集体控股	Collective-owned Holding Enterprises	160107	158091
私人控股	Private Holding Enterprises	7614001	6708930
港澳台商控股	Hongkong, Macao and Taiwan Holding Enterprises	38491	38491
外商控股	Foreign Holding Enterprises	19953	17601
其 他	Others	788511	712330

continued

(10 000 yuan)

#90平方米及以下住房 90 sq.m and Below	#144平方米以上住房 Above 144 sq.m	#别墅、高档公寓 Villas and High-grade Apartment Buildings	办公楼 Office Buildings	商业营业用房 Buildings for Business Operation	其 他 Others
1282270	**2017101**	**188665**	**334819**	**798263**	**130403**
1282230	1974828	162174	244160	795789	130403
41655	7069		3157	18604	118
24651	48356			7016	3683
373035	678234	129383	160065	327845	49324
6093	25314			22725	2421
806653	1179829	32791	80938	407879	73957
30143	36026			11720	900
	38491	26491	90659	122	
			90659	122	
	12000				
	26491	26491			
40	3782			2352	
40	3782			2352	
218836	265278	94274	147252	118231	12382
9800	61634				2016
972057	1409768	45544	177217	615546	112308
	38491	26491			
40	3782			2352	
81537	238148	22356	10350	62134	3697

12-8 房地产开发企业财务状况(2016年)

单位：万元

指　标	Item	固定资产原　价 Original Value of Fixed Assets
总　计	**Total**	**1627807**
按登记注册类型	**Grouped by Type of Registration Status**	
内　资	Domestic-Funded Enterprises	1531474
国　有	State-owned Enterprises	36727
集　体	Collective-owned Enterprises	1736
股份合作	Share Cooperative Enterprises	
国有联营	State Joint Ownership Enterprises	
集体联营	Collective Joint Ownership Enterprises	
国有与集体联营	Joint State-collective Enterprises	
其他联营	Other Joint Ownership Enterprises	
国有独资公司	State-funded Corporations	22707
其他有限责任公司	Other Limited Liability Corporations	345508
股份有限公司	Share Corporations Ltd.	38797
私营独资	Private-funded Enterprises	
私营合伙	Private Partnership Enterprises	
私营有限责任公司	Private Limited Liability Corporations	1053298
私营股份有限公司	Private Share-holding Corporations Ltd.	32701
其　他	Others	
港澳台投资	Enterprises with Investment from Hong Kong, Macao and Taiwan	7083
合资经营	Joint-venture Enterprises	6414
合作经营	Cooperative Enterprises	
独　资	Enterprises with Sole Investment	497
股份有限	Share Corporations Ltd.	169
其　他	Others	3
外商投资	Enterprises with Foreign Investment	89251
合资经营	Joint-Venture Enterprises	3504
合作经营	Cooperative Enterprises	
独　资	Enterprises with Sole Foreign Investment	60977
股份有限	Share Corporations Ltd.	24769
其　他	Others	
按控股情况分	**Grouped by Share Holding**	
国有控股	State Holding Enterprises	196844
集体控股	Collective-owned Holding Enterprises	20377
私人控股	Private Holding Enterprises	1232968
港澳台商控股	Hongkong, Macao and Taiwan Holding Enterprises	1300
外商控股	Foreign Holding Enterprises	86882
其　他	Others	89436

FINANCIAL CONDITION OF REAL ESTATE DEVELOPMENT ENTERPRISES(2016)

(10 000 yuan)

固定资产累计折旧 Accumulative Depreciation of Fixed Assets	#本年折旧 Depreciation of This Year	资产总计 Total Assets	负债合计 Total Liabilities	所有者权益合计 Total Creditors' Equity	#实收资金 Paid-in Capital
470238	**72839**	**81911104**	**72605503**	**9305601**	**7742234**
458196	69311	80119192	71162845	8956347	7421455
8696	1013	1645907	1443398	202509	113491
455	29	39537	36400	3137	3780
5391	895	3400704	2472890	927814	673781
93439	14517	26190952	22707233	3483719	2346127
10095	1215	1208306	1113400	94906	88399
329368	49502	46666117	42501524	4164593	4111376
10753	2141	967670	888000	79669	84501
4343	350	957885	687610	270275	260005
3763	341	602213	454257	147956	141900
430	2	286495	192489	94006	101491
150	8	63987	38643	25344	13613
		5191	2222	2969	3000
7699	3177	834026	755047	78979	60775
1867	99	96851	76591	20261	2665
3178	3078	541008	485016	55992	50110
2654		196168	193441	2727	8000
33727	5701	16265029	13635314	2629715	1738572
8465	560	1056881	933420	123461	50824
389760	60578	57972934	52506170	5466764	5106635
934	124	603015	376293	226722	222105
6842	3103	836953	759816	77138	59741
30511	2774	5176292	4394491	781801	564358

12-8 续表1

单位：万元

指 标	Item	营业收入 Business Revenue
总 计	**Total**	**9039089**
按登记注册类型	**Grouped by Type of Registration Status**	
内 资	Domestic-Funded Enterprises	8944250
国 有	State-owned Enterprises	73274
集 体	Collective-owned Enterprises	2686
股份合作	Share Cooperative Enterprises	
国有联营	State Joint Ownership Enterprises	
集体联营	Collective Joint Ownership Enterprises	
国有与集体联营	Joint State-collective Enterprises	
其他联营	Other Joint Ownership Enterprises	
国有独资公司	State-funded Corporations	322067
其他有限责任公司	Other Limited Liability Corporations	3467700
股份有限公司	Share Corporations Ltd.	226390
私营独资	Private-funded Enterprises	
私营合伙	Private Partnership Enterprises	
私营有限责任公司	Private Limited Liability Corporations	4629051
私营股份有限公司	Private Share-holding Corporations Ltd.	223081
其 他	Others	
港澳台投资	Enterprises with Investment from Hong Kong, Macao and Taiwan	70815
合资经营	Joint-venture Enterprises	6543
合作经营	Cooperative Enterprises	
独 资	Enterprises with Sole Investment	29222
股份有限	Share Corporations Ltd.	35049
其 他	Others	
外商投资	Enterprises with Foreign Investment	24025
合资经营	Joint-Venture Enterprises	44
合作经营	Cooperative Enterprises	
独 资	Enterprises with Sole Foreign Investment	23981
股份有限	Share Corporations Ltd.	
其 他	Others	
按控股情况分	**Grouped by Share Holding**	
国有控股	State Holding Enterprises	1734145
集体控股	Collective-owned Holding Enterprises	116576
私人控股	Private Holding Enterprises	6406643
港澳台商控股	Hongkong, Macao and Taiwan Holding Enterprises	64705
外商控股	Foreign Holding Enterprises	23981
其 他	Others	693039

continued

(10 000 yuan)

#主营业务收入 Revenue of Major Business	土地转让收入 Land Transferred Revenue	商品房屋销售收入 Sales Revenue of Commercial Buildings	房屋出租收入 Revenue from Buildings Leasing	其他收入 Other Revenue
8660816	**95697**	**8003667**	**64500**	**496952**
8565976	95697	7916543	61268	492469
73107	1132	65284	3952	2738
2686		2576	20	90
318429	69669	224117	2310	22333
3163724	17279	2706246	13952	426247
226270		225839	232	200
4559261	7617	4470835	40200	40609
222499		221646	602	251
70815		65118	1232	4465
6543		846	1232	4465
29222		29222		
35049		35049		
24025		22007	2000	18
44		26		18
23981		21981	2000	
1468535	70801	992135	10510	395089
115310		113522	347	1441
6297379	24895	6136353	50158	85973
64705		64419	286	
23981		21981	2000	
690906		675258	1199	14449

12-8 续表2

单位：万元

指 标	Item	营业成本 Business Costs
总 计	**Total**	**7217696**
按登记注册类型	**Grouped by Type of Registration Status**	
内 资	Domestic-Funded Enterprises	7129292
国 有	State-owned Enterprises	59795
集 体	Collective-owned Enterprises	1872
股份合作	Share Cooperative Enterprises	
国有联营	State Joint Ownership Enterprises	
集体联营	Collective Joint Ownership Enterprises	
国有与集体联营	Joint State-collective Enterprises	
其他联营	Other Joint Ownership Enterprises	
国有独资公司	State-funded Corporations	259191
其他有限责任公司	Other Limited Liability Corporations	2696673
股份有限公司	Share Corporations Ltd.	195478
私营独资	Private-funded Enterprises	
私营合伙	Private Partnership Enterprises	
私营有限责任公司	Private Limited Liability Corporations	3725621
私营股份有限公司	Private Share-holding Corporations Ltd.	190661
其 他	Others	
港澳台投资	Enterprises with Investment from Hong Kong, Macao and Taiwan	57943
合资经营	Joint-venture Enterprises	4081
合作经营	Cooperative Enterprises	
独 资	Enterprises with Sole Investment	26299
股份有限	Share Corporations Ltd.	27564
其 他	Others	
外商投资	Enterprises with Foreign Investment	30462
合资经营	Joint-Venture Enterprises	17
合作经营	Cooperative Enterprises	
独 资	Enterprises with Sole Foreign Investment	30445
股份有限	Share Corporations Ltd.	
其 他	Others	
按控股情况分	**Grouped by Share Holding**	
国有控股	State Holding Enterprises	1467322
集体控股	Collective-owned Holding Enterprises	74875
私人控股	Private Holding Enterprises	5023981
港澳台商控股	Hongkong, Macao and Taiwan Holding Enterprises	53665
外商控股	Foreign Holding Enterprises	30445
其 他	Others	567409

continued

(10 000 yuan)

#主营业务成 本 Costs of Major Business	营业税金及附加 Business Tax and Extra Charges	#主营业务税金及附加 Tax and Extra Charges of Major Business	营业利润 Business Profits	利润总额 Total Profits	应交所得税 Income Taxes Payable	从业人员期末人数(人) Number of Employees at The End of Period (person)
6838949	**577734**	**543603**	**304816**	**290414**	**189999**	**56206**
6752055	569415	536023	327909	313250	185359	55425
58809	4420	4400	–3054	–1155	524	2301
1867	135	135	–4	315		313
258934	27276	22402	22776	29228	12546	1187
2381096	211045	201528	308670	307624	85999	12844
195478	10977	10975	–34136	–35259	2464	567
3665704	301407	282663	27717	6921	80687	37247
190167	14156	13920	5940	5575	3140	966
56432	5621	5413	457	908	1128	409
2570	537	328	–2612	–1945	1	313
26299	2787	2787	–1009	–975		66
27564	2298	2298	4109	3858	1128	20
			–30	–30		10
30462	2697	2168	–23549	–23743	3512	372
17			–397	–435		94
30445	2168	2168	–16671	–16732	3512	183
	529		–6482	–6576		95
1242849	94637	88282	–10890	–2754	32872	7137
73245	8285	8282	13020	13387	2896	1048
4872511	425720	398622	247933	225091	138032	44648
53665	5162	5162	2386	2115	1128	192
30445	2697	2168	–22506	–22662	3512	386
566235	41233	41088	74873	75238	11560	2795

主要统计指标解释

房地产开发投资 指各种登记注册类型的房地产开发法人单位统一开发的住宅、厂房、仓库、饭店、宾馆、度假村、写字楼、办公楼等房屋建筑物，配套的服务设施，土地开发工程（如道路、给水、排水、供电、供热、通讯、平整场地等基础设施工程）和土地购置的投资；不包括单纯的土地开发和交易活动。

本年实际到位资金小计 指房地产开发企业在报告期内实际拨入的，用于房地产开发的各种货币资金。包括国内贷款、利用外资、自筹资金和其他资金。

本年土地购置面积 指通过各种方式获得土地使用权的土地面积。

本年土地成交价款 指进行土地使用权交易活动的最终金额。在土地一级市场，是指土地最后的划拨款、“招拍挂”价格和出让价；在土地二级市场是指土地转让、出租、抵押等最后确定的合同价格。土地成交价款与土地购置面积同口径，可以计算土地的平均购置价格。

房屋新开工面积 指报告期内新开工建设的房屋建筑面积，以单位工程为核算对象，即整栋房屋的全部建筑面积，不能分割计算。不包括在上期开工跨入报告期继续施工的房屋建筑面积和上期停缓建而在本期恢复施工的房屋建筑面积。房屋的开工应以房屋正式开始破土刨槽（地基处理或打永久桩）的日期为准。

房屋竣工面积 指报告期内房屋建筑按照设计要求已全部完工，达到住人和使用条件，经验收鉴定合格或达到竣工验收标准，可正式移交使用的各栋房屋建筑面积的总和。

房屋竣工价值 指报告期内按规定已经上报竣工的房屋本身的建造价值。一般按房屋设计和预算规定的内容计算。包括竣工房屋本身的基础、结构、屋面、装修以及水、电、卫等附属工程的建筑价值；也包括作为房屋建筑组成部分而列入房屋建筑工程预算内的设备（如电梯、通风设备等）的购置和安装费用。不包括厂房内的工艺设备、工艺管线的购置和安装，工艺设备基础的建造；室外的水、暖、电、卫、道路工程、挡土墙等环境工程的费用；办公和生活用家具的购置等费用；购置土地的费用；迁移补偿费和场地平整的费用及城市建设配套投资。

房屋竣工价值不仅包括该竣工房屋在报告期内完成的价值，也包括跨年施工的房屋在本期以前完成的价值。未竣工而转让给其他单位的房屋建筑工程，出让单位不计算竣工价值，待接受单位继续施工并符合竣工条件后，由接受单位计算其竣工价值，包括出让单位在出让前所完成的价值。房屋竣工价值一般按结算价格（或中标价）计算。

商品房销售面积 指报告期内出售商品房屋的合同总面积（即双方签署的正式买卖合同中所确定的建筑面积）。商品房销售面积由现房销售面积和期房销售面积两部分组成。

商品房销售额 指报告期内出售商品房屋的合同总价款（即双方签署的正式买卖合同中所确定的合同总价）。该指标与商品房销售面积同口径，由现房销售额和期房销售额两部分组成。

待售面积 指报告期末已竣工的可供销售或出租的商品房屋建筑面积中，尚未销售或出租的商品房屋建筑面积，包括以前年度竣工和本期竣工的房屋面积，但不包括报告期已竣工的拆迁还建、统建代建、公共配套建筑、房地产公司自用及周转房等不可销售或出租的房屋面积。按照商品房待售时间的长短可以划分为待售一年以下、待售一到三年（含一年）和待售三年以上（含三年）。

Explanatory Notes on Main Statistical Indicators

Investment in Real Estate Development refers to investment by real estate development corporation units of various types of ownership in the construction of buildings, such as residential buildings, factory buildings, warehouses, hotels, guesthouses, holiday villages, office buildings, complementary service facilities, land development projects and land purchase, such as roads, water supply, water drainage, power supply, heating supply, telecommunications, land leveling and other infrastructural projects. It does not include activities in pure land transactions.

Total Actual Funds in Place This Year refers to all kinds of monetary funds real estate enterprises actually invested for real estate development in the reference period, including domestic loans, foreign investment, self-raising fund and other funds.

Land Area Purchased This Year refers to the land area which has been got the land use right by all means.

Value of Land Transaction This Year refers to the final value of land use right in the land transaction. It refers to the final appropriations of land, remising price and transfer price in primary land market, while it refers to the contract price of land transfer, lease and mortgage in the secondary land market. Value of land transaction has the same coverage with land area purchased, which can be used to calculate the average price of land purchased.

Floor Space of Buildings under Construction refers to total floor space of all buildings under construction during the reference period, including floor space of newly started buildings during the reference period, floor space of construction extended from the previous period to the current period, and floor space of construction suspended during the previous period and resumed in the current period. Floor space of construction completed in the current period, and floor space of construction started and then suspended in the current period are also included in the floor space under construction of the current year. Floor space of multistoried buildings is the sum of space of every floor.

Floor Space of Buildings Completed refers to the floor space of all buildings completed in the reference period, which has been appraised, accepted or reached the designed standards and transferred to owner units.

Value of Buildings Completed refers to construction value of completed buildings which has been reported in the reference period. It is usually calculated by the contents of building design and budget, including the construction value of completed buildings' backbone, structure, roof, decoration and appurtenant works such as water, electricity and sanitation. The purchasing and installation charges of budgetary facilities, such as elevators and ventilating devices, as a part of the composition of buildings, are also included in the value of completed buildings. The costs of purchasing and installation of plant processing equipments and pipelines and basic construction, costs of environmental projects outdoors, such as water, heating, electricity, sanitation, road projects and retaining walls, costs of purchasing of office and life furniture, costs of land purchasing, costs of residence moving and site formation and costs of supporting investment of urban construction are not included in the value of completed buildings.

Value of buildings completed includes not only value of buildings completed in the reference period, but also includes the previous value of buildings extended the previous period to the current period. The building value of construction projects, which uncompleted and transferred to other units, cannot be calculated by the transferred units. It should be calculated by the receiving units after the projects are completed and reached the relevant standards. Value of buildings completed is usually calculated at the settlement price or the bidding price.

Floor Space of Commercial Buildings Sold refers to total contracted area of commercialized buildings sold, i.e. area of floor space as designated in the formal contracts signed by both sides, during the reference time. It consists of floor space of completed buildings sold and forward delivery buildings sold.

Sales of Commercial Buildings refers to the total contracted value, i.e. value of commercialized buildings as designated in the contract signed by both sides, during the reference period. This indicator has the same coverage with the area of commercialized buildings sold, and it consists of sales of completed buildings and sales of forward delivery buildings.

Floor Space for Sale refers to the floor space of commercial buildings hasn't been sold or leased which is marketable or rentable in the reference period. It includes floor space of building which has been completed in the previous and current period, excluding floor space of completed buildings, such as relocation building, buildings built for employees by the government agencies and institutions units, auxiliary facilities of public buildings, buildings of real estate enterprises for self use, temporary houses, which cannot be sold or rent. Floor space for sale can be divided into floor space for sale less than a year, floor space for sale in 1-3 years, floor space for sale more than 3years according to the sales time.

13 批发和零售业

WHOLESALE AND RETAIL TRADE

资料整理人员

雷士伟　张艳芳　张艳君

批发和零售业
WHOLESALE AND RETAIL TRADE

社会消费品零售总额	Total Retail Sales of Consumer Goods	6480.5	亿元	(100 million yuan)
城　镇	Town	5284.5	亿元	(100 million yuan)
乡　村	Village	1196.0	亿元	(100 million yuan)

社会消费品零售总额构成(%)
Composition of Total Retail Sales of Consumer Goods (%)

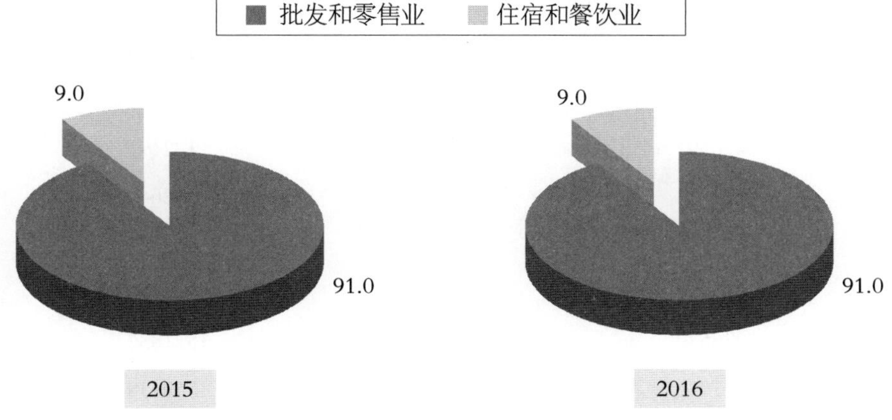

社会消费品零售总额(亿元)
Total Retail Sales of Consumer Goods (100 million yuan)

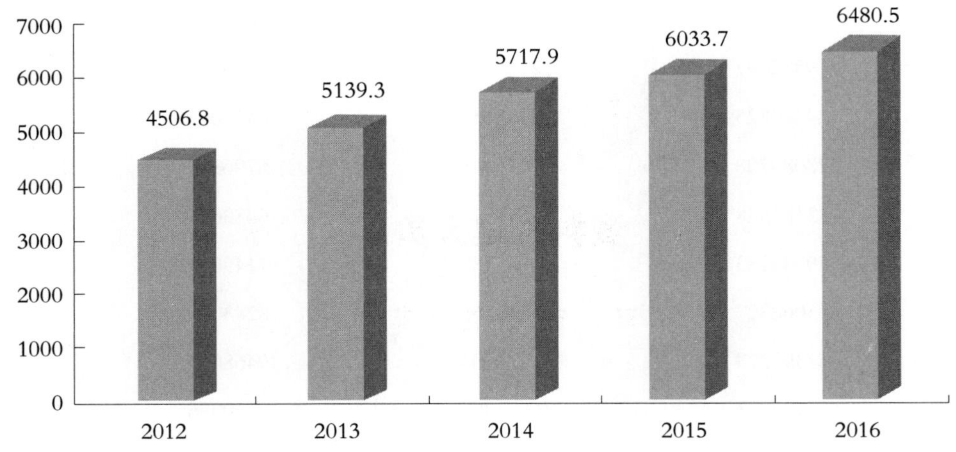

13-1 主要年份社会消费品零售总额
TOTAL RETAIL SALES OF CONSUMER GOODS IN MAJOR YEARS

单位：万元 (10 000 yuan)

年 份 Year	社会消费品零售总额 Total Retail Sales of Consumer Goods	市 City	县 County	县以下 Below County
1952	57436	19536	37900	
1957	119600	52278	67322	
1962	146532	59686	86846	
1965	153257	57252	96005	
1970	190949	63853	127096	
1975	265190	108543	133713	22934
1978	323837	121772	113985	88080
1980	426597	163154	122191	141252
1985	894413	394784	278646	220983
1990	1580415	848543	413831	318041
1995	3759500	2130633	861482	767385
2000	7226579	4240688	1521837	1464054
2001	7811932	4691960	1559178	1560794
2002	8671245	5218448	1720096	1732701
2003	10049972	6495135	1862970	1691867
2004	12190617	8002017	2181917	2006683
2005	14106531	9084606	2637921	2384004
2006	16353948	10630067	3025480	2698401
2007	19532597	12735253	3593998	3203346
2008	24210825	15785458	4479003	3946364
2009	28089708	17476248	5796850	4816610
2010	33181548	26697874	6483674	
2011	39034283	31885231	7149052	
2012	45068327	36825267	8243060	
2013	51393373	41925304	9468069	
2014	57178881	46617895	10560986	
2015	60336646	49172291	11164355	
2016	64805384	52845462	11959922	

注：2010年起分区域划分为城镇和乡村。

Note: Regions are divided into town and village since 2010.

13-2 社会消费品零售总额
TOTAL RETAIL SALES OF CONSUMER GOODS

单位：万元 (10 000 yuan)

指　标	Item	2015	2016
社会消费品零售总额	**Total**	**60336646**	**64805384**
按销售地区分	By Selling Region		
城　镇	Town	49172291	52845462
#城　区	Urban Area	32923522	35385865
乡　村	Village	11164355	11959922
按行业分	By Sector		
批发零售贸易业	Wholesale and Retail Sale Trades	54914900	59003973
限额以上贸易企业	Enterprises above Designated	21994600	22508676
限额以下及个体户贸易业	Enterprises below Designated and Individuals	32920300	36495297
住宿和餐饮业	Hotels and Catering Trade	5421746	5801411
限额以上企业	Enterprises above Designated	743814	748116
限额以下企业及个体户	Enterprises below Designated and Individuals	4677932	5053295
按消费形态分	By Consumption Pattern		
商品零售	Retail Sales	54950015	59044885
餐饮收入	Catering Income	5386631	5760499

13-3 限额以上连锁批发零售业经营情况(2016年)
MANAGEMENT OF CHAIN ENTERPRISES ABOVE DESIGNATED SIZE IN WHOLESALE AND RETAIL TRADE(2016)

指　标	Item	合　计 Total	直营店 Regular Chain	加盟店 Franchise Chain
一、门店总数 (个)	**Number of Store (uint)**	**4001**	**2308**	**1693**
二、年末零售业营业面积 (平方米)	**Areas of Stores (sq.m)**	**2965720**	**2858517**	**107203**
三、年末从业人员 (人)	**Employees (person)**	**38348**	**29971**	**8377**
四、商品购进总额 (万元)	**Total Purchases Value (10 000 yuan)**	**3131311**	**2903206**	**228105**
#统一配送商品购进额	Value of Unified Distribution	2065663	1909299	156365
#自有配送中心配送商品购进额	Disrtibuted by Owned Distribution Center	1289589	1133374	156215
非自有配送中心配送商品购进额	Distributed by Other Distribution Center			
五、商品销售额 (万元)	**Total Sales Value (10 000 yuan)**	**4427747**	**4198598**	**229149**
#零售额	Retail Sales	3523795	3294646	229149

13-4 限额以上批发和零售业法人企业商品购销存情况(2016年)

单位：万元

指　　标	Item	法　人 企业数 (个) Number of Corporation Enterprises (unit)
总　计	**Total**	**2981**
一、批发业	**Wholesale Trade**	**898**
1.按登记注册类型分	Grouped by Registered Kind	
内资企业	Civil Funded Enterprises	892
国有企业	State-owned Enterprises	75
集体企业	Collective-owned Enterprises	30
股份合作企业	Share Cooperative Enterprises	1
联营企业	Joint Ownership Enterprises	1
集体联营企业	Collective Joint Enterprises	1
有限责任公司	Limited Responsibility Corporations	264
国有独资公司	Company Exclusively with Investment from State	54
其他有限责任公司	Other Limited Responsibility Company	210
股份有限公司	Share-holding Limited Corporations	18
私营企业	Private-owned Enterprises	497
私营独资企业	Enterprise Exclusively with Investment from Private	5
私营合伙企业	Private Partnership Enterprises	
私营有限责任公司	Private Limited Responsibility Corporations	480
私营股份有限公司	Private Share-holding Limited Corporations	12
其他企业	Others	6
港澳台商投资企业	Enterprises Funded by HongKong, Macao and Taiwan	5
与港澳台商合资经营企业	Joint Venture Enterprises	2
港澳台商独资企业	Solely Owned Entersprises	2
港澳台商投资股份有限公司	Share Holding Limited Corporation	1
外商投资企业	Foreign Funded Enterprises	1
中外合资经营企业	Joint Venture Enterprises	1
2.按批发行业小类分	Grouped by Wholesale Trade	
农、林、牧产品批发	Wholesale of Agricultural, Forestry and Animal Husbandry Products	35
食品、饮料及烟草制品批发	Wholesale of Food, Beverage and Tobaccos	106
#米、面制品及食用油批发	Rice, Flour and Edible Oil	16
烟草制品批发	Tobacoo Products Manufacturing	12
纺织、服装及家庭用品批发	Wholesale of Textiles, Garments and Family Articles	26
#服装批发	Wholesale of Garments	7
文化、体育用品及器材批发	Wholesale of Culture, Sports Articles and Equipments	13
医药及医疗器材批发	Wholesale of Medicines and Medical Appliances	83
#西药批发	Wholesale of Western Medicine	44
中药批发	Wholesale of Chinese Traditional and Patent Medicine	28

TOTAL VALUE OF COMMODITIES' PURCHASING, SELLING AND INVENTORY OF CORPORATION ENTERPRISES ABOVE DESIGNATED SIZE IN WHOLESALE AND RETAIL TRADE(2016)

(10 000 yuan)

从业人员期末人数（人） Number of Employees at The End of Period (person)	商品购进额 Total Purchases Value	商品销售额 Total Sales Value	#通过公共网络实现的商品销售额 by Public Network	#通过非自营平台实现的商品销售额 by Non-self-operating Platform
235096	**82568805**	**89879271**	**3348698**	**899238**
84755	**65325852**	**69841589**	**2767232**	**720345**
82975	63876805	68355292	2756931	720345
11095	3760461	4900691	2290773	661981
6830	464474	611889		
12		603		
33	1771	2270		
33	1771	2270		
42548	48241660	50328912	37349	560
23327	17024640	17927364	17551	
19221	31217020	32401548	19798	560
1427	3370553	3729798		
20804	7985217	8719042	428809	57804
82	15689	16804		
18732	7429091	8004024	47694	5684
1990	540437	698215	381115	52119
226	52670	62086		
1548	1441296	1478084	10302	
279	1397582	1414544		
1269	43714	63540	10302	
232	7751	8214		
232	7751	8214		
1869	197414	225623		
16053	3634214	4886738	2318976	661974
886	155901	160302		
6758	2117580	3193024	2290716	661924
4209	605979	709969	305744	52119
3098	362972	435967	305744	52119
985	535447	556107		
9417	2177036	2404815	27610	57
5938	1512261	1656431	17608	57
2944	463749	540740	10002	

13-4 续表1

单位：万元

指　　标	Item	法　人 企业数 (个) Number of Corporation Enterprises (unit)
矿产品、建材及化工产品批发	Wholesale of Mineral Products, Building and Chemical Products	510
#煤炭及制品批发	Coal and Related Products	305
石油及制品批发	Petroleum and Related Products	27
金属及金属矿批发	Metals and Metals Materials	109
建材批发	Building Materials	30
化肥批发	Chemical Fertilizer	15
机械设备、五金产品及电子产品	Wholesale of Machinery, Hardwaresand Electronic Products	104
#汽车批发	Motor Vehicles	23
计算机、软件及辅助设备批发	Computer, Sofeware and Accessories	5
贸易经纪与代理	Trade Broker and Agency	1
其他批发业	Other Wholesales	20
3.按控股情况分	Grouped by Share Holding	
国有控股	State Holding Enterprises	270
集体控股	Collective-owned Holding Enterprises	48
私人控股	Private Holding Enterprises	537
港澳台商控股	Hongkong, Macao and Taiwan Holding Enterprises	4
外商控股	Foreign Holding Enterprises	
其　他	Others	39
4.按经营形式分	Grouped by Management Form	
独立门店	Independent Stores	609
连锁总店(总部)	Chain Headquarters	5
连锁门店	Chain Stores	4
其　他	Others	280
5.按单位规模分	Grouped by Enterprise Size	
大　型	Large-size	44
中　型	Medium-size	298
小　型	Small-size	369
微　型	Micro-size	187
二、零售业	**Retail Trade**	**2083**
1.按登记注册类型分组	Grouped by Registered Kind	
内资企业	Civil Funded Enterprises	2063
国有企业	State-owned Enterprises	91
集体企业	Collective-owned Enterprises	70
股份合作企业	Share Cooperative Enterprises	2
联营企业	Joint Ownership Enterprises	
国有联营企业	Collective Joint Enterprises	

continued

(10 000 yuan)

从业人员期末人数(人) Number of Employees at The End of Period (person)	商品购进额 Total Purchases Value	商品销售额 Total Sales Value	#通过公共网络实现的商品销售额 by Public Network	#通过非自营平台实现的商品销售额 by Non-self-operating Platform
47195	52049689	54794212	97816	587
40014	25563379	27229912	89097	560
1390	761251	846935	17	17
3320	11373066	12204414	8703	10
801	10996610	11121152		
416	3088769	3086961		
4250	6024286	6117034	17086	5608
943	604342	634615	4926	4926
71	18336	19601		
5	872	35769		
772	100917	111323		
47055	53856302	57213145	2327562	661981
7964	932484	1101911		
23005	8834908	9665912	429369	58364
1548	85187	106567	10302	
5183	1616970	1754054		
56074	37743250	39971670	1679986	560977
2664	1316071	1550696		
251	30716	34454		
25766	26235815	28284770	1087247	159367
45023	16762460	19820523	2596460	714044
24961	33457850	34701706	145178	5731
10886	3361052	3521205	25594	570
3885	11744490	11798155		
150341	**17242953**	**20037682**	**581466**	**178894**
145911	16855304	19588387	581466	178894
3120	356576	433546		
3295	359512	396881	6695	
65	8414	9873		

13-4 续表2

单位：万元

指　标	Item	法 人 企业数 (个) Number of Corporation Enterprises (unit)
有限责任公司	Limited Responsibility Corporations	342
国有独资公司	Company Exclusively with Investment from State	17
其他有限责任公司	Other Limited Responsibility Company	325
股份有限公司	Share-holding Limited Corporations	44
私营企业	Private-owned Enterprises	1502
私营独资企业	Enterprise Exclusively with Investment from Private	132
私营合伙企业	Private Partnership Enterprises	11
私营有限责任公司	Private Limited Responsibility Corporations	1333
私营股份有限公司	Private Share-holding Limited Corporations	26
其他企业	Others	12
港澳台商投资企业	Enterprises Funded by HongKong, Macao and Taiwan	14
与港澳台商合资经营企业	Joint Venture Enterprises	7
港澳台商独资企业	Solely Owned Entersprises	7
港澳台商投资股份有限公司	Share Holding Limited Corporation	
外商投资企业	Foreign Funded Enterprises	6
中外合资经营企业	Joint Venture Enterprises	2
外资企业	Enterprises with Sole Investment from Foreign	3
其他外商投资企业	Other Foreign Funded Enterprises	1
2.按零售行业小类分	Grouped by Wholesale Trade	
综合零售	General Retail Sales Trade	359
百货零售	Daily Goods	181
超级市场零售	Supermarkets	145
其他综合零售	Others	33
食品、饮料及烟草制品专门零售	Retail of Food, Beverage and Tobaccos	170
纺织、服装及日用品专门零售	Retail of Textiles, Garments and Daily Articles	124
#服装零售	Garments	103
文化、体育用品及器材专门零售	Retail of Culture, Sports Articles and Equipments	111
#图书、报刊零售	Books and Mangzines	74
医药及医疗器材专门零售	Retail of Medicines and Medical Appliances	107
#药品零售	Medicines	103
汽车、摩托车、燃料及零配件专	Retail of Motor Vehicles, Motorcycles, Feuls and Parts	785
#汽车零售	Motor Vehicles	543
机动车燃料零售	Vehicle Feuls	219
家用电器及电子产品专门零售	Retail of Household Electronic Equipments and Products	220
#日用家电设备零售	Household Appliance	120
计算机、软件及辅助设备零售	Computer, Software and Auxiliary Equipments	57
通信设备零售	Communication Equipments	19

continued

(10 000 yuan)

从业人员期末人数(人) Number of Employees at The End of Period (person)	商品购进额 Total Purchases Value	商品销售额 Total Sales Value	#通过公共网络实现的商品销售额 by Public Network	#通过非自营平台实现的商品销售额 by Non-self-operating Platform
34202	3967677	4374148	163530	25284
1839	114358	136506	18391	18391
32363	3853319	4237641	145139	6894
11758	2682607	3252100	2437	2020
93095	9458076	11098105	408258	151439
3470	187813	214763	796	
311	52555	53813		
79733	8800373	9850623	404987	151379
9581	417334	978906	2475	60
376	22442	23734	546	150
3118	323314	379807		
1931	159434	199832		
1187	163881	179976		
1312	64334	69488		
383	10665	12043		
808	41638	41870		
121	12031	15575		
46400	2625116	3514928	30864	22829
18081	1136528	1439361	17017	17001
26222	973163	1552841	1955	631
2097	515425	522726	11891	5196
7426	573001	761715	112017	99608
12717	786937	1144705	31267	1808
10908	632314	955771	9094	1645
4366	313902	352652	1878	75
2486	184917	189493		
14907	1399691	1504854	23293	7903
14797	1390239	1493696	23293	7903
45428	9554412	10584771	166524	29333
28298	6152124	6522955	137469	27753
16703	3240966	3894561	417	
7072	879948	950683	96861	5541
4025	566063	613808	75893	5401
1386	130898	140077	14408	140
710	75398	78993		

13-4 续表3

单位：万元

指　　标	Item	法　人 企业数 (个) Number of Corporation Enterprises (unit)
五金、家具及室内装修材料专门零售	Retail of Hardwares, Furniture and Room Decorative Building	100
货摊、无店铺及其他零售业	Retail of Stall, Non-store and Others	107
3.按控股情况分	Grouped by Share Holding	
国有控股	State Holding Enterprises	226
集体控股	Collective-owned Holding Enterprises	114
私人控股	Private Holding Enterprises	1641
港澳台商控股	Hongkong, Macao and Taiwan Holding Enterprises	12
外商控股	Foreign Holding Enterprises	5
其　他	Others	85
4.按经营形式分	Grouped by Management Form	
独立门店	Independent Stores	1807
连锁总店	Chain Headquarters	90
连锁门店	Chain Stores	59
其　他	Others	127
5.按单位规模分	Grouped by Enterprise Size	
大　型	Large-size	59
中　型	Medium-size	618
小　型	Small-size	1045
微　型	Micro-size	361
6.按零售业态分	Grouped by Retail Format	
#有店铺零售	Store-based	2000
食杂店	Grocery Store	8
便利店	Convenient Store	25
折扣店	Discount Store	
超　市	Supermarket	182
大型超市	Hypermarket	40
仓储会员店	Warehouse Club	5
百货店	Department Store	213
专业店	Specialized Shop	859
专卖店	Exclusive Shop	535
家居建材商店	Home Center	37
购物中心	Shopping Center	49
厂家直销中心	Factory Outlet Center	47
无店铺零售	Non-store	82
#网上商店	Online	55

continued

(10 000 yuan)

从业人员期末人数(人) Number of Employees at The End of Period (person)	商品购进额 Total Purchases Value	商品销售额 Total Sales Value	#通过公共网络实现的商品销售额 by Public Network	#通过非自营平台实现的商品销售额 by Non-self-operating Platform
2987	531796	596054	773	83
9038	578151	627319	117990	11715
30523	4881628	5738422	21614	21165
7735	776385	867652	15016	270
103199	10480037	12182328	503482	156624
2656	283649	315199		
1191	52303	53913		
5037	768951	880167	41355	835
107154	12674424	14824894	349495	153515
20533	2200434	2370001	100802	15386
12236	1200001	1586286	12682	485
10418	1168093	1256501	118487	9508
48816	6594886	8077079	72096	25045
71377	6681348	7612440	270478	35275
26807	3405985	3686685	218777	109402
3341	560733	661478	20116	9172
146818	16975323	19735845	425907	159855
408	21650	25179		
2104	339206	353124	11892	5196
10876	408325	442001	5083	4862
16791	690446	1278276	6543	
212	135477	139104	26853	
23903	1705399	2065675	23904	18196
50563	7818825	8693831	211287	116861
28094	4820046	5288698	118070	14711
1450	258637	294880		
6348	325550	482157	764	29
6069	451764	672923	21511	
3403	267554	301756	155559	19039
2252	182463	192722	152192	16949

13-4 续表4

单位：万元

指　　标	Item	#使用银行卡支付的商品销售额 Paid by Bank Cards
总　计	**Total**	**6550998**
一、批发业	**Wholesale Trade**	**2794520**
1.按登记注册类型分	Grouped by Registered Kind	
内资企业	Civil Funded Enterprises	2786307
国有企业	State-owned Enterprises	2044145
集体企业	Collective-owned Enterprises	6450
股份合作企业	Share Cooperative Enterprises	
联营企业	Joint Ownership Enterprises	
集体联营企业	Collective Joint Enterprises	
有限责任公司	Limited Responsibility Corporations	329132
国有独资公司	Company Exclusively with Investment from State	5641
其他有限责任公司	Other Limited Responsibility Company	323491
股份有限公司	Share-holding Limited Corporations	37396
私营企业	Private-owned Enterprises	369185
私营独资企业	Enterprise Exclusively with Investment from Private	4935
私营合伙企业	Private Partnership Enterprises	
私营有限责任公司	Private Limited Responsibility Corporations	362786
私营股份有限公司	Private Share-holding Limited Corporations	1464
其他企业	Others	
港澳台商投资企业	Enterprises Funded by HongKong, Macao and Taiwan	
与港澳台商合资经营企业	Joint Venture Enterprises	
港澳台商独资企业	Solely Owned Entersprises	
港澳台商投资股份有限公司	Share Holding Limited Corporation	
外商投资企业	Foreign Funded Enterprises	8214
中外合资经营企业	Joint Venture Enterprises	8214
2.按批发行业小类分	Grouped by Wholesale Trade	
农、林、牧产品批发	Wholesale of Agricultural, Forestry and Animal Husbandry Products	10374
食品、饮料及烟草制品批发	Wholesale of Food, Beverage and Tobaccos	942033
#米、面制品及食用油批发	Rice, Flour and Edible Oil	
烟草制品批发	Tobacoo Products Manufacturing	923884
纺织、服装及家庭用品批发	Wholesale of Textiles, Garments and Family Articles	1352
#服装批发	Wholesale of Garments	
文化、体育用品及器材批发	Wholesale of Culture, Sports Articles and Equipments	
医药及医疗器材批发	Wholesale of Medicines and Medical Appliances	143944
#西药批发	Wholesale of Western Medicine	45
中药批发	Wholesale of Chinese Traditional and Patent Medicine	140918

continued

(10 000 yuan)

批发额 Wholesale Value	零售额 Retail Value	#通过公共网络实现的商品零售额 by Public Network	#通过非自营平台实现的商品零售额 by Non-self-operating Platform	期末商品库存额 Total Value of Storing at the End of Period	年末零售营业面积(平方米) Retail Operating Area at Year-end (sq.m)
70168211	**19711059**	**456455**	**60748**	**4816752**	**11420267**
68134396	**1707194**	**8890**		**2400225**	**2131032**
66659208	1696084	5994		2337912	2130602
4744040	156651			388459	85583
575121	36769			47002	32005
603				612	
2270				290	300
2270				290	300
50013976	314936			791492	1182811
17905325	22039			238920	54020
32108651	292897			552572	1128791
3713704	16095			180749	70903
7557547	1161495	5994		924108	754372
14116	2688			381	2833
7220091	783932	5994		876223	749113
323340	374875			47504	2426
51947	10139			5202	4628
1475188	2896	2896		62269	430
1414544				46807	
60644	2896	2896		15462	300
					130
	8214			44	
	8214			44	
215915	9707			106880	79195
4548940	337798	5994		350013	468129
146306	13996			22594	11830
3191809	1216			174601	3300
374352	335617			83151	6543
125529	310438			43517	100
536348	19759			109262	7591
2348218	56597			224860	33516
1625552	30879			165700	21899
531241	9499			39601	8228

13-4 续表5

单位：万元

指　标	Item	#使用银行卡支付的商品销售额 Paid by Bank Cards
矿产品、建材及化工产品批发	Wholesale of Mineral Products, Building and Chemical Products	1650013
#煤炭及制品批发	Coal and Related Products	377894
石油及制品批发	Petroleum and Related Products	103
金属及金属矿批发	Metals and Metals Materials	1135523
建材批发	Building Materials	122741
化肥批发	Chemical Fertilizer	5756
机械设备、五金产品及电子产品批发	Wholesale of Machinery, Hardwaresand Electronic Products	13435
#汽车批发	Motor Vehicles	9339
计算机、软件及辅助设备批发	Computer, Sofeware and Accessories	
贸易经纪与代理	Trade Broker and Agency	
其他批发业	Other Wholesales	33370
3.按控股情况分	Grouped by Share Holding	
国有控股	State Holding Enterprises	2280035
集体控股	Collective-owned Holding Enterprises	56968
私人控股	Private Holding Enterprises	406556
港澳台商控股	Hongkong, Macao and Taiwan Holding Enterprises	
外商控股	Foreign Holding Enterprises	
其　他	Others	50961
4.按经营形式分	Grouped by Management Form	
独立门店	Independent Stores	2049581
连锁总店(总部)	Chain Headquarters	2303
连锁门店	Chain Stores	30288
其　他	Others	712348
5.按单位规模分	Grouped by Enterprise Size	
大　型	Large-size	2255393
中　型	Medium-size	415033
小　型	Small-size	119097
微　型	Micro-size	4997
二、零售业	**Retail Trade**	**3756477**
1.按登记注册类型分组	Grouped by Registered Kind	
内资企业	Civil Funded Enterprises	3659053
国有企业	State-owned Enterprises	17927
集体企业	Collective-owned Enterprises	16443
股份合作企业	Share Cooperative Enterprises	
联营企业	Joint Ownership Enterprises	
国有联营企业	Collective Joint Enterprises	

continued

(10 000 yuan)

批发额 Wholesale Value	零售额 Retail Value	#通过公共网络实现的商品零售额 by Public Network	#通过非自营平台实现的商品零售额 by Non-self-operating Platform	期末商品库存额 Total Value of Storing at the End of Period	年末零售营业面积(平方米) Retail Operating Area at Year-end (sq.m)
54307684	486529			1356878	1287185
26875554	354357			796536	1154285
810069	36866			94384	88928
12127219	77194			397440	18937
11107661	13491			27873	14420
3082340	4620			18638	8490
5663402	453632	2896		119731	246778
222253	412362			11855	191250
18278	1323			1952	362
35769				14577	
103769	7554			34874	2095
56924745	288400			1117947	256808
1024300	77611			87694	55050
8425835	1240077	5994		1057067	1427604
103671	2896	2896		15477	430
1655844	98210			122041	391140
38932654	1039016	5994		1387626	1743802
1548798	1898			239882	2980
34454				1643	
27618490	666280	2896		771073	384250
19008450	812073			793025	201127
34037350	664356	8890		1026921	1002057
3324235	196970			363789	678624
11764361	33794			216490	249224
2033816	**18003866**	**447565**	**60748**	**2416527**	**9289235**
1981655	17606732	447565	60748	2363972	9143943
9262	424284			24833	117600
50448	346432	6695		23713	157263
173	9700			515	3220

13-4 续表6

单位：万元

指 标	Item	#使用银行卡支付的商品销售额 Paid by Bank Cards
有限责任公司	Limited Responsibility Corporations	878366
国有独资公司	Company Exclusively with Investment from State	416
其他有限责任公司	Other Limited Responsibility Company	877949
股份有限公司	Share-holding Limited Corporations	319255
私营企业	Private-owned Enterprises	2427063
私营独资企业	Enterprise Exclusively with Investment from Private	17413
私营合伙企业	Private Partnership Enterprises	463
私营有限责任公司	Private Limited Responsibility Corporations	1923767
私营股份有限公司	Private Share-holding Limited Corporations	485421
其他企业	Others	
港澳台商投资企业	Enterprises Funded by HongKong, Macao and Taiwan	74035
与港澳台商合资经营企业	Joint Venture Enterprises	67019
港澳台商独资企业	Solely Owned Entersprises	7015
港澳台商投资股份有限公司	Share Holding Limited Corporation	
外商投资企业	Foreign Funded Enterprises	23390
中外合资经营企业	Joint Venture Enterprises	3480
外资企业	Enterprises with Sole Investment from Foreign	19910
其他外商投资企业	Other Foreign Funded Enterprises	
2.按零售行业小类分	Grouped by Wholesale Trade	
综合零售	General Retail Sales Trade	857363
百货零售	Daily Goods	286838
超级市场零售	Supermarkets	549889
其他综合零售	Others	20636
食品、饮料及烟草制品专门零售	Retail of Food, Beverage and Tobaccos	55777
纺织、服装及日用品专门零售	Retail of Textiles, Garments and Daily Articles	159482
#服装零售	Garments	135123
文化、体育用品及器材专门零售	Retail of Culture, Sports Articles and Equipments	53682
#图书、报刊零售	Books and Mangzines	1236
医药及医疗器材专门零售	Retail of Medicines and Medical Appliances	32637
#药品零售	Medicines	29833
汽车、摩托车、燃料及零配件专门零售	Retail of Motor Vehicles, Motorcycles, Feuls and Parts	2397865
#汽车零售	Motor Vehicles	1948203
机动车燃料零售	Vehicle Feuls	359287
家用电器及电子产品专门零售	Retail of Household Electronic Equipments and Products	95460
#日用家电设备零售	Household Appliance	43747
计算机、软件及辅助设备零售	Computer, Software and Auxiliary Equipments	17335
通信设备零售	Communication Equipments	21471

continued

(10 000 yuan)

批发额 Wholesale Value	零售额 Retail Value	#通过公共网络实现的商品零售额 by Public Network	#通过非自营平台实现的商品零售额 by Non-self-operating Platform	期末商品库存额 Total Value of Storing at the End of Period	年末零售营业面积(平方米) Retail Operating Area at Year-end (sq.m)
629943	3744205	153498	6598	455653	1928901
769	135737	18391		10210	27917
629173	3608468	135107	6598	445443	1900984
537966	2714134	2437	2020	530862	1151495
753820	10344285	284401	51992	1327176	5753755
13137	201626	796		19408	248720
11705	42108			1019	22350
727717	9122906	281130	51932	1241873	4713453
1261	977645	2475	60	64876	769232
44	23691	534	138	1221	31709
52161	327646			43652	68594
40148	159684			34819	30206
12014	167962			8833	38388
	69488			8904	76698
	12043			1286	38000
	41870			6606	26304
	15575			1011	12394
174768	3340160	30864	22829	327829	3442363
136452	1302909	17017	17001	132319	1872576
1474	1551368	1955	631	178393	1434252
36842	485883	11891	5196	17117	135535
167079	594636	14479	4149	81404	379514
48497	1096208	29438	1361	131964	1003693
45883	909889	7265	1198	109339	940520
31414	321238	1875	75	129277	79285
7074	182419			52955	41544
422132	1082722	11770	7903	161746	172255
418095	1075601	11770	7903	160922	171295
928925	9655847	152111	8869	1409371	2912561
143700	6379255	133063	8862	833225	1257015
661853	3232708	417		565924	1615393
101811	848872	96004	4606	115402	401732
18178	595630	75161	4591	65326	289790
53872	86205	14283	15	22505	28275
29718	49275			9908	10347

13-4 续表7

单位：万元

指 标	Item	#使用银行卡支付的商品销售额 Paid by Bank Cards
五金、家具及室内装修材料专门零售	Retail of Hardwares, Furniture and Room Decorative Building	76164
货摊、无店铺及其他零售业	Retail of Stall, Non-store and Others	28049
3.按控股情况分	Grouped by Share Holding	
国有控股	State Holding Enterprises	539931
集体控股	Collective-owned Holding Enterprises	119023
私人控股	Private Holding Enterprises	2701918
港澳台商控股	Hongkong, Macao and Taiwan Holding Enterprises	74035
外商控股	Foreign Holding Enterprises	23390
其 他	Others	298182
4.按经营形式分	Grouped by Management Form	
独立门店	Independent Stores	2602920
连锁总店	Chain Headquarters	359493
连锁门店	Chain Stores	550151
其 他	Others	243914
5.按单位规模分	Grouped by Enterprise Size	
大 型	Large-size	1820102
中 型	Medium-size	1410542
小 型	Small-size	508389
微 型	Micro-size	17445
6.按零售业态分	Grouped by Retail Format	
#有店铺零售	Store-based	3708442
食杂店	Grocery Store	
便利店	Convenient Store	30223
折扣店	Discount Store	
超 市	Supermarket	21424
大型超市	Hypermarket	528503
仓储会员店	Warehouse Club	91115
百货店	Department Store	342561
专业店	Specialized Shop	1408482
专卖店	Exclusive Shop	1107349
家居建材商店	Home Center	28867
购物中心	Shopping Center	115777
厂家直销中心	Factory Outlet Center	34141
无店铺零售	Non-store	48036
#网上商店	Online	48036

continued

(10 000 yuan)

批发额 Wholesale Value	零售额 Retail Value	#通过公共网络实现的商品零售额 by Public Network	#通过非自营平台实现的商品零售额 by Non-self-operating Platform	期末商品库存额 Total Value of Storing at the End of Period	年末零售营业面积(平方米) Retail Operating Area at Year-end (sq.m)
98243	497811	517	17	30748	496751
60947	566372	110508	10939	28787	401081
990190	4748232	21614	2774	726115	2176869
58908	808744	15016	270	77155	482221
820133	11362196	378272	56935	1445901	6143571
24104	291095			35394	67594
	53913			7892	64304
140481	739686	32664	769	124070	354676
1600854	13224040	223886	37743	1654768	6974334
130037	2239963	100314	15386	346904	1158142
90959	1495327	9565	485	340784	788632
211966	1044535	113800	7134	74071	368127
976998	7100081	72096	25045	950783	3309902
428821	7183619	254590	15937	968979	3098170
569240	3117445	106067	13167	433721	2366701
58757	602722	14812	6599	63044	514462
1978193	17757653	302747	44953	2384752	9155693
4828	20351			1024	16592
48781	304343	11892	5196	14865	101234
5422	436579	5083	4862	62522	411089
166	1278110	6543		126791	1230232
102954	36150	18418		10261	118573
183521	1882153	23904	18196	159501	2135869
1180823	7513008	101557	2855	1218449	2717363
303360	4985338	113075	13815	671743	1319658
20465	274415			13045	344749
3304	478852	764	29	62420	628732
124570	548354	21511		44133	131602
55543	246213	144818	15795	31765	123542
32487	160236	141500	14746	20556	83562

13-5 限额以上批发和零售业法人企业财务状况(2016年)

单位：万元

指　　标	Item	年初存货 Beginning Inventory
总　计	**Total**	**4296571**
一、批发业	**Wholesale Trade**	**2511348**
1.按登记注册类型分	Grouped by Registered Kind	
内资企业	Civil Funded Enterprises	2454692
国有企业	State-owned Enterprises	486976
集体企业	Collective-owned Enterprises	48027
股份合作企业	Share Cooperative Enterprises	1215
联营企业	Joint Ownership Enterprises	293
集体联营企业	Collective Joint Enterprises	293
有限责任公司	Limited Responsibility Corporations	816438
国有独资公司	Company Exclusively with Investment from State	238542
其他有限责任公司	Other Limited Responsibility Company	577896
股份有限公司	Share-holding Limited Corporations	154886
私营企业	Private-owned Enterprises	943605
私营独资企业	Enterprise Exclusively with Investment from Private	240
私营合伙企业	Private Partnership Enterprises	
私营有限责任公司	Private Limited Responsibility Corporations	882992
私营股份有限公司	Private Share-holding Limited Corporations	60373
其他企业	Others	3253
港澳台商投资企业	Enterprises Funded by HongKong, Macao and Taiwan	56507
与港澳台商合资经营企业	Joint Venture Enterprises	45133
港澳台商独资企业	Solely Owned Entersprises	11375
港澳台商投资股份有限公司	Share Holding Limited Corporation	
外商投资企业	Foreign Funded Enterprises	149
中外合资经营企业	Joint Venture Enterprises	149
2.按批发行业小类分	Grouped by Wholesale Trade	
农、林、牧产品批发	Wholesale of Agricultural, Forestry and Animal Husbandry Products	141924
食品、饮料及烟草制品批发	Wholesale of Food, Beverage and Tobaccos	357910
#米、面制品及食用油批发	Rice, Flour and Edible Oil	76458
烟草制品批发	Tobacoo Products Manufacturing	203460
纺织、服装及家庭用品批发	Wholesale of Textiles, Garments and Family Articles	128078
#服装批发	Wholesale of Garments	55889
文化、体育用品及器材批发	Wholesale of Culture, Sports Articles and Equipments	78543
医药及医疗器材批发	Wholesale of Medicines and Medical Appliances	183058
#西药批发	Wholesale of Western Medicine	135588
中药批发	Wholesale of Chinese Traditional and Patent Medicine	37200

FINANCIAL CONDITION OF CORPORATION ENTERPRISES IN WHOLESALE AND RETAIL TRADE ABOVE DESIGNATED SIZE(2016)

(10 000 yuan)

流动资产合计 Total Circulating Assets	#应收帐款 Accounts Receivable	#存货 Inventory	固定资产合计 Total Fixed Assets	累计折旧 Accumulated Depreciation	#本年折旧 Depreciation This Year	资产总计 Total Assets
33199271	**5779180**	**4545080**	**5696787**	**2522047**	**575375**	**49367607**
25681705	**4719402**	**2557807**	**3412953**	**1432941**	**411329**	**37792510**
25435736	4697598	2495371	3397422	1426741	408621	37503090
1545093	133451	381663	249721	220585	21825	2006227
260954	33593	55433	51671	54184	6712	356531
2459	41	612	48	548	69	2507
977	11	435	153	267	223	1130
977	11	435	153	267	223	1130
13176242	2872733	761285	2434921	860071	338018	19621263
5060461	895487	224358	1835454	537117	288416	9271059
8115781	1977246	536927	599466	322954	49603	10350204
3362608	270294	180254	181823	101930	14868	4785261
7075271	1386607	1111889	475589	186556	24587	10713700
4866	3839	256	2922	737	73	9966
5800476	1325107	1035550	434839	176017	22368	7522262
1269929	57662	76083	37828	9803	2146	3181473
12134	869	3800	3497	2600	2319	16470
245380	21494	62399	15343	5770	2607	288645
202124	19734	46804	29	123	0	230039
43256	1761	15595	15314	5647	2607	58606
589	310	38	187	429	101	776
589	310	38	187	429	101	776
205707	19143	119995	73407	24722	1637	302217
1333249	119120	273819	255078	221719	30151	1806776
105745	1539	38590	17387	10379	1362	137565
907203	16019	161830	181312	174427	17782	1160219
1272885	36439	105573	6997	5614	2044	3139003
1163226	24852	67647	5943	4668	1513	3027446
315500	80801	73857	19539	11541	1350	418035
1216109	615792	308010	72858	24891	8106	1403703
770928	384367	215729	49776	16447	5842	904887
295284	135960	56514	21472	6557	2058	343045

13-5 续表1

单位：万元

指　标	Item	年初存货 Beginning Inventory
矿产品、建材及化工产品批发	Wholesale of Mineral Products, Building and Chemical Products	1451459
#煤炭及制品批发	Coal and Related Products	815993
石油及制品批发	Petroleum and Related Products	115448
金属及金属矿批发	Metals and Metals Materials	460185
建材批发	Building Materials	33419
化肥批发	Chemical Fertilizer	10833
机械设备、五金产品及电子产品	Wholesale of Machinery, Hardwaresand Electronic Products	115172
#汽车批发	Motor Vehicles	17352
计算机、软件及辅助设备批发	Computer, Sofeware and Accessories	1767
贸易经纪与代理	Trade Broker and Agency	18217
其他批发业	Other Wholesales	36987
3.按控股情况分	Grouped by Share Holding	
国有控股	State Holding Enterprises	1196309
集体控股	Collective-owned Holding Enterprises	134841
私人控股	Private Holding Enterprises	1053093
港澳台商控股	Hongkong, Macao and Taiwan Holding Enterprises	11386
外商控股	Foreign Holding Enterprises	
其　他	Others	115720
4.按经营形式分	Grouped by Management Form	
独立门店	Independent Stores	1312096
连锁总店(总部)	Chain Headquarters	288510
连锁门店	Chain Stores	2032
其　他	Others	908712
5.按单位规模分	Grouped by Enterprise Size	
大　型	Large-size	891067
中　型	Medium-size	1099669
小　型	Small-size	321940
微　型	Micro-size	198673
二、零售业	**Retail Trade**	**1785223**
1.按登记注册类型分组	Grouped by Registered Kind	
内资企业	Civil Funded Enterprises	1723888
国有企业	State-owned Enterprises	23187
集体企业	Collective-owned Enterprises	21831
股份合作企业	Share Cooperative Enterprises	356
联营企业	Joint Ownership Enterprises	

continued

(10 000 yuan)

流动资产合计 Total Circulating Assets	#应收帐款 Accounts Receivable	#存货 Inventory	固定资产合计 Total Fixed Assets	累计折旧 Accumulated Depreciation	#本年折旧 Depreciation This Year	资产总计 Total Assets
20189815	3354883	1492321	2908002	1101545	359764	29425351
15979386	2488643	899467	2643287	917408	333452	23996138
261815	22611	85477	129086	113845	17034	514469
2586331	350886	444625	74426	35445	5407	3260258
963876	358005	29434	34830	22513	2797	1028661
251963	94651	15291	11450	4329	609	273045
943831	482347	134766	60360	28736	7018	1059890
190302	94278	31285	6450	2617	1130	198158
8371	5643	1896	17	115	15	8391
127612	316	14577	7797	5872	453	146779
76998	10560	34890	8915	8302	807	90755
16269820	2968650	1085186	2465793	1001093	337037	23326425
950150	69116	139183	313484	160119	20252	1708534
7491380	1511533	1199594	539443	222038	38559	11287390
47931	1761	15608	15331	5747	2607	63298
922424	168343	118238	78903	43945	12875	1406863
12915218	2526481	1337365	1876207	665472	109530	19989619
942730	25717	274806	60829	43684	4511	1066964
16540	3369	1672	1713	2165	218	19393
11807217	2163836	943965	1474204	721620	297070	16716534
9746895	1146557	967075	2388545	848074	332838	16774567
11273349	2319127	1093439	658919	402738	59817	15171923
2252896	656078	293359	250310	114428	11913	2972397
2408564	597639	203934	115179	67700	6761	2873623
7517566	**1059779**	**1987273**	**2283834**	**1089107**	**164046**	**11575097**
7353398	1041516	1928573	2195123	1042555	153224	11294059
85051	16824	19868	36598	21932	1533	134865
59856	9132	17380	23079	18336	884	97148
1410	411	244	979	1022	63	11735

13-5 续表2

单位：万元

指　　标	Item	年初存货 Beginning Inventory
有限责任公司	Limited Responsibility Corporations	348976
国有独资公司	Company Exclusively with Investment from State	12012
其他有限责任公司	Other Limited Responsibility Company	336964
股份有限公司	Share-holding Limited Corporations	181394
私营企业	Private-owned Enterprises	1145638
私营独资企业	Enterprise Exclusively with Investment from Private	20025
私营合伙企业	Private Partnership Enterprises	1307
私营有限责任公司	Private Limited Responsibility Corporations	1061023
私营股份有限公司	Private Share-holding Limited Corporations	63282
其他企业	Others	2506
港澳台商投资企业	Enterprises Funded by HongKong, Macao and Taiwan	56389
与港澳台商合资经营企业	Joint Venture Enterprises	
港澳台商独资企业	Solely Owned Entersprises	39815
港澳台商投资股份有限公司	Share Holding Limited Corporation	16574
外商投资企业	Foreign Funded Enterprises	4946
中外合资经营企业	Joint Venture Enterprises	1189
外资企业	Enterprises with Sole Investment from Foreign	3748
其他外商投资企业	Other Foreign Funded Enterprises	10
2.按零售行业小类分	Grouped by Wholesale Trade	
综合零售	General Retail Sales Trade	248344
百货零售	Daily Goods	86079
超级市场零售	Supermarkets	153775
其他综合零售	Others	8490
食品、饮料及烟草制品专门零售	Retail of Food, Beverage and Tobaccos	90526
纺织、服装及日用品专门零售	Retail of Textiles, Garments and Daily Articles	90417
#服装零售	Garments	81700
文化、体育用品及器材专门零售	Retail of Culture, Sports Articles and Equipments	89799
#图书、报刊零售	Books and Mangzines	20276
医药及医疗器材专门零售	Retail of Medicines and Medical Appliances	118792
#药品零售	Medicines	117981
汽车、摩托车、燃料及零配件专门零售	Retail of Motor Vehicles, Motorcycles, Feuls and Parts	978982
#汽车零售	Motor Vehicles	737917
机动车燃料零售	Vehicle Feuls	235200
家用电器及电子产品专门零售	Retail of Household Electronic Equipments and Products	100823
#日用家电设备零售	Household Appliance	61911
计算机、软件及辅助设备零售	Computer, Software and Auxiliary Equipments	18370
通信设备零售	Communication Equipments	7930

continued

(10 000 yuan)

流动资产合计 Total Circulating Assets	#应收帐款 Accounts Receivable	#存货 Inventory	固定资产合计 Total Fixed Assets	累计折旧 Accumulated Depreciation	#本年折旧 Depreciation This Year	资产总计 Total Assets
1874345	388763	335296	664718	329892	43689	3055687
149354	17173	9676	109816	33838	1351	307382
1724991	371591	325621	554901	296054	42338	2748305
796777	26557	335368	427193	216638	39287	1452984
4527576	596970	1218954	1037785	454132	67629	6521146
46749	11266	19076	29643	11361	2356	84119
3027	-3284	1194	1922	1322	50	6243
4273610	580831	1127537	874341	389187	60933	5981374
204189	8157	71146	131879	52262	4290	449411
8384	2858	1464	4772	603	141	20496
150289	18134	51627	69450	29864	7177	238399
87870	13764	33783	54498	21781	4270	158870
62419	4370	17844	14952	8083	2907	79529
13880	129	7073	19262	16688	3645	42639
3573		1286	333	6108	1706	3981
7181	7	5774	2627	3807	518	19220
3126	122	12	16302	6773	1421	19438
1542183	61303	291434	489262	227931	21229	2530986
864612	27780	95276	203002	83874	8988	1302718
553604	31328	161735	260379	136031	10856	1037029
123967	2195	34423	25882	8026	1385	191239
239601	41608	89448	115833	33549	4975	428818
392108	67467	84551	153232	68434	11609	723532
347697	57691	64441	130599	64758	10827	643272
235875	34969	94821	64218	41036	5877	351998
113567	25247	18432	38540	23052	3420	182096
663555	279281	152207	26767	17374	2693	748335
651212	271014	151587	26599	17174	2642	735801
3427284	340673	1096377	827713	455548	79045	4854675
2319686	275917	709062	315134	183917	38035	2871988
1085491	56666	380718	511051	270890	40890	1958924
362572	60533	111842	30214	12345	2201	422827
229435	20307	68626	18008	5441	1058	264493
78898	24124	23381	3016	2893	384	85583
26981	11080	9636	2577	1690	408	30665

13-5 续表3

单位：万元

指　标	Item	年初存货 Beginning Inventory
五金、家具及室内装修材料专门零售	Retail of Hardwares, Furniture and Room Decorative Building	35961
货摊、无店铺及其他零售业	Retail of Stall, Non-store and Others	31580
3.按控股情况分	Grouped by Share Holding	
国有控股	State Holding Enterprises	328167
集体控股	Collective-owned Holding Enterprises	77658
私人控股	Private Holding Enterprises	1254603
港澳台商控股	Hongkong, Macao and Taiwan Holding Enterprises	45719
外商控股	Foreign Holding Enterprises	4937
其　他	Others	74139
4.按经营形式分	Grouped by Management Form	
独立门店	Independent Stores	1418058
连锁总店	Chain Headquarters	183329
连锁门店	Chain Stores	103883
其　他	Others	79954
5.按单位规模分	Grouped by Enterprise Size	
大　型	Large-size	519670
中　型	Medium-size	803948
小　型	Small-size	400545
微　型	Micro-size	61060
6.按零售业态分	Grouped by Retail Format	
#有店铺零售	Store-based	1757255
食杂店	Grocery Store	1865
便利店	Convenient Store	12239
折扣店	Discount Store	
超　市	Supermarket	60291
大型超市	Hypermarket	124446
仓储会员店	Warehouse Club	16576
百货店	Department Store	95130
专业店	Specialized Shop	734421
专卖店	Exclusive Shop	606663
家居建材商店	Home Center	15815
购物中心	Shopping Center	38971
厂家直销中心	Factory Outlet Center	50839
无店铺零售	Non-store	27576
#网上商店	Online	13641

continued

(10 000 yuan)

流动资产合计 Total Circulating Assets	#应收帐款 Accounts Receivable	#存货 Inventory	固定资产合计 Total Fixed Assets	累计折旧 Accumulated Depreciation	#本年折旧 Depreciation This Year	资产总计 Total Assets
213333	90373	34654	75989	19924	3775	363752
441056	83572	31940	500605	212966	32642	1150175
1791277	290405	482148	902800	464755	69074	3311953
242780	65210	68344	82456	50607	7131	402410
5060928	662752	1323440	1150657	496315	70805	7219550
141349	16025	44858	69450	29864	7177	229459
10754	7	7061	2960	9915	2224	23201
270479	25380	61423	75511	37651	7636	388525
5564882	901781	1441977	1455856	676080	110539	8247615
1224181	53994	361949	195068	106966	16416	1648228
233440	13807	104160	209866	102564	8104	625131
495063	90197	79187	423045	203497	28988	1054124
2821812	308055	717646	1037767	504819	67722	4677965
2968330	383898	779946	857639	414002	68651	4534580
1435289	288239	436563	321257	147187	24985	1964589
292135	79586	53118	67172	23098	2688	397964
7311764	1023108	1961794	2178203	1062485	162670	11188253
6983	974	2542	4200	1008	99	11473
77150	10731	8455	22303	12336	1070	146933
180839	24893	63498	48203	29228	3613	279155
433072	19025	125349	197143	101613	6944	824794
29046	3608	18007	3827	2095	266	33217
1026925	47061	128002	319592	139895	16198	1591488
3148558	568539	922762	843446	373936	69078	4656251
1878830	253776	580386	357161	209122	32857	2487281
114387	50022	14325	35522	9634	1671	194236
162426	4604	39260	23518	15129	3678	317467
253547	39875	59207	323287	168490	27196	645960
198602	31460	24656	96791	24517	1376	358343
58100	8850	14799	7856	1827	755	78718

13-5 续表4

单位：万元

指　　标	Item	流动负债合　　计 Total Liquid Liabilities
总　计	**Total**	**32153285**
一、批发业	**Wholesale Trade**	**24027698**
1.按登记注册类型分	Grouped by Registered Kind	
内资企业	Civil Funded Enterprises	23905029
国有企业	State-owned Enterprises	880942
集体企业	Collective-owned Enterprises	234123
股份合作企业	Share Cooperative Enterprises	495
联营企业	Joint Ownership Enterprises	1066
集体联营企业	Collective Joint Enterprises	1066
有限责任公司	Limited Responsibility Corporations	13593323
国有独资公司	Company Exclusively with Investment from State	5714727
其他有限责任公司	Other Limited Responsibility Company	7878596
股份有限公司	Share-holding Limited Corporations	2837281
私营企业	Private-owned Enterprises	6348726
私营独资企业	Enterprise Exclusively with Investment from Private	5753
私营合伙企业	Private Partnership Enterprises	
私营有限责任公司	Private Limited Responsibility Corporations	5652626
私营股份有限公司	Private Share-holding Limited Corporations	690348
其他企业	Others	9073
港澳台商投资企业	Enterprises Funded by HongKong, Macao and Taiwan	120924
与港澳台商合资经营企业	Joint Venture Enterprises	98760
港澳台商独资企业	Solely Owned Entersprises	22164
港澳台商投资股份有限公司	Share Holding Limited Corporation	
外商投资企业	Foreign Funded Enterprises	1746
中外合资经营企业	Joint Venture Enterprises	1746
2.按批发行业小类分	Grouped by Wholesale Trade	
农、林、牧产品批发	Wholesale of Agricultural, Forestry and Animal Husbandry Products	172280
食品、饮料及烟草制品批发	Wholesale of Food, Beverage and Tobaccos	708116
#米、面制品及食用油批发	Rice, Flour and Edible Oil	106922
烟草制品批发	Tobacoo Products Manufacturing	275551
纺织、服装及家庭用品批发	Wholesale of Textiles, Garments and Family Articles	665882
#服装批发	Wholesale of Garments	544823
文化、体育用品及器材批发	Wholesale of Culture, Sports Articles and Equipments	277843
医药及医疗器材批发	Wholesale of Medicines and Medical Appliances	1197245
#西药批发	Wholesale of Western Medicine	777398
中药批发	Wholesale of Chinese Traditional and Patent Medicine	279314

continued

(10 000 yuan)

负债合计 Total Liabilities	所有者权益合计 Total Creditors' Equity	#实收资本 Capital Hold	#国家资本 State	#集体资本 Collective	#法人资本 Legal Person	#个人资本 Individual
37197104	**12170503**	**6173690**	**1846194**	**221595**	**1946844**	**2026063**
28329367	**9463143**	**3595552**	**1367814**	**177640**	**1074070**	**877881**
28206698	9296392	3420858	1291314	177640	1074020	877881
944420	1061807	165723	156414	143	9071	95
241097	115434	48081	147	47756	176	
495	2012	2012				2012
1066	64	46		46		
1066	64	46		46		
16750159	2871104	1570459	874138	121419	513305	61597
7890748	1380311	456502	404603		51676	223
8859411	1490793	1113957	469535	121419	461629	61374
3375812	1409449	335004	258212	527	29661	46604
6883145	3830555	1297386	2234	7250	521548	766355
5753	4213	4373				4373
6179472	1342790	1124043	2234	7250	504837	609723
697920	2483552	168970			16711	152259
10504	5966	2147	169	500	260	1218
120924	167721	174645	76500			
98760	131279	150001	76500			
22164	36442	24644				
1746	-970	50			50	
1746	-970	50			50	
186841	115376	57283	26228		4933	26122
782356	1024420	111768	29626	16525	41736	23881
116227	21338	16333	7747		5229	3356
275551	884668	15522	12917		2606	
671296	2467707	158453		237	3617	150886
547477	2479969	148385			662	144011
278398	139637	29577	16577		7960	5040
1221840	181864	137031	12678	265	43033	81055
790567	114320	80092	4027	175	30951	44939
287709	55336	41813	5735		7398	28680

13-5 续表5

单位：万元

指　　标	Item	流动负债合　　计 Total Liquid Liabilities
矿产品、建材及化工产品批发	Wholesale of Mineral Products, Building and Chemical Products	19936093
#煤炭及制品批发	Coal and Related Products	16075994
石油及制品批发	Petroleum and Related Products	298778
金属及金属矿批发	Metals and Metals Materials	2142555
建材批发	Building Materials	940361
化肥批发	Chemical Fertilizer	229232
机械设备、五金产品及电子产品批发	Wholesale of Machinery, Hardwaresand Electronic Products	912461
#汽车批发	Motor Vehicles	190316
计算机、软件及辅助设备批发	Computer, Sofeware and Accessories	5591
贸易经纪与代理	Trade Broker and Agency	91111
其他批发业	Other Wholesales	66669
3.按控股情况分	Grouped by Share Holding	
国有控股	State Holding Enterprises	15664908
集体控股	Collective-owned Holding Enterprises	891795
私人控股	Private Holding Enterprises	6793937
港澳台商控股	Hongkong, Macao and Taiwan Holding Enterprises	26736
外商控股	Foreign Holding Enterprises	
其　他	Others	650323
4.按经营形式分	Grouped by Management Form	
独立门店	Independent Stores	11816616
连锁总店(总部)	Chain Headquarters	908123
连锁门店	Chain Stores	6476
其　他	Others	11296483
5.按单位规模分	Grouped by Enterprise Size	
大　型	Large-size	8736709
中　型	Medium-size	10818128
小　型	Small-size	2371497
微　型	Micro-size	2101364
二、零售业	**Retail Trade**	**8125587**
1.按登记注册类型分组	Grouped by Registered Kind	
内资企业	Civil Funded Enterprises	7935376
国有企业	State-owned Enterprises	99819
集体企业	Collective-owned Enterprises	59362
股份合作企业	Share Cooperative Enterprises	9955
联营企业	Joint Ownership Enterprises	

continued

(10 000 yuan)

负债合计 Total Liabilities	所有者权益合计 Total Creditors' Equity					
		#实收资本 Capital Hold	#国家资本 State	#集体资本 Collective	#法人资本 Legal Person	#个人资本 Individual
24082095	5343256	2934092	1241422	158170	924580	536418
19879987	4116151	1876993	835166	70024	675481	296322
456436	58033	84915	13028	3919	42599	25368
2257687	1002571	775997	348832	75576	132109	145980
955361	73299	107469	25000	143	45546	36779
231902	41142	29532	13249	3319	10049	2913
924117	135773	147022	39181	900	46361	39648
190316	7841	16721	1417	501	8358	6445
5591	2800	2600				2600
115079	31700	5000				5000
67346	23409	15327	2102	1543	1851	9831
19267779	4058647	1919312	1362868	14926	413424	54593
984849	723685	156634	147	145871	4542	6071
7384638	3902752	1402692	2281	7423	582554	810435
26736	36562	24645				
665366	741498	92270	2518	9420	73550	6782
14403931	5585688	2014314	598367	112561	610924	618962
908180	158784	68602	3002		5000	60600
7230	12162	2219		1919	186	114
13010026	3706509	1510417	766445	63161	457961	198206
11589758	5184810	822337	378612	55855	117708	266450
11894790	3277133	1586376	675502	96995	548111	244835
2541397	431000	558733	111631	12279	215170	219654
2303424	570199	628106	202069	12512	193081	146942
8867736	**2707361**	**2578138**	**478380**	**43955**	**872774**	**1148182**
8674045	2620014	2522880	478380	43955	858359	1141686
104151	30714	25294	13808	106	11319	61
65568	31579	17369	163	16592	160	454
9986	1749	1296	567	729		

13-5 续表6

单位：万元

指 标	Item	流动负债合 计 Total Liquid Liabilities
有限责任公司	Limited Responsibility Corporations	2080964
国有独资公司	Company Exclusively with Investment from State	70592
其他有限责任公司	Other Limited Responsibility Company	2010372
股份有限公司	Share-holding Limited Corporations	872749
私营企业	Private-owned Enterprises	4805765
私营独资企业	Enterprise Exclusively with Investment from Private	36887
私营合伙企业	Private Partnership Enterprises	3014
私营有限责任公司	Private Limited Responsibility Corporations	4442039
私营股份有限公司	Private Share-holding Limited Corporations	323824
其他企业	Others	6762
港澳台商投资企业	Enterprises Funded by HongKong, Macao and Taiwan	131264
与港澳台商合资经营企业	Joint Venture Enterprises	
港澳台商独资企业	Solely Owned Enterspirses	93357
港澳台商投资股份有限公司	Share Holding Limited Corporation	37906
外商投资企业	Foreign Funded Enterprises	58947
中外合资经营企业	Joint Venture Enterprises	18513
外资企业	Enterprises with Sole Investment from Foreign	15894
其他外商投资企业	Other Foreign Funded Enterprises	24540
2.按零售行业小类分	Grouped by Wholesale Trade	
综合零售	General Retail Sales Trade	1869816
百货零售	Daily Goods	875756
超级市场零售	Supermarkets	863843
其他综合零售	Others	130217
食品、饮料及烟草制品专门零售	Retail of Food, Beverage and Tobaccos	261291
纺织、服装及日用品专门零售	Retail of Textiles, Garments and Daily Articles	537672
#服装零售	Garments	493689
文化、体育用品及器材专门零售	Retail of Culture, Sports Articles and Equipments	178301
#图书、报刊零售	Books and Mangzines	87801
医药及医疗器材专门零售	Retail of Medicines and Medical Appliances	537064
#药品零售	Medicines	524990
汽车、摩托车、燃料及零配件专门零售	Retail of Motor Vehicles, Motorcycles, Feuls and Parts	3480308
#汽车零售	Motor Vehicles	2337281
机动车燃料零售	Vehicle Feuls	1125765
家用电器及电子产品专门零售	Retail of Household Electronic Equipments and Products	320359
#日用家电设备零售	Household Appliance	225589
计算机、软件及辅助设备零售	Computer, Software and Auxiliary Equipments	47615
通信设备零售	Communication Equipments	19930

continued

(10 000 yuan)

负债合计 Total Liabilities	所有者权益合计 Total Creditors' Equity	#实收资本 Capital Hold	#国家资本 State	#集体资本 Collective	#法人资本 Legal Person	#个人资本 Individual
2480034	575653	579580	234762	22587	242046	79685
205851	101531	26177	14196		11739	242
2274183	474122	553403	220566	22587	230307	79443
892310	560674	271830	226035	1351	40990	3455
5113852	1407294	1616505	3015	2283	559794	1051413
38763	45355	23145	5	20	11637	11483
3115	3128	1214			553	661
4710428	1270946	1556519	3010	2009	542189	1009310
361545	87865	35627		254	5415	29959
8145	12350	11007	30	307	4050	6620
133572	104827	51064			13615	6296
93357	65513	33643			4295	6296
40215	39314	17421			9321	
60119	-17480	4194			800	199
18513	-14532	996			300	199
17065	2154	2698				
24540	-5103	500			500	
2107768	423217	362004	8164	11107	175738	163017
1056183	246535	211401	3669	6617	138552	58585
905427	131601	116867	3030	246	33356	80235
146158	45081	33736	1465	4244	3830	24197
300133	128684	100917	10907	6024	43326	39941
597199	126332	113715	582	2033	48095	56905
550702	92570	102781	459	1221	42328	53674
179367	172631	101656	6164	1937	64065	28342
87910	94186	58748	6164		51587	997
542725	205610	162990	103901	158	29813	29118
530641	205160	162297	103901	158	29420	28818
3600743	1253932	1010626	262838	12281	384617	335536
2380996	490991	577119	29454	10510	256590	265211
1201653	757272	428638	232972	1721	125593	68352
324481	98346	99109	363	90	40144	58512
230762	33731	43319	212	20	22963	20125
47669	37915	31606	152	70	7349	24035
18437	12228	11537			2612	8925

13-5 续表7

单位：万元

指　　标	Item	流动负债合计 Total Liquid Liabilities
五金、家具及室内装修材料专门零售	Retail of Hardwares, Furniture and Room Decorative Building	249564
货摊、无店铺及其他零售业	Retail of Stall, Non-store and Others	691212
3.按控股情况分	Grouped by Share Holding	
国有控股	State Holding Enterprises	2009312
集体控股	Collective-owned Holding Enterprises	297584
私人控股	Private Holding Enterprises	5345670
港澳台商控股	Hongkong, Macao and Taiwan Holding Enterprises	122577
外商控股	Foreign Holding Enterprises	34407
其　他	Others	316037
4.按经营形式分	Grouped by Management Form	
独立门店	Independent Stores	5644952
连锁总店	Chain Headquarters	1296438
连锁门店	Chain Stores	451646
其　他	Others	732551
5.按单位规模分	Grouped by Enterprise Size	
大　型	Large-size	3221243
中　型	Medium-size	3229743
小　型	Small-size	1408668
微　型	Micro-size	265933
6.按零售业态分	Grouped by Retail Format	
#有店铺零售	Store-based	8007146
食杂店	Grocery Store	7611
便利店	Convenient Store	76067
折扣店	Discount Store	
超　市	Supermarket	200734
大型超市	Hypermarket	724258
仓储会员店	Warehouse Club	15590
百货店	Department Store	1076229
专业店	Specialized Shop	3047469
专卖店	Exclusive Shop	1877624
家居建材商店	Home Center	141281
购物中心	Shopping Center	239016
厂家直销中心	Factory Outlet Center	601266
无店铺零售	Non-store	106020
#网上商店	Online	38437

continued

(10 000 yuan)

负债合计 Total Liabilities	所有者权益合计 Total Creditors' Equity	#实收资本 Capital Hold	#国家资本 State	#集体资本 Collective	#法人资本 Legal Person	#个人资本 Individual
257856	105896	431765	1644	8229	28164	393231
957463	192712	195355	83816	2096	58812	43581
2342878	969075	658856	468832	3371	182163	4490
345209	57201	55035	163	36208	14755	3909
5670914	1548636	1742596	3100	2573	630343	1106580
124886	104573	51064			13615	6296
35579	-12378	3694			300	199
348270	40254	66893	6285	1803	31598	26707
6114015	2133600	2214662	352540	41676	760482	1041634
1360420	287808	124417	42605	403	25290	46800
480333	144798	87835	22799	404	47477	17005
912968	141156	151223	60435	1472	39524	42742
3539339	1138625	663816	380475	3692	126917	140682
3546945	987635	1291363	68378	22365	473830	705210
1497701	466887	512489	22094	11760	232575	245340
283751	114213	110471	7433	6138	39452	56950
8618816	2569438	2517355	464403	43705	852095	1122305
8713	2760	1609		167	582	860
87790	59143	39224	16538	1398	3990	17299
209147	70009	64198	3537	788	30570	29304
772400	52394	76035	528	168	17192	54169
16396	16820	7703			7653	50
1280746	310741	266298	5323	10721	158618	91636
3165357	1490894	982634	349031	10785	299155	321894
1978375	508905	919903	72147	11556	277145	542504
147034	47202	49843		7562	19015	22769
261260	56207	45144		105	13332	26706
691597	-45636	64764	17301	454	24844	15115
236499	121843	55783	13977	250	15679	25877
41333	37386	29851			11695	18157

13-5 续表8

单位：万元

指　标	Item	营业收入 Business Revenue
总　计	**Total**	**81879439**
一、批发业	**Wholesale Trade**	**63695040**
1.按登记注册类型分	Grouped by Registered Kind	
内资企业	Civil Funded Enterprises	62411005
国有企业	State-owned Enterprises	4348096
集体企业	Collective-owned Enterprises	607075
股份合作企业	Share Cooperative Enterprises	703
联营企业	Joint Ownership Enterprises	2270
集体联营企业	Collective Joint Enterprises	2270
有限责任公司	Limited Responsibility Corporations	46357879
国有独资公司	Company Exclusively with Investment from State	16909498
其他有限责任公司	Other Limited Responsibility Company	29448381
股份有限公司	Share-holding Limited Corporations	2960098
私营企业	Private-owned Enterprises	8072924
私营独资企业	Enterprise Exclusively with Investment from Private	14515
私营合伙企业	Private Partnership Enterprises	
私营有限责任公司	Private Limited Responsibility Corporations	7360379
私营股份有限公司	Private Share-holding Limited Corporations	698029
其他企业	Others	61961
港澳台商投资企业	Enterprises Funded by HongKong, Macao and Taiwan	1276923
与港澳台商合资经营企业	Joint Venture Enterprises	1214846
港澳台商独资企业	Solely Owned Entersprises	62078
港澳台商投资股份有限公司	Share Holding Limited Corporation	
外商投资企业	Foreign Funded Enterprises	7112
中外合资经营企业	Joint Venture Enterprises	7112
2.按批发行业小类分	Grouped by Wholesale Trade	
农、林、牧产品批发	Wholesale of Agricultural, Forestry and Animal Husbandry Products	230790
食品、饮料及烟草制品批发	Wholesale of Food, Beverage and Tobaccos	4062009
#米、面制品及食用油批发	Rice, Flour and Edible Oil	152413
烟草制品批发	Tobacoo Products Manufacturing	2802930
纺织、服装及家庭用品批发	Wholesale of Textiles, Garments and Family Articles	685079
#服装批发	Wholesale of Garments	437474
文化、体育用品及器材批发	Wholesale of Culture, Sports Articles and Equipments	464921
医药及医疗器材批发	Wholesale of Medicines and Medical Appliances	2149747
#西药批发	Wholesale of Western Medicine	1452143
中药批发	Wholesale of Chinese Traditional and Patent Medicine	508934

continued

(10 000 yuan)

主营业务收入 Revenue of Major Business	营业成本 Business Costs	主营业务成本 Costs of Major Business	营业税金及附加 Business Taxes and Extra Charges	主营业务税金及附加 Taxes and Extra Charges in Major Business	其他业务利润 Profits of Other Business	销售费用 Costs of Sales
77434668	**77416134**	**73347800**	**516931**	**512676**	**254588**	**1882487**
59671525	**60982655**	**57055514**	**467210**	**465682**	**74898**	**950953**
58388058	59731103	55803975	466880	465352	74274	937858
4335768	3497844	3488539	393121	393085	2059	77951
603787	457546	455388	4500	4488	1797	97485
515	438	438	2	2		135
2270	1831	1831	5	5		310
2270	1831	1831	5	5		310
42409804	45444809	41576929	52914	51597	52016	357289
16849387	16460460	16436249	28404	27328	24889	139605
25560417	28984349	25140681	24511	24268	27127	217684
2950934	2844584	2843881	2201	2201	64	48708
8023019	7432054	7384970	14025	13863	18273	349751
14515	13818	13818	176	176		194
7310474	6875016	6827933	12928	12766	18259	259692
698029	543219	543219	921	921	14	89865
61961	51999	51999	112	112	64	6230
1276446	1245971	1245959	304	304	532	11267
1214403	1199626	1199613	35	35	498	4838
62043	46345	46345	269	269	35	6429
7020	5581	5581	27	27	92	1828
7020	5581	5581	27	27	92	1828
230279	214521	214485	164	145	439	7127
4049635	3124220	3114869	396566	396552	2994	99295
152406	147166	147166	270	270	8	4865
2792613	1993721	1984539	392233	392233	393	46743
683406	537007	535967	780	766	216	89929
437440	298683	298483	495	495	35	78696
461616	423610	423586	547	547	329	11535
2144413	1927494	1926304	4538	4476	7713	116038
1448234	1331594	1331017	2476	2440	2032	54473
507599	429672	429069	1608	1583	5141	52470

13-5 续表9

单位：万元

指　　标	Item	营业收入 Business Revenue
矿产品、建材及化工产品批发	Wholesale of Mineral Products, Building and Chemical Products	50601799
#煤炭及制品批发	Coal and Related Products	25106693
石油及制品批发	Petroleum and Related Products	750682
金属及金属矿批发	Metals and Metals Materials	10563922
建材批发	Building Materials	10804789
化肥批发	Chemical Fertilizer	3085506
机械设备、五金产品及电子产品批发	Wholesale of Machinery, Hardwaresand Electronic Products	5359114
#汽车批发	Motor Vehicles	627150
计算机、软件及辅助设备批发	Computer, Sofeware and Accessories	17907
贸易经纪与代理	Trade Broker and Agency	35843
其他批发业	Other Wholesales	105740
3.按控股情况分	Grouped by Share Holding	
国有控股	State Holding Enterprises	52151766
集体控股	Collective-owned Holding Enterprises	1124513
私人控股	Private Holding Enterprises	8695329
港澳台商控股	Hongkong, Macao and Taiwan Holding Enterprises	99108
外商控股	Foreign Holding Enterprises	
其　他	Others	1624325
4.按经营形式分	Grouped by Management Form	
独立门店	Independent Stores	36942017
连锁总店(总部)	Chain Headquarters	1349338
连锁门店	Chain Stores	29830
其　他	Others	25373856
5.按单位规模分	Grouped by Enterprise Size	
大　型	Large-size	17432844
中　型	Medium-size	32316438
小　型	Small-size	3147553
微　型	Micro-size	10798205
二、零售业	**Retail Trade**	**18184399**
1.按登记注册类型分组	Grouped by Registered Kind	
内资企业	Civil Funded Enterprises	17743193
国有企业	State-owned Enterprises	381807
集体企业	Collective-owned Enterprises	364206
股份合作企业	Share Cooperative Enterprises	7540
联营企业	Joint Ownership Enterprises	

continued

(10 000 yuan)

主营业务收入 Revenue of Major Business	营业成本 Business Costs	主营业务成本 Costs of Major Business	营业税金及附加 Business Taxes and Extra Charges	主营业务税金及附加 Taxes and Extra Charges in Major Business	其他业务利润 Profits of Other Business	销售费用 Costs of Sales
46632049	49339317	45443328	62589	61175	55672	589034
21167400	24066502	20208487	49420	48208	48994	514094
744662	690147	687791	2221	2212	1886	19923
10543188	10460320	10428106	5389	5266	2557	41523
10802361	10770972	10769243	2207	2143	1115	3254
3085504	3074710	3073449	1723	1723	16	4972
5329103	5283767	5265015	1736	1732	7185	32126
611791	592317	580807	693	692	267	17126
17907	17144	17144	14	14		356
35769	35078	35078			74	409
105255	97643	96883	290	290	276	5462
48192454	50535948	46660937	435424	434077	52379	317144
1119627	893595	890139	14864	14852	3151	111008
8641916	7977369	7929159	14968	14805	18766	410644
99073	81782	81782	298	298	102	7920
1618455	1493962	1493498	1657	1651	499	104237
33135372	35643620	31896874	180754	179533	51094	480994
1331800	1172214	1143343	80933	80933	215	18529
29830	25194	25194	83	83		905
25174523	24141627	23990104	205440	205133	23589	450525
17313563	15666389	15590188	438420	437452	40927	472675
32132914	31564617	31423408	19497	19266	28376	374588
3139647	3012345	3010201	4209	4099	3084	81492
7085401	10739304	7031717	5084	4866	2512	22199
17763143	**16433479**	**16292285**	**49721**	**46994**	**179690**	**931534**
17338380	16065738	15931684	47635	45198	173967	883681
380933	351293	323406	800	752	2629	14976
363024	331840	331490	1212	1208	1558	10737
7453	6013	6013	58	58	88	

13-5 续表10

单位：万元

指　标	Item	营业收入 Business Revenue
有限责任公司	Limited Responsibility Corporations	3857518
国有独资公司	Company Exclusively with Investment from State	162254
其他有限责任公司	Other Limited Responsibility Company	3695264
股份有限公司	Share-holding Limited Corporations	2962910
私营企业	Private-owned Enterprises	10144798
私营独资企业	Enterprise Exclusively with Investment from Private	212579
私营合伙企业	Private Partnership Enterprises	52378
私营有限责任公司	Private Limited Responsibility Corporations	8936703
私营股份有限公司	Private Share-holding Limited Corporations	943140
其他企业	Others	24415
港澳台商投资企业	Enterprises Funded by HongKong, Macao and Taiwan	379792
与港澳台商合资经营企业	Joint Venture Enterprises	
港澳台商独资企业	Solely Owned Entersprises	221827
港澳台商投资股份有限公司	Share Holding Limited Corporation	157965
外商投资企业	Foreign Funded Enterprises	61413
中外合资经营企业	Joint Venture Enterprises	9777
外资企业	Enterprises with Sole Investment from Foreign	37096
其他外商投资企业	Other Foreign Funded Enterprises	14540
2.按零售行业小类分	Grouped by Wholesale Trade	
综合零售	General Retail Sales Trade	3115941
百货零售	Daily Goods	1211498
超级市场零售	Supermarkets	1461546
其他综合零售	Others	442897
食品、饮料及烟草制品专门零售	Retail of Food, Beverage and Tobaccos	653085
纺织、服装及日用品专门零售	Retail of Textiles, Garments and Daily Articles	979012
#服装零售	Garments	832156
文化、体育用品及器材专门零售	Retail of Culture, Sports Articles and Equipments	330796
#图书、报刊零售	Books and Mangzines	186146
医药及医疗器材专门零售	Retail of Medicines and Medical Appliances	1289888
#药品零售	Medicines	1278731
汽车、摩托车、燃料及零配件专门零售	Retail of Motor Vehicles, Motorcycles, Feuls and Parts	9802670
#汽车零售	Motor Vehicles	6076878
机动车燃料零售	Vehicle Feuls	3561311
家用电器及电子产品专门零售	Retail of Household Electronic Equipments and Products	824183
#日用家电设备零售	Household Appliance	499416
计算机、软件及辅助设备零售	Computer, Software and Auxiliary Equipments	141711
通信设备零售	Communication Equipments	79063

continued

(10 000 yuan)

主营业务收入 Revenue of Major Business	营业成本 Business Costs	主营业务成本 Costs of Major Business	营业税金及附加 Business Taxes and Extra Charges	主营业务税金及附加 Taxes and Extra Charges in Major Business	其他业务利润 Profits of Other Business	销售费用 Costs of Sales
3661691	3358465	3317555	10027	8731	25156	203737
130749	133234	102213	598	598	904	8435
3530942	3225232	3215342	9429	8133	24252	195302
2919776	2790079	2755820	2783	2246	3013	166365
9981360	9206374	9175791	32058	31507	141522	486858
212416	187732	187709	1117	1096	1003	8628
52378	48712	48712	127	127	172	778
8819868	8148761	8121703	27400	26871	92353	380575
896699	821168	817666	3415	3414	47994	96877
24143	21674	21609	697	697		1009
365519	318207	311069	1694	1580	4427	35881
211393	189379	182422	593	592	2394	19199
154126	128828	128648	1101	988	2032	16683
59245	49534	49533	393	216	1297	11972
9351	7793	7793	52	52		2673
36582	29829	29827	120	120	68	6892
13312	11912	11912	221	44	1229	2407
2998001	2707740	2696004	14653	13401	104455	239456
1172291	1036150	1031657	8597	7642	28763	82077
1383326	1246393	1239150	5273	4980	75237	149615
442384	425197	425197	783	778	455	7764
650525	585486	583540	2962	2921	1992	31248
957994	853435	825920	3913	3472	20180	68139
811439	727733	727276	3348	2928	19154	58514
327788	265248	262421	2905	2808	2896	38879
183219	143837	141013	449	368	2174	27312
1284146	1140842	1138612	2571	2568	2638	82663
1273366	1130545	1128617	2551	2547	2638	82455
9602924	9107853	9062475	12100	11437	34766	363002
6043910	5755199	5745194	7659	7555	30960	153255
3515350	3312162	3276789	4337	3784	3091	208754
812773	732548	728119	2664	2627	2916	53249
494102	442102	441029	1647	1613	1100	35369
140146	125348	124662	315	315	459	7058
75396	72207	69655	524	521	710	4091

13-5 续表11

单位：万元

指　标	Item	营业收入 Business Revenue
五金、家具及室内装修材料专门零售	Retail of Hardwares, Furniture and Room Decorative Building	502241
货摊、无店铺及其他零售业	Retail of Stall, Non-store and Others	686581
3.按控股情况分	Grouped by Share Holding	
国有控股	State Holding Enterprises	5141088
集体控股	Collective-owned Holding Enterprises	738173
私人控股	Private Holding Enterprises	11156363
港澳台商控股	Hongkong, Macao and Taiwan Holding Enterprises	314105
外商控股	Foreign Holding Enterprises	46873
其　他	Others	787797
4.按经营形式分	Grouped by Management Form	
独立门店	Independent Stores	13377984
连锁总店	Chain Headquarters	2037052
连锁门店	Chain Stores	1543472
其　他	Others	1225890
5.按单位规模分	Grouped by Enterprise Size	
大　型	Large-size	7217959
中　型	Medium-size	6955429
小　型	Small-size	3444285
微　型	Micro-size	566726
6.按零售业态分	Grouped by Retail Format	
#有店铺零售	Store-based	17861679
食杂店	Grocery Store	23768
便利店	Convenient Store	305040
折扣店	Discount Store	
超　市	Supermarket	413450
大型超市	Hypermarket	1228200
仓储会员店	Warehouse Club	138783
百货店	Department Store	1698891
专业店	Specialized Shop	7791600
专卖店	Exclusive Shop	4939738
家居建材商店	Home Center	215676
购物中心	Shopping Center	444829
厂家直销中心	Factory Outlet Center	661705
无店铺零售	Non-store	322640
#网上商店	Online	192275

continued

(10 000 yuan)

主营业务收入 Revenue of Major Business	营业成本 Business Costs	主营业务成本 Costs of Major Business	营业税金及附加 Business Taxes and Extra Charges	主营业务税金及附加 Taxes and Extra Charges in Major Business	其他业务利润 Profits of Other Business	销售费用 Costs of Sales
497815	439513	439193	5289	5179	3391	19996
631177	600814	556002	2666	2581	6456	34904
5044646	4733400	4634038	8212	7447	20185	301398
734934	675663	675277	4038	2971	3656	25213
10985058	10126115	10093074	34087	33500	145922	536877
300911	253356	247209	1604	1491	4337	30137
45933	37622	37621	171	171	68	9565
651663	607322	605067	1610	1413	5523	28345
13096866	12130291	12063851	38075	35909	116701	567256
2016066	1802933	1792946	5023	4884	7081	159972
1471720	1381328	1356265	4116	3860	50870	147061
1178491	1118927	1079224	2508	2341	5039	57246
7044946	6568497	6495260	15200	14711	95120	435824
6861128	6292408	6239565	18064	16831	52506	341580
3291294	3044424	3030233	11236	10245	27198	138816
565775	528149	527227	5222	5206	4866	15315
17471668	16162711	16052387	48729	46001	178306	913053
23768	21458	21428	41	40		580
302061	278698	277003	1136	1052	1428	15800
410104	356477	355782	1910	1676	3069	35320
1164472	1048765	1041694	3403	3334	59548	143449
17711	18275	17538	32	32	-1052	537
1637293	1485133	1451105	9977	8603	47774	81095
7728750	7138491	7103519	16016	15531	24169	382883
4890531	4633093	4607561	8170	7843	26148	168209
211769	184585	184405	4532	4422	3232	12315
430672	381819	381758	1870	1844	12667	38561
654537	615917	610594	1641	1624	1324	34305
291396	270708	239838	751	751	1384	18481
191749	162412	162050	441	441	587	14954

13-5 续表12

单位：万元

指　　标	Item	管理费用 Costs of Administration
总　计	**Total**	**1227432**
一、批发业	**Wholesale Trade**	**688608**
1.按登记注册类型分	Grouped by Registered Kind	
内资企业	Civil Funded Enterprises	683836
国有企业	State-owned Enterprises	156759
集体企业	Collective-owned Enterprises	26679
股份合作企业	Share Cooperative Enterprises	38
联营企业	Joint Ownership Enterprises	122
集体联营企业	Collective Joint Enterprises	122
有限责任公司	Limited Responsibility Corporations	341526
国有独资公司	Company Exclusively with Investment from State	174818
其他有限责任公司	Other Limited Responsibility Company	166708
股份有限公司	Share-holding Limited Corporations	17755
私营企业	Private-owned Enterprises	139138
私营独资企业	Enterprise Exclusively with Investment from Private	257
私营合伙企业	Private Partnership Enterprises	
私营有限责任公司	Private Limited Responsibility Corporations	127534
私营股份有限公司	Private Share-holding Limited Corporations	11347
其他企业	Others	1820
港澳台商投资企业	Enterprises Funded by HongKong, Macao and Taiwan	4563
与港澳台商合资经营企业	Joint Venture Enterprises	2262
港澳台商独资企业	Solely Owned Entersprises	2301
港澳台商投资股份有限公司	Share Holding Limited Corporation	
外商投资企业	Foreign Funded Enterprises	209
中外合资经营企业	Joint Venture Enterprises	209
2.按批发行业小类分	Grouped by Wholesale Trade	
农、林、牧产品批发	Wholesale of Agricultural, Forestry and Animal Husbandry Products	7869
食品、饮料及烟草制品批发	Wholesale of Food, Beverage and Tobaccos	169261
#米、面制品及食用油批发	Rice, Flour and Edible Oil	4311
烟草制品批发	Tobacoo Products Manufacturing	134141
纺织、服装及家庭用品批发	Wholesale of Textiles, Garments and Family Articles	13409
#服装批发	Wholesale of Garments	8907
文化、体育用品及器材批发	Wholesale of Culture, Sports Articles and Equipments	10668
医药及医疗器材批发	Wholesale of Medicines and Medical Appliances	57245
#西药批发	Wholesale of Western Medicine	32188
中药批发	Wholesale of Chinese Traditional and Patent Medicine	15304

continued

(10 000 yuan)

财务费用 Costs of Finance	#利息支出 Interest Expenses	营业利润 Business Profits	利润总额 Total Profits	应交所得税 Income Tax Payable	应付职工薪酬 (本年贷方累计发生额) Remuneration Payable (Accumulated Credit Balance of The Year)	应交增值税 Added Taxes Payable
530478	**516495**	**169498**	**338199**	**152892**	**1084965**	**504787**
376159	**433099**	**193085**	**306360**	**117795**	**559916**	**363396**
371919	432149	183021	296145	117586	551630	361653
-18167	6253	239718	259315	67331	114821	151186
2774	2840	15366	15164	1403	18353	20487
		90	83	21	31	12
		4	4		203	39
		4	4		203	39
269982	345281	-170275	-69710	41484	322561	121624
140428	120874	-50225	17335	26396	198626	55590
129554	224407	-120050	-87045	15088	123935	66034
15425	5451	29566	30937	2679	12845	15716
101811	72300	66815	58902	4652	81378	52046
69	8	11	-41	5	148	16
98343	68710	13843	6107	4511	75122	51434
3399	3582	52961	52835	136	6108	596
94	24	1737	1450	16	1437	543
4232	941	10606	10755	209	7366	1527
3276		4828	4967	209	2143	246
957	941	5777	5788		5223	1281
8	8	-542	-539		920	216
8	8	-542	-539		920	216
3309	1841	-5178	4644	42	5874	287
-15738	3837	288021	284595	69838	116221	160938
2176	1855	-6367	-910	6	3026	326
-25379	13	261503	261521	67035	92011	145265
3172	2860	45355	43896	389	15254	4528
1753	1829	51924	51956	9	9831	1311
-927	883	16923	17302	4681	4252	645
24312	13184	20987	20527	5430	50160	31623
17856	8172	14510	14862	3489	29493	16834
5024	3532	4791	3991	1224	18705	12682

13-5 续表13

单位：万元

指 标	Item	管理费用 Costs of Administration
矿产品、建材及化工产品批发	Wholesale of Mineral Products, Building and Chemical Products	400231
#煤炭及制品批发	Coal and Related Products	352120
石油及制品批发	Petroleum and Related Products	4543
金属及金属矿批发	Metals and Metals Materials	23422
建材批发	Building Materials	11066
化肥批发	Chemical Fertilizer	2787
机械设备、五金产品及电子产品批发	Wholesale of Machinery, Hardwaresand Electronic Products	23604
#汽车批发	Motor Vehicles	3011
计算机、软件及辅助设备批发	Computer, Sofeware and Accessories	227
贸易经纪与代理	Trade Broker and Agency	1216
其他批发业	Other Wholesales	5105
3.按控股情况分	Grouped by Share Holding	
国有控股	State Holding Enterprises	448303
集体控股	Collective-owned Holding Enterprises	60990
私人控股	Private Holding Enterprises	154783
港澳台商控股	Hongkong, Macao and Taiwan Holding Enterprises	2359
外商控股	Foreign Holding Enterprises	
其 他	Others	22173
4.按经营形式分	Grouped by Management Form	
独立门店	Independent Stores	358198
连锁总店(总部)	Chain Headquarters	28927
连锁门店	Chain Stores	2979
其 他	Others	298504
5.按单位规模分	Grouped by Enterprise Size	
大 型	Large-size	380954
中 型	Medium-size	208039
小 型	Small-size	71394
微 型	Micro-size	28222
二、零售业	**Retail Trade**	**538823**
1.按登记注册类型分组	Grouped by Registered Kind	
内资企业	Civil Funded Enterprises	523655
国有企业	State-owned Enterprises	11298
集体企业	Collective-owned Enterprises	12285
股份合作企业	Share Cooperative Enterprises	1542
联营企业	Joint Ownership Enterprises	

continued

(10 000 yuan)

财务费用 Costs of Finance	#利息支出 Interest Expenses	营业利润 Business Profits	利润总额 Total Profits	应交所得税 Income Tax Payable	应付职工薪酬（本年贷方累计发生额） Remuneration Payable (Accumulated Credit Balance of The Year)	应交增值税 Added Taxes Payable
351260	401320	-179617	-80090	36815	344425	153266
294870	349002	-224765	-130274	29878	291645	111742
1832	2399	31694	32485	3591	13805	22250
40591	35407	4857	9330	2243	29627	11183
8000	7026	9536	9256	333	3993	3772
417	2920	1037	1220	599	1136	2539
7767	7039	12522	21233	384	20194	10693
-954	57	15123	15445	19	4099	6128
107	50	34	50	10	195	65
2464	1517	-3324	-3162		127	
542	619	-2603	-2585	216	3408	1417
231160	326177	115038	226663	108041	400354	251213
25497	25888	19265	19511	2743	34847	38730
112993	76048	56840	56399	6221	90699	60045
984	941	5766	5841	209	6365	1520
5524	4045	-3823	-2054	581	27650	11888
210978	255023	78388	172463	61109	288093	148858
12662	20240	37396	38624	12810	28674	32275
1		668	747	174	596	547
152518	157836	76632	94526	43703	242553	181716
164026	278239	313295	380958	95896	367766	243406
130844	101575	-21493	9341	18624	129541	102581
62882	40452	-75056	-67805	1739	46483	13397
18408	12833	-23662	-16133	1536	16126	4013
154319	**83396**	**-23587**	**31839**	**35097**	**525049**	**141390**
151184	80563	-26562	30496	31263	506121	135205
881	185	2564	3433	918	9181	1301
817	362	7331	7663	612	6936	1701
15	14	-87	74	18	277	213

13-5 续表14

单位：万元

指　　标	Item	管理费用 Costs of Administration
有限责任公司	Limited Responsibility Corporations	123145
国有独资公司	Company Exclusively with Investment from State	8166
其他有限责任公司	Other Limited Responsibility Company	114979
股份有限公司	Share-holding Limited Corporations	44852
私营企业	Private-owned Enterprises	330223
私营独资企业	Enterprise Exclusively with Investment from Private	10006
私营合伙企业	Private Partnership Enterprises	481
私营有限责任公司	Private Limited Responsibility Corporations	303080
私营股份有限公司	Private Share-holding Limited Corporations	16655
其他企业	Others	310
港澳台商投资企业	Enterprises Funded by HongKong, Macao and Taiwan	13919
与港澳台商合资经营企业	Joint Venture Enterprises	
港澳台商独资企业	Solely Owned Enterspries	8182
港澳台商投资股份有限公司	Share Holding Limited Corporation	5737
外商投资企业	Foreign Funded Enterprises	1250
中外合资经营企业	Joint Venture Enterprises	182
外资企业	Enterprises with Sole Investment from Foreign	508
其他外商投资企业	Other Foreign Funded Enterprises	560
2.按零售行业小类分	Grouped by Wholesale Trade	
综合零售	General Retail Sales Trade	120021
百货零售	Daily Goods	63842
超级市场零售	Supermarkets	49027
其他综合零售	Others	7152
食品、饮料及烟草制品专门零售	Retail of Food, Beverage and Tobaccos	21521
纺织、服装及日用品专门零售	Retail of Textiles, Garments and Daily Articles	58388
#服装零售	Garments	51719
文化、体育用品及器材专门零售	Retail of Culture, Sports Articles and Equipments	14481
#图书、报刊零售	Books and Mangzines	8603
医药及医疗器材专门零售	Retail of Medicines and Medical Appliances	33896
#药品零售	Medicines	33284
汽车、摩托车、燃料及零配件专门零售	Retail of Motor Vehicles, Motorcycles, Feuls and Parts	202129
#汽车零售	Motor Vehicles	131047
机动车燃料零售	Vehicle Feuls	69571
家用电器及电子产品专门零售	Retail of Household Electronic Equipments and Products	30058
#日用家电设备零售	Household Appliance	17445
计算机、软件及辅助设备零售	Computer, Software and Auxiliary Equipments	6735
通信设备零售	Communication Equipments	2585

continued

(10 000 yuan)

财务费用 Costs of Finance	#利息支出 Interest Expenses	营业利润 Business Profits	利润总额 Total Profits	应交所得税 Income Tax Payable	应付职工薪酬(本年贷方累计发生额) Remuneration Payable (Accumulated Credit Balance of The Year)	应交增值税 Added Taxes Payable
31587	16862	14448	30168	15508	132111	41869
1611	53	11986	14204	3809	7376	1030
29976	16808	2462	15965	11699	124735	40840
4860	1216	-33766	-33144	1860	67077	9889
112898	61855	-17660	21745	12340	289816	80194
1010	547	4108	3521	174	7510	1178
6	1	780	756	243	627	275
101994	59038	-21121	3447	11733	250626	75038
9889	2269	-1428	14023	189	31053	3703
126	70	609	557	6	723	38
2387	2229	7964	6906	3789	14315	4904
1759	1725	2718	2085	2235	10395	2664
629	504	5245	4821	1554	3920	2240
747	604	-4989	-5563	46	4613	1282
539	544	-2740	-3252		982	274
147	60	-1606	-1672	46	3030	673
60		-643	-639		602	335
47067	20190	-6484	28316	6720	118877	34696
21300	10378	860	17227	5174	57205	14739
23077	9699	-10055	7510	600	57116	5646
2690	113	2711	3579	945	4557	14312
6126	4874	6011	5114	1111	23324	3999
14398	12274	-22528	-20429	1539	29217	5893
13799	11884	-26917	-25054	599	25001	4190
1514	191	9844	11533	2775	23174	2510
-41	16	7100	7985	2106	15993	95
5502	3894	24322	23991	6501	43508	19471
5495	3894	24310	23992	6492	43161	19354
63871	34623	-54557	-47403	8529	199519	59396
53570	28069	-21535	-16079	5007	111488	41175
10231	6542	-34054	-31860	3375	86942	18066
4234	1375	2866	2113	582	35396	7812
2500	611	1735	1873	44	15542	3644
996	426	1210	981	321	14673	1692
246	65	-486	-966	127	2466	1157

13-5 续表15

单位：万元

指 标	Item	管理费用 Costs of Administration
五金、家具及室内装修材料专门零售	Retail of Hardwares, Furniture and Room Decorative Building	17397
货摊、无店铺及其他零售业	Retail of Stall, Non-store and Others	40933
3.按控股情况分	Grouped by Share Holding	
国有控股	State Holding Enterprises	110518
集体控股	Collective-owned Holding Enterprises	28665
私人控股	Private Holding Enterprises	359297
港澳台商控股	Hongkong, Macao and Taiwan Holding Enterprises	13803
外商控股	Foreign Holding Enterprises	690
其 他	Others	25851
4.按经营形式分	Grouped by Management Form	
独立门店	Independent Stores	407507
连锁总店	Chain Headquarters	57685
连锁门店	Chain Stores	26332
其 他	Others	47300
5.按单位规模分	Grouped by Enterprise Size	
大 型	Large-size	167176
中 型	Medium-size	244281
小 型	Small-size	109410
微 型	Micro-size	17957
6.按零售业态分	Grouped by Retail Format	
#有店铺零售	Store-based	522341
食杂店	Grocery Store	427
便利店	Convenient Store	8964
折扣店	Discount Store	
超 市	Supermarket	19084
大型超市	Hypermarket	28236
仓储会员店	Warehouse Club	1121
百货店	Department Store	87505
专业店	Specialized Shop	195049
专卖店	Exclusive Shop	116255
家居建材商店	Home Center	9341
购物中心	Shopping Center	32593
厂家直销中心	Factory Outlet Center	23766
无店铺零售	Non-store	16208
#网上商店	Online	11217

continued

(10 000 yuan)

财务费用 Costs of Finance	#利息支出 Interest Expenses	营业利润 Business Profits	利润总额 Total Profits	应交所得税 Income Tax Payable	应付职工薪酬 (本年贷方累计发生额) Remuneration Payable (Accumulated Credit Balance of The Year)	应交增值税 Added Taxes Payable
3473	2103	14127	14217	678	7257	3226
8135	3874	2812	14388	6663	44778	4388
14297	7007	–13389	4142	16259	146058	33155
7442	5033	–548	–1280	846	19675	4287
122602	63987	–15788	22880	13407	326464	88206
2351	2229	13111	12705	3771	12320	4678
687	604	–4346	–4924	46	4012	947
6941	4537	–2628	–1684	768	16520	10119
122547	70411	6153	35424	24457	358172	108530
14277	7107	3150	3431	3839	71398	19970
9479	2774	–25265	–8520	957	51511	6484
8015	3105	–7626	1504	5844	43968	6406
50005	21689	–4595	16051	17834	186514	43747
78839	48184	–19258	19677	11584	235630	57054
21770	12426	–642	–5161	5229	91906	37855
3705	1097	907	1272	451	10999	2735
150933	83000	–37630	14553	31422	507732	139593
70	27	1191	928	12	582	141
2187	260	1596	3161	947	7808	1105
3885	1483	–2926	–1192	585	23482	2396
17750	8131	–13568	3636	403	47438	5594
209		–1670	–1297	1	737	103
28309	14390	9808	23999	5330	62366	28574
36907	19644	35139	35859	15793	195922	61188
48458	27983	–29270	–23831	5613	120409	34051
1628	1156	843	761	264	4020	1397
8351	7637	–21222	–19735	318	14783	2330
3178	2290	–17551	–7736	2155	30187	2715
2807	396	14267	17510	3676	17107	1797
952	327	2453	3978	298	15346	1451

13-6 限额以上批发零售业商品销售类值(2016年)

SALES VALUE OF ENTERPRISES ABOVE DESIGNATED SIZE IN WHOLESALE AND RETAIL TRADE BY CATEGORY OF COMMODITIES(2016)

单位：万元 (10 000 yuan)

指标	Item	销售额 Sales Value	批发额 Wholesale	零售额 Retail
总　计	**Total**	**89934625**	**67425949**	**22508676**
一、批发业	**Wholesale Trade**	**67788535**	**66220940**	**1567596**
1.粮油、食品类	Grain, Oil and Food	1657992	1372113	285879
2.饮料类	Beverages	107631	77378	30253
3.烟酒类	Tobacco and Liquor	3559549	3432476	127073
4.服装、鞋帽、针纺织品类	Clothing, Shoes and Hats, Textiles	413363	112463	300900
服装类	Garments	384370	91877	292494
鞋帽类	Shoes and Hats	21942	17520	4422
针纺织品	Textiles	7051	3066	3985
5.化妆品类	Cosmetics	3338	858	2480
6.金银珠宝类	Gold Silver and Jewels	89096	88769	328
7.日用品类	Daily Use Goods	64232	52212	12020
#儿童玩具类	Children Toys	29717	28878	839
8.五金、电料类	Hardware and Electrical Appliances	50608	37405	13203
9.体育、娱乐用品类	Sports and Recreation Articles	19008	18409	599
#照相器材类	Photographic Equipment			
10.书报杂志类	Books Newspapers and Magazines	274210	252915	21295
11.电子出版物及音像制品类	Electronic Publications and Audiovisual Products	9953	9953	
12.家用电器和音像器材类	Household Electrical and Sound Acoustic Appliances	290283	214603	75680
13.中西药品类	Chinese and Western Medicine	2063973	2027000	36973
#西　药	Western Medicine	1451490	1429215	22275
中草药及中成药类	Chinese Medicine	320414	311548	8866
14文化办公用品类	Culture and Office Articles	120737	117540	3197
#计算机及其配套产品	Computer and Corollarty Equipment	6099	5882	217
15.家具类	Furnitures	2587	1027	1560
16.通讯器材类	Communication Equipment	12	12	
17.煤炭及制品类	Coal and Related Products	17843099	17744138	98961
18.木材及制品类	Timber and Related Products	31276	31276	
19石油及制品类	Petroleum and Related Products	554889	533369	21520
20.化工材料及制品类	Chemical Materials	3118899	3118899	
#化肥类	Chemical Fertilizer	662867	662867	
21.金属材料类	Metal Materials	28695136	28695136	
22.建筑及装潢材料类	Building and Decoration Materials	316363	258975	57388
23.机电产品及设备类	Mechanical and Electrical Products and Equipments	5002595	4998749	3846
#农机类	Farm Machineries	18966	18966	
24.汽车类	Motor Vehicles	693168	254810	438358
25.种子饲料类	Seeds and Forages	55304	55304	
26.棉麻类	Cotton and Hemp			
27.其他类	Others	2751236	2715152	36084

13-6 续表 continued

单位：万元 (10 000 yuan)

指 标	Item	销售额 Sales Value	批发额 Wholesale	零售额 Retail
二、零售业	**Retail Trade**	**22146090**	**1205010**	**20941080**
1.粮油、食品类	Grain, Oil and Food	2040152	32312	2007840
2.饮料类	Beverages	238810	3386	235424
3.烟酒类	Tobacco and Liquor	579224	29534	549690
4.服装、鞋帽、针纺织品类	Clothing, Shoes and Hats, Textiles	2543983	15042	2528941
服装类	Garments	1944547	6852	1937695
鞋帽类	Shoes and Hats	386342	432	385910
针纺织品	Textiles	213093	7757	205336
5.化妆品类	Cosmetics	258955	502	258452
6.金银珠宝类	Gold Silver and Jewels	358719	10212	348507
7.日用品类	Daily Use Goods	403164	2459	400705
#儿童玩具类	Children Toys	55989	851	55137
8.五金、电料类	Hardware and Electrical Appliances	218494	21300	197194
9.体育、娱乐用品类	Sports and Recreation Articles	56001	326	55675
#照相器材类	Photographic Equipment	531	1	530
10.书报杂志类	Books Newspapers and Magazines	210904	2881	208023
11.电子出版物及音像制品类	Electronic Publications and Audiovisual Products	11215	142	11073
12.家用电器和音像器材类	Household Electrical and Sound Acoustic Appliances	1029712	18650	1011062
13.中西药品类	Chinese and Western Medicine	1434656	319975	1114681
#西 药	Western Medicine	1022390	268477	753913
中草药及中成药类	Chinese Medicine	238577	50643	187934
14.文化办公用品类	Culture and Office Articles	143446	34019	109427
#计算机及其配套产品	Computer and Corollarty Equipment	48084	20107	27978
15.家具类	Furnitures	409594	1488	408106
16.通讯器材类	Communication Equipment	88137	6373	81764
17.煤炭及制品类	Coal and Related Products	75674	1351	74323
18.木材及制品类	Timber and Related Products	646	646	
19.石油及制品类	Petroleum and Related Products	4163149	535559	3627590
20.化工材料及制品类	Chemical Materials	24594	24594	
#化肥类	Chemical Fertilizer	23155	23155	
21.金属材料类	Metal Materials	612	612	
22.建筑及装潢材料类	Building and Decoration Materials	404430	11263	393167
23.机电产品及设备类	Mechanical and Electrical Products and Equipments	63336	4976	58360
#农机类	Farm Machineries	4987	4987	
24.汽车类	Motor Vehicles	6741309	76951	6664358
25.种子饲料类	Seeds and Forages	174	174	
26.棉麻类	Cotton and Hemp	1342	4	1338
27.其他类	Others	645662	50280	595382

13-7 亿元以上商品交易市场基本情况(2016年)

BASIC STATISTICS ON COMMODITY EXCHANGE MARKETS OF TRANSACTION VOLUME OVER 100 MILLION YUAN(2016)

市 场	Market	市场数量(个) Number of Markets (unit)	年末出租摊位数(个) Number of Stalls at Year-end (unit)	营业面积(平方米) Area of Bussiness (sq.m)	成交额(万元) Volume of Transaction (10 000 yuan)
总 计	**Total**	**32**	**24986**	**2552764**	**6345511**
一、按市场类别分组	Grouped by Market Category				
1.综合市场	Comprehensive Markets	11	15996	1693215	5064695
综合贸易市场	Comprehensive Commercial Markets	11	15996	1693215	5064695
生产资料综合市场	Productive Materials Comprehensive Markets	1	100	23000	10460
工业消费品综合市场	Industrial Consumable Comprehensive Markets	2	1154	111220	20707
农产品综合市场	Farm Products Comprehensive Markets	4	3075	341490	537313
其他综合市场	Others	4	11667	1217505	4496215
2.专业市场	Special Markets	21	8990	859549	1280816
生产资料市场	Productive Materials Markets	3	588	95180	109417
煤炭市场	Coal Markets	1	3	180	18946
建材市场	Building Materials Markets	1	372	15000	37261
金属材料市场	Metal Materials Markets	1	213	80000	53210
农产品市场	Farm Products Comprehensive Markets	7	3206	280680	799597
粮油市场	Grain and Oil Markets	1	132	16000	74280
蔬菜市场	Vegetables Markets	4	2732	224800	677317
干鲜果品市场	Dried and Fresh Melons and Fruits Markets	2	342	39880	48000
食品、饮料及烟酒市场	Food, Beverages, Tobacco and Liquor Markets	1	89	3000	11100
纺织、服装、鞋帽市场	Textiles, Clothing, Shoes and Hats Markets	7	4303	308320	316675
服装市场	Clothing Markets	6	3693	270320	304275
鞋帽市场	Shoes and Hats Markets	1	610	38000	12400
其他纺织服装鞋帽市场	Others				
日用品及文化用品市场	Daily Use Articles and Cultural Goods Markets				
黄金、珠宝、玉器等首饰市场	Gold, Jewellery, Jade Markets				
电器、通讯器材、电子设备市场	Electrical Appliances, Communication Equipments and Electronic Equipments Markets				
家具、五金及装饰材料市场	Furniture, Hardware and Decoration Materials	3	804	172369	44027
家具市场	Markets Furniture Markets	1	571	123563	32691
装饰材料市场	Decoration Materials Markets	2	233	48806	11336
汽车、摩托车及零配件市场	Cars, Motorcycles and Spare Parts Markets				
二、按经营方式分组	Grouped by Business Style				
1.以批发为主	Wholesale mainly	27	22810	2199395	6124909
2.以零售为主	Retail mainly	5	2176	353369	220602
三、按经营环境分组	Grouped by Business Environment				
1.露天式	Open-air Markets	5	2300	325400	292894
2.封闭式	Enclosed Markets	19	18658	1945139	5836888
3.其 他	Others	8	4028	282225	215729

13-8 亿元以上商品交易市场按摊位分类成交情况(2016年)

CLASSIFICATION OF COMMODITY EXCAHNGE MARKETS OF TRANSACTION VOLUME OVER 100 MILLION YUAN(2016)

类　别	Classification	年末出租摊位数(个) Number of Stalls at Year-end (unit)	成交额(万元) Volume of Transaction (10 000 yuan)
总　计	**Total**	**24986**	**6345511**
1.粮油、食品类	Grain, Oil and Food	6963	1964441
#粮油类	Grain and Oil	846	223439
肉禽蛋类	Meat, Poultry and Eggs	361	83320
水产品类	Aquatic Products	425	74756
蔬菜类	Vegetables	3694	966716
干鲜果品类	Dried and Fresh Fruits	1614	613538
2.饮料类	Beverages	127	14650
3.烟酒类	Tobacco and Liquor	349	359247
4.服装、鞋帽、针纺织品类	Clothing, Shoes, Hats and Textiles	9813	977467
服装类	Clothing	6052	703063
鞋帽类	Footwear and Hats	2065	174900
针纺织品类	Knitwear and Textiles	1696	99504
5.化妆品类	Cosmetics	183	4354
6.金银珠宝类	Gold, Silver and Jewellery	5	522
7.日用品类	Articles for Daily Use	1655	566014
8.五金、电料类	Hardware and Electrical Materials	583	237058
9.体育、娱乐用品类	Sports and Recreational Articles	48	1830
10.书报杂志类	Newspapers and Magazines	1	5
11.电子出版物及音像制品类	Electronic Publication and Audiovisual Products	59	740
12.家用电器和音像器材类	Household Appliances and Audiovisual Equipments	113	3488
13.中西药品类	Traditional Chinese and Western Medicine	1	2
14.文化办公用品类	Cultural and Official Articles	183	5973
15.家具类	Furniture	1207	45797
16.通讯器材类	Communication Equipments	5	10
17.煤炭及制品类	Coal and Related Products	3	18946
18.化工材料及制品类	Raw Chemical Materials and Related Products	4	200
19.金属材料类	Metal Materials	333	659183
20.建筑及装潢材料类	Building and Decoration Materials	1806	726913
21.机电产品及设备类	Mechanical and Electrical Products	215	217957
22.汽车类	Automobiles	33	472137
23.其他类	Others	1297	68577

13-9 私营企业基本情况(2016年)

BASIC STATISTICS ON PRIVATE-OWNED ENTERPRISES(2016)

单位：户 (household)

指　标	Item	年末实有户　数 Real Number of Enterprises at Year-end	#本年开业 Openning at This Year	从业人员(人) Employees (person)	注册资金(万元) Registered Capital (10 000 yuan)
总　计	**Total**	**387244**	**85239**	**1747934**	**191083435**
农、林、牧、渔业	Farming, Forestry, Animal Husbandry and Fishery	21521	4303	92115	9442627
采矿业	Mining	4910	306	90937	6464371
制造业	Manufacturing	31021	3586	487735	23735322
电力、热力、燃气及水生产和供应业	Production and Supply of Electricity, Heat, Gas and Water	2470	921	15298	4603669
建筑业	Construction	24987	5910	111832	15309007
交通运输、仓储和邮政业	Transport, Storage and Post	13019	3073	50052	4037858
信息传输、软件和信息技术服务业	Information Transmission, Software and Information Technology Services	23401	5280	42114	7237070
批发和零售业	Wholesale and Retail Trade	158277	35802	539514	58894216
住宿和餐饮业	Hotels and Catering Services	6980	1841	39235	2160590
金融业	Financial Industry	4577	761	21055	7777492
房地产业	Real Estate	11796	1766	46963	11913094
租赁和商务服务业	Lease and Business Affairs Services	41453	9676	100377	23171825
科学研究和技术服务业	Scientific Reseach and Technical Services	13343	3510	24850	7726237
水利、环境和公共设施管理业	Water, Environmental Protection and Public Facility Management	2596	446	9174	1606275
居民服务、修理和其他服务业	Resident Services, Repair and Other Services	16053	4173	42747	3736767
教　育	Education	928	351	4189	236215
卫生和社会工作	Health Care and Social Work	1529	476	6809	673590
文化、体育和娱乐业	Culture, Sports and Recreation	8223	3038	19417	1977719
其他行业	Others	160	20	3521	379491

13-10 个体工商业基本情况(2016年)
BASIC STATISTICS ON INDIVIDUAL BUSSINESS(2016)

单位：户 (household)

指 标	Item	年末实有户数 Real Number of Households at Year-end	#本年开业 Openning at This Year	从业人员(人) Employees (person)	注册资金(万元) Registered Capital (10 000 yuan)
总 计	**Total**	**1401927**	**227947**	**3059657**	**8503908**
农、林、牧、渔业	Farming, Forestry, Animal Husbandry and Fishery	16135	5149	57237	344797
采矿业	Mining	778	59	4700	28615
制造业	Manufacturing	47385	8028	134944	397169
电力、热力、燃气及水生产和供应业	Production and Supply of Electricity, Heat, Gas and Water	365	113	760	3573
建筑业	Construction	3617	807	15961	52789
交通运输、仓储和邮政业	Transport, Storage and Post	52548	26287	99914	537056
信息传输、软件和信息技术服务业	Information Transmission, Software and Information Technology Services	42055	983	78138	129898
批发和零售业	Wholesale and Retail Trade	884918	114099	1725565	4865550
住宿和餐饮业	Hotels and Catering Services	160358	39267	459766	1011221
金融业	Financial Industry	183	62	543	1732
房地产业	Real Estate	320	86	1005	1999
租赁和商务服务业	Lease and Business Affairs Services	9415	1675	22390	86392
科学研究和技术服务业	Scientific Reseach and Technical Services	2041	191	5057	13158
水利、环境和公共设施管理业	Water, Environmental Protection and Public Facility Management	6806	29	15469	25787
居民服务、修理和其他服务业	Resident Services, Repair and Other Services	159911	28589	396209	869433
教 育	Education	359	155	1475	4261
卫生和社会工作	Health Care and Social Work	6749	909	14598	37226
文化、体育和娱乐业	Culture, Sports and Recreation	7839	1421	25582	91904
其他行业	Others	145	38	344	1350

主要统计指标解释

批发业 指向其他批发或零售单位（含个体经营者）及其他企事业单位、机关团体等批量销售生活用品、生产资料的活动，以及从事进出口贸易和贸易经纪与代理的活动。

零售业 指百货商店、超级市场、专门零售商店、品牌专卖店、售货摊等主要面向最终消费者（如居民等）的销售活动，以互联网、邮政、电话、售货机等方式的销售活动，还包括在同一地点，后面加工生产，前面销售的店铺（如面包房）。

批发和零售业法人企业 指具备如下条件的批发零售贸易企业：(1)依法成立，有自己的名称、组织机构和场所，能够承担民事责任；(2)独立拥有和使用资产，承担负债，有权与其他单位签订合同；(3)独立核算盈亏，并能够编制包括资产负债表在内的全部会计帐户。

限额以上批发企业 年主营业务收入2000万元及以上为限额以上批发企业。

限额以上零售企业 年主营业务收入500万元及以上为限额以上零售企业。

社会消费品零售总额 指企业（单位、个体户）通过交易直接售给个人、社会集团非生产、非经营用的实物商品金额，以及提供餐饮服务所取得的收入金额。个人包括城乡居民和入境人员，社会集团包括机关、社会团体、部队、学校、企事业单位、居委会或村委会等。

批发和零售业零售额 指批发和零售业企业、产业活动单位和个体户售给城乡居民用于生活消费和社会集团用于公共消费的商品金额。

门店总数 指该连锁企业所拥有的全部连锁门店数量，包括总店(如果总公司有门店的话)和全部直营分店、加盟分店数。其中，总店作为一个直营店处理。此外，有的地区分出控股店，控股店按直营店统计。

连锁企业（或称连锁店、连锁公司） 指在核心企业或总店的领导下，由分散的、经营同类商品或服务的企业或活动单位，采取共同方针，实行集中采购和分散销售的有机结合，通过规范化经营，实现规模效益的经济联合组织形式。一般连锁店应由若干个分店组成。其经营特征：(1)经营同类商品；(2)使用统一商号；(3)统一采购配送，采购与销售相分离(部分商品可根据物流合理和保质保鲜原则由供应商直接送货到门店，其余均由总部统一配送)。连锁店总店(总部)指连锁店的核心企业或管理中心。连锁店分店指连锁店所属各分散经营的企业或活动单位，也可称分店或成员店。

连锁店包括下列三种形式：

直营连锁 指连锁店铺由连锁公司全资或控股开设，在总部的直接控制下，开展统一经营的连锁经营形式。

特许连锁 指拥有注册商标、企业标志、专利、专有技术等经营资源的企业（特许人），以合同形式将其拥有的经营资源许可其他经营者（被特许人）使用，被特许人按合同约定在统一的经营模式下开展经营，并向特许人支付特许经营费用的连锁经营形式。

自愿连锁 指若干个店铺或企业自愿组合起来，在不改变各自资产所有权关系的情况下，以同一个品牌形象面对消费者，以共同进货为纽带开展的连锁经营形式。

零售业态 指零售企业（单位）为满足不同的消费需求进行相应的要素组合而形成的不同经营形态；分类原则是，零售业态按零售店铺的结构特点，根据其经营方式、商品结构、服务功能，以及选址、商圈、规模、店堂设施、目标顾客和有无固定营业场所进行分类。

零售业态从总体上可以分为有店铺零售业态和无店铺零售业态两类。按照零售业态分类原则分为食杂店、便利店、折扣店、超市、大型超市、仓储会员店、百货店、专业店、专卖店、家居建材商店、购物中心、社区购物中心、市区购物中心、城郊购物中心、厂家直销中心、电视购物、邮购、网上商店、自动售货亭、电话购物等20种零售业态。

商品购进额 指从本企业以外的单位和个人购进(包括从国外直接进口)作为转卖或加工后转卖的商品金额(含增值税)。本指标反映批发和零售业从国内外市场上购进商品的总价。

商品销售额 指对本单位以外的单位和个人出售的商品金额（包括售给本单位消费用的商品，含增值税），本指标反映批发和零售业在国内市场上销售商品以及出口商品的总量。

期末商品库存额 对于批发和零售业法人单位和个体经营户，是指报告期末取得所有权的全部商品金额（含增值税）；对于批发和零售业产业活动单位，是指报告期末实际在库且归属法人具有所有权的全部商品金额（含增值税）。该指标反映批发和零售业商品库存情况，以及对市场商品供应的保证程度。

亿元以上商品交易市场 指年成交额在亿元及以上的商品交易市场。商品交易市场是指经有关部门和组织批准设立，有固定场所、设施，有经营管理部门和监管人员，若干市场经营者入内，常年或实际开业三个月以上，集中、公开、独立地进行生活消费品、生产资料等现货商品交易以及提供相关服务的交易场所，包括各类消费品市场、生产资料市场等。

Explanatory Notes on Main Statistical Indicators

Wholesale Trade refers to the activities of wholesaler selling commodities in bulk for daily use and capital goods to other wholesale and retail enterprises, institutions and government offices, including the activities of wholesaler engaged in import and export and acting as a trade agent.

Retail Trade refers to the activities of department store, supermarket, franchised store, brand store, retail stall and on-the-spot-making-selling store selling commodities to the final consumers (citizens) by any means including internet, post, telephone, sales machine.

Wholesale and Retail Corporation Enterprises refer to the wholesale and retail trade enterprises satisfy the conditions as follow: (1) They are established legally, having their own names, organizations, location, able to take civil liability; (2) They possess and use their assets independently, assume liabilities, and are entitled to sign contracts with other units; (3) They are financially independent and compile their own balance sheets.

Wholesale Enterprise above Designated Size refers to wholesale enterprises whose annual revenue of major business amounts to 20 million yuan and over.

Retail Trade Enterprise above Designated Size refers to retail enterprises whose annual revenue of major business amounts to 5 million yuan and over.

Total Retail Sales of Consumer Goods refer to the amount obtained by enterprises (units, self-employed individuals) through direct sales of non-production and non-business physical commodity to individuals, social institutions, and revenue from providing catering services. Individuals include rural and urban households, population from abroad, and social institutions include government agencies, social organizations, military units, schools, institutions, neighborhood (village) committees.

Total Retail Sales of Wholesale and Retail Trade refer to the amount obtained by wholesale and retail enterprises, active units and self-employed individuals through sales to residents and social groups for mass consumption.

The Number of Stores refers to the total number of enterprises owned by the full number of chain stores, including the headquarters (if there has one) and all direct stores, franchises. The headquarters are counted as a direct store. In addition, there are some share holding stores in some regions, and these stores are also counted as direct stores.

Chain Enterprises (also called chain stores or chain corporations) refer to a form of joint economic entities under which scattered enterprises or establishments engaged in providing homogeneous commodities or services, with the central leadership of core enterprise or headquarters and guided by common policies, conduct centralized purchase and distributed selling of commodities, in order to gain better efficiency through standardized operation. Consisting of a number of branch stores, the chain stores have in general the following features: (1) homogeneous commodities, (2) unique name of stores, (3) centralized purchase and delivery which is separated from distributed selling operation (most commodities are delivered from the headquarters except some items which, for logistics, quality or freshness considerations, might be delivered by suppliers directly). Chain headquarters (HQ) means the core of enterprises or chain management centre. Branch chain store refers the enterprises or active unit that owned by the chain store under decentralized operation, which is also called branch store or member store.

Chain stores include the following three forms:

Regular Chain refers to chain that are invested or controlled by the headquarters. They operate under direct and unified management from the headquarters. Adopting a direct management approach, the headquarters gives orders and controls all retail stores, which follow completely the directives from the headquarters. Large monopolized commercial companies develop and expand their business through purchasing, merging, direct investment and controlling of shares.

Franchise Chain Through contracts, chain stores (or their owners) obtain licenses from the headquarters (franchisee) to use designated trade marks, names, operation know-how, and to sell commodities developed by the headquarters. Under this arrangement, each store in the chain is an independent legal entity and operates under the guidance from the headquarters.

Voluntary Chain refers to the chain business model that several stores or enterprises united together voluntarily to use a same brand image and purchase together under the previous independent property relationship.

Retail Trade Format refers to the different business forms which combined by corresponding factors to satisfy different consumption needs. It is classified according to retail stores' structure characters, such as business form, commodities' structure, service function, address, business circle, scale, store facilities, target customers and whether having a fixed business place.

Retail trade format can be divided into store-based and non-store retail. It can be classified into 20 forms as the following: grocery store, convenient store, discount store, supermarket, hypermarket, warehouse club, department store, specialized shop, exclusive shop, home centre, shopping centre, community shopping centre, urban shopping centre, suburban shopping centre, factory outlet centre, TV shopping, mail shopping, web shop, vending machine and telephone shopping.

Value of Commodities Purchases refers to the value of commodities purchasing by enterprises from other units or individuals with value-added tax, including direct import form abroad, for the purpose of re-selling, either with or without further processing of the commodities purchased. It reflects the total commodities value that wholesale and retail trade purchased from the domestic and abroad market.

Value of Commodities Sales refers to the value of commodities sold by the units to other units or individuals with value-added tax, including goods sold for self consumption. It reflects the total commodities amount that wholesale and retail trade sold and exported in the domestic and abroad market.

Total Value of Storing at the End of Period refers to total possessed commodities value including value-added tax for the wholesale and retail corporation units and individuals at the end of report period. And it refers to the total commodities value at the end of report period, including value-added tax, which are in stock and belong to the corporation units for the wholesale and retail active units. It reflects the goods stock of the wholesale and retail trade and the guarantee degree of goods supply to the market.

Commodities Trading Market over 100 Million Yuan refers to the commodity market with an annual transaction at and above 100 million yuan. Commodities trading market refers market that is approved by related government departments, which has fixed sites, facilities, managers and administration offices, traders, and has operated for more than three months. It is a place where the commodities including the articles for daily consumption, productive materials, goods transactions and services are traded in a centralized, independent and open way. And it includes consumer market, materials market and etc.

14 住宿、餐饮业和旅游

HOTELS, CATERING SERVICES AND TOURISM

资料整理人员

雷士伟　张艳芳　张艳君

住宿、餐饮业和旅游
HOTELS, CATERING SERVICES AND TOURISM

住宿、餐饮业营业额	Business Volume of Hotels and Catering Services	806113	万元	(10 000 yuan)
接待国内游客人数	Domestic Tourists	44330	万人次	(10 000 person-times)
接待入境过夜游客人数	Inbound Overnight Tourists	63.0	万人次	(10 000 person-times)
旅游总收入	Total Income of Tourism	4247.1	亿元	(100 million yuan)
旅游外汇收入	Foreign Exchange Earnings from Tourism	31738	万美元	(USD 10 000)

旅游总收入（亿元）
Total Income of Tourism (100 million yuan)

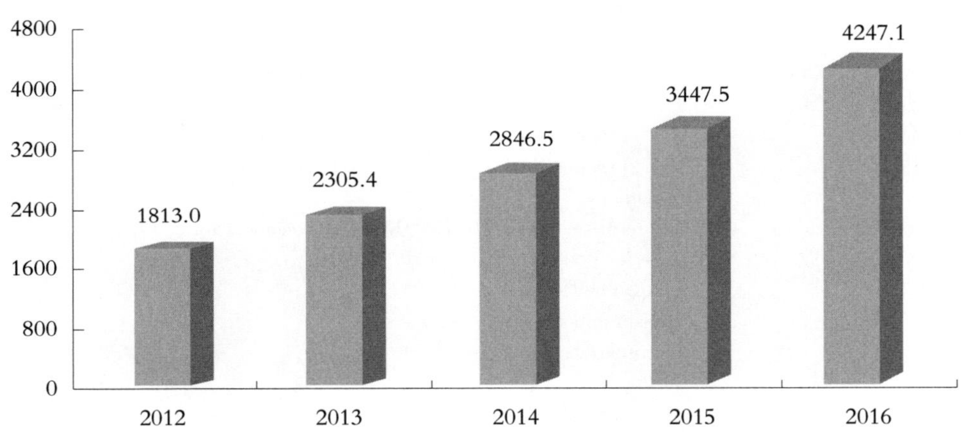

接待国内游客人数（万人次）
Domestic Tourists (10 000 person-times)

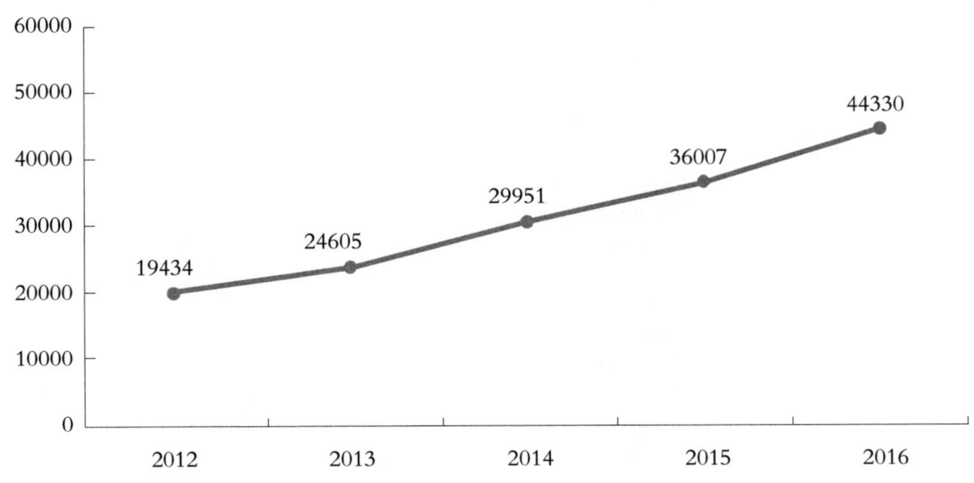

14-1 限额以上住宿和餐饮业法人企业经营情况(2016年)

单位：万元

指 标	Item	法人企业数(个) Number of Corporation Enterprises (unit)
总 计	**Total**	**804**
一、住宿业	**Hotels**	**354**
1.按登记注册类型分	Grouped by Registered Kind	
内资企业	Civil Funded Enterprises	353
国有企业	State-owned Enterprises	64
集体企业	Collective-owned Enterprises	11
有限责任公司	Limited Responsibility Corporations	57
国有独资公司	Company Exclusively with Investment from State	3
其他有限责任公司	Other Limited Responsibility Corporations	54
股份有限公司	Share-holding Limited Corporations	8
私营企业	Private-owned Enterprises	211
私营独资企业	Enterprise Exclusively with Investment from Private	31
私营合伙企业	Private Partnership Enterprises	2
私营有限责任公司	Private Limited Responsibility Corporations	176
私营股份有限公司	Private Share-holding Limited Corporations	2
其他企业	Others	2
港澳台商投资企业	Enterprises Funded by HongKong, Macao and Taiwan	1
与港澳台商合资经营企业	Joint Venture	1
2.按住宿行业小类分组	Grouped by Hotels	
旅游饭店	Resturants for Trip	194
一般旅馆	Ordinary Hotels	146
其他住宿服务	Others	14
3.按控股情况分	Grouped by Share Holding	
国有控股	State Holding Enterprises	84
集体控股	Collective-owned Holding Enterprises	17
私人控股	Private Holding Enterprises	235
港澳台商控股	Hongkong, Macao and Taiwan Holding Enterprises	
外商控股	Foreign Holding Enterprises	
其 他	Others	18
4.按经营形式分	Grouped by Management Form	
独立门店	Independent Stores	310
连锁总店(总部)	Chain Headquarters	2
连锁门店	Chain Stores	10
其 他	Others	32
5.按单位规模分	Grouped by Enterprise Size	
大 型	Large-size	1
中 型	Medium-size	29
小 型	Small-size	285
微 型	Micro-size	39
6.按星级分	Grouped by Stars	
五 星	Five Star	15
四 星	Four Star	52
三 星	Three Star	76
二 星	Two Star	24
其 他	Others	187

MANAGEMENT OF HOTELS AND CATERING CORPORATION ENTERPRISES ABOVE DESIGNATED SIZE(2016)

(10 000 yuan)

从业人员期末人数(人) Number of Employees at The End of Period (person)	营业额 Business Volume	#使用银行卡支付的营业额 Paid by Bank Cards	客房收入 Revenue of Guest Room	#通过公共网络实现的客房收入 by Public Network	通过非自营平台实现的客房收入 by Non-self-operating Platform
74147	**806113**	**123441**	**233304**	**12968**	**3493**
32025	**319409**	**59688**	**150298**	**9400**	**3173**
31948	318961	59581	150085	9382	3173
8693	86239	23783	39944	2995	690
850	6720	1224	3477	26	3
7582	77777	9098	30491	1950	602
349	3756	1141	1599	242	172
7233	74021	7957	28892	1708	429
622	8404	41	3490	94	15
14091	139096	25435	72209	4317	1863
1542	13726	971	8219	168	50
71	608		342		
12270	123092	24464	62964	4149	1814
208	1670		684		
110	725		475		
77	447	107	213	18	
77	447	107	213	18	
22573	230333	44442	100433	6392	2185
8458	82195	14660	46997	2736	950
994	6880	586	2868	273	39
11217	115544	28383	52190	3815	1250
1443	12596	1389	6038	131	29
16444	159763	27858	79805	4935	1863
2921	31506	2058	12265	520	31
28959	292389	57355	134803	7614	2650
108	218		218		
420	7518	1242	6303	1283	511
2538	19284	1091	8974	503	11
600	12819	7902	5543		
9257	116008	25478	43213	2864	499
21441	186703	26216	98769	6442	2611
727	3879	92	2773	94	62
3987	49868	13465	19225	412	292
6769	65628	10909	28435	983	249
7795	75173	16620	32143	1971	641
1436	10571	522	5477	172	51
12038	118168	18173	65019	5863	1940

14-1 续表1

单位：万元

指　标	Item	法人企业数(个) Number of Corporation Enterprises (unit)
二、餐饮业	**Catering**	**450**
1.按登记注册类型分	Grouped by Registered Kind	
内资企业	Civil Funded Enterprises	447
国有企业	State-owned Enterprises	23
集体企业	Collective-owned Enterprises	4
股份合作企业	Share Cooperative Enterprises	1
有限责任公司	Limited Responsibility Corporations	66
国有独资公司	Company Exclusively with Investment from State	1
其他有限责任公司	Other Limited Responsibility Company	65
股份有限公司	Share-holding Limited Corporations	7
私营企业	Private-owned Enterprises	341
私营独资企业	Enterprise Exclusively with Investment from Private	54
私营合伙企业	Private Partnership Enterprises	5
私营有限责任公司	Private Limited Responsibility Corporations	271
私营股份有限公司	Private Share-holding Limited Corporations	11
其他企业	Others	5
港澳台商投资企业	Enterprises Funded by HongKong, Macao and Taiwan	2
港澳台商独资企业	Solely Owned	2
外商投资企业	Foreign Funded Enterprises	1
外资企业	Enterprises Funded by Foreign Invetments	1
2.按餐饮行业小类分组	Grouped by Catering Services	
正餐服务	Dinner	436
快餐服务	Fast Food	10
其他餐饮业	Others	4
餐饮配送服务	Distribution Service	1
其他未列明餐饮业	Other Unlisted Service	3
3.按控股情况分	Grouped by Share Holding	
国有控股	State Holding Enterprises	36
集体控股	Collective-owned Holding Enterprises	9
私人控股	Private Holding Enterprises	383
港澳台商控股	Hongkong, Macao and Taiwan Holding Enterprises	2
外商控股	Foreign Holding Enterprises	1
其　他	Others	19
4.按经营形式分	Grouped by Management Form	
独立门店	Independent Stores	398
连锁总店(总部)	Chain Headquarters	14
连锁门店	Chain Stores	9
其　他	Others	29
5.按单位规模分	Grouped by Enterprise Size	
大　型	Large-size	4
中　型	Medium-size	32
小　型	Small-size	359
微　型	Micro-size	55

continued

(10 000 yuan)

从业人员期末人数(人) Number of Employees at The End of Period (person)	营业额 Business Volume	#使用银行卡支付的营业额 Paid by Bank Cards	客房收入 Revenue of Guest Room	#通过公共网络实现的客房收入 by Public Network	通过非自营平台实现的客房收入 by Non-self-operating Platform
42122	**486705**	**63753**	**83005**	**3568**	**321**
37122	415492	60706	82872	3468	321
1670	12226	1159	4443	143	58
140	1460	156	540		
35	481	111	257		
7217	88861	11907	15848	511	16
165	765	306	628	30	
7052	88096	11601	15220	481	16
655	3772	262	1391	85	
27105	306697	47112	59974	2729	247
2482	29355	2046	5486	90	32
209	1672	55	342		
23382	266743	43547	50683	2435	71
1032	8928	1464	3463	204	144
300	1996		420		
511	13595	3048	134	100	
511	13595	3048	134	100	
4489	57617				
4489	57617				
36207	399295	61096	82602	3562	321
5722	85373	2658			
193	2037		403	5	
85	850				
108	1187		403	5	
4025	31449	5128	11274	203	58
526	15153	168	907	16	
31159	354905	54471	67961	3226	263
511	13595	3048	134	100	
4489	57617				
1412	13986	939	2730	23	
30914	314511	51818	75716	3223	321
8037	123294	7812	2307		
796	8735	3415	327		
2375	40165	708	4656	345	
6585	93369	2658	4465	291	
9262	143453	34888	22313	1167	
25280	246484	25814	55327	2063	321
995	3399	394	900	47	

14-1 续表2

单位：万元

指 标	Item	餐费收入 Revenue of Dining	#通过公共网络实现的餐费收入 by Public Network
总 计	**Total**	**510388**	**16202**
一、住宿业	**Hotels**	**134810**	**4445**
1.按登记注册类型分	Grouped by Registered Kind		
内资企业	Civil Funded Enterprises	134577	4445
国有企业	State-owned Enterprises	40185	1729
集体企业	Collective-owned Enterprises	2980	6
有限责任公司	Limited Responsibility Corporations	34934	557
国有独资公司	Company Exclusively with Investment from State	1723	
其他有限责任公司	Other Limited Responsibility Corporations	33211	557
股份有限公司	Share-holding Limited Corporations	4263	
私营企业	Private-owned Enterprises	52009	2152
私营独资企业	Enterprise Exclusively with Investment from Private	4233	11
私营合伙企业	Private Partnership Enterprises		
私营有限责任公司	Private Limited Responsibility Corporations	46858	2142
私营股份有限公司	Private Share-holding Limited Corporations	918	
其他企业	Others	206	
港澳台商投资企业	Enterprises Funded by HongKong, Macao and Taiwan	234	
与港澳台商合资经营企业	Joint Venture	234	
2.按住宿行业小类分组	Grouped by Hotels		
旅游饭店	Resturants for Trip	105418	3394
一般旅馆	Ordinary Hotels	27185	1028
其他住宿服务	Others	2208	23
3.按控股情况分	Grouped by Share Holding		
国有控股	State Holding Enterprises	52600	1772
集体控股	Collective-owned Holding Enterprises	5496	8
私人控股	Private Holding Enterprises	60399	2628
港澳台商控股	Hongkong, Macao and Taiwan Holding Enterprises		
外商控股	Foreign Holding Enterprises		
其 他	Others	16315	37
4.按经营形式分	Grouped by Management Form		
独立门店	Independent Stores	125222	4091
连锁总店(总部)	Chain Headquarters		
连锁门店	Chain Stores	1095	354
其 他	Others	8494	
5.按单位规模分	Grouped by Enterprise Size		
大 型	Large-size	6305	
中 型	Medium-size	61582	1917
小 型	Small-size	66143	2528
微 型	Micro-size	781	
6.按星级分	Grouped by Stars		
五 星	Five Star	26815	29
四 星	Four Star	31221	602
三 星	Three Star	34810	1688
二 星	Two Star	4636	70
其 他	Others	37328	2055

continued

(10 000 yuan)

其中：通过非自营平台实现的餐费收入 by Non-self-operating Platform	商品销售额收入 Revenue of Sales of Commodities	其他收入 Other Revenue	客房数(间) Rooms (unit)	床位数(个) Beds (unit)	餐位数(位) Tables (unit)	年末餐饮营业面积(平方米) Operating Area of Catering Services at Year-end(sq.m)
2386	**23372**	**39050**	**65964**	**114003**	**340375**	**2019510**
1219	**4193**	**30107**	**40630**	**70981**	**123190**	**831629**
1219	4193	30107	40573	70880	122690	828559
332	315	5796	8114	14350	25878	171036
	11	253	1481	2912	3423	11922
18	972	11379	7704	12981	30760	177569
	197	236	454	742	1300	3290
18	775	11143	7250	12239	29460	174279
	28	624	825	1596	4542	22019
869	2822	12055	22309	38761	57847	441148
10	317	956	2313	4477	5893	52216
		266	140	240		
859	2491	10779	19655	33666	50954	387552
	14	54	201	378	1000	1380
	45		140	280	240	4865
			57	101	500	3070
			57	101	500	3070
695	3241	21242	24759	42617	86330	529437
517	736	7277	14616	26251	32081	274039
8	216	1589	1255	2113	4779	28153
345	599	10155	10846	18888	33150	208591
2	35	1026	2132	4179	5935	28736
869	3061	16498	24804	42960	72885	533164
3	498	2428	2848	4954	11220	61138
1115	3910	28454	35046	61486	110240	709525
			184	320	5	80
104	52	68	1664	2399	1188	19435
	231	1585	3736	6776	11757	102589
		971	401	527	600	4000
686	853	10359	7059	11927	23186	116770
534	3239	18552	31191	55126	94722	657433
	101	224	1979	3401	4682	53426
23	184	3644	4001	6835	12654	71797
104	677	5295	7966	13226	29458	161337
320	1833	6387	8214	15023	31914	205246
40	226	232	1877	3587	7452	54078
732	1272	14549	18572	32310	41712	339171

14–1 续表3

单位：万元

指　　标	Item	餐费收入 Revenue of Dining	#通过公共网络实现的餐费收入 by Public Network
二、餐饮业	**Catering**	**375578**	**11757**
1.按登记注册类型分	Grouped by Registered Kind		
内资企业	Civil Funded Enterprises	304499	11388
国有企业	State–owned Enterprises	7415	
集体企业	Collective–owned Enterprises	650	51
股份合作企业	Share Cooperative Enterprises	224	
有限责任公司	Limited Responsibility Corporations	56810	3696
国有独资公司	Company Exclusively with Investment from State	136	
其他有限责任公司	Other Limited Responsibility Company	56674	3696
股份有限公司	Share–holding Limited Corporations	2195	27
私营企业	Private–owned Enterprises	235630	7614
私营独资企业	Enterprise Exclusively with Investment from Private	22995	574
私营合伙企业	Private Partnership Enterprises	1325	
私营有限责任公司	Private Limited Responsibility Corporations	206331	6467
私营股份有限公司	Private Share–holding Limited Corporations	4979	573
其他企业	Others	1576	
港澳台商投资企业	Enterprises Funded by HongKong, Macao and Taiwan	13462	370
港澳台商独资企业	Solely Owned	13462	370
外商投资企业	Foreign Funded Enterprises	57617	
外资企业	Enterprises Funded by Foreign Invetments	57617	
2.按餐饮行业小类分组	Grouped by Catering Services		
正餐服务	Dinner	289148	11495
快餐服务	Fast Food	85368	2
其他餐饮业	Others	1062	260
餐饮配送服务	Distribution Service	500	260
其他未列明餐饮业	Other Unlisted Service	562	
3.按控股情况分	Grouped by Share Holding		
国有控股	State Holding Enterprises	17612	19
集体控股	Collective–owned Holding Enterprises	1657	51
私人控股	Private Holding Enterprises	274320	7979
港澳台商控股	Hongkong, Macao and Taiwan Holding Enterprises	13462	370
外商控股	Foreign Holding Enterprises	57617	
其　他	Others	10911	3339
4.按经营形式分	Grouped by Management Form		
独立门店	Independent Stores	223718	10590
连锁总店(总部)	Chain Headquarters	120422	501
连锁门店	Chain Stores	8402	134
其　他	Others	23036	532
5.按单位规模分	Grouped by Enterprise Size		
大　型	Large–size	88571	474
中　型	Medium–size	116166	3784
小　型	Small–size	168538	7492
微　型	Micro–size	2303	8

continued

(10 000 yuan)

其中：通过非自营平台实现的餐费收入 by Non-self-operating Platform	商品销售额收入 Revenue of Sales of Commodities	其他收入 Other Revenue	客房数(间) Rooms (unit)	床位数(个) Beds (unit)	餐位数(位) Tables (unit)	年末餐饮营业面积(平方米) Operating Area of Catering Services at Year-end(sq.m)
1167	**19179**	**8943**	**25334**	**43022**	**217185**	**1187881**
1165	19179	8943	25242	42842	204442	1148202
	133	235	1369	2551	8058	36418
	1	269	144	304	1690	9800
			24	50	300	2000
161	12717	3486	4276	7401	32312	211649
		1	166	283	1100	8000
161	12717	3486	4110	7118	31212	203649
	183	4	374	523	3713	14713
1004	6145	4948	18959	31827	157679	868140
417	385	488	1543	2735	20663	91190
	4		160	292	1627	9370
448	5712	4018	16296	26990	128654	714031
139	43	443	960	1810	6735	53549
			96	186	690	5482
2			92	180	3743	12729
2			92	180	3743	12729
					9000	26950
					9000	26950
925	18604	8940	25077	42581	199713	1132313
2	3	3			15946	46369
240	572		257	441	1526	9199
240	350				480	1000
	222		257	441	1046	8199
	133	2430	2940	5195	15568	93275
	12061	528	398	782	3106	20020
1069	6780	5845	21133	35560	176980	985889
2			92	180	3743	12729
					9000	26950
96	205	140	771	1305	8788	49018
593	6504	8573	22279	38972	172837	1009529
242	416	149	260	300	27592	109611
		6	64	110	3185	17583
332	12259	215	2731	3640	13571	51158
2	334		808	1600	15978	48659
	1405	3569	3499	5298	36474	217589
1165	17413	5206	19873	34070	155651	825443
	27	168	1154	2054	9082	96190

14-2 限额以上住宿和餐饮业法人企业主要财务状况(2016年)

单位：万元

指　标	Item	年初存货 Beginning Inventory
总　计	**Total**	**81575**
一、住宿业	**Hotels**	**31587**
1.按登记注册类型分	Grouped by Registered Kind	
内资企业	Civil Funded Enterprises	31423
国有企业	State-owned Enterprises	6620
集体企业	Collective-owned Enterprises	1095
有限责任公司	Limited Responsibility Corporations	6770
国有独资公司	Company Exclusively with Investment from State	500
其他有限责任公司	Other Limited Responsibility Corporations	6270
股份有限公司	Share-holding Limited Corporations	973
私营企业	Private-owned Enterprises	15936
私营独资企业	Enterprise Exclusively with Investment from Private	657
私营合伙企业	Private Partnership Enterprises	4
私营有限责任公司	Private Limited Responsibility Corporations	15226
私营股份有限公司	Private Share-holding Limited Corporations	49
其他企业	Others	29
港澳台商投资企业	Enterprises Funded by HongKong, Macao and Taiwan	164
与港澳台商合资经营企业	Joint Venture	164
2.按住宿行业小类分组	Grouped by Hotels	
旅游饭店	Resturants for Trip	22411
一般旅馆	Ordinary Hotels	8458
其他住宿服务	Others	718
3.按控股情况分	Grouped by Share Holding	
国有控股	State Holding Enterprises	9366
集体控股	Collective-owned Holding Enterprises	1447
私人控股	Private Holding Enterprises	18986
港澳台商控股	Hongkong, Macao and Taiwan Holding Enterprises	
外商控股	Foreign Holding Enterprises	
其　他	Others	1788
4.按经营形式分	Grouped by Management Form	
独立门店	Independent Stores	28789
连锁总店(总部)	Chain Headquarters	5
连锁门店	Chain Stores	243
其　他	Others	2550
5.按单位规模分	Grouped by Enterprise Size	
大　型	Large-size	607
中　型	Medium-size	5857
小　型	Small-size	23577
微　型	Micro-size	1546
6.按星级分	Grouped by Stars	
五　星	Five Star	4387
四　星	Four Star	7964
三　星	Three Star	6562
二　星	Two Star	1575
其　他	Others	11100

FINANCIAL CONDITION OF HOTELS AND CATERING CORPORATION ENTERPRISES ABOVE DESIGNATED SIZE(2016)

(10 000 yuan)

流动资产合计 Total Circulating Assets	#应收帐款 Accounts Receivable	#存货 Inventory	固定资产合计 Total Fixed Assets	累计折旧 Accumulated Depreciation	#本年折旧 Depreciation This Year	资产总计 Total Assets
825269	**114485**	**79745**	**1079649**	**691416**	**84100**	**2511563**
411330	**60452**	**28179**	**606960**	**433487**	**44633**	**1303273**
410468	60439	27981	605287	432605	44633	1298904
120243	13043	5677	169096	152840	15727	380072
8889	4091	959	13391	6225	462	33276
77910	11022	6462	121314	106326	6981	259742
1428	624	434	13941	7678	154	16270
76483	10398	6028	107374	98648	6827	243472
4378	811	837	15787	15440	1051	24501
198534	31384	14027	284026	150538	20145	599125
17608	5026	962	9859	3511	402	31077
232		3	187	67	11	1157
174967	25043	12974	273099	144290	17200	560274
5727	1315	89	881	2670	2532	6617
514	87	18	1673	1236	268	2187
862	14	198	1673	882		4369
862	14	198	1673	882		4369
307398	43132	20590	446016	367333	36543	972296
95373	16458	6645	138052	56639	7594	296130
8559	862	944	22892	9515	496	34847
135689	18389	8085	217854	199612	18199	452884
10961	4869	1362	27902	13856	1030	52765
221453	34224	16809	321683	179940	23306	674531
43227	2970	1923	39522	40078	2098	123093
377751	55282	25870	529214	410948	41499	1177497
281		4	27	62	6	1001
2213	148	217	2286	1884	389	6641
31086	5022	2088	75433	20593	2739	118134
16268	175	626	35493	22051	6622	52241
144768	12245	5781	159445	130786	9616	442577
242799	45041	21196	402727	277895	28175	785970
7495	2992	575	9296	2755	220	22484
75565	6774	3745	138665	81609	10505	253349
104071	15255	7437	104071	117858	11986	294168
95986	12728	6211	91645	116288	7038	256730
7600	2497	1479	35537	12177	2129	51629
128108	23199	9308	237042	105555	12974	447397

14-2　续表1

单位：万元

指　　标	Item	年初存货 Beginning Inventory
二、餐饮业	**Catering**	**49988**
1.按登记注册类型分	Grouped by Registered Kind	
内资企业	Civil Funded Enterprises	48102
国有企业	State-owned Enterprises	1021
集体企业	Collective-owned Enterprises	413
股份合作企业	Share Cooperative Enterprises	6
有限责任公司	Limited Responsibility Corporations	7760
国有独资公司	Company Exclusively with Investment from State	277
其他有限责任公司	Other Limited Responsibility Company	7483
股份有限公司	Share-holding Limited Corporations	812
私营企业	Private-owned Enterprises	37959
私营独资企业	Enterprise Exclusively with Investment from Private	2287
私营合伙企业	Private Partnership Enterprises	40
私营有限责任公司	Private Limited Responsibility Corporations	34830
私营股份有限公司	Private Share-holding Limited Corporations	803
其他企业	Others	131
港澳台商投资企业	Enterprises Funded by HongKong, Macao and Taiwan	200
港澳台商独资企业	Solely Owned	200
外商投资企业	Foreign Funded Enterprises	1686
外资企业	Enterprises Funded by Foreign Invetments	1686
2.按餐饮行业小类分组	Grouped by Catering Services	
正餐服务	Dinner	47739
快餐服务	Fast Food	2162
其他餐饮业	Others	88
餐饮配送服务	Distribution Service	21
其他未列明餐饮业	Other Unlisted Service	66
3.按控股情况分	Grouped by Share Holding	
国有控股	State Holding Enterprises	2773
集体控股	Collective-owned Holding Enterprises	2381
私人控股	Private Holding Enterprises	41849
港澳台商控股	Hongkong, Macao and Taiwan Holding Enterprises	200
外商控股	Foreign Holding Enterprises	1686
其　他	Others	1099
4.按经营形式分	Grouped by Management Form	
独立门店	Independent Stores	42568
连锁总店(总部)	Chain Headquarters	3338
连锁门店	Chain Stores	123
其　他	Others	3960
5.按单位规模分	Grouped by Enterprise Size	
大　型	Large-size	11891
中　型	Medium-size	8157
小　型	Small-size	28132
微　型	Micro-size	1808

continued

(10 000 yuan)

流动资产合计 Total Circulating Assets	#应收帐款 Accounts Receivable	#存货 Inventory	固定资产合计 Total Fixed Assets	累计折旧 Accumulated Depreciation	#本年折旧 Depreciation This Year	资产总计 Total Assets
413939	**54033**	**51566**	**472689**	**257930**	**39467**	**1208290**
409502	54005	50867	465255	250337	39103	1176822
5939	1100	1117	15440	12380	1081	24807
1339	200	382	1561	2487	174	3037
101	10	13	49	56	6	150
68986	11433	7816	144029	72528	15367	308621
1407	65	285	2749	1424		34286
67579	11368	7531	141280	71104	15367	274335
12227	1032	777	287	1372	71	17931
319993	40322	40648	302080	159035	22183	818732
25769	2422	1646	17453	6622	596	49565
419	213	122	1305	118	9	2472
274385	32581	38078	259772	148600	20955	711270
19420	5105	803	23549	3696	623	55425
917	-92	113	1810	2478	223	3544
3445	26	234	4564	679	364	17456
3445	26	234	4564	679	364	17456
992	2	465	2870	6914		14013
992	2	465	2870	6914		14013
402154	52818	50414	456683	247164	38361	1157637
11219	993	1005	8466	9030	846	41809
565	222	148	7540	1736	259	8844
149	1	65	296	3	1	537
417	221	83	7244	1733	258	8308
24599	3297	2867	123929	50361	10114	221713
4698	1191	2355	5769	5395	2375	12229
371881	47650	44660	326030	189979	24800	922454
3445	26	234	4564	679	364	17456
992	2	465	2870	6914		14013
8325	1866	985	9528	4603	1814	20426
364902	49913	45339	430152	222750	32270	1082097
17769	2148	2425	23155	24083	2449	65905
2870	219	328	511	678	94	5387
28397	1753	3473	18871	10420	4653	54902
20844	394	13725	9230	11895	1017	63708
77787	13979	7960	139728	93113	13605	281897
291911	38288	28089	309473	137349	23809	814317
23396	1372	1792	14258	15573	1036	48368

14-2 续表2

单位：万元

指　　标	Item	流动负债合　　计 Liquid Liabilities
总　计	**Total**	**1888759**
一、住宿业	**Hotels**	**932899**
1.按登记注册类型分	Grouped by Registered Kind	
内资企业	Civil Funded Enterprises	927988
国有企业	State-owned Enterprises	192607
集体企业	Collective-owned Enterprises	31094
有限责任公司	Limited Responsibility Corporations	209517
国有独资公司	Company Exclusively with Investment from State	2966
其他有限责任公司	Other Limited Responsibility Corporations	206551
股份有限公司	Share-holding Limited Corporations	11096
私营企业	Private-owned Enterprises	481966
私营独资企业	Enterprise Exclusively with Investment from Private	23780
私营合伙企业	Private Partnership Enterprises	947
私营有限责任公司	Private Limited Responsibility Corporations	454104
私营股份有限公司	Private Share-holding Limited Corporations	3136
其他企业	Others	1708
港澳台商投资企业	Enterprises Funded by HongKong, Macao and Taiwan	4911
与港澳台商合资经营企业	Joint Venture	4911
2.按住宿行业小类分组	Grouped by Hotels	
旅游饭店	Resturants for Trip	674506
一般旅馆	Ordinary Hotels	227469
其他住宿服务	Others	30924
3.按控股情况分	Grouped by Share Holding	
国有控股	State Holding Enterprises	218953
集体控股	Collective-owned Holding Enterprises	42955
私人控股	Private Holding Enterprises	553712
港澳台商控股	Hongkong, Macao and Taiwan Holding Enterprises	
外商控股	Foreign Holding Enterprises	
其　他	Others	117278
4.按经营形式分	Grouped by Management Form	
独立门店	Independent Stores	838603
连锁总店(总部)	Chain Headquarters	1005
连锁门店	Chain Stores	7810
其　他	Others	85481
5.按单位规模分	Grouped by Enterprise Size	
大　型	Large-size	7314
中　型	Medium-size	317822
小　型	Small-size	590194
微　型	Micro-size	17569
6.按星级分	Grouped by Stars	
五　星	Five Star	132073
四　星	Four Star	207022
三　星	Three Star	199743
二　星	Two Star	43603
其　他	Others	350457

continued

(10 000 yuan)

负债合计 Total Liabilities	所有者权益合计 Total Creditors' Equity	#实收资本 Capital Hold	#国家资本 State	#集体资本 Collective	#法人资本 Legal Person	#个人资本 Individual
2231929	**279634**	**754794**	**155086**	**8822**	**272052**	**317067**
1138136	**165136**	**455327**	**130495**	**4590**	**153784**	**166458**
1133225	165678	454827	130495	4590	153784	165958
294035	86038	120517	113214		7304	
31140	2137	3061	10	2596	456	
246183	13560	104870	17272	205	48934	38460
2966	13304	667	428		210	29
243217	255	104203	16843	205	48724	38431
11096	13405	23457		1786	21652	20
549065	50060	202418			75439	126979
24918	6160	8879			6835	2043
947	210	210				210
518623	41651	191290			68304	122985
4577	2040	2040			300	1740
1708	479	503		3		500
4911	-542	500				500
4911	-542	500				500
871055	101241	337001	84619	3104	130611	118667
235968	60162	104388	45876	1486	17034	39992
31114	3733	13938			6139	7799
327868	125016	164283	130485	105	32414	1279
43078	9687	11073	10	4481	6462	120
631996	42535	233508			95159	138349
135194	-12102	46463		3	19750	26710
1025474	152023	429439	121874	2691	149515	155359
1005	-4	5				5
8820	-2179	1750			1570	180
102838	15296	24133	8621	1899	2700	10914
46257	5984	2985	2985			
414582	27995	130970	79733		19762	31475
659334	126636	309541	46443	4496	130434	128168
17963	4521	11830	1334	93	3588	6815
212663	40686	97804	37169	1110	8760	50766
245278	48890	128318	39757	90	51611	36860
263489	-6759	83351	34665	1991	35291	11404
46662	4966	13463	1846	174	7464	3979
370045	77352	132391	17059	1224	50659	63449

14-2 续表3

单位：万元

指　标	Item	流动负债合　计 Liquid Liabilities
二、餐饮业	**Catering**	**955861**
1.按登记注册类型分	Grouped by Registered Kind	
内资企业	Civil Funded Enterprises	936812
国有企业	State-owned Enterprises	14045
集体企业	Collective-owned Enterprises	1163
股份合作企业	Share Cooperative Enterprises	31
有限责任公司	Limited Responsibility Corporations	232325
国有独资公司	Company Exclusively with Investment from State	22830
其他有限责任公司	Other Limited Responsibility Company	209496
股份有限公司	Share-holding Limited Corporations	19331
私营企业	Private-owned Enterprises	666063
私营独资企业	Enterprise Exclusively with Investment from Private	28322
私营合伙企业	Private Partnership Enterprises	305
私营有限责任公司	Private Limited Responsibility Corporations	600726
私营股份有限公司	Private Share-holding Limited Corporations	36710
其他企业	Others	3854
港澳台商投资企业	Enterprises Funded by HongKong, Macao and Taiwan	13221
港澳台商独资企业	Solely Owned	13221
外商投资企业	Foreign Funded Enterprises	5828
外资企业	Enterprises Funded by Foreign Invetments	5828
2.按餐饮行业小类分组	Grouped by Catering Services	
正餐服务	Dinner	927920
快餐服务	Fast Food	26910
其他餐饮业	Others	1030
餐饮配送服务	Distribution Service	368
其他未列明餐饮业	Other Unlisted Service	662
3.按控股情况分	Grouped by Share Holding	
国有控股	State Holding Enterprises	121759
集体控股	Collective-owned Holding Enterprises	6052
私人控股	Private Holding Enterprises	792801
港澳台商控股	Hongkong, Macao and Taiwan Holding Enterprises	13221
外商控股	Foreign Holding Enterprises	5828
其　他	Others	16201
4.按经营形式分	Grouped by Management Form	
独立门店	Independent Stores	860052
连锁总店(总部)	Chain Headquarters	45831
连锁门店	Chain Stores	7610
其　他	Others	42367
5.按单位规模分	Grouped by Enterprise Size	
大　型	Large-size	24569
中　型	Medium-size	215138
小　型	Small-size	677633
微　型	Micro-size	38521

continued

(10 000 yuan)

负债合计 Total Liabilities	所有者权益合计 Total Creditors' Equity	#实收资本 Capital Hold	#国家资本 State	#集体资本 Collective	#法人资本 Legal Person	#个人资本 Individual
1093793	**114498**	**299467**	**24591**	**4233**	**118268**	**150609**
1073995	102827	292701	24591	4233	113268	150609
16610	8198	13671	7050		6615	6
1163	1874	2530		2530		
31	119	100				100
262907	45714	57505	17541	1503	26404	12057
23201	11086	11000			11000	
239707	34628	46505	17541	1503	15404	12057
19572	-1641	4474			1970	2504
767029	51703	213551		200	78279	135072
33621	15944	18521			3592	14930
305	2167	2167			160	2007
682258	29013	182263		200	68800	113263
50845	4580	10600			5728	4872
6684	-3140	870				870
13455	4001	5028			5000	
13455	4001	5028			5000	
6343	7670	1739				
6343	7670	1739				
1061758	95879	284442	24591	4023	112409	143391
27526	14284	9397			5208	2450
4509	4335	5628		210	650	4768
368	168	150			150	
4141	4167	5478		210	500	4768
124694	97019	44240	24591		18573	1076
11783	447	3745		3745		1
920976	1478	237192		200	88359	148633
13455	4001	5028			5000	
6343	7670	1739				
16542	3884	7523		288	6335	900
992040	90057	270602	23531	4133	101000	141911
46358	19547	12030	1000		8310	981
7630	-2243	1066			431	635
47764	7138	15769	60	100	8527	7082
48711	14997	19668			6929	11000
255455	26443	39032	6000		12330	20702
737988	76329	230333	17827	3945	92242	116292
51639	-3271	10435	764	288	6766	2616

14-2 续表4

单位：万元

指　　标	Item	营业收入 Business Revenue
总　计	**Total**	**778291**
一、住宿业	**Hotels**	**313841**
1.按登记注册类型分	Grouped by Registered Kind	
内资企业	Civil Funded Enterprises	313489
国有企业	State-owned Enterprises	86430
集体企业	Collective-owned Enterprises	6563
有限责任公司	Limited Responsibility Corporations	77151
国有独资公司	Company Exclusively with Investment from State	3736
其他有限责任公司	Other Limited Responsibility Corporations	73415
股份有限公司	Share-holding Limited Corporations	8339
私营企业	Private-owned Enterprises	134281
私营独资企业	Enterprise Exclusively with Investment from Private	13829
私营合伙企业	Private Partnership Enterprises	553
私营有限责任公司	Private Limited Responsibility Corporations	118230
私营股份有限公司	Private Share-holding Limited Corporations	1670
其他企业	Others	725
港澳台商投资企业	Enterprises Funded by HongKong, Macao and Taiwan	352
与港澳台商合资经营企业	Joint Venture	352
2.按住宿行业小类分组	Grouped by Hotels	
旅游饭店	Resturants for Trip	224544
一般旅馆	Ordinary Hotels	82544
其他住宿服务	Others	6753
3.按控股情况分	Grouped by Share Holding	
国有控股	State Holding Enterprises	115532
集体控股	Collective-owned Holding Enterprises	12336
私人控股	Private Holding Enterprises	154803
港澳台商控股	Hongkong, Macao and Taiwan Holding Enterprises	
外商控股	Foreign Holding Enterprises	
其　他	Others	31170
4.按经营形式分	Grouped by Management Form	
独立门店	Independent Stores	286847
连锁总店(总部)	Chain Headquarters	163
连锁门店	Chain Stores	7309
其　他	Others	19522
5.按单位规模分	Grouped by Enterprise Size	
大　型	Large-size	12819
中　型	Medium-size	114755
小　型	Small-size	182812
微　型	Micro-size	3455
6.按星级分	Grouped by Stars	
五　星	Five Star	49532
四　星	Four Star	65829
三　星	Three Star	71918
二　星	Two Star	10023
其　他	Others	116539

continued

(10 000 yuan)

主营业务收入 Revenue in Major Business	营业成本 Business Costs	主营业务成本 Costs in Major Business	营业税金及附加 Business Taxes and Extra Charges	主营业务税金及附加 Taxes and Extra Charges in Major Business	其他业务利润 Profits of Other Business	销售费用 Costs of Sales
770185	**359102**	**356775**	**20870**	**20254**	**18523**	**295927**
310650	**119873**	**119569**	**8557**	**8221**	**4814**	**132555**
310298	119738	119433	8531	8195	4814	132358
86085	28912	28827	2455	2455	559	39688
6443	2832	2832	272	272	120	2143
76828	30133	30011	1813	1645	41	31786
3633	1135	1038	12	12	6	1918
73195	28998	28973	1801	1633	35	29867
8312	3504	3497	127	120	315	2479
131904	54141	54050	3836	3675	3778	55802
13829	7376	7370	551	551		5073
553	399	399	11	11		17
115853	45704	45619	3233	3072	3778	49923
1670	662	662	42	42		789
725	216	216	28	28		460
352	135	135	27	27		197
352	135	135	27	27		197
222222	86450	86236	5533	5477	3254	101716
82420	30387	30296	2675	2396	850	28270
6008	3036	3036	349	349	710	2569
114950	41383	41182	3081	3081	567	51495
12153	4453	4441	387	380	152	4495
152377	59988	59897	4462	4133	4093	65325
31169	14049	14048	627	627	2	11240
283680	109414	109110	7639	7351	4422	122026
163	107	107	5	5		
7286	1625	1625	308	259	385	3188
19522	8727	8727	606	606	6	7341
12819	2535	2535	732	732		3928
114600	40124	40097	2528	2521	1668	51770
179795	75908	75631	5148	4819	3094	75057
3436	1305	1305	149	149	52	1800
49375	14808	14783	1457	1450	2031	20183
65624	24656	24539	1391	1391	408	27807
71492	32188	32122	1645	1645	432	29151
10023	4212	4212	387	387	278	4009
114137	44009	43913	3676	3347	1666	51405

14–2 续表5

单位：万元

指　　标	Item	营业收入 Business Revenue
二、餐饮业	**Catering**	**464451**
1.按登记注册类型分	Grouped by Registered Kind	
内资企业	Civil Funded Enterprises	393758
国有企业	State–owned Enterprises	12288
集体企业	Collective–owned Enterprises	1331
股份合作企业	Share Cooperative Enterprises	470
有限责任公司	Limited Responsibility Corporations	75104
国有独资公司	Company Exclusively with Investment from State	668
其他有限责任公司	Other Limited Responsibility Company	74436
股份有限公司	Share–holding Limited Corporations	3713
私营企业	Private–owned Enterprises	298857
私营独资企业	Enterprise Exclusively with Investment from Private	29573
私营合伙企业	Private Partnership Enterprises	1672
私营有限责任公司	Private Limited Responsibility Corporations	258789
私营股份有限公司	Private Share–holding Limited Corporations	8824
其他企业	Others	1996
港澳台商投资企业	Enterprises Funded by HongKong, Macao and Taiwan	13075
港澳台商独资企业	Solely Owned	13075
外商投资企业	Foreign Funded Enterprises	57617
外资企业	Enterprises Funded by Foreign Invetments	57617
2.按餐饮行业小类分组	Grouped by Catering Services	
正餐服务	Dinner	377912
快餐服务	Fast Food	84603
其他餐饮业	Others	1936
餐饮配送服务	Distribution Service	856
其他未列明餐饮业	Other Unlisted Service	1080
3.按控股情况分	Grouped by Share Holding	
国有控股	State Holding Enterprises	32165
集体控股	Collective–owned Holding Enterprises	3112
私人控股	Private Holding Enterprises	344454
港澳台商控股	Hongkong, Macao and Taiwan Holding Enterprises	13075
外商控股	Foreign Holding Enterprises	57617
其　他	Others	14027
4.按经营形式分	Grouped by Management Form	
独立门店	Independent Stores	308084
连锁总店(总部)	Chain Headquarters	122772
连锁门店	Chain Stores	6381
其　他	Others	27214
5.按单位规模分	Grouped by Enterprise Size	
大　型	Large–size	92849
中　型	Medium–size	140733
小　型	Small–size	228184
微　型	Micro–size	2685

continued

(10 000 yuan)

主营业务收入 Revenue in Major Business	营业成本 Business Costs	主营业务成本 Costs in Major Business	营业税金及附加 Business Taxes and Extra Charges	主营业务税金及附加 Taxes and Extra Charges in Major Business	其他业务利润 Profits of Other Business	销售费用 Costs of Sales
459536	**239229**	**237206**	**12313**	**12033**	**13710**	**163372**
388843	207115	205093	10808	10529	13710	137948
12272	6599	6352	405	402	25	3003
1315	339	339	18	18	16	662
470	257	257	7	7		147
73059	42183	41912	2696	2588	861	26335
668	237	235	12	12		678
72390	41946	41677	2685	2577	861	25657
3690	1678	1661	106	65	369	1452
296042	154947	153458	7541	7412	11927	105448
29573	16986	16071	838	772	363	4949
1672	1166	1124	120	120		3
256182	132729	132198	6275	6221	11564	96927
8616	4066	4066	308	300		3569
1996	1114	1114	35	35	512	903
13075	4183	4183	216	216		7576
13075	4183	4183	216	216		7576
57617	27930	27930	1288	1288		17848
57617	27930	27930	1288	1288		17848
372999	197528	195506	10357	10078	13710	133648
84600	40356	40356	1824	1824		29614
1936	1344	1344	131	131		111
856	685	685	84	84		26
1080	659	659	47	47		85
31099	17651	17154	1314	1233	394	12144
3097	1402	1402	94	94	16	1449
340654	181588	180063	9097	8911	13598	118433
13075	4183	4183	216	216		7576
57617	27930	27930	1288	1288		17848
13993	6474	6474	303	290	-298	5922
304178	153933	151910	8859	8582	10969	113324
121948	69370	69370	2502	2502	2261	37207
6381	3013	3013	233	233	261	1966
27029	12913	12913	718	716	218	10875
92849	41702	41702	1791	1791	7717	34778
138232	78238	78187	3970	3872	3477	48379
225900	117662	115691	6466	6288	2356	78835
2555	1626	1626	85	82	160	1380

14-2 续表6

单位：万元

指　　标	Item	管理费用 Costs of Administration
总　计	**Total**	**204566**
一、住宿业	**Hotels**	**103704**
1.按登记注册类型分	Grouped by Registered Kind	
内资企业	Civil Funded Enterprises	103482
国有企业	State-owned Enterprises	30703
集体企业	Collective-owned Enterprises	2136
有限责任公司	Limited Responsibility Corporations	26461
国有独资公司	Company Exclusively with Investment from State	1221
其他有限责任公司	Other Limited Responsibility Corporations	25240
股份有限公司	Share-holding Limited Corporations	2564
私营企业	Private-owned Enterprises	41548
私营独资企业	Enterprise Exclusively with Investment from Private	1852
私营合伙企业	Private Partnership Enterprises	32
私营有限责任公司	Private Limited Responsibility Corporations	39098
私营股份有限公司	Private Share-holding Limited Corporations	566
其他企业	Others	71
港澳台商投资企业	Enterprises Funded by HongKong, Macao and Taiwan	222
与港澳台商合资经营企业	Joint Venture	222
2.按住宿行业小类分组	Grouped by Hotels	
旅游饭店	Resturants for Trip	71445
一般旅馆	Ordinary Hotels	30819
其他住宿服务	Others	1441
3.按控股情况分	Grouped by Share Holding	
国有控股	State Holding Enterprises	40193
集体控股	Collective-owned Holding Enterprises	3834
私人控股	Private Holding Enterprises	49985
港澳台商控股	Hongkong, Macao and Taiwan Holding Enterprises	
外商控股	Foreign Holding Enterprises	
其　他	Others	9692
4.按经营形式分	Grouped by Management Form	
独立门店	Independent Stores	95603
连锁总店(总部)	Chain Headquarters	53
连锁门店	Chain Stores	2012
其　他	Others	6035
5.按单位规模分	Grouped by Enterprise Size	
大　型	Large-size	6780
中　型	Medium-size	29523
小　型	Small-size	65586
微　型	Micro-size	1815
6.按星级分	Grouped by Stars	
五　星	Five Star	20132
四　星	Four Star	26610
三　星	Three Star	20166
二　星	Two Star	4335
其　他	Others	32462

continued

(10 000 yuan)

财务费用 Costs of Finance	#利息支出 Interest Expense	营业利润 Business Profits	利润总额 Total Profits	应交所得税 Income Tax Payable	应付职工薪酬 (本年贷方累计发生额) Remuneration Payable (Accumulated Credit Balance of The Year)
25908	**15876**	**-130721**	**-115166**	**2271**	**214840**
12967	**8383**	**-70498**	**-62507**	**667**	**116524**
12838	8254	-70141	-62218	667	116351
1693	1706	-17669	-13869	32	34965
78	68	-898	-317	2	2375
4231	1563	-24353	-23029	129	24491
9		-559	-614		1489
4221	1563	-23794	-22415	129	23002
34		-243	-515		1610
6798	4916	-26925	-24435	504	52699
100	8	-1127	-1048	38	3300
16		77			78
6673	4908	-25477	-22991	466	48601
10		-398	-396		719
4		-53	-53		212
129	129	-357	-289		174
129	129	-357	-289		174
10887	6761	-57768	-50193	230	70840
2050	1621	-12257	-11727	390	43733
30	1	-473	-587	48	1951
1852	1886	-23145	-19258	95	45713
105	77	-939	-579	2	3854
8096	5065	-39460	-35837	505	57988
2913	1356	-6954	-6833	65	8969
12028	7599	-66782	-58429	573	108244
16		-8	-9		10
51	18	125	-368	28	1141
872	766	-3833	-3701	67	7129
-128		-1029	-1029		5136
6805	4543	-16482	-14116	258	32051
6200	3754	-51514	-45435	406	77667
90	86	-1474	-1928	3	1671
2843	2911	-9657	-7830		17761
3095	1219	-24533	-23157	1	19796
3384	2407	-14154	-13484	150	27629
73	53	-2872	-2457	23	3075
3572	1793	-19283	-15579	494	48264

14-2 续表7

单位：万元

指 标	Item	管理费用 Costs of Administration
二、餐饮业	**Catering**	**100862**
1.按登记注册类型分	Grouped by Registered Kind	
内资企业	Civil Funded Enterprises	95486
国有企业	State-owned Enterprises	5792
集体企业	Collective-owned Enterprises	393
股份合作企业	Share Cooperative Enterprises	36
有限责任公司	Limited Responsibility Corporations	23526
国有独资公司	Company Exclusively with Investment from State	237
其他有限责任公司	Other Limited Responsibility Company	23289
股份有限公司	Share-holding Limited Corporations	1093
私营企业	Private-owned Enterprises	64082
私营独资企业	Enterprise Exclusively with Investment from Private	4685
私营合伙企业	Private Partnership Enterprises	314
私营有限责任公司	Private Limited Responsibility Corporations	56245
私营股份有限公司	Private Share-holding Limited Corporations	2839
其他企业	Others	564
港澳台商投资企业	Enterprises Funded by HongKong, Macao and Taiwan	498
港澳台商独资企业	Solely Owned	498
外商投资企业	Foreign Funded Enterprises	4879
外资企业	Enterprises Funded by Foreign Invetments	4879
2.按餐饮行业小类分组	Grouped by Catering Services	
正餐服务	Dinner	94579
快餐服务	Fast Food	5907
其他餐饮业	Others	376
餐饮配送服务	Distribution Service	24
其他未列明餐饮业	Other Unlisted Service	352
3.按控股情况分	Grouped by Share Holding	
国有控股	State Holding Enterprises	18363
集体控股	Collective-owned Holding Enterprises	741
私人控股	Private Holding Enterprises	73789
港澳台商控股	Hongkong, Macao and Taiwan Holding Enterprises	498
外商控股	Foreign Holding Enterprises	4879
其 他	Others	2594
4.按经营形式分	Grouped by Management Form	
独立门店	Independent Stores	84715
连锁总店(总部)	Chain Headquarters	9706
连锁门店	Chain Stores	1338
其 他	Others	5104
5.按单位规模分	Grouped by Enterprise Size	
大 型	Large-size	9609
中 型	Medium-size	27239
小 型	Small-size	62243
微 型	Micro-size	1772

continued

(10 000 yuan)

财务费用 Costs of Finance	#利息支出 Interest Expense	营业利润 Business Profits	利润总额 Total Profits	应交所得税 Income Tax Payable	应付职工薪酬(本年贷方累计发生额) Remuneration Payable (Accumulated Credit Balance of The Year)
12941	**7493**	**-60223**	**-52660**	**1604**	**98315**
12467	7493	-64569	-56972	727	95295
148	54	-3165	-685	2	4955
2		-83	-81	1	331
2		21	21		112
2070	893	-18509	-18299	129	19335
5		-500	-500		224
2065	893	-18009	-17799	129	19111
385		-1001	-1002		1450
9858	6546	-41229	-36323	595	68468
895	709	1544	366	52	4538
1		68	62	7	423
8489	5752	-40411	-35139	490	60744
472	85	-2430	-1611	47	2764
2		-605	-604		644
439		164	92		1976
439		164	92		1976
35		4182	4220	877	1045
35		4182	4220	877	1045
12420	7489	-65124	-57216	680	93181
517	5	4930	4930	924	4994
4		-29	-373		141
		37			1
4		-66	-373		139
654	77	-14772	-12305	68	12100
5	2	-575	-496	1	1144
11756	7391	-47883	-42900	667	78711
439		164	92		1976
35		4182	4220	877	1045
52	23	-1339	-1271	-9	3340
11723	7489	-59525	-53890	650	79487
1005		1560	1666	911	10689
33	3	-202	12	28	2025
179	1	-2055	-447	15	6115
621		2894	2876	911	7929
4217	2526	-19021	-18716	151	28584
8029	4924	-42058	-34881	536	59872
74	43	-2038	-1938	6	1930

14-3 限额以上连锁住宿餐饮业经营情况(2016年)
MANAGEMENT OF CHAIN ENTERPRISES ABOVE DESIGNATED SIZE IN HOTELS AND CATERING SERVICES(2016)

指标	Item	合计 Total	直营店 Regular Chain	加盟店 Franchise Chain
一、门店总数 (个)	**Number of Stores (uint)**	**107**	**103**	**4**
二、年末餐饮业营业面积 (平方米)	**Business Area of Catering at Year-end (sq.m)**	**62880**	**60780**	**2100**
三、年末从业人员 (人)	**Employees at Year-end (person)**	**5524**	**5453**	**71**
四、年末经营餐饮业务餐位数 (位)	**Number of Catering Tables at Year-end (uint)**	**19704**	**18554**	**1150**
五、商品购进总额 (万元)	**Total Purchases Value (10 000 yuan)**	**34375**	**34184**	**191**
#统一配送商品购进额	Value of Unified Distribution	28070	28070	
#自有配送中心配送商品购进额	Disrtibuted by Owned Distribution Center	28070	28070	
非自有配送中心配送商品购进额	Distributed by Other Distribution Center			
六、营业收入 (万元)	**Business Revenue (10 000 yuan)**	**71817**	**70934**	**884**
#餐费收入	Revenue of Dining	71815	70934	881

14-4 主要年份旅游接待人数
NUMBER OF TOURISTS IN MAJOR YEARS

年份 Year	接待国内游客人数 (万人次) Domestic Tourists (10 000 person-times)	接待入境过夜游客人数 (人次) Inbound Overnight Tourists (person-time)	外国人 Foreigners	华侨 Overseas Chinese	港澳台同胞 Compatriots from Hong Kong, Macao and Taiwan	#台湾同胞 Compatriots from Taiwan
1985	360	34327	26066	1523	6738	2628
1990	465	46777	26983	908	18886	10786
1995	977	71199	51513	1106	18580	10035
2000	2905	165282	116578		48704	21460
2005	6545	421458	253986		167472	64970
2010	12497	1302856	820935		481921	178480
2011	14975	1553208	982522		570686	213088
2012	19434	1891758	1204155		687603	261330
2013	24605	2126372	1350399		775973	296177
2014	29951	564770	361272		203498	82258
2015	36007	593772	380390		213382	86425
2016	44330	629836	404221		225615	91981

注：2014年起，海外旅游相关指标采用新口径，后同。

Note: Oversea tourism and related indicators have adopted a new coverage since 2014. The same applies to the following.

14-5 主要年份旅游收入
TOTAL INCOME OF TOURISM IN MAJOR YEARS

单位：亿元 (100 million yuan)

年 份 Year	旅游总收入 Total Income of Tourism	国内旅游收入 Revenue from Domestic Tourism	旅游外汇收入 (万美元) Foreign Exchange Earnings from Tourism (USD 10 000)	国内旅游人均花费 (元/人次) Per Capita Expenditure of Domestic Tourists (yuan/person-time)
1985	0.48	0.36	146	10.00
1990	2.80	2.22	458	47.74
1995	16.71	15.00	2062	153.53
2000	81.35	77.21	4991	265.78
2005	291.99	281.91	11622	447.41
2010	1083.46	1052.26	46460	861.10
2011	1342.59	1305.10	56720	878.60
2012	1813.01	1766.28	72024	903.00
2013	2305.44	2253.65	82268	966.00
2014	2846.51	2829.29	28073	855.00
2015	3447.50	3428.91	29710	884.00
2016	4247.12	4227.97	31738	962.77

14-6 旅游外汇收入(2016年)
FOREIGN EXCHANGE EARNINGS FROM INTERNATIONAL TOURISM(2016)

单位：万美元 (USD 10 000)

项 目	Item	合 计 Total	外国人 Foreigners	香港同胞 Hong Kong Compatriots	澳门同胞 Macao Compatriots	台湾同胞 Taiwan Compatriots
总 计	**Total**	**31737.6**	**20273.5**	**4313.7**	**2089.4**	**5061.1**
1.长途交通	Long Distance Transportation	8782.3	5609.7	1193.7	578.3	1400.5
飞 机	Air	4126.2	2635.6	560.8	271.8	658.0
火 车	Railway	2856.5	1824.6	388.3	188.0	455.5
汽 车	Highway	1799.6	1149.5	244.6	118.5	287.0
2.住 宿	Accommodation	5015.7	3204.2	681.6	330.1	799.7
3.餐 饮	Catering	4856.0	3101.9	660.1	319.7	774.4
4.景区游览	Visiting	5434.6	3471.8	738.6	357.7	866.6
5.娱 乐	Recreation	2551.8	1630.0	346.9	168.0	407.0
6.购 物	Shopping	3269.2	2088.2	444.4	215.3	521.3
7.市内交通	Urban Transportation	698.3	446.0	94.9	46.0	111.4
8.邮电通讯	Post and Communication	717.3	458.2	97.5	47.2	114.4
9.其 他	Others	412.6	263.6	56.1	27.2	65.8

14-7 旅游四星级以上饭店(2016年)
TOURIST HOTELS ABOVE FOUR STAR GRADE(2016)

名　　称	Name	地　　址	Address
五星级	**5 Star**		
山西国贸大饭店	Shanxi World Trade Hotel	太原市府西街69号	No.69, Fuxi St., Taiyuan
万狮京华大酒店	Grand Metropark Wanshi Hotel	太原平阳路126号	No.126, Pingyang Rd., Taiyuan
晋祠宾馆	Jinci Hotel	太原晋祠路中段669号	No.669, Middle Section of Jinci Rd., Taiyuan
丽华大酒店	Lihua Grand Hotel	太原长风街1号	No.1, Changfeng St., Taiyuan
天贵国际酒店	Tiangui International Hotel	大同新开南路133号	No.133, North Xinkai Rd., Datong
金地豪生大酒店	Howard Johnson Jindi Plaza	大同市平城街88号	No.88, Pingcheng St., Datong
五台山五峰宾馆	Wutaishan Wufeng Hotel	五台县台怀镇龙泉寺	Longquan Temple, Taihuai Town, Wutai County
宏源国际饭店	Hongyuan International Hotel	灵石高速路口	Lingshi Highway Intersection
万豪美悦国际酒店	Wanhaomeiyue International Hotel	榆次迎宾西街中段	West Yingbin St., Yuci
药林会议中心	Yaolin Conference Center	阳泉平定县张庄镇南后峪村	South Houyu Vil., Zhangzhuang Town, Pingding County, Yangquan
益东国际酒店	Yidong International Hotel	长治市西一环路	Weat First Ring Rd., Changzhi
东明国际大酒店	Dongming International Hotel	长治市紫金东街369号	No.369, East Ziji St., Changzhi
万通源大酒店	Wantongyuan Hotel	朔州市开发北路68号	No.68, North Kaifa Rd., Shuozhou
阳城环城凯斯顿酒店	Huancheng Caston Hotel	阳城县南环路	South Ring Rd., Yangcheng
东兴帝豪酒店	Royal Dongxing Hotel	孝义市崇文大街181号	No.181, Chongwen St., Xiaoyi
海纳温泉国际酒店	Haina Wenquan International Hotel	运城永济河东大道南段	South Hedong Av., Yongji, Yuncheng
阳城美韵花园大酒店	Yangcheng Meiyun Garden Hotel	阳城县新阳西街	West Xinyang St., Yangcheng
四星级	**4 Star**		
山西大酒店	Shanxi Grand Hotel	太原新建南路5号	No.5, South Xinjian Rd., Taiyuan
山西愉园大酒店	Shanxi Yuyuan Hotel	太原开化寺街148号	No.148, Kaihuasi St.,Taiyuan
三晋国际饭店	Sanjin International Hotel	太原迎泽大街30号	No.30, Yingze St., Taiyuan
黄河京都大酒店	Yellow River Jingdu Hotel	太原平阳路17号	No.17, Pinyang Rd., Taiyuan
山西阳光大酒店	Shanxi Xinyangguang Hotel	太原北大街47号	No.47, North St., Taiyuan
山西晋协宾馆	Shanxi Jinxie Hotel	太原东缉虎营35号	No.35, Dongjihuying, Taiyuan

14-7 续表1 continued

名 称	Name	地 址	Address
西山大厦	Xishan Hotel	太原西矿街318号	No.318, Xikuang St., Taiyuan
太原铁道大厦	Taiyuan Railway Hotel	太原迎泽南街19号	No.19, South Yingze St., Taiyuan
云水国际大酒店	Yunshui International Hotel	太原平阳路48号	No.48, Pingyang Rd., Taiyuan
太原金辇酒店	Taiyuan Jinnian Hotel	太原滨河东路北段22号	No.22, North Section of East Binhe Rd., Taiyuan
山西滨河饭店	Shanxi Binhe Hotel	太原市府西街103号	No.103, Fuxi St., Taiyuan
泰瑞国际商务酒店	Tairui International Commercial Hotel	太原长风街7号	No.7, Chengfeng St., Taiyuan
宏安国际酒店	Hongan International Hotel	大同迎宾西路28号	No.28, West Yingbin Rd., Datong
大同宾馆	Datong Hotel	大同迎宾西路37号	No.37, West Yingbin Rd., Datong
五洲大酒店	Wuzhou Hotel	大同迎宾西路宾西街88号	No.88, Binxi St., West Yingbin Rd., Datong
大同国宾大酒店	Datong Presidential Hotel	大同御河西路898号	No.898, West Yuhe Rd., Datong
花园大饭店	Huayuan Hotel	大同大南街59号	No.59, Danan St., Datong
浩海国际酒店	Haohai International Hotel	大同新建南路46号	No.46, South Xinjian Rd., Datong
雁北宾馆	Yanbei Hotel	大同御河北路甲1号	No. Jia1, North Yuhe Rd., Datong
晨光国际酒店	Chenguang International Hotel	大同迎宾东路68号	No.68, West Yingbin Rd., Datong
北冰洋大酒店	Beibingyang Hotel	阳泉北大街80号	No.80, North St., Yangquan
山西泉美国际大酒店	Shanxi quanmei International Hotel	阳泉市南大西街15号楼	No.15 Building South West Street, Yangquan
鹏宇国际大酒店	Pengyu International Hotel	长治市长兴中路509号	No.509, Changxing Middle Rd., Changzhi
财苑大厦	Caiyuan Hotel	长治市长兴中路305号	No.305, Changxing Middle Rd., Changzhi
富景国际饭店	Fujing International Hotel	晋城新市东街81号	No.81, East Xinshi St., Jincheng
晋城大酒店	Jincheng Grand Hotel	晋城凤台西街88号	No.88, West Fengtai St., Jincheng
太平洋大厦	Pacific Ocean Hotel	晋城凤台西街59号	No.59, West Fengtai St., Jincheng
颐宾大酒店	Yibin Hotel	晋城前西街58号	No.58, Qianxi St., Jincheng
晋城高都大酒店	Jincheng Gaodu Grand Hotel	晋城新市东街8号	No.8, East Xinshi St., Jincheng
晋城阳光大酒店	Jincheng Sunshine Hotel	晋城市泽州路76号	No.76, Zezhou Rd., Jincheng
棋源山庄	Qiyuan Moutain Village	晋城陵川县棋子山风景区	Qizishan Scenic Spot, Lingchuan, Jincheng
兰花大酒店	Lanhua Hotel	晋城凤台东街2288号	No.2288, East Fengtai St., Jincheng
泽州大酒店	Zezhou Hotel	晋城市凤台西街2839号	No.2839 West Feitai St., Jincheng

14-7 续表2 continued

名 称	Name	地 址	Address
皇城相府贵宾楼	Xianfu Grand Hotel	晋城市阳城北留皇城村	Huangcheng Vil., Beiliu, Yangcheng, Jincheng
万通源平鲁宾馆	Wantongyuan Pinglu Hotel	朔州市平鲁区胜利南路	South Shengli Rd., Pinglu District, Shuozhou
平朔宾馆	Pingshuo Hotel	朔州平朔生活区	Living District , Pingshuo, Shuozhou
圣厚源大酒店	Shenghouyuan Hotel	朔州开发北路安泰街2号	No.2, Antai St., North Kaifa Rd., Shuozhou
玉龙国际酒店	Yulong International Hotel	右玉县新建大街北侧	North of Xinjian St., Youyu
颐景国际大酒店	Yijing International Hotel	晋中市榆次区西顺城街71号	No.71, Xishuncheng St., Yuci District, Youyu
平遥峰岩大酒店	Pingyao Fengyan Hotel	晋中市平遥县曙光路峰岩广场	Fengyan Square, Shuguang Rd., Pingyao, Jinzhong
介休市正达海悦酒店	Jiexiu Zhengdahaiyue Hotel	晋中市介休市北坛东路25号	No.25, East Beitan Rd., Jiexiu, Jinzhong
运城市宾馆	Yuncheng Hotel	运城市红旗东街84号	No.84, East Hongqi St., Yuncheng
天都大酒店	Tiandu Hotel	河津市振兴东路	East Zhenxing Rd., Hejin
桃源国际酒店	Taoyuan International Hotel	运城市圣慧北路2号	No.2, North Shenghui Rd., Yuncheng
芮城惠阳大酒店	Ruicheng Huiyang Hotel	芮城县洞宾东街8号	No.8, East Dongbin St., Ruicheng
新康国际酒店	Xinkang International Hotel	运城市人民南路243号	No.243, South Renmin Rd., Yuncheng
五台山银海山庄	Wutai Moutain Yinhai Moutain Village	忻州五台山台怀镇	Taihuai Town, Wutai Moutain, Xinzhou
原平市宾馆	Yuanping Hotel	忻州原平前进西街57号	No.57, West Qianjin St., Yuanping, Xinzhou
花卉山庄	Huahui Moutain Village	忻州五台山大车沟	Dachegou, Wutai Moutain, Xinzhou
繁峙县嘉盛伦大酒店	Fansi Jiashenglun Hotel	忻州市繁峙县向阳北路	North Xiangyang Rd., Fanshi, Xinzhou
金鼎大酒店	Jinding Grand Hotel	忻州市定襄县晋昌大街	Jinchang St., Dingxiang, Xinzhou
侯马华翔大酒店	Houma Huangxiang Hotel	临汾市侯马市火车站南侧	South of Houma Railway Station, Linfen
金海湾大酒店	Jinhaiwan Hotel	临汾市向阳西路西段	West Section of West Xiangyang Rd., Linfen
思麦尔国际酒店	Smir International Hotel	临汾市鼓楼东大街40号	No.40, East Gulou Dong St., Linfen
山西丁陶国际大酒店	Shixi Dingtao International Hotel	临汾市襄汾县兴农路公园南侧	South of XingnongRd. Park, Xiangfen, Linfen
华强大酒店	Huaqiang Grand Hotel	侯马市呈王东路69号	No.69, East Chengwang Rd., Houma
吕梁国际宾馆	Lvliang International Hotel	离石区滨河南东路2号	No.2, South Binhe Rd. , Lishi District
贾家庄裕和花园酒店	Jiajiazhuang Yuhe Garden Hotel	吕梁市汾阳县贾家庄腾飞路	Tengfei Rd., Jiajia Vil., Fenyang, Lvliang
东兴酒店	Dongxing Hotel	孝义市府前街55号	No.55, Fuqian St., Xiaoyi

主要统计指标解释

住宿业 指为旅行者提供短期留宿场所的活动，有些单位只提供住宿，也有些单位提供住宿、饮食、商务、娱乐一体的服务。

餐饮业 指通过即时制作加工、商业销售和服务性劳动等，向消费者提供食品和消费场所及设施的服务。

限额以上住宿企业 年主营业务收入200万元及以上为限额以上住宿企业。

限额以上餐饮企业 年主营业务收入200万元及以上为限额以上餐饮企业。

住宿和餐饮业零售额 指专门从事提供食宿服务、进行食品烹饪调制的住宿和餐饮业企业、产业活动单位和个体户，直接向居民和社会集团出售主食、菜肴、烟酒饮料和其他商品取得的餐费收入和商品销售额，包括各行业企业或单位附设的对外营业的旅馆、火车餐车、轮船餐厅、机场餐厅的零售额，不包括机关、团体、学校、企事业单位不对外营业的职工食堂所出售的餐费收入。

住宿业企业星级评定情况 星级等级指符合《中华人民共和国星级酒店评定标准》(GB/T14308-2003)，并经过有关旅游管理权威部门评定（验收）后授予“星级”称号的宾馆、饭店等住宿设施的等级划分，分为一星级到五星级5个标准。星级越高，表示企业的档次越高。

营业额 指住宿和餐饮业单位在经营活动中因提供服务或销售商品等取得的全部收入，包括：客房收入、餐费收入、商品销售额（含增值税）和其他收入。

客房收入 指住宿和餐饮业单位在经营活动中因提供住宿服务取得的收入。

餐费收入 指住宿和餐饮业单位因为顾客提供就餐服务取得的收入。

商品销售额 指住宿和餐饮业单位出售商品的销售总额（含增值税）。

其他收入 指营业额中除客房收入、餐费收入、商品销售额（含增值税）以外的其他收入。

入境过夜游客 指在中国（大陆）的旅游住宿单位内至少停留一夜的外国人、港澳台同胞。

国内游客 指报告期内在中国（大陆）观光游览、度假、探亲访友、就医疗养、购物、参加会议或从事经济、文化、体育、宗教活动的中国（大陆）居民，其出游的目的不是通过所从事的活动谋取报酬。

旅游外汇收入 入境游客在中国（大陆）境内旅行、游览过程中用于交通、参观游览、住宿餐饮、购物、娱乐等全部花费。

国内旅游收入 指国内游客在国内旅行、游览过程中用于交通、参观游览、住宿餐饮、购物、娱乐等全部花费。

Explanatory Notes on Main Statistical Indicators

Hotel Services refer to activities provided to travelers a short time accommodation places. Some hotels only provide accommodation, others also provide lodging, business and entertainment services.

Catering Services refer to the activities provided to customers food, consumption places and facilities by on-the-spot making and processing, commercial sales and service-type labor.

Hotel Enterprises Above Designated Size refer to hotel enterprises whose annual revenue of major business amounts to 2 million yuan and over.

Catering Enterprises Above Designated Size refer to catering enterprises whose annual revenue of major business amounts to 2 million yuan and over.

Retail Sales of Hotels and Catering Services refer to the retail sales hotels and catering enterprises, active units and self-employed individuals which specialized in providing accommodation, food services got by directly selling staple foods, cooked foods, beverages, tobacco and other goods to the residents and community groups. It includes retail sales from opening to the public hotels, restaurants, train dining cars, ship and airport dining rooms of all kinds of enterprises or units, while it excludes dining revenue from stuff's dining hall of government agencies, groups, schools, enterprises and institutions, which aren't open to the public.

Star Rating of Hotel Service Enterprises refers to catering enterprises being assessed by the relevant tourism authorities according to GB/T14308-2003 standard. Hotels can be divided into five standards from one-star to five-star. The more stars hotels get, the higher grade they show.

Business Revenue refers to the total revenue hotel and catering service enterprises get from business activities by providing services and commodities selling. It includes room revenue, dinning revenue, commodities sales with value-added tax and other revenue.

Room Revenue refers to business revenue hotel and catering enterprises got by providing lodging services.

Dinning Revenue refers to revenue hotel and catering enterprises got by providing customers catering services.

Commodity Sales refers to revenue hotel and catering enterprises got by selling commodities including value-added tax.

Other Revenue refers to other revenue hotel and catering enterprises get except room revenue, dinning revenue, and commodity sales including value-added tax.

Inbound Overnight Tourists refer to foreigners and compatriots from Hong Kong, Macao and Taiwan who come to China (the mainland) and stay in the tourist accommodation units for at least one night.

Domestic Tourists refer to residents of China (the mainland) who travel within China (the mainland) for sightseeing, vacation, visiting relatives, medical treatment, shopping, attending conference, or engaging in economic, cultural, sports and religious activities. And the purpose of their travelling isn't for profits.

Foreign Exchange Earnings from Tourism refer to the total expenditures of inbound tourists during their stay in the mainland of China on transportation, sightseeing, accommodation, food, shopping and entertainment.

Revenue from Domestic Tourism refers to the total expenditures of domestic tourists during their stay in the mainland of China on transportation, sightseeing, accommodation, food, shopping and entertainment.

15 交通运输、邮电通信业

TRANSPORTATION, POST AND TELECOMMUNICATION SERVICES

资料整理人员

崔旭莲　阮并晶

交通运输、邮电通信业
TRANSPORTATION, POST AND TELECOMMUNICATION SERVICES

铁路营业里程	Length of Railways in Operation	5293	公里	(km)
公路通车里程	Length of Highways	142066	公里	(km)
货物周转量	Turnover Volume of Freight Traffic	3565.5	亿吨公里	(100 million ton-km)
旅客周转量	Turnover Volume of Passenger Traffic	360.5	亿人公里	(100 million person-km)
市话年末到达数	Urban Telephone Subscribers at Year-end	287.7	万户	(10 000 subscribers)
农话年末到达数	Rural Telephone Subscribers at Year-end	55.9	万户	(10 000 subscribers)
移动电话户数	Number of Mobile Telephone Subscribers	3365.7	万户	(10 000 subscribers)

民用汽车拥有量（万辆）
Number of Civil Motor Vihicles (10 000 units)

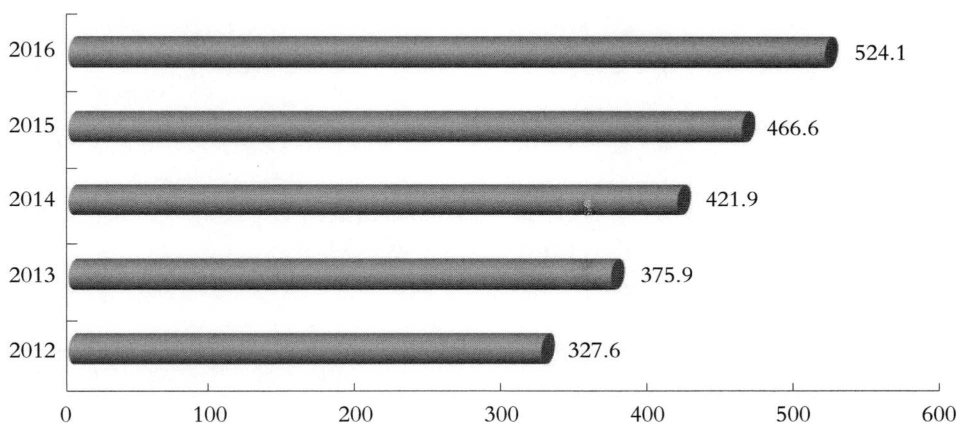

公路通车里程（公里）
Length of Highways (km)

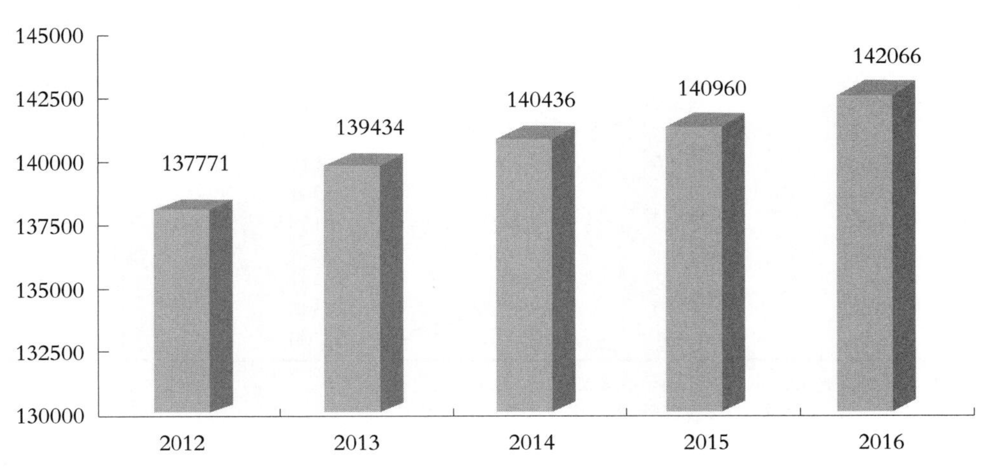

15-1 主要年份运输线路长度

LENGTH OF TRANSPORT ROUTES IN MAJOR YEARS

单位：公里 (km)

年 份 Year	铁路营业里程 Length of Railways in Operation	公路通车里程 Length of Highways	#高速公路 Expressways	每百平方公里平均里程 Average Length Per Square Kilometre 铁 路 Railways	公 路 Highways
1978	2057	31868		1.3	20.3
1980	2129	27261		1.4	17.4
1985	2169	28762		1.4	18.4
1990	2330	30784		1.5	19.6
1995	2435	33644		1.6	21.5
2000	2512	55408	518	1.6	35.4
2005	2512	111227	1686	1.6	71.0
2010	3752	131644	3003	2.4	84.0
2011	3774	134808	4005	2.4	86.0
2012	3774	137771	5011	2.4	87.9
2013	3786	139434	5011	2.4	89.1
2014	4980	140436	5011	3.2	89.9
2015	5086	140960	5028	3.2	90.0
2016	5293	142066	5265	3.4	90.7

注：2005年起公路线路里程包括村道里程数；2006年起铁路营业里程包括国铁、合资和地方铁路。

Note: Length of highways and all-weather highways has included length of roads between villages since 2005. Length of railways has included length of national railways, joint-venture railways and local railways since 2006.

15-2 主要年份货运量

FREIGHT TRAFFIC IN MAJOR YEARS

单位：万吨 (10 000 tons)

年 份 Year	合 计 Total	铁 路 Railways	#中央铁路 National Railways	公 路 Highways	水 运 Water Transport	民 航 Civil Aviation
1978	15620	9166	9166	6443	11	0.09
1980	18080	11067	11067	7004	9	0.15
1985	29181	16110	16092	13071		0.35
1990	50111	23332	23082	26706	72	0.55
1995	65962	26095	25718	39776	90	0.67
2000	86624	28779	28469	57813	31	0.60
2005	125367	49067	47697	76201	95	3.80
2010	124677	63836	60808	60819	18	4.49
2011	137940	69194	65695	65201	41	4.53
2012	144622	71437	68294	73150	30	4.84
2013	156048	73181	69894	82834	28	5.00
2014	164924	76411	75059	88491	17	5.07
2015	161772	70509	68268	91240	17	5.04
2016	167082	64861	62563	102200	16	5.49

注：(1)2000年以前汽车货运量为交通系统内口径，2000年及以后为全社会口径。

(2)2008-2012年，2013年至今，公路运输量相关指标为五年一次专项调查数据，下同。

Notes: (1)The freight traffic of automobile is calculated by the coverage of traffic system before 2000, and refferred to total society from 2000.

(2)Traffic volume of highways and relative data from 2008 to 2012, from 2013 to now are obtained from two special surveys, which are conducted once every 5 years. The same applies to the follwing.

15-3 主要年份货物周转量
TURNOVER VOLUME OF FREIGHT TRAFFIC IN MAJOR YEARS

单位：万吨公里 (10 000 ton-km)

年 份 Year	合 计 Total	铁 路 Railways	#中央铁路 National Railways	公 路 Highways	水 运 Water Transport
1978	1896350	1784790	1784790	111483	77
1980	2253618	2096450	2096450	157126	42
1985	3609795	3086917	3086584	522878	
1990	5948295	4795516	4784200	1152520	259
1995	7179630	5363846	5346060	1815463	321
2000	8679954	5979696	5958000	2700206	52
2005	13625549	9697012	9599369	3927715	822
2010	23324205	13624714	13436905	9698896	595
2011	30827489	20355804	20153949	10471189	496
2012	33458466	21435390	21231815	12022480	596
2013	35923686	23137331	23117075	12785747	608
2014	37108069	23475689	23453328	13631956	423
2015	34385474	20637317	20478663	13747614	543
2016	35654565	21133151	20965576	14520591	823

注：2011年起，铁路为全行业数据，包括国家铁路(含控股)、非控股合资铁路及地方铁路。

Note: Volume of railways is calculated by the whole industry coverage from 2011, which includes national railways, non-shareholding joint venture railways and local railways.

15-4 主要年份旅客运输量和周转量
PASSENGER TRAFFIC AND TURNOVER VOLUME IN MAJOR YEARS

年 份 Year	客运量 (万人) Passenger Traffic (10 000 persons)	#铁 路 Railways	#公 路 Highways	旅客周转量 (万人公里) Passenger Kilometers (10 000 person-km)	#铁 路 Railways	#公 路 Highways
1978	4498	2124	2375	387366	270950	116416
1980	5865	2523	3342	497897	356420	141477
1985	10564	3391	7173	931783	621351	310432
1990	15960	3226	12728	1260441	668100	587953
1995	21337	3308	17956	1750989	806580	861061
2000	31818	2953	28821	2245807	833600	1358962
2005	40209	3433	36456	3295406	1056422	1809406
2010	39059	5746	32606	3715683	1558206	2157019
2011	39932	6219	32865	4158078	1957808	2199108
2012	40839	6208	33662	4229773	1923652	2306121
2013	34781	6294	28487	3864404	1898201	1966203
2014	34040	6949	27091	3843762	2023842	1819920
2015	30676	7393	22085	3799506	2154182	1645324
2016	27619	7530	18702	3604561	2193137	1411424

注：2009年起旅客周转量不包括民航数据。

Note: Passenger turnover volume doesn't include civil aviation data from 2009.

15-5 主要年份民用汽车拥有量
NUMBER OF CIVIL MOTOR VEHICLES IN MAJOR YEARS

单位：辆 (unit)

年份 Year	民用汽车总数 Total	#载货汽车 Trucks	#载客汽车 Buses and Cars	#私人汽车 Private Vehicles	#载货 Trucks	#载客 Buses and Cars	每百公里公路平均汽车数 Average Number of Motor Vehicles Per 100 km
1978	45634	34383	8341				143.2
1980	70730	47872	10329				259.5
1985	129286	102033	20968	23664	21525	1884	449.5
1990	232665	174618	46390	46540	36084	10450	755.8
1995	332886	210157	106924	94987	54806	40131	989.4
2000	550148	278235	253481	235078	98837	135909	992.9
2005	1074350	379599	677746	587721	155570	430314	1056.5
2010	2478905	558169	1899271	1865984	319589	1541432	2315.8
2011	2953253	612696	2316189	2301975	364040	1931590	2190.7
2012	3275805	567788	2708017	2697177	362482	2334695	2377.7
2013	3758528	582913	3175615	3180579	385930	2794649	2695.6
2014	4219470	591108	3628362	3661596	400345	3261251	3004.6
2015	4665842	571789	4094053	4137927	393407	3744520	3310.0
2016	5240814	595149	4645665	4720486	406394	4314092	3689.0

注：民用汽车总数和私人汽车数不包括三轮汽车和低速货车。

Note: Number of civil motor vehicles and number of private cars exclude tricars and lower-speed cars.

15-6 民用汽车拥有量(2016年)
NUMBER OF CIVIL MOTOR VEHICLES(2016)

单位：辆 (unit)

指标	Item	合计 Total	营运 Business	非营运 Non-business	#个人 Individual
一、民用汽车	Civil Motor Vehicles	5306076	547615	4757561	4770247
1.载客汽车	Buses and Cars	4645665	80440	4564325	4314092
大型	Large	30555	21801	8116	580
中型	Medium	13265	4142	8861	2927
小型	Small	4454065	53834	4400231	4169673
微型	Mini	147780	663	147117	140912
#轿车	Cars	3294555	53655	3240900	3114890
2.载货汽车	Trucks	595149	430853	164296	406394
重型	Heavy	243571	240548	3023	119291
中型	Medium	14168	13007	1161	10040
轻型	Light	333130	176645	156485	273271
微型	Mini	4280	653	3627	3792
#普通载货汽车	Ordinary	253693	108711	144982	209963
3.其他汽车	Others	65262	36322	28940	49761
二、拖拉机	Tractors	488620			
三、摩托车	Motorcycles	322766	29145	293621	312148
四、载货挂车	Trailers	140311	139885	426	62292
五、其他类型车	Other Kinds of Vehicles	192	122	70	6

注：民用汽车拥有量包括三轮汽车和低速货车。

Note: Number of civil motor vehicles include tricars and lower-speed cars.

15-7 民用航空航线(2016年)
CIVIL AVIATION ROUTES(2016)

太原-北京	Taiyuan-Beijing
太原-常州-福州	Taiyuan-Changzhou-Fuzhou
太原-长沙	Taiyuan-Changsha
太原-长沙-福州	Taiyuan-Changsha-Fuzhou
太原-长沙-海口	Taiyuan-Changsha-Haikou
太原-长沙-南宁	Taiyuan-Changsha-Nanning
太原-长沙-厦门	Taiyuan-Changsha-Xiamen
太原-长沙-珠海	Taiyuan-Changsha-Zhuhai
太原-长治-武汉	Taiyuan-Changzhi-Wuhan
太原-长治-厦门	Taiyuan-Changzhi-Xiamen
太原-长治-重庆	Taiyuan-Changzhi-Chongqi
太原-成都	Taiyuan-Chengdu
太原-大连	Taiyuan-Dalian
太原-大同	Taiyuan-Datong
太原-福州	Taiyuan-Fuzhou
太原-广州	Taiyuan-Guangzhou
太原-桂林-海口	Taiyuan-Guilin-Haikou
太原-贵阳	Taiyuan-Guiyang
太原-贵阳-南宁	Taiyuan-Guiyang-Nanning
太原-海口	Taiyuan-Haikou
太原-海拉尔	Taiyuan-Hailaer
太原-杭州	Taiyuan-Hangzhou
太原-杭州-福州	Taiyuan-Hangzhou-Fuzhou
太原-杭州-三亚	Taiyuan-Hangzhou-Sanya
太原-合肥-海口	Taiyuan-Hefei-Haikou
太原-合肥-三亚	Taiyuan-Hefei-Sanya
太原-合肥-厦门	Taiyuan-Hefei-Xiamen
太原-呼和浩特	Taiyuan-Hohhot
太原-呼和浩特-乌兰浩特	Taiyuan-Hohhot-Wulanhaote
太原-黄山-厦门	Taiyuan-Huangshan-Xiamen
太原-昆明	Taiyuan-Kunming
太原-昆明-西双版纳	Taiyuan-Kunming-Xishuangbanna
太原-兰州-拉萨	Taiyuan-Lanzhou-Lasa
太原-丽江	Taiyuan-Lijiang
太原-南昌-深圳	Taiyuan-Nanchang-Shenzhen
太原-南京	Taiyuan-Nanjing
太原-南京-福州	Taiyuan-Nanjing-Fuzhou
太原-南京-厦门	Taiyuan-Nanjing-Xiamen
太原-南宁-海口	Taiyuan-Nanning-Haikou
太原-南通-福州	Taiyuan-Nantong-Fuzhou
太原-秦皇岛	Taiyuan-Qinhuangdao
太原-青岛	Taiyuan-Qindao
太原-青岛-温州	Taiyuan-Qindao-Wenzhou
太原-三亚	Taiyuan-Sanya
太原-上海	Taiyuan-Shanghai
太原-深圳	Taiyuan-Shenzhen
太原-石家庄	Taiyuan-Shijiazhuang
太原-天津	Taiyuan-Tianjin
太原-温州	Taiyuan-Wenzhou
太原-温州-三亚	Taiyuan-Wenzhou-Sanya
太原-乌鲁木齐	Taiyuan-Wulumuqi
太原-武汉-桂林	Taiyuan-Wuhan-Guilin
太原-武汉-贵阳	Taiyuan-Wuhan-Guiyang
太原-武汉-温州	Taiyuan-Wuhan-Wenzhou
太原-武汉-厦门	Taiyuan-Wuhan-Xiamen
太原-西安	Taiyuan-Xian
太原-西安-南宁	Taiyuan-Xian-Nanning
太原-西安-三亚	Taiyuan-Xian-Sanya
太原-烟台	Taiyuan-Yantai
太原-榆林-银川	Taiyuan-Yulin-Yinchuan
太原-运城	Taiyuan-Yucheng
太原-郑州-合肥	Taiyuan-Zhengzhou-Hefei
太原-重庆	Taiyuan-Chongqi
太原-重庆-昆明	Taiyuan-Chongqi-Kunming
长春-太原-西安	Changchun-Taiyuan-Xian
长沙-太原-北京	Changsha-Taiyuan-Beijing
长治-太原-天津	Changzhi-Taiyuan-Tianjin
成都-太原-北京	Chengdu-Taiyuan-Beijing
成都-太原-大连	Chengdu-Taiyuan-Dalian
成都-太原-大同	Chengdu-Taiyuan-Datong
成都-太原-唐山	Chengdu-Taiyuan-Tangshan
大连-太原-海口	Dalian-Taiyuan-Haikou
大连-太原-三亚	Dalian-Taiyuan-Sanya
大连-太原-西宁	Dalian-Taiyuan-Xining
大同-太原-昆明	Datong-Taiyuan-Kunming
大同-太原-南京	Datong-Taiyuan-Nanjing
大同-太原-厦门	Datong-Taiyuan-Xiamen
东胜-太原-广州	Dongsheng-Taiyuan-Guangzhou
东胜-太原-杭州	Dongsheng-Taiyuan-Hangzhou
东胜-太原-济南	Dongsheng-Taiyuan-Jinan
广州-太原-北京	Guangzhou-Taiyuan-Beijing
桂林-太原-哈尔滨	Guizhou-Taiyuan-Harbin

15-7 续表 continued

贵阳-太原-北京	Guiyang-Taiyuan-Beijing	北京-大同	Beijing-Datong
哈尔滨-太原-海口	Harbin-Taiyuan-Haikou	大同-上海	Datong-Shanghai
哈尔滨-太原-昆明	Harbin-Taiyuan-Kunming	大同-运城-三亚	Datong-Yuncheng-Sanya
哈尔滨-太原-三亚	Harbin-Taiyuan-Sanya	哈尔滨-大同-厦门	Harbin-Datong-Xiamen
海口-合肥-太原	Haikou-Hefei-Taiyuan	呼和浩特-大同-天津	Hohhot-Datong-Tianjin
合肥-太原-呼和浩特	Hefei-Taiyuan-Hohhot	沈阳-大同-西安	Shenyang-Datong-Xian
呼和浩特-太原-济南	Hohhot-Taiyuan-Jinan	大同-烟台	Datong-Yantai
呼和浩特-太原-昆明	Hohhot-Taiyuan-Kunming	北京-运城	Beijing-Yuncheng
呼和浩特-太原-南昌	Hohhot-Taiyuan-Nanchang	成都-运城	Chengdu-Yuncheng
济南-太原-包头	Jinan-Taiyuan-Baotou	大连-运城-南宁	Dalian-Yuncheng-Nanning
昆明-太原-北京	Kunming-Taiyuan-Beijing	广州-运城	Guangzhou-Yuncheng
兰州-太原-青岛	Lanzhou-Taiyuan-Qingdao	贵阳-运城-沈阳	Guiyang-Yuncheng-Shenyang
满洲里-太原-西安	Manzhouli-Taiyuan-Xian	哈尔滨-运城-三亚	Harbin-Yuncheng-Sanya
南京-太原-银川	Nanjing-Taiyuan-Yinchuan	海口-长沙-运城	Haikou-Changsha-Yuncheng
青岛-太原-乌鲁木齐	Qingdao-Taiyuan-Wulumuqi	海口-重庆-运城	Haikou-Chongqing-Yuncheng
沈阳-太原-昆明	Shenyang-Taiyuan-Kunming	杭州-运城-乌鲁木齐	Hangzhou-Yuncheng-Wulumuqi
沈阳-太原-重庆	Shenyang-Taiyuan-Chongqi	合肥-郑州-运城	Hefei-Zhengzhou-Yuncheng
天津-太原-贵阳	Tianjin-Taiyuan-Guiyang	昆明-运城-天津	Kunming-Yuncheng-Tianjin
天津-太原-呼和浩特	Tianjin-Taiyuan-Hohhot	兰州-运城-青岛	Lanzhou-Yuncheng-Qingdao
天津-太原-兰州	Tianjin-Taiyuan-Lanzhou	南京-运城	Nanjing-Yuncheng
天津-太原-银川	Tianjin-Taiyuan-Yinchuan	上海-运城	Shanghai-Yuncheng
乌鲁木齐-太原-北京	Wulumuqi-Taiyuan-Beijing	深圳-运城	Shenzhen-Yuncheng
西安-太原-北京	Xian-Taiyuan-Beijing	太原-运城	Taiyuan-Yuncheng
西安-太原-海拉尔	Xian-Taiyuan-Hailaer	乌鲁木齐-运城-杭州	Wulumuqi-Yuncheng-Hangzhou
西安-太原-沈阳	Xian-Taiyuan-Shenyang	厦门-武汉-运城	Xiamen-Wuhan-Yuncheng
银川-太原-张家界	Yinchuan-Taiyuan-Zhangjiajie	太原-釜山	Taiyuan-Pusan
张家界-太原-银川	Zhangjiajie-Taiyuan-Yinchuan	太原-海口-新加坡	Taiyuan-Haikou-Singapore
郑州-太原-呼和浩特	Zhengzhou-Taiyuan-Hohhot	太原-济州	Taiyuan-Jeju
重庆-太原-北京	Chongqi-Taiyuan-Beijing	太原-曼谷	Taiyuan-Bangkok
吕梁-北京	Lvliang-Beijing	太原-清州	Taiyuan-Cheongju
吕梁-上海	Lvliang-Shanghai	太原-仁川	Taiyuan-Incheon
吕梁-西安-广州	Lvliang-Xian-Guangzhou	太原-首尔	Taiyuan-Seoul
吕梁-长沙-海口	Lvliang-Changsha-Haikou	太原-襄阳郡	Taiyuan-Yangyang-gun
北京-长治	Beijing-Changzhi	普吉-太原	Phuket-Taiyuan
长治-成都	Changzhi-Chengdu	太原-澳门	Taiyuan-Macau
长治-上海	Changzhi-Shanghai	太原-高雄	Taiyuan-Kaohsiung
大同-长治-广州	Datong-Changzhi-Guangzhou	太原-台北	Taiyuan-Taipei
海口-长治-天津	Haikou-Changzhi-Tianjin	太原-台中	Taiyuan-Taizhong
青岛-长治-银川	Qingdao-Changzhi-Yinchuan	太原-香港	Taiyuan-Hong Kong
包头-大同-海口	Baotou-Datong-Haikou	大同-香港	Datong-Hong Kong

15-8 国家铁路分货类运输量(2016年)
NATIONAL RAILWAY FREIGHT TRAFFIC BY CATEGORY OF CARGO(2016)

指　　标	Item	货运量(万吨) Volume of Freight Traffic (10 000 tons)	货物周转量(万吨公里) Turnover Volume of Freight Traffic (10 000 ton-km)	平均运程(公里) Average Transport Mileage (km)
合　计	**Total**	**51208.9**	**31288761.2**	**482**
#煤　炭	Coal	40703.6	27005676.6	565
石　油	Petroleum	58.1	195264.1	284
焦　炭	Cake	2327.2	1111132.3	372
金属矿石	Metal Ore	1566.2	870864.6	200
钢铁及有色金属	Steel and Nonferrous Metal	1929.4	660299.9	266
非金属矿石	Nonmetal Ores	182.3	58724.2	271
磷矿石	Phosphate Rock	9.4	831.2	88
矿建材料	Mine Construction Materials	2439.1	190304.6	76
水　泥	Cement	0.7	172.5	232
木　材	Timber	3.5	9403.9	356
粮　食	Grain	416.7	171066.5	339
零　担	Sporadic Freight Transport	87.1	38768.0	413
集装箱	Container Transport	1015.6	490943.4	291

注：本表为太原铁路局全部数据。

Note: Data in the table is supplied by Taiyuan Railway Bureau.

15-9 地方铁路营运概况(2016年)
BASIC STATISTICS ON LOCAL RAILWAYS(2016)

地市及线路名称 Regions and Name of Railway Lines	起迄地址 The Beginning and The End	线路长度(公里) Length of Railways (km)		机　车(台) Locomotives (unit)		
		延展里程 Length of Extention	正线里程 Length of the Truck Lines	合　计 Total	电　气 Electrical	内　燃 Diesel
总　计　Total		**295.2**	**208.3**	**33**	**26**	**7**
一、合资铁路		184.8	115.5	26	19	7
Joint Venture Railways						
武沁铁路	武乡-左权；沁县-沁源	141.4	116.2	5		5
Wuqin Railway	Wuxiang-Zuoquan;Qinxian-Qinyuan					
孝柳有限责任公司	孝西-穆村	184.8	115.5	26	19	7
Xiaoliu Railway Co., Ltd.	Xiaoxi-Mucun					
二、地方铁路		110.4	92.8	7	7	
Local Railways						
宁静铁路	宁武-静乐	110.4	92.8	7	7	
Ningjing Railway	Ningwu-Jingle					

地市及线路名称 Regions and Name of Railway Lines	货物运输 Freight Traffic		财务状况 Financial Situation			
	货运量(万吨) Freight Traffic (10 000 tons)	货物周转量(万吨公里) Turnover of Freight Traffic (10 000 ton-kms)	运输收入(万元) Transportation Revenue (10 000 yuan)	运输支出(万元) Transportation Expend (10 000 yuan)	实现利润(万元) Profits (10 000 yuan)	上缴税金(万元) Taxes (10 000 yuan)
总　计　Total	**2298**	**167575**	**49104**	**49380**	**-901**	**4523**
一、合资铁路	1989	160015	45086	45504	-451	4388
Joint Venture Railways						
武沁铁路	309	17894	5340	5249	58	33
Wuqin Railway						
孝柳有限责任公司	1680	142120	39746	40255	-509	4355
Xiaoliu Railway Co., Ltd.						
二、地方铁路	309	7561	4018	3876	-450	135
Local Railways						
宁静铁路	309	7561	4018	3876	-450	135
Ningjing Railway						

15-10 邮电业务总量(2016年)
BUSINESS VOLUME OF POST AND TELECOMMUNICATION SERVICES(2016)

指　标	Item	2016
邮电业务总量 (亿元)	**Business Volume of Post and Telecommunication** Services(10 000 yuan)	**386**
函　件 (万件)	Number of Letters (10 000 pcs)	2650
包　裹 (万件)	Number of Parcels (10 000 pcs)	46
汇　兑 (万笔)	Number of Postal Money Orders (10 000 pcs)	98
机要邮件 (万件)	Number of Confidential Letters (10 000 pcs)	50
快 递 (万件)	Express Mail Services (10 000 pcs)	18665
集邮邮票 (万枚)	Philately (10 000 pcs)	3642
订阅报纸期发数 (万份)	Newspapers Circulation (10 000 copies)	59
订阅报纸累计数 (万份)	Accumulative Total of Newspapers Circulation (10 000 copies)	51797
订阅杂志期发数 (万份)	Magazines Circulation (10 000 copies)	25
订阅杂志累计数 (万份)	Accumulative Total of Magazines Circulation (10 000 copies)	1701
报刊流转额 (万元)	Circulation of Newspapers and Magazines (10 000 yuan)	61646
市话年末到达数 (万户)	Number of Subscribers of Urban Telephone at Year-end (10 000 subscribers)	287.7
农话年末到达数 (万户)	Number of Subscribers of Rural Telephone at Year-end (10 000 subscribers)	55.9
移动电话用户　(万户)	Number of Mobile Telephone Subscribers (10 000 subscribers)	3365.7
移动短信 (亿条)	Mobile Short Information (10 000 pcs)	201

15-11 主要年份邮电通信网
NETWORK OF POST AND TELECOMMUNICATION IN MAJOR YEARS

年 份 Year	邮政支局所 (处) Number of Branch Post Offices (unit)	#在农村 In Rural Area	邮路长度 (公里) Length of Postal Routes (km)	#铁 路 Railway Routes	#汽 车 Highway Routes
1978	1675	1444	143907	6840	17672
1980	1629	1380	141596	7304	17902
1985	1890	1591	146024	7024	21454
1990	1813	1456	146251	9482	20320
1995	1888	1454	157202	11062	30700
2000	1730	1239	203725	11564	45488
2005	1603	1045	181703	13738	48016
2010	1306	759	184998	15200	58698
2011	1526	853	213310	16066	81394
2012	1516	738	169908	16860	82490
2013	1483	773	150648	15358	58770
2014	1518	1072	87520	8306	68938
2015	1582	1158	86946	8392	74542
2016	1636	1194	93323	8306	83107

注：2014年起，邮政实施网运改革，邮路长度采用新口径。

Note: Because of the post reform of network operation, length of postal routes has adopted a new coverage since 2014.

15-12 邮政邮路
POSTAL ROUTES

单位：公里 (km)

指 标	Item	2015	2016
邮路总条数(条)	Number of Postal Routes (route)	460	496
#铁 路	Railway Postal Routes	2	2
汽 车	Highway Postal Routes	416	472
邮路总长度(单程)	Total Length of Postal Routes (one-way)	43473	46662
#铁 路	Railway Postal Routes	4196	4153
汽 车	Automobile Postal Routes	37271	41554
农村邮路条数(条)	Number of Rural Postal Routes (route)	264	250
农村邮路长度(单程)	Length of Rural Postal Routes (one-way)	14584	15141
城市投递路线条数(条)	Number of Rural Delivery Routes (route)	1529	1638
城市投递路线长度(单程)	Length of Rural Delivery Routes (one-way)	33683	36276
农村投递路线条数(条)	Number of Rural Delivery Routes (route)	2399	2211
#摩托车	Motorcycles	1874	1997
自行车	Bicycles	481	68
步 班	On Foot	13	10
农村投递线路长度(单程)	Length of Rural Delivery Routes (one-way)	102496	108813
#摩托车	Motorcycles	88161	97121
自行车	Bicycles	12197	2981
步 班	On Foot	263	277

15-13 邮政局所、房屋、服务点
NUMBER OF POSTAL OFFICES, BUILDINGS AND SERVICE PLACES

单位：处 (unit)

指　标	Item	2015	2016
邮政支局所	Number of Branch Post Offices	1582	1636
#设在农村的	In Rural Area	1158	1194
电子化支局	Electrical Branch Offices	1033	1069
邮政局	Number of Post Offices	108	108
邮政支局	Nmber of Branch Post Offices	401	403
自办邮政所	Number of Post Offices Operated By Post Department	526	525
代办邮政所	Number of Postal Agencies	655	708
邮政信筒信箱(个)	Post Boxes (unit)	1320	1362
自有房屋建筑面积(万平方米)	Floor Space of Self-owned Buildings (10 000 sq.m)	104.5	107.0
邮政生产用房面积	Floor Space of Production Used	60.2	58.9
其他生产用房	Other Productive Buildings	2.6	5.5
非生产用房面积	Floor Space of Non-production	41.8	42.6

主要统计指标解释

铁路营业里程 指办理客货运输业务的铁路正线总长度。凡是全线或部分建成双线及以上的线路，以第一线的实际长度计算；复线、站线、段管线、岔线和特别用途线以及不计算运费的联络线都不计算营业里程。线路营业里程是反映铁路运输业基础设施发展水平的重要指标，也是计算客货周转量、运输密度和机车车辆运用效率等指标的基础资料。

铁路延展里程 可以分为总延展里程以及正线、站线、段管线、岔线和特别用途线的延展里程。总延展里程是各种线路的延展里程之和。正线延展里程是正线第一线、第二线、第三线和其他正线建筑里程之和，站线、段管线、岔线和特别用途线的延展里程，均是各自建筑里程之和。延展里程是作为计算线路上钢轨、枕木及路基砂石需要量的主要依据。

公路网 是由各级公路组成的网状运输系统。它是由连结各城镇、乡村和工矿基地之间主要供汽车行驶的道路形成的网络。我国的公路里程是按其作用及使用管理性质分为国家干线公路、省级干线公路、县级公路、乡公路和专用公路。按其公路工程技术要求分为高速公路和一、二、三、四级公路。

公路里程 也称“公路通车里程”，是指实际达到交通部制定的公路工程技术标准规定的等级公路长度。它包括大中城市的郊区以及通过小城镇街道的公路里程，也包括桥梁、渡口的长度，但不包括城市街道以及厂矿、林区和农业生产用道的里程。两条或多条公路共同径由同一路段，只计算一次，不得重复计算里程长度。公路里程是反映公路建设发展规模的重要指标，也是计算运输网密度等指标的资料。

民用汽车 由公安交通监理部门所掌管的领有本地区民用车辆牌照的机动车辆中的一部分。不包括拖拉机、摩托车、其他机动车等。民用汽车包括普通载货汽车、专用载货汽车、载客汽车、其他专用汽车、特种汽车等。

营运汽车 指领有公安交通监理部门核发的车辆牌照，并经当地工商行政管理机关核准，领取营业执照，参加营业性运输的载客和载货汽车。

货(客)运量 指运输业实际运送的货物（旅客）数量。货运按吨计算。货物不论运输距离长短、货物类别，均按实际重量计算，旅客不论行程远近或票价多少，均按一人一次作为客运量统计。半票价、小孩票也按一人统计。货（客）运量反映运输业为国民经济和人民生活服务的数量指标，也是制定和检查运输生产计划，研究运输发展规模和速度的重要指标。

货物(旅客)周转量 指运输业运送的货物（旅客）数量与其相应运输距离的乘积之总和，通常以吨公里和人公里为计算单位。计算货物周转量通常按发出站与到达站之间的最短距离，也就是计费距离计算。它是反映运输业生产总成果的重要指标，也是编制和检查运输生产计划、计算运输效率、劳动生产率以及核算运输单位成本的主要基础资料。

换算周转量 是综合反映各种运输工具在一定时期内实际完成的旅客、货物周转量的综合指标。具体计算方法是将旅客周转量和货物周转量区分不同运输工具按相应的换算比例，换算成同一计量单位进行加总求得。其计算单位为：吨公里。

公路运输的换算比例是：1 吨公里=10 人公里

内河水运的换算比例是：1 吨公里=3 人公里（座位）　　1 吨公里=1 人公里（带卧铺）

铁路运输的换算比例是：1 吨公里=1 人公里（地方铁路为 5 人公里）

民航运输的换算比例是：1 吨公里=13.9 人公里（国际航线为 13.3 人公里）

邮电业务总量 指以货币表现的邮电部门为用户传递信息和提供其他邮电服务的总量。它用各种邮电分类业务量，如函件件数、电报份数、长话张数、市内电话和农村电话的年均户数、订销报刊累计份数等，分别乘以相应的平均单价（不变价），加总后再加上出租电路和设备的收入、代用户维护电话交换机和线路等设备的收入、其他业务收入求得。邮电业务总量综合反映了一定时期邮电工作的总成果，是研究邮电业务量构成和发展趋势的重要指标。

电话用户数 包括固定和移动电话。固定电话用户指接入国家公众固定电话网，并按固定电话业务进行经营管理的电话用户。移动电话用户指在移动电话营业部门登记，通过移动电话交换机接入移动电话网、占有移动电话号码的用户。

邮路 各邮政局所之间，邮政局所与车站、码头、机场、转运站、邮件处理中心、报刊社之间，邮区中心局与邮政局所及各邮区中心局之间由自办或委办人员按固定班期规定路线交换邮件（包括机要文件，下同）、报刊的路线。包括农村地区运邮兼投递的路线，不包括城市、农村地区纯投递路线。按运输方式可分为航空邮路、铁路邮路、汽车邮路、水路邮路和其他邮路等。

邮路总长度 邮路由起点到终点的长度。单程长度统计法的计算方法是直线算单程，环型算全程；直环混合中直线部分算单程，环型部分算全程；Y 型三段相加算单程。

投递路线 投递路线是指邮政局所或邮政投递机构的自办或委办人员按固定班期（班次）、规定路线为城乡用户投递邮件、报刊的路线。按地域可分为城市投递路线和农村投递路线。按投递方式可分为汽车投递路线、摩托车投递路线、自行车投递路线、马班投递路线和步班投递路线等。

Explanatory Notes on Main Statistical Indicators

Length of Railways in Operation refers to the total length of the trunk line under passenger and freight transportation. The calculation is based on the actual length of the first line even if this line has a full or partial double tracks, excluding double tracks, station sidings, tracks under the charge of stations, branch lines, special-purpose lines and the non-payable connecting lines. The length of railways is an important, traffic density and utilization efficiency of the locomotives and carriages.

Extension Length of Railway it can be divided into total extension length and extension length of main lines, station lines, section lines, branch lines and special lines. Total extension length is the sum of the length of all kinds of lines. Extension length of main lines is the sum of the length of first lines, second lines, third lines and other constructed main lines. Extension length of station lines, section lines, branch lines and special lines, is the sum of their construction length. It provides important information for the calculation of the needs for rails, sleepers, sand and stone for the construction of railways.

Highway Net is a netted communications system, it is composed of various highway. It is a network that linked with carious road of cities, towns, villages and mines. In China, the length of highways, if grouped by its functions and administer characters, can be divided into state highways, provincial highways, county highways, village highways and highways for special purpose. Grouped by its engineering standard, it can be divided into expressways and class I to IV class highways.

Length of Highways it is also be called "opening length of highways". It refers to the length of highways which are built in conformity with the grades specified by the highway engineering standard formulated by the Ministry of Communications. The length of highways includes that of the suburb highways at large and medium-sized cities, highways passing through streets at small cities and towns, and also the length of bridges and ferries. It does not include the length of streets in big and medium-sized cities and highways built for the production purpose at factories, mines, forest areas and agricultural areas. If two or more highway go the same section of the way, the length of the section is only calculated for once and no duplication is allowed. The length of highway is an important indicator to show the development of the highway construction and to provide essential information to calculate the transport network density.

Civil Motor Vehicles refer to a part of motor vehicles that are controlled by public security supervise department and have this locality civil motor vehicles license. Excluding the tractors, motor cycles and other motor vehicles, civil motor vehicles include ordinary trucks, trucks for special use, buses and cars, other trucks for special use, special vehicles.

Business Vehicles refer to the passenger vehicles and trucks for business, which gains vehicle licenses issued by the traffic control department and the business license approved by administration for industry and commerce.

Freight (Passenger) Traffic refers to the volume of freight (passenger) transported with various means within a specific period of time. This indicator reflects the service of the transport industry towards the national economy and people's living conditions, as well as an important indicator used in formulating and monitoring transport production plans and research into the scale and pace of transport development. Freight transport is calculated in tons and passenger traffic is calculated in terms of number of persons. Freight transport is calculated in terms of the actual weight of the goods and takes no account of the type of freight and distance of travel. Passenger traffic is calculated by the principle that one person can be counted only once in one trip and takes no account of the travelling distance and ticket price. The passengers who travel with a half price ticket or a child's ticket is also calculated as one person.

Freight Ton-kilometres (Passenger-kilometres) refers to the sum of the product of the volume of transported cargo (passengers) multiplied by the transport distance. It is an important indicator to reflect the achievement of the transportation industry. This is an important indicator to show the total results of the transport industry; to prepare and examine the transport plan; and to serve as the main basic data for calculating the efficiency, labour productivity and unit cost of transport. Normally, the shortest distance between the departure station and the destination station (i.e., the payable distance) is the basis in calculating the freight ton-kilometres.

Converted into Turnover Volume is a synthesis item which reflect real freight or passenger traffic with various means in a period time. The calculated method as follows: Sum of Freight or passenger traffic which are converted into uniform unit by transport means according to corresponding scaling. The uniform unit is ton-km.

Scaling of highways: 1 ton-km=10 person-km

Scaling of river: 1 ton-km=3 person-km(seat);1 ton-km=1 person-km(sleeper)

Scaling of railway: 1 ton-km=1 person-km(equals 5 person-km on local railways)

Scaling of Civil Aviation: 1 ton –km=13.9 person-km(equals 13.3 person-km on international routes)

Volume of Post and Telecommunication Services refers to the total amount of postal and telecommunication services, expressed in value terms, provided by the post and telecommunications departments for society. Postal and telecommunication services can be classified as letters, parcels, remittance, issue of newspapers and magazines, fast mail service, express mail service, savings deposits, stamps for collection, facsimiles, long-distance telephone service, leasing of telephone lines, mobile telephone service, data transmission, income from leasing, maintenance, etc. The accounting approach is to multiply the service products of all types with their average unit price (constant price) to get the total business value, and to add to it income from other services such as leasing of telephone lines and equipment and maintenance of telephone switchboards and lines on behalf of customers. This indicator reflects the overall results of postal and telecommunication services during a given period, and is important for studying the composition of business service and the trend of development of postal and telecommunication services.

Number of Telephone Subscribers includes fixed-telephone subscribers and mobile telephone subscribers. Fixed-telephone subscribers refer to subscribers that are connected to the state public fixed-telephone net and are managed according to fixed-telephone business. Mobile telephone subscribers refer to subscribers that are registering in business department on mobile phone, connected to the mobile telephone net and owing the number of mobile phone.

Postal Routes refers routes that self-run clerks or clients change mails, newspapers and magazines by fixed schedule and regular routes between post offices, post offices and stations, docks, airports, transfer stations, mail processing centers, newspaper agencies. It includes posting and delivering routes in rural areas, while excludes routes that only delivers in urban and rural areas. It can be divided into airway postal routes, railway postal routes, automobile postal routes, waterway postal routes and other postal routes according to transport means.

Total Length of Post Routes refers length of postal routes from the start point to the end point. The single length is calculated by the following method, that is, straight line route is calculated as single way, circle route as entire way, straight line and circle mixed route is calculated separately, and Y type route is calculated as the sum of three single lines.

Delivery Routes refers routes that self-run clerks or clients of postal offices and postal delivery agencies deliver mails, newspapers and magazines by fixed schedule and regular routes for urban and rural residents. It can be divided into urban delivery postal routes and rural delivery postal routes according to regions. And there are automobile deliver route, motorcycle deliver route, bicycle deliver route, horse deliver route and deliver route on foot.

16 教育、科技

EDUCATION, SCIENCE
AND TECHNOLOGY

资料整理人员

史美荣　吴丹宁

教育、科技

EDUCATION, SCIENCE AND TECHNOLOGY

高等学校数	Institutions of Higher Education	80	所	(unit)
高等学校专任教师数	Full-time Teachers of Higher Education	4.1	万人	(10 000 persons)
高等学校在校学生数	Students Enrollment of Higher Education	75.6	万人	(10 000 persons)
普通中专学校数	Regular Specialized Secondary Schools	92	所	(unit)
普通中专专任教师数	Full-time Teachers of Regular Specilized Secondary Schools	7853	人	(person)
普通中专在校学生数	Students Enrollment of Regular Specilized Secondary Schools	12.1	万人	(10 000 persons)
科学研究机构	Scientific Research Institutions	161	个	(unit)

自然科技人员构成(%)

Composition of Natural Science and Technology Personnels (%)

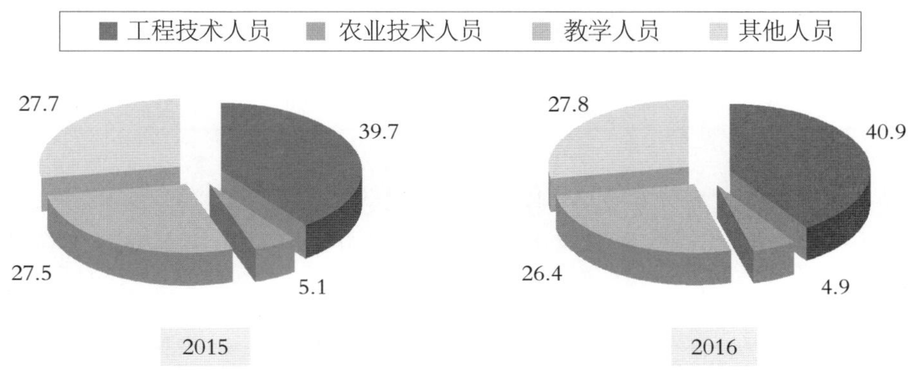

研究生在校学生数（人）

Number of Postgraduate Enrollment (person)

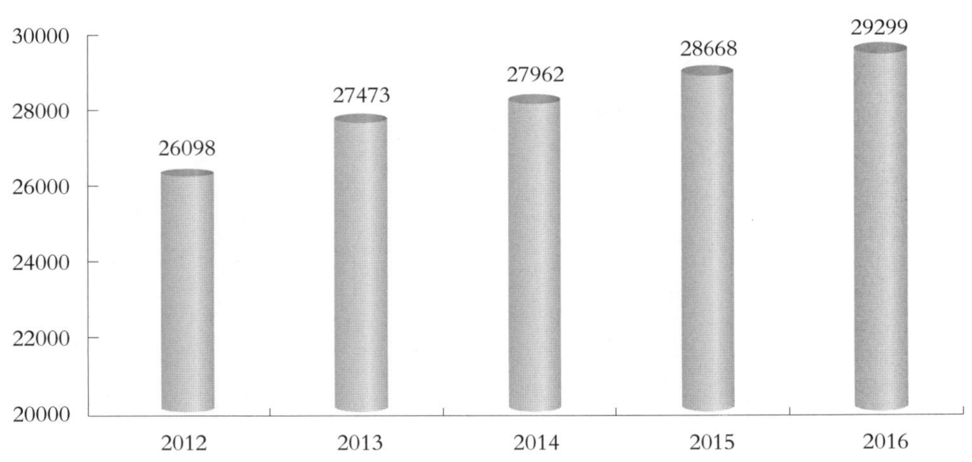

16-1 主要年份各类学校数

SCHOOLS BY LEVEL IN MAJOR YEARS

单位：所 (unit)

年 份 Year	高等学校 Regular Instiutions of Higher Education	中等职业教育 Secondary Vocational Education	#普通中专 Regular Specia-lized Secondary Schools	#职业中学 Vocational Schools	#技工学校 Skilled Workers Schools	普通中学 Regular Secondary Schools	小学 Primary Schools	特殊教育学校 Special Education Schools
1978	16	210	73	87	50	14062	33393	12
1980	16	488	90	337	61	9895	37746	12
1985	22	591	113	408	70	4749	42394	12
1990	26	602	125	380	97	3944	42195	12
1995	26	616	129	377	110	3401	40795	19
2000	24	600	127	339	134	3346	37451	28
2005	59	498	73	309	116	3279	24339	40
2010	65	576	92	259	110	2747	12776	45
2011	66	572	93	249	111	2611	10936	51
2012	67	556	90	246	100	2534	10042	53
2013	70	507	92	234	62	2495	8946	56
2014	71	543	92	233	99	2418	6885	62
2015	79	542	92	233	98	2400	6403	64
2016	80	544	92	235	98	2353	6043	69

16-2 主要年份各类学校专任教师数

NUMBER OF FULL-TIME TEACHERS BY LEVEL OF SCHOOL IN MAJOR YEARS

单位：人 (person)

年 份 Year	高等学校 Regular Instiutions of Higher Education	中等职业教育 Secondary Vocational Education	#普通中专 Regular Specia-lized Secondary Schools	#职业中学 Vocational Schools	#技工学校 Skilled Workers Schools	普通中学 Regular Secondary Schools	小学 Primary Schools
1978	4244	4514	3246	330	938	103772	132785
1980	5077	6423	3991	1046	1386	104075	148255
1985	7099	12621	6176	4512	1933	92619	157251
1990	8963	18975	8295	6976	3704	108774	163693
1995	9140	22855	9161	8632	5062	113216	171860
2000	10466	24845	9823	10343	4679	127582	180362
2005	27862	22319	5687	11132	5500	159803	192271
2010	36492	23440	7437	12461	3542	172793	190538
2011	37527	24816	7877	13051	3888	175443	188820
2012	38124	29295	7903	13597	4365	176319	184326
2013	40764	25401	7943	13806	3652	177344	180548
2014	40317	30744	7793	13671	5803	176853	176840
2015	40406	32652	7830	13997	7485	175053	172957
2016	41301	33058	7853	14199	7583	173503	171535

16-3 主要年份各类学校在校学生数
STUDENTS ENROLLMENT BY LEVEL OF SCHOOL IN MAJOR YEARS

单位：万人 (10 000 persons)

年 份 Year	高等学校(人) Regular Institutions of Higher Education (person)	中等职业教育 Secondary Vocational Education	#普通中专 Regular Specialized Secondary Schools	#职业中学 Vocational Schools	#技工学校 Skilled Workers Schools	普通中学 Regular Secondary Schools	#高中 Senior	小学 Primary Schools
1978	20940	4.73	2.90	0.64	1.19	194.28	58.45	377.36
1980	33104	8.38	4.61	2.12	1.65	179.55	31.06	384.16
1985	41946	14.58	5.14	7.58	1.86	156.97	22.87	335.20
1990	51309	21.47	8.68	8.78	4.01	145.08	22.31	297.40
1995	67420	26.40	10.74	10.51	5.15	150.97	19.04	327.04
2000	125674	37.19	19.65	13.62	3.92	199.75	33.72	343.60
2005	407036	46.58	20.15	17.04	9.39	261.15	71.37	350.26
2010	562924	56.51	20.73	24.65	11.13	253.67	82.29	291.06
2011	594469	61.94	18.33	22.32	11.08	249.55	85.27	277.19
2012	637330	60.00	17.85	21.45	11.68	235.74	85.50	261.76
2013	676817	50.46	16.38	19.40	6.82	213.99	84.85	229.64
2014	713218	51.03	15.37	18.39	11.10	204.68	82.78	224.50
2015	740245	43.59	13.99	17.91	10.62	192.06	79.37	226.95
2016	756287	43.82	12.12	17.83	10.03	184.65	75.38	227.09

16-4 主要年份各类学校招生数
NEW STUDENTS ENROLLMENT BY LEVEL OF SCHOOL IN MAJOR YEARS

单位：人 (person)

年 份 Year	高等学校 Regular Institutions of Higher Education	中等职业教育 Secondary Vocational Education	#普通中专 Regular Specialized Secondary Schools	#职业中学 Vocational Schools	#技工学校 Skilled Workers Schools	普通中学 Regular Secondary Schools	#高中 Senior	小学 Primary Schools	特殊教育学校 Special Education Schools
1978	7951	29399	15531	5708	8160	890626	280473	879737	376
1980	8287	38592	18800	11696	8096	539613	65803	664927	234
1985	14107	67423	20864	37437	9122	529347	75300	548667	390
1990	15710	81787	28615	38566	14606	482926	78749	557803	402
1995	20926	101436	35898	46721	18817	552978	69774	642867	555
2000	48041	134274	67975	52476	13823	726669	137662	631942	856
2005	127514	183008	75240	65842	41926	887403	263159	548755	743
2010	184399	219365	90505	90223	38637	852635	280984	451390	1088
2011	184602	177933	52311	84592	41030	795844	286680	440802	1339
2012	208122	214892	56744	83397	42475	755080	292630	440460	1215
2013	215296	164653	48846	70984	21710	701819	288826	394203	1069
2014	214394	170977	47936	69008	39134	634452	255585	347419	1411
2015	222685	145471	39118	65257	37247	583570	248426	376640	1637
2016	219954	145033	37083	62968	34020	620287	244539	383579	2050

16-5 主要年份各类学校毕业生数
GRADUATES BY LEVEL OF SCHOOL IN MAJOR YEARS

单位：人 (person)

年份 Year	高等学校 Regular Institution of Higher Education	普通中专 Regular Specialized Secondary Schools	职业中学 Vocational Schools	技工学校 Skilled Workers Schools	普通中学(万人) Regular Secondary Schools (10 000 persons)	#高中 Senior	小学(万人) Primary Schools (10 000 persons)	特殊教育学校 Special Education Schools
1978	4523	11766	760	3713	75.26	19.18	62.09	145
1980		13563	4884	10649	34.80	23.40	59.28	95
1985	8499	16773	16941	6383	39.09	5.48	64.67	105
1990	15130	26768	31770	11708	47.63	7.27	51.31	466
1995	20312	31474	38238	15542	43.17	7.08	55.36	402
2000	19785	42356	48364	17652	56.18	7.86	64.09	349
2005	88344	54904	47546	19514	82.95	19.69	63.56	483
2010	165545	54669	78368	48592	83.48	25.94	57.24	895
2011	152680	62044	80175	40296	82.54	27.01	52.78	805
2012	162571	62927	79604	32335	86.39	28.53	54.73	882
2013	173259	53525	73280	25379	82.76	28.61	47.73	1023
2014	174060	55208	68170	37566	72.22	27.35	38.81	832
2015	191273	49198	59597	37876	71.12	28.36	34.11	1060
2016	199259	53182	56541	38454	69.54	28.44	38.03	1296

16-6 普通本科分形式、分学科学生数(2016年)
STUDENTS OF REGULAR UNDERGRADUATE COURSES BY FORM AND BY FIELD OF STUDY(2016)

单位：人 (person)

项目	Item	毕业生数 Number of Graduates	招生数 Number of New Students Enrollment	在校学生数 Number of Students Enrollment
总计	**Total**	**101534**	**125759**	**474271**
#女	Female	55349	71312	261781
按形式分	By Form			
高中起点	Senior as Starting Point	96622	119819	462408
专科起点	Junior College as Starting Point	4912	5940	11863
第二学士学位	Second Bachelor's Degree			
按学科分	By Field of Study			
哲学	Philosophy	37	29	146
经济学	Economics	4502	5270	19780
法学	Law	3733	4443	16443
教育学	Education	4925	6037	23070
文学	Literature	8951	9248	34946
#外语	Foreign Language	4214	3954	14424
历史学	History	1339	1409	5700
理学	Science	9994	11819	45055
工学	Engineering	32784	42608	161146
农学	Agriculture	1894	2283	7888
医学	Medicine	6587	9929	39225
管理学	Administration	17587	20627	77474
艺术学	Art Theory	9201	12057	43398
总计中：师范生	Of the total：Teacher-training	15424	16602	64960

16-7 主要年份研究生数
NUMBER OF POSTGRADUATES IN MAJOR YEARS

单位：人 (person)

年 份 Year	培养研究生的单位数(个) Institutions of Foster Postgraduates (unit)	招生数 New Students Enrollment	毕业生数 Graduates	在校学生数 Students Enrollment
1978	4	151		151
1980	6	15		218
1985	8	399	84	670
1990	9	219	288	688
1995	12	524	263	1336
2000	12	1190	466	2633
2005	12	4929	2069	12059
2010	12	8074	5929	23555
2011	12	8745	7330	24790
2012	12	9212	7771	26098
2013	13	9384	7754	27473
2014	14	9141	8492	27962
2015	14	9769	8795	28668
2016	14	10078	9118	29299

16-8 研究生数(2016年)
NUMBER OF POSTGRADUATES(2016)

单位：人 (person)

项 目	Item	招生数 New Students Enrollment	#攻读硕士学位 Master Degree	毕 业 生 数 Graduates	#攻读硕士学位 Master Degree	在 校 学生数 Students Enrollment	#攻读硕士学位 Master Degree
总 计	**Total**	**10078**	**9547**	**9118**	**8742**	**29299**	**26663**
国家任务	Country Assignment	9994	9534	7838	7591	28439	26537
委托培养	Entrust Foster	84	13	182	64	738	52
自筹经费	Self-raised Funds			1098	1087	122	74
一、中央部门	**Central Departments**	**23**	**23**	**25**	**25**	**69**	**69**
国家任务	Country Assignment	23	23	25	25	69	69
委托培养	Entrust Foster						
自筹经费	Self-raised Funds						
二、地方部门	**Local Departments**	**10055**	**9524**	**9093**	**8717**	**29230**	**26594**
国家任务	Country Assignment	9971	9511	7813	7566	28370	26468
委托培养	Entrust Foster	84	13	182	64	738	52
自筹经费	Self-raised Funds			1098	1087	122	74

16-9 高等教育学校学生数(2016年)

单位：人

指　标	Item	毕业生数 Graduates
研究生	Postgraduates	9118
博　士	Doctor Degree	376
硕　士	Master Degree	8742
普通本科、专科生	Students of Regular Undergraduate Course and Specialized Subject	199259
本　科	Students of Regular Undergraduate Course	101534
专　科	Students of Specialized Subject	97725
成人本科、专科生	Adult Education Students of Regular Undergraduate Course and Specialized Subject	60315
函授本科	Correspondence Education of Regular Undergraduate Course	16802
业余本科	Spare Time Education of Regular Undergraduate Course	6128
脱产本科	Released from Work for Education of Regular Undergraduate Course	436
函授专科	Correspondence Education of Specialized Subject	21879
业余专科	Spare Time Education of Specialized Subject	10269
脱产专科	Released from Work for Education of Specialized Subject	4801
网络本科、专科生	Net Education Students of Regular Undergraduate Course and Specialized Subject	
本　科	Students of Regular Undergraduate Course	
专　科	Students of Specialized Subject	
在职人员攻读硕士学位	Persons Admitted to Master Degree Programme	
学历文凭考试	Academic Credentials Examination	
电大注册视听生	TV Education Students	
自考助学班	Guidance Class for Students Learning Themselves and Examination	
研究生课程进修班	Class for Advanced Studies of Postgraduate Course	
普通预科生	Students for Preparatory Course	
证书教育	Certificate Education	4496
岗位培训	Post Training	19426
进修及培训	Advanced Study and Training	51971
留学生	Student Studing Abroad	152

NUMBER OF STUDENTS IN HIGHER EDUCATION INSTITUTIONS(2016)

(person)

#授予学位数 Award Degree	招生数 New Students Enrollment	在校生数 Students Enrollment
9083	10078	29299
345	531	2636
8738	9547	26663
99604	219954	756287
99604	125759	474271
	94195	282016
3091	26271	108013
	10739	41502
	4479	14306
	366	842
	7432	34870
	1904	12345
	1351	4148
1970	1956	7608
		57
		6383
		18829
		26506
4	261	431

16-10 普通高校分类别专任教师数(2016年)

FULL-TIME TEACHERS OF HIGHER EDUCATION INSTITUTIONS BY TYPE(2016)

单位：人 (person)

类别	Type	专任教师 Full-time Teachers	正高级 Senior	副高级 Sub-senior	中级 Middle	初级 Junior	无职称 No Rank
总计	**Total**	**41301**	**2864**	**10819**	**16094**	**8023**	**3501**
#女	Female	23383	1256	5778	9308	5023	2018
分类型:	By Type						
本科院校	Regular Undergraduate Course	29175	2627	7962	11345	4965	2276
专科院校	Specialized Subject	12126	237	2857	4749	3058	1225
分性质类别:	By Nature						
综合大学	Synthesize Universitys	10423	457	2618	4353	2379	616
理工院校	Science and Engineering Institutes	12696	1006	3486	5299	1980	925
农业院校	Agriculture Institutes	2095	246	494	705	495	155
林业院校	Forestry Institutes	220	4	46	87	54	29
医药院校	Medical Institutes	2962	340	762	1136	475	249
师范院校	Teacher-Training Institutes	5501	328	1597	1979	981	616
语文院校	Chinese Institues	1192	45	253	420	366	108
财经院校	Finance and Economic Institutes	5226	401	1293	1750	1030	752
政法院校	Politics and Law Institutes	431	21	143	140	93	34
体育院校	Sports Institues	140	1	33	70	30	6
艺术院校	Art Institutes	415	15	94	155	140	11
分举办者:	By Owner						
1.地方所属	Departments of Local Government	33908	2230	9078	13839	6235	2526
教育部门	Education Departments	24024	1957	6492	9752	4100	1723
其他部门	Other Departments	9421	273	2494	3896	2013	745
地方企业	Local Enterprises	463		92	191	122	58
2.民　办	Run by Private Institutions	7393	634	1741	2255	1788	975

16-11 普通高校分科专任教师数(2016年)
FULL-TIME TEACHERS OF HIGHER EDUCATION INSTITUTIONS BY FIELD OF STUDY(2016)

单位：人 (person)

类 别	Type	专任教师 Full-time Teachers	正高级 Senior	副高级 Sub-senior	中 级 Middle	初 级 Junior	无职称 No Rank
总 计	**Total**	**41301**	**2864**	**10819**	**16094**	**8023**	**3501**
#女	Female	23383	1256	5778	9308	5023	2018
总计中:哲 学	Of the Total: Philosophy	1146	88	303	444	211	100
经济学	Economics	2062	163	604	755	315	225
法 学	Law	2072	123	457	859	420	213
教育学	Education	4428	158	1237	1754	992	287
文 学	Literature	5756	196	1269	2421	1464	406
历史学	History	565	36	169	200	109	51
理 学	Science	5559	532	1773	1978	754	522
工 学	Engineering	9893	763	2660	3974	1634	862
农 学	Agriculture	1312	168	376	505	191	72
医 学	Medicine	2496	331	689	939	372	165
管理学	Administration	2908	187	696	1161	526	338
艺术学	Artistics	3104	119	586	1104	1035	260

16-12 中等职业教育分科类学生情况(2016年)
STUDENTS IN SECONDARY VOCATIONAL EDUCATION BY FIELD OF STUDY(2016)

单位：人 (person)

类 别	Type	毕业生数 Number of Graduates	#获得职业资格证书 Having Occupation Credentials	招生数 Number of New Students Enrollment	#招收初中毕业生数 Graduates from Junior	在校学生数 Number of Students Enrollment
总 计	**Total**	**129594**	**106991**	**111013**	**99872**	**337947**
#女	Female	66727	55474	52852	47621	165945
农林牧渔类	Farming,Forestry,Husbandry and Fishing	17476	2313	3367	2837	22987
资源环境类	Resource and Environment	3321	3227	897	775	2458
能源与新能源类	Engery and New Energy	110	85	108	108	391
土木水利类	Engineering	4439	4054	2854	2600	10318
加工制造类	Processing and Manufacture	13089	12666	10945	9703	33635
石油化工类	Petroleum Chemical	1318	1105	576	560	1897
轻纺食品类	Textile and Food	1055	1018	834	775	1982
交通运输类	Transportation	6764	6693	7452	6642	22030
信息技术类	Information Technology	24380	22734	27742	25908	76714
医药卫生类	Medicine and Hygiene	11720	10431	9615	8321	30679
休闲保健类	Recreation and Health Care	1586	1582	1351	1307	3456
财经商贸类	Economics,Finance and Business	11081	10030	9565	8508	28938
旅游服务类	Tourism Service	5094	4729	4582	4374	13317
文化艺术类	Culture and Art	11309	10723	15944	14751	44440
体育与健身	Sports and Fitness	2196	2166	2181	1823	7300
教育类	Education	10897	9793	7815	7654	24561
司法服务类	Judicial Service	1486	1411	1358	1215	3571
公共管理与服务类	Public Administration and Service	1094	1052	2276	1518	4410
其 他	Others	1179	1179	1551	493	4863

注：本表不含技工学校数。

Note: The coverage doesn't include skilled workers schools in this table.

16-13 普通中学学校数、班数(2016年)

NUMBER OF REGULAR SECONDARY SCHOOLS AND CLASSES(2016)

项目	Item	学校数(所) Number of Schools (unit)	初级中学 Junior	高级中学 Senior	完全中学 Junior And Senior	九年一贯制学校 9 Year Education	十二年一贯制学校 12 Year Education	班数(班) Classes (class)	初中 Junior	高中 Senior
总计	**Total**	**2353**	**1361**	**250**	**208**	**489**	**45**	**39858**	**24649**	**15209**
教育部门	Education Departments	1992	1272	191	150	373	6	31596	19696	11900
民办	Run by Private Institutions	350	86	59	57	110	38	8226	4917	3309
地方企业	Local Enterprises	3				3		9	9	
其他部门	Other Departments	8	3		1	3	1	27	27	
城区	Urban Areas	570	245	73	146	82	24	14958	8290	6668
教育部门	Education Departments	448	223	55	109	57	4	11530	6398	5132
民办	Run by Private Institutions	118	21	18	36	23	20	3406	1870	1536
地方企业	Local Enterprises	1				1		3	3	
其他部门	Other Departments	3	1		1	1		19	19	
镇区	Township	1030	652	160	44	157	17	19816	12220	7596
教育部门	Education Departments	873	607	127	35	102	2	16259	9974	6285
民办	Run by Private Institutions	152	43	33	9	53	14	3546	2235	1311
地方企业	Local Enterprises	2				2		6	6	
其他部门	Other Departments	3	2				1	5	5	
乡村	Rural Areas	753	464	17	18	250	4	5084	4139	945
教育部门	Education Departments	671	442	9	6	214		3807	3324	483
民办	Run by Private Institutions	80	22	8	12	34	4	1274	812	462
地方企业	Local Enterprises									
其他部门	Other Departments	2				2		3	3	

16-14 普通中学学生数(2016年)
STUDENTS OF REGULAR SECONDARY SCHOOLS(2016)

单位：人 (person)

项　目	Item	毕业生数 Number of Graduates	#高中 Senior	招生数 Number of New Students Enrollment	#高中 Senior	在校学生数 Number of Students Enrollment	#高中 Senior
总　计	**Total**	**695417**	**284423**	**620287**	**244539**	**1846516**	**753777**
#女	Female	344376	147004	307859	127389	916096	394085
教育部门	Education Departments	552199	225465	482517	192271	1448983	595443
民　办	Run by Private Institutions	142671	58757	137498	52268	396706	158334
地方企业	Local Enterprises	89		92		261	
其他部门	Other Departments	458	201	180		566	
城　区	Urban Areas	269712	123969	243371	107287	712422	327920
教育部门	Education Departments	209748	96436	186954	84020	549711	255081
民　办	Run by Private Institutions	59740	27508	56298	23267	162304	72839
地方企业	Local Enterprises	26		6		51	
其他部门	Other Departments	198	25	113		356	
镇　区	Township	353096	144813	313301	121609	940811	379571
教育部门	Education Departments	290615	121566	252376	100408	764199	316368
民　办	Run by Private Institutions	62172	23071	60791	21201	176245	63203
地方企业	Local Enterprises	63		86		210	
其他部门	Other Departments	246	176	48		157	
乡　村	Rural Areas	72609	15641	63615	15643	193283	46286
教育部门	Education Departments	51836	7463	43187	7843	135073	23994
民　办	Run by Private Institutions	20759	8178	20409	7800	58157	22292
地方企业	Local Enterprises						
其他部门	Other Departments	14		19		53	

16-15 中学学校教职工数(2016年)
TEACHERS AND STAFF OF SECONDARY SCHOOLS(2016)

单位：人 (person)

项 目	Item	教职工数 Total	#专任教师 Full-time Teachers	#行政人员 Administrative Personnel	#教辅人员 Teaching Assistants	代课教师 Substitute Teachers	兼任教师 Part-time Teachers
总 计	**Total**	**221095**	**188420**	**5964**	**12100**	**7219**	**1015**
#女	Female	139008	124309	1631	6207	4657	615
#少数民族	Minority Nationality	318	287	12	9	1	
教育部门	Education Departments	175308	155856	4087	9975	4403	299
民 办	Run by Private Institutions	45473	32284	1871	2113	2809	716
地方企业	Local Enterprises	127	117				
其他部门	Other Departments	187	163	6	12	7	
城 区	Urban Areas	78964	66196	3056	4233	3485	753
教育部门	Education Departments	60139	53043	2011	3299	1805	211
民 办	Run by Private Institutions	18717	13052	1043	930	1680	542
地方企业	Local Enterprises	38	37				
其他部门	Other Departments	70	64	2	4		
镇 区	Township	108435	93553	2056	6114	2494	201
教育部门	Education Departments	88461	79109	1501	5146	1762	34
民 办	Run by Private Institutions	19827	14311	554	966	725	167
地方企业	Local Enterprises	89	80				
其他部门	Other Departments	58	53	1	2	7	
乡 村	Rural Areas	33696	28671	852	1753	1240	61
教育部门	Education Departments	26708	23704	575	1530	836	54
民 办	Run by Private Institutions	6929	4921	274	217	404	7
地方企业	Local Enterprises						
其他部门	Other Departments	59	46	3	6		

注：本表包括初级中学、九年一贯制学校、职业初中、完全中学、高级中学、十二年一贯制学校。

Note: Teachers and staff who work in junior schools, 9 year education schools, vocational junior schools, senior schools and 12 year education schools are included in the table.

16-16 职业高中分科类学生数(2016年)
STUDENTS OF VOCATIONAL HIGH SCHOOLS BY FIELD OF STUDY(2016)

单位：人 (person)

学科分类	Subject	毕业生数 Number of Graduates	招生数 Number of New Students Enrollment	在校学生数 Number of Students Enrollment
总　计	**Total**	**70396**	**65749**	**196442**
农林牧渔类	Farming,Forestry,Husbandry and Fishing	13288	2038	16015
资源环境类	Resource and Environment	779	748	1663
能源与新能源类	Engery and New Energy	50		256
土木水利类	Engineering	1347	1205	3640
加工制造类	Processing and Manufacture	7639	7303	21896
石油化工类	Petrochemical Industry	807	574	1704
轻纺食品类	Textile and Food	997	826	1948
交通运输类	Transportation	3865	4541	13309
信息技术类	Information Technology	19910	23117	63557
医药卫生类	Medicine and Public Health	2169	2140	7061
休闲保健类	Recreation and Health Care	729	547	1745
财经商贸类	Economics,Finance and Business	5412	5251	15966
旅游服务类	Tourism Service	3247	2950	8790
文化艺术类	Culture and Art	6843	10763	28717
体育与健身	Sports and Fitness	561	489	1409
教育类	Education	1155	954	3556
司法服务类	Judicial Service	231	435	998
公共管理与服务类	Public Administration and Service	890	1381	2971
其　他	Others	477	487	1241

16–17 职业高中分课程专任教师数

FULL–TIME TEACHERS OF VOCATIONAL HIGH SCHOOLS BY COURSE OF STUDY

单位：人 (person)

项　目	Item	2015	2016
总　计	**Total**	**13997**	**14199**
#女	Female	8391	8611
文化课	Foundation	8047	8108
专业课	Specialized	5663	5745
农林牧渔类	Farming,Forestry,Husbandry and Fishing	165	143
资源环境类	Resource and Environment	54	52
能源与新能源类	Engery and New Energy	46	44
土木水利类	Engineering	136	129
加工制造类	Processing and Manufacture	548	522
石油化工类	Petrochemical Industry	60	78
轻纺食品类	Textile and Food	26	42
交通运输类	Transportation	205	267
信息技术类	Information Technology	1309	1289
医药卫生类	Medicine and Public Health	168	186
休闲保健类	Recreation and Health Care	34	34
财经商贸类	Economics,Finance and Business	401	416
旅游服务类	Tourism Service	248	313
文化艺术类	Culture and Art	1032	1084
体育与健身	Sports and Fitness	283	240
教育类	Education	532	500
司法服务类	Judicial Service	27	35
公共管理与服务类	Public Administration and Service	88	107
其　他	Others	301	264
实习指导课	Practical Courses	287	346

16-18 小学学生情况(2016年)
BASIC STATISTICS ON PRIMARY SCHOOLS(2016)

单位：人 (person)

项目	Item	学校数(所) Number of Schools (unit)	毕业生数 Number of Graduates	招生数 Number of New Students Enrollment	在校学生数 Number of Students Enrollment	预计毕业生数 Expected Number of Graduates
总计	**Total**	**6043**	**380313**	**383579**	**2270899**	**375021**
#女	Female		182886	184565	1088929	179405
教育部门	Education Departments	5850	344304	354357	2082261	339082
民办	Run by Private Institutions	180	34937	28331	182248	34814
地方企业	Local Enterprises	5	190	165	1229	225
其他部门	Other Departments	8	882	726	5161	900
城区	Urban Areas	874	127009	146013	818883	127655
教育部门	Education Departments	809	115496	135036	753347	116485
民办	Run by Private Institutions	58	10719	10353	60939	10369
地方企业	Local Enterprises		6	9	92	14
其他部门	Other Departments	7	788	615	4505	787
镇区	Township	1604	162396	161076	958050	161038
教育部门	Education Departments	1530	144475	147116	865604	142645
民办	Run by Private Institutions	73	17698	13764	91122	18157
地方企业	Local Enterprises	1	166	131	907	174
其他部门	Other Departments		57	65	417	62
乡村	Rural Areas	3565	90908	76490	493966	86328
教育部门	Education Departments	3511	84333	72205	463310	79952
民办	Run by Private Institutions	49	6520	4214	30187	6288
地方企业	Local Enterprises	4	18	25	230	37
其他部门	Other Departments	1	37	46	239	51

16-19 小学学校教职工数(2016年)
TEACHERS AND STAFF OF PRIMARY SCHOOLS(2016)

单位：人 (person)

项　目	Item	教职工数 Total	#专任教师 Full-time Teachers	#行政人员 Adminis-trative Personnel	代课教师 Substitute Teachers	兼任教师 Part-time Teachers
总　计	**Total**	**172627**	**156618**	**3629**	**10620**	**955**
#女	Female	127987	120599	1134	9284	780
#少数民族	Minority Nationality	186	173	9	4	
教育部门	Education Departments	162473	149832	3151	10171	852
民　办	Run by Private Institutions	9842	6499	468	444	46
地方企业	Local Enterprises	42	42			57
其他部门	Other Departments	270	245	10	5	
城　区	Urban Areas	46358	42434	1261	2671	52
教育部门	Education Departments	42814	40055	1061	2636	38
民　办	Run by Private Institutions	3307	2161	190	31	14
地方企业	Local Enterprises					
其他部门	Other Departments	237	218	10	4	
镇　区	Township	64514	58845	1137	3258	404
教育部门	Education Departments	59660	55658	942	3116	342
民　办	Run by Private Institutions	4854	3187	195	142	18
地方企业	Local Enterprises					44
其他部门	Other Departments					
乡　村	Rural Areas	61755	55339	1231	4691	499
教育部门	Education Departments	59999	54119	1148	4419	472
民　办	Run by Private Institutions	1681	1151	83	271	14
地方企业	Local Enterprises	42	42			13
其他部门	Other Departments	33	27		1	

注：本表为小学、教学点数。

Note: The coverage includes primary schools and their relavent teaching schools in this table.

16-20 小学学龄人口入学率(2016年)
RATE OF SCHOOL-AGED CHILDREN ENROLLMENT(2016)

单位：人 (person)

项　目	Item	校内外学龄人口数 Total School-age Children in and out of School	在校学龄人口数 Total School-age Children in School	适龄人口入学率(%) Rate of Enrollment
总　计	**Total**	**2250648**	**2247735**	**99.9**
#女　童	Female Children	1080398	1079162	99.9
城　区	Urban Areas	814427	807459	99.1
镇　区	Township	945372	950232	100.5
乡　村	Rural Areas	490849	490044	99.8

16-21 主要年份幼儿园基本情况
BASIC STATISTICS ON KINDERGARTENS IN MAJOR YEARS

单位：人 (person)

年　份 Year	幼儿园数(所) Number of Kindergartens (unit)	在园幼儿数 Number of Student Enrollment	教职工数 Number of Staff and Teachers	#专任教师 Full-time Teachers	平均每一教师负担幼儿数 Student-Teacher Ratio
1978	5997	305783	13243	6473	47
1980	7461	408471	17363	10390	39
1985	7731	592600	26855	20714	29
1990	7849	816087	38074	28922	28
1995	8477	1026401	45760	37483	27
2000	10856	1025982	51694	42565	24
2005	4619	641470	32666	21711	30
2010	4352	710297	42782	28509	25
2011	4908	820608	51472	33294	25
2012	5489	914797	58666	38194	24
2013	5882	951431	63684	41317	23
2014	6183	968237	68785	44475	22
2015	6450	982943	74823	48285	20
2016	6708	990985	79984	51110	19

16-22 幼儿园基本情况(2016年)
BASIC STATISTICS ON KINDERGARTENS(2016)

单位：人 (person)

项 目	Item	园数(所) Number of Kindergartens (unit)	班数(个) Number of Classes (unit)	在园幼儿数 Number of Students Enrollment	教职工数 Number of Staff and Teachers	#专任教师 Full-time Teachers	平均每一教师负担幼儿数 Student-Teacher Ratio
总 计	**Total**	**6708**	**42909**	**990985**	**79984**	**51110**	**19**
#女	Female			477393	74247	50369	9
教育部门	Education Departments	1888	18276	412686	19883	14482	28
其他部门	Other Departments	79	575	17367	1816	1097	16
地方企业	Local Enterprises	144	1137	33058	5211	2782	12
事业单位	Institutional Units	16	147	4571	646	318	14
部 队	Troops	10	46	1219	209	95	13
集 体	Run by Collectives	1787	5909	116077	7346	4875	24
民 办	Run by Private Institutions	2784	16819	406007	44873	27461	15
城 区	Urban Areas	1581	12068	313721	38492	22634	14
教育部门	Education Departments	198	2287	74012	6116	4327	17
其他部门	Other Departments	39	370	12006	1501	857	14
地方企业	Local Enterprises	112	894	25779	4158	2192	12
事业单位	Institutional Units	14	135	4224	625	299	14
部 队	Troops	7	38	1066	166	72	15
集 体	Run by Collectives	198	903	24189	2017	1268	19
民 办	Run by Private Institutions	1013	7441	172445	23909	13619	13
镇 区	Township	2196	15290	425505	29837	20865	20
教育部门	Education Departments	634	6466	198661	9962	7577	26
其他部门	Other Departments	22	152	4822	288	223	22
地方企业	Local Enterprises	29	222	6706	988	556	12
事业单位	Institutional Units	1	6	174	12	11	16
部 队	Troops						
集 体	Run by Collectives	417	1732	42077	2410	1689	25
民 办	Run by Private Institutions	1093	6712	173065	16177	10809	16
乡 村	Rural Areas	2931	15551	251759	11655	7611	33
教育部门	Education Departments	1056	9523	140013	3805	2578	54
其他部门	Other Departments	18	53	539	27	17	32
地方企业	Local Enterprises	3	21	573	65	34	17
事业单位	Institutional Units	1	6	173	9	8	22
部 队	Troops	3	8	153	43	23	7
集 体	Run by Collectives	1172	3274	49811	2919	1918	26
民 办	Run by Private Institutions	678	2666	60497	4787	3033	20

16-23 特殊教育学校基本情况(2016年)
BASIC STATISTICS ON SPECIAL EDUCATION SCHOOLS(2016)

单位：人 (person)

类 别	Type	班数(个) Number of Classes (unit)	毕业生数 Number of Graduates	招生数 Number of New Students Enrollment	在校学生数 Number of Students Enrollment	教职工数 Number of Staff and Teachers	#专任教师 Full-time Teachers
总 计	**Total**	**708**	**1296**	**2050**	**10770**	**1769**	**1516**
#女	Female		508	809	4260	1296	1172
视力残疾	Vision Deformity	32	96	105	569		
听力残疾	Hearing Deformity	220	488	422	2667		
智力残疾	Intelligence Deformity	430	412	1057	5201		
其他残疾	Others	26	300	466	2333		
特殊教育学校	Special Education School	666	723	1119	5932		
视力残疾	Vision Deformity	32	52	42	211		
听力残疾	Hearing Deformity	217	390	290	1920		
智力残疾	Intelligence Deformity	398	271	763	3643		
其他残疾	Others	19	10	24	158		
小学附设特教班	Class Attached Primary School	37	14	33	189		
视力残疾	Vision Deformity		1	1	1		
听力残疾	Hearing Deformity	3	3	2	18		
智力残疾	Intelligence Deformity	27	10	26	143		
其他残疾	Others	7		4	27		
小学随班就读	Learning with Other Children in Primary School		293	499	3355		
视力残疾	Vision Deformity		14	25	253		
听力残疾	Hearing Deformity		50	82	551		
智力残疾	Intelligence Deformity		85	190	1145		
其他残疾	Others		144	202	1406		
初中附设特教班	CLass Attached Junior Secondary School	5	1	1	14		
视力残疾	Vision Deformity						
听力残疾	Hearing Deformity						
智力残疾	Intelligence Deformity	5	1	1	14		
其他残疾	Others						
初中随班就读	Learning with Other Students in Junior Secondary School		265	398	1280		
视力残疾	Vision Deformity		29	37	104		
听力残疾	Hearing Deformity		45	48	178		
智力残疾	Intelligence Deformity		45	77	256		
其他残疾	Others		146	236	742		

16-24 科学研究机构及人员(2016年)
INSTITUTIONS AND PERSONNELS OF SCIENTIFIC RESEARCH(2016)

项目	Item	机构(个) Institutions (unit)	职工人数(人) Employees (person)	从事科技活动人员(人) Personnels (person)	#大学本科及以上学历 Bachelor Degree and Above
总计	**Total**	**161**	**10507**	**8744**	**6924**
一、自然科学	**Natural Science**	**127**	**9233**	**7642**	**6004**
按隶属关系分	Grouped by Jurisdiction of Management				
中央	Central Government	1	545	541	429
地方	Local Government	126	8688	7101	5575
按国民经济行业分	Grouped by Sector				
农、林、牧、渔业	Farming, Forestry, Animal Husbandry and Fishery	50	3102	2554	2146
采矿业	Mining	2	134	47	47
制造业	Manufacturing	16	815	540	366
建筑业	Construction	1	787	703	659
信息传输、软件和信息技术服务业	Information Transmission , Software and Information Technology Services	1	124	114	104
科学研究和技术服务业	Scientific Reseach and Technical Services	21	1723	1542	1132
水利、环境和公共设施管理业	Water, Environmental Protection and Public Facility Management	17	842	755	567
卫生和社会工作	Health Care and Social Work	16	1607	1327	936
文化、体育和娱乐业	Culture, Sports and Recreation	2	90	51	39
公共管理、社会保障和社会组织	Public Management, Social Security and Social Organization	1	9	9	8
二、社会科学	**Social Science**	**22**	**960**	**802**	**681**
艺术学	Art	6	141	115	80
考古学	Archaeology	2	186	133	103
经济学	Economics	8	402	335	304
社会学	Sociology	1	24	24	24
教育学	Education	2	145	142	125
体育科学	Sport Science	2	53	44	38
统计学	Statistics	1	9	9	7
三、情报科学	**Information Science**	**12**	**314**	**300**	**239**

16-25 主要年份县级以上自然科学研究与技术开发机构数
NATURAL SCIENTIFIC RESEARCH AND TECHNOLOGICAL DEVELOPMENT INSTITUTIONS AT COUNTY LEVEL AND ABOVE IN MAJOR YEARS

单位：个 (unit)

年份 Year	合计 Total	中国科学院直属 Subordinated to CAS	国务院各部门直属 Subordinated to the State Council Departments	省科委及各厅局直属 Subordinated to Provincial Departments	地、市直属 Subordinated to Prefecture and City
1980	134	1	10	54	69
1985	147	1	12	65	69
1990	199	1	12	77	109
1995	180	1	7	75	97
2000	160	1	7	76	76
2005	132	1		66	65
2010	134	1		70	63
2011	133	1		70	62
2012	133	1		72	60
2013	129	1		69	59
2014	128	1		68	59
2015	131	1		71	59
2016	127	1		71	55

16-26 县级以上自然科学研究与技术开发机构人员数(2016年)
PERSONNELS OF NATURAL SCIENTIFIC RESEARCH AND TECHNOLOGICAL DEVELOPMENT INSTITUTIONS AT COUNTY LEVEL AND ABOVE(2016)

单位：人 (person)

项目	Item	机构数(个) Number of Institutions (unit)	职工人数 Number of Employees	#从事科技活动人员 Personnels	#大学本科及以上学历 Bachelor Degree and Above	在职工总数中：从事课题活动人员 Personnels of Projects in Staff and Workers
总计	**Total**	**127**	**9233**	**7642**	**6004**	**5010**
中国科学院属	Subordinated to CAS	1	545	541	429	388
省地市属	Subordinated to Province, Prefecture and City	126	8688	7101	5575	4622
太原市	Taiyuan	69	6382	5337	4209	3533
大同市	Datong	5	220	171	145	136
阳泉市	Yangquan	3	75	43	31	26
长治市	Changzhi	10	268	199	137	106
晋城市	Jincheng	7	60	57	38	12
朔州市	Shuozhou	2	49	34	15	11
晋中市	Jinzhong	4	463	321	286	184
运城市	Yuncheng	6	426	342	242	217
忻州市	Xinzhou	8	207	188	149	130
临汾市	Linfen	7	307	229	189	159
吕梁市	Lvliang	5	231	180	134	108

16-27 主要年份自然科学技术人员数

PERSONNELS OF NATURAL SCIENCE AND TECHNOLOGY IN MAJOR YEARS

单位：人 (person)

年份 Year	总计 Total	工程技术人员 Engineering	农业技术人员 Agriculture	卫生技术人员 Health Care	科学研究人员 Scientific Research	教学人员 Teaching
1952	14558	4764	448	7196	105	2045
1957	48922	20010	3131	19883	379	5519
1962	72683	25777	5111	33155	1417	7223
1965	84527	28591	5498	37877	2174	10387
1975	119357	34998	5778	42016	3391	33174
1978	151951	51127	13671	46557	5906	34690
1980	152781	54683	10825	41755	5602	39916
1985	238276	112064	12641	63502	5837	44232
1990	323808	152920	14608	77013	5218	74049
1995	355452	167114	11808	82407	4789	89334
2000	328936	121751	17074	83886	3681	102544
2001	340230	125134	17549	86843	3463	107241
2002	347760	126244	17705	89348	3442	111021
2003	352384	124547	18596	90826	3794	114621
2004	364246	121807	20011	97924	4637	119867
2005	375556	127236	20191	100160	4118	123851
2006	396904	133263	20456	112702	4006	126477
2007	403813	137329	20280	113775	3903	128526
2008	416572	145019	20507	116453	4007	130586
2009	422416	146990	20840	119458	3958	131170
2010	426966	148829	23269	119979	3652	131237
2011	433546	153618	23823	122011	3613	130481
2012	446840	162442	25613	126525	4930	127330
2013	451492	167161	25931	123205	4077	131118
2014	460218	177869	25313	124146	4442	128448
2015	461163	183053	23736	123148	4597	126629
2016	470156	192515	22836	126100	4500	124205

注：2000年及以后不包括中央驻晋单位自然科学技术人员数。

Note: Data in this table excludes persons belonging to the central unit since 2000.

16-28 省科学技术协会及所属学会工作情况(2016年)
PROVINCIAL SCIENCE AND TECHNOLOGY ASSOCIATION AND ITS BRANCHES(2016)

项　　目	Item	省科协 Provincial Associations	省级学会 Provincial Learned Societies	地(市)科协 Prefectural (civic) Associations
一、机构与从业人员	**Organization and Personnel**			
机　构(个)	Organization (unit)	1		11
机关从业人员(人)	Personnel of Administrative organs (person)	41		161
直属单位从业人员(人)	Personnel of Affiliated Institntions (person)	450		161
二、学术交流	**Academic Exchange**			
学术会议(次)	Academic Meetings (time)		264	53
参加人员(人次)	Participants (person-time)		38420	2300
交流论文(篇)	Papers Presented (piece)		6780	315
#国内学术会议(次)	Domestic Academic Meetings (time)		246	53
参加人员　(人次)	Participants (person-time)		36696	2300
交流论文　(篇)	Papers Presented (piece)		6605	315
国际学术会议(次)	International Academic Meetings (time)		18	
参加人员　(人次)	Participants (person-time)		1724	
交流论文　(篇)	Papers Presented (piece)		175	
三、科学普及	**Science Universal**			
举办科普宣讲活动(次)	Science Universal Lectures (time)	262	1801	787
宣讲活动受众人数(人次)	Participants (person-time)	758110	350216	686027
四、科技培训	**Science and Technology Training**			
举办实用技术培训(次)	Practical Techniques Training (time)	1119	1307	532
培训人数(人次)	Persons Trained (person-time)	6910871	57799	98690
五、青少年科技活动	**Science and Technology Activity for Teenagers**			
举办青少年科普宣讲活动(次)	Science Universal Lectures to teenagers (time)	12	442	154
青少年科技竞赛(次)	Teenagers Participating in Science and Technology Competitions (time)	3	19	25
参加人数(人次)	Number of Participants (person-time)	1000	46070	94701

注：2016年学术交流统计口径变化，与上年数据不可比。

Note: The data of academic exchange in 2016 is not comparable with the last year's because the statistical coverage is changed.

16–29 规模以上工业企业的科技活动基本情况
BASIC STATISTICS ON SCIENCE AND TECHNOLOGY ACTIVITIES OF INDUSTRIAL ENTERPRISES ABOVE DESIGNATED SIZE

指　标	Item	2015	2016
一、企业基本情况	**Statistics on Industrial Enterprises**		
有R&D活动企业数 (个)	Number of Enterprises Having R&D Activities (unit)	295	348
有R&D活动企业所占比重 (%)	Percentage of Enterprises Having R&D Activities to Total Number of Enterprises (%)	7.7	9.8
二、R&D活动情况	**Statistics on R&D Activities**		
R&D人员全时当量 (万人年)	Full–time Equivalent of R&D Personnel (10 000 man–years)	2.9	2.9
R&D经费支出 (亿元)	Expenditure on R&D (100 million yuan)	100.9	97.6
R&D经费支出与主营业务收入之比(%)	Percentage of Expenditure on R&D to Sales Revenue (%)	0.7	0.7
R&D项目数 (项)	R&D Projects (item)	2232	2471
R&D项目经费支出 (亿元)	Expenditure on R&D Projects (100 million yuan)	85.2	83.7
三、企业办R&D机构情况	**Statistics on R&D Institutions**		
机构数 (个)	Number of R&D Institutions (unit)	243	323
机构人员数 (万人)	R&D Personnel (10 000 persons)	2.1	2.3
机构经费支出 (亿元)	Expenditure on R&D (100 million yuan)	34.0	33.3
四、新产品开发及生产情况	**Statistics on New Products Development and Production**		
新产品开发项目数 (个)	Number of New Products (unit)	1910	2206
新产品开发经费支出 (亿元)	Expenditure on New Products Development (100 million yuan)	68.2	69.0
新产品销售收入 (亿元)	Sales Revenue of New Products (100 million yuan)	833.3	1085.0
#新产品出口	Export	158.4	160.7
五、专利情况 (件)	**Statistics on Patents (piece)**		
有效发明专利数	Number of Inventions in Force	4468	5350
六、技术获取和技术改造情况 (亿元)	**Statistics on Technology Acquisition and Technology Reconstruction (100 million yuan)**		
引进国外技术经费支出	Expenditure for Acquisition of Foreign Technology	5.6	4.7
引进技术消化吸收经费支出	Expenditure for Assimilation of Technology	0.8	0.6
购买国内技术经费支出	Expenditure for Purchase of Domestic Technology	2.0	1.5
技术改造经费支出	Expenditure for Technical Renovation	73.9	45.5

16-30 按登记注册类型分规模以上工业企业研究与试验发展(R&D)活动及专利情况(2016年)

STATISTICS ON R&D ACTIVITIES AND PATENTS OF INDUSTRIAL ENTERPRISES ABOVE DESIGNATED SIZE BY REGISTRATION STATUS(2016)

登记注册类型	Status of Registration	R&D人员全时当量(人年) Full-time Equivalent of R&D Personnel (man-year)	R&D经费(万元) Expenditure on R&D (10 000 yuan)	有效发明专利数(件) Number of Inventions in Force (piece)
合　计	**Total**	**29450**	**976283**	**5350**
#大中型工业企业	Large and Medium-sized Industrial Enterprises	27142	918274	4092
内资企业	**Domestic Funded Enterprises**	**27474**	**937389**	**5160**
国有企业	State-owned Enterprises	689	10224	243
集体企业	Collective-owned Enterprises	28	456	
股份合作企业	Cooperative Enterprises	5	243	3
联营企业	Joint Ownership Enterprises			
国有联营企业	State Joint Ownership Enterprises			
有限责任公司	Limited Liability Corporations	21078	788303	3333
国有独资公司	State Sole Funded Corporations	7801	429271	1598
股份有限公司	Share-holding Corporations Ltd.	2630	59545	646
私营企业	Private Enterprises	3046	78618	935
其他企业	Other Enterprises			
港、澳、台商投资企业	**Enterprises with Funds from Hong Kong, Macao and Taiwan**	**259**	**4738**	**90**
合资经营企业	Joint-venture Enterprises	13	460	14
合作经营企业	Cooperative Enterprises			
独资经营企业	Enterprises with Sole Fund	16	1181	27
投资股份有限公司	Share-holding Corporations Ltd.	229	3097	49
外商投资企业	**Foreign Funded Enterprises**	**1717**	**34155**	**100**
中外合资经营企业	Joint-venture Enterprises	125	2973	92
中外合作经营企业	Cooperation Enterprises			
外资企业	Enterprises with Sole Fund	1585	31127	7
外商投资股份有限公司	Share-holding Corporations Ltd.	6	56	1

16-31 按行业分规模以上工业企业研究与试验发展(R&D)活动及专利情况(2016年)

STATISTICS ON R&D ACTIVITIES AND PATENTS OF INDUSTRIAL ENTERPRISES ABOVE DE SIGNATED SIZE BY INDUSTRIAL SECTOR(2016)

行 业	Sector	R&D人员全时当量(人年) Full-time Equivalent of R&D Personnel (man-year)	R&D经费(万元) Expenditure on R&D (10 000 yuan)	有效发明专利数(件) Number of Inventions in Force (piece)
总 计	**Total**	**29450**	**976283**	**5350**
煤炭开采和洗选业	Mining and Washing of Coal	9911	314352	342
石油和天然气开采业	Extraction of Petroleum and Natural Gas	65	5234	42
黑色金属矿采选业	Mining and Processing of Ferrous Metal Ores	4	50	
有色金属矿采选业	Mining and Processing of Non-ferrous Metal Ores	4	74	
非金属矿采选业	Mining and Processing of Non-metal Ores			
农副食品加工业	Processing of Food from Agricultural Products	88	3888	6
食品制造业	Manufacture of Foods	65	1714	27
酒、饮料和精制茶制造业	Manufacture of Liquor, Beverages and Refined Tea	84	2033	17
烟草制品业	Manufacture of Tobacco			1
纺织业	Manufacture of Textile	67	618	8
纺织服装、服饰业	Manufacture of Textile, Wearing Apparel and Accessories	82	980	14
皮革、毛皮、羽毛及其制品和制鞋业	Manufacture of Leather, Fur, Feather and Related Products and Footwear			
木材加工和木、竹、藤、棕、草制品业	Processing of Timber, Manufacture of Wood, Bamboo, Rattan, Palm and Straw Products	5	175	
家具制造业	Manufacture of Furniture			
造纸及纸制品业	Manufacture of Paper and Paper Products	11	1702	
印刷和记录媒介复制业	Printing and Reproduction of Recording Media	43	687	
文教、工美、体育和娱乐用品制造业	Manufacture of Articles for Culture, Education, Arts and Crafts, Sport and Entertainment Activities	27	306	47
石油加工、炼焦及核燃料加工业	Processing of Petroleum, Coking and Processing of Nuclear Fuel	181	8258	51

16-31 续表 continued

行　业	Sector	R&D人员全时当量(人年) Full-time Equivalent of R&D Personnel (man-year)	R&D经费(万元) Expenditure on R&D (10 000 yuan)	有效发明专利数(件) Number of Inventions in Force (piece)
化学原料及化学制品制造业	Manufacture of Raw Chemical Materials and Chemical Products	2120	52792	312
医药制造业	Manufacture of Medicines	1527	33153	353
化学纤维制造业	Manufacture of Chemical Fibre			
橡胶和塑料制品业	Manufacture of Rubber and Plastics Products	130	3618	32
非金属矿物制品业	Manufacture of Non-metallic Mineral Products	1097	19992	205
黑色金属冶炼和压延加工业	Smelting and Pressing of Ferrous Metals	2895	240395	652
有色金属冶炼和压延加工业	Smelting and Pressing of Non-ferrous Metals	475	15968	81
金属制品业	Manufacture of Metal Products	1737	55975	681
通用设备制造业	Manufacture of General Purpose Machinery	648	17711	240
专用设备制造业	Manufacture of Special Purpose Machinery	1636	45741	993
汽车制造业	Manufacture of Automobiles	737	17434	130
铁路、船舶、航空航天和其他运输设备制造业	Manufacture of Railway, Ship, Aerospace and Other Transport Equipments	1843	23925	134
电气机械和器材制造业	Manufacture of Electrical Machinery and Apparatus	1490	62162	286
计算机、通信和其他电子设备制造业	Manufacture of Computers, Communication and Other Electronic Equipment	1835	36628	150
仪器仪表制造业	Instruments and Meters	205	4514	279
其他制造业	Other Manufacturing			
废弃资源综合利用	Utilization of Waste Resources			7
金属制品、机械和设备修理业	Repair Service of Metal Products, Machinery and Equipment	37	1354	10
电力、热力生产和供应业	Production and Supply of Electric Power and Heat Power	375	4640	235
燃气生产和供应业	Production and Supply of Gas	23	211	15
水的生产和供应业	Production and Supply of Water			

16-32 按登记注册类型分规模以上工业企业新产品开发及生产情况(2016年)

NEW PRODUCTS DEVELOPMENT AND PRODUCTION OF INDUSTRIAL ENTERPRISES ABOVE DESIGNATED SIZE BY REGISTRATION STATUS(2016)

登记注册类型	Status of Registration	新产品开发项目数(项) New Products (unit)	新产品开发经费支出(万元) Expenditure on New Products Development (10 000 yuan)	新产品销售收入(万元) Sales Revenue of New Products (10 000 yuan)	#出口 Exports
合　计	**Total**	**2206**	**689735**	**10850063**	**1607254**
#大中型工业企业	Large and Medium-sized Industrial Enterprises	1567	614280	10270124	1576678
内资企业	**Domestic Funded Enterprises**	**2128**	**676880**	**10469646**	**1588798**
国有企业	State-owned Enterprises	74	9932	6750	96
集体企业	Collective-owned Enterprises	6	599	963	100
股份合作企业	Cooperative Enterprises	5	534	1717	
联营企业	Joint Ownership Enterprises				
国有联营企业	State Joint Ownership Enterprises				
有限责任公司	Limited Liability Corporations	1215	528443	9439617	1470860
国有独资公司	State Sole Funded Corporations	424	251265	5611551	1103126
股份有限公司	Share-holding Corporations Ltd.	275	56036	408536	5350
私营企业	Private Enterprises	553	81337	612064	112392
其他企业	Other Enterprises				
港、澳、台商投资企业	**Enterprises with Funds from Hong Kong, Macao and Taiwan**	**55**	**6517**	**168808**	**9736**
合资经营企业	Joint-venture Enterprises	4	452	38807	
合作经营企业	Cooperative Enterprises				
独资经营企业	Enterprises with Sole Fund	29	2778	36259	47
投资股份有限公司	Share-holding Corporations Ltd.	22	3287	93741	9689
外商投资企业	**Foreign Funded Enterprises**	**23**	**6338**	**211610**	**8720**
中外合资经营企业	Joint-venture Enterprises	20	5813	205238	4702
中外合作经营企业	Cooperation Enterprises				
外资企业	Enterprises with Sole Fund	3	525	4351	4019
外商投资股份有限公司	Share-holding Corporations Ltd.			2021	

16-33 按行业分规模以上工业企业新产品开发及生产情况(2016年)

NEW PRODUCTS DEVELOPMENT AND PRODUCTION OF INDUSTRIAL ENTERPRISES ABOVE DESIGNATED SIZE BY INDUSTRIAL SECTOR(2016)

行业	Sector	新产品开发项目数(项) New Products (unit)	新产品开发经费支出(万元) Expenditure on New Products Development (10 000yuan)	新产品销售收入(万元) Sales Revenue of New Products (10 000yuan)	#出口 Exports
总计	**Total**	**2206**	**689735**	**10850063**	**1607254**
煤炭开采和洗选业	Mining and Washing of Coal	215	151954	2161855	220240
石油和天然气开采业	Extraction of Petroleum and Natural Gas	16	4066	35407	
黑色金属矿采选业	Mining and Processing of Ferrous Metal Ores				
有色金属矿采选业	Mining and Processing of Non-Ferrous Metal Ores	1	74	2414	
非金属矿采选业	Mining and Processing of Non-metal Ores				
农副食品加工业	Processing of Food from Agricultural Products	43	7500	43138	
食品制造业	Manufacture of Foods	20	6266	1147	
酒、饮料和精制茶制造业	Manufacture of Liquor, Beverages and Refined Tea	10	1937	33895	
烟草制品业	Manufacture of Tobacco	1	718	454	
纺织业	Manufacture of Textile	3	682	936	276
纺织服装、服饰业	Manufacture of Textile, Wearing Apparel and Accessories	3	623		
皮革、毛皮、羽毛及其制品和制鞋业	Manufacture of Leather, Fur, Feather and Related Products and Footwear				
木材加工和木、竹、藤、棕、草制品业	Processing of Timber, Manufacture of Wood, Bamboo, Rattan, Palm and Straw Products	1	175		

16-33 续表1 continued

行 业	Sector	新产品开发项目数(项) New Products (unit)	新产品开发经费支出(万元) Expenditure on New Products Development (10 000yuan)	新产品销售收入(万元) Sales Revenue of New Products (10 000yuan)	#出口 Exports
家具制造业	Manufacture of Furniture				
造纸和纸制品业	Manufacture of Paper and Paper Products	1	1702		
印刷和记录媒介复制业	Printing and Reproduction of Recording Media	9	609		
文教、工美、体育和娱乐用品制造业	Manufacture of Articles for Culture, Education, Arts and Crafts, Sport and Entertainment Activities	5	462	8991	489
石油加工、炼焦及核燃料加工业	Processing of Petroleum, Coking and Processing of Nuclear Fuel	6	223	20261	
化学原料及化学制品制造业	Manufacture of Raw Chemical Materials and Chemical Products	151	32119	322448	6729
医药制造业	Manufacture of Medicines	273	35944	395815	60242
化学纤维制造业	Manufacture of Chemical Fibres				
橡胶和塑料制品业	Manufacture of Rubber and Plastics Products	35	4583	140680	41205
非金属矿物制品业	Manufacture of Non-metallic Mineral Products	92	21465	150767	5552
黑色金属冶炼和压延加工业	Smelting and Pressing of Ferrous Metals	118	116978	4366517	1002371
有色金属冶炼和压延加工业	Smelting and Pressing of Non-ferrous Metals	61	19149	320408	
金属制品业	Manufacture of Metal Products	266	66802	424650	34878
通用设备制造业	Manufacture of General Purpose Machinery	106	16199	258316	1045

16-33 续表2 continued

行 业	Sector	新产品开发项目数(项) New Products (unit)	新产品开发经费支出(万元) Expenditure on New Products Development (10 000yuan)	新产品销售收入(万元) Sales Revenue of New Products (10 000yuan)	#出 口 Exports
专用设备制造业	Manufacture of Special Purpose Machinery	329	56774	673715	206216
汽车制造业	Manufacture of Automobiles	71	42025	306716	17814
铁路、船舶、航空航天和其他运输设备制造业	Manufacture of Railway, Ship, Aerospace and Other Transport Equipments	80	25461	460035	1035
电气机械和器材制造业	Manufacture of Electrical Machinery and Apparatus	120	56267	643030	2662
计算机、通信和其他电子设备制造业	Manufacture of Computers, Communication and Other Electronic Equipment	36	6899	40079	6501
仪器仪表制造业	Manufacture of Measuring Instruments and Machinery	57	6540	29353	
其他制造业	Other Manufacture				
废弃资源综合利用	Utilization of Waste Resources			300	
金属制品、机械和设备修理业	Repair Service of Metal Products, Machinery and Equipment				
电力、热力生产和供应业	Production and Supply of Electric Power and Heat Power	74	5227	8738	
燃气生产和供应业	Production and Supply of Gas	3	315		
水的生产和供应业	Production and Supply of Water				

主要统计指标解释

普通高等学校　指按照国家规定的审批程序批准举办，通过全国统一招生考试招收高级中等学校毕业生和具有同等学历者，实施高等教育，培养高等专门人材的学校。包括大学、专门学院、专科学院和短期职业大学。

成人高等学校　指按照国家规定的审批程序批准举办，招收在职高中毕业或同等学历者，利用多种形式对成人实施高等教育，培训相当普通高等学校专科或本科毕业水平的专门人才的学校。包括广播电视大学、职工高等学校、农民高等学校、干部管理学院、教育学院、独立函授学院以及普通高等学校举办的函授、夜大等。

小学学龄儿童入学率　指调查范围内已入小学学习的学龄儿童数占全部小学学龄儿童总数（包括弱智儿童在内，但不包括盲聋哑儿童）的比重。计算公式是：

$$\text{小学学龄儿童入学率}=\frac{\text{已入学的小学学龄儿童数}}{\text{校内外小学学龄儿童总数}}\times 100\%$$

科学家和工程师　指大学毕业及以上文化程度和其他具有高、中级职称的从事科技活动人员。

自然科学技术人员　指已取得科学技术职称，或大学、中专的理、工、农、医类系毕业，以及国民经济各部门从工作实践中提拔，从事理、工、农、医等自然科学技术的研究、教学、生产（事业）技术方面工作的专业人员和在机关、企业、事业中从事科学技术业务管理工作的专业人员。

工程技术人员　指在国民经济各行业从事工程技术工作的自然科学技术的专业人员。包括：高级工程师、工程师、助理工程师、技术员和未评定职称的技术人员。

农业技术人员　指在国民经济各行业从事农业技术工作的自然科学技术的专业人员。包括：高级农艺师、农艺师、助理农艺师、技术员和未评定职称的技术人员。

卫生技术人员　指在国民经济各行业从事卫生医务工作的自然科学技术的专业人员。包括：正副主任医师、主治医师、医师、医（护）士和未评定职称的技术人员。

科学研究人员　指在国民经济各行业从事科学技术活动的自然科学技术的专业人员。包括：正副研究员、助理研究员、实习研究员、技术员和未评定职称的技术人员。

教学人员　指在国民经济各行业从事自然科学技术方面的教学活动的专业人员。包括：正副教授、讲师、助教、教师和在小学从事自然科学技术方面的教学活动的人员。

科技活动　指在所有科学技术领域内，即自然科学、工程科学和技术、医学科学、农业科学、社会科学及人文科学中，与科技知识的产生、发展、传播、应用密切相关的全部的、有组织的、系统的活动。包括三类活动：(1)研究与实验发展活动；(2)研究与实验发展成果应用；(3)科技服务活动。

科技服务　指同研究与实验发展活动、研究与实验发展成果应用活动有关的和有助于科技知识的产生、传播和应用的活动。目前我们所统计的科技服务是指调查范围内，除为研究与实验发展活动直接（完全或主要是为某项研究与实验发展而开展的辅助性活动）以外的科技服务，如情报、文献、咨询等。

科学论文　指以书面发表的，最原始的研究与开发成果报道。科学论文应该是：(1)首次或最初发表的研究与开发成果；(2)作者的实验应该能被同行重复并验证；(3)发表后科技界能引用。

科技著作　指经过正式出版部门编印出版的论述科学技术问题的理论性文集或专著。如果著作系与本机构外的同行数人合著，则只统计以本机构科技人员为主的著作。

国外发表　包括在各种国际性学术会议、讨论会、讲座上发表的论文以及编入国际会议文集的论文和我国学术刊物上发表的论文。

R&D 项目　指在当年立项并开展研究工作、以前年份立项仍继续进行研究的研发项目或课题，包括当年完成和年内研究工作已告失败的研发项目或课题。

R&D 人员全时当量　是国际上通用的、用于比较科技人力投入的指标。指 R&D 全时人员（全年从事 R&D 活动累积工作时间占全部工作时间的 90%及以上人员）工作量与非全时人员按实际工作时间折算的工作量之和。例如：有两个 R&D 全时人员和三个 R&D 非全时人员(工作时间分别为 0.2 年、0.3 年和 0.7 年)，则 R&D 人员全时当量为 1+1+0.2+0.3+0.7=3.2 人年。

Explanatory Notes on Main Statistical Indicators

Regular Institutions of Higher Education refer to educational establishments set up according to the government evaluation and approval procedures, enrolling graduates from senior secondary schools and providing higher education courses and training for senior professionals. They include full-time universities, colleges, institutions of higher professional education, institutions of higher vocational education and others.

Institutions of Higher Education for Adults refer to educational establishments, set up in line with relevant rules approved by the government, enrolling staff and workers with senior secondary school or equivalent education, and providing higher education courses in many forms of correspondence, spare time, or full time for adults. Professionals thus trained receive a qualification equivalent to graduates studying regular courses at regular universities, colleges and professional colleges. Institutions of higher learning for adults include schools of higher education for staff and workers, schools of higher education for peasants, colleges for management cadres, pedagogical colleges, independent correspondence colleges, Radio and TV universities and other educational establishments.

Enrollment Rate of Primary School-age Children refers to the proportion of school age children enrolled at schools to the total number of school age children both in and outside schools (including retarded children, but excluding blind, deaf and mute children). The formula is:

$$\text{Enrollment Rate of Primary School-age Children}=\frac{\text{Total Primary School - age Children at School}}{\text{Total Primary School - age Children}}\times 100\%$$

Scientists and Engineers refer to persons engaged in S&T activities either having obtained titles of senior and middle level professional positions, or those without such positions but have completed university or higher education.

Natural Scientific and Technical Personnel refer to those professionals holding scientific and technical titles or taking such positions, or being graduated from departments of science, engineering, agriculture and medicine, and having been promoted in practice in different sectors of the national economy and working on research, teaching and production technique in the scientific and technological fields such as science, engineering, agriculture and medicine, etc. and the professionals doing administrative work related to science and technology in government agencies, enterprises and institutions.

Engineering Personnel refer to the persons who are engaged in engineering science and technology in different sectors of the national economy, including senior engineers, engineers, assistant engineers, technicians and technical personal without professional titles.

Agricultural Personnel refer to the persons who are working on the science of agriculture in different sectors of the national economy, including senior agronomists, agronomists, assistant agronomists, technicians and technical personnel without professional titles.

Public Health Personnel refer to those personnel engaged in medical and health work in different sectors of the national economy, including director doctors and their deputies, doctors in charge, doctors, paramedics, nurses and technical personnel without professional title.

Scientific Research Personnel refers to the persons who are engaged in scientific and technical activities in different sectors of the national economy, including research fellows and their deputies, assistant research fellows, research trainees, technicians and technical personnel without professional titles.

Teaching Personnel refer to those professionals engaged in the teaching in different activities in different sectors of the national economy, including professions, associate professors, lecturers, associate professors, lecturers, teaching assistants, teachers and teaching personnel in science and technology in primary schools.

Scientific and Technological Activities refer to organized activities which are closely related with the creation, development, dissemination and application of the scientific and technical knowledge in the fields of natural sciences, agricultural science, medical science, engineering and technological science, humanities and social sciences. It includes three kind of activities: (1) developing activities of research and experiment; (2) the application of developing results of research and experiment; (3) service activities in science and technology.

Science and Technology Services refer to activities related to activities of research and experiment, to applied activities of developing results of research and experiment, and benefiting the production, spread and application of knowledge of science and technology. Nowadays the services in science and technology we have summed up refer to services in science and technology with in the investigation with the exception of developing activities of research and experiment, such as information, literary data, consultation, etc.

Scientific Paper refer to the most original report on research and developing results published in written form. Scientific papers should be: (1) research and developed results published for the first time or at the first; (2) the author's experiments should be repeated and proved by their fellow craftsmen; (3) these papers should be quoted by the public of science and technology after they are published.

Science and Technology Works refer to theoretical writers' works or personal works demonstrating the question of science and technology edited and published by formal publishing section. If the works are written together by several fellow craftsmen beyond this institution then you should just compile the statistics of works written by the scientific research personnel of this institution.

Published Abroad including the papers published in all kinds of international academic meetings, conferences and lectures and papers compiled into writer's works at the international conference and those published in the academic periodicals abroad.

R&D Projects refers to the R&D projects or subjects set up and implemented at the reference year, and the R&D projects or subjects set up in former years and under implementation, including those finished and failed at the reference year.

Full-time Equivalent of R&D Personnel is an international indicator to compare R&D manpower input. It refers to the sum of the workload of full-time persons, whose work time on R&D isn't less than 90% on the whole work time, and the converted workload of part-time persons according to the actual working time. For instance, if there are 2 full-time persons and 3 part-time persons whose working time are respectively 0.2 year, 0.3 year, and 0.7 year, the full-time equivalent are 1+1+0.2+0.3+0.7=3.2 person-years.

17 文化、体育、卫生、环保

CULTURE, SPORTS, PUBLIC HEALTH AND ENVIRONMENTAL PROTECTION

资料整理人员

史美荣　高宇宏　吕　洁

文化、体育、卫生、环保
CULTURE, SPORTS, PUBLIC HEALTH AND ENVIRONMENTAL PROTECTION

电视台数	Number of TV Stations	2	个	(unit)
文化馆数	Number of Cultural Centers	119	个	(unit)
公共图书馆数	Number of Public Libraries	127	个	(unit)
体育场地数	Number of Sports Grounds	26459	个	(unit)
医院数	Number of Hospitals	1393	个	(unit)
废水排放总量	Total Volume of Waste Water	28513	万吨	(10 000 tons)

卫生技术人员构成 (%)
Composition of Medical Technical Personnels (%)

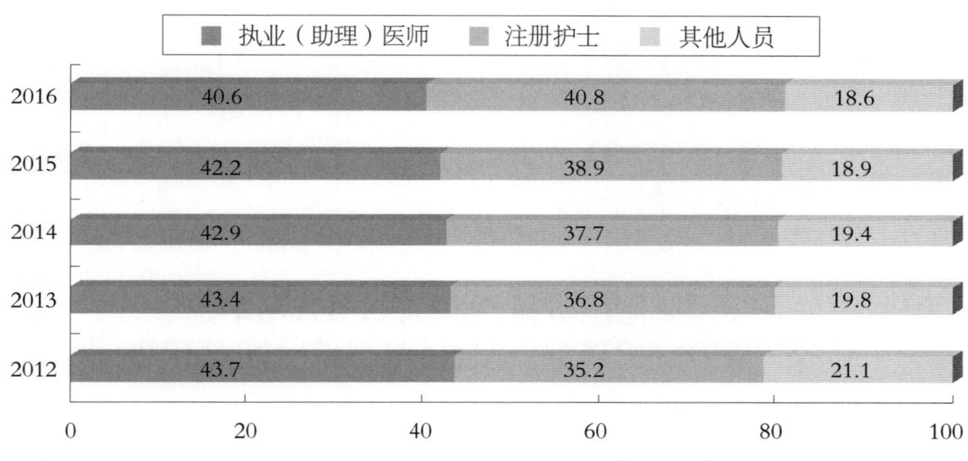

报纸总印数（万份）
Total Printed Copies of Newspapers (10 000 copies)

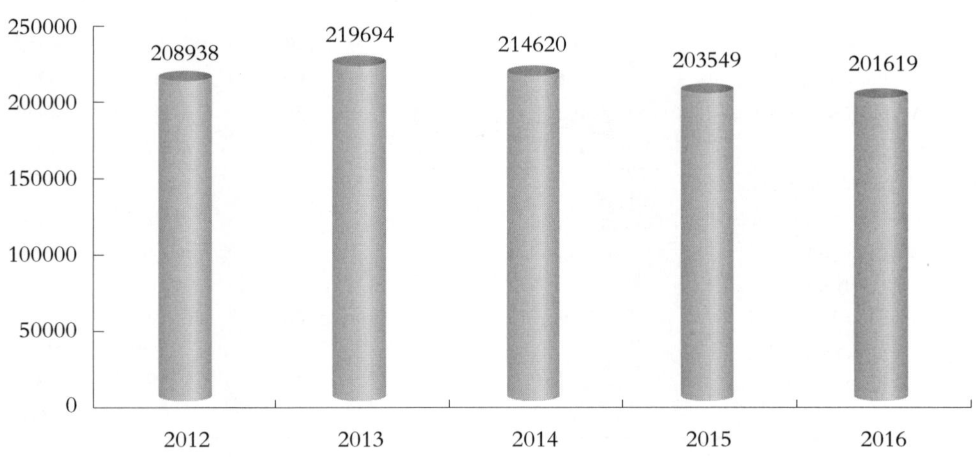

17-1 主要年份广播、电视台(站)数
NUMBER OF RADIO AND TELEVISION STATIONS IN MAJOR YEARS

单位：个 (unit)

年 份 Year	无 线 Radio Broadcast		电视广播 Telecast		人口覆盖率(%) Population Coverage Rate (%)	
	广播电台 Broadcasting Stations	中短波发射台和转播台 Transmission and Relaying Stations of Medium and Short Wave	电视台 Television Stations	一百瓦以上电视发射台 Transmission Stations above 100W	广 播 Radio	电 视 TV
1980	1	10	1	11	44.5	46.6
1985	3	12	6	16	43.0	60.0
1990	14	20	25	36	51.0	78.0
1995	53	21	31	46	68.0	84.1
2000	8	17	12	53	90.0	95.2
2005	10	15	12	309	91.8	95.8
2010	7	15	8	151	93.3	97.5
2011	4	15	6	148	93.6	97.7
2012	2	15	4	148	95.4	98.1
2013	1	15	3	145	96.8	98.5
2014	1	15	2	178	98.0	99.0
2015		13	2	192	98.5	99.3
2016		13	2	190	98.6	99.4

注：2006年以前电视台和转播台为1000瓦以上口径。
Note：Coverage of TV transmission stations and relaying stations before 2006 is above 1000w.

17-2 文化艺术机构和人员数(2016年)
INSTITUTIONS AND PERSONNELS OF CULTURE AND ART(2016)

类 别	Type	机构数(个) Institutions (unit)	国有单位 State-owned Units	非国有单位 Non-state-owned Units	人数(人) Persons (person)	国有单位 State-owned Units	非国有单位 Non-state-owned Units
总 计	**Total**	**7800**	**2362**	**5438**	**60721**	**24352**	**36369**
艺术表演团体	Art Performance Troupes	546	150	396	17619	7783	9836
艺术表演场馆	Art Performance Places	127	93	34	1929	1415	514
图书馆业	Libraries	127	127		1676	1676	
群众文化服务业	Mass Culture Services	1540	1540		4482	4482	
艺术展览机构	Art Exibition Institutions	31	31		269	269	
艺术教育业	Art Education	19	19		1427	1427	
文物业	Culture Relics						
文化市场经营机构	Business Institutions of Culture Market	5008		5008	26019		26019
文艺科研	Art Research	35	35		1398	1398	
其 他	Others	367	367		5902	5902	

注：文化市场经营机构不含非公有制艺术表演团体。
Note: Business institutions of culture market don't include non-public ownership art troupes.

17-3 主要年份广播剧、电视剧、电影故事片制作情况
PRODUCTION OF RADIO PLAYS, TELEVISION PLAYS AND FEATURE FILMS IN MAJOR YEARS

年 份 Year	广 播 剧 Radio Plays		电 视 剧 TV Plays		电影故事片 (部) Feature Films (unit)
	部 Unit	时 长 Hour	部 Unit	集 数 Part	
1985	13	50	18	39	2
1987	12	16	13	46	1
1988	9	37	14	111	2
1989	6	9	24	102	1
1990	5	14	28	122	
1995			12	80	1
2000	5	8	3	42	
2005	7	353	19	371	18
2010	25	1133	2	32	6
2011			2	67	8
2012			1	50	18
2013			7	199	12
2014		4819	8	211	11
2015		5593	7	221	15
2016		6624	9	314	26

注：2014年起，广播剧类广播节目统计口径由集数改为时长。
Note:The coverage of radio plays has changed into length of play from the part of play since 2014.

17-4 主要年份国有文化艺术、文物单位数
INSTITUTION NUMBER OF STATE-OWNED CULTURE, ART AND CULTURAL RELICS IN MAJOR YEARS

单位：个 (unit)

年 份 Year	国有艺术表演团体 State-owned Art Troupes	文化馆(含群众艺术馆) Cultural Centers (including Mass Art Centers)	公共图书馆 Public Libraries	博物馆 Museums
1978	147	124	61	15
1980	162	126	72	19
1985	175	129	103	56
1990	169	130	111	67
1995	162	130	119	67
2000	159	130	121	76
2005	156	131	122	86
2010	167	131	126	89
2011	162	131	126	89
2012	163	131	126	92
2013	155	131	127	98
2014	163	131	126	99
2015	157	131	126	131
2016	150	131	127	140

注：2015年起，博物馆包含民办博物馆、行业博物馆。
Note: Museums include non-state-owned museums and industrial museums from 2015.

17-5 国有艺术表演团体演出情况(2016年)
PERFORMANCE OF STATE-OWNED ART TROUPES(2016)

单位：千场 (1 000 shows)

类　别	Type	国内演出场　次 Number of Performances in Domestic	#到农村演出场次 Shows in Rural Areas	国内演出观众人次(千人次) Number of Spectators (1 000 person-times)
总　计	**Total**	**25.47**	**22.22**	**22423**
按登记注册类型分	**By Types of Registration Status**			
国有经营剧团	Troupes Sponsord by State-owned Units	12.93	10.50	10482
集体经营剧团	Troupes Sponsord by Collective-owned Units	9.41	8.75	8126
其　他	Others	3.58	2.98	3816
按剧种分	**By Art Types**			
话剧、儿童剧、滑稽剧类	Drama, Children Play and Comedy Troupes	0.17		179
其中：儿童剧	Children Play Troupes	0.01		6
歌舞、音乐类	Song and Dance Troupes	1.11	0.54	1184
京剧、昆曲类	Beijing Opera and Kunqu Opera Troupes	0.06		90
其中：京剧	Beijing Opera Troupes	0.06		90
地方戏曲类	Local Opera Troupes	22.61	20.95	20252
杂技、魔术、马戏类	Acrobatics, Magic and Circus Troupes	0.63	0.05	315
曲艺类	Ballad Troupes	0.07	0.42	90
综艺性艺术表演团体	Comprehensive Art Performance Troupes	0.82	0.27	314

17-6 国有艺术表演团体收入和支出(2016年)
REVENUE AND EXPENDITURE OF STATE-OWNED ART TROUPES(2016)

单位：千元 (1 000 yuan)

类　别	Type	剧　团(个) Number of Art Troupes (unit)	#国家经费补贴剧团 Government Subsidies	总收入 Total Revenue	#演出收入 Revenue from Performances	总支出 Total Expenditures
总　计	**Total**	**150**	**130**	**456857**	**154644**	**511225**
按登记注册类型分	**By Types of Registration Status**					
国有经营剧团	Troupes Sponsord by State-owned Units	86	75	370633	102844	411177
集体经营剧团	Troupes Sponsord by Collective-owned Units	52	44	62083	33468	65189
其　他	Others	12	11	24141	18332	34859
按剧种分	**By Art Types**					
话剧、儿童剧、滑稽剧类	Drama, Children Play and Comedy Troupes	3	3	19739	9237	26805
其中：儿童剧	Children Play Troupes	1	1	142	10	13
歌舞、音乐类	Song and Dance Troupes	22	19	103775	31104	112321
京剧、昆曲类	Beijing Opera and Kunqu Opera Troupes	1	1	3539	2260	11304
其中：京剧	Beijing Opera Troupes	1	1	3539	2260	11304
地方戏曲类	Local Opera Troupes	115	98	296371	101902	324894
杂技、魔术、马戏类	Acrobatics, Magic and Circus Troupes	1	1	5332	2339	5445
曲艺类	Ballad Troupes	2	2	1498	1046	3698
综艺性艺术表演团体	Comprehensive Art Performance Troupes	6	6	26603	6756	26758

17-7 群众艺术馆、文化馆(站)业务活动及经费(2016年)
ACTIVITIES AND FUNDS OF MASS ART CENTERS AND CULTURAL CENTERS(2016)

项　目	Item	总　计 Total	#群众艺术馆 Mass Art Centers	#文化馆 Cultural Centers
单位数 (个)	Number of Units (unit)	1540	12	119
举办展览 (个)	Number of Exhibtions (unit)	3431	111	691
举办培训班 (次)	Training Courses (time)	12374	1025	4306
组织文艺活动次数 (次)	Art Performances (time)	22499	1212	5016
总支出 (千元)	Total Expenditures (1 000 yuan)	348795	87404	165959
#商品和服务支出	Expenditures on Goods and Services	75338	15093	29685

17-8 公共图书馆业务活动及经费(2016年)
ACTIVITIES AND FUNDS OF PUBLIC LIBRARIES(2016)

项　目	Item	总　计 Total	省级公共图书馆 Public Libraries at Provincial Level	地市级公共图书馆 Public Libraries at Prefecture Level	县级公共图书馆 Public Libraries at County Level
总藏量(千册)	Total Collections (1 000 volumes)	17271	3295	3883	10093
书架单层总长度(千米)	Total Length of Bookshelves (1 000 m)	206189	36505	57978	111706
有效借书证数(千个)	Number of Valid Library Cards (1 000 unit)	1092227	262374	593432	236421
总流通人次(千人次)	Total Number of Circulation Books (1 000 person-times)	9814	3105	2343	4365
#书刊文献外借人次	Borrowing from Libraries	3615	679	860	2076
为读者服务举办各种活动次数(次)	Number of Service Activities Provided for Readers (time)	3108	252	568	2288
参加人数(千人次)	Number of Readers Involved (1 000 person-times)	1198	366	121	711
电子阅览室终端数(个)	Number of Terminal in Electrical Reading Room (unit)	4653	121	1025	3507
总支出 (千元)	Total Expenditures (1 000 yuan)	338987	73832	130322	134833
#新增藏量及数字资源购置费	Purchase Expenses of New Collections and Digital Resources	48105	9418	22026	16661
本年新增藏量(含电子图书) (千册)	New Collections (including Electronic Books) of The Year (1 000 volumes)	2219	101	786	1332
实际使用公用房屋建筑面积(千平方米)	Actual Usage Floor Space of Public Buildings (1 000 sq.m)	478	80	128	270
#书　库	Stock Rooms	83	13	17	54
阅览室座席(千个)	Seating Capacity of Reading Rooms (1 000 seats)	32	3	8	20

17-9 出版发行、文物、图书馆、群众文化事业机构和人员数(2016年)

INSTITUTIONS AND PERSONNELS OF PUBLISHING, CULTURAL RELICS, LIBRARY AND MASS CULTURE(2016)

项　目	Item	机构数(个) Number of Institutions (unit)	人数(人) Number of Personnels (person)
出版发行事业	Publishing Undertakings		
#出版社	Publishing Houses	8	673
国有书店	State-owned Book Stores	397	5320
文物事业	Cultural Relics Undertakings	383	7632
博物馆	Museums	140	3303
文物机构	Cultural Relics Institutions	243	4329
图书馆事业	Public Libraries Undertakings	127	1676
群众文化服务业	Mass Cultural Service	1540	4482
群众艺术馆	Mass Art Centers	12	369
文化馆	Cultural Centers	119	1429
文化站	Cultural Stations	1409	2684
#乡镇文化站	Cultural Stations of Townships and Towns	1196	2205

17-10 博物馆、文物机构业务活动及经费(2016年)

ACTIVITIES AND FUNDS OF MUSEUMS AND CULTURAL RELICS INSTITUTIONS(2016)

项　目	Item	总计 Total	文物保护管理机构 Protection and Management Institutions	其他文物机构 Other Institutions	博物馆 Museums	文物商店 Cultural Relics Shop	文物科研机构 Research Instituton of Relics
藏　品(件)	Number of Collections (piece)	1458367	188985	90855	984459	130147	63921
#一级品	Grade One	4169	513	256	3102		298
业务活动	Operation Activities						
陈列、展览(个)	Number of Displays and Exhibitions (unit)	352	15		337		
参观人数(千人次)	Number of Visitors (1 000 person-times)	24094	8221		14596		1277
经费收入(千元)	Revenue of Funds (1 000 yuan)	1973610	319423	940222	555516	9965	148484
经费支出(千元)	Total Expenditures (1 000 yuan)	1816694	316510	850410	479400	9858	160516
#商品和服务支出	Expenditures on Goods and Services	729898	106471	321781	200755		100891
项目支出	Project Expenses	1229289	168457	660485	276427		123920

17-11 主要年份图书、期刊和报纸总印数
TOTAL PRINTED COPIES OF BOOKS, MAGAZINES AND NEWSPAPERS IN MAJOR YEARS

年 份 Year	图 书 Books		期 刊 Magazines		报 纸 Newspapers	
	种数(种) Number of Kinds (kind)	总印数(万册) Total Printed Copies (10 000 copies)	种数(种) Number of Kinds (kind)	总印数(万份) Total Printed Copies (10 000 copies)	种数(种) Number of Kinds (kind)	总印数(万份) Total Printed Copies (10 000 copies)
1978	290	6422	16	598	14	17869
1980	361	9055	33	1905	10	17590
1985	550	9991	110	7981	72	55174
1990	989	12166	129	2815	39	54361
1991	1381	14079	130	3086	42	46872
1992	1782	14163	139	3589	49	70047
1993	2261	13058	151	4001	55	73240
1994	2108	12300	158	3948	56	62568
1995	1728	13919	164	3586	59	59254
1996	1783	14654	160	3119	59	58363
1997	1741	15109	158	3199	59	66262
1998	1639	14016	157	2792	56	71954
1999	2214	15487	152	2816	57	69108
2000	1532	10105	165	2657	62	58825
2001	1894	10105	165	2659	59	62815
2002	2177	11800	187	3030	66	101712
2003	2505	13264	195	4290	65	140950
2004	2560	11098	198	4208	67	160553
2005	1683	10081	200	5914	60	329713
2006	1813	9337	199	4441	60	206067
2007	1979	11764	199	5434	60	210541
2008	2586	10535	199	3950	77	163296
2009	2629	11187	200	3402	77	183273
2010	3032	13183	200	4000	77	206698
2011	3401	13887	200	3428	77	202664
2012	4002	14789	198	3733	77	208938
2013	4025	13452	198	3384	77	219694
2014	3458	12866	200	2930	60	214620
2015	3832	12439	200	2573	60	203549
2016	3513	9860	201	2421	60	201619

注：本表2008年至2013年报纸相关数据包含高校校报。

Note: Newspaper data from 2008 to 2013 include college newspaper.

17-12 体育局系统从业人员数(2016年)
EMPLOYEES OF SPORTS BUREAU(2016)

单位：人 (person)

类　别	Type	合　计 Total	行政机关职工合计 Staff and Workers of Administrative Agencies	运动项目管理部门 Administrative Departments of Sports Programmes	职业运动技术学院 Professional Sports Technique College	体育运动学　校 Physical Education and Sports Schools
总　计	**Total**	**1440**	**53**	**799**	**195**	
公务员	Civil Servants	45	45			
教练员	Coaches	136		105	28	
运动员	Athletes	353		353		
科研人员	Scientific and Technical Personnel	32		3		
医务人员	Medical Personnel	15		11	3	
文化教师	Teachers	112			112	
管理人员	Administrative Personnel	491		215	37	
工勤人员	Logistics Personnel	96	8	42	11	
其他人员	Others	160		70	4	

类　别	Type	业余体校 Sparetime Sports Schools	体　育场　馆 Stadiums and Gymnasiums	训　练基　地 Training Bases	科研所 Scientific Research Institutes	其　他 Others
总　计	**Total**		**146**		**34**	**213**
公务员	Civil Servants					
教练员	Coaches					3
运动员	Athletes					
科研人员	Scientific and Technical Personnel				29	
医务人员	Medical Personnel					1
文化教师	Teachers					
管理人员	Administrative Personnel		75		5	159
工勤人员	Logistics Personnel		16			19
其他人员	Others		55			31

17-13 体育场地情况(2016年)
STATISTICS ON SPORTS GROUND(2016)

单位：个 (unit)

项 目	Item	总 计 Total	体育系统 Sports System	教育系统 Education System	高等院校 Regular Institutions of Higher Education	中专中技 Specialized Secondary and Skilled Worker Schools	中小学 Regular Secondary and Primary Schools	其他 Others	其他系统 Other System
总　计	**Total**	**26459**	**839**	**7618**	**724**	**327**	**6390**	**177**	**18002**
体育场	Sports Field	104	33	59	14	2	39	4	12
体育馆	Sports Gym	90	36	23	10	1	10	2	31
游泳馆	Natatorium	123	16	14	7		6	1	93
室内游泳池	Indoor Swimming Pool								
室外游泳池	Outdoor Swimming Pool	29	5						24
室内跳水池	Indoor Diving Pool								
室外跳水池	Outdoor Diving Pool								
有固定看台灯光球场	Illuminated Fields with Fixed Seat								
综合房馆	General Gym	324	23	39	12	1	22	4	262
田径房馆	Track and Field Gym	1	1						
篮球房馆	Basketball Gym	96	9	44	10	4	27	3	43
排球房馆	Valleyball Gym	4		4			4		
手球房馆	Handball Gym	2	1						1
体操房馆	Gymnastics Gym	9	2	4	2		2		3
羽毛球房馆	Badminton Gym	114	8	27	8		17	2	79
乒乓球房馆	Table Tennis Gym	716	28	147	12	7	112	16	541
武术房馆	Wushu Gym	25	4	11	2		5	4	10
摔跤柔道房馆	Wrestling and Judo Gym	43	14	3		1	1	1	26
举重房馆	Weightlifting Gym	6	4	2		1		1	
健身房馆	Body Buildings Gym	207	12	39	12	2	22	3	156
棋牌房馆	Chess and Card Gym	229	2	10	7		3		217
其他训练房馆	Other Training Gym								
保龄球房馆	Bowling Gym	3	1						2
台球房馆	Billiards Gym	295	22	6	4		2		267
田径场	Track and Field	356	11	317	40	20	248	9	28
小运动场	Small Sports Field	1743	8	1658	12	44	1577	25	77
手球场	Handball Field	3	3						
足球场	Football Field	62	1	54	7	3	43	1	7
室内网球场馆	Indoor Tennis Gym	10	6						4
室外网球场馆	Outdoor Tennis Gym	348	75	94	57	4	29	4	179
室内射击场	Indoor Shooting Range	7	4	2	1	1			1

注：2016年数据为第六次全国体育场地普查数据，普查时点为2013年12月31日，下表同。

Note: Data of 2016 are from the Sixth National Sport-site Investigation, with the census time on December 31, 2013. The same applies to the following tables.

17-13 续表 continued

单位：个 (unit)

项 目	Item	总 计 Total	体育系统 Sports System	教育系统 Education System	高等院校 Regular Institutions of Higher Education	中专中技 Specialized Secondary and Skilled Worker Schools	中小学 Regular Secondary and Primary Schools	其 他 Others	其他系统 Other System
室外射击场	Outdoor Shooting Range	3	3						
卡丁车场	Small Car Race Field	3							3
自行车赛车场	Cycling Field	2	1						1
天然游泳场	Natural Swimming Pool	1							1
航空运动机场	Flying Sports Airport	2	2						
室内轮滑场	Indoor Wheel Slide Field	3							3
室外轮滑场	Outdoor Wheel Slide Field	3							3
攀岩场	Climbing Cliff Field	7	2						5
地掷球场	Baseball Ground Ball Field	20	7						13
篮球场	Basketball Field	20593	425	4790	442	226	4029	93	15378
排球场	Valleyball Field	275	4	250	54	8	188		21
门球场	Croquet Field	599	67	21	11	2	4	4	511

17-14 主要年份体育场地数

STADIUMS AND GYMNASIUMS IN MAJOR YEARS

单位：个 (unit)

年 份 Year	体育场 Stadiums	体育馆 Gymnasiums	有看台的灯光球场 Illuminated Fields with Fixed Seating	运动场 Playgrounds	航空机场 Aviation Airporter	射击场 Shooting Range	游泳池 Swimming Pools
1978	16	3	100	61	3	7	30
1980	17	3	127	68	3	7	31
1985	20	2	169	85	3	12	46
1990	29	7	216	140	3	14	72
1995	38	7	239	131	3	15	75
2000	38	7	239	131	3	15	75
2005	104	34	201	189	3	13	142
2010	104	34	201	189	3	13	142
2011	104	34	201	189	3	13	142
2012	104	34	201	189	3	13	142
2013	104	34	201	189	3	13	142
2014	99	87	356	1743	2	9	151
2015	104	90	368	1826	2	9	153
2016	104	90	368	1826	3	9	153

17-15 分项目等级运动员发展人数(2016年)
CERTIFIED ATHLETES BY TYPE OF SPORTS(2016)

单位：人　　(person)

运动项目	Item	人数合计 Number of Persons	国际级运动健将 Master of Sports in International Level	#女 Female	一级 First Grade	#女 Female	二级 Second Grade	#女 Female
总　计	**Total**	**1474**			**420**	**191**	**1054**	**385**
田　径	Track and Field	238			7	1	231	72
游　泳	Swimming	58			16	6	42	16
水　球	Water Polo							
跳　水	Diving							
体　操	Gymnastics							
艺术体操	Artistic Gymnastics	4			4			
蹦　床	Trampoline	5			5	5		
举　重	Weightlifting	5			4	4	1	1
拳　击	Boxing	10			5	4	5	3
国际式摔跤	International Wrestling	35			10	4	25	6
中国式摔跤	Chinese-style Wrestling	40			11	4	29	11
柔　道	Judo	49			40	15	9	1
跆拳道	Kickboxing	62			13	7	49	14
自行车	Cycle Racing	45			28	12	17	7
击　剑	Fencing	17			12	6	5	2
射　击	Shooting	10			2	2	8	3
射　箭	Sport Archery							
足　球	Football	201			77	36	124	69
篮　球	Basketball	179			30	18	149	65
排　球	Volleyball	112			78	40	34	11
乒乓球	Table Tennis	159			65	23	94	33
羽毛球	Badminton	18					18	7
网　球	Tennis	86					86	39
手　球	Handball							
曲棍球	Field Hockey							
棒　球	Baseball							
健美操	Bodybuilding Gymnastics							
街　舞	Hip Hop							
软式网球	Soft Tennis							
武　术	Wushu	138			11	4	127	25
蹼　泳	Fin Swimming							
摩托艇	Motorboat							
围　棋	Weiqi	3			2		1	
国际象棋	International Chess							
中国象棋	Chinese Chess							
橄榄球	Rugby Football							
航空模型	Model Airplane							

17-16 分项目等级裁判员发展人数(2016年)
CERTIFIED REFEREES BY TYPE OF SPORTS(2016)

单位：人 (person)

运动项目	Item	人数合计 Number of Persons	一级 First Grade	#女 Female	二级 Second Grade	#女 Female
总　计	**Total**	**2719**			**2719**	**932**
田　径	Track and Field	319			319	99
游　泳	Swimming	110			110	86
跳　水	Diving					
水　球	Water Polo					
花样游泳	Synchronised Swimming					
体　操	Gymnastics					
艺术体操	Artistic Gymnastics					
蹦　床	Trampoline					
举　重	Weightlifting	11			11	2
拳　击	Boxing	6			6	1
国际式摔跤	International Wrestling	12			12	5
中国式摔跤	Chinese-style Wrestling					
柔　道	Judo	1			1	
跆拳道	Kickboxing	69			69	16
自行车	Cycle Racing	15			15	1
击　剑	Fencing					
马　术	Equestrian					
足　球	Football	435			435	73
篮　球	Basketball	656	1		655	111
排　球	Volleyball	96			96	51
乒乓球	Table Tennis	215			215	99
羽毛球	Badminton	271			271	118
网　球	Tennis	71			71	24
健美操	Bodybuilding Gymnastics	66			66	56
街　舞	Hip Hop					
软式网球	Soft Tennis					
武　术	Wushu	237			237	97
滑　水	Aquaplane					
潜　水	Dive					
蹼　泳	Fin Swimming					
摩托艇	Motorboat					
围　棋	Weiqi	6			6	1
国际象棋	International Chess	2			2	
中国象棋	Chinese Chess	3			3	
桥　牌	Bridge					
台　球	Billiard					
门　球	Croquet	70			70	51
龙　舟	Dragon boat					
钓　鱼	Angling					
风　筝	Kite Flying					
体育舞蹈	Physical Dancing	49			49	41

17-17 主要年份运动员打破纪录情况
RECORDS BROKEN BY ATHLETES IN MAJOR YEARS

年 份 Year	打破世界纪录 World Records Chalked Up			打破全国纪录 National Records Chalked Up			打破省纪录 Provincial Records Chalked Up		
	项数(项) Number of Events (item)	次数(次) Number of Times (time)	人数(人) Number of Persons (person)	项数(项) Number of Events (item)	次数(次) Number of Times (time)	人数(人) Number of Persons (person)	项数(项) Number of Events (item)	次数(次) Number of Times (time)	人数(人) Number of Persons (person)
1978				15	21	10	118	260	95
1980				11	31	4	123	233	132
1985				2	2	2	48	64	35
1990	1	1	1	7	10	7	106	152	62
1995				2	2	5	60	89	84
2000				3	4	6	70	78	57
2005				2	2	2	17	17	25
2010				2	2	2	5	8	8
2011							3	3	3
2012				1	1	1	11	11	3
2013							13	13	18
2014							4	5	4
2015							12	18	12
2016							8	8	7

17-18 体育彩票、福利彩票发行情况
ISSUE OF SPORTS LOTTERY AND WELFARE LOTTERY

单位：万元 (10 000 yuan)

项 目	Item	2015	2016
体育电脑彩票销售点 (个)	Computer Sale Place of Sports Lottery Ticket (unit)	3117	3160
体育彩票销售收入	Sale Revenue of Sports Lottery Ticket	208448	232871
#用于兑奖金额	Value of Exchanging Awards	122758	152432
福利彩票销售点(个)	Sale Place of Welfare Lottery Ticket (unit)	3901	4126
福利彩票销售收入	Sale Revenue of Welfare Lottery Ticket	423735	436400

17-19 主要年份卫生机构数
HEALTH CARE INSTITUTIONS IN MAJOR YEARS

单位：个 (unit)

年 份 Year	总 计 Total	#医 院 Hospitals	#疗养院(所) Sanatoriums	#门诊部(所) Outpatient Departments	#专科疾病防治院（所、站） Specialized Disease Prevention and Treatment Centers
1978	4995	2302	10	2345	7
1980	5190	2346	11	2432	6
1985	5834	2468	15	2910	6
1990	6108	2573	15	3020	10
1995	5922	2590	13	2790	12
2000	3273	716	13	92	15
2005	3009	885	6	52	14
2010	11889	1201	9	106	15
2011	12004	1216	9	291	11
2012	11907	1215	8	317	10
2013	12040	1219	8	297	8
2014	12528	1234	8	284	8
2015	12903	1274	8	312	8
2016	13178	1393	8	355	7

年 份 Year	#疾病预防控制中心 Centers for Disease Control and Prevention	#妇幼保健院(所、站) Maternity and Child Care Centers	#医学科学研究机构 Research Institutes of Medical Science	#其他卫生机 构 Other Institutions
1978	136	128	3	46
1980	137	129	12	89
1985	135	123	19	129
1990	141	123	23	136
1995	153	131	22	58
2000	148	136	23	61
2005	157	131	10	24
2010	147	133	6	67
2011	147	132	7	59
2012	135	132	7	59
2013	134	132	7	71
2014	134	133	7	51
2015	134	132	7	54
2016	136	134	7	50

注：2011年起，卫生机构数不包括村卫生室数，后同。
Note: Rural clinics aren't included in health care institutions from 2011. The same applies to the following.

17-20 主要年份卫生机构床位数
NUMBER OF BEDS IN HEALTH CARE INSTITUTIONS IN MAJOR YEARS

单位：张 (unit)

年 份 Year	总 计 Total	医 院 Hospitals	其他卫生机 构 Other Institutions	平均每千人口拥有医院床位数 Number of Hospital Beds Per 1000 Population
1978	65426	63293	2133	2.69
1980	71702	69141	2561	2.89
1985	87768	82076	5692	3.34
1990	105324	98142	7182	3.45
1995	110422	101936	8486	3.37
2000	111880	77300	34580	2.38
2005	107968	81150	26818	2.42
2010	155973	108333	47640	3.09
2011	158459	111335	47124	3.11
2012	165294	119856	45438	3.32
2013	172620	128294	44326	3.54
2014	177442	133957	43485	3.67
2015	183209	140257	42952	3.83
2016	189778	147096	42682	4.00

17-21 主要年份卫生技术人员数
NUMBER OF MEDICAL TECHNICAL PERSONNELS IN MAJOR YEARS

单位：人 (person)

年 份 Year	卫生技术人 员 Medical Technical Personnels	#执业(助理)医师 Licensed Assistant Doctors	#注册护士 Registered Nurses	平均每千人口拥有卫生技术人员数 Number of Medical Technical Personnel Per 1000 Population
1978	76475	35157	10775	3.16
1980	87815	40479	11561	3.54
1985	109596	48557	16488	4.17
1990	128465	60185	27956	4.52
1995	142239	68658	34907	5.68
2000	136224	64900	37057	4.19
2005	130955	58617	38117	3.90
2010	190917	85376	62251	5.45
2011	189283	82547	64793	5.27
2012	199601	87319	70337	5.54
2013	203385	88182	74849	5.62
2014	209491	89852	79055	5.63
2015	213995	90216	83344	5.84
2016	225770	91748	92139	6.13

17-22 卫生机构、床位、人员数(2016年)

INSTITUTIONS, BEDS AND PERSONNELS IN HEALTH CARE INSTITUTIONS(2016)

类别	Type	机构数(个) Institutions (unit)	床位数(张) Beds (unit)	人员合计(人) Personnel (person)	#卫生技术人员 Medical Technical Personnel
总计	**Total**	**13178**	**189778**	**267809**	**221072**
一、医院合计	**Total Number of Hospitals**	**1393**	**147096**	**184512**	**151931**
综合医院	General Hospitals	692	101098	131932	109514
中医医院	Hospitals of Chinese Medicine	210	16201	18888	15670
中西医结合医院	Hospitals for Chinese and Western Medicine	26	2356	2591	2189
民族医院	Nationality Hospitals				
专科医院	Special Hospitals	464	27251	31067	24528
口腔医院	Stomatological Hospitals	48	495	1724	1311
眼科医院	Ophthalmology Hospitals	31	1482	1931	1461
耳鼻喉科医院	Otolaryngology Hospitals	7	201	285	211
肿瘤医院	Tumor Hospitals	4	2632	3555	3009
心血管病医院	Cardiovascular Hospitals	13	1283	1556	1316
血液病医院	Hematological Hospitals	2	80	66	60
妇产(科)医院	Maternity Hospitals	36	1347	2166	1679
儿童医院	Children Hospitals	5	1123	2424	2102
精神病医院	Mental Hospitals	26	4540	2715	1994
传染病院	Hospitals for Infections Diseases	7	1813	2492	2026
皮肤病医院	Dermatology Hospitals	9	174	181	131
结核病医院	Tuberculosis Hospitals	5	883	950	749
职业病医院	Occupational Disease Hospital	2	435	780	627
骨科医院	Orthopaedics Hospitals	58	2489	2013	1634
康复医院	Recovered Hospitals	21	1247	955	679
整形外科医院	Plastics Hospitals	2	40	48	40
美容医院	Cosmetic Hospitals	6	115	278	148
其他专科医院	Other Specialized Hospitals	182	6872	6948	5351
护理院	Nursing Hospitals	1	190	34	30
二、疗养院	**Sanatoriums**	**8**	**1850**	**408**	**106**
三、社区卫生服务中心(站)	**Community Medical Service Centers and Stations**	**927**	**3977**	**12314**	**10605**
#社区卫生服务中心	Community Medical Service Centers	231	3087	6650	5623
四、卫生院合计	**Total Number Commune Hospitals**	**1621**	**32810**	**26800**	**21827**
街道卫生院	Urban Areas Neighbourhood Hospitals	288	2742	2038	1702
乡镇卫生院	Township Town Hospitals	1333	30068	24762	20125
中心卫生院	Centre Hospitals	421	12837	9885	8137
乡卫生院	Township Hospitals	912	17231	14877	11988
五、门诊部合计	**Total Number of Clinics**	**355**	**249**	**4059**	**3382**
综合门诊部	General Clinics	108	115	1457	1212
中医门诊部	Chinese Medicine Clinics	40	19	383	284
中西医结合门诊部	Chinese and Western Medicine Clinics	17	11	127	123
专科门诊部	Special Clinics	190	104	2092	1763

注：卫生机构、床位、人员数不包括村卫生室等数字；卫生机构床位数为实有数。

Note: The number of health care institutions,beds and personnel exclude rural clinics.The number of beds in health care institutions is an actual data.

17-22 续表1 continued

类 别	Type	机构数(个) Institutions (unit)	床位数(张) Beds (unit)	人员合计(人) Personnel (person)	#卫生技术人员 Medical Technical Personnel
六、诊所、卫生所、医务室	**Clinics, Health Centers and Infirmaries**	**8358**		**17210**	**16763**
诊 所	Clinics	7601		14704	14396
卫生所、医务室	Health Centres and Infirmaries	757		2506	2367
七、急救中心(站)	**First-aid Centers**	**9**	**10**	**565**	**417**
八、采供血机构	**Selection and Supplyment Blood Institutions**	**22**		**1037**	**761**
九、妇幼保健院 (所、站)	**Maternity and Child Care Centers**	**134**	**3616**	**9274**	**7082**
1.省 属	Belong to Province	1			
省辖市(地区)属	Belong to City(prefecture) of Province	14	1347	3138	2462
地辖市属	Belong to City of Prefecture	31	560	1886	1437
县 属	Belong to County	82	1593	3889	2887
其 他	Others	6	116	361	296
2.妇幼保健院	Maternity and Child Care Hospitals	87	3355	7753	5982
妇幼保健所	Maternity and Child Care Institutes	6	5	146	112
妇幼保健站	Maternity and Child Care Stations	40	256	1363	976
生殖保健中心	Reproduction Care Centers	1		12	12
十、专科疾病防治院 (所、站)	**Special Prevention Institutions**	**7**	**160**	**403**	**287**
专科疾病防治院	Special Prevention Hospitals	1	150	207	149
结核病防治院	Tuberculosis Prevention Stations				
职业病防治院	Occupational Disease Preventivetion Stations	1	150	207	149
其 他	Others				
专科疾病防治所 (站、中心)	Special Prevention Institutes	6	10	196	138
口腔病防治所 (站、中心)	Stomatological Prevention Institutes	2		17	11
结核病防治所 (站、中心)	Tuberculosis Prevention Institutes				
职业病防治所 (站、中心)	Prevention Stations of Occupational Diseases	2	10	113	78
地方病防治所 (站、中心)	Endemic Diseases Prevention Stations	1		60	44
其 他	Others	1		6	5
十一、疾病预防控制中心(防疫站)	**Diseases Prevention and Control Center**	**136**		**5033**	**3443**
1.省 属	Belong to Province	1		220	169
省辖市(地区)属	Belong to City (prefecture) of Province	10		833	586
地辖市属	Belong to City of Prefecture	33		1151	834
县 属	Belong to County	79		2288	1458
其 他	Others	13		541	396
2.疾病预防控制中心	Diseases Prevention and Control Centers				
卫生防疫站	Sanitation and Antiepidemic Stations				
预防保健中心	Prevention and Care Centers				

17-22 续表2 continued

类 别	Type	机构数(个) Institutions (unit)	床位数(张) Beds (unit)	人员合计(人) Personnel (person)	#卫生技术人员 Medical Technical Personnel
十二、卫生监督所	**Sanitation Supervision Stations**	**132**		**4075**	**3179**
省 属	Belong to Province	1			
省辖市(地区)属	Belong to City (prefecture) of Province	11		487	353
地辖市属	Belong to City of Prefecture	33		929	719
县 属	Belong to County	87		2659	2107
其 他	Others				
十三、计划生育技术服务机构	**Family Planning Technical Service Institution**	**5**		**136**	**59**
十四、医学科学研究机构	**Research Institutes of Medical Sciences**	**7**		**149**	**120**
十五、医学在职培训机构	**Medical In-service Training Institutes**	**3**		**18**	**14**
十六、健康教育所(站、中心)	**Care Education Institutes**	**11**		**133**	**68**
十七、其他卫生机构	**Other Medical Institues**	**50**	**10**	**1683**	**1028**
卫生监督检验(监测)机构	Sanitary Supervison and Inspection Institution	2		61	60
临床检验中心	Checking Clinic Centers	7	10	253	152
其 他	Others	41		1369	816

17-23 卫生机构分类人员数

NUMBER OF PERSONNELS IN HEALTH CARE INSTITUTIONS BY CATEGORY

单位：人 (person)

人员分类	Type of Personnel	2010	2015	2016
一、各类人员总计	**Total Personnel**	**227897**	**256317**	**267809**
卫生技术人员	Medical Technical Personnel	190925	213995	221072
其他技术人员	Other Technical Personnel	10473	11249	11366
管理人员	Managerial Personnel	11300	11630	13620
工勤人员	Logistics Workers	15199	19443	21751
二、卫生技术人员	**Medical Technical Personnel**	**190925**	**213995**	**221072**
执业(助理)医师	Licensed Assistant Doctors	85376	90216	87488
#执业医师	Licensed Doctors	69976	77314	77023
注册护士	Registered Nurses	62251	83344	91701
药师(士)	Pharmacists	10187	9840	10392
技师(士)	Technicians	10108	11126	11654
其 他	Others	23003	19469	19837

注：本表不包括村卫生室的人员。
Note: Data in the table does not include rural clinic personnel.

17-24 医疗机构医疗服务量情况(2016年)
SERVICES QUANTITY IN HEALTH CARE INSTITUTIONS(2016)

类　别	Item	总诊疗人次 (万人次) Total Diagnosis and Treatment (10 000 person-times)	出院人数 (万人) Discharged Patients (10 000 persons)
总　计	**Total**	**12998.10**	**425.08**
#医　院	Hospital	5380.98	363.43
#综合医院	General Hospitals	3939.35	272.55
中医医院	Hospitals of Chinese Medicine	677.23	32.95
专科医院	Special Hospitals	709.35	53.37
卫生院	Commune Hospitals	1742.28	45.31
#乡镇卫生院	Town and Township Hospitals	1603.68	42.34
门诊部	Clinics	147.89	0.78
妇幼保健院(所、站)	Maternity and Child Care Centers	334.20	10.88
专科疾病防治院(所、站)	Special Disease Prevention Institutions	5.33	0.32

17-25 公证工作和调解
STATISTICS ON NOTARIZATION AND MEDIATION

项　目		Item	2015	2016
公证工作		**Notarization**		
公证处	(个)	Number of Notarization Offices(unit)	112	113
公证员(含公证员助理)	(人)	Notaries (Assistant Notaries) (person)	927	932
办理国内公证	(件)	Handle Civil Affair Notarization (case)	134285	162762
办理涉外公证	(件)	Handle Foreign Nationals Notarization (case)	39819	37675
涉港澳台公证	(件)	Hongkong, Macao and Taiwan Notarization (case)	635	484
调解工作		**Mediation**		
专职人民调解员	(人)	Full-time People's Mediators (person)	18889	17409
人民调解委员会	(个)	Number of People Mediation Committees (unit)	32171	32056
调解人员	(人)	Number of Mediators (person)	103838	106030
调解各类纠纷	(件)	Mediation Various Quarrels (case)	177046	162430
防止民间纠纷引起自杀	(人)	Prevent Civil Quarrel Causing Committing Suicide (person)	158	83
防止民间纠纷转化为刑事案件	(件)	Prevent Civil Quarrel Turning to Criminal Case (case)	541	446

17-26 律师工作
STATISTICS ON LAWYERS

项 目	Item	2015	2016
律师事务所 (个)	Number of Law Offices (unit)	634	687
律师工作人员(注册) (人)	Number of Lawyers (person)	7197	8113
#专职律师	Full-time Lawyers	6258	7031
兼职律师	Part-time Lawyers	345	363
聘请常年法律顾问的单位 (个)	Number of Units with Permanent Legal Advisors (unit)	7560	8149
民事诉讼代理 (件)	Agent of Civil Cases (case)	62261	67240
行政诉讼代理 (件)	Agent of Administrative Action (case)	2419	2709
刑事辨护及代理 (件)	Agent and Defender of Criminal Cases (case)	21036	23411
非诉讼法律事务 (件)	Agent of Non-Litigious Legal Affairs (case)	42284	45671
解答法律咨询 (人次)	Advisory Services (person-time)	112578	149163
代写法律事务文书 (件)	Legal Documents Written on Behalf of Clients (case)	25536	27579

17-27 主要年份婚姻登记数
MARRIAGE REGISTRATION IN MAJOR YEARS

单位：对 (couple)

年 份 Year	登 记 结婚数 Permitting Marriage Registration	#恢复结婚 Resuming Marriage	初婚数 (人) First Marriage (person)	再婚数 (人) Remarriage (person)	男 Male	女 Female	登 记 离婚数 Permitting Divorce Registration
1985	236206	1787	453433	18979	9400	9579	7615
1990	220581	1115	422721	18441	8770	9671	7471
1995	179300	1090	343561	15039	7566	7473	7100
2000	164639	981	313195	16083	8407	7676	7612
2005	189741	1222	354147	25563	12163	13400	17398
2010	360581	4481	675719	45443	24033	21410	26473
2011	339607	3330	633629	45585	21910	23675	31260
2012	362827	4102	677046	48608	22845	25763	35585
2013	384006	4725	710324	57688	26399	31289	41939
2014	350711	5216	637477	63945	29134	34811	47894
2015	346789	8992	623132	70446	31818	38628	54166
2016	300121	6943	530845	69397	31423	37974	58962

17-28 妇联组织状况(2016年)

WOMEN'S FEDERATION ORGANIZATION(2016)

单位：个 (unit)

项　目	Item	2016
地市妇联数	Number of Women's Federation of Prefecture and City	11
县(市)妇联数	Number of Women's Federation of County and City	119
乡妇联数	Number of Women's Federation of Township	1351
街妇联数	Number of Women's Federation for Subdistrict Office	262
基层妇联数中	Number of Women's Federation of Basic Level	
城市 (社区妇联)	Urban Areas (Women's Federation of Community)	1923
农村妇联数	Rural Areas	27899
非公有经济组织中妇女组织	Women's Federation in Non-Public Ownership Economic Organization	12613
直属机关妇工委	Women's Council in Department Directly under Governments	5012
高等院校妇女组织	Women's Orgaization in University	33
省级所属	Provincial Level	3
市级所属	City Level	21
民办高校	University Run by Private Insititutions	9
民主党派妇委会数	Number of Women's Federation in Democratic Party	15

17-29 全省工业企业“三废”排放与治理情况(2016年)

DISCHARGE AND TREATMENT OF WASTE WATER, WASTE GAS AND SOLID WASTES BY INDUSTRIAL ENTERPRISES(2016)

项　目	Item	2016
废　水	**Waste Water**	
废水排放总量 (万吨)	Total Volume of Waste Water (10 000 tons)	28513.4
化学需氧量排放量(吨)	Volume of COD (ton)	22816.4
氨氮排放量(吨)	Volume of Ammonia Nitrogen (ton)	2327.5
废　气	**Waste Gas**	
废气排放量 (亿标立方米)	Total Volume of Waste Gas Emission (100 million cu.m)	30344.8
二氧化硫排放量 (吨)	Volume of Sulphur Dioxide Emission (ton)	385721.0
氮氧化物排放量 (吨)	Volume of Nitrogen Dioxide Emission (ton)	383046.8
固体废物	**Solid Wastes**	
固体废物产生量 (万吨)	Volume of Solid Wastes Produced (10 000 tons)	28881.6
固体废物综合利用量 (万吨)	Volume of Solid Wastes Utilized (10 000 tons)	13972.3
固体废物综合利用率 (%)	Percentage of Solid Wastes Utilized (%)	48.3
固体废物处置量 (万吨)	Volume of Solid Wastes Treated (10 000 tons)	11850.2
固体废物贮存量 (万吨)	Volume of Solid Wastes Accumulated (10 000 tons)	3105.7
污染治理	**Pollution Treatment**	
当年污染治理施工项目总数 (个)	Number of Projects for Pollution Treatment in the Year (unit)	330
污染治理项目本年完成投资额 (万元)	Investment of the Project for Pollution Treatment in the Year (10 000 yuan)	300741.8
治理废水	Treatment of Waste Water	18504.5
治理废气	Treatment of Waste Gas	228806.9
治理固体废物	Treatment of Solid Wastes	2817.1
治理噪声	Noise Abatement	52.5
治理其他	Others	50560.9

注：由于环保部环境统计年报制度改革，2016年数据与之前年份不可比。

Note: Data of 2016 isn't comparable with the previous years' because of the environmental statistical annual report system reform of Ministry of Environmental Protection.

主要统计指标解释

艺术表演团体　指从事戏曲、音乐、舞蹈、杂技等专业艺术表演，有独立帐户，实行单独核算的团体。不包括半工半艺、半农半艺的业余团体。

文化馆　指专门从事群众文化活动的群众文化场馆。不包括临时抽调人员组成、没有编制的农村和街道文化工作队、服务站等。

文化市场经营机构　指经文化市场行政部门审批或已申报登记并领取相关许可证的、从事文化经营和文化服务活动的机构。

图书馆　指各类图书馆的管理与服务（对文献和信息的搜集、整理、存储、利用和管理，向社会公众开放并提供科学、文化等各种知识普及教育）。包括公共图书馆和各类机构内部举办的或单独举办的图书馆的管理与服务。不包括部队系统以及文化馆（文化中心、群众艺术馆）、文化站内设的图书室。

文化艺术研究机构　指有明确的研究方向和任务，有一定水平的学术带头人和一定数量、质量的研究人员，有开展工作的基本条件，主要进行文化艺术研究（含科技）的机构。

博物馆　指为了研究、教育、欣赏的目的，收藏、保护、展示人类活动和自然环境的见证物，向公众开放，非营利性、永久性社会服务机构，包括以博物馆（院）、纪念馆（舍）、美术（艺术）馆、科技馆、陈列馆等专有名称开展活动的单位。

艺术表演观众人数　指售票、包场演出或民族地区免费演出艺术表演观众人次数。不包括彩排审查和内部观摩演出的观看人次数。

等级运动员人数　指经考核正式批准授予等级运动员称号的人数。运动员等级分为国际级运动健将、运动健将、一级运动员、二级运动员、三级运动员、少年级运动员。

等级裁判员人数　指经考核正式批准授予等级裁判员称号的人数。裁判员等级分为国际裁判、国家级裁判、一级裁判、二级裁判、三级裁判。

体育场　指有400米跑道（中心含足球场），有固定道牙，路道6条以上，并有固定看台的田径场。以看台容纳观众人数分：甲级25000人以上，乙级15000–25000人，丙级5000–15000人，丁级5000人以下。

体育馆　指有固定看台可供篮球、排球、羽毛球、乒乓球、体操等项目训练比赛活动用的室内场地。以看台容纳观众人数分：甲级6000人以上，乙级4000–6000人，丙级2000–4000人，丁级2000以下。

工业废水排放量　指经过企业厂区所有排放口排到企业外部的工业废水量。包括生产废水、外排的直接冷却水、超标排放的矿井地下水和与工业废水混排的厂区生活污水，不包括独立外排的间接冷却水(清浊不分流的间接冷却水应计算在内)。

工业废气排放量　指企业厂区内燃料燃烧和生产工艺过程中产生的各种排入空气中含有污染物的气体总量，按标准状态［273 K，101325Pa］计算。

工业二氧化硫排放量　指企业在燃料燃烧和生产工艺过程中排入大气的二氧化硫总质量。工业中二氧化硫主要来源于化石燃料（煤、石油等）的燃烧，还包括硫矿石的冶炼或含硫酸、磷肥等生产的工业废气排放。

工业固体废物产生量　指企业在生产过程中产生的固体状、半固体状和高浓度液体状废弃物的总量、包括危险废物、冶炼废渣、粉煤灰、炉渣、煤矸石、尾矿、放射性废物和其他废物等；不包括矿山开采的剥离废石和掘进废石(煤矸石和呈酸性或碱性的废石除外)。酸性或碱性废石指采掘的废石其流经水、雨淋水的PH值小于4或PH值大于10.5者。

工业固体废物贮存量　指以综合利用或处置为目的，将固体废物暂时贮存或堆存在专设的贮存设施或专设的集中堆存场所内的数量。专设的固体废物贮存场所或贮存设施必须有防扩散、防流失、防渗漏、防止污染大气、水体的措施。

工业固体废物处置量　指将固体废物焚烧或者最终置于符合环境保护规定要求的场所，并不再回取的工业固体废物量(包括当年处置往年的工业固体废物累计贮存量)。处置方法有填埋(其中危险废物应安全填埋)、焚烧、专业贮存场(库)封场处理、深层灌注、回填矿井等。

Explanatory Notes on Main Statistical Indicators

Art Performance Troupes refer to the troupes which are engaged in drama, music, dance, acrobatics or other art performance, have independent accounts with banks and have self-supporting accounting system. Amateur troupes which are engaged partly in industrial or agricultural activities and partly in art performance are not included.

Culture Centers refer to mass cultural centers which specialize in mass cultural activities. They do not include rural and street cultural teams or service stations that comprise of temporary transferred staff or personnel who do not have a personnel quota.

Business Institutions of Cultural Market refer to the institutions dealing in culture and cultural services, which registered and permitted with the relative certificate by cultural market administration.

Libraries refer to management and services of all kinds of libraries, that is, collect, collate, store and manage literature and information, supply various popular knowledge and education of science and culture openly. They include management and service that are carried out internally and singly by public libraries and all kinds of agencies, but don't include library rooms of army and culture centers or stations.

Culture and Art Research Institutions refer to institutions that mainly do research on culture and art. These institutions own academic leaders to a certain degree and research personnel to a certain quantity and quality, have the basic condition to carry out work under definite research direction and task.

Museums refer to social service agencies which collect, protect, exhibit the evidence of human's activities and natural environment in an open, non-profit and permanent way. They include museum, memorial hall, art gallery, science museum, exhibition hall and so on.

Number of Spectators at Art Performance refers to the number of attendants at commercial shows completely booked shows or free shows given in minority national areas and does not include the number of spectators at rehearsals for examination and internal shows for study.

Number of Athletes in Grades refers to the number of athletes who have been given titles through examination. The titles of athletes include international masters of sports, masters of sports, first grade athletes, second grade athletes, third grade athletes and young athletes.

Number of Referees in Grades refers to the number of referees who have been given titles after examination. They are classified into international referees, national referees, first grade referees, second grade referees and third grade referees.

Stadiums refer to athletic field which have 400-meter track around football field, fixed kerbs, road way above six and fixed stands. Stadiums are classified into the following types according to seating capacity: Class A seating 25000 people, Class B 15000 to 25000 people, Class C 5000 to 15000 people and Class D fewer than 5000 people.

Gymnasiums refer to indoor sports grounds with fixed seats for the training or competition of basketball, volleyball, badminton, table tennis, gymnastics and other sports events. Gymnasiums are classified into the following types according to seating capacity: Class A seating over 6000 people, Class B 4000 to 6000 people, Class C 2000 to 4000 people and class D fewer than 2000 people.

Volume of Industrial Waste Water Discharged refers to the volume of industrial waste water discharged through all outlets to the outside of industrial enterprises including waste water produced, direct-cooling water, underground water from mines that does not meet the standard and the domestic sewage mixed up with industrial waste water, excluding indirect-cooling water discharged separately.

Volume of Industrial Waste Gas Emission refers to total emission volume of polluted gas enterprises discharge into atmosphere from fuels burning and production process in the factory. It is measured by standard atmospheric pressure of [273K, 101325Pa].

Volume of Industrial Sulphur Dioxide Emission refers to dioxide emission volume enterprises discharge into atmosphere from fuels burning and production process. Industrial sulphur dioxide is mainly from burning of fossil fuels (coal, petroleum and etc). It is also from the emission of industrial waste gas which is produced during the process of smelting sulphur ores, sulphur acid or phosphate fertilizer.

Volume of Industrial Solid Wastes Produced refers to the total volume of solid semi-solid or high concentration liquid residue produced by industrial enterprises in their production process including dangerous wastes residues, melting waste slag, coal ash, gangue chemical residues, tailings, radioactive residues and other residues, but excluding stripped or dug stones in mining except gangue and acid or alkali stones which are stones washed or soaked by water with PH value smaller than 4 or larger than 10.5.

Volume of Industrial Solid Wastes Accumulated refers to the volume of industrial solid wastes temporarily stored up or piled with special facilities or piled in the special sites for the purpose of utilization or treatment in future. The special facilities or special sites for storing up solid wastes should have the measures against spreading or being washed away to other places, permeating the soil causing air pollution or water contamination.

Volume of Industrial Solid Wastes Treated refers to solid wastes disposed of in a non—recoverable place that meet the requirement of environmental protection such as burying (dangerous wastes should be buried safely), burning, piling in designated sites, pouring water into the deep strata, filling of old mines, etc, (including treatment of solid wastes piled up in the previous years).

18 城市概况

GENERAL SURVEY OF CITIES

资料整理人员

马金兰　李悦榕　杨　磊　杨　敏　白鹏洲
田　丹　韩春光

18-1 地级城市主要经济指标(2016年)
MAJOR ECONOMIC INDICATORS OF CITIES AT PREFECTURE LEVEL(2016)

指　　标	Item	太原市区 Taiyuan Urban District	大同市区 Datong Urban District	阳泉市区 Yangquan Urban District
总户数 (万户)	Number of Households (10 000 households)	85.27	59.95	26.02
常住人口 (万人)	Resident Population(10 000 persons)	364.51	179.10	73.89
出生人数 (人)	Birth Population (person)	36272	15060	5999
死亡人数 (人)	Death Population (person)	7899	5475	2868
城镇从业人员期末人数(人)	Number of Urban Employees at the End of Period (person)	986774	329206	190406
土地面积 (平方公里)	Area of Land (sq.km)	1500	2080	652
地区生产总值 (万元)	Gross Domestic Product (10 000 yuan)	27549377	8186718	4014561
第一产业	Primary Industry	162465	127926	21893
第二产业	Secondary Industry	9693482	3185056	1702769
第三产业	Tertiary Industry	17693430	4873736	2289899
工业经济指标	Industrial Indicators			
工业企业数 (个)	Number of Enterprises (unit)	261	83	47
内资企业	Domestic Capital	244	78	42
港澳台投资企业	Hong kong, Macao and Taiwan Investment	3		2
外商投资企业	Foreign Capital	14	5	3
流动资产合计 (万元)	Total Circulating Funds(10 000 yuan)	18928227	9349702	12358319
固定资产合计 (万元)	Total Fixed Assets (10 000 yuan)	14264058	12458287	3129570
主营业务收入 (万元)	Revenue of Major Business (10 000 yuan)	20979942	16854192	4083500
主营业务税金及附加 (万元)	Tax and Extra Charges of Major Business (10 000 yuan)	349782	35989	136399
本年应交增值税 (万元)	Value Added Tax Payable (10 000 yuan)	572410	331960	184810
利润总额 (万元)	Total Profits (10 000 yuan)	176253	103483	85190
固定电话用户数 (万户)	Number of Telephone Subscribers (10 000 subscribers)	83.72	26.19	9.73
年末移动电话用户数 (万户)	Number of Mobile Phone Subscribers (10 000 subscribers)	691.22	298.23	147.19
互联网宽带接入用户数 (万户)	Internet Subscriber (10 000 subscriber)	135.12	53.18	37.20

注：总户数和总人口相关指标为公安年报数；固定电话、年末移动电话、互联网宽带接入用户数为全市口径。

Note: Number of households and population are from public security department.The coverage of subscribers numbers of telephone,mobile phone and internet are all citywide.

18-1 续表1 continued

指 标	Item	太原市区 Taiyuan Urban District	大同市区 Datong Urban District	阳泉市区 Yangquan Urban District
全社会用电量 (万千瓦小时)	Total Electricity Consumption (10 000 kwh)	2348433	806073	588904
#工业用电	Industry	1513096	550828	478019
城乡居民生活用电	Resident Living	313423	104702	35570
固定资产投资 (不含农户)(万元)	Investment in Fixed Assets (Excluding Rural Household) (10 000 yuan)	18173411	5621904	2321821
#房地产开发投资	Investment in Real Estate	6683142	1633533	305446
#住 宅	Residential Buildings	4845627	1100992	248003
商品房屋销售面积 (万平方米)	Floor Space of Commercial Houses Sold (10 000 sq.m)	581.66	125.02	57.90
商品房屋销售额 (万元)	Sales of Commercial Houses (10 000 yuan)	4569080	584835	242300
社会消费品零售总额 (万元)	Total Retail Sales of Consumer Goods (10 000 yuan)	15438351	4765321	2235047
公共财政收入 (万元)	Public Finance Revenue (10 000 yuan)	839780	777456	323042
公共财政支出 (万元)	Public Finance Expenditure (10 000 yuan)	1322694	1608843	587189
在校学生数	Student Enrollment			
高等学校 (人)	Institutions of Higher Education (person)	432234	28142	10882
中等职业学校 (人)	Vocational Secondary Schools (person)	117951	17505	5731
普通中学 (万人)	Regular Secondary Schools (10 000 persons)	16.57	8.44	3.58
小 学 (万人)	Primary Schools (10 000 persons)	23.69	11.45	3.99
科技活动人员 (人)	Technological Activities Personnel (person)	19882	10259	6191
医院、卫生院数 (个)	Number of Hospitals (unit)	174	129	46
医院、卫生院床位数 (张)	Number of Beds in Hospitals (bed)	33199	13468	6142
医生数 (人)	Number of Doctors (person)	19355	7113	2776
在岗职工平均人数 (万人)	Average Number of Fully Employed Staff and Workers (10 000 persons)	94.32	31.05	18.83
在岗职工工资总额 (万元)	Total Wages of Full Employed Staff and Workers (10 000 yuan)	6222256	1727903	931393
居民储蓄存款余额 (万元)	Balance of Residents Savings Deposits (10 000 yuan)	33098445	13647008	4757046

18-1 续表2 continued

指 标	Item	长治市区 Changzhi Urban District	晋城市区 Jincheng Urban District	朔州市区 Shuozhou Urban District
总户数（万户）	Number of Households (10 000 households)	22.33	13.56	26.74
常住人口（万人）	Resident Population(10 000 persons)	80.04	49.29	73.13
出生人数（人）	Birth Population (person)	8381	4701	8430
死亡人数（人）	Death Population (person)	2123	909	3811
城镇从业人员期末人数(人)	Number of Urban Employees at the End of Period (person)	146121	169475	106113
土地面积（平方公里）	Area of Land (sq.km)	334	143	4107
地区生产总值（万元）	Gross Domestic Product (10 000 yuan)	3720097	2498081	4529330
第一产业	Primary Industry	36373	7446	166969
第二产业	Secondary Industry	1513934	809300	1923779
第三产业	Tertiary Industry	2169790	1681335	2438582
工业经济指标	Industrial Indicators			
工业企业数（个）	Number of Enterprises (unit)	54	40	62
内资企业	Domestic Capital	51	35	59
港澳台投资企业	Hong Kong, Macao and Taiwan Investment	2	2	2
外商投资企业	Foreign Capital	1	3	1
流动资产合计(万元)	Total Circulating Funds(10 000 yuan)	2045255	7846279	2936958
固定资产合计(万元)	Total Fixed Assets (10 000 yuan)	2230937	2866213	7171249
主营业务收入(万元)	Revenue of Major Business (10 000 yuan)	2852397	4197700	3337795
主营业务税金及附加(万元)	Tax and Extra Charges of Major Business (10 000 yuan)	23294	120964	126230
本年应交增值税（万元）	Value Added Tax Payable (10 000 yuan)	88258	186329	197894
利润总额（万元）	Total Profits (10 000 yuan)	98616	323244	80431
固定电话用户数(万户)	Number of Telephone Subscribers (10 000 subscribers)	24.97	16.98	14.91
年末移动电话用户数(万户)	Number of Mobile Phone Subscribers (10 000 subscribers)	306.44	225.03	175.28
互联网宽带接入用户数(万户)	Internet Subscriber (10 000 subscriber)	55.08	54.31	25.16

18-1 续表3 continued

指　　标	Item	长治市区 Changzhi Urban District	晋城市区 Jincheng Urban District	朔州市区 Shuozhou Urban District
全社会用电量 (万千瓦小时)	Total Electricity Consumption (10 000 kwh)	296578	174470	604079
#工业用电	Industry	197235	121596	517436
城乡居民生活用电	Resident Living	46258	17962	30554
固定资产投资 (不含农户)(万元)	Investment in Fixed Assets (Excluding Rural Household) (10 000 yuan)	4133803	4056451	1459099
#房地产开发投资	Investment in Real Estate	354210	496344	198829
#住　宅	Residential Buildings	259848	368519	154558
商品房屋销售面积 (万平方米)	Floor Space of Commercial Houses Sold (10 000 sq.m)	136.77	81.20	58.00
商品房屋销售额 (万元)	Sales of Commercial Houses (10 000 yuan)	646000	392909	206839
社会消费品零售总额 (万元)	Total Retail Sales of Consumer Goods (10 000 yuan)	3736602	2046880	1091799
公共财政收入 (万元)	Public Finance Revenue (10 000 yuan)	401451	387882	336061
公共财政支出 (万元)	Public Finance Expenditure (10 000 yuan)	671598	602948	650068
在校学生数	Student Enrollment			
高等学校 (人)	Institutions of Higher Education (person)	38129	6325	11357
中等职业学校 (人)	Vocational Secondary Schools (person)	23385	17854	6343
普通中学 (万人)	Regular Secondary Schools (10 000 persons)	5.92	3.70	4.37
小　学　(万人)	Primary Schools (10 000 persons)	5.72	3.58	5.49
科技活动人员 (人)	Technological Activities Personnel (person)	997	30216	
医院、卫生院数 (个)	Number of Hospitals (unit)	86	39	66
医院、卫生院床位数 (张)	Number of Beds in Hospitals (bed)	9051	3950	3675
医生数 (人)	Number of Doctors (person)	4035	2616	1702
在岗职工平均人数 (万人)	Average Number of Fully Employed Staff and Workers (10 000 persons)	13.27	15.95	10.49
在岗职工工资总额 (万元)	Total Wages of Full Employed Staff and Workers (10 000 yuan)	655610	937623	5735024
居民储蓄存款余额 (万元)	Balance of Residents Savings Deposits (10 000 yuan)	6595314	6114442	5000453

18-1 续表4 continued

指　标	Item	晋中市区 Jinzhong Urban District	运城市区 Yuncheng Urban District	忻州市区 Xinzhou Urban District
总户数（万户）	Number of Households (10 000 households)	22.04	23.50	23.01
常住人口（万人）	Resident Population(10 000 persons)	65.83	70.12	56.21
出生人数（人）	Birth Population (person)	7809	7882	6414
死亡人数（人）	Death Population (person)	4039	3984	1752
城镇从业人员期末人数(人)	Number of Urban Employees at the End of Period (person)	100817	99201	73448
土地面积（平方公里）	Area of Land (sq.km)	1311	1205	1987
地区生产总值（万元）	Gross Domestic Product (10 000 yuan)	2162832	2248879	1200652
第一产业	Primary Industry	199729	126391	93037
第二产业	Secondary Industry	650836	659710	310888
第三产业	Tertiary Industry	1312267	1462778	796727
工业经济指标	Industrial Indicators			
工业企业数（个）	Number of Enterprises (unit)	91	77	30
内资企业	Domestic Capital	82	75	30
港澳台投资企业	Hong Kong, Macao and Taiwan Investment	5		
外商投资企业	Foreign Capital	4	2	
流动资产合计(万元)	Total Circulating Funds(10 000 yuan)	1251344	2159478	531166
固定资产合计(万元)	Total Fixed Assets (10 000 yuan)	1359189	1133091	600794
主营业务收入(万元)	Revenue of Major Business (10 000 yuan)	1947053	2268289	712530
主营业务税金及附加(万元)	Tax and Extra Charges of Major Business (10 000 yuan)	11664	9375	1415
本年应交增值税（万元）	Value Added Tax Payable (10 000 yuan)	44879	34964	5739
利润总额（万元）	Total Profits (10 000 yuan)	-9354	89231	71169
固定电话用户数(万户)	Number of Telephone Subscribers (10 000 subscribers)	34.00	38.50	56.66
年末移动电话用户数(万户)	Number of Mobile Phone Subscribers (10 000 subscribers)	307.84	459.10	273.30
互联网宽带接入用户数(万户)	Internet Subscriber (10 000 subscriber)	201.35	101.00	40.00

18-1 续表5 continued

指标	Item	晋中市区 Jinzhong Urban District	运城市区 Yuncheng Urban District	忻州市区 Xinzhou Urban District
全社会用电量 (万千瓦小时)	Total Electricity Consumption (10 000 kwh)		362807	122093
#工业用电	Industry		197266	56916
城乡居民生活用电	Resident Living		73290	27365
固定资产投资 (不含农户)(万元)	Investment in Fixed Assets (Excluding Rural Household) (10 000 yuan)	2758083	2948846	1213060
#房地产开发投资	Investment in Real Estate	874118	731070	186840
#住 宅	Residential Buildings	25269	356518	84502
商品房屋销售面积 (万平方米)	Floor Space of Commercial Houses Sold (10 000 sq.m)	55.97	109.74	31.85
商品房屋销售额 (万元)	Sales of Commercial Houses (10 000 yuan)	256778	379509	107838
社会消费品零售总额 (万元)	Total Retail Sales of Consumer Goods (10 000 yuan)	980018	2304419	880336
公共财政收入 (万元)	Public Finance Revenue (10 000 yuan)	120602	95626	45355
公共财政支出 (万元)	Public Finance Expenditure (10 000 yuan)	261559	275279	199312
在校学生数	Student Enrollment			
高等学校 (人)	Institutions of Higher Education (person)	132248	55222	19738
中等职业学校 (人)	Vocational Secondary Schools (person)	16585	22933	5982
普通中学 (万人)	Regular Secondary Schools (10 000 persons)	2.74	5.92	4.17
小 学 (万人)	Primary Schools (10 000 persons)	4.34	5.85	3.63
科技活动人员 (人)	Technological Activities Personnel (person)	1022		2960
医院、卫生院数 (个)	Number of Hospitals (unit)	43	110	57
医院、卫生院床位数 (张)	Number of Beds in Hospitals (bed)	4650	6726	2725
医生数 (人)	Number of Doctors (person)	2216	2339	1135
在岗职工平均人数 (万人)	Average Number of Fully Employed Staff and Workers (10 000 persons)	8.21	15.28	6.98
在岗职工工资总额 (万元)	Total Wages of Full Employed Staff and Workers (10 000 yuan)	484932	472938	290269
居民储蓄存款余额 (万元)	Balance of Residents Savings Deposits (10 000 yuan)	4765107	3642712	3696289

18-1 续表6 continued

指 标	Item	临汾市区 Linfen Urban District	吕梁市区 Lvliang Urban District
总户数（万户）	Number of Households (10 000 households)	27.32	11.07
常住人口（万人）	Resident Population(10 000 persons)	97.63	33.26
出生人数（人）	Birth Population (person)	9827	3420
死亡人数（人）	Death Population (person)	2829	1568
城镇从业人员期末人数(人)	Number of Urban Employees at the End of Period (person)	88773	58131
土地面积（平方公里)	Area of Land (sq.km)	1316	1339
地区生产总值（万元)	Gross Domestic Product (10 000 yuan)	2612024	704473
第一产业	Primary Industry	87516	20261
第二产业	Secondary Industry	569981	165754
第三产业	Tertiary Industry	1954527	518458
工业经济指标	Industrial Indicators		
工业企业数（个）	Number of Enterprises (unit)	44	23
内资企业	Domestic Capital	42	23
港澳台投资企业	Hong Kong, Macao and Taiwan Investment	1	
外商投资企业	Foreign Capital	1	
流动资产合计(万元)	Total Circulating Funds(10 000 yuan)	847990	1662707
固定资产合计(万元)	Total Fixed Assets (10 000 yuan)	1314476	678482
主营业务收入(万元)	Revenue of Major Business (10 000 yuan)	923282	399332
主营业务税金及附加(万元)	Tax and Extra Charges of Major Business (10 000 yuan)	14257	16673
本年应交增值税（万元)	Value Added Tax Payable (10 000 yuan)	31260	18510
利润总额（万元)	Total Profits (10 000 yuan)	-87353	15819
固定电话用户数(万户)	Number of Telephone Subscribers (10 000 subscribers)	20.81	23.80
年末移动电话用户数(万户)	Number of Mobile Phone Subscribers (10 000 subscribers)	411.21	286.10
互联网宽带接入用户数(万户)	Internet Subscriber (10 000 subscriber)	79.63	57.80

18-1 续表7 continued

指 标	Item	临汾市区 Linfen Urban District	吕梁市区 lvliang Urban District
全社会用电量 (万千瓦小时)	Total Electricity Consumption (10 000 kwh)	274214	84650
#工业用电	Industry	142774	28181
城乡居民生活用电	Resident Living	59922	
固定资产投资 (不含农户)(万元)	Investment in Fixed Assets (Excluding Rural Household) (10 000 yuan)	2521124	1185676
#房地产开发投资	Investment in Real Estate	532068	52368
#住 宅	Residential Buildings	380376	46486
商品房屋销售面积 (万平方米)	Floor Space of Commercial Houses Sold (10 000 sq.m)	99.48	19.40
商品房屋销售额 (万元)	Sales of Commercial Houses (10 000 yuan)	482754	86516
社会消费品零售总额 (万元)	Total Retail Sales of Consumer Goods (10 000 yuan)	2394536	670719
公共财政收入 (万元)	Public Finance Revenue (10 000 yuan)	119266	80108
公共财政支出 (万元)	Public Finance Expenditure (10 000 yuan)	350913	206784
在校学生数	Student Enrollment		
高等学校 (人)	Institutions of Higher Education (person)	47585	23000
中等职业学校 (人)	Vocational Secondary Schools (person)	11863	6732
普通中学 (万人)	Regular Secondary Schools (10 000 persons)	6.53	3.16
小 学 (万人)	Primary Schools (10 000 persons)	6.19	3.97
科技活动人员 (人)	Technological Activities Personnel (person)	506	
医院、卫生院数 (个)	Number of Hospitals (unit)	77	232
医院、卫生院床位数 (张)	Number of Beds in Hospitals (bed)	6408	1876
医生数 (人)	Number of Doctors (person)	3596	1246
在岗职工平均人数 (万人)	Average Number of Fully Employed Staff and Workers (10 000 persons)	8.32	4.77
在岗职工工资总额 (万元)	Total Wages of Full Employed Staff and Workers (10 000 yuan)	482774	257816
居民储蓄存款余额 (万元)	Balance of Residents Savings Deposits (10 000 yuan)	5466024	2305893

18-2 地级城市公用事业及设施水平(2016年)
LEVEL OF PUBLIC FACILITIES IN CITIES AT PREFECTURE LEVEL(2016)

指　　标	Item	太原市区 Taiyuan Urban District	大同市区 Datong Urban District
供水综合生产能力 (万立方米/日)	Daily Production Capacity of Tap Water (10 000 cu.m/day)	215.00	66.00
城市供水总量 (万吨)	Total Volume of City Water Supply (10 000 tons)	36499	9517
#居民生活用水量	Residential Use	12597	3320
平均每人生活用水(吨)	Per Capita Consumption of Tap Water for Resiential Use (ton)	31.30	26.40
排水管道长度(公里)	Lenth of Drainage Pipelines (km)	2417	638
年末实有城市道路面积 (万平方米)	Actual Area of City Roads at the Year End (10 000 sq.m)	4903	2151
供气总量 (人工、天然气)(万立方米)	Coal Gas Supply (Munufactured and Natural Gas) (10 000 cu.m)	81156	13973
#家庭用量	Residential Use	21806	4505
液化石油气供气总量 (吨)	Natural Gas Supply (ton)	1352	9157
#家庭用量	Residential Use	968	2833
公共汽(电)车营运车辆数 (辆)	Number of Public Transportation Vehicles (unit)	2671	1009
出租汽车数 (辆)	Number of Taxis (unit)	8726	4705
公共汽(电)车客运总量 (万人次)	Number of Passengers Carried by Public Transportation Vehicles (10 000 person-times)	44719	22000
绿地面积 (公顷)	Green Area (ha)	12655	4684
#公园绿地面积	Green Area of Parks	4099	1417
建成区绿化覆盖面积 (公顷)	Green Coverage of Completed Areas (ha)	14369	5127

18-2 续表1

指　标	Item	阳泉市区 Yangquan Urban District
供水综合生产能力 (万立方米/日)	Daily Production Capacity of Tap Water (10 000 cu.m/day)	30.00
城市供水总量 (万吨)	Total Volume of City Water Supply (10 000 tons)	4662
#居民生活用水量	Residential Use	1615
平均每人生活用水(吨)	Per Capita Consumption of Tap Water for Resiential Use (ton)	28.33
排水管道长度(公里)	Lenth of Drainage Pipelines (km)	429
年末实有城市道路面积 (万平方米)	Actual Area of City Roads at the Year End (10 000 sq.m)	643
供气总量 (人工、天然气)(万立方米)	Coal Gas Supply (Munufactured and Natural Gas) (10 000 cu.m)	88930
#家庭用量	Residential Use	8082
液化石油气供气总量 (吨)	Natural Gas Supply (ton)	700
#家庭用量	Residential Use	580
公共汽(电)车营运车辆数 (辆)	Number of Public Transportation Vehicles (unit)	960
出租汽车数 (辆)	Number of Taxis (unit)	1884
公共汽(电)车客运总量 (万人次)	Number of Passengers Carried by Public Transportation Vehicles (10 000 person-times)	15483
绿地面积 (公顷)	Green Area (ha)	2286
#公园绿地面积	Green Area of Parks	659
建成区绿化覆盖面积 (公顷)	Green Coverage of Completed Areas (ha)	2328

continued

长治市区 Changzhi Urban District	晋城市区 Jincheng Urban District	朔州市区 Shuozhou Urban District	晋中市区 Jinzhong Urban District	运城市区 Yuncheng Urban District	忻州市区 Xinzhou Urban District
28.81	17.00	8.00	20.41	10.00	16.55
8313	3098	2159	5542	2478	2083
5492	1547	981	1815	1643	737
73.28	31.89	29.35	35.32	38.80	24.57
493	367	363	938	378	483
762	584	785	1095	716	641
6569	10988	3938	8458	8865	3269
2119	2995	1436	1531	3651	1446
3772	3540	1300	2560		3700
3650	1350	680	400		3650
450	459	260	390	378	166
1801	1453	1274	1330	1801	713
7384	6177	2676	15281	6800	2632
3162	1806	1400	2460	2104	1160
924	585	511	896	613	384
2771	1915	1553	2889	2420	1344

18-2 续表2 continued

指　　标	Item	临汾市区 Linfen Urban District	吕梁市区 Lvliang Urban District
供水综合生产能力 (万立方米/日)	Daily Production Capacity of Tap Water (10 000 cu.m/day)	9.00	8.00
城市供水总量 (万吨)	Total Volume of City Water Supply (10 000 tons)	2596	1168
#居民生活用水量	Residential Use	1679	749
平均每人生活用水(吨)	Per Capita Consumption of Tap Water for Resiential Use (ton)	27.46	28.21
排水管道长度(公里)	Lenth of Drainage Pipelines (km)	185	306
年末实有城市道路面积 (万平方米)	Actual Area of City Roads at the Year End (10 000 sq.m)	720	360
供气总量 (人工、天然气)(万立方米)	Coal Gas Supply (Munufactured and Natural Gas) (10 000 cu.m)	12191	1890
#家庭用量	Residential Use	2702	1302
液化石油气供气总量 (吨)	Natural Gas Supply (ton)	1333	
#家庭用量	Residential Use	533	
公共汽(电)车营运车辆数 (辆)	Number of Public Transportation Vehicles (unit)	508	170
出租汽车数 (辆)	Number of Taxis (unit)	1862	450
公共汽(电)车客运总量 (万人次)	Number of Passengers Carried by Public Transportation Vehicles (10 000 person-times)	5218	2485
绿地面积 (公顷)	Green Area (ha)		867
#公园绿地面积	Green Area of Parks	783	359
建成区绿化覆盖面积 (公顷)	Green Coverage of Completed Areas (ha)	2222	990

主要统计指标解释

城乡居民生活用电 指市民住宅、集体宿舍、招待所、机关、商店、学校等照明用电。

城市供水总量 指报告期供水企业（单位）供出的全部水量，包括有效供水量和漏损水量，不包括开水直接利用量。

年末实有公共汽（电）车营运车辆数 是指城市公共交通企业可参加营运的全部车辆数。包括技术完好的、在修的、待修的、长期停驶的，以及拟报废尚未经上级主管部门批准报废的运营车辆数。不包括公交企业的油罐车、货车和其他专用车等非运营车，也不包括借入、租入的客运车辆。

全年公共汽（电）车客运总量 指运送乘客的总人数。包括普通票乘客人次，月票乘客人次和包车乘客人次。

供气总量（人工煤气、天然气） 指城市煤气企业向城市生产用户、家庭用户和其他用户供应的全部煤气量，包括外购及损失量。

居民生活用水量 指城市范围内所有居民家庭的日常生活用水。包括城市居民、农民家庭、公共供水站用水。

Explanatory Notes on Main Statistical Indicators

Consumption of Electricity for Residential Use refers to lighting consumption being used in residence, collective dormitory, rest house, department, store and school.

Total Volume of City Water Supply refers to total water volume supplied by waterworks (units) during the reference period. It includes both the effective water supply and loss during water supply, while it doesn't include volume of boil water directly used.

Number of Public Buses (Trolley Buses) Under Operation at Year-end refers to the total number of operational buses available, including the operational vehicles and vehicles in stock. Non-operational vehicles such as tank cars, machine shop cars, trucks and special vehicles and the borrowed passenger vehicles are excluded.

Number of Passengers Carried by Bus (Trolley Bus) in the Year refers to the total person-times of passengers carried by buses and trolley bus, including ordinary tickets passengers, monthly tickets passengers and group passengers.

Volume of (Manufactured and Natural) Gas Supply refers to the total volume of gas sold to city produce users, household users and other users by gas corporations, including volume purchased and loss.

Water Consumption for Residential Use refers to water consumption of total households for daily life in city, including water consumption of urban households, rural households and public water supply stations.

19 地市篇

CITIES AT PREFECTURE LEVEL

19-1 国民经济核算主要指标(2016年)
MAJOR INDICATORS OF NATIONAL ECONOMIC ACCOUNTING(2016)

单位：万元 (10 000 yuan)

市名 City		总产出 Total Output	第一产业 Primary Industry	第二产业 Secondary Industry	#工业 Industry	第三产业 Tertiary Industry	#交通运输、仓储和邮政业 Transportation, Storage and Post	#批发和零售业 Wholesale and Retail Trade
全省	**Total**	**329147500**	**14445000**	**187363800**	**142065200**	**127338700**	**21518100**	**14577300**
太原市	Taiyuan	97762043	729905	58762828	29206255	38269310	3901882	6265519
大同市	Datong	31162694	1081888	15862116	14372243	14218690	4144691	2464470
阳泉市	Yangquan	13411586	200018	7571149	6069090	5640419	1205745	1185395
长治市	Changzhi	29614964	1079925	18382998	15803160	10152041	1354499	1585802
晋城市	Jincheng	21985734	929244	13062489	11138901	7994001	1638768	824603
朔州市	Shuozhou	24667595	1180846	10012333	9453768	13474416	3422154	4638918
晋中市	Jinzhong	26890280	1867126	16319150	12805000	8704004	2288707	1057517
运城市	Yuncheng	32933602	3810456	16427668	14738855	12695478	2144432	2851111
忻州市	Xinzhou	23101152	1148924	11259958	10257266	10692270	1453212	1160775
临汾市	Linfen	35995298	1791712	22661875	19537627	11541712	1854947	2698250
吕梁市	Lvliang	25761791	997936	16486692	15393139	8277163	1247145	805338

市名 City		地区生产总值 Gross Domestic Product	第一产业 Primary Industry	第二产业 Secondary Industry	#工业 Industry	第三产业 Tertiary Industry	#交通运输、仓储和邮政业 Transportation, Storage and Post	#批发和零售业 Wholesale and Retail Trade
全省	**Total**	**129662000**	**7847800**	**49633000**	**40831400**	**72181200**	**9307500**	**10581200**
太原市	Taiyuan	29556045	387731	10674889	7093233	18493425	1525730	3370042
大同市	Datong	10257962	598791	3745947	3023468	5913224	1234423	769235
阳泉市	Yangquan	6228625	103059	2991666	2561432	3133900	444621	489657
长治市	Changzhi	12704767	613589	6469377	5991120	5621801	798394	880938
晋城市	Jincheng	10493406	498569	5543568	5114295	4451270	760837	622846
朔州市	Shuozhou	9180640	562818	3952240	3702600	4665582	883180	776131
晋中市	Jinzhong	10911041	1083479	4686455	3948500	5141107	1071166	796057
运城市	Yuncheng	12222982	2009917	4438494	3527454	5774571	961264	982815
忻州市	Xinzhou	7161357	633000	3159045	2758711	3369312	461958	345336
临汾市	Linfen	12051761	959506	5611125	4870366	5481130	845261	750923
吕梁市	Lvliang	9953079	536696	5552709	5322277	3863674	627041	506028

19-1 续表 continued

单位：万元 (10 000 yuan)

市 名 City	人均地区生产总值(元/人) Per Capita GDP (yuan/person)	资本形成总额 Gross Capital Formation	最终消费 Final Consumption Expenditure	居民总消费水平(元/人) Household Consumption Expenditure (yuan/person)	农村居民 Rural Households	城镇居民 Urban Households
全 省 Total	**35303**	**93717300**	**74547100**	**15065**	**9226**	**19724**
太原市 Taiyuan	68234	15949453	13542170	24660	11257	27123
大同市 Datong	30046	8169097	5169736	11709	6292	15098
阳泉市 Yangquan	44461	4893212	2651936	13357	9419	15361
长治市 Changzhi	37063	8051676	6740336	16231	9833	22433
晋城市 Jincheng	45271	6261178	4742061	16073	9178	20997
朔州市 Shuozhou	51753	5086300	3794317	15396	9953	19994
晋中市 Jinzhong	32646	7091573	6124199	13020	9376	16340
运城市 Yuncheng	23105	9627472	6799637	10892	7584	14639
忻州市 Xinzhou	22747	6707521	3895962	9246	6650	12160
临汾市 Linfen	27102	6680863	6161160	11071	8221	13845
吕梁市 Lvliang	25896	6545343	4827224	9911	6539	13713

19-2 国民经济核算主要指标指数(2016年)

INDICES OF MAJOR INDICATORS OF NATIONAL ECONOMIC ACCOUNTING(2016)

上年=100 (last year=100)

市 名 City	总产出 Total Output	第一产业 Primary Industry	第二产业 Secondary Industry	#工 业 Industry	第三产业 Tertiary Industry	#交通运输、仓储和邮政业 Transportation, Storage and Post	#批发和零售业 Wholesale and Retail Trade
全 省 Total	**103.9**	**103.1**	**101.8**	**100.7**	**107.5**	**109.7**	**102.9**
太原市 Taiyuan	111.9	102.8	114.9	114.6	107.5	110.0	97.6
大同市 Datong	101.5	102.2	99.2	97.8	104.2	99.8	99.0
阳泉市 Yangquan	103.4	103.6	101.4	101.4	106.2	107.9	101.1
长治市 Changzhi	105.2	103.9	104.0	103.7	107.5	109.0	101.7
晋城市 Jincheng	103.3	100.8	101.6	101.9	106.5	111.4	103.0
朔州市 Shuozhou	101.7	103.7	100.4	99.6	102.6	102.8	101.4
晋中市 Jinzhong	105.5	104.9	105.4	105.5	105.7	108.5	102.3
运城市 Yuncheng	103.0	100.3	101.9	102.0	105.2	106.6	100.8
忻州市 Xinzhou	104.8	105.6	103.3	103.2	106.2	110.7	102.1
临汾市 Linfen	103.6	103.9	101.4	100.5	107.8	105.6	103.8
吕梁市 Lvliang	105.1	104.9	104.2	104.3	107.1	109.1	99.6

19-2 续表 continued

上年=100 (last year=100)

市 名 City	地区生产总值 Gross Domestic Product	第一产业 Primary Industry	第二产业 Secondary Industry	#工 业 Industry	第三产业 Tertiary Industry	#交通运输、仓储和邮政业 Transportation, Storage and Post	#批发和零售业 Wholesale and Retail Trade
全 省 Total	**104.5**	**102.8**	**101.5**	**101.1**	**107.0**	**108.7**	**102.0**
太原市 Taiyuan	107.5	103.2	107.3	106.7	107.7	110.0	99.5
大同市 Datong	101.0	103.4	93.6	90.0	106.6	100.0	98.9
阳泉市 Yangquan	103.4	103.5	101.7	102.1	105.1	105.0	99.8
长治市 Changzhi	104.6	103.3	102.7	102.5	106.8	108.6	101.4
晋城市 Jincheng	103.8	100.3	102.4	102.5	106.3	111.4	103.0
朔州市 Shuozhou	104.2	103.1	102.5	102.7	105.8	107.2	101.3
晋中市 Jinzhong	105.1	102.5	104.9	105.0	105.8	108.4	102.4
运城市 Yuncheng	104.0	100.6	102.4	102.2	106.4	109.3	101.1
忻州市 Xinzhou	104.7	105.1	102.8	102.6	106.4	110.0	101.9
临汾市 Linfen	103.4	103.9	100.5	99.7	106.6	102.8	101.9
吕梁市 Lvliang	104.1	104.7	102.5	102.6	106.4	108.8	99.0

市 名 City	资本形成总额 Gross Capital Formation	最终消费 Final Consumption Expenditure	居民总消费水平 Household Consumption Expenditure	农村居民 Rural Households	城镇居民 Urban Households
全 省 Total	**100.6**	**101.3**	**103.7**	**103.7**	**102.5**
太原市 Taiyuan	102.1	108.0	108.0	106.7	108.0
大同市 Datong	103.1	105.0	103.9	104.4	102.8
阳泉市 Yangquan	100.2	106.5	105.4	111.1	103.1
长治市 Changzhi	103.1	105.9	105.8	108.0	103.1
晋城市 Jincheng	99.9	104.8	107.2	114.8	104.1
朔州市 Shuozhou	100.2	106.1	102.3	105.2	101.0
晋中市 Jinzhong	104.0	103.9	104.5	104.5	103.4
运城市 Yuncheng	104.2	102.4	102.7	107.4	98.3
忻州市 Xinzhou	107.2	107.1	106.0	100.8	107.9
临汾市 Linfen	96.4	108.6	112.3	113.8	110.1
吕梁市 Lvliang	101.3	106.0	107.4	106.7	105.9

19-3 基本单位数(2016年)
NUMBER OF BASIC UNITS (2016)

单位：个 (unit)

市名 City		法人单位数 Corporation Units			产业活动单位数 Active Units	
		合计 Total	单产业法人 Single Industry	多产业法人 Multi-industry	合计 Total	#多产业法人所属产业活动单位 Units Belong to Multi-industry Corporation
全省	**Total**	**498902**	**471982**	**26920**	**602197**	**130215**
太原市	Taiyuan	125968	122308	3660	139399	17091
大同市	Datong	28140	26639	1501	35111	8472
阳泉市	Yangquan	16807	15441	1366	21459	6018
长治市	Changzhi	46717	43251	3466	57870	14619
晋城市	Jincheng	35207	32194	3013	43739	11545
朔州市	Shuozhou	25588	24758	830	30023	5265
晋中市	Jinzhong	46552	44334	2218	57868	13534
运城市	Yuncheng	48218	45552	2666	60485	14933
忻州市	Xinzhou	38488	36440	2048	46511	10071
临汾市	Linfen	50007	45541	4466	64187	18646
吕梁市	Lvliang	37210	35524	1686	45545	10021

19-4 按登记注册类型分基本单位数(2016年)
NUMBER OF BASIC UNITS BY REGISTRATION STATUS(2016)

单位：个 (unit)

市名 City		法人单位数 Corporation Units				产业活动单位数 Active Units			
		合计 Total	内资单位 Civil Funded Enterprises	港澳台商投资单位 Enterprises Funded by Hong Kong, Macao and Taiwan	外商投资单位 Foreign Funded Enterprises	合计 Total	内资单位 Civil Funded Enterprises	港澳台商投资单位 Enterprises Funded by Hong Kong, Macao and Taiwan	外商投资单位 Foreign Funded Enterprises
全省	**Total**	**498902**	**498382**	**214**	**306**	**602197**	**600690**	**658**	**849**
太原市	Taiyuan	125968	125808	61	99	139399	138978	174	247
大同市	Datong	28140	28096	18	26	35111	35001	50	60
阳泉市	Yangquan	16807	16784	9	14	21459	21393	31	35
长治市	Changzhi	46717	46674	16	27	57870	57784	38	48
晋城市	Jincheng	35207	35169	13	25	43739	43661	23	55
朔州市	Shuozhou	25588	25573	4	11	30023	30000	8	15
晋中市	Jinzhong	46552	46483	33	36	57868	57726	62	80
运城市	Yuncheng	48218	48180	13	25	60485	60344	63	78
忻州市	Xinzhou	38488	38472	9	7	46511	46446	35	30
临汾市	Linfen	50007	49969	22	16	64187	63913	132	142
吕梁市	Lvliang	37210	37174	16	20	45545	45444	42	59

19-5 按产业分基本单位数及从业人数(2016年)
NUMBER OF BASIC UNITS AND EMPLOYEES BY INDUSTRY(2016)

市名 City	法人单位 Corporation Units							
	单位数(个) Number of Units (unit)	第一产业 Primary Industry	第二产业 Secondary Industry	第三产业 Tertiary Industry	从业人数(人) Employees (person)	第一产业 Primary Industry	第二产业 Secondary Industry	第三产业 Tertiary Industry
全　省 Total	**498902**	**87165**	**62498**	**349239**	**9963653**	**939976**	**3847514**	**5176163**
太原市 Taiyuan	125968	4960	14523	106485	2392863	39031	839136	1514696
大同市 Datong	28140	6401	2965	18774	758810	52283	317623	388904
阳泉市 Yangquan	16807	2608	2479	11720	447176	30898	235093	181185
长治市 Changzhi	46717	11392	4860	30465	867844	109578	351822	406444
晋城市 Jincheng	35207	6274	4021	24912	748623	71348	334683	342592
朔州市 Shuozhou	25588	6497	2402	16689	480422	58003	167020	255399
晋中市 Jinzhong	46552	9331	7418	29803	900125	91467	388016	420642
运城市 Yuncheng	48218	10724	7720	29774	1050610	176385	399787	474438
忻州市 Xinzhou	38488	9308	4668	24512	599213	77336	183343	338534
临汾市 Linfen	50007	11081	6033	32893	893427	120417	304118	468892
吕梁市 Lvliang	37210	8589	5409	23212	824540	113230	326873	384437

市名 City	产业活动单位 Active Units							
	单位数(个) Number of Units (unit)	第一产业 Primary Industry	第二产业 Secondary Industry	第三产业 Tertiary Industry	从业人数(人) Employees (person)	第一产业 Primary Industry	第二产业 Secondary Industry	第三产业 Tertiary Industry
全　省 Total	**602197**	**87465**	**68328**	**446404**	**10725975**	**943486**	**3986956**	**5795533**
太原市 Taiyuan	139399	4983	15916	118500	2609415	39226	907712	1662477
大同市 Datong	35111	6413	3298	25400	800639	52366	273622	474651
阳泉市 Yangquan	21459	2631	2815	16013	528897	31409	281145	216343
长治市 Changzhi	57870	11424	5359	41087	934164	110083	374899	449182
晋城市 Jincheng	43739	6311	4486	32942	795274	71879	334471	388924
朔州市 Shuozhou	30023	6515	2624	20884	506166	58374	175721	272071
晋中市 Jinzhong	57868	9376	8145	40347	975368	91786	405792	477790
运城市 Yuncheng	60485	10749	8126	41610	1100388	176576	413788	510024
忻州市 Xinzhou	46511	9320	5012	32179	646079	77420	197503	371156
临汾市 Linfen	64187	11137	6764	46286	960640	120983	290924	548733
吕梁市 Lvliang	45545	8606	5783	31156	868945	113384	331379	424182

19-6 按行业分法人单位数(2016年)
NUMBER OF CORPORATION UNITS BY SECTOR(2016)

单位：个 (unit)

市名 City	合计 Total	农、林、牧、渔业 Farming, Forestry, Animal Husbandry and Fishery	采矿业 Ming	制造业 Manufacturing	电力、热力、燃气及水生产和供应业 Production and Supply of Electricity, Heat, Gas and Water
全省 Total	**498902**	**94596**	**6965**	**32151**	**3662**
太原市 Taiyuan	125968	5240	538	5309	342
大同市 Datong	28140	6705	388	1517	394
阳泉市 Yangquan	16807	2733	241	1517	172
长治市 Changzhi	46717	12183	627	2412	320
晋城市 Jincheng	35207	6923	426	2080	300
朔州市 Shuozhou	25588	6981	297	1158	225
晋中市 Jinzhong	46552	10115	816	4247	348
运城市 Yuncheng	48218	11867	478	5281	284
忻州市 Xinzhou	38488	10150	1054	2497	392
临汾市 Linfen	50007	12254	1038	2875	591
吕梁市 Lvliang	37210	9445	1062	3258	294

市名 City	建筑业 Construction	批发和零售业 Wholesale and Retail Trade	交通运输、仓储和邮政业 Transport, Storage and Post	住宿和餐饮业 Hotels and Catering Services	信息传输、软件和信息技术服务业 Information Transmission, Software and Information Technology Services
全省 Total	**20372**	**139240**	**11375**	**7109**	**11529**
太原市 Taiyuan	8473	51855	1988	2538	5424
大同市 Datong	756	6441	562	479	318
阳泉市 Yangquan	585	4827	400	226	304
长治市 Changzhi	1562	11842	806	536	526
晋城市 Jincheng	1291	10197	612	414	667
朔州市 Shuozhou	754	6611	712	309	348
晋中市 Jinzhong	2044	10608	1326	636	1116
运城市 Yuncheng	1739	10828	1446	648	858
忻州市 Xinzhou	752	6981	1025	356	470
临汾市 Linfen	1573	11592	1306	625	892
吕梁市 Lvliang	843	7458	1192	342	606

19-6 续表 continued

单位：个 (unit)

市 名 City	金融业 Financial Industry	房地产业 Real Estate	租赁和商务服务业 Lease and Business Affairs Services	科学研究和技术服务业 Scientific Reseach, and Technical Services	水利、环境和公共设施管理业 Water, Environmental Protection and Public Facility Management
全 省 Total	**2883**	**12856**	**36562**	**13141**	**3848**
太原市 Taiyuan	722	4305	15906	5205	709
大同市 Datong	197	652	1518	614	246
阳泉市 Yangquan	120	422	1010	458	138
长治市 Changzhi	166	1143	2247	1053	415
晋城市 Jincheng	211	765	2511	656	406
朔州市 Shuozhou	168	535	1093	499	163
晋中市 Jinzhong	293	1090	2807	1249	383
运城市 Yuncheng	214	1247	2519	1046	371
忻州市 Xinzhou	243	636	1855	717	362
临汾市 Linfen	288	1149	3324	1063	375
吕梁市 Lvliang	261	912	1772	581	280

市 名 City	居民服务、修理和其他服务业 Resident Services, Repair and Other Services	教 育 Education	卫生和社会工作 Health Care and Social Work	文化、体育和娱乐业 Culture, Sports and Recreation	公共管理、社会保障和社会组织 Public Management, Social Security and Social Organization
全 省 Total	**15397**	**11769**	**6400**	**10128**	**58919**
太原市 Taiyuan	7212	2009	1008	2344	4841
大同市 Datong	605	945	538	533	4732
阳泉市 Yangquan	357	387	244	381	2285
长治市 Changzhi	1056	1122	675	1018	7008
晋城市 Jincheng	1209	778	377	885	4499
朔州市 Shuozhou	545	564	335	432	3859
晋中市 Jinzhong	1040	1228	577	1189	5440
运城市 Yuncheng	795	1216	734	1057	5590
忻州市 Xinzhou	579	950	564	692	8213
临汾市 Linfen	1186	1456	838	957	6625
吕梁市 Lvliang	813	1114	510	640	5827

19-7 总户数、常住人口数(2016年)
NUMBER OF HOUSEHOLDS AND RESIDENT POPULATION(2016)

单位：人　　　　　　　　　　　　　　　　　　　　　　　　　　　　　　　　　(person)

市　　名 City		总户数 (户) Number of Households (household)	常住人口 Resident Population	按性别分 by Sex		按城镇乡村分 by Residence	
				男　性 Male	女　性 Famle	城镇人口 Urban	乡村人口 Rural
全　　省	**Total**	**13043537**	**36816393**	**18859609**	**17956784**	**20696309**	**16120084**
太 原 市	Taiyuan	1172286	4344429	2215917	2128512	3673193	671236
大 同 市	Datong	1277668	3421891	1743957	1677934	2121835	1300056
阳 泉 市	Yangquan	537775	1403585	716332	687253	935845	467740
长 治 市	Changzhi	1190620	3435380	1752368	1683012	1770295	1665085
晋 城 市	Jincheng	833256	2320858	1172010	1148848	1354043	966815
朔 州 市	Shuozhou	677666	1768103	915867	852236	958406	809697
晋 中 市	Jinzhong	1307084	3348738	1728275	1620463	1772431	1576307
运 城 市	Yuncheng	1709192	5305178	2709243	2595935	2527808	2777370
忻 州 市	Xinzhou	1327448	3155312	1627835	1527477	1511398	1643914
临 汾 市	Linfen	1532027	4458048	2285317	2172731	2230485	2227563
吕 梁 市	Lvliang	1478515	3854871	1992488	1862383	1840570	2014301

注：本表总户数为公安年报数。

Note: Number of households in the table are obtained from public security department.

19-8 城镇人口增加来源(2016年)
INCREASE SOURCES OF URBAN POPULATION(2016)

单位：人　　　　　　　　　　　　　　　　　　　　　　　　　　　　　　　　　(person)

市　　名 City		合 计 Total	出 生 Birth	城镇人口迁　入 Immigration of Urban Population	农业转移人口落户城镇 Immigration of Rural Population with Urban Residency	退出现役 Out of Commission	港澳台人员和华侨回内地（回国）定居及外国人、无国籍人入籍 Immigration of Hong Kong, Macao, Taiwan Population, Overseas Chinese, Aliens and Stateless Persons	其 他 Others
全　　省	**Total**	**305046**	**173071**	**59294**	**51133**	**2174**	**14**	**19360**
太 原 市	Taiyuan	65907	36593	19222	6826	579	11	2676
大 同 市	Datong	32424	17352	6581	5192	410		2889
阳 泉 市	Yangquan	12396	7463	2381	1972	128		452
长 治 市	Changzhi	23904	14562	2806	5394	206		936
晋 城 市	Jincheng	21073	10618	3100	6690	115		550
朔 州 市	Shuozhou	12029	6474	2917	1752	73		813
晋 中 市	Jinzhong	27718	15578	5494	4818	300	1	1527
运 城 市	Yuncheng	31904	18906	5052	5543	175	1	2227
忻 州 市	Xinzhou	21433	12018	4163	3602	89		1561
临 汾 市	Linfen	29686	16761	4278	5364	65		3218
吕 梁 市	Lvliang	26572	16746	3300	3980	34	1	2511

注：本表为公安年报数。

Note: Data of the table are obtained from public security department.

19-9 非私营单位从业人员(2016年)
NUMBER OF EMPLOYEES IN NON-PRIVATE UNITS(2016)

单位：人 (person)

市 名 City	总 计 Total	#女 性 Female	在岗职工 Fully Employed	其他从业人 员 Others
全 省 Total	**4305525**	**1477117**	**4123482**	**182043**
太 原 市 Taiyuan	1040529	342728	1008794	31735
大 同 市 Datong	402250	126217	380282	21968
阳 泉 市 Yangquan	253662	86565	248050	5612
长 治 市 Changzhi	425665	142819	409061	16604
晋 城 市 Jincheng	355697	117022	342598	13099
朔 州 市 Shuozhou	188946	59500	184051	4895
晋 中 市 Jinzhong	350489	122832	321452	29037
运 城 市 Yuncheng	352202	142787	335385	16817
忻 州 市 Xinzhou	239462	84727	231040	8422
临 汾 市 Linfen	344706	132246	331431	13275
吕 梁 市 Lvliang	351917	119674	331338	20579

19-10 非私营单位从业人员劳动报酬(2016年)
REWARD OF EMPLOYEES IN NON-PRIVATE UNITS(2016)

单位：万元 (10 000 yuan)

市 名 City	从业人员平均人数(人) Average Employees (person)	在岗职工 Fully Employed	其他从业人 员 Others	从业人员劳动报酬 Reward of Employees	在岗职工工资总额 Total Wages of Fully Employed	其他从业人员劳动报酬 Reward of Others	在岗职工平均工资(元) Average Wage of Fully Employed (yuan)
全 省 Total	**4288758**	**4106436**	**182322**	**23032647**	**22575147**	**457500**	**54975**
太 原 市 Taiyuan	1029128	996536	32592	6552044	6459585	92459	64820
大 同 市 Datong	405035	382364	22671	2179233	2120214	59019	55450
阳 泉 市 Yangquan	253379	247845	5534	1206131	1194481	11650	48195
长 治 市 Changzhi	421111	405623	15488	2091674	2058101	33574	50739
晋 城 市 Jincheng	359261	345449	13812	1931415	1899352	32063	54982
朔 州 市 Shuozhou	188544	183604	4940	959112	943304	15808	51377
晋 中 市 Jinzhong	350202	321912	28290	1758932	1691910	67021	52558
运 城 市 Yuncheng	343754	327913	15841	1672593	1624642	47952	49545
忻 州 市 Xinzhou	240006	231296	8710	1114400	1093221	21179	47265
临 汾 市 Linfen	348562	334780	13782	1705209	1673354	31855	49984
吕 梁 市 Lvliang	349776	329114	20662	1861904	1816983	44921	55208

19-11 国有单位从业人员(2016年)
NUMBER OF EMPLOYEES IN STATE-OWNED UNITS(2016)

单位：人 (person)

市名 City	从业人员 Employees	#女性 Female	在岗职工 Fully Employed	其他从业人员 Others
全省 Total	**1998589**	**848224**	**1903284**	**95305**
太原市 Taiyuan	458419	171968	447233	11186
大同市 Datong	170482	67828	154119	16363
阳泉市 Yangquan	86813	39298	84168	2645
长治市 Changzhi	169394	75741	162418	6976
晋城市 Jincheng	106853	46612	101920	4933
朔州市 Shuozhou	96514	37623	94351	2163
晋中市 Jinzhong	169713	75375	154646	15067
运城市 Yuncheng	212340	97227	203390	8950
忻州市 Xinzhou	159679	62958	153923	5756
临汾市 Linfen	199608	93031	193501	6107
吕梁市 Lvliang	168774	80563	153615	15159

19-12 国有单位从业人员劳动报酬(2016年)
REWARD OF EMPLOYEES IN STATE-OWNED UNITS(2016)

单位：万元 (10 000 yuan)

市名 City	从业人员平均人数(人) Average Employees (person)	在岗职工 Fully Employed	其他从业人员 Others	从业人员劳动报酬 Reward of Employees	在岗职工工资总额 Total Wages of Fully Employed	其他从业人员劳动报酬 Reward of Others	在岗职工平均工资(元) Average Wage of Fully Employed (yuan)
全省 Total	**1990495**	**1896231**	**94264**	**11379609**	**11178725**	**200884**	**58952**
太原市 Taiyuan	457763	446368	11395	3458952	3429502	29451	76831
大同市 Datong	169851	153694	16157	892181	852047	40135	55438
阳泉市 Yangquan	87066	84419	2647	468955	464095	4859	54975
长治市 Changzhi	168805	161877	6928	843001	833226	9775	51473
晋城市 Jincheng	106495	101601	4894	592082	581754	10327	57259
朔州市 Shuozhou	96800	94672	2128	451922	446760	5162	47190
晋中市 Jinzhong	168475	154387	14088	879609	852792	26817	55237
运城市 Yuncheng	206898	198257	8641	1081838	1061986	19852	53566
忻州市 Xinzhou	160369	154249	6120	757720	744645	13075	48276
临汾市 Linfen	199318	193221	6097	1034366	1021065	13301	52844
吕梁市 Lvliang	168655	153486	15169	918984	890854	28131	58041

19-13 城镇集体单位从业人员(2016年)

NUMBER OF EMPLOYEES IN URBAN COLLECTIVE-OWNED UNITS(2016)

单位：人 (person)

市 名 City		从业人员 Employees	#女 性 Female	在岗职工 Fully Employed	其他从业人员 Others
全 省	**Total**	**167947**	**71459**	**159179**	**8768**
太原市	Taiyuan	32199	12806	30540	1659
大同市	Datong	16912	9463	16216	696
阳泉市	Yangquan	13283	6800	13032	251
长治市	Changzhi	11816	5462	11023	793
晋城市	Jincheng	11887	5200	11638	249
朔州市	Shuozhou	7314	2215	7127	187
晋中市	Jinzhong	12039	5810	10823	1216
运城市	Yuncheng	14427	6731	13364	1063
忻州市	Xinzhou	15774	5198	14412	1362
临汾市	Linfen	10589	4662	10178	411
吕梁市	Lvliang	21707	7112	20826	881

19-14 集体单位从业人员劳动报酬(2016年)

REWARD OF EMPLOYEES IN COLLECTIVE-OWNED UNITS(2016)

单位：万元 (10 000 yuan)

市 名 City		从业人员平均人数(人) Average Employees (person)	在岗职工 Fully Employed	其他从业人员 Others	从业人员劳动报酬 Reward of Employees	在岗职工工资总额 Total Wages of Fully Employed	其他从业人员劳动报酬 Reward of Others	在岗职工平均工资(元) Average Wage of Fully Employed (yuan)
全 省	**Total**	**168624**	**159906**	**8718**	**751047**	**732277**	**18770**	**45794**
太原市	Taiyuan	32480	30715	1765	134115	129767	4347	42249
大同市	Datong	16923	16202	721	55462	53801	1662	33206
阳泉市	Yangquan	13184	12939	245	49607	49055	552	37912
长治市	Changzhi	11637	10881	756	56178	54822	1356	50383
晋城市	Jincheng	11875	11620	255	58078	57367	711	49369
朔州市	Shuozhou	7462	7313	149	34554	33958	596	46435
晋中市	Jinzhong	12377	11155	1222	62288	60337	1951	54090
运城市	Yuncheng	14363	13275	1088	75133	72386	2747	54528
忻州市	Xinzhou	16167	14928	1239	52253	49625	2628	33243
临汾市	Linfen	10542	10096	446	68582	67573	1008	66931
吕梁市	Lvliang	21614	20782	832	104798	103587	1212	49844

19-15 其他单位从业人员(2016年)
NUMBER OF EMPLOYEES IN OTHER-OWNED UNITS(2016)

单位：人 (person)

市 名 City		从业人员 Employees	#女 性 Female	在岗职工 Fully Employed	其他从业人员 Others
全 省	**Total**	**2138989**	**557434**	**2061019**	**77970**
太 原 市	Taiyuan	549911	157954	531021	18890
大 同 市	Datong	214856	48926	209947	4909
阳 泉 市	Yangquan	153566	40467	150850	2716
长 治 市	Changzhi	244455	61616	235620	8835
晋 城 市	Jincheng	236957	65210	229040	7917
朔 州 市	Shuozhou	85118	19662	82573	2545
晋 中 市	Jinzhong	168737	41647	155983	12754
运 城 市	Yuncheng	125435	38829	118631	6804
忻 州 市	Xinzhou	64009	16571	62705	1304
临 汾 市	Linfen	134509	34553	127752	6757
吕 梁 市	Lvliang	161436	31999	156897	4539

19-16 其他单位从业人员劳动报酬(2016年)
REWARD OF EMPLOYEES IN OTHER-OWNED UNITS(2016)

单位：万元 (10 000 yuan)

市 名 City		从业人员平均人数(人) Average Employees (person)	在岗职工 Fully Employed	其他从业人员 Others	从业人员劳动报酬 Reward of Employmees	在岗职工工资总额 Total Wages of Fully Employed	其他从业人员劳动报酬 Reward of Others	在岗职工平均工资(元) Average Wage of Fully Employed (yuan)
全 省	**Total**	**2129639**	**2050299**	**79340**	**10901991**	**10664144**	**237847**	**52013**
太 原 市	Taiyuan	538885	519453	19432	2958978	2900317	58661	55834
大 同 市	Datong	218261	212468	5793	1231589	1214367	17223	57155
阳 泉 市	Yangquan	153129	150487	2642	687570	681331	6239	45275
长 治 市	Changzhi	240669	232865	7804	1192496	1170053	22443	50246
晋 城 市	Jincheng	240891	232228	8663	1281255	1260231	21025	54267
朔 州 市	Shuozhou	84282	81619	2663	472637	462586	10050	56676
晋 中 市	Jinzhong	169350	156370	12980	817035	778781	38254	49804
运 城 市	Yuncheng	122493	116381	6112	515623	490270	25353	42126
忻 州 市	Xinzhou	63470	62119	1351	304426	298951	5476	48125
临 汾 市	Linfen	138702	131463	7239	602261	584716	17546	44478
吕 梁 市	Lvliang	159507	154846	4661	838121	822543	15579	53120

19-17 私营单位从业人员和劳动报酬(2016年)
NUMBER AND REWARD OF EMPLOYEES IN PRIVATE UNITS(2016)

单位：人 (person)

市 名 City		从业人员 Employees	劳动报酬总额 (万元) Total Reward of Employees (10 000 yuan)	平均劳动报酬 (元) Average Reward of Employees (yuan)
全 省	**Total**	**2168433**	**6600416**	**30501**
太原市	Taiyuan	424351	1473493	34728
大同市	Datong	137476	413344	29000
阳泉市	Yangquan	42724	104508	24300
长治市	Changzhi	233024	636207	28016
晋城市	Jincheng	186715	491768	26181
朔州市	Shuozhou	127020	384046	30713
晋中市	Jinzhong	342292	1005284	29483
运城市	Yuncheng	201294	607239	31248
忻州市	Xinzhou	122479	332245	26250
临汾市	Linfen	142580	441682	31421
吕梁市	Lvliang	208478	710601	33555

19-18 居民家庭生活基本情况(2016年)
BASIC LIVING CONDITIONS OF HOUSEHOLDS(2016)

单位：元 (yuan)

市 名 City		居民人均可支配收入 Per Capita Disposable Income of Households	城镇居民人均可支配收入 Per Capita Disposable Income of Urban Households	城镇居民人均生活消费支出 Per Capita Living Expenditure of Urban Households	农村居民人均可支配收入 Per Capita Disposable Income of Rural Households	农村居民人均生活消费支出 Per Capita Living Expenditure of Rural Households
全 省	**Total**	**19049**	**27352**	**16993**	**10082**	**8029**
太原市	Taiyuan	27169	29632	16775	14591	10929
大同市	Datong	18594	26273	11785	8217	6292
阳泉市	Yangquan	21951	27801	15077	12172	8968
长治市	Changzhi	19117	28094	15724	11863	9025
晋城市	Jincheng	20578	28223	17355	11635	9297
朔州市	Shuozhou	20113	28989	14364	11478	7698
晋中市	Jinzhong	19783	29149	14038	11525	7737
运城市	Yuncheng	16001	25636	11405	9365	7513
忻州市	Xinzhou	14371	24987	12160	7025	6650
临汾市	Linfen	17438	27085	13388	10005	7664
吕梁市	Lvliang	14429	24180	13710	7644	5940

19-19 财政收支情况(2016年)
FINANCIAL REVENUE AND EXPENDITURE(2016)

单位:万元 (10 000 yuan)

市名 City	一般公共预算收入 General Public Budget Revenue	#增值税 Value-added Taxes	#营业税 Operation Taxes	#企业所得税 Enterprises Income Taxes
地区合计 Total	**10546046**	**2391213**	**1007786**	**741134**
太原市 Taiyuan	2826893	593397	326559	282243
大同市 Datong	889263	209776	96530	99868
阳泉市 Yangquan	412776	90442	42571	17883
长治市 Changzhi	985278	246310	71688	59013
晋城市 Jincheng	893229	181295	71431	71589
朔州市 Shuozhou	491229	158091	36094	19076
晋中市 Jinzhong	1008005	201414	92383	52153
运城市 Yuncheng	591100	135693	61405	25768
忻州市 Xinzhou	692427	139605	60589	33644
临汾市 Linfen	859858	159305	89338	38252
吕梁市 Lvliang	895988	275885	59198	41645

市名 City	一般公共预算支出 General Public Budget Expenditure	#一般公共服务 Public Services	#教育 Education	#社会保障和就业 Social Security and Employment
地区合计 Total	**27098641**	**2230497**	**5082209**	**3994178**
太原市 Taiyuan	4240666	283833	703360	532951
大同市 Datong	2858886	209679	542410	394416
阳泉市 Yangquan	957303	90359	205350	133366
长治市 Changzhi	2343437	201957	452597	359335
晋城市 Jincheng	1728079	149242	336436	240737
朔州市 Shuozhou	1276607	120638	240244	176407
晋中市 Jinzhong	2471699	191960	459275	375333
运城市 Yuncheng	2878358	245726	585159	471975
忻州市 Xinzhou	2475508	238560	444686	432544
临汾市 Linfen	3109586	249931	513263	497837
吕梁市 Lvliang	2758512	248612	599429	379277

19-20 金融机构本外币各项存款和贷款余额(2016年)

BALANCE OF DEPOSITS AND LOANS IN FINANCIAL INSTITUTIONS(2016)

单位：亿元 (100 million yuan)

市 名 City	各项存款 Balance of Deposits	#非金融企业存款 Non-financial Enterprises Deposits	#广义政府存款 Broad Government Deposits
全 省 Total	**30869.07**	**7843.18**	**5174.62**
太原市 Taiyuan	11497.49	4138.74	2773.59
大同市 Datong	2638.18	567.86	260.09
阳泉市 Yangquan	1367.99	421.54	125.73
长治市 Changzhi	2122.18	431.21	244.83
晋城市 Jincheng	1961.19	489.52	404.11
朔州市 Shuozhou	1292.95	207.11	170.43
晋中市 Jinzhong	2366.10	527.02	235.33
运城市 Yuncheng	1887.83	232.17	247.52
忻州市 Xinzhou	1785.06	208.04	226.08
临汾市 Linfen	2139.01	357.32	273.12
吕梁市 Lvliang	1811.11	262.65	213.79

市 名 City	各项贷款 Balance of Loans	#非金融企业及机关团体贷款 Loans to Non-financial Enterprises, Government Departments and Orgnizations	#票据融资 Bill Finance
全 省 Total	**20356.50**	**16959.63**	**1544.00**
太原市 Taiyuan	10216.78	8943.84	509.89
大同市 Datong	1225.77	1031.32	188.13
阳泉市 Yangquan	742.64	682.42	36.72
长治市 Changzhi	1196.82	1033.35	137.14
晋城市 Jincheng	1091.82	955.16	77.98
朔州市 Shuozhou	577.33	426.28	74.63
晋中市 Jinzhong	1379.88	1096.59	129.35
运城市 Yuncheng	1013.05	660.87	59.24
忻州市 Xinzhou	777.35	552.57	26.30
临汾市 Linfen	1184.16	861.22	149.69
吕梁市 Lvliang	950.92	716.00	154.94

19–21 原保险保费收入(2016年)
PREMIUM OF PRIMARY INSURANCE(2016)

单位：万元 (10 000 yuan)

市名 City		合计 Total	财产险 Property Insurance	意外险 Accident Insurance	健康险 Health Insurace	寿险 Life Insurance
全省	**Total**	**7005480**	**1741487**	**111710**	**598997**	**4553287**
本级	Provincial	761	58	20	82	602
太原市	Taiyuan	2201660	492807	43595	156754	1508504
大同市	Datong	561491	179868	6790	52977	321856
阳泉市	Yangquan	283842	68096	3526	21876	190344
长治市	Changzhi	505838	139581	6439	60148	299669
晋城市	Jincheng	382400	114420	5260	31630	231090
朔州市	Shuozhou	184141	64765	3438	12436	103502
晋中市	Jinzhong	582857	140273	7317	38745	396521
运城市	Yuncheng	778605	192000	13459	73354	499792
忻州市	Xinzhou	369279	98286	5493	22381	243119
临汾市	Linfen	664739	144770	9488	67162	443320
吕梁市	Lvliang	489867	106562	6884	61453	314967

19–22 单位地区生产总值能源消耗(等价值)情况
ENERGY CONSUMPTION PER UNIT OF GDP(EQUIVALENT VALUE)

单位：吨标准煤/万元 (ton of SCE/10 000 yuan)

市名 City		2013	2014	2015	2016	2016年比上年增长(%) Increase by Percent over Last Year(%)
全省	**Total**	**1.58**	**1.52**	**1.44**	**1.45**	**–4.22**
太原市	Taiyuan	1.08	1.05	0.99	0.91	–5.42
大同市	Datong	1.53	1.48	1.40	1.39	–3.54
阳泉市	Yangquan	1.54	1.45	1.42	1.36	–3.23
长治市	Changzhi	1.74	1.68	1.62	1.69	–3.61
晋城市	Jincheng	1.30	1.26	1.35	1.40	–1.45
朔州市	Shuozhou	1.93	1.86	1.76	1.77	–5.52
晋中市	Jinzhong	1.60	1.54	1.49	1.54	–3.35
运城市	Yuncheng	2.01	1.89	1.81	1.80	–3.22
忻州市	Xinzhou	1.43	1.36	1.30	1.24	–4.33
临汾市	Linfen	2.43	2.31	2.19	2.29	–5.34
吕梁市	Lvliang	1.72	1.67	1.61	1.78	–3.21

注：本表2016年数据为2015年不变价；2016年以前数据为2010年不变价。

Note：Data of 2016 are calculated at the price base year of 2015, and data before 2016 are calculated at the price base year of 2010.

19-23 固定资产投资主要指标(2016年)
MAJOR INDICATORS OF INVESTMENT IN FIXED ASSETS(2016)

单位：万元 (10 000 yuan)

市名 City		施工项目(个) Projects Under Construction(unit)	#本年新开工 Newly Started This Year	本年投产项目(个) Number of Projects Completed and Put into Use This Year(unit)	本年新增固定资产 Newly Increased Fixed Assets This Year
全　省	**Total**	**23321**	**19717**	**18687**	**96652686**
太原市	Taiyuan	1244	686	582	8444594
大同市	Datong	2330	2069	2104	9081295
阳泉市	Yangquan	817	717	634	3133212
长治市	Changzhi	2369	2096	1997	10396017
晋城市	Jincheng	2797	2528	2446	9799299
朔州市	Shuozhou	1390	1245	1286	5273749
晋中市	Jinzhong	2442	2024	1901	8228492
运城市	Yuncheng	2732	2462	2210	12067160
忻州市	Xinzhou	2437	1958	1291	9408535
临汾市	Linfen	3293	2951	3003	12660990
吕梁市	Lvliang	1460	979	1233	8159138

市名 City		本年完成投资 Investment Completed This Year	#住宅 Residential Buildings	建筑工程 Construction Projects	安装工程 Installation Projects
全　省	**Total**	**139463510**	**16654993**	**91168968**	**13052403**
太原市	Taiyuan	20277123	5131343	11667247	2169890
大同市	Datong	12128208	1193083	7384826	2093490
阳泉市	Yangquan	6171379	613190	3738651	1033824
长治市	Changzhi	15144247	2531607	10966220	560359
晋城市	Jincheng	11503657	1480225	8574360	472321
朔州市	Shuozhou	6376804	248175	3386964	691057
晋中市	Jinzhong	13758360	1308767	9279871	1281743
运城市	Yuncheng	14837212	1059218	8597932	1963132
忻州市	Xinzhou	11676598	425903	9329030	567970
临汾市	Linfen	13942534	1215330	10348596	738383
吕梁市	Lvliang	11184608	1448152	6428726	1417209

19-23 续表 continued

单位：万元 (10 000 yuan)

市名 City		设备工器具购置 Purchase of Equipment and Instruments	其他 Others	新建 New Construction	扩建 Expansion	改建和技术改造 Recons-truction	其他 Others
全 省	**Total**	**21169672**	**14072467**	**89574546**	**15778096**	**11811368**	**6325968**
太原市	Taiyuan	1834845	4605141	10418525	899070	1404821	735690
大同市	Datong	1978909	670983	7855683	1331397	911704	352131
阳泉市	Yangquan	954048	444856	4892766	243284	354877	40671
长治市	Changzhi	2503327	1114341	10421088	1072802	819617	2152778
晋城市	Jincheng	1542310	914666	9367871	838692	321626	171820
朔州市	Shuozhou	1270107	1028676	5225623	391277	283778	195396
晋中市	Jinzhong	1581422	1615324	8975443	1505108	1222676	264772
运城市	Yuncheng	3527639	748509	11133124	1568835	800964	171175
忻州市	Xinzhou	1262007	517591	9840304	890555	443333	61448
临汾市	Linfen	1891964	963591	3741971	5022840	3264130	938253
吕梁市	Lvliang	2443390	895283	5239368	2014236	1983842	1241834

注：本表新建项目投资中不含房地产投资。
Note: New construction investment in this table does not include real estate investment.

19-24 固定资产投资房屋面积(2016年)
FLOOR SPACE OF BUILDINGS UNDER INVESTMENT IN FIXED ASSETS(2016)

单位：平方米 (sq.m)

市名 City		本年施工房屋面积 Floor Space of Buildings under Construction	#住宅 Residential Buildings	本年竣工房屋面积 Floor Space of Buildings Completed	#住宅 Residential Buildings
全 省	**Total**	**255578277**	**153429277**	**64967204**	**35798090**
太原市	Taiyuan	68054048	43374235	6380083	4930797
大同市	Datong	21363638	10684105	6451617	2170323
阳泉市	Yangquan	7209852	5575138	1065150	940250
长治市	Changzhi	30849222	21509669	11856737	7804765
晋城市	Jincheng	16973315	9967086	7611045	3450028
朔州市	Shuozhou	8228605	5637546	3222747	2393891
晋中市	Jinzhong	19397807	12025847	2653850	1675925
运城市	Yuncheng	29367485	14088442	7882023	2933293
忻州市	Xinzhou	14585200	8285398	3089738	1688147
临汾市	Linfen	21594148	10980614	9328985	3476151
吕梁市	Lvliang	17954957	11301197	5425229	4334520

19-25 海关进出口情况
IMPORTS AND EXPORTS OF CUSTOMS

单位：万元 (10 000 yuan)

市名 City	2015			2016		
	进出口总额 Total	出口总额 Exports	进口总额 Imports	进出口总额 Total	出口总额 Exports	进口总额 Imports
全省 Total	**9139905**	**5233393**	**3906512**	**10989659**	**6553289**	**4436370**
太原市 Taiyuan	6635169	4097887	2537282	8793832	5497053	3296779
大同市 Datong	257635	176920	80715	236305	194221	42084
阳泉市 Yangquan	127202	94235	32967	85893	64454	21439
长治市 Changzhi	97634	20097	77536	51212	18747	32465
晋城市 Jincheng	557080	179823	377256	395070	108788	286282
朔州市 Shuozhou	36488	18984	17504	52736	24618	28118
晋中市 Jinzhong	128360	120073	8286	138825	119713	19112
运城市 Yuncheng	740945	205089	535856	800872	214461	586411
忻州市 Xinzhou	120941	118320	2622	120434	119221	1213
临汾市 Linfen	187139	103096	84043	123956	87446	36510
吕梁市 Lvliang	251312	98869	152443	190524	104567	85957

19-26 利用外商直接投资额
UTILIZATION OF FOREIGN DIRECT INVESTMENT

单位：万美元 (USD 10 000)

市名 City	2015		2016	
	合同金额 Contract Value	实际使用金额 Actual Value	合同金额 Contract Value	实际使用金额 Actual Value
全省 Total	**98210**	**286985**	**83030**	**233242**
太原市 Taiyuan	2612	85067	28233	46214
大同市 Datong	17330	26461	10689	20110
阳泉市 Yangquan	55	30500	10740	31546
长治市 Changzhi	39457	45118	3147	47502
晋城市 Jincheng	374	25657	350	18000
朔州市 Shuozhou	5646	15420	4500	9833
晋中市 Jinzhong	28153	37077	2049	37870
运城市 Yuncheng	963	1745	2904	2229
忻州市 Xinzhou	61	4280		3321
临汾市 Linfen	817	15660	18226	16616
吕梁市 Lvliang	2742		2192	

19-27 乡村基本情况(2016年)
BASIC CONDITIONS OF RURAL AREAS (2016)

市名 City		乡镇政府(个) Number of Township and Town Governments (unit)	#镇政府 Number of Town Governments	村民委员会(个) Number of Villager's Committees (unit)	乡村户数(户) Number of Rural Households (household)	乡村人口(人) Rural Population (person)
全省	**Total**	**1196**	**564**	**28097**	**8329752**	**24219418**
太原市	Taiyuan	52	21	925	369886	1034676
大同市	Datong	99	33	1969	659576	1675198
阳泉市	Yangquan	32	20	960	300092	714465
长治市	Changzhi	132	68	3443	814006	2455272
晋城市	Jincheng	74	48	2248	596162	1622471
朔州市	Shuozhou	69	19	1624	392078	1042514
晋中市	Jinzhong	118	59	2740	935990	2409044
运城市	Yuncheng	136	81	3197	1228530	4316544
忻州市	Xinzhou	185	59	4890	945417	2424410
临汾市	Linfen	151	75	2968	993761	3365128
吕梁市	Lvliang	148	81	3133	1094254	3159696

市名 City		乡村从业人员(人) Number of Rural Laborers (person)	农、林、牧、渔业 Farming, Forestry, Animal Husbandry and Fishery	工业 Industry	建筑业 Construction	其他行业 Others
全省	**Total**	**11605637**	**6626240**	**1437569**	**952178**	**2589650**
太原市	Taiyuan	487422	237033	73755	26010	150624
大同市	Datong	739624	422996	56393	62737	197498
阳泉市	Yangquan	327819	146285	66550	19767	95217
长治市	Changzhi	1187092	665779	167477	114124	239712
晋城市	Jincheng	822211	433765	133943	70858	183645
朔州市	Shuozhou	484399	327149	37346	27704	92200
晋中市	Jinzhong	1171377	623090	191857	98458	257972
运城市	Yuncheng	2251680	1408262	252145	154335	436938
忻州市	Xinzhou	1105713	690485	83419	109932	221877
临汾市	Linfen	1610432	880745	191823	143543	394321
吕梁市	Lvliang	1417868	790651	182861	124710	319646

19-28 农林牧渔业总产值(2016年)
GROSS OUTPUT VALUE OF FARMING, FORESTRY, ANIMAL HUSBANDRY AND FISHERY(2016)

按当年价格计算 (at current price)

市名 City		农林牧渔业总产值(万元) Total (10 000 yuan)	农业 Farming	林业 Forestry	牧业 Animal Husbandry	渔业 Fishery	农林牧渔服务业 Farming, Forestry, Animal Husbandry and Fishery Service
全省	**Total**	**15340250**	**9581137**	**1003129**	**3761654**	**99131**	**895200**
太原市	Taiyuan	767905	438166	74208	214411	3120	38000
大同市	Datong	1115793	460336	45201	575367	983	33905
阳泉市	Yangquan	204968	102310	17928	78318	1461	4950
长治市	Changzhi	1124347	688013	46481	339881	5550	44422
晋城市	Jinchen	949614	362096	38326	523750	5073	20369
朔州市	Shuozhou	1212844	532981	86250	559430	2187	31997
晋中市	Jinzhong	1906301	1184934	60936	617162	4094	39175
运城市	Yuncheng	4090456	3071746	62504	647511	28695	280000
忻州市	Xinzhou	1184424	545285	91642	507784	4213	35500
临汾市	Linfen	1830059	1231678	88482	457212	14341	38347
吕梁市	Lvliang	1016936	494318	56136	443988	3494	19000

19-29 农林牧渔业中间消耗(2016年)
INTERMEDIATE CONSUMPTION OF FARMING, FORESTRY, ANIMAL HUSBANDRY AND FISHERY(2016)

按当年价格计算 (at current price)

市名 City		农林牧渔业中间消耗(万元) Total (10 000 yuan)	农业 Farming	林业 Forestry	牧业 Animal Husbandry	渔业 Fishery	农林牧渔服务业 Farming, Forestry, Animal Husbandry and Fishery Service
全省	**Total**	**7066939**	**4131468**	**571310**	**1849663**	**44686**	**469811**
太原市	Taiyuan	362833	169500	37000	134220	1454	20659
大同市	Datong	501158	203605	24581	254439	472	18061
阳泉市	Yangquan	99517	48781	10048	37388	742	2558
长治市	Changzhi	487640	263705	23270	176510	2852	21303
晋城市	Jinchen	441267	153485	19181	255687	2323	10592
朔州市	Shuozhou	633153	268362	47878	300458	1332	15124
晋中市	Jinzhong	803572	392560	35971	353376	1741	19925
运城市	Yuncheng	1934559	1400146	37272	346691	16430	134020
忻州市	Xinzhou	531361	254832	47313	211692	1748	15775
临汾市	Linfen	851868	567074	44107	214243	6782	19662
吕梁市	Lvliang	470300	212197	26114	221352	1578	9060

19-30 粮食播种面积
SOWN AREAS OF GRAIN

单位：公顷 (ha)

市名 City		粮食 Grain 2015	粮食 Grain 2016	#小麦 Wheat 2015	#小麦 Wheat 2016	#玉米 Corn 2015	#玉米 Corn 2016
全省	**Total**	**3287190**	**3241420**	**675090**	**672940**	**1676860**	**1624750**
太原市	Taiyuan	75571	73435	114	81	52010	51478
大同市	Datong	280090	277128			161756	157650
阳泉市	Yangquan	55809	54077			47610	46096
长治市	Changzhi	246310	242852	7410	5530	207424	205520
晋城市	Jincheng	178140	169024	46714	43158	88296	88284
朔州市	Shuozhou	268092	265202		15	159720	154348
晋中市	Jinzhong	262474	256779	7863	6084	217341	215201
运城市	Yuncheng	642757	622079	327763	312551	286179	279725
忻州市	Xinzhou	430997	423511	97	119	238930	233573
临汾市	Linfen	517020	512529	219493	209843	253358	258337
吕梁市	Lvliang	354734	351429	2174	1728	179437	177287

19-31 油料和棉花播种面积
SOWN AREAS OF OIL-BEARING CROPS AND COTTON

单位：公顷 (ha)

市名 City		油料 Oil-bearing Crops 2015	油料 Oil-bearing Crops 2016	#葵花籽 Sunflower Seeds 2015	#葵花籽 Sunflower Seeds 2016	棉花 Cotton 2015	棉花 Cotton 2016
全省	**Total**	**121190**	**114701**	**28516**	**32695**	**10617**	**7054**
太原市	Taiyuan	2312	1778	820	650	8	5
大同市	Datong	16115	16934	5264	5753		
阳泉市	Yangquan	81	93	57	64		
长治市	Changzhi	1989	2636	366	320	37	27
晋城市	Jincheng	2055	2135	609	579	143	131
朔州市	Shuozhou	25744	26413	2800	3826		
晋中市	Jinzhong	2108	1829	567	523	54	22
运城市	Yuncheng	9176	11922	4130	6223	10039	6618
忻州市	Xinzhou	24325	24075	4090	5027		
临汾市	Linfen	6616	6477	3259	3550	253	196
吕梁市	Lvliang	23900	20409	6557	6181	85	56

19-32 粮食产量
OUTPUT OF GRAIN

单位：吨 (ton)

市 名 City		粮 食 Grain		#小 麦 Wheat		#玉 米 Corn	
		2015	2016	2015	2016	2015	2016
全 省	**Total**	**12595700**	**13185100**	**2714300**	**2734100**	**8627400**	**8888900**
太原市	Taiyuan	299327	312869	669	476	260059	270572
大同市	Datong	1034978	1126558			842817	904861
阳泉市	Yangquan	249284	259175			230902	238675
长治市	Changzhi	1569961	1617128	34050	26329	1437227	1489520
晋城市	Jincheng	962290	900509	229971	184658	629147	624094
朔州市	Shuozhou	1099692	1270288		73	949147	1076823
晋中市	Jinzhong	1757848	1844217	35050	26364	1607828	1706290
运城市	Yuncheng	3212371	3214711	1573410	1540588	1557335	1586138
忻州市	Xinzhou	1502741	1766844	431	666	1198107	1347083
临汾市	Linfen	2361708	2679013	1071812	1028510	1222465	1550837
吕梁市	Lvliang	723770	1115804	8040	5440	570751	862342

19-33 油料和棉花产量
OUTPUT OF OIL-BEARING CROPS AND COTTON

单位：吨 (ton)

市 名 City		油 料 Oil-bearing Crops		#葵花籽 Sunflower Seeds		棉 花 Cotton	
		2015	2016	2015	2016	2015	2016
全 省	**Total**	**153043**	**154346**	**41192**	**54104**	**14489**	**10324**
太原市	Taiyuan	2995	2375	1295	1033	14	8
大同市	Datong	17268	20171	7580	7694		
阳泉市	Yangquan	150	209	119	132		
长治市	Changzhi	2009	2343	741	651	21	16
晋城市	Jincheng	4494	3932	1507	1173	133	106
朔州市	Shuozhou	24861	29607	4815	7208		
晋中市	Jinzhong	4071	3805	882	883	60	21
运城市	Yuncheng	19660	26138	9606	15042	14089	9997
忻州市	Xinzhou	24673	32281	4885	8161		
临汾市	Linfen	9285	10818	5170	6389	153	155
吕梁市	Lvliang	18636	22668	4593	5739	19	21

19-34 水果、林业及渔业生产情况(2016年)
OUTPUT OF FRUITS, FORESTRY AND FISHERY(2016)

市名 City		全年水果产量(吨) Annual Output of Fruits (ton)	#苹果 Apples	年末果园面积(公顷) Area of Orchards (ha)
全省	**Total**	**7539010**	**4286152**	**355822**
太原市	Taiyuan	90757	14778	9211
大同市	Datong	55832	7186	6522
阳泉市	Yangquan	13206	8593	1735
长治市	Changzhi	40187	20619	3962
晋城市	Jincheng	57759	22118	3829
朔州市	Shuozhou	6481	1355	2312
晋中市	Jinzhong	498189	223725	30535
运城市	Yuncheng	5601987	3293735	170573
忻州市	Xinzhou	120012	21968	17794
临汾市	Linfen	831693	658291	54282
吕梁市	Lvliang	222906	13785	55065

市名 City		当年造林面积(公顷) Afforestation Area (ha)	全年水产品总产量(吨) Annual Aquatic Products (ton)	淡水养殖面积(公顷) Fishery Breeding Area (ha)
全省	**Total**	**266694**	**52279**	**15937**
太原市	Taiyuan	10293	2600	1227
大同市	Datong	21667	1080	1139
阳泉市	Yangquan	3095	621	54
长治市	Changzhi	10552	3700	2490
晋城市	Jincheng	1773	1794	381
朔州市	Shuozhou	11621	851	452
晋中市	Jinzhong	10023	3432	1542
运城市	Yuncheng	13126	24734	3030
忻州市	Xinzhou	47047	2967	1132
临汾市	Linfen	30521	7339	1049
吕梁市	Lvliang	38227	1792	1233

注：本表造林面积不包括省属九大林局数据；渔业数据不包括省属水库的数据。

Note: Coverage of afforestation area in this table doesn't include nine provincal forestry administration data. Fishery data doesn't include data of provincial reservoirs.

19-35 畜牧业生产情况(2016年)

NUMBER OF LIVESTOCK AND LIVESTOCK PRODUCTS(2016)

市名 City		大牲畜年末存栏(头) Large Animals (head)	#牛 Cattle	猪年末存栏(头) Hogs (head)	羊年末存栏(只) Sheep and Goats (head)	禽年末存栏(只) Poultry (heads)
全省	**Total**	**1255027**	**1065452**	**4496784**	**9104066**	**93774851**
太原市	Taiyuan	45866	41303	277720	468930	3652860
大同市	Datong	246327	179163	605540	2016028	4614122
阳泉市	Yangquan	9747	7825	139252	137551	2406269
长治市	Changzhi	65128	52054	603767	835220	14160239
晋城市	Jincheng	16383	16207	1029642	669534	9630924
朔州市	Shuozhou	212039	182958	228244	1762646	2339488
晋中市	Jinzhong	121460	115446	1055151	1220949	19732397
运城市	Yuncheng	48014	47316	1076868	902055	27673492
忻州市	Xinzhou	175130	125720	429710	3300156	5607649
临汾市	Linfen	77105	72102	858257	1044209	12395672
吕梁市	Lvliang	192910	180440	508570	999216	15955437

市名 City		肉类总产量(吨) Output of Meat (ton)	#猪肉 Pork	#牛肉 Beef	#羊肉 Mutton	#禽肉 Poultry
全省	**Total**	**844269**	**575239**	**59165**	**74289**	**124552**
太原市	Taiyuan	56441	38001	2307	7831	8116
大同市	Datong	145436	95923	11756	28659	6624
阳泉市	Yangquan	20221	15157	231	1034	3735
长治市	Changzhi	112213	76796	3793	7226	23372
晋城市	Jincheng	165945	139693	1477	6246	18013
朔州市	Shuozhou	90996	25462	8019	54935	1886
晋中市	Jinzhong	211688	117180	17799	18042	57704
运城市	Yuncheng	177201	120434	3270	10126	42346
忻州市	Xinzhou	122424	59187	8134	46812	6654
临汾市	Linfen	141004	103131	5398	8908	21291
吕梁市	Lvliang	167748	58697	16313	12375	80200

19-35 续表 continued

市名 City		奶类总产量(吨) Output of Milk (ton)	#牛奶 Cow Milk	羊毛总产量(吨) Output of Wool (ton)	禽蛋产量(吨) Output of Poultry Eggs (ton)
全省	**Total**	**958782**	**950883**	**10617**	**892312**
太原市	Taiyuan	111640	111416	422	30929
大同市	Datong	248163	247260	1554	57650
阳泉市	Yangquan	6834	6834	63	33618
长治市	Changzhi	17700	17605	987	138073
晋城市	Jincheng	564	564	844	83255
朔州市	Shuozhou	496121	496121	1894	25655
晋中市	Jinzhong	144116	143261	1055	161100
运城市	Yuncheng	49816	49816	869	263537
忻州市	Xinzhou	58914	58913	1796	78876
临汾市	Linfen	44444	38704	670	125234
吕梁市	Lvliang	28083	28003	464	95316

19-36 农业生产条件(2016年)
CONDITIONS OF AGRICULTURAL PRODUCTION(2016)

市名 City		灌溉机电井(眼) Electromechanical Well for Irrigation (unit)	农村用电量(万千瓦小时) Electricity Consumption in Rural Areas (10 000 kwh)	农用化肥施用量(折纯量,吨) Agricultural Consumption of Chemical Fertilizers (ton)
全省	**Total**	**92663**	**975220**	**1170719**
太原市	Taiyuan	2758	54200	28719
大同市	Datong	8913	35946	81252
阳泉市	Yangquan	134	58732	14452
长治市	Changzhi	9400	82114	125375
晋城市	Jincheng	571	75165	65152
朔州市	Shuozhou	8475	28416	77604
晋中市	Jinzhong	8658	144308	102697
运城市	Yuncheng	25784	249496	287118
忻州市	Xinzhou	8054	60440	131948
临汾市	Linfen	13737	92397	176417
吕梁市	Lvliang	6179	94004	79986

19-37 规模以上主要工业产品产量(2016年)
OUTPUT OF MAJOR INDUSTRIAL PRODUCTS OF ENTERPRISES ABOVE DESIGNATED SIZE(2016)

市 名 City		原 煤 (万吨) Coal (10 000 tons)	发电量 (亿千瓦小时) Electricity (100 million kwh)	粗 钢 (万吨) Crude Steel (10 000 tons)	钢 材 (万吨) Steel Products (10 000 tons)	生 铁 (万吨) Pig Iron (10 000 tons)	焦 炭 (万吨) Coke (10 000 tons)
全 省	**Total**	**81641.5**	**2498.7**	**3936.1**	**4279.0**	**3641.1**	**8186.0**
太原市	Taiyuan	2858.2	279.2	1106.2	1048.8	771.7	1069.2
大同市	Datong	9560.1	361.0	15.3		16.9	11.4
阳泉市	Yangquan	5110.3	98.3				69.3
长治市	Changzhi	10854.3	271.6	523.1	495.3	339.3	1378.2
晋城市	Jincheng	8749.1	226.3	357.8	354.2	416.9	33.2
朔州市	Shuozhou	15201.1	267.5				
晋中市	Jinzhong	7503.6	200.2	165.8	257.6	174.0	1108.6
运城市	Yuncheng	740.3	160.7	500.0	608.2	517.4	880.4
忻州市	Xinzhou	5175.3	283.6	52.8	45.0	59.8	205.5
临汾市	Linfen	5435.3	195.0	931.9	1199.7	946.9	1688.2
吕梁市	Lvliang	10453.9	155.2	283.3	270.1	398.1	1741.9

市 名 City		水 泥 (万吨) Cement (10 000 tons)	平板玻璃 (万重量箱) Plate Glass (10 000-weightcases)	硫 酸 (万吨) Sulfuric Acid (10 000 tons)	化学肥料 (万吨) Chemical Fertilizer (10 000 tons)	工业锅炉 (蒸发量吨) Industrial Boiler (Evaporate Capacity tons)	变压器 (万千伏安) Transformer (10 000 kva)
全 省	**Total**	**3595.4**	**1648.1**	**53.6**	**437.5**	**16430**	**654.8**
太原市	Taiyuan	492.7					
大同市	Datong	501.7					221.9
阳泉市	Yangquan	251.9				113	31.2
长治市	Changzhi	385.9	709.6		34.7		
晋城市	Jincheng	193.3			259.5		
朔州市	Shuozhou	218.1			1.6		
晋中市	Jinzhong	220.9			25.7		
运城市	Yuncheng	484.3		41.4	70.3		401.7
忻州市	Xinzhou	150.7			23.7	16317	0.1
临汾市	Linfen	281.7		12.2	9.3		
吕梁市	Lvliang	414.2	938.5		12.7		

19-37 续表 continued

市名 City	泵(台) Pump (unit)	纱(吨) Yarn (ton)	布(万米) Cloth (10 000 m)	白酒(千升) Alcoholic Drink (kiloliter)	啤酒(千升) Beer (kiloliter)	机制纸及纸板(外购原纸加工除外)(吨) Machine-made Paper and Paperboard (ton)
全省 Total	**92547**	**53769.4**	**4175.9**	**103238.5**	**339597.0**	**416694**
太原市 Taiyuan		3911.2		7319.0	100589.0	25697
大同市 Datong					29958.2	
阳泉市 Yangquan	418					
长治市 Changzhi	1943			880.0		16200
晋城市 Jincheng		4438.0	892.0			
朔州市 Shuozhou				7011.0	34518.0	
晋中市 Jinzhong	15818	1560.6		6467.0	99482.0	341815
运城市 Yuncheng	74368	42333.4	2543.0		75049.8	29212
忻州市 Xinzhou						3770
临汾市 Linfen		1526.3	740.9			
吕梁市 Lvliang				81561.5		

市名 City	煤层气(亿立方米) Coalbed Methane (100 million cu.m)	手机(万台) Mobile Phones (10 000 units)	化学药品原药(吨) Chemical Medicine (ton)	醋(吨) Vinegar (ton)	太阳能电池(千瓦) Solar Cell (kw)	新能源汽车(辆) New Energy Motor Vehicles (set)
全省 Total	**432209**	**2693.4**	**27733.9**	**626955.3**	**1441692**	**12292**
太原市 Taiyuan	4711	2693.4	464.0	463853.0		
大同市 Datong			25417.8			
阳泉市 Yangquan	98168					
长治市 Changzhi			0.3	4804.0	731853	3742
晋城市 Jincheng	324682			9900.0	52222	
朔州市 Shuozhou			1372.7			2797
晋中市 Jinzhong	4647			113922.2		
运城市 Yuncheng			479.1			5753
忻州市 Xinzhou						
临汾市 Linfen						
吕梁市 Lvliang				34476.0	657617	

19-38 工业企业主要经济指标(2016年)

MAIN ECONOMIC INDICATORS OF INDUSTRIAL ENTERPRISES(2016)

单位：亿元　　(100 million yuan)

市 名 City	单位数(个) Number of Enterprises (unit)	#亏损企业 Loss-making Enterprises	工业销售产值 Industrial Sales Output Value	出口交货值 Value of Export Delivery	资产总计 Total Assets
全 省 Total	**3548**	**1234**	**12757.28**	**921.76**	**33621.95**
省直报 Direct Report	2		768.17		839.88
太原市 Taiyuan	355	113	2211.22	658.25	4887.85
大同市 Datong	168	57	668.70	14.85	2664.08
阳泉市 Yangquan	122	55	490.70	1.98	2546.62
长治市 Changzhi	316	110	1445.84	0.68	3290.57
晋城市 Jincheng	241	96	824.33	53.18	3315.64
朔州市 Shuozhou	232	65	715.26	1.36	2290.11
晋中市 Jinzhong	517	224	1124.74	15.57	2885.98
运城市 Yuncheng	454	120	1298.55	19.46	2210.34
忻州市 Xinzhou	339	95	597.44	10.45	1606.06
临汾市 Linfen	354	125	1240.95	137.38	2690.13
吕梁市 Lvliang	448	174	1371.38	8.60	4394.69

市 名 City	流动资产合计 Total Circul-ating Funds	固定资产合计 Total Fixed Assets	固定资产原价 Original Value of Fixed Assets	累计折旧 Total Depreciation	流动负债 Liquid Liabilites
全 省 Total	**13290.44**	**12901.36**	**18364.43**	**7360.03**	**17901.16**
省直报 Direct Report	57.01	749.56	1255.08	586.85	357.02
太原市 Taiyuan	2099.84	1631.66	2811.78	1231.22	2605.05
大同市 Datong	1039.27	1483.68	1323.38	567.93	1072.87
阳泉市 Yangquan	1391.55	542.88	898.89	398.33	1272.37
长治市 Changzhi	1438.23	1300.15	1723.18	723.21	1813.06
晋城市 Jincheng	1337.85	974.05	1559.50	719.06	1707.41
朔州市 Shuozhou	631.36	1075.66	1591.42	552.81	1011.80
晋中市 Jinzhong	1074.50	1098.38	1428.63	457.92	1942.00
运城市 Yuncheng	990.53	830.30	1327.18	548.77	1212.34
忻州市 Xinzhou	523.60	745.09	994.07	336.16	798.24
临汾市 Linfen	1024.36	950.03	1378.96	521.94	1574.11
吕梁市 Lvliang	1682.35	1519.90	2072.38	715.83	2534.90

19-38 续表1 continued

单位：亿元 (100 million yuan)

市 名 City	负债合计 Total Liabilities	年末所有者权益 Creditors' Equity at Year-end	主营业务收入 Revenue of Major Business	主营业务成本 Costs of Major Business	主营业务税金及附加 Tax and Extra Charges of Major Business
全 省 Total	**25579.36**	**8041.22**	**14226.45**	**11915.83**	**236.99**
省直报 Direct Report	561.46	278.43	834.23	730.97	1.45
太原市 Taiyuan	3660.38	1224.04	2346.11	2040.36	36.46
大同市 Datong	2166.21	497.87	1782.83	1559.75	5.16
阳泉市 Yangquan	2047.91	497.85	616.78	528.75	17.02
长治市 Changzhi	2349.47	941.11	1271.96	981.11	34.39
晋城市 Jincheng	2273.70	1041.00	945.07	759.69	28.73
朔州市 Shuozhou	1626.74	668.83	710.64	475.70	21.17
晋中市 Jinzhong	2442.49	443.49	1147.56	986.28	19.72
运城市 Yuncheng	1525.93	684.41	1310.25	1141.14	8.13
忻州市 Xinzhou	1199.50	406.03	510.20	407.73	9.92
临汾市 Linfen	2192.76	496.29	1257.22	1108.83	16.10
吕梁市 Lvliang	3532.81	861.88	1493.61	1195.51	38.72

市 名 City	营业费用 Costs of Business	管理费用 Costs of Administration	财务费用 Costs of Finance	#利息支出 Interest Expenditure	利润总额 Total Profits
全 省 Total	**494.79**	**787.12**	**609.69**	**615.92**	**294.78**
省直报 Direct Report	2.00	25.74	11.77	11.44	18.57
太原市 Taiyuan	57.50	148.21	86.99	90.67	17.48
大同市 Datong	83.54	56.01	61.66	66.56	11.90
阳泉市 Yangquan	7.69	45.12	37.01	63.22	5.26
长治市 Changzhi	36.27	103.39	47.74	51.00	75.56
晋城市 Jincheng	16.74	79.56	64.15	67.03	56.29
朔州市 Shuozhou	93.23	37.62	38.49	32.73	45.85
晋中市 Jinzhong	47.93	60.44	56.73	48.85	-18.63
运城市 Yuncheng	40.13	49.77	35.68	32.10	50.69
忻州市 Xinzhou	14.08	31.69	27.41	22.87	24.23
临汾市 Linfen	27.86	60.17	51.40	46.10	-3.89
吕梁市 Lvliang	67.82	89.40	90.66	83.34	11.46

19-38 续表2 continued

单位：亿元 (100 million yuan)

市 名 City	亏损企业亏损额 Loss of Loss-making Enterprises	利税总额 Total Pre-tax Profits	应付薪酬总额 Total Wages Payable	应交增值税 Value Added Taxes Payable
全 省 Total	**398.70**	**1051.73**	**1170.27**	**501.08**
省直报 Direct Report		43.29	4.03	23.24
太原市 Taiyuan	65.47	116.94	257.61	62.04
大同市 Datong	23.16	64.31	113.07	35.30
阳泉市 Yangquan	10.89	46.18	72.38	23.89
长治市 Changzhi	32.43	177.32	123.71	65.93
晋城市 Jincheng	29.70	134.91	157.82	49.59
朔州市 Shuozhou	28.81	111.62	57.83	44.52
晋中市 Jinzhong	57.78	34.36	89.09	32.73
运城市 Yuncheng	23.08	90.29	73.36	31.03
忻州市 Xinzhou	11.45	61.24	43.68	26.02
临汾市 Linfen	47.47	54.24	72.75	41.76
吕梁市 Lvliang	68.46	117.04	104.94	65.03

市 名 City	总资产贡献率(%) Ratio of Profits, Taxes and Interests to Average Assets (%)	资产负债率(%) Ratio of Debts to Assets (%)	成本费用利润率(%) Ratio of Profits to Total Costs (%)	产品销售率 (%) Ratio of Sales to Gross Output Value (%)
全 省 Total	**4.79**	**76.08**	**2.07**	**95.70**
省直报 Direct Report	6.50	66.85	2.40	100.00
太原市 Taiyuan	4.24	74.89	0.74	100.17
大同市 Datong	4.66	81.31	0.67	83.40
阳泉市 Yangquan	3.14	80.42	0.75	91.69
长治市 Changzhi	6.83	71.40	6.05	93.66
晋城市 Jincheng	5.90	68.57	5.89	97.92
朔州市 Shuozhou	6.25	71.03	7.02	96.32
晋中市 Jinzhong	2.82	84.63	-1.55	93.70
运城市 Yuncheng	5.36	69.04	3.80	96.87
忻州市 Xinzhou	5.18	74.69	4.98	88.69
临汾市 Linfen	3.71	81.51	-0.30	97.12
吕梁市 Lvliang	4.51	80.39	0.78	98.14

19-39 国有控股工业企业主要经济指标(2016年)
MAIN ECONOMIC INDICATORS OF STATE-HOLDING INDUSTRIAL ENTERPRISES(2016)

单位：亿元 (100 million yuan)

市名 City	单位数(个) Number of Enterprises (unit)	#亏损企业 Loss-making Enterprises	工业销售产值 Industrial Sales Output Value	出口交货值 Value of Export Delivery	资产总计 Total Assets
全省 Total	**802**	**333**	**6078.59**	**125.89**	**22133.69**
省直报 Direct Report	2		768.17		839.88
太原市 Taiyuan	93	40	1190.88	101.50	3565.83
大同市 Datong	55	20	566.44	14.10	2370.61
阳泉市 Yangquan	34	21	333.43		2327.40
长治市 Changzhi	89	31	653.01	0.35	2037.86
晋城市 Jincheng	113	44	502.04	0.36	2700.02
朔州市 Shuozhou	60	24	440.99		1747.42
晋中市 Jinzhong	93	40	285.11	1.88	1193.67
运城市 Yuncheng	47	18	350.68	2.15	845.72
忻州市 Xinzhou	71	23	271.25	1.69	1209.72
临汾市 Linfen	84	42	334.68	1.46	1691.19
吕梁市 Lvliang	61	30	381.91	2.42	1604.37

市名 City	流动资产合计 Total Circulating Funds	固定资产合计 Total Fixed Assets	固定资产原价 Original Value of Fixed Assets	累计折旧 Total Depreciation	流动负债 Liquid Liabilites
全省 Total	**7624.88**	**9189.19**	**13364.92**	**5564.50**	**11169.05**
省直报 Direct Report	57.01	749.56	1255.08	586.85	357.02
太原市 Taiyuan	1150.58	1405.42	2426.76	1062.61	1678.97
大同市 Datong	911.49	1360.81	1171.09	519.19	917.24
阳泉市 Yangquan	1280.44	457.53	783.83	365.72	1152.01
长治市 Changzhi	845.95	896.43	1227.20	539.34	1132.51
晋城市 Jincheng	1063.52	723.55	1201.44	578.71	1441.38
朔州市 Shuozhou	420.44	825.56	1295.91	485.45	775.87
晋中市 Jinzhong	231.69	565.85	754.94	240.07	820.36
运城市 Yuncheng	330.77	389.65	666.41	295.93	476.01
忻州市 Xinzhou	342.83	601.86	822.12	281.74	601.84
临汾市 Linfen	562.96	569.09	867.90	321.43	969.69
吕梁市 Lvliang	427.20	643.88	892.24	287.45	846.14

19-39　续表1　continued

单位：亿元　　(100 million yuan)

市　名 City	负债合计 Total Liabilities	年末所有者权益 Creditors' Equity at Year-end	主营业务收入 Revenue of Major Business	主营业务成本 Costs of Major Business	主营业务税金及附加 Tax and Extra Charges of Major Business
全　省 Total	**17119.55**	**5024.22**	**7809.76**	**6364.55**	**178.99**
省直报 Direct Report	561.46	278.43	834.23	730.97	1.45
太原市 Taiyuan	2659.03	903.37	1311.90	1093.86	32.78
大同市 Datong	1965.72	404.89	1671.23	1473.92	4.15
阳泉市 Yangquan	1885.56	441.84	494.84	424.57	14.70
长治市 Changzhi	1508.53	529.33	607.98	438.67	26.41
晋城市 Jincheng	1953.19	746.83	619.71	478.29	23.55
朔州市 Shuozhou	1259.13	498.93	423.62	247.67	17.71
晋中市 Jinzhong	1057.94	135.73	293.80	239.84	10.72
运城市 Yuncheng	659.36	186.36	375.57	316.56	5.45
忻州市 Xinzhou	947.33	262.39	234.65	171.94	7.68
临汾市 Linfen	1450.66	243.39	418.54	362.32	11.33
吕梁市 Lvliang	1211.64	392.73	523.68	385.93	23.05

市　名 City	营业费用 Costs of Business	管理费用 Costs of Administration	财务费用 Costs of Finance	#利息支出 Interest Expenditure	利润总额 Total Profits
全　省 Total	**301.71**	**522.72**	**422.73**	**448.95**	**115.33**
省直报 Direct Report	2.00	25.74	11.77	11.44	18.57
太原市 Taiyuan	39.29	117.80	79.12	79.83	-16.91
大同市 Datong	78.46	45.02	57.55	62.98	6.10
阳泉市 Yangquan	3.57	39.51	32.78	60.03	2.86
长治市 Changzhi	10.94	60.15	32.64	35.87	45.78
晋城市 Jincheng	12.34	62.76	56.78	59.77	42.01
朔州市 Shuozhou	87.62	27.51	30.16	25.18	13.77
晋中市 Jinzhong	9.57	27.28	22.84	19.60	-15.08
运城市 Yuncheng	7.51	19.39	18.22	18.18	17.88
忻州市 Xinzhou	5.62	18.34	23.09	19.40	9.56
临汾市 Linfen	8.61	39.44	33.19	33.14	-21.32
吕梁市 Lvliang	36.19	39.77	24.60	23.52	12.12

19-39 续表2 continued

单位：亿元 (100 million yuan)

市 名 City	亏损企业亏损额 Loss of Loss-making Enterprises	利税总额 Total Pre-tax Profits	应付薪酬总额 Total Wages Payable	应交增值税 Value Added Taxes Payable
全 省 Total	**240.93**	**645.73**	**788.52**	**334.43**
省直报 Direct Report		43.29	4.03	23.24
太原市 Taiyuan	55.69	63.28	164.66	46.46
大同市 Datong	15.72	54.10	103.33	31.97
阳泉市 Yangquan	7.97	39.00	63.09	21.44
长治市 Changzhi	18.44	119.28	90.66	45.67
晋城市 Jincheng	22.94	103.83	109.64	37.98
朔州市 Shuozhou	17.75	61.65	39.92	30.14
晋中市 Jinzhong	29.77	8.31	47.43	12.52
运城市 Yuncheng	13.61	40.08	33.07	16.73
忻州市 Xinzhou	6.11	36.37	32.15	18.07
临汾市 Linfen	38.60	10.56	48.02	20.31
吕梁市 Lvliang	14.30	65.98	52.52	29.90

市 名 City	总资产贡献率(%) Ratio of Profits, Taxes and Interests to Average Assets (%)	资产负债率(%) Ratio of Debts to Assets (%)	成本费用利润率(%) Ratio of Profits to Total Costs(%)	产品销售率(%) Ratio of Sales to Gross Output Value(%)
全 省 Total	**4.68**	**77.35**	**1.46**	**95.10**
省直报 Direct Report	6.50	66.85	2.40	100.00
太原市 Taiyuan	3.87	74.57	-1.25	99.13
大同市 Datong	4.66	82.92	0.36	81.09
阳泉市 Yangquan	2.99	81.02	0.49	90.80
长治市 Changzhi	7.41	74.03	7.60	90.97
晋城市 Jincheng	5.88	72.34	6.50	98.75
朔州市 Shuozhou	4.90	72.06	3.48	98.96
晋中市 Jinzhong	2.29	88.63	-4.87	95.44
运城市 Yuncheng	6.57	77.96	4.56	100.05
忻州市 Xinzhou	4.55	78.31	4.29	89.04
临汾市 Linfen	2.37	85.78	-4.73	99.21
吕梁市 Lvliang	5.52	75.52	2.44	97.11

19-40 外商投资和港澳台投资工业企业主要经济指标(2016年)

MAIN INDICATORS OF INDUSTRIAL ENTERPRISES WITH HONG KONG, MACAO, TAIWAN AND FOREIGN FUNDS(2016)

单位：亿元 (100 million yuan)

市 名 City	单位数(个) Number of Enterprises (unit)	#亏损企业 Loss-making Enterprises	工 业 销售产值 Industrial Sales Output Value	出口交货值 Value of Export Delivery	资产总计 Total Assets
全 省 Total	**133**	**44**	**1283.68**	**615.71**	**2152.74**
太原市 Taiyuan	20	8	712.69	555.90	745.84
大同市 Datong	10	2	18.34	0.07	64.00
阳泉市 Yangquan	7	4	14.15	0.92	46.71
长治市 Changzhi	9	5	65.72	0.00	198.44
晋城市 Jincheng	15	3	181.89	48.91	364.75
朔州市 Shuozhou	4	2	24.38		111.48
晋中市 Jinzhong	28	9	76.60	3.67	159.09
运城市 Yuncheng	15	4	19.01	1.51	27.62
忻州市 Xinzhou	3		3.20	1.78	9.58
临汾市 Linfen	11	3	27.98	2.33	70.80
吕梁市 Lvliang	11	4	139.72	0.62	354.44

市 名 City	流动资产合计 Total Circulating Funds	固定资产合计 Total Fixed Assets	固定资产原价 Original Value of Fixed Assets	累计折旧 Total Depreciation	流动负债 Liquid Liabilites
全 省 Total	**1137.76**	**791.98**	**1297.01**	**573.85**	**1208.94**
太原市 Taiyuan	631.59	86.86	170.05	83.30	578.06
大同市 Datong	23.99	35.82	46.18	11.83	19.05
阳泉市 Yangquan	9.04	31.89	46.41	14.80	15.93
长治市 Changzhi	68.14	89.90	105.95	38.23	126.09
晋城市 Jincheng	163.04	155.82	338.25	205.79	118.26
朔州市 Shuozhou	20.53	88.24	105.13	23.49	33.20
晋中市 Jinzhong	53.25	89.96	153.69	64.29	83.48
运城市 Yuncheng	13.37	9.46	27.68	15.56	11.64
忻州市 Xinzhou	2.15	7.39	7.61	0.61	1.98
临汾市 Linfen	12.87	53.18	90.31	37.54	34.30
吕梁市 Lvliang	139.79	143.46	205.74	78.40	186.95

19-40 续表1 continued

单位：亿元 (100 million yuan)

市 名 City	负债合计 Total Liabilities	年末所有者权益 Creditors' Equity at Year-end	主营业务收入 Revenue of Major Business	主营业务成本 Costs of Major Business	主营业务税金及附加 Tax and Extra Charges of Major Business
全 省 Total	**1489.70**	**663.04**	**1290.78**	**1136.86**	**13.90**
太原市 Taiyuan	582.00	163.84	724.13	678.38	2.21
大同市 Datong	33.36	30.64	18.63	11.08	0.20
阳泉市 Yangquan	35.09	11.62	13.88	10.31	0.67
长治市 Changzhi	137.57	60.87	69.20	51.65	2.84
晋城市 Jincheng	143.83	220.92	182.00	146.60	3.78
朔州市 Shuozhou	86.40	25.07	24.61	23.09	0.41
晋中市 Jinzhong	143.48	15.61	72.69	60.81	1.45
运城市 Yuncheng	11.88	15.74	18.17	15.02	0.12
忻州市 Xinzhou	5.95	3.62	3.20	2.12	0.00
临汾市 Linfen	55.92	14.88	28.41	22.02	0.24
吕梁市 Lvliang	254.20	100.24	135.85	115.78	1.97

市 名 City	营业费用 Costs of Business	管理费用 Costs of Administration	财务费用 Costs of Finance	#利息支出 Interest Expenditure	利润总额 Total Profits
全 省 Total	**17.72**	**38.57**	**20.44**	**24.86**	**72.00**
太原市 Taiyuan	4.76	12.86	0.72	4.74	28.40
大同市 Datong	0.46	1.59	0.57	0.54	4.72
阳泉市 Yangquan	1.01	0.80	0.91	0.89	-0.17
长治市 Changzhi	2.74	4.05	2.90	2.61	3.82
晋城市 Jincheng	0.65	6.84	1.62	2.32	26.06
朔州市 Shuozhou	0.02	0.19	3.36	3.39	-2.38
晋中市 Jinzhong	3.46	4.73	4.09	3.42	1.11
运城市 Yuncheng	0.98	1.36	0.06	0.16	0.65
忻州市 Xinzhou	0.04	0.10	0.21	0.21	0.74
临汾市 Linfen	0.98	1.40	2.11	2.06	1.78
吕梁市 Lvliang	2.63	4.65	3.89	4.52	7.26

19-40 续表2 continued

单位：亿元 (100 million yuan)

市 名 City	亏损企业亏损额 Loss of Loss-making Enterprises	利税总额 Total Pre-tax Profits	应付薪酬总额 Total Wages Payable	应交增值税 Value Added Taxes Payable
全 省 Total	**21.88**	**121.85**	**148.86**	**35.91**
太原市 Taiyuan	1.38	40.26	76.42	9.65
大同市 Datong	0.41	4.76	1.32	-0.16
阳泉市 Yangquan	2.05	0.58	3.33	0.08
长治市 Changzhi	2.11	11.10	6.75	4.41
晋城市 Jincheng	2.94	38.44	37.44	8.60
朔州市 Shuozhou	3.58	-1.83	4.59	0.13
晋中市 Jinzhong	3.09	7.07	8.49	4.52
运城市 Yuncheng	0.98	1.41	1.55	0.63
忻州市 Xinzhou		0.75	0.14	0.01
临汾市 Linfen	1.59	3.78	1.78	1.76
吕梁市 Lvliang	3.74	15.53	7.04	6.30

市 名 City	总资产贡献率(%) Ratio of Profits, Taxes and Interests to Average Assets (%)	资产负债率(%) Ratio of Debts to Assets (%)	成本费用利润率(%) Ratio of Profits to Total Costs(%)	产品销售率(%) Ratio of Sales to Gross Output Value(%)
全 省 Total	**6.93**	**69.20**	**5.86**	**100.76**
太原市 Taiyuan	6.68	78.03	4.06	104.97
大同市 Datong	8.25	52.13	33.93	102.91
阳泉市 Yangquan	3.22	75.12	-1.25	94.52
长治市 Changzhi	6.90	69.32	6.12	94.30
晋城市 Jincheng	10.78	39.43	16.73	95.87
朔州市 Shuozhou	1.35	77.51	-8.91	99.45
晋中市 Jinzhong	6.57	90.19	1.39	94.72
运城市 Yuncheng	5.96	43.02	3.57	77.78
忻州市 Xinzhou	10.05	62.15	30.07	94.60
临汾市 Linfen	8.24	78.98	6.69	96.72
吕梁市 Lvliang	5.41	71.72	5.58	99.26

19-41 大中型工业企业主要经济指标(2016年)
MAIN ECONOMIC INDICATORS OF LARGE AND MEDIUM-SIZE INDUSTRIAL ENTERPRISES(2016)

单位：亿元 (100 million yuan)

市名 City	单位数(个) Number of Enterprises (unit)	#亏损企业 Loss-making Enterprises	工业销售产值 Industrial Sales Output Value	出口交货值 Value of Export Delivery	资产总计 Total Assets
全省 Total	**1066**	**431**	**9695.58**	**893.96**	**28367.09**
省直报 Direct Report	2		768.17		839.88
太原市 Taiyuan	91	36	1957.59	656.50	4379.50
大同市 Datong	48	18	589.26	14.21	2335.89
阳泉市 Yangquan	40	22	354.13	0.18	2434.31
长治市 Changzhi	127	47	1091.89	0.65	2812.67
晋城市 Jincheng	127	50	729.55	52.68	3023.55
朔州市 Shuozhou	72	32	450.84	0.22	1694.17
晋中市 Jinzhong	155	71	616.95	11.40	2149.52
运城市 Yuncheng	97	24	903.02	14.61	1685.60
忻州市 Xinzhou	51	14	351.19	1.74	1011.01
临汾市 Linfen	114	49	857.74	136.41	2302.87
吕梁市 Lvliang	142	68	1025.25	5.36	3698.13

市名 City	流动资产合计 Total Circulating Funds	固定资产合计 Total Fixed Assets	固定资产原价 Original Value of Fixed Assets	累计折旧 Total Depreciation	流动负债 Liquid Liabilites
全省 Total	**11123.68**	**10693.61**	**15533.13**	**6558.71**	**15177.18**
省直报 Direct Report	57.01	749.56	1255.08	586.85	357.02
太原市 Taiyuan	1832.88	1484.06	2586.46	1165.82	2379.00
大同市 Datong	935.84	1298.02	1100.85	518.69	912.63
阳泉市 Yangquan	1338.03	491.69	827.12	380.06	1208.06
长治市 Changzhi	1222.93	1101.98	1452.60	634.94	1557.29
晋城市 Jincheng	1237.47	819.85	1370.28	663.15	1551.31
朔州市 Shuozhou	456.96	751.51	1173.91	435.27	765.63
晋中市 Jinzhong	698.94	829.54	1125.25	376.71	1468.07
运城市 Yuncheng	743.65	623.39	1041.16	450.87	957.96
忻州市 Xinzhou	339.27	465.02	658.35	262.39	520.96
临汾市 Linfen	873.73	821.57	1204.38	462.46	1347.60
吕梁市 Lvliang	1386.98	1257.39	1737.69	621.52	2151.65

19-41 续表1 continued

单位：亿元 (100 million yuan)

市名 City	负债合计 Total Liabilities	年末所有者权益 Creditors' Equity at Year-end	主营业务收入 Revenue of Major Business	主营业务成本 Cost of Major Business	主营业务税金及附加 Tax and Extra Charges of Major Business
全省 Total	**21709.51**	**6655.37**	**11294.72**	**9352.14**	**216.95**
省直报 Direct Report	561.46	278.43	834.23	730.97	1.45
太原市 Taiyuan	3327.08	1052.42	2077.76	1803.57	35.53
大同市 Datong	1919.64	416.25	1701.08	1496.89	4.36
阳泉市 Yangquan	1959.11	475.20	506.12	428.56	16.23
长治市 Changzhi	2006.78	805.89	972.29	717.98	33.01
晋城市 Jincheng	2056.09	967.46	848.58	677.47	28.14
朔州市 Shuozhou	1180.09	514.08	426.24	261.14	18.80
晋中市 Jinzhong	1847.58	301.93	645.35	527.47	16.57
运城市 Yuncheng	1197.51	488.09	934.89	801.41	6.98
忻州市 Xinzhou	769.86	241.15	305.24	238.86	6.35
临汾市 Linfen	1884.86	415.79	897.16	779.18	13.73
吕梁市 Lvliang	2999.45	698.68	1145.78	888.66	35.79

市名 City	营业费用 Costs of Business	管理费用 Costs of Administration	财务费用 Costs of Finance	#利息支出 Interest Expenditure	利润总额 Total Profits
全省 Total	**409.41**	**682.67**	**521.88**	**541.46**	**206.15**
省直报 Direct Report	2.00	25.74	11.77	11.44	18.57
太原市 Taiyuan	49.73	130.94	81.13	85.66	12.24
大同市 Datong	80.68	49.51	54.23	59.36	9.72
阳泉市 Yangquan	5.08	41.91	34.81	61.23	2.49
长治市 Changzhi	27.96	93.87	40.93	44.48	63.33
晋城市 Jincheng	14.33	73.76	59.41	62.73	53.85
朔州市 Shuozhou	84.65	29.90	27.87	23.70	5.39
晋中市 Jinzhong	29.64	46.96	43.70	37.33	-15.91
运城市 Yuncheng	31.31	38.77	27.09	25.57	43.58
忻州市 Xinzhou	9.39	20.21	16.67	15.50	16.16
临汾市 Linfen	19.76	53.02	44.63	40.39	-10.81
吕梁市 Lvliang	54.87	78.09	79.65	74.05	7.51

19-41 续表2 continued

单位：亿元 (100 million yuan)

市 名 City	亏损企业亏损额 Loss of Loss-making Enterprises	利税总额 Total Pre-tax Profits	应付薪酬总额 Total Wages Payable	应交增值税 Value Added Taxes Payable
全 省 Total	**320.35**	**876.27**	**1065.09**	**435.78**
省直报 Direct Report		43.29	4.03	23.24
太原市 Taiyuan	59.59	104.31	243.64	55.62
大同市 Datong	14.66	60.99	107.21	34.97
阳泉市 Yangquan	8.93	41.45	67.73	22.73
长治市 Changzhi	28.96	160.57	116.45	62.81
晋城市 Jincheng	24.08	130.47	151.84	48.20
朔州市 Shuozhou	18.90	54.58	48.17	30.33
晋中市 Jinzhong	44.56	26.49	73.44	25.30
运城市 Yuncheng	15.73	77.81	60.08	27.21
忻州市 Xinzhou	3.82	42.40	33.89	18.86
临汾市 Linfen	41.00	31.49	62.79	28.31
吕梁市 Lvliang	60.11	102.43	95.82	58.22

市 名 City	总资产贡献率(%) Ratio of Profits, Taxes and Interests to Average Assets(%)	资产负债率(%) Ratio of Debts to Assets (%)	成本费用利润率(%) Ratio of Profits to Total Costs (%)	产品销售率(%) Ratio of Sales to Gross Output Value(%)
全 省 Total	**4.80**	**76.53**	**1.81**	**95.65**
省直报 Direct Report	6.50	66.85	2.40	100.00
太原市 Taiyuan	4.33	75.97	0.58	100.92
大同市 Datong	4.87	82.18	0.57	81.94
阳泉市 Yangquan	3.01	80.48	0.42	90.70
长治市 Changzhi	7.13	71.35	6.60	92.45
晋城市 Jincheng	6.18	68.00	6.26	97.86
朔州市 Shuozhou	4.60	69.66	1.33	97.80
晋中市 Jinzhong	2.90	85.95	-2.29	91.52
运城市 Yuncheng	5.91	71.04	4.57	97.85
忻州市 Xinzhou	5.66	76.15	5.57	87.87
临汾市 Linfen	3.11	81.85	-1.17	96.39
吕梁市 Lvliang	4.72	81.11	0.67	98.08

19-42 建筑业企业总产值和竣工产值(2016年)
GROSS OUTPUT VALUE AND COMPLETED VALUE OF CONSTRUCTION ENTERPRISES(2016)

单位：万元 (10 000 yuan)

市 名 City		总产值 Gross Output Value	#建筑工程 Construction	#安装工程 Installation	竣工产值 Completed Value
全 省	**Total**	**33184739**	**28780169**	**3475946**	**12785480**
太原市	Taiyuan	23351248	20358831	2457884	7387088
大同市	Datong	1303673	1033689	203912	702083
阳泉市	Yangquan	550491	471154	71368	270612
长治市	Changzhi	1476357	1320368	133001	814216
晋城市	Jincheng	561178	458193	53288	450348
朔州市	Shuozhou	558565	330741	159281	492726
晋中市	Jinzhong	2236890	2088538	134776	746535
运城市	Yuncheng	1276528	1087253	120815	847596
忻州市	Xinzhou	681198	583962	36393	437684
临汾市	Linfen	732586	634280	72492	385121
吕梁市	Lvliang	456024	413159	32737	251471

19-43 按主要用途分的房屋建筑竣工面积(2016年)
FLOOR SPACE OF BUILDINGS COMPLETED BY MAJOR USE(2016)

单位：平方米 (sq.m)

市 名 City		总 计 Total	#住宅房屋 Residential Buildings	#商业及服务用房屋 Commercial and Service Buildings	#办公用房 Oiffice Buildings	#科研、教育、医疗用房屋 Scientific Research, Education and Healthcare Buildings
全 省	**Total**	**33532617**	**23662087**	**1462378**	**2650152**	**2332121**
太原市	Taiyuan	16614315	11176911	993888	1486435	1563294
大同市	Datong	2917833	2437098	28079	124741	58079
阳泉市	Yangquan	554403	491464	1155		1241
长治市	Changzhi	3115653	2309488	146634	423708	86624
晋城市	Jincheng	1159941	848138	17198	83439	57441
朔州市	Shuozhou	480608	407969	5293	23989	15680
晋中市	Jinzhong	1582205	1022649	7208	67275	123973
运城市	Yuncheng	3011772	2045470	150971	268539	190023
忻州市	Xinzhou	2293912	1930802	43658	81705	103415
临汾市	Linfen	794690	492093	32109	84076	84423
吕梁市	Lvliang	1007285	500005	36185	6245	47928

19-44 按主要用途分的房屋建筑竣工价值(2016年)
VALUE OF BUILDINGS COMPLETED BY MAJOR USE(2016)

单位：万元 (10 000 yuan)

市名 City		总计 Total	#住宅房屋 Residential Buildings	#商业及服务用房屋 Commercial and Service Buildings	#办公用房 Oiffice Buildings	#科研、教育、医疗用房屋 Scientific Research, Education and Healthcare Buildings
全省	**Total**	**5480485**	**3563838**	**240466**	**495377**	**476824**
太原市	Taiyuan	3054972	1852652	170037	276422	336809
大同市	Datong	396898	307977	4790	28440	11678
阳泉市	Yangquan	66494	56776	346		259
长治市	Changzhi	505356	344709	25472	87760	17860
晋城市	Jincheng	138043	102509	2620	6456	14290
朔州市	Shuozhou	72866	60024	554	3123	4556
晋中市	Jinzhong	282220	178220	1585	17906	25732
运城市	Yuncheng	468222	319785	19518	46714	30324
忻州市	Xinzhou	266377	212530	6031	14191	15714
临汾市	Linfen	105670	66896	3672	13350	12682
吕梁市	Lvliang	123368	61762	5840	1016	6921

19-45 建筑业企业房屋建筑面积(2016年)
FLOOR SPACE OF BUILDINGS CONSTRUCTED BY CONSTRUCTION ENTERPRISES(2016)

单位：平方米 (sq.m)

市名 City		房屋建筑施工面积 Floor Space of Buildings Under Construction	#本年新开工面积 Floor Space Started This Year	#投标承包的面积 Floor Space of Enter a Bid Contract
全省	**Total**	**146205756**	**45322426**	**125671517**
太原市	Taiyuan	99369827	25803947	92288115
大同市	Datong	5928686	3391608	4582159
阳泉市	Yangquan	2736067	744951	1730472
长治市	Changzhi	11593667	3702898	10551290
晋城市	Jincheng	3763205	895370	1819551
朔州市	Shuozhou	1081834	883147	727084
晋中市	Jinzhong	6217104	2426521	4687745
运城市	Yuncheng	7171078	3218846	4908007
忻州市	Xinzhou	3353145	1903292	1228652
临汾市	Linfen	1736958	1016695	1150287
吕梁市	Lvliang	3254185	1335151	1998155

19-46 建筑业企业机械设备情况(2016年)

MACHINARY AND EQUIPMENT OF CONSTRUCTION ENTERPRISES(2016)

市 名 City	自有机械设备年末总台数(台) Number of Machinery and Equipment Owned (unit)	自有机械设备年末总功率(千瓦) Total Power of Machinery and Equipment Owned (kw)	自有机械设备净值(万元) Net Value of Machinery and Equipment Owned (10 000 yuan)
全 省 Total	**197334**	**6970480**	**1468913**
太原市 Taiyuan	90345	4365019	836937
大同市 Datong	9272	157172	33721
阳泉市 Yangquan	6140	216377	32098
长治市 Changzhi	7298	205100	51760
晋城市 Jincheng	8446	271092	38016
朔州市 Shuozhou	7179	202806	50132
晋中市 Jinzhong	17297	519261	152519
运城市 Yuncheng	14320	242574	89989
忻州市 Xinzhou	14058	213657	65977
临汾市 Linfen	11977	258779	60867
吕梁市 Lvliang	11002	318643	56896

19-47 建筑业企业劳动生产率(2016年)

LABOR PRODUCTIVITY OF CONSTRUCTION ENTERPRISES(2016)

单位：元/人 (yuan/person)

市 名 City	企业个数(个) Number of Enterprises (unit)	从事建筑业活动的从业人员平均人数(人) Average Number of Employees Engaged in Construction Activities (person)	按总产值计算的劳动生产率 Overall Labor Productivity in Terms of Total Output Value	人均竣工产值 Per Capita Output Value of Completed
全 省 Total	**2532**	**1122660**	**295590**	**113886**
太原市 Taiyuan	1108	739436	315798	99902
大同市 Datong	201	52140	250033	134653
阳泉市 Yangquan	82	23265	236618	116317
长治市 Changzhi	168	46468	317715	175221
晋城市 Jincheng	103	30410	184537	148092
朔州市 Shuozhou	123	25101	222527	196297
晋中市 Jinzhong	180	57364	389947	130140
运城市 Yuncheng	178	59077	216079	143473
忻州市 Xinzhou	137	35250	193248	124166
临汾市 Linfen	154	32935	222434	116934
吕梁市 Lvliang	98	21214	214964	118540

19-48 建筑业企业负债及所有者权益(2016年)
LIABILITIES AND CREDITORS' EQUITY OF CONSTRUCTION ENTERPRISES(2016)

单位：万元 (10 000 yuan)

市名 City		负债合计 Total Liabilities	#流动负债 Liquid Liabilities	#非流动负债合计 Illiquid Liabilities	所有者权益合计 Total Creditors' Equity
全　省	**Total**	**37819762**	**34841097**	**2443714**	**10634135**
太原市	Taiyuan	26907901	24618159	2205654	6327679
大同市	Datong	1386735	1307971	62302	486107
阳泉市	Yangquan	2020325	1939441	29496	185257
长治市	Changzhi	1515896	1456918	12631	697791
晋城市	Jincheng	929507	917880	9532	345730
朔州市	Shuozhou	602193	549821	43138	216677
晋中市	Jinzhong	2192673	2163318	24110	715219
运城市	Yuncheng	748586	688192	41976	526943
忻州市	Xinzhou	442669	403756	748	354338
临汾市	Linfen	549117	538743	2687	458418
吕梁市	Lvliang	524161	256898	11440	319977

19-49 建筑业企业收入及成本情况(2016年)
REVENUE AND COST OF CONSTRUCTION ENTERPRISES(2016)

单位：万元 (10 000 yuan)

市名 City		营业收入 Revenue of Business	#主营业务收入 Revenue of Major Business	主营业务成本 Cost of Major Business
全　省	**Total**	**33340063**	**33029335**	**29379325**
太原市	Taiyuan	23160970	22973777	20503922
大同市	Datong	1466517	1420066	1278080
阳泉市	Yangquan	556197	551981	483826
长治市	Changzhi	1539801	1535503	1358746
晋城市	Jincheng	566664	562521	471553
朔州市	Shuozhou	606949	604081	528340
晋中市	Jinzhong	2352572	2336015	2121132
运城市	Yuncheng	1172387	1157905	1040466
忻州市	Xinzhou	686605	683122	597565
临汾市	Linfen	738073	712034	595437
吕梁市	Lvliang	493328	492331	400258

19-50 建筑业企业资产(2016年)
ASSETS OF CONSTRUCTION ENTERPRISES(2016)

单位：万元 (10 000 yuan)

市 名 City	资产总计 Total Assets	#流动资产合计 Total Circulating Assets	#固定资产合计 Total Fixed Assets
全 省 Total	**48453897**	**40457188**	**2958614**
太原市 Taiyuan	33235579	27659005	1448082
大同市 Datong	1872842	1660001	138401
阳泉市 Yangquan	2205582	1858623	109893
长治市 Changzhi	2213687	1855346	180933
晋城市 Jincheng	1275237	1087887	104157
朔州市 Shuozhou	818870	658293	108464
晋中市 Jinzhong	2907891	2610512	230343
运城市 Yuncheng	1275529	989478	188513
忻州市 Xinzhou	797007	606487	161015
临汾市 Linfen	1007536	806155	150120
吕梁市 Lvliang	844138	665404	138693

市 名 City	固定资产原价 Original Value of Fixed Assets	本年折旧 Depreciation This Year	实收资本 Capitals Hold
全 省 Total	**4806771**	**333113**	**7240168**
太原市 Taiyuan	2625751	195341	4190007
大同市 Datong	168596	17894	386691
阳泉市 Yangquan	188356	14203	200119
长治市 Changzhi	228769	12043	460180
晋城市 Jincheng	166907	8217	226808
朔州市 Shuozhou	161409	9793	178215
晋中市 Jinzhong	364576	29139	444618
运城市 Yuncheng	290537	14699	344719
忻州市 Xinzhou	216055	12557	237022
临汾市 Linfen	224751	13955	323632
吕梁市 Lvliang	171062	5273	248157

19-51 建筑业企业费用情况(2016年)
EXPENSES OF CONSTRUCTION ENTERPRISES(2016)

单位：万元 (10 000 yuan)

市名 City		销售费用 Sales Expenses	管理费用 Administrative Expenses	财务费用 Financial Expenses
全省	**Total**	**97429**	**1565024**	**214893**
太原市	Taiyuan	52114	1110353	136202
大同市	Datong	6699	62433	13091
阳泉市	Yangquan	363	32896	9136
长治市	Changzhi	4245	54711	13393
晋城市	Jincheng	4121	34379	5476
朔州市	Shuozhou	6405	36739	1937
晋中市	Jinzhong	2733	93777	20794
运城市	Yuncheng	6404	52312	7641
忻州市	Xinzhou	5442	25406	3047
临汾市	Linfen	7192	45201	1946
吕梁市	Lvliang	1713	16818	2230

19-52 建筑业企业薪酬及利润情况(2016年)
REMUNERTION AND PROFITS OF CONSTRUCTION ENTERPRISES(2016)

单位：万元 (10 000 yuan)

市名 City		应付职工薪酬 Remuneration Payable	营业利润 Business Profits	其他业务利润 Profits of Other Business
全省	**Total**	**2513761**	**950924**	**33556**
太原市	Taiyuan	1302118	678841	20457
大同市	Datong	164330	24549	2427
阳泉市	Yangquan	58847	20526	1086
长治市	Changzhi	119328	56169	1317
晋城市	Jincheng	107620	15770	1147
朔州市	Shuozhou	66700	12396	1139
晋中市	Jinzhong	296305	54220	1614
运城市	Yuncheng	170046	25872	1987
忻州市	Xinzhou	86291	23756	22
临汾市	Linfen	90242	20776	2298
吕梁市	Lvliang	51933	18049	63

19-53 建筑业企业利润及税金情况(2016年)
PROFITS AND TAXES OF CONSTRUCTION ENTERPRISES(2016)

单位：万元 (10 000 yuan)

市 名 City	利润总额 Total Profits	税金总额 Total Taxes	主营业务税金及附加 Taxes and Extra Charges of Major Business	管理费用中的税金 Taxes in Costs of Administration	应交增值税 Value-added Taxes Payable
全 省 Total	**972077**	**506539**	**477373**	**29166**	**396567**
太原市 Taiyuan	692816	286983	272089	14894	275459
大同市 Datong	25167	33730	32384	1346	18818
阳泉市 Yangquan	21022	7700	6482	1218	10231
长治市 Changzhi	58120	34277	32464	1813	19887
晋城市 Jincheng	18679	7434	6609	825	7279
朔州市 Shuozhou	13444	17380	15408	1972	6080
晋中市 Jinzhong	53674	32982	31094	1888	14691
运城市 Yuncheng	26109	31008	28999	2009	18070
忻州市 Xinzhou	23797	21098	20119	979	12831
临汾市 Linfen	21435	16438	14953	1485	7734
吕梁市 Lvliang	17813	17508	16772	736	5487

19-54 房地产开发投资(2016年)
INVESTMENT IN REAL ESTATE DEVELOPMENT(2016)

单位：万元 (10 000 yuan)

市 名 City	本年完成投资 Investment Completed This Yesr	#住 宅 Residential Buildings	建筑工程 Construction Projects	安装工程 Installation Projects	设备工器具购置 Purchase of Equipment and Instruments	其他费用 Others Expenses
全 省 Total	**15973532**	**11410813**	**10516027**	**2419144**	**221372**	**2816989**
太原市 Taiyuan	6819017	4955449	4124695	721835	82391	1890096
大同市 Datong	1677293	1124348	1201517	341408	19166	115202
阳泉市 Yangquan	639781	518305	467094	111493	19176	42018
长治市 Changzhi	677962	489227	549309	66772	15515	46366
晋城市 Jincheng	803648	589152	572458	108227	2176	120787
朔州市 Shuozhou	280730	205592	149501	95642	23631	11956
晋中市 Jinzhong	1790361	1137871	1202406	268112	12378	307465
运城市 Yuncheng	1163114	884876	798982	275864	8684	79584
忻州市 Xinzhou	440958	285964	350692	70216	5749	14301
临汾市 Linfen	975340	682008	602356	230576	20002	122406
吕梁市 Lvliang	705328	538021	497017	128999	12504	66808

19-55 房地产开发房屋销售额(2016年)
SALES OF BUILDINGS IN REAL ESTATE DEVELOPMENT(2016)

单位：万元 (10 000 yuan)

市名 City	商品房销售额 Sales of Commercial Buildings	住宅 Residential Buildings	#90平方米及以下住房 90 sq.m and Below	#144平方米以上住房 Above 144 sq.m
全　省 Total	**10271364**	**9007879**	**1282270**	**2017101**
太原市 Taiyuan	4684106	4096946	581019	1245964
大同市 Datong	632368	545021	61926	113233
阳泉市 Yangquan	385312	342519	70185	75304
长治市 Changzhi	933308	800826	149767	158968
晋城市 Jincheng	602788	581767	53775	77771
朔州市 Shuozhou	242209	159018	49356	32139
晋中市 Jinzhong	621586	541844	82882	58006
运城市 Yuncheng	871567	768207	50580	97874
忻州市 Xinzhou	351957	329737	72605	39687
临汾市 Linfen	676195	601437	57087	90203
吕梁市 Lvliang	269968	240557	53088	27952

市名 City	#别墅、高档公寓 Villas and High-grade Apartment Buildings	办公楼 Office Buildings	商业营业用房 Buildings for Business Operation	其他 Other Buildings
全　省 Total	**188665**	**334819**	**798263**	**130403**
太原市 Taiyuan	171979	290814	249541	46805
大同市 Datong			60352	26995
阳泉市 Yangquan			34865	7928
长治市 Changzhi		11107	105558	15817
晋城市 Jincheng	3034		18756	2265
朔州市 Shuozhou		2128	68274	12789
晋中市 Jinzhong		6370	70401	2971
运城市 Yuncheng	3187	3851	94549	4960
忻州市 Xinzhou	160		17948	4272
临汾市 Linfen	10305	18386	51301	5071
吕梁市 Lvliang		2163	26718	530

19-56　房地产开发房屋销售面积(2016年)

FLOOR SPACE OF BUILDINGS SOLD IN REAL ESTATE DEVELOPMENT(2016)

单位：平方米　　　　(sq.m)

市　名 City	商品房销售面积 Floor Space of Commercial Buildings Sold	住　宅 Residential Buildings	#90平方米及以下住房 90 sq.m and Below	#144平方米以上住房 Above 144 sq.m
全　省 Total	**20610554**	**18815060**	**3006168**	**3318801**
太原市 Taiyuan	6137253	5603347	912411	1647249
大同市 Datong	1433867	1270247	175747	191752
阳泉市 Yangquan	956806	872135	203389	145038
长治市 Changzhi	2190447	1979114	425175	294851
晋城市 Jincheng	1305620	1267851	121578	136592
朔州市 Shuozhou	714686	533189	158566	98388
晋中市 Jinzhong	1504911	1398005	199744	147547
运城市 Yuncheng	2758309	2540175	185540	262585
忻州市 Xinzhou	1137022	1077478	281067	98060
临汾市 Linfen	1580580	1456968	140686	212022
吕梁市 Lvliang	891053	816551	202265	84717

市　名 City	#别墅、高档公寓 Villas and High-grade Apartment Buildings	办公楼 Office Buildings	商业营业用房 Buildings for Business Operation	其　他 Other Buildings
全　省 Total	**188823**	**386227**	**986882**	**422385**
太原市 Taiyuan	164106	304510	168352	61044
大同市 Datong			75352	88268
阳泉市 Yangquan			60728	23943
长治市 Changzhi		20800	104106	86427
晋城市 Jincheng	3472		23020	14749
朔州市 Shuozhou		7000	119913	54584
晋中市 Jinzhong		13000	79485	14421
运城市 Yuncheng	7706	3439	186444	28251
忻州市 Xinzhou	313		36028	23516
临汾市 Linfen	13226	32626	66172	24814
吕梁市 Lvliang		4852	67282	2368

19-57 房地产开发施工、竣工面积及价值(2016年)
FLOOR SPACE AND VALUE OF BUILDINGS UNDER CONSTRUCTION AND COMPLETED IN REAL ESTATE DEVELOPMENT(2016)

单位：平方米 (sq.m)

市　　名 City	房屋施工面积 Floor Space of Buildings Under Construction	#住宅 Residential Buildings	房屋竣工面积 Floor Space of Buildings Completed	#住宅 Residential Buildings	房屋竣工价值(万元) Value of Buildings Completed (10 000 yuan)	#住宅 Residential Buildings
全　省 Total	**170692512**	**122223158**	**38547826**	**26542830**	**26835885**	**20422192**
太原市 Taiyuan	58733324	42042733	14487675	9859828	5722047	4689077
大同市 Datong	15892327	9301924	3200455	1860973	2882061	1748969
阳泉市 Yangquan	6284818	5134802	1520455	1244022	970000	850350
长治市 Changzhi	11560085	8472931	1791029	1361683	3232215	2485020
晋城市 Jincheng	8990483	6362726	1806952	1253082	837034	664510
朔州市 Shuozhou	7205051	5462547	1269774	887672	3108448	2347872
晋中市 Jinzhong	15746607	11240403	5719542	3974495	2071678	1520344
运城市 Yuncheng	16776854	12720216	2338886	1655897	3029519	2356642
忻州市 Xinzhou	9071760	6656115	1248460	941966	1979372	1536293
临汾市 Linfen	11698905	8247421	2565807	1509133	1585809	1132500
吕梁市 Lvliang	8732298	6581340	2598791	1994079	1417702	1090615

19-58 社会消费品零售总额(2016年)
TOTAL RETAIL SALES OF CONSUMER GOODS(2016)

单位：万元 (10 000 yuan)

市　　名 City	社会消费品零售总额 Total Retail Sales of Consumer Goods	城镇 Town	乡村 Village
全　省 Total	**64805384**	**52845462**	**11959922**
太原市 Taiyuan	16662362	15482102	1180260
大同市 Datong	6090130	4978702	1111428
阳泉市 Yangquan	3062665	2768699	293966
长治市 Changzhi	5666196	4598305	1067891
晋城市 Jincheng	3861943	3264588	597355
朔州市 Shuozhou	2910719	2075982	834737
晋中市 Jinzhong	5692111	3638534	2053578
运城市 Yuncheng	7047230	5510494	1536736
忻州市 Xinzhou	3380208	2365359	1014849
临汾市 Linfen	6094418	4851247	1243172
吕梁市 Lvliang	4337402	3311451	1025951

19-59 旅游事业发展情况(2016年)
DEVELOPMENT OF TOURISM(2016)

市名 City		接待入境过夜游客人数(人次) Inbound Overnight Tourists (person-time)	旅游外汇收入(万美元) Foreign Exchange Earnings from Tourism (USD 10 000)	接待国内游客人数(万人次) Domestic Tourists (10 000 person-times)	国内旅游收入(亿元) Revenue from Domestic Tourism (100 million yuan)
全省	**Total**	**629836**	**31738**	**44330**	**4228**
太原市	Taiyuan	153644	8446	5666	679
大同市	Datong	69658	4022	4041	361
阳泉市	Yangquan	4823	107	2733	226
长治市	Changzhi	25170	1561	3751	368
晋城市	Jincheng	12819	714	3885	356
朔州市	Shuozhou	6405	219	1717	161
晋中市	Jinzhong	227075	12125	6335	651
运城市	Yuncheng	31832	914	5322	434
忻州市	Xinzhou	54697	1828	3411	326
临汾市	Linfen	38196	1588	4024	374
吕梁市	Lvliang	5517	214	3444	293

19-60 公路通车里程(2016年)
LENGTH OF HIGHWAYS(2016)

单位：公里 (km)

市名 City		公路通车里程 Length of Highways	在通车里程中 In Length of Highways					
			国道 State Class	省道 Province Class	县公路 County Class	乡公路 Township Class	专用公路 Special Purpose	村道 Village Class
全省	**Total**	**142066**	**11096**	**6701**	**19961**	**48896**	**546**	**54865**
太原市	Taiyuan	7401	618	253	1010	1711	102	3707
大同市	Datong	12574	742	774	2048	5348	4	3657
阳泉市	Yangquan	5656	419	274	799	879	4	3281
长治市	Changzhi	11643	949	692	1662	3875	47	4418
晋城市	Jincheng	9135	505	510	1159	3561	28	3372
朔州市	Shuozhou	10216	789	415	1373	3908	36	3695
晋中市	Jinzhong	15988	1276	681	2190	6632	63	5146
运城市	Yuncheng	16088	1247	695	2620	6257	84	5185
忻州市	Xinzhou	17443	1739	847	2126	6608	117	6005
临汾市	Linfen	18541	1514	718	2421	5537	60	8290
吕梁市	Lvliang	17382	1298	842	2553	4579		8108

19-61 公路等级里程(2016年)
LENGTH OF HIGHWAYS BY CLASS(2016)

单位：公里 (km)

市 名 City	等级里程 Expressway and Class I to IV Expressways	高 速 Express -way	一 级 First Class	二 级 Second Class	三 级 Third Class	四 级 Fourth Class	等外里程 Highway Below class IV	等级里程占总里程的百分比 Percentage to Total Length of Highways
全 省 Total	**139110**	**5265**	**2576**	**15397**	**18891**	**96980**	**2956**	**97.9**
太原市 Taiyuan	7283	287	221	951	1255	4570	118	98.4
大同市 Datong	12534	549	129	1067	2257	8532	40	99.7
阳泉市 Yangquan	5656	282	107	423	586	4257		100.0
长治市 Changzhi	11248	339	121	1359	1401	8028	395	96.6
晋城市 Jincheng	8918	319	155	682	1493	6269	217	97.6
朔州市 Shuozhou	10118	389	205	1037	1434	7054	98	99.0
晋中市 Jinzhong	15919	625	508	2250	1457	11080	69	99.6
运城市 Yuncheng	16066	601	333	1903	2017	11211	23	99.9
忻州市 Xinzhou	16891	822	46	1790	1756	12477	552	96.8
临汾市 Linfen	18030	518	412	1919	3016	12165	510	97.2
吕梁市 Lvliang	16447	534	338	2017	2219	11338	935	94.6

19-62 公路路面里程(2016年)
LENGTH OF PAVED HIGHWAYS(2016)

单位：公里 (km)

市 名 City	有铺装路面里程 Length of Paved Highways	占总里程(%) Percentage to Total Length of Highways	简易铺装路面里程 Length of Simply Paved Highways	占总里程(%) Percentage to Total Length of Highways	未铺装路面里程 Length of Non-paved Highways
全 省 Total	**103844**	**73.1**	**20949**	**14.7**	**17273**
太原市 Taiyuan	5845	79.0	732	9.9	824
大同市 Datong	10818	86.0	317	2.5	1439
阳泉市 Yangquan	5274	93.2	169	3.0	212
长治市 Changzhi	8633	74.1	2180	18.7	830
晋城市 Jincheng	8279	90.6	574	6.3	281
朔州市 Shuozhou	7369	72.1	935	9.2	1912
晋中市 Jinzhong	10415	65.1	2007	12.5	3566
运城市 Yuncheng	9681	60.2	6269	39.0	139
忻州市 Xinzhou	13622	78.1	1410	8.1	2411
临汾市 Linfen	11100	59.9	4177	22.5	3263
吕梁市 Lvliang	12808	73.7	2179	12.5	2395

19-63 公路绿化里程(2016年)
LENGTH OF AFFOREST HIGHWAYS(2016)

单位：公里 (km)

市名 City	绿化里程 Length of Afforest Highways	占总里程(%) Percentage	在绿化里程中 In Length of Afforest Highways 国道 State Class	省道 Province Class	县公路 County Class	乡公路 Township Class	专用公路 Special Purpose	村道 Village Class
全省 Total	**60882.6**	**42.9**	**8268.6**	**4879.4**	**13958.5**	**20657.2**	**253.6**	**12865.4**
太原市 Taiyuan	2272.8	30.7	476.2	171.0	673.2	615.3	86.4	250.8
大同市 Datong	4282.2	34.1	515.3	615.6	1278.9	1494.9		377.5
阳泉市 Yangquan	1641.0	29.0	311.9	165.6	601.4	254.1	3.5	304.4
长治市 Changzhi	5897.2	50.7	723.4	539.0	1177.1	1784.5	13.7	1659.4
晋城市 Jincheng	2711.0	29.7	346.2	387.6	528.4	827.7	17.6	603.6
朔州市 Shuozhou	4196.0	41.1	620.4	310.9	929.8	1649.2	20.6	665.2
晋中市 Jinzhong	8320.4	52.0	1058.3	550.5	1903.2	3141.4	34.6	1632.4
运城市 Yuncheng	14918.7	92.7	1048.6	590.7	2508.7	5998.1	21.3	4751.4
忻州市 Xinzhou	4760.5	27.3	1301.1	518.8	1247.0	1554.0	38.9	100.8
临汾市 Linfen	7711.2	41.6	1056.3	541.8	2023.8	2630.0	17.1	1442.3
吕梁市 Lvliang	4171.4	24.0	810.9	488.0	1087.0	708.0		1077.4

19-64 公路客货运输量(2016年)
HIGHWAY PASSENGER AND FREIGHT TRAFFIC(2016)

市名 City	客运量(万人) Passenger Traffic (10 000 persons)	旅客周转量(万人公里) Passenger-kilometers (10 000 person-km)	货运量(万吨) Freight Traffic (10 000 tons)	货物周转量(万吨公里) Freight Ton-kilometers (10 000 ton-km)
全省 Total	**18702**	**1411424**	**102200**	**14520591**
太原市 Taiyuan	876	225380	15043	1436331
大同市 Datong	1381	86688	10315	1028180
阳泉市 Yangquan	1104	71225	3709	322228
长治市 Changzhi	3295	211229	8713	1116132
晋城市 Jincheng	1416	116678	5990	493715
朔州市 Shuozhou	1210	55806	3244	333380
晋中市 Jinzhong	2065	128282	11021	1911230
运城市 Yuncheng	2921	144975	13432	3261467
忻州市 Xinzhou	1579	100313	7906	1640804
临汾市 Linfen	1463	150552	14669	2102416
吕梁市 Lvliang	1391	120297	8159	874708

19-65 镇(乡)村通公路、通油路情况(2016年)
TRAFFIC CONNECTION OF TOWNS, TOWNSHIPS AND VILLAGES(2016)

单位：个 (unit)

市名 City	乡、镇总数 Number of Townships and Towns	#通油路数 Connect With Asphalt Highways	镇总数 Number of Towns	#通油路数 Connect With Asphalt Highways	#占镇总数的比例(%) Percentage (%)	乡总数 Number of Townships	#通油路数 Connect With Asphalt Highways	#占乡总数的比例(%) Percentage (%)
全省 Total	**1196**	**1196**	**563**	**563**	**100.0**	**633**	**633**	**100.0**
太原市 Taiyuan	52	52	21	21	100.0	31	31	100.0
大同市 Datong	99	99	33	33	100.0	66	66	100.0
阳泉市 Yangquan	32	32	20	20	100.0	12	12	100.0
长治市 Changzhi	132	132	68	68	100.0	64	64	100.0
晋城市 Jincheng	74	74	48	48	100.0	26	26	100.0
朔州市 Shuozhou	69	69	18	18	100.0	51	51	100.0
晋中市 Jinzhong	118	118	59	59	100.0	59	59	100.0
运城市 Yuncheng	136	136	81	81	100.0	55	55	100.0
忻州市 Xinzhou	185	185	59	59	100.0	126	126	100.0
临汾市 Linfen	151	151	75	75	100.0	76	76	100.0
吕梁市 Lvliang	148	148	81	81	100.0	67	67	100.0

市名 City	行政村 Administration Villages					
	总数 Total	通公路 Connect with Highways	#通油路 Connect with Asphalt Highways	通公路村比重(%) Percentage of Connect with Highways	通油路村比重(%) Percentage of Connect with Asphalt Highways	不通公路 Non-connect with Highways
全省 Total	**27972**	**27953**	**27843**	**99.93**	**99.54**	**19**
太原市 Taiyuan	894	894	892	100.00	99.78	
大同市 Datong	1969	1969	1967	100.00	99.90	
阳泉市 Yangquan	960	960	960	100.00	100.00	
长治市 Changzhi	3446	3444	3444	99.94	99.94	2
晋城市 Jincheng	2212	2211	2211	99.95	99.95	1
朔州市 Shuozhou	1624	1624	1623	100.00	99.94	
晋中市 Jinzhong	2712	2712	2708	100.00	99.85	
运城市 Yuncheng	3196	3196	3196	100.00	100.00	
忻州市 Xinzhou	4888	4872	4771	99.67	97.61	16
临汾市 Linfen	2961	2961	2961	100.00	100.00	
吕梁市 Lvliang	3110	3110	3110	100.00	100.00	

19-66 邮电业务总量及电话数(2016年)

BUSINESS VOLUME OF POST AND TELECOMMUNICATION SERVICES AND NUMBER OF TELEPHONE SUBSCRIBERS(2016)

单位：万元 (10 000 yuan)

市 名 City		邮电业务总量 Business Volume of Post and Telecommunication Services	邮 政 Post	电 信 Telecommunication Services	电话数(万户) Number of Telephone Subscribers (10 000 subscribers)	固 定 Fixed Telephone	移 动 Mobile Telephone
全 省	**Total**	**3856028**	**568744**	**3287284**	**3709**	**344**	**3366**
太原市	Taiyuan	866245	206127	660118	747	95	652
大同市	Datong	352934	52707	300228	324	24	300
阳泉市	Yangquan	141412	18235	123177	153	13	140
长治市	Changzhi	276787	33778	243009	326	30	296
晋城市	Jincheng	200856	20492	180364	250	23	227
朔州市	Shuozhou	196272	15851	180421	161	12	148
晋中市	Jinzhong	305241	37370	267871	335	38	296
运城市	Yuncheng	427400	64325	363075	449	38	411
忻州市	Xinzhou	281092	38414	242678	265	19	246
临汾市	Linfen	456105	44169	411936	391	28	362
吕梁市	Lvliang	351684	37277	314407	310	24	286

注：本表邮政分市数据中不含民营业务量。

Note: Post data of 11 cities doesn't contain volume of private enterprises.

19-67 小学基本情况(2016年)

BASIC STATISTICS ON PRIMARY SCHOOLS(2016)

单位：人 (person)

市 名 City		学校数(所) Number of Schools (unit)	毕业生数 Number of Graduates	招生数 Number of New Students Enrollment	在校学生数 Number of Students Enrollment	专任教师数 Number of Full-time Teachers
全 省	**Total**	**6043**	**380313**	**383579**	**2270899**	**171535**
太原市	Taiyuan	433	42072	52229	286678	17093
大同市	Datong	436	30975	32280	199172	17629
阳泉市	Yangquan	265	14104	12929	83015	5382
长治市	Changzhi	643	37159	36392	207548	15107
晋城市	Jincheng	494	23599	18486	118011	9227
朔州市	Shuozhou	182	21565	20754	128849	9024
晋中市	Jinzhong	678	34806	37768	236867	15054
运城市	Yuncheng	820	52341	51414	286986	25517
忻州市	Xinzhou	504	32156	31001	185781	16234
临汾市	Linfen	1012	48231	44875	272412	21404
吕梁市	Lvliang	576	43305	45451	265580	19864

注：本表专任教师数不包括九年一贯制学制学校和十二年一贯制学校。

Note: Primary full-time teachers in the table don't include teachers who work in 9-year system or 12-year system schools.

19-68 普通中学基本情况(2016年)
BASIC STATISTICS ON REGULAR SECONDARY SCHOOLS(2016)

单位：人 (person)

市名 City	学校数(所) Number of Schools (unit)				毕业生数 Number of Graduates		
	合计 Total	#初级中学 Junior	#高级中学 Senior	#完全中学 Junior and Senior	合计 Total	初中 Junior	高中 Senior
全 省 Total	**2353**	**1361**	**250**	**208**	**695417**	**410994**	**284423**
太原市 Taiyuan	218	107	15	63	73467	44039	29428
大同市 Datong	212	88	11	30	59721	35833	23888
阳泉市 Yangquan	82	50	7	7	24249	14189	10060
长治市 Changzhi	209	110	14	29	68249	39319	28930
晋城市 Jincheng	156	114	23	9	51542	27888	23654
朔州市 Shuozhou	89	47	17	8	48363	27605	20758
晋中市 Jinzhong	226	155	24	8	53903	35056	18847
运城市 Yuncheng	330	190	53	9	104438	58618	45820
忻州市 Xinzhou	260	144	27	8	55531	34297	21234
临汾市 Linfen	283	172	25	29	81327	48557	32770
吕梁市 Lvliang	288	184	34	8	74627	45593	29034

市名 City	招生数 New Students Enrollment			在校学生数 Number of Students Enrollment		
	合计 Total	初中 Junior	高中 Senior	合计 Total	初中 Junior	高中 Senior
全 省 Total	**620287**	**375748**	**244539**	**1846516**	**1092739**	**753777**
太原市 Taiyuan	67417	40105	27312	200083	117861	82222
大同市 Datong	52183	31234	20949	153758	91776	61982
阳泉市 Yangquan	22629	14001	8628	66576	39504	27072
长治市 Changzhi	59953	36487	23466	174684	102687	71997
晋城市 Jincheng	40354	23331	17023	126228	69745	56483
朔州市 Shuozhou	41111	24583	16528	126054	74679	51375
晋中市 Jinzhong	54986	35689	19297	159213	102651	56562
运城市 Yuncheng	88535	53179	35356	262893	153532	109361
忻州市 Xinzhou	49290	29718	19572	149058	88225	60833
临汾市 Linfen	75054	45904	29150	223655	132071	91584
吕梁市 Lvliang	68775	41517	27258	204314	120008	84306

19–68 续表 continued

单位：人 (person)

市 名 City	专任教师数 Number of Full-time Teachers 合 计 Total	初 中 Junior	高 中 Senior
全 省 Total	**173503**	**110164**	**63339**
太原市 Taiyuan	18911	11601	7310
大同市 Datong	15744	10431	5313
阳泉市 Yangquan	5780	3813	1967
长治市 Changzhi	15367	9629	5738
晋城市 Jincheng	11118	6792	4326
朔州市 Shuozhou	10339	5931	4408
晋中市 Jinzhong	15272	10099	5173
运城市 Yuncheng	26344	16426	9918
忻州市 Xinzhou	14236	9355	4881
临汾市 Linfen	21330	13663	7667
吕梁市 Lvliang	19062	12424	6638

19–69 村卫生室情况(2016年)
MAIN INDICATORS OF RURAL CLINICS (2016)

单位：人 (person)

市 名 City	机构数(个) Institutions (unit)	执业(助理)医师 Licensed (Assistant) Doctors	注册护士 Registered Nurses	乡村医生 Rural Doctors	卫生员 Health Workers
全 省 Total	**29027**	**4260**	**438**	**35797**	**2832**
太原市 Taiyuan	965	294	23	1332	54
大同市 Datong	1823	275	27	2361	146
阳泉市 Yangquan	927	131	12	1293	156
长治市 Changzhi	3751	478	33	3917	358
晋城市 Jincheng	2250	312	19	2643	148
朔州市 Shuozhou	1652	48	7	1642	130
晋中市 Jinzhong	2799	345	67	4159	233
运城市 Yuncheng	3518	717	76	4451	493
忻州市 Xinzhou	4188	392	40	5269	176
临汾市 Linfen	3540	791	59	4287	393
吕梁市 Lvliang	3614	477	75	4443	545

19-70 卫生机构数(2016年)
HEALTH CARE INSTITUTIONS(2016)

单位：个 (unit)

市　名 City	总　计 Total	#医　院 Hospitals	#疾病预防控制中心 Diseases Prevention and Control Centre	#妇幼保健院(所、站) Maternity and Child Care Centres
全　省 Total	**13178**	**1393**	**136**	**134**
太原市 Taiyuan	2759	185	14	13
大同市 Datong	1402	141	13	14
阳泉市 Yangquan	596	51	6	6
长治市 Changzhi	872	101	14	15
晋城市 Jincheng	852	80	7	7
朔州市 Shuozhou	475	64	7	6
晋中市 Jinzhong	969	103	12	12
运城市 Yuncheng	1787	263	14	14
忻州市 Xinzhou	1015	114	15	15
临汾市 Linfen	1281	192	20	18
吕梁市 Lvliang	1170	99	14	14

19-71 卫生机构床位数和人员情况(2016年)
BEDS AND PERSONNELS IN HEALTH CARE INSTITUTIONS(2016)

单位：人 (person)

市　名 City	卫生机构床位数(张) Beds (unit)	卫生技术人员 Medical Technical Personnels	#执业(助理)医师 Licensed (Assistant) Doctors	#注册护士 Registered Nurses
全　省 Total	**189778**	**225770**	**91748**	**92139**
太原市 Taiyuan	37891	55389	20835	26172
大同市 Datong	19445	21692	9389	8390
阳泉市 Yangquan	7280	9893	3843	4364
长治市 Changzhi	16888	19650	7840	8122
晋城市 Jincheng	11257	12891	5532	4741
朔州市 Shuozhou	7684	6492	2827	2234
晋中市 Jinzhong	15501	17581	6813	7285
运城市 Yuncheng	29002	27406	10937	10522
忻州市 Xinzhou	12813	13816	5877	4827
临汾市 Linfen	19815	25147	10587	9858
吕梁市 Lvliang	12202	15813	7268	5624

19–72 主要城市空气质量情况 (2016年)
AIR QUALITY IN MAJOR CITIES(2016)

市 名 City	空气质量达标天数(天) Days Reach the Standard of Air Quality (day)	细颗粒物($PM_{2.5}$)年平均浓度 ($\mu g/m^3$) Annual Average Concentration of $PM_{2.5}$	可吸入颗粒物(PM_{10})年平均浓度 ($\mu g/m^3$) Annual Average Concentration of PM_{10}	二氧化硫年平均浓度 ($\mu g/m^3$) Annual Average Concentration of SO_2
全 省 Total	**249**	**60**	**109**	**66**
太原市 Taiyuan	232	66	125	68
大同市 Datong	320	37	78	48
阳泉市 Yangquan	202	63	131	62
长治市 Changzhi	219	69	114	61
晋城市 Jincheng	237	62	111	70
朔州市 Shuozhou	247	57	97	67
晋中市 Jinzhong	226	62	109	88
运城市 Yuncheng	252	65	108	67
忻州市 Xinzhou	269	56	103	49
临汾市 Linfen	244	74	120	83
吕梁市 Lvliang	287	49	98	62

市 名 City	二氧化氮年平均浓度 ($\mu g/m^3$) Annual Average Concentration of NO_2	一氧化碳日均值第95百分位浓度 (mg/m^3) Daily Average 95th Percentile Concentration of CO	臭氧(O_3)日最大8小时第90百分位浓度 ($\mu g/m^3$) Daily Maximum 8 Hours Average 90th Percentile Concentration of O_3
全 省 Total	**37**	**3.4**	**138**
太原市 Taiyuan	46	3.3	140
大同市 Datong	29	2.7	134
阳泉市 Yangquan	48	2.7	168
长治市 Changzhi	40	3.7	155
晋城市 Jincheng	40	4.1	128
朔州市 Shuozhou	33	2.0	160
晋中市 Jinzhong	36	3.1	142
运城市 Yuncheng	36	4.0	110
忻州市 Xinzhou	39	3.5	138
临汾市 Linfen	34	5.0	136
吕梁市 Lvliang	25	3.1	106

20 县（市、区）篇

COUNTIES, CITIES AND DISTRICTS AT COUNTY LEVEL

20-1 常住人口数(2016年)
RESIDENT POPULATION(2016)

单位：人 (person)

县(市、区)	Region	总户数(户) Number of Households (household)	常住人口 Resident Population	按性别分 by Sex		按城镇、乡村分 by Residence	
				男 Male	女 Female	城镇人口 Urban	乡村人口 Rural
太 原 市	**Taiyuan**						
小店区	Xiaodian	178461	834814	424647	410167	764397	70417
迎泽区	Yingze	155923	610358	299327	311031	593109	17249
杏花岭区	Xinghualing	179633	663272	334006	329266	638750	24522
尖草坪区	Jiancaoping	109647	430465	221569	208896	404316	26149
万柏林区	Wanbailin	164074	779038	405592	373446	760121	18917
晋源区	Jinyuan	64985	230090	117678	112412	150881	79209
清徐县	Qingxu	122842	353186	180961	172225	118514	234672
阳曲县	Yangqu	64277	122511	63672	58839	43368	79143
娄烦县	Loufan	52316	108442	57004	51438	43243	65199
古交市	Gujiao	80128	212253	111461	100792	156494	55759
大 同 市	**Datong**						
城　区	Chengqu	250709	745951	369291	376660	745951	
矿　区	Kuangqu	164844	514611	258290	256321	514611	
南郊区	Nanjiao	134391	419136	215457	203679	194848	224288
新荣区	Xinrong	49560	111263	58020	53243	37518	73745
阳高县	Yanggao	119205	279954	143243	136711	113269	166685
天镇县	Tianzhen	96294	212620	109103	103517	85408	127212
广灵县	Guangling	79131	188813	100453	88360	56606	132207
灵丘县	Lingqiu	103571	241968	126541	115427	76267	165701
浑源县	Hunyuan	136307	353945	181176	172769	142250	211695
左云县	Zuoyun	61980	161417	84020	77397	77415	84002
大同县	Datongxian	81676	192213	98363	93850	77692	114521
阳 泉 市	**Yangquan**						
城　区	Chengqu	72802	198093	98504	99589	198093	
矿　区	Kuangqu	86174	250033	124592	125441	250033	
郊　区	Jiaoqu	101245	290527	148878	141649	212448	78079
平定县	Pingding	143764	343985	177865	166120	142673	201312
盂　县	Yuxian	133790	320947	166493	154454	132598	188349
长 治 市	**Changzhi**						
城　区	Chengqu	123126	510961	258228	252733	510961	
郊　区	Jiaoqu	100132	289397	147325	142072	200877	88520
长治县	Changzhixian	121509	351613	175811	175802	136564	215049
襄垣县	Xiangyuan	88963	277945	141597	136348	133611	144334
屯留县	Tunliu	101598	272423	142343	130080	108696	163727
平顺县	Pingshun	57376	151539	76392	75147	48982	102557
黎城县	Licheng	67061	161930	82803	79127	68616	93314
壶关县	Huguan	113488	298591	152110	146481	96734	201857
长子县	Zhangzi	130400	362286	182642	179644	118973	243313
武乡县	Wuxiang	76409	184638	98348	86290	65986	118652
沁　县	Qinxian	67362	176639	95148	81491	73332	103307
沁源县	Qinyuan	64282	162864	84958	77906	72303	90561
潞城市	Lucheng	78914	234554	114663	119891	134660	99894

注：本表总户数为公安年报数。

Note: Number of households are obtained from public security department.

20-1 续表1 continued

单位：人 (person)

县(市、区)	Region	总户数(户) Number of Households (household)	常住人口 Resident Population	按性别分 by Sex		按城镇、乡村分 by Residence	
				男 Male	女 Female	城镇人口 Urban	乡村人口 Rural
晋城市	**Jincheng**						
城　区	Chengqu	135637	492880	248136	244744	492880	
沁水县	Qinshui	82069	215866	110350	105516	90992	124874
阳城县	Yangcheng	170072	391986	198114	193872	182597	209389
陵川县	Lingchuan	92335	235317	120138	115179	96566	138751
泽州县	Zezhou	193617	491789	248402	243387	230250	261539
高平市	Gaoping	159526	493020	246870	246150	260758	232262
朔州市	**Shuozhou**						
朔城区	Shuocheng	181426	521827	269388	252439	333525	188302
平鲁区	Pinglu	85936	209476	108678	100798	111078	98398
山阴县	Shanyin	104821	246549	128982	117567	130028	116521
应　县	Yingxian	131351	338445	176163	162282	129121	209324
右玉县	Youyu	50342	115498	59906	55592	61080	54418
怀仁县	Huairen	123790	336308	172750	163558	193574	142734
晋中市	**Jinzhong**						
榆次区	Yuci	220362	658289	328826	329463	505580	152709
榆社县	Yushe	57576	139132	73194	65938	54176	84956
左权县	Zuoquan	68176	165796	87916	77880	73131	92665
和顺县	Heshun	56321	147620	76868	70752	68147	79473
昔阳县	Xiyang	103731	231496	118975	112521	85274	146222
寿阳县	Shouyang	87392	214332	117837	96495	84725	129607
太谷县	Taigu	118195	308233	160107	148126	145424	162809
祁　县	Qixian	111382	273592	141216	132376	109247	164345
平遥县	Pingyao	211077	519058	268558	250500	229890	289168
灵石县	Lingshi	105448	271402	140070	131332	143136	128266
介休市	Jiexiu	167424	419788	214708	205080	273701	146087
运城市	**Yuncheng**						
盐湖区	Yanhu	234994	701178	351467	349711	498267	202911
临猗县	Linyi	172160	591050	299892	291158	250517	340533
万荣县	Wanrong	139211	454040	230292	223748	140951	313089
闻喜县	Wenxi	132440	417342	214577	202765	204100	213242
稷山县	Jishan	117530	359490	183798	175692	140822	218668
新绛县	Xinjiang	101409	344636	176033	168603	150591	194045
绛　县	Jiangxian	86040	290965	148008	142957	157259	133706
垣曲县	Yuanqu	88348	238550	124101	114449	118642	119908
夏　县	Xiaxian	111846	364550	188002	176548	121741	242809
平陆县	Pinglu	97601	266328	137204	129124	89458	176870
芮城县	Ruicheng	151613	408628	209068	199560	199077	209551
永济市	Yongji	143526	458920	232328	226592	233321	225599
河津市	Hejin	132474	409501	214473	195028	223062	186439
忻州市	**Xinzhou**						
忻府区	Xinfu	230123	562131	284438	277693	347273	214858
定襄县	Dingxiang	102746	224407	115003	109404	90560	133847
五台县	Wutai	140939	306154	157288	148866	114931	191223
代　县	Daixian	96338	220617	113423	107194	97091	123526

20-1 续表2 continued

单位：人 (person)

县(市、区)	Region	总户数(户) Number of Households (household)	常住人口 Resident Population	按性别分 by Sex		按城镇、乡村分 by Residence	
				男 Male	女 Female	城镇人口 Urban	乡村人口 Rural
繁峙县	Fanshi	115261	275299	142592	132707	122369	152930
宁武县	Ningwu	69582	165168	86791	78377	81180	83988
静乐县	Jingle	58875	160885	84229	76656	64095	96790
神池县	Shenchi	46089	108882	56456	52426	43300	65582
五寨县	Wuzhai	53389	110924	57732	53192	51659	59265
岢岚县	Kelan	37841	86845	45679	41166	41894	44951
河曲县	Hequ	65517	149313	77664	71649	73848	75465
保德县	Baode	65103	165231	86328	78903	69165	96066
偏关县	Pianguan	46882	115597	60006	55591	54496	61101
原平市	Yuanping	198763	503859	260206	243653	259537	244322
临汾市	**Linfen**						
尧都区	Yaodu	273182	976259	499312	476947	676548	299711
曲沃县	Quwo	65474	245397	125564	119833	98850	146547
翼城县	Yicheng	102242	321017	163619	157398	124144	196873
襄汾县	Xiangfen	179685	458179	234746	223433	186595	271584
洪洞县	Hongtong	272459	756682	385382	371300	318629	438053
古　县	Guxian	34957	95039	48824	46215	39451	55588
安泽县	Anze	34831	84869	43875	40994	35020	49849
浮山县	Fushan	49199	130780	67122	63658	51184	79596
吉　县	Jixian	40899	109586	55904	53682	39988	69598
乡宁县	Xiangning	81601	240705	126392	114313	90358	150347
大宁县	Daning	25478	66737	35539	31198	29663	37074
隰　县	Xixian	41266	107236	56285	50951	47139	60097
永和县	Yonghe	25101	65682	33957	31725	27515	38167
蒲　县	Puxian	37629	110810	56550	54260	51192	59618
汾西县	Fenxi	56445	149746	78130	71616	66303	83443
侯马市	Houma	82714	247756	125803	121953	161998	85758
霍州市	Huozhou	128865	291568	148313	143255	185908	105660
吕梁市	**Lvliang**						
离石区	Lishi	110714	332616	170966	161650	273459	59157
文水县	Wenshui	169271	436437	222478	213959	162056	274381
交城县	Jiaocheng	87460	237382	121796	115586	123850	113532
兴　县	Xingxian	103202	289506	151338	138168	115775	173731
临　县	Linxian	246617	600397	311310	289087	197423	402974
柳林县	Liulin	128548	330468	173539	156929	137664	192804
石楼县	Shilou	44606	115732	60675	55057	50239	65493
岚　县	Lanxian	68828	180002	93831	86171	64870	115132
方山县	Fangshan	62410	147555	77056	70499	53232	94323
中阳县	Zhongyang	57875	145953	76364	69589	90402	55551
交口县	Jiaokou	46606	123968	63951	60017	51545	72423
孝义市	Xiaoyi	186404	483612	247921	235691	322183	161429
汾阳市	Fenyang	165974	431243	221263	209980	197872	233371

20-2 非私营单位从业人员和在岗职工工资(2016年)

单位：人

县(市、区)	Region	从业人员 Employees	在岗职工 Fully Employed	国有单位 State-owned Units	城镇集体单位 Urban Collective -owned Units
太原市	**Taiyuan**				
小店区	Xiaodian	145733	141836	72794	788
迎泽区	Yingze	161551	151845	87312	9311
杏花岭区	Xinhualing	269669	261413	192138	5324
尖草坪区	Jiancaoping	67659	66229	7966	9207
万柏林区	Wanbailin	193770	188230	35635	3312
晋源区	Jinyuan	16374	14982	5588	436
清徐县	Qingxu	22867	22582	12341	544
阳曲县	Yanqu	8812	8764	5378	421
娄烦县	Loufan	5658	5319	4579	415
古交市	Gujiao	16418	16083	10095	636
经济区	Economic Zone	91596	91383	2321	18
高新区	High-tech Zone	38845	38626	10812	111
工业园区	Industrial Park	1577	1502	274	17
大同市	**Datong**				
市辖	Jurisdiction of the City	125088	125088		
城区	Chengqu	114779	101697	53996	3070
矿区	Kuangqu	25797	24014	10986	11055
南郊区	Nanjiao	44655	40202	24565	967
新荣区	Xinrong	9619	8691	6132	8
阳高县	Yanggao	10326	10326	7661	
天镇县	Tianzhen	6205	6205	5867	
广灵县	Guangling	8111	7481	6066	387
灵丘县	Lingqiu	11551	11119	9038	43
浑源县	Hunyuan	12333	12321	11710	53
左云县	Zuoyun	16200	15950	9941	191
大同县	Datongxian	8318	8102	6692	8
开发区	Development Zone	9268	9086	1465	434
阳泉市	**Yangquan**				
城区	Chengqu	52665	51459	31250	935
矿区	Kuangqu	104308	103594	12761	6819
郊区	Jiaoqu	24453	24110	13245	1517
平定县	Pingding	24902	22495	9691	1359
盂县	Yuxian	38276	37917	11497	2267
开发区	Development Zone	9058	8475	5724	135
长治市	**Changzhi**				
城区	Chengqu	110371	102526	68018	1012
郊区	Jiaoqu	35750	34737	8464	1607
长治县	Changzhixian	37611	36696	8915	639
襄垣县	Xiangyuan	71576	71115	9629	1153
屯留县	Tunliu	30061	28339	7539	668
平顺县	Pingshun	9079	7736	6185	774
黎城县	Licheng	7719	7679	5035	294
壶关县	Huguan	14886	14579	8002	1215
长子县	Zhangzi	28477	27676	10693	1376
武乡县	Wuxiang	15772	15570	7559	903
沁县	Qinxian	6418	6300	5081	312
沁源县	Qinyuan	27850	26318	7746	994
潞城市	Lucheng	29610	29305	9552	76
高新区	High-tech Zone	485	485		

NUMBER OF EMPLOYEES AND WAGE OF FULLY EMPLOYED STAFF AND WORKERS IN NON–PRIVATE UNITS(2016)

(person)

其他单位 Other Units	其他从业人员 Other Employees	在岗职工工资总额（千元） Total Wages of Fully Employed (1 000 yuan)	#国有单位 State–owned Units	#城镇集体单位 Urban Collective –owned Units	在岗职工平均工资（元） Average Wages of Fully Employed (yuan)
68254	3897	9201905	5541204	26716	65022
55222	9706	10132060	6042138	640663	68351
63951	8256	20687618	17108699	151565	79793
49056	1430	3892893	525551	299038	59265
149283	5540	11104775	2346991	84131	58611
8958	1392	821161	389993	18759	54454
9697	285	833588	515269	16069	36788
2965	48	422538	298443	15957	48679
325	339	283304	253686	14493	52600
5352	335	833862	525956	21845	50211
89044	213	3935461	107275	332	46969
27703	219	2358078	621148	7701	61046
1211	75	88611	18662	403	57765
125088		7781783			61842
44631	13082	5559523	3094172	132980	54267
1973	1783	1118785	700463	350483	46901
14670	4453	2228577	1342618	22377	55140
2551	928	457432	321554	244	52153
2665		588049	470351		55676
338		243090	225706		39246
1028	630	419860	362673	9462	56433
2038	432	416683	353127	1280	38422
558	12	758657	721214	499	60106
5818	250	745237	425696	5048	46688
1402	216	450513	395601	380	54847
7187	182	433947	107290	15252	47153
19274	1206	2692494	1876868	17604	51995
84014	714	4958854	563974	196100	48194
9348	343	1338419	786308	98708	54993
11445	2407	1169791	586387	94099	52062
24153	359	1431199	584406	81791	37723
2616	583	354052	243008	2246	42044
33496	7845	4983674	3528995	25768	49267
24666	1013	1700703	452438	75549	48311
27142	915	1952464	463280	48562	54503
60333	461	3714989	482646	62912	52538
20132	1722	1589051	400528	47751	57645
777	1343	383849	333020	30208	50807
2350	40	371771	247730	28096	48282
5362	307	604413	406979	49630	42137
15607	801	1705905	487708	74735	61122
7108	202	749523	396710	39671	48838
907	118	330168	278901	21989	52575
17578	1532	1241549	382604	41146	47884
19677	305	1229337	470723	2200	41654
485		23611			40155

20-2 续表1

单位：人

县(市、区)	Region	从业人员 Employees	在岗职工 Fully Employed	国有单位 State-owned Units	城镇集体单位 Urban Collective -owned Units
晋城市	**Jincheng**				
城　区	Chengqu	65889	64586	36822	3576
沁水县	Qingshui	32638	30918	11278	946
阳城县	Yangcheng	46543	44464	13055	2641
陵川县	Lingchuan	13868	12779	8495	850
泽州县	Zezhou	40051	39812	16341	2269
高平市	Gaoping	53122	51878	13864	1276
市直管	City-administered	69538	64230	2065	
开发区	Development Zone	34048	33931		80
朔州市	**Shuozhou**				
朔城区	Shuocheng	66647	66103	38036	3678
平鲁区	Pinglu	30938	30823	11838	78
山阴县	Shanyin	20371	19660	11108	377
应　县	Yingxian	13249	12648	8731	87
右玉县	Yuoyu	9606	9522	5566	69
怀仁县	Huairen	39607	37171	16784	2838
开发区	Development Zone	8528	8124	2288	
晋中市	**Jinzhong**				
榆次区	Yuci	100817	88805	44930	936
榆社县	Yushe	11386	11315	6258	243
左权县	Zuoquan	13787	13687	7842	430
和顺县	Heshun	17984	17943	8207	481
昔阳县	Xiyang	21425	20320	7883	799
寿阳县	Shouyang	30601	30337	8948	834
太谷县	Taigu	19279	18575	14515	983
祁　县	Qixian	17788	17680	10837	2413
平遥县	Pingyao	20753	19410	16116	150
灵石县	Lingshi	27057	26747	11147	65
介休市	Jiexiu	48994	47102	14792	3403
开发区	Development Zone	20618	9531	3171	86
运城市	**Yuncheng**				
盐湖区	Yanhu	78886	76289	49588	3196
临猗县	Linyi	32142	32138	20489	1336
万荣县	Wanrong	13562	13560	12845	466
闻喜县	Wenxi	18874	17604	10912	693
稷山县	Jishan	12675	12243	10589	333
新绛县	Xinjiang	11741	11211	8509	1293
绛　县	Jiangxian	10914	10835	9299	303
垣曲县	Yuanqu	23533	22573	9014	276
夏　县	Xiaxian	12703	12189	9184	523
平陆县	Pinglu	11580	10833	8175	744
芮城县	Ruicheng	18484	18033	10062	755
永济市	Yongji	26582	25963	14516	1918
河津市	Hejin	56055	49630	24574	862
开发区	Development Zone	11929	10107	1550	109
风陵渡开发区	Fenglingdu Development Zone	1039	1039	451	
绛县开发区	Jiangxian Development Zone	3117	3025	2268	
空港开发区	Konggang Development Zone	8386	8113	1365	557

continued

(person)

其他单位 Other Units	其他从业人员 Other Employmees	在岗职工工资总额(千元) Total Wages of Fully Employed (1 000 yuan)	#国有单位 State-owned Units	#城镇集体单位 Urban Collective -owned Units	在岗职工平均工资(元) Average Wages of Fully Employed (yuan)
24188	1303	3657028	2153370	206396	56307
18694	1720	1718584	622759	52031	55152
28768	2079	2256074	710047	121893	50763
3434	1089	640198	493713	29845	50409
21202	239	2047953	996289	98339	50949
36738	1244	2740229	738272	63886	52847
62165	5308	4409420	103093		67524
33851	117	1524035		1279	43735
24389	544	3303121	1956729	243137	50189
18907	115	1946075	476231	2088	63380
8175	711	877797	428891	13086	45848
3830	601	584106	456423	3321	45866
3887	84	502346	245902	2972	52690
17549	2436	1733769	794556	74973	46484
5836	404	485828	108869		58023
42939	12012	5062568	2823713	37426	57546
4814	71	598479	345678	19518	53321
5415	100	624610	388774	38947	45695
9255	41	811140	386841	41044	45677
11638	1105	1103426	410989	54327	53648
20555	264	1643185	458319	48355	53666
3077	704	952641	778511	72236	50729
4430	108	862310	588307	92567	48839
3144	1343	987967	792950	6390	50322
15535	310	1239972	570703	2559	46344
28907	1892	2329447	763942	186827	48787
6274	11087	703357	219191	3176	73820
23505	2597	4235884	3018788	207281	55451
10313	4	1268558	861473	75323	45209
249	2	644538	615030	21444	47581
5999	1270	960044	651675	48648	54458
1321	432	587039	517603	23101	48090
1409	530	563967	458930	55523	49851
1233	79	545057	495250	18323	47612
13283	960	1058084	464464	19799	47091
2482	514	589633	483431	27410	48342
1914	747	544462	427600	39406	50052
7216	451	976685	607066	23159	54811
9529	619	1411210	750677	102802	54080
24194	6425	2049712	1020553	27679	44166
8448	1822	338897	82864	4930	32935
588		72149	25403		71153
757	92	112087	67920		36052
6191	273	288679	71129	29302	40918

20-2 续表2

单位：人

县(市、区)	Region	从业人员 Employees	在岗职工 Fully Employed	国有单位 State-owned Units	城镇集体单位 Urban Collective -owned Units
忻州市	**Xinzhou**				
忻府区	Xinfu	73448	70666	46800	3817
定襄县	Dingxiang	9357	8472	6812	655
五台县	Wutai	13688	13451	11542	1363
代　县	Daixian	8155	8083	6866	1025
繁峙县	Fanshi	15335	14884	12005	2396
宁武县	Ningwu	20257	20250	10130	350
静乐县	Jingle	12698	11538	7992	379
神池县	Shenchi	6322	5734	4686	171
五寨县	Wuzhai	5990	5934	5217	377
岢岚县	Kelan	4655	4606	4180	326
河曲县	Hequ	12652	12569	6791	234
保德县	Baode	13861	13532	9326	289
偏关县	Pianguan	7480	7063	5616	652
原平市	Yuanping	33611	32323	14497	2120
五台山风景名胜区	Wutai Mount Scenic Area	1953	1935	1463	258
临汾市	**Linfen**				
尧都区	Yaodu	88773	86122	52361	3201
曲沃县	Quwo	10764	10502	9040	374
翼城县	Yicheng	19435	18778	11676	514
襄汾县	Xiangfen	13604	11955	10000	550
洪洞县	Hongtong	46923	46725	20772	1542
古　县	Guxian	9766	9511	5643	310
安泽县	Anze	8897	8304	6192	263
浮山县	Fushan	8985	8128	5605	453
吉　县	Jixian	7820	7764	5616	279
乡宁县	Xiangning	23476	23155	10677	548
大宁县	Daning	5086	4994	4713	191
隰　县	Xixian	7725	7195	6625	329
永和县	Yonghe	4265	3759	3352	151
蒲　县	Puxian	14914	14872	9272	554
汾西县	Fenxi	6029	6029	5823	146
侯马市	Houma	28668	27557	15748	252
霍州市	Huozhou	39576	36081	10386	521
吕梁市	**Lvliang**				
离石区	Lishi	58131	49381	33451	1187
文水县	Wenshui	24264	22468	12166	1268
交城县	Jiaocheng	27712	27584	7854	1647
兴　县	Xingxian	20217	19255	9775	1097
临　县	Linxian	20580	20321	12788	819
柳林县	Liulin	41684	40473	10393	7471
石楼县	Shilou	6359	5392	5048	246
岚　县	Lanxian	11201	11181	6841	231
方山县	Fangshan	12566	11898	5041	86
中阳县	Zhongyang	21899	21840	9147	452
交口县	Jiaokou	9326	9084	5864	209
孝义市	Xiaoyi	62074	59193	22686	1676
汾阳市	Fenyang	35904	33268	12561	4437

continued

(person)

其他单位 Other Units	其他从业人员 Other Employmees	在岗职工工资总额（千元） Total Wages of Fully Employed (1 000 yuan)	#国有单位 State-owned Units	#城镇集体单位 Urban Collective -owned Units	在岗职工平均工资（元） Average Wages of Fully Employed (yuan)
20049	2782	2902685	2078825	133692	41585
1005	885	360688	303111	26493	42369
546	237	580450	500188	51831	43541
192	72	376461	332336	37874	45439
483	451	606689	536957	47120	39687
9770	7	1007803	549448	12315	49195
3167	1160	552379	398397	13164	47842
877	588	337800	295598	15376	58483
340	56	322653	290732	18632	52201
100	49	212713	186978	20050	44971
5544	83	878497	395205	18525	69617
3917	329	691459	454238	10095	51702
795	417	425049	309173	10139	59959
15706	1288	1598524	753304	71703	49588
214	18	78356	61959	9241	38391
30560	2651	5025724	3126709	294918	56674
1088	262	551911	479823	26810	52573
6588	657	785538	533677	27179	41532
1405	1649	736387	628868	56258	60813
24411	198	1958035	876414	94094	41549
3558	255	510915	322670	15349	52423
1849	593	418053	315529	17438	51169
2070	857	430115	307383	21566	56916
1869	56	398208	294323	18925	51085
11930	321	1122967	488258	19126	47835
90	92	282751	273335	7875	57121
241	530	351949	329671	18724	48666
256	506	221927	204513	9529	59339
5046	42	722660	412232	20516	49064
60		280408	275528	1424	45848
11557	1111	1189620	750532	7073	42871
25174	3495	1746374	591188	18930	48249
14743	8750	2635956	1861502	68396	53741
9034	1796	1156399	734854	61312	51966
18083	128	1437057	472222	88251	52080
8383	962	1301362	529182	26747	67974
6714	259	1187872	771247	53357	59148
22609	1211	2199038	467148	447450	54324
98	967	314782	300601	11323	57726
4109	20	597321	335603	14823	53721
6771	668	654999	289216	3699	54848
12241	59	1185692	562881	23948	54196
3011	242	436749	297122	15959	48164
34831	2881	3187108	1401975	80263	54173
16270	2636	1875496	884985	140338	58211

20-3 地区生产总值(2016年)
GROSS DOMESTIC PRODUCT(2016)

单位：万元 (10 000 yuan)

县(市、区)	Region	地区生产总值 Gross Domestic Product	第一产业 Primary Industry	第二产业 Secondary Industry	第三产业 Tertiary Industry	人均地区生产总值(元) Per Capita GDP (yuan)
太原市	**Taiyuan**					
小店区	Xiaodian	7388145	82329	3620730	3685086	87598
迎泽区	Yingze	6022009	3318	805920	5212771	98988
杏花岭区	Xinghualing	5091806	4971	953517	4133318	76987
尖草坪区	Jiancaoping	2456869	35721	1484264	936884	57240
万柏林区	Wanbailin	3527703	4788	1795453	1727462	45435
晋源区	Jinyuan	571632	40827	203418	327387	24930
清徐县	Qingxu	1224624	136223	640271	448130	34792
阳曲县	Yangqu	334743	50396	176830	107517	27337
娄烦县	Loufan	183388	19653	70093	93642	16920
古交市	Gujiao	263913	18994	94213	150706	12446
大同市	**Datong**					
城区	Chengqu	1448503		438506	1009997	
矿区	Kuangqu	230141		31009	199132	
南郊区	Nanjiao	3339481	81217	2121662	1136602	79635
新荣区	Xinrong	243852	41457	102454	99941	21909
阳高县	Yanggao	302967	104681	56338	141948	10840
天镇县	Tianzhen	229721	66381	64722	98618	10804
广灵县	Guangling	224041	54319	59944	109778	12110
灵丘县	Lingqiu	304772	37778	98279	168715	12632
浑源县	Hunyuan	371526	104633	101664	165229	10513
左云县	Zuoyun	369038	27037	120835	221166	22907
大同县	Datongxian	269206	76082	59109	134015	15124
阳泉市	**Yangquan**					
城区	Chengqu	1604590		221025	1383565	81220
矿区	Kuangqu	995017		713436	281581	39899
郊区	Jiaoqu	826221	21894	467965	336362	35114
平定县	Pingding	949682	42572	524460	382650	27644
盂县	Yuxian	1264382	38594	764437	461351	39450
长治市	**Changzhi**					
城区	Chengqu	2064141	6100	432653	1625388	40561
郊区	Jiaoqu	1655956	30273	1081281	544402	57408
长治县	Changzhixian	1331694	65111	717711	548872	37959
襄垣县	Xiangyuan	1473907	59597	950120	464190	53129
屯留县	Tunliu	866816	66508	576562	223746	31891
平顺县	Pingshun	211379	23691	77848	109840	13972
黎城县	Licheng	317688	31937	106347	179404	19630
壶关县	Huguan	479004	52708	206778	219518	16065
长子县	Zhangzi	1122551	119477	688747	314327	31047
武乡县	Wuxiang	517371	32542	238585	246244	28074
沁县	Qinxian	234923	58790	36124	140009	13333
沁源县	Qinyuan	1027856	26482	719925	281449	63297
潞城市	Lucheng	905406	46547	561536	297323	38718
晋城市	**Jincheng**					
城区	Chengqu	2498081	7446	809300	1681335	50783
沁水县	Qinshui	1720483	59972	1199570	460942	79802

注：由于部分市属区尚未实行在地GDP统计，所以有的区的GDP数据不完整，有的区人均GDP数据空缺。

Notes: Some districts haven't implemented statistical investigation of GDP by the regional statistics. Therefore, the data of GDP in some districts are inperfect and the data of per capita GDP in some districts are vacancy.

20-3 续表1 continued

单位：万元 (10 000 yuan)

县(市、区)	Region	地区生产总值 Gross Domestic Product	第一产业 Primary Industry	第二产业 Secondary Industry	第三产业 Tertiary Industry	人均地区生产总值(元) Per Capita GDP (yuan)
阳城县	Yangcheng	1665181	96862	900779	667540	42512
陵川县	Lingchuan	352685	49177	95998	207510	15005
泽州县	Zezhou	2185348	140083	1344554	700711	44485
高平市	Gaoping	2002904	145030	1205038	652836	40675
朔州市	**Shuozhou**					
朔城区	Shuocheng	2433839	128217	543308	1762314	46716
平鲁区	Pinglu	1617671	34923	1080995	501753	77362
山阴县	Shanyin	1430972	117027	504126	809819	58134
应　县	Yingxian	660300	134499	169370	356431	19545
右玉县	Youyu	565058	57095	261603	246360	49012
怀仁县	Huairen	2049374	87228	1146401	815745	61030
晋中市	**Jinzhong**					
榆次区	Yuci	2162832	199729	650836	1312267	32190
榆社县	Yushe	275966	46299	102540	127127	19880
左权县	Zuoquan	447904	35636	211055	201213	27064
和顺县	Heshun	461097	28376	237972	194749	31281
昔阳县	Xiyang	578858	47687	291889	239282	25026
寿阳县	Shouyang	911217	130115	436811	344291	42560
太谷县	Taigu	800007	174420	202847	422740	26023
祁　县	Qixian	717370	171842	195003	350526	26291
平遥县	Pingyao	1007343	140212	339987	527144	19451
灵石县	Lingshi	1791916	49778	1085139	656999	66159
介休市	Jiexiu	1439804	62440	764458	612906	34378
运城市	**Yuncheng**					
盐湖区	Yanhu	2248834	135119	659711	1454004	32168
临猗县	Linyi	1351885	433553	375582	542750	22942
万荣县	Wanrong	637683	166982	200289	270412	14080
闻喜县	Wenxi	722359	112212	241424	368723	17356
稷山县	Jishan	747449	128248	273344	345857	20621
新绛县	Xinjiang	737199	160501	295784	280914	21456
绛　县	Jiangxian	547212	92189	196243	258780	18856
垣曲县	Yuanqu	481336	44381	219233	217722	20224
夏　县	Xiaxian	485700	190409	107949	187342	13358
平陆县	Pinglu	375703	95753	121870	158080	14145
芮城县	Ruicheng	768168	225519	231085	311564	18851
永济市	Yongji	1340707	212843	664054	463810	29305
河津市	Hejin	1777369	75158	1067122	635089	43531
忻州市	**Xinzhou**					
忻府区	Xinfu	1200652	93037	310888	796727	21359
定襄县	Dingxiang	357658	35823	164246	157589	15981
五台县	Wutai	427035	49099	109966	267970	14024
代　县	Daixian	530838	28268	294282	208288	24107

20-3 续表2 continued

单位：万元 (10 000 yuan)

县(市、区)	Region	地区生产总值 Gross Domestic Product	第一产业 Primary Industry	第二产业 Secondary Industry	第三产业 Tertiary Industry	人均地区生产总值(元) Per Capita GDP (yuan)
繁峙县	Fanshi	535618	49303	306091	180224	19498
宁武县	Ningwu	436531	19845	247959	168727	26472
静乐县	Jingle	245779	36638	88230	120911	15304
神池县	Shenchi	203062	69936	28079	105047	18689
五寨县	Wuzhai	195490	37848	18732	138910	17659
岢岚县	Kelan	208859	36264	40191	132404	24050
河曲县	Hequ	740559	30037	473544	236978	49702
保德县	Baode	660948	32549	469273	159126	39741
偏关县	Pianguan	254965	38238	84284	132443	22056
原平市	Yuanping	1168137	122079	473840	572218	23237
临 汾 市	**Linfen**					
尧都区	Yaodu	2612024	87516	569981	1954527	26823
曲沃县	Quwo	906899	131704	504583	270612	37054
翼城县	Yicheng	728099	89750	278174	360175	22747
襄汾县	Xiangfen	1171709	138590	556444	476675	25636
洪洞县	Hongtong	1648397	109653	941080	597664	21852
古 县	Guxian	442554	23707	315398	103448	46658
安泽县	Anze	428065	39577	294315	94174	50577
浮山县	Fushan	446009	44280	293446	108284	34174
吉 县	Jixian	198909	59569	81996	57344	18170
乡宁县	Xiangning	836927	31423	585053	220451	34814
大宁县	Daning	51739	12850	5568	33321	7775
隰 县	Xixian	146627	37801	23676	85150	13710
永和县	Yonghe	79455	24404	13933	41118	12127
蒲 县	Puxian	556843	21713	419929	115201	50349
汾西县	Fenxi	209154	29227	64311	115616	14020
侯马市	Houma	947048	33525	240231	673292	38317
霍州市	Huozhou	708396	36622	432159	239615	24348
吕 梁 市	**Lvliang**					
离石区	Lishi	704473	20261	165754	518458	21239
文水县	Wenshui	600192	113617	315643	170932	13807
交城县	Jiaocheng	528776	30322	293882	204572	22334
兴 县	Xingxian	604451	32790	436044	135617	20949
临 县	Linxian	417167	67869	114586	234712	6971
柳林县	Liulin	1218193	20004	790792	407397	36969
石楼县	Shilou	86888	24670	1482	60736	7525
岚 县	Lanxian	276951	22476	153409	101066	15424
方山县	Fangshan	240891	15696	131589	93606	16356
中阳县	Zhongyang	459892	14039	291179	154674	31581
交口县	Jiaokou	357226	17241	261058	78927	28895
孝义市	Xiaoyi	3387764	96019	2088052	1203693	70236
汾阳市	Fenyang	1059682	71840	515739	472103	24640

20-4 城乡居民收入(2016年)
INCOME OF URBAN AND RURAL HOUSEHOLDS(2016)

单位：元 (yuan)

县(市、区)	Region	居民人均可支配收入 Per Capita Disposable Income of Residents	城镇居民人均可支配收入 Per Capita Disposable Income of Urban Households	农村居民人均可支配收入 Per Capita Disposible Income of Rural Households
太原市	**Taiyuan**			
小店区	Xiaodian	29613	30560	19851
迎泽区	Yingze	30084	30421	19112
杏花岭区	Xinghualing	29856	30463	16816
尖草坪区	Jiancaoping	28686	29724	13714
万柏林区	Wanbailin	29224	29472	19937
晋源区	Jinyuan	23996	29877	13300
清徐县	Qingxu	19410	28492	16752
阳曲县	Yangqu	11824	21572	7648
娄烦县	Loufan	10616	18702	6033
古交市	Gujiao	23772	27412	13916
大同市	**Datong**			
城　区	Chengqu	29200	29200	
矿　区	Kuangqu	28223	28223	
南郊区	Nanjiao	17081	23518	13309
新荣区	Xinrong	11786	22009	8185
阳高县	Yanggao	11001	19352	6730
天镇县	Tianzhen	10615	19647	6060
广灵县	Guangling	9147	19656	6400
灵丘县	Lingqiu	10784	24093	6701
浑源县	Hunyuan	11320	20484	6633
左云县	Zuoyun	16527	24215	10714
大同县	Datongxian	11470	18242	8189
阳泉市	**Yangquan**			
城　区	Chengqu	28813	28813	
矿　区	Kuangqu	28403	28403	
郊　区	Jiaoqu	20275	23549	12815
平定县	Pingding	16756	25692	11669
盂　县	Yuxian	17649	27713	12170
长治市	**Changzhi**			
城　区	Chengqu	30136	30136	
郊　区	Jiaoqu	28160	35086	16240
长治县	Changzhixian	19070	28346	14941
襄垣县	Xiangyuan	21100	31686	13641
屯留县	Tunliu	17033	23884	13672
平顺县	Pingshun	9054	20675	5494
黎城县	Licheng	11061	16956	7790
壶关县	Huguan	8951	20620	5243
长子县	Zhangzi	16059	26193	12574
武乡县	Wuxiang	10199	21058	5950
沁　县	Qinxian	9708	17489	5650
沁源县	Qinyuan	19397	30438	12745
潞城市	Lucheng	19116	25785	12199

20-4 续表1 continued

单位：元 (yuan)

县(市、区)	Region	居民人均可支配收入 Per Capita Disposable Income of Residents	城镇居民人均可支配收入 Per Capita Disposable Income of Urban Households	农村居民人均可支配收入 Per Capita Disposible Income of Rural Households
晋城市	**Jincheng**			
城　区	Chengqu	30168	30168	
沁水县	Qinshui	15599	24825	10098
阳城县	Yangcheng	17589	26037	11488
陵川县	Lingchuan	11257	17256	7929
泽州县	Zezhou	19826	29333	13129
高平市	Gaoping	20036	28235	12168
朔州市	**Shuozhou**			
朔城区	Shuocheng	23229	29911	12925
平鲁区	Pinglu	15485	22365	8824
山阴县	Shanyin	22013	30470	14199
应　县	Yingxian	13481	21962	9331
右玉县	Youyu	13735	21132	6588
怀仁县	Huairen	23100	30812	14017
晋中市	**Jinzhong**	19783	29149	11525
榆次区	Yuci	26733	30815	15624
榆社县	Yushe	9734	20020	4693
左权县	Zuoquan	12207	23687	4745
和顺县	Heshun	12508	22069	5638
昔阳县	Xiyang	12238	22720	7743
寿阳县	Shouyang	18111	30720	11834
太谷县	Taigu	20907	27385	16368
祁　县	Qixian	19524	28619	14841
平遥县	Pingyao	16852	26815	10885
灵石县	Lingshi	23498	33364	15072
介休市	Jiexiu	23436	30650	12333
运城市	**Yuncheng**			
盐湖区	Yanhu	21922	27610	10634
临猗县	Linyi	16493	25565	11408
万荣县	Wanrong	11644	22565	8210
闻喜县	Wenxi	15934	25721	8641
稷山县	Jishan	14301	23742	9654
新绛县	Xinjiang	15787	25206	10229
绛　县	Jiangxian	15524	23177	8425
垣曲县	Yuanqu	13699	23289	6236
夏　县	Xiaxian	11077	22923	6858
平陆县	Pinglu	10209	21279	6222
芮城县	Ruicheng	16655	25980	9806
永济市	Yongji	18171	26366	11640
河津市	Hejin	18608	25695	11993
忻州市	**Xinzhou**			
忻府区	Xinfu	18583	26792	8923
定襄县	Dingxiang	16245	26712	11296
五台县	Wutai	11047	23802	5765
代　县	Daixian	12306	23706	5169

20-4 续表2 continued

单位：元 (yuan)

县(市、区)	Region	居民人均可支配收入 Per Capita Disposable Income of Residents	城镇居民人均可支配收入 Per Capita Disposable Income of Urban Households	农村居民人均可支配收入 Per Capita Disposible Income of Rural Households
繁峙县	Fanshi	14557	26664	6940
宁武县	Ningwu	12310	21713	4825
静乐县	Jingle	10758	20837	6004
神池县	Shenchi	11244	20825	6732
五寨县	Wuzhai	12593	21567	6616
岢岚县	Kelan	13746	23940	5898
河曲县	Hequ	14005	24343	5895
保德县	Baode	13251	26106	6400
偏关县	Pianguan	11923	19929	6030
原平市	Yuanping	17115	27202	9290
临 汾 市	**Linfen**			
尧都区	Yaodu	24130	30371	12956
曲沃县	Quwo	18359	28431	13135
翼城县	Yicheng	15587	26852	10274
襄汾县	Xiangfen	17181	27397	11752
洪洞县	Hongtong	15585	24605	10467
古 县	Guxian	15715	27888	9065
安泽县	Anze	14336	25195	8335
浮山县	Fushan	14271	26674	8031
吉 县	Jixian	8766	18478	4661
乡宁县	Xiangning	14115	26251	8744
大宁县	Daning	8789	17484	2905
隰 县	Xixian	11473	21063	5129
永和县	Yonghe	9154	19366	3221
蒲 县	Puxian	14651	24252	7871
汾西县	Fenxi	11239	23582	3374
侯马市	Houma	20783	25725	13177
霍州市	Huozhou	20851	26998	12143
吕 梁 市	**Lvliang**			
离石区	Lishi	22705	26349	5474
文水县	Wenshui	12239	19695	9050
交城县	Jiaocheng	14085	19751	8763
兴 县	Xingxian	8885	19061	4006
临 县	Linxian	7345	16169	4446
柳林县	Liulin	16883	28415	10583
石楼县	Shilou	6786	13063	2877
岚 县	Lanxian	8512	18109	4689
方山县	Fangshan	8451	19087	4142
中阳县	Zhongyang	14537	20187	6208
交口县	Jiaokou	10966	18292	6829
孝义市	Xiaoyi	24398	30416	14978
汾阳市	Fenyang	15834	21328	12397

20-5 财政收支情况(2016年)
FINANCIAL REVENUE AND EXPENDITURE(2016)

单位：万元 (10 000 yuan)

县(市、区)	Region	一般公共预算收入 General Public Budget Revenue	#增值税 Value-added Taxes	#营业税 Operation Taxes	#企业所得税 Enterprises Income Taxes	一般公共预算支出 General Public Budget Expenditure
太原市	**Taiyuan**					
小店区	Xiaodian	246035	61074	38815	9177	375279
迎泽区	Yingze	139219	39305	22746	6759	193940
杏花岭区	Xinghualing	147489	35665	21590	6679	218239
尖草坪区	Jiancaoping	73287	21273	16216	1881	132819
万柏林区	Wanbailin	174766	32841	35476	7903	254909
晋源区	Jinyuan	58984	14303	12021	1735	147508
清徐县	Qingxu	64146	18510	8607	5182	180097
阳曲县	Yangqu	36095	4856	5166	1531	133653
娄烦县	Loufan	26482	6087	2355	517	112482
古交市	Gujiao	53304	8936	4500	1523	166210
不锈钢产业区	Stainless Steel Industrial Zone	19765	3625	1867	368	17162
高新区	High-tech Zone	119429	35941	19293	6736	75843
经济区	Economic Zone	168262	57213	11264	14306	185534
民营区	Private Zone	32121	7539	7545	969	33798
大同市	**Datong**					
城　区	Chengqu	35316	7757	4725	2464	222810
矿　区	Kuangqu	8123	2335	746	329	129410
南郊区	Nanjiao	81215	19232	6868	6260	224078
新荣区	Xinrong	13506	5180	763	286	71818
阳高县	Yanggao	10857	1983	1825	369	181819
天镇县	Tianzhen	8077	1663	1579	335	169032
广灵县	Guangling	8673	1751	1620	877	176115
灵丘县	Lingqiu	11218	2253	2000	517	204802
浑源县	Hunyuan	23253	1898	2006	511	236390
左云县	Zuoyun	33529	8822	3233	2644	124789
大同县	Datongxian	16200	3221	1718	345	157096
开发区	Development Zone	44416	7278	12626	4320	48709
阳泉市	**Yangquan**					
城　区	Chengqu	20589	3681	3701	2225	54632
矿　区	Kuangqu	22782	3857	2820	4921	67232
郊　区	Jiaoqu	42420	7066	8576	1108	119977
平定县	Pingding	36284	7600	4821	1890	192996
盂　县	Yuxian	53450	10675	4923	1817	177118
开发区	Development Zone	20351	4161	5469	1076	34378
长治市	**Changzhi**					
城　区	Chengqu	45918	4463	3162	2084	99765
郊　区	Jiaoqu	39550	5948	1439	1154	110137
长治县	Changzhi	105571	30666	4982	5094	193150
襄垣县	Xiangyuan	124521	20582	5190	2869	201368
屯留县	Tunliu	52382	12295	4501	3119	132934
平顺县	Pingshun	8452	741	1718	892	123573
黎城县	Licheng	16144	3517	1664	567	110680
壶关县	Huguan	21081	1981	1499	1244	171397
长子县	Zhangzi	75640	19303	3475	5283	170611
武乡县	Wuxiang	29416	7273	1841	453	142171
沁　县	Qinxian	8789	820	918	211	120593
沁源县	Qinyuan	62996	15825	3533	5233	129038
潞城市	Lucheng	56693	11291	3159	3922	113623
高新区	High-tech Zone	22142	7213	1469	1212	62701

20-5 续表1 continued

单位：万元 (10 000 yuan)

县(市、区)	Region	一般公共预算收入 General Public Budget Revenue	#增值税 Value-added Taxes	#营业税 Operation Taxes	#企业所得税 Enterprises Income Taxes	一般公共预算支出 General Public Budget Expenditure
晋城市	**Jincheng**					
城　区	Chengqu	88567	7776	6376	5453	167482
沁水县	Qinshui	117105	23442	7540	5613	181487
阳城县	Yangcheng	123548	29416	4908	16457	240161
陵川县	Lingchuan	14352	2327	2101	353	158780
泽州县	Zezhou	123756	27748	6096	5181	279410
高平市	Gaoping	126586	23933	8489	2624	265293
开发区	Development Zone	28453	1928	985	1655	20796
朔州市	**Shuozhou**					
朔城区	Shuocheng	79336	16378	7551	1863	192306
平鲁区	Pinglu	52957	10789	4645	2733	149125
山阴县	Shanyin	57359	24970	4166	2955	182647
应　县	Yingxian	13906	2120	2196	729	168692
右玉县	Youyu	28875	6821	3067	1594	106344
怀仁县	Huairen	55028	17381	3668	3481	168856
开发区	Development Zone	21148	3829	1909	791	26396
晋中市	**Jinzhong**					
榆次区	Yuci	120602	22612	18227	9240	261559
榆社县	Yushe	19688	3820	1911	575	122100
左权县	Zuoquan	45366	3838	3661	1727	137318
和顺县	Heshun	43029	5444	3628	1192	150025
昔阳县	Xiyang	52088	9768	4534	1128	160608
寿阳县	Shouyang	61050	15637	3929	3994	153783
太谷县	Taigu	44320	7731	3571	2025	169946
祁　县	Qixian	33401	5321	3514	1265	163385
平遥县	Pingyao	45345	7187	6961	3211	243760
灵石县	Lingshi	112166	38043	4652	2937	224057
介休市	Jiexiu	107077	16746	6689	3678	230611
开发区	Development Zone	55354	7808	5625	4289	62077
运城市	**Yuncheng**					
盐湖区	Yanhu	85686	13299	9172	4120	257704
临猗县	Linyi	23712	3390	2525	1895	219571
万荣县	Wanrong	14710	3465	2781	1036	209061
闻喜县	Wenxi	23891	4556	2006	790	207257
稷山县	Jishan	17470	5823	1935	831	147224
新绛县	Xinjiang	17333	3896	1634	989	158213
绛　县	Jiangxian	8972	1658	1209	610	159112
垣曲县	Yuanqu	18880	4324	2586	604	162208
夏　县	Xiaxian	13539	1624	1825	1332	159891
平陆县	Pinglu	19852	4222	1947	104	150469
芮城县	Ruicheng	27809	4859	2340	1457	198371
永济市	Yongji	40634	9759	3081	2449	197214
河津市	Hejin	75808	28982	4758	445	196573
开发区	Development Zone	16350	1633	1878	332	25270
风陵渡开发区	Fenglingdu Development Zone	4830	1711	220	70	5171
华信开发区	Huaxin Development Zone	1849	557	47	169	6499
空港经济开发区	Konggang Economic Development Zone	9940	1928	1175	212	17575
忻州市	**Xinzhou**					
忻府区	Xinfu	45355	7529	6889	2615	199312

20–5 续表2 continued

单位：万元 (10 000 yuan)

县(市、区)	Region	一般公共预算收入 General Public Budget Revenue	#增值税 Value-added Taxes	#营业税 Operation Taxes	#企业所得税 Enterprises Income Taxes	一般公共预算支出 General Public Budget Expenditure
定襄县	Dingxiang	16616	6003	1549	432	130424
五台县	Wutai	28602	5744	2556	2013	198568
代　县	Daixian	21768	4582	1417	375	143812
繁峙县	Fanshi	21380	3323	2237	1526	172929
宁武县	Ningwu	59190	9415	5414	812	143041
静乐县	Jingle	38685	853	2504	425	150412
神池县	Shenchi	15343	1882	1706	1561	97506
五寨县	Wuzhai	17622	4779	1230	507	108990
岢岚县	Kelan	11403	1968	1792	305	107081
河曲县	Hequ	51564	13545	2694	1340	121737
保德县	Baode	37197	9803	4666	1038	130197
偏关县	Pianguan	9804	1674	1397	210	100824
原平市	Yuanping	63566	17294	5434	2643	272520
开发区	Development Zone	15559	4956	2715	303	7661
临汾市	**Linfen**					
尧都区	Yaodu	119266	19273	17847	4968	350913
曲沃县	Quwo	25000	4705	2130	528	132783
翼城县	Yicheng	25368	3454	2466	488	156177
襄汾县	Xiangfen	36920	6300	4048	3177	209590
洪洞县	Hongtong	65981	9681	7367	2855	305075
古　县	Guxian	21286	4888	1142	1050	88390
安泽县	Anze	30005	8261	903	890	85744
浮山县	Fushan	9051	873	602	80	97872
吉　县	Jixian	11087	1416	1587	572	113298
乡宁县	Xiangning	89176	18896	4500	6049	158617
大宁县	Daning	3101	526	533	126	86492
隰　县	Xixian	7361	814	2179	329	123926
永和县	Yonghe	7629	1345	2127	88	79068
蒲　县	Puxian	71106	11715	2802	669	155055
汾西县	Fenxi	6593	414	630	150	104618
侯马市	Houma	40858	6913	4309	3272	133693
霍州市	Huozhou	58547	14324	2808	764	165031
开发区	Development Zone	18012	2121	3196	1331	44495
侯马开发区	Houma Development Zone	8127	892	817	223	18893
吕梁市	**Lvliang**					
离石区	Lishi	80108	17037	8752	1741	206784
文水县	Wenshui	20988	4601	1659	1066	211710
交城县	Jiaocheng	41071	9425	5215	1995	141994
兴　县	Xingxian	71191	23573	4378	3512	205113
临　县	Linxian	40260	10352	2884	933	333552
柳林县	Liulin	106994	42271	5035	3235	202943
石楼县	Shilou	2876	479	572	88	108708
岚　县	Lanxian	32452	10954	3191	1041	143017
方山县	Fangshan	31423	9286	2125	359	138779
中阳县	Zhongyang	37568	11724	2318	–185	120652
交口县	Jiaokou	46300	14885	1133	3306	115188
孝义市	Xiaoyi	155569	46268	6280	8512	262445
汾阳市	Fenyang	72432	15913	2965	7118	212149

20-6 固定资产投资
INVESTMENT IN FIXED ASSETS

单位：万元 (10 000 yuan)

县(市、区)	Region	2012	2013	2014	2015	2016
太 原 市	**Taiyuan**					
小店区	Xiaodian	2852251	3228904	1908681	2541980	2654293
迎泽区	Yingze	1121913	1387901	1530465	1909744	2182485
杏花岭区	Xinghualing	1582201	1799379	1493174	1918814	1562781
尖草坪区	Jiancaoping	1220648	1646793	1291150	1600006	1513933
万柏林区	Wanbailin	2030999	2466003	3124845	3816427	3080783
晋源区	Jinyuan	785204	882779	1353999	1662222	1441372
清徐县	Qingxu	851799	699579	730611	914867	745499
阳曲县	Yangqu	254501	357220	457242	575996	503718
娄烦县	Loufan	87705	136310	194905	271514	306336
古交市	Gujiao	543044	693493	512806	642663	548159
大 同 市	**Datong**					
城 区	Chengqu	1920335	2172000	1512084	939864	1059263
矿 区	Kuangqu	44458	202706	172550	209041	235101
南郊区	Nanjiao	1332086	1594588	2101129	2452499	2666799
新荣区	Xinrong	315290	497389	596162	730299	816418
阳高县	Yanggao	392935	576567	715798	860801	976147
天镇县	Tianzhen	315521	487387	621167	751090	840763
广灵县	Guangling	304298	488148	592308	757132	852531
灵丘县	Lingqiu	492732	697709	822225	976171	850085
浑源县	Hunyuan	467577	803720	981693	1162222	1312148
左云县	Zuoyun	984107	1187296	1228367	1085700	800138
大同县	Datongxian	907380	1214027	1380597	1234444	874492
阳 泉 市	**Yangquan**					
城 区	Chengqu	556862	669382	316675	317360	288149
矿 区	Kuangqu	781843	938212	941027	990293	852228
郊 区	Jiaoqu	783104	986793	1073565	1135147	960595
平定县	Pingding	891025	1123635	1360752	1631218	1709206
盂 县	Yuxian	900045	1137428	1481666	1772253	1881286
长 治 市	**Changzhi**					
城 区	Chengqu	1087962	1345088	1550785	1738331	1995963
郊 区	Jiaoqu	1148811	1502468	1601336	1865614	2137840
长治县	Changzhixian	834196	1085775	1250506	1463978	1494296
襄垣县	Xiangyuan	1050479	1513797	1756094	1925012	1977316
屯留县	Tunliu	764527	992216	1150371	1340352	738916
平顺县	Pingshun	205132	269514	313931	365799	412410
黎城县	Licheng	299137	400505	481029	569807	620984
壶关县	Huguan	291940	382000	458182	540754	628148
长子县	Zhangzi	652285	883470	1053782	1229285	1432405
武乡县	Wuxiang	396007	200258	252086	310470	349858
沁 县	Qinxian	292548	388527	329759	383172	435556
沁源县	Qinyuan	583277	771547	909282	1070192	1083686
潞城市	Lucheng	810581	1085976	1288055	1511315	1706141

注：各县(市、区)投资不含跨省、市项目投资和农村农户投资。

Note: Investment in city and county doesn't include investment across provinces and cities, aparting from investment of rural pesant household.

20-6 续表1 continued

单位：万元 (10 000 yuan)

县(市、区)	Region	2012	2013	2014	2015	2016
晋 城 市	**Jincheng**					
城 区	Chengqu	2001736	2642932	3315092	3735221	3508091
沁水县	Qinshui	968038	1094989	1363300	1500260	1593121
阳城县	Yangcheng	908764	1190421	1406627	1600716	1647973
陵川县	Lingchuan	228419	299758	329968	390491	416491
泽州县	Zezhou	1270980	1437999	1833898	2103402	2260420
高平市	Gaoping	1047032	1381702	1262073	1493576	1504814
朔 州 市	**Shuozhou**					
朔城区	Shuocheng	1662074	2257179	2280870	1458602	954840
平鲁区	Pinglu	1299322	1507644	1715612	2470408	1909500
山阴县	Shanyin	950941	1213229	834106	1570160	945391
应 县	Yingxian	359007	482110	551369	666120	471350
右玉县	Youyu	587567	658768	800680	867649	456622
怀仁县	Huairen	869061	1124742	1365549	1571246	1134842
晋 中 市	**Jinzhong**					
榆次区	Yuci	1505611	1999982	2599942	2690002	2758083
榆社县	Yushe	75049	98876	124096	146579	154540
左权县	Zuoquan	579462	769838	800634	881227	994000
和顺县	Heshun	450006	511343	539850	652378	685595
昔阳县	Xiyang	596043	818132	939491	1099114	1113241
寿阳县	Shouyang	789016	844757	975024	1157217	1293931
太谷县	Taigu	350212	483734	650049	787134	828884
祁 县	Qixian	330370	446502	563030	671781	739180
平遥县	Pingyao	510457	682960	860659	1018132	1106345
灵石县	Lingshi	1016290	1329720	1583696	1862458	1987592
介休市	Jiexiu	758290	1000213	1192200	1417015	1495790
运 城 市	**Yuncheng**					
盐湖区	Yanhu	1801033	2198362	2524748	2827890	1947027
临猗县	Linyi	603271	775311	940202	1095443	1271133
万荣县	Wanrong	432610	542976	680546	789230	909908
闻喜县	Wenxi	732119	903665	730199	946701	1088682
稷山县	Jishan	433753	531918	651594	767607	882729
新绛县	Xinjiang	470067	582059	720481	831110	630290
绛 县	Jiangxian	532828	631319	791451	934049	843323
垣曲县	Yuanqu	301446	406954	520300	650031	749314
夏 县	Xiaxian	342394	419872	544354	572287	659541
平陆县	Pinglu	340802	411975	575197	675017	780057
芮城县	Ruicheng	402926	515243	697890	823223	688760
永济市	Yongji	632651	816671	1015754	1156273	1279832
河津市	Hejin	976512	1227982	1486567	1490025	1501094
忻 州 市	**Xinzhou**					
忻府区	Xinfu	830209	953564	1055163	1250134	1638170
定襄县	Dingxiang	224997	296173	356331	418972	466189
五台县	Wutai	260229	349317	486448	572155	613169
代 县	Daixian	210464	335944	456537	534759	564243

20-6 续表2 continued

单位：万元 (10 000 yuan)

县(市、区)	Region	2012	2013	2014	2015	2016
繁峙县	Fanshi	460201	588927	742006	877867	928506
宁武县	Ningwu	407988	553757	722511	844215	898520
静乐县	Jingle	379891	528176	652513	767689	843845
神池县	Shenchi	194966	272422	314604	331142	201264
五寨县	Wuzhai	158650	233201	269699	248919	279683
岢岚县	Kelan	244871	332497	397812	419116	462517
河曲县	Hequ	600468	813395	1163157	1358566	1462459
保德县	Baode	581214	796069	1039753	1214337	1255029
偏关县	Pianguan	130073	193459	225793	264430	290458
原平市	Yuanping	1146229	1345878	1400926	1635931	1748644
临 汾 市	**Linfen**					
尧都区	Yaodu	1786611	2390728	2675255	2546938	2521124
曲沃县	Quwo	423866	571272	728178	874090	791040
翼城县	Yicheng	406024	545450	689293	827247	883687
襄汾县	Xiangfen	618613	833563	1051813	1262726	1187698
洪洞县	Hongtong	1014008	1389402	1411611	1638015	1680217
古 县	Guxian	280236	394625	502385	603867	563304
安泽县	Anze	308203	416447	527786	633538	558759
浮山县	Fushan	224646	299759	380241	456759	456428
吉 县	Jixian	166116	224898	290660	349437	365075
乡宁县	Xiangning	382002	509870	607431	720658	847611
大宁县	Daning	59694	80593	104018	120888	183689
隰 县	Xixian	114923	169200	221997	265816	225736
永和县	Yonghe	65183	70654	109624	127310	169516
蒲 县	Puxian	250022	367574	504001	605088	701545
汾西县	Fenxi	150885	209366	269942	327461	419279
侯马市	Houma	404073	460766	689802	829151	959163
霍州市	Huozhou	891003	1194852	1516723	1648586	1396129
吕 梁 市	**Lvliang**					
离石区	Lishi	753499	664875	871072	1184018	1185676
文水县	Wenshui	143453	199838	439832	601682	567369
交城县	Jiaocheng	303591	399058	531000	721174	715514
兴 县	Xingxian	363546	484582	620114	828727	659858
临 县	Linxian	281374	407407	556611	786071	712677
柳林县	Liulin	929911	1166411	1483730	1819556	1648676
石楼县	Shilou	71613	72671	80523	120023	146362
岚 县	Lanxian	605347	530122	284678	399327	399560
方山县	Fangshan	146164	142164	167466	232394	246846
中阳县	Zhongyang	282511	375864	529114	671726	647473
交口县	Jiaokou	243020	322295	443320	573031	638425
孝义市	Xiaoyi	2212497	2801624	3230706	2680188	2700745
汾阳市	Fenyang	457550	530259	640309	848796	886727

20-7 乡村基本情况(2016年)

县(市、区)	Region	乡镇政府(个) Number of Township and Town Governments (unit)	#镇政府 Number of Town Governments	村民委员会(个) Number of Villager Committees (unit)	乡村户数(户) Number of Rural Households (household)
太原市	**Taiyuan**				
小店区	Xiaodian	3	1	64	46018
迎泽区	Yingze	1	1	25	8211
杏花岭区	Xinghualing	2		32	9187
尖草坪区	Jiancaoping	5	2	84	34438
万柏林区	Wanbailin	1		42	12341
晋源区	Jinyuan	3	3	85	42294
清徐县	Qingxu	9	4	188	99394
阳曲县	Yangqu	10	4	117	45004
娄烦县	Loufan	8	3	142	33548
古交市	Gujiao	10	3	146	39451
大同市	**Datong**				
南郊区	Nanjiao	10	3	189	115957
新荣区	Xinrong	7	1	140	40643
阳高县	Yanggao	13	7	262	91683
天镇县	Tianzhen	11	5	222	62645
广灵县	Guangling	9	2	180	59810
灵丘县	Lingqiu	12	3	255	80477
浑源县	Hunyuan	18	6	315	106653
左云县	Zuoyun	9	3	228	41906
大同县	Datongxian	10	3	175	54978
开发区	Development Zone			3	4824
阳泉市	**Yangquan**				
郊　区	Jiaoqu	8	4	184	82955
平定县	Pingding	10	8	318	112468
盂　县	Yuxian	14	8	453	100367
开发区	Development Zone			5	4302
长治市	**Changzhi**				
城　区	Chengqu			28	18393
郊　区	Jiaoqu	6	5	122	50069
长治县	Changzhixian	11	6	254	93973
襄垣县	Xiangyuan	11	8	323	63813
屯留县	Tunliu	11	7	294	79488
平顺县	Pingshun	12	5	262	46053
黎城县	Licheng	9	5	243	45936
壶关县	Huguan	12	5	390	93933
长子县	Zhangzi	12	7	399	106006
武乡县	Wuxiang	14	5	377	62025
沁　县	Qinxian	13	6	306	47742
沁源县	Qinyuan	14	5	254	49178
潞城市	Lucheng	7	4	191	57397

BASIC CONDITIONS OF RURAL AREAS(2016)

乡村人口 (人) Rural Population (person)	乡村从业人员 (人) Number of Rural Employees (person)	农林牧渔业 Farming, Forestry, Animal Husbandry and Fishery	工业 Industry	建筑业 Construction	其他行业 Others
130364	67148	34936	7861	5133	19218
21609	10530	1170	1317	762	7281
25574	13845	2477	3829	1067	6472
103071	49662	16699	6899	2893	23171
32730	13480	2394	1104	497	9485
134937	67791	27373	11155	5027	24236
268647	128976	70871	23060	4797	30248
109547	53902	31930	6540	2918	12514
102149	48750	31533	4405	2258	10554
106048	33338	17650	7585	658	7445
276564	130094	43099	11639	9304	66052
89205	44251	22764	7739	1217	12531
251478	94252	64944	4381	7541	17386
167450	69974	51293	2685	5253	10743
154011	59331	41423	3974	4678	9256
209091	100564	61341	6749	12086	20388
288105	129541	66049	9544	15869	38079
102600	47098	30362	5394	1927	9415
125397	58382	40547	3353	4194	10288
11297	6137	1174	935	668	3360
200035	86073	18917	29773	3414	33969
259441	112826	47958	18888	9839	36141
243476	122906	79406	16178	5885	21437
11513	6014	4	1711	629	3670
63031	33110	4551	4525	1770	22264
172154	84404	25604	25482	6952	26366
305838	150093	71326	29862	15718	33187
191182	85198	51998	12026	3163	18011
234917	117119	73100	12552	13124	18343
133114	66123	35468	5366	12381	12908
127179	61844	35688	9378	5724	11054
267747	137955	76012	14683	22430	24830
328647	171545	121508	12391	10514	27132
177452	79143	54389	5839	6609	12306
136805	55306	36742	4080	4998	9486
137401	57806	32076	12674	2922	10134
179805	87446	47317	18619	7819	13691

20-7 续表1

县(市、区)	Region	乡镇政府(个) Number of Township and Town Governments (unit)	#镇政府 Number of Town Governments	村民委员会(个) Number of Villager Committees (unit)	乡村户数(户) Number of Rural Households (household)
晋城市	**Jincheng**				
城　区	Chengqu	1	1	72	25149
沁水县	Qinshui	14	7	250	59470
阳城县	Yangcheng	17	10	469	141447
陵川县	Lingchuan	12	7	378	77214
泽州县	Zezhou	17	14	627	158527
高平市	Gaoping	13	9	445	131965
开发区	Development Zone			7	2390
朔州市	**Shuozhou**				
朔城区	Shuocheng	11	2	299	94788
平鲁区	Pinglu	13	2	286	29125
山阴县	Shanyin	13	4	257	61038
应　县	Yingxian	12	3	298	98880
右玉县	Youyu	10	4	321	28392
怀仁县	Huairen	10	4	162	77882
开发区	Development Zone			1	1973
晋中市	**Jinzhong**				
榆次区	Yuci	10	6	272	105050
榆社县	Yushe	9	4	271	45171
左权县	Zuoquan	10	5	203	52616
和顺县	Heshun	10	5	287	41819
昔阳县	Xiyang	12	5	335	82326
寿阳县	Shouyang	14	7	206	65760
太谷县	Taigu	9	3	198	92800
祁　县	Qixian	8	6	156	86017
平遥县	Pingyao	14	5	273	164860
灵石县	Lingshi	12	6	291	71552
介休市	Jiexiu	10	7	231	111796
开发区	Development Zone			17	16223
运城市	**Yuncheng**				
盐湖区	Yanhu	13	7	314	137166
临猗县	Linyi	14	9	375	131255
万荣县	Wanrong	14	4	281	105965
闻喜县	Wenxi	13	7	343	97773
稷山县	Jishan	7	5	200	90587
新绛县	Xinjiang	9	8	220	78512
绛　县	Jiangxian	10	8	205	63887
垣曲县	Yuanqu	11	5	189	52889
夏　县	Xiaxian	11	6	257	89925
平陆县	Pinglu	10	6	228	78119
芮城县	Ruicheng	10	7	172	117594
永济市	Yongji	7	7	265	98861
河津市	Hejin	7	2	148	85997

continued

乡村人口 (人) Rural Population (person)	乡村从业人员 (人) Number of Rural Employees (person)	农林牧渔业 Farming, Forestry, Animal Husbandry and Fishery	工 业 Industry	建筑业 Construction	其他行业 Others
60487	31123	9279	4223	2572	15049
158509	86615	57232	8439	4880	16064
317490	163589	81878	31455	16030	34226
229369	108998	55363	13350	12682	27603
441500	215236	117214	39274	12627	46121
409181	213525	111719	36367	21852	43587
5935	3125	1080	835	215	995
258544	116357	80470	5649	7844	22394
88223	50996	34123	5690	1242	9941
165413	65142	46891	5022	3591	9638
251298	123002	94944	5658	8246	14154
80630	41199	22932	3173	1615	13479
193444	87297	47718	12114	5161	22304
4962	406	71	40	5	290
265739	132074	81553	12143	7650	30728
118501	50715	31126	3049	4929	11611
137312	62413	41991	4740	5343	10339
110410	53420	34365	6204	3608	9243
198379	99674	62338	8919	7534	20883
169498	83586	57322	8282	2567	15415
226038	114525	57635	24309	9275	23306
212773	107811	55126	20400	10289	21996
444619	207042	99506	39429	21962	46145
183912	89953	38252	23348	4069	24284
300371	146846	56714	34735	19526	35871
41492	23318	7162	6299	1706	8151
444251	241179	150441	21119	14908	54711
504345	255127	182966	16842	9764	45555
409608	175216	119359	13712	12970	29175
369123	188088	84903	56991	14110	32084
327320	168327	100537	30450	10932	26408
290854	153235	99570	17341	10379	25945
233972	137089	88976	13870	9327	24916
166150	78531	42524	8561	7541	19905
330298	195259	136231	16227	17146	25655
214255	111633	80331	8549	6262	16491
352828	191556	121876	13999	15525	40156
360631	208347	126687	11348	9387	60925
312909	148093	73861	23136	16084	35012

20-7 续表2

县(市、区)	Region	乡镇政府(个) Number of Township and Town Governments (unit)	#镇政府 Number of Town Governments	村民委员会(个) Number of Villager Committees (unit)	乡村户数(户) Number of Rural Households (household)
忻 州 市	**Xinzhou**				
忻府区	Xinfu	17	6	394	141436
定襄县	Dingxiang	9	3	155	77043
五台县	Wutai	16	5	510	103959
代　县	Daixian	11	6	377	68262
繁峙县	Fanshi	13	3	402	90385
宁武县	Ningwu	14	4	464	45975
静乐县	Jingle	14	4	381	46450
神池县	Shenchi	10	3	241	30630
五寨县	Wuzhai	12	3	250	34743
岢岚县	Kelan	12	2	202	22197
河曲县	Hequ	13	4	340	46923
保德县	Baode	13	4	341	50147
偏关县	Pianguan	10	4	248	32907
五台山风景名胜区	Wutai Mount Scenic Area	3	1	63	5956
原平市	Yuanping	18	7	522	148404
临 汾 市	**Linfen**				
尧都区	Yaodu	16	10	372	135669
曲沃县	Quwo	7	5	158	50836
翼城县	Yicheng	10	6	212	74547
襄汾县	Xiangfen	13	7	348	133497
洪洞县	Hongtong	16	9	463	205080
古　县	Guxian	7	4	111	24997
安泽县	Anze	7	4	104	20612
浮山县	Fushan	9	2	185	33075
吉　县	Jixian	8	3	79	30943
乡宁县	Xiangning	10	5	182	62243
大宁县	Daning	6	2	84	17889
隰　县	Xixian	8	3	97	29418
永和县	Yonghe	7	2	79	13257
蒲　县	Puxian	9	4	93	26091
汾西县	Fenxi	8	5	126	41130
侯马市	Houma	3		76	32032
霍州市	Huozhou	7	4	199	62445
吕 梁 市	**Lvliang**				
离石区	Lishi	5	2	194	62723
文水县	Wenshui	12	7	199	140837
交城县	Jiaocheng	10	6	150	66765
兴　县	Xingxian	17	7	376	84187
临　县	Linxian	23	13	631	210357
柳林县	Liulin	15	8	257	101858
石楼县	Shilou	9	4	134	30456
岚　县	Lanxian	12	4	167	50449
方山县	Fangshan	7	5	169	46995
中阳县	Zhongyang	7	5	93	34396
交口县	Jiaokou	7	4	95	33048
孝义市	Xiaoyi	12	7	379	107769
汾阳市	Fenyang	12	9	289	124414

continued

乡村人口 (人) Rural Population (person)	乡村从业人员 (人) Number of Rural Employees (person)				
		农林牧渔业 Farming, Forestry, Animal Husbandry and Fishery	工　业 Industry	建筑业 Construction	其他行业 Others
351284	175177	97453	11786	24424	41514
180331	93956	54676	13559	9322	16399
251890	105590	67938	6305	18951	12396
160311	76402	60176	4503	5293	6430
242201	96430	70986	7417	5025	13002
118894	58256	36475	3810	3215	14756
138421	58731	28894	4538	7731	17568
79909	32186	26575	1095	793	3723
93416	44853	35317	1162	1933	6441
66382	32598	22561	3042	3006	3989
115602	47376	31466	4100	3674	8136
146328	67741	38424	6384	6326	16607
92654	39422	22299	2212	4321	10590
15178	7843	3177	139	451	4076
371609	169152	94068	13367	15467	46250
490889	250853	112739	29824	24834	83456
196797	108376	59688	15100	11373	22215
270151	119611	59225	26675	12538	21173
449205	228756	130172	32869	15452	50263
677878	346732	181989	35369	37320	92054
74272	25097	15971	3637	1041	4448
66450	24093	16306	1800	898	5089
109334	39292	22568	3193	2704	10827
96040	37164	25909	1921	2937	6397
201458	86414	58897	8559	4941	14017
56567	27357	18350	451	2261	6295
90288	38051	28331	909	3018	5793
49681	19486	14999	537	977	2973
86630	43307	25520	6762	2039	8986
133120	63250	38723	4705	3621	16201
114829	59365	18780	10167	10211	20207
201539	93228	52578	9345	7378	23927
177120	77350	36299	6323	9707	25021
398851	197166	109357	24617	12736	50456
191029	85470	31089	30341	5706	18334
257345	117579	72776	10110	11640	23053
591628	259868	176365	11649	28702	43152
299331	123202	56626	18017	11140	37419
99106	42193	29375	1745	1823	9250
166527	77535	49745	6775	4672	16343
130718	54785	39358	3757	5060	6610
110600	47134	21444	8939	5127	11624
101932	45118	30015	4666	1089	9348
292727	122976	46030	36860	8593	31493
342782	167492	92172	19062	18715	37543

20-8 农林牧渔业总产值(2016年)

GROSS OUTPUT VALUE OF FARMING, FORESTRY, ANIMAL HUSBANDRY AND FISHERY(2016)

按当年价格计算 (at current price)

县(市、区)	Region	农林牧渔业总产值(万元) Total (10 000 yuan)	农业产值 Farming	林业产值 Forestry	牧业产值 Animal Husbandry	渔业产值 Fishery	农林牧渔服务业产值 Farming, Forestry, Animal Husbandry and Fishery Service
太原市	**Taiyuan**						
小店区	Xiaodian	154162	102059	9893	37646	64	4500
迎泽区	Yingze	7052	319	5694	979	60	
杏花岭区	Xinghualing	10843	1570	4698	4575		
尖草坪区	Jiancaoping	69027	36422	9616	22007	232	750
万柏林区	Wanbailin	10398	1054	5139	3143	30	1033
晋源区	Jinyuan	77594	51232	2065	22889	299	1110
清徐县	Qingxu	259839	173418	4052	71001	2168	9200
阳曲县	Yangqu	95184	45654	8765	38096	69	2600
娄烦县	Loufan	40268	18103	6995	12946	525	1700
古交市	Gujiao	43482	13367	8455	17317	143	4200
大同市	**Datong**						
南郊区	Nanjiao	126172	50663	772	68911	27	5800
新荣区	Xinrong	76144	27744	4452	38967	62	4920
阳高县	Yanggao	219982	100961	3393	109502	125	6000
天镇县	Tianzhen	123734	50424	2269	70711		330
广灵县	Guangling	115104	56020	3568	50016	109	5391
灵丘县	Lingqiu	84919	29908	5397	47657	168	1790
浑源县	Hunyuan	164575	60928	8544	91150	55	3900
左云县	Zuoyun	57207	18378	9404	28126		1300
大同县	Datongxian	141308	63705	2935	69754	432	4482
阳泉市	**Yangquan**						
郊　区	Jiaoqu	42544	17402	3956	20217	19	950
平定县	Pingding	83944	38251	7137	36174	1182	1200
盂　县	Yuxian	78480	46658	6836	21927	260	2800
长治市	**Changzhi**						
城　区	Chengqu	11480	5213	2029	3883		355
郊　区	Jiaoqu	55788	28753	1628	22197	413	2798
长治县	Changzhixian	132638	57531	4115	67973	120	2899
襄垣县	Xiangyuan	111351	80724	3411	17889	428	8900
屯留县	Tunliu	123202	81425	3539	30245	594	7400
平顺县	Pingshun	52855	27394	5639	13103	320	6400
黎城县	Licheng	53591	29002	7716	15439	234	1200
壶关县	Huguan	92869	53779	3526	34642	122	800
长子县	Zhangzi	206736	137606	2289	63676	966	2200
武乡县	Wuxiang	61216	41819	2683	13848	566	2300
沁　县	Qinxian	101015	65523	3677	28669	1197	1950
沁源县	Qinyuan	49332	31224	6006	6930	152	5020
潞城市	Lucheng	82084	47026	5937	26561	360	2200

20-8 续表1 continued

按当年价格计算 (at current price)

县(市、区)	Region	农林牧渔业总产值(万元) Total (10 000 yuan)	农业产值 Farming	林业产值 Forestry	牧业产值 Animal Husbandry	渔业产值 Fishery	农林牧渔服务业产值 Farming, Forestry, Animal Husbandry and Fishery Service
晋城市	**Jincheng**						
城　区	Chengqu	15758	6978	3425	4389	134	832
沁水县	Qinshui	110720	49481	11005	46010	1741	2484
阳城县	Yangcheng	174731	71223	6177	92753	216	4362
陵川县	Lingchuan	93792	37729	4230	48331	951	2551
泽州县	Zezhou	274512	96791	6856	163940	1749	5176
高平市	Gaoping	280102	99893	6634	168327	283	4964
朔州市	**Shuozhou**						
朔城区	Shuocheng	221943	119988	27087	63218	1097	10552
平鲁区	Pinglu	77249	39857	8925	21875	61	6530
山阴县	Shanyin	241898	89482	8293	142026	238	1860
应　县	Yingxian	312313	174656	8642	121205	400	7410
右玉县	Youyu	128128	28867	24725	72212	184	2140
怀仁县	Huairen	223018	77964	8578	133068	208	3200
晋中市	**Jinzhong**						
榆次区	Yuci	319333	226241	9485	74195	613	8800
榆社县	Yushe	73416	48063	2663	19163	1127	2400
左权县	Zuoquan	62797	46488	1766	12566	467	1511
和顺县	Heshun	51427	31886	1164	16867		1510
昔阳县	Xiyang	86766	59523	2414	23721	108	1000
寿阳县	Shouyang	222523	188344	3334	26331	614	3900
太谷县	Taigu	331102	186279	5174	135877	268	3503
祁　县	Qixian	284630	168572	8316	101844	97	5800
平遥县	Pingyao	256252	137504	9607	104245	579	4318
灵石县	Lingshi	93621	48598	9921	34186	46	870
介休市	Jiexiu	124436	43437	7091	68169	176	5564
运城市	**Yuncheng**						
盐湖区	Yanhu	256861	203103	6684	28604	965	17505
临猗县	Linyi	877894	747868	6270	35671	85	88000
万荣县	Wanrong	357533	268949	4496	57063	7225	19800
闻喜县	Wenxi	239557	179714	8568	42273	82	8920
稷山县	Jishan	245931	135380	3008	96285	57	11200
新绛县	Xinjiang	362341	259400	3352	79638	172	19780
绛　县	Jiangxian	181626	129373	13008	27190	55	12000
垣曲县	Yuanqu	99802	58104	5064	27430	1704	7500
夏　县	Xiaxian	385580	316267	4823	34322	168	30000
平陆县	Pinglu	187856	139520	4120	30165	52	14000
芮城县	Ruicheng	436895	339194	4490	59156	1410	32646
永济市	Yongji	424021	330419	4925	46632	15214	26832
河津市	Hejin	148993	99100	2963	31859	571	14500

20-8 续表2 continued

按当年价格计算 (at current price)

县(市、区)	Region	农林牧渔业总产值(万元) Total (10 000 yuan)	农业产值 Farming	林业产值 Forestry	牧业产值 Animal Husbandry	渔业产值 Fishery	农林牧渔服务业产值 Farming, Forestry, Animal Husbandry and Fishery Service
忻州市	**Xinzhou**						
忻府区	Xinfu	150544	93178	6778	44079	498	6011
定襄县	Dingxiang	64347	45645	3366	12965	471	1900
五台县	Wutai	91862	38510	6937	41223	1192	4000
代县	Daixian	56743	34181	4858	14381	423	2900
繁峙县	Fanshi	89727	22527	11669	51992	453	3086
宁武县	Ningwu	36608	11843	2797	20886	82	1000
静乐县	Jingle	62755	29788	8515	23039	175	1238
神池县	Shenchi	130581	52424	3634	72401		2122
五寨县	Wuzhai	70341	49007	4984	13899	147	2304
岢岚县	Kelan	70132	28204	3324	36405		2200
河曲县	Hequ	58817	29308	7852	18936	321	2400
保德县	Baode	57820	34119	3712	18415	144	1430
偏关县	Pianguan	75090	25266	7752	39805	68	2200
原平市	Yuanping	218942	98290	5121	105747	785	9000
临汾市	**Linfen**						
尧都区	Yaodu	171075	114885	6668	42504	4722	2296
曲沃县	Quwo	234614	185145	4364	39824	3273	2007
翼城县	Yicheng	171874	95345	4675	68595	1092	2168
襄汾县	Xiangfen	266255	198705	4729	55435	2206	5180
洪洞县	Hongtong	211764	130622	6689	70574	1288	2590
古县	Guxian	44684	34786	3224	6020	2	652
安泽县	Anze	72062	52162	4725	12611	4	2560
浮山县	Fushan	79833	56940	4095	17099	12	1688
吉县	Jixian	108628	89245	4564	9848	4	4968
乡宁县	Xiangning	64777	34445	6455	22491	6	1380
大宁县	Daning	24776	15567	4719	2982	8	1500
隰县	Xixian	81340	63927	6284	8616	1	2512
永和县	Yonghe	53565	37670	5123	9099	3	1670
蒲县	Puxian	48659	31016	6394	9695	14	1540
汾西县	Fenxi	57958	27810	3589	25439		1120
侯马市	Houma	62986	42329	5517	12239	900	2000
霍州市	Huozhou	67919	38378	4950	23898	82	612
吕梁市	**Lvliang**						
离石区	Lishi	36279	14749	3027	17417	86	1000
文水县	Wenshui	212747	83437	1153	124006	1151	3000
交城县	Jiaocheng	59875	18686	2272	38174	144	600
兴县	Xingxian	61879	36074	5377	18936	73	1420
临县	Linxian	121046	67881	2780	47705	281	2400
柳林县	Liulin	37517	20568	2510	12996	143	1300
石楼县	Shilou	43176	29420	2867	10322	67	500
岚县	Lanxian	40608	24175	4549	9939	384	1560
方山县	Fangshan	30388	16191	3370	9934	243	650
中阳县	Zhongyang	27132	14737	1885	10079	146	285
交口县	Jiaokou	33246	20611	1566	10849		220
孝义市	Xiaoyi	174441	78071	4410	81743	218	10000
汾阳市	Fenyang	132885	55000	5000	66288	398	6200

20-9 农林牧渔业中间消耗(2016年)

INTERMEDIATE CONSUMPTION OF FARMING, FORESTRY, ANIMAL HUSBANDRY AND FISHERY(2016)

按当年价格计算 (at current price)

县(市、区)	Region	农林牧渔业中间消耗(万元) Total (10 000 yuan)	农业 Farming	林业 Forestry	牧业 Animal Husbandry	渔业 Fishery	农林牧渔服务业 Farming, Forestry, Animal Husbandry and Fishery Service
太原市	**Taiyuan**						
小店区	Xiaodian	69533	40619	5400	21280	34	2200
迎泽区	Yingze	3734	142	2950	611	31	
杏花岭区	Xinghualing	5872	620	2359	2893		
尖草坪区	Jiancaoping	32941	14430	5000	13000	126	385
万柏林区	Wanbailin	5132	328	2364	1870	15	555
晋源区	Jinyuan	36225	20200	990	14305	161	568
清徐县	Qingxu	119486	70400	2260	40580	1176	5070
阳曲县	Yangqu	43448	15650	4200	22300	38	1260
娄烦县	Loufan	19797	6820	3465	8350	281	882
古交市	Gujiao	22573	5310	4020	10880	78	2285
大同市	**Datong**						
南郊区	Nanjiao	41805	22540	367	16234	15	2650
新荣区	Xinrong	33768	8474	2774	18481	39	4000
阳高县	Yanggao	112900	56460	1620	51164	56	3600
天镇县	Tianzhen	57143	23236	1512	32275		120
广灵县	Guangling	58190	20257	2843	32213	82	2796
灵丘县	Lingqiu	46471	15277	4288	25739	47	1120
浑源县	Hunyuan	57092	23642	2104	30268	29	1050
左云县	Zuoyun	29451	8842	5883	14146		580
大同县	Datongxian	62889	24421	2634	33484	204	2145
阳泉市	**Yangquan**						
郊　区	Jiaoqu	20178	8927	1948	8812	13	478
平定县	Pingding	40752	17862	3404	18320	587	580
盂　县	Yuxian	38586	21993	4695	10255	142	1500
长治市	**Changzhi**						
城　区	Chengqu	5216	1800	1464	1761		191
郊　区	Jiaoqu	23998	13264	892	8321	240	1281
长治县	Changzhixian	65910	26044	2288	36241	56	1282
襄垣县	Xiangyuan	47694	30492	2065	10112	185	4840
屯留县	Tunliu	52897	31760	1920	15312	303	3602
平顺县	Pingshun	25254	11869	3518	7187	189	2490
黎城县	Licheng	21049	10259	3220	6861	114	595
壶关县	Huguan	39726	18434	1958	18898	70	365
长子县	Zhangzi	86009	50448	1258	32966	388	950
武乡县	Wuxiang	27548	15998	1658	8403	315	1175
沁　县	Qinxian	41286	21469	1850	16401	555	1010
沁源县	Qinyuan	20251	11121	2155	4468	86	2422
潞城市	Lucheng	34438	16141	2173	14844	180	1100

20–9 续表1 continued

按当年价格计算 (at current price)

县(市、区)	Region	农林牧渔业中间消耗(万元) Total (10 000 yuan)	农业 Farming	林业 Forestry	牧业 Animal Husbandry	渔业 Fishery	农林牧渔服务业 Farming, Forestry, Animal Husbandry and Fishery Service
晋城市	**Jincheng**						
城　区	Chengqu	7913	3001	1883	2519	77	433
沁水县	Qinshui	49556	21079	4897	21671	618	1292
阳城县	Yangcheng	75776	30199	3601	39605	102	2268
陵川县	Lingchuan	43390	15922	2286	23344	511	1327
泽州县	Zezhou	131945	41330	3462	83610	852	2692
高平市	Gaoping	132689	41955	3052	84938	163	2581
朔州市	**Shuozhou**						
朔城区	Shuocheng	88527	49026	9515	24335	697	4954
平鲁区	Pinglu	38199	20841	3403	11515	38	2403
山阴县	Shanyin	123797	40470	3399	78982	159	786
应　县	Yingxian	174006	95533	4953	69713	205	3602
右玉县	Youyu	69898	14663	15907	38124	99	1105
怀仁县	Huairen	134407	47711	4318	80426	136	1817
晋中市	**Jinzhong**						
榆次区	Yuci	117906	69184	5507	38235	230	4750
榆社县	Yushe	25937	12703	2371	9363	280	1220
左权县	Zuoquan	27474	16654	1708	7806	316	990
和顺县	Heshun	22121	11392	1072	9078		580
昔阳县	Xiyang	38659	22404	1322	14321	32	580
寿阳县	Shouyang	90038	71141	3126	13883	358	1530
太谷县	Taigu	154624	47578	2079	103409	114	1445
祁　县	Qixian	110269	50818	6024	50098	49	3280
平遥县	Pingyao	114012	53367	5037	53054	264	2290
灵石县	Lingshi	43383	17074	4943	20936	20	410
介休市	Jiexiu	59282	20262	2911	33180	79	2850
运城市	**Yuncheng**						
盐湖区	Yanhu	112587	85386	3419	14875	557	8350
临猗县	Linyi	397541	332787	3818	19694	43	41200
万荣县	Wanrong	180057	134993	2562	29294	3902	9306
闻喜县	Wenxi	129125	96616	5444	22565	49	4450
稷山县	Jishan	112033	55073	1884	49493	32	5550
新绛县	Xinjiang	182527	129041	2358	41140	99	9890
绛　县	Jiangxian	83287	55131	8204	14068	33	5850
垣曲县	Yuanqu	51282	28931	3050	15061	880	3360
夏　县	Xiaxian	179471	144062	2819	18194	97	14300
平陆县	Pinglu	84403	58771	2510	16792	31	6300
芮城县	Ruicheng	193730	142194	2425	33312	800	15000
永济市	Yongji	197347	149408	2496	23312	9131	13000
河津市	Hejin	66196	40386	1702	16882	366	6860

20-9 续表2 continued

按当年价格计算 (at current price)

县(市、区)	Region	农林牧渔业中间消耗(万元) Total (10 000 yuan)	农 业 Farming	林 业 Forestry	牧 业 Animal Husbandry	渔 业 Fishery	农林牧渔服务业 Farming, Forestry, Animal Husbandry and Fishery Service
忻 州 市	**Xinzhou**						
忻府区	Xinfu	54040	28870	3114	19314	198	2544
定襄县	Dingxiang	28757	20160	1709	5754	233	900
五台县	Wutai	40513	15640	3454	19195	474	1750
代 县	Daixian	26976	16779	2203	6416	177	1400
繁峙县	Fanshi	38700	9463	5464	22216	194	1363
宁武县	Ningwu	15780	5124	1225	8942	39	450
静乐县	Jingle	25378	9501	3387	11896	96	499
神池县	Shenchi	59483	20512	1710	36301		960
五寨县	Wuzhai	31189	21638	2300	6197	54	1000
岢岚县	Kelan	30584	11470	1673	16351		1090
河曲县	Hequ	22451	9643	3662	7913	113	1120
保德县	Baode	24440	13258	1927	8592	64	599
偏关县	Pianguan	35603	12530	4645	17452	26	950
原平市	Yuanping	91462	39398	2677	45462	325	3600
临 汾 市	**Linfen**						
尧都区	Yaodu	82381	56795	3436	18731	2301	1117
曲沃县	Quwo	101935	79105	2140	18144	1515	1032
翼城县	Yicheng	80985	43039	2363	34009	546	1028
襄汾县	Xiangfen	125087	91265	2537	27719	964	2602
洪洞县	Hongtong	100800	65268	3176	30517	560	1280
古 县	Guxian	20627	16018	1702	2603	1.2	303
安泽县	Anze	31265	22170	2457	5297	2	1339
浮山县	Fushan	34767	23477	2051	8332	6	902
吉 县	Jixian	46654	37894	1975	4220	2	2562
乡宁县	Xiangning	32620	18933	3254	9785	3	646
大宁县	Daning	11172	6709	2436	1276	4	747
隰 县	Xixian	42255	33899	3368	3759	1	1228
永和县	Yonghe	28302	20563	2764	4163	1	811
蒲 县	Puxian	26152	16945	3607	4848	7	746
汾西县	Fenxi	28165	13811	1681	12120		554
侯马市	Houma	28412	18439	2770	5836	415	952
霍州市	Huozhou	30974	16421	2674	11549	41	289
吕 梁 市	**Lvliang**						
离石区	Lishi	15449	5704	1604	7666	44	430
文水县	Wenshui	97600	30484	587	64484	575	1470
交城县	Jiaocheng	29223	7835	1204	19836	78	270
兴 县	Xingxian	28280	15235	2742	9658	35	611
临 县	Linxian	51808	25044	1251	24329	152	1032
柳林县	Liulin	16773	8506	1280	6357	70	559
石楼县	Shilou	18235	11312	1491	5173	30	230
岚 县	Lanxian	17306	8819	2502	5071	181	733
方山县	Fangshan	14346	7065	1787	5066	124	306
中阳县	Zhongyang	12945	6450	952	5332	74	137
交口县	Jiaokou	15882	9297	846	5642		97
孝义市	Xiaoyi	73022	24621	1984	41713	104	4600
汾阳市	Fenyang	57635	18545	2650	33475	175	2790

20-10 主要粮食作物播种面积(2016年)

单位：公顷

县(市、区)	Region	粮食作物播种面积 Sown Area of Grain Crops	秋收粮食 Sown Area of Autumn Grain Crops	谷物 Cereal	#小麦 Wheat	#玉米 Corn	#谷子 Millet
太原市	**Taiyuan**						
小店区	Xiaodian	7604	7545	7566	59	7484	
迎泽区	Yingze	172	172	131		90	24
杏花岭区	Xinghualing	570	570	401		275	49
尖草坪区	Jiancaoping	4328	4328	3924		3473	311
万柏林区	Wanbailin	415	415	342		289	44
晋源区	Jinyuan	2666	2666	2601		2393	2
清徐县	Qingxu	20458	20436	20242	22	19625	3
阳曲县	Yangqu	20579	20579	19145		14647	3501
娄烦县	Loufan	9179	9179	4590		1642	1515
古交市	Gujiao	7465	7465	3609		1560	817
大同市	**Datong**						
南郊区	Nanjiao	14573	14573	13139		10409	653
新荣区	Xinrong	20870	20870	14304		4517	1341
阳高县	Yanggao	50802	50802	45839		34893	4518
天镇县	Tianzhen	37721	37721	29779		24936	2412
广灵县	Guangling	27657	27657	24201		17092	2624
灵丘县	Lingqiu	30733	30733	24181		17068	3813
浑源县	Hunyuan	35701	35509	28527		22441	1997
左云县	Zuoyun	21881	21881	13809		2563	1413
大同县	Datongxian	36807	36807	29420		23368	1987
开发区	Development Zone	385	385	383		364	5
阳泉市	**Yangquan**						
郊　区	Jiaoqu	5205	5205	4924		4561	341
平定县	Pingding	20426	20426	19408		17671	1606
盂　县	Yuxian	28446	28134	26194		23863	2014
长治市	**Changzhi**						
城　区	Chengqu	203	203	203		203	
郊　区	Jiaoqu	8096	8088	8011	8	7979	24
长治县	Changzhixian	18283	17990	17751	293	16819	516
襄垣县	Xiangyuan	28361	28200	27710	162	25403	2061
屯留县	Tunliu	33950	33355	33035	595	32061	345
平顺县	Pingshun	9981	8842	8958	1139	6912	881
黎城县	Licheng	14726	13377	13599	1349	11640	580
壶关县	Huguan	16081	16079	15562	2	15013	467
长子县	Zhangzi	30429	29582	29336	847	28227	222
武乡县	Wuxiang	26839	26622	23691	216	16885	5551
沁　县	Qinxian	25518	25455	24554	63	21322	2377
沁源县	Qinyuan	13940	13940	10081		8145	1283
潞城市	Lucheng	16446	15590	16148	856	14911	292

SOWN AREAS OF MAJOR GRAIN CROPS(2016)

(ha)

#高　梁 Sorghum	#燕　麦 Oats	#荞　麦 Buckwheat	豆　类 Beans	#大　豆 Soybean	薯　类 Tubers	#马铃薯 Potato
24			36	7	2	2
9	2	3	9	1	31	25
12		51	122	108	47	34
51			285	250	119	94
6		1	13	3	59	59
67			34	15	31	26
592			65	50	152	3
137		195	1033	786	401	385
217	240	976	1238	666	3351	3351
32	151	150	1840	1302	2016	2013
448	55	134	943	236	491	491
1352	1712	743	2800	2554	3767	3767
755			2714	697	2248	2248
448	147		1985	790	5957	5957
138	694	835	1417	142	2039	2039
117	591	142	3665	2322	2887	2887
76	1754		4078	963	3096	3096
52	5638	2832	4284	2383	3788	3788
195			6159	1221	1227	1227
			1		1	1
8		1	128	38	154	49
55			465	342	553	219
12	17	15	597	218	1655	1588
			69	64	16	16
			170	87	363	362
22			266	189	386	204
33			291	278	625	564
			172	151	851	807
22			1056	1052	71	51
3			82	65	437	429
40			257	204	836	664
635	53		769	687	2379	2270
791			405	349	560	401
3	128	105	833	432	3026	2981
88			193	187	105	73

20-10 续表1

单位：公顷

县(市、区)	Region	粮食作物播种面积 Sown Area of Grain Crops	秋收粮食 Sown Area of Autumn Grain Crops	谷 物 Cereal	#小 麦 Wheat	#玉 米 Corn	#谷 子 Millet
晋 城 市	**Jincheng**						
城 区	Chengqu	1555	393	1468	1162	288	18
沁水县	Qinshui	25427	23064	23792	2364	19779	1400
阳城县	Yangcheng	31458	23774	30065	7683	18988	3341
陵川县	Lingchuan	20343	20239	18831	104	17311	1349
泽州县	Zezhou	58697	29067	37909	29630	6604	1625
高平市	Gaoping	30954	29011	28336	1943	25287	1090
开发区	Development Zone	590	318	339	273	27	39
朔 州 市	**Shuozhou**						
朔城区	Shuocheng	54461	53773	48457	15	41208	1419
平鲁区	Pinglu	37427	33076	18895		4122	719
山阴县	Shanyin	51411	50052	45429		34524	1635
应 县	Yingxian	49155	48345	44725		39544	1940
右玉县	Youyu	30789	28390	17768		4286	850
怀仁县	Huairen	41195	41195	36003		29901	1537
开发区	Development Zone	764	764	764		764	
晋 中 市	**Jinzhong**						
榆次区	Yuci	29546	29412	28547	134	26194	1617
榆社县	Yushe	15882	15882	14182		10439	2876
左权县	Zuoquan	11537	11523	10101	13	7782	1968
和顺县	Heshun	11962	11962	9850		7861	1173
昔阳县	Xiyang	22094	22094	21288		19700	1341
寿阳县	Shouyang	45706	45706	43338		40693	2119
太谷县	Taigu	25167	23795	22979	1372	20284	944
祁 县	Qixian	23426	22537	22297	889	21075	306
平遥县	Pingyao	37054	36913	35392	79	34145	789
灵石县	Lingshi	11819	10188	11229	1631	8618	525
介休市	Jiexiu	21597	19631	19760	1966	17426	278
开发区	Development Zone	990	990	987		985	2
运 城 市	**Yuncheng**						
盐湖区	Yanhu	44998	25345	40339	19653	20647	1
临猗县	Linyi	52360	28181	46560	24179	22380	
万荣县	Wanrong	50339	27539	44990	22800	22092	92
闻喜县	Wenxi	68586	27391	66442	41195	24498	235
稷山县	Jishan	44338	20820	44130	23519	20605	6
新绛县	Xinjiang	49151	23771	48612	25380	23207	15
绛 县	Jiangxian	40107	18038	39347	22069	17210	34
垣曲县	Yuanqu	25207	10508	24417	14699	8996	590
夏 县	Xiaxian	49887	28940	49306	20947	27982	335
平陆县	Pinglu	30719	13818	28972	16901	12018	52
芮城县	Ruicheng	64994	31525	62737	33469	28814	414
永济市	Yongji	70165	38054	68663	32111	36238	
河津市	Hejin	31229	15599	30693	15630	15038	17

continued

(ha)

#高 粱 Sorghum	#燕 麦 Oats	#荞 麦 Buckwheat	豆 类 Beans	#大 豆 Soybean	薯 类 Tubers	#马铃薯 Potato
			67	60	20	3
236			1208	1138	427	227
3			1237	1162	155	63
			223	190	1289	1260
49			20364	20363	424	86
16			2070	2059	549	38
			248	248	3	
936	2062	111	3108	637	2895	2895
	10783	1978	9356	1510	9177	9177
452	2407	643	4240	1871	1743	1743
469	3		1979	325	2451	2451
48	9599	2587	5453	2985	7569	7569
958			4664	1358	528	528
202	1	258	859	668	140	90
565	2	17	1368	1163	332	264
67	70	84	640	629	795	748
33	179	304	897	831	1214	1214
27		9	396	338	410	355
108		371	383	348	1986	1983
325			1621	1582	567	351
28			729	710	400	106
218	59	12	725	649	938	556
195	2	32	337	246	254	142
89			1464	1408	374	84
					2	
39			4283	503	376	
			3972	1379	1829	
6			4254	666	1094	
514			1574	284	570	111
1			149	54	59	23
9			481	262	59	
35			414	287	345	21
132			299	260	491	24
41			264	120	317	46
1			975	857	773	87
39			1741	384	516	31
314			1251	1209	251	15
8			424	51	112	16

20-10 续表2

单位：公顷

县(市、区)	Region	粮食作物播种面积 Sown Area of Grain Crops	秋收粮食 Sown Area of Autumn Grain Crops	谷物 Cereal	#小麦 Wheat	#玉米 Corn	#谷子 Millet
忻州市	**Xinzhou**						
忻府区	Xinfu	47302	47302	46522		43535	2436
定襄县	Dingxiang	25172	25172	24197		22113	1576
五台县	Wutai	28151	28151	23875		19440	3013
代　县	Daixian	23214	23214	21607		18842	1523
繁峙县	Fanshi	34885	34885	28764		18971	3651
宁武县	Ningwu	13840	13840	6617		1366	210
静乐县	Jingle	22103	22103	11015		2864	2650
神池县	Shenchi	39220	39220	26140		12297	7448
五寨县	Wuzhai	36058	36058	31531		22883	7586
岢岚县	Kelan	26400	26400	12294		6376	3050
河曲县	Hequ	24091	24091	16866		7710	5030
保德县	Baode	21529	21529	12136		5257	4208
偏关县	Pianguan	25504	25504	17612		5294	6235
原平市	Yuanping	56043	55925	51909	119	46625	2899
临汾市	**Linfen**						
尧都区	Yaodu	48667	23156	47643	25511	21839	200
曲沃县	Quwo	34491	17644	33965	16847	17118	
翼城县	Yicheng	45481	22146	45155	23334	21223	573
襄汾县	Xiangfen	83840	40190	82538	43650	38484	384
洪洞县	Hongtong	78357	36115	76286	42242	33779	191
古　县	Guxian	13709	12279	12739	1430	10432	837
安泽县	Anze	23081	23081	22617		21878	655
浮山县	Fushan	25523	10723	24653	14800	9290	484
吉　县	Jixian	7040	6981	5963	59	5109	669
乡宁县	Xiangning	25533	13807	21992	11726	8021	1018
大宁县	Daning	9777	9747	8243	30	7022	1101
隰　县	Xixian	20923	20783	18862	140	16346	1714
永和县	Yonghe	23697	23528	19843	170	14558	4412
蒲　县	Puxian	14525	14505	12601	20	10982	677
汾西县	Fenxi	24175	12808	22645	11367	8640	895
侯马市	Houma	15003	7337	15000	7666	7334	
霍州市	Huozhou	18709	7857	17485	10852	6284	280
吕梁市	**Lvliang**						
离石区	Lishi	14453	14453	7495		4651	2080
文水县	Wenshui	31288	31198	29989	90	29612	201
交城县	Jiaocheng	8284	8243	6703	41	6013	288
兴　县	Xingxian	50650	50650	28124		13412	11419
临　县	Linxian	78910	78910	51142		35736	11830
柳林县	Liulin	20555	20555	12262		6417	3590
石楼县	Shilou	26140	25979	20800	161	12460	5110
岚　县	Lanxian	29425	29425	15909		8771	3456
方山县	Fangshan	14472	14472	7577		6032	942
中阳县	Zhongyang	9244	9244	4853		2861	1356
交口县	Jiaokou	9491	9491	7582		5794	987
孝义市	Xiaoyi	18935	17532	15719	1403	10685	1731
汾阳市	Fenyang	39584	39544	37883	34	34844	2123

continued

(ha)

#高　粱 Sorghum	#燕　麦 Oats	#荞　麦 Buckwheat	豆　类 Beans	#大　豆 Soybean	薯　类 Tubers	#马铃薯 Potato
371	1		508	446	273	82
309		14	526	283	449	279
124	421		1544	901	2732	2654
258	92	11	821	192	786	759
	453		4106	3629	2015	2008
	5036	5	4329	503	2894	2894
145	3194		5325	2121	5764	5764
	4308		7962	2116	5119	5119
63	128	1	1774	824	2754	2754
	2064		7753	764	6353	6353
19	129		2971	1833	4254	4222
322	143		4319	1382	5074	4869
	1055	246	2996	2293	4896	4896
392	955		2409	1020	1725	1635
40			638	573	387	308
			135	47	392	
24			242	229	84	35
4			957	673	346	10
32			1148	782	923	34
39			506	315	465	429
84			222	198	242	126
47			587	384	283	105
11		9	776	413	301	224
			2400	1053	1141	1056
3	10		1195	638	339	204
18		87	719	468	1341	1311
199			2946	692	908	569
	358	231	340	320	1584	1584
69		127	602	360	928	469
					3	
69			755	670	469	214
28	19		4684	2993	2274	2245
85			593	216	706	581
70			802	183	778	772
816	420		14182	9925	8343	7992
244			13376	9566	14392	13467
382			6358	6137	1935	1780
472	287	155	3562	2338	1777	1300
1841	736		3982	585	9534	9534
37			2547	989	4349	4316
35	331	158	2842	2117	1550	1489
6	288	176	1063	821	846	757
994	238	298	2650	2456	567	434
579	80	15	913	739	788	555

20-11 主要粮食作物产量(2016年)

单位：吨

县(市、区)	Region	粮食总产量 Output of Grain	秋粮产量 Output of Autumn Grain	谷物 Cereal	#小麦 Wheat	#玉米 Corn	#谷子 Millet
太原市	**Taiyuan**						
小店区	Xiaodian	62440	62100	62372	340	61850	
迎泽区	Yingze	409	409	352		269	57
杏花岭区	Xinghualing	881	881	642		480	64
尖草坪区	Jiancaoping	14896	14896	14247		13157	754
万柏林区	Wanbailin	1592	1592	1479		1369	95
晋源区	Jinyuan	21534	21534	21227		19622	11
清徐县	Qingxu	104105	103969	103052	136	99277	6
阳曲县	Yangqu	79270	79270	76829		66733	8319
娄烦县	Loufan	16820	16820	7980		4515	1780
古交市	Gujiao	10923	10923	5868		3300	1322
大同市	**Datong**						
南郊区	Nanjiao	68743	68743	66798		60987	1554
新荣区	Xinrong	55423	55423	43253		22182	3153
阳高县	Yanggao	264672	264672	255368		228436	12299
天镇县	Tianzhen	170895	170895	157882		146487	5295
广灵县	Guangling	167670	167670	160330		147270	5807
灵丘县	Lingqiu	91546	91546	80922		63946	10536
浑源县	Hunyuan	169396	169021	154298		142904	4651
左云县	Zuoyun	35544	35544	23518		9783	2536
大同县	Datongxian	99709	99709	92037		80000	4389
开发区	Development Zone	2960	2960	2956		2867	24
阳泉市	**Yangquan**						
郊　区	Jiaoqu	23026	23026	22441		21548	857
平定县	Pingding	92798	92798	89176		84687	4190
盂　县	Yuxian	143350	142258	137712		132440	4748
长治市	**Changzhi**						
城　区	Chengqu	1555	1555	1555		1555	
郊　区	Jiaoqu	54995	54955	54706	40	54538	127
长治县	Changzhixian	134883	133233	132429	1650	127724	2466
襄垣县	Xiangyuan	176926	176415	174688	510	167240	6674
屯留县	Tunliu	264230	260639	260857	3592	255662	1368
平顺县	Pingshun	53642	47450	50894	6192	42137	2487
黎城县	Licheng	68542	62903	66459	5639	59246	1416
壶关县	Huguan	123300	123292	121305	8	119572	1592
长子县	Zhangzi	245082	239620	239191	5461	232856	649
武乡县	Wuxiang	111820	111173	106855	648	86678	16286
沁　县	Qinxian	186252	186047	182016	205	167678	8501
沁源县	Qinyuan	75216	75216	64118		58925	4027
潞城市	Lucheng	120686	118302	119608	2383	115710	1024

OUTPUT OF MAJOR GRAIN CROPS(2016)

(ton)

#高 粱 Sorghum	#燕 麦 Oats	#荞 麦 Buckwheat	豆 类 Beans	#大 豆 Soybean	薯 类 Tubers	#马铃薯 Potato
182			47	11	21	21
18		2	16	2	42	25
22		49	122	97	117	97
141			557	500	92	68
12			23	2	90	90
710			114	56	193	154
3633			99	74	954	5
644		250	1397	1057	1043	1012
220	365	1100	1840	990	7000	7000
97	400	700	1856	1331	3200	3190
1221	158	147	1093	325	852	852
4491	1524	696	3243	2999	8927	8927
2607			3605	1212	5699	5699
1969	173		1798	813	11215	11215
182	833	807	1984	236	5356	5356
480	1091	155	3997	2496	6627	6627
301	2232		5086	1028	10012	10012
140	5679	3485	4588	2862	7439	7439
539			5734	1299	1938	1938
			2		3	3
12		1	187	44	399	155
175			622	523	3000	1243
39	29	16	705	272	4934	4812
			191	178	98	98
			481	305	1973	1968
116			499	352	1738	788
236			1155	1124	2218	2005
			446	425	2301	2199
145			1756	1750	327	205
8			225	171	1770	1748
225			864	646	5026	4106
2373	94	1	1144	1053	3821	3556
5632			1088	952	3148	2270
5	156	114	1683	873	9415	9302
487			473	468	604	442

20-11 续表1

单位：吨

县(市、区)	Region	粮食总产量 Output of Grain	秋粮产量 Output of Autumn Grain	谷物 Cereal	#小麦 Wheat	#玉米 Corn	#谷子 Millet
晋城市	**Jincheng**						
城区	Chengqu	7073	2340	6788	4733	1990	63
沁水县	Qinshui	144848	136502	140802	8346	126840	4006
阳城县	Yangcheng	165937	131823	162754	34114	117560	10962
陵川县	Lingchuan	102128	101673	97263	455	93302	3376
泽州县	Zezhou	236668	108913	195709	127756	60772	6892
高平市	Gaoping	241770	233719	235323	8051	223412	3760
开发区	Development Zone	2085	883	1527	1202	218	106
朔州市	**Shuozhou**						
朔城区	Shuocheng	312337	310798	296774	73	279512	3970
平鲁区	Pinglu	75677	68267	40127		19625	1162
山阴县	Shanyin	265010	263723	257212		239736	4557
应县	Yingxian	345420	340514	330341		314900	8750
右玉县	Youyu	35183	33716	20157		9185	968
怀仁县	Huairen	230360	230360	224282		207566	5388
开发区	Development Zone	6300	6300	6300		6300	
晋中市	**Jinzhong**						
榆次区	Yuci	197336	196489	195453	847	187781	4912
榆社县	Yushe	87768	87768	82474		68142	10776
左权县	Zuoquan	56729	56686	53110	44	46620	6002
和顺县	Heshun	67132	67132	61773		55958	3875
昔阳县	Xiyang	162465	162465	161007		155616	4570
寿阳县	Shouyang	382451	382451	373927		363411	7970
太谷县	Taigu	215222	207061	206887	8161	193377	3077
祁县	Qixian	212364	208196	209773	4168	204532	906
平遥县	Pingyao	271941	271370	267299	348	262628	2783
灵石县	Lingshi	62606	58440	61482	4166	53710	1716
介休市	Jiexiu	122145	113514	118289	8631	108476	691
开发区	Development Zone	6057	6057	6046		6041	5
运城市	**Yuncheng**						
盐湖区	Yanhu	205610	116190	201081	89420	111492	2
临猗县	Linyi	300123	175277	277927	124846	153081	
万荣县	Wanrong	180144	100480	166936	79665	87122	136
闻喜县	Wenxi	356349	165411	348936	190938	154977	501
稷山县	Jishan	241284	119310	240702	121974	118716	10
新绛县	Xinjiang	261018	126344	259944	134674	125188	54
绛县	Jiangxian	196160	115058	192773	81103	111399	76
垣曲县	Yuanqu	101766	41944	96648	59821	35109	1353
夏县	Xiaxian	272265	149883	270482	122382	147221	770
平陆县	Pinglu	129328	59667	122818	69661	53031	124
芮城县	Ruicheng	353149	175436	347881	177713	167764	2151
永济市	Yongji	427323	233211	422312	194112	226142	
河津市	Hejin	190192	95913	189240	94279	94898	49

continued

(ton)

#高粱 Sorghum	#燕麦 Oats	#荞麦 Buckwheat	豆类 Beans	#大豆 Soybean	薯类 Tubers	#马铃薯 Potato
			196	187	89	10
1569			2092	1971	1954	989
10			2277	2168	906	416
			443	395	4421	4310
287			38090	38088	2870	517
100			3858	3841	2589	172
			548	548	10	
2648	4533	217	5003	928	10560	10560
	15647	1864	12742	2116	22808	22808
1159	1987	517	4155	1771	3644	3644
1196	1		2939	792	12140	12140
107	7736	1839	4215	2695	10811	10811
3626			4958	1729	1121	1121
1316	3	390	1530	1318	353	223
2722	2	27	3981	3454	1312	1025
165	105	127	1254	1242	2366	2255
64	663	621	1745	1636	3614	3614
100		22	850	769	609	542
744		1625	763	734	7760	7744
2170			3795	3733	4540	2865
167			1605	1591	986	305
1259	89	19	1580	1480	3061	1716
898	6	72	832	648	292	143
490			2518	2429	1338	208
			1	1	11	
168			2610	1193	1918	
			8481	4264	13716	
13			5289	785	7920	
2519			2073	526	5340	1018
2			194	83	388	88
29			851	543	223	
196			789	597	2599	71
365			536	481	4581	86
110			314	198	1469	124
2			1688	1544	4822	525
250			2469	619	2799	156
2058			3395	3305	1616	101
15			494	81	458	67

20-11 续表2

单位：吨

县(市、区)	Region	粮食总产量 Output of Grain	秋粮产量 Output of Autumn Grain	谷物 Cereal	#小麦 Wheat	#玉米 Corn	#谷子 Millet
忻州市	**Xinzhou**						
忻府区	Xinfu	304803	304803	302907		294516	6432
定襄县	Dingxiang	175786	175786	173160		166885	4450
五台县	Wutai	110043	110043	100849		90148	7208
代县	Daixian	86866	86866	84531		78049	3556
繁峙县	Fanshi	81330	81330	74613		65164	4655
宁武县	Ningwu	24413	24413	12239		6217	499
静乐县	Jingle	57820	57820	32853		17423	6984
神池县	Shenchi	138384	138384	109016		63026	32193
五寨县	Wuzhai	210080	210080	197048		153310	40399
岢岚县	Kelan	62125	62125	35210		23543	8631
河曲县	Hequ	67414	67414	58001		34082	13522
保德县	Baode	46728	46728	31073		16885	8714
偏关县	Pianguan	54132	54132	40536		13533	15568
原平市	Yuanping	346919	346253	338129	666	324302	7733
临汾市	**Linfen**						
尧都区	Yaodu	253323	130128	250651	123195	126758	415
曲沃县	Quwo	209575	113295	206980	96280	110700	
翼城县	Yicheng	236451	122501	235732	113950	119560	2140
襄汾县	Xiangfen	497259	250036	493064	247222	244696	1081
洪洞县	Hongtong	468841	242279	461418	226562	234078	609
古县	Guxian	72006	67172	69506	4834	61805	2725
安泽县	Anze	154258	154258	152390		150576	1403
浮山县	Fushan	101051	51032	98686	50019	46672	1696
吉县	Jixian	29627	29446	28139	181	25973	1411
乡宁县	Xiangning	81508	42842	76602	38665	34094	2359
大宁县	Daning	43961	43899	41819	61	38976	2610
隰县	Xixian	111083	110721	103528	363	96204	5945
永和县	Yonghe	82243	81986	78293	257	68018	9250
蒲县	Puxian	82507	82448	77700	59	74029	1969
汾西县	Fenxi	77685	41448	75601	36237	35838	1494
侯马市	Houma	92658	44028	92633	48629	44004	
霍州市	Huozhou	84979	42984	81972	41996	38857	866
吕梁市	**Lvliang**						
离石区	Lishi	26223	26223	19528		15432	3183
文水县	Wenshui	249028	248496	244970	532	243434	416
交城县	Jiaocheng	44240	43996	40468	244	38448	721
兴县	Xingxian	101263	101263	73610		39865	28473
临县	Linxian	155348	155348	132077		112492	15330
柳林县	Liulin	46837	46837	36008		24977	8158
石楼县	Shilou	70935	70707	64736	228	51064	9565
岚县	Lanxian	65344	65344	48186		37518	5109
方山县	Fangshan	43116	43116	31052		28315	1836
中阳县	Zhongyang	23057	23057	18265		14375	3015
交口县	Jiaokou	34843	34843	32292		30388	1298
孝义市	Xiaoyi	78830	74479	74378	4351	60005	5469
汾阳市	Fenyang	176740	176594	174252	86	166030	5016

continued

(ton)

#高　粱 Sorghum	#燕　麦 Oats	#荞　麦 Buckwheat	豆　类 Beans	#大　豆 Soybean	薯　类 Tubers	#马铃薯 Potato
1595	2		545	475	1351	291
1281		11	941	553	1685	816
588	761		2644	1821	6550	6382
847	117	20	890	352	1446	1407
	340		3695	3266	3023	3012
	5517	5	4624	691	7551	7551
459	3578		6122	2388	18845	18845
	7979		13411	3093	15957	15957
365	261	1	3395	1685	9638	9638
	2080		12828	1068	14087	14087
160	240		2714	1806	6699	6672
963	436		5996	1655	9659	9311
	910	307	3921	2851	9675	9675
2440	1144		3052	1591	5738	5423
110			1162	1053	1510	1058
			176	39	2419	
82			403	383	316	43
18			2416	2061	1779	35
110			2708	2073	4716	58
138			1109	709	1391	1278
411			550	462	1318	666
235			835	583	1529	467
11		22	1138	593	351	315
			2571	1469	2335	2145
5	20		1576	868	566	435
94		67	1123	914	6432	6315
441			2418	716	1533	1049
	600	405	433	408	4373	4373
74		70	640	415	1444	566
					24	
254			1655	1557	1353	571
30	11		4109	3189	2586	2556
588			872	462	3185	2552
540			1240	278	2532	2508
1714	375		17449	13392	10204	9876
300			8016	5718	15255	14251
875			7642	7439	3187	2971
1084	401	209	4513	3081	1687	1233
3735	586		3551	354	13606	13606
125			2543	1001	9521	9502
118	199	124	2350	1767	2442	2385
6	163	93	1051	892	1500	1313
3407	244	259	3682	3343	771	569
2792	74	11	1216	1060	1272	714

20-12 棉花生产基本情况(2016年)
BASIC STATISTICS ON COTTON PRODUCTION(2016)

县(市、区)	Region	播种面积(公顷) Sown Area (ha)	总产量(吨) Total Output (ton)	每公顷产量(公斤) Output per ha (kg)
太原市	**Taiyuan**			
清徐县	Qingxu	5	8	1778
长治市	**Changzhi**			
平顺县	Pingshun	4	4	977
黎城县	Licheng	7	4	560
潞城市	Lucheng	16	8	516
晋城市	**Jincheng**			
沁水县	Qinshui	119	97	818
阳城县	Yangcheng	8	6	782
泽州县	Zezhou	5	3	639
晋中市	**Jinzhong**			
榆次区	Yuci	5	2	408
太谷县	Taigu	13	16	1212
平遥县	Pingyao	4	3	915
运城市	**Yuncheng**			
盐湖区	Yanhu	899	1308	1455
临猗县	Linyi	4022	6659	1656
万荣县	Wanrong	599	515	860
闻喜县	Wenxi	18	22	1253
新绛县	Xinjiang	2	2	1151
绛　县	Jiangxian	9	7	800
垣曲县	Yuanqu	82	138	1682
夏　县	Xiaxian	69	79	1137
平陆县	Pinglu	56	110	1976
芮城县	Ruicheng	300	434	1446
永济市	Yongji	561	722	1286
河津市	Hejin	1	1	1001
临汾市	**Linfen**			
尧都区	Yaodu	11	8	738
曲沃县	Quwo	1	4	4400
襄汾县	Xiangfen	11	20	1779
洪洞县	Hongtong	4	3	776
浮山县	Fushan	15	25	1707
大宁县	Daning	22	24	1097
永和县	Yonghe	106	55	515
汾西县	Fenxi	3	1	467
霍州市	Huozhou	23	14	614
吕梁市	**Lvliang**			
兴　县	Xingxian	1	2	1500
临　县	Linxian	13	1	96
柳林县	Liulin	23	10	429
石楼县	Shilou	19	8	410
中阳县	Zhongyang			666

20-13 油料生产基本情况(2016年)
BASIC STATISTICS ON OIL-BEARING CROPS(2016)

县(市、区)	Region	油料合计 Oil-bearing Crops		胡麻籽 Benne		葵花籽 Sunflower Seeds	
		播种面积(公顷) Sown Area (ha)	总产量(吨) Total Output (ton)	播种面积(公顷) Sown Area (ha)	总产量(吨) Total Output (ton)	播种面积(公顷) Sown Area (ha)	总产量(吨) Total Output (ton)
太原市	**Taiyuan**						
小店区	Xiaodian						
迎泽区	Yingze	3	6			3	6
杏花岭区	Xinghualing	3	3			3	3
尖草坪区	Jiancaoping	41	57			41	57
万柏林区	Wanbailin						
晋源区	Jinyuan						
清徐县	Qingxu	32	62			12	23
阳曲县	Yangqu	225	425	95	177	108	205
娄烦县	Loufan	726	974	477	518	189	351
古交市	Gujiao	747	848	306	370	295	388
大同市	**Datong**						
南郊区	Nanjiao	415	323	263	190	35	44
新荣区	Xinrong	2739	3009	2739	3009		
阳高县	Yanggao	3069	3891			2766	3622
天镇县	Tianzhen	1335	2005			959	1505
广灵县	Guangling	1777	2072	882	939	692	920
灵丘县	Lingqiu	2299	2891	1209	1485	773	1016
浑源县	Hunyuan	1729	2061	1006	1223	432	464
左云县	Zuoyun	3419	3740	2760	2547	18	30
大同县	Datongxian	153	178			78	93
阳泉市	**Yangquan**						
郊　区	Jiaoqu						
平定县	Pingding	47	119			27	56
盂　县	Yuxian	46	91			36	76
长治市	**Changzhi**						
长治县	Changzhixian	15	24				
襄垣县	Xiangyuan	1139	254			39	56
屯留县	Tunliu		1				1
平顺县	Pingshun	36	69	1	2	8	15
黎城县	Licheng	72	135			67	122
壶关县	Huguan	202	63			2	4
长子县	Zhangzi						
武乡县	Wuxiang	537	641			107	251
沁　县	Qinxian	8	69			1	1
沁源县	Qinyuan	545	888	5	7	86	175
潞城市	Lucheng	82	200			10	27

20-13 续表1 continued

县(市、区)	Region	油料合计 Oil-bearing Crops		胡麻籽 Benne		葵花籽 Sunflower Seeds	
		播种面积 (公顷) Sown Area (ha)	总产量 (吨) Total Output (ton)	播种面积 (公顷) Sown Area (ha)	总产量 (吨) Total Output (ton)	播种面积 (公顷) Sown Area (ha)	总产量 (吨) Total Output (ton)
晋城市	**Jincheng**						
城　区	Chengqu	4	18			4	18
沁水县	Qinshui	566	960			147	250
阳城县	Yangcheng	839	1717			357	767
陵川县	Lingchuan	278	485			2	5
泽州县	Zezhou	370	695			69	133
高平市	Gaoping	77	58				
朔州市	**Shuozhou**						
朔城区	Shuocheng	3579	5974	2741	4466	796	1475
平鲁区	Pinglu	8547	8865	7368	7332	59	172
山阴县	Shanyin	2913	3740	1267	1090	1590	2548
应　县	Yingxian	1187	2717	112	50	1072	2662
右玉县	Youyu	9631	7742	7389	5507	42	55
怀仁县	Huairen	556	569	43	43	268	296
晋中市	**Jinzhong**						
榆次区	Yuci	128	184			104	157
榆社县	Yushe	49	274			28	68
左权县	Zuoquan	301	436			84	131
和顺县	Heshun	703	1598	531	1354	4	3
昔阳县	Xiyang	71	206	8	18	62	185
寿阳县	Shouyang	20	32			20	32
太谷县	Taigu	2	3				
祁　县	Qixian	10	25			4	9
平遥县	Pingyao	418	850		1	159	224
灵石县	Lingshi	112	152	8	6	58	73
介休市	Jiexiu	14	44			1	1
运城市	**Yuncheng**						
盐湖区	Yanhu	1043	2483			703	1967
临猗县	Linyi	1345	4048			1209	3613
万荣县	Wanrong	1684	2996			703	1132
闻喜县	Wenxi	870	1961			709	1618
稷山县	Jishan	117	246			89	195
新绛县	Xinjiang	280	609			192	442
绛　县	Jiangxian	312	760			242	570
垣曲县	Yuanqu	429	1003			35	129
夏　县	Xiaxian	830	1662			341	736
平陆县	Pinglu	2055	3500			589	972
芮城县	Ruicheng	1704	3401			571	1352
永济市	Yongji	1011	2598			726	1894
河津市	Hejin	243	873			112	423

20-13 续表2 continued

县(市、区)	Region	油料合计 Oil-bearing Crops		胡麻籽 Benne		葵花籽 Sunflower Seeds	
		播种面积 (公顷) Sown Area (ha)	总产量 (吨) Total Output (ton)	播种面积 (公顷) Sown Area (ha)	总产量 (吨) Total Output (ton)	播种面积 (公顷) Sown Area (ha)	总产量 (吨) Total Output (ton)
忻州市	**Xinzhou**						
忻府区	Xinfu	49	133	1	2	35	106
定襄县	Dingxiang	341	618			315	563
五台县	Wutai	96	160	9	8	37	83
代　县	Daixian	370	723	121	132	124	239
繁峙县	Fanshi	2280	1744	1134	884	613	460
宁武县	Ningwu	2180	2367	2166	2345	2	8
静乐县	Jingle	3831	4904	3310	4037	289	607
神池县	Shenchi	5044	7478	3558	4946	1486	2532
五寨县	Wuzhai	545	889	76	108	467	777
岢岚县	Kelan	3452	3742	2909	3091	543	651
河曲县	Hequ	1795	3127			210	225
保德县	Baode	798	1672			402	1011
偏关县	Pianguan	2461	3599	1325	1995	278	470
原平市	Yuanping	832	1126	601	689	227	429
临汾市	**Linfen**						
尧都区	Yaodu	130	240	4	5	68	134
曲沃县	Quwo	190	317			140	253
翼城县	Yicheng	143	326			138	312
襄汾县	Xiangfen	465	1294	3	6	177	432
洪洞县	Hongtong	142	448	1	2	57	199
古　县	Guxian	338	519			249	510
安泽县	Anze	230	653			107	308
浮山县	Fushan	417	1215			353	1025
吉　县	Jixian	705	948			431	651
乡宁县	Xiangning	928	1586			582	930
大宁县	Daning	446	529			234	267
隰　县	Xixian	387	575	1	5	360	549
永和县	Yonghe	1054	1131			335	455
蒲　县	Puxian	379	430	207	244	170	184
汾西县	Fenxi	381	370	102	69	96	94
侯马市	Houma	17	33			17	33
霍州市	Huozhou	127	204			37	56
吕梁市	**Lvliang**						
离石区	Lishi	555	466	39	29	136	136
文水县	Wenshui	148	528			27	86
交城县	Jiaocheng	83	199	29	37	3	6
兴　县	Xingxian	9478	11417	262	224	3192	2944
临　县	Linxian	3726	3185	47	28	2210	1802
柳林县	Liulin	1076	1228	16	17	353	418
石楼县	Shilou	1757	2221	44	57	180	258
岚　县	Lanxian	1464	1330	992	877	4	4
方山县	Fangshan	668	746			55	64
中阳县	Zhongyang	428	281	278	168	18	18
交口县	Jiaokou	808	573	461	362		
孝义市	Xiaoyi	132	153	63	10	2	1
汾阳市	Fenyang	87	342		1	2	3

20-14 药材、蔬菜、瓜果生产情况(2016年)
PRODUCTION OF MEDICINAL MATERIALS, VEGETABLES AND MELONS(2016)

县(市、区)	Region	药材类 Medicinal Materials		蔬 菜 Vegetables		瓜果类 Melons	
		播种面积 (公顷) Sown Area (ha)	总产量 (吨) Total Output (ton)	播种面积 (公顷) Sown Area (ha)	总产量 (吨) Total Output (ton)	播种面积 (公顷) Sown Area (ha)	总产量 (吨) Total Output (ton)
太原市	**Taiyuan**						
小店区	Xiaodian			5034	274100	6	382
迎泽区	Yingze			8	255		3
杏花岭区	Xinghualing			47	2200		
尖草坪区	Jiancaoping	2		831	56981	25	786
万柏林区	Wanbailin	4	4	46	1293		
晋源区	Jinyuan			2394	163576		
清徐县	Qingxu	203	218	9660	663012	45	853
阳曲县	Yangqu	301	2232	2362	93841	24	530
娄烦县	Loufan	416	939	260	9970	43	1621
古交市	Gujiao	271		544	42569	8	110
大同市	**Datong**						
南郊区	Nanjiao			1872	105596	103	3454
新荣区	Xinrong			425	19230	184	7315
阳高县	Yanggao	22	3	3791	221713	423	11288
天镇县	Tianzhen	13	173	1069	50963	260	7181
广灵县	Guangling			922	40161	41	1776
灵丘县	Lingqiu	77		215	9902	59	1396
浑源县	Hunyuan	622		1005	61481	54	1459
左云县	Zuoyun	142	107	167	16992	77	1226
大同县	Datongxian	3	10	4129	80715	765	20671
开发区	Development Zone			28	1050		
阳泉市	**Yangquan**						
郊　区	Jiaoqu	314	62	471	27000	1	27
平定县	Pingding	239	21	401	25623	1	6
盂　县	Yuxian	167	940	468	22709	9	160
长治市	**Changzhi**						
城　区	Chengqu			247	21241		
郊　区	Jiaoqu	275	1047	795	60248		1
长治县	Changzhixian	67	78	2193	138941	5	600
襄垣县	Xiangyuan	297	172	1851	110481	187	8261
屯留县	Tunliu	20	239	1611	98494	41	2210
平顺县	Pingshun	949	1901	555	15073	9	53
黎城县	Licheng	366	339	500	9771	13	440
壶关县	Huguan	66	189	860	76050	8	154
长子县	Zhangzi	4030	1061	6578	389159	4	180
武乡县	Wuxiang	97	162	1060	25300	266	6815
沁　县	Qinxian	127	513	716	29586	45	1582
沁源县	Qinyuan	1240	1015	781	17924	67	906
潞城市	Lucheng	87	766	1149	70489	2	67

20-14 续表1 continued

县(市、区)	Region	药材类 Medicinal Materials		蔬 菜 Vegetables		瓜果类 Melons	
		播种面积 (公顷) Sown Area (ha)	总产量 (吨) Total Output (ton)	播种面积 (公顷) Sown Area (ha)	总产量 (吨) Total Output (ton)	播种面积 (公顷) Sown Area (ha)	总产量 (吨) Total Output (ton)
晋城市	**Jincheng**						
城 区	Chengqu	1	5	266	16199	3	107
沁水县	Qinshui	364	1291	1085	50297	37	1709
阳城县	Yangcheng	520	731	985	53393	17	549
陵川县	Lingchuan	991	3340	826	37143		
泽州县	Zezhou	227	2063	1683	79828	15	171
高平市	Gaoping	234	83	1709	117815	5	151
开发区	Development Zone						
朔州市	**Shuozhou**						
朔城区	Shuocheng	273	282	1628	93151	262	5789
平鲁区	Pinglu			8	455	2	22
山阴县	Shanyin	5	7	1691	77579	129	6074
应 县	Yingxian	53	175	7924	369829	2540	70008
右玉县	Youyu			94	5347	42	1537
怀仁县	Huairen	2		2950	145177	1557	39816
开发区	Development Zone			53	5540		
晋中市	**Jinzhong**						
榆次区	Yuci	116	168	13200	927883	365	14871
榆社县	Yushe	37	110	740	56399	17	2187
左权县	Zuoquan	338	144	542	21431	3	13
和顺县	Heshun	121	802	532	28187		
昔阳县	Xiyang	461	1750	1000	64805		
寿阳县	Shouyang	3	22	7894	800156	71	4969
太谷县	Taigu			6598	573323	324	19654
祁 县	Qixian	7	90	3243	280835	64	3405
平遥县	Pingyao	382	1352	3424	127328	283	4807
灵石县	Lingshi	47	14	1330	37927	8	367
介休市	Jiexiu	69	18	470	23861	18	654
开发区	Development Zone			69	4040	2	124
运城市	**Yuncheng**						
盐湖区	Yanhu	610	4578	2833	158373	777	20208
临猗县	Linyi	259	3917	2817	97500	682	19971
万荣县	Wanrong	3419	22505	3568	184256	384	10100
闻喜县	Wenxi	3954	65227	6751	286387	839	22193
稷山县	Jishan	1868	8425	522	30463	3	68
新绛县	Xinjiang	1024	5894	10536	585107	18	1145
绛 县	Jiangxian	1932	38229	1081	52479	357	12241
垣曲县	Yuanqu	408	420	1506	55995	267	16487
夏 县	Xiaxian	2808	20474	13764	720248	628	36664
平陆县	Pinglu	107	400	1916	83496	210	7420
芮城县	Ruicheng	1029	9900	3785	143613	559	27862
永济市	Yongji	28	851	3051	88866	665	24977
河津市	Hejin	513	20003	2329	92253	55	3004

20–14 续表2 continued

县(市、区)	Region	药材类 Medicinal Materials		蔬 菜 Vegetables		瓜果类 Melons	
		播种面积 (公顷) Sown Area (ha)	总产量 (吨) Total Output (ton)	播种面积 (公顷) Sown Area (ha)	总产量 (吨) Total Output (ton)	播种面积 (公顷) Sown Area (ha)	总产量 (吨) Total Output (ton)
忻州市	**Xinzhou**						
忻府区	Xinfu	21	600	2894	69585	401	16786
定襄县	Dingxiang	67	709	1708	27697	810	27623
五台县	Wutai	115	1500	309	15661	4	124
代 县	Daixian	1	1	126	3875	106	2939
繁峙县	Fanshi	75	12	459	19921	250	8131
宁武县	Ningwu			81	3476	22	200
静乐县	Jingle	723	21	573	11505	46	1179
神池县	Shenchi	46	708	2725	57388		
五寨县	Wuzhai			92	5119	3	90
岢岚县	Kelan			183	5003		
河曲县	Hequ			550	20138	204	7982
保德县	Baode			694	6159	134	1711
偏关县	Pianguan			68	1838	53	742
原平市	Yuanping	72	80	751	47395	97	5905
临汾市	**Linfen**						
尧都区	Yaodu	229	5812	1650	119076	140	5189
曲沃县	Quwo	539	8927	5620	348489	195	9009
翼城县	Yicheng	799	2430	613	34056	196	7968
襄汾县	Xiangfen	1036	12164	4372	261802	410	13439
洪洞县	Hongtong	786	6864	2027	70328	47	858
古 县	Guxian	693	5115	197	5240	54	827
安泽县	Anze	734	4859	963	43501	62	2972
浮山县	Fushan	125	5331	943	41280	401	25595
吉 县	Jixian	14	116	959	19956	414	6725
乡宁县	Xiangning			610	2892	29	197
大宁县	Daning	25	174	376	6694	561	11775
隰 县	Xixian	44	58	218	4541	254	4077
永和县	Yonghe	208	94	355	13526	165	3943
蒲 县	Puxian	385	1536	251	14317	12	230
汾西县	Fenxi	292	1100	450	10517	11	261
侯马市	Houma	114	1065	679	50032	80	2652
霍州市	Huozhou	2	56	1010	57694	50	1104
吕梁市	**Lvliang**						
离石区	Lishi	62	13	465	4345	62	386
文水县	Wenshui	1		968	36193	139	2699
交城县	Jiaocheng	59		472	23851	1	16
兴 县	Xingxian	90	4	244	3914	93	1221
临 县	Linxian	3		3551	43126	86	2605
柳林县	Liulin			1059	15362	207	2691
石楼县	Shilou			458	4795	107	1378
岚 县	Lanxian	1		168	3536	10	147
方山县	Fangshan	74	156	440	10054	33	806
中阳县	Zhongyang	595	45	323	5160	1	5
交口县	Jiaokou	263	165	567	6995		
孝义市	Xiaoyi	143	36	1315	43370	4	105
汾阳市	Fenyang	7	15	335	8746	16	220

20-15 农业生产条件(2016年)
CONDITIONS OF AGRICULTURAL PRODUCTION(2016)

县(市、区)	Region	灌溉机电井 (眼) Electromechanical Well for Irrigation (unit)	农村用电量 (万千瓦小时) Electricity Consumption in Rural Areas (10 000 kwh)	农用化肥施用量 (折纯量, 吨) Agricultural Consumption of Chemical Fertilizers (ton)
太 原 市	**Taiyuan**			
小店区	Xiaodian	350	5912	3220
迎泽区	Yingze	52	2360	3
杏花岭区	Xinghualing		5165	32
尖草坪区	Jiancaoping	184	7266	982
万柏林区	Wanbailin	34	1889	45
晋源区	Jinyuan	325	3977	912
清徐县	Qingxu	1388	19564	13184
阳曲县	Yangqu	245	4010	8744
娄烦县	Loufan	35	662	852
古交市	Gujiao	145	3395	746
大 同 市	**Datong**			
南郊区	Nanjiao	1019	11498	3302
新荣区	Xinrong	388	1148	1503
阳高县	Yanggao	2365	4021	17507
天镇县	Tianzhen	1507	2928	15593
广灵县	Guangling	490	3067	7816
灵丘县	Lingqiu	377	3524	12815
浑源县	Hunyuan	1253	4691	14424
左云县	Zuoyun	176	1411	1623
大同县	Datongxian	1338	3501	6517
阳 泉 市	**Yangquan**			
郊　区	Jiaoqu	44	40064	782
平定县	Pingding	8	8907	3455
盂　县	Yuxian	82	9224	10214
长 治 市	**Changzhi**			
城　区	Chengqu	184	3341	291
郊　区	Jiaoqu	741	14740	5125
长治县	Changzhixian	1525	14225	15128
襄垣县	Xiangyuan	405	7461	10779
屯留县	Tunliu	2405	7065	26355
平顺县	Pingshun	7	2317	4484
黎城县	Licheng	104	2548	5428
壶关县	Huguan		6251	8881
长子县	Zhangzi	3577	8438	21849
武乡县	Wuxiang	88	3505	7487
沁　县	Qinxian	80	2367	8145
沁源县	Qinyuan	72	3767	2237
潞城市	Lucheng	212	6090	9185

20–15 续表1 contiuned

县(市、区)	Region	灌溉机电井(眼) Electromechanical Well for Irrigation (unit)	农村用电量(万千瓦小时) Electricity Consumption in Rural Areas (10 000 kwh)	农用化肥施用量(折纯量,吨) Agricultural Consumption of Chemical Fertilizers (ton)
晋城市	**Jincheng**			
城　区	Chengqu	20	4474	619
沁水县	Qinshui	54	4200	9231
阳城县	Yangcheng	372	25235	12129
陵川县	Lingchuan	32	5891	14028
泽州县	Zezhou	74	17905	10194
高平市	Gaoping	19	17421	18848
朔州市	**Shuozhou**			
朔城区	Shuocheng	1396	4645	17140
平鲁区	Pinglu	25	772	5003
山阴县	Shanyin	1571	4428	13751
应　县	Yingxian	3301	9133	26508
右玉县	Youyu	192	1104	2171
怀仁县	Huairen	1990	7679	13030
晋中市	**Jinzhong**			
榆次区	Yuci	2533	18983	13072
榆社县	Yushe	91	948	3036
左权县	Zuoquan	233	5207	2704
和顺县	Heshun	77	2014	1917
昔阳县	Xiyang	48	3882	5019
寿阳县	Shouyang		6543	20270
太谷县	Taigu	2873	14369	17519
祁　县	Qixian	2184	16706	16558
平遥县	Pingyao		13470	14634
灵石县	Lingshi	81	11378	1990
介休市	Jiexiu	538	47905	5692
运城市	**Yuncheng**			
盐湖区	Yanhu	3620	23646	21329
临猗县	Linyi	3140	35169	60353
万荣县	Wanrong	1048	22858	15702
闻喜县	Wenxi	1366	29337	26231
稷山县	Jishan	1470	37285	16266
新绛县	Xinjiang	1788	19245	24144
绛　县	Jiangxian	795	5588	27317
垣曲县	Yuanqu	276	3610	5727
夏　县	Xiaxian	4142	15878	25329
平陆县	Pinglu	572	6365	14403
芮城县	Ruicheng	1911	14617	21461
永济市	Yongji	4406	18268	17193
河津市	Hejin	1250	17631	11662

20-15 续表2 contiuned

县(市、区)	Region	灌溉机电井(眼) Electromechanical Well for Irrigation (unit)	农村用电量(万千瓦小时) Electricity Consumption in Rural Areas (10 000 kwh)	农用化肥施用量(折纯量, 吨) Agricultural Consumption of Chemical Fertilizers (ton)
忻州市	**Xinzhou**			
忻府区	Xinfu	2763	12230	18141
定襄县	Dingxiang	1219	10764	9855
五台县	Wutai	166	3967	6434
代　县	Daixian	851	3457	10592
繁峙县	Fanshi	678	7349	8123
宁武县	Ningwu	12	1715	1060
静乐县	Jingle	129	1337	5002
神池县	Shenchi	86	717	14753
五寨县	Wuzhai	120	1214	13768
岢岚县	Kelan	47	443	5678
河曲县	Hequ	147	1582	6006
保德县	Baode	120	6226	3646
偏关县	Pianguan	38	977	5376
原平市	Yuanping	1678	8150	23318
临汾市	**Linfen**			
尧都区	Yaodu	4049	15243	18518
曲沃县	Quwo	1216	11203	14189
翼城县	Yicheng	1944	5424	13668
襄汾县	Xiangfen	3838	25158	25957
洪洞县	Hongtong	1638	12772	34004
古　县	Guxian		1285	5008
安泽县	Anze	15	512	7214
浮山县	Fushan	61	2723	6520
吉　县	Jixian		307	6918
乡宁县	Xiangning	8	3680	9419
大宁县	Daning		290	3500
隰　县	Xixian		732	7625
永和县	Yonghe	3	378	3497
蒲　县	Puxian	4	2289	5427
汾西县	Fenxi	6	1653	1457
侯马市	Houma	747	4862	8802
霍州市	Huozhou	208	3887	4694
吕梁市	**Lvliang**			
离石区	Lishi	20	5634	3382
文水县	Wenshui	1958	18433	10060
交城县	Jiaocheng	546	15061	3344
兴　县	Xingxian	132	3284	4519
临　县	Linxian	188	5905	18828
柳林县	Liulin	200	3887	5115
石楼县	Shilou	14	1219	4894
岚　县	Lanxian	311	2390	6187
方山县	Fangshan	43	1986	3346
中阳县	Zhongyang	18	6453	1787
交口县	Jiaokou		6855	952
孝义市	Xiaoyi	696	9439	7019
汾阳市	Fenyang	2053	13457	10554

20-16 畜牧业生产情况(2016年)

县(市、区)	Region	大牲畜年末存栏(头) Large Animals at Year-end (head)	#牛 Cattle and Buffaloes	猪年末存栏(头) Hogs at Year-end (head)	羊年末存栏(只) Sheep and Goats at Year-end (head)	禽年末存栏(只) Poultry at Year-end (head)
太原市	**Taiyuan**					
小店区	Xiaodian	8709	8684	17514	18273	549656
迎泽区	Yingze	130	130	2922	6156	82621
杏花岭区	Xinghualing	53	26	13095	7356	108608
尖草坪区	Jiancaoping	10217	10153	28500	25807	168010
万柏林区	Wanbailin	151	146	8838	872	56700
晋源区	Jinyuan	2421	2378	17359	15876	559691
清徐县	Qingxu	7514	7421	119811	108997	927564
阳曲县	Yangqu	8258	6917	35234	140144	581879
娄烦县	Loufan	4816	3015	12430	69843	115410
古交市	Gujiao	3597	2433	22017	75606	502721
大同市	**Datong**					
南郊区	Nanjiao	17383	16780	42564	85438	794715
新荣区	Xinrong	16750	14450	16523	116120	136520
阳高县	Yanggao	40906	30043	248719	305239	418447
天镇县	Tianzhen	39811	21285	70104	145960	219652
广灵县	Guangling	24851	13585	58403	275104	434437
灵丘县	Lingqiu	38717	27151	45943	416693	329742
浑源县	Hunyuan	35973	30341	63621	337693	360503
左云县	Zuoyun	12150	10755	10156	158716	89520
大同县	Datongxian	19649	14636	48777	174330	1824126
开发区	Development Zone	137	137	730	735	6460
阳泉市	**Yangquan**					
郊　区	Jiaoqu	1091	1012	31215	17264	889756
平定县	Pingding	2212	1017	51930	24465	990428
盂　县	Yuxian	6444	5796	56107	95822	526085
长治市	**Changzhi**					
城　区	Chengqu	1267	1247	6737	2375	96000
郊　区	Jiaoqu	2144	2037	35994	13838	652192
长治县	Changzhixian	2127	1927	141624	36553	2996439
襄垣县	Xiangyuan	3393	2681	26505	54500	586407
屯留县	Tunliu	4545	4488	40871	96528	812136
平顺县	Pingshun	4453	2250	33790	29559	264285
黎城县	Licheng	4900	3955	47653	57238	470936
壶关县	Huguan	276	234	83098	31177	1479385
长子县	Zhangzi	5631	5328	87414	79943	3206594
武乡县	Wuxiang	10137	7978	24363	143050	1723496
沁　县	Qinxian	16417	14572	15328	67338	1160479
沁源县	Qinyuan	4945	3227	5728	190190	288100
潞城市	Lucheng	4893	2130	54662	32931	423790

NUMBER OF LIVESTOCK AND LIVESTOCK PRODUCTS(2016)

奶类总产量(吨) Output of Milk (ton)	#牛奶 Cow Milk	肉类总产量(吨) Output of Meat (ton)	#猪肉 Pork	#牛肉 Beef	#羊肉 Mutton	禽蛋产量(吨) Poultry Eggs (ton)
42500	42500	4462	2100	260	212	4100
18	18	258	178	4	65	226
34	34	1704	1471	4	149	394
26666	26659	4302	3708	57	277	1719
323	323	977	856	13	11	717
12159	12159	4624	3235	155	147	5735
12631	12416	23390	16902	987	2580	7277
17051	17048	8802	5000	425	2691	6735
		2623	1245	236	839	815
259	259	5298	3306	166	859	3211
73466	73430	9789	6583	945	1156	12360
10690	10650	5988	2409	1138	1926	1726
52811	52811	37988	32849	1216	2952	3710
33121	33121	17131	11901	1543	2738	4275
14604	13820	13538	7886	982	3592	4143
5585	5575	10944	5721	1503	2671	5790
24199	24175	26077	18739	1817	4877	4512
4415	4415	9076	2266	720	5817	1068
28539	28530	14799	7503	1875	2915	20027
733	733	108	66	16	15	40
3873	3873	4069	3173	13	186	11676
2954	2954	10186	7068	36	310	14425
7	7	5966	4916	182	537	7517
2228	2202	1008	798	37	19	1185
5059	5008	5479	4503	108	179	10400
3040	3022	25018	20937	81	426	33190
		6369	3756	320	762	4497
34	34	9492	6361	458	1461	9259
		4659	3848	104	316	3172
1212	1212	5030	4216	126	396	4230
101	101	12735	9579	25	217	11863
174	174	17131	11237	535	1022	43972
439	439	6565	1573	410	896	2494
236	236	8264	1940	1431	435	6588
2757	2757	1605	579	65	573	2203
2420	2420	8859	7470	93	524	5021

20-16 续表1

县(市、区)	Region	大牲畜年末存栏(头) Large Animals at Year-end (head)	#牛 Cattle and Buffaloes	猪年末存栏(头) Hogs at Year-end (head)	羊年末存栏(只) Sheep and Goats at Year-end (head)	禽年末存栏(只) Poultry at Year-end (head)
晋城市	**Jincheng**					
城 区	Chengqu	370	370	5609	9483	114300
沁水县	Qinshui	2188	2055	47102	233907	1398093
阳城县	Yangcheng	2446	2434	170770	102015	3319045
陵川县	Lingchuan	745	731	118753	57285	1123096
泽州县	Zezhou	9880	9880	358851	210625	1949482
高平市	Gaoping	754	737	325807	56219	1726908
开发区	Development Zone			2750		
朔州市	**Shuozhou**					
朔城区	Shuocheng	23906	15486	21736	212295	830732
平鲁区	Pinglu	10062	4415	19918	178715	57669
山阴县	Shanyin	76647	72612	25514	176209	498704
应 县	Yingxian	58778	56309	84515	250682	231151
右玉县	Youyu	27211	19752	31297	329918	73093
怀仁县	Huairen	13067	12016	45019	614605	648139
开发区	Development Zone	2368	2368	245	222	
晋中市	**Jinzhong**					
榆次区	Yuci	11741	11081	115829	149845	1540513
榆社县	Yushe	6752	6006	16041	158156	631001
左权县	Zuoquan	4976	4477	15146	144807	455350
和顺县	Heshun	23664	22911	13760	44340	377637
昔阳县	Xiyang	4418	2936	68777	88510	196957
寿阳县	Shouyang	2391	1868	37737	92129	504958
太谷县	Taigu	6844	6451	429112	126930	3838158
祁 县	Qixian	43714	43456	89968	80458	1958790
平遥县	Pingyao	13368	13138	102089	161058	4801589
灵石县	Lingshi	429	309	72115	82717	1484539
介休市	Jiexiu	3056	2706	85650	82895	3690105
开发区	Development Zone	107	107	8927	9104	252800
运城市	**Yuncheng**					
盐湖区	Yanhu	3259	3205	79986	94189	971988
临猗县	Linyi	1302	1265	110800	87635	1515280
万荣县	Wanrong	2346	2236	99518	69917	2604436
闻喜县	Wenxi	2719	2622	78087	91450	3869605
稷山县	Jishan	1890	1837	78442	54902	7606515
新绛县	Xinjiang	9063	8927	118389	53639	4279908
绛 县	Jiangxian	4924	4924	63943	72972	743302
垣曲县	Yuanqu	5428	5426	67202	100259	431255
夏 县	Xiaxian	2639	2582	94078	59943	1704657
平陆县	Pinglu	4000	4000	61676	65800	292322
芮城县	Ruicheng	2933	2891	143806	66650	965913
永济市	Yongji	4785	4774	128508	62492	2074778
河津市	Hejin	2719	2620	56660	43134	849955

continued

奶类总产量(吨) Output of Milk (ton)	#牛奶 Cow Milk	肉类总产量(吨) Output of Meat (ton)	#猪肉 Pork	#牛肉 Beef	#羊肉 Mutton	禽蛋产量(吨) Poultry Eggs (ton)
		920	636	70	102	1293
		14716	4471	119	2194	4647
13	13	24519	18205	323	1070	28715
		15095	12878	37	697	9676
480	480	52331	47687	879	1598	22768
71	71	58081	55559	49	575	16123
		284	256		10	35
52471	52471	5936	1827	523	2995	10984
4845	4845	6055	3151	425	2266	555
233700	233700	7501	2921	2132	2026	6561
153410	153410	14972	6984	1368	6359	2184
18251	18251	12894	3638	2477	6469	1138
21263	21263	43292	6904	783	34821	4232
12180	12180	347	37	310		
41494	41494	26100	15676	392	2041	12926
		6440	1170	222	963	4730
19	19	3652	1535	231	1139	4903
		4519	1429	2351	350	5016
2166	2166	7139	6012	255	690	3788
1050	1050	5499	3459	243	1222	7980
13720	13720	59268	43782	864	2670	27345
51301	51017	31959	12453	11924	3425	22879
23621	23072	32798	12741	1206	3060	37481
148	148	17565	10347	8	1005	6499
10120	10098	15548	7906	103	1315	24811
478	478	1200	670	1	163	2741
13864	13864	9704	6106	139	927	8800
3350	3350	16128	13177	37	701	9741
940	940	15129	11064	691	468	37020
1387	1387	18618	6869	354	674	11879
706	706	12424	6012	108	519	122110
7790	7790	18228	12986	620	418	53580
278	278	11894	8108	400	1393	4440
58	58	11281	7874	228	1378	2660
248	248	14057	9201	323	938	12851
2851	2851	10381	8213	456	1145	3506
3952	3952	21411	17816	362	1148	4119
15099	15099	24553	13795	233	803	9357
1535	1535	9603	7704	141	424	10789

20-16 续表2

县(市、区)	Region	大牲畜年末存栏(头) Large Animals at Year-end (head)	#牛 Cattle and Buffaloes	猪年末存栏(头) Hogs at Year-end (head)	羊年末存栏(只) Sheep and Goats at Year-end (head)	禽年末存栏(只) Poultry at Year-end (head)
忻州市	**Xinzhou**					
忻府区	Xinfu	11885	10579	44280	143482	498700
定襄县	Dingxiang	7369	5326	38135	88115	68191
五台县	Wutai	21354	19421	24255	164276	260243
代　县	Daixian	18150	16525	12587	157808	95342
繁峙县	Fanshi	26062	18935	75557	351407	800000
宁武县	Ningwu	15289	10925	4607	223125	85435
静乐县	Jingle	14456	6616	10705	231814	275483
神池县	Shenchi	8634	4832	17950	447274	70807
五寨县	Wuzhai	8887	5400	11384	220455	90807
岢岚县	Kelan	10708	7916	17658	402873	71772
河曲县	Hequ	9193	4770	17581	144220	385668
保德县	Baode	1829	1545	25725	99857	224577
偏关县	Pianguan	4879	2021	8256	285301	60563
原平市	Yuanping	16435	10909	121030	340149	2620061
临汾市	**Linfen**					
尧都区	Yaodu	4836	4601	108455	78942	1832129
曲沃县	Quwo	3590	3342	90123	74741	1484530
翼城县	Yicheng	9445	9244	140916	107357	765425
襄汾县	Xiangfen	5066	4322	160119	98764	2028062
洪洞县	Hongtong	8533	8404	110282	128838	2119820
古　县	Guxian	3439	3308	8998	35831	160638
安泽县	Anze	3791	3711	9409	62082	328472
浮山县	Fushan	3759	3458	29253	68320	220499
吉　县	Jixian	3137	2259	29314	10987	112434
乡宁县	Xiangning	7018	6920	35160	98532	840303
大宁县	Daning	1506	991	3599	13191	82045
隰　县	Xixian	1947	1714	16957	27092	261512
永和县	Yonghe	3342	2712	11275	90580	154204
蒲　县	Puxian	8446	8402	15988	5863	299599
汾西县	Fenxi	3898	3894	24066	81655	892650
侯马市	Houma	1664	1664	18720	26708	264750
霍州市	Huozhou	3688	3156	45623	34726	548600
吕梁市	**Lvliang**					
离石区	Lishi	7321	7294	36102	63358	605434
文水县	Wenshui	91007	90974	50728	92455	3793072
交城县	Jiaocheng	22678	21915	41900	44853	929843
兴　县	Xingxian	6783	6273	22018	167858	322348
临　县	Linxian	3503	3464	87561	248751	1766950
柳林县	Liulin	1586	1432	33895	44718	358546
石楼县	Shilou	4575	3970	29577	8432	235184
岚　县	Lanxian	17468	8495	16396	96379	65732
方山县	Fangshan	13985	13507	11829	27646	578247
中阳县	Zhongyang	7494	7143	22598	22489	310443
交口县	Jiaokou	4132	4091	27888	60616	329290
孝义市	Xiaoyi	2258	2029	36352	39667	4113636
汾阳市	Fenyang	10120	9853	91726	81994	2546712

continued

奶类总产量(吨) Output of Milk (ton)	#牛奶 Cow Milk	肉类总产量(吨) Output of Meat (ton)	#猪肉 Pork	#牛肉 Beef	#羊肉 Mutton	禽蛋产量(吨) Poultry Eggs (ton)
32718	32718	8411	6411	356	1051	7326
3362	3362	5338	4215	242	787	621
		10478	5499	1866	2712	3550
283	283	2779	738	586	1184	451
9246	9246	15017	10303	454	3778	5358
36	36	5030	656	659	2214	2830
51	51	4388	1264	189	2647	1689
591	591	20553	5840	1907	11834	704
112	112	3948	798	186	2832	908
268	268	5817	1492	480	3635	905
4992	4992	3396	1662	103	1198	4024
183	183	4298	2460	53	1606	2021
		8104	1640	391	5825	862
7072	7072	24866	16211	661	5509	47626
7568	7562	12426	9537	218	616	18310
4942	4919	12636	8139	381	660	12269
14505	14505	27055	24956	503	693	9642
1141	1141	20427	17298	170	751	22420
8795	3940	17676	12900	772	1314	25562
121		1522	808	240	275	1519
		1829	778	307	253	2965
608	520	4935	3376	619	550	3866
6	6	3450	2658	410	138	1679
1079	1079	5389	3398	430	654	9407
24	24	846	418	73	259	630
326	315	2390	1754	108	224	3530
68	68	2355	1423	137	633	1750
32	32	3245	1673	472	446	1077
79	66	11203	2530	306	731	3800
2374	2374	3890	3370	105	204	3002
2777	2154	9728	8115	148	506	3807
525	525	6482	4395	187	514	3723
5401	5388	27092	6069	10705	1414	28256
1178	1178	12002	5431	1610	2356	6921
110	110	4308	2087	322	1694	2070
6742	6742	13289	9258	121	2152	14299
1415	1415	3889	3193	95	443	3515
184	184	4016	3569	148	75	2162
34	34	2447	1402	108	762	882
210	210	2724	805	443	275	4456
29	29	3336	2067	279	206	3006
50	50	4622	2930	275	370	1344
2891	2891	60062	4750	661	550	7623
9314	9247	23478	12742	1358	1565	17059

20-17 水果、林业及渔业生产情况(2016年)
PRODUCTION OF FRUITS, FORESTRY AND FISHERY(2016)

县(市、区)	Region	全年水果产量(吨) Annual Output of Fruits (ton)	#苹果 Apples	年末果园面积(公顷) Area of Orchards at Year-end (ha)	当年造林面积(公顷) Afforestation Area in the Year (ha)	全年水产品总产量(吨) Annual Aquatic Products(ton)	年末养殖面积(公顷) Fishery-breeding Area at Year-end (ha)
太原市	**Taiyuan**						
小店区	Xiaodian	1042	280	303		46	22
迎泽区	Yingze	178	60	63		50	167
杏花岭区	Xinghualing	1129	571	629	270		
尖草坪区	Jiancaoping	24905	8140	1315		166	20
万柏林区	Wanbailin	603	12	86		20	11
晋源区	Jinyuan	3807	1126	492	86	261	77
清徐县	Qingxu	52448	1696	2712	612	1355	314
阳曲县	Yangqu	4314	2335	2587	2193	43	37
娄烦县	Loufan	1705	450	259	3421	477	33
古交市	Gujiao	626	108	765	3578	143	20
大同市	**Datong**						
南郊区	Nanjiao	9213	51	365	514	48	13
新荣区	Xinrong	196	91	472	733	46	10
阳高县	Yanggao	14240	379	2406	3533	208	66
天镇县	Tianzhen	12405	2360	612	3574		
广灵县	Guangling	787	10	121	3356	136	85
灵丘县	Lingqiu	3239	789	591	3087	140	41
浑源县	Hunyuan	5342	3119	404	2381	42	8
左云县	Zuoyun	449		34	1860		
大同县	Datongxian	9963	388	1517	2482	460	916
阳泉市	**Yangquan**						
郊区	Jiaoqu	7506	5360	1175	640	6	1
平定县	Pingding	2662	1446	297	1962	405	9
盂县	Yuxian	3038	1788	264	493	210	44
长治市	**Changzhi**						
城区	Chengqu	347	290	102			
郊区	Jiaoqu	2476	1776	235		250	103
长治县	Changzhixian	884	588	105	3	100	12
襄垣县	Xiangyuan	4960	1944	423	1014	285	454
屯留县	Tunliu	214	146	23	708	540	426
平顺县	Pingshun	8199	4237	186	3076	160	27
黎城县	Licheng	5250	3448	304	1132	90	24
壶关县	Huguan	2214	1037	372	449	40	1
长子县	Zhangzi	5508	2555	516	573	750	460
武乡县	Wuxiang	3338	824	1132	1082	390	423
沁县	Qinxian	2354	562	183	1036	855	530
沁源县	Qinyuan	193	56	44	1119	40	5
潞城市	Lucheng	4251	3156	338	360	200	25

注：本表造林面积不包括省属九大林局、市直单位数据；渔业生产情况不包括省属渔业单位、市直单位数据。

Note: The coverage of afforestation area in this table doesn't include data of nine privincial forestry administration and municipal units. Fishery production indicators don't include privincal and municipal fishery units data.

20-17 续表1 continued

县(市、区)	Region	全年水果产量(吨) Annual Output of Fruits (ton)	#苹果 Apples	年末果园面积(公顷) Area of Orchards at Year-end (ha)	当年造林面积(公顷) Afforestation Area in the Year (ha)	全年水产品总产量(吨) Annual Aquatic Products(ton)	年末养殖面积(公顷) Fishery-breeding Area at Year-end (ha)
晋城市	**Jincheng**						
城　区	Chengqu	789	152	51		50	3
沁水县	Qinshui	8593	5685	458	719	655	43
阳城县	Yangcheng	7213	777	337	425	81	63
陵川县	Lingchuan	3178	2539	333	287	247	32
泽州县	Zezhou	18723	6149	669	181	655	184
高平市	Gaoping	19264	6816	1981	161	106	56
朔州市	**Shuozhou**						
朔城区	Shuocheng	462	40	297	3607	389	53
平鲁区	Pinglu				2394	16	1
山阴县	Shanyin	1299	153	164	487	12	13
应　县	Yingxian	1160	715	389	2660	203	32
右玉县	Youyu				2340	36	24
怀仁县	Huairen	3559	447	1462	133	33	20
晋中市	**Jinzhong**						
榆次区	Yuci	103138	77343	7329	1100	557	42
榆社县	Yushe	2033	78	182	2501	805	461
左权县	Zuoquan	558	95	32	445	301	309
和顺县	Heshun	21		4	417	40	61
昔阳县	Xiyang	7652	6713	894	1228	90	36
寿阳县	Shouyang	5415	1198	638	917	558	208
太谷县	Taigu	69091	20043	4243	566	389	263
祁　县	Qixian	159086	60547	9374	667	85	26
平遥县	Pingyao	139327	51102	6690	495	435	125
灵石县	Lingshi	3367	1909	480	1297	55	3
介休市	Jiexiu	5337	2680	431	390	117	8
开发区	Development Zone	3164	2017	238			
运城市	**Yuncheng**						
盐湖区	Yanhu	495294	86658	16707	1583	630	1289
临猗县	Linyi	2377570	1701283	61355	669	45	16
万荣县	Wanrong	558156	490132	22176	957	5492	400
闻喜县	Wenxi	31318	12216	1366	860	60	5
稷山县	Jishan	156138	30721	7967	1135	40	5
新绛县	Xinjiang	90496	17761	2818	800	115	23
绛　县	Jiangxian	94199	26043	3563	966	46	15
垣曲县	Yuanqu	23689	12817	467	695	1415	46
夏　县	Xiaxian	240309	70557	7567	1021	140	10
平陆县	Pinglu	334685	212681	10256	2260	37	23
芮城县	Ruicheng	581560	483238	16656	934	1092	256
永济市	Yongji	566467	139214	17618	433	15214	908
河津市	Hejin	52106	10413	2059	813	408	34

20-17 续表2 continued

县(市、区)	Region	全年水果产量(吨) Annual Output of Fruits (ton)	#苹 果 Apples	年末果园面积(公顷) Area of Orchards at Year-end (ha)	当年造林面积(公顷) Afforestation Area in the Year (ha)	全年水产品总产量(吨) Annual Aquatic Products(ton)	年末养殖面积(公顷) Fishery-breeding Area at Year-end (ha)
忻州市	**Xinzhou**						
忻府区	Xinfu	9738	4321	1296	2400	415	113
定襄县	Dingxiang	10222	2651	670	335	362	68
五台县	Wutai	6025	225	838	861	596	137
代　县	Daixian	18542	3879	1081	2371	302	68
繁峙县	Fanshi	1570	756	950	3873	221	270
宁武县	Ningwu	200		22	1475	51	75
静乐县	Jingle	198	67	138	4525	140	47
神池县	Shenchi				3591		
五寨县	Wuzhai				5744	105	60
岢岚县	Kelan	1191	245	150	4675	4	25
河曲县	Hequ	3565	352	2103	5907	100	15
保德县	Baode	27276	736	5338	2039	96	14
偏关县	Pianguan	1270	199	812	5710	52	
原平市	Yuanping	40215	8537	4396	3541	523	240
临汾市	**Linfen**						
尧都区	Yaodu	70289	42245	2805	1248	1557	239
曲沃县	Quwo	71281	36240	2376	120	1894	359
翼城县	Yicheng	122239	114188	5408	213	590	92
襄汾县	Xiangfen	124891	103140	3906	1604	1309	142
洪洞县	Hongtong	13685	7056	600	736	1288	125
古　县	Guxian	1410	649	151	113	3	2
安泽县	Anze	2368	1127	179	373	2	1
浮山县	Fushan	14098	11381	549	113	10	8
吉　县	Jixian	248396	246700	11031	2539	3	3
乡宁县	Xiangning	21938	18260	1936	3170	3	10
大宁县	Daning	5052	3664	4875	3914	8	3
隰　县	Xixian	82189	43144	8176	5091	1	1
永和县	Yonghe	21294	4311	9983	3779	3	1
蒲　县	Puxian	1645	1327	545	4498	8	3
汾西县	Fenxi	5672	4338	526	1484		
侯马市	Houma	8463	4548	390	533	600	51
霍州市	Huozhou	16786	15976	845	993	60	9
吕梁市	**Lvliang**						
离石区	Lishi	889	425	382	3244	54	52
文水县	Wenshui	119098	504	4010	1066	822	316
交城县	Jiaocheng	9712	974	512	1533	80	98
兴　县	Xingxian	17153	1616	7854	6137	50	14
临　县	Linxian	45673	3623	25141	4803	170	95
柳林县	Liulin	7140	836	5456	3103	68	14
石楼县	Shilou	13797	881	10481	4164	42	20
岚　县	Lanxian	24	9	17	3962	96	63
方山县	Fangshan	1061	654	192	3454	162	453
中阳县	Zhongyang	359	272	225	426	91	40
交口县	Jiaokou	117	107	36	2064		
孝义市	Xiaoyi	1399	555	425	1725	75	44
汾阳市	Fenyang	6487	3329	334	2546	82	24

20-18 社会消费品零售总额(2016年)
TOTAL RETAIL SALES OF CONSUMER GOODS(2016)

单位：万元 (10 000 yuan)

县(市、区)	Region	社会消费品零售总额 Total Retail Sales of Consumer Goods	城镇 Town	乡村 Village
太原市	**Taiyuan**			
小店区	Xiaodian	4423982	4287168	136814
迎泽区	Yingze	4401717	4203614	198103
杏花岭区	Xinghualing	2044306	1926212	118094
尖草坪区	Jiancaoping	914496	842924	71572
万柏林区	Wanbailin	2244762	2054281	190481
晋源区	Jinyuan	365797	329217	36580
清徐县	Qingxu	557684	271411	286273
阳曲县	Yangquan	133595	95436	38159
娄烦县	Loufan	43653	28664	14989
古交市	Gujiao	489117	399922	89195
高新区	High-Tech Zone	402086	402086	
经济区	Economic Zone	275406	275406	
民营区	Private Zone	365762	365762	
大同市	**Datong**			
城　区	Chengqu	2419666	2419666	
矿　区	Kuangqu	945403	945403	
南郊区	Nanjiao	1057281	684704	372578
新荣区	Xinrong	101386	49735	51651
阳高县	Yanggao	114580	69281	45299
天镇县	Tianzhen	95643	56256	39387
广灵县	Guangling	99468	54073	45395
灵丘县	Lingqiu	302095	181979	120117
浑源县	Hunyuan	321589	190362	131228
左云县	Zuoyun	232169	104682	127488
大同县	Datongxian	159265	41952	117313
开发区	Development Zone	241585	180611	60974
阳泉市	**Yangquan**			
城　区	Chengqu	1678784	1678784	
矿　区	Kuangqu	243968	243968	
郊　区	Jiaoqu	167472	61709	105763
平定县	Pingding	341083	235165	105919
盂　县	Yuxian	486535	404251	82284
开发区	Development Zone	144824	144824	
长治市	**Changzhi**			
城　区	Chengqu	3258061	3258061	
郊　区	Jiaoqu	478541	409807	68734
长治县	Changzhixian	297111	124243	172868
襄垣县	Xiangyuan	268510	181796	86714
屯留县	Tunliu	156159	68661	87498
平顺县	Pingshun	87186	40996	46190
黎城县	Licheng	134406	67321	67085
壶关县	Huguan	185173	66096	119077
长子县	Zhangzi	182038	70528	111510
武乡县	Wuxiang	133816	70632	63184
沁　县	Qinxian	98340	33892	64448
沁源县	Qinyuan	233613	113122	120491
潞城市	Lucheng	153243	93149	60095

20–18 续表1 continued

单位：万元 (10 000 yuan)

县(市、区)	Region	社会消费品零售总额 Total Retail Sales of Consumer Goods	城镇 Town	乡村 Village
晋城市	**Jincheng**			
城　区	Chengqu	2046880	2046880	
沁水县	Qinshui	224373	116368	108005
阳城县	Yangcheng	430122	364743	65380
陵川县	Lingchuan	175078	95069	80009
泽州县	Zezhou	386410	215975	170435
高平市	Gaoping	599080	425554	173526
朔州市	**Shuozhou**			
朔城区	Shuocheng	1091800	776156	315643
平鲁区	Pinglu	324696	210414	114281
山阴县	Shanyin	373641	287010	86631
应　县	Yingxian	297912	205091	92821
右玉县	Youyu	157299	118180	39120
怀仁县	Huairen	665372	479131	186240
晋中市	**Jinzhong**			
榆次区	Yuci	1792932	1210034	582898
榆社县	Yushe	121632	77990	43642
左权县	Zuoquan	143482	88126	55356
和顺县	Heshun	144300	90227	54073
昔阳县	Xiyang	251912	167278	84635
寿阳县	Shouyang	264777	173896	90882
太谷县	Taigu	362427	241687	120740
祁　县	Qixian	406040	220478	185562
平遥县	Pingyao	589177	308725	280453
灵石县	Lingshi	714967	441064	273903
介休市	Jiexiu	900466	619029	281437
运城市	**Yuncheng**			
盐湖区	Yanhu	2294047	2012587	281460
临猗县	Linyi	632334	443107	189226
万荣县	Wanrong	319127	220849	98278
闻喜县	Wenxi	423858	356960	66898
稷山县	Jishan	289092	191145	97947
新降县	Xinjiang	429555	245131	184425
绛　县	Jiangxian	241573	169850	71723
垣曲县	Yuanqu	239527	185038	54489
夏　县	Xiaxian	254796	187189	67607
平陆县	Pinglu	275807	217182	58626
芮城县	Ruicheng	325992	264386	61606
永济市	Yongji	579514	538080	41434
河津市	Hejin	742009	478990	263020
忻州市	**Xinzhou**			
忻府区	Xinfu	1054742	787367	267375
定襄县	Dingxiang	211257	139928	71329
五台县	Wutai	253797	176907	76890
代　县	Daixian	130324	71557	58767

20-18 续表2 continued

单位：万元 (10 000 yuan)

县(市、区)	Region	社会消费品零售总额 Total Retail Sales of Consumer Goods	城 镇 Town	乡 村 Village
繁峙县	Fanshi	176117	110888	65229
宁武县	Ningwu	114104	68798	45306
静乐县	Jingle	94347	60119	34228
神池县	Shenchi	87448	60981	26468
五寨县	Wuzhai	85148	57068	28080
岢岚县	Kelan	86283	57274	29010
河曲县	Hequ	149928	107733	42195
保德县	Baode	173413	118523	54891
偏关县	Pianguan	89436	63582	25854
原平市	Yuanping	673863	484635	189228
临汾市	**Linfen**			
尧都区	Yaodu	2394536	1944810	449727
曲沃县	Quwo	224679	167708	56970
翼城县	Yicheng	407389	286205	121184
襄汾县	Xiangfen	435418	372923	62495
洪洞县	Hongdong	563436	337452	225984
古　县	Guxian	99366	66717	32649
安泽县	Anze	90480	70240	20240
浮山县	Fushan	86017	53559	32459
吉　县	Jixian	73630	50770	22860
乡宁县	Xiangning	201734	165648	36086
大宁县	Daning	31711	27093	4618
隰　县	Xixian	97006	81612	15394
永和县	Yonghe	45468	36468	9000
蒲　县	Puxian	77963	68298	9664
汾西县	Fenxi	117716	92169	25547
侯马市	Houma	814916	770364	44552
霍州市	Huozhou	332954	259210	73744
吕梁市	**Lvliang**			
离石区	Lishi	670719	556493	114226
文水县	Wenshui	203137	140771	62366
交城县	Jiaocheng	180534	128179	52355
兴　县	Xingxian	147496	95872	51624
临　县	Linxian	419614	327392	92222
柳林县	Liulin	379667	305130	74537
石楼县	Shilou	30731	21512	9219
岚　县	Lanxian	109559	67926	41633
方山县	Fangshan	91089	54653	36436
中阳县	Zhongyang	132064	95520	36544
交口县	Jiaokou	76670	53669	23001
孝义市	Xiaoyi	1288947	970687	318260
汾阳市	Fenyang	607176	493648	113528

20-19 工业主要指标(2016年)

单位：万元

县(市、区)	Region	单位数(个) Number of Enterprises (unit)	工业销售产值 Industrial Sales Output Value	资产总计 Total Assets
太 原 市	**Taiyuan**			
小店区	Xiaodian	39	489076	990638
迎泽区	Yingze	6	634532	1705217
杏花岭区	Xinhualing	22	342447	1362561
尖草坪区	Jiancaoping	53	6962393	14269111
万柏林区	Wanbailin	18	2174820	10563638
晋源区	Jingyuan	18	198703	1206772
清徐县	Qingxu	55	1486265	3236545
阳曲县	Yangqu	23	566716	747872
娄烦县	Loufan	8	83207	128157
古交市	Gujiao	8	237857	1985178
高新区	High-tech Zone	41	1496678	3441193
开发区	Development Zone	52	7372094	8923644
民营区	Private Zone	12	67409	317939
大 同 市	**Datong**			
市　直	Jurisdiction Area	1	3586418	17383909
城　区	Chengqu	18	460480	1198549
矿　区	Kuangqu	10	60489	272344
南郊区	Nanjiao	27	914595	2126324
新荣区	Xinrong	12	114045	401234
阳高县	Yanggao	15	161022	563680
天镇县	Tianzhen	10	61785	273263
广灵县	Guangling	7	104298	453155
灵丘县	Lingqiu	18	90517	553383
浑源县	Hunyuan	7	164353	302134
左云县	Zuoyun	14	167645	1579958
大同县	Datongxian	14	205016	307766
开发区	Development Zone	15	596319	1225134
阳 泉 市	**Yangquan**			
城　区	Chengqu	6	159136	663768
矿　区	Kuangqu	2	1629647	18803156
郊　区	Jiaoqu	25	424159	1212220
平定县	Pingding	49	1082371	2017803
盂　县	Yuxian	27	1454166	2426652
开发区	Development Zone	13	157537	342644
长 治 市	**Changzhi**			
城　区	Chengqu	21	520210	903724
郊　区	Jiaoqu	38	3435355	4302658
长治县	Changzhixian	48	1357843	5059230
襄垣县	Xiangyuan	39	2340580	6726133
屯留县	Tunliu	29	876319	3089812
平顺县	Pingshun	13	178334	244668
黎城县	Licheng	12	694543	355926
壶关县	Huguan	12	757825	728257
长子县	Zhangzi	29	1011762	2576151
武乡县	Wuxiang	15	523781	1237292
沁　县	Qinxian	5	78556	262095
沁源县	Qinyuan	21	1274171	3562093
潞城市	Lucheng	34	1409107	3857624

MAJOR INDUSTRIAL INDICATORS(2016)

(10 000 yuan)

主营业务收入 Revenue of Major Business	利税总额 Total Pre-tax Profits	利润总额 Total Profits	应交增值税 Value Added Taxes Payable
473249	4077	-2133	5031
637618	276774	39707	49483
357647	12391	-11841	20851
7585385	431361	171237	220979
2326795	-136614	-349537	125595
624795	-47983	-72872	17942
1614694	67279	33364	26288
535264	12232	6190	4892
71370	565	-1930	967
259854	-16843	-39039	15803
1431153	132777	101020	27035
7466516	430676	300244	103889
76785	2729	427	1605
14607480	283828	-48371	213452
509012	14968	-7854	18661
123830	-9146	-13112	3086
908153	206354	114345	71334
125630	16778	218	10137
170209	-14515	-13279	-1473
57673	21030	20347	374
120753	33131	27636	4784
94618	-19044	-21324	1666
140256	16063	4418	9933
199794	4017	-9032	2374
190812	11574	6716	3430
580088	78081	58257	15289
209435	32385	7012	15607
3365790	291362	62220	130218
361647	61544	3461	36830
1004357	-11885	-39337	22248
1079930	67286	6742	31868
146629	21133	12498	2155
510255	44109	33599	7204
2443935	173951	64803	87461
1390330	366855	148072	135820
2068764	321203	110263	125251
1168500	113226	14592	67941
167122	9352	6731	321
476877	12050	5966	4811
760957	34980	29606	3937
973219	369046	201949	99209
539992	89944	36180	38171
78786	888	-2209	3047
724751	176766	86364	53925
1416098	60861	19719	32222

20-19 续表1

单位：万元

县(市、区)	Region	单位数(个) Number of Enterprises (unit)	工业销售产值 Industrial Sales Output Value	资产总计 Total Assets
晋 城 市	**Jincheng**			
市　直	Jurisdiction Area	3	1667912	13451940
城　区	Chengqu	22	321291	1443455
沁水县	Qinshui	37	892853	5101444
阳城县	Yangcheng	57	1230430	4080786
陵川县	Lingchuan	11	88230	281531
泽州县	Zezhou	45	1776966	3026821
高平市	Gaoping	51	1162369	4133354
开发区	Development Zone	15	1103275	1637090
朔 州 市	**Shuozhou**			
朔城区	Shuochengqu	28	2352150	8720318
平鲁区	Pinglu	25	524541	3399401
山阴县	Shanyin	40	1250663	4156335
应　县	Yingxian	41	493777	423312
右玉县	Youyu	16	351445	2155875
怀仁县	Huairen	73	1725973	2276983
经济开发区	Economic Development Zone	9	454051	1768828
晋 中 市	**Jinzhong**			
榆次区	Yuci	91	2304489	3218676
榆社县	Yushe	7	322122	427594
左权县	Zuoquan	17	310578	1919375
和顺县	Heshun	15	329679	1445727
昔阳县	Xiyang	16	513496	2554877
寿阳县	Shouyang	29	702028	2966905
太谷县	Taigu	51	523117	569382
祁　县	Qixian	31	616932	442507
平遥县	Pingyao	40	933498	1728483
灵石县	Lingshi	98	2220750	5783980
介休市	Jiexiu	87	2107581	7283440
开发区	Development Zone	35	363135	518894
运 城 市	**Yuncheng**			
盐湖区	Yanhu	77	2084633	3861934
临猗县	Linyi	44	897316	1370339
万荣县	Wanrong	24	322574	430892
闻喜县	Wenxi	27	662341	1517577
稷山县	Jishan	21	664461	826572
新绛县	Xinjiang	29	1018178	1371025
绛　县	Jiangxian	37	604494	1003430
垣曲县	Yuanqu	12	567669	1947618
夏　县	Xiaxian	20	172113	334822
平陆县	Pinglu	19	342180	688959
芮城县	Ruicheng	27	371290	1054342
永济市	Yongji	47	2348083	2545086
河津市	Hejin	70	2930126	5150790

continued

(10 000 yuan)

主营业务收入 Revenue of Major Business	利税总额 Total Pre-tax Profits	利润总额 Total Profits	应交增值税 Value Added Taxes Payable
2779700	527867	256843	162406
321185	19363	5190	11531
932906	234349	126710	65935
1239617	320944	170858	100595
90454	4382	-3290	5283
1852802	111566	14914	73311
1137234	47163	-69533	64440
1096815	83493	61211	12391
2374979	261236	16427	149413
533669	68742	17606	34919
1254950	138665	32812	68828
484659	25087	15817	5374
329960	43375	6294	20503
1699067	504197	323131	152614
429147	74898	46399	13562
1947053	47540	-9354	44879
322120	12003	-5859	15506
269635	-22409	-43204	10724
304419	-10539	-50017	19912
494821	33167	-10004	9841
687161	126272	38794	49921
514206	45988	18481	24122
637640	70099	50985	14901
851389	4406	-24811	23366
2394537	82910	-24322	56304
2711919	-83046	-150645	46044
340682	37172	23677	11751
2268289	137326	89231	34964
816150	31142	25704	4866
270473	28705	19338	8391
678310	31272	11376	18664
711169	28244	5870	20206
1026316	52033	40802	9850
490718	9238	2166	6460
650584	12152	-11190	20276
177670	13792	10007	2655
353177	23104	24854	-2453
422189	36033	4046	27277
2246095	118189	81259	29925
2991344	381633	203478	129215

20–19 续表2

单位：万元

县(市、区)	Region	单位数 (个) Number of Enterprises (unit)	工业销售产值 Industrial Sales Output Value	资产总计 Total Assets
忻 州 市	**Xinzhou**			
忻府区	Xinfu	30	779462	1244851
定襄县	Dingxiang	33	311589	346927
五台县	Wutai	12	224017	731019
代　县	Daixian	60	506390	666893
繁峙县	Fanshi	57	764913	990460
宁武县	Ningwu	19	332920	2686355
静乐县	Jingle	14	154451	777782
神池县	Shenchi	5	66720	446443
五寨县	Wuzhai	10	84508	168248
岢岚县	Kelan	13	204550	207190
河曲县	Hequ	26	805234	2152580
保德县	Baode	19	557436	1301581
偏关县	Pianguan	5	83758	604031
原平市	Yuanping	36	1098481	3736280
临 汾 市	**Linfen**			
尧都区	Yaodu	44	872230	3198957
曲沃县	Quwo	22	1970328	2282791
翼城县	Yicheng	24	650894	716187
襄汾县	Xiangfen	28	1564443	1699661
洪洞县	Hongtong	58	2388369	5083514
古　县	Guxian	24	668660	1386437
安泽县	Anze	10	579882	856813
浮山县	Fushan	21	473396	270322
吉　县	Jixian	5	74456	148550
乡宁县	Xiangning	34	612223	2988328
大宁县	Daning	1	4724	6606
隰　县	Xixian			
永和县	Yonghe	1	30089	84985
蒲　县	Puxian	31	897801	2592548
汾西县	Fenxi	7	155634	16887
侯马市	Houma	25	704518	940248
霍州市	Huozhu	19	761872	4628449
吕 梁 市	**Lvliang**			
离石区	Lishi	23	424852	3524670
文水县	Wenshui	31	1154322	2050725
交城县	Jiaocheng	41	1051141	2678873
兴　县	Xingxian	17	1045523	3600144
临　县	Linxian	22	264348	2001848
柳林县	Liulin	45	1929823	9754292
石楼县	Shilou	2	8780	9156
岚　县	Lanxian	11	518128	1795755
方山县	Fangshan	14	300194	966410
中阳县	Zhongyang	28	895024	3255303
交口县	Jiaokou	26	864140	1551797
孝义市	Xiaoyi	162	4352097	10378419
汾阳市	Fenyang	26	905380	2379471